THE ANNUAL REGISTER
Vol. 244

THE ANNUAL REGISTER ADVISORY BOARD

CHAIRMAN
JAMES BISHOP
Former Editor of The Illustrated London News
and Foreign News Editor of The Times

EDITOR
D. S. LEWIS

DEPUTY EDITOR
WENDY SLATER

PHILIP M. H. BELL
Senior Research Fellow, University of Liverpool
NOMINATED BY
THE ROYAL HISTORICAL SOCIETY

MICHAEL KASER
*Emeritus Fellow of St Antony's College, Oxford,
and Honorary Professor, University of Birmingham*
NOMINATED BY
THE ROYAL INSTITUTE OF INTERNATIONAL AFFAIRS

ALASTAIR NIVEN, OBE
*Principal, King George VI and Queen Elizabeth
Foundation of St Catharine's*
NOMINATED BY
THE BRITISH COUNCIL

RICHARD O'BRIEN
Partner, Outsights
NOMINATED BY
THE ROYAL ECONOMIC SOCIETY

LORELLY WILSON
Honorary Teaching Fellow, University of Manchester
NOMINATED BY
THE BRITISH ASSOCIATION FOR THE ADVANCEMENT OF SCIENCE

Anticipating Victory (3 October): "Lula"'s supporters celebrate in Rio de Janeiro on the eve of the presidential election. (Popperfoto).

[Top] *Uniting Europe* (1 September 2001): Packages of euros are prepared by the European Central Bank in Brussels for the launch of the new currency on 1 January 2002. (Popperfoto/Reuters).

[Bottom] *Camp X-Ray* (6 February): Prisoners of war from Afghanistan, designated "unlawful combatants", are interned and interrogated at the US Naval Base, Guantanamo Bay, Cuba. (Popperfoto/Reuters).

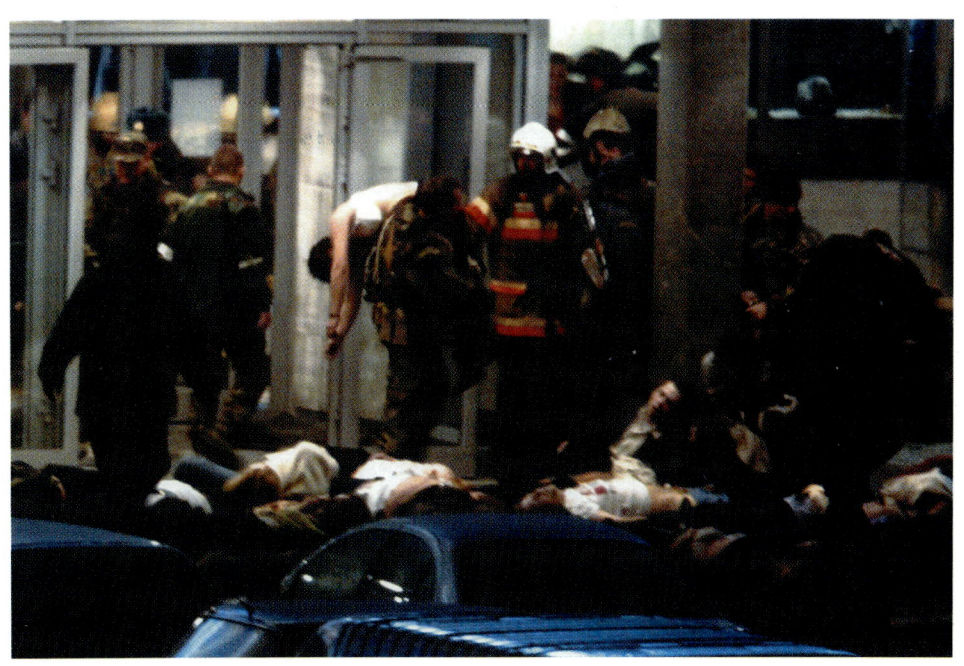

[Top] *Act of Remembrance* (14 October): Mourners hold candlelight vigil on a beach in Bali for victims of the nightclub bombing by Islamic extremists. (Popperfoto).

[Bottom] *Costly Rescue* (26 October): Russian special forces remove the bodies of hostages from a besieged Moscow theatre, after using incapacitating gas to overcome the Chechen separatists. (Popperfoto).

Called to Account (23 January): Massive accounting fraud is uncovered by federal investigators at the headquarters of the US energy giant, Enron Corp., in Houston, Texas. (Popperfoto/Reuters).

THE
ANNUAL REGISTER

A Record of World Events
2002

Edited by
D. S. LEWIS

Deputy Editor
WENDY SLATER

assisted by
LAURA CLIFTON

FIRST EDITED IN 1758
BY EDMUND BURKE

Keesing's Worldwide
PRINT · CD-ROM · ONLINE

THE ANNUAL REGISTER 2002
Published by Keesing's Worldwide, LLC, 4905 Del Ray Avenue, Suite 402,
Bethesda, MD 20814-2557, United States of America

ISBN 1-886994-46-3

©Keesing's Worldwide, LLC 2003
All rights reserved; no part of this publication may be reproduced,
stored in a retrieval system, or transmitted in any form or by any
means, electronic, mechanical, photocopying, recording or otherwise
without either the prior permission of the Publishers or a licence
permitting restricted copying issued by the Copyright Licensing Agency,
90 Tottenham Court Road, London, W1P 9HE, UK

British Library Cataloguing in Publication Data
The Annual Register—2002
1. History—Periodicals
909.82'8'05 D410

Library of Congress Catalog Card Number: 4-17979

Set in Times Roman by
NEW AGE GRAPHICS, BETHESDA, MD, USA

Printed in the USA by
PORT CITY PRESS, BALTIMORE, MD, USA

CONTENTS

	CONTRIBUTORS	viii
	IGO ABBREVIATIONS	xiv
	PREFACE TO 244th VOLUME	xv
	EXTRACTS FROM PAST VOLUMES	xvii

I OVERVIEWS OF THE YEAR

1	Global Issues and Regional Realities	1
2	The International Economy	9

II WESTERN AND SOUTHERN EUROPE

1	i United Kingdom 17 ii Scotland 39 iii Wales 41 iv Northern Ireland 43	17
2	i Ireland 47 ii Germany 50 iii France 54 iv Italy 59 v Belgium 63 vi The Netherlands 64 vii Luxembourg 66	47
3	i Denmark 67 ii Iceland 68 iii Norway 69 iv Sweden 70 v Finland 72 vi Austria 73 vii Switzerland 75 viii European Mini-States 77	67
4	i Spain 80 ii Gibraltar 84 iii Portugal 84 iv Malta 86 v Greece 88 vi Cyprus 90 vii Turkey 93	80

III CENTRAL AND EASTERN EUROPE

1	i Poland 97 ii Baltic States 99 iii Czech Republic 103 iv Slovakia 105 v Hungary 107 vi Romania 109 vii Bulgaria 112	97
2	i Albania 114 ii Bosnia & Herzegovina 116 iii Croatia 118 iv Macedonia 120 v Slovenia 122 vi Yugoslavia 123	114
3	i Russia 126 ii Belarus, Ukraine and Moldova 131 iii Armenia, Georgia and Azerbaijan 137	126

IV AMERICAS AND THE CARIBBEAN

1	United States of America	140
2	Canada	158
3	i Mexico 162 ii Guatemala 163 iii El Salvador 164 iv Honduras 165 v Nicaragua 165 vi Costa Rica 166 vii Panama 167	162
4	i Cuba 167 ii Jamaica 168 iii Dominican Republic and Haiti 169 iv Windward and Leeward Islands 171 v Barbados 173 vi Grenada 173 vii Trinidad & Tobago 174 viii The Bahamas 174 ix Guyana, Belize and Suriname 175 x UK Dependencies 177 xi Netherlands Antilles and Aruba 179 xii US Dependencies 179	167
5	i Brazil 180 ii Argentina 184 iii Paraguay 187 iv Uruguay 189 v Chile 190 vi Peru 191 vii Bolivia 192 viii Ecuador 194 ix Colombia 196 x Venezuela 198	180

V MIDDLE EAST AND NORTH AFRICA

1	Israel	202
2	i Palestine and the Arab World 205 ii Egypt 208 iii Jordan 212 iv Syria 214 v Lebanon 216 vi Iraq 218	205
3	i Saudi Arabia 224 ii Yemen 226 iii Arab States of the Gulf 227	224
4	i Sudan 233 ii Libya 235 iii Tunisia 237 iv Algeria 239 v Morocco 241 vi Western Sahara 243	233

VI EQUATORIAL AFRICA

1	i Horn of Africa 245 ii Kenya 250 iii Tanzania 252 iv Uganda 253	245
2	i Ghana 254 ii Nigeria 256 iii Sierra Leone 258 iv The Gambia 260 v Liberia 261	254
3	i West African Francophone States 262 ii Central African Franc Zone States 269	262

VII CENTRAL AND SOUTHERN AFRICA

1	i Democratic Republic of Congo 274 ii Burundi and Rwanda 277 iii Guinea-Bissau, Cape Verde and São Tomé and Príncipe 280 iv Mozambique 282 v Angola 284	274
2	i Zambia 286 ii Malawi 287 iii Zimbabwe 288 iv Botswana, Lesotho, Namibia and Swaziland 291	286
3	South Africa	298

VIII SOUTH ASIA AND INDIAN OCEAN

1	i Iran 302 ii Afghanistan 304 iii Central Asian Republics 309	302
2	i India 315 ii Pakistan 319 iii Bangladesh 321 iv Nepal 323 v Bhutan 325 vi Sri Lanka 325	315
3	i Mauritius 327 ii Seychelles, Comoros and Maldives 328 iii Madagascar 330	327

IX SOUTH-EAST AND EAST ASIA

1	i Myanmar (Burma) 332 ii Thailand 333 iii Malaysia 335 iv Brunei 337 v Singapore 337 vi Indonesia 338 vii East Timor 342 viii Philippines 342 ix Vietnam 344 x Cambodia 346 xi Laos 347	332
2	i China 348 ii Hong Kong SAR 352 iii Taiwan 353 iv Japan 356 v South Korea 360 vi North Korea 361 vii Mongolia 363	348

X AUSTRALASIA AND THE PACIFIC

1	i Australia 365 ii Papua New Guinea 369	365
2	i New Zealand 371 ii Pacific Island States 374	371

XI INTERNATIONAL ORGANISATIONS

1	United Nations	380
2	i Defence Organisations 393 ii Economic Organisations 399	393
3	i The Commonwealth 405 ii Francophonie and CPLP 407 iii Non-Aligned Movement and Developing Countries 411 iv Organisation of the Islamic Conference 413	405
4	European Union	414
5	i Council of Europe 423 ii Organisation for Security and Co-operation in Europe 425 iii European Bank for Reconstruction and Development 428 iv Nordic, Baltic and Arctic Organisations 429 v Other European Organisations 431	423
6	i Arab Organisations 433 ii African Organisations and Conferences 436 iii Asia-Pacific Organisations 438 iv American and Caribbean Organisations 443	433

CONTENTS vii

| XII | RELIGION | 447 |

XIII THE SCIENCES

1	Scientific, Medical and Industrial Research	452
2	Information Technology	458
3	The Environment	462

XIV THE LAW

1	i International Law 469 ii European Union Law 473	469
2	Law in the United Kingdom	476
3	Law in the USA	481

XV THE ARTS

1	i Opera 484 ii Music 486 iii Ballet & Dance 489 iv Theatre 492	484
	v Cinema 495 vi Television & Radio 498	
2	i Visual Arts 502 ii Architecture 505	502
3	Literature	508

| XVI | SPORT | 513 |

XVII DOCUMENTS AND REFERENCE

1	UN Security Council Resolution on Iraq	522
2	Durban Declaration on Launch of African Union	528
3	Key Outcomes of the UN World Summit on Sustainable Development	531
4	Preamble to the Constitution of the Democratic Republic of East Timor	535
5	UK Labour Government	536
6	United States Republican Administration	538
7	International Comparisons: Population, GDP and Growth	539

| XVIII OBITUARY | 540 |

| XIX | CHRONICLE OF PRINCIPAL EVENTS IN 2002 | 578 |

| INDEX | 603 |

MAPS AND TABLES

North Caucasus	136
United States Congressional Elections	145
Indonesia: East Timor, Bali	341
Net Recipients and Contributors to EU Budget	417
United Nations Political and Peace-building Missions	388
United Nations Peacekeeping Missions	390

CONTRIBUTORS

EXTRACTS FROM PAST VOLUMES	**Philip M. H. Bell**, Senior Research Fellow, University of Liverpool
PART I	
GLOBAL ISSUES AND REGIONAL REALITIES	**John M. Roberts,** Former Vice-Chancellor of the University of Southampton and Warden of Merton College, Oxford
THE INTERNATIONAL ECONOMY	**Thomas C. Muller,** Co-editor, *Political Handbook of the World*, Binghamton University.
	Robert L. Ostergard Jr., Ph.D, Associate Director, Institute of Global Cultural Studies; Assistant Professor, Departments of Political Science and African Studies Binghamton University
PART II	
UNITED KINGDOM	**Institute of Contemporary British History** (Harriet Jones, BA, MSc, PhD, Director, ICBH; Michael Kandiah, BA, MA, PhD, Director, Witness Seminar Programme; Virginia Preston, BA, Deputy Director)
SCOTLAND	**Charlotte Lythe**, MA, Senior Lecturer in Economic Studies, University of Dundee
WALES	**Gwyn Jenkins**, MA, Keeper of Manuscripts and Records, National Library of Wales, Aberystwyth
NORTHERN IRELAND	**Thomas Hennessey,** BA, MA, PhD, FRHistS, Lecturer in History, Canterbury Christ Church University College
REPUBLIC OF IRELAND	**Mary E. Daly**, MA, D Phil, MRIA, Chair of the Humanities Institute of Ireland; Professor of Irish History, University College Dublin
GERMANY, AUSTRIA, SWITZERLAND	**Rüdiger Wink,** PhD, Senior Research Fellow at European Research Institute, Institute for German Studies, University of Birmingham
FRANCE	**Martin Harrison,** Professor of Politics, University of Keele
ITALY	**Mark Donovan,** PhD, Senior Lecturer in Politics, Cardiff University of Wales; Editor, *Modern Italy*
BELGIUM, NETHERLANDS, LUXEMBOURG	**Marc Cole-Bailey,** Writer on European affairs
DENMARK, ICELAND, NORWAY, SWEDEN, FINLAND	**Torbjörn Nilsson,** PhD, Assistant Professor in History, Centre for Contemporary History, Södertörn University College, Sweden
EUROPEAN MINI-STATES	**Wendy Slater,** MA, PhD, Lecturer in Contemporary Russian History, University College London; Deputy Editor, *The Annual Register.*
SPAIN, GIBRALTAR	**Elisenda Fenés,** Freelance writer specialising in Spanish affairs
PORTUGAL	**Martin Eaton,** BA, PhD, FRGS/IBG, Lecturer in European Regional Development, University of Ulster at Coleraine

CONTRIBUTORS ix

MALTA	**Dominic Fenech,** BA, DPhil, Professor of History, University of Malta
GREECE	**Susannah Verney,** PhD, Lecturer in Department of Political Science and Public Administration, University of Athens; Visiting Research Fellow, University of Bradford; co-editor, *South European Society and Politics*
CYPRUS	**Robert McDonald,** Writer and broadcaster on Cyprus, Greece and Turkey
TURKEY	**A. J. A. Mango,** BA, PhD, Orientalist and writer on current affairs in Turkey and the Near East

PART III

POLAND	**A. Kemp-Welch,** BSc(Econ), PhD, Senior Lecturer, School of Economic and Social Studies, University of East Anglia
ESTONIA, LATVIA, LITHUANIA	**Mel Huang,** Research Associate, Conflict Studies Research Centre (CSRC), Sandhurst, UK; former Baltics analyst; Radio Free Europe; former Baltics editor, *Central European Review*.
CZECH REPUBLIC, SLOVAKIA	**Sharon Fisher,** MA, Analyst specialising in East European political and economic affairs
HUNGARY	**Marietta Stankova,** MA, PhD, Freelance writer on Eastern European contemporary history
ROMANIA	**Gabriel Partos,** South-East Europe Analyst, BBC World Service
BULGARIA, ALBANIA	**Richard Crampton,** PhD, Professor of East European History and Fellow of St Edmund Hall, University of Oxford
FORMER YUGOSLAV REPUBLICS	**William Bartlett,** MA, MSc, PhD, Reader at School for Policy Studies, University of Bristol
RUSSIA, BELARUS, UKRAINE, MOLDOVA AND CAUCASUS	**Stephen White,** PhD, DPhil, Professor of Politics, University of Glasgow

PART IV

UNITED STATES OF AMERICA	**Neil A. Wynn,** MA, PhD, Reader in History and American Studies, University of Glamorgan
CANADA	**David M. L. Farr,** MA, DPhil, LLD, Emeritus Professor of History, Carleton University, Ottawa
SOUTH AMERICA, CENTRAL AMERICA AND MEXICO	**Peter Calvert,** MA, PhD, Professor of Comparative and International Politics, University of Southampton
CARIBBEAN	**Peter Clegg,** MSc, PhD, Lecturer in Politics, University of the West of England, Bristol

PART V

ISRAEL, JORDAN, SYRIA, LEBANON, IRAQ	**Darren Sagar,** MA, Freelance writer specialising in Middle Eastern and South-East Asian affairs
PALESTINE AND THE ARAB WORLD, EGYPT	**Anoush Ehteshami,** Professor of International Relations and Director of the Institute for Middle Eastern and Islamic Studies, University of Durham

SAUDI ARABIA, YEMEN, ARAB STATES OF THE GULF	**George Joffé,** Senior Research Fellow, School of Oriental and African Studies, University of London
SUDAN	**Ahmed Al-Shahi,** MLitt, DPhil, Former lecturer in Social Anthropology, University of Newcastle Upon Tyne
LIBYA, TUNISIA, ALGERIA, MOROCCO, WESTERN SAHARA	**Richard Lawless,** PhD, Emeritus Reader in Modern Middle Eastern Studies, University of Durham; Research Associate, Queen Elizabeth House, University of Oxford.

PART VI

HORN OF AFRICA	**Patrick Gilkes,** Writer and broadcaster on the Horn of Africa
KENYA, TANZANIA, UGANDA	**William Tordoff,** MA, PhD, Emeritus Professor of Government, University of Manchester
GHANA, SIERRA LEONE, THE GAMBIA, LIBERIA	**Jeffrey Haynes,** BA, PhD, Professor of Politics, London Guildhall University
NIGERIA	**Guy Arnold,** Writer specialising in Africa and North-South affairs
FRANCOPHONE AFRICA	**Kaye Whiteman,** Former publisher, *West Africa*

PART VII

DEMOCRATIC REPUBLIC OF CONGO, BURUNDI & RWANDA, MOZAMBIQUE	**Patrick Harries,** PhD, Professor of African History, University of Basel, Switzerland
GUINEA BISSAU, CAPE VERDE, SÃO TOMÉ AND PRÍNCIPE, ANGOLA, ZAMBIA, MALAWI	**Christopher Saunders,** DPhil, Professor in Department of Historical Studies, University of Cape Town
ZIMBABWE	**R. W. Baldock,** BA, PhD, Editorial Director, Yale University Press; writer on African affairs
BOTSWANA, LESOTHO, NAMIBIA, SWAZILAND, SOUTH AFRICA	**Elizabeth Sidiropoulos,** BA Hons, MA, Director of Studies, South African Institute of International Affairs, Johannesburg

PART VIII

IRAN	**Keith McLachlan,** BA, PhD, Emeritus Professor, School of Oriental and African Studies, University of London
AFGHANISTAN	**D. S. Lewis,** PhD, Editor, *The Annual Register*; Editor, *Keesing's Record of World Events*
CENTRAL ASIAN REPUBLICS	**Shirin Akiner,** PhD, Lecturer in Central Asian Studies, School of Oriental and African Studies, University of London
INDIA, BANGLADESH, NEPAL, BHUTAN, SRI LANKA	**Peter Lyon,** BSc (Econ), PhD, Reader Emeritus in International Relations and Senior Research Fellow, Institute of Commonwealth Studies, University of London; editor, *The Round Table*, the Commonwealth journal of international affairs
PAKISTAN	**David Taylor,** Senior Lecturer in Politics with reference to South Asia, School of Oriental and African Studies, University of London
MAURITIUS, SEYCHELLES, COMOROS, MALDIVES, MADAGASCAR	**Malyn Newitt,** BA, PhD, JP, Charles Boxer Professor of History, Department of Portuguese, King's College, London

CONTRIBUTORS xi

PART IX

MYANMAR (BURMA), THAILAND, MALAYSIA, BRUNEI, SINGAPORE VIETNAM, CAMBODIA, LAOS **Robert H. Taylor,** PhD, former Professor of Politics, School of Oriental and African Studies, University of London; consultant on South East Asian affairs

INDONESIA, PHILIPPINES **Norman MacQueen,** BA, MSc, DPhil, Head of Department of Politics, University of Dundee

CHINA, HONG KONG, TAIWAN **Phil Deans,** BA, PhD, Lecturer in Chinese Politics, School of Oriental and African Studies, University of London

JAPAN **Ian Nish,** Emeritus Professor of International History, London School of Economics and Political Science

NORTH AND SOUTH KOREA **Sanjay Sharma,** MA, MPhil, PhD, Professor of Korean and International Studies, Changwon National University, Republic of Korea

MONGOLIA **Alan Sanders,** FIL, Former Lecturer in Mongolian Studies, School of Oriental and African Studies, University of London

PART X

AUSTRALIA **James Jupp,** MSc (Econ), PhD, FASSA, Director, Centre for Immigration and Multicultural Studies, Australian National University, Canberra

PAPUA NEW GUINEA **Norman MacQueen,** (see Pt. IX. Indonesia, Philippines)

NEW ZEALAND, PACIFIC ISLAND STATES **Stephen Levine,** PhD, Associate Professor and Head of School, School of Political Science and International Relations, Victoria University of Wellington

PART XI

UNITED NATIONS **David Travers,** BA, Lecturer in Politics and International Relations, Lancaster University; Specialist Advisor on UN to House of Commons' Foreign Affairs Committee

DEFENCE ORGANISATIONS **Paul Cornish,** PhD, Research Director, Centre for Defence Studies, King's College, London

ECONOMIC ORGANISATIONS **Thomas C. Muller and Robert Ostergard Jr,** (see Pt. I, The International Economy)

COMMONWEALTH **Derek Ingram,** Consultant Editor of *Gemini News Service*; author and writer on the Commonwealth

FRANCOPHONIE **Kaye Whiteman,** (see Pt. VII, Francophone Africa)

COMMUNITY OF PORTUGUESE-SPEAKING COUNTRIES **Martin Eaton,** (see Pt. II, Portugal)

NON-ALIGNED MOVEMENT AND GROUP OF 77 **Peter Willetts,** PhD, Professor of Global Politics, Department of Sociology, The City University, London

ORGANISATION OF THE ISLAMIC CONFERENCE **Darren Sagar,** (see Pt. V, Israel etc.)

EUROPEAN UNION **Michael Berendt,** Expert on affairs of the European Union

COUNCIL OF EUROPE **James Rhys,** MA, Secretary to UK delegation to Parliamentary Assembly of the Council of Europe

ORGANISATION FOR SECURITY AND CO-OPERATION IN EUROPE **Adrian G. V. Hyde-Price,** BSc (Econ), PhD, Institute of German Studies, University of Birmingham

xii   CONTRIBUTORS

EUROPEAN BANK FOR RECONSTRUCTION AND DEVELOPMENT	**Michael Kaser,** MA, DLitt, DSocSc, Emeritus Fellow of St Antony's College, Oxford, and Honorary Professor, University of Birmingham
NORDIC/BALTIC/ARCTIC ORGANISATIONS	**Torbjörn Nilsson,** (see Pt. II, Denmark, etc.)
OTHER EUROPEAN ORGANISATIONS	**Marc Cole-Bailey,** (see Pt. II, Belgium, etc.)
ARAB ORGANISATIONS	**George Joffé,** (see Pt. V, Saudi Arabia, etc.)
AFRICAN ORGANISATIONS AND CONFERENCES	**Christopher Saunders,** (see Pt. VII, Angola, etc.)
ASIA-PACIFIC ORGANISATIONS	**Darren Sagar,** (see Pt. V, Iraq)
AMERICAN AND CARIBBEAN ORGANISATIONS	**Peter Calvert,** (see Pt. IV, Latin America, etc.)

PART XII
RELIGION	**Geoffrey Parrinder,** MA, PhD, DD, Emeritus Professor of the Comparative Study of Religions, University of London

PART XIII
MEDICAL, SCIENTIFIC AND INDUSTRIAL RESEARCH	**Tim Curtis,** Regional Editor, *Keesing's Record of World Events*; writer on international affairs
INFORMATION TECHNOLOGY	**Kristian Saxton,** Freelance writer on Information Technology; IT professional
ENVIRONMENT	**Julian Coleman,** Journalist, broadcaster and radio producer specialising in the environment, development and science

PART XIV
INTERNATIONAL LAW	**Christine Gray,** MA, PhD, Fellow in Law, St John's College, Cambridge
EUROPEAN COMMUNITY LAW	**Neville March Hunnings,** LLM, PhD, Editor, *Encyclopedia of European Union Law: Constitutional Texts*
LAW IN THE UK	**David Ibbetson,** MA, PhD, Fellow and Tutor in Law, Magdalen College, Oxford
LAW IN THE USA	**Robert J. Spjut,** ID, LLD, Member of the State Bars of California and Florida

PART XV
OPERA	**Charles Osborne,** Author; opera critic, *The Jewish Chronicle*
MUSIC	**Francis Routh,** Composer and author; founder director of the Redcliffe Concerts
BALLET & DANCE	**Jane Pritchard,** Archivist, Rambert Dance Company and English National Ballet
THEATRE	**Matt Wolf,** London theatre critic, *Variety* and the Associated Press
CINEMA	**Derek Malcolm,** Cinema critic, *The Guardian*
TV & RADIO	**Raymond Snoddy,** Media Editor, *The Times*
VISUAL ARTS	**Anna Somers Cocks,** Editor, *The Art Newspaper*
ARCHITECTURE	**Rory Coonan,** Honorary Fellow, Royal Institute of British Architects; member, Franco-British Council
LITERATURE	**Alastair Niven,** OBE, Principal, King George VI and Queen Elizabeth Foundation of St Catharine's; formerly Director of Literature, British Council

PART XVI
SPORT   Paul Newman, Sports Editor of *The Independent*

PART XVII
DOCUMENTS AND REFERENCE

PART XVIII
OBITUARY   James Bishop, Former Editor of *The Illustrated London News* and Foreign News Editor of *The Times*

PART XIX
CHRONICLE OF 2002   Tim Curtis, (see Pt. XIII, Science etc.)

MAPS AND DIAGRAMS   Michael Lear, MJL Graphics, N. Yorks, YO14 9BE

ACKNOWLEDGMENTS

THE editor gratefully acknowledges his debt to a number of individuals and institutions for their help with sources, references and documents. Acknowledgment is also due to the principal sources for the national and IGO data sections (showing the situation at end 2002 unless otherwise stated), namely *Keesing's Record of World Events* (Keesing's Worldwide), the *2002/2003 World Development Report* (Oxford University Press for the World Bank) and the *Financial Times* (London). The Board and the bodies which nominate its members disclaim responsibility for any opinions expressed or the accuracy of facts recorded in this volume.

ABBREVIATIONS OF NON-UN INTERNATIONAL ORGANISATIONS

AC	Arctic Council
ACP	African, Caribbean and Pacific states associated with EU
ACS	Association of Caribbean States
AL	Arab League
ALADI	Latin American Integration Association
AMU	Arab Maghreb Union
ANZUS	Australia-New Zealand-US Security Treaty
APEC	Asia-Pacific Economic Co-operation
ASEAN	Association of South-East Asian Nations
AU	African Union
Benelux	Belgium-Netherlands-Luxembourg Economic Union
BSEC	Black Sea Economic Co-operation
CA	Andean Community of Nations
Caricom	Caribbean Community and Common Market
CBSS	Council of the Baltic Sea States
CE	Council of Europe
CEEAC	Economic Community of Central African States
CEFTA	Central European Free Trade Agreement
CEI	Central European Initiative
CIS	Commonwealth of Independent States
COMESA	Common Market of Eastern and Southern Africa
CPLP	Community of Portuguese-Speaking Countries
CWTH	The Commonwealth
EBRD	European Bank for Reconstruction and Development
ECO	Economic Co-operation Organisation
ECOWAS	Economic Community of West African States
EEA	European Economic Area
EFTA	European Free Trade Association
EU	European Union
G-8	Group of Eight
GCC	Gulf Co-operation Council
IOC	Indian Ocean Commission
Mercosur	Southern Cone Common Market
NAFTA	North American Free Trade Agreement
NAM	Non-Aligned Movement
NATO	North Atlantic Treaty Organisation
NC	Nordic Council
OAPEC	Organisation of Arab Petroleum Exporting Countries
OAS	Organisation of American States
OECD	Organisation for Economic Co-operation and Development
OECS	Organisation of Eastern Caribbean States
OIC	Organisation of the Islamic Conference
OPEC	Organisation of the Petroleum Exporting Countries
OSCE	Organisation for Security and Co-operation in Europe
PC	Pacific Community
PFP	Partnership for Peace
PIF	Pacific Islands Forum
SAARC	South Asian Association for Regional Co-operation
SADC	Southern African Development Community
SELA	Latin American Economic System
UEMOA	West African Economic and Monetary Union

PREFACE

The terrorist attacks of 11 September 2001 cast their long shadow over a year which began with the final throes of a US-led military campaign in Afghanistan and ended with preparations for an attack upon Iraq. In that sense the year 2002 neatly encapsulated a period when the US-led "war against terrorism" slipped from its hunt for Osama bin Laden, the architect of the 11 September atrocity, to a war against Iraqi President Saddam Hussein, whose secular dictatorship was fundamentally opposed by bin Laden and his followers. This change of focus was widely criticised and, as the year progressed, US allies fell away and the huge groundswell of sympathy which had been so evident in the aftermath of 11 September was dissipated.

The reasons behind the USA's decision to go to war against Iraq will doubtless be much debated by historians. In part it sprang from the need to assuage the pain and humiliation of 11 September, an attack which a disturbingly large number of US citizens believed was the work of the Iraqi dictator. In truth, however, influential neo-conservatives connected to the Bush administration had been calling for the removal of Saddam even before the Twin Towers had burned and crumpled in front of a stunned global audience. Thus, whilst the USA lurched inexorably to war, dragging its loyal UK ally in its wake, there was the unmistakeable feeling that this was a war which had been germinating since the last Gulf conflict in 1991. It had about it an air of unfinished business as well as the unmistakeable whiff of oil.

Almost in slow motion, the year unfolded with a diplomatic charade which never seemed likely to deflect the bloody course of future events. In what appeared to be a search by the US administration for a *casus belli*, the justification for attacking Iraq was subject to frequent amendment and variation. Ostensibly it was the need to rid Iraq of weapons of mass destruction, although with no such weapons yet discovered—and the UN inspectors back in the country by the year's end and eager to continue monitoring Iraq's compliance with its obligations to disclose such weapons—this appeared an increasingly inadequate justification. Other reasons were cited by proponents of war on both sides of the Atlantic. These included "regime change" and a war to liberate the Iraqi people from tyranny, aims which overlooked the West's earlier support for Saddam at a time when the deficiencies in his regime's human rights record were already well known. Also cited was the need to protect Iraq's neighbours from aggression and, ironically, to maintain the authority of the UN by enforcing its resolutions; arguments undermined by the US administration's unconditional support for Israel which not only itself possessed illegal weapons of mass destruction but which had also attacked more neighbouring states than had Iraq and had defied more UN resolutions over a much longer period. The justifications for war also included constructing a democratic government in Iraq, a desirable aim but one fraught with a host of practical difficulties and uncertainties.

The USA, in part persuaded by its UK ally, pursued the route of UN diplomacy, but only for as long as this promised to produce the desired result: the legitimisation of an invasion of Iraq. As allied forces were being assembled in the Gulf, the widespread opposition to the war strained and tore at the established patterns of international diplomacy. These divisions were only partially concealed by UN Resolution 1441 which was passed unanimously precisely because it did not sanction the use of force against Saddam. In an attempt to produce a majority for a second resolution explicitly sanctioning war, countries on the Security Council were bribed, bullied and cajoled. When it became clear that the US-UK position did not command even a simple majority on the 15-member Council, the UN route was abandoned (its failure being blamed on the French threat to veto any second resolution) in favour of unilateral military action.

The results of the war are as yet unclear, but some possibilities appear more rather than less likely. Terrorism in Western cities seems more not less imminent. "Imperial power", "arrogance", and "over-reach" are terms which have coalesced rather than diverged since the fighting began. The war has, ironically, made alliances between secular dictatorship and Islamic fundamentalism more rather than less likely. It has brought closer a "clash of civilisations", the Western war against Islam which bin Laden sought but had hitherto only prophesied. The conflict may also have caused irreparable damage to the UN, fractured the EU, and undermined the very concept of international law.

After three weeks of fighting the war appears almost won, albeit at a cost in civilian deaths which remains unclear but could be appallingly high. The superiority of allied firepower has been decisive: "precision weapons" but weapons which proved able to kill and maim the innocent just the same. The deaths of civilians and combatants alike have led to the freeing of Iraq from a vile tyranny, a liberation greeted by some with wild jubilation on the streets of Baghdad. The war may be won, however, but the victors will be judged by what follows: the length of military occupation (and its cultural sensitivity), the financial transparency of the process of reconstruction, and the role granted in post-war Iraq to the UN. From an illegal war there is the opportunity for the world's superpower to make an unprecedented contribution to peace in the Middle East and, in so doing, to build bridges with Islam and the Arab world. This requires not just the construction of a democratic Iraq but also of a just and viable Palestinian state living in peace with a secure Israel. It will be a key test of US intentions. The whole world is watching.

D.S. Lewis
Cambridge, April 2003.

EXTRACTS FROM PAST VOLUMES

225 years ago

1776-7. *Washington winters at Valley Forge.* In the mean time, Washington removed his camp from White Marsh to Valley Forge, upon the Schuylkill, about 15 or 16 miles from Philadelphia, in a very strong, and consequently secure position. Nothing could afford a stronger proof, to whoever considers the nature and disposition of those people, of the unbounded influence on the minds both of his officers and men which that General possessed, than his being able, not only to keep them together, but to submit to the incommodities and distresses incident to living in a hutted camp, during the severe winter of that climate, and where all his supplies of provision and stores must come from a great distance, at much expence and no small hazard. It was also a proof, with many others, of the general strong disposition of America, to suffer all things rather than submit to force.

200 years ago

1802. *Account of a Diving Boat.* Citizen St. Aubin, a man of letters at Paris, and a member of the tribunate, has given the following account of the bateau plongeur, a diving boat, lately discovered by Mr. Fulton, an American: "I have", says he, "just been to inspect the plan and section of a nautilus, or diving boat, invented by Mr. Fulton, similar to that with which he lately made his curious and interesting experiment at Havre and Brest. The diving boat, in the construction of which he is now employed, will be capacious enough to contain eight men, and provisions enough for twenty days, and will be of sufficient strength and power to enable him to plunge 100 feet under water, if necessary. He has contrived a reservoir for air, which will enable eight men to remain under water for eight hours. . . what will become of maritime wars, and where will sailors be found to man ships of war, when it is a physical certainty, that they may every moment be blown into the air by means of a diving boat, against which no human foresight can guard them?"

175 years ago

1827. *The Battle of Navarino.* [20 October] The battle continued with unabated fury during four hours. At the end of that period, the Turkish and Egyptian fleets had disappeared; the Bay of Navarino was covered with their wrecks; only a few of the smaller vessels, or some battered and useless hulks, escaped into the security of the inner harbour. The carnage on board the crowded ships of the enemy was destructive. In two of their ships of the line alone, two thirds of their crews were killed or wounded. The severest loss on the side of the allies [Britain, France and Russia] was sustained by the British squadron, which had seventy-five men killed, and one hundred and ninety-seven wounded.

150 years ago

1852. *The wreck of the Birkenhead.* [26 February] ... in the beginning of April, intelligence was received of the wreck of Her Majesty's steam troopship, Birkenhead, near the Cape of Good Hope, with frightful loss of life. . . . Mr. Salmond gave orders to Colonel Seton to send troops to the chain-pumps:- the orders were implicitly obeyed, and perfect discipline maintained. The women and children were calmly placed in the cutter, which lay alongside, in the charge of an officer, and pulled off to a short distance to be free from the danger of a rush; two other boats were also manned . . . When the vessel was about to go down, the commander called out "all those who can swim jump overboard, and make for the boats". We [the military officers] begged the men not to do as the commander said, as the boat with the women must be swamped. Not more than three made the attempt. Under this heroic obedience to discipline the whole mass were engulphed in the waves by the sinking of the ship.

125 years ago

1877. *The United States.* In the United States the year 1877 opened gloomily amid the difficulties and uncertainties, the turmoil and strife, of a disputed Presidential Election. . . The votes of the Presidential Electors were almost equally balanced, and whether Mr. Tilden and Mr. Hendricks, the Democratic Candidates, or Mr. Hayes and Mr. Wheeler, the Republican Candidates, would be declared President and Vice-President for the next four years, depended on the admission or rejection of the votes of three of the Southern States, viz., Florida, Louisiana, and South Carolina. In these States Republican Legislatures had appointed partisan returning Boards, and these were accused by the opposite party of falsifying the returns. The Democrats, therefore, demanded an investigation; but the Republicans maintained that, according the Constitution, the certificate of the Governor of a State legalised the returns and could not be upset. How could the dispute be adjusted? In what way might a peaceful settlement be arrived at?. . . In this dilemma the common sense and political sagacity of the practical and law-respecting people of the United States devised a means of escape. The Senate and the Lower House agreed to appoint an Electoral Commission, composed of five members taken from each branch of the Legislature and the five Judges of the Supreme Court. The functions of this Committee of Fifteen were intended to be judicial; but the members of it, whether senators, deputies or judges voted simply for the interests of their respective parties, without any reference whatever to the merits of the case. It was ruled by a majority of one that Congress should not inquire into the credentials of a Presidential Elector. This at once gave the victory to the Republicans.

100 years ago

1902. *Russia.* The year 1902 was chiefly remarkable in Russia for the alarming spread of the revolutionary movement, by which it became clear that a considerable part of the whole social, economic, and political fabric of the Empire was undermined. No disturbances, indeed, occurred which could not be easily suppressed by the employment of soldiery if the latter were entirely to be relied on. But, on the one hand, there began to be symptoms of indisposition on the part of existing Russian troops to use their weapons for the suppression of popular movements; and on the other hand it was evident that the classes from whom the Army was for the most part annually replenished were becoming increasingly subjected to revolutionary influences. The principal active agents in the diffusion of those influences were university students and the members of the liberal professions—teachers, doctors, barristers and the like; but also, as was pointed out in a circular issued in June by M. Plehve, the recently appointed Minister of the Interior, much use was made of clever and energetic peasants, who were first trained in courses of instruction in sociology and in such subjects as the history of political and economic movements and then sent forth to carry on an anti-governmental propaganda among their fellows. . . It must be added that even the clergy, the strongest bulwark of Russian autocracy, were beginning to be penetrated with revolutionary opinions.

75 years ago

1927. *Lindbergh's Flight.* In May began the series of trans-Atlantic flights. On the 8th, two French airmen, Nungesser and Coli, set off from Le Bourget in the "Oiseau Blanc". There were contradictory reports, but never again was there authentic news of these daring pioneers. The French were greatly disappointed and grieved. It was known that the Americans were preparing flights from the United States to France—and it was held by some experts that the eastward flight was perhaps better favoured by the prevailing winds than the westward flight. Foolish reports were sent to America pleading for the postponement of all attempts until French chagrin had disappeared. Captain—afterwards Colonel—Charles A. Lindbergh ignored these warnings and, forestalling his rivals, who had been preparing in the full blaze of publicity to cross the Atlantic by air, he set off unheralded, without notice, in his "Spirit of Saint Louis", and after a solitary thirty-three-hour journey over the ocean, arrived safely at his destination, Le Bourget, 3,600 miles away from his starting-point at Roosevelt Field, near New York, on Saturday evening, May 21. Lindbergh's performance was extraordinarily spectacular, and the quiet demeanour of the flier won the hearts of the French.

50 years ago

1952. *Mr. Eden in New York.* On 11 January Mr. Eden, after receiving an honorary degree at Columbia University, New York, delivered a "lecture" which was in effect a statement of British foreign policy in all parts of the world. Defending British policy towards the European Union movement he declared that Britain had given all possible evidence of her solidarity with Western Europe and had contributed much more than her fair share towards its rearmament, but that "joining a European federation is something that we know in our bones we cannot do".

The European Coal and Steel Community. M. Monnet was appointed president of the High Authority, and at its first meeting on 10 August he emphasised both the supra-national and the experimental nature of the new Community, when he said, "All these institutions can be changed and improved by experience. What will not be changed is their supra-national and—let us say it—federal character."

25 years ago

1977. *The USSR.* The sixtieth anniversary of the Bolshevik Revolution saw Lenin's heirs forced more frequently on the defensive than had been usual in the previous few years. The anniversary was marked, it is true, by the adoption of a new Constitution. It was also marked by the adoption of a new President (or at any rate an almost-new President, since Mr Brezhnev had occupied this ceremonial post once before). On the other hand, the Kremlin's treatment of its unofficial internal opposition was subjected to far more public criticism by foreign governments than had previously been the case; Eurocommunists continued to make similar attacks, and the expulsions of Soviet advisers from the Sudan and Somalia were significant setbacks. On the economic front, growth was relatively slow; there was a mediocre harvest, and machinery orders to Western suppliers had to be cut back.

THE ANNUAL REGISTER
FOR THE YEAR 2002

I OVERVIEWS OF THE YEAR

1. GLOBAL ISSUES AND REGIONAL REALITIES

INEVITABLY 2002 passed in the shadow of its predecessor (see AR 2001, pp. 1-15), but it was not altogether a bad year. The situation in Angola and Sri Lanka seemed to be improving and East Timor became an independent state at last, even if some Muslims deplored it. Nor were there wars in Macedonia or, in spite of much provocation, in Kashmir. But this was almost all that could be entered on the credit side. The shadow of war in the Middle East hung over the whole year, although no war broke out there; and so did that cast by the spectre of terrorism, which, even more profoundly, obsessed international attention and darkened counsel throughout 2002.

The term "terrorism" was used and abused in many different contexts. Turning a blind eye to its own history, Israel drew the largest dividend on the universal alarm, while Russia exploited the term in Chechnya, India accused Pakistan of it, and China blamed it on its dissidents. This loose but widespread application merely recognised reality. To name only a few widely scattered examples, in 2002 bombs went off in South Africa, Corsica, the Basque country, Thailand, and Jordan. In Israel, the Palestinian intifada continued its bloody course. Its long-running violence, though, was temporarily eclipsed by spectacular events towards the end of the year. After a sea borne attack on a French tanker off the Yemen there followed the worst atrocity since 11 September 2001, with a tourist resort in Bali as its target. Then, a band of Muslims seized a theatre in Moscow and held its audience hostage while demanding Russian withdrawal from Chechnya. Kenya, already the scene of terrorist violence in the past, came back into the news in November with an unsuccessful attempt in Mombasa to bring down an Israeli airliner and, almost simultaneously, an all too successful and murderous car-bomb attack on a hotel frequented by Israeli tourists but which killed mostly Kenyans. Finally, after Christmas, a car-bomb destroyed the building of the Russian-supported administration in Grozny, the Chechen capital, with another heavy toll of lives.

Islamic terrorists were blamed for much of the year's violence and, indeed, often claimed responsibility for it, as did, for example, al-Qaida, now driven from

Afghanistan. Great efforts were made to gather intelligence about the organisation and to pick off its adherents, but its significance and strength remained uncertain and it seemed successful in recruiting and training Muslim supporters in many countries. Messages purporting to be from its leader, Osama bin Laden, were aired by al Jazeera, a Gulf television station, and continued to arouse alarm. The view came to be even more widely held (not only by US citizens) that terrorism was above all an Islamic phenomenon. But this encouraged a counter-assumption amongst Muslims that the war which had been proclaimed against terrorism was really a war against Islam.

Such simplicities obscured important and even obvious facts. Muslims might attack Christian churches in Islamabad, but Pakistani Shi'ites attacked Suni Muslims as well. Iran was named in May by the US State Department as "the most active state sponsor of terrorism" but Iranian police arrested Taliban sympathisers just the same. Islam was too complicated a notion to be of great explanatory value without context, despite the continued talk about conflicts of civilisations. Yet the cause of the Palestinians fuelled anti-US feeling and consolidated support for terrorism amongst Muslims in all the Arab lands.

As the year opened, the US-led war against terrorism (Operation Enduring Freedom) was ending in Afghanistan. Taliban resistance was soon said to be over, even if, months later, a US general spoke of "unfinished business" there. By then, though, Afghan recovery (or "nation-building", as it was often characterised) was a greater preoccupation than the continuing military operations. The economy of what had long been one of the poorest countries in the world lay in ruins, and the war had left the country littered with uncharted landmines. Yet huge numbers of refugees sought to return to Afghanistan. Fantasies of democracy crumbled before tribal and local rivalries, however, while warlords exploited US patronage and the plentiful arms left behind by the combatants. There were small grounds for optimism in having put girls back in school and promises of international aid. Yet a victorious, if limited, campaign against terrorism had indeed been fought and won, eliminating Muslim terrorist bases and training sites, and scattering the Taliban.

This was, nonetheless, the only obvious victory over terrorism, for all the alarmed responses that violence elicited. In the USA, popular support facilitated the inauguration of a new Department of Homeland Security. US forces were sent to the Philippines, Georgia, and the Horn of Africa on counter-terrorist tasks. Police action was launched against al-Qaida suspects and Islamic extremists in the UK, France, Germany, Turkey, the Philippines, and Singapore. In Muslim countries, too, there were forceful responses. Arrests were made in Pakistan, Indonesia, Morocco, Algeria, and even Libya; and Saudi Arabia claimed to have frozen resources on which terrorists might draw.

The main focus of US anti-terrorist policy, though, came to be Iraq. In the first instance this was because of Saddam Hussein's supposed connection with and support for al-Qaida. Yet no new information emerged to confirm this link. Preoccupation with the Weapons of Mass Destruction (WMD)—chemical, biological and nuclear—which Saddam was believed to possess and to wish to develop instead loomed larger in US policy. This drew attention to a paradox, and suggested double standards, given that the USA and several of her allies possessed such weapons. In Iraq's case, they were seen both as an affront to UN resolutions in the past and as a threat to the balance of power in the Middle East in the present (which meant Israel). In response, Saddam played a long game. While fanning the anti-Israeli sentiment of fellow-Arabs, he stressed his readiness for "dialogue" with the UN and the renewal of arms inspection. Yet by the summer speculation focused upon whether US military action against him—unilateral and possibly pre-emptive—was inevitable. Domestic support for it was strong, in spite of occasional reservations by Democratic politicians, and mid-term congressional elections produced Republican majorities in both houses of Congress in November. The President's authority and freedom of action were thereafter greater than ever. What this might prompt his administration to do, of course, frightened foreign observers, even in countries which were potential allies.

In his State of the Union message in January President George Bush, while conceding that the war on terror was "only beginning", had already caused some dismay by identifying an "axis of evil" states. It included North Korea, Iran, and Iraq. Yet although using an ominous phrase about not waiting on events, he did not explicitly advocate action. Soon his Secretary of State, General Colin Powell, announced that there was no intention of going to war with Iran or North Korea, but that "regime change" in Iraq would be in the best interests of the Middle East. That, too, was given a further rider: Iraq, said Powell, could avoid confrontation with the USA if it would readmit the UN inspectors who had been withdrawn in 1998. Then came leaks in the US press of a Nuclear Posture Review which envisaged pre-emptive US action with nuclear weapons in unspecified circumstances to stop the spread of WMD. When in May the President declared that he had "no war plans on my desk" much of the world remained unconvinced, alarmed, and confused.

Two perceptions were widespread. One, fed by the rhetoric of some members of the administration and those close to it, was that whatever was said, US policy was bent on war with Iraq. The other perception—less defined but perhaps more reasonably based—was psychological: of an administration which enjoyed its new "imperial" role, careless of other interests and callous in weighing them. The roots of this went back to the Clinton years at least, but Bush's tariff concessions and agricultural subsidies at home, without regard to the interests of allies or undeveloped countries, confirmed it. It became known, too, that the US army, which had in 1961 undertaken to abandon biological weapons, had been for years conducting research into the production and management of weapons-grade anthrax. When notice came of the abandonment of "MAD" (the doctrine of Mutually Assured Destruction) which had underpinned containment and peace for so much of the Cold War, such a change in US strategic thinking seemed to confirm that a pre-emptive war was in the making.

Yet continued harping on Iraq's WMD did not produce evidence to convince sceptics that the danger was real or more than a smokescreen for US ambition. For many, the real motives behind a determination to attack Iraq were ambitions to seize control of more oil-producing areas and to humiliate Islam. Meanwhile, US failure to restrain Israel continued to make conciliation of Muslim feeling impossible. Any uneasiness which might be felt by Muslim governments about Saddam's intentions was silenced amid the revulsion aroused by the US collusion with Israel's oppression of the Palestinians. Even Saudi Arabia refused the US assistance such as it had given in the Gulf War.

The intifada, meanwhile, spectaculaly conducted by suicide bombers (the first woman among them died in February) stoked the fire. The attacks were unpredictable and were often directed against defenceless targets; the death-toll of Israeli civilians, including women and children, steadily rose. The punitive Israeli response, however, seen by many as a form of terrorism, ensured that the numbers of Palestinian civilians killed was rising faster still. Israel, too, lost moral ground through its military incursions into Palestinian areas, collective punishments, targeted killings of alleged Arab terrorist leaders, and the further entrenchment of Jewish settler enclaves in the occupied territories. Its relentless efforts to damage and possibly destroy the infrastructure of effective government in the Palestinian areas, and especially the refugee camps, gave rise to allegations of massacre and the torture of prisoners. Meanwhile, the intifada was driving the Israeli economy (already dependent on US subvention) into recession.

Although increasingly disillusioned by the Palestinian leadership, the USA made occasional gestures towards even-handedness. The President spoke of Israeli and Palestinian states living side by side and said that further Israeli settlement in non-Israeli territory should stop. He welcomed peace initiatives by King Abdullah of Jordan. Yet Israeli Prime Minister Ariel Sharon, unrestrained and apparently unquestioned by his superpower ally, continued to assert that he was only resisting terrorism whilst behaving in a way which seemed illustrative of the mistaken belief that Palestinian aspirations for statehood could be forever suppressed by brute force. That he was able to do so made it clear that the USA could neither much influence Israel nor, perhaps, wished to. In spite of occasional posturing by the US government (after two sieges of Arafat's compound, which Bush said were "not helpful"), nothing was done to dispel Arab impressions that the Israeli tail would always wag the American dog. Full explanations of US ties with Israel must await the verdicts of future historians, but Bush was soon saying that he was not yet ready to name a date for the Palestinian statehood which he had previously endorsed.

Foreign criticism of the USA mounted. It was particularly blatant in the German electoral campaign in the autumn. Yet US diplomacy had its successes too, for all its unhelpful entanglement with Israel's interests. The USA never lost the UK's support, even if differences in tone emerged from the two countries. Vigorous efforts to keep the Pakistani government on side bore fruit in co-operative, if not wholly unembarrassed, intelligence relations without finally antagonising India. Above all, there was success in the UN. The changing tone of US diplomacy began to make it evident that the Bush administration was prepared to work through the Security Council. After a speech to the General Assembly by Bush in September, and weeks of intensive negotiation, these efforts won unanimous support in the Security Council for Resolution 1441 in November. This declared Iraq to be in breach of her obligations under earlier resolutions, authorised the return of an unfettered inspection mission, and gave the Iraqi government thirty days to provide a list of WMD and its facilities for their manufacture. The resolution also envisaged an immediate reconvening of the Security Council in the event of further non-compliance by the Iraqis.

Saddam Hussein agreed to re-admit UN inspectors with greatly enhanced powers, and the first of them quickly arrived (to occupy their predecessors' now heavily-bugged premises) and began work. Within a few days Iraq was complaining that they were spying for the USA, and the US government that they were being insufficiently rigorous. Nonetheless, on 8 December the Iraqis delivered a formal statement as required; it ran to 12,000 pages and denied the existence of any WMD. Yet to have achieved this much was a major success, even if it was unclear whether military action to follow non-compliance with resolution 1441 would follow automatically or would require further authorisation. The USA continued to prepare for war without revealing whether it would seek such UN authorisation to act in the event. Then, as Christmas approached, the USA, the UK and the head of the UN mission all denounced Iraq's document for its omissions; it seemed that the long-expected attack on Saddam was a step nearer.

So intense was international attention to the Middle East and Islam that it was easy to lose sight of matters less obviously pressing. One arose in North Korea, when the country's archaic and secretive regime announced its intention to reactivate a nuclear reactor said by the USA to be capable of producing enriched uranium for weapons. The US administration cut off oil supplies from December by way of riposte, thus appearing to threaten the derelict North Korean economy with complete breakdown. Other unsolved political problems remained in Kashmir and, in spite of rising hopes, Cyprus. At a much more fundamental level, though, the year again brought alarming reports of ice melting at the poles with increasing rapidity, of the ravages caused by commercial logging of hardwoods, and of increasing pollution of water resources. The world's demands, some said, had at last outrun its regenerative capacity. There was further evidence too, of the mounting menace of AIDS/HIV, above all in Africa (where there were 28.5 million out of the world's 40 million cases), although governments elsewhere were also showing alarm. Probably over-optimistically, the Chinese conceded that there would be a million cases in that country by the end of the year, and rates of infection were also rising rapidly in India, Indonesia, and Russia.

Environmental and health problems were not all that tested governments' capacities. Still-developing countries, especially the two potential giants, India and China, reacted strongly against outside interference with their domestic plans, of course. Yet even they were beginning to feel the effects, marginal as they might be, of new limitations on and erosions of their independence of action. This remains hard to assess for the process had begun years before and had many sources. Some lay in internal divisions increasingly difficult to reconcile with aspirations to democracy and self-determination (as in the drawn-out and costly war of Russia in Chechnya or the brutalities of ETA in Spain), others in external infringements of sovereignty (as prefigured in Somalia, Bosnia, and Kosovo). Even prosperity, so often seen as the proper aim of government, created troubling expectations. Globalisation was often a scapegoat too. Such themes transcend calendar years.

More precise and familiar uncertainties hung over the EU. Its further enlargement and actual constitutional working had long aroused misgiving. In some of the countries applying to join, there was now a new uneasiness about what lay ahead, only slightly relieved at the Copenhagen summit of EU leaders in December. Questions of constitutional change had meanwhile been shunted into the siding of a special commission which seemed likely to produce highly contentious conclusions. But both areas of uncertainty inevitably awoke divisions among member states, and they had to be dealt with whilst unemployment rose, industrial investment fell, and budgetary problems proliferated in almost every country. The successful introduction of a new currency (the Euro) on 1 January for cash transactions in 12 states of the Union (and a handful of associated micro-states) was dimmed as other difficulties began to appear, among them the self-denying restriction imposed in the new currency zone on individual countries' freedom to run budgetary deficits. By September enough governments were in trouble for the rules to have to be relaxed. This led to further divisions and another obstacle to the much-needed reform of the Common Agricultural Policy (CAP). The French won a significant victory when President Jacques Chirac and Chancellor Gerhard Schröder of Germany agreed bilaterally to put off any reform of the system until 2013 and to slow down the extension of the CAP's anticipated bounty to new members of the EU.

Europe's democratic electorates also worried about immigration, especially that from potential future members. A striking symptom came in the first round of the French presidential election when an ultra-nationalist, anti-immigration, and anti-EU candidate inflicted wounding blows on both his right-wing and socialist opponents. Traditional political tendencies seemed to lose their grip when confronted by so plausible a populist alternative. In France, matters corrected themselves in the next electoral round, and after a few more right-wing electoral triumphs (in the Netherlands and Greece, for example), the trend seemed to slacken by the autumn. Nonetheless, several governments found it prudent or necessary to restrict immigration or regulate it more closely. Like measures against terrorism, this aroused worry over possible threats to civil liberties. Fears of mass migrations, however, soured the atmosphere in which enlargement had to be discussed, especially Turkey's application, consideration of which remained blocked after Copenhagen until 2004.

The troubles of other continents registered less strongly with Europeans than did their own preoccupations. Sub-Saharan Africa's story was still often one of continuing civil and cross-border strife amid deepening poverty. The Ivory Coast was absorbed in the atrocities of its civil war, while the Democratic Republic of Congo remained the prey of its own rulers. Ethiopia and Malawi faced famine and Zambia declared a national disaster in June. In Zimbabwe, human agency seemed particularly culpable. Robert Mugabe's re-election as President by manipulation and intimidation awoke strong criticism in the Commonwealth (although some African members rallied to his support). Meanwhile, serious food shortages were made worse by his policies of selling grain reserves and evicting white farmers from their properties. The surrendered farms, often given to influential supporters of the ruling party, were invariably abandoned as productive units. There followed a collapse in output. Whatever the rights or wrongs of redistribution it was in practice disastrous. Refugees began to leave Zimbabwe in search of food. The EU meanwhile imposed modest sanctions to fall on members of the ruling elite as retribution for Mugabe's unconstitutional and dictatorial acts, while the US conceded that regime change in Zimbabwe would be welcome. It was small alleviation of Africa's plight that at the end of the year Kenya successfully held elections which provided a peaceful transition of power after decades of one-party domination.

Some thought promising the inauguration in July of a new African Union which was launched as a successor to the Organisation of African Unity (OAU). Its announced aim was to build an Africa "governed on the basis of democracy", but given Africa's past record this promised little. The African renaissance which had once provoked enthusiasm still seemed in abeyance when there met at Johannesburg at the end of August a huge conference on Sustainable Development which Bush, unlike other Western leaders, pointedly did not attend. It was indeed almost without positive achievement. That could hardly be blamed on the USA, but Bush's absence was taken as another sign of US preoccupation with narrowly-defined national goals.

The Americas south of the Rio Grande were disturbed and unhappy too, but experienced less violence than sometimes in the past. There were a few, not very important, expressions of anti-US feeling but little evidence of US intervention. Speculation awoke over the possible role of the CIA in a failed coup in Venezuela, but by the end of the year that country seemed on the verge of a popular revolution to rid itself of its President. Indigenous terrorism survived in Peru, where Shining Path was still active. Colombia remained de facto partitioned between government and Marxist guerrilla armies. The main preoccupations of the continent, however, were once more deepening economic and financial problems. In Argentina, a succession of ministers (several removed by riots) grappled in vain with misdirected government expenditure, international capital flows, and the self-enrichment of the governing classes. As the year advanced, startled middle-class citizens of what had once been one of the world's most prosperous nations faced empty food shops, child malnutrition, local barter economies and, often, the evaporation of savings. Nowhere else in the region were things quite so bad. Other countries were not refused, as was Argentina, international assistance and loans.

Of two potential superpowers other than the USA, Russia continued to look more and more like one industrial state among many. The summer was a good one for Vladimir Putin, bringing as it did an arms reduction agreement with the US, association with NATO, and the formal acknowledgement by the EU that Russia had a market economy. At home, its behaviour in Chechnya was helpfully glossed by the sanitising label of "anti-terrorism". Yet Russia remained in many ways a place apart, shaped by its special history. The handling of the Moscow theatre siege cost the lives of over a hundred hostages (thanks to the security forces' use of poison gas) and showed how acceptable still to Russians were old standards of governmental ruthlessness, whatever foreign commentators might think. Putin's standing at home had in fact been enhanced by his uncompromising response to the terrorists.

China, as ever, was harder to read. Astonishing economic growth continued in parallel with the expansion of foreign trade and investment, whatever challenges they might imply for ideology and the governing monopoly of the Communist Party. Yet relations with the USA hardly improved, encumbered as they were by Taiwan and Chinese misgivings over US strategic policy. Even given the stimulus of the two countries' common concern with danger in North Korea, this remained true. The Chinese leadership may have been immobilised by fear of a North Korean economic collapse and the subsequent meltdown of a communist regime such as had occurred in Eastern Europe in the 1980s. Meanwhile the leadership underwent a renovation, or at least a reshuffle, from which emerged in the ascendant the obscure figure of Hu Jintao, and an enlarged Politburo.

Almost at once it had to face a crisis over North Korea. There had already occurred a mysterious and not fully explained incident when a shipment of ballistic missiles from North Korea had been detected on its way to the Yemen. Now, in December, the North Korean government denounced the restraints imposed by the UN on its nuclear programme and expelled the UN inspectors charged with maintaining them. It also accused the USA of planning a pre-emptive attack on it. The motive for this new stridency remained obscure, but it was alarming. China's relations with Russia, South Korea, and Japan, as well as those with the USA, were bound to be tangled in any imbroglio over North Korea.

Clearly, as the year ended, world history was once more going to roll forward as a blend of the familiar (sometimes long familiar) and the surprising. The existence of an ultimate US hegemony was incontestable, but revealed little in itself. Problems old and new would, unsolved, complicate 2003. Perhaps most symbolic of the uncertainties that lay ahead, a claim was made from Canada as the year closed that the first successful cloning of a human being had been achieved by a religious cult. True or false, that should have awoken deep uncertainties and anxieties, even if it was not yet the business of international leaders.

2. THE INTERNATIONAL ECONOMY

AT the end of 2001 global economic analysts had been reluctant to use the word "recession". A year later they were just as hesitant about uttering another "r" word—"recovery"—at least without attaching a string of qualifiers such as "tepid", "unbalanced", "fragile", or "stuttering". From senior policy-makers to average people on the street, many heads were being scratched concerning the state of affairs in 2002. Had the USA and other major national economies embarked on a genuine turnaround? If so, why did it feel so "joyless", and where were the new jobs that would normally be associated with recovery? In many respects, the statistics demonstrated improvement, albeit modest, over 2001. The IMF estimated that global economic growth had improved to 2.8 per cent in 2002 (up from 2.2 per cent in 2001), while the World Bank, which calculated it differently, measured the 2002 rate at 1.7 per cent (up from 1.1 per cent in 2001). In addition, overall world trade, which had contracted in 2001, expanded by about 2 per cent in 2002, according to preliminary figures. However, on the negative side, foreign investment to developing countries declined significantly, and the world continued to exhibit a potentially dangerous "over-dependence" on conditions in the USA. The final verdict on 2002 would probably depend ultimately on how matters proceeded in 2003 and beyond. If progress ensued, 2002 was likely to be characterised as an acceptable beginning. Should the economic ship founder, however, many would write off 2002 as a false start, full of anomalies and startling challenges to several of the global system's most basic tenets.

Notwithstanding this uncertainty, some aspects of 2002 were all too clear. For instance, investors hated it. They suffered losses for the third year in a row, the worst such sequence since the Great Depression. World stock market indexes plunged 20 per cent (the biggest decline since 1974), and their cumulative losses since the start of 2000 reached some 43 per cent. The Dow Jones Industrial Average in the USA fell 16.8 per cent, while the Nasdaq composite index of high technology stocks plummeted 22 per cent, pushing its three-year loss to a stunning 67 per cent.

Surprisingly, considering the possible repercussions from the terrorist attacks on 11 September 2001, financial markets were relatively stable in the first part of 2002. However, they proved less resilient in withstanding the shock waves emanating from the series of corporate scandals that erupted in the spring. Even though the Enron collapse of late 2001 had alerted investors to the fact that corporations were capable of chicanery of unprecedented magnitude in the wake of the collapse of the high-tech "bubble", the breadth and depth of the malfeasance uncovered in 2002 was of a scale greater than even the most ardent anti-capitalist might have dared to dream. WorldCom, Inc., previously a darling of many investment analysts, was revealed to be a house of cards, its disgraced officers ultimately admitting that more than US$10 billion in expenses had gone unreported in recent company statements. The Chief Executive Officers (CEOs) of several major corporations were accused of "looting" hundreds of millions of dollars from company coffers, while others apparently profited immensely from illegal insider trading of stock. The reputations of large accounting firms were also severely tarnished when it became apparent that they had presented tainted, "blue sky" audits for corporations in fear that accurate but negative reports would cost them valuable consulting contracts with those same corporations. Finally, top investment banks acknowledged that their supposedly unbiased research departments had provided "overly rosy" analyses of new companies being handled by the banks. Not surprisingly, stock prices fell relentlessly as one mind-boggling revelation followed another. For its part, the US Congress quickly passed reform legislation that required CEOs and Chief Financial Officers (CFOs) to attest that corporate financial reports were accurate, a notion many investors were probably stunned to hear was not already part of the equation. In any event, by "oath day" in August, more than 200 companies had "restated" their earnings. In addition, regulators in December announced an agreement whereby investment banks would pay US$1.4 billion in fines and other costs and insulate their research activities from other bank functions. Meanwhile, by year's end, it was reported that some 186 US companies had declared bankruptcies totalling US$346 billion, up more than 40 per cent (in volume) from the previous record high set in 2001.

Amidst the market anxiety and distractions from the "year of CEO infamy", it was easy to lose sight of the fact that the US economy had rebounded significantly in several regards in 2002, with GDP growth of 2.5-2.8 per cent being achieved. The cornerstone of the advance was what one analyst called the US consumer's "unquenchable enthusiasm for spending", spurred on by record low interest rates that supported sales of expensive items such as houses and cars. In addition, worker productivity was up an estimated 5 per cent, largely a result of continued technological advances. (The high-tech revolution had not been all hype; the sale of the 1 billionth computer was commemorated in July 2002.) However, pessimists noted that most of the US acceleration had occurred in the first half of the year and that momentum had been lost in the last quarter as the realities of, among other things, severe pension fund losses, finally appeared to put a check on consumer spending. Joblessness was also a sobering influence, unemployment having reached 6 per cent of the workforce. Democrats attempted to make the economy the main issue in the November legislative elections, but they were trumped by the Republican emphasis on the "war on terrorism". Nevertheless, the Bush administration subsequently appeared to recognise the magnitude of the problem, the President installing a new team of economic advisors and promising to propose an extensive stimulus package in the near future.

Although most of Europe had joined the USA in the 2001 slide, it lost contact during the return trip in 2002. For those who had been waiting patiently for the "hour of Europe" to arrive, 2002 was yet another disappointing year. The "eurozone" managed GDP growth of only 0.8 per cent as European consumers proved much more frugal than their "indefatigable" US counterparts. Meanwhile, exports declined, already high unemployment rose even further in the face of the weak investment climate, and many countries faced difficulty in addressing long-standing inflexibility in labour and product markets. Germany, the continent's largest economy, again proved to be its weakest link. German GDP advanced by only 0.2 per cent for the year, while the country's leading stock market index fell 44 per cent, distinguishing itself as the worst performer in the world. As a result, the national budget deficit rose to 3.7 per cent of GDP, placing Germany in danger of becoming the first country to face action from the European Commission for violating the 3 per cent limit imposed through the Stability and Growth Pact of the 12-member European Monetary Union (EMU). (Such a rebuke would prove particularly ignominious for Germany, one of the most ardent supporters of the EMU during its formative stages.) France and Italy also experienced difficulty controlling their public finances in 2002, contributing to a continent-wide reassessment of the proper role for collective fiscal and monetary policies. For example, the European Commission argued that "too many rules" were impeding economic advancement and that insufficient attention was being given to trying to improve the manufacturing sector. Others criticised the European Central Bank for worrying inordinately about inflation and thereby implementing stimulus plans that were "too little, too late", especially in regard to interest rate cuts. (By contrast, interests rates in the United Kingdom reached a 38-year low in 2002 and were credited with supporting relatively liberal consumer spending and GDP growth of 1.6 per cent which, although down from 2001, still permitted the government to increase spending on a number of its favourite projects.) On a more positive note for the EMU, the replacement of national currencies with euro notes and coins on 1 January 2002 went as smoothly as euro-enthusiasts had hoped. The euro also strengthened by some 16 per cent against the dollar by the end of the year.

Russia registered another solid year of growth (about 4 per cent) in 2002 based primarily on relatively high oil prices, increased worker productivity, and surging disposable income. However, the latter also contributed to an ongoing high inflation rate of almost 15 per cent. In the broad view, Russia in 2002, as one journalist put it, took another major step toward becoming "a respected member of the world economic community", a fact underlined by the EU's decision in October to recognise the country formally as operating a market economy. As for the former Soviet republics and satellite states, the European Bank for Reconstruction and Development (EBRD) reported that, despite the global economic sluggishness, its funding to the central and eastern European countries had increased by 6 per cent to US$4.1 billion in 2002 in conjunction with a similar rise in the flow of private capital to the region. However, the EBRD decried the ongoing high level of corruption in the former communist states, the EU seconding that analysis by demanding that the Balkan states in particular act quickly to address the problem or face cuts in aid. Double-digit unemployment also continued to plague Bulgaria, Croatia, Romania, Poland, and Slovakia.

Asia was by far the top regional performer in 2002 (4.7 per cent growth with Japan excluded), led by another remarkable 8 per cent expansion of GDP in China, now recognised as the region's main engine for economic growth. (For example, China in 2002 moved past Japan as the top Asian exporter to the USA.) Advances in 2002 were attributed to China's developing status as the "world's assembly line", its inexpensive labour attracting factories from its Asian neighbours as well as from other countries around the world, such as Mexico, which were formerly the prime targets for industrial migration. A leader in nearly every category of manufactured goods, China benefited from a reported US$50 billion in foreign investment in 2002. Collaterally, it "soaked up" commodities from around the globe, imports such as steel soaring as the result of the lowering of tariffs associated with accession to the WTO in late 2001. Growing urban wealth underpinned a housing boom, while the burgeoning middle class also became a surprising source of growth for the regional tourism sector. In view of the obvious initial success of its decision to join the WTO, the Chinese government late in 2002 agreed to draft laws that would formally protect private investment, which had hitherto enjoyed only de facto protection. That action had been approved by a congress of the Chinese Communist Party in November which also accepted entrepreneurs into its central committee for the first time and pledged additional free-market reforms. Although still only one-ninth the size of the US economy, the Chinese economy appeared on track to meet projections that it would become the world's largest by the middle of the 21st century. However, analysts noted that widespread corruption in official circles could still prove a barrier to that goal. Meanwhile, although Taiwan reportedly jobs lost to the mainland in 2002, it returned to positive growth after suffering contraction in 2001.

Although Japan, depending on final fourth quarter figures, may have just crawled out of a formal recession in 2002, its performance was still a bitter disappointment to the international community, which had for several years been searching for a candidate to take the pressure off the USA regarding responsibility for the global economy. The Nikkei share price in Japan fell 19 per cent to its lowest point in nearly two decades, while official unemployment reached a record high of 5.5 per cent. Deflation also continued, sapping corporate profits and increasing the debt burdens that have been stifling the banking sector for more than 10 years. It seemed clear to most analysts that aggressive restructuring was required on the part of the banks, which had been funnelling money to inefficient corporations rather than face debt cancellations. Although the government of Prime Minister Junichiro Koizumi, installed in 2001, had promised reform and aggressive stimulus efforts, "political gridlock" subsequently hampered the implementation of these aims. In contrast, South Korea prospered in 2002 (achieving growth of over 6 per cent), but the overall small size of its economy precluded any significant offset of Japan's malaise.

After a dismal performance in 2001, most of the South Asian countries rebounded well in 2002. Malaysia, Singapore, and Thailand were all expected to finish the year with growth rates in excess of 4 per cent. Underachievers included Indonesia, which struggled with political upheaval. Burma remained internationally isolated and constrained by Western economic sanctions imposed in response to the country's abysmal human rights record. Rocketing prices for food and basic goods combined with a failing currency to apply added pressure on the government. In the sub-continent, India posted another good year with growth of 5 per cent, despite drought conditions in a number of northern agricultural states. Meanwhile, Bangladesh was named the most corrupt country in the world by

Transparency International, which noted in its annual report that corruption was a significant issue in about 70 per cent of the 102 countries that it had reviewed and that the position had deteriorated substantially in 2002. (Nigeria and Paraguay followed Bangladesh in the negative ranking, while Finland registered as the least corrupt in the world; the USA finished in 16th place.)

The Middle East and North Africa overcame a number of problems (poor weather, unstable currencies, and a precipitous drop in tourist arrivals arising from terrorism concerns) to post growth of about 2.5 per cent. As always, most of the region's fortunes rested on oil prices, which remained relatively high in 2002 under the influence of OPEC production cuts implemented in 2001. In a tangential development, the United Nations Development Program (UNDP) strongly criticised Arab governments for having failed in many cases to transform oil wealth into prosperity for all of their citizens. (Growth in per capita income in Arab countries had barely surpassed that of sub-Saharan Africa, the UNDP argued.) Meanwhile, Israel suffered its worst economic performance in over 50 years in 2002 as GDP declined more than 1 per cent and unemployment rose to almost 10.5 per cent of the workforce. A second year of the Palestinian intifada was deemed widely responsible for the contraction, as Israel continued to impose sanctions within the occupied territories which damaged its own economy, whilst also increasing military spending in pursuit of a seemingly unwinnable war. Even with the traditional infusion of huge amounts of US aid, the result was unsupportable deficits and austerity measures which contributed to the collapse of the national unity government.

By far the most troubled region in 2002 was South America, which to some observers was "falling apart" in the wake of Argentina's ongoing massive debt default, high financial anxiety in Brazil, and tumult in Venezuela. Capital flows to the region fell nearly 50 per cent, contributing to economic contraction for Latin America and the Caribbean of 1.1 per cent and the worst recession in two decades. As in 2001, attention focused on Argentina, which was forced to freeze billions of dollars in bank deposits for most of the year as it unsuccessfully attempted to negotiate a new debt agreement with the IMF. (Argentina's total debt was estimated at US$141 billion; about US$115 billion of that amount was in commercial debt, of which Argentina had defaulted on at least US$95 billion.) The "nightmare" also included a 70 per cent devaluation of the peso, a 10-11 per cent decline in GDP, and widespread emigration. Brazil, which had been bravely resisting contagion since 2001, appeared to lose that battle in mid-2002 when investor uncertainty precipitated a 30 per cent drop in the value of the real against the dollar. In September the IMF agreed to a 15-month, US$30 billion stand-by credit for Brazil (the largest such single IMF credit to date), and a meltdown was averted. However, the accord was contingent on the acceptance of strict economic targets by the leftist government elected in October. Paraguay and Uruguay, the two other members of the Southern Cone Common Market (Mercosur), were also adversely affected by the upheavals in their larger neighbours. Uruguay required emergency financing to stave off default in the face of its three-year recession, while Paraguay was described as "nearly broke". Chile, on the other hand, emerged as the region's "most open and vibrant economy" and was rewarded with a free trade agreement with the EU, effective 1 January 2003.

Although political factors were also at play, economic distress contributed to the brief overthrow of Venezuelan President Hugo Chávez in April 2002 by the military and, following his return to office, continuing efforts to force his resignation late in the year. The most alarming offshoot of the political chaos, as far as the international community was concerned, was the strike of national oil company workers in December, which reduced production from 3 million barrels per day to 200,000-400,000 barrels per day in the world's fifth leading oil-producing country. As a result of the sudden loss of oil revenue, GDP in Venezuela fell by nearly 1 per cent for the year.

Chávez's election in 2001 had been the first in a series of leftist victories in South America that in 2002 saw like-minded candidates gain national control in Brazil and Ecuador and local dominance in Peru. In addition, a Marxist performed very well in the Bolivian presidential election. Some analysts attributed the leftward shift to a growing sentiment among a significant segment of the population that the free-market reforms which had been trumpeted in the 1990s had failed, or at least not lived up to expectations. This was supported by evidence that the maldistribution of wealth in Latin America had in 2002 reached its worst proportion in 10 years. Analysts also contended that rampant corruption not only had undermined support for economic reform but also had drained confidence in democratic structures.

Africa "limped painfully on" in 2002, its 2.5 per cent growth rate failing by far to reach the level at which its myriad problems could be effectively addressed. The most positive development for the continent was a global increase in many commodity prices which, combined with favourable weather, contributed to agricultural expansion in Africa. However, conflict in and around the Democratic Republic of the Congo continued to hamper development efforts, in part due to UN sanctions against the sale of diamonds and other precious stones (which had in the past been used by rebel groups to buy arms) by several countries in that resource-rich area. Political turmoil in Zimbabwe also proved to be an economic hindrance to southern Africa as well as an embarrassing issue for the continent's leaders, who in 2001 had announced ambitious plans to include good governance as one of the primary pillars of the New Partnership for Africa's Development. Critics accused the Partnership of failing its first "peer review" test on the issue by choosing not to condemn the land seizures in Zimbabwe and other grave human rights abuses by the Mugabe administration. Also bothersome to analysts eager for a different approach to development were the initial aid requests from the Partnership, which appeared to comprise, as one reporter described it, "the same old shopping list of large infrastructure projects" that had produced inconsistent results, at best, for decades.

For its part, the Bush administration in Washington announced that it would establish a separate US agency, led by Secretary of State Colin Powell (who was well respected internationally), to disburse an additional US$5 billion in aid to developing countries over the next three years based in part on applicants' adherence to the rule of law, support for the democratic process, and endorsement of other good governance concepts. The new US plan was announced in March shortly before the UN's International Conference on Financing for Development, which reconfirmed the goal established in 2000 of reducing the number of people in the world living in poverty (currently estimated at 1.2 billion) by 50 per cent by 2015. Significantly, President Bush, in his address to the Conference, acknowledged the role that poverty could play in fomenting terrorism.

Another major international conference that attracted significant attention in 2002 was the August-September UN World Summit on Sustainable Development, at which the USA was harshly criticised for retreating from environmental targets established in 1992, particularly in regard to greenhouse gas emissions. Little of substance was accomplished at the session, although guidelines were published for corporations to provide an analysis of the social and environmental impact of their activities in annual reports. (More than 2,500 corporations reportedly were including such analyses as of the end of the year.) A degree of progress in international economic cooperation was also apparent in a July agreement by central bankers and regulators from most developed countries to increase the amount of money that banks were required to set aside for emergency use in case of extensive loan defaults. The measure was designed to guard against potential financial meltdowns such as those that occurred in several regions in the second half of the 1990s, requiring massive rescue packages from the IMF, World Bank, and creditor countries.

On a less positive note from the perspective of global integrationists, most observers concluded that enthusiasm for new global trade negotiations, launched with great fanfare at the WTO's meeting in Doha, Qatar, in 2001, had dwindled by the end of 2002. Retrenchment was noticeable in the EU's insistence on maintaining its extensive agricultural subsidies and the Bush administration's decisions to impose tariffs to protect the US steel industry and to boost government payments to US farmers (both measures reflected significant domestic political concerns). Emphasis appeared to be turning toward bilateral talks, the USA, for example, signing a free trade agreement with Chile and preliminarily endorsing a similar accord with Singapore. More than 20 other negotiations toward bilateral or limited multilateral free trade agreements were reportedly underway around the globe. It was unclear what effect such strategy would eventually have on overall global economic development. In any event, as of the end of 2002, global attention was appropriately more concerned about the short term which, among other things, offered the potential for a US-led attack on Iraq (and possible collateral disruption of oil supplies), further disruption in Venezuela, additional terrorist attacks throughout the world, and increased tension in East Asia resulting from North Korea's renewed nuclear weapons programme. At best, the crystal ball was obscured by some glowering clouds.

The 2002 Nobel Prize for Economics was shared by Daniel Kahneman (a dual US-Israeli citizen and professor of psychology and public affairs at Princeton University) and Vernon L. Smith (a US citizen and professor of economics and law at George Mason University) for their separate work in the field of evaluating economic behaviour, particularly that which appeared to violate long-held economic theories. Both men have also been prominent in applying laboratory experiments to economics, a concept that remained controversial among some traditionalists who argue that only "real-world" actions should be evaluated. Kahneman, much of whose research was done in collaboration with the late Amos Tversky, had conducted experiments that demonstrated that people routinely made seemingly irrational economic decisions, often depending on the language used in presenting the available options. The Royal Swedish Academy of Sciences lauded Kahneman for having laid the groundwork for a "new field of research" by bringing psychological insights to bear on economics. Analysts described Kahneman's research as valuable in explaining why, for example, people continue to pump money into a stock market "bubble" long after the point where rational analysis would call for a halt to such investment. Smith, also well-known for arguing that traditional economic textbooks failed adequately to predict behaviour, had concentrated on trade and "bargaining" decisions by, among other things, "testing" alternative market designs in a laboratory setting prior to their implementation.

II WESTERN AND SOUTHERN EUROPE

1. UNITED KINGDOM—SCOTLAND—WALES—NORTHERN IRELAND

i. UNITED KINGDOM

CAPITAL: London   AREA: 245,000 sq km   POPULATION: 58,800,000 ('01 census)
OFFICIAL LANGUAGES: English; Welsh in Wales   POLITICAL SYSTEM: multiparty monarchy
HEAD OF STATE: Queen Elizabeth II (since Feb '52)
RULING PARTY: Labour Party (since May '97)
HEAD OF GOVERNMENT: Tony Blair, Prime Minister (since May '97)
MAIN IGO MEMBERSHIPS (NON-UN): NATO, CWTH, EU, OSCE, CE, PC, OECD, G-8
CURRENCY: pound sterling (end-'02 US$1=£0.6244, €1=£0.6498)
GNI PER CAPITA: US$24,230, US$24,460 at PPP ('01)

THERE was much to celebrate in the UK in 2002, in spite of unease over both the world economy and the threat of terrorism. Queen Elizabeth II celebrated her Golden Jubilee, marking 50 years on the throne, and the depth of popular support evident throughout those celebrations came as a surprise to many commentators. The economy performed well relative to many other developed countries, a dramatic change from the days when the UK was known as the "sick man of Europe". In international affairs, the UK enjoyed a high profile through its close alliance with the USA. Taken together, such factors helped to account for the fact that historians were beginning to write about the "end of declinism" in the UK, or the perception that the nation had been in a century-long decline from great power status.

PARTY POLITICS. The Labour Party remained dominant in UK politics in 2002; its lead in the opinion polls fell to five points in September, perhaps due to fears about war with Iraq, but was back up to 11 points in October (with Labour on 43 per cent, the Conservatives on 32 per cent, and the Liberal Democrats on 20 per cent). The Conservatives, under their new leader Iain Duncan Smith, failed to make a comeback. In the local council elections in May, however, the Conservatives did gain some 220 seats and regain control of several councils, including Richmond, Barnet, Redbridge, and Enfield in London. They polled slightly more votes than Labour on a turnout of 35 per cent. In experiments with all-postal voting in some wards, turnout went up an average of 28 per cent (to 57.38 per cent in Gateshead, for example), although similar experiments with online voting and voting via mobile phones produced much smaller increases in turnout. As a result of the elections, the Labour Party ended up with control of 63 councils, a net loss of eight, and the Conservatives with control of 42 councils, a net gain of nine. The Liberal Democrats were in control of 15 councils, a net gain of two, although they unexpectedly lost control in Sheffield where Labour regained some of the seats which it had lost in recent years. Other parties had control of two councils (including Wyre Forest district council, where the Kidderminster Health Concern party took control, after its success returning an MP to Parliament in 2001) and there were 52 councils with no party in overall control, a net decline of five. The Labour party had a total of 2,402 councillors, a net loss of 339, while the Conservatives were up 237 at 2,005, and the Liberal Democrats up 45 at 1,263. The number of independent councillors fell 79 to 136 and there were 101 councillors from other parties, a net increase of two. In general, commentators considered that all the parties had had successes and failures in these elections, but that the Conservatives had not done enough to constitute a breakthrough or to suggest a serious challenge to Labour's dominance. Conservative and Labour Party shares of the vote were about equal, at 34 and 33 per cent respectively, with the Liberal Democrats polling 27 per cent.

The "other party" councillors included three members of the far-right British National Party (BNP). These were the first seats which the party had won since a council by-election in Tower Hamlets' Millwall ward in the mid-1990s. The three BNP councillors were elected in Burnley, out of the 66 BNP candidates standing in various wards around England, and the party's share of the vote in Burnley went up from that in the 2001 general election. However, the BNP failed to win any seats in nearby Oldham, although it took an average share of 28 per cent of the vote in the five wards which it contested. In Millwall its share of the vote was only 3.7 per cent. In November, however, the party made a further gain at a Blackburn council by-election, winning Mill Hill ward by 16 votes.

In seven places, the first direct elections for mayors were held, with Labour candidates winning in Doncaster, Lewisham, and Newham; a Liberal Democrat in Watford; a Conservative in North Tyneside; and independents in Hartlepool and Middlesbrough. The Hartlepool winner, Stuart Drummond, had campaigned as H'Angus, the monkey mascot of the local football club, with the promise of free bananas for schoolchildren, although when elected he said he would be working to improve children's nutrition and to crack down on hard drug users.

Over the rest of the year, the Conservative Party's showing in council by-elections was not very encouraging under Duncan Smith's leadership. The party suffered a net loss of council seats in English local by-elections. In 243 local by-elections the Tories gained 24 and lost 31 seats, an overall loss of seven seats, and in particular they had gained only nine seats from the Liberal Democrats while losing 18 to them. In contrast, the Liberal Democrats gained 14 seats from Labour whilst losing only two. At the Liberal Democrat conference at the end of September Charles Kennedy, their leader, called upon party supporters to eclipse Conservatives and thereby become the second party of British politics. The conference also agreed to ringfence national insurance contributions to fund the National Health Service (NHS), with pensions coming instead from general taxation, and set out plans for public service reform with a large-scale devolution of power to regional and local levels.

In a shadow Cabinet reshuffle in July, Iain Duncan Smith removed party chairman David Davis, who had been accused of disloyalty and of hindering the party's modernisation, appointing him instead to shadow the Deputy Prime Minister, John Prescott, and replacing him with the party's first-ever female chair, Theresa May. Addressing the Tory conference in October, she told the party that it had to change. "Twice we went to the country unchanged, unrepentant, just plain unattractive. And twice we got slaughtered." The party's base was "too narrow and so, occasionally, are our sympathies. You know what some people call us? The nasty party." She called on Tories to reach out "to all areas of our society", and upon local associations to appoint more women and ethnic minority candidates. By the end of the year, however, she was still calling for this as just nine women and one ethnic minority candidate had been chosen to contest 60 winnable seats at the next general election.

In his own speech at the conference, Iain Duncan Smith said that people should "not underestimate the determination of a quiet man", suggested that the Conservatives had begun the "slow, hard road back to power", and received a seven-minute ovation from the hall. Twenty-five policy proposals were announced at the conference, including the scrapping of Advanced (AS/A2) Levels, giving schools control of budgets and policies, charging for abuses of the NHS, imposing longer sentences on young offenders and New York-style neighbourhood policing, extending the right-to-buy to housing association tenants, and reducing means-testing for pensioners. However, the leopard-print shoes which Theresa May wore when delivering her speech received almost as much press coverage as any of these ideas.

At the Labour party conference, Tony Blair set out his vision of an "enabling state", calling on the party to support him in speeding up reform of health, education, and criminal justice. He said that Labour was best when it was boldest and argued that state schools and hospitals should be able to offer the choices which had been assumed to be available only in the private sector. The government suffered a defeat, however, on 30 September, when delegates voted 67 per cent to 33 per cent for a review of the private finance initiative (PFI), currently being used to fund improvements in public services such as health. Despite Paul Boateng's speech saying that the review would "hold up those schools and hospitals we promised at the last election" and it being clear that the review would not be implemented, a compromise statement supporting PFI but calling for talks to avoid a two-tier workforce was rejected by 54 to 46 per cent.

There were continuing arguments within the Conservative Party in the latter part of the year, and suggestions that there might be another leadership contest, especially when Michael Portillo and Kenneth Clarke were among eight Tory MPs who rebelled against the leadership on 4 November to vote in favour of government proposals to allow gay and unmarried heterosexual couples to adopt children. Duncan Smith had imposed a three-line whip on Conservative MPs to vote against the government, but as well as the eight voting for the measure, 35 Tory MPs stayed away altogether and shadow pensions minister John Bercow resigned because he could not support the three-line whip. The following day Duncan Smith made a statement calling on the party to "unite or die" behind his leadership and saying that "the Conservative Party wants to be led. It elected me to lead it in the direction that I am now going. It will not look kindly on people who put personal ambitions before the interests of the entire party."

Just before the Conservative Party conference in October, what would once have been an enormous scandal had broken when former Conservative Cabinet minister Edwina Currie published her diaries, revealing that she had had a four-year affair with former Conservative Prime Minister John Major from 1987 until he became a Cabinet minister. Her diaries were serialised in *The Times*, causing enormous surprise and provoking Major to say that it was the event in his life of which he was "most ashamed".

The biggest political scandal of the year, however, did not concern an actual politician, but the Prime Minister's wife, Cherie Blair, who was accused of covering up her connection with a convicted fraudster, Peter Foster—the boyfriend of her friend, Carole Caplin—who had helped negotiate the purchase of property in Bristol for her. She initially denied any relationship with him, but e-mails proved that he had been involved in the flat purchase. After several days of successive revelations and hostile press coverage, she made a personal statement saying that she had acted instinctively to protect her family's privacy. The furore eventually died down, although a mid-December poll found that two-thirds of voters thought that the government had been damaged by the affair. But however unpopular Cherie Blair might have been, and whatever damage was done to her husband by association, voters were not turning to the Tories for comfort. A *Guardian*/ICM poll on 17 December put the Conservatives at 27 per cent, 14 points behind the Labour Party and only four points ahead of the Liberal Democrats, their lowest showing for four years.

At the beginning of the year, the scandal over special advisers at the Department of Transport, Local Government and the Regions ran on, with claims that political advisor, Jo Moore, who had famously suggested that 11 September, 2001 was a good day to bury bad news, had meant to release bad rail statistics on the day of Princess Margaret's funeral, but was blocked by communications director Martin Sixsmith. On 15 February Moore resigned and it was also announced that Sixsmith had resigned, although later it was disputed whether he had, in fact, agreed to resign or not.

Legislation promised in the Queen's Speech at the State Opening of Parliament on 13 November included several bills on reforming the criminal justice system: ending the "double jeopardy" rule so that criminals could be retried after acquittal in cases "where new and compelling evidence emerges"; further controlling anti-social behaviour; reforming the laws on sexual offences; and improving international co-operation against crime. In the public services, there would be greater freedom for successful hospitals and more power and resources devolved to NHS frontline staff, and local authorities would be given the duty to support older people waiting to be discharged from hospital. There would be reform of railway regulation and a railway accident investigation branch would be established. Legislation would be put forward to allow referendums on regional governance in England, and there would be a decision by June 2003 on whether to recommend UK entry to the European single currency after an assessment of the five economic tests. The UK's aid budget would be increased, and there would be reform of secondary schools to "promote opportunity and choice through greater diversity for parents and pupils" and of universities to "improve access and build on excellence".

In Scotland, the image of its Parliament was not improved when the First Minister, Labour MSP Jack McConnell, was accused of obstructing enquiries into his constituency party's accounts, after £11,000 was claimed to be missing. An internal investigation cleared McConnell of wrongdoing, but exposed infighting in the local Labour Party. There was also criticism of the cost of the new Scottish Parliament building at Holyrood, which had originally been estimated at £40 million but was costing over £300 million, including £28 million of extra bomb-proofing put in after 11 September.

The National Assembly in Wales, like the Scottish Parliament, rejected the possibility of top-up fees for university students, instead introducing a means-tested "student support grant" which would average about £935 a year for about 55,000 students. They also went their own way on the NHS, abolishing prescription charges for under-25s and over-60s and rejecting in November the idea of autonomous foundation hospitals as inappropriate for Wales. The First Minister, Rhodri Morgan, said in October, however, that the Assembly still had "a long way to go" in convincing Welsh voters that it was worthwhile. In the Cabinet changes following the resignation of Estelle Morris as Education Secretary in October, Peter Hain, MP for Neath, became the Welsh Secretary. He had been a junior minister in the Welsh office when devolution was being introduced.

In Northern Ireland, the peace process was stalled, if not going backwards. Distrust between Unionists and Nationalists came to a head in October when police raided Sinn Féin's Stormont offices and other places in Belfast, on suspicion of an IRA spy ring. Denis Donaldson, Sinn Féin's head of administration and a former IRA prisoner, was among those arrested. Sinn Féin denounced the raid as a politically motivated attack on the "Good Friday" Agreement, but the Democratic Unionist Party removed its two ministers from the power-sharing executive on 11 October, and the First Minister, David Trimble, threatened to withdraw Ulster Unionist ministers if Sinn Féin were not removed from the executive. The Social Democratic and Labour Party (SDLP) would have opposed Sinn Féin's exclusion, and without its support such a measure could not have been passed by the assembly. On 14 October the Northern Ireland Secretary, John Reid, signed an order suspending devolved government in Northern Ireland. Intensive discussions with the political parties and the Irish government had failed to find a way through the problems, and he believed this was the only way "to safeguard the progress made and tackle the remaining challenges". The Northern Ireland Office therefore took over the departments previously run by the executive, and devolution there was back on hold; it was the fourth suspension in less than three years, although two of these had only been for one day.

Barbara Castle, Baroness Castle of Blackburn, died on 4 May 2002 (see XVIII). She was a Labour MP from 1945 to 1979, and had served as a Cabinet minister under Prime Minister Harold Wilson. After leaving Westminster she spent some time at the European Parliament in the 1980s, and was an active campaigner for pensioners' rights. Among other political figures who died during the year was Baroness Young of Farnworth, who died in September 2002 (see XVIII). She had held a variety of offices in Conservative governments, including serving as Leader of the House of Lords from 1981-83.

THE GOLDEN JUBILEE AND THE ROYAL FAMILY. 2002 marked the Golden Jubilee to celebrate the 50th anniversary of the reign of Queen Elizabeth II. The first half of the year was one of sadness for the monarch, however, who lost her sister in February and her mother at the end of March (see XVIII). Princess Margaret, 71, died peacefully in her sleep in the early hours of 9 February due to complications following the third stroke that she had suffered in recent years. Her funeral, held on 15 February in Windsor, was a relatively subdued and private affair, attended by the royal family and around 450 other mourners. The service was held in St George's Chapel on the 50th anniversary of the burial of her father, King George VI. A frail but determined Queen Elizabeth, the Queen Mother, was present at the burial of her younger daughter. Princess Margaret had expressed a wish to be cremated, and her ashes were later interred in the royal vault under the chapel near her father's tomb.

Queen Elizabeth, the Queen Mother, died on 30 March aged 101. Born Lady Elizabeth Bowes-Lyon on 4 August 1900, she married the Duke of York (later King George VI) on 23 April 1923, becoming Queen following the abdication crisis in December 1936. Prince Charles spoke movingly in public following his grandmother's death. "She was quite simply the most magical grandmother you could possibly have, and I was utterly devoted to her," he said. On the eve of her funeral on 9 April, her four grandsons held a symbolic vigil around her coffin in Westminster Hall. For days, thousands of mourners had queued for hours to pay their respects, a mark of the deep popular affection in which she was held. It was estimated that around one million people lined the route of the funeral procession.

Close attention was paid to the protocol surrounding the death and funeral of the Queen Mother, which had long been expected and prepared for. This did not pass without controversy. BBC presenter, Peter Sissons, attracted criticism when he appeared on camera the morning following her death wearing a maroon rather than a black tie. Public anger was aroused in India when the 108 carat Koh-i-noor diamond, at the centre of a royal crown, was placed on top of the coffin. The Koh-i-noor had originally been presented to Queen Victoria in 1849 by Lord Dalhousie. It had been taken from Duleep Singh, the young maharajah of the Punjab, following the British annexation that resulted from the Sikh army rebellion of the mid-19th century.

A row blew up between the press and the Prime Minister's office in the weeks following the funeral, over allegations that the Prime Minister's private secretary, Clare Sumner, had sought to inflate his role during the lying-in-state. An official complaint made by the Prime Minister's office on 23 April to the Press Complaints Commission was later dropped, however, when it became clear that the government's version of the story was at odds with the recollection of Sir

Michael Willcocks, the former general who was currently serving as Black Rod in the House of Lords.

Bowing to pressure, Buckingham Palace made public the outline of the Queen Mother's will in mid-May. Full disclosure was not made, however. As a result of a deal struck with John Major's government in the 1990s, the Queen would not have to pay inheritance tax on her mother's estate, valued at between £50 million and £70 million. Normal rates of tax would have been levied at 40 per cent once the value of an estate exceeded £250,000. The sovereign's tax arrangements were based on the need to preserve her financial independence as well as to compensate her for not being able to earn her own living. However, this news generated further controversy over the constitutional role of the royal family.

The extent of genuine popular participation in the Golden Jubilee celebrations, for which two days' national holiday were declared on Monday 3 and Tuesday 4 June, came as a welcome relief to the royal family. Coinciding with the soccer World Cup (see XVI), the weekend was billed as the UK's biggest royal celebration for a generation, and was marked by more than 4,000 parties registered up and down the country, including street parties, garden parties, parties in the pub and on the village green. A series of 1,952 beacons was lit across the UK, the Channel Islands, and the Commonwealth. In London, the Queen hosted concerts in the gardens of Buckingham Palace for which a lottery of tickets had been held and large screens set up in the Mall. This included a pop event on Monday evening, complete with guitarist, Brian May, from the group Queen performing on the roof of the palace, the heavy metal artist, Ozzy Osborne, and a group rendition of the Beatles' classic "All You Need is Love". On Tuesday, celebrations reached a climax with a ceremonial procession from Buckingham Palace to St Paul's Cathedral for a service of thanksgiving. Parades in the afternoon culminated in a balcony appearance of the royal family and an RAF flypast down the Mall. It was estimated that over a million people were out on the streets of central London for this, and the sight of the Queen in her Golden Coach was broadcast around the world. It was, for a change, a masterpiece of public relations for the monarchy, and was widely viewed as a reminder of the deep popular affection in which this institution was still held by many.

The collapse of the trials of two former palace butlers in the autumn, however, marked a return to the gossip and scandal which were the more normal royal fare in the UK tabloid press. Both trials had been delayed in order not to coincide with the Golden Jubilee celebrations. The trial of Princess Diana's former butler, Paul Burrell, who had been charged in August 2001 with stealing 342 items belonging to Princess Diana, Prince William, and Prince Charles, collapsed on 1 November after the Queen came forward with information which undermined the prosecution. Why the Queen did not intervene at an earlier stage of the prosecution remained an intriguing and unanswered question, with some commentators suggesting that she had halted the trial in order to prevent Burrell from entering the witness box and giving evidence that would have been embarrassing or damaging to the royal family. Burrell, cleared of all charges, subsequently sold his story to the press. The related trial of Princess Margaret's former butler, Harold Brown, over similar allegations, collapsed on 3 December. Several weeks of intense press coverage of these events revealed a disturbing picture of life inside the royal household.

On 21 November Princess Anne, the Princess Royal, became the first member of the royal family to be convicted of a criminal offence when she pleaded guilty to a charge under the Dangerous Dogs Act. Dotty, a three-year-old English bull terrier, bit two children as they walked in Windsor Great Park on 1 April. The Princess was fined £500 for the attack and ordered to pay £250 in compensation and £148 in costs at a magistrates court in Slough. After hearing evidence of Dotty's "placid" nature from royal dog psychologist Roger Mugford, district judge Penelope Hewitt spared the animal's life but ordered that it must undergo training and be kept on a lead in all public places.

RELIGIOUS AFFAIRS. 2002 was a year in which religious leaders called for mutual understanding and dialogue between faith groups, often in the face of hostility from fundamentalist believers. The Queen made her first visit to a mosque when she visited the Pakistani Social Cultural and Islamic Centre in Scunthorpe at the beginning of August. This was one of many initiatives designed to lend support to the 1.8 million British Muslims, and to promote interfaith understanding. On the first anniversary of the terrorist attacks of 11 September 2001, the Muslim Council of Britain repeated its condemnation of terrorism. However, it also acknowledged that the preceding year had been a difficult one for Muslims in the UK. Muslim leaders complained about the unfair impact of anti-terrorist legislation, which permitted suspected terrorists to be incarcerated indefinitely without trial.

Britain's Chief Rabbi, Jonathan Sacks, attracted controversy in the second half of the year with the publication of a book entitled *The Dignity of Difference*, which argued in favour of dialogue between even extremist religious groups. Difference, he wrote, was not a problem to be managed, but an "essential" part of creation and something to be celebrated as coming from God. Some passages in the book, however, outraged conservative rabbis, who interpreted his remarks as an attack upon Israeli government policy at a time of deep crisis for the state of Israel. Sacks called for understanding on both sides, and revealed for the first time that he had been engaged in secret discussion with Muslim clerics through the offices of the UN since 2000.

On 27 July it was announced that Rowan Williams, the Archbishop of Wales, had been appointed by Tony Blair to succeed George Carey as Archbishop of Canterbury. Widely viewed as a bold choice, Williams soon lived up to predictions that he would take an active view of his role in public life as well as in the life of the Anglican communion. Although in some ways a theological conservative, Williams was known to take a liberal view on homosexuality—an issue which threatened to divide the Anglican Church internationally—and his appointment drew criticism from conservative evangelical elements within the Church of England. The appointment was formally confirmed at the beginning of December at a ceremony in St Paul's Cathedral, although the new Archbishop would not take up his public ministry in his new role until February 2003 after his installation at Canterbury Cathedral. An indication of his new approach came on 18 December when he delivered the 2002 Dimbleby Lecture, broadcast on BBC television. "If it is true that the nation state has had its day and that we are—whether we like it or not—already caught up in a political system both more centralised and more laissez-faire," he declared, "we are bound to ask whether there is a future for the reasonable citizen, for public debate about what is due to human beings, for intelligent argument about goals beyond the next election. My conclusion is that this future depends heavily on those perspectives that are offered by religious belief."

As in the USA, Roman Catholic Church leaders in the UK faced public criticism in 2002 over their past handling of child abuse allegations. In November, a former priest, Michael Hill, was jailed for five years for child abuse. The case attracted attention particularly because of the controversial decision in 1985 of Cormac Murphy-O'Connor, currently serving as the Cardinal who led the Catholic Church community in the UK, to appoint Hill as chaplain at Gatwick Airport, in spite of his past history. However, it was unclear at the end of 2002 whether the Catholic Church in the UK would succumb to the extent of controversy that had befallen the Catholic Church community in the USA. UK church officials appeared to have followed a relatively robust policy towards offenders, with 21 priests convicted between 1995 and 1999 and others cautioned.

INDUSTRIAL UNREST. Industrial relations deteriorated during the second half of 2002, reviving memories of the 1978-79 "Winter of Discontent" which had doomed the Callaghan government to electoral destruction. Attention focused particularly on the Fire Brigades Union (FBU), which balloted in favour of a series of strikes, beginning on 13 November, over a 40 per cent pay claim. FBU leaders argued that a rise of such magnitude was necessary because of the extent to which pay in the fire service had fallen behind the rest of the economy in recent years. The initial 48-hour walkout led to a new round of negotiations between the FBU and local authority employers. With only hours to go before the eight-day stoppage that began on 22 November, it appeared that a deal had been struck, based on a 16 per cent settlement in return for modernisation. However, talks broke down when the government refused to approve the deal. From this point, the dispute escalated into an outright confrontation between the union movement and the government.

FBU leader Andy Gilchrist claimed that the government had intervened to prevent the deal from proceeding. The government alleged that the FBU was not serious about changing its restrictive working practices. It was clear that the Treasury feared that a generous settlement would trigger a series of inflationary pay claims in the public sector, undermining confidence in Chancellor of the Exchequer Gordon Brown's economic policy. The Cabinet was determined to demonstrate that it could be "tough" on union militancy. As industrial action threatened to spread to the other sectors, including transport and education, John Monks, the normally loyal leader of the Trades Union Congress (TUC) warned on 23 November that pressure for further public sector wage rises would continue to grow unless government plans to reform working practices were matched by a long-term public sector pay policy. By the beginning of December, the confrontation had become overtly political. At a rally in Manchester, Gilchrist declared "I'm quite prepared to work to replace New Labour with what I'm prepared to call Real Labour".

During the period of the strikes, the army rolled out its 800 "green goddess" fire tenders, acknowledged to be less effective than the far larger pool of modern equipment normally at the disposal of the fire service. Predictions that this would lead to a serious breakdown in emergency cover proved ungrounded, and striking firefighters proved willing to assist during serious incidents. However, Admiral Sir Michael Boyce, chief of the defence staff, spoke publicly of his concern about the effect that the strike was having on morale in the armed forces. Leave was postponed as a result of the dispute, and many soldiers were sent from service in the Balkans to train as firefighters. With the prospect of a war with Iraq looming in the new year, this would mean a long uninterrupted stretch of service in extremely stressful circumstances. Basic pay for junior service personnel, moreover, started at £12,000 per year, far lower than the wages under dispute by the FBU.

Meanwhile, the government-appointed fire services review, under the chairmanship of Sir George Bain, was boycotted by the FBU. Reporting on 15 December, it called for an 11 per cent pay rise over two years, and a package of reform in working practices that would imply a loss of more than 3,000 jobs in the service. The report was dismissed by the FBU. Deputy Prime Minister John Prescott, however, was determined to proceed with the implementation of many of the recommendations in the report, including the controversial introduction of charges to insurance companies for the costs of attending road traffic accidents, to commercial operators for fire safety advice, and to recover the costs of false callouts. Prescott also refused to rule out the closure of many stations in order to improve efficiency in the service.

Meanwhile the FBU continued to prove willing to negotiate with employers through the Advisory, Conciliation and Arbitration Service (Acas). This process, running in parallel with the government response to the Bain report, successfully averted a third walkout, scheduled for 16 December. However, by this time the government and FBU were virtually ignoring one another.

On 18 December veteran union leader Brendan Barber was named as the next general secretary of the TUC, replacing John Monks in May 2003 when the latter was due to take over the leadership of the European TUC in Brussels. Barber had built his reputation as a "fixer" in the labour movement, and had played an extremely active role in keeping open channels of communication during the fire dispute. Considered to be a Blairite, he nevertheless did not hesitate to criticise the government for its role in exacerbating the dispute. Barber, who had been a TUC insider for more than 25 years, faced the tough challenge of rebuilding a constructive relationship between the government and the country's 70 unions and seven million union members. By the end of 2002, this looked far from likely in the short term.

RURAL AFFAIRS. Animal welfare lobbyists began 2002 determined to pressure the government to honour its commitment to introduce a bill banning fox hunting in England and Wales. Their cause received an historic victory on 13 February, when the Scottish Parliament voted by 83 to 36 votes in favour of the Protection of Wild Mammals (Scotland) Bill. This made mounted fox-hunting, fox-baiting, and hare-coursing criminal offences punishable by a £5,000 fine or up to six months in jail. Rural protestors vowed to challenge the new law, warning that there would be revolution in the countryside if similar legislation were introduced in other parts of the UK.

In spite of such threats, at the end of February Blair announced his intention to permit a free vote on hunting, apparently hoping to find a middle way between an outright ban on hunting and a continuation of the status quo. However, hunting remained an issue that deeply divided public opinion as well as Westminster, where MPs were overwhelmingly opposed to blood sports and peers just as firmly in favour. On 18 March MPs backed a full ban on hunting by 386 to 175 votes. In the House of Lords on the following day, peers voted for hunting to continue under licence by 366 to 59 votes, a sign that the upper house had softened its earlier intransigent opposition to any change in the status quo. However, peers were infuriated several days later when Rural Affairs Minister Alun Michael announced his willingness to use the Parliament Act to impose the Commons' will and force an outright ban.

The government planned six months of consultation in order to seek a compromise that would prove acceptable to the majority on both sides. In September, a three-day public consultation was organised at Westminster in co-operation with pro- and anti-hunting groups. The extent of rural opposition to a ban was underscored on 22 September, when an estimated 400,000 protestors attended the "Liberty and Livelihood" march in central London, organised by the Countryside Alliance. Organisers presented Tony Blair with a list of 10 demands on hunting, farming, and the provision of local services. Of these, the right to hunt was promoted as the "touchstone" of rural unrest.

With public debate still highly polarised, the government introduced an amended hunting bill at the beginning of December that attempted to offer MPs and peers a compromise position. The bill proposed a ban on hare-coursing and stag-hunting, while protecting other forms of hunting, such as angling and falconry. Fox-hunting with dogs could continue under the terms of the bill, with the permission of an independent registrar, provided that packs could demonstrate a need to carry out the hunt and meet standards of minimum cruelty. On 16 December MPs voted by 368 votes to 155 in favour at the second reading.

ASYLUM AND IMMIGRATION. In February Home Secretary David Blunkett presented his white paper on immigration, "Secure Borders, Safe Haven", containing a package of measures. These included a range of initiatives designed to encourage immigration among skilled workers and young people to cover areas where there were labour shortages. Regarding asylum seekers, he proposed to establish gateways abroad in co-operation with the UN High Commission for

Refugees, to encourage legal entry into the UK. The controversial voucher scheme would be phased out by the end of 2002, and a four-tier system of refugee centres would provide for induction, accommodation, reporting, and removal, as appropriate for individual cases. The white paper also proposed to introduce a citizenship "test", requiring applicants to demonstrate knowledge of the English language and British politics and culture. The use of arranged marriages as a means of entry from the Indian subcontinent was to be curtailed, by extending the probation period for new marriages to two years in order to detect fraudulent claims. Strengthened immigration service teams would help to identify illegal workers and their employers. Trafficking for sexual or labour exploitation would be made a criminal offence.

On 15 February, the £100 million Yarl's Wood detention centre in Bedfordshire was destroyed when asylum seekers awaiting deportation lit a series of fires. The incident was allegedly triggered by the mistreatment of a woman resident of the centre, and unease grew later in the spring when it became clear that many of the potential witnesses had subsequently been deported before their evidence could be recorded. The incident embodied growing concern over the treatment of asylum seekers, as the Home Office tried to balance fair treatment with firmness.

In July, the Home Office announced that an agreement had been secured with the French to close the controversial Sangatte refugee camp near the entrance to the Channel tunnel at Calais. The camp had been used as a base for attempts to enter the UK illegally by many of its residents, causing regular disruption to train services through the tunnel. Housed in a warehouse complex owned by Eurotunnel, the camp was run by the Red Cross. Pressure for its closure increased at the beginning of the year after nearly 500 refugees from the camp had attempted to storm the tunnel at Christmas 2001. In December it was announced that the centre would close at the end of the month, four months ahead of schedule. As part of this deal, Blunkett agreed to accept 1,200 asylum seekers from Sangatte. The remaining 3,600 would remain in France.

TRANSPORT. Transport continued to be a topic of public controversy in 2002. In January Lord Birt, former director of the BBC and unpaid advisor to the government's Policy and Innovation Unit, was invited by the Prime Minister to provide long-term "blue sky" thinking on transportation policy. His appointment was widely interpreted as a vote of diminishing confidence in Transport Secretary Stephen Byers. Birt subsequently angered the House of Commons transport select committee by refusing to appear before it to discuss his views. Byers' position continued to weaken throughout the spring. In late May, the Commons' transport select committee published a damning report on the government's 10-year transport plan, which it labelled "ill-balanced" and "over-optimistic". Coming on top of a series of problems in the department (see AR 2001, p. 34), this proved to be the final straw for Byers, who announced his decision to resign on 28 May. His defenders within the government would subsequently charge that the chairwoman of the select committee, Gwyneth Dunwoody, had unfairly labelled him a failure after a relatively short period in office. His successor, Alistair Darling, was appointed Transport Secretary with the local government brief passing to John Prescott's Office of the Deputy Prime Minister.

Attention in 2002 continued to focus on the nation's railways. On 25 March Byers announced that £300 million would be set aside for the shareholders in Railtrack, the railway infrastructure company which he had put into administration in 2001 after a series of controversial failures. This enabled shareholders to be paid 244-255 pence per share when the government announced the sale of Railtrack to Network Rail on 27 June. On 3 October, the responsibility for the railways passed formally to Network Rail from Railtrack, ending its troubled six year record of stewardship of the country's track, stations, and bridges.

The railways suffered another tragic setback on 10 May, when seven passengers were killed in an accident at Potter's Bar in Hertfordshire. Blame was subsequently focused on the chaotic structure of the privatised system. Jarvis, the company sub-contracted by Railtrack to maintain the track, at first had claimed that the line might have been sabotaged, and subsequently blamed deficient track repairs on an incorrectly reported fault from Railtrack. Rail safety campaigners and trade unions expressed fury when it was announced in July that Jarvis's profits were up 85 per cent, from £24.8 million to £45.8 million. The surge was partly due to the award of a £250 million five-year contract from Railtrack to maintain the east coast main line, on which the Potters Bar accident had taken place. An interim report on the crash, published at the beginning of July, found that the accident had been caused by a set of points which had moved as a train passed over it, causing a derailment. Investigators found that 40 out of 300 nuts on other points around Potters Bar were not fully tightened, and that the points responsible for the crash had been wrongly assembled. On 30 September, relatives of victims killed in the Potters Bar train crash began legal proceedings against Railtrack, Jarvis, and the Health and Safety Executive, accusing the rail industry of going to "absurd lengths" to avoid admitting liability. Nina Bawden, the award-winning novelist whose husband, Austen Kark, died in the accident and who had herself sustained serious injuries, said the government owed it to the victims to launch a public inquiry.

With air travel growing at around 5 per cent per year in spite of the aftermath of 11 September 2001, long-term planning included the expansion of airport provision, particularly in the south east. At the beginning of the year, the government indicated its intention to produce a white paper by the end of the year, with provision for three new runways in the London region, including the possibility of a new airport at Cliffe, in the Kent marshlands. This latter idea was strongly opposed by environmentalists because of the area's importance as a bird habitat. By the autumn, it was clear that planning for expansion would be delayed for a year. The delay was partly due to a high court ruling in November that Gatwick must be included in the white paper, in spite of a previous agreement with the local council that there should be no expansion there before 2019.

Following a positive report from accountants Ernst and Young in February, the government announced its support for a partial privatisation of London's underground ("tube") system. But a public-private partnership (PPP) solution to the future development of the network continued to face strong opposition, led by London mayor Ken Livingstone and his transport commissioner Robert Kiley, who believed that the arrangements were potentially unsafe and would create a "funding gap" of £1.5 billion, which would need to be paid for by large fare increases or from public money. Under PPP the tube would be split into three main sections: two private consortiums, Metronet and Tube Lines Group, would control the lines and infrastructure under 30-year contracts; while the public transport authority, Transport for London, would continue to run trains and operate signals. At the end of December the Tube Lines Group took over responsibility for the Jubilee, Northern, and Piccadilly lines, with Metronet set to follow within weeks. The PPP deal would inject £16 million of investment in the underground system over the next 15 years.

There was a shift in government attitudes towards road building in 2002. In December, Alistair Darling presented a new transport plan, based on 23 studies of key transport problem areas commissioned by the government in 1998. Some £3 billion of the £5.5 billion investment programme was earmarked for new road schemes, including a £200 million tunnel to be built under Stonehenge. Environmentalists claimed that this represented a "U-turn" in transport policy, which had previously focused on investment in public transport.

EDUCATION CONTROVERSY. 2002 saw controversy focus on the credibility of the Advanced (AS/A2) Level examination system that prepared 16 to 18-year old secondary school students for university entrance. The administration of the examinations had been the subject of criticism in previous years, but came to a head in September when headteachers claimed that exam grades were being manipulated in order to limit grade inflation. Teachers were concerned in particular that many students predicted to receive top marks had fallen short of those levels. A report held by the exam watchdog body, the Qualifications and Curriculum Authority (QCA), concluded that teachers did not sufficiently understand the curriculum coursework. This only inflamed feelings in the schools and calls grew for an independent inquiry.

The government announced a full inquiry headed by Mike Tomlinson, retired head of the Office for Standards in Education (Ofsted). Reporting after only two weeks, the Tomlinson inquiry concluded that the crisis had been exacerbated by confusion and lack of clarity in the rush to deliver the new curriculum. QCA chairman Sir William Stubbs resigned after publicly criticising Education Secretary Estelle Morris. In October 300,000 papers were re-marked, but fewer than 2,000 students had their grades adjusted. Ron McLone, head of the Oxford, Cambridge, and RSA Examinations Board, stated that the crisis had proved to be "a storm in a teacup". But doubts remained over the future of the examinations, which were proving to be increasingly cumbersome in an expanded university sector. When Tomlinson's final report was published in December, however, it made few substantial recommendations for change.

The A-level affair was followed in October by a row over pupil exclusions. Teachers threatened to go on strike when an independent appeals panel overturned the decision of a school and its governors to exclude two pupils who had made death threats against a teacher. Morris intervened by demanding that the boys should be placed elsewhere, a step which exceeded her legal powers. The subsequent press attention proved to be the final straw for the Minister, who resigned as Education Secretary on 23 October. "If I am really honest with myself I was not enjoying the job. I could not accept being second best. I am hard at judging my own performance. I was not good at setting the priorities. I had to know I was making a difference, and I do not think I was giving the Prime Minister enough," she said.

Labour Party chairman Charles Clarke took her place. His first months in office were dominated by public debate over the future funding of the university sector. The government's target of getting 50 per cent of 18 to 30-year olds into some form of higher education by 2010, and increasing the number of university students from "non-traditional backgrounds", had been imposed without significant new investment in the sector. It had been clear for several years that the higher education system was seriously underfunded. The universities themselves estimated that the sector needed £10 billion of investment over the next three years in order to remain competitive and solvent; 50 institutions had been in deficit in the 2001-02 financial year. This was beginning to have a major impact on the sector. By the autumn of 2002 spending per student had halved since the 1970s, while academic pay had risen by only 6 per cent since the 1980s, compared to the labour market's 44 per cent . More and more staff members were employed on short term or part time contracts. Crisis-led management throughout the sector was found by the Commons select committee on education to be largely untrained, incompetent, and a major factor in the deteriorating morale of academic staff. Several institutions had proceeded with or were planning mergers in order to save through economies of scale. In London alone, the University of North London and Guildhall University merged in October 2002 to become London Metropolitan University. Controversial proposals presented in October to merge Imperial and University College, two of the constituent colleges of the federal University of London, and to introduce fees as high as £15,000, were dropped in the face of staff and student protests. But radical restructuring of the sector was bound to continue without new sources of revenue. It was estimated that there was an annual £1 billion shortfall just to keep university buildings and equipment in working order.

While there was general agreement about the need for increased revenue, the future structure of university financing was a major political problem. A white paper due in November was delayed by the new minister until the new year while a range of alternative funding methods were floated in public. Most experts agreed that some form of differentiated "top-up fee" was likely, so that student tuition would pay for a larger proportion of the highly subsidised university sector in the UK, which had traditionally been entirely public. Critics charged, however, that increased fees were incompatible with widening participation. In fact, middle-class families (who would not be exempt from tuition fees) were at the root of the problem. Government leaders recognised that this could be a potent source of dissatisfaction with government performance at the next election, and were wary of risking a middle-class revolt. British families, used to a higher education system paid largely out of general taxation, were understandably angry over the thousands of pounds it seemed likely to cost to send their children through the system. By the end of the year Clarke had indicated that he was likely to opt for a system of post-graduate payment in order to avoid this scenario, either through a loan system or some form of graduate tax.

THE ECONOMY IN 2002. Despite persistent fears and anxieties to the contrary, the UK economy fared comparatively well in 2002 as, unlike most other Western economies, it did not drift into recession. The economy performed not too far from its historical average of 2 per cent growth. Nevertheless, GDP growth did not match the 2 to 2.5 per cent predicted by Chancellor of the Exchequer Gordon Brown; instead, it grew at an estimated rate of around 1.6 per cent. GDP growth was strongest in the third quarter of the year, up by 0.9 per cent from the previous quarter. This distortion was due to the "Jubilee effect". The impact of the Queen's Golden Jubilee celebrations, which included extra bank holidays on 3 and 4 June, on the economy during the second quarter was statistically significant.

The Jubilee effect exaggerated the statistical recovery of the manufacturing sector, which appeared to show an increase of 0.7 per cent in the third quarter, breaking the trend of decline in the six previous quarters. Without the Jubilee effect, manufacturing output would have remained broadly stable through to October. Within the manufacturing sector there were positive increases, such as in motorcar manufacturing (up by 10.8 per cent), which had been strong for much of the year (with output mostly going to overseas markets); and in telecommunications, which did not appear to have been affected at all by the Jubilee. However, after October 2002 the manufacturing sector showed clear signs of contraction. According to the Confederation of British Industry (CBI), by December around half of all manufacturers estimated output to be below normal and only a minority believed that output had actually increased during the final months of 2002. This contraction was the result of several factors, some domestic, but mostly because of the continuation of poor international economic performance by the UK's main trading partners, the USA and the EU, as UK manufacturing industries exported a high proportion of their output to these regions. The UK's manufacturing exports to the USA declined by £400 million over the year, and largely contributed to the UK's historically worst goods deficit of £10.3 billion in November. This deficit was partly offset by a £1.2 billion monthly surplus on trade in services, leaving the overall trade deficit at £2.8 billion for the month. For this reason, business confidence at the end of 2002 was the worst it had been for a decade and business investment figures for the end of the year showed a drop of 9.8 per cent when compared to 2001. Even so, production remained broadly flat during 2002, with a slide beginning to become increasingly manifest in the last quarter of the year.

The construction sector continued to expand, with more new dwellings being built, and this sector registered its eighth successive quarterly increase. This condition was a reflection of the continuing strength of the property market, which had underpinned and fuelled the growth of the UK's economy during the year 2002. Despite some conflicting data, it would appear that house prices increased steadily until around August or September 2002, and then remained unchanged until the end of the year. The average price of a house was between £110,000 and £120,000, indicating an increase of between 24 and 30 per cent over the year. House price increases were most noticeable in the south east of England (around London), with most other regions showing more modest increases. In early December the UK's central bank, the Bank of England, indicated that it thought the property boom was unsustainable over the long run.

The substantial overall increases in property prices brought considerable liquidity into the UK economy. Mortgage and, more importantly, re-mortgage lending showed month-on-month increases, and during the middle of the year it was estimated that around £12.5 billion of mortgage equity had been withdrawn by home owners between July and September. It was estimated that re-mortgaging had paid for around two-thirds of the growth in consumer spending during 2002, the rest going to service household debt. Consumer borrowing was facilitated by low interest rates, with the Bank of England leaving its base interest rate unchanged at 4 per cent for the entire year. The Bank's decision not to alter the base rate reflected the uncertainty which it felt towards the rising cost of homes against its fear that an interest rate hike and the curbing of consumer spending would plunge the economy into recession. The strength of consumer spending during the year was the principal reason why the UK did not slip into recession during 2002. However, the sustainability of this trend was questionable, with the December financial stability review of the Bank of England showing that the household sector's debt-to-income ratio was at an all time high of 120 per cent during the year.

The dismal performance of the stock markets, both in London and abroad, contributed to the continuing property boom in 2002 as people saw high returns on property investment compared with negative growth in investments in stocks and shares. The London FTSE-100 share index of top companies roller-coastered up and down throughout the year, and ended valued at less than three-quarters of what it had been worth at the beginning of the year. Additionally, corporate scandals in the USA—in particular Enron and WorldCom (see IV.1)—cast a long shadow across the Atlantic, because of the close links between the London and New York stock markets, and because of the high volume of UK investment in US stocks and shares. Fear of war with Iraq also contributed to investor nervousness. A rally of the London stock market in October was greeted with relief by investors and, although the general bearishness of the market was not entirely dispelled, its performance for the rest of year was relatively stable.

A factor indirectly influencing the strong demand for property was the pensions crisis brought about by the revelation of mis-selling of personal pension schemes by brokers, the inability of Equitable Life (a important provider of pensions) to pay out promised levels of pensions to its shareholders, the closure of final salary pension schemes by many companies (including the pension provider Prudential), and changes to tax laws that deprived relief to company pension funds. At the same time, the government announced its intention that the burden on the public purse for pensions would not increase beyond the current 5 per cent of GDP, and it urged people to save more for their old age. To this end, the government produced a green paper in October 2002, which suggested, among other things, that the retirement age should be extended to 70 and that the pensions system should be simplified to encourage people to save. However, with a property market steadily outperforming all other methods of saving, housing continued to appear to be one of the safest places to invest savings for many.

The high cost of property, particularly in the south east of England, led to fears of possible wage-push inflation. The firefighters strike in October 2002, with a demand for a basic pay of £30,000 (which would have meant an increase of 40 per cent), appeared to give credence to such fears. However, overall public sector pay increases were modest. Evidence from the CBI suggested that private sector pay increases were only running slightly ahead of inflation because of firms' determination to keep costs down.

At the end of 2002, the UK inflation rate had risen to 2.8 per cent, its highest level for more than four years and higher than the Bank of England's target rate of 2.5 per cent. According to National Statistics, much of this increase could be accounted for by rising property prices. Even so, higher motoring costs and higher costs of clothing and footwear contributed to the trend, and there was a suspicion that, taking into account cheap credit and low interest rates, retailers had put up their prices, particularly towards the end of the year. However, consumers showed that they were discriminating when spending money, leading to disappointing retail sales before the Christmas season, traditionally the highest of the year. Reports of poor trading depressed share prices in some retail firms; the clothes retailer Next was worst affected with a £200 million reduction of its share value. Dixons, the largest electrical chain, posted a profits warning after lower than average December sales. In all events, retail sales actually rose by 1.1 per cent compared to November.

The UK's tourist industry, which had been hit hard the previous year by the 11 September terrorist attacks and by the foot and mouth disease crisis, stagnated in 2002 with only a 1 per cent increase in the numbers of visitors from abroad. However, in consequence of the growing "tourism deficit", with more than 15 million people leaving the UK for their holidays, the British airline industry showed strength, with consolidation (notably EasyJet with Go in May) and the growth of low cost airlines. EasyJet's £4 billion order for 120 aircraft from Airbus Industrie was the largest aircraft purchase of the year by any airline. Additionally, British Airways, Europe's largest airline, which was heavily dependent on transatlantic travel, actually showed a modest pre-tax profit of £65 million in August 2002 after suffering massive losses in the final quarter of 2001. The airline had undertaken a radical restructuring programme over the year, including staff redundancies and aggressive cost cutting, which appeared to be paying off.

During 2002 unemployment drifted upwards, although there was a drop in the numbers claiming unemployment benefits. The fall in the claimant count in October led to an historic 27 year low in the unemployment rate of 3.1 per cent. However, the labour force survey, which included those not claiming benefits, suggested that in September the jobless figure was 1.5 million, the highest for two years. These apparently contradictory figures reflected sectoral lay-offs, particularly in banking where the recently unemployed did not tend to claim state benefits. Generally high consumer spending had meant that the service sector had absorbed many of those who found themselves unemployed in other sectors, but not by enough to prevent the slightly upward unemployment trend.

Rising unemployment and the performance of the UK economy led to lower than expected tax revenues for the government. In November Chancellor Brown, in his pre-budget report to the House of Commons, announced that the government would downgrade its estimate of the UK's economic growth and double its expected borrowing to £20 billion in 2002, and to over £100 billion over the next five years. The increases in borrowing would help fund the increases in public spending, which the Chancellor had announced earlier in the year, and the military build-up in advance of a possible war with Iraq.

The prospect of the UK's adoption of the euro remained in the balance. During the middle of the year, the slippage in the value of sterling against the euro led to the hope that conditions would become more propitious for UK entry. In December, the banking and financial sectors were disappointed that the government had not indicated more firmly its intentions on this matter. Government quiescence was the result of continuing hostility to the adoption of the single currency by most British voters and its preoccupation with averting a domestic recession in the midst of a worldwide one.

EXTERNAL RELATIONS AND DEFENCE. At the beginning of 2002, UK troops who had taken part in military operations in Afghanistan against the Taliban and al Qaida took the lead for the first six months of the new International Security Assistance Force (ISAF) set up to support the Afghan Interim Authority (see VIII.1.ii). In that six month period ISAF, which was made up of troops from 19 countries, mounted 2,185 joint patrols with Afghan security forces in and around Kabul; disposed of nearly 3 million munitions (of which 80 per cent were anti-personnel landmines); trained the 1st Battalion of the new Afghan National Guard, which helped to ensure the security of the Loya Jirga; and completed about 200 humanitarian aid projects, many in response to the earthquake in northern Afghanistan in late March. ISAF was led by Major General McColl, who signed the agreement for its deployment with the then Afghan Interior Minister, Mohammad Yunis Qanouni, on 4 January 2002. The leadership of the force was handed over to Turkey on 20 June and "Task Force Jacana" was withdrawn, reducing the number of UK troops in Afghanistan from over 4,000 to about 2,000. One British soldier from the Royal Anglian Regiment died on 9 April 2002 after an incident during a security patrol in Kabul, but not due to hostile action.

Elsewhere, there were UK troops serving in Kosovo as part of the NATO-led Kosovo Force (K-For) peacekeeping troops, with about 3,000 people working there in the capital, Pristina, and an area extending up to the north-east boundary with Serbia. Norway, Finland, Sweden, and the Czech Republic also contributed personnel to that area, where the aim was to support the UN interim administration, build security, tackle organised crime, corruption and extremism, and help displaced people to return. In Bosnia, about 1,900 UK personnel were working with the NATO-led Stabilisation Force (S-For) operations in Banja Luka and the north west of Bosnia, with troops from Canada and the Netherlands. Their tasks included reforming the armed forces and arresting people indicted for war crimes, as well as providing support for the UN High Representative and help for displaced people, and working against organised crime, corruption, and extremism.

International attention had long left the Balkans, however, and early in 2002 it shifted away from Afghanistan after US President George Bush's 29 January speech describing Iraq, Iran, and North Korea as an "axis of evil" (see IV.1). Jack Straw, the UK Foreign Secretary, was initially cautious in his response to this phrase. However, by February the Prime Minister, on his way to the Commonwealth Heads of Government Meeting (see XI.3.i), said the President "is right to raise these issues and certainly he has our support in doing so". UK troops, of course, were already serving in the Gulf, with RAF Tornados and Jaguars continuing to take part in patrolling the no-fly zones in southern and northern Iraq. They came under periodic attack from Iraqi forces, to which they responded with what the Ministry of Defence called "accurate and measured military actions to deter further attacks". The Royal Navy was also involved in the effort to intercept vessels breaking UN sanctions against Iraq.

During the year, the likelihood of a war against Iraq in which the UK would be involved grew, despite mixed feelings among the UK population and politicians about whether such a war would be justified, especially in the absence of full UN backing. By early July there were reports that the UK would contribute 30,000 troops to the campaign, and Bush and Blair were believed to be discussing what should happen in Iraq if Saddam Hussein were removed from power. In December, London hosted a conference of Iraqi opposition leaders to discuss this problem, which agreed "guiding principles" for constructing a democratic Iraq. On 24 September the UK government had published its "dossier" on Iraq, which had been promised for some time. In Blair's foreword to the dossier, he stated firmly that he believed "the assessed intelligence has established beyond doubt . . . that Saddam has continued to produce chemical and biological weapons, that he continues in his efforts to develop nuclear weapons, and that he has been able to extend the range of his ballistic missile programme. I also believe that, as stated in the document, Saddam will now do his utmost to try to conceal his weapons from UN inspectors." In consequence, it was argued, the UN inspectors must be allowed back to complete their work, and if they were not, or were impeded, "the international community will have to act". Commentators were not all convinced by the dossier, however, as it did not present much new evidence of Iraqi capabilities and intentions. A further dossier, on Iraqi human rights abuses, published by Jack Straw on 2 December, was also criticised, not because the abuses were doubted but because it was thought to be a propaganda effort in advance of a military campaign; an Amnesty International spokesman called it "opportunistic and selective". Public opinion remained divided at the end of the year, with a December survey of European opinion by the US Pew Research Group finding that 75 per cent of Britons asked believed that Saddam Hussein must be removed; but when asked if this should be done by force 47 per cent said "no", and 47 per cent "yes". This compared with 71 per cent saying "no" in Germany and 64 per cent in France.

Within the Labour Party there was considerable unease about war with Iraq. Former US President Bill Clinton attempted to allay this when he spoke to the Labour Party conference in October, arguing in favour of acting against Iraq via the UN and telling delegates to trust Tony Blair. An emergency debate in the Commons on 24 September saw 53 Labour MPs vote against the government's position on Iraq, and in a Commons debate on a government motion on 25 November, 32 Labour MPs voted for a Liberal Democrat amendment which sought to preclude military action without explicit UN authority. There was also speculation that Cabinet ministers like Development Secretary Clare Short, who had questioned the wisdom of the war, might resign if the UK participated in an attack upon Iraq without UN authority.

Other European leaders were not as supportive as Blair of President Bush's stance on Iraq. The French, for example, fought hard in the UN Security Council for a resolution which would not allow the USA and UK to act against Iraq without UN authorisation. Eventually unanimous agreement was reached on 8 November for a US-UK resolution warning Iraq of "serious consequences" if it failed to disarm itself of weapons of mass destruction. Anglo-French relations, however, had already suffered another blow when French President Chirac and Blair had a public row over the EU's Common Agricultural Policy and the UK rebate at a European Union summit on 25 October. The following week, the Anglo-French summit due to take place in December was postponed.

By contrast, the strength of the Franco-German alliance, when it worked, was shown again at the EU's Copenhagen summit on 12-14 December (see XI.4). The summit successfully agreed the enlargement of the European Union by 10 additional member states, including the Greek-controlled part of Cyprus, but the UK's arguments for an early date for negotiations with Turkey—something also supported by Spain, Italy, and Greece—were unsuccessful. It was finally agreed that these should begin "without delay" after a progress review in December 2004, and the final summit statement described Turkey as "a candidate state destined to join the union", but this was much less than had been hoped for by advocates of Turkish entry (see II.4.vii).

The possibility of continuing terrorist attacks, and whether one might take place in the UK, hit headlines again in December. The Foreign Office had been criticised for failing to warn tourists about the dangers of travelling to Indonesia before the Bali bomb in which 26 Britons were among the nearly 200 who died (see IX.1.vi), and announced that it would review the way that it gave travel advice.

Alongside the Iraqi issue, Tony Blair attempted to push the Middle East peace process during the second half of the year, telling the Labour Party conference at the beginning of October that "by this year's end, we must have revived final status negotiations and they must have explicitly as their aims an Israeli state free from terror, recognised by the Arab world, and a viable Palestinian state based on the boundaries of 1967". US unconditional support for Israel and opposition to any such settlement, however, meant that by the end of the year such negotiations had not been revived; but on 16 December Blair announced a conference to be held in January 2003 to attempt to help the Palestinians prepare for running their own viable state. Representatives of Saudi Arabia, Egypt, and Jordan were invited, as well as the Quartet group—the US, the UN, the EU, and Russia—which had been discussing a comprehensive peace settlement. Tony Blair announced the conference after a meeting with the Syrian President, Bashar al-Assad. A year previously, al-Assad had criticised Tony Blair at a joint press conference over Israel and the attacks on Afghanistan; the meeting in 2002 marked an improvement in their relationship.

As part of her Golden Jubilee celebrations, the Queen visited Jamaica, New Zealand, and Australia in late February and early March, despite the recent death of her sister, Princess Margaret. There were suggestions that the visits would not be very successful, given the discussions in Australia about becoming a republic, and comments from the New Zealand Prime Minister at the start of the Queen's visit that she fully expected New Zealand to be a republic in 10 or 20 years' time. However, 57 per cent of Jamaicans reportedly believed the Jubilee to be important, and the Queen received a warm welcome there. She was also well received in New Zealand and in Australia, where over 30,000 people came to hear her address at Queensland's "People's Day" fair in Brisbane on 3 March. In the autumn, coverage in the UK of her visit to Canada concentrated mainly on the day that her water taxi broke down while crossing the freezing Red River in Winnipeg, but she was once again well received, and a poll published to coincide with her visit showed that 84 per cent of Canadians thought she did a good job, although 48 per cent were in favour of ending Canada's formal ties with the monarchy.

As part of her visit to Australia, the Queen was present in Coolum on 2 March for the Commonwealth Heads of Government meeting (CHOGM). One of the issues discussed there was whether and what action should be taken against Zimbabwe. Relations between the UK and the Zimbabwean government under Robert Mugabe did not improve during the year. Tony Blair argued at the CHOGM meeting on 2-3 March that Zimbabwe should be suspended from the Commonwealth immediately, but the meeting agreed instead to defer the decision until the presidential elections had taken place. When the elections did take place the following weekend, Commonwealth observers declared that they had been deeply flawed, and condemned the violence and intimidation which had taken place, much of it instigated by Mugabe's supporters (see VII.2.iii). On 19 March, South African and Nigerian Presidents Thabo Mbeki and Olusegun Obasanjo, and Australian Prime Minister John Howard met in London on behalf of the Commonwealth and agreed to suspend Zimbabwe from the councils of the Commonwealth for one year. In June the British High Commissioner in Zimbabwe, Brian Donnelly, was accused of supporting insurrection against Mugabe's government; and in July a *Guardian* correspondent was ordered to leave the country although he had been acquitted of breaking a new press law. At the beginning of September Mugabe attacked Blair in his speech to the Earth Summit in Johannesburg. Overshadowing Blair's comments, in which he had said that he had a passion for Africa, Mugabe responded that "we do not mind having and bearing sanctions banning us from Europe; we are not Europeans; we have not asked for any square inch of that territory. So, Blair, keep your England and let me keep my Zimbabwe." By the end of the year, there were calls for the English cricket team to boycott World Cup matches scheduled to be held in Zimbabwe in 2003.

ii. SCOTLAND

CAPITAL: Edinburgh   AREA: 78,313 sq km   POPULATION: 5,062,000 ('01 census)
OFFICIAL LANGUAGES: English/Gaelic   POLITICAL SYSTEM: devolved administration within UK
HEAD OF STATE: Queen Elizabeth II (since Feb '52)
RULING PARTIES: Labour & Liberal Democrats (since May '99)
HEAD OF GOVERNMENT: Jack McConnell (Labour), First Minister (since Nov '01)

THE legal processes following from the 1988 Lockerbie bombing (see AR 1988, p. 38) were completed during the year. Abdel Baset Al-Megrahi lost his appeal against his conviction, and was transferred to Barlinnie Prison in Glasgow to serve the remainder of his life sentence. Accommodation was arranged in Glasgow to enable Al Megrahi's family to visit him. In March Camp van Zeist in the Netherlands, which had been legally part of Scotland during Al Megrahi's trial and initial detention, was formally transferred back to Dutch sovereignty.

In July the final administrative steps were taken to the creation of Scotland's first national park, in the Loch Lomond and Trossachs area. This was an area of natural beauty, close to the central belt of Scotland and so both popular with visitors but under threat of unsuitable development. There was considerable debate throughout the year about the boundaries of the proposed Cairngorm National Park, with some arguing for the inclusion of areas of upland Angus and Perthshire. Advocates of narrower boundaries said that a tighter definition of the Park would facilitate planning processes.

In December a serious fire destroyed some of the historic buildings in the Canongate area of the old town of Edinburgh. Fortunately, the fire was contained before it spread to the better known parts of the World Heritage Site. As the year ended, the cause of the fire was unknown but it was thought to be accidental. There was an active debate about whether the rebuilding should seek to replicate the lost buildings or should be modern in style.

The Scottish Parliament and Executive made little impact on the strong feeling of political apathy in Scotland. One cause was the continuing rise of the cost of the new Scottish Parliament building, calculated by the end of the year to be at least £325 million, with the opening of the building delayed until at least August 2003. However, Parliament did deliberate on some innovative legislation, including one bill to provide permanent accommodation for all homeless people by 2012. Attempts were made to associate the First Minister, Jack McConnell, with financial improprieties in his Motherwell and Wishaw constituency office. These concerned questions about the accuracy of accounting in the office and the declaration of trade union subscriptions. An enquiry exonerated him from personal involvement. He thus became the first First Minister to hold office for a full calendar year. With the resignation on personal grounds in May of Wendy Alexander from her post as Enterprise Minister, the Scottish Executive lost one of its more popular and higher profile members. There were no major by-elections during the year. In the council by-elections, the only perceptible trend was low turnout and a small swing to the Conservatives, who gained three seats, and against Labour, which lost five.

A significant shift in the social structure of Scotland was brought about by the decision of council house tenants, in Glasgow in April and in Dumfries and Galloway in July, to accept the transfer of their housing from local authority control to non-profit housing partnerships. Historically, council tenancy had accounted for a high proportion of the Scottish housing stock, especially in the industrial cities, and the decision, therefore, represented a major privatisation. The decision of the Scottish Executive to buy the Health Care International private hospital at Clydebank, which was in some financial difficulties, and to transfer its administration to the National Health Service, however, represented a shift towards public rather than private sector provision of services.

On the economy, there was an important positive development with the opening of the Rosyth-Zeebrugge ferry service, saving transport costs between Scotland and continental Europe for freight and passengers. Throughout the year, however, the future prospects of the fishing industry and associated food processing activities became increasingly bleak. Successive reports to the European Commission had made it clear that the stocks of certain white fish, particularly cod, haddock, and whiting, in the North Sea were becoming too small to ensure the sustainability there of these species, and some had argued for a complete ban on fishing for cod in 2003. In the event, a deal under the EU Common Fisheries Policy was struck in mid-December, with UK white fishing vessels restricted to 15 days at sea each month. Permitted cod catches were cut by 45 per cent, haddock by 50 per cent, and whiting by 60 per cent. Much of the UK white fishing fleet operated out of Scottish harbours, particularly from north-east Scotland where fish processing was also a significant source of employment. Initial reactions from Scottish fishing leaders were that, unless the EU produced significant compensation, up to 20,000 jobs could be at risk in Scotland with little immediate prospect of alternative employment.

In the run-up to the celebrations of the Golden Jubilee of Queen Elizabeth II, Stirling was selected as Scotland's sixth city. The choice was controversial, with other candidates, particularly Paisley, feeling that they had at least as strong a case. The death of Queen Elizabeth, the Queen Mother, had a strong resonance in Scotland because her childhood home was at Glamis Castle, in Angus, and latterly she had bought and restored the Castle of Mey, in Caithness. She had been a regular visitor to Scotland throughout her life. The Scottish Parliament was recalled from recess on 3 April to enable it to pay tribute to her.

In sport, the year started on a high note with the UK women's curling team, all from Scotland, winning a gold medal at the Winter Olympic Games in Salt Lake City, (Britain's first Winter Olympics Gold Medal since 1984), but ended with some recriminations as the joint Scottish-Irish bid to host the Euro 2008 Football Championships was unsuccessful.

iii. WALES

CAPITAL: Cardiff   AREA: 20,755 sq km   POPULATION: 2,903,000 ('01 census)
OFFICIAL LANGUAGES: Welsh & English   POLITICAL SYSTEM: devolved administration within UK
HEAD OF STATE: Queen Elizabeth II (since Feb '52)
RULING PARTIES: Labour & Liberal Democrats (since Oct '00)
HEAD OF GOVERNMENT: Rhodri Morgan, First Secretary (since Feb '00)

ON the political front, this was a largely uneventful year. Although general criticism of the National Assembly for Wales increased, there was also evidence of considerable support for enhancing the Assembly's powers so that it might become comparable to the Scottish Parliament. The Welsh Assembly government, with the Labour-Liberal Democrat coalition still intact, continued under the leadership of the First Minister Rhodri Morgan. The Liberal Democrat leader, Mike German, returned to the Assembly's Cabinet in June after a year-long investigation into allegations of financial irregularities relating to a previous post, the crown prosecution service having decided that there was insufficient evidence to prosecute him.

The Welsh Assembly government was prepared, where possible and appropriate, to pursue policies which were at variance with those of central government. This was particularly true in education and health. Education Minister Jane Davidson announced in February that grants for students from low income families would be reintroduced in Wales, at a cost of £44 million. The average grant was likely to be only £935, however, and only the very poorest students (an estimated 55,000 of the student population) would be eligible to apply.

There was also a different agenda pursued for health service reorganisation in Wales to that proposed for England. From April 2003 the existing five health authorities would be replaced by 22 health boards, matching local authority boundaries, with the aim of improving healthcare by streamlining bureaucracy. It was expected that the restructuring would be cost-neutral but grave doubts were expressed from within the National Assembly and externally that this would not be the case. In December the Auditor General, Sir John Bourn, cast doubt on the viability of the restructuring and in the same month the Health Minister responsible for the reforms, Jane Hutt, was heavily criticised when it was announced that targets for reducing hospital waiting lists had not been achieved.

In November the Minister for Culture, Jenny Randerson, announced a new plan for promoting a bilingual Wales, with the aim of increasing the number of Welsh speakers by 5 per cent by 2011. Some £27 million was to be spent on schemes to support the Welsh language over the next three years, with the introduction of the language to pre-school children being given a high priority.

The October reshuffle of the Westminster Cabinet saw the appointment of Peter Hain as Secretary of State for Wales in place of Paul Murphy. That Hain continued to hold his existing European portfolio, however, was an indication of the diminishing role of the post of Secretary of State in the governance of Wales.

In a speech in December, and with an eye on the forthcoming Assembly election campaign in 2003, Rhodri Morgan stated that he favoured equity over choice and the "fundamentally socialist aim of equality of outcome". He opposed Prime Minister Tony Blair's plans for foundation hospitals and specialist schools and suggested that there should be "clear red water between Wales and Westminster".

The Welsh economy, with its high dependence on the manufacturing sector, was increasingly exposed by the continuing global economic stagnation. The closure of clothing factories in small towns such as Cardigan and Fishguard during the year had a devastating effect on local economies. The company involved, Dewhirst, transferred its operations to Morocco on the grounds that labour costs there were substantially cheaper. Traditional industries continued to suffer, with the expected demise of the Ebbw Vale steelworks being followed by the unexpected closure of the Allied Steel and Wire factory in Cardiff. The Welsh Assembly government emphasised the need to invest in new technology and, following the success of the Swansea Technium, another technium was planned for St Asaph in north-east Wales, with the aim of boosting the optoelectronic industry in the area. Some £100 million was also to be spent on improving broadband communications in Wales, an investment believed to be crucial to future prosperity.

One economic indicator, property prices, suggested a more prosperous outlook. According to the Principality Building Society, Wales's largest independent financial organisation, house prices rose by nearly 17 per cent during the year and the average cost of a home in Wales was £83,246. However, concern was expressed about the limited opportunities for local young people to enter the housing market in the face of competition from incomers from more prosperous areas. This problem was particularly acute in Welsh-speaking communities and the pressure group, Cymuned, continued to gather support, particularly over opposition to local authority unitary development plans such as that proposed by Ceredigion County Council.

The effects of the outbreak of Foot and Mouth disease in 2001 (see AR 2001, p. 53) continued to cast a shadow over the agricultural industry. The 20-day rule on the movement of livestock was criticised by farmers as being unnecessarily restrictive and members of rural communities throughout Wales were active in protests organised by the Countryside Alliance. The holding once more of agricultural shows, including the Royal Welsh Show at Llanelwedd in July, was welcomed.

In the summer, the announcement that a Welsh-speaking Welsh bishop, Rowan Williams, was to be the next Archbishop of Canterbury caused much celebration in Wales but consternation in some quarters. The first Welshman for a thousand years to be so appointed, Williams was seen by some traditionalists as being too radical in his views, although many others recognised his breadth and vision and his capacity to communicate effectively.

The most dramatic event of the year was the kidnapping of a south Wales businessman, Peter Shaw, by rebels in the former Soviet republic of Georgia. Shaw, who had been living in Georgia for six years as a financial adviser for Agrobiznesbank, escaped from his captors in November, having been incarcerated in a hole in the ground for five months.

On the sporting front, Welsh rugby continued in disarray but, under the astute managership of Mark Hughes, the Welsh soccer team remained unbeaten during the year. Creditable draws against the Czech Republic and Argentina and a 1-0 win against Germany earlier in the year were followed by an autumn campaign which saw Wales win all three of its opening qualifiers for the European Championship, including a memorable and thoroughly deserved 2-1 victory against Italy in front of a capacity crowd at Cardiff's Millennium Stadium. These successes opened the possibility that Wales could qualify for a major international football tournament for the first time since the 1958 World Cup.

iv. NORTHERN IRELAND

CAPITAL: Belfast   AREA: 18,843 sq km   POPULATION: 1,685,000 ('01 census)
OFFICIAL LANGUAGES: English, Irish & Ulster Scots   POLITICAL SYSTEM: devolved administration within UK
HEAD OF STATE: Queen Elizabeth II (since Feb '52)
RULING PARTIES: Ulster Unionist Party (UUP), Social Democratic and Labour Party (SDLP), Democratic Unionist Party (DUP) & Sinn Féin (since Dec '99)
HEAD OF GOVERNMENT: David Trimble, First Minister (since July '98)

NORTHERN Ireland's political landscape continued to be dominated by the uncertain future of the 1998 "Good Friday" Agreement (officially known as the Belfast Agreement—see AR 1998, pp. 44-51; 556-67) and the institutions created by it. On a day-to-day level the Northern Ireland executive, containing the Ulster Unionist Party, the Democratic Unionist Party, Sinn Féin, and the Social and Democratic Labour Party, functioned well. The North-South Ministerial Council and the British-Irish Council met regularly with intergovernmental co-operation proceeding in a number of fields.

Notwithstanding this, however, the underlying problems of Northern Irish society were never far beneath the surface. It took only two days into the new year for terrorism to claim its first victim: an Ulster Defence Association (UDA) member was killed while assembling a pipe bomb in Coleraine. Soon afterwards, a young Catholic postman was murdered by Loyalist paramilitaries. In a particularly grizzly punishment attack in November Loyalists crucified a man by nailing him to a fence. A new Loyalist feud was sparked off by the murder of a Loyalist Volunteer Force (LVF) member by the UDA apparently in a dispute over drugs. Several days later an east Belfast UDA brigadier was shot in the head. The attendance of the UDA's Johnny Adair, recently released from prison, at the LVF man's funeral sowed further dissension within the former organisation. In November the UDA and LVF declared a fragile truce. Dissident Republicans remained active as well. In February a Ministry of Defence civilian worker was critically injured in a bomb explosion at an army training camp; and in August a Protestant man was killed in a booby-trap blast at a Territorial Army centre in Londonderry. The Real IRA, however, seemed to be increasingly in disarray. In October, jailed members of the Real IRA issued a statement calling for the leadership of the organisation to stand down. It claimed that the leadership had "forfeited all moral authority" to lead the organisation: the Real IRA was at an end and only a few "corrupt" members of the group were "fraternising with criminal elements".

Communal tensions continued to erupt into violence in the sectarian interfaces of north Belfast. In May, significant sectarian confrontations spread into east Belfast. As the marching season began, the police alleged that Republicans were planning to orchestrate a riot on 12 July on Belfast's Ardoyne Road after the Parades Commission had ruled that an Orange Order march should be allowed to pass through a Nationalist area. A huge security force operation kept Catholics and Protestants separated. However, there was a riot on the Springfield Road in the west of the city. More rioting broke out in Portadown between Protestants and the police after the Orange march was banned for the fifth consecutive year from proceeding along the Nationalist Garvaghy Road. A dramatic example of the ongoing tensions was the decision of Neil Lennon, a Catholic playing for Glasgow Celtic football club, to announce his retirement from the Northern Ireland football team after receiving a death threat from Loyalists.

The Police Service of Northern Ireland (PSNI), which found itself in the forefront of these sectarian clashes, got its first Chief Constable when Hugh Orde, who had been probing allegations of security force collusion with Loyalists, was appointed. There was concern that too few Catholics were joining the new force. As part of future policing arrangements Catholic-Protestant recruitment had to be on a 50:50 basis. But instead of a maximum of 60 officers graduating, some of the classes had been as low as 34 because of a failure of Catholics to take up places. Tom Constantine, the US police officer monitoring the reform programme within the PSNI, claimed that potential recruits had been frightened off. Sinn Féin refused to endorse the revised policing arrangements and some political leaders appeared to be steering supporters away from considering careers as police officers. A review carried out by Her Majesty's Inspectorate of Constabulary into the PSNI's controversial Special Branch recommended a major overhaul of the unit. Special Branch had come under intense criticism for intelligence failures in the run up to the Omagh bomb in 1998 (see AR 2001, p. 56). Among the key recommendations was the need for early consultation with a senior CID officer on all proactive Special Branch operations. Regional police officers were also to be more closely involved in decisions about intelligence led operations. Chief Constable Orde accepted the recommendations but emphasised that he had no intention of dismantling Special Branch.

Politically, the Westminster Parliament lifted a ban on Sinn Féin's MPs using parliamentary facilities. Although the four Sinn Féin MPs continued to refuse to take their seats and would not make the oath of allegiance to the Queen, they were now able to use House of Commons facilities and receive office allowances. On 8 April, the Independent International Commission on Decommissioning (IICD) announced that it had witnessed an event in which the Provisional IRA leadership had put a varied and substantial quantity of ammunition, arms, and explosive material beyond use. The IICD made an inventory of the arms concerned. While the Democratic Unionist Party (DUP), which opposed the Good Friday Agreement, dismissed the event as insignificant, First Minister David Trimble, of the Ulster Unionist Party (UUP), argued that this second act showed that Republicans were involved in a process of decommissioning and made anti-Agreement Unionists look "foolish". In another conciliatory gesture, on the 30th anniversary of "Bloody Friday", when nine people were killed after a series of bombs exploded in Belfast in a single day, the Provisional IRA apologised for "all the deaths and injuries of non-combatants" caused by the organisation.

Concern still remained, however, as to whether the Republican movement was wholly committed to a lasting peace. Three alleged Provisional IRA members went on trial in Colombia for aiding terrorism there. Gerry Adams, the president of Sinn Féin, declined an invitation to testify before a US Congressional committee into terrorist activity in Colombia. The House international relations committee concluded that international terrorists had exploited a rebel-controlled safe haven in Colombia to create a new threat to international security. The report stated that members of the Provisional IRA had helped to train the Revolutionary Armed Forces of Colombia (FARC) in the guerrillas' former haven, together with members of groups from Cuba, Iran, and possibly the Basque separatist organization ETA. Back in Northern Ireland, on St Patrick's Day, three masked men raided a first floor office at Castlereagh police station in Belfast. A Special Branch officer was bound, gagged, and beaten during the raid and a number of documents were taken. The Provisional IRA denied involvement as police questioned senior Republicans.

In response to mounting pressure from Trimble, the Prime Minister, Tony Blair, set out new conditions to judge whether paramilitaries were holding to their ceasefires. In July, Blair said that paramilitary organisations should be stood down while the development of weapons and targeting of individuals should also cease. But he stopped short of outlining any new sanctions against parties linked to paramilitary groups. It was "no longer sufficient that there should be no terrorist violence—we have to be clear that preparations for violence have ceased. It is right that with the passage of time these judgments should become increasingly rigorous." To the anger of Sinn Féin and the Provisional IRA the government announced an independent monitor to assess the status of paramilitary ceasefires. This was not enough for the UUP, which announced in September that unless the Republican movement demonstrated that it was fully committed to non-violence, it would withdraw from the Northern Ireland executive in January 2003.

A full blown political crisis developed in October when police raided a number of Sinn Féin offices at the seat of the Northern Ireland executive, Stormont, as well as private addresses in Belfast, seizing hundreds of documents and arresting four people. Among those arrested was Sinn Féin's head of administration at Stormont. Documents seized included confidential correspondence between the Secretary of State for Northern Ireland and the Prime Minister. Allegations of a Provisional IRA spying ring at the heart of government brought the announcement of Trimble's resignation as First Minister. Before this could take effect, the UK government suspended devolution and reintroduced direct rule. Paul Murphy became the new Secretary of State for Northern Ireland with John Reid moved to the chairmanship of the Labour Party.

In a keynote speech in Belfast, Tony Blair stated that the Provisional IRA must remove its threat of violence in order for Northern Ireland's political process to succeed. The Prime Minister said "we cannot carry on with the IRA half in, half out of this process. Not just because it isn't right anymore. It won't work anymore... To this blunt question: 'How come the Irish government won't allow Sinn Féin to be in government in the south until the IRA ceases its activity, but unionists must have them in government in the North?' there are many sophisticated answers. But no answer was as simple, telling and direct as the question." Blair indicated that further inch-by-inch negotiation would not work and that symbolic gestures no longer built trust. It was "time for acts of completion". Effectively, therefore, Blair had raised the stakes with what amounted to a call for the disbandment of the Provisional IRA. The Provisional IRA, however, rejected this and refused to accept the "imposition of unrealisable demands". The institutions went into cold storage as the politicians once more tried to hammer out another deal.

The year ended with the publication of the census results in Northern Ireland. Sinn Féin had predicted that Protestants would fall below 50 per cent of the population for the first time thus bringing their dream of a united Ireland closer. In the event, Unionists were delighted when the figures revealed a narrowing of the denominational divide but by a smaller margin than many Nationalists had predicted. Protestants made up 53.1 per cent of the population while the proportion of Catholics was 43.8 per cent. Increased migration—probably of Protestants returning from the UK—and converging fertility rates between the two communities, was believed to account for the surprising result. In terms of the geographical distribution there was evidence of the west and south of Northern Ireland becoming more Catholic with a declining Protestant population, while Protestants were increasingly concentrated in the east.

2. REPUBLIC OF IRELAND—GERMANY—FRANCE—ITALY—BELGIUM—
THE NETHERLANDS—LUXEMBOURG

i. REPUBLIC OF IRELAND

CAPITAL: Dublin   AREA: 70,000 sq km   POPULATION: 2,900,000 ('02 census)
OFFICIAL LANGUAGES: Irish & English   POLITICAL SYSTEM: multiparty republic
HEAD OF STATE: President Mary McAleese (since Nov '97)
RULING PARTIES: coalition of Fianna Fáil (FF) & Progressive Democrats (PD)
HEAD OF GOVERNMENT: Bertie Ahern (FF), Prime Minister/Taoiseach (since June '97)
MAIN IGO MEMBERSHIPS (NON-UN): EU, OSCE, CE, OECD, PFP
CURRENCY: euro (end-'02 £1=€1.5391, US$1=€0.9610)
GNI PER CAPITA: US$22,960, US$25,470 at PPP ('00)

THE 2002 census recorded the population of the Republic of Ireland at 2.9 million, the highest figure since the 1870s. The rise in population reflected the remarkable success of the Irish economy, which continued to attract a steady flow of returning emigrants and new immigrants. In 2002 GNP rose by approximately 2 per cent, with GDP (inflated by the profits of multi-national firms) rising by over 4 per cent. Although the growth rate was quite respectable by international standards, and unemployment at 4.4 per cent was half the EU average, 2002 marked the end of the era of the "Celtic tiger". Farm incomes fell because of a wet summer and falling livestock prices; tourism was hit by a lack of US visitors and allegations of high prices. Several Irish businesses experienced serious setbacks during the year. In January the *Wall Street Journal* questioned the accountancy practices of the pharmaceutical company Elan, prompting a spectacular fall in the company's share price and the resignation of chief executive and chairman Donal Geaney. Allied Irish Banks (AIB), the country's largest quoted company, also captured international headlines for the wrong reasons when it emerged that a rogue trader in its US subsidiary Allfirst had incurred losses of $691 million. AIB's main rival, the Bank of Ireland, failed in its bid to take over the UK's Abbey National bank. However the low-cost airline Ryanair had another triumphant year, with profits projected to rise by 49 per cent to €257 million and the state-owned airline Aer Lingus bounced back from the post 11 September crisis, transforming a loss of €2 million into a profit of more than €40 million.

A general election in May, two referendums, and two leadership contests made 2002 an eventful year in Irish politics. The outgoing minority coalition of Fianna Fáil (FF) and the Progressive Democrats (PD) was returned to office with a secure majority, becoming the first government to be re-elected since 1969. FF gained four seats and, with 81 seats, was only three short of an overall majority. The Progressive Democrats doubled their representation from four to eight, having campaigned on the dangers of a single-party FF government. Fine Gael, the main opposition party, was returned with 31 seats, a loss of 23. Labour was unchanged with 21 seats. Labour had refused to enter a pre-election pact with Fine Gael, a decision that left the electorate without a clear alternative to the outgoing government and one that deprived both parties of preference vote transfers that were vital under Ireland's system of proportional representation. Fine Gael leader Michael Noonan announced his resignation before the election count had ended; Labour leader Rory Quinn stepped down some months later. The new Fine Gael leader was Mayo deputy Enda Kenny, which reflected the party's electoral base in rural constituencies. Labour party members elected two former members of the Democratic Left, Pat Rabbitte and Liz McManus, as leader and deputy leader respectively. Smaller parties and independents reaped benefit from the general election: the Green Party increased its representation from two to six deputies; whilst Sinn Féin won five seats, compared with one in the outgoing Dáil. They formed a "technical" alliance with a majority of the 15 independent deputies, a move that posed a greater threat to Labour and Fine Gael than to the government. The upheaval in the opposition did not extend to the government. Although Prime Minister Bertie Ahern promised major changes to his Cabinet, his legendary caution prevailed, and there were only four new faces in the Cabinet.

During the election campaign, the opposition warned that public spending was seriously off target. With the election safely won, Finance Minister Charlie McCreevy used gloomy predictions of a budget deficit to strengthen his control over public spending and ended the year with a marginal surplus. McCreevy indicated that there would be no return to the heavy borrowing of the 1980s, and he reiterated his commitment to a low tax regime, but the brunt of the corrective measures fell on expenditure. Public borrowing had been held at 0.79 per cent, which most commentators believed was too low, given the demand for more investment in public transport, roads, housing, schools, and high-speed telecommunications to meet the needs of an expanding population and a growing economy. However the budget did provide for the first phase of awards to public servants averaging 8.9 per cent as recommended by the benchmarking commission to bring their pay into line with the private sector.

The National Spatial Strategy, a key element in the National Development Plan 2002-7, finally appeared in December. The most contentious planning issue in 2002, however, was the proliferation of one-off rural houses, which accounted for 36 per cent of all new dwellings. Rural lobby groups, farmers, and most local councillors supported this trend, and rejected criticism by the environmental lobby group, An Taisce, as an attack on rural life. The proposed crack-down by Transport Minister Seamus Brennan on the estimated 300,000 drivers who did not hold a full licence, was also condemned as another assault on rural life, but Brennan's measures were credited with reducing the number of road deaths to the lowest level since 1965.

The child sexual abuse scandal in the Roman Catholic Church (see II.3.viii) seriously damaged the standing of the Church in Ireland. Demands for the resignation of the Archbishop of Dublin, Cardinal Desmond Connell, were ignored, but in April, Brendan Comiskey, Bishop of Ferns, became the first Catholic bishop to resign over the issue of child sexual abuse by a priest under his jurisdiction after the screening of a television documentary, *Suing the Pope*. A clearly-shaken hierarchy established a commission, chaired by retired judge

Gillian Hussey, to establish the extent of child sexual abuse by clergy and the response of church authorities to complaints of sexual abuse, but critics noted that the commission was wholly dependent on the co-operation of the church. A second television documentary screened in November revealed that the archdiocese of Dublin had repeatedly ignored reports of sexual abuse by clergy, and had failed to report them to the police. When Justice Minister Michael McDowell announced that he would establish a statutory inquiry into the allegations, the hierarchy bowed to the inevitable and the Hussey Commission was disbanded. Under an agreement brokered by the outgoing government, the Catholic Church would transfer cash and land valued at €127 million to the state; in return the state would assume responsibility for compensating those who were abused by Catholic clergy in industrial schools and other state-controlled residential institutions. The Catholic Church suffered another blow in March when a referendum to reverse the 1992 Supreme Court judgement that the risk of suicide was grounds for abortion was narrowly defeated.

The outcome of the second referendum on the EU Nice Treaty in October was much more decisive, with over 62 per cent voting in favour. An active "Yes" campaign by the government parties, plus Fine Gael, Labour, and the umbrella group Alliance For Europe, whose star performer was the 75-year old former Taoiseach Garret FitzGerald, persuaded many who had abstained in 2001 to vote in favour. Turnout increased from 35 per cent to 49 per cent; the number of "No" votes was almost unchanged. The debate over Ireland's continued neutrality persisted, despite a declaration by EU ministers that it would remain unaffected by the Nice Treaty.

Sport and politics were intertwined on many occasions during the year. Bertie Ahern pressed forward with plans to build a national sports stadium (dubbed "the Bertie Bowl") despite mounting evidence that the cost of the plan had been seriously underestimated. Shortly after the election, however, as the public finances came under pressure, the plans were abandoned. The Republic of Ireland soccer team fared better in the World Cup than many had predicted given the pre-match dispute between manager Mick McCarthy and captain Roy Keane, which resulted in the latter returning home. A subsequent inquiry vindicated Keane's claims of poor management of the preparations for the World Cup. A joint Scotland-Ireland bid to host the 2008 European Championship was unsuccessful.

ii. GERMANY

CAPITAL: Berlin   AREA: 357,000 sq km   POPULATION: 82,200,000
OFFICIAL LANGUAGE: German   POLITICAL SYSTEM: multiparty republic
HEAD OF STATE: President Johannes Rau (since July '99)
RULING PARTIES: Social Democratic Party (SPD) Alliance '90/Greens
HEAD OF GOVERNMENT: Gerhard Schröder (SPD), Federal Chancellor (since Oct '98)
MAIN IGO MEMBERSHIPS (NON-UN): NATO, EU, OSCE, CE, CBSS, AC, OECD, G-8
CURRENCY: euro (end-'02 £1=€1.5391, US$1=€0.9610)
GNI PER CAPITA: US$23,700, US$25,530 at PPP ('01)

As in several other European countries, a general election lay at the core of German politics in 2002. Four main topics dominated the political agenda at different times during the year: economic crisis and the necessity for institutional reform; natural catastrophes; foreign policy and, particularly, the Iraq crisis; and the credibility and integrity of politicians.

The year began with the leader of the Christian Social Union (CSU), Edmund Stoiber, convincing Angela Merkel, the leader of the larger opposition party, the Christian Democratic Union (CDU), to stand aside from being a joint candidate for Chancellor at the 2002 election (see AR 2001, p. 64). The decision meant the choice of a more conservative figure, but one who could emphasise economic competence, as Bavaria, where Stoiber served as governor, had been the state with highest growth and lowest unemployment rates in Germany during recent years.

In contrast with most experts' forecasts, no improvement in the German economy could be observed in 2002. After years of slow decline, unemployment rose sharply, and Federal Chancellor Gerhard Schröder, who had promised in 1998 to reduce unemployment to 3.5 million by 2002, found himself faced with some 4 million unemployed. Furthermore, the success story of Hans Eichel, who, as the SPD Finance Minister, had reduced the high public debts which had followed German reunification, came to an end as the European Commission proposed sending a formal "early warning" to Germany for failing to meet the standards of annual public debt ratios (3 per cent of GDP) that were contained within the EU's 1997 Stability and Growth Pact. Although the government succeeded in preventing the early warning from being issued (by promising to eliminate its budget deficit by 2004), doubts remained whether Germany was still one of the foundations of budgetary stability.

On 1 January, the euro was introduced as the country's new currency and was accompanied by fears of "hidden" price increases. Popular examples of higher prices in restaurants served to confirm such apprehension, although there was no empirical evidence on the inflationary effects of the new currency. Nevertheless, "Teuro", a combination of the German word for "expensive" (*teuer*) and the name of the new currency, was chosen as the "word of the year".

The opposition used this discontent with the economy as its main argument for political change. The increasingly antagonistic political climate between federal government and opposition was heightened by a clash in the Bundesrat, the upper chamber of the legislature which represented the states of the German federation. The new immigration bill, which aimed to modernise immigration rules by providing for the admission of controlled numbers of skilled workers and more rigorous action against illegal immigrants, was passed by the Bundesrat on 22 March by 35 votes to 34, but in highly controversial circumstances. The SPD president of the Bundesrat, Klaus Wowereit, ruled that the votes of the two Brandenburg representatives—one an SPD member supporting the bill and the other a CDU member who was opposed to it—should both be counted in favour on the grounds that each state should vote as a bloc and that the SPD representative (Brandenburg's Minister President) was senior to his CDU colleague.

The state elections in the eastern state of Saxony Anhalt on 21 April served as the year's first electoral test of the parties as they prepared for the federal elections in September. The SPD, which had led a minority government supported by the ex-communist Party of Democratic Socialism (PDS), lost nearly half of its seats in the state. By contrast, the PDS maintained its level of representation. The election was won by the CDU and the liberal Free Democratic Party (FDP). The former increased its vote by 15.3 per cent and won 48 of the 115 seats. It interpreted this triumph, in a state with the highest level of unemployment in the country, as confirmation of its strategy for the forthcoming federal election campaign of attacking the government's economic competence.

As for the FDP, after eight years of being out of state legislatures in eastern Germany, the party celebrated its comeback by more than trebling its share of votes. This result was seen as a consequence of positioning the FDP as a liberal populist party, which absorbed protest votes formerly taken by right-wing parties like the German People's Party (DVU). This strategy was introduced by FDP vice chairman Jürgen Möllemann during the successful state election campaign in North Rhine-Westphalia in 2000 (see AR 2000, pp. 49-50) and led to the objective of achieving 18 per cent in the federal election (the so-called "Project 18"). In May, the FDP nominated its chairman, Guido Westerwelle, as candidate for Chancellor at the federal election, thereby underlining its independence from the two big parties (CDU/CSU and SPD) as possible coalition partners.

Saxony Anhalt State Election (21 April 2002)

Party	% of vote 2002	Seats 2002	% of vote 1998	Seats 1998
SPD	20.0	25	35.9	47
CDU	37.3	48	22.0	28
PDS	20.4	25	19.6	25
FDP	13.3	17	4.2	-
Alliance '90/Greens	2.0	-	3.2	-
Others	7.0	-	15.1	16
Total	100	115	100	116
Turnout	56.5	-	71.5	-

The election coincided with a series of scandals which enveloped the SPD. Party representatives in several municipalities in North Rhine-Westphalia, the former industrial heartland of Germany which had been a foundation of Schröder's electoral success in 1998, were found to have accepted bribes in return for public works contracts. Further damage was done to the party when the federal Minister of Defence, Rudolf Scharping, was dismissed in July amidst allegations that he had improperly accepted payments from a lobbyist. At the beginning of summer the SPD was far behind the CDU in the opinion polls.

During the summer months, however, the political situation changed dramatically. A commission on the modernisation of employment services, led by a manager of the automobile manufacturer Volkswagen, presented a programme on labour market reforms which gave fresh blood to the reformist image of Schröder. Heavy rain in August in central and eastern Europe led to massive floods in Bavaria and eastern Germany, causing deaths, the destruction of thousands of homes, and total damage estimated at up to €10 billion. The floods caused unprecedented private charitable initiatives and many examples of voluntary assistance. The sense of national pride which this provoked was accompanied by media plaudits for the federal government in its response to the catastrophe.

Federal Chancellor Schröder used the public support which followed the floods to introduce a new issue to the federal election campaign: opposition to the US campaign for an attack upon Iraq. After 11 September 2001 Germany had quickly offered "unqualified support" to the USA (see AR, 2001, p. 59) and had committed troops to peacekeeping as well as anti-terrorist duties. In April 2002, 14 German tourists died in a terror attack by members of al-Qaida in Tunisia. Even during a visit by US President George W. Bush to Berlin in early summer, the federal government demonstrated its willingness to participate in a close anti-terrorist partnership. But in August, Schröder launched a campaign not to support any military action by the USA or its allies in Iraq regardless of any UN decision. The US government reacted sharply to this and, in the words of US Defence Secretary Donald Rumsfeld, relations between the two allies rapidly became "poisoned". Rumsfeld's remark followed an interview in which the federal Minister of Justice, Herta Däubler-Gmelin, compared the motivation of Bush towards Iraq with the strategy of the Nazi regime in trying to switch public awareness away from domestic problems by initiating foreign wars. Despite US anger, Schröder gained popularity by his clear anti-war position, particularly in eastern Germany where the SPD took support from the traditionally pacifist PDS.

The federal election saw an extremely close result between government and opposition parties. For some hours, the leader of the opposition, Stoiber, was presented as the winner and the new Chancellor, before being overtaken in the count by the SPD. The CDU/CSU performed well in the south and in rural regions, but lost votes to the SPD in eastern Germany and the big municipalities of the north. In the east, the SPD gained votes from the PDS. The latter fared particularly badly, and emerged from the election with only two constituency seats, a result so poor that it was ineligible to receive a share of the seats distributed through proportional representation. By contrast, the Greens achieved an unexpected success and strengthened their position as the third biggest party and the coalition partner of the SPD. This success was a personal triumph for the Foreign Minister, Joschka Fischer, who was one of Germany's most popular politicians and acted as sole anchorman in the election campaign despite the Greens' preference for collectivism. The FDP failed to reach any of its objectives and remained behind the Greens. The party's disappointing performance was blamed on the resurgence of charges of anti-Semitism following the criticism by deputy chairman Jürgen Möllemann of Israel's "militaristic" policies towards the Palestinians.

Federal election (22 September 2002)

Party	% of votes 2002	Seats	% of votes 1998	Seats
SPD	38.5	251	40.9	298
CDU/CSU	38.5	248	35.1	245
Greens	8.6	55	6.7	47
FDP	7.4	47	6.2	43
PDS	4.0	2	5.1	36
Schill/PRO	0.8	-	-	-
Others	2.7	-	5.9	-
Total	100	603	100	669
Turnout	79.1	-	82.2	-

In the state election, held the same day as the federal election, in the northeastern state of Mecklenburg-West Pomerania the outcome was similar to that of the federal election in eastern Germany. The incumbent SPD/PDS coalition was returned to office, but the PDS lost a third of its votes, whilst the Greens and the FDP failed once more to achieve legislative representation in an eastern German state.

State Election Mecklenburg- West Pomerania (22 September 2002)

Party	% of votes 2002	Seats	% of votes 1998	Seats
SPD	40.6	33	34.3	27
CDU	31.4	25	30.2	24
PDS	16.4	13	24.4	20
Greens	2.6	-	2.7	-
FDP	4.7	-	1.6	-
Others	4.4	-	6.8	-
Total	100	71	100	71
Turnout	70.6	-	79.4	-

As in 1998, the new government had a weak start. Following the federal election, the state of the economy once more dominated public awareness. Decreasing tax revenue resulting from the recession and a change in corporate tax law caused the budget deficit to rise to 3.7 per cent of GNP. Thus, Germany failed to remain within the parameters of the EU's Stability and Growth Pact and the European Commission instigated a formal investigation. Plans to increase taxes to cut the deficit caused public discontent, as did the increasing costs of the country's social security system. Furthermore, the Constitutional Court ruled that the Bundesrat had not passed the Immigration Act correctly. This meant that in future a state's voting behaviour in the upper chamber could not be determined by the will of its most senior member, a development which strengthened the role of coalition partners in the states. The government's attempt to smooth over the conflict with the US administration over its Iraq policy forced concessions, including allowing US military aircraft to fly over German territory in case of war with Iraq, and the offer of German technological support and specialists to assist the war effort. The CDU/CSU opposition responded by launching a campaign on "election fraud" which was designed to prove that Schröder had lied in his campaign pledges over taxes and Iraq.

At the end of the year, Germany faced a demanding agenda: to overcome a poor economic performance; to reduce the budget deficit; to modernise the healthcare and pension systems in the context of demographic change and an ageing society; to reform the education sector after the shock of its poor performance in an OECD comparison of students' competencies (PISA) and violent attacks in schools (most notably the killing of 18 people in a school in Erfurt in April); to implement a new immigration law; to support the development of a European Constitutional Treaty; and to help define a strategy on Iraq as a member of the UN Security Council.

iii. FRANCE

CAPITAL: Paris   AREA: 552,000 sq km   POPULATION: 59,200,000
OFFICIAL LANGUAGE: French   POLITICAL SYSTEM: multiparty republic
HEAD OF STATE AND GOVERNMENT: President Jacques Chirac (UMP), since May '95
RULING PARTY: Union for a Popular Movement (UMP) (since Nov '02)
PRIME MINISTER: Jean-Pierre Raffarin (DL) (since May '02)
MAIN IGO MEMBERSHIPS (NON-UN): NATO, EU, OSCE, CE, OECD, G-8, PC, Francophonie
CURRENCY: euro (end-'02 £1=€1.5391, US$1=€0.96190)
GNI PER CAPITA: US$22,690, US$25,280 at PPP ('01)

ONE event touched every home in France in 2002: the adoption of the euro. The demise of the franc after 650 years gave rise to only muted obsequies. The new currency arrived with strikingly few hitches and without the feared surge in prices, although, for many, calculating in euro came only slowly.

Domestic politics focused on the presidential election, at long last in its final phase. A record 16 candidates had acquired the requisite 500 nominations from elected officials in 30 departments, but it was universally assumed that only two had a real chance of victory: incumbent President Jacques Chirac, and Prime Minister Lionel Jospin. They had been locked in an uneasy cohabitation for the previous five years, with first one and then the other leading in the opinion polls. It was considered a foregone conclusion that they would emerge from the first ballot in April as the two leading candidates, and then compete decisively in the second round in May.

Both men had talents and liabilities. A formidable campaigner, Chirac was dogged by allegations of impropriety during his time as mayor of Paris, and fresh evidence of this emerged during the election campaign. He steadfastly refused to address the allegations and, as President, he was immune from questioning and charges. In January the judge investigating the allegations resigned in protest at the delays and obstruction which he was encountering.

Jospin was generally seen as "clean" if dour, with a reasonable economic record. However, the economic climate was deteriorating and discontent growing. Small employers particularly were incensed by the 35-hour working week, as were medical auxiliaries who claimed that it had been introduced without extra funds to take on more staff, while doctors struck over deteriorating pay and conditions. In January, the Constitutional Council disallowed parts of the government's social modernisation legislation, making redundancies more difficult and costlier for employers, as a "manifestly excessive attack on freedom of enterprise". The Council also rejected plans to grant extensive devolution of power to the troubled island of Corsica. A former prefect of Corsica, who was sentenced to a year's imprisonment for ordering an arson attack by police on two illegal beach restaurants, alleged that he had acted on instructions from Jospin's office.

Competing for centrist votes, the two men offered fairly similar programmes. Chirac promised a 5 per cent cut in income tax, lower taxes on businesses, higher social spending and "zero tolerance" for crime. Jospin also promised tax cuts, new child-care allowances, housing for all, reduced unemployment, and a tough line on crime. Already a major preoccupation with the public, crime moved up the agenda when a succession of killings and violent attacks culminated in a disturbed loner shooting eight councillors dead in the Paris suburb of Nanterre. (The perpetrator leaped to his death from a fourth-floor window at police headquarters.) Public concern was fanned by Jean-Marie Le Pen, the veteran far-right candidate whose message on "insecurity" was steeped in anti-immigrant and racist sentiments.

Though dismissed by Jospin as old (69) and "clapped out", Chirac fought a fast and flexible campaign with energy and charm, under the umbrella of Union pour la Majorité Présidentielle. By contrast, constrained by a divided party and a heterogeneous coalition, Jospin's campaign was lacklustre and he steadily lost ground. Nevertheless, the outcome of the first ballot was a stunning political shock. Despite the record field of candidates, at 71.6 per cent the turnout was a record low for the Fifth Republic. Chirac, as expected, topped the poll with 5,666,440 votes (19.88 per cent). But that Le Pen had beaten Jospin into third place with 4,805,307 votes (16.86 per cent) to the Prime Minister's 4,610,749 (16.18 per cent)—an outcome that no leading polling organisation had predicted—sent shock waves through the political system, not least for the disaffection with conventional politics that it implied. More than a third of those who voted had supported candidates from outside the political mainstream. The result led to protest demonstrations in many cities, and voters now agonised over the choice between "a crook or a fascist" in the run-off ballot. The result was never in doubt. With the turnout up to 80.14 per cent, Chirac took the presidency by 25,316,647 votes (82.15 per cent) to Le Pen's 5,502,314 (17.85 per cent). Jospin immediately resigned, withdrew from public life, and departed on holiday, leaving his party to fight the legislative elections leaderless and demoralised.

Chirac had moved from the lowest ever score for a first-ballot leader to the most numerically compelling victory. Recognising the ambiguity of his triumph, he named a relatively little-known senator, Jean-Pierre Raffarin, as Prime Minister. Raffarin projected himself as an affable provincial, in touch with "grass roots France", in contrast to an arrogant, alienating Parisian elite. Action and modesty would be his watchwords. Chirac promised that his government would "respond to the concerns of the French people", especially over law and order, taxation, and pensions. He pledged that the nation should unite and that politics should change. The new Cabinet was very much his choice. Nicolas Sarkozy, heading a revamped Ministry of the Interior, launched highly-publicised measures to fight crime. Michèle Alliot-Marie became France's first female Defence Minister. Civil society was recognised in the choice of Francis Mer, co-chairman of the giant steel corporation Arcelor, as Minister for Finance, Economy, and Industry; and a philosopher, Luc Ferry, to head the notoriously intractable Education Ministry. Chirac's chief-of-staff, Dominique de Villepin, became Foreign Minister.

Turnout in the June elections to the National Assembly (the lower house of the bicameral legislature) reached fresh lows: 64.41 per cent in the first ballot and 60.32 per cent in the second. The Right swept to victory with 399 of the 577 seats—355 of them Chirac supporters. The Socialists lost half of their seats, while the Communists and Greens lost their respective leaders, Robert Hue and Dominique Voynet. Le Pen's National Front, fresh from its success in the presidential contest, failed to win a single seat. A reshaped 39-strong Raffarin government included 10 women, amongst them France's first female astronaut.

Thus, Chirac stood in an unprecedented position. The first President elected for a five-year term (following an amendment to the constitution), he and his supporters controlled every major state institution. He also moved swiftly to place loyalists at the head of both the foreign and domestic intelligence services, their predecessors having paid the price of indulging the Jospin government's curiosity about actions during Chirac's earlier premiership. With the opposition parties scattered and demoralised, the bulk of the mainstream Right merged into a single party, the UMP (now standing for Union pour un Mouvement Populaire), headed by former Prime Minister Alain Juppé. Yet the fate of the government, it seemed, might be determined less by its formal majorities than by opinion on the street. The previous right-wing government had lost its reforming zeal in the face of a wave of strikes and demonstrations. An unsuccessful attempt by an extreme right-wing zealot to assassinate the President during the Bastille Day parade could be discounted as a lone act, but demonstrations by doctors soon forced the government into increasing their fees. With this early warning, the new administration advanced towards its less popular objectives with caution.

The government faced the challenge of honouring its election pledges to spend more and tax less at the same time as the flagging economy was making the assumption of 3 per cent growth increasingly unrealistic. Moreover, in his Bastille Day interview Chirac spoke of raising defence expenditure from 1.8 per cent of GDP to 2.3 per cent, providing more help to the handicapped, cutting the appalling toll of road deaths, and improving cancer survival rates. Mer soon warned that some commitments would have to be deferred until the economy rallied. Even so, the budget made the promised 5 per cent across-the-board cut in income tax, reduced corporate taxation, and introduced measures to make it easier to start new companies. Inevitably, the budget deficit would increase, conceivably to take France through the 3 per cent limit prescribed in the EU's Growth and Stability Pact. Mer brushed aside warnings from the European Commission that the increased budget deficit would inevitably lead France to breach the Pact and rejected the requirement to restore the budget to balance by 2006.

In most respects the economy performed no worse than the Eurozone's uninspiring average; GDP rose by about 1.0 per cent, with industrial production up slightly. Unemployment edged up from 8.8 per cent to 9.1 per cent but the rise in earnings, at 3.4 per cent, ran comfortably ahead of consumer prices, up by 2.3 per cent. The stock market fell just over 35 per cent. Though painful, this was also in line with the Eurozone's general performance. However, some major companies ran into serious trouble. The giant conglomerate Vivendi Universal reported the biggest annual loss in French corporate history of €13,600 million. Its chief executive, Jean-Marie Messier (who had also stirred widespread criticism by declaring "the Franco-French cultural exception dead"), was ousted in a boardroom revolt. France-Télécom, with huge losses and massive debts, proposed shedding 20,000 jobs and still required a €15,000 million bailout. Other major companies, like Alstom, Alcatel, and LVMH, also had serious problems.

The government quickly pushed through legislation scrapping the 35-hour week. However, the parlous state of the financial markets led it to defer, at least, promises to introduce pensions based on private pension funds. It also decided against further privatisations, which threatened furious union opposition, preferring to sell shares in 13 state companies, notably gas and electricity, while promising that the state would retain a majority holding. It disappointed many by declining to raise the minimum wage more than strictly required, while infuriating some by allowing a 70 per cent rise in the salaries of government ministers. This was justified on the grounds that they were no longer receiving unofficial bonuses, which had disappeared when the Jospin government abolished customary payments from secret funds.

The fight against crime and the reform of the judicial system produced a spate of measures. In July, Sarkozy announced plans to recruit 13,500 new police and gendarmes, create a corps of recently retired police officers to deal with major law and order crises, introduce more closed-circuit television camera surveillance, allow easier police access to private information, and embark on a big prison building programme with a special junior minister to carry it through. (The prison population already stood at a record 56,000). There would be legislation to clamp down on prostitution; punishments for parents who let their children skip school; new secure units for juvenile offenders; and new offences of offensive begging, loitering in communal areas of apartment blocks, and insulting behaviour towards teachers. Civil libertarians criticised what they termed a "frenzy of repression", but Sarkozy claimed that "zero tolerance" was cutting crime dramatically.

In July President Chirac declared the moment had come to "resume the long march towards decentralisation". The cause was also close to the Prime Minister's heart. This was to be the "key reform" of the next five years. In October, plans were agreed to pass control of transport, health, and education to the 26 regional assemblies. It was claimed that this would reduce bureaucracy, give the public a greater say in public services, and combat the widespread public disaffection from politics. Subject to a referendum approving the requisite constitutional amendments, the transfer of powers should begin during 2003. Public sector unions were deeply suspicious that the result might be job cuts and damage to the educational system, while reaction in Corsica offered no great hope that the proposals would provide a solution to the island's problems.

Liberated from the constraints of cohabitation, the President now had a freer hand in foreign policy and was at pains to assert that France was a force to be reckoned with. Over Iraq, he made it plain in a variety of ways that France would not swing automatically behind the USA, while also steering a course that kept him in line to join possible coalition action. Indeed, France felt herself to be very much in the front line in "the war against terrorism" after 11 French naval contractors were killed by a terrorist bomb in the Pakistani city of Karachi in May, and a French oil tanker was attacked by suicidal terrorists off Yemen in October. The French security services were particularly active in detecting and disrupting terrorist cells. Iraq apart, efforts were made to repair the poor state of foreign relations that had developed under the Socialists. Bridge-building was also called for within the Franco-German alliance in the EU, which had more than its usual share of tensions. However, Chirac was able to secure German support for blocking early reform of the Common Agricultural Policy, whilst acquiescing in enlargement and, after a long rearguard action, accepting the phased opening of the EU energy market. France also opposed extension of the mandate of the NATO peacekeeping force in Macedonia, arguing that the role should be handed over to the EU to inaugurate its new defence role. Meanwhile, in December, 2,500 paratroopers were dispatched to the Ivory Coast, ending a period during which France appeared to have withdrawn from her willingness to act as "Africa's policeman". In October, plans were announced to spend €14,640 million over six years on military hardware, including a second aircraft carrier, new spy satellites and reconnaissance drones, and heavy-lift transport aircraft. This marked the President's intention to match the UK in terms of equipment and fighting efficiency.

iv. ITALY

CAPITAL: Rome   AREA: 301,000 sq km   POPULATION: 57,700,000
OFFICIAL LANGUAGE: Italian   POLITICAL SYSTEM: multiparty republic
HEAD OF STATE: President Carlo Azeglio Ciampi (since May '99)
RULING PARTIES: Casa delle Libertà coalition
HEAD OF GOVERNMENT: Silvio Berlusconi (Forza Italia), Prime Minister (since June '01)
MAIN IGO MEMBERSHIPS (NON-UN): NATO, EU, OSCE, CE, CEI, OECD, G-8
CURRENCY: euro (end-'02 £1=€1.5391, US$1=€0.9610)
GNI PER CAPITA: US$19,470, US$24,340 at PPP ('01)

INTERNATIONAL circumstances, natural disasters, and continuing political antagonism made 2002 a difficult year for Italy. After a number of terrorist alarms, the threat from al-Qaida was made specific to Italy, among other countries, in a taped message ostensibly from Osama bin Laden himself; and whilst the global economy proved to be less depressed than many had feared, Europe's sluggish performance was mirrored in Italy, leaving the government little room for fiscal manoeuvre.

The storms which flooded large parts of Central Europe in August caused €172 million-worth of agricultural losses in northern Italy, and in late November the area experienced the wettest weather, and worst consequent flood damage, for 25 years. More natural disasters occurred in the south where a series of eruptions at Mount Etna, beginning in late October, covered large areas with ash, eventually leading to the temporary closure of Messina airport. On 30 December, the volcanic island of Stromboli produced a *tsunami* when a recent lava flow collapsed into the sea. Flooding, and the danger of more to come, provoked the evacuation of the island's 400-strong population. The worst natural disaster, however, took place in the Molisan village of San Giuliano di Puglia where, on 31 October, an earthquake caused the collapse of a school building, killing 26 pupils and one teacher. Further gloom was provided by a major crisis in FIAT, the country's leading industrial enterprise. In early October the company announced that major redundancies would be necessary. By the end of the year no restructuring plan had been adopted, and the first job losses were implemented. All told, for most Italians 2002 was a year best forgotten.

The government did little to reverse this judgment. For its supporters, the performance of the Home of Freedom (Casa delle Libertà) coalition, led by Silvio Berlusconi, was below expectations, whilst much of the opposition remained unreconciled to the Right's electoral triumph. Despite the appeals of the President of the Republic, Carlo Azeglio Ciampi, for the contending sides to recognise each other's democratic legitimacy, the year ended with the country still bitterly divided. This acute political fracture exacerbated the danger, highlighted by the assassination of a labour market policy adviser, Marco Biagi, on 19 March, that otherwise minor domestic terrorist activities could bloom into a substantial resurrection of left-wing terrorism, even if not on the scale of the 1970s. Biagi's murder, like a number of other outrages, was claimed to be the work of the extreme left-wing Red Brigades, the most effective of the many terrorist organizations active in that decade. An echo of this period also came on 17 November when the Perugia appeal court found former Prime Minister

Giulio Andreotti guilty of complicity in the murder of an investigative journalist in 1979. The defendant launched an appeal against his conviction.

Politically, the year began with the resignation on 5 January of the Foreign Minister, Renato Ruggiero. Most commentators had interpreted the appointment of this non-parliamentary technocrat as providing a guarantee that the new government would maintain Italy's pro-European stance, notwithstanding the prominence of eurosceptics within its ranks. In fact, criticism by fellow ministers of his allegedly unquestioning enthusiasm for the EU provoked his departure after only eight months in office. Partly because of the difficulty of reshuffling the coalition, Prime Minister Berlusconi initially assumed the vacant portfolio himself, retaining it until 4 November. The new minister, Franco Frattini, eventually came from the Prime Minister's party, Forza Italia, and confirmed that party's dominant role in the government. The year also saw the resignation of a junior culture minister and, more seriously, of the Interior Minister, Claudio Scajola, on 3 July. Guilty of a tasteless remark regarding the assassination of Biagi, Scajola was forced to resign by the pressure of public opinion, much to the Prime Minister's displeasure.

Industrial relations, along with foreign policy and judicial reform, were a key area of development in 2002, even if only to the extent of producing a hard-fought stalemate. Nevertheless, the Prime Minister's apparent acknowledgement of this in his end-of-year speech, where he invoked a return to a co-operative approach to social and economic reform in 2003, was highly significant. In fact, 2002 was a year of confrontation in which the number of hours lost in strikes quadrupled compared with 2001. At the start of the year, President Ciampi had promoted the resumption of dialogue between the government and the unions. This had broken down in late 2001 when the government targeted, as a major cause of market rigidity, Article 18 of the 1970 Workers' Statute, a symbolically highly significant clause which defended workers (at least those to whom it applied) against unfair dismissal. In 2002 the government sought union co-operation whilst still challenging Article 18. The results were mixed. On the one hand, on 5 July a "Pact for Italy" was signed by the government and most leading economic associations, providing a basis for the resumption of co-operation. The Pact also agreed a package of reforms to improve labour market flexibility largely independently of Article 18. On the other hand, the largest trade union confederation, the left-wing CGIL, opposed the pact. Indeed, a general strike promoted by the CGIL on 16 April was very successful and followed hard on the heels of nationwide demonstrations in defence of Article 18 on 26 March. These, coming just a week after Biagi's assassination, were particularly politically significant. Although the signing of the Pact split the unions badly, the moderate confederations (CISL and UIL), like the moderate parliamentary Left, were concerned not to provoke an explicitly political confrontation with the CGIL. Indeed, so successful had been the CGIL's mobilisation, and so lacklustre the party Left, that the CGIL's leader, Sergio Cofferati, was widely promoted as a possible future leader of the Left. This speculation apart, by the end of the year it looked as though the government's stumbling offensive against Article 18, inspired by Confindustria, the industrialists' association, had backfired. Almost certainly unnecessary from a narrow policy perspective, the government had apparently sought to gain what would have been a hugely significant symbolic victory against the industrial Left, reinforcing the rout already effected at the parliamentary level. However, polls showed one-third even of government supporters opposed the reform of Article 18, and this was in effect abandoned.

It was in the field of foreign policy that the government claimed its greatest successes. Even before becoming Foreign Minister, Berlusconi had been active in promoting Italian interests and even participation in operations in Afghanistan, via the European Council. As Foreign Minister, he built on this to obtain a strong presence for Italy in the European Convention, with Giuliano Amato being appointed—outside the Italian quota—as a representative of the European Left to the Convention's right-wing chairman, French President Jacques Chirac. Beyond Europe, Berlusconi promoted relations with President Vladimir Putin of Russia and with the USA, leading to Italy's hosting of the NATO-Russia summit at the end of May at Pratica di Mare, outside Rome. Earlier that month, on 7 May, Italy ratified the Nice Treaty, with only the Communist Refoundation voting against it. This confirmed the split in the Left, whilst the Right maintained a united front, with even the Northern League (LN) foregoing its normally vitriolic criticism of the EU. The division within the Left was further underlined in a parliamentary vote on 2 October on the sending of an additional 1,000 specialist mountain troops to Afghanistan. The year also saw the government shift its position to a more pro-Israeli one, a matter of particular concern for the far-right National Alliance (AN) which sought thereby finally to bury its predecessor party's anti-Semitism.

Judicial reform was the most controversial area of the government's activity, as it had been in 2001. On 14 February Switzerland suspended its ratification of an accord on rogatory matters pending clarification of controversial Italian legislation on the subject. On 20 June the national association of magistrates (ANMI) undertook a one-day strike in defence of its independence and constitutional role. In August, the newly appointed Higher Council of the Judiciary failed to elect, as its vice-president—and de facto chair, since its president was the President of the Republic—the government's nominee. This unprecedented decision signalled the judiciary's lack of confidence in the government. In the legislature, much time was taken up by the so-called "Cirami bill", the nub of which was the possibility of transferring trials out of a jurisdiction in which the impartiality of the judiciary could not be guaranteed. The proposal was taken by critics as another law made by a "clan" government in defence of the private interests of Silvio Berlusconi and his allies, notably Cesare Previti, particularly with regard to the IMI-SIR case underway in Milan. The legislation allegedly saw the office of the President of the Republic take a direct role in drafting its final content. Such intervention was seen by many as reflecting a shift in the behaviour of the President, as his attempts at moral suasion were supplemented by more direct measures. However, he remained formally impartial, even in his first official message to the legislature, on 23 July, which addressed the issue of media pluralism and freedom of information. Internationally distinguished Italian scholars voiced concern that Italy was leading the trend towards modern Western political systems becoming illiberal democracies, yet by the end of the year legislation regarding Berlusconi's conflicts of interests had still not been passed.

The centrality of the relationship between the media, politics, and democracy was highlighted by the controversial appointment in February of the management board of RAI, the state broadcasting service. The appointment of its five members by the speakers of the two parliamentary chambers—both of whom were from the majority, albeit institutionally independent—was heavily influenced by the parties and three of the board members apparently represented the government. Berlusconi thus seemed to have asserted his domination over public broadcasting, thereby reinforcing his near monopoly of the private sector. Coming as it did after "jesting" comments by the Prime Minister that a clutch of RAI's political commentators and satirists should be sacked, this development was the crux of the argument that Italy was becoming an illiberal regime. At the end of November, three members of the board resigned in protest at the inadequate management of the company. The year ended with the rump board morally illegitimate but still legally constituted.

The crucial third resignation, in addition to those of the two RAI board members identified with the opposition, was of Marco Staderini, of the small Christian Democratic party (UDC), the fourth party in Berlusconi's coalition. The UDC was founded in early December 2001 from three fragments of the Christian Democratic party which had collapsed in 1993. A degree of party regrouping also took place on the left in 2002, with the formal constitution of the Margherita, on 24 March. This centrist, liberal Catholic party comprised three of four party fragments which had successfully presented themselves as an alliance in the 2001 election—the Italian People's Party (PPI), Republican Party (RI), and the Democrats, but not the Union of Democratic European Reformers (UDEUR). Despite this amalgamation, the Left remained badly fragmented at the party level and divided strategically between those favouring intransigent opposition to the government and those seeking to promote the development of a democracy based on government alternation. Pessimists, however, doubted that the Left could win an election in Italy in the near future, notwithstanding its strong performance in local elections in May and June. Certainly the parliamentary left's performance had been lamentable, provoking a grass-roots movement that, starting in February, grew to be a major political phenomenon in support of Cofferati's more radical opposition to the government.

The Prime Minister concluded the year by relaunching the theme of institutional reform, in particular reinforcing the powers of his own office. For some, this renewed emphasis reflected the government's difficulties in making progress in social and economic reform; for others, it demonstrated the government's need to redeem its election campaign promises now that it had dealt with its more immediately pressing judicial reforms. It was also the case that many saw a need to reinforce central government, as the complex processes of administrative and legislative decentralisation continued to unroll, jealously overlooked by Umberto Bossi of the LN. Whether the Left would be able to respond constructively to the argument that the Italian constitution, which had been partially demolished over recent years, could neither be left to stagnate nor abandoned to the government majority, was one of the main questions awaiting resolution in 2003.

v. BELGIUM

CAPITAL: Brussels   AREA: 33,000 sq km   POPULATION: 10,300,000
OFFICIAL LANGUAGES: French, Flemish & German   POLITICAL SYSTEM: multiparty monarchy
HEAD OF STATE: King Albert II (since Aug '93)
RULING PARTIES: Flemish Liberals and Democrats (VLD/Flemish), Liberal Reform Party (PRL/Walloon), Socialist Party (SP/Flemish), Socialist Party (PS/Walloon), Flemish Greens (Agalev) & Walloon Greens (Ecolo)
HEAD OF GOVERNMENT: Guy Verhofstadt (VLD), Prime Minister (since July '99)
MAIN IGO MEMBERSHIPS (NON-UN): NATO, EU, Benelux, OSCE, CE, OECD, Francophonie
CURRENCY: euro (end-'02 £1=€1.5391, US$1=€0.9610)
GNI PER CAPITA: US$23,340, US$28,210 at PPP ('01)

HUMAN rights issues both in the contemporary world and in Belgium's own colonial history dominated political and judicial affairs during 2002. On 26 June an appeals court in Brussels dismissed an attempt to try Israeli Prime Minister Ariel Sharon for alleged crimes against humanity in connection with the massacre of Palestinian civilians in the Lebanese refugee camps of Chatila and Sabra in 1982, (for background to the case see AR 2001, p. 76). The appeals court ruled that, according to Belgium's criminal code, alleged crimes against humanity committed outside the country could be pursued only when the alleged perpetrator was in Belgium. The court affirmed this view in a second case, rejecting a complaint against President Laurent Gbagbo of Côte d'Ivoire who had been accused of crimes against humanity relating to the killing of civilians during unrest in the country in 2000. In an earlier development on 14 February, the UN International Court of Justice (the ICJ, also referred to as the World Court) ruled that Belgium (as a foreign state) did not have the right to try, on human rights charges, former and current government ministers and leaders who were protected by diplomatic immunity.

Belgium's own human rights record continued to come under scrutiny during 2002. On 6 February Louis Michel, the Belgian Deputy Prime Minister and Minister of Foreign Affairs, expressed the government's "profound and deepest regrets" for Belgium's role in the murder of Patrice Lumumba, the Prime Minister of the then Belgian Congo in 1961 (see AR 1961, p. 316). A Belgian parliamentary inquiry into the killing had concluded in November 2001 that Belgium bore "moral responsibility", as the colonial power, for the events which led to Lumumba's murder, (see AR 2001, p. 76).

In a separate development, the government survived a vote of confidence by 87 votes to 38 on 31 August over a controversial deal to supply arms to the government of Nepal, which was engaged in a conflict against Maoist rebels. The deal to sell thousands of automatic rifles to Nepal was opposed by the Flemish Greens (Agalev) party, which was a key member of the ruling six-party coalition, and by critics who claimed that the sale was illegal under the Belgian constitution. Prime Minister Guy Verhofstadt insisted, however, that the deal would be honoured, but made a number of concessions before the vote of confidence, including a commitment to postpone any shipments of the weapons until after the Nepalese general election, scheduled for November. On 26 August the Health Minister, Magda Aelvoet, a member of Agalev, resigned from her post because of the arms deal, declaring that it was incompatible with her personal convictions.

In social policy, following two days of heated debate, the Chamber of Representatives (the lower house of the bicameral federal legislature) voted on 16 May to adopt a bill which legalised physician-assisted suicide. The legislation had been approved by the Senate (the upper house) in October 2001, (see AR 2001, p. 76). The legislation set out strict conditions governing assisted suicide, including a stipulation that no request for euthanasia could be granted without having been reviewed by a special commission.

In an apparent resolution to a long-running scandal, Alain Van der Biest, a former federal Pensions Minister and, until 1992, the Interior Minister in the French-speaking region of Wallonia, committed suicide on 18 March. Van der Biest had been re-arrested in December 2001 in connection with the assassination of the former Socialist Party (PS) Deputy Prime Minister André Cools in 1991. Van der Biest had been charged in 1996 with masterminding the assassination, but had been released by authorities because of insufficient evidence to link him to the murder (see AR 1996, p. 56). According to press reports, Van der Biest had denied involvement in the assassination in his suicide note.

vi. THE NETHERLANDS

CAPITAL: Amsterdam   AREA: 41,000 sq km   POPULATION: 16,000,000
OFFICIAL LANGUAGES: Dutch   POLITICAL SYSTEM: multiparty monarchy
HEAD OF STATE: Queen Beatrix (since April '80)
RULING PARTIES: Christian Democratic Appeal (CDA) leads minority coalition with People's Party for Freedom and Democracy (VVD) (since Oct '02)
HEAD OF GOVERNMENT: Jan Pieter Balkenende (CDA), Prime Minister (since July '02)
MAIN IGO MEMBERSHIPS (NON-UN): NATO, EU, Benelux, OSCE, CE, OECD
CURRENCY: euro (end-'02 £1=€1.5391 US$1=€0.9610)
GNI PER CAPITA: US$24,040, US$26,440 at PPP ('01)

THE government of Prime Minister Jan Pieter Balkenende resigned on 16 October after 87 days in office, when bitter in-fighting within the Lijst Pim Fortuyn (LPF), a junior coalition partner of Balkenende's Christian Democratic Appeal (CDA), resulted in the paralysis of the ruling coalition. Balkenende announced that he would remain as leader of a minority government coalition with the People's Party for Freedom and Democracy (VVD) until new elections could be held in January 2003. The collapse of the ruling coalition had been precipitated by the resignations of Eduard Bomhoff, the Deputy Prime Minister, and his LPF colleague Herman Heinsbroek, the Minister for Economic Affairs. Bomhoff had been infuriated by a series of statements by Heinsbroek in which the latter had declared his intention to depose Harry Wijnschenk, the leader of the LPF.

The CDA had entered into the coalition in July with the LPF and the VVD after two months of negotiations following the general election of May 15. In the elections to the 150-member lower house of the Staten Generaal, the bicameral legislature, the LPF had secured 26 seats and 17 per cent of the vote whereas the CDA had won 43 seats and 27.9 per cent of the vote. The next largest bloc in the legislature was the VVD which secured 24 seats and 15.4 per cent of the popular vote. The remaining 57 seats were won by seven parties, the largest of which was the Labour Party (PvdA) which secured 23 seats—a disastrous net loss of 22 seats (see AR 1998, p. 67 for the results of the previous election in May 1998).

The general election had been overshadowed by the assassination on 6 May of Pim Fortuyn, the leader of the LPF, who was shot dead as he emerged from a radio interview in Hilversum (see XVIII). Although the motives of Fortuyn's assassin, Volkert van der Graaf, were not clear, der Graaf was reported to be an animal rights campaigner incensed by Fortuyn's criticism of the Green movement. Fortuyn had been a flamboyant and charismatic politician who defied the conventional political labels of left and right. Whilst he campaigned to halt immigration into the Netherlands, Fortuyn was an open homosexual who had criticised Islamic culture for its intolerance of homosexuality. Fortuyn had been widely expected to do well in the May election since the LPF, capitalising on a sense of disillusionment with the established political parties, had, as the Leefbaar Rotterdam (LR), secured control of that city in municipal elections held on 7 March. Fortuyn's assassination, which was unprecedented in modern Dutch history, made headlines around the world and led to an outburst of sympathy for the murdered man and the LPF in general amongst the Dutch electorate.

The May general election had been called following the resignation of the government of Prime Minister Wim Kok on 16 April. The three party coalition led by the PvdA had resigned following the publication of a report by the Netherlands Institute for War Documentation which condemned the UN, the Dutch government, and senior Dutch officers for sending a small force of troops to perform an impossible mission to guard the UN designated "safe haven" of Srebrenica, in eastern Bosnia in July 1995. The authors concluded that the outgunned Dutch troops had been "unwittingly" complicit in the massacre of an estimated 8,000 Muslim civilians by Bosnian Serb forces which overran the enclave (see AR 2000, p. 62).

Prince Claus of the Netherlands died from the effects of Parkinson's disease and pneumonia on 6 October, aged 76. A German by birth, Claus von Amsberg had served as a West German diplomat before adopting Dutch nationality. In 1966 he had married Queen Beatrix, then Crown Princess. Prince Claus had overcome initial resentment at his childhood membership of the Hitler Youth movement to become a popular and influential figure. During the 1970s he chaired the national committee for development strategy and, despite criticism of his openly left-wing views, remained as a special advisor to the government on international development issues until his death.

vii. LUXEMBOURG

CAPITAL: Luxembourg   AREA: 3,000 sq km   POPULATION: 444,000
OFFICIAL LANGUAGE: Letzeburgish   POLITICAL SYSTEM: multiparty monarchy
HEAD OF STATE: Grand Duke Henri (since Oct '00)
RULING PARTIES: Christian Social People's (PCS) & Democratic (DP) parties
HEAD OF GOVERNMENT: Jean-Claude Juncker (PCS), Prime Minister (since Jan '95)
MAIN IGO MEMBERSHIPS (NON-UN): NATO, EU, Benelux, OSCE, CE, OECD, Francophonie
CURRENCY: euro (end-'02 £1=€1.5391, US$1=€0.9610)
GNI PER CAPITA: US$41,770, US$48,080 at PPP ('01)

LUXEMBOURG was one of six EU countries that on 14 February unexpectedly announced their intention to introduce a new European arrest warrant one year ahead of schedule, in early 2003. France, Belgium, Spain, Luxembourg, Portugal, and the UK promised to adopt the necessary legislation in 2002 in order to send a clear signal that European countries were determined to tackle terrorism and organised crime. The introduction of the European-wide arrest warrant had been agreed at the Laeken EU Summit in December 2001 (see AR 2001, p. 438).

Luxembourg's relations with its European partners were strained during 2002 by the perception that it was not fully co-operating with EU measures to control money laundering and financial crime. A French parliamentary committee released a report on 21 January which argued that EU efforts to control such crimes were being obstructed by Luxembourg's culture of banking secrecy and its general reluctance to co-operate with the authorities in other EU states. Tension over the matter had increased after a deal to tax the savings of non-resident non-EU citizens had collapsed on 4 December 2001 when, at a meeting of European Finance Ministers, Austria, Belgium, and Luxembourg had objected to measures which would have reduced banking secrecy in their jurisdictions. Luxembourg and its allies argued that the competitiveness of EU banking regimes would be jeopardised if they agreed to reduce secrecy when non-EU jurisdictions, such as Switzerland, were not bound by the same rules.

Pierre Werner, who had dominated politics in Luxembourg by serving as the leader of the Christian Social Party (PCS) and Prime Minister between 1959 and 1974 and again from 1979 until 1984, died on 24 June, aged 88 (see XVIII). Werner, an early advocate of European monetary union, was the author of the 1971 Werner Plan which, had it been implemented, would have led to economic and monetary union in 1980. Werner was widely credited with diversifying Luxembourg's economy during his tenure as Prime Minister, in response to the decline in the viability of the steel industry.

DENMARK—ICELAND—NORWAY—SWEDEN—FINLAND—AUSTRIA—SWITZERLAND—EUROPEAN MINI-STATES

i. DENMARK

CAPITAL: Copenhagen   AREA: 43,000 sq km   POPULATION: 5,400,000
OFFICIAL LANGUAGE: Danish   POLITICAL SYSTEM: multiparty monarchy
HEAD OF STATE: Queen Margrethe II (since Jan '72)
RULING PARTY: Liberal (V) party
HEAD OF GOVERNMENT: Anders Fogh Rasmussen (V), Prime Minister (since Dec '01)
MAIN IGO MEMBERSHIPS (NON-UN): NATO, EU, NC, CBSS, AC, OSCE, CE, OECD
CURRENCY: Danish krone (end-'02 £1=DKr11.4314, US$1=DKr7.1378
GNI PER CAPITA: US$31,090, US$27,950 at PPP ('01)

IMMIGRATION policy dominated the Danish political agenda in 2002. On 17 January the government, led by Prime Minister Anders Fogh Rasmussen of the Liberal Party (V), presented a series of measures aimed at drastically cutting the number of refugees granted entry into Denmark. New immigrants would be allowed to remain only if their claims precisely matched guidelines in the international conventions on the treatment of refugees. Danish citizenship would be granted at the earliest after nine years' (previously seven years') residence. Applicants were also required to pass a test on their knowledge of the Danish language and Danish society, and no immigrant under 24 years of age would automatically receive citizenship through marriage to a Danish citizen. The proposals had been anticipated after the victory of centre-right parties in the legislative elections of 20 November 2001 (see AR 2001, pp. 84-85). On 31 May the new legislation was passed by the Folketinget (the unicameral legislature). It was supported by the far-right anti-immigration Danish People's Party (DF). The legislation caused tensions between Denmark and Sweden: open criticism came from the Swedish Immigration Minister Mona Sahlin and the leader of the Swedish Liberal Party (FP), Lars Leijonborg (see II.3.iv).

The Danish Presidency of the EU, which ended in December, was described as a success, both for Prime Minister Fogh Rasmussen and for Danish diplomacy. The negotiations concerning the enlargement of the EU were completed, including the difficult question of a timetable for Turkish entry. A summit of EU heads of government was held in Copenhagen on 12-13 December (see XI.4), and although the capital saw large demonstrations, there were few problems for the police.

On 31 December, in his new year's speech, Prime Minister Fogh Rasmussen declared that Denmark would hold a referendum on European and Monetary Union in 2004 or 2005. The referendum would thus take place after a new EU treaty had been approved. In 2000 the Danish people had voted against the adoption of the euro (see AR 2000, p. 67), but some opinion polls in 2002 showed a clear rise in the level of support for the currency since then.

On 3 December the Chechen politician Akhmed Zakayev was released after spending five weeks in a Copenhagen prison. He had been detained after a request from the Russian authorities who accused him of terrorism. Zakayev was closely connected with Aslan Maskhadov, the elected President of Chechnya, and at the time of his arrest had been a delegate at a congress of Chechen exiles held in Copenhagen. However, Danish law courts did not accept the Russian accusations. Zakayev, and the Danish Minister of Justice, Lene Espersen, openly criticised the Russian handling of the case.

On 18 December the leader of the mysterious Tvind-movement, Mogens Amdi Petersen, was put on trial. In the 1970s Tvind had founded socialist schools in Denmark, but it later became an aid organisation which collected clothes for sale abroad. Over the ensuing years, former members and the press had revealed many anomalies within the movement, which was more usually described as an authoritarian sect. Amdi Petersen, who had been in hiding, was extradited from the USA, to face charges of fraud and tax crimes amounting to more than 100 million kroner.

After the legislative election in the Faroe Islands in April, Prime Minister Anfínn Kallsberg remained in office. However, his ruling three-party coalition, comprising the Republican Party, the conservative People's Party, and the Independence Party, obtained only half of the seats. The election was, instead, a success for the Union Party, the leading opponent of total independence from Denmark, which achieved 26 per cent of the vote. The turnout in the election was high, at 91.1 per cent.

The regional election in Greenland in December resulted in a victory for the leftwing party Inuit Ataqatigiit (IA). However, the social democratic Siumut maintained its position as the strongest party. Greenland had left the EU after a referendum in 1982, mainly because of widespread concern about the fishing industry. Subsequently, however, Greenland had reversed its attitude towards the EU, and on 28 August an EU ministerial summit in Ilulissat had accepted Greenland's proposal for an "Arctic window" inside the EU. Formally Denmark would represent Greenland in discussions about trade, the Arctic environment, and telecommunications.

ii. ICELAND

CAPITAL: Reykjavík   AREA: 103,000 sq km   POPULATION: 284,000
OFFICIAL LANGUAGE: Icelandic   POLITICAL SYSTEM: multiparty republic
HEAD OF STATE: President Ólafur Ragnar Grímsson (since Aug '96)
RULING PARTIES: Independence (IP) & Progressive (PP) parties
HEAD OF GOVERNMENT: Davíd Oddson (IP), Prime Minister (since April '91)
MAIN IGO MEMBERSHIPS (NON-UN): NATO, EFTA/EEA, NC, AC, OSCE, CE, OECD
CURRENCY: króna (end-'02 £1=IKr130.254, US$1=IKr81.3300)
GNI PER CAPITA: US$28,880, US$29,830 at PPP ('01)

ENVIRONMENTAL issues were foremost amongst Iceland's concerns during 2002. An extensive plan to build a series of hydroelectric power stations in a vast area in the highlands of the country led to the formation of a growing protest movement. The decision, taken by Environment Minister Siv Fridleifsdottir in December 2001, was unpopular not only amongst environmentalists but also amongst intellectuals and artists, including the popular singer Björk. During the autumn, demonstrators met daily at mid-day outside the Alltinget (the legislature) in Reykjavík to protest against the dam project. Many international organisations similarly demanded that the government protect the unique wilderness area. The Prime Minister, David Oddsson, however, strongly defended the plan and characterised its opponents as traditionalists who threatened the country's modernisation and popular welfare.

On 15 October Iceland unexpectedly rejoined the International Whaling Commission (IWC), an organisation which it had left in 1991 in protest at the radical anti-whaling stance of some of the IWC's members. Iceland had several times failed in its attempts to rejoin the IWC because other members objected to the country's apparent intention to ignore the ban on commercial whaling. The decision to readmit Iceland, taken at a special meeting in Cambridge (UK) in October, was attributed to an error by the Swedish delegation. In the complicated voting procedure, Sweden erroneously voted for the Icelandic proposal which allowed Iceland to re-enter the IWC and to continue commercial whaling from 2006.

iii. NORWAY

CAPITAL: Oslo AREA: 324,000 sq km POPULATION: 4,500,000
OFFICIAL LANGUAGE: Norwegian POLITICAL SYSTEM: multiparty monarchy
HEAD OF STATE: King Harald V (since Jan '91)
RULING PARTIES: Christian Democratic Party (KrF), Conservative (H) and Liberal (V) parties
HEAD OF GOVERNMENT: Kjelle Magne Bondevik (KrF), Prime Minister (since October '01)
MAIN IGO MEMBERSHIPS (NON-UN): NATO, EFTA/EEA, NC, CBSS, AC, OSCE, CE, OECD
CURRENCY: Norwegian krone (end-'02 £1=K11.2333, US$1=K7.0140)
GNI PER CAPITA: US$35,530, US$30,440 at PPP ('01)

THE Norwegian economy experienced some problems during the year. Although to a large extent the economy remained insulated by the oil industry from the growing threat of recession, the ruling centre-right government remained wary of the risk of inflation. The strong Norwegian krone also led to a rise in the real estate market in the Swedish boarder districts as many Norwegians continued to move to Sweden where the cost of living as well as house prices were much lower than in their homeland. Due to the combination of a strong currency, high interest rates, and increasing wages, unemployment rose slightly, although at 3.9 per cent it remained low by wider European standards. The budget was presented as a thrift budget by the conservative Finance Minister Per-Kristian Foss, with public expenditure rising by only 0.5 per cent, the lowest increase since the middle of the 1990s.

Politically the government remained dependent on parliamentary support from the populist Progress Party (FrP). Party chairman Carl Hagen demanded a more expansionary budget, and opinion polls during the summer suggested that the FrP's popularity was increasing as a result of its traditional anti-immigration policy which proposed to halt the admittance of non-Western asylum seekers. Meanwhile, after a long period of internal conflict and decreasing support in elections and opinion polls, the Labour Party appointed Jens Stoltenberg as its party chairman, with the hope that the former Prime Minister could revive the party's flagging popular support.

On 2 May the government launched a package of legislation in order to introduce a total ban on smoking in public places by early 2004. If carried through, it promised to be the world's strictest anti-tobacco policy. The legislation was inspired by reports which maintained that passive smoking was responsible for more deaths within the country than road traffic accidents.

On 20-24 May the International Whaling Commission (IWC) held its 54th annual meeting in Japan. The Japanese and Norwegian proposal to resume commercial whaling—after a 16 year moratorium—was defeated on 23 May by 25 votes to 16. The proposal required a three-quarters majority for approval. In a separate but related development, on 8 September the killer whale Keiko, better known as Willy in a series of popular US feature films, was discovered in Skaalvikfjorden, a Norwegian fjord, having been released from Iceland six weeks earlier. In order to protect the world famous Keiko from harm, the authorities banned all boats from approaching him.

On 12 November Russian President Vladimir Putin made an official visit to Oslo. The main focus of the visit concerned the lengthy negotiations over the Russo-Norwegian maritime boundary in the Barents Sea. Having been a key operating ground for Soviet submarines during the Cold War, the 175 square kilometre stretch of water remained economically important because of its cod stocks and potential gas and oil resources. The visit did not result in any further steps to resolve the boundary dispute which had been under discussion for 30 years.

On 24 May Princess Märtha Louise married Ari Behn, a writer and media personality. In keeping with tradition the wedding took place in the Nidaros Cathedral in Trondheim, although the Princess relinquished her royal title and was no longer to receive a financial allowance from the state.

iv. SWEDEN

CAPITAL: Stockholm AREA: 450,000 sq km POPULATION: 8,900,000
OFFICIAL LANGUAGE: Swedish POLITICAL SYSTEM: multiparty monarchy
HEAD OF STATE: King Carl XVI Gustav (since Sept '73)
RULING PARTIES: Social Democratic Labour Party (SAP) in coalition with Left Party (Vp) and
    Green Party (MpG) (since Oct '02)
HEAD OF GOVERNMENT: Göran Persson, Prime Minister (since March '96)
MAIN IGO MEMBERSHIPS (NON-UN): EU, NC, CBSS, AC, PFP, OSCE, CE, OECD
CURRENCY: Swedish krona (end-'02 £1=K14.1186, US$1=K8.8156)
GNI PER CAPITA: US$25,400, US$24,670 at PPP ('01)

THE result of the general election of 15 September to the Riksdag (the unicameral legislature) was described as a personal victory for Prime Minister Göran Persson, chairman of the Social Democratic Labour Party (SAP). Contrary to the prevailing European trend, the ruling party increased its share of the vote, attaining nearly 40 per cent and remaining in power. As before, Persson refused demands for government posts from the Left Party (Vp) and the Green Party (MpG), which had co-operated with the social democratic government over the previous two years. After complicated negotiations an agreement was finally reached whereby the Social Democrats made some concessions to the other two parties in return for their support for the government. The government accepted, for example, the Green Party's proposal for a unilateral ban on Swedish cod fishing in the Baltic Sea, at an estimated cost of 700 million kronor. The government also promised to try to persuade other countries to follow the ban. However, the co-operation did not extend to European Monetary Union or defence and security issues.

Among the opposition parties, the Liberal Party (FpL) was a clear winner, increasing its share of seats from 17 to 48 (13.3 per cent of the vote). The result was a victory particularly for the party's leader, Lars Leijonborg, who had been widely criticised by senior party members a couple of months before the election. In the election campaign the Liberals had stressed the immigration issue. At the same time Leijonborg demanded a more generous policy towards immigrants, but proposed language tests for those who wished to become Swedish citizens. The liberal-conservative Moderate Unity Party (MUP) suffered severe electoral losses, relinquishing one-third of its seats. After the election, party leader Bo Lundgren succeeded in retaining his position, but many other senior politicians lost their posts or retired. Industry Minister Björn Rosengren, for example, left the government for the commercial sector, joining the media company Tele2, formerly led by the controversial "media mogul" Jan Stenbeck (who died on 19 August). When Leni Björklund was appointed Defence Minister, Sweden got its first woman in that post. Former Defence Minister Björn von Sydow was appointed speaker of the Riksdag, a prestigious office second only to the monarch in constitutional precedence.

On 20 November the Riksdag with a clear majority (248 votes to 47) approved a constitutional change concerning EU membership. The new constitutional provisions made it possible for the Riksdag to devolve decision-making powers on a wider spectrum of issues to the EU than before, for example police co-operation and security policy. After negotiations between the political parties, an agreement was reached in December on holding a referendum on 14 September 2003 over whether or not Sweden should adopt the euro.

One of the most controversial social issues before and after the election was the rapidly rising number of citizens taking sick leave. Although Sweden was characterised in many studies as one of the most healthy nations in Europe, the increase in the number of people taking sick leave was the most rapid in Europe. In September the government presented a plan for a 50 per cent reduction in sick leave entitlement over six years. Another significant social issue surfaced when, on 5 June, the Riksdag approved the right for homosexual couples to apply to adopt children from abroad as well as from within Sweden. The political parties were divided over the question, but the strongest opposition came from the Christian Democrats (KD). Adoption organisations were also critical, fearing that many countries would not permit adoption in Sweden if homosexuals were allowed as adoptive parents.

On 29 August a man was arrested on suspicion of hijacking an airliner destined for London at Västerås airport, 100 km north west of the capital Stockholm, after security officials discovered a gun in his hand luggage. The suspected hijacker, Kerim Chatty, had Tunisian parents and was an active Muslim who had planned to follow a group of Muslims to a conference in Birmingham, UK. Earlier he had received commercial flying lessons in the USA. Under such circumstances, and only two weeks before the first anniversary of the 11 September attack on the World Trade Centre, there was, unsurprisingly, worldwide speculation that another such attack had been narrowly prevented, and journalists from many countries came to Västerås. However, the police investigation showed no evidence that the 29-year old had been planning a terrorist attack, and he was subsequently sentenced only to three months in prison for illegally carrying a gun.

On 17 December the Security Service Commission presented its official report. The main work had been done by recognised historians who had spent three years investigating the controversial surveillance of left-wing and other radical groups that had taken place over previous decades. The report criticised the extent of the operation (100,000 individuals were monitored in the 1960s), the continued registration of political views even many years after this method had been banned, and the murky relationship between the state security organs and the ruling Labour Party.

v. FINLAND

CAPITAL: Helsinki   AREA: 338,000 sq km   POPULATION: 5,200,000
OFFICIAL LANGUAGE: Finnish   POLITICAL SYSTEM: multiparty republic
HEAD OF STATE: President Tarja Halonen (SSDP), since February '00
RULING PARTIES: Social Democratic Party (SSDP), National Coalition (KOK), Left-Wing Alliance
   (VAS), Swedish People's Party (SFP)
HEAD OF GOVERNMENT: Paavo Lipponen (SSDP), Prime Minister (since April '95)
MAIN IGO MEMBERSHIPS (NON-UN): EU, NC, CBSS, AC, PFP, OSCE, CE, OECD
CURRENCY: euro (end-'02 £1=€1.5391, US$1=€0.96190)
GNI PER CAPITA: US$23,940, US$25,180 at PPP ('01)

ON 1 January Finland became the only Nordic country to adopt the euro. The decision had clear popular support, but the apparent increase in the prices of some products led to criticism a few months into the euro experiment. The introduction of the new currency was a sign of Finland's rapid reorientation towards the West since the 1990s when the sensitive relationship with the former Soviet Union had ended. President Tarja Halonen also expressed the value to Finland of NATO during the NATO-summit in Prague in November (see XI.2.i). In contrast with official statements from Finland's Western neighbour, Sweden, nothing was said about nonalignment in her speech. However, membership of NATO was still only supported by a small minority in Finland.

On 17 January the government approved a controversial plan to construct Finland's fifth nuclear reactor, thereby making the country the only one in Western Europe that planned to expand its nuclear energy programme. The reactor would have a capacity of 1500 megawatts and would be ready in 2009 at an estimated cost of 2.6 billion euros. After intense debate, the Eduskunta (the unicameral legislature) on 24 May approved the plan by a relatively small margin (107 votes to 92). One of the plan's main opponents, the Green Party, subsequently left the five-party coalition government, led by the Social Democratic (SSDP) Prime Minister Paavo Lippone, in protest at the decision.

The year also saw crises in the telecommunications industry. On 4 August the government initiated an inquiry concerning a disastrous investment made by Sonera, the Finnish telecommunications company in which the state was a majority shareholder. The company had lost 4.3 billion euros after buying German 3G telephone licences. Sonera's investment was labelled the biggest corporate failure in Finnish history and the sum lost was said to be higher than the war reparations paid by Finland to the Soviet Union after World War II—an allegation which provoked severe criticism in the media. In November another scandal hit the company when three of its top managers were arrested for the illegal telephone tapping of employees who were suspected of having leaked information to the media. After complicated negotiations, Sonera in November reached an agreement with its Swedish equivalent, Telia. The merger between the two state-dominated companies was seen as a rescue package which, together with the continuing problems of the leading telecommunications company, Nokia, seemed to mark the end of Finland's long period of fast economic growth.

On 11 October the capital, Helsinki, was struck by an explosion, which at first seemed to be a terrorist attack. Seven people were killed and 80 injured when a homemade bomb exploded in a shopping centre. The perpetrator, however, who died in the explosion, was found to be a 19-year-old chemistry student. Although his motives were unclear, the student had no criminal record and the police found no links with terrorist or other extreme organisations.

vi. AUSTRIA

CAPITAL: Vienna   AREA: 84,000 sq km   POPULATION: 8,100,000
OFFICIAL LANGUAGE/S: German   POLITICAL SYSTEM: multiparty republic
HEAD OF STATE: Federal President Thomas Klestil (since Aug '92)
RULING PARTIES: People's (ÖVP) and Freedom (FPÖ) parties
HEAD OF GOVERNMENT: Wolfgang Schüssel (ÖVP), Federal Chancellor (since Feb '00)
MAIN IGO MEMBERSHIPS (NON-UN): EU, OSCE, CE, PFP, OECD
CURRENCY: euro (end-'02 £1=€1.5391, US$1=€0.9610)
GNI PER CAPITA: US$23,940, US$27,080 at PPP ('01)

NEARLY three years after the end of the "grand coalition" in February 2000 (see AR 2000, p. 73), the balance of power between the parties in the Nationalrat (the lower house of the bicameral national legislature) was once again overturned. The collapse of the "black-blue" coalition of the conservative People's Party (ÖVP) and the radical right-wing Freedom Party (FPÖ) led to a general election in November 2002 which saw a personal triumph for Federal Chancellor Wolfgang Schüssel. His ÖVP increased its share of the vote by more than 15 per cent to become the strongest party in the Nationalrat, having previously been the third largest; whilst the second largest party, the FPÖ, lost more than half of its share of the vote, achieving only 10 per cent. The biggest party in opposition, the Social Democrats (SPÖ), made weaker gains than expected and fell behind the ÖVP. The Greens, who had started the election campaign with ambitions of achieving a political shift to a Red (SPÖ)-Green coalition, as in Germany, managed only a slight increase, and were left with no opportunity of gaining office.

Austrian General Election (24 November 2002)

Party	% of votes 2002	Seats 2002	% of votes 1999	Seats 1999
ÖVP	42.3	79	26.9	52
SPÖ	36.5	69	33.2	65
FPÖ	10.0	18	26.9	52
Greens	9.4	17	7.4	14
Total	-	183	-	183
Turnout	84.3	-	80.4	-

The collapse of the FPÖ's vote was seen as the result of a deep crisis of identity within the party. After defeats in provincial elections (see AR 2000, p. 74; AR 2001, p. 91), which were attributed to discontent with the FPÖ's performance in national government, Jörg Haider, the FPÖ's leader and the strategic brain behind the party's right-wing orientation, tried to sharpen the FPÖ's profile in opposition to the national government. Although only holding office as governor of Carinthia, Haider worked to set a national political agenda. In January he initiated a plebiscite campaign on the closure of the Czech nuclear reactor at Temelin, which greatly concerned the Austrian public because of reports of its poor safety standards and its location only 56 km away from the Austrian border. The campaign found more than 900,000 supporters. Haider tried to force the Austrian government to veto the accession of the Czech Republic to the EU for as long as Temelin continued to operate. The government refused, however, and referred to a 2001 agreement with Czech Prime Minister Milos Zeman on safety improvements (see AR, 2001, p. 92). Further attempts by Haider to launch populist campaigns—including a visit to Iraqi leader Saddam Hussein in Baghdad and demands for the repeal by the Czech legislature of the Benes Decrees on the violent expulsion of German speakers from former Czechoslovakia after World War II—failed to mobilise large numbers of supporters but caused ongoing difficulties between Haider and FPÖ representatives both within government and inside the legislature.

Unprecedented floods in Central and Eastern Europe in August caused catastrophic damage to much of Austria. The Austrian government announced a €650 million programme of direct subsidies to the affected regions. As the original objective of a zero-deficit budget had already been postponed due to lower than expected tax revenues, the government looked for ways to compensate for this additional expenditure and decided to cancel a planned tax cut in 2003. This reduction had been a major theme of the FPÖ election campaign in 1999 and had served to bolster its image as the party of the "ordinary man in the street". Haider urged the government to go ahead with the tax reform and to cancel instead its planned purchase of Eurofighter combat aircraft. Conflict between FPÖ ministers and Haider escalated in September when a party conference in Knittelfeld was used to tear up a compromise paper between Haider and the FPÖ Vice Chancellor, Susanne Riess-Passer. One day after the conference, Riess-Passer, the FPÖ Minister of Finance, Karl-Heinz Grasser, and the FPÖ leader in the Nationalrat, Peter Westerthaler, all resigned. The next day, Chancellor Schüssel announced the break-up of the coalition and called for a general election.

The election campaign started with a lead in the polls for a potential Red-Green coalition between the SPÖ and the Greens. The FPÖ found it hard to make up for the loss of its three leading personalities on the national level. Haider refused to lead the campaign, and instead Infrastructure Minister Mathias Reichhold assumed this role. Meanwhile, Chancellor Schüssel succeeded in portraying himself as an experienced political leader who had left Austria in comparatively good economic shape, particularly compared with the Red-Green government in Germany. Shortly before the election, Finance Minister Grasser announced that he would support Schüssel and the ÖVP against his own party, the FPÖ.

At the end of 2002, negotiations on a new government coalition remained inconclusive. There was no doubt that Schüssel would once again be Federal Chancellor, and it was expected that he would again lead a black-blue coalition, but this time with a much weaker junior partner.

vii. SWITZERLAND

CAPITAL: Berne   AREA: 41,000 sq km   POPULATION: 7,200,000
OFFICIAL LANGUAGES: German, French, Italian & Rhaeto-Romanic   POLITICAL SYSTEM: multiparty republic
RULING PARTIES: Christian Democratic People's (CVP), Radical Democratic Party (FDP), Social Democratic Party (SPS); and Swiss People's Party (SVP)
HEAD OF GOVERNMENT: Kaspar Villiger (FDP), 2002 President of Federal Council and Minister of Finance
MAIN IGO MEMBERSHIPS (NON-UN): OECD, OSCE, CE, EFTA, PFP, Francophonie
CURRENCY: Swiss franc (end-'02 £1=SFr2.2393, US$1=SFr1.3982)
GNI PER CAPITA: US$36,970, US$31,320 at PPP ('01)

IN 2002, Swiss politics had to cope with the increasing challenges posed by international relations and a loss of trust in Swiss institutions and corporate governance. After decades of restraints on formal international relations, Switzerland became the 190th member of the UN, although more than 45 per cent of the population voted against membership in the referendum in March. Here, as in several other referendums, there emerged a greater willingness for international involvement in the French speaking parts of the country but a greater reluctance in the German speaking cantons. Further co-operation with the EU was impeded by conflicts over the secrecy of Swiss banks concerning the identity of their depositors. The international image of Switzerland was also affected by the report of an experts' commission, named after its chairman, Jean-François Bergier, on the role of the Swiss political and corporate establishment during World War II, and, in particular, the economic involvement of Swiss authorities and banks in the politics of Nazi Germany.

In autumn 2001, three domestic events—the bankruptcy of Swissair, the killing of people in a cantonal parliament, and a major truck accident in the Gotthard tunnel—had shocked Switzerland (see AR, 2001, pp. 93-94). In 2002, additional shocks occurred. A plane crash on the border between Switzerland and Germany caused the death of all 71 Russian passengers (many of them schoolchildren) and crew members. Initial attempts by the Swiss authorities to blame the accident on the pilot of the Russian plane were followed by reports implicating the deficiencies of the Swiss air traffic control system in giving a late and fatally erroneous order to the Russian pilot. The unwillingness of the Swiss authorities to shoulder the blame for the accident was widely criticised and the Swiss Federal President was even excluded from a funeral service for the victims in Russia.

The global economic slowdown also affected Switzerland. The main sectors of the Swiss economy found themselves in deep trouble, and several leaders of big companies had to resign. News of high severance payments to former chief executives shattered public confidence in the Swiss system of corporate governance. The major pharmaceutical companies and UBS, the largest company in the financial sector, maintained their position, but only by strengthening their multinational orientation.

One year before the next federal election, Swiss domestic politics revealed growing competition between the parties. In particular, the Swiss People's Party (SVP) tried to sharpen its profile by initiating several controversial referendums, including more restrictive rules for asylum seekers, an initiative which was rejected by a mere 3,300 votes. Social Democratic Party (SPS) Federal Councillor Ruth Dreyfus, responsible for many initiatives in the social security system, resigned after nine years and was replaced by party colleague Micheline Calmy-Rey, who was given the Foreign Affairs portfolio in the reshuffled Cabinet. The former Foreign Minister Joseph Deiss became Minister for Economic Affairs, and Pascal Couchepin took the Department of the Interior. The leader of the Radical Democratic Party (FPD), Gerold Bührer, resigned. He was a board member of the life insurance company Rentenanstalt/Swiss Life, which lost more than 80 per cent of its shareholder value during the year. The image of the FPD as the party of economic competence was also damaged by several other instances of failure by companies led by FPD party members. The overall effect was to threaten the FPD's eclipse as the country's leading liberal-conservative party by the SVP.

The results of the referendums did not reveal a clear picture. Comparatively liberal reforms—membership of the UN, a law allowing the termination of a pregnancy within the first three months, reform of unemployment insurance, refusal of stricter restrictions on asylum seekers—were approved, as were decisions to protect the status quo, such as the refusal to liberalise energy markets or to sell gold reserves. Nevertheless, despite symptoms of uncertainty and instability, economic and social conditions in Switzerland remained favourable. Unemployment rose only moderately, and social problems remained comparatively minor. The 6th Swiss national exposition, Expo 02, held in Murten, Biel, Neuenburg, and Yverdon, which attracted more than 10 million visitors, was seen as having had an important impact on national unity.

viii. EUROPEAN MINI-STATES

Andorra

CAPITAL: Andorra la Vella   AREA: 445 sq km   POPULATION: 67,000
OFFICIAL LANGUAGE: Catalan   POLITICAL SYSTEM: multiparty monarchy (co-principality)
HEAD OF STATE: President Jacques Chirac of France & Bishop Joan Martí Alanis of Urgel (co-princes)
HEAD OF GOVERNMENT: Marc Forné Molné, President of Executive Council (since Dec '94)
MAIN IGO MEMBERSHIPS (NON-UN): CE, OSCE
CURRENCY: euro (end-'02 £1=€1.5391, US$1=€0.9610)

Holy See (Vatican City State)

CAPITAL: Vatican City   AREA: 0.44 sq km   POPULATION: 880
OFFICIAL LANGUAGES: Italian & Latin   POLITICAL SYSTEM: non-party papacy
HEAD OF STATE: Pope John Paul II (since '78)
HEAD OF GOVERNMENT: Cardinal Angelo Sodano, Secretary of State (since Dec '90)
MAIN IGO MEMBERSHIPS (NON-UN): OSCE
CURRENCY: euro (end-'02 £1=€1.5391, US$1=€0.9610)

Liechtenstein

CAPITAL: Vaduz   AREA: 160 sq km   POPULATION: 32,000
OFFICIAL LANGUAGE: German   POLITICAL SYSTEM: multiparty monarchy
HEAD OF STATE: Prince Hans Adam II (since Nov '89)
RULING PARTY: Progressive Citizens' Party (FBP)
HEAD OF GOVERNMENT: Otmar Hasler, Prime Minister (since April '01)
MAIN IGO MEMBERSHIPS (NON-UN): EFTA/EEA, OSCE, CE
CURRENCY: Swiss franc (end-'02 £1=SFr2.2393, US$1=SFr1.3982)
GNI PER CAPITA: US$45,000 ('98 est.)

Monaco

CAPITAL: Monaco-Ville   AREA: 1.95 sq km   POPULATION: 32,000
OFFICIAL LANGUAGE: French   POLITICAL SYSTEM: non-party monarchy
HEAD OF STATE: Prince Rainier III (since '49)
HEAD OF GOVERNMENT: Patrick Leclercq, Minister of State (since Jan '00)
MAIN IGO MEMBERSHIPS (NON-UN): OSCE, Francophonie
CURRENCY: euro (end-'02 £1=€1.5391, US$1=€0.9610)

San Marino

CAPITAL: San Marino   AREA: 60.5 sq km   POPULATION: 27,000
OFFICIAL LANGUAGE: Italian   POLITICAL SYSTEM: multiparty republic
HEAD OF STATE AND GOVERNMENT: Captains-Regent Antonio Giuseppe Maria Morganti and Mauro Chiaruzzi
RULING PARTIES: Christian Democratic and Socialist parties
MAIN IGO MEMBERSHIPS (NON-UN): OSCE, CE
CURRENCY: euro (end-'02 £1=€1.5391 US$=0.9610)

ANDORRA, like Liechtenstein and Monaco, appeared in the OECD's list (published on 18 April) of states or territories which continued to protect offshore financial operations that were considered "harmful" to the international economy. The states' continued refusal to meet the OECD's standards on financial transparency and effective exchange of information opened the possibility of the imposition of financial sanctions upon them by the OECD's member-states in

2003. The OECD had first compiled its list of tax havens in 2000 (see AR 2000, p. 386). Monaco objected to its inclusion in the OECD's list, saying in a statement on 18 April that the principality had taken steps to increase the exchange of information on tax and was being treated differently from neighbouring countries. This statement appeared to refer to OECD members Luxembourg and Switzerland that had not been included on the OECD blacklist, despite their retention of secretive banking practices.

The HOLY SEE (Vatican City State) was shaken in 2002 by the worldwide condemnation of the Roman Catholic Church's handling of the proliferating allegations of sexual abuse of minors by Roman Catholic priests and other clergy. A number of measures were taken during the year in an attempt to deal with the crisis, but these were widely perceived as inadequate for both the scale and gravity of the problem. Pope John Paul II had issued an apology on 22 November 2001 to victims of sexual abuse by priests and clergy that acknowledged the church's failure to eradicate such abuse, and he made a further papal statement on 22 March 2002 which condemned the sexual abuse of minors by priests as "grievously evil". On 8 January the Vatican published new rules on how to deal with such allegations. These stipulated that local church tribunals of priests, convened in secrecy but under direct Vatican supervision, would decide on a priest's future in the Church and whether or not he would be relieved of his ministry. The rules did not preclude initiating civil prosecutions, but did not make them mandatory, leading to criticism that the Church was evading the issue.

Bishops in the USA, Poland, and Ireland resigned over allegations that they had themselves sexually abused minors. Some of the severest criticism amongst both Catholics and non-Catholics, however, was reserved for senior church figures who had allegedly permitted priests under their jurisdiction suspected of having committed sexual abuse to continue working with young people. On 13 December, mounting pressure amongst US Roman Catholics led to the resignation as Archbishop of Boston of the most senior figure in the Catholic Church in the USA, Cardinal Bernard Law. His original offer to resign, at a special summit of 12 US cardinals held in the Vatican on 23-24 April to discuss the problem, had been rejected by Pope John Paul II. Observers suggested that Law's resignation signalled a new confidence amongst the laity to challenge a Roman Catholic hierarchy that had appeared callous towards the victims of sexual abuse by priests and secretive in tackling the issue. On 19 November, the US Conference of Catholic Bishops made an apparent challenge to the Vatican's stance by adopting at its General Meeting a "Charter for the Protection of Children and Young People" which stated unequivocally that any clergyman convicted under canon law of the sexual abuse of a minor would be removed from his ministry and possibly defrocked.

The Roman Catholic Church made several controversial canonisations during 2002. These included, on 16 June, Padre Pio, a controversial but immensely popular Capuchin friar personally known to the Pope. Padre Pio, who had died at the age of 81 in 1968, had a large personal following but caused unease in the Vatican which had twice investigated him for faking miracles—including the stigmata that he was said to have borne from 1918 until his death—and for immoral behaviour. A second controversy surrounded the canonisation on 31 July at a ceremony in Mexico City (the capital of Mexico) of a 16th-century Aztec Indian, who was believed to have seen in 1531 a vision of Our Lady of Guadalupe (a dark-skinned Virgin Mary, the Patron of the Americas since 1910). Juan Diego Cuauhtlatoatzin (1474-1548)—already a popular figure in Mexico—thus became the first indigenous Latin American saint. However, some Mexican clergy claimed that his very existence had been invented by the Spanish conquerors to assist the subjugation and conversion of indigenous peoples. Finally, the canonisation of Josemaría Escrivá de Balaguer, Spanish founder of Opus Dei, in October caused consternation in Spain (see II.4.i).

The Pope had visited Mexico during his 10-day tour of Canada, Guatemala, and Mexico in July, during which he participated in the celebrations of World Youth Day in Toronto. In August, the visibly frail John Paul II made a four-day visit to Poland where he hinted that this, his ninth visit to his homeland, might be his last.

In LIECHTENSTEIN the 10-year long constitutional dispute over the role of the princely house continued unabated. The amended constitution, which had been rejected by the Landtag (the 25-seat legislature) in December 2001, was redrafted by a constitutional commission of the Landtag with the participation of the Reigning Prince Hans-Adam II and the Hereditary Prince Alois. However, by the end of the year, the constitutional amendments had still not been adopted, and the princely house reiterated its threat to move to Vienna if its powers were reduced by constitutional changes which it found unacceptable.

In MONACO, male nurse Theodore "Ted" Maher was convicted on 2 December of having caused the fire that had killed his employer, billionaire banker Edmond Safra, and another nurse in Safra's penthouse in December 1999 (see AR 1999, p. 90). Maher, who was sentenced to 10 years in prison, continued to insist that Safra's death had been "a terrible accident" which had resulted from his (Maher's) attempt to curry favour with Safra by rescuing him from danger.

In SAN MARINO, the 12-member coalition government of the Christian Democratic Party (PDCS) and Socialist Party (PSS) remained in power following the elections to the Great and General Council in June 2001 (see AR 2001, p. 97). The regular six-monthly rotation of Captains-Regent (the two heads of state and government), nominated by the Council, brought Antonio Lazzaro Volpinari (PSS) and Giovanni Francesco Ugolini (PDCS) to power between 1 April and 30 September, 2002, (replacing Alberto Cecchetti (PSS) and Gino Giovagnoli (PDCS)—in office since 1 October 2001). On 1 October 2002 Giuseppe Maria Morganti (PDCS) and Mauro Chiaruzzi (PSS) were installed as Captains Regent for the next six months.

4. SPAIN—GIBRALTAR—PORTUGAL—MALTA—GREECE—CYPRUS—TURKEY

i. SPAIN

CAPITAL: Madrid   AREA: 506,000 sq km   POPULATION: 39,500,000
OFFICIAL LANGUAGE: Spanish   POLITICAL SYSTEM: multiparty monarchy
HEAD OF STATE: King Juan Carlos (since Nov '75)
RULING PARTY: Popular Party (PP)
HEAD OF GOVERNMENT: José María Aznar López, Prime Minister (since May '96)
MAIN IGO MEMBERSHIPS (NON-UN): NATO, EU, OSCE, CE, OECD
CURRENCY: euro (end-'02 £1=€1.5391, US$1=€0.9610)
GNI PER CAPITA: US$14,860, US$20,150 at PPP ('01)

IN 2002 Spain's centre-right government entered a more turbulent period in office, characterised by weaker economic growth, higher unemployment, tense labour relations, and widespread public dissatisfaction over its performance.

The harmonious climate of labour relations that had characterised the Popular Party (PP)'s six years in office was brought to an end by a general strike on 20 June, in protest at the government's reform of the unemployment benefit system. It was no accident that the strike had been called for the day before the Seville summit that was meant to mark a triumphant end to Spain's presidency of the EU. The government's error had been to try and push the proposed reform through the legislature without explaining it properly to those affected. That sort of haste was a leitmotif of Jose María Aznar López's ambitious second term as Prime Minister. The result was the emergence of a period of wider and deeper discontent with the government. The year saw other protests: 300,000 people demonstrated in Barcelona on 16 March against the current political and economic dogmas; plans to reform education took students and teachers onto the streets of 34 towns across Spain on 28 October; and tens of thousands of people went to Valencia on 24 November to denounce the National Hydrological Plan (PHN) (see AR 2001, p. 100).

The political cost of the general strike was considerable. Only 19 days after the protest, Labour Minister Juan Carlos Aparicio Pérez and Government Spokesman (Minister without Portfolio) Pío Cabanillas, who had officially declared that the strike had not taken place, were replaced in a major Cabinet reshuffle. The new Labour Minister, Eduardo Zaplana, who had presided successfully over the region of Valencia, was charged with putting into effect the new labour reforms while rebuilding relations with the trade unions. Prime Minister Aznar also changed his Foreign and Interior Ministers. Ana Palacio, a prominent member of the European Parliament, was appointed to replace outgoing Foreign Minister Josep Piqué i Camps, and former Justice Minister Ángel Acebes was named as the new Interior Minister. Former Interior Minister Mariano Rajoy Brey remained in the Cabinet with the new post of Deputy Prime Minister. Rajoy also took on the roles of Minister in charge of the Prime Minister's office and Government Spokesman. In all, six ministers were removed from the Cabinet, five new figures were brought in, and three others switched portfolios.

Reporting the changes, the Spanish daily *El País* said that Aznar's objective had been "to regain the political initiative and stop the forward progress of the main opposition Socialist Workers' Party (PSOE)". The PSOE had gained ground in the polls because of Spain's economic problems and a major banking scandal surrounding secret accounts of the Banco Bilbao Vizcaya Argentaria (BBVA) in which Spanish news reports said some government members might have been implicated. José Luis Rodríguez Zapatero consolidated his leadership of the PSOE when he was named as the Socialist challenger for the premiership at the next general election due in the spring of 2004. Aznar had previously announced at a Popular Party congress in January that he would step down in 2004 when his second four-year term ended.

The year was also marked, once more, by conflict in the Basque country. The separatist terrorist group Basque Homeland and Freedom (ETA) continued with its campaign of political murders and bomb attacks. The death toll, however, was the lowest since the violence had restarted in 2000 (see AR 2000, p. 81). Five people were killed, and two ETA activists died while handling explosives. The comparatively low figure was attributed to the success of anti-terrorist measures. On the political level, the Basque country ended the year in the same way in which it had started it: with tension and lack of unity. Protest marches after ETA attacks showed an ever more angry public response not just to the violence but to the politicians' squabbles. Relations between the government in Madrid and the main Basque party, the Basque Nationalist Party (PNV), which ran the region's government, had rarely been worse. In particular, the central government insisted that ETA could be defeated by tough police and legal action and, in an effort to silence ETA's supporters, it started moves to outlaw ETA's political mouthpiece (since 2001 called Batasuna), which received official funding as a political party. The PNV fiercely opposed the ban, however, calling the idea anti-democratic, and launched its own plan for the future of the Basque country which would redefine the region's relationship with the central state in a "free association" under shared sovereignty.

In June amendments to the law on political parties had opened the way to the banning of Batasuna. The law allowed the government to ban any political group deemed to "promote hatred, violence, and civil confrontation". It also made it illegal to challenge Spain's existing democratic institutions. After some vigorous arm-twisting by the government, the PSOE and the nationalist coalition which ran Catalonia voted for the bill, while the PNV, along with the United Left coalition and the Galician nationalists, voted against. Many Basques, including some of those opposed to ETA and its terrorism, were against the ban on Batasuna. They feared that it would mean more, rather than less, violence, while simultaneously stripping the separatist cause of legitimacy. The influential bishops of the Basque region's three largest cities, Bilbao, Vitoria, and San Sebastian, signed a pastoral letter full of misgivings. In their letter the bishops were careful to denounce violence, but also said that it was "wrong to create a climate where 'anything goes' in the fight against terrorism". Outraged, the government called on the Vatican to reprimand the bishops.

The opportunity actually to ban Batasuna arrived in August. The party provoked national criticism for failing to condemn the killing of a six-year old girl in an ETA bomb attack on a police barracks at a resort on the southeast coast, which also killed a 57-year old man. At a special session of the legislature, recalled from recess on 26 August, members passed a motion asking the Supreme Court to outlaw the party. The motion received the support of the PSOE, but the Catalan Nationalists and United Left coalition abstained, and the PNV voted against. The full process was expected to take several months, but investigating magistrate Baltasar Garzón moved immediately to suspend the activities of Batasuna. The idea behind both moves was to prevent Batasuna from participating in the local elections due in 2003. Garzón froze Batasuna's bank accounts and forbade its leaders to organise demonstrations. On 27 August the Basque regional police began to implement a legal order to close Batasuna offices throughout the Basque country.

The Basque premier, Juan José Ibarretxe, did his best to obey Garzón's order that Batasuna's headquarters be closed down whilst simultaneously challenging his ruling in the higher courts. Meanwhile, the Basque regional assembly, also controlled by the PNV, went a step further by declaring Garzón's ruling invalid. This in turn prompted calls in the Spanish legislature, mainly by conservatives but also by some Socialists, to suspend part or all of the self-government that Basques enjoyed under the system of regional devolution enshrined in the constitution. With the declared aim of eradicating ETA violence, Ibarretxe proposed on 27 September a radical redefinition of the political status of the Basque country which, if implemented, would lead to de facto independence from Spain. Although the proposal had no legal basis, the regional government committed itself to holding a referendum during the current legislative period. This caused a further deterioration in relations with central government, which denounced the idea as contrary to the constitution.

As the year moved to a close, the single-hulled tanker *Prestige*, carrying 77,000 tonnes of heavy fuel oil, split apart in rough seas and sank off the northwestern coast of Spain on 19 November, causing the country's worst ever environmental disaster with potentially dire political consequences for the Galician and central governments, both of which were run by the People's Party. The clamour against the government's sluggish and ill-equipped official response to the crisis, which had spread the pollution more widely than necessary, reached its climax when, in the largest demonstration in the history of the region, some 200,000 angry citizens marched in the rain through Santiago de Compostela, Galicia's capital, on 1 December, calling for political heads to roll. The government not only ignored the petition but also accused the opposition of disloyalty and of taking advantage of the disaster. It was not until a month after the accident that Aznar visited Galicia, announced a package of economic aid, and admitted that his government had made some errors in its response. In the face of the government's lack of initiative, civil society demonstrated its own vitality as thousands of volunteers went on pilgrimage to clean up the beaches. Experts calculated that it would take months and cost many millions of euros to clean up the coast. In addition to the environmental costs, Spain was counting the cost to its fishing fleet—a vital part of the Galician economy—and to the tourist industry in the region. Meanwhile, the European Commission rushed out proposals to tighten the rules of maritime transport.

An uninhabited islet off the Moroccan coast, lying some 10 km from the Spanish north African city enclave of Ceuta, became the focus of an international diplomatic row when on 11 July a 12-member Moroccan police unit occupied the islet, called Perejil by Spain and Leila by Morocco. Spain responded by deploying five warships and saying it wanted to resolve the dispute through negotiations. On 17 July, however, Spanish armed forces evicted the Moroccans by force. The Spanish troops withdrew from the island after mediation from the USA. The island's status was unclear. Perejil had been controlled by Spain since the 17th century, but Morocco insisted that it had inherited the island when it gained independence in 1956. Spain believed that Morocco was using Perejil to highlight other differences, such as fishing rights, illegal immigration, and the issue of Western Sahara. Morocco had also frequently called on Spain to cede control over the enclaves of Ceuta and Melilla. Relations between the two countries had come under increasing strain since October 2001, when Morocco recalled its ambassador from Madrid (see AR 2001, p. 255). Talks between the two countries were resumed at foreign ministerial level in December.

In social affairs, the year saw further moves towards the normalisation of homosexuality. The Guardia Civil, Spain's militarised police force, amended the ruling which limited the right to live in barracks to heterosexual couples following a request from a homosexual officer; and a parish priest challenged church doctrine twice by admitting that he was a practising homosexual.

Spain's reassessment of its recent history took an important step when, 27 years after the death of Gen. Francisco Franco y Bahamonde, the Spanish legislature passed official condemnation of his fascist regime and offered recognition to the victims of the 1936-39 civil war which brought him to power (see AR, 1939, pp. 262-69). The motion was the result of growing pressure in Spain for public recognition of repression under Franco, which had remained a taboo subject since the country's transition to democracy in the mid-1970s. In addition, the canonisation of Josemaría Escrivá de Balaguer, Spanish founder of Opus Dei (an extremely conservative Catholic lay order), at a ceremony in Rome on 6 October before an estimated 300,000 people including several Spanish government ministers, provoked criticism in Spain because of Opus Dei's support for the Franco regime.

ii. GIBRALTAR

CAPITAL: Gibraltar   AREA: 6.5 sq km   POPULATION: 27,000
OFFICIAL LANGUAGE: English   POLITICAL SYSTEM: semi-autonomous UK overseas territory
HEAD OF STATE: Queen Elizabeth II
GOVERNOR-GENERAL: David Durie
RULING PARTY: Gibraltar Social Democrats (GSD)
HEAD OF GOVERNMENT: Peter Caruana, Chief Minister (since May '96)
CURRENCY: Gibraltar pound (at a par with UK pound)

ANGLO-SPANISH talks over the future of Gibraltar continued as scheduled over the first half of 2002 (see AR 2001, pp. 101-02), but, as had been expected, no agreement was reached by the summer. The summer target was missed as talks became bogged down, mainly on the question of joint sovereignty, but also on the issue of access to the territory's military base. The UK wanted any settlement to be a permanent arrangement, but Spain refused to give up its hope of one day regaining full sovereignty.

A referendum called by Gibraltar's Chief Minister, Peter Caruana, and held on 7 November found that 99 per cent of voters opposed the principle of shared sovereignty. Turnout was 85 per cent. Although the result carried no legal weight, the Gibraltarian authorities hoped that it would demonstrate the strength of local feeling against any change in the Rock's current status as a British dependent territory.

iii. PORTUGAL

CAPITAL: Lisbon   AREA: 92,000 sq km   POPULATION: 10,200,000
OFFICIAL LANGUAGE: Portuguese   POLITICAL SYSTEM: multiparty republic
HEAD OF STATE: President Jorge Sampaio (since March '96)
RULING PARTIES: Social Democrats (PSD) and People's Party (PP) form coalition
HEAD OF GOVERNMENT: José Manuel Durão Barroso , Prime Minister (since April '02)
MAIN IGO MEMBERSHIPS (NON-UN): NATO, OECD, EU, OSCE, CE, CPLP
CURRENCY: euro (end-'02 £1=€1.5391, US$1=€0.9610)
GNI PER CAPITA: US$10,670, US$17,270 at PPP ('01)

PORTUGAL'S introduction of the euro on 1 January was expected to confirm the country's acceptance into an elite group of 12 adopting member states. However, the difficulties in complying with the fiscal controls imposed by the EU meant that Portugal struggled, for much of 2002, to control its budgetary deficit and to avoid censure from the European Commission. Amidst acrimonious debate, Portugal experienced significant political change, severe financial austerity, and heightened economic upheaval; all played out against a backdrop of frustration associated with the national pastime—football.

The year began with preparations for an early general election scheduled for 17 March. Following a series of embarrassing defeats for the Socialist Party (PS) in the municipal elections of December 2001, Prime Minster António Guterres tendered his resignation. On 26 January, he was replaced by former Cabinet Minister for Social Affairs and Employment, Eduardo Ferro Rodrigues, who became leader after two other front-runners—António Vitorino and Jaime Gama—withdrew for personal reasons.

The Social Democratic Party (PSD), under the leadership of José Manuel Durão Barroso, began the campaign with a lead in the opinion polls and hopes of gaining an overall majority in the Assembly of the Republic (the unicameral legislature). The PSD manifesto included cutting corporate taxes to encourage foreign investment, reducing public spending, and the privatisation of several state-run services. One of the more unusual aspects of the election debate concerned an unlikely combination of sport and politics, with football taking centre stage. Newly elected PSD mayors in Lisbon and Oporto inherited plans (and costs) from their socialist predecessors for the construction of 10 new stadiums associated with the staging of the 2004 European football championships. The PSD officials questioned the major financial commitments involved and the football clubs, in turn, threatened to suspend building work unless assurances were given by government. UEFA, European football's governing body, warned that the championships would be switched to another venue and President Jorge Sampaio convened talks, which resolved the matter. Many commentators, however, felt that the general election was relegated to the level of terrace banter and that more important issues had been overshadowed by the dispute.

On the day of the general election, the public's disillusionment with the political situation led to an abstention rate of around 38 per cent. The low turn-out contributed to a narrow victory for the PSD with Durão Barroso securing 40 per cent of the vote and 105 seats in the 230-seat Assembly of the Republic. The outgoing PS party gained 38 per cent of the vote and 96 seats in the legislature. This result was not enough, however, to secure an overall majority and so the PSD was forced into a coalition (thereby gaining the support of a further 14 legislators) with the conservative People's Party (PP) under the tutelage of Paulo Portas.

On 6 April Prime Minister Durão Barroso unveiled a new centre-right coalition government with an expanded 18 member Cabinet and, as part of the PSD/PP pact, Paulo Portas secured control of the Defence Ministry. One of the most significant appointments was that of Manuela Ferreira Leite as Minister for what became the pivotal Finance portfolio.

At the beginning of May, a package of emergency financial measures was announced, aimed at dramatically reducing Portugal's budget deficit. Dubbed the "Iron Lady", Ferreira Leite outlined a series of essential, if unpopular, decisions. These included an increase in value added tax (VAT) from 17 per cent to 19 per cent, an abolition of state-subsidised mortgage rates for home-buyers, a freezing of recruitment to the civil service, a prohibition of local authorities incurring further debt, and a closure or merger of more than 70 state institutions. On 30 May Durão Barroso announced an additional package aimed at revitalising the national economy and including plans to privatise the state-owned national airline (TAP) together with a number of public utilities.

Government concern over the state of the economy was linked to an announcement on 25 July that the budget deficit for 2001 had far exceeded the maximum stipulated in the EU's Stability and Growth Pact. Provoking widespread controversy, the PSD government revealed that the deficit had risen in 2001 (under the Socialists), to 4.1 per cent of GDP—well above the 3.0 per cent limit permitted.

The threat of sanctions loomed large because the European Commission had the option to impose heavy fines and, more importantly, could prevent Portugal from applying for financial assistance via the cohesion funds. Such a move would have enormous implications for a country that had grown used to improvements based on major infrastructure and public works schemes financed by the EU's largesse. Ferreira Leite argued that her spending cuts would reduce the budget deficit to 2.8 per cent and bring the economy back under control.

Whilst few doubted that Portugal needed to implement austerity measures of this magnitude, the revised budget provoked widespread anger and protests. The largest demonstrations came with a one-day general strike on 16 October. Much of the country was brought to a standstill by public sector workers as hundreds of offices, hospitals, and schools closed. The strike was called by the main trade unions in protest against radical government proposals. These included the introduction of salary grading, an imposition of restricted wage levels, and increased private sector involvement in the social security system, particularly in relation to retirement pension schemes. On 21 October the most prominent dissenter, Chief of Staff of the Armed Forces Gen. Alvarenga Sousa Santos, was dismissed having publicly criticised a proposed "insignificant" 2 per cent increase in government expenditure on the military.

On a lighter note, the country's obsession with the staging of the 2004 European football championship was brought into focus on 28 November. It was announced that Luiz Felipe Scolari had agreed to take over as coach of the national team. Scolari, popularly known as "Big Phil", had previously coached Brazil to World Cup triumph in June 2002 and was set to sign an 18-month contract in January 2003. The appointment was greeted with optimism, particularly given Portugal's own poor performance in Japan and South Korea where the team had failed to qualify from the first phase of the tournament.

iv. MALTA

CAPITAL: Valletta   AREA: 316 sq km   POPULATION: 392,000
OFFICIAL LANGUAGES: Maltese & English   POLITICAL SYSTEM: multiparty republic in British Commonwealth
HEAD OF STATE: President Guido de Marco (since April '99)
RULING PARTY: Nationalist Party (NP)
HEAD OF GOVERNMENT: Edward Fenech Adami, Prime Minister (since Sep '98)
MAIN IGO MEMBERSHIPS (NON-UN): NAM, CWTH, OSCE, CE
CURRENCY: Maltese lira (end-'02 £1=ML0.6430, US$1=ML0.4015)
GNI PER CAPITA: US$9,450, US$15,800 at PPP ('00 est.)

As was to be expected, the issue of EU membership dominated public debate and events during the year, since Malta, like all applicant states for the next enlargement, had to conclude accession negotiations in 2002. Having closed 20 *acquis communautaire* chapters by the end of 2001 (see AR 2001, p. 104), Malta closed the remaining 11 chapters before or at the EU summit held in Copenhagen on 13 December. The hardest chapters to negotiate were those on the environment (because of bird hunting and trapping), taxation (because of

Value Added Tax (VAT) on food and medicines), and competition policy (because of state subsidies to the shipyards).

Bird hunters and trappers, a numerous, vociferous, and powerful lobby, were perceived by the political parties to be sufficiently devoted to their pastime to sway an election result. Much to the annoyance of environmentalists—who tended to be in favour of Maltese accession to the EU in the belief that membership would force the authorities to take the environment more seriously—the government pleaded the case for hunters and trappers and succeeded in securing permission for bird hunting and trapping to take place during the spring months.

VAT, introduced in Malta by the Nationalist (PN) government in 1994 (see AR 1994, pp. 99-100), had since then been a constant bone of contention, with the opposition Malta Labour Party (MLP) only very recently and begrudgingly agreeing to retain it if re-elected. It was, therefore, particularly important for the government to secure a concession exempting food and medicines from even the reduced minimum rate of 5 per cent required by EU law. After lengthy negotiations, Malta was allowed to continue exempting food and medicines until 2010, on the basis of the precedent set by the UK and Ireland, or even later if these two countries were to succeed in retaining their exemption beyond that date.

The most significant concession wrung from the EU, however, was that allowing the government to continue subsidising the state-owned shipyards at current rates until the end of 2008, by which time the ongoing restructuring should have been completed. This notable exception to EU practice, achieved after two years of hard negotiation, was underlined by the caveat that "this unique case can in no way be regarded as a precedent". Its political significance lay in the fact that it assuaged fears for the immediate future of the industry, which had been the grounds on which its militant workforce had prevailed on the powerful General Workers Union (GWU) to oppose EU membership. The GWU continued to oppose membership nonetheless.

The financial package announced at the Copenhagen summit made Malta a net beneficiary of EU funding to the tune of €194 million over the first three years of membership. Nevertheless, the MLP remained unmoved by the outcome of the negotiations and adamant in its commitment to withdraw Malta's application if returned to office before accession. It equally maintained that it would disregard the outcome of the referendum on membership, and would recognise only the popular verdict delivered in the next general election, due after the referendum but before the date set for accession (1 May 2004).

As the political parties battled it out, a number of pro and anti-membership groups proliferated. None attracted more attention than the anti-membership front established by former Prime Minister Dom Mintoff, who had brought down the Labour government in 1998 after falling out with its leader (see AR 1998, p. 100). Evidently sensing that the reason for the EU's eagerness to admit Malta concerned European security issues and the progress of the Common Foreign and Security Policy (CFSP), Mintoff re-emerged from retirement to campaign against membership on the grounds that it violated Malta's constitutional neutrality and threatened its sovereignty. That Malta in recent years had become a factor in Europe's security considerations, meanwhile, was amply illustrated by the extraordinary stream of illegal migrants who were stranded, intercepted, or shipwrecked on and around the island during 2002, the bulk of them bound for southern Europe.

v. GREECE

CAPITAL: Athens   AREA: 132,000 sq km   POPULATION: 10,600,000
OFFICIAL LANGUAGE: Greek   POLITICAL SYSTEM: multiparty republic
HEAD OF STATE: President Kostas Stephanopoulos (since March '95)
RULING PARTY: Pan-Hellenic Socialist Movement (PASOK)
HEAD OF GOVERNMENT: Kostas Simitis, Prime Minister (since Jan '96)
MAIN IGO MEMBERSHIPS (NON-UN): NATO, EU, OSCE, CE, BSEC, OECD
CURRENCY: euro (end-'02 £1=€1.5391, US$1=€0.9610)
GNI PER CAPITA: US$11,780, US$17,860 at PPP ('01)

THE year began with the triumphal introduction of the euro, the reward for Greece's striking achievement in meeting the tough criteria for entry to Economic and Monetary Union. As the EU's easternmost member, Greece, the Eurozone's latest entrant, actually became the first state formally to introduce the new currency on 1 January. Initial public enthusiasm was soon tempered by discontent, however, as the currency change apparently fuelled inflation, provoking two unprecedented consumer boycotts in September.

The question of pension reform, which had dominated the political agenda in 2001, was resolved—at least temporarily—by the passage of Law 3029/2002, which omitted previous controversial proposals to raise the retirement age. Public protest focused on a general strike in May, but died away once the law was passed on 19 June.

The event of the year occurred 10 days later, when the accidental detonation of a bomb in the hands of icon painter Savvas Xyros led to the uncovering of the notorious 17 November (17N) terrorist group. Throughout the hot summer, Greeks remained glued to their television screens, following the sensationalist media coverage of the 17N saga. Particular excitement was generated by the arrest on 17 July of Alexandros Yotopoulos, the group's alleged founder and ideologue, and the voluntary surrender to the police of Dimitris Coufoudinas, the apparent "second generation" leader, on 6 September. After 27 years during which the group had eluded capture, conducting over 100 attacks against targets ranging from foreign diplomats to strike-breaking tugboats, the myth of 17N was finally exploded. Belying the intellectual pretensions of the group's lengthy political manifestos, the suspects proved to be a surprisingly unglamorous group who had apparently evolved into an extortion and bank-robbing enterprise. In true Greek fashion, it also seemed to be largely a family affair. The 18 suspects arrested by year's end included four brothers, two cousins, and the current and former partners of the only woman arrested, Angeliki Sotiropoulou. Further revelations were expected at the trial, scheduled for 2003.

Basking in the achievement of the 17N roundup, the government avoided the predicted defeat in the first and second tier local government elections on 13 and

20 October. The polls were conducted using new electoral registers, which for the first time listed voters in the municipality where their family was registered rather than in their place of birth. Electoral gender segregation was also abolished, with men and women from now on voting in the same polling centres.

Unusually for Greece's traditionally male-dominated political scene, women were the major winners in Athens (the capital), with Dora Bakogianni from the opposition Nea Dimokratia (ND) elected mayor of the city, while Fofi Gennimata of the ruling Pan-Hellenic Socialist Movement (PASOK) won the Athens-Piraeus "super-prefecture". Although PASOK lost three prefectures and a number of important municipalities, ND's gains were overshadowed by its resounding defeat in the Athens-Piraeus "super-prefecture". The choice of a non-party candidate, journalist Yannis Tzannetakis, well known for his pro-secular stand during the Church-State identity cards controversy in 2000-01 (see AR 2001, p. 107), prompted many ND supporters to defect in the first round. While the 13.6 per cent vote for a far-right populist, Georgios Karatzaferis, excited speculation that Greece might be following the West European trend of rising right-wing extremism, it seemed more likely that this was a protest against a particular ND candidate rather than a seachange in political life.

A more lasting result of the election appeared to be the reinforced role of Archbishop Christodoulos, now restored to political prominence despite the earlier identity cards defeat. Between the two rounds of the elections, ND openly canvassed the Archbishop's support, with two of the party's candidates making a much-publicised visit to seek his blessing. Following the announcement of the UN's peace plan for Cyprus on 11 November (see II.4.vi), socialist Foreign Minister George Papandreou also took care to brief the Archbishop and ensure his support. Church involvement in secular affairs, an issue resolved by many other West European states in the 19th century, was apparently flourishing in 21st century Greece.

In contrast, a judgment by the European Court of Human Rights (ECHR) emphasised that the question of the monarchy, abolished after the 1974 referendum, was definitively closed. In November 2000, the ECHR had decided that expropriation of the royal estates without compensation had violated the ex-King's right of private property. On 28 November, deeming that the compensation did not need to reflect the value of the properties concerned, the Court awarded the former royal family a total of 13.7 million euros. As this was less than 3 per cent of the sum demanded by ex-King Constantine, the judgment was regarded by the Greek government as a moral victory.

The most significant government victory of 2002 occurred on 13 December when the major foreign policy aim of the previous decade—Cyprus' accession to the EU—was approved at the Copenhagen summit (see XI.4). If negotiations on the UN's plan did not bear fruit by 28 February, only the Republic of Cyprus (the Greek entity) would be admitted, leaving the Turkish north of the island outside the EU. It thus remained an open question if accession would create a new dynamic for the resolution of the Cyprus problem. The Greek government tried to facilitate Turkish concessions by supporting negotiations on the UN plan and campaigning actively for an EU commitment to a date for opening accession negotiations with Turkey. Within Greek society, initial opposition to the Cyprus plan abated once it appeared that the UN proposal might act as a catalyst for change in northern Cyprus.

In contrast to these successes, a major policy failure concerned the second regularisation of undocumented migrants, launched in 2001. Faced with the inability of the public administration to process the applications in time, in April the government automatically extended all temporary residence permits until the end of the year. One day before they expired, on 30 December, a further 6-month extension had to be granted for all permit-holders who had submitted renewal applications. That the development of a coherent immigration policy had become one of the major challenges facing the Greek state was tragically underlined by the 24 "boat people" who drowned in Greek waters in December alone.

Trafficking in human beings, which had assumed major dimensions, was the subject of a law passed on 2 October. Also on the legislative front, a draft law enacting one of the 2001 constitutional revisions forbidding legislators from exercising a profession whilst in office sparked controversy concerning the anticipated impact on the political independence of parliament. Other legislative innovations included prohibitions on fruit machines and smoking in government offices. As the non-smoking law did not specify sanctions for transgressors, it remained to be seen how effective it would be in a society with the highest per capita cigarette consumption in the EU.

vi. CYPRUS

CAPITAL: Nicosia AREA: 9,250 sq km   POPULATION: 875,300 ('01 est): 671,300 Greek Cypriots and others; 204,000 Turkish Cypriots and Turkish immigrants in the north
POLITICAL SYSTEM: separate multiparty republics: Republic of Cyprus (recognised by UN), Turkish Republic of Northern Cyprus (TRNC—recognised only by Turkey)
HEAD OF STATE AND GOVERNMENT: President Glafkos Clerides (since Feb '93); in the north, Rauf Denktash has been the community leader since Feb '75 (self-styled President since '83); Dervis Eroglu, Prime Minister (since Dec '98)
RULING PARTIES: Democratic Rally (DISY) heads coalition with United Democrats (EDI) and independents in Greek Cyprus; National Unity Party (UPB) and Communal Liberation Party (TKP) form coalition in TRNC
MAIN IGO MEMBERSHIPS (NON-UN): NAM, OSCE, CE, CWTH
CURRENCY: Cyprus pound (end-'02 £1=C£0.8813, US$1=C£0.5502); Turkish lira in the north
GNI PER CAPITA: Greek Cyprus US$12,230, US$19,530 at PPP ('98 est.); TRNC US$4,000 at PPP ('00 est.)

AFTER more than a year of no negotiations (see AR 2001, pp. 109-110), the Greek and Turkish Cypriot leaders, Glafkos Clerides and Rauf Denktash, agreed to intensive talks under UN auspices commencing on 16 January 2002. The process was sparked by the prospect of Cypriot accession to the EU at the end of 2002. The format called for the two leaders to meet, face-to-face, together with a limited number of advisers, at the UN headquarters in the buffer zone at the former Nicosia airport. The meetings were presided over by Alvaro de Soto, special advisor on Cyprus to UN Secretary General Kofi Annan. However, despite more than 60 sessions, plus meetings with Annan himself in May (in Cyprus), September

(Paris), and October (New York), no agreement could be reached.

The UN urged the two sides to concentrate on practical matters of governance, security, territory, and property but the Turkish Cypriots insisted on prior resolution of the nature of the state. The Greek Cypriots sought a federal arrangement in which a strong central government would devolve powers to two provinces. The Turkish Cypriots demanded a sovereignty association between two internationally recognised states: the Republic of Cyprus (founded in 1960 as a power-sharing state but since 1963 with a government consisting solely of Greek Cypriots—see AR 1960, pp. 132-34) and the Turkish Republic of Northern Cyprus (declared in 1983 in the northern territory which lay under Turkish military control—see AR 1983, p. 171).

On 11 November 2002 with the EU's decision on the accession of Cyprus looming, Annan sought to break the stalemate by advancing a comprehensive, 137-page settlement proposal and calling upon the parties to agree in principle to its main points ahead of the EU heads of government summit in Copenhagen on 12-13 December. He proposed negotiations to produce a final agreement by 28 February 2003 and referendums in both communities by 30 March 2003 with a view to Cyprus acceding to the EU as a united island at the formal enlargement ceremony to be held in Athens on 16 April 2003.

The Annan compromise called for a confederal constitutional arrangement consisting of a "common state" and two largely autonomous "component states". The common state would have a power-sharing government responsible for external relations, citizenship and immigration, central bank functions, and matters concerning the whole island such as aviation, navigation, and communications. The component states would exercise authority in all other matters. The reunified state would speak and act with one voice internationally and in fulfilment of its EU obligations. However, in addition to citizenship of the common state, each of the component states would also have the right to confer citizenship and this would be used as the basis for derogations from rights of freedom of settlement and ownership of property. The number of citizens of one state who could live in the territory of the other would be capped at approximately 30 percent of the total. This would ensure that the Turkish Cypriot character of the north would not be unduly diluted. In exchange, the Turkish Cypriots would cede substantial territory, allowing some 85,000 of 200,000 Greek Cypriot refugees to return to their former homes. (Maps accompanying the plan suggested that the present distribution of land—Greek Cypriots 60 per cent, Turkish Cypriots 37 per cent, and UN 3 percent in the buffer zone—should be amended to approximately 71.5 per cent Greek Cypriot and 28.5 per cent Turkish Cypriot. The UN presented two maps with possible scenarios.) Of the 204,000 inhabitants of the north, some 129,000 were Turkish immigrants. Although the agreement would not require their repatriation, it was expected that many of them would return to the mainland.

The common state would have a bicameral parliament consisting of a Senate and a Chamber of Deputies each with 48 members elected for five-year terms. The Chamber would be elected in proportion to population, with neither state ever having fewer than 12 members, while each state would have equal representation in the Senate. There would be complex voting procedures to ensure the support of both states for controversial bills. The executive would consist of a six-member Presidential Council, elected by the Senate, from which a president and a vice-president—each from a different component state—would be drawn in rotation at 10-month intervals with neither component state holding the presidency for more than two consecutive terms.

The EU heads of government summit agreed to admit Cyprus as one of 10 new member states effective from May 2004. The summit conclusions determined that the whole island would be admitted and that, if there were no prior settlement, the application of the *acquis communautaire* would be considered "suspended" in the northern territory until such time as there was one. The heads of government declared, however, that it was their "strong preference" that the island should join the EU as a united entity. Efforts to get the Greek and Turkish Cypriots to commence talks in Copenhagen failed. On New Year's eve, however, Denktash was reported to have agreed to begin negotiations in January 2003, although he rejected the proposals for the cession of territory. There was a positive development when the Turkish Cypriots appointed delegates to joint committees who were to meet on the island to flesh out details of the UN's proposals.

The Turkish government sent mixed signals about the way forward. Members of the Islamist Justice and Development Party, elected in November (see II.4.vii), made statements suggesting that Denktash should be prepared to make compromises to achieve a settlement. The military and foreign policy establishment in Ankara, however, continued to back Denktash's rejectionist stance. Ironically, public opinion polls in the TRNC showed overwhelming support for the UN plan, whilst a majority of Greek Cypriots were opposed to accepting a settlement based on the UN terms.

In the TRNC during 2002, the hegemony of the nationalist camp supporting Denktash and his separatist views faced its first serious challenge in more than a quarter of a century. In June, municipal elections gave the conservative and anti-federalist National Unity Party (UBP) control of 16 out of 28 municipalities, but control of the three main towns—Nicosia, Famagusta, and Kyrenia—was secured by the pro-federalist and pro-European Republican Turkish Party (CTP) which took five municipalities overall.

In August, 86 Turkish Cypriot non-governmental organisations, said to represent some 38,000 people, issued a joint statement declaring a "common vision" for a new partnership state on the island leading to membership of the EU. Moreover, on 26 December, a reported 30,000 people (nearly the entire Turkish Cypriot—as opposed to the settler—adult population of the north) demonstrated in favour of a settlement that would allow Cyprus to enter the EU as a united island. The demonstrators called for the resignation of Denktash unless he agreed to negotiate.

vii. TURKEY

CAPITAL: Ankara AREA: 775,000 sq km POPULATION: 67,800,000 ('00 census)
OFFICIAL LANGUAGE/S: Turkish POLITICAL SYSTEM: multiparty republic
HEAD OF STATE: President Ahmet Necdet Sezer (since May '00)
RULING PARTY: Justice and Development Party (AKP) (since Nov '02)
HEAD OF GOVERNMENT: Abdullah Gül (AKP), Prime Minister (since Nov '02)
MAIN IGO MEMBERSHIPS (NON-UN): NATO, OSCE, OECD, CE, OIC, ECO, BSEC
CURRENCY: Turkish lira (end-'02 £1=TL2,650,565.5, US$1=TL1,655,000.00)
GNI PER CAPITA: US$2,540, US$6,640 at PPP ('01)

IN mid-2002, the coalition government headed by 77-year old Bülent Ecevit, leader of the centre-left Democratic Left Party (DSP), collapsed after three and a half years in office, precipitating early elections to the Grand National Assembly (GNA—the unicameral legislature). These elections in November redrew the country's political map, ending some 15 years of unstable coalition government and bringing an Islamic-inspired party into government.

Relations between the coalition partners had deteriorated in the first months of the year as the government pushed forward with legislation designed to meet the political criteria for the commencement of negotiations on Turkey's accession to the EU. Immediate liberalisation was advocated by Deputy Prime Minister Mesut Yilmaz, leader of the centre-right Motherland Party (ANAP), the smallest of the three coalition parties, and was supported by Prime Minister Ecevit. But the third coalition partner, the right-wing Nationalist Action Party (MHP), opposed measures such as the abolition of the death penalty (which had not been applied for more than fifteen years) and instruction and broadcasting in Kurdish and other minority languages. The situation was complicated by the fact that, whilst Ecevit and MHP leader Devlet Bahçeli both opposed any concessions in Cyprus, Yilmaz favoured a more flexible approach.

At first it seemed that the coalition would survive these disagreements, as all of the partners realised that their electoral support had been eroded by the hardships resulting from the financial crisis of the previous year (see AR 2001, pp. 111-12), and all wanted to see the major economic reform programme agreed with the IMF bear fruit before going to the country. The MHP thus let it be known that it would remain in the governing coalition even if the reforms which it opposed were approved in the GNA with the help of the opposition, as happened on 6 February. However, government cohesion was fatally undermined when Bülent Ecevit fell seriously ill in May and yet refused to give way to a successor. A statement by the leaders of the three coalition parties on 1 July that they were determined to stay in office until the end of the legislative term in April 2004 failed to restore confidence. Between 8 and 11 July, six ministers, including Foreign Minister Ismail Cem, resigned from Ecevit's DSP, taking with them more than half of the party's deputies, and depriving the government of its majority in the GNA. Bahçeli saw this as a prelude to the formation of an alternative coalition, from which his MHP would be excluded in favour of the centre-right True Path Party (DYP). In order to frustrate this move, he said that he would withdraw from the government unless elections were held in November. Mesut Yilmaz agreed to early elections, hoping to profit from his stance as the main champion of EU membership. Ecevit continued to argue that elections were unnecessary, but had to concede that his government had disintegrated. On 13 July the GNA voted overwhelmingly to hold elections on 3 November. Sensing the popularity of the prospect of EU membership, the outgoing GNA went on to approve on 3 August a wide-ranging package of amendments to align the constitution and the statute book with EU standards. This included the abolition of the death penalty, a move which allowed the death sentence which had been passed against the Kurdish rebel leader Abdullah Öcalan to be commuted to life imprisonment in October. The MHP, however, once again opposed the changes. The state of emergency in south-eastern Turkey, imposed in the fight against Kurdish separatist, was lifted in November.

The final blow against Ecevit was delivered by the resignation on 10 August of Kemal Dervish, the minister who had negotiated the economic rescue package with the IMF. Dervish had been expected to join DSP dissidents in the New Turkey Party (YTP), headed by the former Foreign Minister Ismail Cem. Instead, he chose to lend his weight to Deniz Baykal, leader of the opposition centre-left Republican People's Party (CHP), the country's oldest party formed by the republic's founding father Mustafa Kemal Atatürk.

Public opinion surveys predicted a massive win by the Justice and Development Party (AKP) which had been formed in 2001 by the former Istanbul mayor, Recep Tayyip Erdogan, as one of the two successors of the banned Virtue Party (FP), which was of Islamic inspiration. Therefore, many deputies changed their minds and tried to postpone the elections or to amend the electoral law which limited representation in the GNA to parties that obtained at least 10 per cent of the countrywide poll. But the President of the Republic, Ahmet Necdet Sezer, opposed a postponement, and the parties could not agree on electoral reform. The decision of the electoral board to ban Erdogan from standing for the GNA because of his conviction in 1999 for inciting religious animosity (by reciting a poem in praise of militant Islam), and the filing of a petition to the Constitutional Court to ban the AKP, did not affect the result which fully vindicated the pre-electoral polls.

In the elections on 3 November, the AKP won an absolute majority of 362 seats in the 550-member single-chamber legislature, with 34.3 per cent of the total vote. The CHP was the only other party to cross the 10 per cent threshold, receiving 19.4 per cent of the poll and winning 177 seats. Eight independents were also elected. One was later disqualified for voting irregularities, and another, the former police chief Mehmet Agar, rejoined the DYP and was elected party leader in December, replacing the former Prime Minister Tansu Çiller who resigned the leadership when her party obtained a meagre 9.5 per cent of the vote. The three coalition parties received less than 15 per cent between them: the MHP 8.3 per cent, ANAP 5.1 per cent, and Ecevit's DSP only 1.3 per cent. The Felicity Party (SP), the more radical of the two parties of Islamic inspiration, could muster only 2.5 per cent and Cem's New Turkey Party only 1.2 per cent. Yilmaz and Bahçeli both resigned as party leaders, whilst Ecevit faded away. One significant result was the rise from 4.8 to 6.3 per cent in the votes cast for the thinly veiled Kurdish nationalist party, the Democratic People's Party (DEHAP), formerly the People's Democracy Party (HADEP). As it failed to reach 10 per cent threshold, however, no Kurdish nationalists were elected to the GNA although DEHAP led the poll in the main Kurdish-speaking provinces of south-eastern Turkey. The Young Party (GP), formed by the controversial millionaire Cem Uzan, who faced legal proceedings in a number of countries and who campaigned on an unapologetically xenophobic platform, received a surprising 7.3 per cent of the poll.

As Erdogan remained outside parliament, AKP deputy leader Abdullah Gül formed the new government which the President approved on 18 November and which was endorsed by the GNA 10 days later by 346 votes to 170. The prospect of a stable single-party administration after some 15 years of rule by discordant coalitions, and the return of a two-party legislature after half-a-century of fragmentation, raised confidence in the country. The Istanbul stock exchange index, which had started the year at 14,077 points and had dipped to 8,748 on 9 July, rose to 14,058 points on 18 November. Market enthusiasm wore off quickly, however, and the index ended the year at 10,369, in spite of strong signs that the IMF programme was proving successful with the rise in consumer prices down from 68.5 to 29.7 per cent, the lowest level for 20 years, and growth during the first nine months rising to 6.2 per cent after a record dip of 9.4 per cent in GDP the previous year. One reason for market unease was the impression that, in Erdogan's absence, Abdullah Gül lacked authority over his Cabinet colleagues. This concern was somewhat allayed when, on 31 December, President Sezer signed constitutional amendments allowing Erdogan to stand for the GNA.

The President had earlier approved another package of reforms which, the government hoped, would have persuaded the EU Council of Ministers meeting in Copenhagen on 12 December to fix a date for the beginning of accession negotiations. Erdogan visited all the EU capitals and Washington DC, immediately after the Turkish elections and canvassed strongly for a firm date to begin negotiations in 2003 or 2004. Yet neither his efforts nor strong US support had the desired result, and the EU Council contented itself with the promise to examine in December 2004 the report which the Commission was to prepare on Turkey's progress and to commence negotiations without delay if that report was favourable. Erdogan subsequently hailed this decision as another milestone on Turkey's path to EU membership.

In the run-up to the Copenhagen summit, the new Turkish government had tried hard to persuade the Turkish Cypriot leader, Rauf Denktash, to engage in negotiations to settle the Cyprus dispute on the basis of the plan which had been presented in November by the UN Secretary General Kofi Annan, and, together with the Greek President of Cyprus Glafkos Clerides, to sign a framework agreement during the summit (see II.4.vi). When this proved impossible, the UN extended its deadline for agreement on the framework to 28 February 2003. As the year ended, Erdogan continued to press for negotiations, although he was careful to add that the interests of Turkey and of Turkish Cypriots had to be safeguarded.

By the end of the year, Turkey's stance in the event of a war with Iraq became the main preoccupation of the new government. Faced with US requests for active support—voiced by Assistant Defence Secretary Paul Wolfowitz and Assistant Secretary of State Mark Grossman during visits to Ankara in December—Turkey agreed to an inspection by the USA of air bases and harbours which would be used in military operations, but did not promise to allow US ground troops into Turkey nor to participate in a ground offensive. At the same time, the Turks reinforced their military presence in northern Iraq. As the year ended, negotiations with the USA on economic aid and the post-war settlement in Iraq were continuing, whilst the official Turkish position remained that war could and should still be averted and that, in any case, international legality must be respected.

In December, natural gas began to flow through the Blue Stream pipeline laid under the Black Sea from Russia to Turkey (see map III.3.iii). However as this underwater pipeline, the deepest in the world to date, was completed, doubts were expressed about Turkey's ability to consume all of the gas shipments expected from Russia in addition to the gas flowing through the newly completed pipeline from Iran.

III CENTRAL AND EASTERN EUROPE

1. POLAND—BALTIC STATES—CZECH REPUBLIC—SLOVAKIA—HUNGARY—
ROMANIA—BULGARIA

i. POLAND

CAPITAL: Warsaw   AREA: 323,000 sq km   POPULATION: 38,700,000
OFFICIAL LANGUAGE: Polish   POLITICAL SYSTEM: multiparty republic
HEAD OF STATE: President Aleksander Kwasniewski (since Dec '95)
RULING PARTIES: coalition of Democratic Left Alliance (DLA) and Union of Labour (UP)
HEAD OF GOVERNMENT: Leszek Miller (DLA), Prime Minister (since Oct '01)
MAIN IGO MEMBERSHIPS (NON-UN): NATO, OSCE, CE, CEI, CEFTA, CBSS, OECD, Francophonie
CURRENCY: zloty (end-'02 £1=Zl6.1540, US$1=Zl3.8425)
GNI PER CAPITA: US$4,240, US$9,280 at PPP ('01)

EUROSCEPTICISM grew markedly during 2002 as Poland moved towards EU membership. While President Kwasniewski, in a speech on 18 February, envisaged a "Europe of homelands" rather than a federal super-state, many counted the predicted economic costs of enlargement. In general, educated youth eagerly anticipated the advantages of EU membership, whilst many other social groups expressed their fears through extra-parliamentary protests. Nonetheless, the December Copenhagen summit (see XI.4) set a date for entry, to be preceded by a Polish referendum.

Protests against EU membership were led by Polish farmers, who still constituted almost a quarter of the country's workforce. They objected to an EU draft that offered a mere 25 per cent subsidy on food products at the date of entry, and was scheduled to reach 100 per cent only in 2013. Despite vigorous diplomatic representations, this was not an issue over which Poland was able to achieve concessions. There was, however, agreement between the Polish government and the European Commission on most other matters, including taxation, the free movement of capital, and the contentious question of land sales to foreigners (to be allowed after three years in eastern and southern Poland, and seven years elsewhere). It was also agreed, on 30 July, to tighten border crossings with Belarus and Ukraine in an effort to keep illegal immigrants and criminals out of the enlarged EU.

The background to anti-EU protests was an ailing economy. Following the success in the 1990s of "shock therapy", economic growth had stagnated, with the 2002 forecast cut to 1 per cent from 1.2 per cent in 2001. At the same time inflation was forecast to remain around 5 per cent. Unemployment rose to a record 18 per cent by the end of January, with 3.25 million officially unemployed. A new political party capitalising on the phenomenon, the All-Poland Unemployed Alliance, was registered on 26 February.

One response by the government, a centre-left coalition elected in September 2001 (see AR 2001, p. 115), was to halt bank privatisation and to pause in order to reorganise state-owned industrial companies before launching any further sales of state assets. Those utilities held back from sale included the monopoly gas supply and the electricity grid. On 2 April the Polish government withdrew from the sale of a majority stake in a state-owned insurance company to a Netherlands-based company on the grounds of the "protection of state interests".

A further government measure, introduced on 16 May, aimed to re-nationalise the bankrupt Szczecin Shipyard, whose 7,000 workers had not been paid since February. The Economy Ministry called for banks to resume deficit financing as soon as they saw plans for the enterprise to return to profitability. When banks did not deliver, the government's Industrial Development Agency stepped in to underwrite loans for a New Szczecin Shipyard to resume production. On 13 July, the workforce in Szczecin formed a National Protest Committee (OKP) to represent workers in other industries also facing bankruptcy.

The most dramatic protests were rural, often under the rubric of the Farmers' Self-Defence Committee (*Samo-obrona*) whose energetic leader, Andrzej Lepper, engaged in many anti-government activities. On 25 January the Sejm (the lower house of the legislature) lifted his immunity from prosecution, following which a Gdansk court imposed fines on him for insulting the President and various politicians and former ministers whom he had accused of having mafia connections. On 18 February he was arraigned for slander before a Warsaw court. Undeterred, he led 200 protestors into the Ministry of Agriculture on 15 May, demanding talks with the Minister, who had the intruders ejected by the police. Road blockages, planned for 25 June, were forestalled by the militia. Vociferous protests were also held outside the Central Bank against cheap grain imports from the EU and demanding the resignation of Central Bank governor Leszek Balcerowicz (the original architect of "shock therapy").

Whilst ignoring these protests as irritants, the government announced a reshuffle of finance ministers and an anti-crisis package in early July. Shortly afterwards, Lech Walesa, the founder of the Solidarity trade union and the first post-communist President (1990-95) announced that he would contest the presidency again. Since he had gained just 1 per cent of the vote in 2000 (see AR 2000, p. 100) this looked a somewhat forlorn quest, but Walesa gained backing from a new political group, Solidarity Convention (KS), of which he became chairman on 18 August.

The same day, Pope John Paul II held a mass for more than 2 million Catholics in the Blonia Meadow outside Krakow. On his ninth, and possibly last, pilgrimage to his homeland, the frail and ailing Pope endorsed EU accession but also issued coded warnings against the "illusory ideology of freedom" represented by unfettered capitalism. Although this view cut across political divisions, an increasingly vociferous League of Polish Families sought to build on public support (standing at 9 per cent in the 2001 election) for a platform of Catholic nationalist fundamentalism. It proposed an external role for Poland as part of an east European free trade alliance with the USA as a buffer against both the EU and Russia.

For his part, Russian President Putin, on his first official visit to a former "eastern bloc" state (on 16-17 January), regretted the last decade of "lost opportunities" in bilateral relations. He stated that Russia would try to redress its vast trade surplus of US$3 billion with Poland, caused largely by the sale of natural gas. Specific measures to achieve this, however, were not revealed

More significant steps were taken towards repairing relations with world Jewry. Poland's Institute of National Memory published archival research on the participation of some 40 Polish citizens in the World War II massacre of Polish Jews at Jedwabne in 1941, leaving the question of "German instigation" undetermined. In addition to the state's formal apologies for this and other massacres of the period, civil society considered an appropriate memorial to Poland's Jews. As a result, the city of Warsaw donated a 13,000 square metre plot on the site of the former Warsaw Ghetto for a fitting memorial: Eastern Europe's first major museum celebrating the everyday life of the region's Jews. A US$60 million project, designed by Western architects and museum curators, it was due to open in 2006.

ii. ESTONIA—LATVIA—LITHUANIA

Estonia

CAPITAL: Tallinn   AREA: 45,000 sq km   POPULATION: 1,400,000
OFFICIAL LANGUAGE: Estonian   POLITICAL SYSTEM: multiparty republic
HEAD OF STATE: President Arnold Rüütel (since Sept. '01)
RULING PARTIES: Pro Patria Union, Moderate & Reform parties
HEAD OF GOVERNMENT: Siim Kallas (Reform), Prime Minister (since Jan '02)
MAIN IGO MEMBERSHIPS (NON-UN): OSCE, CE, PFP, BC, CBSS
CURRENCY: kroon (end-'02 £1=K24.0813, US$1=K15.0362)
GNI PER CAPITA: US$3,810, US$10,020 at PPP ('01)

Latvia

CAPITAL: Riga   AREA: 65,000 sq km   POPULATION: 2,300,000
OFFICIAL LANGUAGE: Latvian   POLITICAL SYSTEM: multiparty republic
HEAD OF STATE: President Vaira Vike-Freiberga (since July '99)
RULING PARTIES: coalition of New Era, Union of Greens and Farmers (ZZS), Latvia First Party (LPP), & Fatherland and Freedom Union (TB-LNNK) (since Nov '02)
HEAD OF GOVERNMENT: Einars Repse (New Era) (since Nov '02)
MAIN IGO MEMBERSHIPS (NON-UN): OSCE, CE, PFP, BC, CBSS, WTO
CURRENCY: lats (end-'02 £1=L0.9412, US$1=L0.5877)
GNI PER CAPITA: US$3,260, US$7,870 at PPP ('01)

Lithuania

CAPITAL: Vilnius   AREA: 65,000 sq km   POPULATION: 3,500,000
OFFICIAL LANGUAGE: Lithuanian   POLITICAL SYSTEM: multiparty republic
HEAD OF STATE: President Valdas Adamkus (since Feb '98)
RULING PARTY: Lithuanian Social Democratic Party (LSDP)
HEAD OF GOVERNMENT: Algirdas Brazauskas (SDP), Prime Minister (since July '01)
MAIN IGO MEMBERSHIPS (NON-UN): OSCE, CE, PFP, BC, CBSS, Francophonie
CURRENCY: litas (end-'02 £1=L5.3134, US$1=L3.3177)
GNI PER CAPITA: US$3,270, US$7,610 at PPP ('01)

NOT since the restoration of independence in 1991 had the three Baltic states experienced a year as momentous as 2002, marked by symbolic invitations to all three countries to re-unite with the European mainstream. The issuing of invitations to join NATO (at Prague in November, see XI.2.i) and the EU (at Copenhagen in

December, see XI.4) marked the fulfilment of the two main foreign policy goals of all three Baltic countries: the recognition that they were firmly back amongst the Western family of nations.

ESTONIA entered 2002 in mild political disorder, as Prime Minister Mart Laar had already announced his intention to resign in December 2001 (see AR 2001, p. 118). When Laar dismantled his three-party centre-right coalition in January, one of the junior partners, the ultra-liberal Reform Party, took the helm and forged a deal with its former rival, the populist Centre Party, to form the next government. Reform Party leader and outgoing Finance Minister Siim Kallas was confirmed as Prime Minister in late January.

Although the two parties had had an acrimonious relationship for years, they chose to run a "caretaker" regime and avoided their major dispute: whether to keep and lower the flat income tax system, as the Reform Party proposed, or to create a progressive tax system, as advocated by the Centre Party. Although the Centre Party held more seats in the Riigikogu (the unicameral legislature), its controversial leader, transition-era Prime Minister Edgar Savisaar, remained in his post as mayor of Tallinn (the Estonian capital) in order to deflect any possible international criticism over his role in the illegal recording of politicians' conversations in 1995 that had led to his resignation as Interior Minister (see AR 1995, p. 141).

The October local elections, especially for the Tallinn city council, served as a trial run for the parliamentary vote in March 2003. The Centre Party performed strongly throughout the country, taking advantage of the weakness of the Left. Savisaar led his party to an outright majority in Tallinn (winning with 32 of the 63 seats), but entered a coalition with the Reform Party (which won 11 seats) to give the city its most stable administration for many years.

However, the political story of the year was the spectacular rise in popularity of the new centre-right party, Res Publica. Taking advantage of the downturn in the fortunes of other centre-right groups, Res Publica scored victories in many councils around the country and came second in Tallinn with 17 seats. Even the controversial resignation of state auditor Juhan Parts to take over the party's leadership did not dent its rising popularity in the run-up to the 2003 legislative elections.

The collapse of the coalition in January did not improve the position of the conservative Pro Patria Union of former Prime Minister Laar, nor of the social democratic Moderates' Party of former Foreign Minister Toomas Hendrik Ilves. Both parties fared poorly in the local elections, failing most miserably in Tallinn where they won no seats. Both Laar and Ilves resigned as the leaders of their respective parties as fears ran high in both camps of facing a similar fate in March 2003.

Aside from politics, the event of the year was Tallinn's successful hosting of the Eurovision Song Contest at the brand-new Saku Arena in May. The expensive task of organising the spectacle paid off with the arrival of hordes of tourists from throughout Europe, and the country's success in securing third place in the competition.

The country's love affair with technology continued in 2002. By the end of the year, nearly half of all Estonians were banking on-line and about half of income tax returns were being submitted via the Internet. Mobile telephones were commonly used to pay fares on public transport in Tallinn, as well as to pay for purchases in shops and for public parking.

In LATVIA, 2002 saw a dramatic change in the political scene, marked by the victory of a political novice and the collapse of two major parties in the autumn legislative elections. At the climax of a heated and unpleasant campaign, the 5 October elections continued the trend of voters' faith in new political voices: of the six parties that gained seats, three had either won none in the previous elections in 1998 or had not even existed at that time.

Former Central Bank governor Einars Repse, credited with playing a major role in Latvia's economic revival, led his new centre-right party, the New Era (JL), to a spectacular victory with 26 of the 100 seats in the Saeima (the unicameral legislature). Together with three other parties—the Green and Farmers Union (ZZS) with 12 seats, Latvia's First Party (LPP) with 10 seats, and the nationalist For Fatherland and Freedom (TB) with seven seats—Repse was nominated and confirmed as Prime Minister of an unwieldy coalition a month later after acrimonious squabbles among the personalities involved.

Much as after the 1998 elections, the centre-right People's Party (TP) of controversial two-term Prime Minister Andris Skele, failed to turn electoral success into power. Running an aggressive populist campaign, Skele once again alienated other centre-right forces and could not turn his party's 20 seats into more than an agitated right-leaning opposition. Finally realising the inevitable, Skele dramatically bowed out of politics at the end of the year, leaving the party without its unifying and most prominent figure.

During the late days of the campaign, the dismissal of Interior Minister Mareks Seglins (TP) by Prime Minister Andris Berzins of the centrist Latvia's Way (LC)—for police seizures of anti-TP leaflets—marred the entire campaign. It also helped to seal the fate of the ailing LC, which had taken part in every ruling coalition since the restoration of independence, as it failed to win any seats. The most vocal opposition to Repse came from the 25 seats won by the left-wing For Equal Rights in a United Latvia (PCTVL) coalition, which included elements which had campaigned against independence a decade earlier. It remained the only opposition from the Left, as the Latvian Social Democratic Workers Party (LSDSP), the most popular party during a large part of the legislative cycle, also spectacularly failed to cross the 5 per cent threshold for representation in the legislature.

However, the event that most marked Latvia's year was the victory of Marie N (Marija Naumova) in the 2002 Eurovision Song Contest, held in Tallinn in May (see above). Though squabbling about the venue to host the contest in 2003 had dampened the mood a little, the victory brought immense pride to Latvia which had been hoping to achieve the same kind of success as Estonia had enjoyed by hosting the high-profile event.

The political year in LITHUANIA did not heat up until its very end when President Valdas Adamkus faced re-election in late December. Having successfully won invitations to join both NATO and the EU, the ultra-popular Adamkus was viewed as a certain winner by analysts and politicians alike, especially as his predecessor as President, current Prime Minister Algirdas Brazauskas, chose not to compete. However, Adamkus did not win outright in the 22 December vote, in which 17 candidates took part. His 35 per cent required a run-off, to be held in early January 2003.

There was some surprise when twice Prime Minister Rolandas Paksas, of the populist right-wing Liberal Democratic Party, came second with nearly 20 per cent of the vote after a flamboyant and aggressive campaign. Many had predicted a second round between the right-leaning centrist Adamkus and the centre-left chairman of the Seimas (legislature), Arturas Paulauskas, leader of the New Alliance (Social Liberals). However, Paulauskas finished a poor third, far behind Paksas, and in the January 2003 run-off, in which most analysts had predicted a smooth victory for Adamkus, Paksas shocked the establishment by winning.

The flashy campaign style of Paksas, including a stunt flying display under a Vilnius bridge with only a seven-metre clearance, alongside his populist rhetoric, brought him support among those who had not benefited from the "return to Europe" led by Adamkus. However, with none of the main political parties backing him, questions were raised concerning his tactics and sources of finance, and even his party's symbol, which curiously resembled the Nazi swastika.

Despite this election upset, for the first 11 months of the year the political world remained relatively stable. Under the left-leaning coalition of Algirdas Brazauskas, the government made significant progress in privatisation, especially in two problematic areas. The last state-owned bank, Zemes Ukio Bankas (Agriculture Bank) was sold to Germany's Norddeutsche Landesbank. The state also finalised the privatisation process for the utility company Lietuvos Dujos (Lithuanian Gas), and sold the 34 per cent stake allocated to strategic investment to German energy giants Ruhrgas and E.ON Energie.

However, the energy world brought Lithuania its main headache of the year. US energy company Williams, the operator of the national oil company Mazeikiu Nafta (MN), and the Lithuanian government agreed in April to sell a 28.65 per cent stake in MN to Russia's Yukos in order to guarantee supply for the under-exploited export and refining facilities. But Lithuania became a victim of the collapse of the energy sector in the USA, as Williams shockingly pulled out of Lithuania in September, and sold its operating stake in MN to Yukos, thereby making Russia's second largest oil company the majority owner and operator in Lithuania. As the original privatisation terms for MN had endeavoured to keep the company out of Russian hands, this spectacular reverse caused universal political anger, together with a reluctant recognition of Lithuania's impotence to alter the decision.

Finally, the Central Bank completed its re-pegging of the litas to the euro from the US dollar, locking it into the exchange rate as of 1 February 2002.

iii. CZECH REPUBLIC

CAPITAL: Prague   AREA: 79,000 sq km   POPULATION: 10,300,000
OFFICIAL LANGUAGE: Czech   POLITICAL SYSTEM: multiparty republic
HEAD OF STATE: President Václav Havel (since Jan '93)
RULING PARTIES: Czech Social Democratic Party (CSSD), Christian Democrats (KDU-CSL) and Freedom Union (US)
HEAD OF GOVERNMENT: Vladimir Spidla (CSSD), Prime Minister (since June '02)
MAIN IGO MEMBERSHIPS (NON-UN): NATO, OSCE, CE, CEI, CEFTA, OECD, Francophonie
CURRENCY: koruna (end-'02 £1=Kor48.3036, US$1=Kor30.1605)
GNI PER CAPITA: US$5,270, US$14,550 at PPP ('01)

THE year was a difficult one for the Czech Republic, as massive floods in August inflicted tremendous damage on Prague and other important centres of tourism and industry. The flooding also complicated the country's already strained fiscal position.

The political Left achieved a victory in 2002, winning a parliamentary majority for the first time since the fall of communism in 1989. The Social Democrats (CSSD), who had ruled since 1998 in a power-sharing "opposition agreement" with the right-wing Civic Democratic Party (ODS), emerged victorious in the elections to the Chamber of Deputies (the lower house) on 14-15 June, winning 30.2 per cent of the vote and 70 seats in the 200-member chamber. Although the two parties had been neck-and-neck in the opinion polls in the months preceding the election, the ODS finished a somewhat distant second, with 24.5 per cent and 58 seats. The only other groups that surpassed the 5 per cent threshold needed for entry into the legislature were the Communists, with 18.5 per cent of the vote and 41 seats, and the Coalition, with 14.3 per cent and 31 seats. At just under 58 per cent of the electorate, voter turnout was disappointingly low.

The CSSD would have had considerable leeway in forming leftist-oriented policy had it created a minority government with tacit support from the Communists, particularly given the two parties' relatively strong legislative majority. However, the CSSD chose instead to govern with the centre-right Coalition, which subsequently broke down into its separate parts: the Christian Democrats (KDU-CSL) and the Freedom Union (US). That decision was in part due to the Czech Republic's ongoing talks on accession to the EU, as it was feared that the government's reliance on the Communists might hinder negotiations. Czech President Václav Havel appointed CSSD chairman Vladimir Spidla as Prime Minister on 12 July, and the rest of the Cabinet was installed on 15 July. The ruling coalition had an overall legislative majority of just one seat.

The KDU-CSL and US had little influence on policy making with the CSSD filling 11 of the 17 Cabinet positions, including most of the important ones. In entering the new Cabinet, the KDU-CSL and US wanted both to confirm their reliability as negotiating partners and to prevent other options that could damage the country's interests. Nonetheless, the situation remained precarious, as demonstrated most notably on 13 September, when the legislature narrowly defeated the government's proposed tax measures which were designed to funnel new revenues toward flood relief in 2003 and 2004. The bill failed when former US chairwoman Hana Marvanova voted together with the opposition, thereby throwing the government into crisis. The government's collapse was averted five days later, when the leaders of the three ruling parties signed an addendum to the coalition agreement guaranteeing that their legislators would unanimously back key government legislation. The addendum also stated that if the US failed to garner the support of all its deputies, it must voluntarily leave the government, but at the same time refrain from backing a vote of no-confidence in the Cabinet.

The three ruling parties suffered a crushing defeat in the Senate elections, held in two rounds in late October and early November. The parties lost their majority in the 81-member upper house, with unaffiliated candidates and representatives of the opposition ODS pulling ahead in the second-round runoff. Of the 27 seats being contested, just seven were won by CSSD candidates, compared with nine for the ODS and eight for independents and candidates from non-parliamentary parties. The CSSD's junior partners each won one seat, as did the opposition Communists. The only candidate to win an absolute majority in the first round was Vladimir Zelezny, a political independent who owned the popular television station TV Nova. The government parties needed to win at least 16 constituencies in order to maintain a Senate majority. With a total of 34 seats in the Senate, the ruling coalition found itself dependent on support from unaffiliated members for the approval of government bills. The ODS controlled a total of 26 Senate seats, compared with three for the Communists and 18 for unaffiliated members.

Another major political development in 2002 was the replacement of former Prime Minister Vaclav Klaus as ODS chairman during a December party congress. Klaus, a key player in the economic reform process in Czechoslovakia and later in the Czech Republic, had been ODS chairman since its founding congress in 1991. He first served as Czech Prime Minister following the June 1992 elections, and he led the Czechs to independence in January 1993. Klaus was the last of the senior Czech party leaders from the 1990s to give up his position, and many argued that the step came too late, as his arrogance had alienated many former sympathisers at home and abroad, triggering divisions within the party and diminishing the ODS's potential as a coalition partner. Klaus was replaced by the 46-year old Mirek Topolanek, the deputy chairman of the Senate.

The biggest economic concerns in 2002 related to fiscal and exchange rate policy. The country's budget deficit had been mounting because of the high cost of bank restructuring and rising mandatory payments for pensions and social benefits, but the CSSD was reluctant to implement reforms. Throughout much of the year, currency traders were undeterred by the government's lack of fiscal responsibility, and the Czech koruna reached new heights against the euro in 2002. With exporters expressing anxiety that the stronger currency was hindering sales abroad, the Czech National Bank cut interest rates several times and intervened against the koruna in an effort to halt its appreciation.

In foreign affairs, the Czech Republic hosted the NATO summit on 21-22 November (see XI.2.i), signalling that the country had become a fully-fledged member of that organisation. Relations with the EU were strained during much of 2002, however, partly over the issue of the Benes decrees, which had facilitated the expulsion of ethnic Germans and Hungarians from Czechoslovakia following World War II. Nonetheless, the Czech Republic managed to complete accession negotiations with the EU during the Copenhagen summit on 12-13 December (see XI.4). Along with nine other candidate countries, the Czech Republic was expected to join the organisation on 1 May 2004.

iv. SLOVAKIA

CAPITAL: Bratislava   AREA: 49,000 sq km   POPULATION: 5,400,000
OFFICIAL LANGUAGE: Slovak   POLITICAL SYSTEM: multiparty republic
HEAD OF STATE: President Rudolf Schuster (since June '99)
RULING PARTIES: Slovak Democratic Coalition and Christian Union (SDKU), Hungarian Coalition Party (SMK), Christian Democratic Movement (KDH) & New Citizen's Alliance (ANO) form ruling coalition
HEAD OF GOVERNMENT: Mikulas Dzurinda (SDKU), (since Oct '98)
MAIN IGO MEMBERSHIPS (NON-UN): OSCE, CE, PFP, CEI, CEFTA, OECD
CURRENCY: Slovak koruna (end-'02 £1=K64.3068, US$1=K40.1529)
GNI PER CAPITA: US$3,700, US$11,610 at PPP ('01)

THE legislative elections on 20-21 September were the major event of 2002 in Slovakia. The election results were considered crucial for the future direction of the country, particularly in light of the forthcoming decisions on the enlargement of NATO and the EU. It was feared that Slovaks would turn away from the reformist, pro-Western government that had held office since 1998 and would instead support the return of populist and nationalist forces who could lead the country to international isolation.

Much to the surprise of everyone (including the parties themselves), four centre-right parties won a majority in the elections, with 78 of the 150 seats in the National Council (the unicameral legislature). The new ruling parties included the Slovak Democratic and Christian Union (SDKU), which won 15.1 per cent of the vote and 28 seats; the Party of the Hungarian Coalition (SMK), with 11.2 per cent and 20 seats; the Christian Democratic Movement (KDH), with 8.3 per cent and 15 seats; and the New Citizen's Alliance (ANO), with 8 per cent and 15 seats. All but the ANO had worked together in government over the previous four years, and within just two weeks of the elections they had formed a new Cabinet and had agreed on the basic policies that they would pursue. SDKU chairman Mikulas Dzurinda was reappointed as Prime Minister on 15 October, and the remaining ministers were installed the following day. In addition to Dzurinda, a number of other key players were retained, marking a sign of continuity. Foreign policy was arguably the most important impetus behind voters' decisions. At 70 per cent, turnout was boosted by a Western-funded "get-out-the-vote" campaign.

The election results may have finally brought foreign observers' scepticism regarding the Slovak political scene to a halt by signalling an end to the political career of former Prime Minister Vladimir Meciar. Although Meciar's party, the Movement for a Democratic Slovakia (HZDS), won 19.5 per cent of the vote and

36 seats, its support was lower than expected and its coalition-forming potential was negligible. Moreover, the far-right Slovak National Party (SNS) failed to gain election to the National Council, while the populist Smer (Direction) fared considerably worse than expected. The HZDS and Smer were thus joined in opposition by the Communist Party (KSS), which won seats for the first time since 1989, shutting out the democratic left-wing parties which had participated in the 1998-2002 Cabinet.

Dzurinda's new centre-right government was one of the most progressive in Central Europe, and it promised to push forward rapidly with economic and social reforms, unhampered by the left-wing parties that had blocked many of the proposed changes between 1998 and 2002. The Cabinet promised to implement much-needed reforms in the areas of pensions, social welfare, healthcare, and education, as well as to improve the business environment in an effort to attract more foreign investment and reduce the unemployment rate. Although many of the reform measures advocated by the government were expected initially to be unpopular, it was hoped that their positive effects would be felt by the time of the next elections so that the populists would have no chance to re-emerge.

The first test for the new government came in local elections on 6-7 December. While the ruling parties fared well, the populist opposition was disappointed. The four centre-right ruling parties won 21.5 per cent of all mayoral posts and 30.9 per cent of the seats in district assemblies. In contrast, the three opposition parties gained 16.6 per cent of mayoral positions and 23.2 per cent of local assembly seats. Independent candidates won the largest share of mayoral posts (32.7 per cent) and controlled 13.5 per cent of the seats in district assemblies.

In terms of the economy, Slovakia had one of the highest growth rates in the region in 2002. Moreover, low inflation helped to boost real wages substantially, giving consumers more leeway to spend. On a negative note, however, the country continued to struggle with high fiscal and current account deficits, although the reforms proposed by the new government were expected to alleviate these problems in the medium-term.

Thanks to the positive outcome of the September elections, Slovakia, together with six other countries from Central and Eastern Europe, was invited to become a full member of NATO during the alliance's Prague summit on 21-22 November (see XI.2.i). Meanwhile, negotiations on accession to the EU were completed during the Copenhagen summit on 12-13 December (see XI.4). Along with nine other candidate countries, Slovakia was expected to join the EU on 1 May 2004.

v. HUNGARY

CAPITAL: Budapest AREA: 93,000 sq km POPULATION: 10,200,000
OFFICIAL LANGUAGE: Hungarian POLITICAL SYSTEM: multiparty republic
HEAD OF STATE: President Ferenc Madl (since Aug '00)
RULING PARTIES: coalition of Hungarian Socialist Party (MSzP) with Alliance of Free Democrats (SzDSz)
HEAD OF GOVERNMENT: Peter Medgyessy (MSzP), Prime Minister (since May '02)
MAIN IGO MEMBERSHIPS (NON-UN): NATO, OSCE, CE, CEFTA, CEI, PFP, OECD
CURRENCY: forint (end-'02 £1=Ft362.831, US$1=Ft226.550)
GNI PER CAPITA: US$4,800, US$12,570 at PPP ('01)

THERE was significant political change in Hungary during 2002, as both national and local elections were won by the Hungarian Socialist Party (MSzP) although not without the eruption of political scandal.

In elections to the National Assembly (the unicameral legislature) in April, the governing Federation of Young Democrats (Fidesz) and Hungarian Democratic Forum (MDF) ran jointly; while the main opposition party, the MSzP, united with the Alliance of Free Democrats (SzDSz). During the campaign, Prime Minister Viktor Orban played the nationalist card, calling for the abolition of the "Benes decrees" by which Czechoslovakia had expelled ethnic Germans and Hungarians at the end of World War II. This briefly complicated relations with the rest of the Visegrad countries, but Orban attracted support from Italian Prime Minister Silvio Berlusconi and former German Chancellor Helmut Kohl. Simultaneously, Orban warned that the opposition would exclusively favour international capital over Hungarian interests. Indeed, nationalism strongly coloured government propaganda. The main pillar of government policy, the Status Law that had been adopted the previous year (see AR 2001, p. 124), had been presented as an "investment project" reflecting the strategic goal of improving conditions for ethnic Hungarians in the entire Carpathian Basin. Orban himself whipped up the tone of the campaign, claiming that those Hungarians who did not support the principles of the Status Law should not be active in public life. He and others from the ruling coalition labelled the MSzP—which had voted for the law but disagreed with the subsequent memorandum on its implementation between Hungary and Romania—"traitors", prompting them to boycott the National Assembly from February until the April elections.

The Socialists also played the nationalist card, claiming that Fidesz had not sufficiently protected the interests of ethnic Hungarians in neighbouring countries. The MSzP programme was mainly socially-oriented. It stressed fiscal prudence but simultaneously promised tax cuts and lower inflation, the creation of new jobs, real wage increases, the strengthening of local government, and increased representation for ethnic minorities.

With smaller parties also stepping into the fray, the electoral campaign frequently assumed an unpleasant tone which even the mediation of President Ferenc Madl was unable to soften. Although the opposition tried to link Orban with the leader of the notorious far-right Hungarian Life and Justice Party (MIÉP), István Csurka, no pre-electoral agreement between the two had been reached. In the single debate held between the incumbent Prime Minister and the MSzP challenger, the former appeared to gain the upper hand and opinion polls predicted a government victory.

On 7 April there was a record 70.5 per cent election turnout. The MSZP won 42.03 percent of the vote compared with 41.07 per cent for the governing Fidesz-MDF alliance. The only other political force to obtain legislative representation was the SzDSz, with 5.56 per cent. The MIÉP, which had attracted some of the largest crowds in rallies, unexpectedly failed to pass the 5 per cent electoral hurdle; as did the Independent Smallholders Party (FKgP). In the second round, turnout was even higher at 73.5 per cent and although the Fidesz-MDF alliance ended up with 188 seats, it fell short of achieving an overall majority as the MSzP won 178 seats and the Free Democrats 20.

The new Prime Minister was the MSzP nominee Peter Medgyessy, who formed a Cabinet in late May and set out to fulfil his electoral promises. The new government's programme for its first 100 days in office was a mixture of social and liberal measures, the highlights of which were a twofold increase in family allowances, a one-off compensation for pensioners, significant increases in public sector pay and university student grants, as well as the introduction of a minimum salary for graduates.

Orban, who did not occupy a formal position in Fidesz (and after the election professed to have lost interest in traditional party politics), proclaimed his objective to be a right-wing merger and announced the formation of a new broad centre-right movement, Hajra Magyarorszag! (Go Hungary!), to serve as the focus for numerous civic groups. One express aim of the movement would be to bar the foreign ownership of farmland.

The local election campaign was dominated by the scandal that erupted following press revelations about Medgyessy's secret work in the past for the Communist Interior Ministry. Quick to admit this, the Prime Minister apologised to the nation for not having come clean earlier and claimed that he had actually protected Hungarian interests from the Soviet Union. (Only at the end of the year was it proven in court that some of the allegations against him had been false.) The matter of collaboration was stirred up by further revelations that politicians of different affiliations had collaborated with the former secret services and, significantly, high-profile figures in both Fidesz and the MDF were implicated. However, the majority of Hungarians seemed to agree with the Prime Minister's view that such matters were not relevant to the present. On 20 October, with turnout at 46 per cent, the MSzP together with the SzDSz obtained 45 per cent of the vote while Fidesz and the MDF gained 33 per cent.

Abroad, the generally positive image of Hungary was marred only by reports of unequal treatment of the Roma minority and outbursts of anti-Semitism. Both the outgoing administration and the new government acknowledged the problem and made clear their commitment to resolve it. The Council of Europe and the European Commission urged Hungary and Slovakia to reach agreement over the contentious Status Law—which the MSzP retained with some amendments—but no proper negotiations took place between the two neighbours.

The EU commended Hungary for progressing towards the completion of the criteria for accession and encouraged stricter budgetary discipline, the curbing of inflation, and more efforts towards the elimination of regional inequalities. However, the Orban government and the European Commission disagreed on the length of the transition period before Hungary would become eligible for full EU agricultural subsidies to new members and on the length of the ban on foreign purchase of arable land. The Medgyessy government continued the policies of its predecessor on these issues, until accepting a compromise on the eve of the December Copenhagen summit at which Hungary was invited to join the EU as of 1 May 2004. In opposition, Orban linked Fidesz support in the forthcoming referendum on EU accession to domestic conditions such as granting loans to farmers. He increasingly voiced concern about the loss of Hungary's sovereignty under what he saw as unfavourable conditions for accession.

Although the deficit figures had to be corrected, thus demolishing Orban's concept of his "Hungarian miracle", the economy performed well in 2002 and in June annual inflation fell to 4.8 per cent, the lowest rate in 16 years.

The Nobel Prize for Literature was awarded to Hungary's Imre Kertesz for his accounts of his experience as survivor of Nazi concentration camps at Auschwitz and Buchenwald. In a further reminder of the legacy of World War II, the Medgyessy Cabinet announced compensation payments to the families of Holocaust victims as well as to the heirs of those killed in Soviet forced-labour camps.

vi. ROMANIA

CAPITAL: Bucharest   AREA: 238,000 sq km   POPULATION: 21,700,000 ('02 census)
OFFICIAL LANGUAGE: Romanian   POLITICAL SYSTEM: multiparty republic
HEAD OF STATE: President Ion Iliescu (since Dec '00)
RULING PARTY: Social Democratic Party (PSD)
HEAD OF GOVERNMENT: Adrian Nastase (PSD), Prime Minister (since Dec '00)
MAIN IGO MEMBERSHIPS (NON-UN): OSCE, CE, CEI, PFP, CEFTA, BSEC, Francophonie
CURRENCY: leu (end-'02 £1=L53,643.9, US$1=L33,495.0)
GNI PER CAPITA: US$1,710, US$6,980 at PPP ('01)

THE formal invitation by NATO to Romania to join the alliance, followed by the EU's confirmation that Romania appeared ready to become a member in 2007, were the two outstanding events of the year. The fact that both decisions had been expected for some time did little to temper the satisfaction of Romania's leaders at what they portrayed as their country's return to Europe and the West in general. These successes—against a background of solid, if unspectacular, economic growth—boosted the government's popularity and prompted Prime Minister Adrian Nastase at the end of the year to moot the idea of holding early elections. However, he dropped his proposal in the face of opposition from President Ion Iliescu.

Nastase's Social Democratic Party (PSD) continued to dominate Romania's political scene throughout 2002. In January the PSD renewed its 12-month co-operation agreement with the Democratic Union of Hungarians in Romania (UDMR) for a further year. That arrangement provided Nastase's administration—formally a minority government—with a continued working majority in the legislature. The ethnic Hungarian community benefited from the deal and several additional Hungarian-language schools were opened during the year. The dispute over providing Hungarian-language university education, however, was not fully resolved.

To consolidate its appeal, the PSD also reached out to several organisations representing minority or regional interests. In June the PSD absorbed the Moldovan Party, thereby strengthening its position in the north-east. During the same month the PSD also signed co-operation agreements with organisations representing the Roma and ethnic German communities. These moves were designed to improve Romania's image abroad, particularly as the treatment of the Roma had been criticised in the EU's earlier progress reports on Romania's compliance with the accession requirements.

The PSD's strong showing in opinion polls throughout the year was matched by the decline in support for the main opposition grouping, the radical nationalist Greater Romania Party (PRM), and for its leader, Corneliu Vadim Tudor. Isolated in the legislature by both the governing and mainstream opposition parties, the PRM—with its xenophobic platform—was losing its popular appeal at a time when the government's success in forging closer links with the rest of the world was promoting a more cosmopolitan outlook across Romanian society.

The PRM's loss of momentum did not, on the whole, translate into greater public support for the other opposition parties which remained largely incapable of overcoming their internal divisions, let alone being able to establish a united front against the government. The only partial exception to this trend was the National Liberal Party (PNL), whose popularity increased after August when it elected former Prime Minister (1991-92) Theodor Stolojan as its new leader. Stolojan had done considerably better than his party in the elections of 2000 when he stood as a presidential candidate. However, PNL plans to form an alliance with the Democratic Party (PD), the other mainstream opposition group in the legislature, made little headway.

Nastase's administration was widely criticised for its failure to deal effectively with corruption. Yet with the opposition making little impression, the government succeeded in coping relatively easily with problems that could have sorely tested a weaker administration. At the beginning of the year Nastase faced widespread allegations in the media that linked him with Sorin Ovidiu Vintu, a financier at the centre of a web of political donations. The Prime Minister managed to ride out the storm without any noticeable impact on his personal standing. Nor was his administration adversely affected by the controversy that had arisen in the UK during the spring over the British government's support during the previous year for the privatisation of Sidex-Galati, Romania's largest steel plant, which had been acquired by LNM Holdings, a company with somewhat tenuous UK links.

Much of the year was spent in preparation for the NATO summit in Prague (see XI.2.i) where Romania was hoping to reverse its failure five years earlier in Madrid to be invited to join the Alliance (see AR 1997, p. 438). To this end, Romania continued to transform its armed forces. It updated the military's air control system, increased the proportion of professional officers, and boosted the number of army personnel who spoke English.

On the diplomatic front, in August Romania became the first country to conclude an agreement with the USA not to extradite US citizens accused of war crimes to the newly-established International Criminal Court (ICC). That decision put Romania at odds with the EU which was, at that stage, still trying to formulate a collective response to the US request for exemption from the ICC's jurisdiction. Romania's willingness to accommodate the USA over the ICC was not the only issue where Romania found itself caught between the conflicting requirements of the USA and the EU. Also in August, the government announced that it was lifting its ban on the adoption of Romanian children by foreigners. The ban had been introduced in 2001 at the prompting of the European Parliament, which had argued that the lack of controls in Romania meant that adoptions amounted to child trafficking. However, the moratorium on adoptions proved very unpopular in the USA which was the destination for many of the Romanian orphans. As part of its attempts to manoeuvre between its two main foreign partners, Romania subsequently extended the ban until 2003.

Romania's policies paid off. At the Prague summit it was among the seven formerly communist-ruled republics—and the only one with a substantial army, albeit one with largely obsolete equipment—to be invited to join NATO. The day after the summit, on 23 November, US President George W. Bush paid a lightning visit to Bucharest where he addressed tens of thousands of jubilant Romanians in the city's historic Revolution Square. President Iliescu described NATO's decision as signalling Romania's return to the family of Western nations. Nastase called it the final end of the "iron curtain". Within three weeks formal talks on Romania's accession got underway, and it was expected that Romania would join NATO around the middle of 2004.

There was more good news for Romania at the EU's summit in Copenhagen in December (see XI.4). Although the summit confirmed that Romania would not be included within the first wave of enlargement in 2004, it was made clear that Romania (along with Bulgaria) would be able to join relatively soon after that, in 2007, if it met the requirements for membership. The summit provided a detailed "road map" for accession and also a very substantial increase in pre-accession funding. The "road map" stipulated, inter alia, that Romania should, in the years ahead, improve the administrative capacity of its civil service, guarantee the independence of the judiciary, reduce the rate of inflation, and enforce more effective bankruptcy procedures.

The economy performed reasonably well during 2001, against a background of a slow-down in global trade, with GDP growth, on preliminary figures, reaching 4.5 per cent, only slightly less than in the previous year. There were signs, too, that inflation was gradually being tamed: the annual rate dropped by over one-third to about 18 per cent. Unemployment was down by 1 per cent to 8 per cent of the labour force. By contrast, the slow pace of structural reforms and the uneven pace of privatisation delayed for several months the disbursement of a World Bank loan. Overall, though, it appeared that Romania was heading for sustained economic growth for the first time since the fall of communism.

However, the extent of the long-term economic dislocation and decline in living standards in the aftermath of the communist era was highlighted by the publication of preliminary results from the census of March 2002. Over the previous 10 years the population had declined by 1.1 million to 21.7 million, amounting to a reduction of 4.2 per cent, which was largely attributed to increased emigration and a falling birth rate. The census figures confirmed that Romania had a long way to go before the majority of its citizens could enjoy a degree of prosperity.

vii. BULGARIA

CAPITAL: Sofia   AREA: 111,000 sq km   POPULATION: 8,100,000
OFFICIAL LANGUAGE: Bulgarian   POLITICAL SYSTEM: multiparty republic
HEAD OF STATE: President Georgi Pûrvenov (since Nov '01)
RULING PARTIES: Simeon II National Movement (NDSV), Movement for Rights and Freedoms (MRF), & Bulgarian Socialist Party (BSP)
HEAD OF GOVERNMENT: Simeon Saxecoburggotski (NDSV), Prime Minister (since June '01)
MAIN IGO MEMBERSHIPS (NON-UN): OSCE, CE, PFP, CEI, CEFTA, BSEC, Francophonie
CURRENCY: lev (end-'02 £1=L3.0060, US$1=L1.8769)
GNI PER CAPITA: US$1,560, US$5,950 at PPP ('01)

THE most important events in Bulgaria came towards the end of year: the invitation to join NATO, issued at the alliance's conference in Prague on 21 November (see XI.2.i), and the decision of the EU conference in Copenhagen on 12-13 December that Bulgaria should join the union in 2007 (see XI.4).

The accession processes had dominated Bulgarian political life throughout the year. Early in the year the government launched what Foreign Minister Solomon Pasi called a "spring offensive" to promote the country's bid to join NATO. The campaign included a visit to Washington DC by the Prime Minister, Simeon Saxecoburggotski. Internally Bulgaria did much to meet NATO requirements. Reforms of the military structure contained in "Plan 2004" were approved by the Sûbranie (the legislature) in April, and involved cutting the armed forces from 65,000 to 45,000 personnel and the transfer of responsibility for the National Protection Service and the National Intelligence Service to the Council of Ministers. In January Bulgaria also agreed to send a decontamination shower unit to serve with the International Security Assistance Force (ISAF) in Afghanistan. Another important step towards making itself acceptable to NATO was the destruction of all former Soviet missiles on Bulgarian territory. Despite concerns that this might pose environmental and health hazards, the last missile was disabled in October.

Satisfying the EU that the country was an acceptable entrant was more difficult. On 7 February the government approved a six-month "action plan" aimed at catching up with other candidate countries. The plan insisted that a functioning market economy would be introduced and that measures would be put in place to improve the judicial system, eradicate corruption, and lessen discrimination against the Roma minority. The plan was updated in July to include action against money-laundering and the trafficking of human beings. The EU reacted with differing enthusiasm. On 22 April EU Enlargement Commissioner Guenther Verheugen described Bulgaria's achievements in the preceding months as unprecedented. In June Bulgaria closed another three chapters of the *acquis communautaire*—meaning it had completed 20 of the 30 currently under discussion—including the vitally important issues of the free movement of goods, the free movement of people, and taxation. Additionally, Bulgaria agreed that, for a period of seven years following accession, EU member states would have the right to restrict the access of Bulgarian citizens to their labour markets. Furthermore, five major bills aimed at harmonising Bulgarian practices with those of the EU were drafted or enacted. Despite this, however, Verheugen later criticised Bulgaria's achievement, calling it "artificial"; his remarks raised grave doubts as to whether 2007 was a realistic accession date for Bulgaria. Given this equivocation, Bulgaria's relief at the Copenhagen decision was understandable.

An issue which was to prove contentious both in the accession negotiations and in domestic politics was that of the nuclear power complex at Kozlodui. The complex consisted of six reactors. It had already been agreed between the EU and Bulgaria that the two oldest reactors should be closed by the end of 2002 and that Bulgaria would receive €400 million in compensation. The EU also insisted, for safety reasons, that two more reactors should be closed with a similar sum to be paid in compensation. To this the government eventually agreed, but in doing so it provoked considerable protest from a public fearful of yet more energy price increases.

The Kozlodui debate was one of a number in which differences of opinion appeared between the government and President Georgi Pûrvanov, who had been installed on 22 January. Pûrvanov, a former chairman of the Bulgarian Socialist Party (BSP), did not accept the arguments in favour of closing the further two reactors, and complicated the government's position when he wrote to the 15 EU member states telling them so. There had been other points of tension between the President and the government. Even before he assumed office Pûrvanov had criticised the Cabinet for not consulting him on military reforms. In February he vetoed the recently passed Privatisation and Post-Privatisation Act, although the Sûbranie subsequently overrode the veto. Later in the year Pûrvanov questioned the assertion of the government and the majority party—the Simeon II National Movement (NDSV)—that accession to NATO necessitated a constitutional change to abolish the provision under which only the Sûbranie, and not the government alone, could sanction the transit of foreign troops through Bulgaria.

The government was embarrassed by the fact that two major privatisation projects, for Bulgartabak and for the Bulgarian Telecommunications Company (BTK), were annulled by the courts after complaints by the opposition parties of irregularities in the privatisation processes. The case of Bulgartabak was particularly sensitive. The mainly Turkish Movement for Rights and Freedoms (MRF), a member of the ruling coalition, was anxious to ensure that privatisation would not inflict too much harm on the nation's tobacco growers, most of whom were ethnic Turks. Another potential problem was that at least one of the consortia bidding for Bulgartabak included in its leadership a Russian expelled from Bulgaria in August 2000 who was thought to have connections with illegal organisations.

There was further embarrassment in October when police at the Bulgarian-

Turkish border intercepted a shipment of tractor parts manufactured by the Bulgarian state-owned firm, Terem. The shipment was destined for Syria but the parts could also be used in Soviet-made armoured personnel carriers and did not have the necessary government approval for such exports. A number of arrests followed but the possibility that the goods were ultimately destined for Iraq raised fears that Bulgaria's bid to join NATO would be compromised.

A more positive international event was the four-day visit of Pope John Paul II in May. It was the first time that the head of the Catholic Church had set foot in the country and he delighted Bulgarians by announcing that he did not believe that Bulgaria had been involved in the 1981 plot to assassinate him (see AR 1982, p. 124).

There was also good economic news as Bulgaria's credit rating was upgraded five times during the year, and Milen Velchev won the *Euromoney* "Finance Minister of the Year" award.

2. ALBANIA—BOSNIA AND HERZEGOVINA—CROATIA—MACEDONIA—
SLOVENIA—YUGOSLAVIA

i. ALBANIA

CAPITAL: Tirana   AREA: 29,000 sq km   POPULATION: 3,400,000
OFFICIAL LANGUAGE: Albanian   POLITICAL SYSTEM: multiparty republic
HEAD OF STATE: President Gen. (retd.) Alfred Moisiu (since June '02)
RULING PARTY: Socialist Party of Albania (PPS) holds presidency and heads government coalition
HEAD OF GOVERNMENT: Pandeli Majko (PS), Prime Minister (since Feb '02)
MAIN IGO MEMBERSHIPS (NON-UN): OSCE, PFP, CE, CEI, BSEC, OIC, Francophonie
CURRENCY: lek (end-'02 £1=AL214.608, US$1=AL134.000)
GNI PER CAPITA: US$1,230, US$3,880 at PPP ('01)

THE first half of the year was characterised by persistent political instability. On 29 January Ilir Meta resigned as Prime Minister following continued feuding within his own Socialist Party of Albania (PSS) (see AR 2001, p. 132). The party leader and former Prime Minister, Fatos Nano, argued that government policy should be determined by the party, whereas Meta insisted that this was the prerogative of the Cabinet, which included some non-PSS members. These differences were aggravated by deep personal antagonisms. Meta also painted his opponents as "Stalinists", whereas his own objective, he claimed, was to "Europeanise" the Socialist Party. Meta's successor was Pandeli Majko, whose efforts to create a Cabinet acceptable to both factions within the PSS—a task which took 10 days to achieve—were helped by Meta's decision not to seek office. Sali Berisha, the leader of the main opposition party, the Democratic Party of Albania (PDS), made capital out of the feud within the PSS. After Meta's resignation, the PDS ended the boycott of the People's Assembly (the legislature) which it had imposed since the elections of 2000 and, in March, PDS deputies formed an alliance with the pro-Meta PSS faction to secure a majority in a vote calling for the dismissal of the Prosecutor-

General, Arben Rakipi, who was accused of incompetence and of having links to organised crime.

The first sign that political instability might be overcome was seen on 8 April when the PSS agreed to unite behind the government of Majko and to back its own candidate for the presidential elections due in the summer. The latter was a crucial issue. The incumbent, Rexhep Mejdani, was not eligible for re-election and Nano's own presidential ambitions had fuelled the dispute within the PSS. In the event, the party did not present its own candidate. Much to the surprise of many observers, the two main political parties buried their differences and agreed to support a "neutral" candidate, retired army General Alfred Moisiu, who received 97 out of a possible 140 votes when the issue was placed before the People's Assembly on 24 June. Moisiu was sworn in on 24 July and the following day Majko resigned, to be replaced by Nano.

With the appointment of an apolitical President and the combining of the premiership with the leadership of the strongest party in government and the legislature, Albania seemed, at last, to be moving towards the stability which it needed if it were to modernise and achieve closer integration with international organisations.

External agencies had for some time been emphasising to Albania that further aid and international integration depended on establishing political stability, on the resumption of the process of economic and political reform, and on further steps to combat crime and corruption. In February the IMF postponed US$30 million of aid until the political feuding had ended, whilst the World Bank threatened suspension of a further US$70 million. It was also believed that behind-the-scenes influence had been exerted in favour of Moisiu by, amongst others, the representative of the Organisation for Security and Co-operation in Europe (OSCE) in Tirana, Geert-Hinrich Ahrens. In Brussels, too, it had been made clear that any move towards closer ties between the EU and Albania would depend on the latter's resuming the reform process (which had been disrupted since February by the political crisis) and on a more rigorous battle against crime and corruption.

This pressure continued after the apparent return to stability in July. On 21 October EU foreign ministers agreed that negotiations should begin with Albania on a stabilisation and association agreement but, said EU Commissioner for Foreign Affairs Chris Patten, "we will be looking at the Albanians . . . to make clear without any doubt that the reform process that was interrupted earlier this year has been resumed effectively."

The government in Tirana (the capital) took a number of steps to combat crime, focusing particularly on the traffic in human beings. In August a new, elite anti-smuggling unit was formed in Vlore, the centre of the smuggling trade; it was to conduct operations with police forces from Italy and Greece. Nevertheless, after the collapse of the pyramid schemes in 1997 (see AR 1997, pp. 122-24) many Albanians in the Vlore area saw smuggling as the only available livelihood and it was estimated that in the summer months the number of persons taken across the Adriatic was still between 2,500 and 3,000.

On other fronts the government could record some successes. The Foreign Minister, Arte Dada, stated in April that there had been a 60 per cent reduction in the drug traffic through Albania, and in November police broke up a drug smuggling ring operating in Albania and Italy. Despite these and other successes, however, the conjoined problems of crime and corruption continued to influence foreign attitudes to Albania. When Patten announced in December that he hoped to begin talks on the EU association agreement in February 2003, he stated once again that the outcome of any negotiations would be linked to Albania's progress in fighting these two evils.

Albania's need to achieve closer association with international organisations, most importantly the EU and NATO, also dominated its relations with other Balkan states. In November Moisiu and the Presidents of Croatia and Macedonia stated that they would deepen regional co-operation and co-ordinate their efforts to join NATO, and a month later a meeting between the Albanian and Macedonian Presidents concentrated on the two countries' efforts to achieve EU accession and resulted in promises of co-operation to combat smuggling.

A desire to move closer towards NATO was also one motive in a thoroughgoing reform of the Albanian military announced in April, and in the decision to send a platoon of 30 specially-trained Albanian soldiers to serve with the International Security Assistance Force in the Afghan capital, Kabul.

ii. BOSNIA & HERZEGOVINA

CONSTITUENT REPUBLICS: Federation of Bosnia & Herzegovina and Republika Srpska (Serb Rebublic)
CAPITAL: Sarajevo AREA: 51,129 sq km POPULATION: 4,060,000
OFFICIAL LANGUAGES: Serbo-Croat POLITICAL SYSTEM: multiparty republic
HEAD OF STATE AND GOVERNMENT: Mirko Sarovic (SDS) (chairman of the presidency, Serb);
 Sulejman Tihic (SDA) (Bosniak); Dragan Covic (HDZ) (Croat), all elected Oct. '02
PRESIDENTS OF REPUBLICS: Safet Halilovic (Muslim-Croat Federation, since Jan '02); Dragan Cavic
 (SDP), (Republika Srpska, since Nov '02)
PRIME MINISTERS: Adnan Terzic (SDA) (Republic of Bosnia & Herzegovina, since Dec '02); Alija
 Behmen (SDP) (Muslim-Croat Federation, since March '01); Mladen Ivanic (PDP) (Republika
 Srpska, since Jan '01)
MAIN IGO MEMBERSHIPS (NON-UN): OSCE, CEI
CURRENCY: marka (end-'02 £1=M3.0141, US$1=M1.8820)
GNI PER CAPITA: US$1,240 ('01)

CONSTITUTIONAL changes were introduced in April which required that national minorities should be ensured minimum representation in all three of Bosnia's legislatures: the state federal parliament and the parliaments of the two "entities"—the ethnically based regional governments of the Muslim-Croat Federation of Bosnia and Herzegovina (FBiH), and Republika Srpska (RS). These reforms were pushed through by the High Representative of the international community, Wolfgang Petritsch, against opposition from the nationalist political parties before he left his post in mid-year. He was replaced by the former leader of the UK Liberal Democratic Party, Paddy Ashdown, who took over the position of High Representative in Bosnia-Herzegovina in June. Soon after he arrived, a corruption scandal gripped the RS as it was revealed that customs officers had stolen some €15 million through false documentation and bribery. Ashdown called for the resignation of the RS Finance Minister, who duly stepped down, and 27 customs officials were also dismissed. It was believed that some of the money was used to provide security protection for the indicted war criminal Radovan Karadzic. Not surprisingly, opinion surveys, carried out in anticipation of the October elections, revealed that the public distrusted the elected politicians. The failure of the international community to create a viable multi-ethnic state was indicated by the high level of support among Bosnian Serbs for the independence of the RS and among Bosnian Croats for the independence of the largely Croat populated Herzegovina region.

General elections to all three parliaments were held on 5 October. The wide support for the main nationalist parties was demonstrated by the results of the elections, which ensured that nationalist hard-line parties became the largest in all three legislatures. The moderate Social Democratic Party (SDP) fared badly in the elections, frustrating the hopes of the international community that this widely based multi-ethnic party could lead the country forward into a new phase of European integration. A similar picture emerged in the presidential elections, which returned Mirko Saravic of the Serbian Democratic Party (SDS), Sulejman Tihic of the Bosniak Party of Democratic Action (SDA), and Dragovan Covic of the Croatian Democratic Union (HDZ) to the collective Presidency. A poor turnout of just 55 per cent of the electorate aided the nationalist parties in achieving their victories. Ashdown announced that he was willing to work with the nationalists as long as they were willing to implement reforms. This represented something of a turnaround from the position of previous High Representatives who had attempted to undermine the nationalist parties wherever possible and favour the moderates. However, Ashdown's tactic appeared to work as the new governments supported reforms promoted by him, including the introduction of value added tax, and making changes in the federation intelligence services.

A further scandal came to light at the end of October when it was discovered that Orao Aviation Institute in Bijeljina was involved in smuggling arms to Iraq in collaboration with the Yugoslav state-owned company Yugoimport. The Institute had acted as a conduit for spare parts for Iraqi MiG-21 aircraft produced in various factories in Republika Srpska. The Bosnian authorities immediately imposed a ban on armaments exports and two senior officials in RS, the Defence Minister and an army commander, resigned, whilst the director of the Institute was dismissed.

Economic growth in Bosnia-Herzegovina had slowed down after several years of sustained rapid growth following the Dayton Peace agreement in the mid 1990s. In 2002, growth of real GDP was just 2.3 per cent. Growth was uneven between the two entities, being more rapid in the FBiH where industrial output growth of 12 per cent was achieved, while industrial output fell in RS by 14 per cent. Inflation remained subdued in the FBiH at just 1.7 per cent, while it was significantly higher in RS at 7.3 per cent. The weakness of the overall economy of Bosnia-Herzegovina was reflected in a government budget deficit of 6.3 per cent of GDP and in the large current account deficit of 23 per cent of GDP.

At the end of December the UN international police task force (UNMIBH—UN Mission in Bosnia-Herzegovina) came to the end of its mandate, and handed over its responsibilities to the EU Police Mission. The UNMIBH had been the largest police reform operation in the history of the UN, involving over 10,000 officers from more than 50 countries over the seven years of its operation since the Dayton peace agreement was signed in 1995 (see AR 1995, pp. 126-28). The mission had been responsible for restructuring and retraining the police forces in Bosnia-Herzegovina and had succeeded in creating a trained and slimmed-down police force and a unified State Border Service which assumed full control of the external borders in September 2002. The border control had tightened significantly, with cases of illegal entry across borders falling from 25,000 in 2000 to just a few hundred in 2002.

iii. CROATIA

CAPITAL: Zagreb   AREA: 57,000 sq km   POPULATION: 4,437,460 ('02 census)
OFFICIAL LANGUAGE: Croatian   POLITICAL SYSTEM: multiparty republic
HEAD OF STATE AND GOVERNMENT: President Stipe Mesic (HNS) (since Feb '00)
RULING PARTIES: Social Democratic Party (SDP) leads coalition which also includes Croatian Peasant Party (HSS); Croatian People's Party (HNS); and the Liberal Party (LS)
PRIME MINISTER: Ivica Racan (SDP), since Feb '00
MAIN IGO MEMBERSHIPS (NON-UN): OSCE, CE, CEI, PFP
CURRENCY: kuna (end-'02 £1=K11.4615, US$1=K7.1565)
GNI PER CAPITA: US$4,550, US$8,440 at PPP ('01)

THE coalition government led by Ivica Racan of the Social Democrats (SDP) collapsed in June, as disputes between the main coalition partners, the SDP and the Croatian Social Liberal Party (HSLS), led by Drazen Budisa, came to a head. After a short interlude, the government was reconstituted without the participation of the HSLS. A new coalition government comprising the SDP, the Croatian Peasant Party (HSS), the Liberal Party (LS), and Croatian People's Party (HNS), to which the President, Stipe Mesic, belonged, was supported by a majority of legislators: 84 out of a total of 151. The HSS became the second largest party in the government, and one of its members, Ante Simonic, became Deputy Prime Minister. The government was also supported by a number of smaller regional parties, the most important of which was the Istrian Democratic Forum (IDS).

Among the surprise appointments in the new government were a female Minister of Defence, Zeljka Antunovic of the SDP, and two non-party experts. These were Ljubo Jurcic, the new Minister of Economy, formerly a little-known professor at the University of Zagreb economics faculty, and Gvozden Flego, an academic from the philosophy faculty, who became Minister for Science and Technology. The appointment of the latter minister followed the earlier rejection of Racan's first choice by HSS politicians on the grounds that he was insufficiently supportive of the Catholic Church, which played an important role in Croatia's social and political affairs.

The main opposition party, the Croatian Democratic Community (HDZ), had been relatively ineffective and had suffered from internal dissension between a moderate faction, headed by party leader Ivo Sanader, and a more hard-line extreme right-wing faction led by Ivic Pasalic. Following his defeat at a party leadership election in July, Pasalic left the party and in September established his own grouping called the Croatian Bloc. The HSLS, now in opposition, was also weakened by an internal split as several legislators loyal to the governing coalition also left their party and established a new, third, liberal party known simply as Libra.

Despite the apparent weakness of the opposition, a number of events conspired to improve the popularity of the HDZ during the autumn. Two main factors were at work. The first was the continuing high level of unemployment (rising above 22 per cent in 2002) and the low living standards of a large proportion of the population. The government did not have an effective economic policy to tackle the problem, particularly in the Dalmatian coastal area around Split where the old shipyards and chemical industries were ailing despite heavy government subsidies to the former. However, economic growth had begun to pick up in 2001 and accelerated in 2002 so that unemployment appeared to have been stabilised and looked likely to fall in 2003.

The second factor which led to an increase in support for the Right was the indictment of a popular army General, Janko Bobetko, by the International Criminal Tribunal for the Former Yugoslavia (ICTY). The indictment covered war crimes allegedly committed in the 1990s when Croatia was recovering territory from the rebel Serb communities which had set up an independent breakaway state in the Krajina regions of Croatia. Although not supposedly directly involved in the killing of civilians, Bobetko was indicted on the grounds of his "command responsibility". The indictment put the government in a difficult position. The extradition of the General was fiercely opposed by his right-wing supporters, who mobilised public opinion in his support. The government stalled the extradition proceedings, while the ailing and elderly General, in his eighties, was taken to hospital where he was examined by a specialist medical team from the ICTY early in the new year. The increase in right-wing sentiment played into the hands of Sanader who presented himself as a moderate, and modern, centre-right politician. Consequently his popularity grew whilst that of the apparently dithering Ivica Racan fell.

The bright spot for the government was the turnaround in the economy. Real GDP had been growing at a rate above 4 per cent per annum over the year, while industrial production increased by 9 per cent per annum in the third quarter of the year compared to the same period in 2001. Tourism receipts rose after a successful season which saw Western tourists returning to the Croatian coast after a period in which the area was considered too dangerous to visit following the civil wars of the early 1990s. The increased tourist revenue financed a growing balance of trade deficit. Whilst the deficit was caused by increased imports of consumer goods, there was also an increase in imports of machinery and investment goods by Croatian industries. The banking system also stabilised as foreign investors continued to buy significant holdings in most of the Croatian banks. The new owners were mainly banks from Italy and Austria. This provided a much-needed influx of banking expertise as well as improved access to international capital markets, which helped to drive down interest rates, thus further stimulating investment and growth.

The main cloud on the horizon was the high level of government debt. Following pressure from the IMF, the government took steps to curb the debt, mainly by reducing defence expenditure and cutting the growth of public sector wages below the rate of inflation. The latter policy provoked resentment among public sector workers and led to strikes by hospital staff and teachers towards the end of the year. The part privatisation of the pension system further reduced pressure on the government budget, however, and the government's plans to reduce the deficit to below 5 per cent of GDP appeared to be realistic. Within this overall limitation, the government switched expenditure towards a major road-building programme, with highway construction well advanced on the Zagreb-Split and Zagreb-Rijeka highways. Once completed, these would further stimulate tourism in the coastal regions.

iv. MACEDONIA

CAPITAL: Skopje   AREA: 26,000 sq km   POPULATION: 2,000,000
OFFICIAL LANGUAGE: Macedonian   POLITICAL SYSTEM: multiparty republic
HEAD OF STATE AND GOVERNMENT: President Boris Trajkovski (VMRO-DPMNE) (since Dec '99)
RULING PARTIES: coalition of Social Democratic Alliance for Macedonia (SDSM), Liberal
   Democratic Party (LDP), and Party for Democratic Integration (BDI)
PRIME MINISTER: Branko Crvenkovski (SDSM) (since Nov '02)
MAIN IGO MEMBERSHIPS (NON-UN): OSCE, PFP, CE, CEI, Francophonie
CURRENCY: Macedonian denar (end-'02 £1=D94.9870, US$1=D59.3094)
GNI PER CAPITA: US$1,690, US$4,860 at PPP ('01)

THE year began in a state of uncertainty as to whether the Ohrid Framework Peace Agreement between the government and the rebel Albanian forces (see AR 2001, p.139) would hold, or whether the country would again be plunged into civil conflict with the potential to escalate into a major crisis. In the event, the planned re-entry of the Macedonian police forces—using ethnically mixed police patrols—into the areas previously held by the rebels went relatively smoothly. The presence of international monitors and an international military presence, "Operation Amber Fox", undoubtedly helped to calm the situation. By June, the former paramilitary Albanian insurgents had transformed themselves into a non-violent political party, the Party for Democratic Integration (BDI), ready for the September general election. A new Law on Local Self-Government was passed, with the intention of implementing a more effective devolution of power to local administrative units, and other measures were introduced to ensure improved civic and linguistic rights for the minority Albanian community.

The legislative elections held on 15 September resulted in a victory for the Zaedno (Together) coalition of opposition parties. The main partners in the coalition were the Social Democratic Party of Macedonia (SDSM) and the Liberal Democratic Party (LDP), together with a number of smaller ethnically based parties of Bosniaks, Roma, Turks, Serbs, and Vlachs. The coalition gained 40.5 per cent of the vote on a high turnout of 74 per cent of the electorate. As a result, the coalition won 59 of the 120 seats in the Sobranje (the unicameral legislature), of which the SDSM took 46. SDSM leader Branko Crvenkovski led negotiations to form a new government with the largest Albanian party, the recently formed BDI, which was led by Ali Ahmeti, formerly the leader of the Albanian insurgents. The negotiations lasted until the end of October when the new government was eventually formed. Major appointments in the administration included (from the SDSM) Hari Kostov, an independent economist and former commercial bank director, as Interior Minister, and old hands Vlado Buckovski as Defence Minister and Ilinka Mitreva as Foreign Minister; while Radmila Sekerinska was appointed Deputy Prime Minister in charge of European Integration. From the BDI ranks, Musa Xhaferi was appointed Deputy Prime Minister in charge of political reform, and other BDI deputies headed the Ministries of Justice, Health, and Education and Science. The other two Albanian parties—the Democratic Party of Albanians (PDSH), which had been a partner in the previous government, and the Party for Democratic Prosperity (PPD), which had been a partner in the first post-independence government in the early 1990s—both fared badly at the polls and failed to secure inclusion in the new government. It was a considerable achievement that the SDSM had found it possible to form a coalition with the BDI as even as late as 2001 the party's leadership was looked upon as terrorists. Such compromises suggested that the political system in Macedonia was entering a period of stability, and that the Ohrid Agreement, forged with the support, and indeed insistence, of the EU and other key international players, had succeeded, at least in the short term, in stabilising the country and averting another Balkan-style civil conflict along ethnic lines.

The incoming government found an economy in a state of collapse and a public treasury stripped bare by the excesses and corruption of the previous administration, led by the Internal Macedonian Revolutionary Organisation-Democratic Party for Macedonian National Unity (VMRO-DPMNE). The former director of the state health fund was prosecuted for taking money from the fund for personal use. An early crisis that greeted the new government was a strike by employees of the main newspaper publishing company, NIP, which published the daily newspaper *Nova Makedonija*. A Slovenian consortium had bought the company for US$2.25 million, but it emerged that the new owners had financed the deal from the employees' wage fund, and that the employees had consequently been unpaid for several months. Many industrial workers, including miners and railway workers, also went on strike to protest over unpaid wages. Reversing the parlous state of the economy would be a major test for the new government in the year ahead.

Following a year of negative GDP growth, attributed to the Kosovo war and the civil conflict which had badly affected the Macedonian economy after signs of growth in the late 1990s, the economy picked up a little in 2002 and GDP grew, albeit at a relatively slow rate of just 1 per cent over the year. Industrial output, however, continued to decline at a rate of 8 per cent. In November, the new Minister of Labour and Social Affairs, Jovan Manasievski, announced that almost one quarter of Macedonian citizens lived in poverty and that over one-fifth of the state budget was spent on income support and unemployment benefits. Economic stagnation kept unemployment at chronically high levels, and in 2002 registered unemployment reached 30.5 per cent of the labour force. Partly because of the high burden of social expenditure, but also a result of heavy spending on defence and military equipment following the rebel insurgency in 2001, the budget deficit amounted to 3.9 per cent of GDP. The current account continued its chronic deficit and reached €480 million, or 12 per cent of GDP, in 2002, while gross foreign debt reached 43 per cent of GDP. Nevertheless, following the political developments of 2002 international donor organisations stepped in to offer support to the incoming government, and the EU announced a US$46 million aid package. Much, therefore, depended on whether the government would be able to negotiate a new standby arrangement with the IMF in 2003.

Although Macedonia had signed a Stabilisation and Association Agreement with the EU, its progress towards European integration was held back by the civil conflict and consequent poor economic performance. Macedonia was admitted to the World Trade Organisation (WTO) at a meeting of the organisation in Geneva on 17 September. Accession was expected both to open up new export opportunities, but also to lead to increased competition for domestic firms.

v. SLOVENIA

CAPITAL: Ljubljana AREA: 20,000 sq km POPULATION: 2,000,000
OFFICIAL LANGUAGE: Slovene POLITICAL SYSTEM: multiparty republic
HEAD OF STATE AND GOVERNMENT: President Janez Drnovsek (LDS) (since Dec '02)
RULING PARTIES: Liberal Democracy of Slovenia (LDS), United List of Social Democrats (ZLSD), Slovenian People's Party (SLS&SKD), & Democratic Party of Pensioners (DeSUS)
PRIME MINISTER: Anton Rop (since Dec '02)
MAIN IGO MEMBERSHIPS (NON-UN): OSCE, CE, PFP, CEI, CEFTA, Francophonie
CURRENCY: tolar (end-'02 £1=T354.103 US$1=T221.100)
GNI PER CAPITA: US$9,780, US$18,160 at PPP ('01)

SLOVENIA, unlike Serbia, saw its population participating actively in political life in 2002, to the extent that an extraordinary 2.5 per cent of the electorate (40,000 candidates) contested the local elections held on 10 November for seats in 193 municipalities. (The biggest surprise in the municipal elections was the victory of Danica Simsic of the United List of Social Democrats (ZLSD), who beat the incumbent Vika Potocnik for the post of mayor of Ljubljana.) No less significant was the first round of the presidential elections held the same day, in which about 71 per cent of the electorate took part. In the presidential contest, incumbent Prime Minister Janez Drnovsek of the Liberal Democracy of Slovenia party (LDS) gained 44 per cent of the vote, and his main opponent, state prosecutor and centre-right politician Barbara Brezigar, gained just 31 per cent. Drnovsek's tally, however, was insufficient for an outright victory and the elections went to a second round on 1 December. On this occasion, Drnovsek beat Brezigar by a narrow margin with 56 per cent of the vote on a 64 per cent turnout. Anton Rop, also of the LDS, replaced Drnovsek as Prime Minister and immediately announced a government reshuffle, appointing Dusan Mramor as Finance Minister and creating a new Ministry for Regional Development.

Economic growth slowed in 2002. Real GDP grew at a rate of 2.8 per cent over the year, while industrial output increased by just 2.5 per cent. This was partly due to slow growth within the EU, which represented Slovenia's main export market. However, exports to the Federal Republic of Yugoslavia and to Russia increased, leading to an overall surplus in the balance of payments current account of 1.8 per cent of GDP. Foreign direct investment, which had been relatively low in Slovenia compared to other countries in central-eastern Europe, also improved in 2002. Unemployment remained relatively low at 6.5 per cent, while the government budget deficit was held to just 2.8 per cent of GDP. The most serious problem facing the Slovenian economy was a relatively high rate of inflation, which reached 7.3 per cent in 2002. The National Bank followed a relaxed monetary policy, which was balanced by a willingness to allow a gradual nominal depreciation of the currency, the tolar, in order to maintain international competitiveness.

Slovenia began accession talks with NATO at the organisation's Prague summit meeting on 21 November (see XI.2.i). Later, US Secretary of Defence Donald Rumsfeld paid a visit to Slovenia to discuss its accession and the contribution that Slovenia could make to NATO, with special skills in mountain combat, peace-keeping, and mine clearing. A referendum on NATO membership was planned for early in 2003. In December the EU announced that Slovenia's application for membership had been accepted (see XI.4), and that the country was expected to join the union in May 2004.

vi. FEDERAL REPUBLIC OF YUGOSLAVIA

CONSTITUENT REPUBLICS: Montenegro (13,812 sq km), Serbia (88,316 sq km)
CAPITAL: Belgrade   AREA: 102,128 sq km   POPULATION: 10,600,000
OFFICIAL LANGUAGES: Serbo-Croat   POLITICAL SYSTEM: multiparty republic
HEAD OF STATE AND GOVERNMENT: President Vojislav Kostunica (since Oct '00)
RULING PARTIES: Democratic Opposition of Serbia (DOS) & Socialist People's Party of Montenegro (SNP)
PRESIDENTS OF REPUBLICS: Natasa Micic (interim President of Serbia, since Dec '02); Filip Vujanovic (interim President of Montenegro, since Dec '02)
PRIME MINISTERS: Dragisa Pesic (SNP) (since July '01); Zoran Djindjic (DOS DS) (Serbia, since Jan '01); Milo Djukanovic (DPS) (Montenegro, since Oct '02)
MAIN IGO MEMBERSHIPS (NON-UN): OSCE (suspended), CEI, EBRD
CURRENCY: new Yugoslav dinar (end-'02 £1=YD94.8153, US$1=YD59.2022)
GNI PER CAPITA: n/a

AFTER months of discussions, Serbia and Montenegro came to a new constitutional agreement to restructure their federal state along more decentralised lines under the name of "Serbia and Montenegro", consigning the failed label of "Yugoslavia" to history. The change, agreed in December, was due to come into effect in early 2003. The new arrangement envisaged that the federal government would retain powers only over joint defence and foreign affairs, while devolving wide autonomy on other matters to each component state. The deal had been supported by the EU, under the guidance of Javier Solana, the EU High Representative for Common Foreign and Security Policy. The new arrangement would last for three years, after which it would be renewed, or Montenegro would become an independent state. By increasing the powers of the presidencies in both Serbia and Montenegro, the new constitutional agreement gave increased significance to the presidential elections which occurred in both Serbia and Montenegro in 2002.

The Serbian presidential elections were held on 29 September, and saw most votes cast for Vojislav Kostunica, the incumbent President of the Federal Republic of Yugoslavia and leader of the small Democratic Party of Serbia (DSS). Kostunica gained 31 per cent of the vote, closely followed by Miroljub Labus, the candidate of the governing coalition, the Democratic Opposition of Serbia (DOS), who polled 27 per cent. Labus had been a liberal economics professor from Belgrade's law faculty before becoming a politician, and had acted as Minister of Foreign Trade in the federal Yugoslav government. He was also a founder member of the influential G17 group of dissident economists which was active during the Milosevic regime. The far right-wing nationalist, Vojislav Seselj of the Serbian Radical Party (SRS), came third with a sizeable 23 per cent of the vote. Voter turnout in the first round of the elections was 55 per cent, above the 50 per cent threshold for validating the election.

In the 13 October run-off between Kostunica and Labus, however, only 46 per cent of the electorate participated, thus invalidating the result and necessitating a further round of voting. The low turnout was partly in response to an election boycott called by Seselj, but was also attributed to the lukewarm support proffered by Labus's supposed ally and fellow DOS member, Zoran Djindjic, the Serbian Prime Minister. It was not in Djindjic's interest to see the election succeed since, if elected to the Serbian presidency, Kostunica was expected to call new parliamentary elections which Djindjic's Democratic Party (DS) would have been likely to lose. Labus decided to drop out of the electoral contest after polling only 31 per cent in the invalid second round, and subsequently abandoned the DS to establish his own party, known as "G17 Plus". This move effectively split the reformist forces and strengthened the right-wing parties in Serbian politics.

The third round of voting, held on 8 December, was thus contested by Kostunica and Seselj. Once again, Kostunica won a clear majority of the votes cast (58 per cent), but the voter turnout was again too low (45 per cent) to validate the election results. Since there was no provision in the constitution for a fourth round of presidential elections, a little-known politician, Natasa Micic, the youthful speaker of the legislature, became acting President of Serbia. Micic was a member of the Alliance for Change, and an ally of Djindjic. Kostunica contested the election results, alleging that Djindjic's supporters had packed the electoral register with fictitious voters. A more serious problem, however, was the continued inclusion of Kosovar Albanian citizens on the register of voters, although for many years Albanians in the disputed region of Kosovo had refused to participate in elections for the Serbian legislature.

Part of the reason for the low voter turnout and the relatively high level of support for the extreme right-wing nationalist party led by Seselj was the growing disillusionment of voters with the politicians who had done little to bring about economic recovery in Serbia. The economy remained at a low ebb after years of sanctions and NATO's 1999 bombing campaign. The economic reforms that had been introduced, although necessary, had merely made hidden unemployment a visible phenomenon. Serbia's GDP grew at just 3 per cent in 2002, down from the 6.2 per cent recorded in 2001, a rate that was insufficient to make significant inroads into unemployment, which remained persistently high at 30 per cent. With average monthly gross wages at just €219 (compared to €2,300 in the EU), poverty was a real and persistent concern. On the positive side, the Yugoslav federal government concluded a US$850 million agreement with the IMF in May, which was a precondition of debt forgiveness by the Paris Club of international bankers, and inflation fell to 20 per cent, down from 91 per cent in 2001. Economic development in Yugoslavia was also supported by the European Investment Bank which provided loans for several projects, including €85 million for the restoration of the railway line between Belgrade, Podgorica, and Bar on the Montenegrin coast; €95 million to repair major roads and motorways in Serbia; and €70 million to restore and upgrade the electricity infrastructure in Serbia and Montenegro.

In an embarrassing scandal for the government, the Yugoslav authorities were discovered to be implicated in the same Iraqi arms smuggling operation which had led to dismissals and resignations in Bosnia (see III.2.ii). A Serbian daily newspaper revealed that Yugoslav army experts from the Sava Kovacevic Navy Technical Association in Tivat, Montenegro, had visited Iraq to negotiate an arms deal. Although no contract was ever signed, the affair undermined the authority of President Kostunica. It was suggested that the information was known to US secret services who had leaked it just ahead of the third round of the presidential election in order to damage Kostunica's candidacy.

Presidential elections held in Montenegro in December also yielded an inconclusive result. Despite the clear majority (84 per cent) of the vote for Filip Vujanovic of the Democratic Party of Montenegrin Socialists (DPS), the turnout, as in Serbia, was below the 50 per cent requirement for validating the vote. Vujanovic nevertheless was named interim President, pending a second round of voting. Legislative elections in Montenegro on 21 October attracted a larger voter turnout (at 75 per cent) than in the presidential elections. The Democratic List for European Montenegro topped the polls with 48 per cent of the vote, giving the coalition 39 of the 75 parliamentary seats. The DPS gained 30 seats to become the largest single party in the legislature. The opposition coalition, "Together for Changes" (ZzJ), led by the Socialist People's Party of Montenegro (SNP), gained 38 per cent of the vote and won 30 seats, of which the SNP took 19. DPS leader Milo Djukanovic, formerly President of Montenegro, became Prime Minister in the new legislature.

The agreement on the constitutional status of Serbia and Montenegro had some significance for Kosovo, since under the 1999 peace agreement Kosovo was considered to be a province of Yugoslavia. The demise of Yugoslavia raised the question of the final status of Kosovo, and its eventual independence as a sovereign state.

Voting for a new President took place in the Kosovo Assembly on 10 January. Ibrahim Rugova, the leading candidate, failed to win the required 81 votes in the assembly to secure victory. Municipal elections, which were held in October, began the process of transferring power from the UN Interim Administration Mission in Kosovo (UNMIK) overseers to local politicians. Voting took place in 30 municipalities, and there was a 54 per cent turnout. Altogether, 40 different political parties gained seats in the various municipal assemblies. However, the province remained a problem for the international community, having become a base for organised crime syndicates which dealt in human trafficking and drug smuggling, and whose malign influence extended throughout the EU.

Although NATO had announced a cut in its garrison in Kosovo from 38,000 to 33,000 troops, to take effect in early 2003, the province remained unstable, with over 200,000 Serbian refugees unable to return to the homes which they had left at the end of the 1999 war. A major flashpoint was the town of Mitrovica, which marked a boundary between the mainly Albanian south of the province and an area in the north populated mostly by Serbs. The town was divided between the two ethnic groups on either side of the river Ibar. In November, following an election boycott by Serbian residents, the head of UNMIK, Michael Steiner, introduced direct UNMIK rule over the northern part of the city. The aim was to promote the gradual integration of the two communities, but critics argued that UNMIK could do little more than provide institutionalised cover for de facto partition.

3. RUSSIA, EASTERN EUROPE AND THE CAUCASUS

i. RUSSIA

CAPITAL: Moscow   AREA: 17,075,000 sq km   POPULATION: 145,100,00 ('02 census)
OFFICIAL LANGUAGE: Russian   POLITICAL SYSTEM: multiparty republic
HEAD OF STATE AND GOVERNMENT: President Vladimir Putin (since May '00)
RULING PARTIES: United Russia party
PRIME MINISTER: Mikhail Kasyanov (since May '00)
MAIN IGO MEMBERSHIPS (NON-UN): CIS, APEC, OSCE, G-8, CE, PFP, CBSS, BSEC, AC
CURRENCY: rouble (end-'02 £1=R50.9693, US$1=R31.8250)
GNI PER CAPITA: US$1,750, US$8,660 at PPP ('01)

RUSSIA had a relatively stable 2002, and its President—to judge from the opinion polls—continued to enjoy a remarkable level of popular support. There were even signs of a modest personality cult, which reached a peak in October 2002 when Vladimir Putin celebrated his 50th birthday. Putin had an equally harmonious relationship with the Russian legislature, and there was little to suggest that a credible challenger might appear by the end of his first term in March 2004. But there was little evidence that the President and his government had developed a coherent strategy for sustaining the economic recovery that had begun in 1999, despite the passage of legislation that extended the 2001 land code to permit the sale of agricultural as well as urban land (see AR, 2001, pp. 145-46), and Putin showed some impatience during the year with the apparent inability of his ministers to provide the kind of growth rate that would be necessary if Russia were to catch up at least with Portugal (the EU's poorest country, and a target which he had identified at the start of his presidency). Nor was there any sign of an end to the bloody Chechen conflict; casualties continued at a high level and a dramatic hostage crisis in Moscow in late October underlined the failure of the authorities to provide a secure environment for ordinary citizens, whether in Chechnya or the country at large. Putin's future appeared to rest on a complex calculus between the satisfaction that Russians appeared to feel with a political leader who continued to represent a great improvement on his unpredictable predecessor, and their growing dissatisfaction with his performance in most areas of domestic policy.

One of the areas in which government policy was regarded as least successful by ordinary Russians was law and order. Putin issued a public rebuke to the country's senior law enforcement officers in February for their failure to tackle rising levels of violent crime. More than 7,000 murderers had "escaped justice" in 2001, he said; murder, kidnapping, robbery and burglaries had become a "fact of life"; and three million crimes had been committed in 2001, half of them serious. A number of particularly savage murders took place in the course of the year, which lent weight to these concerns. A growing body of opinion favoured the restoration of the death penalty, suspended in 1996 in compliance with Russia's membership of the Council of Europe, but not removed from the statute book. The lower house of the legislature, the State Duma, sent an appeal to the President in February urging him to lift the moratorium, although there was no sign that he would be willing to do so. Inevitably, most media attention focused on the murders of politicians, of which there were a number, most of them apparently contract killings. A second, unsuccessful, attempt was made on the life of the deputy mayor of Moscow in June, and a Duma deputy was shot dead in August while walking his dog near his home. The same month a deputy governor of the Smolensk region was killed, and in October the governor of Magadan region, Valentin Tsvetkov, was shot dead in central Moscow. He was the most senior politician to have been killed during the Putin presidency.

The problems of crime and disorder also assumed a racist aspect. There was serious rioting in central Moscow in June, following Russia's defeat by Japan in a match at the finals of the soccer World Cup (see XVI); one person was killed and more than 20 injured. Foreigners and national minorities were targeted for beatings by racist thugs, including, in November, the ambassador of Ghana. The Duma adopted legislation at the end of June that was intended to prevent such "extremism". The new law allowed the authorities to suspend groups suspected of such activities before a court had judged them guilty; but there were concerns among human rights activists that the law might be used to target non-violent groups which had incurred the displeasure of the authorities.

The year saw further developments that were detrimental to the independent media, and which appeared to reflect the wish of the presidential administration to establish firm control over the flow of information, particularly on national television, Russians' main source of news. TV6, Russia's last remaining independent television station with national coverage, went off the air in January when its equipment was impounded, electricity cut off, and telephone lines severed. Most TV6 journalists had come from NTV, the independent station formerly owned by the oligarch (rich financier with political ambitions), Vladimir Gusinsky, but taken over in April 2001 by a subsidiary of the state-owned gas company, Gazprom (see AR 2001, pp. 146-47). The closure of TV6 followed its defeat in a complex ongoing legal battle against liquidation, which many commentators thought had been brought at the instigation of the Russian presidency. Moves against the independent media were part of a wider battle against the oligarchs, and particularly against the majority shareholder in TV6, Boris Berezovsky, once an ally of Putin and, particularly, of his predecessor, Boris Yeltsin, but now a critic of the government.

The tender to broadcast on the TV6 frequency was eventually won by a new consortium, Media-Sotsium, headed by the former director of TV6, Evgenii Kiselev. It brought together his group of journalists with a number of leading business and political leaders, including some who were known to be close to the presidency, such as Anatolii Chubais, head of the Russian electricity company, and Roman Abramovich, governor of the Chukotka autonomous district and principal shareholder in the Sibneft oil group. For Kiselev, the outcome was a victory for freedom of speech; for other commentators, it was a decision that gave the oligarchs who had taken part in the bid a new outlet for their opinions. It was certainly a defeat for TV6's previous majority shareholder, Berezovsky, who remained abroad and in opposition to Putin. At a press conference in London in March he produced new evidence that the Russian authorities had themselves instigated the apartment bombings of 1999 that had prompted the armed intervention in Chechnya and through which Putin had come to power (see AR 1999, pp. 146-7). The Russian President, Berezovsky claimed, "definitely knew that such things were taking place".

There were several other developments during the year that underlined the fragility of the independent media. The Federal Security Service (FSB), for instance, made repeated attempts to damage the reputation of a journalist, Anna Politkovskaya, who was best known for her outspoken reporting from Chechnya, particularly on human rights abuses there by the Russian military. She was accused of being motivated by financial gain and the newspaper for which she worked, *Novaya gazeta*, was fined US$1.5 million in two libel actions, which the paper insisted were part of a government campaign to close it down. In June the Supreme Court upheld the punishment that had been imposed on military journalist Grigorii Pasko, who had been sentenced in December 2001 to four years' imprisonment for "intending" to pass state secrets to Japan. In October Putin repealed a 1991 decree that had guaranteed the status of the Moscow bureau of the US-funded Radio Liberty, which had recently established a Chechen-language broadcasting service: the decision had little immediate effect but was consistent with the larger attempt to bring the news agenda under political control.

The attention of party politicians began to shift during the year towards the elections which were due in December 2003 to the new Duma, and in March 2004 for the presidency. One sign of this reorientation was the restructuring of political parties, prompted in part by the need to satisfy the requirements of the law on political parties which had been adopted in the summer of 2001 with the aim of creating a more manageable party system. The most important of these developments was the dissolution of three of the main contenders in the 1999 Duma election—Fatherland, All Russia, and Unity—and the formation in February of a new, merged entity entitled United Russia. Plans to merge the three "parties of power" had been under way since April 2001 and the new party had been formally established in December 2001. Fatherland leader and Moscow mayor Yuri Luzhkov promised that the new party would be the "largest and most influential in the country", and made clear that it would offer its broad support to Putin.

There were splits, rather than mergers, on the left of the political spectrum. In a dramatic coup in April, the Communist Party of the Russian Federation (KPRF) and its ally, the Agro-Industrial Union, were stripped of their chairmanships of Duma committees. The presidential administration appeared to be behind these developments, in an attempt to deprive its main opponents of the administrative resources they would otherwise have commanded in advance of the December 2003 elections. The KPRF's Central Committee responded by ruling that all of its members should relinquish their Duma positions in these circumstances, but two of them refused to do so and were eventually expelled. The party member in the most invidious position was Gennadii Seleznev, the Duma's long-standing speaker and a politician of national standing. In the end, Seleznev chose to remain as speaker and, after being expelled from the KPRF in May, he formed his own political party, Russian Revival. This was to be a party of the centre left and, it seemed, one that was likely to deprive the Communists of a section of their more moderate electoral support.

The most obvious policy failure during the year was the long-running dispute with the separatist Chechen republic in the northern Caucasus (see map, III.3.iii). The Russians authorities appeared to have achieved one of their most important objectives when, in April, it was announced that Omar ibn al-Khattab, a Saudi national who had been one of the Chechens' leading field commanders, had been killed in somewhat mysterious circumstances the previous month. The Russian authorities insisted that Khattab had contacts with the al-Qaida network and was a channel for funding the Chechen separatists from abroad. Russia's own military losses, however, continued at a high level. In August a transport helicopter was shot down near the main Russian military base outside Grozny, the capital of Chechnya, killing 117 of the 147 personnel on board. It was the worst single incident of its kind since the resumption of hostilities in 1999, and the head of the army's air services was suspended immediately afterwards. According to official figures made available in December, over 4,700 Russian servicemen had lost their lives since the conflict resumed in 1999 and over 14,000 Chechen "fighters" had reportedly been killed.

The Chechen crisis made its impact felt in Moscow on the evening of 23 October when about 40 heavily armed male and female Chechen separatists took hostage the entire cast and audience at one of Moscow's most popular musicals, *Nord Ost* (North East). The hostage-takers demanded an end to the war in Chechnya, and threatened to blow up the theatre (and its 800 occupants) if their demands were not met. The siege came to a violent end on the early morning of 26 October when Russian special forces seized the building after flooding it with an incapacitating gas. The action became deeply controversial when it emerged that only two of the 129 hostages who died had been shot and that the rest had succumbed to the effects of the gas, whose precise nature was not immediately disclosed. All 41 hostage-takers were killed during the assault. Despite the loss of life, Putin's handling of the crisis was widely praised by foreign and (still more so) domestic commentators. The hostage-takers had been led by Movsar Baraev, the nephew of a Chechen warlord who had been killed the previous year; the Chechen President, Aslan Maskhadov, had immediately dissociated himself from the action.

As part of an intended settlement to the Chechen problem, Putin announced in December that a new constitution establishing Chechnya as a "self-ruling" republic within the Russian Federation would be put to a referendum in March 2003, to be followed by elections to the Chechen presidency and legislature. But there was no sign, in spite of appeals from some leading Russian politicians, of any attempt to develop a dialogue with the separatists. Their defiance of federal authority was underlined in late December when two trucks loaded with explosives rammed the headquarters of Chechnya's pro-Russian government and almost entirely demolished it, killing at least 80 people.

International affairs were at the top of the political agenda in May, with a series of summit meetings between the Russian President and representatives of the USA, NATO, and the EU. President Bush's visit to Russia was his first, and it included a side-trip to Putin's native St Petersburg. The two Presidents signed a Strategic Offensive Reduction Treaty on 24 May, committing both countries to reduce their stockpiles of nuclear weapons from "between 6,000 and 7,000" to between 1,700 and 2,200 by the end of 2012. They also agreed to co-operate over energy policy and anti-terrorist measures, although it was clear that significant differences remained over trade and nuclear non-proliferation. Putin, in particular, strongly defended Russia's participation in the construction of a nuclear power station in Iran, insisting that it presented no danger of accelerating nuclear proliferation. A Russia-EU summit took place in Moscow shortly afterwards, at which the EU formally recognised Russia as a market economy; and there was a further summit in Brussels in November at which a compromise was reached over the movement of Russian citizens between the enclave of Kaliningrad (from 2004 to be surrounded by new EU members) and the rest of Russia.

In another significant development NATO heads of state and Putin signed a declaration near Rome on 28 May which inaugurated a new relationship between the former adversaries, and established a NATO-Russia Council. The new Council was intended to allow Russia to participate in discussions with NATO members on matters of common interest, including fighting terrorism, crisis management, peacekeeping, and preventing the spread of weapons of mass destruction. The agreement had already been approved in principle at a meeting of NATO and Russian Foreign Ministers in mid-May in the Icelandic capital, Reykjavik. It was made clear at the same time that Russia would have no veto over the intended expansion of the alliance to new member states, including some that were former Soviet republics. At the NATO Prague summit in November, when the accession of seven former Soviet-bloc states was agreed, Russian Defence Minister Sergei Ivanov reiterated that Russia was "absolutely calm" about the expansion of the alliance to include those countries, although it was hoped that the three Baltic republics (Estonia, Latvia, and Lithuania) would sign the Treaty on Conventional Forces in Europe before they became members. Putin held another summit with Bush immediately afterwards, near St Petersburg; in a joint statement the two

Presidents agreed that Iraq would face serious consequences if it did not comply completely with UN Resolution 1441 on Iraq (see XVII) and co-operate unconditionally with UN weapons inspectors.

Putin made a state visit to China at the start of December, underlining Russia's interest in a closer relationship with its eastern as well as its western neighbours (one of his own daughters, he told the press, was studying Chinese). A joint declaration committed both countries to "deepening their strategic partnership" (Russia was the only country with which China had a relationship of this nature), although the development of trade continued to fall below expectations. The Russian President also visited India in December where he concluded eight bilateral agreements, including a declaration on the two countries' strategic partnership.

ii. BELARUS—UKRAINE—MOLDOVA

Belarus

CAPITAL: Minsk   AREA: 208,000 sq km   POPULATION: 10,000,000
OFFICIAL LANGUAGES: Belarusian & Russian   POLITICAL SYSTEM: multiparty republic
HEAD OF STATE AND GOVERNMENT: President Alyaksandr Lukashenka (since July '94)
RULING PARTY: Belarussian Patriotic Movement (BPR)
PRIME MINISTER: Henadz Navitski (since Oct '01)
MAIN IGO MEMBERSHIPS (NON-UN): CIS, OSCE, PFP, CEI, NAM
CURRENCY: Belarusian rouble (end-'02 £1=BR3094.20, US$1=BR1932.00)
GNI PER CAPITA: US$1,190, US$8,030 at PPP ('01)

Ukraine

CAPITAL: Kyiv (Kiev)   AREA: 604,000 sq km   POPULATION: 48,457,000 ('01 census)
OFFICIAL LANGUAGE: Ukrainian   POLITICAL SYSTEM: multiparty republic
HEAD OF STATE AND GOVERNMENT: President Leonid Kuchma (since July '94)
RULING PARTIES: For a United Ukraine (ZYU) bloc links ruling circle
PRIME MINISTER: Viktor Yanukovych (since Nov '02)
MAIN IGO MEMBERSHIPS (NON-UN): CIS, OSCE, CE, PFP, BSEC, CEI
CURRENCY: hryvna (end-'02 £1=H8.5511, US$1=H5.3393)
GNI PER CAPITA: US$720, US$4,150 at PPP ('01)

Moldova

CAPITAL: Chisinau (Kishinev)   AREA: 34,000 sq km   POPULATION: 4,300,000
OFFICIAL LANGUAGE: Moldovan   POLITICAL SYSTEM: multiparty republic
HEAD OF STATE AND GOVERNMENT: President Vladimir Voronin (since April '01)
RULING PARTY: Communist Party of Moldova (PCM)
PRIME MINISTER: Vasile Tarlev (since April '01)
MAIN IGO MEMBERSHIPS (NON-UN): CIS, OSCE, CE, PFP, BSEC, CEI, Francophonie
CURRENCY: leu (end-'02 £1=ML22.2616, US$1=ML13.9000)
GNI PER CAPITA: US$380, US$2,420 at PPP ('01)

IN BELARUS the year saw mounting pressure upon opposition politicians and the independent media. In addition, a series of arrests of factory managers, which had begun in late 2001, extended in January 2002 to the manager of the Minsk Tractor Works, one of the world's largest. He was accused of abuse of office, negligence and bribery, but the action appeared to have a closer connection with his criticism of President Lukashenka's economic policies. The director of a radio factory was accused of similar charges. In May, a case was opened against the director of a state oil concern, and there were bribery charges against the director of a Minsk wine factory. The tractor plant director received a non-custodial five year sentence in May in the first of these cases to be brought to court.

There was also continuing government pressure throughout the year on opposition activists, in the form of border detentions, arrests, and police sentences. Arrests were made at demonstrations held to commemorate Freedom Day, 24 March, which was the anniversary of the proclamation of the Belarusian Democratic Republic in 1918. Also in May, Aleksander Chygyr, son of a former Prime Minister and opposition politician, was given a seven year sentence with confiscation of property; he had been accused of car theft but the sentence was widely seen as a political one. His father, Mikhail Chygyr, was himself sentenced to three years' imprisonment and confiscation of property in July on charges of tax evasion. In April an unauthorised demonstration of about a thousand people demanding increased wages and pensions, and compensation for lost savings, was attacked by riot police and 85 were arrested. Two journalists on the banned opposition newspaper, *Pahonya*, were given sentences in June for defaming the Belarusian President. The opposition newspaper *Svobodnye novosti* was closed in August, and another opposition paper, *Nasha svoboda*, announced that it would cease publication. In September the editor of the opposition paper *Rabochii* was sentenced to two years in a corrective labour camp for attempting to defame Lukashenka.

The authorities themselves acquired a powerful new instrument with the opening of a new, second television channel (BT-2) in May, which was to be 51 per cent state-owned. Lukashenka made clear in this connection that "ideology. . . should remain under the state's influence". No less significant was the election in September of the deputy head of the presidential administration, Leanid Kozik, as head of the Trade Union Federation of Belarus. The Federation had been critical of the government's economic policy, and had been the primary support of opposition candidate Vladimir Goncharik at the presidential election of September 2001 (see AR 2001, p. 151).

Foreign relations became increasingly fraught throughout the year, not only with the Western nations but also with Russia. There was controversy in February when Belarusian officials fiercely denied US claims that the country was engaging in illegal arms sales to countries that were accused of terrorism, and might also be giving military training to terrorist groups. The Belarusian authorities themselves continued to deny requests from the Organisation for Security and Co-operation in Europe (OSCE) that its Advisory and Monitoring Group (AMG) be allowed to resume its work in the country. The Belarusian security service, the KGB, issued a statement blaming the former head of the AMG, German diplomat Hans-Georg Wieck, for attempting to "encourage the country to conduct domestic reforms in the interests of the West and the USA"; in June the AMG's acting head was required to leave the country. By 30 December, however, both sides had agreed to replace the AMG with an OSCE representative office in Minsk. The difficult character of Belarusian relations with the outside world was underlined in November when Lukashenka and seven leading officials were denied visas by 14

EU member states, and by the USA, which meant that they were unable to attend NATO's Euro-Atlantic Partnership meeting in Prague (see XI.2.i).

Relations with Slavic neighbour Russia, were more turbulent than they had been during the Yeltsin years. In June, following a meeting with Lukashenka in St Petersburg, Russia's President Vladimir Putin declared himself dissatisfied with Belarusian proposals for the new Belarus-Russia union state. Belarusian demands for a veto in the new state were unacceptable, he said, and the restoration of Soviet-era structures was undesirable. Lukashenka himself made clear that Belarus could not agree to any arrangement that compromised its sovereignty. A summit meeting in Moscow in August ended acrimoniously after the Belarusian President rejected Putin's plans to amend the structure of the proposed Belarus-Russia Union. At the summit's concluding news conference, Putin proposed a detailed timetable for integration, including the formation of a federal state on the basis of the Russian constitution, for which approval would be sought by referendum in May 2003; and the election of a President for the new state in March 2004. Lukashenka's reaction to these proposals, which he claimed would amount to Belarus' integration into the Russian Federation, was increasingly hostile, and later in the month he described them as "insulting".

UKRAINIAN public life in 2002 revolved around the legislative elections that took place at the end of March, and a mounting wave of opposition to President Leonid Kuchma. The Ukrainian unicameral legislature, the Supreme Council, was composed of 450 deputies of whom 225 were elected by a national party-list competition, with seats allocated proportionally to all of the parties that cleared the 4 per cent threshold. A further 225 single-member constituencies were filled on the basis of a simple majority. The campaign officially began on 9 February, marked by a variety of corruption scandals and accusations that "doublers" (parties or individuals with the same name as established groups or politicians) were undermining the entire process. In all, there were 33 parties or movements on the ballot paper. International observers thought the election was an improvement on that of 1998 but were sharply critical of several aspects of its conduct, including pressure from the authorities to vote in favour of pro-presidential parties and candidates, partisan state media, and overcrowded polling stations (turnout was 69.7 per cent).

The outcome of the election was an apparent victory for the opponents of Kuchma, but the opposition was split between the centre-right Our Ukraine bloc, led by former Prime Minister Viktor Yushchenko, and the Communist Party of Ukraine (KPU), led by Petro Symonenko. Yushchenko, his opponents alleged, was in effect the candidate of the West, which might even entertain longer-term ambitions to use him to replace Kuchma. His support was disproportionately strong in the country's western regions. Symonenko's support, by contrast, was concentrated in the Russian-speaking east. A further bloc, For a United Ukraine (ZYU), included five pro-presidential parties and had the strong support of the state machine including the state-run media. Three other parties cleared the threshold for representation in the legislature: the Yulia Tymoshenko bloc, the Socialist Party (both in opposition to Kuchma), and the pro-presidential Social Democratic Party of Ukraine (United).

The final results showed that Our Ukraine had won the largest share of the party-list vote, forcing the KPU into second place, but the single-member seats were mostly won by independents who had, in practice, enjoyed the support of the pro-presidential For a United Ukraine bloc. The future composition of the legislature, accordingly, was somewhat uncertain. Our Ukraine had won 24 per cent of the party-list vote, and 112 seats overall; the KPU had won 20 per cent of the party-list vote, and a total of 66 seats; ZYU took 12 per cent of the party-list vote, but 101 seats; the Tymoshenko Bloc had 12 per cent and 22 seats; the Socialist Party 9 per cent and 23 seats; and the Social Democratic Party (United) 6 per cent and 24 seats. Candidates who were at least nominally independent, however, won by far the largest share (93) of the single-member constituencies. The new Supreme Council, when it assembled, formed six factions: United Ukraine was the largest, with 175 of the seats that had so far been declared, followed by Our Ukraine with 119, and the KPU with 63.

After tortuous negotiations, Volodymyr Lytvyn, the former head of the presidential administration and leader of ZYU, was elected parliamentary speaker at the end of May in what was seen as a victory for Kuchma. The President appointed Viktor Medvedchuk, an oligarch (powerful businessman with political ambitions) and head of the pro-presidential Social Democratic Party of Ukraine (United), as head of his administration in June, in succession to Lytvyn. In late August, in a television address marking the 11th anniversary of Ukrainian independence, Kuchma called for constitutional change in the direction of a "parliamentary-presidential model" with a stronger local government, describing this as "our European choice". The opposition, for its part, called for national protests on 16 September, which was the second anniversary of the disappearance of journalist Heorhiy Gongadze (see AR 2000, p. 135), and began to press for Kuchma's resignation.

The anti-Kuchma campaign acquired substantial dimensions when, on 16 September, about 20,000 demonstrators converged on the centre of Kiev to initiate a nationwide protest. Smaller meetings were held throughout the country. The demonstration took place in spite of a ban prohibiting the rally in central Kiev; protestors responded by setting up tents around the presidential administration, which were then dismantled by the police. On 23 September about 30 deputies, including opposition leaders, entered the headquarters of the state-owned television company and demanded the opportunity to announce a forthcoming, still larger demonstration. Their demands were refused, and a blank screen was shown instead of the regular news broadcast. The following day, 24 September, about 5,000 people gathered in front of the Supreme Council building to demand a debate on Kuchma's impeachment. The crowd then moved to the presidential administration, where a group of opposition leaders handed over a demand for the President's resignation. Demonstrations continued in October, though on a smaller scale, and Kuchma appeared to have weathered the immediate crisis although his political authority had been seriously diminished.

There were further upheavals in November, when Kuchma dismissed Anatolii Kinakh and his government (appointed in May 2001), and nominated Viktor Yanukovych as Prime Minister. The nomination was approved by the Supreme Council on 21 November and the formation of the new government was completed on 1 December. Yanukovych was seen as a malleable ally of Kuchma; and the President's victory over the opposition appeared complete when, in December, pro-presidential deputies in the Supreme Council succeeded in removing from office remaining senior opposition figures, including the head of the Central Bank and 19 legislative committee chairmen.

Kuchma made official visits during the year to China and Italy. He also visited the Euro-Atlantic Partnership meeting in Prague in November, although it was made clear that his presence would not be welcomed. The president of the European Commission, Romano Prodi, himself made clear to the Italian press that he did not envisage Moldova, Belarus, or Russia as possible members of the EU; and, speaking to the Dutch press in November, said that he saw "no reason whatever why Morocco, Ukraine, or the Republic of Moldova" should join. His remarks were received with little enthusiasm in the Ukrainian capital. Relations with the USA were also placed under some strain in September when the US authorities announced they were in possession of evidence that the Ukrainian President had authorised the sale of a military radar system to Iraq—allegations denied by the Ukrainians—and froze the USA's annual aid package to Ukraine.

In MOLDOVA demonstrations led by the opposition Christian Democratic Popular Party (CDPP) were held throughout January to protest against the introduction of compulsory Russian language lessons in primary schools. Prime Minister Vasile Tarlev accused the protestors of trying to destabilise the country and on 22 January the Moldovan Justice Ministry banned the CDPP from taking part in political activities for a month on the grounds that it had held unauthorised rallies. The following month the government decided to suspend the regulation (the Education Minister, Ilie Vancea, who had introduced compulsory Russian, was himself dismissed), but protests continued. In late February about 15,000 people picketed the parliament building, up to 80,000 protested two days later against "communist dictatorship". The Supreme Court ruled that the protests were illegal and ordered their immediate cessation; the following day, however, about 2,000 protestors marched to the national television headquarters, alleging that it had become the mouthpiece of the ruling Communist Party.

Public opposition continued into March, including a rally attended by an estimated 60,000 people. But the protests were called off in April following intervention by the Parliamentary Assembly of the Council of Europe (PACE), which recommended that there should be a moratorium on actions relating to compulsory foreign-language instruction in schools, and also that anti-government demonstrations should cease. In other developments, the Parlamentul (the unicameral legislature) adopted a new civil code in June, replacing a Soviet-era text of 1964; on the basis of the new code the World Bank agreed to resume lending, and two substantial credits for structural adjustment and rural development were approved. President Voronin appeared to find a sympathetic audience for his concerns when he visited the USA in December; both sides agreed on the importance of finding a basis for agreement with the secessionist regime in Transdniester, with which negotiations had made little progress during the year.

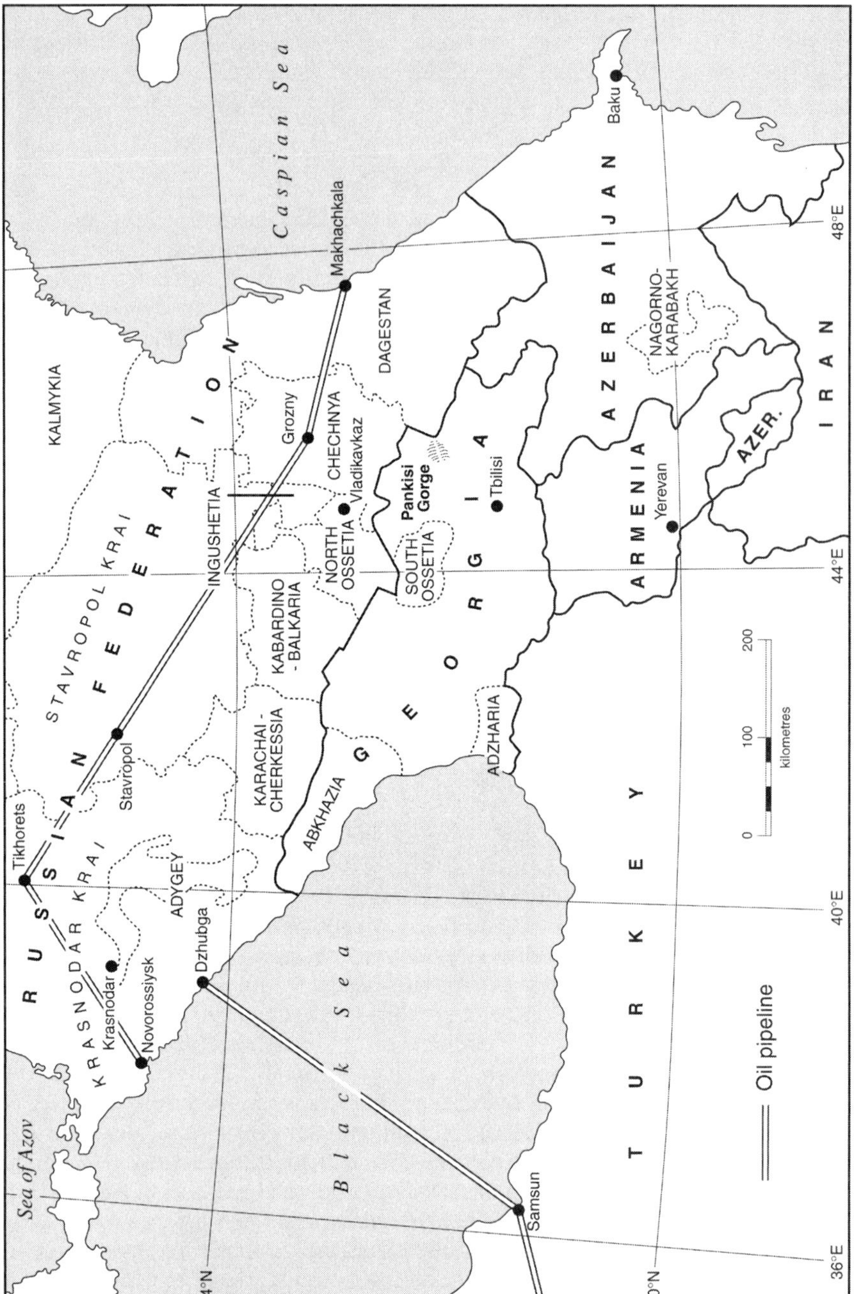
Sea of Azov
Caspian Sea
Black Sea
RUSSIAN FEDERATION
KALMYKIA
STAVROPOL KRAI
KRASNODAR KRAI
ADYGEY
KARACHAI - CHERKESSIA
KABARDINO - BALKARIA
NORTH OSSETIA
INGUSHETIA
CHECHNYA
DAGESTAN
ABKHAZIA
SOUTH OSSETIA
ADZHARIA
GEORGIA
Pankisi Gorge
AZERBAIJAN
NAGORNO-KARABAKH
AZER.
ARMENIA
IRAN
TURKEY
Tikhorets
Stavropol
Krasnodar
Novorossiysk
Dzhubga
Grozny
Makhachkala
Vladikavkaz
Tbilisi
Yerevan
Baku
Samsun
44°N
40°N
36°E
40°E
44°E
48°E
0
100
200
kilometres
Oil pipeline

iii. ARMENIA—GEORGIA—AZERBAIJAN

Armenia

CAPITAL: Yerevan   AREA: 30,000 sq km   POPULATION: 3,800,000
OFFICIAL LANGUAGE: Armenian   POLITICAL SYSTEM: multiparty republic
HEAD OF STATE AND GOVERNMENT: President Robert Kocharian (since Feb '98)
RULING PARTY: Pan-Armenian National Movement heads coalition
PRIME MINISTER: Andranik Markarian (since May '00)
MAIN IGO MEMBERSHIPS (NON-UN): CIS, OSCE, PFP, BSEC, CE, CEI
CURRENCY: dram (end-'02 £1=D932.423, US$1=D582.200)
GNI PER CAPITA: US$560, US$2,880 at PPP ('01)

Georgia

CAPITAL: Tbilisi   AREA: 70,000 sq km   POPULATION: 5,000,000
OFFICIAL LANGUAGE: Georgian   POLITICAL SYSTEM: multiparty republic
HEAD OF STATE AND GOVERNMENT: President Eduard Shevardnadze (since Oct '92)
RULING PARTIES: Citizens' Union of Georgia (SMK) co-ordinates fluid coalition
MAIN IGO MEMBERSHIPS (NON-UN): CIS, CE, OSCE, PFP, BSEC
CURRENCY: lari (end-'02 £1=L3.3823, US$1=L2.1119)
GNI PER CAPITA: US$620, US$2,860 at PPP ('01)

Azerbaijan

CAPITAL: Baku   AREA: 87,000 sq km   POPULATION: 8,100,000
OFFICIAL LANGUAGE: Azeri   POLITICAL SYSTEM: multiparty republic
HEAD OF STATE AND GOVERNMENT: President Geidar Aliyev (since June '93)
RULING PARTY: New Azerbaijan Party (YAP)
PRIME MINISTER: Artur Rasizade (since July '96)
MAIN IGO MEMBERSHIPS (NON-UN): CIS, OSCE, PFP, BSEC, OIC, ECO, CE
CURRENCY: manat (end-'02 £1=M7,837.99, US$1=M4,894.00)
GNI PER CAPITA: US$650, US$3,020 at PPP ('01)

IN ARMENIA there were continuing tensions between the authorities and their opponents, in advance of elections that were scheduled for the following year. The independent A1+ television channel, which had frequently broadcast harsh criticism of the government of President Kocharian, was forced to close down on 3 April after losing a tender for its frequency to Sharm TV, an entertainment company with reported links to a member of the presidential administration. Tens of thousands of people attended a rally in the capital, Yerevan, to protest against the outcome of the tender. The protests continued throughout the month, but opposition attempts to force the reinstatement of A1+ were unsuccessful.

In August Kocharian approved legislation which altered the electoral system, increasing the number of single-member constituencies at national level from 37 to 56 and decreasing the number elected on a party-list basis from 94 to 75. The Central Electoral Commission was also restructured; at its first meeting it called new presidential elections for February and parliamentary elections for May 2003. The leaders of 16 opposition parties signed a statement on 4 September establishing a union to put forward a single candidate and programme at the presidential election. The government, meanwhile, in November approved the sale of five state-owned factories to Russia in payment of its

US$95 million debt. Armenia was accepted as a member of the World Trade Organisation in December.

In GEORGIA there were mounting tensions in relations with Russia, which accused the Georgian authorities of harbouring Chechen terrorists in the remote Pankisi Gorge in the country's north-east (see map, III.3.iii). The Georgians themselves sought the military advice of the USA, which sent advisors to the republic in February in connection with its larger "war on terrorism". A US presence, warned Russian Foreign Minister Igor Ivanov, would "further aggravate the situation", although President Shevardnadze described it as fulfilling one of his country's strategic objectives. The strains continued, however, with the Russian authorities insisting that Chechen separatists were being allowed to use Georgian territory to launch cross-border attacks on Russian troops operating in Chechnya.

Relations deteriorated sharply during August, with Russia claiming the right to extend its military operations against Chechnya over the Georgian border. Georgia accused Russia of an "explicit act of aggression" in late August, after what it said had been a fifth bombing raid in a month, and Shevardnadze promised that Georgia would use "all possible means" to repel any future attacks. For his part, Putin wrote to his Georgian counterpart in September to insist on "focused and forceful action" aimed at "neutralising" the rebels. He also accused the Georgian authorities of harbouring individuals responsible for planning the 11 September 2001 attacks on the USA and for carrying out the 1999 Moscow apartment bombings (see AR 1999, p. 146). If the Georgians themselves took no "concrete actions" against the Chechen rebels, warned Putin, Russia would take "appropriate measures". Relations improved during October, assisted by a meeting between the two Presidents at which it was agreed that they would take co-ordinated action to detain the remaining Chechen militants in the Pankisi Gorge area, and to co-operate more closely in border protection.

Municipal elections in early June resulted in a severe setback for Shevardnadze and his ruling party, the Citizens' Union of Georgia (SMK), which failed to win any seats on councils in the capital, Tbilisi. The New Right Party, formed by dissidents who had left the SMK, won more seats throughout the republic than all of its major rivals combined, but by far the largest share of seats was won by independent candidates.

In a separate development, Shevardnadze, attending the Euro-Atlantic Partnership meeting in Prague in November (see XI.2.i), announced that Georgia would be seeking NATO membership, although it was a decision that could not be implemented for some time.

In AZERBAIJAN an August referendum overwhelmingly approved a series of constitutional amendments, which appeared calculated to strengthen the hand of President Geidar Aliyev. One of the amendments specified that the Prime Minister, rather than the Speaker of the legislature, would exercise executive power if the President became unable to discharge his functions. The Prime Minister, however, was a presidential nominee, and it was feared that this new mechanism could allow the President to appoint his politically ambitious son or another loyal ally as his successor. Foreign observers complained of "widespread irregularities" in the conduct of the referendum.

Aliyev visited Moscow in January for talks with Russian President Vladimir Putin, and visited Iran in May. Pope John Paul II was an unusual visitor to Azerbaijan in May, where he was primarily concerned to make contact with the country's small Roman Catholic community. Incumbent President Arkadii Gukasyan was re-elected President of the self-proclaimed Republic of Nagorno-Karabakh in August, despite criticisms of the entire exercise by the Azerbaijani authorities. Aliyev, the new Nagorno-Karabakh President retorted, was a "politician on his way out". To judge from his preparations for the forthcoming election, however, the Azerbaijani President had other ideas.

IV THE AMERICAS AND THE CARIBBEAN

1. UNITED STATES OF AMERICA

CAPITAL: Washington, DC   AREA: 9,364,000 sq km   POPULATION: 284,000,000
OFFICIAL LANGUAGE: English   POLITICAL SYSTEM: multiparty republic
HEAD OF STATE AND GOVERNMENT: President George W. Bush, Republican (since Jan '01)
RULING PARTY: Congress is controlled by the Republicans
MAIN IGO MEMBERSHIPS (NON-UN): NATO, OSCE, OECD, G-8, OAS, NAFTA, APEC, AC, CP, PC, ANZUS
CURRENCY: dollar (end-'02 £1=US$1.6016, €1=US$1.0406)
GNI PER CAPITA: US$34,870

THE year following the terrorist attacks of 11 September on the USA (see AR 2001, pp. 1-16; 157-60) and the successful conclusion of the war in Afghanistan, was dominated by the "war on terror" and its escalation to include Iraq, which was identified as part of an "axis of evil" by President George W. Bush at the start of the year. These issues overshadowed growing concerns about the state of the US economy—a fact reflected in the Republican Party's successes in the congressional elections in November. Support for Bush's international policies remained strong and his public opinion ratings continued to be high. Even an accident on 13 January in which he apparently struck his head in a fall, allegedly after choking on a piece of pretzel and briefly losing consciousness whilst watching football on television, did not diminish his popularity.

The last piece of debris from the site of the World Trade Centre, destroyed in the 11 September attacks, was removed on 30 May. In September authorities put the final official death toll for the attacks at the World Trade Centre as 2,801. The figure for the attack on the Pentagon was 184, with a further 44 deaths in the fourth hijacked plane which crashed in Pennsylvania. The anniversary of the attacks was marked by ceremonies across the country.

POLITICAL DEVELOPMENTS. President Bush delivered his first State of the Union address before Congress on 29 January. In his opening reference to the response after the 11 September terrorist attacks, the President said the country had "rallied a great coalition, captured, arrested, and rid the world of thousands of terrorists, destroyed Afghanistan's terrorist training camps, saved a people from starvation, and freed a country from brutal oppression".

Bush's main subject was "our war against terror" which, he said, "is only beginning". He said the USA would "shut down terrorist camps, disrupt terrorist plans, and bring terrorists to justice". Secondly, the country would prevent those who sought chemical, biological, or nuclear weapons from threatening the USA. The President identified an "axis of evil" formed by Iran, Iraq, and North Korea, all of which he claimed were developing weapons of mass destruction and posed "a grave and growing danger". While continuing to work with coalition partners, Bush assured his audience that "America will do what is necessary to ensure our nation's security".

Pointing to the cost of the war against terrorism Bush indicated that he had asked for the largest increase in defence spending in two decades. Spending on homeland security was to be doubled and would focus on "bioterrorism, emergency response, airport and border security, and improved intelligence".

Bush said that his final priority was "economic security for the American people". He said that there would be a small, short-term budget deficit "so long as Congress restrains spending and acts in a fiscally responsible manner". He promised "we will defeat this recession". In order to ensure good jobs, the President said, the country should continue to improve education and provide good schools with "a quality teacher in every classroom". Good jobs also required reliable and affordable energy and he said that the USA "must act to increase energy production at home so America is less dependent on foreign oil". The President also called for an expansion in trade and he asked Congress to approve "trade promotion authority" and an economic "stimulus package", and for previous tax cuts to be made permanent.

Amongst the other measures Bush called upon Congress to enact were "a patients' bill of rights to give uninsured workers credits to help buy health coverage", an increase in spending on veterans' health provision, and a sound Medicare system covering the cost of prescription drugs for the elderly. Social security reform, a productive farm policy, environmental measures, and broader home-ownership were also cited.

Pointing to the impact of 11 September in bringing out "a culture of responsibility", Bush called upon every US citizen to commit "4,000 hours over the rest of your lifetime" to public service, and announced the creation of the USA Freedom Corps to mobilise such action. In addition the President called upon the USA to extend compassion to every part of the world and, in an attempt to assuage Islamic critics of US policy, he referred to the positive elements of "Islam's own rich history" in this respect. The USA would continue "with friends and allies from Europe to Asia, and Africa to Latin America" to demonstrate "that the forces of terror cannot stop the momentum of freedom".

Some measures referred to in the President's message had been enacted earlier in the month. On 8 January Bush had signed the "No Child Left Behind" education reform bill, passed by Congress in December. The legislation, regarded as the most important measure in education reform since the 1960s, extended federal authority in education through the introduction of national standardised tests in reading and mathematics for children between the ages of eight and 14 from 2004. Federal funds would be provided for schools that could not show an improvement in pupils' performance over a two-year period.

On 10 January Bush signed a US$317.5 billion defence bill for fiscal 2002, approved by Congress the previous December. The bill increased military spending by 10 per cent, with a 5 per cent increase in military salaries. Some US$7.8 billion was provided for the development of a national missile defence system (NMD). Amendments to the bill provided US$8.2 billion in emergency aid to the areas of New York, Pennsylvania, and Washington DC affected by the 11 September attacks. A further US$8.3 billion was provided for homeland security measures.

On 19 April the Senate (the upper house) voted to accept a comprehensive energy bill, but in a major setback for the President, rejected an amendment to allow drilling for oil in the Arctic National Wildlife Refuge in Alaska. The amendment, defeated as a consequence of a Democratic filibuster, was a central plank in the energy strategy drawn up by Vice President Dick Cheney. The House of Representatives (the lower chamber) had approved exploratory drilling in Alaska, and the two versions of the bill remained to be reconciled.

In a televised address on 6 June Bush called upon Congress to make the Office of Homeland Security, established in the aftermath of the 11 September attacks, a Cabinet-level department. The Department would review intelligence collected by the CIA and FBI, and co-ordinate national, state, and local domestic defence measures. The new Department would have an annual budget of US$37.5 billion and would incorporate all or part of a number of agencies, including the Coast-guard, Secret Service, and Immigration and Naturalisation Service. The new Department came into being when the President signed the Homeland Security Act on 25 November.

In the aftermath of the Enron scandal (see below), Bush announced on 9 July that he would establish a corporate fraud task force headed by Deputy Attorney General Larry Thompson to assist federal investigations of corporate fraud. On 30 July the President signed into law the corporate fraud bill passed by Congress five days earlier. The act required immediate disclosure of stock sales by corporate executives, doubled the penalty for corporate fraud from five to 10 years in prison, restricted the services provided to corporate clients by accountancy firms, and established a five-member board to set accounting standards.

Both Bush and Cheney faced questioning throughout July about their activities as senior executives in the oil industry. Cheney declined to comment on a Securities and Exchange Commission (SEC) inquiry into financial irregularities at Halliburton Co., a Dallas-based oil company of which he had been chairman. A lawsuit filed on 10 July by the Judicial Watch law firm charged Cheney with accounting fraud. In response to repeated press questions Bush refused to discuss a SEC inquiry into his sale in 1990 of his shareholdings in the Texan oil and gas exploration company, Harken, shortly before it was announced that the company was in financial difficulty. Although an SEC memo stated that Bush did not appear to have engaged in "illegal insider dealing", the White House subsequently admitted that Bush had been aware that there would be losses, but not of their extent. It also transpired that he had bought the shares with money lent to him by Harken itself.

Bush secured the trade promotion authority that he had requested in his State of the Union address when on 6 August he signed the measure approved earlier by Congress. The act, which enabled the President to negotiate international trade agreements, won sufficient Democratic votes to pass in the Senate only after measures had been approved to provide subsidised health insurance and job training for workers who lost their jobs because of foreign competition.

Concerns about the mounting possibility of conflict with Iraq found expression in different forms in September. Bush indicated on 4 September that he would not take any action without the endorsement of a congressional resolution. In his speech before the UN Security Council on 12 September he indicated that he would work with delegates to secure the "necessary resolutions" to approve military action.

Although leaders of both parties had expressed backing for a congressional resolution in a meeting with the President on 18 September, the support of the Democratic Party was not unequivocal. Towards the end of September former Vice President Al Gore made a number of speeches critical of the President's policies and suggesting that a war against Iraq would undermine international support in the "war against terrorism". Gore also indicated he would not support the congressional resolution as presented by the White House. The fragility of the political consensus was further revealed on 25 September when, in a speech in the Senate, Democratic majority leader Tom Daschle condemned White House attempts to question the patriotism of war critics. He said that "we ought not politicise the rhetoric about war and life and death".

On 19 September the White House presented a draft resolution to Congress to authorise the President "to use all means that he determines to be appropriate, including force, in order to enforce the United Nations Security Council resolutions". The tone of the resolution reflected the determination of the Bush administration to act against Iraq even if the UN failed to agree new, stronger resolutions. On 10 October the House of Representatives approved the resolution by 296 votes to 133. The Senate passed it the following day by 77 votes to 23. Bipartisan support for the resolution had been secured by agreeing that any such action would be limited to Iraq, and undertaken only when all other methods to resolve the crisis had been exhausted. Furthermore, Congress required prior notification of any military action and progress reports every 60 days once initiated.

The mid-term congressional elections were watched eagerly to determine whether Bush would receive a mandate for his policies. The 34 Senate campaigns were particularly crucial as the Democrats had a majority of only one seat in the upper house. The Republicans held a majority in the House of Representatives of 223 to 208, with three vacant seats and one independent. There were also 36 gubernatorial contests taking place, including a challenge to the President's brother, Jeb Bush, in Florida. Bush made several visits to the state in support of his brother, while Al Gore, Jesse Jackson, and Bill Clinton tried to mobilise the Democratic, and particularly African-American, voters in the state. Problems with the voting machines in Florida during the Democratic Party primary brought new claims of vote fixing, but former Attorney General Janet Reno conceded defeat to her rival for the gubernatorial nomination, Bob McBride, on 18 September.

Robert Torricelli, the Democratic senator for New Jersey who had been admonished in July by the Senate ethics committee for accepting questionable gifts, announced on 30 September that he would not seek re-election. Although state laws officially prohibited changes to candidates listed less than 51 days before the election, the New Jersey Supreme Court ruled to make an exception to allow a "full and fair ballot choice" for voters. Seventy-eight year old Frank Lautenberg, who had retired in 2000 after 18 years in the Senate, agreed to run again. On 27 October the Democratic Party quickly selected 74-year old Walter Mondale, Vice-President under Jimmy Carter, to stand as the candidate for election to the Senate for Minnesota following the death of Senator Paul Wellstone in an air crash on 25 October.

The elections on 5 November strengthened Bush's position as the Republicans won three seats in the Senate to give them a majority of 51. Mondale failed to hold Minnesota, and the Republicans also won in Missouri and Georgia. Elizabeth Dole, wife of former Senator and presidential contender Robert Dole, held on to the seat formerly held by the conservative Republican Jesse Helms in North Carolina. Frank Lautenberg was elected in New Jersey.

The Republican majority in the House increased by four. Jeb Bush secured a convincing majority in the gubernatorial campaign in Florida, and Sonny Perdue became the first Republican governor of Georgia since the 1870s when he defeated the incumbent, Roy Barnes. Maryland elected its first Republican governor since Spiro Agnew in 1966 when Robert Ehrlich defeated Robert Kennedy's daughter, Kathleen Kennedy Townsend. The only positive results for the Democrats were in Arkansas, where Mark Pryor defeated Senator Tim Hutchinson, and in the gubernatorial contests where they won seven victories including those in the crucial states of Pennsylvania, Michigan, and Illinois. The 50 states were evenly divided in terms of governors from each party. However, for the first time since 1954 the Republicans controlled more state legislatures than the Democrats (21 to 17).

In the wake of the poor election results the Democratic leader in the House of Representatives, Dick Gephardt, resigned on 7 November. On 14 November the Democratic representatives elected Nancy Pelosi from San Francisco as his successor. The Republicans had chosen Tom DeLay of Texas as majority leader the day before. Some questions were raised about Pelosi's suitability due to her liberal record. However, she declared that "people elected me to be a leader not an advocate for my own point of view".

On 27 November Bush appointed Henry Kissinger to chair the independent commission charged with investigating the 11 September terrorist attacks. The appointment of the 79-year old former Secretary of State under Richard Nixon was greeted with some criticism because of his previous policies toward Vietnam, Cambodia, and Chile, and questions about his own personal integrity. Former Senator George Mitchell who had been named as vice chairman, resigned on 11 December, citing a desire to continue his legal practice. Observers felt, however, that Mitchell was uncomfortable working with Kissinger. Kissinger himself resigned on 13 December rather than reveal details of his business interests that might have included links with Saudi Arabia.

Earlier, the celebration of the Republican Party's success in the polls was soured by remarks made by Senate majority leader Trent Lott in a speech to celebrate the 100th birthday of fellow senator Strom Thurmond on 5 December.

IV.1. UNITED STATES OF AMERICA 145

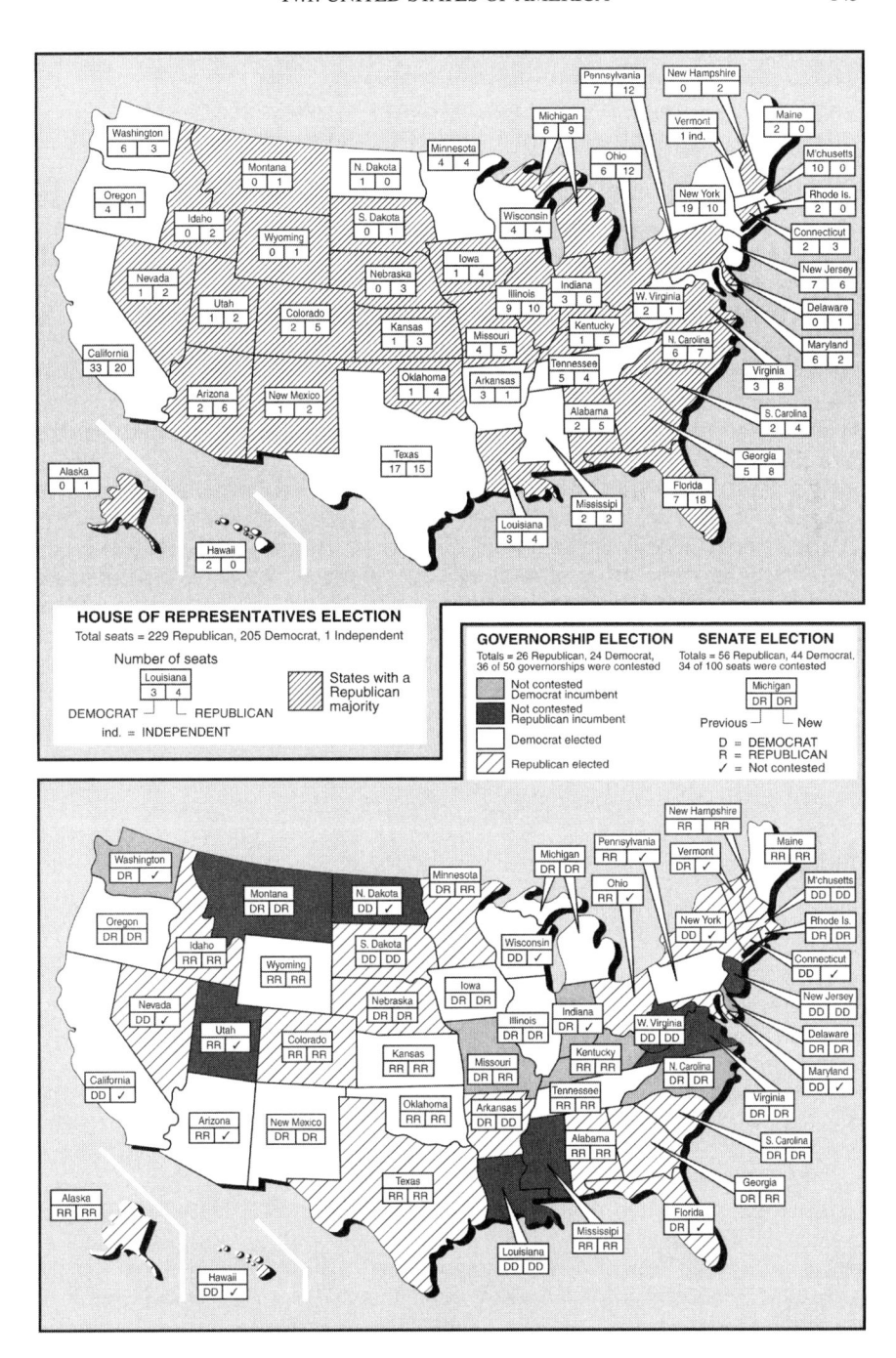

HOUSE OF REPRESENTATIVES ELECTION
Total seats = 229 Republican, 205 Democrat, 1 Independent

Number of seats
Louisiana
3 | 4
DEMOCRAT — REPUBLICAN
ind. = INDEPENDENT

States with a Republican majority

GOVERNORSHIP ELECTION
Totals = 26 Republican, 24 Democrat, 36 of 50 governorships were contested

Not contested Democrat incumbent
Not contested Republican incumbent
Democrat elected
Republican elected

SENATE ELECTION
Totals = 56 Republican, 44 Democrat, 34 of 100 seats were contested

Michigan
DR | DR
Previous — New

D = DEMOCRAT
R = REPUBLICAN
✓ = Not contested

House of Representatives (Democrat | Republican)

State	D	R
Washington	6	3
Oregon	4	1
Montana	0	1
Idaho	0	2
Wyoming	0	1
N. Dakota	1	0
S. Dakota	0	1
Minnesota	4	4
Nevada	1	2
Utah	1	2
Colorado	2	5
Nebraska	0	3
Iowa	1	4
Wisconsin	4	4
California	33	20
Arizona	2	6
New Mexico	1	2
Kansas	1	3
Missouri	4	5
Illinois	9	10
Indiana	3	6
Michigan	6	9
Ohio	6	12
Oklahoma	1	4
Arkansas	3	1
Tennessee	5	4
Kentucky	1	5
W. Virginia	2	1
Pennsylvania	7	12
New York	19	10
Vermont	1 ind.	
New Hampshire	0	2
Maine	2	0
M'chusetts	10	0
Rhode Is.	2	0
Connecticut	2	3
New Jersey	7	6
Delaware	0	1
Maryland	6	2
Virginia	3	8
N. Carolina	6	7
S. Carolina	2	4
Georgia	5	8
Alabama	2	5
Mississippi	2	2
Louisiana	3	4
Texas	17	15
Florida	7	18
Alaska	0	1
Hawaii	2	0

Governorship and Senate (Previous | New)

State	Gov	Sen
Washington	DR	✓
Oregon	DR	DR
Montana	DR	DR
Idaho	RR	RR
Wyoming	RR	RR
N. Dakota	DD	✓
S. Dakota	DD	DD
Minnesota	DR	RR
Nevada	DD	✓
Utah	RR	✓
Colorado	RR	RR
Nebraska	DR	DR
Iowa	DR	DR
Wisconsin	DD	✓
California	DD	✓
Arizona	RR	✓
New Mexico	DR	DR
Kansas	DR	RR
Missouri	RR	RR
Illinois	DR	✓
Indiana	DR	✓
Michigan	DR	DR
Ohio	DR	✓
Oklahoma	RR	RR
Arkansas	DR	DD
Tennessee	RR	RR
Kentucky	RR	RR
W. Virginia	DD	DD
Pennsylvania	RR	✓
New York	DD	✓
Vermont	DR	✓
New Hampshire	RR	RR
Maine	RR	RR
M'chusetts	DD	DD
Rhode Is.	DR	DR
Connecticut	DD	✓
New Jersey	DD	DD
Delaware	DR	DR
Maryland	DD	✓
Virginia	DR	DR
N. Carolina	DR	DR
S. Carolina	DR	DR
Georgia	DR	RR
Alabama	RR	RR
Mississippi	RR	RR
Louisiana	DD	DD
Texas	RR	RR
Florida	DR	✓
Alaska	RR	RR
Hawaii	DD	✓

Lott said that if others had voted like him for Thurmond in the 1948 presidential election "We wouldn't have had all these problems over the years". Thurmond had stood as the candidate for the States' Rights Party on a platform to maintain racial segregation. Lott's remarks, which were picked up and circulated by internet "bloggers", were condemned by leaders of the Democratic Party and civil rights organisations. Speaking to a largely black audience in Philadelphia on 12 December, Bush said that the remarks were "wrong" and "offensive" and did not "reflect the spirit of our country". Lott made several television appearances to apologise, and denied that he "embraced the discarded policies of the past". However, in the face of continued criticism he announced his resignation as majority leader on 20 December. He did not resign as a senator, however, and thus avoided jeopardising the Republican majority in the Senate. Lott was replaced by David Frist of Tennessee on 23 December. Frist, a former doctor, was regarded as more moderate than his predecessor.

The campaign for the Democratic Party's nomination for the 2004 presidential race formally began on 1 December when Senator John Kerry of Massachusetts announced his candidacy. Kerry, a Vietnam veteran and senior member of the Senate foreign relations committee, had positive ratings in the opinion polls. On 15 December former Vice President Al Gore announced that he would not be seeking the Democratic nomination as presidential candidate in 2004. After two weeks travelling the country and appearing on television talk shows it was clear that Gore's candidacy would not have generated much enthusiasm. In November Gary Hart, the former Democratic senator whose presidential campaign in 1988 had collapsed because of a sex scandal, indicated he might run again.

SOCIAL, LEGAL, AND GENERAL. On 2 January a plea of not guilty was entered for Zacarias Moussaoui, a French citizen of Moroccan descent, who had been charged in the Federal District Court in Alexandria, Virginia, with conspiracy to commit terrorist acts in connection with the 11 September attacks (see AR 2001, p. 172). Moussaoui had declined to enter a plea. In July Moussaoui pleaded guilty, but when his claim of insanity was rejected, he withdrew the plea. Richard Reid, the "shoe-bomber" detained in December (see AR 2001, p. 172), pleaded not guilty to nine charges, including the attempted use of a weapon of mass destruction, in a US District Court in Boston on 18 January.

A third man, Mokhtar Haouari, an Algerian, was sentenced to 24 years' imprisonment by a US District Court in New York on 16 January following his conviction in July 2001 (see AR 2001, p. 168) for his part in a bomb attack on Los Angeles international airport in 1999.

In a chilling re-enactment of the 11 September attacks, a 15-year old boy, Charles Bishop, flew a Cessna light aircraft into the 28th floor of the Bank of America building in central Tampa, Florida, on 5 January. Bishop, who was the only fatality in the incident, left a note indicating that he had done so out of sympathy for Osama bin Laden.

During January different congressional investigations were underway into the collapse in December of the Enron Corp., which, with debts of US$15 billion, represented the largest corporate bankruptcy in US history (see AR 2001, p. 22). On 9 January the Justice Department announced that a criminal investigation was to be led by Deputy Attorney General Larry Thompson. Attorney General John Ashcroft removed himself from the investigation because he had received substantial contributions from Enron in his unsuccessful bid for a Senate seat in 2000.

The Enron auditors, Arthur Andersen LLP, announced on 10 January that a "significant" number of documents had been deliberately destroyed in October and November 2001, and on 15 January the company dismissed David Duncan, the partner responsible. Duncan subsequently invoked his right under the Fifth Amendment not to testify during an appearance before a congressional investigating committee.

Papers made public on 14 January revealed that Sherron Watkins, an Enron executive, had warned the company's chief executive, Kenneth Lay, in August that Enron was about "to implode in a wave of accounting scandals". This suggested that senior executives within the company had prior knowledge of the financial problems and were able to sell their stocks at a profit before bankruptcy proceedings put an end to stock dealing.

Charges of collusion between the Bush administration and Enron were rebutted on 10 January when the President said he had not discussed the company's financial problems although he had met Lay on several occasions during 2001. Requests for help from the company to the Treasury and Commerce Departments had been refused. Other suspicions about links between the company and the Bush administration focused on the influence exercised by Enron as a major donor to the Republican Party in shaping the report of Vice President Cheney's energy task force in 2001. It was revealed that Enron executives had met with members of the Vice President's staff on several occasions and that Cheney was present at some of those meetings.

Kenneth Lay resigned as chairman and chief executive of Enron on 23 January. Two days later the body of Clifford Baxter, a former Enron vice president, was found in his car after he had apparently committed suicide. A report by a special committee of directors of the Enron Corp. in February found that company executives had deliberately exaggerated profits and disguised debts.

On 14 March the Justice Department announced that it would bring charges of obstructing justice against Arthur Andersen LLP following the shredding of documents at a number of the company's offices after the launch in December of investigations into the Enron collapse. Andersen's chief executive, Joseph Beradino, announced his resignation on 26 March, and on 9 April David Duncan pleaded guilty in a court in Houston to charges that he had intentionally destroyed documents in response to inquiries into the Enron collapse.

On 14 March a federal grand jury in Trenton, New Jersey, issued indictments against Ahmad Omar Sayeed Shaikh in connection with the kidnapping and murder of the journalist Daniel Pearl in Pakistan. Another indictment filed against Shaikh in Washington, DC, on the same day charged him with the kidnapping of Bela Nuss in Pakistan in 1994.

Federal courts in New York and Detroit ruled in April that the Justice Department had exceeded its powers by imprisoning people as material witnesses in relation to the 11 September attacks before any indictments were issued, and that immigration hearings held in secret on grounds of national security were illegal. However, the authorities detained 104 people on 23 April on suspicion of having supplied false information to obtain jobs at various international airports in the USA. In a later ruling, a US federal judge in Washington DC required the federal government to release the names of the more than 1,000 people detained after 11 September, mostly on minor immigration charges, within 15 days. Most of those detained had been released or deported.

A series of measures to reform the Federal Bureau of Investigation (FBI) was announced by the director Robert Mueller on 29 May. Increased priority was to be given to counter-terrorist operations and the number of staff in such areas was to be tripled to about 3,000. Mueller admitted that the 11 September attacks might have been averted if the FBI had correctly interpreted intelligence collected by its various offices. This was seen as a reference to leaked reports that in July 2001 an FBI agent in Phoenix had suggested routine sweeps of aviation training schools, and that agents involved in the case of Zacarias Moussaoui, the so-called "20th hijacker", had apparently also speculated that he could be involved in a suicide attack and had even identified the World Trade Centre as a possible target. Attorney General John Ashcroft announced on 30 May that, rather than being split between New York and Washington DC, analysis of intelligence material would henceforth be centralised in Washington.

Suggestions that Bush had failed to heed warnings of the 11 September attacks were denied on 17 May. Although it was acknowledged that in August 2001 the President had received CIA briefings of plans to hijack planes, it was claimed that the briefings were a vague repetition of previous warnings. Vice President Cheney described suggestions of prior knowledge of the 11 September attacks as "thoroughly irresponsible and totally unworthy of national leaders in time of war". Demands by members of both parties in Congress for full details of the CIA briefing to be released were denied on grounds of security.

Criticism of the FBI's intelligence gathering and analysis in connection with the events of 11 September continued during congressional hearings in June. On 4 June FBI director Mueller insisted that the various warnings received before the event had not been sufficiently detailed or precise to prevent the attacks. However, two days later Coleen Rowley, the FBI's General Counsel in the Minneapolis field office, testified before a Senate committee that FBI bureaucracy and infighting discouraged local initiatives and had sabotaged investigations of Zacarias Moussaoui. Further embarrassment about intelligence failures was caused by revelations that the CIA had been monitoring the activities of two of the 11 September hijackers for 18 months prior to the attacks. The agency apparently failed to pass the information on to either the FBI or the Immigration Service. A preliminary report of the House and Senate intelligence committees, issued on 18 September, reiterated many of these accusations and led to calls for an independent investigation.

Robert Hanssen the former FBI agent convicted on charges of espionage in June 2001 (see AR 2001, p.168) was sentenced to life imprisonment without parole on 10 May by a US District Court judge in Alexandria, Virginia. Hanssen had agreed to provide the authorities with details of his activities in return for a life sentence rather than face the death penalty.

On 22 May the decomposed remains of Chandra Levy, the Washington intern who had disappeared in April 2001 (see AR 2001, p. 167), were found in the undergrowth in Rock Creek Park, Washington DC. It was later announced that she had been murdered although the exact cause of death could not be determined. Levy's disappearance had provoked a scandal when it emerged that she had been having an affair with a Californian congressman, Gary Condit.

The Attorney General, John Ashcroft, announced on 10 June that a US citizen, Abdullah al-Mujahir (also known as Jose Padilla), had been arrested on 8 May, following his arrival from Pakistan at O'Hare International Airport, on suspicion of terrorist activities. It was claimed that al-Mujahir was involved in a plot to explode a bomb containing radioactive material in the USA. The suspect was declared an "enemy combatant" enabling the authorities to detain him indefinitely without charge and without legal representation, treatment that raised some criticism from civil liberties groups. There was also some suggestion that, given an apparent lack of evidence against al-Mujahir, the attorney general was scare mongering. In December a Federal Court judge in Manhattan ruled that al-Mujahir did have rights and was entitled to legal representation.

Various newspapers reported in June that investigations into the anthrax attacks in 2001 (see AR 2001, p. 170-1) indicated that the anthrax spores had been grown rather than stolen, and that the likely perpetrator was probably an individual working alone, unaided by any foreign group or terrorist network. It was believed the individual had been employed in US government-financed biological weapons programmes and it was revealed that the homes of 20 biological warfare experts in the USA had been searched. Considerable attention focused on Steven Hatfill, a former worker at the army's biological warfare laboratory in Maryland. Despite intensive searches of his property, no charges were brought. In July reports indicated that the government would only administer anthrax vaccine to individuals at high risk rather than to all military personnel. It was also announced that stockpiles of anthrax vaccine would be stored at locations around the USA for use in the event of any future attack.

A jury in the US District Court in Houston found the accounting company Arthur Andersen LLP guilty of obstructing justice in the investigations of the Enron collapse on 15 June. The company announced it would cease to conduct company audits as of the end of August. In the wake of the Enron collapse and the panic that ensued in business circles, a number of corporations issued revised financial statements. On 25 June WorldCom Inc., the country's second-largest long-distance communications company and one audited by Arthur Andersen LLP, announced that its profits had been overstated by

US$3.8 billion over the previous five quarters and that the chief financial officer, Scott Sullivan, had been dismissed.

Following further revelations that another US$3 billion in liabilities had been concealed, WorldCom Inc. filed for bankruptcy in July. This represented the largest bankruptcy filing in US history. Sullivan and Buford Yates, former director of general accounting in WorldCom, were indicted in a federal District Court in Manhattan on 28 August on charges relating to the collapse of the company, including securities fraud. Charges of securities fraud were also filed against officials of Tyco International in the same court on 12 September. John Rigas, chief executive of the cable television company Adelphia Communications Corp., had been arrested in July on charges of fraud along with several of the company's executives. In August it was announced that the Justice Department had opened an investigation into the accounting practices of AOL Time Warner, the world's largest media company. On 2 October the former chief financial officer of Enron Corp., Andrew Fastow, was charged with several offences in relation to the company's collapse.

The Supreme Court issued a landmark ruling on the death penalty on 20 June when it ruled by six votes to three in *Atkins v. Virginia* that it was unconstitutional to execute mentally retarded individuals found guilty of capital offences. This overturned a previous ruling in 1989 when the Court had found insufficient "national consensus" on the issue to declare such executions "cruel and unusual". The position had changed as 16 states had since prohibited executions of mentally retarded people. In a second ruling, in *Ring v. Arizona*, on 24 June, the Supreme Court ruled by seven to two that a jury rather than a judge should determine whether a convicted person should be sentenced to death. In a separate decision, a judge in a US District Court ruled on 1 July that the Federal Death Penalty Act of 1994 was unconstitutional because the "undue risk" that innocent people could be executed was contrary to the due process clause of the 14th Amendment.

Widespread fears of a terrorist attack to mark US Independence Day celebrations proved largely unfounded. However, an Egyptian, later identified as Hesham Mohamed Hadayet, shot and killed two people in an attack on an El Al ticket counter at Los Angeles Airport on 4 July before he was shot dead by an El Al security guard. Hadayet was apparently angered by the proliferation of US flags in his neighbourhood. It was announced subsequently that armed federal guards would in future patrol public access areas at airports.

The first batch of 25 payments from the federal government to victims of the 11 September attacks was announced on 23 August. The payments, ranging from US$300,000 to US$3 million determined by victims' earning power and age, were to go to the families of police officers, firefighters, and people working in the World Trade Centre's twin towers.

In September five men in Detroit were charged with conspiring to provide "material support and resources" for terrorist attacks in the USA. Another five men, all US citizens of Yemeni descent, were arrested outside Buffalo, New York, on similar charges on 14 September. The FBI claimed that the suspects were a cell trained by al-Qaida in Kandahar although there appeared to be little evidence of any specific threat from the men. Attorney General John Ashcroft announced on 4 October that a further six people, including five US citizens, in Portland, Oregon, had been charged for conspiring to wage war against the USA and with aiding al-Qaida. Another person was indicted on 9 October in Chicago for illegally diverting charitable funds to the terrorist group.

Sweeping new security measures were introduced at airports and border crossings on 1 October. All visitors to the USA from certain (predominantly Muslim) countries were to be photographed and fingerprinted. The measures were denounced by some groups as ethnic profiling.

Richard Reid, the British man accused of trying to explode a shoe bomb on board a flight from Paris to Miami, pleaded guilty to eight charges, including attempting to use a weapon of mass destruction and attempted murder, in a Boston court on 5 October. Reid said he did not recognise the court, but admitted that he had "got on the plane with a bomb" and tried to ignite it. He was, he said, "a follower of Osama bin Laden. I'm an enemy of your country and I don't care." Reid faced a jail sentence of 60 years to life in prison.

On 4 October John Walker Lindh, a US citizen who had fought for the Taliban and been captured in Afghanistan, was sentenced to 20 years in prison by a US District Court judge in Alexandria, Virginia. Lindh received the relatively light sentence after pleading guilty to fighting alongside an enemy of the USA and in exchange for giving intelligence information to the authorities.

A security shut down was imposed on the UN building in New York on 3 October after a man fired several shots in the air outside the building before being overcome by guards. The man scattered leaflets concerning the situation in North Korea.

Residents of Washington DC and the neighbouring suburbs in Maryland and Virginia were terrorised for much of October by an unknown sniper. The gunman killed 10 people including one person outside a supermarket, two people on garage forecourts, and a bus driver in his parked bus in apparently random motiveless shootings between 2 and 22 October. The assailant also wounded three more people, including a 13-year old boy outside his school. As fear swept the area the police, led by Charles Moose, chief of police in Montgomery County, Maryland, for some time seemed to have few leads to follow. However, it appeared that the killer had left messages (including one saying "Dear Policeman: I am God.") near to the scenes of shootings, taunting the police.

Eventually negotiations were opened through the media and then by telephone. In the course of these communications, a remark by the sniper led the police to examine evidence in a murder in Tacoma, Alabama. Fingerprint evidence there enabled them to identify a suspect and his vehicle. The crisis came to an end on 24 October when a former army marksman, John Allen Muhammad, and a 17-year old Jamaican boy, John Lee Malvo, were arrested while they slept in their car. A high power rifle was found in the vehicle which had been modified to enable shots to be fired from inside the car through a hole in the boot without the sniper being seen. The motive for the shootings was unknown, but Muhammad was a convert to Islam who had voiced some sympathy for the 11 September attackers. Several states claimed the right to charge the two suspects.

On 15 November, in the first case of its kind, a court in West Palm Beach, Florida, found that the gun manufacturer Valor was partially responsible for the death of a school teacher shot dead by one of his pupils, Nathan Brazill, in 2000. The court ordered the company to pay more than US$1 million to the teacher's widow, Pam Grunow.

On 7 December the Archbishop of Boston, Cardinal Bernard Law tendered his resignation to Pope John Paul II. Once the most influential figure in the Catholic church in the USA, Law had been much criticised for covering up and failing to remove priests involved in sexual abuse cases that became public in January. The Archdiocese in Boston had agreed in March to pay about US$20 million to settle 84 civil cases against a former priest, John Geoghan, who had been employed despite his record as a known paedophile. In an apparent change of strategy by the church, the settlement was later withdrawn. On 13 March it was announced that the Pope had accepted the resignation of a Florida bishop, Anthony O'Connell, after he admitted sexually abusing a teenager during the 1970s. On 24 May the Archbishop of Milwaukee, Rembert Weakland, resigned for similar reasons.

On 19 December the five men jailed in 1989 for the brutal attack and rape of a jogger in New York's Central Park had their convictions overturned in the state Supreme Court after Matias Reyes, a serial rapist and murderer, confessed to the crime. His confession was confirmed by DNA evidence. The five men, all of whom were in their teens when the offence took place, had been associated with an outbreak of "wilding"—indiscriminate mugging attacks that terrorised people using the park. The teenagers confessed to the crime after being held for more than 20 hours without contact with their parents. Sentenced to periods ranging from five to 15 years in prison, they had all completed their sentences and were expected to claim substantial damages.

In October a jury in Los Angeles awarded Betty Bullock a record US$28 billion in damages against the tobacco company Philip Morris. Bullock was suffering from lung and liver cancer as a consequence of cigarette smoking. On 19 December a superior court judge declared the award "legally excessive" and reduced it to US$28 million. However, the judge denied the company's request for a new trial and said that it had "constantly lied to its customers" concerning the links between smoking and cancer.

In December it was reported that up to 700 immigrants from the Middle East had been detained by US officials in southern California when they turned up to register as required under rules introduced following the 11 September attacks.

ECONOMIC DEVELOPMENTS. The US economy continued to hover on the brink of recession throughout much of the year. On 11 January the Ford Motor Co. announced it would cut 22,000 jobs in the USA and 13,000 worldwide. On 17 January the company announced a loss of US$5.45 billion in 2001, its first recorded loss since 1992.

Bush presented his proposed US$2,130 billion budget for fiscal 2003 to Congress on 4 February. The budget projected a deficit of approximately US$80 billion. Democratic Party leaders were particularly critical of the proposed 13.7 per cent increase in defence spending to US$378.6 billion in 2003. Spending on homeland security was almost doubled, to US$37.7 billion, and US$98 million was provided to assist the Colombian army in counter-insurgency operations against leftist rebels in Colombia.

Spending on non-military domestic programmes was limited to an average increase of 2 per cent, a cut in real terms given an anticipated rate of inflation of 2.2 per cent. The Democrats were critical of the cuts in domestic spending and argued that the tax cuts introduced in 2001 would force the government to raid the surpluses in Social Security and Medicare trust funds. Democratic opposition to tax cuts contributed to the defeat in the Senate on 6 February of the economic stimulus bill previously passed by the House of Representatives.

At the beginning of February it was reported that unemployment in January had fallen to 5.6 per cent from December's 5.8 per cent. On 28 February it was also announced that GDP in the last quarter of 2001 had grown by 1.4 per cent because of higher consumer spending in October and November. Technically this meant that the US economy was not in recession, i.e. it had not experienced two consecutive quarters of negative growth.

On 5 March Bush announced that he accepted the findings of the International Trade Commission and would impose tariffs on imported steel for a period of four years starting on 20 March. The measure, intended to protect US steel industries in West Virginia, Pennsylvania, and Ohio, was seen by some observers as a political move in the run up to the congressional elections. It was met with loud protests and in some cases retaliatory tariffs from the EU, China, Japan, New Zealand, and Australia. After a summit meeting with European representatives at the White House on 2 May, both sides agreed to settle the dispute through the World Trade Organisation (WTO).

Bush signed an economic stimulus bill on 9 March which provided for a 13-week extension of unemployment coverage to be funded by a US$8 billion block grant to the states. Also included in the package was US$43 billion in investment incentives. On 13 May the President signed a farm bill that increased federal expenditure on agriculture by 80 per cent over 10 years by substantially raising subsidies on crops such as cotton, wheat, and corn. Both US and overseas critics saw this as a measure aimed to win support in the November congressional elections, and one that was against the spirit of international agreements to reduce agricultural subsidies.

Despite attempts by Bush and others to "talk up" the economy, worries about the stability of corporate USA and concerns about possible conflict with Iraq all contributed to a drastic downturn in the markets on 15 July. As the Dow Jones index fell by 300 points, the US dollar dropped to its lowest level for 30 months and reached parity with the euro.

The first victim of the downturn in airline passenger numbers in the aftermath of the 11 September attacks appeared on 12 August when US Airways filed for bankruptcy. The sixth largest airline in the USA, US Airways had lost US$2 billion in the last year. Two smaller companies, Vanguard Airlines and Midway Airlines, had filed for bankruptcy earlier.

In an attempt to encourage economic optimism, the Bush administration led an economic forum at Baylor University, Texas, on 13 August. The President admitted that "times are kind of tough right now" and called for further tax-cutting measures from Congress. Figures released by the Department of Commerce earlier, however, indicated that contrary to earlier reports the country was in fact in recession. Bush also used the forum to warn that the government would crack down on fraudulent corporate accounting.

The prospect of a war with Iraq caused uncertainty in the stock market which triggered a period of turbulent trading at the end of September, despite a slight drop in the unemployment rate. The US Federal Reserve admitted on 24 September that the threat of war with Iraq could upset the economic recovery in the USA, but refused to cut interest rates to boost confidence. The rate remained at a 40-year low of 1.75 per cent. Figures published by the census bureau on 25 September showed that the number of people living below the poverty line had risen for the first time in eight years. The number had increased by 1.3 million to 32.9 million, 11.7 per cent of the population.

On 7 October Bush ordered the formation of a three-man board to determine whether the economic impact of a strike that had closed 29 major Pacific ports in September warranted federal intervention. When the board found there was little possibility of a quick settlement being reached, an injunction approving an 80-day cooling off period under the terms of the 1947 Taft-Hartley Act was issued by a San Francisco court. Under the terms of the injunction the employees re-opened the docks on 9 October and union members were instructed to return to work the following day. It was estimated that the strike had cost the US economy about US$1 billion per day.

On 23 October Bush approved a US$355.4 billion defence spending bill for the fiscal year 2003. This represented a rise of US$37.5 billion, or 12 per cent, and was the largest increase since the Reagan era.

Following the release of figures showing a continuation in the economic slowdown, Bush sacked his Treasury Secretary, Paul O'Neill, and the White House economic advisor, Larry Lindsey, on 6 December. The unemployment rate had reached a nine-year high of 6 per cent despite successive cuts in interest rates which had fallen to 1.75 per cent. O'Neill, who had attracted considerable criticism for a succession of optimistic remarks despite all the evidence to the contrary, had been reluctant to cut taxes to stimulate the economy. Later in December Bush announced the appointment of John Snow, chairman of the rail-freight company CSX, as US Secretary of the Treasury to replace O'Neill. Bush also nominated William Donaldson, a former head of the New York Stock Exchange, to head the Securities and Exchange Commission to replace Harvey Pitt who had resigned in November, and Stephen Friedman, a former chief executive of Goldman Sachs, to become chief economic adviser. The nominations would come before the Senate for approval in January.

Indicative of the state of the US economy was the announcement in December that the fast-food chain, McDonalds, was to close 175 outlets in the face of falling sales.

FOREIGN AFFAIRS. Bush's warning in his State of the Union address that the USA might take unilateral action against countries in the "axis of evil" caused considerable international alarm, prompting Secretary of State Colin Powell to state before the Senate budget committee on 12 February that "with respect to Iran and North Korea, there is no plan to start a war with these nations". However, Powell stated that "regime change" in Iraq was part of the policy of the USA.

The treatment of the al-Qaida and Taliban prisoners captured in Afghanistan and transferred to the US base on Guantanamo Bay, Cuba, in January also caused some friction within the allied coalition. The US authorities refused to grant the 158 detainees prisoner-of-war status under the Geneva Convention, but instead classed them as "unlawful combatants" or "battlefield detainees". As such, the prisoners faced the possibility of trial by military tribunal rather than courts martial or civil courts. Shocking images of those detained, naked, blindfolded, and bound and shackled on the aircraft transporters, or later kneeling under armed guard in Cuba, added to the criticism. On 7 February Bush announced that full protection of the Geneva Convention would be extended to captured Taliban fighters, but that the US would not grant them full prisoner-of-war status. Furthermore, neither the protection of the Convention nor POW status would be extended to al-Qaida fighters who were regarded as terrorists. A US federal judge ruled on 31 July that US courts had no jurisdiction to hear lawsuits brought on behalf of the Taliban and al-Qaida prisoners as they were not held in the USA, nor were they US citizens.

During a White House ceremony on 11 March to mark six months since the 11 September attacks, Bush announced "a second stage of the war on terror". The aim of this programme was to prevent members of al-Qaida from regrouping outside Afghanistan and to prevent "rogue states" from developing weapons of mass destruction. Although the President did not specify any particular countries, it was widely assumed that the speech referred particularly to Iraq because of its refusal to admit UN weapons inspectors.

On 4 April Bush delivered a major speech in response to the deteriorating situation in the Middle East. Saying "enough is enough", he urged all in the region to move decisively against terrorist acts and criticised Palestinian President Yasser Arafat for failing to control terrorism. The President also urged Arab states to "accept Israel as a nation and a neighbour" and called upon Israel to stop "settlement activity in occupied territories", to respect the rights of Palestinian people under its control, and to halt incursions into Palestinian-controlled areas. The speech was followed by a lengthy visit by Powell to the Middle East to try to restart the peace talks, but this ended on 17 April without having secured either an Israeli withdrawal from Palestinian-controlled areas or a cease fire.

Following a tour to bolster support for US policies against Iraq in 12 countries in Europe and the Middle East by Vice President Cheney, President Bush embarked on a similar tour of European capitals in May, visiting Germany, France, and Italy. Speaking in Berlin on 23 May he compared the "war on terrorism" with the struggle against Nazism and Communism in the twentieth century, but denied he had any plans for war on Iraq "on my desk". On 24 May Bush met Russia's President Vladimir Putin in Moscow and signed the Strategic Offensive Reduction Treaty to reduce the number of nuclear warheads from between 6,000 and 7,000 to between 1,700 and 2,200 by December 2012.

Attempts to mitigate foreign criticism of US policies were not improved when, earlier in May, the USA formally withdrew its signature from the Rome Treaty establishing an International Criminal Court (ICC) to try war crimes or crimes against humanity. The USA wanted to exempt members of its own armed forces from the possibility of prosecution by the court. Foreign disquiet further increased on 13 May when the US negotiator on climate change, Harlan Watson, indicated that there was no prospect of the USA participating in the Kyoto Protocol on reducing greenhouse gas emissions before 2012 (see AR 2001, pp. 175-76).

In June the USA tabled two resolutions at the UN Security Council to exempt all UN-mandated peacekeepers from the jurisdiction of the ICC and specifically those forces in Bosnia-Herzegovina. When these resolutions were rejected, the USA vetoed a resolution to extend the UN mission in Bosnia-Herzegovina until 31 December 2002.

In a speech at West Point Military Academy on 1 June, Bush stated that, faced by "shadowy terrorist networks" or "unbalanced dictators with weapons of mass destruction" rather than conventional nation states, the traditional doctrine of mutually assured destruction no longer applied. Instead, Bush suggested, the USA would have to consider the use of pre-emptive strikes. In response to criticism of such views from senior Republicans, the President was reported to have promised that he would consult both Congress and foreign allies before authorising any attack on Iraq.

On 16 June the press reported that Bush had ended the moratorium on covert assassinations by US agents which had been in force since the 1970s, and had issued an order authorising the CIA to use "all available tools" to topple President Saddam Hussein of Iraq.

In a long-awaited speech on the Middle East situation on 24 June, Bush called upon the Palestinian people to seek "new leadership, new institutions, and new security arrangements". Without explicitly mentioning President Arafat, Bush said that the Palestinians should elect "leaders not compromised by terror". Although Bush also repeated his call for Israel to withdraw to positions held before September 2000 and to stop further settlement activity, his speech indicated a hardening of his position following the latest wave of suicide bombings. The President made no mention of plans for a peace conference which had been earlier proposed by Powell. Later that month the administration warned that aid to the Palestinian National Authority (PNA) would be cut off if it failed to reform or re-elected Arafat in polls scheduled for January 2003.

Bush addressed the General Assembly of the UN on 12 September on the subject of Iraq's compliance with UN resolutions and weapons inspection. Declaring that Iraq had broken every aspect of the "fundamental pledge" to stop developing and destroy all existing weapons of mass destruction, the President referred to Saddam Hussein as "a grave and gathering danger" whose regime posed "a threat to the authority of the United Nations, and a threat to peace". Furthermore, Bush made it clear that UN resolutions would be complied with "or action will be unavoidable". The President called upon the UN to stand with the USA to preserve "our security, and. . . the permanent rights and the hopes of mankind".

In the course of his address to the UN, Bush announced that the USA would rejoin the UN's educational, scientific, and cultural organisation (Unesco) as a "symbol of our commitment to human dignity". The USA had left the organisation in 1984 on the grounds that it had strayed from its original purpose and was suffering from mismanagement.

Despite Saddam Hussein's agreement to re-admit UN weapons inspectors, on 17 September Bush described the Iraqi government as a "barbaric regime" and urged the UN not to be fooled by a man who had already "delayed, denied, and deceived the world". In October the Bush administration made it clear that it would not accept the return of UN weapons inspectors before Iraq had agreed to free and unfettered access to all areas.

In November Bush attended the NATO summit in Prague. In a speech made while meeting Czech President Václav Havel, the President said that contrary to popular opinion he was not a Texan "with two guns on my side", but that he was more comfortable "with a posse". Discussing the situation with regard to Iraq, Bush said Saddam Hussein would "be disarmed, one way or the other, in the name of peace". Following the summit Bush travelled to Russia, Lithuania, and Romania, to get more support for his policy against Iraq.

Bush outlined the administration's case against Saddam Hussein in a televised address to the nation on 6 October. The President stated that while war was not "imminent or unavoidable", Iraq "stands alone" in the threat to world peace because its "weapons of mass destruction are controlled by a murderous tyrant". Bush claimed that the Iraqi regime had "produced thousands of tonnes of chemical agents, including mustard gas, sarin nerve gas, VX nerve gas", and he cited examples in which these weapons had been used. Furthermore Bush declared that US intelligence pointed to Iraqi capabilities to "disperse chemical or biological weapons across broad areas". The President explicitly linked Iraq with al-Qaida but offered no proof to support this assertion. In order to avert conflict Bush said that the UN Security Council had to approve, and Iraq had to agree to, a new tough weapons inspection policy.

2. CANADA

CAPITAL: Ottawa   AREA: 9,971,000 sq km   POPULATION: 31,000,000
OFFICIAL LANGUAGES: English & French   POLITICAL SYSTEM: multiparty system in British Commonwealth
HEAD OF STATE: Queen Elizabeth II (since Feb '52)
GOVERNOR-GENERAL: Adrienne Clarkson (since Oct '99)
RULING PARTY: Liberal Party (since Oct '93)
HEAD OF GOVERNMENT: Jean Chrétien, Prime Minister (since Oct '93)
MAIN IGO MEMBERSHIPS (NON-UN): NATO, OECD, OSCE, G-7, OAS, NAFTA, APEC, CP, AC, CWTH, Francophonie
CURRENCY: Canadian dollar (end-'02 £1=C$2.5147 US$1=C$1.5702)
GNI PER CAPITA: US$21,340, US$27,870 at PPP ('01)

THE year 2002 was one of transition for Canada as political parties sought new leadership, federal and provincial ministers grappled with plans to strengthen an ailing public healthcare system, and the country pondered its role in a possible US military strike against Iraq.

While the three principal opposition parties moved to appoint new leaders, the governing Liberal Party, traditionally disciplined and cohesive, was disrupted by problems of leadership. Since 1993, under the experienced Jean Chrétien, the Liberals had won three successive general elections. Chrétien, who had been a member of Parliament (with a short break) since 1963, was now 69 years old and personal traits consequent upon a long span of office-holding were becoming apparent. He showed little vision in governing, his deeply-inborn pragmatism causing him to react to change rather than seek to manage it. He had become increasingly authoritarian, dominating his party and Cabinet. With the Liberals holding 169 of the 301 seats in the House of Commons (the lower chamber of the bicameral legislature) and with a fractured opposition, he could afford to be complacent. Yet this attitude, characterised publicly by a refusal to state when he would step down, created dissatisfaction within his party. By the end of 2002 polls indicated that 60 per cent of Canadians believed that he should retire from politics.

Within the Liberal Party discontent gathered around the Minister of Finance, Paul Martin. Martin had been one of the most successful Finance Ministers in Canadian history, responsible for an unprecedented series of balanced budgets since 1998. Yet he had always been an uneasy colleague of Chrétien. The two had been rivals for the leadership of the party in 1990 and Chrétien apparently believed that Martin was too sympathetic towards Québec nationalism. For years Martin had been quietly garnering support among Liberals for a bid to win the leadership when Chrétien retired. The Prime Minister had ordered his ministers to stop campaigning to succeed him, declaring that it was damaging party unity. But Martin refused to restrain his activities and on 2 June, citing "irreconcilable differences" between them, Chrétien dismissed him from his Cabinet. Martin remained in the legislature, continuing to solicit support for an eventual leadership bid. A convention to review party leadership had been scheduled for February 2003, at which the Martin forces were thought likely to challenge Chrétien's position. With the possibility of a humiliating rebuke before him, Chrétien took defensive action. At a party meeting in Québec on 21 August, he announced that he would step down as leader of the party in February 2004. The intervening 18 months, he said, would give him time to bring forward a legislative agenda which would constitute his legacy.

That agenda was unveiled on 30 September in the Speech from the Throne which opened the second session of the 37th Parliament. It was a programme emphasising Chrétien's attachment to liberal policies directed towards the improvement of Canadian society. More funding for public healthcare, an attack on child poverty, and plans to improve the living conditions of the aborigines were stressed as priorities. The environment was to be safeguarded through the ratification of the Kyoto Protocol on greenhouse gas emissions. Official development assistance was to be increased, with an emphasis on aid to Africa. Canadians were to be provided with enhanced security, especially through control of the long border with the USA, Canada's principal trading partner. All of these measures were to be implemented without plunging the country into budget deficits. As a plan of action, the agenda was devoid of funding commitments and target dates.

Chrétien's favoured successor emerged through a number of Cabinet reshuffles during 2002. John Manley, an Ottawa MP, had been a loyal member of the Chrétien administration. Late in 2000 he had been appointed Minister for Foreign Affairs and International Trade and had thus been in office at the time of the terrorist attacks on the USA on 11 September 2001. He had shown a firmness in dealing with US security concerns which Chrétien admired. In January 2002 the Prime Minister carried out a major reshuffle of his Cabinet. Manley was promoted to Deputy Prime Minister with many responsibilities, including the management of relations with the USA. In June, following Martin's departure, Manley became Finance Minister, while retaining his position as Deputy Prime Minister. It was evident that he was Chrétien's most trusted colleague and preferred successor.

Aside from the turmoil within the Liberal Party, the opposition parties also grappled with problems of succession. The western-based Canadian Alliance, with 63 seats in Parliament, had gone through a year of damaging in-fighting in 2001. Its leader, Stockwell Day, a former Alberta provincial Cabinet Minister, had encountered a mutiny within the party. Day had met the challenge by authorising a new leadership election. In the vote, held in March, he was defeated by a former party strategist, Stephen Harper, who favoured increased powers to the provinces and a leaner role for government. In a by-election on 13 May Harper was elected to the House of Commons for a seat in Calgary, Alberta. Hurt by past divisions, the Alliance was at a low ebb in the polls, and Harper sought to co-operate with the Progressive Conservative Party (PCP), but the latter rejected his overtures.

The PCP was also going through leadership difficulties. Its leader, Joe Clark, a former Prime Minister and a senior minister under Prime Minister Brian Mulroney, had determinedly attempted to rebuild the party after its crushing defeat by the Liberals in 1993. He had achieved only modest success, however, and the party held only 14 seats in the house of Commons. In August Clark announced that he would retire from politics, with a successor to be chosen before the autumn of 2003.

Canada's social democratic party, the New Democratic Party, which had vainly struggled to find a role in the 1990s, also moved to select a new leader. Since 1995 it had been headed by Alexa McDonough, a Nova Scotian MP, who had attempted to move the party to the political centre, but had managed to secure only a modest 14 seats in the Commons. McDonough's successor was to be chosen at a party convention in January 2003.

Canada's fifth party, the Bloc Québécois, the federalist wing of the separatist movement in Québec, seemed to be treading water in 2002. Although it held 37 seats, the largest number from Québec for any party, the movement for the independence of the province showed signs of being in decline.

Aside from party politics, Canada experienced robust economic growth in 2002. It was not affected by the US economic decline, nor by the volatile movements of the stock exchanges. Canada also was spared the corporate scandals which marked US business during the year (see IV.1). There was strong job creation, with the unemployment rate hovering around 7 per cent. The consumer price index remained steady, although a temporary spike caused by higher electricity prices pushed the rate to 4.3 per cent in November. Overall the gross domestic product was thought likely to increase by 3.3 per cent in 2002, well above the growth expected in the USA. Canada enjoyed the highest level of economic growth among the G-7 industrialized countries in 2002. The healthy state of Canada's finances was reflected in a return to a Triple A credit rating for the country's bonds in 2002. This favourable position had last been achieved in 1993-94.

There was no federal budget in 2002. John Manley, the new Finance Minister, announced that no changes were planned in the strict financial management initiated by his predecessor, Paul Martin. The budget surplus for the year 2002 was expected to come in at about C$7 billion.

Canada's prized structure of public healthcare, a system founded 40 years ago, came under examination in a report commissioned by the federal government and released on 28 November. The report was prepared by Roy Romanov, a respected former premier of Saskatchewan. Romanov, acknowledging the problems that had developed in the national system, recommended a massive infusion of an additional C$15 billion before 2006. Deeply committed to the principle that Canadians should not be required to purchase healthcare directly, Romanov rejected the introduction of a private system to supplement the national plan. His report was to be taken up by a meeting of first ministers—federal, provincial and territorial—early in 2003.

Canada's principal contribution to the international struggle against terrorism came in the form of a combat mission sent to assist US forces in Afghanistan. In February 850 soldiers were sent to the troubled country to guard the airport in Kandahar. The Canadian troops were placed under US command and represented the largest fighting contingent sent abroad by Canada since the Korean War (1950-53). Six naval vessels and transport and reconnaissance aircraft, operated by

1,600 personnel, were also dispatched to the area of the Arabian Sea. The combat mission had to be withdrawn in August, however, because of the strain which it imposed on the country's military capability, which was heavily committed to peacekeeping duties in Bosnia-Herzegovina. On 17 April four Canadian soldiers were killed and eight wounded in a "friendly fire" accident brought about by pilots of the US Air National Guard who, not realising the Canadians were on a night training exercise, dropped a 200-kilogram laser-guided bomb on the detachment. Military enquiries were instituted by both countries, which concluded that the US pilots had not followed prescribed rules of engagement in their action.

Canada, nervous over the unilateralist policies pursued by the USA under President George W. Bush, hesitated before the prospect of a US strike against Iraq. Since 1998 Canada had criticised the regime headed by Saddam Hussein for expelling UN inspectors sent to report on whether or not Iraq was manufacturing weapons of mass destruction. While believing that the USA had not yet presented a convincing case against the Iraqi regime, Canada gave its support to the concept of a multilateral force under UN auspices.

Prime Minister Jean Chrétien hosted the 2002 meeting of the G-7 industrialised nations, held on 26-27 June at Kananaskis, a remote resort in Alberta's Rocky Mountains. Counter-demonstrations were avoided because of the difficulty of gaining access to the mountain site. Chrétien's chief objective was to expand official development assistance over the next year by US$12 billion, of which half would go to Africa. The money would be dependent upon the institution of democratic reforms and protection of human rights. The G-7 leaders approved half the sum requested, without commitments on how and when it would be expended. The G-7 states also pledged to lower tariffs on imports from Africa, with some exceptions. The meeting made no commitments to a sweeping plan put forward by President Bush to eliminate stocks of nuclear weapons over the next 10 years.

The House of Commons approved the Kyoto Protocol, designed to reduce the output of heat-trapping greenhouse gases, in a vote on 10 December. Canada agreed to cut its emission of carbon dioxide and other gases by 6 per cent below 1990 levels by 2012. Canada was the 98th country to sign the accord, which was due to come into effect with its ratification by Russia, expected in 2003. Implementation of the protocol by Canada would be difficult since there was no consensus concerning action to be taken. Many provinces, especially energy-rich Alberta, opposed the plan and sections of Canadian industry feared their competitive position would suffer if it was implemented.

An old trade dispute with the USA dragged on during 2002. This concerned imports of Canadian construction lumber to the USA, the subject of a 27 per cent duty imposed by the US Commerce Department on 22 March. Canada vigorously protested against the imposition and was upheld in several of its arguments by panels set up under the World Trade Organisation. By reducing production costs, Canadian lumber firms continued to sell in the USA but the industry was severely disturbed by the tariff. The federal government offered C$247 million in assistance to hard-pressed lumber companies and their communities, mostly in British Columbia.

3. MEXICO AND CENTRAL AMERICA

MEXICO—GUATEMALA—EL SALVADOR—HONDURAS—NICARAGUA—
COSTA RICA—PANAMA

i. MEXICO

CAPITAL: Mexico City   AREA: 1,958,000 sq km   POPULATION: 99,400,000
OFFICIAL LANGUAGE: Spanish   POLITICAL SYSTEM: multiparty republic
HEAD OF STATE AND GOVERNMENT: President Vincente Fox Quesada (since Dec '00)
RULING PARTY: National Action Party (PAN)
MAIN IGO MEMBERSHIPS (NON-UN): OAS, SELA, ALADI, ACS, APEC, NAFTA, OECD
CURRENCY: Mexican peso (end-'02 £1=MP16.5320, US$1=MP10.3225)
GNI PER CAPITA: US$5,540, US$8,770 at PPP ('01)

ON 1 January Congress, the bicameral legislature dominated by the former ruling party, the Institutional Revolutionary Party (PRI), finally passed the 2002 budget and enacted a tax reform package that would substantially increase revenue. Proposals by the government to extend the scope of value added tax (IVA) were blocked, however, as were other fiscal and regulatory reforms requested by President Vicente Fox Quesada. On 9 February, José Sarukhan Kermez, the Cabinet's social policy co-ordinator, resigned; and at the beginning of April Finance Minister Francisco Gil Díaz was forced to announce cuts of US$1,100 million in current year public expenditure as a result of the shortfall in IVA and the decline in oil revenue. Increasing hostility from both the PRI and the opposition Democratic Revolutionary Party (PRD) led on 9 April to the unprecedented refusal of the Senate (the upper house) to grant the President the permission required by the constitution to travel to the USA and Canada.

On 8 May the federal electoral tribunal (FEI) reopened its investigation into allegations of illegal foreign funding for President Fox's 2000 campaign. The investigation stemmed from a complaint made at the time but dropped in 2001 when it was stated that the FEI had no evidence. At the same time a federal judge ordered the arrest of six former officials of Pemex, the state oil company. They were charged with illicitly raising funds for the PRI. The party's president, Roberto Madrazo Pintado, who had himself been chosen on 24 February in a hotly disputed election marred by irregularities, claimed that the charges had been held back since April in order to maximise their political impact. The re-election on 21 March of the president of the National Action Party (PAN), Luis Felipe Bravo Mena, confirmed his role as one of President Fox's strongest critics within his own party. In June, however, three Cabinet members announced that they had joined five of their colleagues as members of PAN, thereby strengthening the President's hand against his critics.

On 9 March, in a suburb of Puebla, Mexican special forces captured Benjamín Arrellano Félix, alleged to be the head of the Tijuana cocaine cartel; his brother, Ramón Arrellano Félix, was believed to have been killed in a shoot-out by police in Mazatlán the previous month. The alleged head of the Gulf cartel, Adán

Medrano, was arrested in a separate operation on 27 March; and on 26 May the army captured another leader of the cartel, Jesús Albino Quintero Meraz ("El Beto"), in Veracruz.

Other significant events of the year included the missing on 31 May of a deadline to present to the US government plans to pay back some of the deficit of 1.5 million acre/feet of water alleged to be due to the USA under the 1944 treaty on the sharing of the waters of the Rio Bravo (Rio Grande). The deficit had built up because of Mexico's failure since 1993 to honour its obligation to allow the USA a minimum of 350,000 acre/feet from the river in exchange for 1.75 million acre/feet annually due to Mexico from the Rio Colorado. On the same day, 26 Zapotec inhabitants of Santiago Texitlán, Oaxaca, were shot dead in a land dispute by Mexicans of European extraction from a neighbouring village. Sixteen people were later arrested. On 10 June President Fox approved a freedom of information bill which had been unanimously approved by both houses of Congress, and on 29 July Foreign Minister Jorge Castañeda, while admitting that the use of torture was still commonplace in Mexico, restated the President's election pledge to improve human rights.

On 31 July in the vast concrete basilica of Guadalupe, the third to stand on the site, Pope John Paul II canonised Juan Diego, the Indian peasant who reportedly saw an apparition of the Virgin there in 1531 (see II.3.viii). The following day the government agreed to abandon its project to construct a huge new international airport at Texcoco, in the state of Mexico. This had been strongly opposed by both environmental and indigenous groups, some of whom had taken a number of local officials and police officers hostage during disturbances the previous month. In September the Supreme Court rejected more than 300 legal challenges to the Indigenous Rights Act passed in 2001, confirming its status as a constitutional amendment.

On 11-12 November President Fox paid a state visit to the UK.

ii. GUATEMALA

CAPITAL: Guatemala City   AREA: 109,000 sq km   POPULATION: 11,700,000
OFFICIAL LANGUAGE: Spanish   POLITICAL SYSTEM: multiparty republic
HEAD OF STATE AND GOVERNMENT: President Alfonso Antonio Portillo Cabrera (since Jan '00)
RULING PARTY: Guatemalan Republican Front (FRG)
MAIN IGO MEMBERSHIPS (NON-UN): OAS, SELA, CACM, ACM, ACS, NAM
CURRENCY: quetzal (end-'02 £1=Q12.4304. US$1=Q7.7615)
GNI PER CAPITA: US$1,670, US$3,850 at PPP ('01)

EARLY in January the director of the national civil police (PNC), Ennio Rivera Cardona, accused powerful interests of shielding former budget director Gil Muñoz, who was wanted for questioning in connection with alleged embezzlement. On 15 January Cardona was dismissed and replaced by Luis Arturo Paniagua. Subsequently the former Interior Minister, Byron Barrientes, was arrested on similar charges after being formally stripped of his congressional immunity. Shortly afterwards opposition deputies resigned from the congressional committee investigating accusations of corruption against President Alfonso Portillo in protest at its control by members of the ruling Guatemalan Republican Front (FRG), and tensions were heightened when, in March, Jorge Rosal Zea, a member of the opposition Patriotic Party (PP), who had publicly demanded the President's resignation, was assassinated.

Former President Ramiro de Leon Carpio, who had resigned as Vice President of Congress in March, died on 14 April in Miami, Florida, from the effects of diabetes. As President he had played a key role in negotiating the 1996 peace accords, in support of which the IMF on 5 April approved a one-year standby credit. At the beginning of May the former guerrilla Guatemalan National Revolutionary Unity (URNG) party withdrew from the leftist New Nation Alliance (ANN) formed in 1999.

In June several thousand former members of the right-wing paramilitary Civil Defence Patrols (PACs) demonstrated across a wide area for payment which they believed was due to them after their disbandment in 1996. Widespread anger was aroused by the proposal to grant their request, however, and on 26 August the Defence Minister, Gen. Alvaro Mendez Estrada, was replaced by Gen. Robin Moran Muñoz. Meanwhile, on 16 July the Interior Minister, Gen. (retd) Eduardo Arévalo Lacs, whose appointment in November 2001 had been seen as confirming the continued role of the armed forces in politics, had been forced to resign. He had come under increasing criticism after the president of the Central Bank, Lizardo Sosa, had been kidnapped on 25 February while jogging near his home, although he was released unharmed three days later.

Heavy rains triggered a landslide which overwhelmed the village of El Porvenir, some 120 km south of the capital, on 12 September, killing at least 17 people.

iii. EL SALVADOR

CAPITAL: San Salvador   AREA: 21,000 sq km   POPULATION: 6,400,000
OFFICIAL LANGUAGE: Spanish   POLITICAL SYSTEM: multiparty republic
HEAD OF STATE AND GOVERNMENT: President Francisco Flores Pérez (since June '99)
RULING PARTY: National Republican Alliance (Arena)
MAIN IGO MEMBERSHIPS (NON-UN): OAS, SELA, CACM, ACS
CURRENCY: Salvadorian colón (end-'02 £1=C14.0088, US$1=C8.7470)
GNI PER CAPITA: US$2,050, US$4,500 at PPP ('01)

IN early January, the secession of six members from the Faramundo Martí Liberation Front (FMLN) left the President's National Republican Alliance (Arena) as the largest bloc in the 84-member Congress (legislature).

On 19 February the government proclaimed a state of emergency following a new outbreak of dengue fever, some 130 people having died of the disease in 2001. In July a US Federal Court ordered two former Defence Ministers, Gens. (retd) José Guillermo García and Eugenio Vides Casanova, to pay US$54.6 million in damages to three US citizens tortured by Salvadoran troops during the civil war in the early 1980s.

iv. HONDURAS

CAPITAL: Tegucigalpa   AREA: 112,000 sq km   POPULATION: 6,600,000
OFFICIAL LANGUAGE: Spanish   POLITICAL SYSTEM: multiparty republic
HEAD OF STATE AND GOVERNMENT: President Ricardo Maduro (since Jan '02)
RULING PARTY: National Party of Honduras (PNH)
MAIN IGO MEMBERSHIPS (NON-UN): OAS, SELA, CACM, ACS, NAM
CURRENCY: lempira (end-'02 £1=L27.0662, US$1=L16.9000)
GNI PER CAPITA: US$900, US$2,450 at PPP ('01)

FOLLOWING his victory in the November 2001 elections (see AR 2001, pp. 186-87), President Ricardo Maduro, of the centre-right National Party of Honduras (PNH), took office on 27 January and appointed a Cabinet in which Guillermo Perez became Minister of Foreign Affairs and Arturo Alvarado Minister of Finance. The country remained in serious economic difficulties, however, and was acutely dependent on support from the enhanced Caribbean Basin Initiative and the Heavily Indebted Poor Countries Initiative.

Lawlessness remained an issue throughout the year. On 1 June the body of 72-year old former Economy Minister Reginaldo Panting Peñalba was found on waste ground near San Pedro Sula; he had apparently been the victim of an unsuccessful kidnapping. At the beginning of September, Interior Minister Oscar Alvarez announced the establishment of a special team to investigate the deaths of some 1,300 street children murdered by death squads who were believed to be composed largely of police officers.

In July the President proclaimed a state of emergency covering five of the country's 18 provinces following an outbreak of dengue fever which had claimed five children's lives.

v. NICARAGUA

CAPITAL: Managua   AREA: 130,000 sq km   POPULATION: 5,200,000
OFFICIAL LANGUAGE: Spanish   POLITICAL SYSTEM: multiparty republic
HEAD OF STATE AND GOVERNMENT: President Enrique Bolanos Geyer (since Jan '02)
RULING PARTY: Liberal Constitutionalist Party (PLC)
MAIN IGO MEMBERSHIPS (NON-UN): OAS, SELA, CACM, ACS, NAM
CURRENCY: gold córdoba (end-'02 £1=C23.3346, US$1=C14.5700)
GNI PER CAPITA: US$420, US$2,100 at PPP ('00)

PRESIDENT Enrique Bolanos, of the centre-right Liberal Constitutionalist Party (PLC), was sworn in on 10 January. He appointed a Cabinet with Norman Caldera Cardenal as Minister of Foreign Affairs and Eduardo Montealegre Rivas as Minister of Finance and Public Credit. Shortly afterwards, on 19 February, for the first time since 1979, the US government agreed to resume military aid to the Nicaraguan armed forces with a grant of US$1 million to combat drug-smuggling and terrorism.

The election on 17 January of former President Arnaldo Alemán Lacayo of the ruling PLC, as President of the unicameral National Assembly, was seen as a clear challenge to the power of Bolanos. A judge ruled on 21 March that there was sufficient evidence for criminal charges of corruption against Alemán to proceed, but that they could not do so until his congressional immunity had been lifted. So, when on 8 August he was formally charged—along with other members of his family—with misappropriating some US$10 million during his term as President of the Republic, and with defrauding the state of some 10 times that amount, the National Assembly declared a recess from 19 August to 10 September to forestall any vote upon the issue. However, following the conviction of a number of his associates on money laundering and embezzlement charges, the deputies finally agreed on 12 December by 48 votes to 47 to dismiss Alemán as President of the National Assembly and thus lift his immunity from prosecution.

Charges of rape and sexual assault made against former President Daniel Ortega Saavedra by his step-daughter, which had ensured his defeat in the 2001 presidential elections, were dismissed by the courts on 2 January on the grounds that they had expired under the statute of limitations. Later in March Ortega was re-elected leader of the opposition Sandinista National Liberation Front (FSLN).

vi. COSTA RICA

CAPITAL: San José   AREA: 51,000 sq km   POPULATION: 3,900,000
OFFICIAL LANGUAGE: Spanish   POLITICAL SYSTEM: multiparty republic
HEAD OF STATE AND GOVERNMENT: President Abel Pacheco de la Espriella (since May '02)
RULING PARTY: Social Christian Unity Party (PUSC)
MAIN IGO MEMBERSHIPS (NON-UN): OAS, SELA, CACM, ACS
CURRENCY: colón (end-'02 £1=C605.915, US$1=C378.330)
GNI PER CAPITA: US$3,950, US$8,080 at PPP ('01)

IN the second round of the presidential elections on 7 April, the 69-year old psychiatrist and poet Abel Pacheco de la Espriella of the Social Christian Unity Party (PUSC) won 57.96 per cent of the votes cast to defeat Rolando Araya Monge of the National Liberation Party (PLN), who obtained 42.04 per cent. In the first round on 3 February, and for the first time since the current constitution was adopted in 1949, neither of the two leading candidates had secured the necessary 40 per cent of the vote to win outright, as a third candidate, Ottón Solís Fallas of the Citizens' Action Party (PAC), had obtained a record 26.2 per cent (with two other candidates getting less than 3 per cent between them). In concurrent elections on 3 February for the 57-seat Legislative Assembly, the results were similarly indecisive, being: PUSC 19 seats, PLN 17, PAC 14, Libertarian Movement (PML) 6, and Costa Rican Renewal Party (PRC) 1.

The new President was sworn in on 8 May and, in pursuit of his goal of eradicating corruption from public life, appointed a Cabinet with an unusually large number of younger members trained in economics. Responsible for tackling the country's continuing economic crisis were Jorge Walter Bolanos as Minister of Finance and Danilo Chaverri as Minister of National Planning and Economic Policy. On 14 May the Assembly approved a bill allowing the President, the Assembly itself, or any citizen supported by 5 per cent of the electorate to call a referendum on any aspect of policy (other than economic policy), and, if approved by a sufficient majority, for it to become law.

vii. PANAMA

CAPITAL: Panama City   AREA: 76,000 sq km   POPULATION: 2,900,000
OFFICIAL LANGUAGE: Spanish   POLITICAL SYSTEM: multiparty republic
HEAD OF STATE AND GOVERNMENT: President Mireya Elisa Moscoso de Gruber (since Sept '99)
RULING PARTIES: Anulfist Party (PA) heads Union for Panama coalition
MAIN IGO MEMBERSHIPS (NON-UN): OAS, SELA, NAM
CURRENCY: balboa (end-'02 £1=B1.6016, US$1=B1)
GNI PER CAPITA: US$3,290, US$5,720 at PPP ('01)

AFTER a member of the opposition Democratic Revolutionary Party (PRD) had admitted accepting bribes to support construction projects, there were mass street protests in the capital in January and February and a formal inquiry was launched. In response, on 25 March a total of 26 members of the Legislative Assembly voluntarily renounced their parliamentary immunity from prosecution. Following daily clashes between police and unemployed workers, a state of social emergency was declared in Colón on 6 June.

On 11 June it was reported that an international warrant had been issued for the arrest on fraud and corruption charges of the former President of Guatemala, Jorge Serrano Elías, who was living in the country; three previous requests having been refused by the Panamanian authorities.

4. THE CARIBBEAN

CUBA—JAMAICA—DOMINICAN REPUBLIC AND HAITI—WINDWARD & LEEWARD ISLANDS—BARBADOS—GRENADA—TRINIDAD & TOBAGO—THE BAHAMAS—GUYANA, BELIZE AND SURINAME—UK DEPENDENCIES—NETHERLANDS ANTILLES AND ARUBA—US DEPENDENCIES

i. CUBA

CAPITAL: Havana   AREA: 115,000 sq km   POPULATION: 11,222,000
OFFICIAL LANGUAGE: Spanish   POLITICAL SYSTEM: one-party republic
HEAD OF STATE AND GOVERNMENT: President Fidel Castro Ruz (since Jan '59)
RULING PARTY: Cuban Communist Party (PCC)
MAIN IGO MEMBERSHIPS (NON-UN): OAS (suspended), ALADI, ACS, SELA, NAM
CURRENCY: Cuban peso (end-'02 £1=Cub33.6326, US$1=Cub21.0000)

THE long-standing trade embargo between Cuba and the USA remained, but there were signs of a fresh approach in certain sections of US society. In May, during an historic six-day visit to Cuba, former US President Jimmy Carter called for the lifting of the embargo. In August the majority leader in the House of Representatives, Dick Amery, also acknowledged that congressional support for the embargo was fading. Despite such sentiments, however, the US government made clear that President George W. Bush would only countenance easing the ban on trade and travel if the Cuban government took "concrete steps toward democracy". At the end of May Bush announced his government's "Initiative for a New Cuba" which included a number of measures to encourage opposition to the regime of President Fidel Castro, while also providing assistance for potential future leaders in a post-Castro Cuba.

Notwithstanding the trade ban, during the year "emergency" purchases of food continued from the USA. On 9 July, for example, Cuba received its first shipment of US apples, onions, and beans in 42 years. Food shipments during the year totalled some US$175 million, meaning that the USA was Cuba's 10th-largest trading partner. Further purchase contracts, for delivery in 2003, were agreed at a US Food and Agribusiness Exhibition held in Havana during October.

Issues relating to the 11 September terrorist attacks and the US "war against terror" also shaped Cuban-US relations during the year. In January the Cuban Defence Minister and Fidel Castro's younger brother, Gen. Raul Castro, stated that Cuba had no objection to the USA holding prisoners from the war in Afghanistan at the Guantanamo US naval base (located in the east of the island). In May, US Undersecretary of State for Arms Control John Bolton alleged that Cuba "has at least a limited offensive biological warfare research and development effort [and had] provided dual use technology to other rogue states". It was also suggested that Cuba was one of the countries involved in the so-called "axis of evil" identified by President Bush in January 2001 (see IV.1). Both allegations were vehemently denied by the Cuban government, and a significant number of politicians in the USA also questioned the accuracy of such claims.

In other developments, Cuba launched an emergency campaign to counter the worst outbreak of dengue fever since 1981. At a special session of the National Assembly on 26 June, a number of constitutional amendments were enacted, one of which made socialism irrevocable. The amendments, which according to official reports had the support of 99.5 per cent of the population, were introduced after 11,000 Cubans had signed a petition demanding democratic reform. During November, it was announced that the number of AIDS-related deaths in Cuba had dropped significantly over the previous 18 months following the development of a series of domestically-produced anti-retroviral drugs. In December, meanwhile, leading Cuban dissident Oswaldo Payá received the European Parliament's Sakharov Prize for Freedom of Thought.

ii. JAMAICA

CAPITAL: Kingston AREA: 11,000 sq km POPULATION: 2,700,000
OFFICIAL LANGUAGE: English POLITICAL SYSTEM: multiparty system in British Commonwealth
HEAD OF STATE: Queen Elizabeth II
GOVERNOR-GENERAL: Sir Howard Cooke
RULING PARTY: People's National Party (PNP)
HEAD OF GOVERNMENT: Percival J. Patterson, Prime Minister (since March '92)
MAIN IGO MEMBERSHIPS (NON-UN): OAS, SELA, ACS, Caricom, ACP, CWTH, NAM
CURRENCY: Jamaican dollar (end-'02 £1=J$79.8373, US$1=J$49.8500)
GNI PER CAPITA: US$2,720, US$3,650 at PPP ('01)

IN elections held in October 2002, the ruling People's National Party (PNP), led by Prime Minister Percival J. Patterson, made history by winning a fourth consecutive term of office. During the election campaign a total of 80 murders was committed, although this number was down on previous campaigns. The decline was partly attributable to a code of conduct signed in June between Patterson and opposition leader Edward Seaga. However, by the year's end there had been 1,045 murders, a similar number to the record toll of 2001 (see AR 2001, p. 191). This continuing high murder rate, together with an upsurge in general criminal activity, precipitated a call from some sections of Jamaican society for the government to declare a state of emergency. Patterson refused to countenance such a move, but in December he announced a joint army and police offensive against crime. In addition, the Prime Minister made clear his support for a resumption of the death penalty after a 14-year hiatus.

A period of heavy rain in late May caused serious flooding and landslides, killing 11 people and making hundreds homeless. Roads, bridges, and crops were also destroyed, with a total cost estimated at US$42 million. In September the Senate approved a new oath of allegiance, which excised any mention of the British monarchy. In December Jamaica received an emergency shipment of oil from Ecuador to compensate for the shortfall from Venezuela which resulted from action by opponents of President Hugo Chavez (see IV.5.x).

iii. DOMINICAN REPUBLIC AND HAITI

Dominican Republic
CAPITAL: Santo Domingo   AREA: 49,000 sq km   POPULATION: 8,500,000
OFFICIAL LANGUAGE: Spanish   POLITICAL SYSTEM: multiparty republic
HEAD OF STATE AND GOVERNMENT: President Hipólito Mejía (since Aug '00)
RULING PARTY: Dominican Revolutionary Party (PRD)
MAIN IGO MEMBERSHIPS (NON-UN): OAS, SELA, ACS, ACP, NAM
CURRENCY: Dominican Republic peso (end-'02 £1=DP32.0310, US$1=20.0000)
GNI PER CAPITA: US$2,230, US$5,870 at PPP ('01)

Haiti
CAPITAL: Port-au-Prince   AREA: 28,000 sq km   POPULATION: 8,100,000
OFFICIAL LANGUAGE: French   POLITICAL SYSTEM: multiparty republic
HEAD OF STATE AND GOVERNMENT: President Jean-Bertrand Aristide (since Nov '00)
RULING PARTY: Lavalas Family (FL) movement
PRIME MINISTER: Yvon Neptune (since March '02)
MAIN IGO MEMBERSHIPS (NON-UN): OAS, SELA, Caricom, ACS, ACP, Francophonie
CURRENCY: gourde (end-'02 £1=G57.6558, US$1=G36.0000)
GNI PER CAPITA: US$480, US$1,450 at PPP ('01)

IN the DOMINICAN REPUBLIC there was a standoff between President Hipólito Mejía and the Chamber of Deputies (the lower chamber of the National Congress, the legislature) during the third quarter of 2002, concerning the balance of the electoral tribunal given the task of preparing for the 2004 presidential elections. Mejía had appointed a strongly pro-government tribunal, the composition of which was heavily criticised by the opposition. Indeed, the main opposition party, the Dominican Liberation Party (PLD), together with the Social Christian Reformist Party (PRSC), boycotted the National Congress until a more balanced tribunal was chosen. In October government and opposition reached an agreement, with two additional members being appointed to the group. In return the opposition ended its boycott. Nevertheless, the situation prior to the compromise had been potentially very serious, with the legislature sitting for only two days between mid-August and mid-October, and the President threatening to rule by decree if the deadlock was not resolved.

Other significant developments during the year included a prison riot in September which left 27 inmates dead and 48 others injured; most of the deaths were caused by smoke inhalation. In November the head of presidential security, Col. Pedro Julio Goica, was arrested in connection with a US$2 million credit card fraud. The detention was an embarrassment to President Mejía who had appointed Goica as head of security despite concerns over his conduct in a previous fraud case involving the country's National Lottery.

In July, seven times President Joaquín Balaguer died aged 95 (see XVIII).

HAITI witnessed further political and social unrest during the year. Although the Organisation of American States (OAS) helped to facilitate a meeting between President Jean-Bertrand Aristide and the opposition Democratic Convergence in June, little progress was made towards halting the worsening public security situation. The major issues of disagreement between the two sides were the status of the disputed 2000 legislative elections (see AR 2000, p. 177); President Aristide's unwillingness to prosecute those responsible for the acts of violence immediately after the attack on the presidential palace in December 2001; and his reluctance to provide financial compensation to the victims (see AR 2001, p. 192). The absence of any effective political dialogue exacerbated social tensions. In August thousands of protesters in the city of Gonaives hurled stones and attacked riot police, whilst in November the unrest worsened with a series of protest marches by opposition and student groups on the one hand, and pro-Aristide elements on the other. On 25 November, six people were shot during pro-government rallies. The opposition called for Aristide's resignation, but the President refused to step down, arguing that a "coup d'état is not a solution to Haiti's problems". The crisis blocked the formation of the Provisional Electoral Council which had the role of organising new elections. At the end of November the terms of a majority of senators and all of the House Representatives expired, leaving Haiti without a mandated legislature.

iv. WINDWARD AND LEEWARD ISLANDS

Antigua & Barbuda
CAPITAL: St John's   AREA: 440 sq km   POPULATION: 68,000
OFFICIAL LANGUAGE: English   POLITICAL SYSTEM: multiparty system in British Commonwealth
HEAD OF STATE: Queen Elizabeth II
GOVERNOR-GENERAL: Sir James B. Carlisle
RULING PARTY: Antigua Labour Party (ALP)
HEAD OF GOVERNMENT: Lester Bird, Prime Minister (since March '94)
MAIN IGO MEMBERSHIPS (NON-UN): OAS, OECS, Caricom, ACS, ACP, CWTH
CURRENCY: East Caribbean dollar (end-'02 £1=EC$4.3242, US$1=EC$2.7000)
GNI PER CAPITA: US$9,070, US$9,870 at PPP ('01)

Dominica
CAPITAL: Roseau   AREA: 48,400 sq km   POPULATION: 73,000
OFFICIAL LANGUAGE: English   POLITICAL SYSTEM: multiparty republic in British Commonwealth
HEAD OF STATE: President Vernon Shaw (since Oct '98)
RULING PARTIES: Dominica Labour (DLP) & Dominica Freedom (DFP) parties
HEAD OF GOVERNMENT: Pierre Charles, Prime Minister (since Oct '00)
MAIN IGO MEMBERSHIPS (NON-UN): OAS, ACS, OECS, Caricom, ACP, CWTH, Francophonie
CURRENCY: East Caribbean dollar (see above)
GNI PER CAPITA: US$3,060, US$5,640 at PPP ('01)

St Christopher (Kitts) & Nevis
CAPITAL: Basseterre   AREA: 260 sq km   POPULATION: 41,000
OFFICIAL LANGUAGE: English   POLITICAL SYSTEM: multiparty system in British Commonwealth
HEAD OF STATE: Queen Elizabeth II
GOVERNOR-GENERAL: Sir Cuthbert Sebastian
RULING PARTY: St Kitts-Nevis Labour Party (SKNLP)
HEAD OF GOVERNMENT: Denzil Douglas, Prime Minister (since July '95)
MAIN IGO MEMBERSHIPS (NON-UN): OAS, ACS, Caricom, OECS, ACP, CWTH
CURRENCY: East Caribbean dollar (see above)
GNI PER CAPITA: US$6,880, US$11,730 at PPP ('01)

St Lucia
CAPITAL: Castries   AREA: 616 sq km   POPULATION: 158,000
OFFICIAL LANGUAGE: English   POLITICAL SYSTEM: multiparty system in British Commonwealth
HEAD OF STATE: Queen Elizabeth II
GOVERNOR-GENERAL: Perlette Louisy
RULING PARTY: St Lucia Labour Party (SLP)
HEAD OF GOVERNMENT: Kenny D. Anthony, Prime Minister (since May '97)
MAIN IGO MEMBERSHIPS (NON-UN): OAS, ACS, OECS, Caricom, ACP, CWTH, NAM, Francophonie
CURRENCY: East Caribbean dollar (see above)
GNI PER CAPITA: US$3,970, US$5,200 at PPP ('01)

St Vincent & the Grenadines
CAPITAL: Kingstown   AREA: 390 sq km   POPULATION: 116,000
OFFICIAL LANGUAGE: English   POLITICAL SYSTEM: multiparty system in British Commonwealth
HEAD OF STATE: Queen Elizabeth II
GOVERNOR-GENERAL: Freddy Ballantyne (since Sept '02)
RULING PARTY: Unity Labour Party (ULP)
HEAD OF GOVERNMENT: Ralph Gonsalves, Prime Minister (since April '01)
MAIN IGO MEMBERSHIPS (NON-UN): OAS, ACS, OECS, Caricom, ACP, CWTH
CURRENCY: East Caribbean dollar (see above)
GNI PER CAPITA: US$2,690, US$5,250 at PPP ('01)

IN ANTIGUA & BARBUDA several thousand people protested on 5 September, demanding the resignation of Prime Minister Lester Bird and his Antigua Labour Party government. The standing of Prime Minister Bird's government had been undermined by a number of scandals. The most significant of these was the publication in August of a report by the public enquiry established to consider allegations of fraud concerning the Medical Benefits Scheme (MBS—see AR 2001, p. 194). It stated that several former ministers and MBS senior employees had benefited illegally from MBS money, and called on the director of public prosecutions to investigate those accused of wrongdoing.

In September the People's Republic of China's 1st Pharmaceutical Company (Antigua) Limited began operating on the island. The company, which produced generic drugs for major diseases, was the first pharmaceutical business to be established in the Eastern Caribbean.

The carnival held in DOMINICA during February suffered its worst violence in almost 40 years, when four people were killed. At the end of July, Dominica's government recommenced the sale of passports to non-national "economic citizens". Sales were suspended in 2001 after the 11 September attacks, with Canada and the USA expressing concern that terrorists and other criminals could abuse the scheme. The decision to restart sales was based on the need to raise additional revenue for an economy in serious difficulties. In October the Financial Action Task Force (FATF)—established by the G-7 and Organisation of Economic Co-operation and Development (OECD)—removed Dominica from the list of countries deemed to have failed to co-operate fully in combating money laundering. In December Prime Minister Pierre Charles travelled to Taiwan in order to strengthen economic ties between the two countries. Taiwan was Dominica's largest single donor of aid.

In June ST CHRISTOPHER (KITTS) & NEVIS was removed from the FATF's list of non-cooperative countries in the fight against money laundering. During November, meanwhile, Prime Minister Denzil Douglas stated for the first time that closing the country's long-standing sugar industry might be considered as part of any future economic restructuring effort. In the past few years, sugar exports had declined, and the industry's losses had mounted.

An issue that returned to the agenda was the political status of Nevis after a dispute occurred between the Nevis Island Administration and the federal government over the division of national revenue. On 6 September the two sides met and subsequently agreed to establish a joint consultative committee to consider possible constitutional changes to provide Nevis with greater autonomy. However, in October Nevis Prime Minister Vance Amory refused to discount secession as a future option.

The economy of ST LUCIA recovered slowly during the year, after it had contracted by 5.4 per cent in 2001. In a statement on 6 August, Prime Minister Kenny Anthony described the country's macroeconomic fundamentals as "sound", while highlighting new investments in the telecommunications sector and a recovering tourist market. However, progress was halted somewhat in late September when Tropical Storm Lili destroyed almost 50 per cent of the island's banana crop.

Despite a number of anti-money laundering provisions instituted in 2002, ST VINCENT & THE GRENADINES remained on the FATF's list of non-cooperative countries. In April it was announced that Kuwait would provide US$8 million in assistance for the expansion of the country's international airport.

v. BARBADOS

CAPITAL: Bridgetown   AREA: 430 sq km   POPULATION: 268,000
OFFICIAL LANGUAGE: English   POLITICAL SYSTEM: multiparty system in British Commonwealth
HEAD OF STATE: Queen Elizabeth II
GOVERNOR-GENERAL: Sir Clifford Husbands
RULING PARTY: Barbados Labour Party (BLP)
HEAD OF GOVERNMENT: Owen Arthur, Prime Minister (since Sept '94)
MAIN IGO MEMBERSHIPS (NON-UN): OAS, SELA, ACS, Caricom, ACP, CWTH, NAM
CURRENCY: Barbados dollar (end-'02 £1=Bd$3.1871, US$1=Bd$1.9900)
GNI PER CAPITA: US$9,280, US$14,770 at PPP ('00)

A new Anti-Terrorism Bill was passed in May, which included a mandatory fine of up to US$1 million for anyone convicted of being involved in terrorist activity. The government also introduced an amendment to the constitution for the application of the death penalty or life imprisonment where a death had occurred as a result of a terrorist-related incident. The changes were a direct response to the 11 September 2001 attacks on the USA.

In other developments, Barbados was removed from the list of countries considered to be uncooperative tax havens by the Organisation for Economic Cooperation and Development, while the World Bank provided a US$15 million loan over five years to provide treatment for the country's HIV and AIDS patients.

vi. GRENADA

CAPITAL: St George's   AREA: 344 sq km   POPULATION: 99,000
OFFICIAL LANGUAGE: English   POLITICAL SYSTEM: multiparty system in British Commonwealth
HEAD OF STATE: Queen Elizabeth II
GOVERNOR-GENERAL: Sir Daniel Williams
RULING PARTY: New National Party (NNP)
HEAD OF GOVERNMENT: Keith Mitchell, Prime Minister (since June '95)
MAIN IGO MEMBERSHIPS (NON-UN): OAS, SELA, ACS, Caricom, OECS, ACP, CWTH, NAM
CURRENCY: East Caribbean dollar (end-'02 £1=EC$4.3242, US$1=EC$2.7000)
GNI PER CAPITA: US$3,720, US$6,720 at PPP ('01)

IN July a major fire destroyed three historic buildings in the capital, St George's, with damage put at a cost of US$19 million. In October, Humberto Rivero Rosario became Cuba's first ambassador in Grenada for almost 20 years. Grenada had severed links with Cuba after the 1983 military coup which had precipitated the US invasion. During November, meanwhile, the government announced that the nutmeg industry would be opened to private investment, a decision which ended 55 years of state control.

The government failed in its attempt during 2002 to get Grenada removed from the Financial Action Task Force blacklist.

vii. TRINIDAD & TOBAGO

CAPITAL: Port of Spain   AREA: 5,128 sq km   POPULATION: 1,310,000
OFFICIAL LANGUAGE: English   POLITICAL SYSTEM: multiparty republic in British Commonwealth
HEAD OF STATE: President Arthur N.R. Robinson (incapacitated); Ganace Ramdial, acting president (since Feb '98)
RULING PARTY: People's National Movement (PNM) (since Oct '02)
HEAD OF GOVERNMENT: Patrick Manning (PNM), Prime Minister (since Dec '01)
MAIN IGO MEMBERSHIPS (NON-UN): OAS, SELA, ACS, Caricom, ACP, CWTH, NAM
CURRENCY: Trinidad & Tobago dollar (end-'02 £1=TT$9.8656, US$1=TT$6.1600)
GNI PER CAPITA: US$5,540, US$9,080 at PPP ('01)

IN a general election held on 7 October, the People's National Movement (PNM), led by incumbent Prime Minister Patrick Manning, broke the political deadlock which had existed since the December 2001 tied election (see AR 2001, p. 196), by winning 20 of the 36 seats in the House of Representatives (the lower chamber of the bicameral Parliament). The opposition United National Congress (UNC) won the remaining 16 seats. The election was precipitated by Parliament's failure to elect a Speaker on 28 August, after the UNC had blocked the PNM's candidate. Without a Speaker, the government was unable to present the budget that was required for the new financial year beginning in November. Furthermore, the legitimacy of the PNM government was being increasingly questioned as Parliament had met only twice since the December 2001 election.

The role of two Islamic organisations based in Trinidad was of concern during the year. The group Jamaat-al Muslimeen came under scrutiny when allegations were made of a link between Jamaat and Islamic terrorism; while another organisation, Waajihatul Islaamiyyah, was accused of being behind plans to attack local US and UK interests in the country.

viii. THE BAHAMAS

CAPITAL: Nassau   AREA: 14,000 sq km   POPULATION: 307,000
OFFICIAL LANGUAGE: English   POLITICAL SYSTEM: multiparty system in British Commonwealth
HEAD OF STATE: Queen Elizabeth II
GOVERNOR-GENERAL: Sir Orville Turnquest
RULING PARTY: Progressive Liberal Party (PLP)
HEAD OF GOVERNMENT: Perry Christie, Prime Minister (since May '02)
MAIN IGO MEMBERSHIPS (NON-UN): OAS, SELA, ACS, Caricom, ACP, CWTH
CURRENCY: Bahamian dollar (end-'02 £1=B$1.6016 US$1=B$1)
GNI PER CAPITA: US$15,010, US$16,490 at PPP ('00)

A general election was held in the Bahamas on 2 May, with the opposition Progressive Liberal Party (PLP), led by Perry Christie, gaining a convincing victory and putting an end to 10 years of Free National Movement (FNM) rule. On 19 August the government outlined plans to reduce the number of illegal immigrants from

Haiti, after 700 had been arrested in the preceding three weeks. In September, the government declared that the national airline, Bahamas Air, would be privatised. In December a joint operation between the Bahamas and the USA successfully dismantled a significant cocaine smuggling network linking the Bahamas to Florida.

ix. GUYANA, BELIZE AND SURINAME

Guyana

CAPITAL: Georgetown   AREA: 215,000 sq km   POPULATION: 766,000
OFFICIAL LANGUAGE: English   POLITICAL SYSTEM: multiparty republic
HEAD OF STATE AND GOVERNMENT: President Bharrat Jagdeo (since Aug '99)
RULING PARTY: People's Progressive Party-Civic (PPP-C)
PRIME MINISTER: Samuel Hinds (since Dec '97)
MAIN IGO MEMBERSHIPS (NON-UN): OAS, SELA, AP, ACS, Caricom, ACP, CWTH, NAM
CURRENCY: Guyana dollar (end-'02 £1=G$286.678, US$1=G$179.000)
GNI PER CAPITA: US$840, US$3,750 at PPP ('01)

Belize

CAPITAL: Belmopan   AREA: 23,000 sq km   POPULATION: 247,000
OFFICIAL LANGUAGE: English   POLITICAL SYSTEM: multiparty system in British Commonwealth
HEAD OF STATE: Queen Elizabeth II
GOVERNOR-GENERAL: Sir Colville Young
RULING PARTY: People's United Party (PUP)
HEAD OF GOVERNMENT: Said Musa, Prime Minister (since Aug '98)
MAIN IGO MEMBERSHIPS (NON-UN): OAS, SELA, ACS, Caricom, ACP, CWTH, NAM
CURRENCY: Belize dollar (end-'02 £1=Bz$3.1551, US$1=Bz$1.9700)
GNI PER CAPITA: US$2,910, US$5,350 at PPP ('01)

Suriname

CAPITAL: Paramaribo   AREA: 163,000 sq km   POPULATION: 420,000
OFFICIAL LANGUAGE: Dutch   POLITICAL SYSTEM: multiparty republic
HEAD OF STATE: President Ronald Venetiaan (since Aug '00)
RULING PARTIES: New Front for Democracy (NF) heads coalition
HEAD OF GOVERNMENT: Vice-President Jules Ajodhia (since Sept '00)
MAIN IGO MEMBERSHIPS (NON-UN): OAS, SELA, AP, ACS, Caricom, ACP, OIC, NAM
CURRENCY: Surinam guilder (end-'02 £1=SG3,488.98, US$1=SG2,178.50)
GNI PER CAPITA: US$1,690, US$3,310 at PPP ('01)

THE political cooperation arrangements in GUYANA between President Bharrat Jagdeo and opposition leader Desmond Hoyte (see AR 2001, p. 198) continued into the early part of the year. However, the contacts between the two ended acrimoniously in March, with Hoyte expressing dissatisfaction over the government's alleged failure to implement decisions reached in the dialogue process. The breakdown in discussions was particularly serious because the National Assembly (the legislature) had not met since October 2001. The clearest manifestation of the serious nature of the crisis came on 3 July, when anti-government protesters attacked the presidential complex in Georgetown. Two people were shot dead by the police, while shops and cars were set on fire by rioters. Hoyte and other leaders of the People's National Congress-Reform (PNC-R) opposition condemned the violence, but insisted that the grievances of the protesters were legitimate. The governing People's Progressive Party-Civic coalition, meanwhile, accused the PNC-R of being centrally involved in the violence, and charged the party with launching an "unprecedented" attempt "to assassinate the President and remove the elected government from office".

Efforts were then made to re-start the dialogue process involving the two party leaders, but the deep animosity between them prevented any immediate resumption of talks. The situation was made worse by the increasing number of violent crimes and kidnappings. For example, in August gunmen shot and killed the deputy head of Guyana's anti-drug agency; while in September, four people were killed and 10 others wounded, including the director of public prosecutions, after shots were fired in a Georgetown bar. In protest against the increasing lawlessness and the political deadlock, the association of regional chambers of commerce, supported by other sectors of civil society, organised a shut down of businesses in early October. However the killings continued, with the number of murders exceeding 150 in 2002, a fourfold increase compared with the year before. A way out of the crisis became even less clear, with the unexpected death of Hoyte in December, creating a leadership vacuum at the head of the PNC-R.

In BELIZE during April there were riots and clashes with police as a result of commuter unhappiness following increases in bus fares. Two protesters were shot dead, a number of police officers were injured, and dozens of arrests were made. In September the government faced its most serious political crisis since coming to power. The difficulties arose after serious allegations of corruption were made against the immigration department, particularly in relation to a contentious scheme for the sale of Belizean passports to foreigners. The practice, which had provided the Belizean government with a significant revenue stream over the last 20 years, was criticised after the 11 September attacks on the USA. As a result, the authorities promised to end the scheme in January, but in fact the immigration authorities continued selling passports until July. The revelations cost the Minister of Police and Immigration his post, while the director of immigration was suspended.

In September proposals were agreed for achieving a "just, equitable and definitive resolution" to the 143-year old border dispute between Belize and Guatemala. In the wide-ranging agreement, Guatemala finally recognised Belize's land boundary based on the treaty signed by the UK and Guatemala in 1859. However, plans to hold referendums on the agreement by 30 November were delayed because of practical difficulties.

In December SURINAME was advised by the IMF to take "quick and decisive actions" to correct a growing deterioration in public finances. The IMF criticised the government's decision earlier in the year to award a 60 per cent pay increase to public sector workers, and advised the government to cut expenditure, move ahead with the privatisation of state assets, and rationalise the remaining state sector.

Earlier in the year, Suriname and Guyana formally agreed to set up a joint border commission to investigate the shared exploitation and management of oil reserves in disputed maritime areas.

x. UK DEPENDENCIES

Anguilla
CAPITAL: The Valley   AREA: 96 sq km   POPULATION: 11,560 (est.)
OFFICIAL LANGUAGE: English   POLITICAL SYSTEM: semi-autonomous UK overseas territory
GOVERNOR-GENERAL: Peter Johnstone
RULING PARTIES: Anguilla National Alliance (ANA) & Anguilla Democratic Party (ADP) form United Front coalition
HEAD OF GOVERNMENT: Osbourne Fleming (ANA), Chief Minister (since March '00)
MAIN IGO MEMBERSHIPS (NON-UN): Caricom (obs.)
CURRENCY: East Caribbean dollar (end-'02 £1=EC$4.3242, US$1=EC$2.7000)

Bermuda
CAPITAL: Hamilton   AREA: 53 sq km   POPULATION: 63,000
OFFICIAL LANGUAGE: English   POLITICAL SYSTEM: semi-autonomous UK overseas territory
GOVERNOR-GENERAL: John Vereker
RULING PARTY: Progressive Labour Party (PLP)
HEAD OF GOVERNMENT: Jennifer Smith, Prime Minister (since Nov '98)
MAIN IGO MEMBERSHIPS (NON-UN): Caricom (obs.)
CURRENCY: Bermudian dollar (end-'02 £1=Bm$1.6016, US$1- Bm$1)

British Virgin Islands
CAPITAL: Road Town   AREA: 153 sq km   POPULATION: 20,700
OFFICIAL LANGUAGE: English   POLITICAL SYSTEM: semi-autonomous UK overseas territory
GOVERNOR-GENERAL: Thomas Townley Macan (since Oct '02)
RULING PARTIES: Virgin Islands Party (VIP)
HEAD OF GOVERNMENT: Ralph O'Neal, Chief Minister (since May '95)
MAIN IGO MEMBERSHIPS (NON-UN): OECS (assoc.), Caricom (assoc.)
CURRENCY: East Caribbean dollar (see above)

Cayman Islands
CAPITAL: George Town, Grand Cayman   AREA: 259 sq km   POPULATION: 35,000
OFFICIAL LANGUAGE: English   POLITICAL SYSTEM: semi-autonomous UK overseas territory
GOVERNOR-GENERAL: Peter John Smith
MAIN IGO MEMBERSHIPS (NON-UN): Caricom (obs.)
CURRENCY: East Caribbean dollar (see above)

Montserrat
CAPITAL: Plymouth   AREA: 102 sq km   POPULATION: 4,500
OFFICIAL LANGUAGE: English   POLITICAL SYSTEM: semi-autonomous UK overseas territory
GOVERNOR-GENERAL: Anthony John Abbott
HEAD OF GOVERNMENT: John Osborne, Chief Minister (since April '01)
MAIN IGO MEMBERSHIPS (NON-UN): OECS, Caricom, ACS
CURRENCY: East Caribbean dollar (see above)

Turks & Caicos Islands
CAPITAL: Cockburn Town   AREA: 430 sq km   POPULATION: 19,300 ('00 est.)
OFFICIAL LANGUAGE: English   POLITICAL SYSTEM: semi-autonomous UK overseas territory
GOVERNOR-GENERAL: Jim Poston (since Nov '02)
RULING PARTY: People's Democratic Movement (PDM)
HEAD OF GOVERNMENT: Derek H. Taylor, Chief Minister (since Jan '95)
MAIN IGO MEMBERSHIPS (NON-UN): Caricom (assoc.)
CURRENCY: US dollar (end-'02 £1=US$1.6016)

ANGUILLA hosted a visit of the IMF in October which had the aim of evaluating the country's anti-money laundering legislation and offshore banking policies. Earlier in the year, Anguilla had imposed visa requirements for citizens of Jamaica and Guyana, a decision criticised by Jamaica as being outside the "spirit" of regional travel and immigration agreements among Caribbean Community members.

In June BERMUDA officially took back possession of land that had been leased to the USA by the British in 1941. The agreement had allowed the US Navy to lease two bases and a NASA tracking station for 99 years. However, the USA withdrew from the islands at the beginning of 2002, 38 years ahead of schedule.

The government of the BRITISH VIRGIN ISLANDS was undermined by allegations of corruption in the early part of the year. In March, Financial Secretary L. Allen Wheatley, along with two other high ranking officials and a prominent businessman, were arrested and charged with attempting to defraud the government in connection with a development project at the international airport.

The CAYMAN ISLANDS witnessed the creation of an opposition party for the first time. The People's Progressive Movement, led by former leader of government business Kurt Tibbetts, was established to challenge the United Democratic Party, which itself had been formed only in November 2001. The advent of party politics came at a time when a new constitution was being formulated for the territory. In early December, representatives from the Cayman Islands met with officials from the UK's Foreign and Commonwealth Office in London to review the proposals.

In February the government confirmed that it would provide assistance to US authorities investigating the bankrupt energy giant, Enron Corp. (see IV.1). The US corporation had reportedly used 692 subsidiary companies in the Cayman Islands, while also having other subsidiaries elsewhere in the Caribbean.

Heavy rainfall in October caused a series of mudflows from the Soufriere Hills volcano in MONTSERRAT. The mudflows buried trees, cars, and buildings in Belham Valley, from which 300 people had been recently evacuated after concerns over increasing volcanic activity.

A decision was taken in the TURKS & CAICOS Legislative Council in late August to abolish the death penalty for treason and piracy. The London based Privy Council formalised the resolution in October.

xi. NETHERLANDS ANTILLES AND ARUBA

Netherlands Antilles
CAPITAL: Willemstad (Curaçao)   AREA: 800 sq km   POPULATION: 217,000
OFFICIAL LANGUAGES: Dutch, Papiamento & English   POLITICAL SYSTEM: autonomous dependency of the Netherlands
GOVERNOR-GENERAL: Jaime M. Saleh
RULING PARTIES: Antillean Restructuring Party (PAR) heads coalition
HEAD OF GOVERNMENT: Miguel Pourier (PAR), Prime Minister (since Nov '99)
CURRENCY: Neth. Antilles guilder (end-'02 £1=AG2.8508, US$1=AG1.7800)
GNI PER CAPITA: n/a

Aruba
CAPITAL: Oranjestad   AREA: 193 sq km   POPULATION: 104,000
OFFICIAL LANGUAGE: Dutch   POLITICAL SYSTEM: autonomous dependency of the Netherlands
GOVERNOR-GENERAL: Olindo Koolman
RULING PARTY: People's Electoral Movement (MEP)
HEAD OF GOVERNMENT: Nelson O. Oduber (MEP), Prime Minister (since Sept '01)
CURRENCY: florin (end-'02 £1=AFI2.8668, US$1=AFl1.7900)
GNI PER CAPITA: GDP per capita US$16,900 ('00 est.)

THE Refineria Isla based in Curaçao, in the NETHERLANDS ANTILLES, which received most of its oil from Venezuela, suspended the production of gasoline, jet fuel, and propane on 16 December. The move was precipitated by the general strike in Venezuela (see IV.5.x), which prevented shipments of oil reaching the refinery.

The government of ARUBA implemented strict immigration controls from July in an attempt to reduce the number of illegal immigrants from Colombia and Venezuela. Prime Minister Nelson Oduber claimed that if Aruba's population growth was not curbed the island would suffer serious social dislocation.

xii. US DEPENDENCIES

Puerto Rico
CAPITAL: San Juan   AREA: 9,103 sq km   POPULATION: 3,950,000
OFFICIAL LANGUAGES: Spanish & English   POLITICAL SYSTEM: multiparty system in US Commonwealth
GOVERNOR-GENERAL: Sila María Calderón
RULING PARTY: New Progressive Party (PNP) has majority in Senate
CURRENCY: US dollar (end-'02 £1=US$1.6016)

US Virgin Islands
CAPITAL: Charlotte Amalie   AREA: 342 sq km   POPULATION: 122,000
OFFICIAL LANGUAGE: English   POLITICAL SYSTEM: semi-autonomous overseas territory of the USA
GOVERNOR-GENERAL: Charles Turnbull (Democratic Party)
RULING PARTY: Democrats
MAIN IGO MEMBERSHIPS (NON-UN): n/a
CURRENCY: US dollar (end-'02 £1=US$1.6016)

WITH official celebrations taking place in PUERTO RICO to mark the island's 50th anniversary of Commonwealth status on 25 July, Governor Sila María Calderón called for a reconsideration of Puerto Rico's governing structures. A "unity and consensus" commission was subsequently established to find ways of increasing the island's autonomy in political and economic matters. However, the probity of the government had been dealt a blow earlier in the year, when 17 people (including a former Education Secretary) were accused a range of crimes, including stealing federal funds, extortion and money laundering.

The use of Vieques Island for US naval operations continued to be an issue of controversy during the year. There were angry protests when the US navy conducted exercises in April and September, but Calderón remained hopeful that President George W. Bush's commitment to end the military exercises on the island by May 2003 would be honoured.

The Governor of the US VIRGIN ISLANDS, Charles Turnbull, announced a raft of new measures on 17 May to combat crime. These included a reduction in the age at which a minor could be prosecuted as an adult for murder, and the enforcement of curfew laws for minors. The move followed an announcement by Carnival Cruise Lines that its ships would no longer stop at St Croix because of "an ongoing problem with crimes against passengers".

5. SOUTH AMERICA

BRAZIL—ARGENTINA—PARAGUAY—URUGUAY—CHILE—PERU—BOLIVIA—ECUADOR—COLOMBIA—VENEZUELA

i. BRAZIL

CAPITAL: Brasília   AREA: 8,547,000 sq km   POPULATION: 172,600,000
OFFICIAL LANGUAGE: Portuguese   POLITICAL SYSTEM: multiparty republic
PRESIDENT ELECT: Luiz Inácio "Lula" da Silva (from Jan '03)
RULING PARTIES: Brazilian Social Democratic Party (PSDB) heads coalition with Liberal Front Party (PFL), Brazilian Progressive Party (PPB), Popular Socialist Party (PPS), & Brazilian Democratic Movement Party (PMDB)
MAIN IGO MEMBERSHIPS (NON-UN): OAS, ALADI, SELA, Mercosur, AP, CPLP
CURRENCY: real (end-'02 £1=R5.6903, US$1=R3.5530)
GNI PER CAPITA: US$3,060, US$7,450 at PPP ('01)

WITH legislative and presidential elections scheduled for October, and incumbent President Fernando Henrique Cardoso ineligible to serve a third term, 2001 promised to be a year of political change for Brazil. In the event, the degree of change proved greater than most had imagined at the start of the year as Luiz Inácio ("Lula") da Silva, the candidate of the leftist Workers' Party (PT) and previously unsuccessful presidential contender, was elected President.

The election campaign proceeded against a gloomy economic backdrop. The government had failed to meet its 6 per cent inflation target for 2001, and on 9

February it announced spending cuts of a further R12,400 million in the current year to meet IMF requirements. Public unease over the economy was heightened by growing concern over the rise of violent crime, particularly in São Paulo. This was dramatically illustrated by the kidnapping on 18 January of Celso Daniel, the PT mayor of the suburb of Santo Andre; Daniel was found dead two days later.

In February the government announced that price controls on electrical power would be lifted, and consumers compensated for price rises by a tax on state-owned generating companies. It was also announced that from 1 March the emergency water rationing measures imposed in May 2001 were to be lifted as adequate rain in the south had replenished reservoirs. Nevertheless, rising prices continued to cause concern and the Central Bank had to step in to calm fears when consumer prices rose by 0.8 per cent in April. This brought the annual rate for the preceding 12 months to 8 per cent, well above the 5 per cent target for the current year. At the same time the real weakened against the US dollar, despite a bank base rate of 18.5 per cent.

Brazil's victory in the football World Cup in June (see XVI) lifted spirits and was an occasion for national rejoicing. But the economy was already feeling the effects of the Argentinian crisis (see IV.5.ii) and the imminence of recession forced the authorities to raise interest rates still further. On 14 May the government had announced extraordinary cuts in the 2002 budget, and on 13 June Finance Minister Pedro Malan announced measures to support the real, the IMF having agreed that Brazil could draw down two-thirds of the stand-by facility agreed in August 2001. As pressure continued, the government on 30 July announced a further US$1.38 billion of cuts in the 2002 budget. US Treasury Secretary Paul O'Neill, however, vetoed IMF support for the real in what was widely seen as one manifestation of the overt pressure from the US administration to forestall the election of Lula. On 6 September, however, the IMF finally agreed to a package which was designed to support the real until the end of 2003, subject to the new government accepting a 3.5 per cent inflation target.

With all eyes focussed on the forthcoming elections, the popularity of the various candidates in the opinion polls was keenly observed. By March, Roseana Sarney, the governor of Maranhao state and the presidential candidate of the right-wing Liberal Front Party (PFL), was enjoying a substantial lead over her rivals, including Cardoso's chosen successor, José Serra, candidate of the President's Brazilian Social Democratic party (PSDB). Her candidacy ran into trouble, however, when she was investigated in connection with corruption allegations. On 7 March the PFL, the largest party in the Chamber of Deputies (the lower house of the bicameral legislature), formally withdrew from the ruling coalition as a protest against what it saw as a government attempt to damage Sarney's candidature through the investigation. Attempts to salvage Sarney's candidacy failed, however, and on 13 April she withdrew from the contest after the polls indicated a collapse in her level of support.

As the campaign progressed further it became clear that the leading candidate was Lula. His "peace and love" campaign was shrewdly fought, for whilst he made a vague commitment to establish an alternative to the free-market "Washington consensus" (neo-liberal) economic model which had been pursued by most South American governments in recent years, he was careful not to alienate foreign investors or the IMF. He also succeeded in building support among some industrialists, whose businesses in such sectors as textiles and electronics had suffered from Brazil's recent policy of reducing tariffs on imported goods. His vice presidential running-mate, José Alencar, was a textile tycoon and a member of the centre-right Liberal Party (PL). Lula also offered to reform the country's labour laws and to pursue "market friendly socialism".

In the first round of the presidential elections, on 6 October, Lula polled over 46 per cent of the vote, comfortably beating Serra. Anthony Garotinho and Ciro Gomes finished in third and fourth places respectively, and endorsed Lula's candidacy in the run-off contest on 27 October. Lula's victory was thus ensured, and he won decisively, with 61.2 per cent of the vote compared with 38 per cent for Serra, who got only a lukewarm endorsement from the PFL.

Results of presidential elections in Brazil

First Round

Candidate	Party	Votes	% of vote
Luiz Inácio "Lula" da Silva	Workers' Party (PT)	39,443,867	46.44
José Serra	Brazilian Social Democratic Party (PSDB)	19,700,470	23.2
Anthony Garotinho	Brazilian Socialist Party (PSB)	15,175,776	17.87
Ciro Gomes	Popular Socialist Party (PPS)	10,167,650	11.97
José Maria de Almeida	United Socialist Workers' Party (PSTU)	402,038	0.47
Rui Costa Pimenta	Workers' Cause Party (PCO)	38,608	0.05
Total		84,928,409	100.00

Turnout: 82.23 per cent (94,774,749 total votes cast; 115,253,816 registered voters).

Second Round

Candidate	Party	Votes	% of vote
Luiz Inácio "Lula" da Silva	Workers' Party (PT)	52,793,364	61.27
José Serra	Brazilian Social Democratic Party (PSDB)	33,370,379	38.73
Total		86,163,743	100.00

Turnout: 79.53 per cent (91,664,259 total votes cast; 115,257,461 registered voters).

Serra's defeat was widely attributed to his lack of personal charisma and to frustration with the PSDB-led coalition, which had stabilised the economy after the financial crisis of 1999, but (arguably) had failed to deliver a sustained increase in standards of living. The PT, on the other hand, had responded to da Silva's successive defeats in the presidential elections of 1989, 1994, and 1998 by abandoning many of its hard left policies, such as the renationalisation of privatised utilities and the suspension of Brazil's foreign debt repayments.

Simultaneous elections to Congress (the bicameral federal legislature) and gubernatorial elections were also held on October 6. In the elections to the Chamber of Deputies, in which all 513 seats were contested under a system of proportional representation, the PT increased its representation to become the single largest party. In the elections to the 81-member Senate (the upper house), in which 54 seats (two thirds) were contested, the PT succeeded in increasing its overall representation to 14 but, as with the lower house, would be dependent on prospective coalition partners to ensure a working majority.

Results of legislative elections in Brazil

Party	Seats in the Chamber of Deputies	Seats in Senate	Overall Seats in the Senate
Workers' Party (PT)	91	10	14
Liberal Front Party (PFL)	84	14	19
Brazilian Democratic Movement (PMDB)	74	9	19
Brazilian Social Democratic Party (PSDB)	71	8	11
Brazilian Progressive Party (PPB)	49	0	1
Liberal Party (PL)	26	2	3
Brazilian Labour Party (PTB)	26	2	3
Brazilian Socialist Party (PSB)	22	3	4
Democratic Labour Party (PDT)	21	4	5
Popular Socialist Party (PPS)	15	1	1
Communist Party of Brazil (PCB)	12	0	0
Others	22	1	1
Total	513	54	81

In a disappointing performance in the gubernatorial elections held in 27 states on October 6, and in 15 run-offs held on October 27, the PT secured just three governorships: those of the states of Acre, Piauí, and Mato Grosso do Sul. The major prizes of São Paulo and Minas Gerais, the most populous states, went to the PSDB.

ii. ARGENTINA

CAPITAL: Buenos Aires AREA: 2,780,000 sq km POPULATION: 37,500,000
OFFICIAL LANGUAGE: Spanish POLITICAL SYSTEM: multiparty republic
HEAD OF STATE AND GOVERNMENT: President Eduardo Duhalde (since Jan '02)
RULING PARTY: Partido Justucialista (Peronist)
MAIN IGO MEMBERSHIPS (NON-UN): OAS, SELA, ALADI, Mercosur
CURRENCY: peso (end-'02 £1=AP5.4693, US$1=AP3.4150)
GNI PER CAPITA: US$6,960, US$11,690 at PPP ('01)

ON 1 January a joint assembly of the Peronist-dominated Congress (the bicameral legislature) and provincial governors chose Eduardo Duhalde to serve out the remaining part of Fernando De la Rúa Bruno's presidential term. The fifth person to wear the presidential sash in a fortnight, the 60-year old Duhalde had been the unsuccessful presidential candidate in 1999, but as a former Vice President and twice elected governor of the Province of Buenos Aires, he had a strong record of public service. Jorge Capitanich became chief of the Cabinet and Carlos Ruckauf Minister of Foreign Affairs. Yet the new Economy Minister, Jorge Remes Lenicov, wrestled unsuccessfully with the task of reconciling internal political demands with the requirements of the IMF. He was unable to find a majority in Congress for the harsh measures demanded and periodic riots in the streets were a reminder that although the banks had re-opened, most of their customers were allowed to draw no more than a few hundred pesos per week from their accounts (a restriction known as the *corralito*, or fence) for fear that the banking system would collapse. The restriction, although gradually eased during the course of the year, caused widespread public fury and precipitated numerous legal challenges by those anxious to recover their money.

The Supreme Court ruled on 1 February that the *corralito* restrictions on cash withdrawals from bank current and deposit accounts were unconstitutional. This view was upheld by further legal rulings during the year. However, the problem of how to scrap the *corralito* without causing a fatal run on the banks was one which exercised the government throughout the year. It was not entirely resolved, despite several attempts to open the way for the abolition of the *corralito* by converting bank deposits into government bonds.

The economic situation that Duhalde inherited was unenviable. In December 2001 the government had defaulted on its foreign debt repayments although, for the present at least, it continued to honour its debts to multilateral lending institutions. Congress granted the President emergency powers and the peso was devalued on 7 January for international trade by 40 per cent and allowed to float for domestic purposes as part of a package which included decoupling utility prices from those of the USA, allowing credit card debts to be settled at the old rate at the banks' expense, re-denominating dollar debts under US$100,000 in pesos, strengthening unemployment benefit, and imposing a tax on oil exports. But the peso's value could not be sustained in what was effectively a dual exchange rate system. The stock market re-opened on 17 January to a sharp fall and violent demonstrations continued across the country against the strict limits on bank withdrawals. When on 9 February the government unveiled plans to cut the budget by

US$370 million, there were widespread protests. In response the government restored convertibility by allowing the peso to float from 11 February, and agreed to allow people to cash their pay cheques in full, although the *corralito* remained in place in relation to bank deposits. An outbreak of riots followed on 20 February in which the unemployed blocked roads and bridges while the middle classes continued to demand full access to their money.

At the beginning of April Argentina was given the uncompromising message that no further international help would be available unless drastic reforms were forthcoming. The Supreme Court ruling and subsequent court orders had partially disabled the *corralito* and led to withdrawals from the banking system of US$100 million per day in April. In a desperate attempt to stem capital outflows from the banks, the Central Bank ordered the closure of all banks and foreign exchange houses on 22 April. The banking holiday was not fully lifted until 29 April (after Congress had enacted the emergency legislation to restrict court orders against the *corralito*) and then only for five hours for non-cash transactions.

On 23 April Economy Minister Remes Lenicov resigned together with most of the rest of the Cabinet after failing to win support for an emergency plan to convert frozen bank deposits into government bonds. By this point the peso had lost approximately 70 per cent of its value since the beginning of the year, inflation had risen to 20 per cent, public sector workers were rioting, and half of the population was said to be living below the national poverty line. In consequence there had also been a steep rise in robberies, kidnappings, and other crimes which the underpaid police were either unable or unwilling to combat. Thieves who stole nearly 3,000 miles of copper wire between January and September seriously disrupted the telephone service, and utility workers were physically attacked when they tried to carry out repairs.

Roberto Lavagna, 60, a former Ambassador to the EU and to the World Trade Organisation (WTO), became the sixth Economy Minister to hold office within a year. The President was able on 24 April to negotiate a 14-point economic programme with government and opposition congressional leaders and provincial governors. The programme incorporated many of the reforms sought by the IMF, including the abolition of the 1974 "economic subversion" law and the amendment of the bankruptcy law. This legislation was passed by Congress during May, but only after the President had threatened to resign if it were not approved. The governors also promised to implement within 15 days an austere revenue-sharing pact between the government and the provinces, which had been announced in February and the immediate implementation of which had been demanded by the IMF.

On 6 May an agreement was reached for the phased lifting of the *corralito*, but this was blocked by the banks. The government's attempts to convince the IMF that it could meet the conditions established for the resumption of further lending were also jeopardised when Felipe Solá, the governor of Buenos Aires province (the wealthiest and most populous of Argentina's provinces), announced on 20 May that he would not sign the new austerity pact. At the end of the month a further plan for ending the *corralito* was formulated which offered depositors the opportunity to convert into bonds their frozen savings. This plan differed from the two previous bond swap proposals—rejected by the Senate (the upper house of the bicameral legislature) and by the banks—in that it would be optional rather than compulsory.

Notwithstanding the revision of the bankruptcy code and the repeal of the "economic subversion" law, negotiations with the IMF regarding the resumption of lending, which had been suspended in December 2001, showed little sign of progress. The IMF had two major concerns, first that the government did not have a credible anti-inflation policy in the wake of the devaluation of the peso and, secondly, that the provincial governors could not be relied upon to honour a commitment to reduce provincial government budget deficits. Without additional IMF loans, the government faced the possibility that it would be forced to default on loan repayments to its multilateral creditors in July.

In such a situation, it was hardly surprising that many took comfort from the expectation that the national football team was widely fancied to win the World Cup; Argentina's shock elimination in the first round, therefore, was a bitter blow (see XVI). Opinion polls confirmed the widespread disillusion with Argentina's political establishment, placing Elisa Carrió, of the small Alternative for a Republic of Equals (ARI) party, as the front-runner for the 2003 presidential elections on the strength of her vigorous campaign against official corruption. Her party, founded by Domingo Cavallo, welcomed his release in June after he had been held for 65 days on unsubstantiated charges of dereliction of duty and aggravated smuggling of weapons to Croatia and Ecuador while a member of the Menem administration.

On 2 July the President announced that the elections originally scheduled for September 2003 would be brought forward to 30 March, following which the government sought to postpone repayment of some US$7 billion to multilateral lenders. However on 29 July the IMF announced that in the absence of a political consensus no further loans would be forthcoming and no timetable existed for resuming them. Meanwhile a series of court rulings increased the pressure on the government. On 26 July a federal appeals court overrode a decree banning legal challenges to the *corralito*, and on 20 August another appeals court upheld a judgement that the *corralito* was unconstitutional. The restriction was relaxed somewhat on 30 September, but to the fury of depositors withdrawals could still only be made in pesos. Further legal blows followed as on 22 August the Supreme Court ruled that the 13 per cent pay cut imposed on public sector workers by the Radical Civic Union (UCR) administration in July 2001 was also unconstitutional, a decision which would cost the government an additional US$1.4 billion. On 1 October an appeals court in Buenos Aires effectively suspended proposed price increases for public utilities.

On 29 August the IMF confirmed that it would not resume lending to Argentina, thereby dashing the government's hopes that it could secure a deal to defer the US$7 billion in debt repayments due in 2002 to multilateral lenders. However, on 5 September the IMF announced that, in an attempt to prevent Argentina from defaulting on its loan repayments to multilateral lenders, such as the Fund itself and the World Bank, it had formalised an agreement to postpone for one year a US$2.7 billion payment due to be paid to the IMF by Argentina on 9 September. The concession, however, fell short of the Argentinian government's request to be allowed to defer all payments to the IMF due in 2002-03. Consequently, on 24 September Economy Minister Roberto Lavagna announced that the government was not prepared to diminish its foreign reserves in order to keep servicing loans from multilateral lenders and that it was possible that Argentina would be unable to make repayments in the near future.

Lavagna announced by decree on 10 September that the government would, with effect from October, offer depositors the opportunity to convert some savings frozen by the *corralito* into bonds. Under the terms of the new voluntary scheme, up to 60 per cent of savings in "term deposits" (higher rate, long-term bank accounts holding up to US$1,990) would be freed from the restrictions if savers purchased government bonds, which would mature in 2013. As an inducement, the bond holders would receive repayment in US dollars upon maturity at the rate of one dollar for every 1.8 pesos invested.

The government announced on 14 November that it would pay only a small proportion of a US$805 million loan repayment due to be paid to the World Bank, thus putting the country into a state of default under World Bank rules (the repayment was already more than 30 days overdue). The default meant that Argentina joined the company of only a handful of countries to have defaulted on a loan repayment to a multilateral lender. The IMF announced on 20 November that it would allow Argentina an extra year to make a US$141 million repayment due to the Fund on 22 November under the Supplemental Reserve Facility (SRF).

In January Foreign Minister Carlos Ruckauf repeated his country's claim to the Falkland Islands, calling on the UK to open negotiations over their future. At a parade in Ushuaia, held on 2 April to commemorate the 20th anniversary of the Argentinian occupation of the Falkland Islands, President Duhalde reaffirmed his country's determination to recover the islands, but only by peaceful means.

iii. PARAGUAY

CAPITAL: Asunción   AREA: 407,000 sq km   POPULATION: 5,600,000
OFFICIAL LANGUAGE: Spanish   POLITICAL SYSTEM: multiparty republic
HEAD OF STATE AND GOVERNMENT: President Luís González Macchi (since March '99)
RULING PARTIES: Colorado Party (ANR-PC) heads coalition with National Encounter (EN)
MAIN IGO MEMBERSHIPS (NON-UN): OAS, ALADI, SELA, Mercosur
CURRENCY: guaraní (end-'02 £1=G11,282.9, US$1=G7,045.00)
GNI PER CAPITA: US$1,300, US$4,400 at PPP ('01)

IN the first months of the year political manoeuvring continued, ahead of the presidential elections scheduled for May 2003. The government of President Luís González Macchi, having survived the opposition attempt to impeach him in September 2001 (see AR 2001, p. 208), continued to be harassed by accusations of corruption. Although on 8 January the President and his chief rival, Vice President Julio César Franco, of the Authentic Radical Liberal Party (PRLA), agreed to enter into a dialogue, they remained bitterly at odds with other. Relations between them worsened during the year and Franco resigned on 22 October in order to contest the presidential elections.

González Macchi managed to survive in office, despite a fresh attempt to impeach him in April, which failed to gain the necessary two-thirds majority in the Chamber of Deputies (the lower house of the legislature). It remained unclear, however, whether the increasingly divided ruling Colorado Party (ANR-PC) would unite behind him since, despite some attempt to bring the economy under control, both the fiscal deficit and, in consequence, government borrowing, continued to rise.

Paraguay's dark past also cast its shadow over the administration. On 12 February Interior Minister Julio César Fanego was forced to resign following allegations that he had known of the abduction and torture of two alleged members of the leftist insurgent group, the Free Fatherland Movement (MPL). He was succeeded by Finance Minister Francisco Oviedo, who was in turn replaced at Finance by James Spalding. The President also announced that the National Intelligence Service (SIN) would be disbanded. Soon afterwards former President Raúl Cubas Grau, who had been in Brazil since his resignation in 1999 (see AR 1999, p. 183), voluntarily returned to the country to face trial in connection with the deaths of four demonstrators.

Another shadow from the past was cast by Gen. (retd) Lino César Oviedo who, although he remained in exile in Brazil, continued to be a key political player. His supporters remained active throughout the year, and in March a faction of the ANR-PC seceded to form a new organisation, the National Unity Movement of Ethical Colorados (UNACE), to support his candidature for the 2003 presidential elections. Oviedo had previously stated that he intended to contest the elections despite the fact that he faced outstanding arrest warrants in Paraguay relating to his alleged role in the assassination of Vice President Luis María Argaña Ferraro in March 1999, and further charges relating to his alleged involvement in an attempted coup in May 2000. Widespread demonstrations in the middle of the year, in which several people were killed, were blamed on the supporters of Oviedo and Vice President Franco, and led to the brief imposition of a state of emergency in mid-July.

Economic worries were exacerbated by fears that Paraguay could suffer from the "Argentinian contagion" (see IV.5.ii), and in June legislation was approved to increase the state guarantee of private bank deposits in order to stem a run on the banks following the placing of Banco Alemán (Paraguay's second-largest private bank) under Central Bank administration on 23 June. Corruption also remained an endemic problem, a fact underlined by an international report published in September which rated the country the most corrupt in South America and the third most corrupt in the world. The need to investigate allegations of corruption within Coapaco, the state-owned telecommunications company, delayed its privatisation. In May the Chamber of Deputies (the lower house of the bicameral legislature) approved a bill suspending the authority for privatisations and, after this had passed the Senate (the upper house) on 14 June, the privatisation was postponed indefinitely, with significant implications for the country's $300 million fiscal deficit.

iv. URUGUAY

CAPITAL: Montevideo   AREA: 177,000 sq km   POPULATION: 3,400,000
OFFICIAL LANGUAGE: Spanish   POLITICAL SYSTEM: multiparty republic
HEAD OF STATE AND GOVERNMENT: President Jorge Batlle Ibáñez (since March '00)
RULING PARTIES: Colorado Party (PC) holds presidency and heads a government which includes the National (Blanco) Party (PN)
MAIN IGO MEMBERSHIPS (NON-UN): OAS, ALADI, SELA, Mercosur, NAM
CURRENCY: peso Uruguayo (end-'02 £1=UP43.6823, US$1=UP27.2750)
GNI PER CAPITA: US$5,670, US$8,710 at PPP ('01)

THE economic crisis in Argentina (see IV.5.ii) adversely affected the government of President Jorge Batlle Ibáñez, and undermined international confidence in the Uruguayan economy. On 17 January the Minister of Economy and Finance, Alberto Benisón, announced emergency measures to keep the fiscal deficit for the year under 2.5 per cent. These steps included a surtax on high incomes; the extension of the IVA value added tax to milk, fruit, and vegetables; and a tax on international telephone calls. Some state-owned land was also to be sold. On 25 March the IMF approved a two-year standby credit from 1 April to support these policies and to help protect the country from the "contagion effects" of the Argentinian crisis, noting that Uruguay had not so far needed to draw on the standby facility approved in May 2000.

When on 13 May the President announced on television a further package of "urgent measures" to reduce the fiscal deficit, the initiative led to large-scale protests accompanied by the beating of empty pots and pans, a tactic widely used in Argentina. Soon afterwards Batlle Ibáñez made a tearful public apology to the people of Argentina after his comment that they were "a bunch of thieves from start to finish" who had only themselves to blame for their economic problems (an opinion widely shared in Uruguay) was accidentally broadcast on television. Although the IMF continued to try to shield Uruguay from the contagion, on 20 June the government abandoned attempts to manage the exchange rate and allowed the peso to float. Also, having lost the confidence of the National (Blanco) Party (PN), the junior party in the ruling coalition, Benisón resigned on 22 July.

On the following day a senior Colorado Party (PC) Senator, 50-year old Alejandro Atchugarray, was appointed as Minister of Economy and Finance. But on 29 July, when the peso had lost about half its value, the government had to follow the example of Argentina and close the banks to halt the run on their reserves. A general strike called on 2 August was punctuated by rioting and some systematic looting, before the USA, in a sharp policy reversal, agreed to give the country a US$1,500 million bridging loan ahead of the visit of US Treasury Secretary Paul O'Neill, whose warmth towards Uruguay was in striking contrast to his coolness towards Argentina. On 5 August, therefore, the banks were able to re-open, even before the international lending agencies had finalised a rescue package.

v. CHILE

CAPITAL: Santiago   AREA: 757,000 sq km   POPULATION: 15,400,000
OFFICIAL LANGUAGE: Spanish   POLITICAL SYSTEM: multiparty republic
HEAD OF STATE AND GOVERNMENT: President Ricardo Lagos Escobar (since March '00)
RULING PARTIES: Concertación coalition composed of Party for Democracy (PPD), Socialist (PS),
    Christian Democratic (PDC), & Social Democratic Radical (PRSD) parties
MAIN IGO MEMBERSHIPS (NON-UN): OAS, ALADI, SELA, APEC, NAM, Mercosur
CURRENCY: Chilean peso (end-'02 £1=Ch1,142.23, US$1=Ch713.200)
GNI PER CAPITA: US$4,350, US$9,420 at PPP ('01)

ON 8 January President Ricardo Lagos reshuffled his Cabinet. Jorge Rodríguez of the Christian Democrats (PDC) was appointed Minister of the Economy, while Michelle Bachelet, of the President's Socialist Party (PS), became the first woman in the world to hold the position of Minister of Defence. On 30 January she announced that the government would buy 10 F-16 fighter-bombers from the Lockheed Martin Corporation of the USA, the first such purchase since the lifting of the US ban on the export of advanced military technology to the region by President Bill Clinton in 1998. This met not only with criticism from within the ruling coalition, but also a formal protest from the President of Peru, Alejandro Toledo.

Chile's dark recent past continued to cast a shadow upon the present as all possibility of further proceedings against the former military dictator Augusto Pinochet Ugarte ended on 1 July when, by a majority of four to one, the Supreme Court ruled that he was suffering from incurable and irreversible dementia. Apparently safe from ever having to answer for the grave crimes committed under his brutal regime, three days later Pinochet resigned his seat as Senator-for-life and retired from public life. On a brighter note, however, there were some instances where those who had abused human rights were called to account. On 5 August a criminal court in Santiago found 12 former officers and one non-commissioned officer guilty of murder and conspiracy relating to the death of Tucapel Jiménez, a trade union leader, in 1982. Four other officers were acquitted. Furthermore, on 8 October the Commander of the Air Force, Gen. Patricio Rios, was arrested on charges of obstructing justice in his evidence to the Truth Commission which was investigating human rights abuses committed under Pinochet's dictatorship. Rios resigned a week later, a move which was seen as a triumph for President Lagos, who, under the terms of the constitution, as amended in 1989, was not empowered to dismiss a commander of one of the armed forces.

By September a combination of regional economic crisis and low commodity prices had forced Finance Minister Nicolás Eyzaguirre to announce spending cuts totalling US$250 million in the current fiscal year in order to meet economic targets. Whilst giving cause for some concern, however, the economy did not suffer from the "contagion" which had caused such damage in Argentina (see IV.5.ii) and some of its neighbours.

In February the worst forest fires for many years destroyed 37,000 acres of forest in the foothills of the Andes, some 800 km south of Santiago.

vi. PERU

CAPITAL: Lima AREA: 1,285,000 sq km POPULATION: 26,100,000
OFFICIAL LANGUAGES: Spanish, Quechua, Aymará POLITICAL SYSTEM: multiparty republic
HEAD OF STATE AND GOVERNMENT: President Alejandro Toledo (since '01)
RULING PARTY: Perú Possible party
PRIME MINISTER: Luis Maria Solari de la Fuente (since July '02)
MAIN IGO MEMBERSHIPS (NON-UN): OAS, APEC, ALADI, SELA, CA, AP, NAM
CURRENCY: new sol (end-'02 £1=S5.6431, US$1=S3.5235)
GNI PER CAPITA: US$2,000, US$4,680 at PPP ('01)

ON 18 January President Alejandro Toledo appointed Aurelio Loret de Mola as Minister of Defence in place of David Waisman. The ruling coalition, Perú Possible—whose secretary-general, Luis María Solari de la Fuente, lost his post as Minister of Health in the reshuffle—criticised Loret de Mola's appointment, as the new Minister was not a member of the coalition.

Widespread demonstrations in April and May led to the postponement on two occasions of the planned privatisation of two state-owned electricity generating companies, Etecen and Etesur. On 16 June a state of emergency was proclaimed in Arequipa after rioting broke out there at the news that the government had sold both companies to the Belgian company Tractebel; three days later it was obliged to suspend the sale for the third time. The Interior Minister, Fernando Rospigliosi, resigned in protest and was replaced by Gino Costa Santolalla. The privatisation programme was, in fact, so unpopular that in a Cabinet reshuffle on 12 July President Toledo replaced the two key advocates of the policy. In the new Cabinet Luis María Solari de la Fuente became Prime Minister and Javier Silva Ruete Minister of Economy and Finance, while a former member of the Aprista Party (PA), Allan Wagner Tizón, was appointed to the vacant post of Foreign Minister.

Although on 3 September Etecen and Etesur were sold to a Colombian company, further decisions about privatisation were postponed until after the country's regional elections on 17 November, in which the government took only one of the 25 regional presidencies. More surprisingly, 12 of the presidencies were won by the long moribund PA, reviving the presidential ambitions of its discredited leader, former President Alan García. In advance of the regional elections in November, the President admitted in mid-October to having fathered a daughter, now 14 years old, while separated from his wife in the 1980s.

Security remained an issue throughout the year. Two bomb attacks on 20 March, one close to the US Embassy in Lima which killed nine people and injured many more, preceded the state visit of US President George W. Bush. The attacks were widely seen as marking the revival of the left-wing guerrilla movement Shining Path (Sendero Luminoso), which US sources claimed had developed links in 2001 with the Colombian Revolutionary Armed Forces (FARC), a leftist guerrilla group, and the drug traffickers who were responsible for FARC's estimated income of some US$300 million a year. In September police captured three Shining Path members whom they suspected of masterminding the March attack.

Past human rights abuses continued to cause echoes in the present as on 9 April the Supreme Court ruled that the state was responsible for the massacre in 1991 of 15 civilians whom the security forces had allegedly mistaken for guerrillas.

Furthermore, in May eight senior army officers faced charges after forensic examination showed that eight of the guerrillas who had been captured alive during the storming of the Japanese Embassy in 1997 (see AR 1997, p. 175) had been shot in the back of the head. The reputation of the then President, Alberto Keinya Fujimori, was further tarnished by the revelation on 24 July that in the four years after 1996 his officials had deceived some 215,227 poorly educated indigenous women into undergoing sterilisation. Later, in September, four former generals who had been associates of Fujimori's notorious intelligence chief, Vladimiro Montesinos, were formally charged with corruption.

Former President Fernando Belaúnde Terry died on 4 June, aged 89.

vii. BOLIVIA

CAPITAL: La Paz and Sucre   AREA: 1,099,000 sq km   POPULATION: 8,500,000
OFFICIAL LANGUAGES: Spanish, Quechua, Aymará   POLITICAL SYSTEM: multiparty republic
HEAD OF STATE AND GOVERNMENT: President Gonzálo Sánchez de Lozada (since Aug. '02)
RULING PARTIES: Nationalist Revolutionary Movement (MNR) heads coalition with Civic Solidarity Union (UCS), Movement of the Revolutionary Left (MIR), Free Bolivia Movement (MBL), Democratic Nationalist Action (ADN), & Unity and Progress Movement (MUP)
MAIN IGO MEMBERSHIPS (NON-UN): OAS, ALADI, SELA, AG, CA, NAM, Mercosur
CURRENCY: boliviano (end-'02 £1=B12.0116, US$1=B7.5000)
GNI PER CAPITA: US$940, US$2,380 at PPP ('01)

THE main political development of 2002 was the election to the presidency of former President Gonzálo Sánchez de Lozada of the centre-right Revolutionary Nationalist Movement (MNR), who in his previous term had presided over the destruction of the tin industry. Sánchez de Lozada's election by members of the two houses of Congress (the legislature) on 4 August came after an inconclusive first round on 30 June in which he had secured 22.46 per cent of the vote compared with the 20.94 per cent achieved by the charismatic, 42-year old president of the coca-growers association, Evo Morales, representing the Movement Towards Socialism (MAS). A close third place (20.91 per cent) was secured by Manfred Reyes Villa of the New Republican Force (NFR), whilst Jaime Paz Zamora of the Movement of the Revolutionary Left (MIR) won 16.32 per cent. Sánchez de Lozada won the run-off elections after the MIR decided to back the millionaire former President, and was joined by the Civic Solidarity Union (UCS), the Free Bolivia Movement (MBL), and the right-wing Democratic Nationalist Action (ADN). Congress's deliberations over which of the two highest-placed candidates to choose were also influenced by a warning from the US ambassador that the election of Morales would, under new US anti-terrorist "fast-track" legislation, endanger US aid and trade. Sánchez de Lozada was eventually chosen by 84 votes to 43 on the morning of 4 August, following more than 24 hours of debate.

Concurrently with the presidential elections in June, elections were held to both houses of the Congress. The MNR emerged as the largest party, but did not secure an overall majority in the Senate or the Chamber of Deputies. The MAS performed well in both contests, and there was a sharp increase in indigenous representation with the six seats won by the Pachakuti Indigenous Movement (MIP) meaning that, for the first time, facilities had to be installed for simultaneous translation into the country's three main indigenous languages, Aymará, Quechua, and Guaraní

Final results of legislative elections in Bolivia

Party	Seats in Chamber of Deputies	Seats in Senate
Ruling coalition		
Nationalist Revolutionary Movement (MNR)*	36	11
Movement of the Revolutionary Left (MIR)	26	5
Democratic Nationalist Action (ADN)	4	1
Civic Solidarity Union (UCS)	5	0
Opposition		
Movement Towards Socialism (MAS)	27	8
New Republican Force (NFR)	25	2
Pachakuti Indigenous Movement (MIP)	6	0
Socialist Party (PS)	1	0
Total	130	27

*Includes seats won by Free Bolivia Movement (MBL) candidates.

The Cabinet announced by the new President in August was dominated by the MNR, with Carlos Saavedra Bruno (MIR) as Minister of Foreign Affairs, Javier Comboni (MNR) as Finance Minister, and Alberto Gasser Vargas (MNR) as Minister of the Interior. In an important concession to the indigenous peoples, on 1 September the decision was reported to redistribute some 500,000 ha of agricultural and 700,000 ha of forestry land to 11,000 landless families. The programme would cost an estimated US$2,500 million.

The ongoing problem of the coca trade continued, with clashes between security forces and coca farmers angry at being deprived of their livelihoods by the US-backed eradication programme. On 15 January farmers at Sacaba, in the department of Cochabamba, attempted to re-open a coca leaf market closed under the terms of a presidential decree; seven people were subsequently killed in confrontations between the farmers and police. Congress voted on 24 January to strip Morales, the president of the coca growers' association, of his parliamentary immunity from prosecution for his alleged incitement of the violence. However on 9 February, with the assistance of mediation efforts by Roman Catholic leaders, the government agreed to suspend the decree closing the markets, pending a review, to allow limited legal dealings in coca leaves.

General Hugo Bánzer Suarez, Bolivia's military dictator between 1971 and 1978, who had served as President from 1997 until his resignation in 2001 when diagnosed with cancer, died of a heart attack at his home in Santa Cruz on May at the age of 75. Despite his tough stance against the cocaine trade, his presidency had seen a significant increase in the power of the coca growers.

viii. ECUADOR

CAPITAL: Quito   AREA: 284,000 sq km   POPULATION: 12,900,000
OFFICIAL LANGUAGE: Spanish   POLITICAL SYSTEM: multiparty republic
HEAD OF STATE AND GOVERNMENT: President Gustavo Noboa Bejarano (since Jan '00)
   PRESIDENT ELECT: Lucio Gutiérrez
RULING PARTIES: Popular Democracy (DP) heads coalition
MAIN IGO MEMBERSHIPS (NON-UN): OAS, ALADI, SELA, AG, CA, NAM
CURRENCY: US dollar (end'02 £1=1.6016)
GNI PER CAPITA: US$1,240, US$3,070 at PPP ('01)

WITH presidential and legislative elections scheduled for October, and President Gustavo Noboa Bejarano of the centre-right Popular Democracy (DP) party deciding not to stand for re-election, 2002 promised to be a year of political change. Notwithstanding the forthcoming elections, however, in its final year in office the Noboa administration faced popular protests, corruption, and scandals.

Early in the year a loose coalition of indigenous farmers and civic groups mounted protests against the lack of investment in the Amazonian departments. They seized drilling facilities and refineries belonging both to Petroecuador and private companies in the Aucas, Sacha, and Shushufindi oilfields, and reduced petroleum production by some 50 per cent in February. Hence, on 22 February the President proclaimed a state of emergency in the Departments of Sucumbíos and Orellana and threatened to send in troops. There were further difficulties in April when the government ordered the arrest of environmentalists who had chained themselves to trees in the Mindo-Nambillo forest on the route of a proposed new crude oil pipeline from the Amazonian fields to the Pacific. In the same month there was widespread popular unrest at plans to privatise electricity supply in the lowlands, which led first to the cancellation of proposed price increases and then, on 11 April, to the abandonment of the planned sale.

On 22 May the National Congress (the unicameral legislature) approved a fiscal reform package that was designed to raise a stabilisation fund, 70 per cent of which was reserved for external debt reduction required by the IMF before renewing the country's standby facility.

Finance Minister Carlos Julio Emanuel resigned on 23 June after several senior ministry officials had been implicated in a corruption scandal. He was replaced by Francisco Arosemena. On 3 July Marcelo Merlo resigned as Interior Minister because of policy differences and was replaced by Rodolfo Barniol, previously president of Petroecuador. On 2 August, the portfolio of Foreign Trade, previously held by Richard Moss, who had resigned to take up the post of secretary general of the Andean Community (ANCOM), was given to the Foreign Minister, Heinz Moeller, who had decided not to contest the elections.

In the run up to the elections, the leading candidate for the presidency was the wealthy banana magnate Alvaro Noboa Pontón, of the rightist New Party for

National Action (PRIAN). He was challenged, however, by a late surge from Lucio Gutiérrez, the joint candidate of the leftist Popular Socialist Party (PSP) and the New Country-Pachakutik Movement (NMN-PP), whose campaign had also been endorsed by the political wing of the Confederation of Indian Nationalities of Ecuador (Conaie). Gutiérrez, 45, an admirer of Hugo Chávez Frías, the controversial President of Venezuela, had been a leading participant in the coup against President Jamil Mahuad Witt in January 2000 (see AR 2000, p. 169). In the event, in the election on 20 October, Gutiérrez secured over 20 per cent of the vote, forcing Noboa Pontón into second place.

Results of first round of presidential elections in Ecuador

Candidate	Party	Number of votes	Percentage of votes
Col. Lucio Edwin Gutiérrez	Popular Socialist Party (PSP)/New Country-Pachakutik Movement (NMN-PP)	899,492	20.3
Alvaro Fernando Noboa Pontón	New Party for National Action (PRIAN)	770,270	17.4
Leon Roldos Aguilera	Socialist Party (PS)	685,508	15.5
Rodrigo Borja Cevallos	Democratic Left (ID)	622,232	14.0
Antonio Xavier Neira Menendez	Social Christian Party (PSC)	541,408	12.2
Jacobo Bucaram Ortiz	Ecuadorian Roldosist Party (PRE)	525,539	11.9
Jacinto Velazquez Herrera	Movimiento Transformación Social Independiente (TSI)	165,811	3.7
Ivonne Leyla Juez Abuchakra	Liberal Radical Party (PLR)	78,434	1.8
Cesar Augusto Alarcon Costa	Liberal Party (PL)	53,342	1.2
Osvaldo Hurtado Larrea	Patriotic Solidarity Movement (MPS)	47,621	1.1
Carlos Antonio Vargas Guatatuca	Indigenous Movement Amauta Jatari (MIAJ)	36,992	0.8
Total		4,426,649	99.9

Turnout 62.9 per cent (8,154,425 registered voters).

Gutiérrez's lead proved unassailable, and in the run-off election on 24 November he won 54.3 per cent of the poll compared with Noboa's 45.7 per cent.

ix. COLOMBIA

CAPITAL: Santa Fe de Bogotá AREA: 1,139,000 sq km POPULATION: 43,000,000
OFFICIAL LANGUAGE: Spanish POLITICAL SYSTEM: multiparty republic
HEAD OF STATE AND GOVERNMENT: President Alvaro Uribe Velez (since Aug. '02)
RULING PARTIES: Government is supported by Liberal Party (PL)
MAIN IGO MEMBERSHIPS (NON-UN): OAS, ALADI, SELA, AG, CA, ACS, NAM
CURRENCY: Colombian peso (end-'02 £1=Col4,557.55, US$1=Col2,858.20)
GNI PER CAPITA: US$1,910, US$5,980 at PPP ('01)

THREE frustrating years of peace talks with the Revolutionary Armed Forces of Colombia (FARC), the largest of Colombia's guerrilla movements, broke down on 13 January when the FARC refused to agree to a cease-fire. The talks definitively ended at midnight on 20 February, when troops entered the demilitarised zone that the government of President Andrés Pastrana Arango had conceded to the rebels in 1998 (see AR 1998, p. 189). The troops quickly seized the town of San Vicente del Caguán, meeting with no resistance from the retreating guerrillas, who had precipitated the breakdown by hijacking a civil airliner and kidnapping Senator Jorge Eduardo Gechem Turbay, president of the Senate peace commission. However, government forces were unable to mount an effective presence throughout the whole of the 16,000 square mile area with a population of about 100,000.

Thousands fled in well-founded fear of reprisals from right-wing paramilitaries, and the rebels quickly resumed their guerrilla tactics, blocking roads and kidnapping Ingrid Betancourt, presidential candidate of the Green Oxygen Party, on the road near Florencia. At least 117 civilians, some 40 of them children, were killed at Bojaya, Department of Choco, on 2 May when a mortar round fired by FARC guerrillas at right-wing paramilitaries who had occupied the town towards the end of April, demolished the church. The guerrillas subsequently overran the town.

The 10 March elections to both the Senate and the Chamber of Deputies (the upper and lower house of the bicameral legislature) were characterised by apathy and widespread abstention. In the new Senate, the Liberals (PL) increased their representation, but only secured a total of 28 seats to the Social Conservatives' (PSC) 13, the Coalition Party's six, and the National Movement's six; the balance of power being held by no fewer than 38 minor parties which each gained at least one of the 49 remaining seats. The distribution of seats in the 161-member Chamber of Deputies followed a similar pattern, the PL gaining only 42 seats and the PSC 21.

Presidential elections followed in May. Promising tough action against the rebels, the 49-year old Alvaro Uribe Velez, running as candidate of the right-wing Colombia First coalition, on 26 May secured 53.04 per cent of the votes to win an unprecedented outright victory in the first round. The official candidate of the outgoing Liberal Party (PL), Horacio Serpa Uribe, secured only 31.72 per cent. The Social Conservative Party (PSC) candidate, Juan Camilo Restrepo, had withdrawn after the legislative elections on 10 March and the party then endorsed Uribe. On 11 June the PL agreed to support the new government, ensuring it a large majority in both houses of Congress.

Voters already disillusioned by the comprehensive failure of the three-year "peace process" had also been subjected to threats by both the FARC guerrillas and the right-wing paramilitary United Defence Forces of Colombia (AUC). Although Uribe had been mayor of Medellín at the time of the rise of the notorious drug cartel, his father had been killed by the rebels on his farm in Antioquia in 1983, and he himself had already survived some 15 attempts on his life, most recently in April when a massive car bomb exploded as his convoy was passing, killing four and wounding 13 but leaving the candidate himself unscathed. Uribe promised a no holds-barred approach to tackling the guerrillas, securing more help from the USA, doubling the fighting strength of the army, and giving judicial functions to the armed forces. The US ambassador, Anne Patterson, rapidly welcomed him as the latest recruit to President Bush's "war on terror"; the US President having in the meanwhile asked the US Congress for funds to support anti-terrorist operations as well as anti-drug operations in Colombia. But on 1 July thousands of local officials resigned their offices after being declared military targets by the FARC, despite pressure from the AUC not to do so. On 18 July the leader of the 10,000-strong AUC, Carlos Castaño, announced that he had disbanded his organisation to purge it of the associations which had led the US government to regard it as a terrorist organisation which financed its operations from drug trafficking. A new, reformed organisation would support the new government if it was unable to fight the guerrillas alone.

In the 24 hours before the new President's inauguration on 7 August, which for security reasons took place in the Congress building, at least 36 people were killed in clashes between troops and guerrillas and four bombs exploded in Bogotá. On the day itself, a volley of mortar bombs fell on the capital, killing 15 and injuring 40. In the new Cabinet, Roberto Junguito Bonnet became Minister of Finance, Carolina Barco Isakson Minister of Foreign Affairs, and Marta Lucía Ramírez Minister of Defence, the first woman to hold that position in Colombia. The following day the President fulfilled his promise to create a network of civilian informers, similar to the *convivirs* which he had established as governor of Antioquia between 1995 and 1997, but subsequently banned when many had degenerated into vigilante movements. On 12 August he proclaimed a 90-day state of emergency, and on 15 August the President appointed Gen. Carlos Alberto Ospina Ovalle as commander of the army and Gen. Teodoro Campo Gomez as national police director. On 10 September a decree extended the emergency powers of the security forces to search properties, tap telephones, and detain suspects indefinitely, while a major military operation was launched against guerrilla strongholds on the Ecuadorian border. When at the end of October Congress finally approved the 2003 budget, defence expenditure was increased by 12 per cent though other expenditure was frozen or reduced.

The rival guerrilla group to FARC, the National Liberation Army (ELN), was also active during the year As a result of 170 bomb attacks by the ELN on the El Caño-Limón pipeline in 2001, the US Administration in March asked Congress for US$98 million to raise additional troops to guard it. The attacks, mainly in the Department of Arauca, had cost the Colombian government US$430 million and substantially reduced the profits of the US corporation, Occidental Petroleum.

On 16 March, contract killers gunned down the Archbishop of Cali, Mgr. Isaias Duarte Cancino. The 63-year old Archbishop, who had just emerged from conducting a wedding service, was shot twice in the head, by an assailant who escaped on a motorcycle ridden by an accomplice. Duarte had consistently been outspoken in condemning violence and had excommunicated a large part of the ELN after guerrillas had burst into a church in May 1999 and kidnapped 150 worshippers. Recently he had denounced local candidates for accepting campaign donations from drug traffickers in the legislative elections of 10 March. No organisation claimed responsibility for his murder.

x. VENEZUELA

CAPITAL: Caracas   AREA: 912,000 sq km   POPULATION: 24,600,000
OFFICIAL LANGUAGE: Spanish   POLITICAL SYSTEM: multiparty republic
HEAD OF STATE AND GOVERNMENT: President Hugo Chávez Frias (since Feb '99)
RULING PARTY: Patriotic Front coalition
MAIN IGO MEMBERSHIPS (NON-UN): OAS, ALADI, SELA, CA, ACS, OPEC, NAM
CURRENCY: bolívar (end-'02 £1=Bs2,215.74, US$1=Bs1383.50)
GNI PER CAPITA: US$4,760, US$5,890 at PPP ('01)

ON 11 April President Hugo Chávez Frías was deposed by a military coup. A massive anti-Chávez demonstration in support of striking oil workers had begun to march on the presidential palace when gunfire broke out and clashes between supporters and opponents of the government—encouraged by agents provocateurs—killed at least 13 and left more than 100 wounded. Amid the deteriorating security situation, Gen. Lucas Rincón, chief of the armed forces, and a number of other senior military officers, requested the President's resignation. The officers claimed that Chávez agreed to stand down, a suggestion which he subsequently denied. In any event he was placed under arrest and, at 3 am on 12 April, he left the palace under guard and was transferred to Orchila Island. Senior officers said that he would not be allowed to leave the country as he had requested, and would face charges. Meanwhile a 60-year old businessman, Pedro Carmona, president of the Venezuelan Chamber of Commerce, was appointed as interim President. This change was welcomed by the US government which had done little to conceal its distrust of Chávez's populist style, and which was widely believed to have helped prepare the coup by providing intelligence material to its architects.

Prior to the coup, tension between the President and army traditionalists had been rising for some months. A videotape broadcast on television on 31 January, which purported to show Venezuelan army units operating in Colombia in support of Colombian FARC rebels, had been dismissed by Rincón as propaganda. The mission, he said, had been approved by the Colombian government in order to secure the release of a kidnapped Venezuelan. The tension had increased further when, on 18 February, a senior naval officer, Rear Adml Carlos Molina Tamayo, publicly accused the President of trying to impose a left-wing tyranny. He called upon him to resign or face impeachment. Like many other senior officers, Molina argued that in cultivating relations with Cuba and Iraq, Chávez—who was chosen as president of the Group of 77 in New York on 11 January—was damaging Venezuela's relations with the USA. Relations between the USA and Venezuela, the fourth largest oil exporter in the world, had been soured in recent years by the Venezuelan government's willingness to cut oil production to comply with OPEC production quotas (thus raising oil prices), and the increasing of taxes in the hydrocarbons sector, as well as by Chávez's disapproval of current US foreign policy, describing it as "fighting terror with terror". Nevertheless, Chávez's removal was not welcomed by the lower and middle ranks of the armed forces, who—like many members of the industrial and agricultural working classes—tended to sympathise with the President's "Bolivarian revolution", which had emphasised, although not necessarily delivered, land reform and redistributive social policies.

Clashes between the President's supporters and an informal alliance of business and labour interests had become increasingly violent. The choice on 24 January of Diosdado Cabello as Vice President and Capt. (retd) Ramón Rodríguez Chacón as Minister of Interior in succession to Luis Miquilena had followed a similar pro-business demonstration, and was itself followed by the decision to confine land redistribution to state-owned land for the time being at least. On 24 February Finance Minister Nelson Merentes had been replaced by Gen. Francisco Ursón. Six days previously, in response to protests by workers' organisations, the government had allowed the bolivar to float, whereupon it fell by some 15 per cent against the US dollar in two weeks. This in turn had led to further protests and a one-day general strike on 20 March, accompanied by looting and violence in Barquisimeto and Valera as well as in the capital. The situation had been worsened by a partial strike of the managers of the state oil monopoly, Petroleos de Venezuela (PDVSA), backed by the unions, who were angered by the terms of the November 2001 hydrocarbons law and the imposition of political appointees on the Board of Directors. Then, after weeks of anti-government strikes and protests, an indefinite national general strike had been called, extending a national strike which had begun on 9 April.

Following the overthrow of Chávez, interim President Carmona appointed a right-wing Cabinet headed by Foreign Minister José Rodríguez Iturbe, a member of the secretive conservative Roman Catholic organisation, Opus Dei. Carmona also ended the general strike, but issued a series of decrees which, by dissolving both the National Assembly (the legislature) and the Supreme Court, and suspending the constitution (which had been approved by referendum in December 1999), cast considerable doubt upon his democratic credentials. As it turned out, the new regime was short-lived. Prior to the coup it appeared that the secretary general of OPEC, Ali Rodríguez Araque, had given Chávez advance warning of the conspiracy to overthrow him. As a result, several hundred pro-Chávez members of the armed forces, led by José Raúl Baduel, had been placed in readiness and were able to come to the aid of the deposed President. With the coup faltering, Carmona was forced to recall the National Assembly on 13 April, but it immediately appointed Diosdado Cabello, who had served as Vice President under Chávez, as President in place of Carmona. Chávez then returned to the Miraflores presidential palace at about 2.50 am on April 14, whereupon Cabello returned the presidency to him in a televised ceremony. Carmona fled the country on 29 May and was granted political asylum in Colombia; while Rear Adml Molina Tamayo was given political asylum in El Salvador. By contrast Rodríguez was appointed head of the Venezuelan state oil monopoly, PDVSA. In the USA President Bush found it hard to conceal his disappointment at the turn of events, stating bitterly that he hoped that Chávez had "learned his lesson" from the events.

Although Chávez did not engage in widespread reprisals, personnel changes inevitably followed the coup. Cabello was quickly replaced by Defence Minister José Vicente Rangel and then, in a Cabinet reshuffle on 5 May, he himself replaced Ramón Rodríguez Chacín in the key post of Minister of Interior. Rincón was excused on the grounds that he had been "confused" during the coup attempt, and was appointed Defence Minister in place of Rangel, although he then retired in July and was replaced by Gen. (retd) José Luis Prieto. Felipe Pérez succeeded Jorge Giordiani as Planning Minister, and Tobías Nóbrega was appointed Economy Minister, a post which had been held by Jesús Bermúdez on an acting basis since April. Nóbrega quickly announced a further cut in the 2002 budget package, including an increase in IVA value added tax from 14.5 per cent to 16 per cent, a move approved by the National Assembly in August.

Despite Chávez's triumphant return, tension remained high, and mass demonstrations continued to destabilise the regime. A number of public figures, together with US Secretary of State Colin Powell, urged both government and opposition to accept meditation from the Organisation of American States (OAS). On the advice of former US President Jimmy Carter, on 16 June Chávez did agree to receive an OAS mission and offered to hold a referendum in August 2003, the earliest date provided for in the constitution, on whether or not he should continue in office.

Surprisingly, on 14 August the Supreme Court ruled that there was insufficient evidence to proceed with charges of rebellion against four senior military officers who had taken part in the coup. This led to further clashes in the streets of Caracas between police and supporters of the President, who demanded that Congress begin impeachment proceedings against the judges. In September security zones were established in the capital after disaffected elements in the armed forces had called for a another coup; some 12 officers were arrested as a result.

The opposition rejected the President's offer of a referendum and demanded immediate elections. On 21 October the Venezuelan Federation and Association of Chambers of Commerce and Industry (Fedecameras) held a one-day strike, and the following day a group of 14 senior military officers, led by Gen. Enrique Medina Gómez, established a camp in Plaza Altamira (a square in a suburb of Caracas), proclaimed themselves in "legitimate rebellion", and called for a campaign of civil disobedience in their support. They were speedily joined by thousands of anti-government demonstrators. After more than a month of demonstrations and counter-demonstrations, oil workers in alliance with Fedecameras went on strike on 1 December and speedily brought petroleum production to a near standstill, costing the government and the country billions of dollars in lost revenue. The President, however, refused to yield to their unconstitutional demands, dismissed executives of PDVSA and ordered troops to move oil tankers. A frustrated opposition on 30 December threatened a tax strike. Thus, although the crisis had helped force up the world price of crude oil to over $30 a barrel, the stand-off continued unresolved at the year's end.

V MIDDLE EAST AND NORTH AFRICA

1. ISRAEL

CAPITAL: Jerusalem   AREA: 21,000 sq km   POPULATION: 6,400,000
OFFICIAL LANGUAGE: Hebrew   POLITICAL SYSTEM: multiparty republic
HEAD OF STATE: President Moshe Katzav (since July '00)
RULING PARTIES: Likud-led coalition
HEAD OF GOVERNMENT: Ariel Sharon (Likud), Prime Minister (since March '01)
CURRENCY: shekel (end-'02 £1=Sh7.6747, US$1=Sh4.7920)
GNI PER CAPITA: US$19,320 at PPP ('00)

FOR Israel 2002 was marked by an unprecedented escalating spiral of violence as the government of Prime Minister Ariel Sharon resorted to increasingly brutal military methods to try and halt Palestinian attacks on Israeli targets on both sides of the "green line" separating the Jewish state from the Palestinian territories. During the first months of the year Palestinian militants carried out frequent suicide bomb attacks on Israeli civilian and military targets and Israel responded by launching heavy military strikes on Palestinian targets, killing large numbers of people and causing widespread destruction. Despite limited diplomatic intervention by the USA and EU, the two sides failed to agree on the terms of a ceasefire and by the end of March Israeli forces had laid siege to the beleaguered Palestinian leader, Yassir Arafat, in his Ramallah compound, the mukaata. During April, Israel carried out a massive military offensive—"Operation Defensive Shield"— in the West Bank, occupying all major Palestinian-controlled towns with the exception of Jericho in the Jordan Valley. The Sharon government claimed that the campaign was aimed at halting Palestinian suicide bombers who had wreaked havoc in Israel during March, killing large numbers of civilians. (In the most brutal attack, at the end of the month a Hamas bomber blew himself up in a hotel dining room in the Israeli coastal resort of Netanya as guests gathered for a Passover Sedar, the ritual evening meal ushering in the Jewish holiday. At least 22 people died in the attack and more than 100 were wounded, making it the deadliest attack on Israel since the start of the Intifada.) Israel insisted that the sole purpose of "Operation Defensive Shield" was to prevent such terrorist outrages and uproot the terrorist infrastructure. Accordingly, the army's main tactic was to carry out house-to-house searches designed to round up radical Palestinians and militant leaders. However, in the refugee camp in Jenin the army met stiff resistance from Palestinian militiamen (losing 13 men in one elaborate ambush) and the destruction caused by Israel's response led to allegations of a massacre. A UN attempt to send a fact-finding mission to Jenin to investigate allegations of an Israeli massacre failed to materialise because of Israeli obstruction.

Many Arabs believed that Sharon had launched "Operation Defensive Shield" in order to destroy Arafat and his Palestine National Authority (PNA) and impose a settlement that fell well short of Palestinian aspirations for statehood. However, the high Palestinian death toll and the apparently wanton destruction wrought by the operation served only to increase the willingness of young volunteers— including a growing number of women—to die for the Palestinian cause. This view was grimly vindicated by the fact that there were at least two major suicide bomb attacks against Israeli civilian targets during the course of "Operation Defensive Shield", and that such attacks continued with depressing regularity throughout the year. Israel declared its offensive over in late April, but its forces remained around Arafat's compound and the Church of the Nativity in Bethlehem until May. Troops were also stationed on the outskirts of key Palestinian towns and cities and, throughout the remainder of the year, they continued to mount frequent incursions into Palestinian territory to capture and detain "terrorist" suspects, thereby effectively taking over the PNA's security role.

Israel also continued to target key Palestinian militants for assassination, including, in late July, Salah Shihada, the leader of the military wing of Hamas, who was blown to pieces along with nine children when a large bomb was dropped into a densely populated area of Gaza City. The carnage caused by the attack led even the US government, traditionally a source of unconditional support for Israel, to criticise the attack as a "heavy-handed action". Nonetheless, US President George W. Bush had in late June lined up firmly behind Sharon when he delivered a much-anticipated speech on the Middle East in which he effectively called for the removal of Arafat as a necessary precursor to Palestinian statehood. The Israeli army staged one of its biggest raids into the Gaza Strip in late September, killing nine Palestinians, all but three of them civilians. The assault followed criticism of Sharon in the Israeli press for focusing retaliation for recent suicide bomb attacks on Arafat, rather than on the Gaza-based Hamas, which had claimed responsibility for many of the attacks. There was further bloodshed in Gaza in early October when an Israeli helicopter gunship fired a rocket into a crowd in Khan Yunis, killing 15 people. Inevitably, the Palestinians responded with a suicide bomb attack a few weeks later, targeting a bus full of soldiers near the northern city of Hadera. The year ended, as it had started, with both sides engaged in a relentless and bloody cycle of "tit-for-tat" attacks. Ten Palestinians were killed when Israeli troops backed by tanks and helicopter gunships swept into the Bureij refugee camp in the Gaza Strip in early December, sparking a three-hour gun battle. At the end of the month two members of Islamic Jihad slipped into a Jewish settlement near Mount Hebron and shot dead four Israelis.

As the year drew to a close the government and people of Israel also had to deal with the growing likelihood of a US-led war on Iraq and the role of Israel in any such conflict. During the 1991 Gulf War, the government of Yitzhak Shamir had bowed to pressure from the USA not to retaliate after Iraqi Scud missiles fell on Israel, for fear it would weaken the support of Arab governments for the war. It was far from certain that a government led by Sharon would prove to be as compliant and, accordingly, the USA made great efforts to make Israel feel protected. In October US officials were reported to have told Sharon that Special Operations Forces would be deployed in the western Iraqi desert at the start of any conflict to destroy facilities that could be used to launch missiles at Israeli targets. By the end of the year Israel had also deployed the Arrow missile defence system to protect major population centres against Iraqi missile attack. The Arrow system, which cost more than US$2 billion and was partly financed by the USA, was designed to avoid the pitfalls of the US Patriot system, which had proved largely ineffective in stopping Iraqi Scud missile attacks in 1991. Furthermore, Israeli officials confirmed in December that more than 15,000 soldiers and public health workers had been vaccinated against smallpox under a crash programme designed to protect the country from a possible Iraqi attack with smallpox or other biological weapons. As a result of the programme, thousands of Israeli public health officials were prepared to immunise the entire country against the smallpox virus within four days should a single smallpox case be diagnosed anywhere in the world.

Domestically, the major story of the year was the collapse of Sharon's Likud-led "national unity" government in late October when the Labour Party withdrew from the 19-month old coalition in a dispute over the 2003 budget. Labour pulled out of the coalition after it had opposed the allocation of funds to Jewish settlements in the West Bank and Gaza Strip, arguing that the funds should be diverted to social welfare programmes. The withdrawal of Labour gave Sharon control of only 55 seats in the 120-seat Knesset and in early November the Prime Minister abandoned plans to build a working majority through the inclusion of extreme right-wing parties, and instead called a general election to take place in late January 2003. Intriguingly, prior to announcing the elections, Sharon had brought his main political rival, former (Likud) Prime Minister Binyamin Netanyahu (1996-99), into the Cabinet as the new Foreign Minister to replace the veteran Labour "dove", Shimon Peres. The appointment of Netanyahu, and the earlier appointment of Lt-Gen. Shaul Mofaz, the recently retired chief of staff, as Defence Minister in place of Labour leader Binyamin Ben-Eliezer, reinforced the new government's sharp drift to the right. Netanyahu, in particular, had repeatedly attacked Sharon's failure to halt Palestinian attacks on Israeli targets. Within hours of his appointment, Netanyahu renounced the possibility of an independent Palestinian state, backed the expansion of Jewish settlements in the occupied territories and threatened to expel Arafat from the West Bank. However, Netanyahu's attempt to outflank Sharon on the right failed miserably when the latter swept to an easy victory in Likud party leadership elections held in late November. After his defeat Netanyahu promised to work alongside the Prime Minister to ensure a Likud victory in the forthcoming elections.

The Labour Party changed leadership ahead of the elections, ditching Ben-Eliezer (who had only replaced former Prime Minister Ehud Barak in late 2001) for Maj.-Gen. (retd) Avraham Mitzna in mid-November. Mitzna was a dovish former head of the army's central command and he promised to take Labour into the elections on a radical peace agenda, promising to order an immediate unilateral Israeli withdrawal from the Gaza Strip and the dismantling of settlements within the strip. If renewed peace talks with the Palestinians failed, he said that he would order a similar withdrawal from much, but not all, of the West Bank and dismantle many, but again, not all, of the settlements there. Opinion polls indicated that Israelis were strongly opposed to Mitzna's radical approach and would support another term for Sharon, despite the launch in mid-December of a police investigation into potentially damaging allegations of corruption within the Likud. The inquiry focused on allegations of vote-buying, bribery, and the possible involvement of criminal elements in the recent Likud primary elections. Among those tainted by the scandal was Sharon's son, Omri Sharon, who had been selected as a Likud candidate for the forthcoming elections. Despite continued widespread support for Sharon, a vocal minority opposed his government's hardline policies towards the Palestinians, including a group of over 500 reservist soldiers (Courage to Refuse) who drew up a much-publicised petition opposing Israel's military presence in the West Bank and Gaza Strip. The reservists lost their challenge to avoid serving in the occupied territories when the Supreme Court ruled in late December that they did not have the right to decide where they would serve.

The dire security situation and the continued fallout from the events of 11 September 2001 continued to have a critical impact on the Israeli economy during 2002. The Intifada was believed to have played a major role in plunging Israel into its worst recession for 25 years. Foreign investment and tourism had virtually collapsed, whilst unemployment had risen to the 10 per cent mark and the shekel was losing value by the month. The bursting of the so-called "dotcom bubble" had further compounded the crisis by damaging the hi-tech industries, the engine of Israel's growth. Reports late in the year indicated that the government was pressing the USA for billions of dollars of emergency aid to shore up the ailing economy.

2. PALESTINE AND THE ARAB WORLD—EGYPT— JORDAN—SYRIA—LEBANON—IRAQ

i. PALESTINE AND THE ARAB WORLD

THE economic, security, and political situation in Palestine continued to worsen in 2002, as it had ever since the beginning of the "al-Aqsa" Intifada in 2000 (see AR 2000, p. 198). Once again the Palestinians, both the leadership and the wider population, had to bear the cost of suicide bombing and the brutality of the Israeli military machine.

While the Israeli leadership had already attempted to condemn Palestinian President Yassir Arafat to the dustbin of history and had moved the Israeli army into Palestinian towns and territories, it remained unprepared to offer any insights into its long-term thinking about Israeli-Palestinian relations and the final status talks with the Palestinians. Despite conceding that there may emerge a Palestinian state "some time in the future", Prime Minister Ariel Sharon gave no signs at the beginning of the year that his government was prepared to countenance any such development. By the end of the year he was too involved in electioneering and domestic political matters to give any value to a peace initiative, thus condemning the stalemate to continue into 2003.

The Palestinian leadership was increasingly marginalised during the year as the unwillingness of Israel to make any concessions towards peace eroded its authority over the Palestinian population. This was exacerbated by the wanton destruction of Israel's military operations which, by the middle of the year, had effectively destroyed the coercive and administrative machinery of the Palestinian National Authority (PNA) and thereby rendered it incapable of dealing with its internal security problems. The combined effect of this was to create greater moral legitimacy as well as logistical freedom for militant activity.

The grim cycle of violence and counter-violence—involving Palestinian suicide bombings and guerrilla attacks upon military and civilian targets; and Israeli incursions into PNA territories, assassinations, and collective punishments—increased significantly in March. In that month alone, Palestinian suicide bombers and gunmen were responsible for over 120 Israeli deaths and many more serious injuries, and Israel responded with heavy military strikes against Palestinian targets, which killed even greater numbers. With the security situation sliding out of control, on 1 April Sharon launched "Operation Defensive Shield", the largest Israeli offensive since its invasion of Lebanon in 1982, which saw the Israeli army effectively reoccupy the territories hitherto administered by the PNA. The most intensive parts of the military operation lasted for three weeks, and climaxed in Jenin's main refugee camp, where not only was severe damage inflicted on Palestinian-owned property but several hundred Palestinians may have also been killed. The full extent of the casualties will probably never been known for Israel refused to allow journalists access to the camp during the operation or, following its conclusion, to co-operate with a UN enquiry into the events which had occurred in Jenin. Israel's refusal increased speculation that its forces had engaged in a massacre in the camp. Although by late April Israeli forces had pulled back from Palestinian towns, they remained in control of the transportation, communication, and the economic and environmental infrastructure of the Palestinian territories. Israeli armour remained stationed on the outskirts of the major Palestinian urban centres; and the hearts of towns and cities such as Bethlehem, Gaza, Nablus, Jenin, Ramallah, and Birzeit remained but a tank shell away from the reach of the Israeli army.

The backdrop to this violent convulsion was a spate of intensive diplomatic activity which culminated in the 27-28 March Arab League summit in Beirut—the first time that the League had visited Lebanon since that country's civil war—at which Saudi Arabia launched a major peace initiative endorsed by virtually all Arab states (see XI.6.i). The plan was based upon the formula of a two-state solution, with Israel withdrawing from the territories occupied since 1967, in return for peace and the normalisation of diplomatic relations with the Arab world. In a keynote speech on the Middle East on 4 April, US President George W. Bush described the peace plan as "promising" and "hopeful, because it acknowledges Israel's right to exist". The plan, however, was doomed to fail for on the day that Crown Prince Abdullah delivered it to the Arab League, a Hamas suicide bomber killed 22 Israeli guests at a Passover dinner reception at a hotel in Netanya. The Israeli public was outraged and endorsed the Prime Minister's response, which came 24 hours after the Arab leaders had signed up in support of the Abdullah peace initiative. Israeli tanks smashed their way into Arafat's compound in Ramallah and occupied all but a small section of the complex, effectively imprisoning the Palestinian leader. The Arab world interpreted Sharon's actions as a clear rejection of Prince Abdullah's peace plan.

Israel's actions did not improve its security. Indeed, the high Palestinian death toll and the wanton destruction wrought by "Operation Defensive Shield" convinced many that it would serve only to increase the willingness of young volunteers to sacrifice their lives for the cause of Palestinian freedom and statehood. This view was grimly vindicated by the fact that there were at least two major suicide bomb attacks against Israeli civilian targets during the course of the Israeli operation. Israel's actions also did nothing to improve its image in the Arab world, as the public and officials reacted to the military offensive with utter outrage. From Morocco to Yemen, huge pro-Palestinian rallies were organised, all demanding an Arab response. These came swiftly, but were varied: Yemen called for an emergency Arab summit in order for the Arab states "to formulate an appropriate response"; Iraq introduced an oil embargo for a month to deprive the West of this vital resource; King Mohammed VI of Morocco greeted the US Secretary of State Colin Powell on 8 April with a badge bearing the words "We are all Palestinians"; Libya urged the frontline Arab states to allow volunteers to enter Israel/Palestine and fight alongside the Palestinian militia; several thousand people took to the usually quiet streets of all the major Gulf Arab cities; and, in Egypt, President Mohammed Hosni Mubarak announced that his country was halting all government-to-government contacts with Israel.

While Palestine burned during April, key members of Western governments were galvanised by the Abdullah Plan and by the sheer magnitude of the violence in the region. Bush's speech led to a new round of diplomatic activity, the highlights of which were a summit with UK Prime Minister Tony Blair in Texas on 7 April and a visit to the Middle East by US Secretary of State Colin Powell. Starting his trip with a visit to Morocco on 8 April, Powell went on to Egypt, Spain, and Jordan, before finally arriving in Israel on 12 April. Powell was looking to prepare the ground for new peace talks and for a way of kick-starting the stalled dialogue. The message given to him in every Arab capital, however, was that so long as the violence against the Palestinian population continued, the Arab side would not be able to deliver state-to-state level contact with the Israeli government. Furthermore, with large demonstrations and rallies in so many Arab countries in early April, Powell had already got a taste of Arab reactions even before arriving in Israel. His arrival was greeted with two suicide bomb attacks in Haifa and Jerusalem which killed 14 people. Any hope of a compromise which he might still have harboured after visiting the Arab capitals must surely have evaporated on the evening of 13 April. Despite several meetings with Sharon during his stay, a three-hour long meeting with Arafat in his besieged headquarters in Ramallah on 14 April, and flying visits to Syria, Lebanon, and Egypt, Powell left the region on 17 April without having achieved any tangible results, and with the Israeli offensive still in progress. Although Sharon had supported the convening of a new US-hosted international peace conference with all the parties (bar Arafat himself), lack of serious commitment from Israel and its Arab counterparts meant that Powell failed to secure an immediate Israeli ceasefire or a timetable for the withdrawal of Israeli armour from Palestinian territories.

The violence continued during the remainder of the year, and there were further Israeli incursions into PNA territory. Having failed to stop the suicide bombings, the Israelis began the construction of a security barrier around the West Bank in an effort to prevent suicide attackers from gaining access to Israel. On the diplomatic front, in June Bush declined to support a proposal by Egyptian President Mubarak for the declaration of a Palestinian state in 2003, saying that the USA was "not ready to lay down a specific calendar". Shortly afterwards Sharon travelled to Washington, DC where Bush endorsed his demand that the Palestinian leadership be overhauled before meaningful peace talks could resume. Such reforms were already underway: on 9 June Arafat reshuffled and pared down his Cabinet, and later in the month it was confirmed that presidential and legislative elections would take place in January 2003 and that constitutional reforms were under discussion for the creation of a post of Prime Minister which would, in effect, limit Arafat's powers as President.

In September Israeli forces once again surrounded Arafat's headquarters but, as with Israel's earlier siege, the effect was to increase the standing of Arafat and, thereby, to undermine the reformists within the PNA. After the siege was lifted, Arafat emerged triumphant having persuaded his dominant Fatah movement to shelve plans for the appointment of a Prime Minister until statehood had been achieved. In December the planned elections were also postponed, on the grounds that it was impossible to go ahead with the poll while Israeli forces continued to occupy West Bank towns. Meanwhile the killing continued and the international community, particularly the USA, seemed too fixated on the growing crisis with Iraq to give any new impetus to the stalled peace process.

ii. EGYPT

CAPITAL: Cairo AREA: 1,001,000 sq km POPULATION: 65,200,000
OFFICIAL LANGUAGE: Arabic POLITICAL SYSTEM: multiparty republic
HEAD OF STATE AND GOVERNMENT: President Mohammed Hosni Mubarak (since '81)
RULING PARTY: National Democratic Party (NDP)
PRIME MINISTER: Atif Mohammed al Ubayd (since Oct '99)
MAIN IGO MEMBERSHIPS (NON-UN): AL, OAPEC, AU, COMESA, OIC, NAM, Francophonie
CURRENCY: Egyptian pound (end-'02 £1=E£7.4192, US$1=E£4.6325)
GNI PER CAPITA: US$1,530, US$3,790 at PPP ('01)

IN Egypt four issues continued to dominate the agenda: Palestine-Israel, Iraq, the consequences of the 11 September attacks, and the struggle against homegrown Islamists. The year got off to a good start as Egypt geared up for the technical negotiations in its vitally important association agreement with the EU. Although in its November 2001 declaration the European Parliament had imposed some conditions on the proposed agreement, largely concerning human rights and political freedoms in Egypt, it was clear that the main focus of EU and Egyptian negotiators would remain the economic dimensions of the association. Egypt was keen to secure easier access to the markets of its most important trading partner, as well as gaining access to badly needed EU funds. The EU, on the other hand, recognised that with the association agreement in place it would be much better placed to guide the Egyptian economy towards reform and to encourage democratisation.

Domestically, too, the government was delighted to be able to inflict serious reverses on its domestic Islamists, which it did through the trial of 94 militants by a military tribunal. In January the idea of a ceasefire had already taken shape and the jailed leaders of the Gema'a movement were stating that armed struggle against the government was bad for Muslims. In June several Islamist leaders again repeated this line to the press. They repented for past deeds and said that the armed struggle was behind them. The government's ability to split the Gema'a leadership so fundamentally was seen by many in Egypt as a major breakthrough for President Mohammed Hosni Mubarak's fight against radical Islam. The next target of the government was the Muslim Brotherhood, several of whose members were arrested in the summer months of 2002 and given fairly stiff prison sentences for public unrest and state security offences. On 21 July, 34 members of the Muslim Brotherhood were arrested for holding a meeting in a private house. In September a total of 51 alleged members of the al-Wa'ad organisation were sentenced to between two and 15 year terms in prison for allegedly plotting to assassinate Mubarak.

At the same time, however, the government was careful not to alienate conservative forces in society and, while jailing Islamist leaders, it also clamped down hard on homosexual conduct, corruption, and other "immoralities". To prove its point, 52 gay men on board a boat were charged with "habitual debauchery"; and several cases of corruption amongst high officials were exposed. Thus, on 18 July the former head of the state-owned Nasr Castings Company went on trial for corruption.

Taking comfort in the tough new anti-terrorism legislation introduced in the UK and the USA in 2001, Mubarak reminded his compatriots that Egypt's "resolute" line on Islamic terrorists had been not only justified but also necessary in view of the threats that such groups posed to domestic and international security. In his implementation of anti-terror measures Mubarak was confident of US support, but he also badly needed a substantial injection of hard currency to alleviate the catastrophic impact that the 11 September attacks had wrought upon tourism, the country's main foreign exchange earner. The Bush administration's promise of nearly US$1 billion at the beginning of the year provided urgent relief and encouraged other potential donors to adopt a conciliatory posture towards Egypt. Thus, by the year's end, Egypt had promises of over US$10 billion in economic aid or grants from Arab and non-Arab sources. Representatives of 34 donor countries met in Sharm al-Shaykh in early February to pledge some US$10.3 billion in economic assistance over a three-year period starting in 2002.

Despite the government's gallant efforts to continue with the liberalisation of the economy, encourage exports, and reduce nonessential imports, the ongoing Palestinian-Israeli conflict and the prospects of a major war in Iraq could not help but pressurise the Egyptian economy which was still in recovery mode from the aftermath of 11 September. These regional tensions did, however, provide much diplomatic trade for the Egyptian government. Until April, when the government severed any meaningful contact with Israel in response to the Israeli army's reoccupation of Palestinian territories (see V.2.i), the Egyptian government found itself at the heart of mediation efforts between the Palestinians and the Israeli government.

The precarious nature of politics in Egypt was demonstrated by public reaction to the country's worst train disaster in February. The tragedy, caused by an on-board fire on a decrepit inter-city train, left many hundreds of people dead (the official death toll was put at 373) and countless others injured. As news of the accident in the third class carriages—which by all accounts could have been prevented had the train been fitted with some elementary safety features— spread, so anti-government demonstrations spread throughout Upper Egypt and days of violence followed. At the mass burial of the victims at Cairo's Martyrs' Cemetery many hundreds of locals gathered to mourn the dead and to vent their anger at the indifference of their "corrupt and uncaring government". As the scale of the tragedy unfolded and public anger deepened, Mubarak appeared on national television promising action: "We will permit no attempt to hide the truth or even a part of the truth because the lives of our citizens are more important than our own". The tragedy resulted in several resignations, including that of the Transportation Minister, Ibrahim al-Dumayri, and the head of the state-owned railways, Ahmad al-Sharif.

Egypt's religious politics fell victim to the "war on terrorism" as the country's top two religious figures, the Grand Mufti, Shaykh Nasser Farid Wasel and his al-Azhar counterpart, Shaykh Mohammed Seyyed Tantawi, publicly fought a battle over when a suicide bombing could be deemed acceptable by Islam. The former, who was junior to the al-Azhar sheikh, had announced that civilian targets were legitimate so long as the aim was the liberation of one's country. Tantawi publicly contradicted this edict in March and declared that it was only legitimate for a Muslim to carry out such acts of suicide if one was attacking military targets. By Tantawi's pronouncement, Hamas and Islamic Jihad suicide bombing attacks against Israeli civilians were contrary to Islam and, therefore, condemnable. If it had to choose between them, the government would have preferred to accept the latter fatwa, but its official position was that any attack on innocent civilians was unacceptable and divorced from religion. Nonetheless, the fact that Egypt's most senior religious figures did not condemn suicide bombings outright did create some difficulties for the government which had declared itself an ally in the USA's "war on terrorism". Wasel's replacement in March may have been a result of behind-the-scenes pressure from outside as well as the government's own decision to act swiftly in order to bring to an end the career of one who had proved to be a maverick Mufti on the occasion of his reaching retirement age.

The discussions about Palestinian suicide bombings were still raging in Egypt when Israel's April offensive against the Palestinians began. The public was shocked by what it saw on television and massive street demonstrations followed. The government again found itself in an unenviable position: condemning Israel's actions while having to use force against its own people demonstrating in support of the Palestinians; not preventing inflammatory coverage of the crisis in Palestine, while blocking its own Islamists from capitalising on street protests to foment dissent and mobilise mass support for the Palestinian Islamist organisations such as Hamas and Islamic Jihad. It was not hard for cheerleaders to draw parallels between Israel's treatment of "heroic Palestinian living martyrs" and their own government's brutal suppression of Islamic activists for supporting the Palestinian cause. In view of public anger, the President could not afford not to be patriotic and pro-Arab, but at the same time he could even less afford to incur the wrath of the USA by being seen to endorse suicide bombings.

In the tense climate which followed April's violence in the Occupied Territories, the regime's impotence in not being able to assist the Palestinians in their hour of need further undermined its legitimacy. The Islamists repeatedly made the case that not only did the regime not represent the Egyptian people, for it was attacking them for supporting the Palestinian cause, but it was also an impediment to the realisation of Palestinian aspirations. Mubarak's ultimate response was to play down the suppression of demonstrations at home, and focus on the resurrection of his traditional mediatory role in the conflict. At the same time, however, he had little option but to allow public anger to be vented against Israel and its backer, the USA. However, demands for military action to defend the Palestinians were summarily dismissed.

The year also saw Egypt begin to discuss the thorny issue of President Mubarak's successor. On the one hand, his son Gamal Mubarak, continued to rise through the ruling party's ranks, and on the other the local press began increasingly to highlight the national and foreign policy influence of the country's General Intelligence director, Omar Sulayman. This gave rise to some speculation that Sulayman was being "groomed" for the succession. Mubarak, who had pointedly refused to appoint a Vice President, gave no indication of his views on the subject.

Succession was also an issue for the Muslim Brotherhood. The death of Mustafa Mashhur in October provided the opportunity for one of modern Egypt's oldest political movements to repackage itself as a new force. The appointment of Ma'mun al-Hudaybi, the son of the movement's founder, to lead the Brotherhood, however, signalled that it, too, did not have the appetite for root and branch reform. In this at least the government and its main opposition force were united.

iii. JORDAN

CAPITAL: Amman   AREA: 89,000 sq km   POPULATION: 5,000,000
OFFICIAL LANGUAGE: Arabic   POLITICAL SYSTEM: multiparty monarchy
HEAD OF STATE: King Abdullah ibn al-Husain (since Feb '99)
PRIME MINISTER: Ali Abu al-Rageb (since June '00)
MAIN IGO MEMBERSHIPS (NON-UN): AL, OIC, NAM
CURRENCY: Jordanian dinar (end-'02 £1=JD1.1363, US$1=JD0.7095)
GNI PER CAPITA: US$1,750, US$4,080 at PPP ('01)

IN a televised address to the nation in mid-August, King Abdullah announced that legislative elections due to have been held in late 2002 had been postponed until the spring of 2003. The King said that "difficult regional circumstances"—an oblique reference to the intractable and bloody Israeli-Palestinian conflict and the looming showdown between the USA and Iraq—had dictated the postponement. The legislature had been dissolved in June 2001 (see AR 2001, p. 227), and although no official date had been set, some Jordanians had expected elections to be held in November 2002. However, the postponement of the elections came as little surprise given the government's inevitable concentration on matters of security in the aftermath of the events of 11 September 2001.

A car bomb exploded in Amman (the capital) in late February, killing two bystanders. The bomb had been placed in a car belonging to the wife of Lt-Col Ali Burjak, leader of the country's Anti-Terrorism Unit. Commentators linked the blast to the government's crackdown on Islamist militants, which had picked up pace after the 11 September attacks on the USA. Reports in July claimed that the authorities had recently foiled a fresh plot to attack US and Israeli interests in the country. The attacks were reportedly averted after 10 Jordanians armed with weapons and explosives were arrested between April and June in raids in and around Amman. Government concern over an Islamist backlash against its support for the US "war on terrorism" became more intense when Lawrence Foley, a senior US diplomat, was shot dead by an unidentified gunman outside his home in Amman in late October. Foley was killed at a time of rising anti-US sentiment in the region over perceived US bias toward Israel and the threat of military action against Iraq. An unconfirmed claim of responsibility for the killing came from a group calling itself the Honourable Men of Jordan. Foley's assassination was the first ever of a Western official in Jordan. The security forces responded by rounding up scores of political activists, including many from fringe Islamic groups and Jordanians who had returned from Afghanistan after the fall of the Taliban regime in late 2001. Eventually, in mid-December, the authorities announced the arrest of two members of Osama bin Laden's al-Qaida organisation in connection with the Foley killing. The government claimed that the two suspects, a Jordanian and a Libyan, had both been trained in al-Qaida camps in Afghanistan and had received their orders from a Jordanian fugitive and senior al-Qaida member, Fadel Nazzal Khalayla (also known as Abu Misab Zarqawi), who in 2000 had been sentenced in absentia to 15 years' imprisonment on charges of recruiting militants and plotting a series of attacks on foreign tourists during Millennium celebrations.

Once again the southern Jordanian town of Maan was at the centre of Islamist- and pro-Iraqi-led protest against the government. Maan had also been the scene of serious rioting and unrest in 1989 and 1996 and, more recently, demonstrations in the city in support of Iraq had repeatedly spiralled into rioting. Serious unrest had erupted in the city in late January in protest at the alleged police torture of a youth who later died. One police officer died in the rioting and 11 others were injured. In November the security forces stormed the city in what proved to be a failed attempt to arrest a local Islamist preacher, Mohammed Shalabi (also known as Abu Sayyaf). The government denied reports that the attempted arrest of Abu Sayyaf was related to the Foley assassination or was a crackdown on Islamist activists. Instead, the authorities said that Abu Sayyaf was wanted in connection with the January riots and insisted that he led a gang of outlaws wanted for armed robbery and drugs and arms trafficking. During a week-long security operation three civilians and two police officers were killed, dozens of "armed gang members" arrested, and large volumes of weaponry seized. However, when most of the police units, which had been joined by military ones, pulled out of the city, the authorities had failed to apprehend Abu Sayyaf and his close supporters.

Tujan Faysal, the only woman ever elected to the House of Representatives (the lower house of the Jordanian legislature), was sentenced to 18 months' imprisonment in May after being convicted on four counts of seditious libel. The court ruled that Faysal, who had sat in the House from 1993 to 1997, had made statements and published articles containing false accusations considered "beyond the boundaries of criticism". Faysal had criticised Jordanian policy towards Iraq and had also accused Prime Minister Ali Abu al-Ragheb of seeking personal gains by doubling vehicle insurance premiums and amending the Income Tax Law. Faisal was pardoned by King Abdullah in late June after serving some five weeks of her sentence.

King Abdullah carried out a Cabinet reshuffle in mid-January. The surprise reshuffle came only a day after the government had passed a 2.35 billion dinar budget for 2002 that aimed to reduce the budget deficit and help combat poverty and unemployment. Prime Minister Rageb left his economic and financial team intact. The main changes were the appointment of Qaftan Majali, hitherto secretary general of the Ministry of Interior, as the new Interior Minister in place of Awad Khulayfat; and of Marwan Muasher as the new Minister of Foreign Affairs, replacing Abdul Illah al-Khatib. Muasher had served as Information Minister (1996) and as Jordan's (first) ambassador to Israel (1995) and as ambassador to the USA (1997-2002).

Jordan's economy, already suffering from the fall in tourism caused by the escalating military conflict in the West Bank, suffered further as the prospect of a US-led war on Iraq increased. In October it was reported that the USA had announced a further US$85 million grant to Jordan, in a move designed to shore up its alliance with the kingdom ahead of a prospective strike on Iraq. Jordanian ministers said that all but US$10 million would be allocated to augment hard currency reserves, providing a vital cushion against the economic fallout of an Iraqi war. In July the IMF had approved a two-year standby credit for SDR 85.28 million for Jordan in support of its economic programme.

Field Marshal Sharid Zaid ibn Shaker, who served as Prime Minister under King Hussein in 1989, 1991, and 1995-96, died in August (see XVIII).

iv. SYRIA

CAPITAL: Damascus   AREA: 185,000 sq km   POPULATION: 16,600,000
OFFICIAL LANGUAGE: Arabic   POLITICAL SYSTEM: multiparty republic
HEAD OF STATE AND GOVERNMENT: President Bashar al-Assad (since July '00)
RULING PARTY: Baath Arab Socialist Party
PRIME MINISTER: Mohammed Mustafa Mero, since March '00
MAIN IGO MEMBERSHIPS (NON-UN): AL, OAPEC, OIC, NAM
CURRENCY: Syrian pound (end-'02 £1=S£82.6000, US$1=S£51.5750)
GNI PER CAPITA: US$1,000, US$3,440 at PPP ('01)

SYRIA'S election in October 2001 to the UN Security Council as a non-permanent member ensured that the country maintained a relatively high profile on the international stage throughout 2002. As the sole Arab voice on the Council, Syria's stance on issues affecting the Middle East, and in particular the question of Iraq, were much scrutinised. Syria's approval of UN Security Council Resolution 1441 (2002) in early November threatening Iraq with "serious consequences" if it failed to disarm (see XVII.1) surprised many commentators, as Syria had hitherto resolutely opposed a US-led military strike on Iraq. It appeared that Syria had backed the US-sponsored resolution because it did not want to be isolated from European and Arab states which believed that the UN alone could restrain the USA from attacking Iraq. Nonetheless, the Syrian vote caused some disquiet within Arab ranks, whilst serving to highlight further the level of Iraq's international isolation.

The question of Iraq was high on the agenda during President Bashar al-Assad's visit to the UK in mid-December. After talks with UK Prime Minister Tony Blair, the two leaders held a joint press conference at which they sought to emphasise the common ground between them over the need for peace in the Middle East and demands that Iraq should disarm. However, Assad made clear his concerns about military action against Iraq, telling reporters: "No one is seeking war . . . Anybody who looks for war as a goal in itself is psychologically ill." The President also dismissed Blair's call that he rein in radical Palestinian factions operating in Syria, insisting that there were no Palestinian "terrorists" in Syria, only Palestinian "press officers". Earlier in the year, in February, Assad had visited Italy where he held talks with senior Italian officials, including President Carlo Ciampi and Prime Minister Silvio Berlusconi. Talks between the two sides centred on the US-led "war on terrorism" and the Israeli-Palestinian conflict, although the presence of businessmen in Assad's party reflected the trip's economic dimensions.

The year saw a number of notable developments regarding Syria's relations with "sister" Lebanon, although Syrian control of its neighbour remained firm. In early March President Assad visited Lebanon for talks with his Lebanese counterpart, Emile Lahoud. Visits to Lebanon by Syrian Presidents were rare and Assad was the first Syrian head of state to pay an official visit to the Lebanese presidential palace at Ba'abda. The two sides agreed a unified position ahead of the Arab summit in Beirut in late March, at which, amongst other things, a Saudi Arabian "land-for-peace" initiative to address the Arab-Israeli conflict was approved. During his visit to Ba'abda, Assad also agreed a number of economic measures designed to help Lebanon's ailing economy (see V.2.v).

The threat of open conflict with Israel appeared to increase during April when Israel carried out a major military offensive—"Operation Defensive Shield"—in the West Bank (see V.2.i). The Israeli offensive led to an upsurge in fighting between Israel and Syrian-backed Islamic militants of Hezbollah in southern Lebanon, particularly around the disputed Shabaa farms area, on the slopes of Mt Hermon immediately adjacent to the Golan Heights. Some Israeli officials believed that Syria was aiming to open a "second front" in order to put military pressure on the Israeli army in the north, while forces to the south undertook their offensive against Palestinians in the West Bank. The USA called on Syria to restrain Hezbollah before the conflict expanded. Israeli Prime Minister Ariel Sharon was less circumspect, warning that Syria was "not immune" from Israeli military action in the region. Syria responded by deploying its estimated 20,000 troops in Lebanon to areas near the Syrian border.

Lt-Gen. Ghazi Kan'an, chief of Syrian military intelligence in Lebanon since 1982, was in October appointed as head of Syria's Political Security Agency, replacing Adnan Badr Hasan. Kan'an had long enjoyed a position of unrivalled authority in Lebanon, and it was thought that he would continue to "supervise" operations in the country. He was replaced by his deputy, Col Rustum Ghazali. In another notable appointment, Lt-Gen. Hasan Turkmani was promoted in January to the post of chief of staff of the army and armed forces. He replaced Lt-Gen. Ali Aslan, who had served in the posts since 1998.

Domestically, the government continued to maintain a firm grip on dissent and there was little sign of a resurgence of the so-called "Damascus spring" which had witnessed greater democratic expression following the accession of Bashar al-Assad to the presidency in 2000. In April Riyad Sayf and Mamum al-Homsi, independent members of the legislature, were sentenced to five years' imprisonment after they were found guilty of violating the constitution with demands for broader political freedoms and criticism of the government. Sayf and Homsi were among a group of opposition figures detained in September 2001 as part of a government crackdown. In June the National Security Court sentenced human rights activist Habib Saleh to three years' imprisonment for inciting sectarian strife through his criticism of the ruling Baath Party. Two days after Saleh's conviction, the most prominent of Syria's eight detained dissidents, Riyad al-Turk, the secretary general of the anti-government faction of the Communist Party of Syria, was sentenced to 30 months' imprisonment after being convicted of attacking the constitution, insulting the state and undermining national consciousness. Turk was released from prison in mid-November for "humanitarian reasons" after serving less than five months of his sentence. His release followed that of Haitham Naal, Syria's longest-serving political prisoner, in August. Naal had been released some 28 years after being imprisoned for membership of the banned Arab Communist Organisation. The release of Turk and Naal was, however, accompanied by the imposition of heavy prison sentences on other opposition figures. In September it was revealed that the State Security Court had recently sentenced economist Arif Dalila to 10 years' imprisonment; engineer Fawaz Tillu, and human rights activists Walid al-Bunni and Habib Issa to five years'; and physician and human rights activist Kamal Labwani and teacher Hassan Sa'dun to three years', both reduced from five years'.

There were two notable disasters during the year. In June the Zeyzoun dam near the town of Idlib, north of Hama, in northern Syria collapsed killing at least 22 people and causing widespread damage. In the days after the disaster police arrested a number of employees of the state-owned company that built and operated the dam. Saudi billionaire Prince Alwaleed ibn Talal pledged to rebuild the entire village of Zeyzoun which had been devastated by the collapse of the dam. In October mountain homes in the northern city of Aleppo collapsed when caves beneath gave way, killing over 30 people and injuring over 20 others.

v. LEBANON

CAPITAL: Beirut   AREA: 10,000 sq km   POPULATION: 4,400,000
OFFICIAL LANGUAGE: Arabic   POLITICAL SYSTEM: multiparty republic
HEAD OF STATE AND GOVERNMENT: President Émile Lahoud (since Nov '98)
PRIME MINISTER: Rafiq al-Hariri (since Oct '00)
MAIN IGO MEMBERSHIPS (NON-UN): AL, OIC, NAM, Francophonie
CURRENCY: Lebanese pound (end-'02 £1=L£2,403.93, US$1=L£1,501.00)
GNI PER CAPITA: US$4,010, US$4,640 at PPP ('01)

THERE was an upsurge of fighting between Hezbollah (the Shi'ite Islamic militia) and Israel in southern Lebanon in early April, particularly around the Shabaa farms area, on the slopes of Mount Hermon immediately adjacent to the Golan Heights. Israeli officials expressed concern that Hezbollah planned to open a "second front" to put military pressure on the Israeli army in the north while forces to the south undertook their Operation Defensive Shield offensive against Palestinians in the West Bank and Gaza Strip. The two sides exchanged fire on a daily basis during the early part of the month, although Israel appeared to adopt a relatively cautious approach, possibly out of concern that Hezbollah might fire long-range rockets into northern Israel. In mid-April Hezbollah fighters fired anti-tank missiles at Israeli positions on Mount Hermon and Shabaa farms whilst US Secretary of State Gen. (retd) Colin Powell was visiting Israel's Northern Command base at Safed. Tension in southern Lebanon remained high during May and on one occasion Syrian troops based in the Bekaa Valley fired anti-aircraft guns at Israeli aircraft overflying their positions. A dispute between Lebanon and Israel over access to fresh water supplies in the former Israeli occupation zone of south Lebanon heightened tension between the two countries during September. The dispute involved a Lebanese project to pipe water supplies to frontier villages from the Wazzani tributary flowing into the Hasbani river, which ultimately flowed into the Jordan and Lake Tiberias, one of Israel's main sources of water. Israeli Prime Minister Ariel Sharon insisted that the project should not be allowed to proceed and warned that "measures" would be taken if the flow of water into Israel was affected. Despite such threats President Emile Lahoud in mid-October officially inaugurated the pumping station.

Reports in the middle of the year accused Hezbollah of increasingly close links with Osama bin Laden's al-Qaida network on logistics and training. It was claimed that co-operation between the two groups was ad hoc and tactical, involved mid- and low-level operatives, and included co-ordination of explosives and training, money-laundering, weapons smuggling, and acquiring forged documents. Sheikh Allamah Mohammed Husayn Fadlallah, Hezbollah's spiritual leader, insisted that allegations of co-operation were "unreasonable", largely because al-Qaida, according to its ideology and proclamations by most of its leaders, did not consider Shi'ites to be true Muslims. In early September the Israeli newspaper *Ha'aretz*, citing various intelligence sources, reported that Syria had sanctioned the entry of as many as 200 al-Qaida operatives into the biggest Palestinian refugee camp in Lebanon, Ain al-Hilweh, near Sidon. The newspaper claimed that gun battles between Islamist elements and members of Fatah, the mainstream Palestinian faction of Yassir Arafat, in August had stemmed from the efforts of al-Qaida to take control of the camp. It was reported in early October that three suspected members of al-Qaida had been arrested in Lebanon on suspicion of trying to establish a new camp for members who had recently fled Afghanistan. The two Lebanese and a Saudi national had been arrested after being kept under prolonged surveillance by Lebanese military intelligence.

Relations with Syria—the power-broker in Lebanon—continued to dominate foreign affairs during 2002. Syrian President Bashar al-Assad visited in early March for talks aimed at achieving a common and united front at the forthcoming Arab League summit in Beirut at the end of the month. Visits to Lebanon by Syrian presidents were rare—Lebanese leaders usually having to make the trip to Damascus—and Assad was the first Syrian head of state to pay an official visit to the Lebanese presidential palace at Ba'abda (see V.2.iv). The symbolism of Assad's visit to Ba'abda was undoubtedly directed at the growing number of Lebanese who openly expressed unease at the "irregularities" in the Syrian-Lebanese relationship.

In a joint statement issued at the end of their meeting, Presidents Assad and Lahoud said that current "circumstances" in the Middle East required "effective and unified Arab stands and solidarity . . . to exert every possible effort to achieve co-operation that serves the common interests of the Arab states and maintains their security, rights and dignity". Assad agreed to a number of economic measures designed to help Lebanon's ailing economy. Syria agreed to eliminate certain barriers to "the process of exchanging commodities of national origin between the two countries" and to pursue a Lebanese proposal to dam the Orontes and the Al-Nahr al-Kabir rivers. Syria would also "restudy" Electricité du Liban's schedule of debts to Syria and deduct half of that amount, and reconsider the price of natural gas being sold to Lebanon. It was also agreed to study a number of joint agricultural and industrial projects, including oil refineries in Tripoli and Sidon.

The year saw a number of high-level assassinations in Lebanon. Elie Hobeika, aged 45, one of Lebanon's most notorious Maronite Christian militia commanders from the civil war of 1975-90, was killed by a car bomb in Beirut in late January. Speculation centred on whether Hobeika's murder was linked to his willingness to testify if a court case was brought in Belgium against Israeli Prime Minister Sharon over his involvement in the massacre of Palestinians in the Chatila and Sabra refugee camps (see II.2.v). The assassination in March in Brazil of Michael Nasser, an arms dealer and a former associate of Hobeika, only served to increase speculation over possible Israeli involvement.

Jihad Jibril, the 38-year-old son of Ahmed Jibril, leader of the Popular Front for the Liberation of Palestine (General Command) (PFLP-GC), was killed by a car bomb in Beirut in May. Jihad Jibril was believed to have planned one of the PFLP-GC's most daring attacks—a raid on the Israel town of Kiryat Shemona in 1987 when a guerrilla killed six Israeli soldiers after floating over the border from Lebanon on a powered hang-glider. PFLP-GC officials claimed that the "technology" of the bomb which killed Jibril showed that Israel was behind the killing. However, Israeli officials insisted that Israel had no connection to the attack. A US nurse, Bonnie Weatherall, was shot dead in the southern port city of Sidon in late November, one of a number of US citizens targeted for attack in the region as tension heightened over a possible US attack on Iraq. No group claimed responsibility for the killing, but some reports claimed that Weatherall had been warned to leave Sidon by Sunni extremists.

vi. IRAQ

CAPITAL: Baghdad   AREA: 438,000 sq km   POPULATION: 23,750,000
OFFICIAL LANGUAGE: Arabic   POLITICAL SYSTEM: one-party republic
HEAD OF STATE: President Saddam Hussein (since July '79), also Prime Minister & Chairman of Revolutionary Command Council
RULING PARTY: Ba'ath Arab Socialist Party
MAIN IGO MEMBERSHIPS (NON-UN): AL, OPEC, OAPEC, OIC, NAM
CURRENCY: Iraqi dinar (end-'02 £1=ID0.4981 US$1=ID0.3110)
GNI PER CAPITA: n/a

THE year was dominated by the growing threat of US-led military action against the regime of President Saddam Hussein. The momentum for US military action to facilitate a "regime change" began to increase markedly in the aftermath of US President George W. Bush's State of the Union address on 29 January in which he singled out Iraq as part of an "axis of evil", along with North Korea and Iran (see IV.1). British Prime Minister Tony Blair quickly indicated that the UK would line up with the USA in any military confrontation to depose Saddam. Interviewed at the Commonwealth heads of government conference in Australia in March, Blair claimed that Iraq was developing weapons of mass destruction and was capable of using them. He further indicated that the West was not planning to repeat the mistakes which it had made by responding slowly to the threat posed by Osama bin Laden and his al-Qaida network—blamed for the 11 September 2001 terrorist attacks on the USA (see AR 2001, pp. 1-15; 157-60)—and insisted that the threat posed by Iraq was not a matter for the USA alone.

Iraq responded to the mounting US threat by launching a "charm offensive" aimed at rallying Arab support against a military attack. Hence, a matter of days after Bush had delivered his State of the Union address, the Iraqi government expressed its willingness to hold talks "without conditions" with the UN over the possible resumption of weapons inspections after a four year absence. Iraq had hitherto refused to allow the UN's weapons inspection agency, the UN Monitoring, Verification and Inspection Commission (UNMOVIC), to enter the country, having previously insisted on the lifting of sanctions, imposed after its invasion of Kuwait in August 1990, as a precondition for continued dialogue. The UN Security Council had refused to lift the sanctions until Iraq could demonstrate that it was no longer seeking to build its chemical, nuclear or biological weapons capability.

In early March Iraqi Foreign Minister Naji Sabri Ahmad al-Hadithi (appointed in government changes in August 2001) held a round of talks in New York with UN Secretary-General Kofi Annan and Hans Blix, the head of UNMOVIC. Subsequent talks took place in New York in early May and in Vienna in early July. Meanwhile, in late March the Arab League held a summit meeting in Beirut (Lebanon) which was dominated by two main, interdependent issues, the Arab-Israeli conflict and Iraq's relations with Kuwait, and new initiatives were discussed and approved in regard to both (see XI.6.i). The question of Iraq's relations with Kuwait was a subject that had divided Arab ranks since Iraq's invasion of its neighbour in 1990. The two states had been seriously estranged since the invasion, but the Beirut summit moved to bridge that divide, with Iraq pledging to respect Kuwaiti sovereignty. Iraq had previously been ambivalent about Kuwait's borders and sovereignty. In an impressive display of Arab unity, the summit rejected the prospect of a US attack on Iraq. Much attention was focused on a highly symbolic public embrace between Saudi Arabian Crown Prince Abdullah ibn Abdul Aziz (the kingdom's de facto leader) and the head of the Iraqi delegation to the summit, Izzat Ibrahim, the vice chairman of the Iraqi Revolutionary Command Council (RCC). Not surprisingly, the USA expressed grave doubts about the accord between Iraq and Kuwait.

Following Iraq's successful reintegration into Arab ranks at the Arab League's Beirut summit, and in light of the overwhelming focus of world attention on the escalating Israeli-Palestinian conflict (see V.2.i), the threat of immediate US military action against Saddam's regime appeared to diminish. In late April Iraq was bold enough to organise lavish national celebrations to mark Saddam's 65th birthday. More than 1 million Iraqis were reported to have taken to the streets, many waving Iraqi and Palestinian flags. However, by the middle of the year international debate over a possible US attack had again reached boiling point and Iraq responded in early August by inviting Hans Blix and members of his UNMOVIC team to visit Iraq for talks on the possible resumption of weapons inspections.

Iraqi Deputy Prime Minister Tariq Aziz held a round of talks with UN Secretary-General Annan in early September on the sidelines of the World Summit on Sustainable Development in Johannesburg. Aziz told Annan that Iraq would consider allowing the return of UN weapons inspectors, but only as part of a comprehensive framework and schedule designed to bring about the eventual lifting of UN sanctions. However, in a keynote speech delivered at the 57th UN General Assembly on 12 September, Bush set stiff and immediate conditions for the Iraqi regime to meet in order to avoid being toppled by US-led forces. The US President, putting aside much of the unilateralist rhetoric that had marked his administration throughout the growing crisis, insisted that he was eager to work with the UN to confront the "grave and gathering danger" posed by Iraq. If Saddam's regime "wishes peace" it must, Bush said, "immediately and unconditionally" give up all weapons of mass destruction; end its support of terrorism; stop the suppression of its people; release Gulf War prisoners; and allow UN administration of the "oil-for-food" programme (see below). UN Secretary-General Annan announced four days later that Iraq had agreed to the unconditional return of UNMOVIC inspectors.

Iraq's sudden agreement to permit the unconditional return of UN weapons inspectors produced a split among key UN Security Council members, complicating the US campaign for a tough new UN resolution threatening military action. US and British officials immediately dismissed the Iraqi announcement as a tactic of delay and diversion. Other countries, however, gave a cautious welcome to the Iraqi move. Russian Foreign Minister Igor Ivanov said that the Iraqi action had served to "deflect the threat of a military scenario and to steer the process back to the political channel". A senior French official said that France was willing to "try inspectors as a real step forward". A Chinese Foreign Ministry spokesman welcomed the Iraqi move as "a positive step". In what appeared to be an attempt to weaken international opposition to military action, the British government on 24 September published a long-awaited dossier on the threat apparently posed to the world by Saddam's regime. The report warned that Iraq could deploy chemical and biological weapons at 45 minutes' notice. Although the policy of containing Iraq's nuclear ambitions appeared to be working, the regime could also, it was claimed, develop a nuclear bomb within two years should it secure essential components from foreign sources.

In early October Iraq agreed to provide UNMOVIC inspectors unfettered access to sites in Iraq (including presidential palaces, which had been a bone of contention in the past), a move which only served to intensify the time pressure for the USA to garner support for a new Security Council resolution that toughened the rules under which inspectors would operate. Russian President Vladimir Putin in early October acknowledged for the first time the need for a fresh Security Council resolution to counter Iraq's weapons of mass destruction. Putin's new line meant that Russia was taking a similar approach to the French position, which called for a resolution demanding the return of weapons inspectors, and then a second resolution in the event of failure. French officials insisted that such a "two-step" process was necessary to justify war in Iraq.

The UN Security Council on 8 November unanimously approved Resolution 1441 (2002) which provided Saddam with a last chance to comply with commitments to disarm or face "serious consequences" (see XVII.1). The surprising show of international unity—even Syria, the lone Arab voice on the Security Council, backed the resolution—sent an unequivocal message to Saddam's regime, leaving it without serious potential allies if it chose to defy the resolution. The text represented a compromise between France and Russia on one side and the USA and the UK on the other. Although it did not provide the USA with overt authority to attack Iraq, the resolution nonetheless sent a very strong message to Saddam that he must comply with UNMOVIC or face the real possibility of war. It effectively acknowledged France's "two-step system", stating that the Security Council would assess any failure by Iraq to comply with the strict new weapons inspections regime outlined by the resolution. It did not oblige the USA to seek further authority for war from the Security Council, however, a previous requirement of both France and Russia.

The immediate key demands of Resolution 1441 were as follows: (i) Iraq had to confirm within seven days of the adoption of the resolution its intention to "comply fully" with its demands and co-operate with UNMOVIC; (ii) Iraq had to declare within 30 days all weapons of mass destruction programmes and related materials, including items that could also be used for civilian purposes; (iii) weapons inspectors should resume their work no later than 45 days after the adoption of the resolution; (iv) inspectors would update the Security Council 60 days after the adoption of the resolution, but could report any Iraqi violations sooner; (v) inspectors would be allowed unconditional and unrestricted access to any place they wished to examine, including Saddam Hussein's palace compounds; (vi) inspectors could, "at their discretion", interview Iraqi scientists and other officials as well as facilitate travel for interviews to be held outside the country; (vii) inspectors could "freeze" a site to be surveyed by declaring exclusion zones within which Iraq would be obliged to suspend "ground and aerial" movements; (viii) the resolution recalled that the Security Council had repeatedly warned Iraq that it would face "serious consequences" as a result of continued violations of its obligations; (ix) the resolution declared that Iraq had been and still was in "material breach" of its obligations, but was being given a "final opportunity" to comply with those obligations; (x) "false statements and omissions" in declarations submitted by Iraq and failure to co-operate fully in the implementation of the resolution would constitute a "further material breach" of Iraq's obligations and "will be reported to the council for assessment"; and (xi) inspectors would report immediately to the Security Council any "interference by Iraq with inspection activities as well as any failure by Iraq to comply with its disarmament obligations".

On 13 November the RCC, Iraq's highest decision making body, formally and unconditionally accepted the resolution. In his letter of acceptance to Kofi Annan, Iraqi Foreign Minister Naji Sabri Ahmad al-Hadithi restated Iraq's long-held assertion that it was not hiding any biological, chemical, nuclear or long-range missile programmes. The Bush administration gave a guarded welcome to Iraq's acceptance of the resolution, but warned that Saddam would be judged on his actions. Hans Blix, the head of UNMOVIC, and Muhammad al-Baradei, head of the International Atomic Energy Agency (IAEA), arrived in the Iraqi capital, Baghdad, on 18 November to re-establish the weapons inspectors' headquarters after a four-year absence. A team of 17 UNMOVIC inspectors arrived in the Iraqi capital a week later and had launched their first inspections before the end of the month.

On 8 December Iraqi government officials delivered to UNMOVIC a 12,000-page declaration on weapons of mass destruction and dual-use equipment. Delivery of the declaration by 8 December had been one of the key demands of Resolution 1441. Handing over the declaration to UNMOVIC officials, Amer al-Saadi, senior weapons adviser to Saddam, insisted that the "complete and accurate" declaration would show that Iraq had no illegal weapons programme. However, after its officials had examined the declaration, the USA on 19 December declared Iraq to be in "material breach" of Resolution 1441. US Secretary of State Colin Powell said that the Iraqi weapons declaration "totally fails" to meet the UN's demand for an accurate and complete account of its weapons programmes. The non-compliance, he said, brought Iraq "closer to the day when it would have to face the consequences" threatened in Resolution 1441. Powell said that "thousands of the document's pages are merely a re-submission of material it [Iraq] gave the UN years ago, material that the UN has already determined was incomplete". He cited several omissions, including Iraq's failure to account for stockpiles of anthrax and other biological weapons as well as its development of mobile chemical weapons production units.

Aside from the growing threat of US-led military action, the year again witnessed much diplomatic manoeuvring over the oil component of the UN sanctions regime against Iraq. The UN Security Council in mid-May adopted Resolution 1409 (2002) which constituted the most sweeping overhaul of the UN's "oil-for-food" programme since its inception in 1996. The new regime allowed Iraq to import with little scrutiny all humanitarian goods except those specifically listed by the Security Council as having military uses. Among goods that would no longer be banned were personal computers; tractors; X-ray equipment for airports and hospitals; irrigation, sewerage, and water filtration systems; and cars for personal use. The UN Security Council in early December approved Resolution 1447 (2002) extending the "oil-for-food" programme for a new period of 180 days. The programme had previously been extended in late November for only a limited nine-day period after Russia and several other council members had opposed US efforts to add to the so-called Goods Review List (GRL) of items that Iraq was prohibited from importing using its oil revenues. Under the terms of the new resolution, it was agreed to consider adjustments to the list of restricted goods within 30 days. Accordingly, a new resolution (1454) was approved on 30 December which expanded the list to include items with potential military applications. The resolution was passed 13 to 0, with Russia and Syria abstaining.

Throughout the year US and UK fighter aircraft continued to carry out air attacks on military targets in the northern and southern "no-fly zones" in Iraq. In early September US and UK aircraft attacked an Iraqi command and control facility and a military airfield some 390 km west of Baghdad. Although the attack was within the southern "no-fly zone" routinely targeted by the US and UK fighters, it was the first reported incident in the western sector since the Desert Fox operation launched in December 1998 to "degrade" Saddam's military capabilities. The scale of the attack—dozens of aircraft were involved—was larger than usual and it was noted that it came after weeks of increased activity in the southern and northern "no-fly zones" after bombing by US and UK aircraft had fallen to very low levels in early 2002. Donald Rumsfeld, the US Defence Secretary, said in mid-September that he had ordered targeting changes in recent air strikes in Iraq, a move that had, he claimed, degraded its air defence capabilities. The USA, he said, had switched from mobile targets, such as radar, to fixed air defence and communications facilities. For their part the Iraqis had little success against the US-UK coalition, although they did manage to shoot down a small number of unmanned reconnaissance aircraft (or "drones") throughout the year.

Despite the massive international campaign being waged against him, Saddam Hussein continued to maintain his iron grip on power. According to official figures, he won 100 per cent of the votes in a national referendum held in mid-October to approve a further seven-year term of office as President. Shortly after the vote Saddam ordered a general amnesty "in gratitude for his 100 per cent victory". Prisons throughout the country were apparently emptied, although there were reports of demonstrations organised by families of prisoners who had not been released, amid opposition claims that thousands of political detainees remained behind bars.

Strenuous efforts were made throughout the year to forge unity between the divided anti-Saddam opposition in exile. These efforts culminated in a gathering of representatives of more than 50 opposition groups in London in mid-December. At the meeting it was agreed to establish a 65-member committee to formulate unified policies and to act as a conduit between Iraqi dissidents and the international community. The committee was regarded in some quarters as the basis for a post-Saddam transitional government. It was agreed that the exiles would reconvene in mid-January 2003 in Kurdish controlled northern Iraq. Shi'ite Muslims, who represented 60 per cent of the Iraqi population but had been largely denied political power under Saddam, held nearly half of the seats on the committee. The list included key leaders including Ahmed Chalabi (head of the Iraqi National Congress); Ayad Allawi (leader of the Iraqi National Accord); and Abdelaziz Hakim, whose brother, Ayatollah Baqir Hakim, headed the Iranian-based Shi'ite Supreme Council for the Islamic Revolution in Iraq (SCIRI). However, the closing session of the conference was marred by a walkout of delegates representing five Shi'ite groups, who said that they were opposed to the apparent dominance of the SCIRI.

For the first time in eight years, Iraq's rival Kurdish factions had in early October held a joint session of their National Assembly (legislature) in Arbil in northern Iraq, some 10 km from the front line with Iraqi forces. The meeting followed concerted pressure from the Bush administration on the Kurds to bury their differences and establish their democratic credentials. The Assembly had not met in full session since 1994, when fighting had erupted between the Patriotic Union of Kurdistan (PUK) and the rival Kurdish Democratic Party (KDP), leading to the territorial division of the north. Masoud Barzani, leader of the KDP, and Jalal Talabani, leader of the PUK, put on a display of friendship at the ceremonial opening of the Assembly and apologised to the Kurdish people for the warfare of the mid-1990s that had divided their movement. Both leaders told a joint news conference, their first in a decade, that the USA had not, as yet, requested any military co-operation with the Kurds. However, Barzani did reveal that the US administration had given an assurance of military support should Iraq launch a pre-emptive strike against the Kurds. For his part, Talabani claimed that the USA had plans to launch a military strike against Islamic militants in the Kurdish-controlled north with links to both the Iraqi government and Osama bin Laden's al-Qaida organisation. Claims of suspected links between Iraq and al-Qaida had been made in late September by Rumsfeld, but they had been discounted by most analysts as unfounded.

3. SAUDI ARABIA—YEMEN—ARAB STATES OF THE GULF

i. SAUDI ARABIA

CAPITAL: Riyadh   AREA: 2,150,000 sq km   POPULATION: 21,400,000
OFFICIAL LANGUAGE: Arabic   POLITICAL SYSTEM: non-party monarchy
HEAD OF STATE: King Fahd ibn Abdul Aziz (since June '82), also Prime Minister
HEAD OF GOVERNMENT/HEIR APPARENT: Crown Prince Abdullah ibn Abdul Aziz (since June '82).
   Also First Deputy Prime Minister
MAIN IGO MEMBERSHIPS (NON-UN): AL, OPEC, OAPEC, GCC, OIC, NAM
CURRENCY: Saudi riyal (end-'02 £1=SR6.0065, US$1=SR3.7505)
GNI PER CAPITA: US$6,910, US$11,080 ('00 est.)

THE year for Saudi Arabia was dominated by the growing crisis in relations with the USA as a result of the attacks of 11 September 2001. In the first half of the year, US resentment rose in the face of a perceived Saudi lack of co-operation in the "war against terror", culminating in a leaked briefing to Defence Department officials by a Rand Corporation analyst which claimed that the Kingdom was the "kernel of evil". The State Department subsequently had to reassure a ruffled Saudi government that this was not the administration's official view.

In Saudi Arabia itself, anxieties over US policy increased and, as early as January, officials began privately to make it clear that the 4,500-strong American forces in the Kingdom had overstayed their welcome and should be relocated elsewhere. Senior Saudi figures, including Second Deputy Prime Minister and Minister of Defence and Aviation Prince Sultan bin Abdul Aziz, and the former intelligence chief and new ambassador to the UK, Turki bin Faisal, also faced a threatened US$600 billion law suit by the families of US victims of terrorism.

At the same time, official anxiety over the decline in relations increased and, in the face of US irritation, pressures mounted for a change in the succession process. By July, the King's health had deteriorated and leading members of the Royal Family met in Geneva to debate the succession, given US disapproval of Crown Prince Abdullah ibn Abdul Aziz's policies towards Israel and Iraq. At the end of March, the Crown Prince had proposed a new Middle East peace plan (see V.2.i) which was adopted by an extraordinary Arab League summit and which received considerable public support within the Middle East and elsewhere. The US government reacted unenthusiastically, however, and no progress was achieved in resolving the Palestinian issue.

Popular support for al-Qaida appeared to mount alarmingly and an unofficial boycott of US goods contributed towards a 43 per cent drop in US exports to the Kingdom. Claims in August, however, that Saudis had withdrawn up to US$200 billion from investments in the USA, estimated to total US$400-US$600 billon, proved to be wildly exaggerated. In June the authorities announced the arrest of 12 suspected al-Qaida militants alleged to be plotting attacks in the Kingdom. More than one hundred further arrests were reported in November.

The US Council on Foreign Relations in October published a report highly critical of Saudi attempts to prohibit private funding of al-Qaida and a furore developed the following month over evidence of charitable donations by the wife of the Saudi ambassador to Washington DC to relatives of the 11 September hijackers. Relations, however, improved by the end of the year, particularly when the Kingdom made it clear that it would co-operate over anti-terrorism measures. This was strengthened by Saudi willingness to co-operate with the USA's policy towards Iraq, provided it was sanctioned by the UN Security Council.

Forty pilgrims were killed in an accident during the *hajj* in February, and the muttawa's refusal to allow emergency services to intervene in a fire at a girls' school in June led to education being removed from religious control. The long-running scandal over bombings allegedly connected with the illegal trade in alcohol culminated in April in sentences, including two death sentences, on the five UK nationals held. However, suspicion that this was an official cover for unacknowledged extremist attacks on Westerners mounted when a British banker was killed by a car bomb in Riyadh in June and a German died in similar circumstances in late September. A British national was arrested in connection with the second incident in November.

The economy continued to cause anxiety, with the IMF demanding cuts in public spending and structural reform. The Kingdom, however, successfully managed OPEC production to ensure a rise in oil prices, despite a projected budget deficit of SR45 billion on revenues of SR157 billion for the year and a domestic debt of SR675 billion,110 per cent of GDP. The US$25 billion natural gas project (the Master Gas System) was stalled throughout the year because of international oil companies' dissatisfaction with proposed rates-of-return and Aramco's unwillingness for foreign upstream participation. Despite declines in non-oil foreign investment, Saudi Basic Industries Corp. (Sabic) sought investment opportunities in Europe and Saudi Telecom offered private investors a 30 per cent stake, with promises of similar deals for Sabic and Saudi Airlines to come.

ii. YEMEN

CAPITAL: Sana'a   AREA: 528,000 sq km   POPULATION: 18,000,000
OFFICIAL LANGUAGE: Arabic   POLITICAL SYSTEM: multiparty republic
HEAD OF STATE AND GOVERNMENT: President (Field Marshall) Ali Abdullah Saleh (since May '90)
RULING PARTIES: General People's Congress (GPC) & Yemeni Alliance for Reform (Islah)
PRIME MINISTER: Abd al-Qadir Abd al-Rahman Bajammal (since April '01)
MAIN IGO MEMBERSHIPS (NON-UN): AL, OIC, NAM
CURRENCY: Yemeni rial (end-'02 £1=YR284.900, US$1=YR177.890)
GNI PER CAPITA: US$460, US$770 at PPP ('01)

EVENTS in Yemen during 2002 were entirely dominated by the aftermath of the 11 September 2001 attacks on New York and Washington DC and the subsequent US-led war with Afghanistan. By the beginning of the year, President Ali Abdullah Salih's government had made a strategic decision that it would have to co-operate closely with the USA in the "war against terror" and the President, on a visit to the USA, reportedly signed a security pact. However, the practical difficulties had been made clear the previous December when Yemeni forces tried to arrest two suspected al-Qaida sympathisers who had sought tribal protection. The mission ended in failure and 20 people were left dead. Throughout the year, Yemeni officials tried unsuccessfully to negotiate, through mediators, with the two men who stated that they were prepared to surrender provided they were not handed over to the USA.

Despite this failure, the authorities made great efforts to satisfy US demands throughout the year, including allowing three teams of US investigators to search the country for al-Qaida sympathisers from March onwards. In February, US intelligence information led to the arrest of five more people, out of 17 said to be involved in anti-US plots. One suspect, Sameer Mohamed Ahmed al-Hada, killed himself rather than allowing himself to be arrested. He was linked with one of the 11 September hijackers and to the attack on the *USS Cole* (see AR 2000, p. 214). Some 800 US special forces, together with an assault ship, were also based in Djibouti in September to help the search, after Ramzi bin al-Shibhi, suspected of involvement in the 11 September attacks, was arrested in Pakistan and an alleged al-Qaida cell in Bahrain and New York state was dismantled. Other arrests were also made in Yemen as a result, but the US government threatened to use "snatch squads" because Yemen refused to extradite suspects. In August, President Salih created a new National Security Agency, answerable to his office, whilst in June a sophisticated electronic surveillance system was installed to improve border security. The proposed reform of the Yemeni education system ground to a halt, however, when the Iman university was allowed to continue to operate. Nonetheless, 115 foreigners studying in unregistered education establishments were arrested in February and later expelled from the country.

US Vice President Dick Cheney visited Yemen in late March, as part of his tour of the Middle East, and discussed the regional situation. He was the first senior US official to visit Yemen since 1986 and his primary concern was Yemeni control of potential violence. (The 21 Yemenis held by the USA in the camp at Guantanamo Bay in Cuba represented the second largest national community held there.) Cheney's visit provoked an angry response from eight political parties and two grenades were thrown into the US embassy compound. By May, a backlash against the intrusive US presence in Yemen seemed to be brewing, with Islamist-organised demonstrations against Israeli policy in Palestine, attacks on the security police headquarters where more than 173 suspected al-Qaida members were held, and bombs in the capital, Sana'a. The US ambassador, Edward Hull, was a particular object of dislike.

In October, a French oil tanker, the *Limburg*, was attacked in Yemeni waters, apparently by an al-Qaida group, although it was claimed by the Islamic Army of Aden-Abayan. One month later, a US Predator "drone" (an unmanned aircraft), operating from Djibouti, killed a leading al-Qaida suspect, Qaed Salim Sinan al-Harithi, together with five of his companions, whilst he was travelling in a car in Marib in what appeared to have been a premeditated US assassination. At the end of December, in an embarrassing incident, the North Korean cargo ship, *So San*, was intercepted by a Spanish warship at US behest and was found to be carrying Scud missiles. It transpired, however, that they had been legitimately purchased by the Yemeni government, so the ship was released.

iii. ARAB STATES OF THE GULF

United Arab Emirates (UAE)
CONSTITUENT MONARCHIES: Abu Dhabi, Dubai, Sharjah, Ras al-Khaimah, Fujairah, Umm al-Qaiwin, Ajman
CAPITAL: Abu Dhabi   AREA: 77,000 sq km   POPULATION: 2,976,000
OFFICIAL LANGUAGE: Arabic   POLITICAL SYSTEM: non-party republic, comprising federation of monarchies
HEAD OF STATE AND GOVERNMENT: Shaikh Zayad bin Sultan al-Nahayyan (Ruler of Abu Dhabi), President of UAE (since Dec '71)
PRIME MINISTER: Shaikh Maktoum bin Rashid al-Maktoum (Ruler of Dubai), Vice-President and Prime Minister of UAE (since Nov '90)
MAIN IGO MEMBERSHIPS (NON-UN): AL, OPEC, OAPEC, GCC, OIC, NAM
CURRENCY: UAE dirham (end-'02 £1=Dh5.8825, US$1=Dh3.6730)
GNI PER CAPITA: US$18,100, US$19,420 at PPP ('00 est.)

Kuwait
CAPITAL: Kuwait   AREA: 18,000 sq km   POPULATION: 2,000,000
OFFICIAL LANGUAGE: Arabic   POLITICAL SYSTEM: non-party monarchy
HEAD OF STATE: Sheikh Jabir al-Ahmad al-Jabir al-Sabah (since Dec '77)
HEIR APPARENT: Crown Prince Sheikh Saad al-Abdullah al-Salim al-Sabah, Prime Minister (since Feb '78)
MAIN IGO MEMBERSHIPS (NON-UN): AL, OPEC, OAPEC, GCC, OIC, NAM
CURRENCY: Kuwaiti dinar (end-'02 £1=KwD0.4804, US$1=KwD0.3000)
GNI PER CAPITA: GDP PER CAPITA US$22,110, US$24,270 at PPP ('98)

Oman
CAPITAL: Muscat   AREA: 300,000 sq km   POPULATION: 2,452,000
OFFICIAL LANGUAGE: Arabic   POLITICAL SYSTEM: non-party monarchy
HEAD OF STATE: Shaikh Qaboos bin Said (since July '70)
MAIN IGO MEMBERSHIPS (NON-UN): AL, GCC, OIC, NAM
CURRENCY: rial Omani (end-'02 £1=RO0.6168, US$1=RO0.3851)
GNI PER CAPITA: US$6,720 ('00 est.)

Qatar

CAPITAL: Doha   AREA: 11,400 sq km   POPULATION: 598,000
OFFICIAL LANGUAGE: Arabic   POLITICAL SYSTEM: non-party monarchy
HEAD OF STATE: Sheikh Hamad bin Khalifa al-Thani (since June '95)
MAIN IGO MEMBERSHIPS (NON-UN): AL, OPEC, OAPEC, GCC, OIC, NAM
CURRENCY: Qatar riyal (end-'02 £1=QR5.8309, US$1=QR3.6408)
GNI PER CAPITA: US$11,570 ('97)

Bahrain

CAPITAL: Manama   AREA: 685 sq km   POPULATION: 714,000
OFFICIAL LANGUAGE: Arabic   POLITICAL SYSTEM: constitutional monarchy
HEAD OF STATE: Sheikh Hamad bin Isa al-Khalifa (since March '99)
HEAD OF GOVERNMENT/HEIR APPARENT: Sheikh Khalifa bin Sulman al-Khalifa, Prime Minister (since Jan '70)
MAIN IGO MEMBERSHIPS (NON-UN): AL, OAPEC, GCC, OIC, NAM
CURRENCY: dinar (end-'02 £1=BD0.6038, US$1=BD0.3770)
GNI PER CAPITA: US$9,370, US$12,170 at PPP ('00 est.)

FOR the Arab states of the Gulf, 2002 was dominated by the issues of Western policy towards Iraq and the Arab-Israeli crisis. Even KUWAIT, traditionally the most antagonistic state towards Iraq, was reluctant to support the US-led threat of war over Iraq's alleged weapons of mass destruction without explicit UN sanction, as it made clear in October. In March, Kuwait and Iraq were formally reconciled at the Arab League summit in Beirut (see XI.6.i), after Iraq had offered to discuss the issue of the 640 Kuwaitis who had remained missing since the 1991 war. By the end of the year, however, it had had to accept the bulk of the US and UK forces moving into the region, despite isolated protests. In October, one US marine was killed and another wounded when their unit, training on Falaika Island, was fired on by two Kuwaiti al-Qaida sympathisers. The two attackers were killed and 50 of their supporters were later arrested.

Later that month, shots were fired at US troops and in late November a policeman attacked two US soldiers near their camp. In the middle of the month, another al-Qaida suspect, together with two others, was arrested for financing an attack on a French oil tanker off Yemen and for planning to bomb a hotel in the Yemen capital, Sana'a, used by US personnel (see V.3.ii). Despite claims that such hostility was confined to isolated groups in the population, there was mounting concern over the growth of sympathy with Osama bin Laden. At the start of the year, 42 per cent of Kuwaitis saw him as a "holy warrior", only 34 per cent considered him a terrorist, and most Kuwaitis had not supported the war in Afghanistan the previous year.

The UNITED ARAB EMIRATES took a critical stance over Western policy towards the region, particularly as far as support for Israel was concerned. As a result of Israeli incursions into the Gaza Strip in February, the UAE called for Israeli Premier Ariel Sharon to be charged with terrorism. In April, in the wake of the adoption of the Saudi peace plan by the Arab League (see V.2.i) at the end of March, the UAE called for US support for the plan and for the US administration to use its influence with the Israeli government. In May, although promising not to use its oil production as a weapon to force a change in Western policy, the UAE called for Sharon to be charged under international law, whilst popular demands for a boycott of US goods and companies increased. Although there was no official reaction to US President George W. Bush's Middle East peace plan in June, leading newspapers in the Federation condemned it. At the end of the year, the UAE government called for the UN to accept Iraq's offer to readmit weapons inspectors and put forward a five point plan for peace in the region, calling for a full solution to the Iraq-Kuwait border dispute, US non-interference in Iraq, full Iraqi compliance with UN resolutions, and the removal of all sanctions together with the removal of weapons of mass destruction from all states in the region, including Israel, in accordance with paragraph 14 of UN Security Council Resolution 687.

In BAHRAIN, where most attention was directed towards political liberalisation during the year, the presence of the headquarters of the US Fifth Fleet led to demonstrations with at least one death, and to calls for an end to Israeli atrocities in the Occupied Territories. There were even two rare demonstrations in Muscat, one outside the US embassy, in protest against events in Palestine in May.

Only QATAR seemed to handle the Iraqi question with equanimity, as in September the USA began to transfer its CENTCOM command headquarters from Florida to the al-Udeid base. This duplicated facilities which were located in Saudi Arabia but which were no longer available for any war against Iraq. The base had been expanded since 1999 and was now set to be the major command centre for any regional hostilities. Echoes of the past emerged in July when the UN reparations commission paid out US$708 million, US$490 million to Kuwaiti companies and individuals and US$60 million to the Kuwaiti state, with the balance going to individuals, organisations, and companies in 33 countries, including three UN agencies. The UAE also tightened its control of the hawala money transfer system, alleged to have been used by terrorists, in November.

The other major regional issue—tensions between Iran and the UAE over the control of the Thunbs islands and Abu Musa—improved during the year. In February, Iran threatened to end economic co-operation with the Gulf Cupertino Council if it supported the UAE's attempt to place the dispute before the International Court of Justice in The Hague, a proposal which had also enjoyed European support. In June, however, the visit by the UAE's Foreign Minister to the Iranian capital, Teheran—the first since 1979—and the promise of a return visit to the UAE by Iran's President, Mohammad Khatami, led to a thaw in relations and negotiations on the issue were set to start in December in Abu Dhabi. The UAE also concluded its border treaty with OMAN when Sultan Qaboos signed it whilst on a visit to the Federation in June.

Domestic political change was striking, particularly in Bahrain where the enthusiasm engendered by the National Charter debate in 2001 (see AR 2001,

p. 243) had begun to wane, given rumours of conservative resistance within the royal family. In February, however, constitutional reforms were announced on the anniversary of the referendum on the Charter the previous year. Bahrain was to become a constitutional monarchy and municipal elections were set for May. In the elections, the first for 30 years, in which women were able to vote for the first time, there were 304 candidates for the 50 seats on five councils, 31 of them women. In the 51.3 per cent turnout, Islamists were the victors, although formal party affiliations were not allowed. They won all 50 seats, although the minority Sunni population won 27 seats, leading the 70 per cent majority Shi'a population to criticise the alignment of electoral boundaries. The General Directorate of Criminal Investigation, long criticised for its abuse of the Shi'a population, was replaced by a new National Security Agency in June.

Legislative elections in Bahrain took place in October, after the ban on political campaigning was lifted in September and despite the decision by the three main opposition groups—the National Democratic Party, the Association for Democratic Action, and the Islamic Association for National Reconciliation—to boycott them. In the 53.2 per cent turnout, moderate Sunni Islamists and independents won 21 of the 40 seats, with three seats being returned unopposed. Some 174 candidates, including eight women, stood in the elections but no woman won, either in the legislative or the municipal elections. At the end of October, in the wake of the elections, a new Cabinet was appointed, as was a new shura council which included six women. New legislation, guaranteeing the freedom of the press was also introduced, in which newspapers were only subject to court order and journalists were only subject to the Press Law.

Developments were not so hopeful in Kuwait, where the Amir returned in January after four months of treatment in London for a stroke, having made a complete recovery. The Constitutional Court in March ruled that the first paragraph of the electoral law, which allowed women to take part in elections, was unconstitutional. The case had been brought by a woman's group, in protest at the decision of the National Assembly in 1999 which had rejected a government amendment designed to give women the vote, as promised by the Amir in May 1999 (see AR 1999, p. 232). Women had demonstrated in February in protest at their continued inability to vote. Tensions between the government and the National Assembly continued as, in February, the Assembly sought to question the Interior Minister over a case of infanticide. The Oil Minister resigned in February, in the wake of an explosion in the al-Randhatain oil gathering centre as the result of a leaking crude pipeline which killed four people and injured 19 at the end of January. The murderer of a leading journalist, Hidaya Sultan, a police officer, was sentenced to death in the same month.

At the end of the year, Kuwaiti relations with Qatar declined as a result of the closure of the al-Jazeera office in Kuwait because the television station's reports were said to "lack objectivity". The decision followed a similar decision by Jordan, which had closed its local office of the station for being "seditious", and growing tensions between Qatar and Saudi Arabia over the station's activities and reports on the Kingdom. In Qatar itself, cautious moves towards political liberalisation were announced by the Amir whilst on a visit to Poland in June. There would be elections for a new legislature within two-and-a-half years and the commission set up in 1999 to consider constitutional change was due to report soon.

Gulf Air, the regional airline financed by Abu Dhabi, OMAN and Bahrain, was close to collapse after incurring a US$800 million debt and after Qatar pulled out from its 25 per cent stake. Oman, in response, was considering building a national airline, based on Oman Air. Emirates Airlines, meanwhile, had bucked the industry trend by showing rising profits and an aggressive expansion strategy, spending US$15 billion over 10 years to acquire 25 Boeing 777 aircraft, eight Airbus 340-600, and three Airbus 330 aircraft, together with 22 Airbus 380 jumbo aircraft under development. This would take its fleet to over 100 aircraft. Airport usage in the UAE, which saw 16 million passengers in 2000, was set to rise to 32 million passengers in 2006 and airport usage fees were being cut in all six of the region's international airports. In the UAE, in particular, where international tourists rose from 600,000 in 1989 to 3.42 million in 2000 and where the ambitious US$3 billion Palm Beach development was nearing completion, this was in part to attract tourism. The UAE, particularly Dubai, was also laying great emphasis on information technology as part of its push for non-oil-based development and was applying World Intellectual Property Organisation standards to its electronic sector, thus allowing for international arbitration. However, the telecom sector needed improvement if this strategy was to succeed. Oman announced that it intended to develop its own information technology sector.

Oil, however, continued to dominate the Gulf scene—representing 73 per cent of government revenue in Oman, 70 per cent in the UAE, and 75 per cent in Kuwait—and the region benefited from generally buoyant oil prices during the year, despite Organisation of the Petroleum Exporting Countries (OPEC) production cuts. Kuwait and the UAE continued to produce over-quota towards the end of the year but this did not adversely affect oil prices. In the UAE and Qatar, GDP in 2001 had fallen by 2.5 per cent and 1.8 per cent respectively because of weak oil prices; but in both countries, the non-oil sector had seen significant gains, rising by 6.6 per cent and 3.5 per cent respectively.

Budget forecasts, however, tended to be too pessimistic because they were based on low oil price forecasts. Thus Kuwait's budget surplus for the first half of the financial year at KD1.15 billion (US$3.75 billion) contrasted with a forecasted deficit of KD721 million (US$2.31 billion). In Oman the projected 2002 budget deficit, at US$974 million—2.5 per cent of GDP and 17 per cent greater than in 2001 when it rose by 20 per cent—was expected to decline, given strong oil prices. The UAE budget for the financial year 2002 anticipated a deficit of US$591 million on revenue of US$5,718 billion. Qatar reported a budget surplus for the 2001-02 financial year of US$157.5 million and this was expected to increase in 2002-03. Debt servicing had risen rapidly, however, by 200 per cent over 1999 levels to US$1.5 billion in 2001.

Trade and investment, however, were stagnant during the year. In Bahrain, non-oil exports fell by 6 per cent in the first quarter of 2002 whilst imports rose by 14.9 per cent and the trade surplus declined by 80 per cent. The trade surplus in Oman was expected to be around US$2 billion in 2002 because of a rise in oil revenue despite a 6.3 per cent decline in production in the first quarter of the year. The Omani government sought to strengthen the non-oil sector and was proposing to privatise OmanTel with a 40 per cent foreign and 9 per cent local stake.

Foreign investment in Qatar remained buoyant, with news of a new Exxon-Mobil-Qatar Petroleum LGN joint venture in June to supply gas to the UK. In Bahrain, where unemployment rose to a record 5.6 per cent (13.6 per cent for the indigenous population) during the year, funding was found for the US$340 million second stage of the Hidd power plant. Difficulties arose for the ARIG insurance group at the end of the year when both the UAE and Libya abruptly refused to subscribe to a new US$100 million rights issue. The group had lost US$283 million in the last three years, mainly in the airlines sector.

In the UAE, which was currently the Arab world's third largest economy, with the second highest per capita income at US$21,280 compared with Qatar (US$28,000), and where international accounting standards were introduced at the start of the year, the new levels of transparency ensured that foreign investment did not fall. There were fears, however, that a boycott of US goods could adversely affect the situation. The UAE also announced that it would authorise no more foreign banks until 2005, to the World Trade Organisation's (WTO) displeasure. Foreign debt there remained low at US$16.5 billion—27.2 per cent of GDP—and with a debt service ratio of 5.9 per cent.

In Kuwait, investment income fell because of the weakness of international stock markets but the current account surplus was expected to improve on the back of rising oil prices which were expected to generate US$14.63 billion in revenue during the year. Foreign investment stagnated largely because the government's 2001-06 economic development plan had not prioritised privatisation. The government also faced an employment dilemma as it provided employment for all nationals who requested it and currently employed 220,000 people, 60 per cent of them in non-productive jobs, with 14,000 new entrants to the employment market each year. At the end of the year, it was announced that the Kuwaiti dinar would be pegged to the US dollar from 1 January 2003, rather than, as in the past, to a currency basket.

4. SUDAN—LIBYA—TUNISIA—ALGERIA—MOROCCO—WESTERN SAHARA

i. SUDAN

CAPITAL: Khartoum   AREA: 2,500,000 sq km   POPULATION: 31,687,000
OFFICIAL LANGUAGE: Arabic   POLITICAL SYSTEM: multiparty republic
HEAD OF STATE AND GOVERNMENT: President (Gen.) Omar Hasan Ahmed al-Bashir (since Oct '93), previously Chairman of Revolutionary Command Council (since June '89)
RULING PARTY: National Congress Party (NCP)
MAIN IGO MEMBERSHIPS (NON-UN): AL, AU, COMESA, OIC, ACP, NAM
CURRENCY: Sudan dinar (end '02 £1=SD414.321, US$1=SD258.700)
GNI PER CAPITA: US$330, US$1,610 at PPP ('01)

INTENSIVE efforts to end the civil war in southern Sudan occurred in January. Clare Short, UK Secretary of State for International Development and Hilde Frafjord Johnson, Norwegian Minister for International Development and Human Rights, met President Omar Hasan Ahmed al-Bashir and Col. John Garang, leader of the Sudan People's Liberation Army Movement (SPLM), the political wing of the rebel Sudan People's Liberation Army (SPLA), in an exploratory attempt to bring together the two warring parties. More successful was John Danforth, special US presidential envoy to Sudan, whose efforts at mediation produced a six-month ceasefire agreement in the Nuba Mountains between the SPLA and the government. It was signed in Switzerland and was endorsed by the African Union (AU).

Egypt and Libya also lobbied for their joint peace initiative, as did the Inter-governmental Authority for Development (IGAD), which advocated rights of self-determination for southern Sudanese and the separation of state and religion. IGAD Foreign Ministers (from Somalia, Sudan, Ethiopia, Kenya, Uganda, Eritrea, and Djibouti) together with representatives from Egypt, Libya, Qatar, the Arab League, and the Organisation of the Islamic Conference (OIC) met in Khartoum (the Sudanese capital) in January to discuss the prospects for peace. Pressure from the USA led the Sudan government to begin peace negotiations with the SPLA on the principle of creating separate systems in the predominantly Muslim north and the Christian south within a confederate state. Egypt and Libya and the Arab League, however, expressed concern that the proposal might endanger the unity of Sudan by exacerbating religious and ethnic divisions.

The possibility of bringing the war to an end and the prospects for power sharing resulted in a reconciliation between Garang and his old rival Riek Machar, leader of the Sudan People's Democratic Front (SPDF). The two leaders signed an agreement in Nairobi on 6 January to merge the SPLM and the SPDF in order to pursue the war more effectively.

Despite efforts to end the civil war, military operations continued. In February, 17 civilians were reported killed by a government helicopter attack on a UN food aid distribution centre in western Upper Nile in southern Sudan. In June the SPLA scored a significant victory by capturing the garrison town of Kapoeta, in Equatoria state, some 50 km north of the border with Kenya. Although government forces recaptured Gaisan, a small town on the border with Ethiopia, this success did not offset the significance of the fall of Kapoeta, which represented the SPLA's biggest battlefield triumph for two years.

Mounting political pressure on Sudan to end the war by the USA, the UK, the EU, and Norway led to serious negotiations in June between the SPLM and the government under the auspices of IGAD in the Kenyan town of Machakos. Supporting this initiative, Kofi Annan, the UN Secretary-General, visited Khartoum in July in order to discuss humanitarian aid and progress in the negotiations. The Machakos talks, chaired by Lt-Gen. Lazaro Sumbeiyow, the special IGAD envoy, resulted in the signing on 20 July of a memorandum which offered the prospect of southern Sudan achieving self-determination and freedom from the Islamic Shari'a law practised in the north. The accord did not include a ceasefire agreement, although the government and SPLM agreed to further talks to try and arrange a halt to hostilities. Following the implementation of a ceasefire, the accord offered the south the option of seceding after a six-year transitional period. During that time, a joint administration of government and rebel leaders would rule from Khartoum, and the south would also be given a degree of autonomy yet to be decided, but which would include religious freedoms.

The commitment of both sides to pressing ahead with the agreement was underlined in late July when President al-Bashir travelled to Uganda for an historic first meeting with Col Garang. However, the issues left outstanding by the Machakos memorandum proved to be a major stumbling block to the achievement of a ceasefire agreement. Furthermore, the memorandum was opposed by Egypt which feared that it would lead to the cession of southern Sudan.

The peace negotiations were suspended by the government following the SPLA's capture of the strategically and symbolically important town of Torit, the capital of Eastern Equatoria state on 30 August. For much of the current conflict Torit had served as the headquarters of the SPLA, until its capture by the government in 1992. Its recapture by the rebels threatened Juba, the largest and most important southern city still under government control. The capture of Torit also underlined the fact that the SPLA was not operating as a guerrilla army, but was making full use of tanks and heavy artillery. Although government troops recaptured Torit in early October, the government's military presence on the eastern bank of the White Nile remained precarious.

Furthermore, the government was under pressure from the US administration to resume participation in the peace process. This increased when President George W. Bush signed the Sudan Peace Act in October which provided for the imposition of economic sanctions against Sudan and US financial assistance to the SPLA if a peace agreement were not signed by March 2003. The resumed Machakos negotiations led to the signing of a temporary ceasefire, to begin at noon on 17 October, which would last as long as the Machakos negotiations continued, or until the end of December. However, the ceasefire was soon violated when government troops launched an assault on rebel-held positions near the border with Eritrea. Although the talks continued until the end of the year, there was little sign of progress, particularly with regard to the vexed issues of power sharing and the division of the country's oil revenues between north and south.

Relations between the Sudanese government and Egypt became closer during the year and protocols were signed to co-operate in the economic, political, and medical fields. In December Uganda and Sudan signed an agreement to allow the former to pursue the forces of the rebel Lord's Resistance Army (LRA) inside Sudan (see VI.1.iv). Relations between the two countries had been improving since April when diplomatic links had been resumed for the first time since 1995. By contrast, relations with Eritrea remained strained as the Sudanese government accused its neighbour of supporting the SPLA and the opposition umbrella group, the National Democratic Alliance (NDA).

Notwithstanding some Cabinet appointments, in terms of domestic politics there was little significant change during the year. In June three leading members of the ruling National Congress Party (NCP) resigned on the grounds that the party was being dominated by a power-hungry clique which was undermining basic freedoms. The three—Minister of Transport Lam Akol, former presidential peace adviser Mekki Ali Balyel, and former deputy Justice Minister Amin Bannani—issued a statement which said that the NCP was "too deformed to be reformed". Although a presidential decree allowed political parties that had been represented in the legislature prior to 1989 to resume their activities, Hasan al-Turabi, the leader of the Popular National Congress Party (PNCP) and al-Bashir's chief rival, remained under house arrest (see AR 2001, p. 245).

The cost of prosecuting the war in the south escalated Sudan's international debt from US$21.5 billion to US$22.7 billion during the year. Nevertheless the government continued to spend heavily on arms, and signed a US$200-US$300 million agreement with Russia for the purchase of fighter aircraft, helicopters, and troop carriers.

ii. LIBYA

CAPITAL: Tripoli   AREA: 1,760,000 sq km   POPULATION: 5,410,000
OFFICIAL LANGUAGE: Arabic   POLITICAL SYSTEM: one-party republic
HEAD OF STATE: Col Moamer Kadhafi, "Leader of the Revolution" (since '69)
HEAD OF GOVERNMENT: Mubarak Abdullah al-Shamikh, Secretary General of General People's Committee (since Dec '97)
MAIN IGO MEMBERSHIPS (NON-UN): AL, OPEC, OAPEC, AMU, AU, OIC, NAM
CURRENCY: Libyan dinar (end-'02 £1=LD1.9691, US$1=LD1.2295)
GNI PER CAPITA: n/a

IN late January Abdel-Baset Al-Megrahi mounted an appeal against his conviction for the 1988 Lockerbie bombing before a panel of five Scottish judges sitting, as before, at Camp Zeist in the Netherlands. At the centre of the appeal was new evidence from a former security guard at London's Heathrow Airport who claimed that on the night that flight PanAm 103 departed, a door giving access to the loading area of Terminal 3 had been tampered with. This suggested that the bomb which destroyed the aircraft (see AR 1988, p. 38) could have been planted in London and not in Malta, thus casting doubt on Megrahi's conviction. On 16 March, however, the judges ruled that none of the grounds put forward by the defence were well-founded and Megrahi's appeal was refused. He was immediately transferred to Barlinnie prison in Glasgow to begin his life sentence. Libya condemned the ruling as a "political verdict" and pledged to continue efforts to free Megrahi.

Notwithstanding Libya's condemnation of the appeal verdict, rumours circulated that a deal with the Libyan government on compensation for the families of Lockerbie victims, involving several billions of dollars, was imminent. In May a partner in the US legal firm representing the Lockerbie families stated that Libya had made an offer of US$2,700 million, but that certain conditions were attached, namely that the money should be paid into a UN escrow account and released in tranches—40 per cent after the permanent lifting of UN sanctions, 40 per cent after the lifting of US sanctions, and the final 20 per cent after Libya was removed from the US list of states believed to be sponsoring terrorism. Libya immediately denied the allegations. Later in the year there were conflicting statements from Libya's Secretary for Foreign Liaison Mohammed Chalgam on whether or not the Libyan state would pay compensation.

Relations with the USA remained cool, and although President George W. Bush did not include Libya in his "axis of evil" speech (see IV.1), the US administration later accused Libya of trying to obtain a nuclear capacity and expertise in ballistic missiles, as well as resuming the manufacture of chemical weapons, allegations firmly rejected by the Libyan authorities. In contrast, relations with the UK and France continued to improve. In early August a British Foreign Office Minister visited Libya for talks with Col Moamer Kadhafi, the first visit at that level for some 20 years. The Minister welcomed statements by the Libyan leader that he was willing to cooperate with the international community on issues such as weapons of mass destruction and the "war against terrorism", but emphasised that there had to be clear proof that Kadhafi intended to deliver on his promises. In early September UK Prime Minister Tony Blair expressed the hope that Libya would become a "fully-fledged member of the international community" and said that, despite concerns relating to Libya's past, he was prepared to extend the hand of friendship. The French Foreign Minister, Dominique de Villepin, visited Tripoli in mid-October and reported that progress had been made regarding further compensation for the families of victims of the 1989 bombing of a UTA airliner. Later that month Chalgam visited Paris for the first meeting of the Franco-Libyan Commission in 20 years, a clear sign that bilateral relations were being normalised.

In July Kadhafi travelled to Durban, South Africa for a heads of state summit to inaugurate the new African Union (see XI.6.ii). He was accompanied by a large entourage and, according to the South African press, "enough weapons to start a small war". In early August Human Rights Watch criticised Kadhafi's appointment to the steering committee of the New Partnership for African Development (NEPAD) and condemned the organisation for nominating Libya to chair the next session of the UN Commission on Human Rights, pointing to its record of human rights abuses. Libyan troops and aircraft continued to help keep President Ange-Félix Patassé in power in the Central African Republic, but by the end of the year his authority was limited to the capital, Bangui (see VI.3.ii). In late August a former Libyan diplomat was expelled from Zimbabwe, accused of working with the opposition Movement for Democratic Change (MDC). The Libyan was believed to have co-operated closely with Zimbabwe's secret services for many years, and unconfirmed reports from the Zimbabwean capital, Harare, alleged that he was being punished for refusing to take part in a plot to murder MDC leader Morgan Tsvangirai. In November, after reports that the 2001 oil agreement between Libya and Zimbabwe had collapsed, the Libyan ambassador to Harare insisted that the reasons for this were commercial rather than political.

At the beginning of March the secretary-general of the Arab League, Amr Moussa, visited Tripoli after Kadhafi threatened to withdraw from the organisation in protest at what he regarded as its ineptitude in the face of the escalating Israeli-Palestinian conflict (see V.2.i). Kadhafi did not attend the League's Beirut summit in late March, but the Libyan delegation eventually supported the Saudi peace plan and pledged US$50 million in assistance to the Palestinians. In late October, however, Libya again gave notice that it wanted to quit the Arab League, but after hectic diplomacy at a meeting of Arab Foreign Ministers in Cairo in mid November, Libya agreed to put its threat on hold (see XI.6.i).

Growth in GDP in 2002 was projected at around 6.5 per cent. Oil companies, notably ENI of Italy, continued to lead the investment drive, the authorities finally decided to devalue the dinar and Libya applied to join the World Trade Organisation.

iii. TUNISIA

CAPITAL: Tunis   AREA: 164,000 sq km   POPULATION: 9,700,000
OFFICIAL LANGUAGE: Arabic   POLITICAL SYSTEM: multiparty republic
HEAD OF STATE AND GOVERNMENT: President (Gen.) Zine el-Abidine Ben Ali (since Nov '87)
RULING PARTY: Constitutional Democratic Rally (RCD)
PRIME MINISTER: Mohammed Ghannouchi (since Nov '99)
MAIN IGO MEMBERSHIPS (NON-UN): AL, AMU, ICO, AU, OIC, NAM, Francophonie
CURRENCY: Tunisian dinar (end-'02 £1=TD2.1390, US$1=TD1.3356)
GNI PER CAPITA: US$2,070, US$6,450 at PPP ('01)

AT the end of February the Chamber of Deputies (the legislature) met in special session to examine proposals for revisions to the constitution. The most controversial proposal was that which recommended that no limits should be placed on the number of times that the president could be re-elected, although all presidential elections had to involve more than one candidate. The revisions were to be put to a referendum which President Zine el-Abidine Ben Ali announced would be held in conditions of transparency, with observers and journalists from neighbouring and friendly countries allowed to monitor the proceedings. The political bureau of Ettajid (the former Communist Party) deplored the fact that the proposals had been presented to the Chamber without prior consultation with opposition parties or civil society, and later was the only party represented in the legislature to condemn the referendum. The opposition group, the National Council for Liberties in Tunisia (CNLT), described the proposals as a manoeuvre to reinforce the absolute powers of the President. There was particular concern that under the proposed changes the head of state would enjoy legal immunity during his term of office and, after the end of his mandate, for actions carried out during that term of office.

At the beginning of April the Chamber of Deputies adopted the proposals which were put to a referendum (Tunisia's first) held on 26 May. Commentators noted that in the final draft the maximum age for presidential candidates had been increased from 70 to 75 years, thereby giving Ben Ali the opportunity to seek two additional terms and fuelling speculation that he intended to make himself "President for life". Despite calls for a boycott by opponents of the changes, the first official results of the referendum indicated that 99.52 per cent of voters had approved them, with voter participation put at 95 per cent. An editorial in the French daily *Le Monde* declared that Ben Ali had used the referendum to mount his own coup d'etat without incurring criticism from the West.

The crackdown on political opponents continued. In February Hamma Hammami, the leader of the Tunisian Communist Workers' Party (POCT), and two party members came out of hiding to protest against the nine-year prison sentences imposed on them in absentia in 1999 for belonging to a banned political party. Brought before a Tunis court, the proceedings were a fiasco. The original sentences were confirmed without the men being given an opportunity to speak and in the absence of their lawyers. There were violent scenes involving plainclothes police both inside and outside the court. Although a court of appeal subsequently reduced the sentences, at the end of June Hammami's wife, lawyer Radia Nasraoui, went on a much-publicised hunger strike to try and secure the immediate release of her husband. At the beginning of June the authorities closed down the popular website *TUNeZINE* and arrested its founder, Zouhair Yahyaoui, for "disseminating false information". As Tunisia's most celebrated "cyber-dissident", Yahyaoui's website had become extremely popular, especially among young people. In early September human rights activists expressed disquiet when the Ministry of Human Rights and Communications was abolished and its functions transferred to the Ministry of Justice as part of a radical Cabinet reshuffle by Ben Ali in which the number of posts was reduced from 54 to 40. In September Hammami and one of his associates were granted conditional release, and in November two other POCT members together with four members of the banned Islamist party, Nahda, were also released. In October the President finally legalised the Democratic Forum for Work and Freedoms (FDTL). Mustapha Ben Jaafer, the party's leader, welcomed the decision but condemned what he described as "made-to-measure pluralism". Mokhtar Trifi, president of the Tunisian Human Rights' League (LTDH), declared that these presidential gestures were totally inadequate and insisted that Tunisia needed instead the liberalisation of political life, a general amnesty, and an independent judiciary.

In early April Tunisia was the target of a serious terrorist attack when a tanker lorry exploded outside the Ghriba synagogue on the island of Djerba killing 19 people, most of whom were German tourists. At first the Tunisian government insisted that the explosion was an accident—this was, no doubt, an exercise in damage limitation because of the importance of the tourist industry to the country's economy—but the German authorities, who sent police investigators to the scene, were convinced that it was a suicide bomb attack. In late June the al-Jazeera television station broadcast a statement by Soulaiman Abou Ghaith, spokesman for al-Qaida, confirming that the attack had been carried out by a young member of al-Qaida "who could not see his Palestinian brothers killed while Jews walked freely in Djerba to enjoy themselves and practice their religion". Later, a number of alleged associates of the young Tunisian suicide bomber, including his brother, were arrested in Germany and France. Shortly after the attack Ben Ali replaced his Interior Minister and the director of the Sûreté National, the most senior officials responsible for internal security.

In January Habib Boulares, a former Tunisian Foreign Minister, was appointed secretary-general of the Arab Maghreb Union (AMU), but despite continued diplomatic efforts, Ben Ali failed to breathe new life into the organisation (see XI.6.i).

In November the government revised GDP growth for 2002 from a projected 4.6 per cent down to 1.9 per cent, blaming the severe drought, a reduction in tourist receipts, and falling exports. The privatisation process received a boost in October when Société Générale of France purchased a 52 per cent stake in the Union Internationale de Banques.

iv. ALGERIA

CAPITAL: Algiers AREA: 2,382,000 sq km POPULATION: 30,900,000
OFFICIAL LANGUAGE: Arabic POLITICAL SYSTEM: multiparty republic
HEAD OF STATE: President Abdelaziz Bouteflika (since April '99)
RULING PARTIES: National Liberation Front (FLN) heads coalition which also includes National Democratic Rally (RND), and Movement for a Peaceful Society (MSP)
PRIME MINISTER: Ali Benflis (since Aug '00)
MAIN IGO MEMBERSHIPS (NON-UN): AL, OPEC, OAPEC, AMU, AU, OIC, NAM
CURRENCY: dinar (end-'02 £1=AD127.620, US$1=AD79.6850)
GNI PER CAPITA: US$1,630, US$5,150 at PPP ('01)

THE National Liberation Front (FLN), formerly the country's single party, swept to victory in legislative elections held at the end of May, securing 199 out of a total of 389 seats and achieving thereby an absolute majority in the new National Assembly. The FLN had come third in the 1997 elections when it won only 62 seats (see AR 1997, p. 235). Political commentators attributed the FLN's success to the energetic leadership of Ali Benflis and to the changes introduced since he became secretary-general, notably his efforts to open the party to young people and women. The National Democratic Rally (RND), widely regarded as the voice of the military "décideurs", was relegated to second place, gaining only 48 seats compared with 155 in 1997. Of the two Islamist parties, the Movement for a Peaceful Society (MSP), which had come second in 1997 with 69 seats, secured only 38 seats, while the National Reform Movement (MRN) led by Sheikh Abdallah Djaballah, took third place with 43 seats (Djaballah's former party, Nahdah, had won 34 seats in 1997). Independent candidates won 29 seats compared with only 11 in 1997, while the Workers' Party (PT) increased its representation from four to 21.

Turnout, however, was low, officially 46 per cent, with the lowest rates recorded in Berber-speaking Kabylia in the north east, where a boycott called by the two main political parties active in the region—the Socialist Forces' Front (FFS) and the Rally for Culture and Democracy (RCD)—and the citizens' movement, the Coordination des aarchs, des diaras et des communes (CADC), proved effective.

Despite concessions by the central government, including a constitutional amendment making Tamazight a national language, the withdrawal of gendarmerie units from the region, and a promise of compensation for victims of rioting during the "black spring" of 2001, Kabylia had continued to descend into anarchy. During the elections most polling stations in the region remained closed and some came under attack by rioters who burnt ballet boxes. Disturbances occurred throughout the region as riot police clashed with demonstrators.

In mid June Benflis formed a new coalition government drawn mainly from the FLN but with the RND and MSP retaining some portfolios. He failed to persuade other political parties, notably the PT and MRN, to join the new administration. About half of the Ministers were new appointments, among them leading feminist and anti-Islamist, Khalida Messaoudi (Communications and Culture and government spokesperson), one of five women appointed to the Cabinet.

In local elections held in October the FLN repeated its success, winning control of 668 of the 1,541 municipal assemblies and 43 of the 48 provincial assemblies. The RND, which had controlled half of the country's municipalities following the 1997 local elections, suffered another crushing defeat, gaining control of only 171 municipal assemblies and not one provincial assembly. The two main Islamist parties together won control of 58 municipal assemblies, the MRN 39 and the MSP 19. The MRN also gained control of one provincial assembly. Turnout was officially given as 50.1 per cent, excluding the provinces of Tizi Ouzou and Bejaia in Kabylia where participation was 7.6 per cent and 15.6 per cent respectively. Although the FFS had decided to take part in these elections, winning control of 66 municipal assemblies, the CADC again succeeded in disrupting voting in many places, and there were violent clashes between protesters and police across Kabylia. A political solution to the crisis engulfing the region remained elusive.

Armed Islamist groups, although smaller and much weaker, were still capable of mounting successful attacks against the security forces and civilians. By the end of the year independent estimates suggested that there were about 1,000 armed Islamists compared with over 25,000 in the mid 1990s. In February the security forces killed Antar Zouabri, emir of the Group islamique armé (GIA) since 1996. Rachid Abu Tourab was named "national emir" and pledged to continue the violent policies of his predecessor, but many believed that the GIA had no more than 100 men and had fragmented into a number of small splinter groups incapable of co-ordinated action. The Groupe salafiste pour la prédication et le combat (GSPC) and the Protecteurs de la prédication salafiste remained well-organised, each with around 350 men. Both groups were believed with have close links with al-Qaida. The fourth group, led by Abdel Khader Souane, with only 100 fighters, was believed to be close to the new head of the Front islamique du salut's executive, Mourad Dhina, based in Geneva, who was considered to be a hardliner.

In foreign relations Algeria continued to emerge from a decade of diplomatic isolation. Jacques Chirac's victory in the French presidential election (see II.2.ii) and the success of the centre-right in legislative elections were welcomed in most political and media circles in Algeria. Relations between the French Socialists and Algeria had always been strained. On his visit to the capital, Algiers, in mid

December the new French Foreign Minister, Dominique de Villepin, called for a "new phase" in Franco-Algerian relations and expressed support for the government's reform programme. In mid October President Abdelaziz Bouteflika had attended the 9th Francophone summit held in Beirut, the first time that an Algerian head of state had taken part (see XI.3.ii). Close co-operation with the USA in the "war against terrorism" continued, and in December the US government lifted its ban on arms sales to Algeria and agreed to supply some military equipment for use in the government's anti-terrorist campaign.

Relations with neighbouring Morocco, however, remained strained and the long-awaited heads of state summit of the Arab Maghreb Union (AMU), scheduled to take place in Algiers in late June, was postponed after King Mohammed announced that he would not attend (see XI.6.i). As relations between Spain and Morocco deteriorated sharply over their disputed territorial claims to a small island (see II.4.i), the former drew closer to Algeria. Bouteflika made an official visit to Spain in October, the first by an Algerian President for 17 years.

In a highly critical report published in mid December, the National Economic and Social Council stated that economic growth in 2002 was probably around 2.5 per cent, well below the 6 per cent officially projected. Despite accumulating reserves of US$21,000 million in 2002, the economy remained sluggish and unemployment continued to rise, aggravating social tensions. It was imperative, said the report, that economic decision-making be centralised and made more transparent. Finally it recommended a return to greater state involvement in the economy.

v. MOROCCO

CAPITAL: Rabat   AREA: 447,000 sq km   POPULATION: 29,200,000
OFFICIAL LANGUAGE: Arabic   POLITICAL SYSTEM: multiparty monarchy
HEAD OF STATE AND GOVERNMENT: King Mohammed VI (since July '99)
RULING PARTIES: Socialist Union of Popular Forces (USFP) heads broad coalition
PRIME MINISTER: Driss Jettou (non-party), Prime Minister (since Oct '02)
MAIN IGO MEMBERSHIPS (NON-UN): AL, AMU, OIC, NAM, Francophonie
CURRENCY: dirham (end-'02 £1=D16.3631, US$1=D10.2170)
GNI PER CAPITA: US$1,180, US$3,690 at PPP ('01)

IN the run-up to legislative elections in September the government, led by Prime Minister Abderrahmane el-Yousifi, agreed important changes to the electoral system, abandoning the first-past-the-post system used since 1955 in favour of proportional representation. Some 10 per cent of the 325 seats in the lower house (the House of Representatives) were reserved for women. Electoral boundaries were redrawn, new electoral rolls were prepared, and millions of new identity cards were issued. Audio-visual awareness campaigns using new technologies such as the Internet and mobile telephone text messages were launched, stressing citizens' free choice and the importance of their vote in contributing to the management of public affairs. At a news conference to mark the beginning of the election campaign, the Interior Minister, Driss Jettou, declared that the vote "must contribute to the building of a democratic society" and would be conducted with "transparency, credibility and sincerity". He renewed his pledge that the administration would remain neutral in all phases of the election. Before stepping down as Prime Minister, el-Yousifi defended the record of his government, but his critics accused him of poor economic management and of giving priority to a smooth royal transition instead of negotiating a new division of powers between the monarchy and the government.

The elections were held in a relatively calm atmosphere marred by only a few isolated violent incidents and accusations of fraud in a few places. Leaders from across the political spectrum and most of the press stated that the elections had, on the whole, been fair and transparent. The official results put turnout at between 52 and 55 per cent, compared with 58.3 per cent in 1997. Press reports during the election campaign had pointed to widespread voter apathy especially in the main urban centres. The leading Islamist group, Al Adl wa-'l Ihsan (Justice and Charity), and the extreme left-wing Democratic Socialist Avant-Garde Party (PADS), had both announced that they would boycott the elections. The Socialist Union of Popular Forces (USFP) came first with 50 seats (down from 57 in 1997) followed by Istiqlal (up from 32 to 48 seats). The Islamist Justice and Development Party (PJD) came third with 42 seats compared with only nine in 1997, a remarkable result as the party had presented candidates in only 56 of the 91 constituencies. The growing appeal of the PJD was widely interpreted as a sign of protest at the failure of the mainstream parties to address the country's deep-seated social and economic problems. The centrist National Rally of Independents (RNI) came fourth with 41 seats, compared with 46 in 1997. Among the other parties the main losers were the right-wing Constitutional Union (UC) (16 seats as against 50 in 1997) and the Popular Movement (MP) (27 seats against 40)—their success in the past had been widely attributed to support from the administration—and the centre-right Social Democratic Movement (MDS) down from 32 to seven seats. In contrast the smaller left-wing parties slightly increased their representation.

King Mohammed VI who had been expected to choose a new Prime Minister from the USFP leadership, instead named technocrat and former Interior Minister Driss Jettou as premier and called upon him to consult with all parties in order to form a new government. Some commentators argued that whereas King Hassan had ruled by manipulating the political parties, his son appeared to want to rule without them in the name of addressing urgent social and economic problems. In early November, after almost a month of negotiations, a new government was appointed composed of six political parties—USFP (eight ministers), Istiqlal (eight), RNI (six), MP (three), Party for Progress and Socialism (PPS) (two), and the National Popular Movement (MNP) (two). Two small left-wing parties, the Front of Democratic Forces (FFD) and the Democratic Socialist Party (PSD), which had been part of the outgoing administration, were not represented in the new government. The new administration remained firmly under the control of the monarchy.

The Israeli military offensive into Palestinian-controlled areas of the West Bank in April (see V.2.i) aroused strong passions among Moroccans. On 7 April, over a million protesters took to the streets in the capital, Rabat, to express solidarity with the Palestinian people. When US Secretary of State Colin Powell visited

Morocco the next day as the first stop on his Middle Eastern peace mission, King Mohammed politely suggested that, given the urgent crisis in the West Bank, it might have been advisable for him to visit Jerusalem first. The incident did not appear to sour relations with the USA, however, and in May the US Deputy Defence Secretary, Paul Wolfowitz, praised Morocco as one of the Muslim states most closely engaged in the "war against terrorism". In June the Moroccan authorities announced that they had arrested three Saudi nationals and seven Moroccans linked to al-Qaida accused of planning attacks against US and UK warships in the Straits of Gibraltar and tourist sites in Marrakech. Later the security forces launched a campaign to crackdown on Islamist extremists, making numerous arrests, closing Islamic bookshops and seizing literature and cassettes.

Relations with Spain deteriorated even further in mid July when a small detachment of Moroccan troops occupied the uninhabited islet of Perejil (Leila) near the Spanish enclave of Ceuta (see II.4.i). Morocco claimed sovereignty over the islet and insisted that it was merely establishing a surveillance post there as part of its campaign against illegal emigration and drug smuggling. Spain protested, recalled its ambassador to Rabat, and a few days later Spanish special forces removed the Moroccan troops from the islet. Following US mediation Spanish forces withdrew from the islet, and during talks in Rabat at the end of July it was agreed that neither Spain nor Morocco should occupy the islet permanently. Further talks were scheduled for September to address other issues causing friction between the two countries, but tensions remained high and it was not until December that an agreement was reached in the Spanish capital, Madrid, to normalise relations. The incident put further strains on Morocco's relations with the EU.

The economy remained sluggish with growth around 2.5 per cent in 2002 compared with an officially projected 4.5 per cent. Prime Minister Jettou, addressing the legislature in late November, stated that economic development was one of the top priorities of his new administration. He pointed to a series of measures to curb unemployment but admitted that growth would have to exceed 6 per cent to reduce the high unemployment rate.

vi. WESTERN SAHARA

CAPITAL: Al Aaiún   AREA: 284,000 sq km   POPULATION: 244,900
STATUS: regarded by Morocco as under its sovereignty, whereas independent Sahrawi Arab Democratic Republic (SADR) was declared by Polisario Front in 1976
MAIN IGO MEMBERSHIPS (NON-UN): AU

IN a new report to the UN Security Council in February on the future of the peace process in the Western Sahara, Secretary-General Kofi Annan stated that in his opinion there were only four options available: (i) to proceed with the long-delayed referendum on self-determination; (ii) for the Western Sahara to become a semi-autonomous province of Morocco—an option rejected by both Polisario and Algeria; (iii) for the UN to end its peace mission in the disputed territory and withdraw its military observers, risking a possible confrontation between Morocco and Algeria; and (iv) the most controversial proposal, to divide the territory between Morocco and Polisario. The Annan report pointed out that while Algeria and Polisario might be willing to discuss this option, Morocco was firmly opposed to it. Morocco attributed the partition plan to Algeria, and claimed that the Algerian government wanted to create a Sahrawi mini-state under its protection in order to provide Algeria with an outlet to the Atlantic. Although Algeria's representative at the UN denied putting forward the plan, there was speculation that it had been a personal initiative of Algerian President Abdelaziz Bouteflika. The Security Council rejected the option of a UN withdrawal from the disputed territory. During further discussions in April and July, however, it remained deeply divided and was unable to agree upon any of the remaining three options put forward by the Secretary-General, efforts by US diplomats having failed to persuade a majority of Council members to accept the autonomy plan favoured by Morocco.

Nevertheless, all members agreed that the UN should not walk away from the problem and passed a resolution renewing the mandate of the UN Mission for the Referendum in Western Sahara (MINURSO) for another six months. The Secretary-General's special envoy, James Baker, was invited to continue his efforts to seek a political solution to the dispute, and the Council expressed its readiness to consider any approach which provided for self-determination for the people of Western Sahara. UN sources, however, stated that it would be virtually impossible to find even sufficient common ground for the parties to begin talks and that Baker's room to manoeuvre was extremely limited. Six months later, the Security Council was likely to be facing exactly the same problems.

At the end of February Bouteflika had made an unexpected visit to the Sahrawi refugee camps around Tindouf in western Algeria. Morocco described the visit, the first by an Algerian President, as "provocative". At the beginning of March King Mohammed VI of Morocco made a two day visit to the Western Sahara, his third in four months, and convened a meeting of the Council of Ministers at the southern port of Dakhla. In a televised address in early November marking the 27th anniversary of the "Green March" (when several hundred thousand Moroccans crossed into Western Sahara in an attempt to legitimise their country's claim to the territory—see AR 1975, p. 206), the King stated that the proposed referendum outlined in the UN settlement plan had become "out-of-date" since it was absolutely impossible to implement it effectively.

In October the UN High Commissioner for Refugees, Ruud Lubbers, stated that the "shameful situation" of Sahrawi refugees was not the result of lack of assistance but the lack of political solutions, and that Morocco and Algeria had better realise the gravity of the situation and talk.

In May Polisario signed an agreement with Fusion Oil of Australia to undertake, at its own cost, an integrated study of all relevant geological and geophysical data available on "Sahrawi territorial waters".

VI EQUATORIAL AFRICA

1. HORN OF AFRICA—KENYA—TANZANIA—UGANDA

i. ETHIOPIA—ERITREA—SOMALIA—DJIBOUTI

Ethiopia

CAPITAL: Addis Ababa   AREA: 1,104,000 sq km   POPULATION: 65,800,000
OFFICIAL LANGUAGE: Amharic   POLITICAL SYSTEM: multiparty republic
HEAD OF STATE: President Girma Woldegiorgis (since Oct '01)
RULING PARTIES: Ethiopian People's Revolutionary Democratic Front (ERPDF) coalition
HEAD OF GOVERNMENT: Meles Zenawi, Prime Minister (since Aug '95)
MAIN IGO MEMBERSHIPS (NON-UN): AU, COMESA, ACP, NAM
CURRENCY: birr (end-'02 £1=Br13.2929, US$1=Br8.3000)
GNI PER CAPITA: US$100, US$710 at PPP ('01)

Eritrea

CAPITAL: Asmara   AREA: 118,000 sq km   POPULATION: 4,200,000
OFFICIAL LANGUAGES: Arabic & Tigrinyam   POLITICAL SYSTEM: transitional government
HEAD OF STATE AND GOVERNMENT: President Isayas Afewerki (since May '93)
RULING PARTY: People's Front for Democracy and Justice (PFDJ)
MAIN IGO MEMBERSHIPS (NON-UN): AU, COMESA, ACP, NAM
CURRENCY: nakfa, at par with Ethiopian birr (see above)
GNI PER CAPITA: US$190, US$970 at PPP ('01)

Somalia

CAPITAL: Mogadishu   AREA: 638,000 sq km   POPULATION: 9,089,000
OFFICIAL LANGUAGES: Somali & Arabic   POLITICAL SYSTEM: transitional government
HEAD OF STATE AND GOVERNMENT: President Abdiqasim Salad Husein (since Aug '00)
PRIME MINISTER: Hasan Abshir Farah (since Nov '01)
MAIN IGO MEMBERSHIPS (NON-UN): AL, AU, ACP, OIC, NAM
CURRENCY: Somalia shilling (end-'02 £1=Ssh4,196.06, US$1=Ssh2,620.00)
GNI PER CAPITA: n/a

Djibouti

CAPITAL: Djibouti   AREA: 23,000 sq km   POPULATION: 644,000
OFFICIAL LANGUAGES: Arabic & French   POLITICAL SYSTEM: multiparty republic
HEAD OF STATE AND GOVERNMENT: President Ismail Omar Guellah (since April '99)
RULING PARTY: Popular Rally for Progress (RPP)
PRIME MINISTER: Dilleita Mohamed Dilleita (since March '01)
MAIN IGO MEMBERSHIPS (NON-UN): AL, AU, COMESA, ACP, OIC, Francophonie, NAM
CURRENCY: Djibouti franc (end-'02 £1=DFr280.271, US$1=DFr175.000)
GNI PER CAPITA: US$890, US$2,120 at PPP ('01)

IN ETHIOPIA throughout 2002 Prime Minister Meles Zenawi and the ruling Ethiopian People's Revolutionary Democratic Front (ERPDF) government continued to have problems in implementing the programme of renewal announced the previous October.

Zenawi re-committed the government to making progress on good governance and reducing poverty when opening the legislature on 8 October. In December, the country hosted the first Ethiopian Consultative Group meeting for six years; its Sustainable Development and Poverty Reduction Programme (SDPRP) was well received. Donors accepted the effects of collapsing world coffee prices and the drought on levels of poverty in the country. Late and insufficient rains meant that 11 million people needed food aid by the end of the year. In March Ethiopia was also identified as one of the four countries in the world most affected by AIDS/HIV, with an estimated 3 million people (7.3 per cent of the population) living with the virus.

Prime Minister Zenawi successfully negotiated his own Tigrai Peoples Liberation Front (TPLF) congress in September, but there were difficulties in most regional states. In March, an outbreak of student unrest in Western Oromo over academic issues compounded the effects of falling coffee and low grain prices. The government response was tough, with five students killed and hundreds of community leaders, farmers, and students arrested. Officials from the state's ruling party, the Oromo Peoples Democratic Organisation (OPDO), were dismissed and arrested. The government claimed involvement by the Eritrean-based opposition Oromo Liberation Front (OLF), which had infiltrated several groups of fighters across the western border. By mid-year most of these had been killed or captured, but small-scale OLF activity continued. The government also accused the OLF of responsibility for a bomb in an Addis Ababa hotel in September. This the OLF denied, but it did admit to bombing a railway office in Dire Dawa in June.

Ethnic clashes occurred in several regions throughout 2002. In the Southern Peoples Regional State, at Tepi, demonstrators clashed with police in March. In the unrest, 24 people were killed and subsequent security force actions left at least 128 others dead. Hundreds more were arrested. In May, armed police fired on several thousand people demonstrating in Awasa against a proposed change of status for the town, leaving up to 40 dead; over 1,000 others were arrested. After international protests at the brutality, a number of officials were detained, but no trials had been held by the end of the year. Extensive purges also took place in the state's ruling party, the Southern Ethiopian Peoples Democratic Front (SEPDF), at its October conference, with its chairman forced to retire and nearly half of the central committee dismissed.

In Gambella Regional State, after a series of clashes between Nuer and Anuak over several months which left thousands displaced and over 200 dead, the ruling party was dissolved and 20 officials arrested. Two new political parties and a new administration were set up. In the Somali State, in May, 71 members of the ruling party and over half of the bureau and zonal heads were dismissed. In November, the Addis Ababa city administration was dissolved with 13 members sacked for inefficiency and corruption. Also in November, the president and vice-presidents of Addis Ababa University resigned over government interference in university management and academic freedom.

Relations between Ethiopia and Eritrea remained uneasy. In February, in an unprecedented visit, a 15-member delegation from the UN Security Council visited Ethiopia and Eritrea to encourage acceptance of the peace process. On

13 April, the independent Border Commission—established by the Permanent Court of Arbitration based in The Hague, the Netherlands, following the December 2000 peace agreement (see AR 2000, p. 232)—released its "final and binding decision" on the Ethiopian-Eritrean border, which both countries were committed to accept. Each side lost and gained substantial areas of territory, but their propaganda continued. Badme, the original flash point of the war, was not on the commission's published maps. Both sides claimed it, although its exact position would only become clear once the border had been demarcated by the United Nations Mission to Ethiopia and Eritrea (UNMEE). Ethiopia promptly asked for clarification of the ruling but the commission rejected the request in July. In May, Ethiopia demanded the removal of UNMEE commander, Maj.-Gen. Patrick Cammaert, accusing him of bias after the UN took a group of journalists to Badme via Eritrea. The UN refused to remove him, and Cammaert ended his tour of duty in October. In April, after the Border Commission report, Eritrea demanded the removal of the Temporary Security Zone (TSZ), accusing Ethiopia of settling people on Eritrean territory. UNMEE ignored the request. In September, Eritrea expelled most demining companies, accusing them of delays and excessive costs. The release of prisoners of war continued, however, with Ethiopia returning the final group on 29 November.

In ERITREA, the first session of the National Assembly since September 2000 was held in January. It formally condemned the "G15", the members of the central committee of the ruling People's Front for Democracy and Justice (PFDJ), who had been arrested in September 2001 (see AR 2001, p. 259). Arrests of supporters and sympathisers continued throughout the year. In September 2001, 10 journalists had been arrested when the privately owned press was banned; by December 2002 there were 18 detained, and another 20 had fled the country. In February, a European Parliamentary resolution expressed concern over the authoritarian trends in Eritrea, but a new Italian ambassador was appointed in September, after President Issayas Aferwerki had visited Italy. The previous ambassador had been expelled in October 2002 after protesting against the journalists' arrests. Eritrea offered the USA a base for its "war against terrorism". The US State Department opposed the idea because of Eritrea's human rights record, but the US military showed interest. US Secretary of State for Defence Donald Rumsfeld, visiting Eritrea in December, did not rule it out. Concerned by his response, Human Rights Watch wrote to US President George W. Bush to express concern over Eritrea's "gross abuses of civil and political rights". The National Assembly did ratify a draft law on elections but political parties other than the PFDJ were prohibited.

In January, Mesfin Hagos, of the G15, who had been out of the country in September 2001, set up the Eritrean People's Liberation Front-Democratic Party (EPLF-DP) in the USA. He received considerable support from Eritrean civil society forums in the USA and Europe. In July, student leader Semere

Kesete, who escaped after a year's detention in Asmara, set up a Movement for Democracy and Change (MDC). In October, these two parties announced their co-operation, but little effort was made to reach any accommodation with the Alliance of Eritrean National Forces (AENF). Backed by Ethiopia and Sudan, the AENF held a conference in Addis Ababa in October, changing its name to the Eritrean National Alliance (ENA). Abdullah Idris, of the Eritrean Liberation Front (ELF), was elected chairman with, more controversially, Herui Tedla Bairu of the Eritrean Co-operative Movement becoming secretary-general and joining the ENA.

Eritrea, like Ethiopia, was hit by a major drought in 2002. Rainfall was the lowest for a decade. In November the government estimated that 1.4 million out of the total population of 4.2 million were affected by drought, and that another 900,000 internally displaced people and returnees needed assistance; it appealed for 477,000 tonnes of food aid. The continued mobilisation of nearly 300,000 troops and national service conscripts contributed to food production shortfalls. The government launched a three month pilot demobilisation programme for 5,000 troops in May. However, despite promises of another 70,000 demobilisations, only 20,000 more had been released from military service by December. In May the government launched a controversial reconstruction and development programme, "Warsai-Yikealo", using national service conscripts. In August, Aferwerki placed the civilian administration in the provinces under the commanders of the country's four military districts.

In mid-year, the UN estimated that AIDS/HIV had become the second highest cause of death in Eritrea and affected 3 per cent of the population.

In November, Abune Yacob was enthroned as the second Patriarch of the Eritrean Orthodox Church after his predecessor, Abune Filipos, died, aged 102, in September.

During the year, reconciliation efforts over SOMALIA made some advance. In January a summit of the Inter-Governmental Authority for Development (IGAD) in Khartoum set up a Technical Committee of Djibouti, Ethiopia, and Kenya to organise a Somali Peace and Reconciliation Conference. Differences between the members of the committee, and conflicts among Somali factions, meant that the conference only started at Eldoret, in Kenya, on 15 October. The Transitional National Government (TNG) was present with its allies, as was the opposing Somali Reconciliation and Restoration Council (SCCR). The still unrecognised Republic of Somaliland continued its refusal to participate in southern Somali reconciliation.

The aim was the establishment of a broad-based and all-inclusive government before the end of the year, but disagreements slowed progress. There were disputes over the numbers of delegates, the role of the Kenyan chairman, and the tactics of the Technical Committee. By the end of the year the only positive outcome was a largely ignored ceasefire; conflict continued in Puntland, in the central regions, and in Mogadishu. Committees were set up to look at federalism, land and property, demobilisation, reconciliation, regional relations, and economics. After their reports had been delivered, the conference was due to set up a power-sharing government.

Security in Somalia remained poor. The TNG Prime Minister, Hassan Abshir Farah, appointed in November 2001, announced a new Cabinet in February, but the TNG failed to expand its authority outside Mogadishu and even lost ground within the city during serious fighting in May. Conflict increased as faction leaders attempted to establish their credentials in advance of the Peace and Reconciliation Conference. In Puntland, the former President, Col Abdullahi Yusuf of the SRRC, took Bossaso in May and forced his rival, President Col Jama Ali Jama, an ally of the TNG, to flee to Djibouti. In central Somalia, Col Mohamed Nur Shatigudud, the head of the Rahenweyne Resistance Army (RRA), a faction of the SRRC, announced the creation of a South Western Regional Administration in March, with himself as President. His two deputies, Shaykh Adan Madobe and Muhammad Ibrahim Habsade, launched an effort to remove him. At the end of the year, they held the regional capital of Baidoa, though the town had changed hands several times. With Somalia also suffering from drought in 2002, the UN expressed its deep concern over the way that fighting disrupted deliveries of aid and assistance; the UN Security Council voted to enforce its ban on weapons and established an expert panel to monitor infringements.

In the Republic of Somaliland, President Mohamed Ibrahim Egal, after controversially obtaining a year's extension for his presidency in February, died in a hospital in South Africa on 3 May. Within a few hours, Vice President Dahir Riyale Kahin had been sworn in as President. He accepted that the promised electoral process of municipal, presidential, and assembly elections should go ahead. Nine parties registered to fight the municipal elections. These were held in December and observers considered them largely successful. The three leading parties, the Allied People's Democratic Party (UDUB), of President Kahin; KULMIYE, headed by Ahmed Mohamed Silanyo; and UCID, led by Faisal Ali Waraabe, were consequently able to put forward candidates for the presidential elections in May 2003. In December, Kahin survived an assassination attempt, apparently organised from Puntland—which claimed part of the Somaliland regions of Sool and Sanaag—in an unsuccessful effort to disrupt the elections.

IN DJIBOUTI, President Ismail Omar Guellah in September lifted the limits on the numbers of permitted parties. Nine parties—organised into two blocs, one backing the President and the other opposing him—registered to participate in legislative elections which had been postponed until January 2003. In June the former chief of police, Gen. Yacin Yabeh Galab, was sentenced to 15 years in prison for an attempted coup in December 2000. Relations with Ethiopia, despite disagreements over Somalia, remained good. In April, for the first time, the two countries signed an agreement regulating port usage. It guaranteed Ethiopia rights of access and transit, free of tax and customs duties.

Djibouti became a centre for the US "war on terrorism" in the Red Sea area and the Horn of Africa, and headquarters for Task Force 150, which included Spanish, German, and US forces. In October, 800 US soldiers arrived, and by the end of the year there were 1,500; US Secretary of State for Defence, Donald Rumsfeld, visited in December.

ii. KENYA

CAPITAL: Nairobi   AREA: 580,000 sq km   POPULATION: 30,700,000
OFFICIAL LANGUAGES: Kiswahili & English   POLITICAL SYSTEM: multiparty republic in British Commonwealth
HEAD OF STATE AND GOVERNMENT: Mwai Kibaki (NARC) (since Dec '02)
RULING PARTIES: National Rainbow Coalition (NARC) (since Dec '02)
MAIN IGO MEMBERSHIPS (NON-UN): AU, COMESA, ACP, CWTH, NAM
CURRENCY: Kenya shilling (end '02 £1=Ks127.443, US$1=Ks79.5750)
GNI PER CAPITA: US$340, US$1,020 at PPP ('01)

THE expectation that Daniel arap Moi, President since 1978, would stand down when his constitutional term in office ended, increased political tension and heightened ambitions amongst his potential successors. The President tried to control events. In March the Kenya African National Union (KANU) and the National Development Party, its junior partner in the coalition government formed in June 2001, merged to form a "new" KANU with Moi as national chairman; Raila Odinga, the Minister of Energy, as secretary-general; and Uhuru Kenyatta, son of the country's revered first President, as one of four vice presidents. In July Moi named Kenyatta as his "preferred" successor with the intention, it was feared, of retaining the substance of power after leaving public office. This ploy failed, however, as it split the ruling party and caused the defection of several Ministers and prominent members. Odinga formed the Liberal Democratic Party, which in October joined other opposition groups in a new super alliance, the National Rainbow Coalition (NARC), with the 70-year old Mwai Kibaki—a former national Vice President and Minister of Finance—as its presidential candidate. Like Kenyatta, Kibaki was a member of Kenya's largest ethnic group, the Kikuyu. The election campaign began in earnest following the dissolution of the National Assembly (the legislature) on 25 October. It was marred by some violence, though this was on a much lesser scale than in the two previous elections. Kibaki pledged, if elected, to tackle the rampant corruption which, five years earlier, had led Western donors to freeze aid (see AR 1997, p. 245); to end Kenya's "period of dictatorship"; and to revive the ailing economy.

In the elections, which began on 27 December, some 56 per cent of the country's 10.5 million registered voters cast their ballots. Kibaki secured over 62 per cent of the vote in the presidential election; while NARC trounced KANU in the legislative elections, gaining 132 seats to KANU's 68 in the 224-seat National Assembly. In addition, 14 Cabinet Ministers lost their seats.

Results of presidential elections in Kenya

Candidate	Party	Votes	% of vote
Mwai Kibaki	National Rainbow Coalition (NARC)	3,578,972	62.3
Uhuru Kenyatta	Kenya African National Union (KANU)	1,758,212	31.3
Simeon Nyachae	Forum for the Restoration of Democracy-People (FORD-People)	374,730	5.9
James Orengo	Social Democratic Party	23,975	0.4
David Ng'ethe	Chama Cha Uma	9,781	0.1
Total		5,745,670	100.0

Turnout: 56.1 per cent (5,792,910 votes cast; 10,495,469 registered voters).

Results of legislative elections in Kenya

Party	Seats
National Rainbow Coalition (NARC)	132
Kenya African National Union (KANU)	68
Forum for the Restoration of Democracy-People (FORD-People)	15
Sisi Kwa Sisi	2
Safina	2
Forum for the Restoration of Democracy-Asili	2
Shirikisho Party of Kenya	1
Ex officio members	2
Total	224

Turnout: 56.1 per cent.

Despite this overwhelming victory, Kibaki's easy-going (some would say indolent) nature, the presence within NARC of discredited former Ministers, and the difficulty of accommodating the interests of 15 discordant parties within a fractured coalition meant that the government faced an uphill task in effecting the radical change which ordinary Kenyans—many of whom were unemployed and lived in dire poverty—expected. The new President undertook to seek legislative approval for the draft constitution prepared by the constitutional review commission, headed by Professor Yash Ghai. Issued in September, this had called for fundamental changes to the country's system of government, including the transfer of executive power from the President to a Prime Minister, the decentralisation of government, and reform of the judiciary.

In June Chris Obure, the Finance Minister, announced that, because of the huge budget deficit and because foreign creditors were continuing to withhold aid, consumer taxes would be increased; the tax exemptions given to legislators, judges, and army officers reduced; and tax administration tightened. Reciprocal duties would be charged on Tanzanian and Ugandan exports to Kenya. The money saved would benefit small businesses, finance rural electrification and AIDS/HIV treatment, and provide educational bursaries. Help would also be given to the ailing manufacturing industry, and the privatisation programme would be accelerated, with loss-making and non-strategic parastatal companies targeted. The divestiture of the Kenya Commercial Bank would be completed and Kenya Railways prepared for sale.

In July the UK Ministry of Defence agreed to pay £4.5 million in compensation to 228 Masai and Samburu pastoralists for the deaths and injuries inflicted on them or their families by unexploded munitions left behind by British army personnel after exercises in northern Kenya.

In late November a suicide car bomb at the Paradise Hotel, Mombasa, killed 16 people, including members of a Kenyan dance group. Israeli holiday-makers were probably the intended victims, a supposition borne out by the unsuccessful attempt the same day to bring down an Israeli airliner leaving Mombasa.

iii. TANZANIA

CAPITAL: Dar es Salaam/Dodoma   AREA: 945,000 sq km   POPULATION: 34,500,000
OFFICIAL LANGUAGES: Kiswahili & English   POLITICAL SYSTEM: multiparty republic in British Commonwealth
HEAD OF STATE AND GOVERNMENT: President Benjamin Mkapa (since Nov '95)
RULING PARTY: Chama cha Mapinduzi (CCM)
PRESIDENT OF ZANZIBAR: Amani Abeid Karume (since Oct '00)
PRIME MINISTER: Frederick Sumaye (since Nov '95)
MAIN IGO MEMBERSHIPS (NON-UN): AU, SADC, ACP, CWTH, NAM
CURRENCY: Tanzanian shilling (end-'02 £1=Tsh1,555.11, US$1=Tsh971.000)
GNI PER CAPITA: US$270, US$540 at PPP ('01)

IN March Tanzanian observers declared the presidential election in Zimbabwe to be "free and fair" (see VII.2.iii); President Benjamin Mkapa warmly congratulated Robert Mugabe on his re-election and praised his defence of "free, democratic and sovereign governance". Trade links with Zimbabwe were also growing, though not all of them were creditable. Elites of the two countries were alleged to be supplying military arms and logistics to political factions in the Democratic Republic of Congo (DRC), Burundi, and Rwanda, and to be profiting from the smuggling of gems. These suspicions, together with widespread corruption, continuing unrest in Zanzibar, mounting instances of Muslim extremism on the mainland, and concern about the purchase from British Aerospace of a sophisticated and expensive air traffic control system against World Bank advice, were endangering foreign aid and investment.

The President, however, did gain credit by seeking to avoid a repeat of the contentious Zanzibari elections of October 2000 (see AR, 2000, p. 236-37). An independent electoral commission for the islands (to include judges and opposition members) was established and eight CUF leaders were attached to Zanzibari Ministries in order to gain experience of government. Though the 14 or so other opposition parties attracted little national support, the CUF claimed to have branches throughout Tanzania; it appealed especially to Muslims and unemployed youths. In October the CCM congress, which was attended by some 1,600 delegates, held elections to its 85-member national executive committee and the 25-strong central committee, the party's key policy-making body. Mkapa was returned as national chairman; and although his constitutional term as state President did not end until 2005, manoeuvring to succeed him was already under way.

The country continued to benefit economically from the pursuit of sound macro-economic policies, donor support, and debt relief. In his June budget Basil Mramba, the Finance Minister, said that the government aimed to raise economic growth from 5.9 to 6.3 per cent by June 2003, and at the same time to lower inflation. The collection of value added tax (VAT) would be improved, the rate remaining at 20 per cent, as against 18 per cent in Kenya and 17 per cent in Uganda. Money made available under the IMF's Heavily Indebted Poor Countries (HIPC) initiative was to be directed towards improving education, health, water, and rural roads. There would be support for the agricultural sector and a credit guarantee scheme would provide loans to farmers and livestock keepers; civil service salaries would also be improved. The budget incorporated some of the demands made by the private sector, including the Confederation of Tanzania Industries. Together with Kenya and Uganda—fellow members of the East African Commission (EAC) (see XI.6.ii)—a common external tariff was to be imposed on goods coming from non-EAC members.

A serious economic and social setback occurred in June when a train crashed south-east of Dodoma, the capital, killing over 280 people and injuring 800 others.

iv. UGANDA

CAPITAL: Kampala   AREA: 241,000 sq km   POPULATION: 22,800,000
OFFICIAL LANGUAGE: English   POLITICAL SYSTEM: non-party republic in British Commonwealth
HEAD OF STATE AND GOVERNMENT: President Yoweri Museveni (since Jan '86)
RULING PARTIES: National Resistance Movement (NRM) heads broad-based coalition
PRIME MINISTER: Apolo Nsibambi (since April '99)
MAIN IGO MEMBERSHIPS (NON-UN): AU, COMESA, ACP, CWTH, OIC, NAM
CURRENCY: new Uganda shilling (end-'02 £1=Ush2,965.27, US$1=Ush1,851.50)
GNI PER CAPITA: US$280, US$1,250 at PPP ('01)

THE renewal for a short period in April of an agreement with the Sudanese government allowed some 10,000 Ugandan soldiers, who had been withdrawn from the Democratic Republic of Congo (DRC), to enter southern Sudan in order to combat the Lord's Resistance Army (LRA)—the nominally fundamentalist Christian group which had terrorised the Acholi and other people in northern Uganda since 1988. In return, the government undertook to withhold support for the rebel Sudanese People's Liberation Army (SPLA). The failure of "Operation Iron Fist", coupled with an LRA attack in August on a UN refugee camp in northern Uganda which killed 50 civilians, and the threat posed to citizens in western Uganda by other rebel forces, underlined the urgent need for reform of the Ugandan military.

Security was a sensitive issue and was endangered by the close involvement of senior army officers in politics. In mid-October the government closed *The Monitor*, the country's only independent newspaper, for several days after it reported—falsely, it was alleged—that the LRA had shot down an army helicopter; charges were also brought against a reporter and two editors. There were investigations to ascertain whether the story had originated with dissatisfied elements within the army, and if they had links with supporters of Kizza Besigye who had unsuccessfully opposed President Yoweri Museveni in the March 2001 presidential election (see AR 2001, p. 264).

The June budget allowed for a 7 per cent increase in expenditure over the previous financial year despite a significant revenue shortfall caused by the drop in coffee earnings. It sought to stimulate the economy and achieve a 6.6 per cent growth rate, strengthen tax administration and raise tax revenue, while reducing dependence on donor aid, which provided 52 per cent of budget resources. Gerald Ssendawula, the Finance Minister, announced that overall social spending would rise by 35 per cent, with 25 per cent going to education, 16.2 per cent to public administration (some 600,000 people were employed in the public sector), 13.1 per cent to security, and 9.8 per cent to health; agriculture was to receive only 2.3 per cent. In September the IMF granted Uganda a three-year loan for SDR (special drawing rights) 13.5 million under the poverty reduction and growth facility (PRGF). However, the discovery two months earlier that a British engineering company (the subsidiary of a Norwegian multinational) had made an "unauthorised payment" of US$10,000 to a Ugandan government minister halted the construction of the World Bank-financed Bujagali dam on the river Nile.

2. GHANA—NIGERIA—SIERRA LEONE—THE GAMBIA—LIBERIA

i. GHANA

CAPITAL: Accra   AREA: 239,000 sq km   POPULATION: 19,700,000
OFFICIAL LANGUAGE: English   POLITICAL SYSTEM: multiparty republic in British Commonwealth
HEAD OF STATE AND GOVERNMENT: President John Agyekum Kufuor (since Jan '01)
RULING PARTY: New Patriotic Party (NPP)
MAIN IGO MEMBERSHIPS (NON-UN): AU, ECOWAS, ACP, CWTH, NAM
CURRENCY: cedi (end-'02 £1=C13,355.3, US$1=C8.339.00)
GNI PER CAPITA: US$290, US$1,980 at PPP ('01)

THE IMF and World Bank agreed to provide a US$893 million debt-relief package in February, which would partly cover Ghana's debt-service obligations to international financial institutions. In May the African Development Bank (ADB) agreed to write off US$131 million in debt: 80 per cent of the money that Ghana owed it. The debt cancellation came a few days after a visit to the country by the managing director of the IMF, Horst Köhler.

In March, Ghana's ruling New Patriotic Party (NPP) won a by-election, giving it an absolute majority (101) of the 200 seats in the legislature. The NPP took the seat, in the northern constituency of Bimbilla, from the former ruling party, the National Democratic Congress (NDC), by a margin of about 7,000 votes.

President John Kufuor declared a state of emergency in the Dagbon region in April, following the killing of more than 30 people, including the King of the Dagombas, the biggest ethnic group in the northern region. The violence, involving the Andani and the Abudu clans, led to the resignation of two senior government ministers: Interior Minister Malik al-Hassan Yakubu, and Imoro Andani, the Minister for the Northern Region. They stood down amid accusations that Andani had backed one of the warring clans. Two people were arrested in November in connection with the King's death.

Former President Jerry Rawlings stood down as head of Ghana's main opposition party, the NDC, in late April, but retained a ceremonial role as NDC "founder". The new chairman, Obed Asamoah, who had served as Foreign Minister and attorney-general under Rawlings, was elected at the NDC's first congress since the party lost the December 2000 elections. Asamoah beat his main rival, former Defence Minister Alhaji Iddrisu, who was supported by Rawlings, by 334 votes to 332.

President Kufuor inaugurated a National Reconciliation Commission (NRC) in May, to examine past human rights violations. Modelled on similar panels in South Africa and Nigeria, the NRC would grant immunity to those who testified before it. It was mandated to investigate abuses committed during the five military regimes that had ruled Ghana for a total of 22 years after the first coup in 1966. Most hearings were expected to highlight alleged atrocities committed during the 1980s, when Rawlings was military head of state. The Ghana Bar Association claimed that some 300 people had disappeared during those years, many of them alleged victims of politically-motivated killings. A number of businessmen were also thought likely to come forward to reclaim properties confiscated by the then government. Hearings were also expected to focus on the murder in 1982 of three judges and a retired officer at an army shooting range (see AR 1982, p. 230). A number of people connected to Rawlings' government had been executed for the crime at the time, but relatives of some of the victims claimed that its real architects were still alive and retained prominent positions in politics and society. The NRC began its work in September. More than 120 petitions were filed on the first day, and over 2,000 had been filed by the end of the year. As expected, most concerned the period 1982-92, during which Rawlings was in power.

Rawlings was once again in the news in August, following a speech that he made in the central city of Kumasi. Accusing Kufuor's government of corruption, he urged Ghanaians to practise what he termed "positive defiance". He stated that: "We don't have to wait for the next election [due in 2004] to prevent the rot." Rawlings, who had staged military coups in 1979 and 1981, accused Kufuor's New Patriotic Party of lying and called it "the worst government the country has ever had".

In November, the Foreign Minister, Hackman Owusu Agyeman, rejected allegations by rebels in the Côte d'Ivoire that Kufuor had agreed to allow Ivoirian troops to attack rebel positions from within Ghana.

ii. NIGERIA

CAPITAL: Abuja   AREA: 924,000 sq km   POPULATION: 129,900,000
OFFICIAL LANGUAGE: English   POLITICAL SYSTEM: multiparty republic in British Commonwealth
HEAD OF STATE AND GOVERNMENT: President (Gen. Retd) Olusegun Obasanjo (since May '99)
MAIN IGO MEMBERSHIPS (NON-UN): AU, ECOWAS, OPEC, ACP, OIC, NAM, CWTH
CURRENCY: naira (end-'02 £1=N208.922, US$1=N130.450)
GNI PER CAPITA: US$290, US$830 at PPP ('01)

PROBLEMS associated with the imposition of Sharia law in 12 northern states, discontent with economic shortcomings, and mounting political tensions over the forthcoming elections characterised 2002.

A rise in fuel prices led to an illegal general strike in mid-January which paralysed Lagos and disrupted business in Abuja, Ibadan, Kano, Kaduna, and Makurdi. The strike followed price rises of 18 per cent on petrol and diesel, and 40 per cent prices on kerosene, imposed on 2 January. At a rally in Abuja the police detained 10 leading officials of the Nigerian Labour Congress (NLC) in a dispute over government plans to deregulate the downstream fuel sector and end the annual US$2 billion subsidy. A strike by police in Cross River State at the end of January over wage arrears and improved conditions spread to Lagos and other cities; President Obasanjo was obliged to approve the immediate release of funds to pay for outstanding salary arrears. Discontent also surfaced in February with an eruption of ethnic rioting in Lagos between Muslim Hausas and Christian Yoruba, in which an estimated 100 people died.

On 3 January the first execution under Sharia law (of a man sentenced to death for the murder of his wife and two children) was carried out in Kaduna. On 22 March a federal high court in Lagos ruled that the 1999 constitution was superior to all laws, acts, or decrees passed under earlier regimes and that any decree had to be consistent with the provisions of the constitution in order to be valid under democratic rule. The Justice Minister and attorney-general, Kanu Godwin Agabi, wrote to the 12 northern states that operated Sharia law to tell them "a Muslim should not be subjected to a punishment more severe than would be imposed on other Nigerians for the same offence", and warned that any court, which imposed "discriminatory punishment", was deliberately flouting the constitution. In this context the case of Amina Lawal made international headlines. She was condemned to death by stoning for having sex outside marriage and lost her appeal against the sentence at Katsina. However, her execution was postponed to January 2004 so that she could breastfeed her baby daughter. Death by stoning was opposed by the EU and the USA and on 22 August the Justice Minister said the federal government was "totally opposed" to the sentence and that state lawyers would assist her with further appeals. On 29 October the Minister of State for Foreign Affairs, Dubem Onyia, said the federal government would never allow the execution by stoning to be carried out. Other Sharia death sentences were passed in Niger and Jigawa states.

The extent to which Sharia law and Muslim-Christian antagonisms had become a dangerous aspect of Nigerian life was highlighted by the aborted Miss World Contest, which was due to be held in Lagos. The supreme council of Islam said that the beauty contest should not be held in Nigeria because it was immoral. During November anti-Miss World riots occurred in Kaduna and Abuja, apparently prompted by an article published in a national newspaper, *This Day*, saying that the Holy Prophet would have approved of the contest. The riots led to 215 deaths and forced the resignation of the editor of *This Day*. The riots were also politically motivated and underlined northern suspicions of southern domination. Criticism was levelled at President Obasanjo for not taking firm action and Christians argued that he was too ready to appease the Muslims.

Much of the year was taken up with political manoeuvring in readiness for the 2003 elections. An amendment to the electoral law laid down that the only requirement for the registering of a new party was that it could field candidates for at least 15 per cent of seats in municipal elections in two-thirds of the country's 36 states. On 25 April Obasanjo announced that he would seek re-election in 2003. For much of the rest of the year a bitter contest between the Independent National Electoral Commission (INEC) and the National Assembly (the bicameral legislature) focused upon the number of parties that would be permitted to contest the elections; in the end 28 political parties were registered. At the same time, moves were made by his opponents to bar Obasanjo from standing for a second presidential term. These included the threat of impeachment. The House of Representatives (the lower chamber), dominated by Obasanjo's People's Democratic Party, accused the President of "monumental inadequacies, ineptitude, and persistent disrespect for the rule of law". These accusations reflected mounting rivalries and political tensions as the elections came nearer. Obasanjo stated that he would ignore the resolution and continue as normal. Although the crisis over the impeachment of Obasanjo subsided, he continued to be regarded with suspicion, and was seen as presiding over a corrupt administration which had little regard for the rights of the legislature. The opposition came principally from within Obasanjo's own party.

In traditional fashion, Nigeria fell out with the IMF, which, on 6 March, discontinued the informal monitoring of the government's economic policies on the grounds that key targets relating to the implementation of its macro-economic policies had been missed. The Minister of State for Finance, Djibril Martins-Kuye, said that "we now have the power to run our economy as we deem best and not to take dictation from any institution no matter how technically competent". On the other hand, the *Financial Times* reported that the IMF decision had been greeted with dismay by many Nigerian economists, who believed politicians wanted to increase expenditure prior to the elections scheduled for 2003. At the end of July the World Bank decided to halve its lending capacity to Nigeria because it was worried that public spending in the run-up to the 2003 elections might be increased. The cutback by US$200 million reflected the strained relations between Nigeria and the global financial institutions.

On 27 August Joseph Sanussi, the governor of the Central Bank, deferred payments on foreign debts because of falling foreign exchange reserves. Debts stood at approximately US$28.5 billion, mainly owed to the Paris Club. Nigeria's oil revenues had decreased sharply because of OPEC production curbs. The economy was generally sluggish with high unemployment and excessive imports of consumer items that should have been produced locally. Although the government was still committed to privatisation and liberalisation, the privatisation of the National Electric Power Authority (NEPA) had not been achieved and there were huge problems with supply, for example to municipal authorities for street lighting. The ongoing efforts to retrieve the large sums of money spirited out of the country by the late ruler, Sani Abacha, continued throughout the year; but although an agreement appeared to have been reached with the Abacha family to return US$1 billion in return for the dropping of charges against Mohammed Abacha, the dictator's son, this agreement collapsed in September.

In July 150 women besieged a Chevron-Texaco oil terminal on Escravos Island in the Delta to support demands for jobs for their sons and electricity for their villages. After two weeks Chevron-Texaco agreed to provide more jobs and social amenities. The women then began a further series of sit-ins. The old dispute about the distribution of oil revenues between states and the central government led, at the end of the year, to a decision that offshore oil should be related to the nearest onshore state which should receive 13 per cent of the revenues from it.

Nigeria and Cameroon were in dispute through the year about the Bakassi Peninsula which Nigeria occupied and Cameroon claimed. An International Court of Justice (ICJ) hearing resulted in a ruling in Cameroon's favour, but this was rejected by Nigeria. Later, the UN established a committee to defuse tension between the two countries.

On 1 June Brig. Joseph Garba, the former Commissioner for External Affairs (1975-78) and a principal architect of the bloodless coup of July 1975, died, aged 58.

iii. SIERRA LEONE

CAPITAL: Freetown   AREA: 72,000 sq km   POPULATION: 5,100,000
OFFICIAL LANGUAGE: English   POLITICAL SYSTEM: multiparty republic in British Commonwealth
HEAD OF STATE AND GOVERNMENT: President Ahmad Tejan Kabbah (since March '96)
RULING PARTY: Sierra Leone People's Party (SLPP)
MAIN IGO MEMBERSHIPS (NON-UN): AU, ECOWAS, OIC, ACP, CWTH (suspended), NAM
CURRENCY: leone (end-'02 £1=Le3,219.12, US$1=Le2,010.00)
GNI PER CAPITA: US$140, US$480 at PPP ('01)

IN January, President Ahmad Tejan Kabbah officially declared that the civil war, after a decade of fighting and 50,000 deaths, was over. The UN Mission in Sierra Leone (UNAMSIL) said that the disarmament of 45,000 fighters was complete and agreed, along with the government, to set up a war crimes court. Sierra Leonean troops and armed UK military advisers were deployed near Sierra Leone's sensitive borders with Liberia and Guinea ahead of presidential and legislative elections scheduled for May. Voters began registering for the elections, but initially with little enthusiasm. There were considerable problems in preparing for the polls, not least the absence of an accurate census. The head of the National Electoral Commission, Walter Nicol, claimed, however, to be confident that security measures would prevent any large-scale fraud during registration.

UK Prime Minister Tony Blair visited Sierra Leone in February and paid tribute to the efforts of British troops to help end the civil war. Blair met Gurkhas near the capital, Freetown, and told them that they had given Sierra Leone "a chance to get back on its feet again". About 300 refugees returned home from Liberia under a UN voluntary repatriation programme, although there were still a further 70,000 Sierra Leonean refugees left in the country.

In March, Kabbah lifted the four-year state of emergency. Foday Sankoh, leader of the rebel group, the Revolutionary United Front (RUF), and 49 other RUF members were charged with murder. Sankoh had been in detention in secret locations since his arrest in June 2000. During the civil war, the RUF was responsible for widespread atrocities, including the mutilation of thousands of civilians, including many children. The RUF, which had transformed itself into a political party and was due to contest the May elections, announced in April that it would not take part in the presidential poll, in protest at Sankoh being deemed ineligible to vote or stand as a candidate in the elections.

President, Kabbah was re-elected for a new five-year term in May, beating his nearest rival, Ernest Koroma of the All People's Congress, by a comfortable margin. His party, the Sierra Leone Peoples' Party (SLPP), won 83 of the 112 seats in the National Assembly (the unicameral legislature), while Koroma's supporters took 27 and the remaining two went to the party of a one-time junta leader, Johnny Paul Koroma, who had briefly deposed Kabbah in May 1997 (see AR 1997, pp. 253-54). After the victory, Kabbah named a new 22-member Cabinet. He replaced the key Foreign, Interior, and Finance Ministers, while keeping for himself the Defence portfolio; and also appointed three women to the Cabinet.

In July, a newly inaugurated Truth and Reconciliation Commission began work. Loosely modelled on the commission set up in South Africa to investigate apartheid era crimes, the Sierra Leone version aimed to help heal divisions caused by years of brutal civil war. In December, judges, appointed to sit in Sierra Leone's Special Court for war crimes committed during the civil war, were sworn in.

The IMF announced it would make more aid available to Sierra Leone because of its improved economic and financial performance. The IMF said that Sierra Leone, having made "remarkable progress" in advancing the peace process, would be able to draw US$12 million in low-interest loans. The World Bank and the IMF in March also promised US$950 million in debt relief (a figure representing 80 per cent of Sierra Leone's external debts), provided that the country abided by financial and economic programmes prescribed by the two institutions.

A low-key ceremony sent British soldiers on their way from Sierra Leone in late July, more than two years after they had been sent to assist in restoring peace. However, while much stability had returned to the country, it was widely accepted that civil war could yet reignite. In September, the UN Security Council agreed unanimously to extend the mandate of its military mission (UNAMSIL) until at least mid-2003. Measures to reduce the size of the 17,300-member force would begin after eight months.

iv. THE GAMBIA

CAPITAL: Banjul   AREA: 11,300 sq km   POPULATION: 1,341,000
OFFICIAL LANGUAGE: English   POLITICAL SYSTEM: multiparty republic in British Commonwealth
HEAD OF STATE AND GOVERNMENT: President (Col) Yahya Jammeh (since Sept '96), previously Chairman of Armed Forces Provisional Revolutionary Council (from July '94)
RULING PARTIES: Alliance for Patriotic Reorientation and Construction (APRC)
MAIN IGO MEMBERSHIPS (NON-UN): AU, ECOWAS, ACP, CWTH, OIC, NAM
CURRENCY: dalasi (end-'02 £1=D35.8347, US$1=D22.3750)
GNI PER CAPITA: US$330, US$1,730 at PPP ('01)

IN January, the ruling Alliance for Patriotic Reorientation and Construction (APRC) decisively won legislative elections which were marked by an opposition boycott and widespread voter apathy. Turnout was well down on the presidential elections of October 2001 which President Yahya Jammeh had won comfortably (see AR 2001, p. 271-72). The boycott by the main opposition party, the United Democratic Party, was instigation by its leader, Ousainou Darboe, who accused the government of fraud. It paved the way for a landslide victory for the APRC, which won 45 seats in the 53-seat legislature, having run unopposed in 33 of the 48 constituencies. Jammeh—with power to appoint the five remaining members in the 53-member assembly—thus easily secured the two-thirds majority needed to pass legislation. Two small opposition parties held the remaining three seats between them.

The legislature passed a controversial media law in May designed to regulate the operations of journalists. Opposition deputies and journalists condemned the legislation, calling it "draconian" and designed to silence the country's independent press. The law required all journalists to register with a special media commission which had wide-ranging powers, including the authority to close down media outlets or have journalists imprisoned for contempt. The government accused the press of negative reporting.

The first post-independence leader of the Gambia, Dawda Kairaba Jawara, ousted in July 1994 in a military coup led by Jammeh (see AR 1994, p. 275), flew home from exile in June. It was the first time that he had been allowed to return since his overthrow, Jammeh having granted him an unconditional amnesty in December 2001. Upon his arrival, security forces escorted Jawara to his private residence in Banjul; family, friends, and journalists were prevented from accompanying him.

Later in the year the government made an effort to woo foreign investors, after upgrading the country's transportation infrastructure, including the international airport. The move was designed to encourage diversification away from agriculture and tourism, the two sectors upon which the Gambian economy was heavily dependant.

v. LIBERIA

CAPITAL: Monrovia   AREA: 97,750 sq km   POPULATION: 3,216,000
OFFICIAL LANGUAGE: English   POLITICAL SYSTEM: multiparty republic
HEAD OF STATE AND GOVERNMENT: President Charles Taylor (since July '97)
RULING PARTY: National Patriotic Party of Liberia (NPPL)
MAIN IGO MEMBERSHIPS (NON-UN): AU, ECOWAS, ACP, NAM
CURRENCY: Liberian dollar (end-'02 £1=L$1.6016, US$1=L$1)
GNI PER CAPITA: n/a

IN January, tens of thousands of Liberians fled from the north of the country to escape fighting between government forces and rebels from the Liberians United for Reconciliation and Democracy (LURD). The rebels were thought to be led by Charles Julu, who had served as Chief of Staff under Samuel Doe, the President who was assassinated in 1990. Fighting also took place in other parts of the country, and LURD briefly captured the village of Sawmill just 80 km from the capital, Monrovia.

President Charles Taylor responded by declaring a state of emergency in February, and as the military situation deteriorated further, in April he ordered the suspension of all mass political gatherings. Although in March LURD announced that it was willing to hold peace talks with government or opposition officials, but not with Taylor himself, the President dismissed the offer and preferred to seek a military solution to the insurgency. Defence Minister Daniel Chea, however, claimed that efforts to defeat the rebels were being undermined because the government could not acquire new military supplies owing to the international arms embargo.

Nevertheless, the UN Security Council voted in May to renew sanctions on Liberia for a further 12 months. This was because Taylor's government was said to have "not yet complied fully" with UN demands to end its support for rebels in neighbouring Sierra Leone. In July, UN Secretary-General Kofi Annan warned that the Liberian conflict threatened the UN's peacekeeping work in neighbouring Sierra Leone (see VI.2.iii).

In early September an explosion rocked Monrovia, leaving at least four people dead. However, later in the same month, government forces claimed significant successes against the rebels, and Taylor lifted the state of emergency. He also announced that all areas previously occupied by LURD had been retaken, with the exception of parts of the northern city of Voinjama.

At the end of the year the government rejected allegations that it had helped members of Osama bin Laden's al-Qaida movement to operate an illegal diamond trade in Liberia. A *Washington Post* article claimed that an investigation into al-Qaida financing had uncovered evidence that the governments of Liberia and Burkina Faso had dealt with two senior al-Qaida operatives who bought diamonds there worth US$20 million.

3. WEST AFRICAN FRANCOPHONE STATES—CENTRAL AFRICAN FRANC ZONE

i. SENEGAL—MAURITANIA—MALI—GUINEA—CÔTE D'IVOIRE— BURKINA FASO—TOGO—BENIN—NIGER

Senegal

CAPITAL: Dakar   AREA: 197,000 sq km   POPULATION: 9,800,000
OFFICIAL LANGUAGE: French   POLITICAL SYSTEM: multiparty republic
HEAD OF STATE AND GOVERNMENT: President Abdoulaye Wade (since April '00)
RULING PARTIES: Front for Changeover (FAL) coalition
PRIME MINISTER: Idrissa Seck (since Nov '02)
MAIN IGO MEMBERSHIPS (NON-UN): AU, ECOWAS, UEMOA, ACP, OIC, NAM, Francophonie
CURRENCY: CFA franc (end-'02 £1=CFAFr1,009.56, US$1=CFAFr630.370)
GNI PER CAPITA: US$480, US$1,560 at PPP ('01)

Mauritania

CAPITAL: Nouakchott   AREA: 1,026,000 sq km   POPULATION: 2,800,000
OFFICIAL LANGUAGES: French & Arabic   POLITICAL SYSTEM: multiparty republic
HEAD OF STATE AND GOVERNMENT: President (Col) Maaouiya Ould Sid Ahmed Taya (since Jan '92), previously Chairman of Military Council of National Salvation (from Dec '84)
RULING PARTY: Democratic and Social Republican Party (PRDS)
PRIME MINISTER: Cheikh El-Avia Ould Mohamed Khouna (since Nov '98)
MAIN IGO MEMBERSHIPS (NON-UN): AU, ECOWAS, UEMOA, AMU, AL, ACP, OIC, NAM, Francophonie
CURRENCY: ouguiya (end-'02 £1=O429.576, US$1=O268.225)
GNI PER CAPITA: US$350, US$1,680 at PPP ('01)

Mali

CAPITAL: Bamako   AREA: 1,240,000 sq km   POPULATION: 11,100,000
OFFICIAL LANGUAGE: French   POLITICAL SYSTEM: multiparty republic
HEAD OF STATE AND GOVERNMENT: President Gen. (retd) Amadou Toumani Touré (since June '02)
RULING PARTIES: government is drawn from all parties in National Assembly
PRIME MINISTER: Mohammed Ag Amani (since June '02)
MAIN IGO MEMBERSHIPS (NON-UN): AU, ECOWAS, UEMOA, AL, ACP, OIC, NAM, Francophonie
CURRENCY: CFA franc (see above)
GNI PER CAPITA: US$210, US$810 at PPP ('01)

Guinea

CAPITAL: Conakry   AREA: 246,000 sq km   POPULATION: 7,600,000
OFFICIAL LANGUAGE: French   POLITICAL SYSTEM: multiparty republic
HEAD OF STATE AND GOVERNMENT: President (Gen.) Lansana Conté (since Dec '93); previously Chairman of Military Committee for National Recovery (from April '84)
RULING PARTY: Party of Unity and Progress (PUP)
PRIME MINISTER: Lamine Sidimé, since March '99
MAIN IGO MEMBERSHIPS (NON-UN): AU, ECOWAS, ACP, OIC, NAM, Francophonie
CURRENCY: Guinean franc (end-'02 £1=GFr3179.08, US$1=GFr1,985.00)
GNI PER CAPITA: US$400, US$1,980 at PPP ('01)

VI.3.i. WEST AFRICAN FRANCOPHONE STATES

Côte d'Ivoire
CAPITAL: Abidjan AREA: 322,000 sq km POPULATION: 16,400,000
OFFICIAL LANGUAGE: French POLITICAL SYSTEM: multiparty republic
HEAD OF STATE AND GOVERNMENT: President Laurent Gbagbo (since Oct '00)
RULING PARTY: Ivorian Popular Front (FPI)
PRIME MINISTER: Affi N'Guessan, since Oct '00
MAIN IGO MEMBERSHIPS (NON-UN): AU, ECOWAS, UEMOA, ACP, OIC, NAM, Francophonie
CURRENCY: CFA franc (see above)
GNI PER CAPITA: US$630, US$1,470 at PPP ('01)

Burkina Faso
CAPITAL: Ouagadougou AREA: 274,000 sq km POPULATION: 11,600,000
OFFICIAL LANGUAGE: French POLITICAL SYSTEM: multiparty republic
HEAD OF STATE AND GOVERNMENT: President (Capt.) Blaise Compaoré (since Dec '91); previously Chairman of Popular Front (from Oct '87)
RULING PARTY: Congress for Democracy and Progress (CDP)
PRIME MINISTER: Paramanga Ernest Yoli (since Nov '00)
MAIN IGO MEMBERSHIPS (NON-UN): AU, ECOWAS, UEMOA, ACP, OIC, NAM, Francophonie
CURRENCY: CFA franc (see above)
GNI PER CAPITA: US$210, US$1,020 at PPP ('01)

Togo
CAPITAL: Lomé AREA: 57,000 sq km POPULATION: 4,700,000
OFFICIAL LANGUAGES: French, Kabiye & Ewem POLITICAL SYSTEM: multiparty republic
HEAD OF STATE AND GOVERNMENT: President (Gen.) Gnassingbe Eyadéma (since '67)
RULING PARTY: Rally of the Togolese People (RPT)
PRIME MINISTER: Messan Agbeyome Kodjo (since Aug '00)
MAIN IGO MEMBERSHIPS (NON-UN): AU, ECOWAS, ACP, OIC, NAM, Francophonie
CURRENCY: CFA franc (see above)
GNI PER CAPITA: US$270, US$1,420 at PPP ('01)

Benin
CAPITAL: Porto Novo AREA: 113,000 sq km POPULATION: 6,400,000
OFFICIAL LANGUAGE: French POLITICAL SYSTEM: multiparty republic
HEAD OF STATE AND GOVERNMENT: President Mathieu Kérékou (since March '96)
MAIN IGO MEMBERSHIPS (NON-UN): AU, ECOWAS, UEMOA, ACP, OIC, NAM, Francophonie
CURRENCY: CFA franc (see above)
GNI PER CAPITA: US$360, US$1,030 at PPP ('01)

Niger
CAPITAL: Niamey AREA: 1,267,000 sq km POPULATION: 11,200,000
OFFICIAL LANGUAGE: French POLITICAL SYSTEM: multiparty republic
HEAD OF STATE AND GOVERNMENT: President Mamadou Tanja (since Dec '99)
RULING PARTY: National Movement for a Society of Development (MNSD)
PRIME MINISTER: Hama Amadou (since Jan '00)
MAIN IGO MEMBERSHIPS (NON-UN): AU, ECOWAS, UEMOA, ACP, OIC, NAM, Francophonie
CURRENCY: CFA franc (see above)
GNI PER CAPITA: US$170, US$770 at PPP ('01)

THE early part of the year was a buoyant time for SENEGAL, especially visible in the boost to the country's international image given by the successes of its national football team, the Lions. The domestic climate, always volatile, was soured by the *Joola* ferry disaster in September, and the year ended with a cluster of anxieties, both over the continued Casamance conflict, and diplomatic frustrations in the west African sub-region.

President Abdoulaye Wade, now a dynamic 76, took full political advantage from the country's footballing successes. Although the team lost in the final of the Africa Cup of Nations in Mali in February (narrowly beaten by Cameroon), the event brought football mania to fever pitch. This was seen at its height in the World Cup held in South Korea and Japan in June (see XVI), in which the Lions of Senegal astonished the world by defeating the cup holders, France, in the first match of the contest and battling their way through to the knock out stages of the competition. Wade ensured that he was there to welcome the team back home. Some of Senegal's independent papers were critical of his obvious attempts to make political capital from the country's sporting success, but he responded with the retort that "football is politics and politics is football".

The *Joola*, a government-run coastal ferry plying a route between Ziguinchor in the southern province of Casamance and the capital, Dakar, capsized in a freak storm on 26 September, with a death toll that eventually reached over 1,800. It was clear that the vessel had been seriously overloaded, and, following an inquiry, both the Transport Minister, Youssouph Sakho, and the Armed Forces Minister, Youba Sambou, resigned. An association of some of the families of *Joola* victims campaigned against what was considered to be inadequate compensation and delays in the identification of corpses, and a demonstration by them in December was suppressed by police. The country's first woman Prime Minister, Mame Madior Boye, was also, in part, a casualty of the *Joola* affair, as she was dismissed in November to be replaced by Idrissa Seck, Secretary-General to the presidency and second-in-command in Wade's party, the Senegalese Democratic Party (PDS).

Moreover, the fact that many of the *Joola* dead came from the rebellious province of Casamance highlighted the impasse in peace discussions between the government and the rebels of the Movement of Democratic Forces of Casamance (MFDC). These had stalled because of divisions within the MFDC, which were reportedly resolved in September; and negotiations resumed in October. There were reports that grievances over the *Joola* affair were exacerbated by the difficulties experienced at the Gambian border, where traffic from Casamance to Dakar was the most affected, one reason for the overcrowding on the boat. Frictions with the Gambia related to Senegal's long-standing suspicions that the Gambian government was clandestinely supporting the rebels.

Wade continued his multi-faceted high-level diplomacy, scoring an important success in May when he mediated in the conflict in Madagascar. He also maximised his position as chairman of the Economic Community of West African States (ECOWAS) to become involved in a series of mediations in the conflict in Côte d'Ivoire which broke out in September. His involvement alongside, and to some extent in competition with, President Gnassingbe Eyadéma of Togo (the most senior of west Africa's politicians) was important in helping to organise a ceasefire in October. An attempt to engage in further mediation by calling an emergency summit in Dakar towards the end of December, however, collapsed amid recriminations.

It was a year without elections in MAURITANIA, but beneath the surface political change continued to ferment. At the beginning of the year the government decided to dissolve the Action for Change (AC), a coalition of four opposition parties that had been formed to fight the elections to the National Assembly in 2001 and which had gained 28 per cent of its seats. AC leader Messaoud Ould Boulkheir said that the decision to dissolve the coalition compromised the multiparty system and went against the spirit of the constitution. He claimed that the ban had been imposed because of the AC's campaign to raise issues like the "cultural question" and slavery.

Also in January, one of the parties in the AC, the Rally of Democratic Forces (RDF), chose as its leader Ahmed Ould Daddah, son of Mauritania's first President. The RDF had been formed in 2001 from elements of the Union of Democratic Forces which had been banned in October 2000 for "subversion and continuous appeals for intolerance" (see AR 2000, p. 250).

In October, several opposition combined to create a new framework for dialogue, called the Unified Opposition Framework. The structure included the RDF, and two parties banned in 2001 for plotting to overthrow the government. Human rights organisations continued to protest at the government's harassment of the opposition. In December, Amnesty International produced a new report saying that it had gathered fresh information to support the contention that slavery continued to exist in Mauritania, despite its legal abolition in 1981.

The key event in MALI was the presidential election held over two rounds on 28 April and 12 May. This was won on the second round by the former military ruler who had handed over power to civilians in 1992, Amadou Toumani Touré. He won with 1,099,653 votes (64.35 per cent of the total), while his only opponent Soumaila Cissé secured 609,320 votes (35.65 per cent). As always in Mali, because of the size of the country and the fragility of the election administration, there was a low turnout, with only 30.17 per cent of the electorate participating in the poll. There were also numerous complaints of confusion at polling stations. The situation was much more fluid in the first round, as Touré obtained only 28 per cent of the poll, with Cissé winning 23 per cent, and the former Prime Minister, Ibrahim Boubacar Keita (known as IBK), obtaining 21 per cent. Although the latter had criticised the poll as a fraud, he decided to call on his supporters to support Touré in the second round. The general view of the elections was that, in spite of poor administration, it was a genuine reflection of the popular will, as Touré was a widely respected figure for the manner in which he had handed power back to civilians after only a year of military rule. Following the legislative elections in August, in which no party achieved an overall majority, a group of parties elected Keita as Speaker of the National Assembly (the unicameral legislature); and President Touré, who ran with no party backing, said he would rule with a majority drawn from an alliance of parties in the National Assembly. All parties in the National Assembly were represented in the government of national union formed in October.

If GUINEA had, to some extent, stabilised its relations with its conflict-prone neighbours, Liberia and Sierra Leone, there were continuing questions concerning the country's political future. Elections in June had indeed brought an increased number of seats in the National Assembly (the unicameral legislature) to the ruling party, the Party for Unity and Progress (PUP); in the main because of the election boycott by the main group of opposition parties, the Republic Front for Democratic Change (FRAD). The participation of one of the other major opposition parties, the Union for Progress and Renewal (UPR) of Siradiou Diallo, led to its subsequent split after it obtained only 20 of the 114 seats. The other parties, notably the Union of Republic Forces (UFR) of former Prime Minister Sidya Touré, alleged widespread vote rigging in the elections. Towards the end of the year, as rumours of the poor health of 68-year old President Lansana Conté grew, speculation increased on who might be his successor. Despite almost 19 years in power, Conté had made no provision for the succession, and seemed to be preparing to contest presidential elections in 2003.

The most serious crisis to have been seen in francophone west Africa since independence hit CÔTE D'IVOIRE after the attempted coup of 19 September. Although this apparently began as a mutiny by disgruntled soldiers, it subsequently became clear from the level of planning and co-ordination that it was an attempt to take over the country by military means. The mutiny broke out in at least five cities concurrently, and although it failed in Abidjan, it succeeded in Bouaké in the centre-north, and in Korhogo in the far north. It was said to have been a pre-emptive move by about 750 recent recruits who had been warned that they would be dismissed from the army.

The coup involved serious fighting in Abidjan, with nearly 300 deaths reported. Among the dead were the Interior Minister, Emile Boga Doudou, one of the hardliners of the regime of President Laurent Gbagbo; but the events also involved the revenge killing of former head of state Gen. Robert Gueï. Although it was initially reported that he had been on his way to the television station to make a coup broadcast, it subsequently emerged that he had been killed by an assassination squad, along with his wife and aide de camp. He was blamed for having been behind the mutiny, as most of the 750 mutineers were reputed to be loyal to him. Some saw the trigger for action as the withdrawal of Gueï supporters in September from a coalition government of five parties which Gbagbo had put together in August as part of his long-running bid for national reconciliation. Subsequent events showed that these had been vain hopes, and that the conflicts of 1999-2000 had created uncontrollable long term tensions.

It rapidly became clear that if the original movers had been the 750, they had been joined by an equally tough collection of dissidents: a group of ex-soldiers, who had defected at various stages in the troubled three years between 1999 and 2002, and had been gathered in Burkina Faso, plotting their own return. While it was unclear whether they had actually been involved in the mutiny or coup conspiracy, their own leadership rapidly imposed itself on the mutineers in the north, and in the space of a few weeks they were able to establish control over a wide swathe of northern Côte d'Ivoire. Attempts by the army loyalists to retake Bouaké proved unsuccessful, and the rebels were only prevented from advancing on the national administrative capital, Yamoussoukro, by the interposition of French troops. These were stationed in the country under a defence agreement, and after the mutiny were deployed in the evacuation of those French citizens who wanted to leave. A special arrangement with the rebels also permitted the troops to enter Bouaké to evacuate French nationals there.

By the beginning of November a ceasefire negotiated under the aegis of the Economic Community of West African States (ECOWAS), was more or less holding, with the country divided between the south, under the control of the Gbagbo government, and the north, under rebel control. The leadership was initially shadowy, but by November a political wing, called the Patriotic Movement of Côte d'Ivoire (MPCI), under secretary-general Guillaume Soro, had emerged, although a number of military commanders continued to be the most important players.

There were disturbing developments in the south, as popular frustration at the impasse spilled over into xenophobic street demonstrations, and attacks on both northerners and foreigners from neighbouring northern countries such as Burkina Faso and Mali, who had been accused of colluding with the rebels. This led to increased tension between Côte d'Ivoire and Burkina Faso in particular, which complicated a coherent ECOWAS position; although at the end of November it was agreed in principle that an ECOWAS peace force from a number of countries (Senegal, Ghana, Niger, Benin, Guinea-Bissau) would be sent to replace the French, who had been playing a vital neutral role in policing the ceasefire. There were also reports that Gbagbo had been recruiting support from Angola, as well as from South African mercenaries. At the end of November, the former Prime Minister and most important northern leader, Alassane Ouattara, was allowed to leave the French embassy where he had sought asylum on 19-20 September, after the torching of his house by government loyalists.

At the end of the year, the French forces, which had increased in numbers from 600 in September to over 1,500, were the main military presence and stabilising force, although their situation was rendered more unpredictable by fresh attacks across the Liberian border by two new movements, the Popular Ivoirian Movement of the Great-West (MPIGO) and the Movement for Justice and Peace (MJP). These were said to be sympathisers of the late General Gueï, but there were rumours of English-speaking west Africans fighting with them, although Liberian President Charles Taylor denied any connection. So the year ended with gloomy prognostications of worsening civil conflict, involving an explosive mix of xenophobia and anarchy, as well as concern that Gbagbo, despite his apparent good intentions and his willingness to continue to seek peace, was in full control neither of his supporters nor of his army.

The regional crisis in West Africa, which worsened after the events of 19 September in Côte d'Ivoire, came to dwarf the internal problems of BURKINA FASO.

Although the opposition continued to protest against the human rights offences of the dictatorial regime of President Blaise Compaoré, the new flood of Burkinabe refugees from the tensions in the south, and the reports of killings and harassment of those remaining in Côte d'Ivoire, brought a stronger movement of national solidarity which Compaoré knew how to orient to his political advantage. Earlier in the year, a measure of political détente had already occurred in the legislative elections, in which opposition parties reduced the majority of the ruling party, the Congress for Democracy and Progress (CDP), in the National Assembly (the lower house of the bicameral legislature) from 104 out of 111 seats in the previous house to only 57.

A meeting between Compaoré and President Gbagbo of Côte d'Ivoire, held under pressure from the French, ended with superficial cordialities but did little to ease the deep rooted hostilities at the popular level. Ivoirians continued to blame Compaoré for an alleged role in the coup, and for supporting the rebellion. Meanwhile the economic effect of the crisis began to bite in Burkina, not only because of the cost of sustaining thousands of refugees and the halt to a part of the remittances sent home by Burkina cocoa and coffee plantation workers in Côte d'Ivoire, but also because the rebellion cut Burkina Faso off from its main route to the sea. Alternative outlets through Ghana, Togo and Benin, although available, were a more expensive substitute.

The sour and stalemated political situation in TOGO saw some evolution in the second part of the year, but not necessarily in a positive direction. In July, Prime Minister Agbeyome Kodjo, who had been seen as a loyal supporter of President Gnassingbe Eyadéma, was removed from office amid a torrent of recriminations and accusations, to be replaced by another southerner, Kofi Sama, the secretary-general of the ruling party, the Togolese Peoples Rally (RPT). Kodjo later fled to Paris, saying that he feared for his life.

This was a prelude to movement on the front of the legislative elections, which had been postponed several times in an attempt to fulfil conditions set by the EU, which had attempted over a four year period to defuse political tensions. Elections to the National Assembly (the unicameral legislature) were finally held on 27 October and, because of a boycott by the main coalition of opposition parties, the ruling RPT—the only party to field candidates in all constituencies—won 72 of 81 seats. The new rubber-stamp legislature at the end of the year approved an amendment to the constitution permitting Eyadéma to stand in the 2003 presidential elections, thereby reversing a commitment he had made to French President Jacques Chirac and the EU.

It was a quiet year in BENIN, although local elections at the end of the year were interpreted as a sign of the passing of an old political order, and the harbinger of a new politics. This was because by the time of the next presidential elections in 2006, both President Mathieu Kérékou and his main rival Nicéphore Soglo would be over 70 years old, and thus barred by the constitution from standing. New leaders and groupings were therefore given a chance to show their paces.

Meanwhile the small and unpretentious economy was showing signs of comfortable growth, likely to be over 5 per cent in 2002. This was mainly because of the difficulties in the Ivoirian economy, as Sahelian states took advantage of the rail link from Niger to Cotonou port.

NIGER'S struggle to survive with an impoverished landlocked economy were worsened by a serious mutiny in the army, based in barracks in the eastern town of Diffa and two other nearby barracks, at the end of July. The cause was reportedly overdue pay and poor living conditions. Loyal government troops recaptured Diffa 10 days later, and the other two centres of dissidence soon afterwards, releasing a number of hostages captured by the mutineers. The Defence Ministry said that about 217 mutineers were arrested, including 29 in Niamey where an attempt at a mutiny was put down on 5 August. Although officially there were only two dead, human rights organisations alleged that many of the mutineers had been killed. Heavy-handed treatment of newspaper journalists who tried to uncover the facts of the mutiny by the government of President Mamadou Tandja (democratically elected in 1999), provoked further criticism, and in September the president and vice-president of the Constitutional Court, Sani Koutoubi and Lawal Ari Gremah, resigned in protest at two draconian decrees issued in August (one imposing a state of emergency and the other restricting information published on the mutiny). The two judges said that the decrees were unconstitutional.

ii. CHAD—CAMEROON—GABON—CONGO— CENTRAL AFRICAN REPUBLIC—EQUATORIAL GUINEA

Chad
CAPITAL: Ndjaména   AREA: 1,284,000 sq km   POPULATION: 7,900,000
OFFICIAL LANGUAGES: French & Arabic   POLITICAL SYSTEM: multiparty republic
HEAD OF STATE AND GOVERNMENT: President (Col.) Idriss Déby (since Dec '90)
RULING PARTIES: Patriotic Salvation Movement (MPS), Union for Renewal and Democracy (URD) & National Union for Development and Renewal (UNDR)
PRIME MINISTER: Haroun Kabadi (since Jun '02)
MAIN IGO MEMBERSHIPS (NON-UN): AU, CEEAC, ACP, OIC, NAM, Francophonie
CURRENCY: CFA franc (end-'02 £1=CFAFr1,009.56, US$1=CFAFr630.370
GNI PER CAPITA: US$200, US$930 at PPP ('01)

Cameroon
CAPITAL: Yaoundé   AREA: 475,000 sq km   POPULATION: 15,200,000
OFFICIAL LANGUAGES: French & English   POLITICAL SYSTEM: multiparty republic in British Commonwealth
HEAD OF STATE: President Paul Biya (since Nov '82)
RULING PARTY: Cameroon People's Democratic Movement (CPDM)
PRIME MINISTER: Peter Mafany Musonge (since Sept '96)
MAIN IGO MEMBERSHIPS (NON-UN): AU, CEEAC, ACP, OIC, CWTH, NAM, Francophonie
CURRENCY: CFA franc (see above)
GNI PER CAPITA: US$570, US$1,670 at PPP ('01)

Gabon

CAPITAL: Libreville   AREA: 268,000 sq km   POPULATION: 1,261,000
OFFICIAL LANGUAGE: French   POLITICAL SYSTEM: multiparty republic
HEAD OF STATE AND GOVERNMENT: President Omar Bongo (since March '67)
RULING PARTY: Gabonese Democratic Party (PDG)
PRIME MINISTER: Jean-François Ntoutoume-Emane (since Feb '99)
MAIN IGO MEMBERSHIPS (NON-UN): AU, CEEAC, ACP, OIC, NAM, Francophonie
CURRENCY: CFA franc (see above)
GNI PER CAPITA: US$3,160, US$5,460 at PPP ('01)

Congo

CAPITAL: Brazzaville   AREA: 342,000 sq km   POPULATION: 3,100,000
OFFICIAL LANGUAGE: French   POLITICAL SYSTEM: transitional government
HEAD OF STATE AND GOVERNMENT: President Denis Sassou-Nguesso (since Oct '97)
RULING PARTIES: Congolese Movement for Democracy and Integral Development (MCDDI) is now included in ruling coalition
MAIN IGO MEMBERSHIPS (NON-UN): CEEAC, ACP, NAM, Francophonie
CURRENCY: CFA franc (see above)
GNI PER CAPITA: US$700, US$580 at PPP ('01)

Central African Republic

CAPITAL: Bangui   AREA: 623,000 sq km   POPULATION: 3,800,000
OFFICIAL LANGUAGE: French   POLITICAL SYSTEM: multiparty republic
HEAD OF STATE AND GOVERNMENT: President Ange-Félix Patassé (since Sept '92)
RULING PARTY: Central African People's Liberation Party (MPLC) heads broad coalition
PRIME MINISTER: Martin Ziguele (since Apr '01)
MAIN IGO MEMBERSHIPS (NON-UN): AU, CEEAC, ACP, OIC, NAM, Francophonie
CURRENCY: CFA franc (see above)
GNI PER CAPITA: US$270, US$1,180 at PPP ('01)

Equatorial Guinea

CAPITAL: Malabo   AREA: 28,000 sq km   POPULATION: 1,014,999 (2002 census)
OFFICIAL LANGUAGES: Spanish & French   POLITICAL SYSTEM: multiparty republic
HEAD OF STATE AND GOVERNMENT: President (Brig.-Gen.) Teodoro Obiang Nguema Mbasogo (since Aug '79)
RULING PARTY: Equatorial Guinea Democratic Party (PDGE)
PRIME MINISTER: Candido Muatetama Rivas (since Feb '01)
MAIN IGO MEMBERSHIPS (NON-UN): AU, CEEAC, ACP, NAM, Francophonie
CURRENCY: CFA franc (see above)
GNI PER CAPITA: US$700, US$5,640 at PPP ('01)

CHAD'S expectations in 2002 were focused on the planned completion of the pipeline, from Doba in the far south of the country to Kribi in Cameroon, expected before the end of 2003. In the meantime, political tensions were increasing and becoming more complex, in spite of the death in September of Youssouf Togoïmi, the leader of the northern rebel movement, the Movement for Democracy and Justice in Chad (MJDT). After his death, which occurred several weeks after driving over a landmine in the Tibesti plateau, the divisions within his movement worsened, with a hardline faction taking over the leadership, which led to a bout of intensified fighting after a long period of quiet. A new movement called the National Resistance Army, under former army chief-of-staff Mahamat Garfa, also engaged the Chad army in combat, using bases in Sudan.

The complexity also came from rising insecurity on the southern border, with a sharp deterioration in relations with the Central African Republic, because of the suspected complicity by Chadians in attempts to overthrow the government in Bangui. The coup-maker, François Bozizé, who had been given asylum in Chad, left for Paris early in October; but in spite of joint border patrols there was a series of border skirmishes which worsened after the 26 October coup attempt in the Central African Republic (see below).

Domestic politics remained fairly low key, although the legislative elections in April saw the ruling Patriotic Safety Movement (MPS) of President Idris Déby take 110 of the 155 seats in the unicameral National Assembly, with the vote split evenly between a number of parties, none of which emerged dominant. The most vocal of the opposition politicians, human rights activist Ngarléjy Yorongar, secured few seats for his party.

There was a hiccup in May in relations with the IMF following the reported misuse of funds provided under an international debt alleviation scheme. Corrective measures were taken, and in September the IMF commended Chad's performance, but the country remained under close international surveillance through mechanisms set up by the World Bank in connection with the loans which it provided for the oil pipeline scheme.

In CAMEROON, the landslide victory for the ruling party, the Cameroon People's Democratic Movement (CPDM), in the legislative elections of 30 June, was generally seen as consolidating the position of President Paul Biya. The ruling party increased its representation in the 180-seat National Assembly from 116 to 133, while the main opposition party, the Social Democratic Front (SDF) won only 21 seats, less than half its 1997 total. The municipal elections held at the same time recorded a similarly decisive CPDM victory. Although local observers noted election irregularities, international observers said that they were satisfied with the conduct of the elections. The mainstream opposition parties contested the results in the Supreme Court and 17 results were annulled; but when they were re-run in September the CPDM again swept the board, winning 16 of the 17 with only one going to the SDF.

Although following the victory the anglophone Prime Minister Peter Mafany Musonge was reappointed, there was still a residual malaise in the anglophone areas of south-western Cameroon, which remained alienated from the mainstream of Cameroon politics. Secessionist sentiment, it would appear, was still not dead.

Reaction was muted in the anglophone areas to the October judgment of the International Court of Justice (ICJ) on the dispute with Nigeria over the Bakassi peninsula, which was favourable to Cameroon. The government was obviously satisfied with the verdict, but subsequent reactions were restrained in view of the clear difficulty which it presented to neighbouring Nigeria. Following a meeting prior to the judgment between President Biya and his Nigerian counterpart, Olusegun Obasanjo, in Paris, mediated by UN Secretary-General Kofi Annan, both parties agreed to not use violence in connection with the dispute.

A second meeting, after the verdict had been announced, however, saw Nigeria decline to accept the judgment because of the position of the majority Nigerian population in the peninsula. Tensions remained throughout the year, with both sides maintaining troops in the vicinity of the disputed territory, but there were no incidents of violence.

It was another troubled year in CENTRAL AFRICAN REPUBLIC, where the hold on power of President Ange-Félix Patassé looked increasingly precarious. In the early part of the year there was increasing concern at the dependence of Patassé on Libyan troops for his security, as pay arrears in the army grew more serious and fears of mutiny grew. On 26 October supporters of ex-army commander François Bozizé (who had twice previously attempted coups) launched an attack on Bangui. It was only with support from Libyan troops and elements of one of the Democratic Republic of Congo (DRC) rebel movements, that Patassé was able to regain control of the capital after six days, but it had been a very close run thing. Even by the end of the year, elements of Bozizé's supporters continued to control areas of the north-west, with support from inside Chad. In 2003, a peace-keeping force from the Economic and Monetary Community of Central Africa (CEMAC) was due to replace the Libyans, who had proved unpopular with the locals, especially after their bombing of parts of northern Bangui.

This was the year in which the President of the Republic of CONGO, Denis Sassou-Nguesso, intended to re-legitimise his rule. He achieved this first with a referendum on a new authoritarian constitution, which abolished the position of Prime Minister and increased the presidential term from five years to seven. The provisions were approved in January by 84.26 per cent of the voters. Armed with this mandate, the President, who had returned to power in a coup in 1997, called presidential elections in March which he easily won after the main challenger, André Milongo, withdrew a few days before the poll, claiming irregularities. Sassou-Nguesso obtained over 85 per cent of the vote, and proceeded to organise legislative elections at the end of May. This was when his plan began to fail, however, as there was serious violence in the Brazzaville area at the time of the vote, which led to a recrudescence of activity from the Ninja militia loyal to former Prime Minister Bernard Kolélas. Nevertheless, this neither prevented Sassou-Nguesso from being sworn in amid great pomp and ceremony in August, nor from visiting French President Jacques Chirac in Paris in September with a large delegation.

After the elections of 2001, this proved to be a quiet year politically in GABON, especially as a role was found for opposition parties in government. This led to some complaints that the country was increasingly returning to a one-party state, as it had been previously under the current President, Omar Bongo, who had ruled since 1967. The longevity of his regime gave him increasing impulses to play the elder statesman, which did not work in relation to attempts to mediate in the fighting in Côte d'Ivoire, when a summit that he had tried to organise in Morocco failed to materialise. His mediation was more successful in the Central African Republic, where he brokered a peace force from central Africa, including troops from Gabon, Equatorial Guinea and Cameroon, to replace the Libyans upon whom the government relied for security.

EQUATORIAL GUINEA received international attention that was in part critical of its politics, and in part approving of its remarkable growth rate. The political record was subject to consistent broadsides of disapproval for the poor human rights record of the government of President Teodoro Obiang Nguema. Throughout the year there were reports of arrests and the maltreatment of opposition politicians, especially after a "threat to the security of the state" was uncovered in March, when more than 200 people were arrested. Another political leader was detained in April for "insulting the head of state". A show trial in June convicted a number of opposition activists for allegedly plotting a coup d'etat. This did not prevent several of those political figures still at large from standing in the presidential elections in December. These, however, were easily won by the President who obtained 99.5 per cent of the votes cast, following the withdrawal of all opposition candidates two hours after voting began, because of serious irregularities in the polls.

The expanding oil-based economy recorded an amazing 20 per cent growth in 2001 and the same—or even higher, according to some calculations—was expected in 2002. Plans to develop reserves of natural gas were expected to add further to GDP. As well as the oil boom, there was also a population boom. Figures released in July indicated that the population was officially 1,014,999, compared with the 1994 census figure of around 500,000. The increase, if accurate, was attributable not only to increased reproduction, but also to the rise in immigration associated with the oil boom, especially from Cameroon and Gabon.

VII CENTRAL AND SOUTHERN AFRICA

1. DEMOCRATIC REPUBLIC OF CONGO—BURUNDI AND RWANDA—
GUINEA-BISSAU, CAPE VERDE AND SÃO TOMÉ AND PRÍNCIPE—
MOZAMBIQUE—ANGOLA

i. DEMOCRATIC REPUBLIC OF CONGO

CAPITAL: Kinshasa   AREA: 2,345,000 sq km   POPULATION: 52,400,000
OFFICIAL LANGUAGE: French   POLITICAL SYSTEM: multiparty republic
HEAD OF STATE AND GOVERNMENT: President Maj.-Gen. Joseph Kabila (since Jan '01)
RULING PARTIES: fluid
MAIN IGO MEMBERSHIPS (NON-UN): AU, SADC, COMESA, CEEAC, ACP, Francophonie, NAM
CURRENCY: Congo franc (end-'02 £1=CFr576.558 US$1=CFr360.000)
GNI PER CAPITA: US$100, US$685 at PPP ('00 est.)

THE year started on a bad note when Mount Nyiragongo erupted in January and streams of molten lava engulfed the streets of Goma. In the same month, 60 km south-west of Goma, up to 40 men were killed when, following heavy rains, a gallery in a coltan mine collapsed. It seemed as though nature had joined in the four-year war that, with Goma on the Rwandan border at its centre, had divided the Democratic Republic of Congo (DRC). Despite these setbacks, the shaky cease-fire cobbled together in 2001 held in the north and east of the country (see AR 2001, pp. 285-89). Meanwhile, the representatives of the belligerent forces met at Sun City in South Africa to negotiate a peace accord with the government of President Joseph Kabila in Kinshasa. The object of this Inter-Congolese National Dialogue (ICND) was to establish a broadly representative transitional government that would end the war and open the way to democratic elections. But reconciling the interests of the various parties engaged in the war was to prove a difficult and tortuous undertaking.

The peace process faltered in March when the Goma-based Congolese Rally for Democracy (RCD) took control of Moliro on the border with Zambia and Tanzania. This caused the representatives of the Kinshasa government to quit the talks in Sun City and led the UN Security Council to criticise the Rwandan-backed RCD. Talks resumed when the RCD abandoned Moliro. An accord was eventually reached in April but, despite pressure from South African President Thabo Mbeki, the agreement excluded the RCD. By drawing up a power-sharing agreement with the Ugandan-backed Congolese Liberation Movement (MLC) of Jean-Pierre Bemba, the Kinshasa government hoped to limit the war to the east and to isolate the RCD and its Rwandan backers.

The agreement was criticised by the ICND facilitator, Botswana's former President Ketumile Masire, and drew the ire of the Rwandans. By the end of April, Rwandan troop reinforcements were starting to cross the border to add their support to the RCD's military drive. A particularly brutal massacre in RCD-held Kisangani in mid-May indicated a rise in tensions within the movement and gave the UN another reason to criticise the Rwandan proxy forces in the DRC. At the same time, heavy tribal fighting in the north-east, occasioned by the withdrawal of Ugandan forces, indicated that a formal agreement between the belligerents might not be sufficient to end the war. As the Rwandans had long claimed, the removal of disciplined foreign soldiers threatened to leave large parts of the DRC under the control of feuding, local militias. Many of these groups had acquired sophisticated weaponry during the war and were anxious to use this equipment to strengthen their local claims to land and natural resources.

As the peace effort ground to a halt in South Africa, the UN extended the mandate of its MONUC (United Nations Organisation Mission) observers of the cease-fire and promised to reinforce their numbers. At the same time, the Kabila government in Kinshasa received substantial loans that reinforced its standing as the formal government of the country. These included a loan of US$750 million in June from the IMF and, in August, a World Bank loan of US$410 million plus a grant of US$44 million from the Bank's International Development Association.

While international support for Kabila's government gathered, the South African President, as the chairperson of the new African Union, put pressure on the Rwandans to enter direct negotiations with representatives of the Kabila government. On 30 July negotiations in Pretoria (the South African capital) resulted in a peace agreement being signed by Presidents Paul Kagame of Rwanda and Joseph Kabila of the DRC. This significant development committed the Kabila government to disarm, arrest, or repatriate the rebel forces in the DRC who were responsible for the Rwandan genocide of 1994. In return, the Rwandan government promised to withdraw the 22,000 troops which it had stationed in the DRC in an attempt to prevent the Interahamwe Hutu militia based in the DRC, and members of the ex-Rwandan Armed Forces (FAR), from attacking Rwanda. The implementation of the agreement was far from guaranteed as the Kabila government was dependent on the support of the Interahamwe and FAR to "liberate" the eastern third of the country occupied by Rwandan troops. The Rwandans, on the other hand, were nervous about leaving the defence of the territory bordering on the eastern frontier of their country in the hands of their proxy movement, the RCD.

Despite these fears, the Rwandan army started to withdraw from the DRC on 17 September. At the same time, the last 2,000 Zimbabwean troops in the DRC prepared to return home. The Kabila government attempted to facilitate the peace process when it banned a political party, the Democratic Liberation Forces of Rwanda, that represented the interests of Hutu exiles in the DRC. Another major step towards peace had been taken on 10 September when the DRC and Uganda signed a separate agreement and Ugandan troops started to vacate the north east. By early October most foreign troops had left the DRC. Another sign of normality emerged when Etienne Tshisekedi, the veteran Congolese politician based in Kinshasa, toured the eastern parts of the country held by the RCD.

South Africa sought to assist the peace accord by promising to augment its 200-strong contingent of peacekeepers with a further 1,500 troops. In October the UN increased the pressure for peace when its panel on the illegal exploitation of natural resources and other forms of wealth drew the world's attention to the large-scale pillaging that had accompanied the war. This underlined the self-reproducing nature of a war in which local and foreign troops fought as much over the exploitation of rich natural resources as over questions of sovereignty and defence. The report called on the Security Council to impose financial sanctions on 29 named companies, and recommended that action should be taken against various well-known figures on both sides of the conflict. It reported that the DRC government and its foreign allies, particularly Zimbabwe, had acquired US$5 billion worth of state assets without making payments to the DRC Treasury. The report caused the Kabila government, later in the year, to sack three of its Ministers and to dismiss several other highly-placed functionaries.

By mid-October the security situation was becoming increasingly uncertain as pro-government militias attempted to take advantage of the withdrawal of Rwandan and Ugandan troops. On Lake Tanganyika, the important town of Uvira fell into the hands of the Mayi-Mayi opposition militia before being reoccupied six days later by the RCD. The growing insecurity in the north east, however, threatened to draw Rwanda and Uganda back into the conflict.

As thousands of refugees fled the renewed fighting, Presidents Kabila and Kagame met in November in Pretoria. Under the auspices of South Africa's President Mbeki, they reviewed the July peace accord and discussed a power-sharing agreement. The following month, representatives of the principal movements engaged in the war met in Pretoria to negotiate the establishment of a shared, transitional government. The formula arrived at gave Joseph Kabila the presidency of the DRC for a transitional period of two years. During that time he was to be assisted by four vice presidents drawn from the RCD, MLC, the (unarmed) opposition, and the governing party. Democratic elections were to be held at the end of the two-year period.

As the year ended, fighting continued to flare up in the north-eastern border areas controlled by the RCD and MLC; and an outbreak of influenza caused the death of several hundred people in the north of the country. But the peace process had marked an important new development as the different parties agreed on the outlines of a government of national unity and on the prospect of democratic elections. The achievement of these goals, however, remained a problem for the future.

ii. BURUNDI AND RWANDA

Burundi
CAPITAL: Bujumbura   AREA: 28,000 sq km   POPULATION: 6,900,000
OFFICIAL LANGUAGES: French & Kirundi   POLITICAL SYSTEM: multiparty republic
HEAD OF STATE AND GOVERNMENT: President (Maj.) Pierre Buyoya (since July '96)
MAIN IGO MEMBERSHIPS (NON-UN): AU, COMESA, CEEAC, ACP, NAM, Francophonie
CURRENCY: Burundi franc (end-'02 £1=BrF1,713.66, US$1=BrF1070.00)
GNI PER CAPITA: US$100, US$590 at PPP ('01)

Rwanda
CAPITAL: Kigali   AREA: 26,000 sq km   POPULATION: 8,700,000
OFFICIAL LANGUAGES: French, Kinyarwanda & English   POLITICAL SYSTEM: multiparty republic
HEAD OF STATE AND GOVERNMENT: President Paul Kagame (since April '00)
RULING PARTIES: Rwandan Patriotic Front (FPR) & Republican Democratic Movement (MDR) head coalition
PRIME MINISTER: Bernard Mazuka (since April '00)
MAIN IGO MEMBERSHIPS (NON-UN): AU, COMESA, CEEAC, ACP, NAM, Francophonie
CURRENCY: Rwanda franc (end-'02 £1=RFr800.775, US$1=RFr500.000)
GNI PER CAPITA: US$220, US$1,000 at PPP ('01)

A power-sharing agreement brokered in July 2001 by the government of BURUNDI and the political opposition (see AR 2001, pp. 290-91) was implemented in November. This created a transitional government under Pierre Buyoya—the Tutsi President of the country since 1996—and a Hutu Vice-President, Domitien Ndayizeye. It also created the space for democratic politics which, within the first few months of 2002, led to the establishment of several new political parties. But the power-sharing agreement had excluded the two major armed movements, the Forces for the Defence of Democracy (FDD)—with some 10,000 fighters—and the smaller National Liberation Forces (FNL). An upsurge of fighting in May, despite the presence of South African peacekeepers, underlined the point that peace could not be achieved without the participation of the armed movements in the transitional government.

On 22 May, members of the Hutu-aligned FNL killed a member of the Senate (the upper chamber of the bicameral legislature) belonging to the minority Twa ethnic group, mounted ambushes on roads leading to Bujumbura in the south, and brought the fighting to the edge of the capital. Within a few weeks, thousands of residents were fleeing their homes in the northern suburbs of Bujumbura. The fighting developed into the most serious clashes seen since the 1993 seizure of power by Tutsi soldiers (see AR 1993, pp. 278-79). In July two columns of FDD rebels moved out of camps in Tanzania and crossed the border. Clashes were soon reported from the neighbourhood of the central town of Gitenga, 100 km east of Bujumbura. As the fighting escalated, and casualties mounted, the government agreed to meet with FDD representatives in the Tanzanian capital, Dar es Salaam, in August. The Tanzanian President called unsuccessfully for a ceasefire to be respected during negotiations aimed at including the FDD in the power-sharing agreement.

The massacre of 173 civilians by government soldiers at Itaba, near Gitenga, momentarily drew the attention of the world to a war that had killed over 200,000 people in less than 10 years. The massacre led to the arrest of two army officers and produced a government commission. This showed that Itaba was on a corridor used by the FDD and that the civilians had given sanctuary to members of the rebel movement. It also underlined the ethnic nature of the conflict which pitted Tutsi soldiers against Hutu rebels and civilians. For the latter, the army was an oppressive and hostile force while, for the Tutsi community, the army represented its only guarantee of survival.

The negotiations in Dar es Salaam were followed by intensive mediation on the part of South Africa and Uganda. This pressure on the belligerents eventually led to the drafting of a ceasefire, signed in Arusha, Tanzania, on 3 December by Pierre Buyoya for the government, and Pierre Nkurunziza for the FDD rebels. Once the ceasefire was implemented on 30 December, further negotiations would follow over how to share power between the Tutsi minority (representing 14 per cent of the population) and the Hutu majority (85 per cent). It was also intended that the ceasefire would lead to the eventual disarmament of the armed opponents and the reorganisation (or reconstitution) of the Tutsi-dominated army.

The next stage of negotiations would require the participation of the FNL in the transitional government, or lead to its political isolation. It would also demand the establishment of democratic norms which, for example, would force the FDD to accept the existence of other Hutu-based parties, most notably the Front for Democracy in Burundi (FRODEBU), which formed a part of the government. The transition towards peace and democracy was also contingent on Buyoya stepping down as President in May 2003 in favour of his Hutu colleague Ndayizeye, a process which was far from assured given that the failure to implement the ceasefire on 30 December was followed by renewed fighting in January 2003.

In RWANDA in early February, the Defence Minister met his Ugandan counterpart in an attempt to bridge the hostility that divided their two countries. In 2001, fighting between units of their respective armies in the Democratic Republic of Congo had brought Rwanda and Uganda close to war. It took a meeting between President Paul Kagame of Rwanda and Ugandan President Yoweri Museveni, later in February, to re-establish peace between their two countries.

Pasteur Bizimungu, the former President of Rwanda and symbol of reconciliation between Hutus and Tutsis, was imprisoned in April. Bizimungu had joined the Rwandan Patriotic Front (FPR), led by exiled Tutsis, in 1990. As a Hutu married to a Tutsi wife, Bizimungu stood out as a symbol of reconciliation between the two ethnic groups and, after the seizure of power by the FPR in July 1994, he was named President. But his role in government was more symbolic than real and, after six years in office, he was replaced by the strong man behind the throne, Paul Kagame. In June 2001 he attempted to form a new political party, but this was immediately banned and Bizimungu started to receive threats. He was finally arrested on 19 April 2002 and brought before the courts in May, accused of civil disobedience and of sowing ethnic hatred—offences that carried a 10 year jail sentence.

On the economic front, privatisation continued to be an important issue. At the end of the previous year, several important tea estates were added to the list of companies to be privatised. In November, it was reported that the state-owned fixed-line phone service (Rwandatel) was for sale. It was hoped that privatisation would contribute US$100m to state revenue.

It was again the trials of genocide suspects that, during 2002, held the attention of the world. The International Criminal Tribunal for Rwanda (ICTR) at Arusha in Tanzania attracted growing criticism. After seven years the ICTR had tried only nine cases. Rwandan courts, by contrast, had tried over 6,000 suspects between December 1996 and June 2001.

Those brought before the ICTR in the early months of 2002 included a former permanent secretary in the Ministry of Defence, a former Minister of Information, a priest, a youth leader, and several senior army officers. The suspects had been arrested in Cameroon, Kenya, and Belgium and faced a range of charges, including genocide, conspiracy to commit genocide, complicity in genocide, direct and public incitement to commit genocide, crimes against humanity (murder and extermination), rape, and persecution. In June the US Ambassador at Large for War Issues, Pierre-Richard Prosper, tried to speed up the process by offering a US$5 million bounty for information leading to the arrest of suspects responsible for the 1994 genocide in Rwanda. This action contributed to the arrest of Gen. Augustin Bizimungu, the former chief-of-staff of the Rwandan army, in Angola on 2 August. He had been fighting alongside the rebel National Union for the Total Independence of Angola (UNITA) in eastern Angola and had been recognised during the demobilisation of UNITA forces following the April ceasefire in that country (see VII.1.v).

Another important development occurred in September when the government of the Democratic Republic of Congo, in a goodwill gesture that recognised the importance of the withdrawal of Rwandan forces from the DRC, repatriated eight Hutu refugees to Rwanda. These men included Jean-Baptiste Gatete, a former mayor of Murambi commune in Kibungo prefecture and an Interahamwe (Hutu militia) leader in the DRC; and Col Tharcisse Renzaho, the former prefect of Kigaliville. When these men were brought to court in Arusha, another courtroom was occupied by the trial of two of the men who had established Radio Mille Collines as a source of propaganda aimed at dehumanising the Tutsis during the 100-day genocide in 1994, and as a centre of control directing the actions of Hutu death squads. A conviction in this trial would establish a precedent for the rules to be used in the judgment of the media in similar cases elsewhere in the world.

The *Gacaca* community courts were launched in June as an attempt to use traditional, village justice to deal with the 115,000 prisoners awaiting trial in overcrowded and unsanitary jails. Some 11,000 courts, each with 19 "people's judges", were created. The first 12 were initiated in June and a further 100 started to function in December.

iii. GUINEA-BISSAU—CAPE VERDE—SÃO TOMÉ & PRÍNCIPE

Guinea-Bissau
CAPITAL: Bissau   AREA: 36,000 sq km   POPULATION: 1,226,000
OFFICIAL LANGUAGE: Portuguese   POLITICAL SYSTEM: multiparty republic
HEAD OF STATE AND GOVERNMENT: President Kumba Yalla (since Feb '00)
RULING PARTY: none
PRIME MINISTER: Mario Pires, (since Nov '02)
MAIN IGO MEMBERSHIPS (NON-UN): AU, ECOWAS, UEMOA, ACP, OIC, NAM, CPLP, Francophonie
CURRENCY: CFA franc (end-'02 £1=CFAFr1,009.56, US$1=CFAFr630.370)
GNI PER CAPITA: US$160, US$710 at PPP ('01)

Cape Verde
CAPITAL: Praia   AREA: 4,000 sq km   POPULATION: 454,000
OFFICIAL LANGUAGE: Portuguese   POLITICAL SYSTEM: multiparty republic
HEAD OF STATE: President Pedro Pires (since March '01)
RULING PARTY: African Party for the Independence of Cape Verde (PAICV)
HEAD OF GOVERNMENT: José Maria Pereira Neves, Prime Minister (since Feb '01)
MAIN IGO MEMBERSHIPS (NON-UN): AU, ECOWAS, ACP, NAM, CPLP, Francophonie
CURRENCY: CV escudo (end-'02 £1=CVEsc174.489, US$1=CvEsc108.950)
GNI PER CAPITA: US$1,310, US$4,870 at PPP ('01)

São Tomé & Príncipe
CAPITAL: São Tomé   AREA: 965 sq km   POPULATION: 151,000
OFFICIAL LANGUAGE: Portuguese   POLITICAL SYSTEM: multiparty republic
HEAD OF STATE AND GOVERNMENT: President Fradique de Menezes (since Sept. '01)
RULING PARTY: Independent Democratic Alliance (ADI)
PRIME MINISTER: Maria das Neves de Sousa (since Oct '02)
MAIN IGO MEMBERSHIPS (NON-UN): AU, CEEAC, ACP, NAM, CPLP, Francophonie
CURRENCY: dobra (end-'02 £1=Db14,445.5, US$1=Db9,019.70)
GNI PER CAPITA: US$280 ('01)

POLITICS in GUINEA-BISSAU remained extremely volatile in 2002. After the failed December 2001 coup attempt against President Kumba Yalla (see AR 2002, p. 294), the alleged coup-plotters remained under arrest but various judicial and court officials were released in February, as well as some human rights activists. Two independent newspapers, forced to close in October 2001, were allowed to resume publishing. Then in May the government claimed that there had been another coup attempt. Under pressure from the UN, Yalla in June proposed an amnesty for soldiers who were involved in the coup attempts of December and May, in the interests of national reconciliation. But he also threatened to invade The Gambia if coup plotters who he claimed were living in the Gambian capital, Banjul, were not handed over. A prominent journalist arrested for criticising this threat went on a hunger strike. After the UN Secretary-General Kofi Annan had sent an envoy to mediate, Yalla withdrew his threat.

In July the UN Security Council reviewed the latest report on the country by the head of the UN Peace-Building mission (UNOGBIS), and supported the need for national dialogue. The Council called on Yalla to work for national reconciliation; to hasten the demobilisation, reintegration, and reinsertion of former combatants; to keep a watchful eye on public finances; and to improve international relations, particularly with The Gambia. But the political scene remained chaotic, with the President and National Assembly (the legislature) unable to agree on the extent of presidential powers in a new constitution. In November Yalla accused the legislature of "subversion" and the minority Social Renewal Party government of having been corrupt. He dismissed the government of Prime Minister Alamara Nhasse, appointing Mario Pires as caretaker Prime Minister; dissolved the National Assembly; and announced that legislative elections would be held early in 2003. With the country's institutions so fragile, and the judiciary so weak, many feared that it would not be possible to hold a free and fair election. The continuing political instability impeded any efforts to pull the country out of poverty.

Economic and political problems continued to plague the island nation of CAPE VERDE. In his New Year's message, President Pedro Pires praised workers for not demanding higher wages in a difficult economic climate and appealed to Cape Verdeans living abroad to help their country. He then promulgated the budget, without having secured the necessary two-thirds support in the legislature, claiming that he had to act because projects contained within the finance bill could not be delayed. The main opposition party, the Movement for Democracy (MPD), reacted with outrage and claimed that Pires had become a de facto dictator, but none could deny the country's economic problems.

Cape Verde produced only 10 per cent of its annual food requirements, and a particularly dry season in 2002 greatly reduced the corn (maize) crop. The government had to request help from the UN World Food Programme, which in June launched a US$1.3 million emergency food operation to help feed some 30,000 Cape Verdeans on the islands of Santiago and Santo Antão. In September the government created an inter-ministerial committee to help minimise the anticipated impact of a bad food harvest. The food crisis was exacerbated, however, by the continuing rapid spread of AIDS/HIV among food-producers. The country remained heavily dependent on international aid, though some revenue was derived from South African Airways, which continued to use Sal Island as a refuelling stop for planes en route to and from the USA. Cape Verde remained an active member of the Community of Portuguese-Speaking Countries (CPLP—see XI.3.ii).

In SÃO TOMÉ AND PRÍNCIPE, President Fradique de Menezes had called an election for 3 March, after failing to agree with Prime Minister Guilherme Posser da Costa of the Movement for the Liberation of São Tomé and Príncipe (MLSTP) over the composition of the Cabinet (see AR 2001, p. 295). In the campaign, each side accused the other of receiving financial backing from outside the country: the MLSTP from Angola's ruling MPLA party and its opponents from those in Taiwan and Nigeria interested in offshore oil possibilities. No party received an absolute majority: the MLSTP won 24 seats, the Democratic Movement Force for Change/Party of Democratic Governance (MDFM/PCD) 23, and a coalition of other parties eight. The President appointed Gabriel Costa, who had been Ambassador to Portugal, to head a coalition government. But at the end of September, de Menezes dissolved the government after complaints from the army over his promotion of two officers to the rank of Lieutenant Colonel, one of them a former Defence Minister. Regular officers complained that they had been sidelined. While the Costa government remained in office, the President held discussions to find a new Prime Minister. In October he asked Maria das Neves, who had been Minister for Trade, Industry and Tourism, to form a government. The archipelago's first woman Prime Minister was able to put together another coalition government. But when the 55-member legislature approved a constitutional reform package limiting presidential powers, the President vetoed it, and the year ended with relations between him and the legislature very strained.

iv. MOZAMBIQUE

CAPITAL: Maputo   AREA: 802,000 sq km   POPULATION: 18,100,000
OFFICIAL LANGUAGE: Portuguese   POLITICAL SYSTEM: multiparty republic in British Commonwealth
HEAD OF STATE AND GOVERNMENT: President Joachim Alberto Chissano (since Nov '86)
RULING PARTY: Front for the Liberation of Mozambique (Frelimo)
PRIME MINISTER: Pascoal Mocumbi (since Dec '94)
MAIN IGO MEMBERSHIPS (NON-UN): AU, SADC, ACP, CWTH, OIC, NAM, CPLP
CURRENCY: metical (end-'02 £1=M37,385.0, US$1=M23,343.0)
GNI PER CAPITA: US$210, US$1,000 at PPP ('01)

THE Mozambican economy continued to post solid gains during 2002. In the first six months of the year the economy grew at an annual rate of 11.7 per cent. From January to September, inflation rose by only 2.5 per cent and the currency, the metical, devalued by less than 1 per cent against a strong US dollar. In 2001 the country had attracted foreign direct investment worth US$255 million. This made Mozambique, a country with few natural resources, the third most successful under-developed nation in the world after oil-rich Sudan and Angola. Some of this income had filtered down to the villages. The rapid growth that followed the end of the civil war and the transition to democratic rule in 1994 (see AR 1994, pp. 296-98) almost doubled the purchasing power of the average Mozambican and extended life expectancy by three years, to 47 years for men and 50 for women.

Over nearly a decade, Mozambique had undergone a social revolution, based on neo-liberal economics, that was as far-reaching as the Marxist revolution, based on centralised economic planning, which shook the country in the late 1970s and 1980s. However, impressive economic growth was accompanied by troubling signs that wealth was being accumulated in restricted geographical areas and in the hands of a limited number of people. The old colonial structure of economic development and dependence had also re-emerged in post-civil war Mozambique. Some were concerned that the Front for the Liberation of Mozambique (Frelimo) government, which received a quarter of its budget in the form of aid, was unable to manage the running of social services in an efficient manner. Others feared that

Frelimo had lost control of the economy to foreign investors, aid agencies, and non-governmental organisations.

Economic development was concentrated in the south of the country, an area that benefited from its proximity to mineral-rich South Africa. In the previous five years, South Africa had invested over US$3 billion in this region. Although this investment had reinforced the economic infrastructure in the south (especially the building of a new toll-road between Maputo and Nelspruit and the modernisation of the rail system), it tended to be concentrated in restricted projects. The most famous was the Mozal aluminium smelter, in Matola outside Maputo, which produced ingots worth US$400 million each year. Having employed 10,000 people during its construction phase, and being responsible for half the country's exports in 2002, Mozal paid virtually no tax and employed a much reduced workforce of only 1,000 people. A second major, capital-intensive project was nearing completion at Chibuto, in Gazaland, to the north of Maputo. This was the Corridor Sands titanium project that, it was estimated, would require an investment of US$1 billion before becoming fully operational during 2004. When it reached its peak production, Corridor Sands was expected to become the world's largest titanium producer. Another important source of export earnings was the natural gas pipeline being built from Inhambane on the coast to Secunda, the oil-from-coal producer in South Africa's Mpumalanga province. Critics said that these showcase projects involved one-off investments and concealed the decline of older industries. The liberalisation of trade had caused the processing of cashew nuts, for example, to shift to India. The lifting of protective barriers had also adversely affected the production of textiles in Mozambique. The concentration of economic growth in the south of the country had led to political problems as marginalised areas voted increasingly for the National Resistance Movement (Renamo) opposition.

Perhaps most importantly, the economic growth of the past decade had done little to reduce the level of malnourishment in the country, which still amounted to about 54 per cent of the population. Under-nourishment of the population in 2002 was, as in much of southern Africa, accentuated by drought and the failure of the harvests. By mid-year, food was becoming scarce in many areas and some 500,000 people were reported to be in need of food aid. AIDS/HIV also emerged as a major, long-term problem, particularly as the government was unable to supply anti-retroviral drugs to, and in many cases could not even afford to test, those inflicted by this scourge (roughly estimated at 11-14 per cent of the population).

The liberalisation of the economy also provoked an unseemly scramble for wealth that resulted in some high-profile criminal cases. In March the Attorney General denounced corruption in a speech before the national parliament in Maputo. Most notoriously, Anibal dos Santos, the man held responsible for the assassination in November 2000 of the anti-corruption campaigning journalist Carlos Cardoso, escaped in September from a high security prison in Maputo. Despite this setback, the six accomplices of dos Santos went on trial for murder in November. The case rapidly became a national soap opera, particularly after the President's son, Nyimpine Chissano, was implicated in Cardoso's killing. In December the Minister of Justice asked for the President's son to be investigated.

This downturn in the fortunes of the Chissano family had begun in June when, at the 8th Frelimo congress, Gen. Armando Emilio Guebuza was elected secretary general of the ruling party and became its candidate for the elections due in 2004. President Joachim Chissano, who was to stand down after 17 years in office, had wanted a younger man to lead the party away from its Marxist past. It remained to be seen whether Guebuza, a party stalwart turned business tycoon, was willing to perform this function. Shifts within Frelimo were accompanied by a similar shake-up in the opposition, Renamo. In July the party president, Alfonso Dhlakama, dismissed the secretary general of Renamo and several of his close confidants. The move confirmed that both parties seemed to be preparing a new face for the 2004 elections.

v. ANGOLA

CAPITAL: Luanda   AREA: 1,247,000 sq km   POPULATION: 13,500,000
OFFICIAL LANGUAGE: Portuguese   POLITICAL SYSTEM: multiparty republic
HEAD OF STATE: President José Eduardo dos Santos (since Sept '79)
RULING PARTY: Popular Movement for the Liberation of Angola-Workers' Party (MPLA-PT) heads nominal coalition
PRIME MINISTER: Fernando da Piedade Dias dos Santos (since Dec '02)
MAIN IGO MEMBERSHIPS (NON-UN): AU, COMESA, SADC, CEEAC, ACP, NAM, CPLP
CURRENCY: readj kwanza (end-'02 £1=Kw93.2951, US$1=Kw58.2530)
GNI PER CAPITA: US$500, US$1,550 at PPP ('01)

PEACE came to Angola in 2002, after four decades of war. The crucial event was the killing by government forces on 22 February, in the central-eastern province of Moxico, of Jonas Savimbi. Leader of the rebel National Union for the Total Independence of Angola (UNITA), Savimbi had led his forces against the ruling party from before independence in 1975 and had, after the contested election of 1992, gone back to war. After his death, and then that of his likely successor, Gen. Antonio Dembo, the government offered amnesty to rebel fighters and the country moved towards a ceasefire, which was signed in Luanda on 4 April after two weeks of talks in Luena in eastern Angola. Though many feared that the ceasefire would not hold, it did. UNITA soldiers were offered assistance in reintegrating into civilian life, and some 50,000 of them, with up to 300,000 family members, moved into government-run assembly areas. Many of these lacked clean water and sanitation, as well as sufficient food and medicines, and UNITA officials alleged that considerable numbers of those in the quartering camps died unnecessarily. Perhaps 30,000 left the camps to return to their home provinces, forfeiting the promised government aid to help their return to civilian life. When the government announced that the camps would be closed, aid agencies said that this was premature, fearing that those still in the camps were not ready to move back to the areas where they had previously lived. One of the arguments for closing the camps was that there should no longer be any UNITA enclaves in the country.

The government faced a colossal task in rebuilding the nation after the war. The infrastructure was devastated, with innumerable roads, bridges, and sections of railway needing repair or rebuilding. Millions of anti-personnel mines littered the countryside, making the distribution of food aid difficult or impossible in many parts of the country, and inhibiting a return to agricultural production in areas affected by the war. Up to four million people, a third of the total population, were displaced within the country. From April a considerable number of these began to move back to where they had originally lived. As the humanitarian agencies began to gain access to areas affected by the war, they reported an appalling situation. The UN World Food Programme, which helped to feed a large proportion of the population, estimated that some two million Angolans were threatened with famine. Only perhaps a quarter of the urban population—which included some two million refugees living in squalor on the outskirts of the capital, Luanda—had access to clean water; in the countryside an even smaller proportion had such access. Half of all children did not attend school.

In the far-north oil-rich province of Cabinda, the armed forces continued to fight different groups of the Front for the Liberation of the Cabinda Enclave (FLEC). President Jose Eduardo dos Santos said that he was prepared to consult on Cabinda's status, but could not negotiate while fighting continued and FLEC was divided into so many factions. Some of the perhaps half-a-million Angolans living as refugees in neighbouring states now also began to make their way home. After the peace agreement was signed with UNITA, tensions eased on the Zambian border in the east, and skirmishes along the border with Namibia in the south came to an end. In September the annual meeting of the Southern African Development Community (SADC) took place in Luanda, and Angola assumed the chair of the organisation.

Angola was the second largest oil producer in sub-Saharan Africa after Nigeria and provided almost 10 per cent of the USA's oil imports. Four companies—ChevronTexaco, TotalfinaElf, ExxonMobil, and British Petroleum—produced about 900,000 barrels per day of crude oil. Oil provided 80 percent of state revenues. In the aftermath of the war, and with Middle East sources increasingly precarious, oil production was expected to increase dramatically. As new deep water fields came on stream, and with new finds onshore expected, there were hopes that Angola's oil production could double by 2008 to reach 1.8 million barrels per day. With the end of the war it seemed that a proposed liquefied natural gas plant would be built, not in Luanda but in Soyo, in the northern Zaire province. But with the oil companies failing to reveal their financial dealings, it was impossible to track revenue flows, and so to know the extent of the large-scale corruption involved in the oil industry. One estimate was that US$3 from each barrel of oil sold went into the pockets of the ruling clique, the small circle of people around the presidency.

Angola was the fourth largest diamond producer in the world, and with the government taking control of the diamond trade, much of which had been in the hands of UNITA, there was the possibility that the trade in illegal diamonds would be stopped. De Beers, the largest diamond company in the world, began talks with the Angolan national diamond company to that end. In November the UN Security Council lifted the travel ban on UNITA, as a step towards the lifting of the other sanctions imposed on the rebel movement since 1993, but UNITA remained divided, with the Renovada (Renewal) faction, which had broken with Savimbi in 1998 and gained seats in the legislature, unwilling to accept the leadership of Gen. Lukamba "Gato". It remained to be seen if UNITA could establish itself as an effective national political party.

Ties between the government and the USA strengthened, with visits by Dos Santos to Washington DC in February, and by US Secretary of State Colin Powell to Luanda in September, but though the USA pressed the Angolan government to set a timetable for elections, this was not done. Dos Santos had said that he would not stand in the presidential election, not thought likely to take place before 2004 at the earliest, but others in the ruling Popular Movement for the Liberation of Angola (MPLA) indicated that he might be a candidate. As peace returned, the institutions of civil society began to revive, and non-governmental groups challenged the government. The Land Forum, for example, claimed a victory when the government agreed to reconsider a controversial draft law relating to land which, the Forum argued, failed to safeguard the interests of rural peasant communities. But the key question remained whether Angola's vast resources would now be used to rebuild the country and promote political stability and multiparty democracy.

2. ZAMBIA—MALAWI—ZIMBABWE—BLNS STATES

i. ZAMBIA

CAPITAL: Lusaka   AREA: 753,000 sq km   POPULATION: 10,300,000
OFFICIAL LANGUAGE: English   POLITICAL SYSTEM: multiparty republic in British Commonwealth
HEAD OF STATE AND GOVERNMENT: President Levy Patrick Mwanawasa (since Jan '02)
RULING PARTY: Movement for Multi-Party Democracy (MMD)
MAIN IGO MEMBERSHIPS (NON-UN): AU, COMESA, SADC, ACP, CWTH, NAM
CURRENCY: Zambian kwacha (end-'02 £1=Kw7,287.06, US$1=Kw4,550.00)
GNI PER CAPITA: US$320, US$790 at PPP ('01)

As a result of the bitterly contested election held in late December 2001 (see AR 2001, p. 299), Levy Mwanawasa of the Movement for Multiparty Democracy (MMD) was able to take office as successor to Frederick Chiluba, though he gained only 28.9 per cent of the vote and beat his main rival by a mere 35,000 votes. In his inauguration speech the new President accused Western donors, and especially the EU, which had funded the election, of "fanning anarchy" in Zambia. Notwithstanding Mwanawasa's inauguration, the election results were challenged in the courts, and during 2002 damning evidence emerged of large-scale corruption and fraud which cast serious doubt upon the legitimacy of his victory. He ignored calls for his resignation, however, and instead turned his attention to exposing acts of corruption by his predecessor and other officials. As the opposition parties together had more seats in the legislature than the ruling party, passing legislation proved difficult. A number of opposition politicians then joined the MMD, which won a series of by-elections. As the year ended, Mwanawasa's political future remained uncertain.

Zambia's was one of the southern African countries most affected by drought in 2002, and a serious food crisis developed, with an estimated 2.3 million of its people threatened with starvation. Yet the Zambian government rejected donations of genetically modified maize from the USA. Announcing this in August, the Information Minister said that the consequences of consuming genetically modified food were uncertain, and that the genetically modified maize posed a long-term risk to the country's food security, because it would contaminate local seed. To help boost agricultural productivity, some of the white farmers who had been forced off their land in Zimbabwe (see VII.2.iii) were offered land in Zambia.

In January Anglo American, which had bought the Zambian copper mines for US$90 million two years before, and promised to invest US$1 billion in the mines, suddenly announced that it would abandon its investment because production in Zambia was too expensive at current world prices for copper. It offered US$30 million in compensation but the government wanted US$200 million. The withdrawal put more than 10,000 jobs at risk, at a time when one in four Zambians was unemployed, and the government was quick to insist that the loss making Konkola, Nchanga, and Nampundwe mines would not be closed. Copper accounted for two-fifths of the country's export earnings, and donor funds enabled the mines to continue operating while a new buyer was sought.

ii. MALAWI

CAPITAL: Lilongwe   AREA: 118,000 sq km   POPULATION: 10,500,000
OFFICIAL LANGUAGE: English   POLITICAL SYSTEM: multiparty republic in British Commonwealth
HEAD OF STATE AND GOVERNMENT: President Bakili Muluzi (since May '94)
RULING PARTIES: United Democratic Front (UDF) heads coalition with Malawi National Democratic Party (MNDP) & United Front for Multi-Party Democracy (UFMD)
MAIN IGO MEMBERSHIPS (NON-UN): AU, COMESA, SADC, ACP, CWTH, NAM
CURRENCY: Malawi kwacha (end-'02 £1=Kw138.790, US$1=Kw86.6600)
GNI PER CAPITA: US$170, US$620 at PPP ('01)

IN 2002 Malawi became even more impoverished, and by the end of the year, an estimated 65 per cent of the population was living on less than US$1 per day. Drought and AIDS/HIV helped to produce a food crisis; an estimated 70,000 people were thought to be dying from AIDS/HIV annually. In the first three months of the year some 500 people starved to death, and malnutrition was rife. By December the UN World Food Programme estimated that the number of hungry people had increased to 3.3 million, almost a third of the population. The EU gave US$3 million that month to Malawi to help feed malnourished children and pregnant and breast-feeding mothers, but that was only enough for 6,000 tonnes of maize (the staple food) to be processed and distributed in a country which needed 600,000 tonnes to stave off the threatened famine.

Meanwhile the IMF refused to resume lending to Malawi until the government brought down its rising wage bill. Sales of tobacco, which had brought in 70 per cent of the country's foreign exchange earnings, were disappointing, and by December Malawi's commercial banks had run out of foreign exchange. Investigations continued into why the country's strategic grain reserves, which had amounted to 166,000 tons in 2000, had been sold off. While the government blamed the sale on poor advice from the IMF, a local anti-corruption bureau established that most of the maize had been bought by senior politicians. No action was taken against such people, although President Bakili Muluzi did dismiss the Minister responsible for poverty alleviation, Leonard Mangulama, after he had been named as the person who had presided over the sale of the maize reserves when he was Agriculture Minister. He had also been one of those who had benefited personally from the sale.

The main political issue continued to be whether the constitution would be amended to enable Muluzi to run for a third presidential term in 2004. After the long years of the Banda dictatorship it had been agreed that a two term limit for Presidents would constitute the cornerstone of the new democratic political system. Many Malawians thought Muluzi should devote his attention to the food crisis rather than his political future, and in July the legislature voted down his Open Term Bill, a constitutional amendment that would have allowed him to stay in office indefinitely. But Muluzi would not give up, despite mounting opposition from the donor community, churches, and human rights groups. His party, the United Democratic Front, amended the draft legislation and produced a Third Term Bill, which proposed to allow him another five year term. Furthermore, Muluzi issued a decree banning all demonstrations relating to his bid for a third term. Vocal opponents of this were imprisoned and, when the courts struck down his decree, Muluzi recommended the dismissal of three judges. As the year ended, the issue remained unresolved, but political violence was on the increase, with the ruling party's militant "Young Democrats" involved in widespread intimidation of opposition supporters.

iii. ZIMBABWE

CAPITAL: Harare   AREA: 391,000 sq km   POPULATION: 12,800,000
OFFICIAL LANGUAGE: English   POLITICAL SYSTEM: multiparty republic in British Commonwealth
HEAD OF STATE AND GOVERNMENT: President Robert Mugabe (since Dec '87); previously Prime Minister (from April '80)
RULING PARTY: Zimbabwe African National Union-Patriotic Front (ZANU-PF)
MAIN IGO MEMBERSHIPS (NON-UN): AU, COMESA, SADC, ACP, CWTH, NAM
CURRENCY: Zimbabwe dollar (end-'02 £1=Z$88.8060, US$1=Z$55.4500)
GNI PER CAPITA: US$480, US$2,340 at PPP ('01)

THE presidential election, scheduled for 9-10 March, was the most important event of the year. Robert Mugabe, head of the country's Zimbabwe African National Union-Patriotic Front (ZANU-PF) government since 1980, faced the most potent challenge of his career in the form of Morgan Tsvangirai, leader of the opposition Movement for Democratic Change (MDC).

The determination of the 78-year-old President to win a fourth term at almost any cost was revealed by the obstacles placed in the way of Tsvangirai's campaign. Opposition rallies were routinely disrupted by ZANU-PF "war veterans", or prohibited by the police through selective use of public order legislation. MDC supporters were widely intimidated and threatened, while draconian curbs on the press undermined fair reporting of the contest. Tsvangirai was briefly detained at Harare airport on returning from a visit to South Africa, and on 22 February a vehicle in which he was travelling to an election meeting was fired upon by the police. Most seriously on 25 February he was charged with treason following an accusation that he had engaged a Canadian public relations company to assassinate the President. The charge, which carried the death penalty, was categorically denied, and trial proceedings were subsequently postponed until February 2003.

International reaction to news of election intimidation was severe. Desmond Tutu, former Archbishop of Cape Town and Nobel peace laureate, declared that Zimbabwe was "sliding towards dictatorship". On 18 February the EU imposed "smart sanctions" on Mugabe and 19 of his close associates, curtailing individual travel and freezing external bank accounts as well as banning weapon sales to the country. Five days later the US government announced similar penalties "because conditions for a transparent election process in Zimbabwe have eroded". On 3 March the Commonwealth Heads of Government meeting, postponed from the previous October (see AR 2001, p. 303) deferred a decision on the suspension of Zimbabwe pending a report by Commonwealth election observers. A triumvirate of Commonwealth leaders—Olusegun Obasanjo of Nigeria, Thabo Mbeki of South Africa, and John Howard of Australia—confirmed the suspension on 19 May.

In the run-up to the election, opinion polls forecast a Tsvangirai victory. Three days before the vote the Zimbabwean Electoral Supervisory Commission had still not announced the location of polling stations, indicated the number of ballot papers printed, or enumerated the postal votes received from Zimbabwe's forces in the Democratic Republic of Congo. The reason became clear when voting began. In urban areas—MDC strongholds—there were 50 per cent fewer polling stations than at the 2000 general election. Given heavy voter turnout, the result was long queues in the hot sun by those wishing to cast a vote. In rural areas, where ZANU-PF expected maximum support, the number of polling stations was augmented. By the close of the second day only 28 per cent of registered voters in Harare had been able to vote, and the MDC applied to the High Court for an extension. A desultory and disorganised third day left ballot boxes in the control of the armed forces, with reports of ballot stuffing, missing boxes and other irregularities.

The result of the election, announced after Registrar-General Tobaiwa Mudede had twice revised the total number of votes cast, gave Mugabe victory by 56.2 per cent to 41.9 per cent, a margin of 463,000 votes. The percentage turnout was conspicuously high in constituencies favourable to ZANU-PF, and correspondingly low in opposition areas. A subsequent analysis by the Helen Suzman Foundation in Johannesburg revealed that 700,000 votes had been "discovered" and added to Mugabe's total following the close of the polls, indicating that Mugabe had lost the vote but won the count. In a simultaneous local government election in Harare, the MDC won 44 out of 46 wards.

Despite the reports of violence and intimidation, African nations were quick to accept the result of the election. South African election observers, though themselves assaulted by ZANU-PF thugs during the campaign, declared it free "to a degree". An observer mission sent by the EU had been withdrawn before the poll after Zimbabwe expelled its Swedish head, Pierre Schori. But the verdict of the Commonwealth team was that the will of the electorate had not been fairly represented. The US government declared the election flawed and declined to recognise Mugabe as the legitimate President. Attempts by Nigeria and South Africa to engineer talks between ZANU-PF and the MDC about the possibility of a government of national unity were called off in mid-May.

Mugabe's stolen victory did not mark the end of violence, but rather saw it increase as retribution was exacted in constituencies which had favoured the MDC candidate. Opposition supporters, or anyone without a ZANU-PF party card, were vulnerable. Teachers lost their jobs, industries sympathetic to the opposition were victimised, and elected MDC legislators were abducted, detained, and tortured. On 22 October the death in prison was revealed of Learnmore Jongwe, a member of the House of Assembly (the unicameral legislature) and Information Secretary of the MDC. Though an official postmortem confirmed poisoning, the government declared Jongwe's death to be suicide. At his funeral on 29 October, hundreds of mourners were gratuitously tear-gassed by the police.

The government's confiscation of white-owned farms, begun in 2000 (see AR 2001, p. 301), reached its climax on 8 September when 2,900 of the remaining 4,500 white farmers were ordered off their land, without compensation. Prime farms were appropriated by political leaders and relatives of the President. On 20 August, Grace Mugabe, the wife of the President, abruptly commandeered a farm 30 miles north-west of Harare from its elderly white owners. The result of the confiscations was a sharp decline in agricultural production. Exacerbated by poor rainfall and the failure of government resettlement schemes, food shortages worsened and a state of disaster was declared on 1 May. By August a third of Zimbabwe's population was at risk of starvation. The government declared the distribution of food aid by foreign agencies illegal, and took control of rationing. Officials of the World Food Organisation reported that ZANU-PF supporters were receiving preferential access to grain, and during two by-election campaigns, food was unashamedly being traded for votes. Didymus Mutasa, a Mugabe confidant and former Speaker of the House of Assembly (the unicameral legislature), made the chilling observation that "we would be better off with only 6 million . . . of our own people who support the liberation struggle". By the close of the year two million Zimbabweans were estimated to have emigrated or migrated illegally to neighbouring countries, some opting for imprisonment in South Africa in return for regular meals.

By December the country appeared close to economic meltdown. With inflation at 175 per cent and a ruinous discrepancy between the official exchange rate of Z$55 to the US dollar compared with a "parallel market" rate of Z$2,000, foreign earnings were extinguished. Tamoil Trading Ltd of Libya, hitherto a major source of fuel, refused further supply in the face of an outstanding government debt of US$48 million. A bilateral trade agreement with Malaysia, one of Zimbabwe's few remaining allies, collapsed pending repayment of a similar obligation. Basic commodities such as flour, maize, cooking-oil, and salt were unobtainable except at inflated prices on the black market. In Harare disruption to the water supply followed power cuts as the municipality ran out of water-purification chemicals. Even banknotes were in short supply, given the scarcity of paper on which to print them.

Notwithstanding the moral and economic bankruptcy of his regime, the cult of Mugabe continued to dominate political life. Apart from "Professor" Jonathan Moyo, the comedic Minister of Information, few of the President's colleagues dared raise their head above the parapet. Simba Makoni, the Minister of Finance, argued for devaluation of the country's exchange rate and was sacked on 24 August. In December Joseph Made, Minister of Lands and Agriculture, publicly admitted the government's failure to ensure adequate supplies of grain. On 17 December Emmerson Mnangagwa, Speaker of the House of Assembly and a man often seen as Mugabe's chosen successor, travelled to Cape Town to meet South African President Thabo Mbeki. Despite rumours of his imminent retirement, however, Mugabe remained the dominant and uncompromising symbol of the devastation of his country. Tsvangirai's advice was simple: "Just resign".

iv. BOTSWANA—LESOTHO—NAMBIA—SWAZILAND

Botswana

CAPITAL: Gaborone   AREA: 582,000 sq km   POPULATION: 1,600,000
OFFICIAL LANGUAGES: English and Setswana   POLITICAL SYSTEM: multiparty republic in British Commonwealth
HEAD OF STATE AND GOVERNMENT: President Festus Mogae (since March '98)
RULING PARTY: Botswana Democratic Party (BDP)
MAIN IGO MEMBERSHIPS (NON-UN): AU, SADC, SACU, ACP, CWTH, NAM
CURRENCY: pula (end-'02 £1=P8.8729, US$1=P5.5402)
GNI PER CAPITA: US$3,630, US$8,810 at PPP ('01)

Lesotho

CAPITAL: Maseru   AREA: 30,000 sq km   POPULATION: 2,100,000
OFFICIAL LANGUAGES: English & Sesotho   POLITICAL SYSTEM: multiparty monarchy in British Commonwealth
HEAD OF STATE: King Letsie III (since Jan '96)
RULING PARTY: Lesotho Congress for Democracy (LCD)
HEAD OF GOVERNMENT: Bethuel Pakalitha Mosisili, Prime Minister (since June '98)
MAIN IGO MEMBERSHIPS (NON-UN): AU, SADC, SACU, ACP, CWTH, NAM
CURRENCY: maloti (end-'02 £1=M13.9984, US$1=M8.7405)
GNI PER CAPITA: US$550, US$2,670 at PPP ('01)

Namibia
CAPITAL: Windhoek   AREA: 824,000 sq km   POPULATION: 1,800,000
OFFICIAL LANGUAGES: Afrikaans & English   POLITICAL SYSTEM: multiparty republic in British Commonwealth
HEAD OF STATE: President Sam Nujoma (since March '90)
RULING PARTY: South West Africa People's Organisation (SWAPO)
HEAD OF GOVERNMENT: Theo-Ben Gurirab, Prime Minister (since August '02)
MAIN IGO MEMBERSHIPS (NON-UN): AU, SADC, COMESA, SACU, ACP, CWTH, NAM
CURRENCY: Namibian dollar (end-'02 £1=N$13.9984, US$1=N$8.7405)
GNI PER CAPITA: US$1,960, US$6,700 at PPP ('01)

Swaziland
CAPITAL: Mbabane   AREA: 17,350 sq km   POPULATION: 1,068,000
OFFICIAL LANGUAGES: English & Siswati   POLITICAL SYSTEM: non-party monarchy in British Commonwealth
HEAD OF STATE: King Mswati III (since '86)
HEAD OF GOVERNMENT: Sibusiso Barnabas Dlamini, Prime Minister (since July '96)
MAIN IGO MEMBERSHIPS (NON-UN): AU, COMESA, SADC, SACU, ACP, CWTH, NAM
CURRENCY: lilangeni/pl. emalangeni (end-'02 £1=E13.9984, US$1=E8.7405)
GNI PER CAPITA: US$1,300, US$4,690 at PPP ('01)

Two key challenges during 2002 were the AIDS/HIV epidemic and the food shortages in Lesotho, Swaziland, and Namibia. While the end of the civil war in Angola in April 2002 (see VII.1.v) had positive ramifications for its neighbours and for accelerated regional economic linkages, the continuing political and economic crisis in Zimbabwe (see VII.2.iii) created negative perceptions of the region. In a positive vein the much-awaited new Southern African Customs Union (SACU) agreement was finally signed in October 2002. It made provision for a new institutional framework, which would include a secretariat, a tariff board, and a tribunal for the settlement of disputes. The agreement also provided for the development of common policies and strategies to enhance industrial development, as well as for co-operation on agricultural and competition policies, and on anti-dumping principles. The revenue-sharing formula, which had been the most contentious issue in negotiations, had a built-in bias in favour of the four smaller countries of the customs union: Botswana, Lesotho, Namibia, and Swaziland.

BOTSWANA had reached a critical stage in its economic development. It had long been regarded as an example to be emulated in Africa, with consistently high economic growth rates, one of the highest GDPs per capita on the continent, and sound political and economic governance. Its exchange reserves in 2001, for example amounted to US$5.9 billion. However, Botswana also had the highest AIDS/HIV infection rate among adults in the world (38.8 per cent), and its economy continued to rely heavily on its diamond industry.

A study conducted by the Botswana Institute for Development and Policy Analysis (BIDPA) estimated that AIDS-related income poverty would add 5 per cent to the overall rate of income poverty over a 10-year period, and economic growth would be reduced by 1.5 per cent over 20 years. The estimated annual cost of AIDS/HIV was about US$25-50 million, but this was set to treble over the next 15 years. According to UN agencies, some 70 per cent of all orphans were AIDS orphans. However, Botswana had been one of the most active countries in developing and implementing a strategy to combat AIDS/HIV, with the help of international agencies and companies.

The economic impact of AIDS/HIV was made more acute by the peaking of diamond production capacity following the completion of the Orapa diamond mine expansion project, coupled with the slowdown in growth in global demand upon which Botswana was dependent. Thus the conditions under which Botswana had realised phenomenal economic growth from the early 1970s onwards had begun to change.

The greatest challenge to Botswana in the short- to medium-term would therefore be its ability to convert its commitment to economic diversification into reality and to enhance its global competitiveness. There was potential in tourism, which had emerged as the country's second largest foreign exchange earner (about US$240 million annually). Growth was expected to be 3.8 per cent in fiscal 2002-03, up from a revised estimate of 1.2 per cent in 2001-02. However, investment was needed in non-traditional agriculture, manufacturing, tourism, financial and business services, and mining outside the diamond sector.

The International Financial Services Centre, which began operation in 2001, formed part of the government's diversification plans. It was established with the intention of attracting foreign companies by offering favourable corporate tax rates. By the end of 2002 there were 10 international companies operating under the scheme, including Barclays Africa. There were also three South African companies.

Although privatisation was a stated government policy, its pace had been very slow. The privatisation of Air Botswana had been scheduled for 2002, but was delayed yet again. The government announced that the airline would be privatised by mid-2003. The Botswana Telecommunications Corporation was also targeted for privatisation.

The eighth six-year National Development Plan (NDP) ended in March 2003 and the proposed 9th NDP (from April 2003) was presented to parliament in November 2002. Key priority areas included the battle against AIDS/HIV; reducing unemployment (currently estimated at about 19.6 per cent); combating poverty; achieving sustainable economic diversification; and public sector reform.

A rising budget deficit—3 per cent of GDP in 2001—was expected to remain a feature of the fiscal position in the short to medium terms given the increasing costs in the health and education budgets, together with demands by public servants for higher salaries.

In August 2002, the US Africa Growth and Opportunity Act (AGOA) was amended to allow, among other things, Botswana and Namibia to benefit from the "lesser developed beneficiary sub-Saharan African country" provision. The amendment also granted AGOA lesser developed beneficiary country status to Botswana, allowing producers there to use third country fabric in qualifying apparel. This would result in increased exports in the future, but would be insufficient to absorb the declines recorded in traditional export categories, particularly in the key sectors of mining and beef.

Although Botswana continued to be one of the more stable and democratic countries in the region, the government had had a strained relationship with the media for several years. Since 1997 the government had tried to table a Media Communications Bill to tighten its control. This had been strongly opposed by local media in Botswana. In October 2002 the Press Council of Botswana was established by the Botswana Chapter of the Media Institute of Southern Africa and the Media Consultative Council. This media self-regulatory instrument would set up an independent complaints committee to receive petitions from the public, adjudicate on such matters, and apply appropriate remedies or sanctions. It was hoped that this initiative would pre-empt any legislation from the government.

In the region, Botswana, like South Africa, had to cope with the large number of illegal immigrants crossing the border from Zimbabwe, primarily because of the land crisis and food shortages in that country. The Zimbabwe crisis affected Botswana's tourism sector negatively. President Festus Mogae was the only leader openly to criticise the policies of Zimbabwe President Robert Mugabe, characterising the crisis in Zimbabwe as a "drought of good governance".

In LESOTHO in 2002 there were two positive developments, notwithstanding the political uncertainty of the last few years. The first was the successful conduct of legislative elections in May. The second was the prosecution on corruption charges of the chief executive officer of the Lesotho Highlands Development Authority, Masupha Ephraim Sole, and of the Canadian company Acres International.

In contrast to the controversy-dogged presidential elections in Zimbabwe in March 2002, Lesotho's proceeded with no allegations of impropriety or fraud. The various international election observer missions in Lesotho described the elections as free and fair. Electoral reforms, which combined the previous constituency-based, first-past-the-post system—which had ensured in 1998 that the Lesotho Congress for Democracy (LCD) won all but one seat in the legislature (with only 60 per cent of the votes)—with proportional representation (PR) provided for a fairer electoral system. The number of seats in the legislature was increased to 120, with 80 constituency-based and 40 to be decided by PR. Nineteen parties contested the election.

The ruling LCD won an absolute majority, taking 77 constituency seats. The Basotho National Party, with the second highest number of votes (but no constituency seats), won 21 PR seats. The new legislature included nine opposition parties.

According to IMF estimates in October 2002, GDP rose by 4 per cent in fiscal 2001-02 (April to March). This reflected primarily the strong performance in construction and manufacturing. There had been a significant rise in textile exports under AGOA. In 2000 the value of Lesotho apparel exports to the USA was US$140.3 million. In 2001 this had increased by 53 per cent to US$215.3 million.

In April 2002 the government declared a state of famine, affecting close to 900,000 people or nearly half the population. The relief plan would cost about US$37 million, of which 78 per cent would be funded by donors. By the end of the year, about 445,000 people were in need of assistance, according to World Food Programme (WFP) estimates, following two consecutive poor harvests. This had been compounded by the reduction by 60 per cent in the area planted because of heavy rains. (The WFP assessment did not cover every region.)

The effect of AIDS/HIV on the population weakened many of the most productive members of households and compounded the acute food shortage. UNAIDS estimated that 31 per cent of Lesotho's adults were HIV positive. Although the government had begun implementing programmes to address the AIDS/HIV epidemic, these had yet to make an impact. The Lesotho AIDS Programme Co-ordinating Authority (LAPCA) was established in 2001 in the Prime Minister's office and 2 per cent of each Ministry's budget was set aside for dealing with AIDS/HIV.

Developments in NAMIBIA raised concerns about the emergence of negative governance trends in the state. These related to the erosion of various freedoms enshrined in the constitution, illustrated in the alleged contravention of detention laws, the rights of detainees, and the continued attacks on media independence. In addition, President Sam Nujoma sent out mixed messages regarding land reform, taking the lead, as many observers saw it, from President Robert Mugabe's land reform measures in Zimbabwe.

The Namibian National Society for Human Rights in its annual report accused the armies of both Namibia and Angola of indulging in ongoing extra-judicial killings in the north of the country. There were at least 21 acts of summary execution, mostly committed by Namibian forces against real or perceived collaborators of the Angolan rebel movement UNITA. The report also said that some 2,300 citizens were living in forced exile in Botswana because of human rights abuses in the Caprivi region. Furthermore, a group of alleged UNITA members, who had been arrested in 2000 by the Namibian Defence Force (NDF), had remained in detention without being charged or brought before a court. Following an agreement between the Angolan and Namibian governments they were handed over to Angola in December. Lack of adherence to constitutional provisions on detainees was also a factor in regard to 123 people implicated in the attacks on Katima Mulilo in the Caprivi region in 1999 who were still awaiting trial.

In August Nujoma reshuffled his Cabinet, removing his Prime Minister Hage Geingob, who had held that position since independence in 1990, and replacing him with the Foreign Minister, Theo-Ben Gurirab. The demotion of Geingob, who subsequently resigned from government, was regarded by observers as a possible indication of Nujoma's intention to run for a fourth presidential term, although the constitution prohibited this. In 2001 Nujoma declared that he would not run, but during the course of 2002 he remained quiet when in

August eight traditional leaders from the ruling South West African People's Organisation's (SWAPO) power base in the north organised a march calling for another constitutional amendment to allow Nujoma to stand again after the expiry of his third term. A few weeks before the Cabinet reshuffle Nujoma had warned members of SWAPO of the danger of "factionalism" and the need to maintain unity within its ranks. There was speculation that these comments had been aimed at Geingob, who had apparently fallen out with the President in recent months.

In the Cabinet reshuffle the Information and Broadcasting portfolio became the responsibility of the President, where previously it was part of the Foreign Affairs portfolio. This was considered a further move to consolidate Nujoma's control of the state media organs, the politicisation of which had never been a secret. Previously, the President accused the Namibian Broadcasting Corporation (NBC) of serving "the enemy". Similar charges were levelled against journalists who had been critical of the actions of his government. In many ways, Nujoma's increasing hostility to the media and his attempts to suppress its freedom mirrored Mugabe's actions. In September Nujoma banned all foreign programming on the NBC saying that it was a bad influence on Namibian youth.

The ongoing land crisis in Zimbabwe continued to have ripple effects in Namibia, where some 30.5 million hectares of land was owned by white farmers, compared with 2.2 million hectares by blacks. In April the government tabled legislation proposing a 0.75 per cent land tax on each hectare of land owned by commercial farmers and 1 per cent for each hectare owned by absentee landlords in an attempt to free up more land for redistribution and to raise revenue. However, the move was opposed by the Namibian Agricultural Union which said that revenue raised from such a tax should not be used to purchase land, but for its redevelopment. Over US$2 million was being spent every year to buy farms for redistribution. However, of 173 farms offered to the state during 2000-01 only 18 were purchased, as the government said that the others were not suitable for resettlement.

Economic growth in 2001 was only 1.6 per cent compared with 2.9 per cent in 2000. This was partly the result of the global economic downturn and the local supply constraint of certain exports. The primary industries experienced negative growth during 2001, a trend which was expected to be only marginally better in 2002. The drought that hit the region during 2002 affected commercial agricultural production severely. While there were a number of projects in the primary and manufacturing sectors which helped the economy, Namibia continued to be plagued by high unemployment of about 20 per cent.

According to the latest UN figures, Namibia's HIV rate was 22.5 per cent among adults, making it one of five countries in the world worst affected by the pandemic. Notwithstanding this, the Namibian government provided nevirapine to expectant mothers and immune-boosting drugs to AIDS patients. As with other countries facing drought in Southern Africa, AIDS/HIV compounded the dire need for food assistance for about 345,000 people. The government set aside US$14 million for the procurement of maize meal, beans, cooking oil, and tinned fish to help lessen the impact of the drought that had affected the northern regions in particular.

Regionally, the tentative steps towards conflict resolution in the Democratic Republic of Congo (DRC) and Angola meant that Namibia could begin to reduce the costs associated with its troop presence in the DRC and its assistance to the Angolan government in pursuing UNITA rebels on its northern borders. Namibia was the first of the foreign forces in the DRC to withdraw its troops in early 2002. The end of the civil war in Angola in April 2002 also created an opening for Namibia to rekindle its trade and investment links with its northern neighbour.

SWAZILAND, the Southern African region's sole remaining absolute monarchy, witnessed an intensification of the ongoing tension between its traditional monarchical system and the forces of democratisation. In a country, with a high HIV infection rate and close to a third of the population facing famine, 2002 was also characterised by governmental excess both in terms of spending on luxury items, such as a private jet for King Mswati (estimated to cost US$45 million compared with the US$20 million national health budget), as well as in asserting that the King was above the law and the courts.

A report published by the Health Ministry at the end of the year estimated that 38.6 per cent of adults in Swaziland were HIV positive and that one quarter of the population would have died from AIDS/HIV by 2010. Although it was declared a national crisis, very little additional funding was allocated to combat the disease and there was no comprehensive national policy. However, the government launched a National Emergency Response Committee on HIV and AIDS (NERCHA), whose purpose was the distribution of government and donor funds to organisations active in anti-AIDS initiatives.

Swaziland's annual GDP growth rate fell from 7 per cent in the 1980s to 3 per cent in the 1990s, to 1.8 per cent in 2002. This was primarily because of a lack of competitiveness compared with other countries in the region. Unemployment in 2002 was estimated at about 40 per cent, although some 80 per cent of the population continued to rely on subsistence agriculture. The problem was compounded by the fact that only about 1 per cent of the land where peasant farmers grew their crops was irrigated. Much of the irrigation water was diverted to industrial agriculture, sugar cane, and timber, which were Swaziland's top exports.

The Constitutional Review Commission (CRC), which was established in 1996 (see AR 1996, pp. 281-82), submitted its findings to the King in 2001. Its report concluded that most Swazis wanted a continuation of the status quo, a strengthening of the King's powers, a continued ban against political parties, a greater emphasis on traditional law and custom, and stiffer penalties for those who spoke out against the state. However, no records of any of the submissions made to the CRC were published, nor was it revealed how many Swazis had presented their views to the Commission. The new constitution had not been unveiled by the end of 2002, but during the year the King promulgated the Internal Security Act, which sought to reinforce a royal ban on opposition political activity. In August 2002 the pro-democracy movement presented a draft alternative constitution, which would strip the King of all legislative and judicial powers, but it was ignored

The government refused to implement two judgments of the Court of Appeal, which ruled that King Mswati had no legal power to make laws outside the legislature and that he had illegally evicted two chiefs and 200 of their subjects from ancestral lands when they opposed the appointment of a brother of the King as their new chief. The six appeal court judges (all South Africans), resigned in November in protest. In addition, three High Court judges demanded the government issue assurances that it would honour all court decisions. Prime Minister Sibusiso Dlamini ignored the demand. The palace's interference with the justice system was condemned by international legal bodies as well as the UN, South Africa, the UK, and the USA.

In a manifesto issued by the Swaziland Coalition of Concerned Civil Organisations (made up of business groups, the law society, a teachers' association, and religious groups), the umbrella body called for the government to recognise immediately the independence of the judiciary, and "desist from making threats against judicial officers"; to rein in the security forces; drop plans to purchase the King's jet; and stop threatening to withhold funding from NGOs with "progressive" political views. This more vocal criticism of the monarchy from a broad spectrum of organisations signified mounting internal pressure on the regime to change which, together with stronger international condemnation, could bring about the necessary momentum for reform.

3. SOUTH AFRICA

CAPITAL: Pretoria   AREA: 1,221,000 sq km   POPULATION: 43,200,000
OFFICIAL LANGUAGES: Afrikaans, English & nine African languages   POLITICAL SYSTEM: multiparty republic in British Commonwealth
HEAD OF STATE AND GOVERNMENT: President Thabo Mbeki (since June '99)
RULING PARTIES: African National Congress (ANC) & Inkatha Freedom Party (IFP)
MAIN IGO MEMBERSHIPS (NON-UN): AU, SADC, SACU, CWTH, NAM
CURRENCY: rand (end-'02 £1=R13.9984, US$1=R8.7405)
GNI PER CAPITA: US$2,900, US$9,510 at PPP ('01)

DURING 2002, South Africa played a leading role on the African stage in promoting the New Partnership for Africa's Development (NEPAD) to the world. In July, it assumed the chairmanship of the newly established African Union, and in September it hosted the World Summit on Sustainable Development (see XVII).

South Africa's foreign policy focused strongly on Africa, and South African troops were deployed in the Democratic Republic of Congo (DRC), in the context of the Lusaka Peace Accords; as well as in the form of a VIP protection force in Burundi, following the signing of a peace agreement there brokered by South Africa. President Thabo Mbeki, Deputy President Jacob Zuma, and other

Cabinet Ministers were involved in facilitating talks and peace agreements in Burundi, the DRC, and Rwanda. South Africa hosted the Inter-Congolese Dialogue at Sun City between February and April, where the President in particular played a pivotal role in breaking the negotiating deadlock that had emerged among the various parties (see VII.1.i). However, closer to home, in Zimbabwe, the South African government maintained its "quiet diplomacy" approach to the crisis there. Its two observer missions to the presidential elections both declared that these had been a legitimate expression of the will of the people, notwithstanding the widespread irregularities and violence that were noted by them and other observer missions (see VII.2.iii).

Domestically, the government's fairly cautious economic and fiscal policy since it came into office in 1994 ensured that the macro-economic indicators were stable. In its 2002 staff report on South Africa, the IMF said that the economy was poised for recovery, but that this was partly dependent on attracting higher foreign investment, which in turn depended on reforms and progress in privatisation and trade liberalisation. (The partial privatisation of Telkom, the telecommunications parastatal, was scheduled for early 2003.)

However, the government's effectiveness in addressing the socio-economic challenges of poverty, unemployment, AIDS/HIV, and crime, was not as successful. Poverty levels remained high. Disparities between urban and rural, and employed and unemployed had, in many cases, overtaken racial inequalities. Among blacks, urban residents earned 89 per cent more than those living in the rural areas. Unemployment was estimated at between 29.4 per cent (strict definition) and 40.9 per cent (expanded definition). The economy's ability to create sufficient jobs to absorb the current unemployed as well as new entrants into the labour market continued to be minimal. However, since 1994 the number of upwardly mobile black people had grown and the country's middle class now accounted for about 25 per cent of the entire population.

Some 4.7 million of the population, or one in nine, was HIV positive, with a higher mortality rate among women than among men. A study by Statistics SA found that the overall proportion of deaths due to AIDS/HIV had nearly doubled from 4.6 per cent in 1997 to 8.7 per cent in 2001. From a policy perspective, the government continued to send out mixed signals on the means to fight the disease. (There were 18 pilot sites around the country providing anti-retroviral drugs to pregnant mothers, but these were not freely available at all public health facilities.) In December 2001 the High Court had ruled that the state initiate mother-to-child-transmission (MTCT) prevention programmes. The Treatment Action Campaign (TAC), one of the most effective lobby groups advocating MTCT programmes and the administering of anti-AIDS drugs at state hospitals, took the government to the Constitutional Court. In August the Constitutional Court agreed with the ruling of the High Court, and ordered that the state make nevirapine available in public health facilities "where, in the opinion of the attending medical practitioner in consultation with the medical superintendent of a clinic or hospital, it is medically indicated and the preconditions for its prescription already exist".

Both former President Nelson Mandela and Archbishop Desmond Tutu had publicly supported the use of anti-AIDS drugs for mothers in public hospitals. However, many in the ruling party and in government, including the Health Minister, continued to maintain that there was no proven link between HIV and AIDS—some even going so far as to attribute the assertion that there was a link to a "racist conspiracy".

The first report of the UN Office for Drug Control and Crime Prevention in South Africa, published in November, described the country as a regional hub for drug trafficking, and as the largest transit zone for illicit drugs in Southern Africa. In addition, the UN report said that reported rates of rape were "at the most serious levels in the world". Generally, it concluded, "the effects of apartheid on crime are still enormous". (The government had not released official crime figures for the year.)

On the political scene, the forging of an alliance between the New National Party and the African National Congress (ANC) in 2001 was consolidated further during 2002, with the passing of floor crossing legislation in June. This allowed national, provincial, and local public representatives to retain their seats despite defecting from the parties under whose banner they had been elected. Whereas floor-crossing had previously been prohibited, the new legislation limited it to two "window" periods during the life of the legislature.

In the latter part of the year there were attempts by right-wing elements to destabilise the government. However, the police made a number of arrests and seized a truckload of arms, ammunition, and explosives. The alleged plot was condemned by the Freedom Front, a party in the legislature which advocated the rights of white Afrikaners. Indeed, there was an overwhelming condemnation from all sectors of society and political parties of the incidents of violence perpetrated by right wingers.

Tensions within the tripartite alliance of the ANC, the Congress of South African Trade Unions (COSATU), and the South African Communist Party continued to brew, especially over the government's stated privatisation policy and the continuing high level of unemployment. However, at the ANC's 51st national conference in Stellenbosch in December, there was no substantial opposition expressed to the leadership and many of the COSATU office holders gained fewer votes in the elections for the national executive committee than in the past. President Mbeki made it quite clear that dissent against official decisions would not be tolerated. At the conference he criticised party members and civil servants who were "careerists" or who were corrupt and he stressed that the "internal accountability of our leadership as a whole" would have to be strengthened. Late in the year, the Scorpions investigation unit began investigations into Deputy President Zuma for an alleged attempt to secure a bribe from a French defence company seeking an arms procurement contract.

In October a mining charter was agreed between government and business, which was seen as a key feature of accelerated black business empowerment. Some of the targets of the charter included channelling an estimated 26 per cent of the value of the mining industry into black empowerment deals over the next 10 years (15 per cent in five years). These deals would be based on a "willing buyer/willing seller principle" and would be financed by the mining houses. Other provisions included literacy training, conversion of hostels into family units, and the development of communities from where the miners originated. However, concern was expressed at the impact that this might have on the ability of the state to attract foreign investment.

The confiscation of land in Zimbabwe had an impact in South Africa. While the government had repeatedly stated that Zimbabwe-style land invasions would not occur in South Africa, the slow progress on land reform and redistribution had been criticised by among others the National Land Committee and the landless movement. The Landless People's Movement, a largely rural-based organisation, also threatened to invade unoccupied or under utilised land (both state-owned and private), which could then be expropriated for the landless. It called on government to expropriate land, failing which it would commence a national campaign to occupy land in 2003. The former Minister of Land Affairs and Agriculture, Derek Hanekom, however, said that unlike Zimbabwe, which had failed to implement a coherent land reform policy after independence, the various land programmes of the South African government, including tenure reform, would ensure that it did not follow the same route as its neighbour.

VIII SOUTH ASIA AND INDIAN OCEAN

1. IRAN—AFGHANISTAN—CENTRAL ASIAN STATES

i. IRAN

CAPITAL: Tehran   AREA: 1,633,000 sq km   POPULATION: 64,600,000
OFFICIAL LANGUAGES: Farsi (Persian)   POLITICAL SYSTEM: multiparty republic, under religious leadership
SPIRITUAL GUIDE: Ayatollah Seyed Ali Khamenei (since June '89)
HEAD OF STATE: President Mohammad Khatami (since Aug '97)
MAIN IGO MEMBERSHIPS (NON-UN): OPEC, ECO, CP, OIC, NAM
CURRENCY: Iranian rial (end-'02 £1=IR12,799.6, US$1=IR7,992.00)
GNP PER CAPITA: US$1,750, US$6,230 at PPP ('01)

IRAN experienced severe shocks in its foreign and domestic politics during 2002 following the State of the Union address in January by US President George W Bush which designated the country part of "an axis of evil", carrying with it the threat of military action (see IV.1). In Tehran the US statement was viewed with consternation and it forced a radical re-evaluation by reformists and hardliners alike of all policies deemed directly offensive to the USA.

The long-standing debate within the regime on the question of dialogue with the USA became a crucial issue as the year progressed. On 26 May hardliners attempted to ban discussion of Iranian-US relations in the press, but the perception that the USA might intervene in Iranian affairs, possibly on the model of its Afghan campaign, kept the matter alive. By mid-year there were reports of talks already having taken place between senior Iranian and US officials. Although later in the year the focus of US concern switched away from Iran towards Iraq, there was a continuing profound impact on domestic policies from the US threats of military intervention.

US preoccupation with disarmament and possible regime-change in Iraq was interpreted in Tehran as a strategic move to contain Iran. A statement by the Bush administration on 12 July indicating sympathy with students protesting against the Islamic regime reinforced Iranian fears concerning US intentions. Iran meanwhile declared its opposition to any military attack on Iraq. It was obliquely indicated, however, that the overthrow of Saddam Hussein would be welcomed and that Iran would not resist a US attack on Iraq—in effect adopting a policy of "active neutrality"—providing it was endorsed by a UN mandate. Iran urged Iraq to co-operate fully with the UN weapons inspectors. The Iranian armed forces in October increased their readiness in case of hostilities through a series of large-scale military exercises. The Iranian Defence Minister, Ali Shamkhani, stated that the Islamic republic would respond firmly to any violation of its territory. On 30 October US Secretary of Defence Donald Rumsfeld suggested that he "expected an early overthrow of the Iranian government by its own people". This negative US view of the Islamic republic persisted, despite Iranian efforts at appeasement, and on 12 December Richard

Boucher, of the US State Department, inflamed sensitivities further by claiming that Iran was directly involved in the development of nuclear weapons. This was rejected by the Iranian Foreign Minister, Kamal Kharrazi.

Significantly, the Iranian government allowed a meeting of Iraqi opposition groups to take place in Tehran in December, including representatives of the Kurdish Democratic Party, the Iraqi National Congress, and the Supreme Council Islamic Revolution in Iraq, although any military invasion of Iraqi territory from Iranian soil was ruled out. At the end of the year Iranian-US relations remained ambivalent. Although there were several levels of diplomatic contact between Iran and the USA, in what amounted to a competition between Iranian political factions to lead a move towards rapprochement with the USA, there was no constructive response by the Bush administration.

Foreign policy was largely overtaken by the US inclusion of the Islamic republic in the "axis of evil" and its growing threat to invade Iraq. The Ministry of Foreign Affairs intensified its rapprochement with the EU in the hope that Europe would act as a mediator on its behalf with the USA. The EU remained supportive of reformist policies and pressed for an end to practices such as execution by stoning. Iran responded to EU concerns on terrorism and the development of weapons of mass destruction. Russia retained its position as an important supplier of arms and technical equipment for the nuclear power industry. A symbol of this link was the visit to Iran on 22 December by the Russian Atomic Energy Minister, Aleksandr Rumyantsev, who announced that the Busehr nuclear power station would be completed and that Russia would continue to assist Iran with the installation of new nuclear capacity. Iran would return to Russia spent nuclear fuel from the plant. The vexed question of oil exploitation in the Caspian Sea area remained a cause of friction. An April summit meeting of the Caspian Sea Littoral States disappointed Iran since it was allocated only 13 per cent of estimated oil resources in the Caspian basin, despite a strong claim for 20 per cent (see VIII.1.iii). Nonetheless, the Russians promised on 10 December that problems arising in this area would be settled by bilateral talks.

Iranian policies towards Afghanistan and the Persian Gulf were adversely affected by the intervention of the USA against Iraq. The long-term attempt by Iran to eliminate non-regional powers from the area was severely set back. The Persian Gulf region was altogether preoccupied with the US military build-up, in which Iran was relegated to a role as onlooker. Relations with Turkey were destabilised by a three-month tussle over the unsatisfactory quality of gas delivered via pipeline from Iran.

The sudden emergence of US threats to the Islamic republic in Bush's State of the Union address had repercussions throughout the Iranian domestic political system. The major factions within the regime were forced to define their positions on negotiations with the USA and review their stances on issues that concerned the Bush administration such as human rights, development of nuclear armaments, and the Middle East peace process.

Inevitably there was an increase in other tensions within the regime, of which the most urgent was the question of the legitimacy of Islamic government. Internal debate focused firstly on the undemocratic structure of government in which members of non-elected institutions, such as the Guardian Council, could block the policies of the President and the majlis (legislature). Secondly, there was dispute over the operation in Iran of "rogue elements" affiliated to the extreme conservative wing that acted violently against liberals in the press and government without legal authority. The strong factional divisions arising on these questions were exacerbated by a growing tide of sentiment and demonstrations, especially in the universities, against the arbitrary nature of a government structure steered by the rumps of revolutionary committees without a popular base. The upper echelons of the 'ulema (religious classes), including many of the most senior clerics in the country such as Ayatollah Jalaleddin Taheri of Isfahan, were moved to support the reformists' point of view. Student unrest on the campuses was made worse by a death sentence imposed on a university professor, Hashem Aghajeri, who in June had called for a withdrawal of clerical rule from secular affairs.

In effect, the legitimacy of the 'ulema to rule the country was roundly attacked. There were counter threats of a coup d'etat against President Mohammad Khatami by hardline leaders in the armed forces to stop the apparent slide towards Western democracy. Ayatollah Ibrahim Amini, the deputy head of the Assembly of Experts, suggested on 15 May that "if popular discontent increases, society and the regime will be in peril".

An encouragingly strengthened economy grew at over 4.5 per cent in the year 1380 (year ending 20 March 2002) despite a modest performance by the oil sector. Inflation ran at 18 per cent; the annual rate of increase in the 64.6 million population was 1.6 per cent; unemployment stood at 14.2 per cent. Foreign exchange reserves rose by US$3 billion, while foreign indebtedness was reported at US$7.8 billion. Civil imports grew strongly against exports of US$1.8 million barrels per day. The 1381 budget (year 2002-03) was forecast at US$86 billion, assuming an oil income of US$13 billion. The principal economic objectives were job-creation, privatisation, and unification of the country's exchange rates, targets which had in the past eluded the authorities.

ii. AFGHANISTAN

CAPITAL: Kabul   AREA: 650,000 sq km   POPULATION: 27,248,000
OFFICIAL LANGUAGE/S: Pushtu, Dari (Persian)   POLITICAL SYSTEM: Transitional government
HEAD OF STATE: Acting Head of State Gen. Mohammad Qasem Fahim
HEAD OF GOVERNMENT: Chairman of the Ruling Council, Hamed Karzai
MAIN IGO MEMBERSHIPS (NON-UN): ECO, CP, OIC, NAM
CURRENCY: afgani (end-'02 £1=Af7,607.36, US$1=Af4,750.00)
GNI PER CAPITA: n/a

ALTHOUGH the Taliban regime had been removed from power, Afghanistan faced a formidable array of problems during 2002. Operating within a country which had been effectively destroyed by years of civil war and by the US-led military campaign against the Taliban, the interim government of Hamid Karzai, assisted by the international community, attempted to focus on reconstruction. It did so, however, against a background of factional fighting and widespread lawlessness, in addition to the problems posed by a tide of returning refugees and rising drug production. Above all, there loomed the continuing presence of the Taliban, defeated but not eradicated, and of the remnants of the al-Qaida terrorist network, the prime suspect in the 11 September attacks on the USA, whose elimination had been the spur for the US-led attack upon Afghanistan (see AR 2000, pp. 318-25).

Throughout the year US-led forces continued military operations against small pockets of Taliban resistance and tried unsuccessfully to locate former Taliban leaders, such as Mullah Mohammed Omar, and al-Qaida figures, especially the movement's leader, Osama bin Laden. On 1 March US troops launched "Operation Anaconda" against enemy positions in the Shah-i-kot valley in the south-eastern Paktia province. The operation, which had been planned as a three-day mission, developed into a 17-day conflict which saw the bloodiest fighting since the arrival of US troops in the country in October 2001. Further operations followed, but the enemy proved elusive and used the rugged Afghan terrain, ideal for guerrilla warfare, to great advantage. By the end of the year there was little to show for the expenditure of so much military effort. In addition to ground forces, the US also relied upon air power to flush out remaining pockets of resistance, but here, too, there were few tangible successes. Moreover, there were several unfortunate incidents when civilians or friendly forces were mistakenly attacked. The worst instance of the latter occurred in April when four Canadian soldiers were killed and eight others wounded when attacked by US F-16 fighters. A tragic example of civilian deaths occurred on 1 July in Urzugan province where as many as 80 people were killed when US aircraft erroneously bombed a wedding party.

Despite these military efforts, Osama bin Laden could not be found. Speculation that he had been killed during the initial assault or had died from ill health was dampened by Al-Jazeera, the Qatar-based Arabic satellite television station. On 12 November it broadcast an audio tape-recording thought to have been made by the al-Qaida leader. In it the speaker referred to a number of attacks against Western targets by Islamists during 2002 as "reactions and reciprocal actions". He promised further actions, threatening that "you will be killed just as you kill, and will be bombed just as you bomb. And expect more that will further distress you. The Islamic nation. . . has started to attack you."

Whilst the USA remained willing to continue fighting in Afghanistan, it was reluctant to engage in nation-building and remained aloof from the International Security Assistance Force (ISAF) force, deployed in mid-January with the task of providing security for the interim government. The 5,500-strong force, drawn from 18 countries and initially led by the UK, was designed not to carry out a peacekeeping role, but to build public confidence in the interim government by providing a visible military presence in the capital, Kabul. Faced with a continuing threat from regrouping Taliban forces and from increasing fighting between rival factions, based on ethnicity or on territorial disputes between local warlords, Karzai visited the USA and UK in late January and appealed for the expansion of ISAF and for its mandate to be widened to include areas outside Kabul. The pleas were rejected, although US President George W. Bush used the occasion of Karzai's visit to defend the US treatment of battlefield detainees from the conflict. Widespread concern over the US treatment of prisoners had emerged in mid-January following the publication of photographs showing hundreds of suspected al-Qaida or Taliban members chained, bound, and gagged as they were transported from Afghanistan to a US military base at Guantanamo Bay, Cuba. Bush repeated his earlier insistence that those in US custody in Afghanistan and Cuba were "illegal combatants" who did not qualify for official prisoner of war status. In consequence, it was argued, they could be kept incarcerated indefinitely, without charge and without access to legal representation.

The insecurity of the new government was underlined on 14 February by the assassination of Tourism and Aviation Minister Abdul Rahim Wardak by elements loyal to a rival faction within the interim government. On 8 April an assassination attempt was made on Mohammad Fahim, the Defence Minister and Vice Chairman of the interim government. The government proved powerless in the face of such threats, and although on 23 May the UN Security Council adopted resolution 1413 (2002) which extended the mandate of ISAF for an additional six months from 20 June (with Turkey taking over command of the force), it reiterated that responsibility for internal Afghan security outside the capital remained with the interim government.

Even within the capital security could not be guaranteed, however, and on 6 July Vice President and Minister of National Reconstruction Haji Abdul Qadeer was assassinated by a group of unidentified gunmen as he left his office in Kabul, only 10 days after his appointment to the Cabinet. Qadeer had been one of three Vice Presidents appointed by Karzai; the others were Defence Minister Mohammad Fahim, a Tajik, and Abdul Karim Khalili, a Hazara. As the second most prominent Pashtun in the interim government (after Karzai himself), Qadeer had assumed a pivotal role by acting as a link between his fiefdom in the east (he was governor of Nangarhar province) and the government in Kabul. His death threw the stability of the interim government into further doubt.

A marked increase in fighting amongst different factions throughout the country in late June and July raised concerns that the fragile peace was in danger of unravelling. Most of the country's regional and national airports were attacked by unknown assailants, most notably at Kabul, Kandahar, Khost, and Jalalabad. In many northern and central provinces renewed factional fighting hampered humanitarian operations and caused a number of international relief organisations to withdraw their staff. At least 15 people were killed when suspected al-Qaida gunmen attacked an army base in the southern outskirts of Kabul on 7 August. The fighting lasted for over three hours until the attack, which occurred outside the ISAF peacekeeping zone, was eventually repulsed by Afghan troops. Two days later a powerful car bomb exploded in Jalalabad, killing 25 people and injuring 80 others. On 5 September Karzai narrowly survived an assassination attempt in Kandahar, the spiritual home of the Taliban. On the same day, a bomb explosion in Kabul killed at least 26 people.

Although the UN Security Council on 27 November approved Resolution 1444 (2002), extending the mandate of ISAF for one year beyond the 20 December deadline, there was little evidence at the end of the year that any improvement in the security situation was imminent.

Despite such levels of insecurity, some progress was made towards constructing a secular and representative government. The interim government on 25 January announced the convening of a 21-member special commission to formulate rules for the meeting of an emergency *Loya Jirga* (council of tribal elders) which was due to convene before 22 June in order to create a transitional government to replace the current interim administration. (The transitional government would then rule for no longer than 18 months before holding UN-monitored elections.) The selection rules were published on 31 March and abandoned the idea of a directly elected *Loya Jirga* in favour of one derived from indirect elections and appointed members.

On 18 April former King Mohammed Zahir Shah, who had lived in exile in Italy since being deposed in 1973 (see AR 1973, p. 300), returned to Kabul. In a statement broadcast on national television he said that he had returned as a private citizen and had no ambition to resurrect the monarchy. He expressed his "full support" for Karzai and praised his leadership of the Afghan people. Buoyed by the ex-King's support, Karzai was the overwhelming favourite to win the presidency when the 1,575-member *Loya Jirga* assembled in Kabul on 11-19 June. He was duly elected interim President by secret ballot on 13 June, winning 1,295 of the votes. He announced a Cabinet which included Taj Mohammad Wardak, a relatively unknown Pashtun leader, as Interior Minister, in what was the most obvious concession to widespread Pashtun demands that the new administration not be dominated by Tajiks.

One of the most pressing issues facing the new government was the return of refugees who had fled from Afghanistan prior to the US-led attack. Even before the mid-point of the year, an estimated 200,000 refugees had poured into Kabul, driving the population of the city above 2 million. This rapid population growth exacerbated an already severe housing shortage and put enormous pressure on the city's water and sanitation services, leading to an increasing incidence of cholera. By the end of the year it was estimated that 1.7 million refugees had returned from neighbouring countries. But with only 20-30 per cent of the country's agricultural land under cultivation in 2002, and a fourth successive year of drought, even with international aid there were difficulties in meeting even the most basic needs of the refugees.

Another pressing issue was drugs. It was reported in mid-February that the planting of opium poppies (from which heroin was derived) had increased dramatically since the fall of the Taliban regime. An ambitious programme designed to destroy the opium crop was launched by the government in April. In reality, however, it proved impossible to implement as farmers resisted the destruction of their highly valued cash crop and local warlords jealously protected the revenue source which enabled them to finance their fiefdoms and arm their followers. In October the UN Office for Drug Control and Crime Prevention published a report which confirmed that, since the fall of the Taliban, Afghanistan had re-emerged as the world's biggest producer of opium.

Notwithstanding the local profits derived from the drugs trade, Afghanistan was economically dependent upon outside aid. On 21-22 January representatives from more than 60 countries and global institutions met in Tokyo for an international donor conference (see IX.2.iv). In total, donors pledged US$4.5 billion in aid, with the bulk of the funding coming from Japan, the EU, the USA, Iran, and Saudi Arabia. Although the aid was conditional upon continued progress towards democracy, many observers expressed grave concerns about security in the country and the ability to distribute aid.

The interim government announced an ambitious plan of currency reform on 4 September, designed to end years of hyperinflation and simultaneously to remove a source of funding from anti-government regional warlords. Over a two-month period, old afghani notes were exchanged for new afghani notes, at an exchange rate of 1,000 old afghanis to one new afghani. The new currency was designed to give the government more control over monetary policy as, until recently, a number of regional warlords had freely printed their own banknotes, thereby devaluing the currency and causing massive inflation.

At a conference in Kabul on 22 December Karzai signed a non-aggression pact with six neighbouring countries, committing all signatories to the principles of territorial integrity, mutual respect, and non-interference in each other's internal affairs. The Kabul Declaration on Good Neighbourly Relations was signed by Karzai and Foreign Ministers from China, Iran, Pakistan, Tajikistan, Turkmenistan, and Uzbekistan. Five days later, Karzai attended a meeting in Ashgabat, the capital of Turkmenistan, where, together with Turkmen President Saparmurad Niyazov and Pakistani Prime Minister Zafarullah Khan Jamali, he signed an accord to establish the legal framework for foreign companies to invest in a planned 1,500 km trans-Afghan pipeline. The US$3.2 billion project would transport liquid gas from Turkmenistan's Dovletabad-Donmez gas field to Pakistan.

Even with so much manufactured misery to endure, Afghanistan did not escape natural disasters during 2002. The worst of these was a powerful earthquake measuring 6.1 on the Richter scale which struck the Hindu Kush region of the country on 25 March, killing as many as 1,800 people and leaving thousands homeless. The city of Nahrin, some 160 km north of Kabul, was hit hardest by the earthquake with 90 per cent of its housing destroyed. Violent aftershocks continued for several days, hampering rescue efforts and causing further damage to buildings.

iii. KAZAKHSTAN—TURKMENISTAN—UZBEKISTAN—KYRGYZSTAN—TAJIKISTAN

Kazakhstan

CAPITAL: Astana AREA: 2,717,000 sq km POPULATION: 14,800,000
OFFICIAL LANGUAGES: Kazakh & Russian POLITICAL SYSTEM: multiparty republic
HEAD OF STATE AND GOVERNMENT: President Nursultan Nazarbayev (since Feb '90)
RULING PARTIES: Fatherland Party (Otan) leads ruling alliance
PRIME MINISTER: Imangali Tasmagambetov (since Jan '02)
MAIN IGO MEMBERSHIPS (NON-UN): CIS, PFP, OSCE, OIC, ECO
CURRENCY: tenge (end-'02 £1=T249.442, US$1=T155.750)
GNI PER CAPITA: US$1,360, US$6,370 at PPP ('01)

Turkmenistan

CAPITAL: Ashgabat AREA: 488,000 sq km POPULATION: 5,300,000
OFFICIAL LANGUAGE: Turkmen POLITICAL SYSTEM: multiparty republic
HEAD OF STATE AND GOVERNMENT: President (Gen.) Saparmurat Niyazov (since Jan '90)
RULING PARTY: Democratic Party of Turkmenistan (DPT)
MAIN IGO MEMBERSHIPS (NON-UN): CIS, PFP, OSCE, OIC, ECO, NAM
CURRENCY: Turkmen manat
GNI PER CAPITA: US$950, US$4,580 at PPP ('01)

Uzbekistan

CAPITAL: Tashkent AREA: 447,000 sq km POPULATION: 25,100,000
OFFICIAL LANGUAGE: Uzbek POLITICAL SYSTEM: multiparty republic
HEAD OF STATE AND GOVERNMENT: President Islam Karimov (since March '90)
RULING PARTY: People's Democratic Party (PDP)
PRIME MINISTER: Otkir Sultonov (since Dec '95)
MAIN IGO MEMBERSHIPS (NON-UN): CIS, PFP, OSCE, OIC, ECO, NAM
CURRENCY: sum (end-'02 £1=S1519.78, US$1=S948.940)
GNI PER CAPITA: US$550, US$2,470 at PPP ('01)

Kyrgyzstan

CAPITAL: Bishkek AREA: 199,000 sq km POPULATION: 5,000,000
OFFICIAL LANGUAGES: Kyrgyz & Russian POLITICAL SYSTEM: multiparty republic
HEAD OF STATE AND GOVERNMENT: President Askar Akayev (since Oct '90)
RULING PARTIES: Democratic Movement of Kyrgyzstan heads loose ruling coalition
PRIME MINISTER: Nikolay Tanayev (since June '02)
MAIN IGO MEMBERSHIPS (NON-UN): CIS, PFP, OSCE, OIC, ECO
CURRENCY: som (end-'02 £1=S73.9819, US$1=S46.1939)
GNI PER CAPITA: US$280, US$2,710 at PPP ('01)

Tajikistan

CAPITAL: Dushanbe AREA: 143,000 sq km POPULATION: 6,200,000
OFFICIAL LANGUAGE: Tajik POLITICAL SYSTEM: multiparty republic
HEAD OF STATE AND GOVERNMENT: President Imamoli Rahmonov (since Nov '92)
RULING PARTIES: People's Democratic Party of Tajikistan & United Tajik Opposition head coalition
PRIME MINISTER: Akil Akilov (since Dec '99)
MAIN IGO MEMBERSHIPS (NON-UN): CIS, OSCE, OIC, ECO, PFP
CURRENCY: somoni (end-'02 £1=4.4603, US$1=2.7850)
GNI PER CAPITA: US$170, US$1,150 at PPP ('01)

IN autumn 2001, the US-led "Operation Enduring Freedom" aimed at eradicating the military bases of al-Qaida and the Taliban in Afghanistan highlighted the strategic importance of the Central Asian states. The Central Asian leaders promptly confirmed their willingness to support the campaign. TAJIKISTAN offered access to its airports, while KAZAKHSTAN opened its air space to allied aircraft and later, in July 2002, agreed to allow the use of the Almaty international airport in emergency conditions. TURKMENISTAN, mindful of its status as a neutral country, provided facilities for conveying humanitarian aid to Afghanistan. However, the key US partners in the region were UZBEKISTAN and KYRGYZSTAN. By mid-2002, an estimated 1,800 US troops were stationed at Khanabad, a former Soviet air base close to the Uzbek-Afghan border; it was reported that the US military was preparing to spend some US$5 million on refurbishing this facility. Another base was established in Kyrgyzstan, at Manas, formerly the international civilian airport (close to the capital, Bishkek, and less than 500 km from the Chinese border). Within a few months, just under 2,000 troops, mainly US but also units from other Western allies, were assembled there. The Uzbek and Kyrgyz governments evidently hoped that co-operation with the USA would yield significant benefits, including greater financial assistance and less international criticism of their records on human rights and corruption. To some extent they were rewarded in this way (Kyrgyzstan alone received US aid totalling over US$90 million in 2002), but this did not satisfy their expectations. Moreover, there was anger, especially in Kyrgyzstan, over the way in which the bases seemed to be fuelling corruption by the granting of lucrative contracts to highly placed individuals.

In March, US Secretary of State Colin Powell and Uzbek Foreign Minister Abdulaziz Kamilov signed a political and strategic partnership agreement which set out practical goals for mutual co-operation in military and economic areas. Uzbekistan reaffirmed its commitment to furthering the process of democratisation. Yet human rights organisations, local and foreign, reported numerous violations of civil liberties during this period, suggesting that conditions were deteriorating rather than improving. An analogous agreement on strategic partnership and co-operation was concluded between Japan and Uzbekistan, when President Islam Karimov made an official visit to Japan in July.

The Western presence in Central Asia prompted a flurry of high-level visits to the region. In October, UN Secretary-General Kofi Annan made his first ever visit to the Central Asian states. Prior to this, several leading military and political figures had visited Central Asia. In April, US Secretary of Defence Donald Rumsfeld visited Kyrgyzstan, Turkmenistan, and Kazakhstan. Concurrently, Iranian President Mohammad Khatami was also touring Central Asia. Issues under discussion included bilateral trade agreements and energy export routes via Iran; however, Khatami also strongly criticised "the presence of armed forces of large non-local states" in Central Asia. Chinese and Turkish military delegations likewise visited the region during this period. In June, Indian Prime Minister Atal Behari Vajpayee, accompanied by a large business delegation, held talks in Kazakhstan on matters of mutual interest. In August,

US General Tommy Franks, head of US Central Command, undertook a week-long tour of the Central Asian states; he stressed that the US government had a long-term commitment to the region. Russia, too, actively sought support in Central Asia during the year, bilaterally as well as within the framework of regional organisations such as the Eurasian Economic Community, the Shanghai Cooperation Organisation, and the Commonwealth of Independent States (CIS) Collective Security Treaty. Relations with Kazakhstan were particularly cordial; in December, following a two-day visit to Moscow, President Nursultan Nazarbayev hailed 2002 as a "breakthrough year" in relations between the two countries.

There were some changes also in regional co-operation structures. In March, the Central Asian Economic Community was officially transformed into the Central Asian Co-operation Organisation (comprising Kazakhstan, Kyrgyzstan, Tajikistan, and Uzbekistan, with Turkmenistan as observer). Several summit meetings were held during the year, focusing on such issues as trade, transport, security, and water management. Grave concern was expressed about the situation in Afghanistan. As Tajik President Imamoli Rahmonov pointed out, much aid had been promised, but very little had been delivered. His own country had suffered a similar fate, he added; donor nations had pledged over US$1billion to assist Tajikistan's post-conflict reconstruction, but after seven years, less than 1 per cent of that sum had been received. In June the inaugural meeting of the Conference on Interaction and Confidence-Building Measures in Asia was held in Almaty, attended by senior representatives of 15 states, among them all the Central Asian states except Turkmenistan, also Pakistan, India, Iran, and Israel. Originally conceived by Kazakh President Nazarbayev in 1992 as an Asian counterpart to the CSCE, later the Organisation for Security and Co-operation in Europe (OSCE), it evolved slowly. The chief issues raised on this occasion were security threats arising from drugs and arms trafficking, terrorism, extremism, and separatism.

On a bilateral level, treaties were signed which resolved some of the outstanding border issues. On 17 May Tajikistan signed a "comprehensive" border agreement with China, whereby Tajikistan ceded to China some 1,000 sq km of unpopulated territory in the Murghab region. In September, Karimov and Nazarbayev finalised the demarcation of the last section (measuring no more than a few kilometres) of the Uzbek-Kazakh border. Earlier that month, the Kyrgyz legislature finally ratified the 1999 Sino-Kyrgyz treaty on border delimitation, whereby Kyrgyzstan received 70 per cent of the disputed territory, but ceded some 95,000 hectares to China. This agreement was one of the factors behind the civil disorders that plagued Kyrgyzstan for much of the year.

Attempts to resolve the legal status of the Caspian Sea progressed haltingly. The long-awaited and much postponed summit meeting of the leaders of the Caspian littoral states (Azerbaijan, Iran, Kazakhstan, Russia, and Turkmenistan) finally took place in Ashgabat, Turkmenistan, on 23-24 April. The stated aim of the summit was to decide on a legal regime for the Sea. Azerbaijan, Kazakhstan, and Russia had, by this time, reached a common position, based on the principle that the surface of the Sea should be used in common, but that the seabed be divided into national sectors, corresponding to each country's coastline, along a median line. Iran rejected the idea of such a division, advocating instead an equal division of the seabed and the surface of the Sea into national sectors, with each littoral state to hold 20 per cent. The Turkmen stance for the most part appeared to be close to that of Iran. The April summit did not yield conclusive results. The assembled heads of state failed to sign any agreements; not even a joint declaration was produced. However, on the sidelines, Russian President Vladimir Putin and Turkmenistan President General Saparmurat Niyazov held a bilateral meeting during which they signed a treaty of friendship and co-operation. Iran, too, actively developed bilateral contacts with the other littoral states. Kazakhstan and Russia had for some time been working towards a full resolution of demarcation issues. On 13 May, the leaders of these two countries signed a protocol on the equal division of three oil fields in the northern Caspian; this supplemented the landmark agreement of 1998 on the bilateral demarcation of the seabed. A similar agreement was concluded with Azerbaijan. These were subsequently brought together in a tripartite agreement. Thus, despite the appearance of a deadlock on progress towards resolving the status of the Caspian Sea, behind the scenes there were some encouraging developments.

During 2002, the trend in domestic affairs in the Central Asian states was towards increasingly repressive, autocratic rule. In some places, however, there were signs of protest and even confrontation. The scandals which had rocked political circles in Kazakhstan at the end of 2001 continued to reverberate. On 28 January Prime Minister Qasymzhomart Toqayev resigned and, as required by the constitution, the entire government followed suit. The following day Toqayev was appointed Minister of Foreign Affairs. The Deputy Prime Minister, 45-year old Imangali Tasmagambetov, was thereupon elevated to the post of Prime Minister. A few weeks later, there was a crackdown on those who had originally started the crisis by criticising Nazarbayev's son-in-law. In late 2001, a number of politicians had joined forces to create a new opposition party, the Democratic Choice of Kazakhstan. In March 2002, two of its leaders, Mukhtar Ablyazov (Minster of Energy, Trade and Industry 1998-99) and Ghalymzhan Zhakiyanov (former governor of Pavlodar province) were arrested and accused of abuse of power, embezzlement, and numerous other offences. Supporters of both men claimed that the charges were politically motivated. Subsequently they were tried and received prison sentences of six and 10 years respectively; in addition, a fine of US$3.6 million was imposed on Ablyazov, whose property was also confiscated.

In June a controversial law on the regulation of political parties in Kazakhstan was passed. It included the requirement that parties seeking registration (a necessary precondition for political activity) should have branches in each of the country's regions and a minimum of 7,000 members in each branch (a total of 50,000 members instead of 3,000, as previously). Only two parties, both pro-presidential, had the necessary geographical spread and size of membership to qualify for registration. The OSCE envoy pointed out that the new ruling would make it almost impossible for opposition parties to operate legally; consequently political pluralism in Kazakhstan would be seriously jeopardised. Pressure on the media was also intensified. This coincided with allegations in the press that a sum of more than US$1 billion of state money was being held in Swiss banks in Nazarbayev's name. Journalists who expressed criticism of the government were subjected to official and unofficial harassment, including street muggings and beatings, and arrests for alleged tax violations and other financial irregularities. In October, Sergei Duvanov, editor of a human rights bulletin, was arrested and charged with the rape of a minor. A few months earlier, he had been charged with impugning the dignity and honour of the President after publishing an article accusing Nazarbayev and his associates of massive corruption. On that occasion, however, the case had stalled. Many commentators believed that the new charge was merely a ploy to re-start legal proceedings against him.

During much of 2002 Kyrgyzstan experienced confrontations of unprecedented violence and hostility between the public and the police. The first clash came in mid-March. Demonstrators gathered in the Djalalabad region, in southern Kyrgyzstan, to call for the release of a popular parliamentary deputy, Azimbek Beknazarov, who had been arrested in January on charges that many regarded as politically motivated. On 17 March the police opened fire, without warning, on a 2,000-strong crowd, killing six people and injuring 62. A large contingent of police reinforcements was immediately drafted into the area to restore law and order, and as a placatory measure Beknazarov was freed, although the charges against him were not dropped. In May, there were further disturbances, including hunger strikes, picketing of government buildings, and a blockade of the main highway between the capital, Bishkek, and the south. The ostensible cause for the protest movement was the ratification by the legislature of the Sino-Kyrgyz border treaty. However, the underlying issue was popular anger at the increasingly authoritarian nature of President Askar Akayev's rule. The government resigned on 22 May, but the situation was not resolved. In August, opposition parties, non-governmental organisations, and other public bodies combined forces to create the Movement for the Resignation of President Akayev. The new grouping found strong support in the south of the country, from where, in early September, protesters set off on a march to the capital. The demonstrators, numbering some 800 people, were halted well before they reached Bishkek. Government officials and opposition spokesmen held talks and signed a memorandum setting out terms and conditions for a peaceful end to the protest. The government acceded to some of the demands of the opposition, giving assurances, among other undertakings, that those who were responsible for the tragedy in March would be punished. However, little action was taken. There were further disturbances in October, triggered by the appeal court's decision to uphold the sentence previously imposed on Feliks Kulov, a former Vice President and Minister of National Security, and founder of the opposition party Ar-Namys.

In Turkmenistan, an anticorruption campaign was launched in March, which led to the purging of several senior officials. In May, criminal charges (including murder, torture, embezzlement, and drug-trafficking) were brought against the former head of the National Security Committee, Muhammad Nazarov, and members of his staff. They were sentenced to between 15 and 20 years imprisonment. Nazarov had previously been regarded as the most powerful figure in Turkmenistan after the President. The former Minister of Defence, the chairman of the National Bank, and the head of the main television channel were likewise removed from office and charged with serious offences. It was rumoured that at least some of these individuals had links with the Turkmen opposition abroad. Meanwhile, the Turkmen government was demanding the extradition from the USA of former Foreign Minister Boris Shikhmuradov; in 2001 he had gone into self-imposed exile and thereafter had been an outspoken critic of the Turkmen regime. On 25 November there was an assassination attempt on the life of Niyazov. This prompted a new wave of dismissals and arrests. Turkmen special forces raided the Uzbek embassy in Ashgabat, claiming that Turkmen nationals who had taken part in the attack were hiding there. They did not find anyone on that occasion, but a week later, at a separate location, they captured Shikhmuradov. It was alleged by some that Uzbekistan had indeed been implicated, at least indirectly, in the assassination plot.

In Tajikistan, there were fears of a resurgence of Islamic radicalism. In July Rahmonov criticised local officials in the northern province of Soghd for allowing militant Islamist groups to operate locally. He pointed to the proliferation of mosques, now numbering over 190 in an area with a population of 200,000, in contravention of the law which permitted one mosque per 15,000 citizens. The majority of the activists were said to be members of the banned Hizb ut-Tahrir (Party of Liberation), a transnational Islamist organisation of Middle Eastern origin that had been present in Central Asia since the mid-1990s. There were also reports that the Islamic Movement of Uzbekistan was regrouping along the Tajik-Afghan border and attempting to re-establish bases in the Garm region of Tajikistan. Fears of rising Islamic militancy were exacerbated by the news that three Tajiks from Soghd province had been captured in Afghanistan among the Taliban, and were now being held in the US camp at Guantanamo Bay, Cuba.

In Uzbekistan presidential rule was strengthened yet further by a nationwide referendum, held on 27 January, to seek the electorate's approval for the extension of the President's term of office from five to seven years. Support for the creation of a bicameral legislature was sought at the same time. A "yes" vote of over 90 per cent was returned on both issues. However, there was little public understanding of the implications of these constitutional changes. Even senior officials were not clear as to how the President's extended term of office was to be calculated (i.e. from the date of the previous election, from the date of the referendum, or from the next election). The US-based organisation Human Rights Watch characterised the referendum as a "blatant grab for power" by Karimov.

2. INDIA—PAKISTAN—BANGLADESH—NEPAL—BHUTAN—SRI LANKA

i. INDIA

CAPITAL: New Delhi   AREA: 3,288,000 sq km   POPULATION: 1,033,400,000
OFFICIAL LANGUAGES: Hindi & English   POLITICAL SYSTEM: multiparty republic in British Commonwealth
HEAD OF STATE: President A.P.J. Abdul Kalam (since July '02)
RULING PARTIES: Bharatiya Janata Party (BJP) heads multi-party coalition
HEAD OF GOVERNMENT: Atal Behari Vajpayee (BJP), Prime Minister (since March '98)
MAIN IGO MEMBERSHIPS (NON-UN): SAARC, CP, CWTH, NAM
CURRENCY: rupee (end-'02 £1=Rs76.8104, US$1=Rs48.22)
GNI PER CAPITA: US$460, US$2,450 at PPP ('01)

AT the beginning of the year more than one million Indian and Pakistani troops faced each other across the ceasefire line in the disputed province of Kashmir. Gen. S. Padmanabhan, India's most senior general, said on 11 January that his armed forces were "fully prepared" for war, including the retaliatory use of nuclear weapons. This point was underlined on 25 January, the day before Republic Day, when India test-fired a nuclear-capable short-range Agni ballistic missile from an island off Orissa. The test caused some international alarm, as did the laying of massive numbers of landmines along both sides of the India-Pakistan border, throwing into reverse the worldwide gains made when the international landmines treaty was signed in Ottawa in 1997 (see AR 1997, pp. 442-43; 566-68). An area stretching almost 3,000 kms and up to five kms deep was affected.

In February there were strong signs that both Russia and the USA were strengthening their weapons' links with India. India signed protocols with its traditional military supplier, Russia, on bilateral defence co-operation. India, having recently placed large orders with Russia for fighter aircraft and tanks, was also negotiating to buy a Russian aircraft carrier. Gen. Richard Myers, chairman of the US joint chiefs of staff, at the end of a two-day visit to India, said that negotiations were underway to finalise a sale by the USA of a weapon-seeking radar system. If completed, it would be the first sale to India of US military equipment since the lifing of the sanctions imposed after the Indian nuclear tests in 1998 (see AR 1998, p. 328).

China's Prime Minister, Zhu Rongji, visited India in mid-January, the first such trip by a Chinese Prime Minister for a decade. China was thought to be adopting a more even-handed approach between India and Pakistan, partly because of its growing fear of Islamic terrorism. Direct air links between Beijing and New Delhi re-started in March.

Domestic affairs were again overshadowed by sectarian violence between Muslims and Hindus. A campaign of savage attacks on Muslims in the western state of Gujerat lasted from February to April and killed up to 2,000 people. There was evidence that the riots and massacres in Gujerat had been prepared in advance and were not, as had first appeared, a spontaneous reaction to an incident on 27 February in which a train carrying Hindus returning from the disputed religious shrine of Ayodhya, in the northern state of Uttar Pradesh, was set on fire killing 58 people. The state authorities failed to intervene, or in some cases helped organise the riots, and there were calls for Narendra Modi, the chief minister of Gujerat and an outspoken Hindu nationalist, to resign. His Bharatiya Janata Party (BJP)—the only surviving BJP administration in a major state—chose instead to dissolve the Gujerat assembly and call early elections. However, when the Election Commission visited Gujerat in August, it ruled that early elections could not be held in the riot-torn state because "communal wounds have still not healed". The Indian government asked President A.P.J. Abdul Kalam to appeal to the Supreme Court against the ruling, on the grounds that the constitution required elections to be held by October, six months after the state assembly's last sitting in April. Opposition parties said that the BJP had called the elections five months early in order to capitalise on the bitter divisions between Hindus and Muslims in Gujerat. Elections were eventually held in December and resulted in a landslide victory for Modi and the BJP. Some analysts saw the victory as marking the demise of the secular basis of Indian politics.

In February Vajpayee replaced the hitherto highly regarded Power Minister, Suresh Prabhu, after pressure from Bal Thackeray, leader of Shiv Sena, a Hindu fundamentalist party based in Maharashtra which was the second-largest of the 23 groups which comprised the BJP-led governing coalition. Thackeray accused his Shiv Sena colleague of spending too much time on his ministerial job and too little on his party's financial needs. Leaders of industry were dismayed by the move because poor power supply was holding up investment. In October police began investigating Thackeray's activities after he had called on Hindus to form suicide squads to be used against Pakistan and other Islamic countries.

Elections were held in the disputed territory of Kashmir in four stages between 12 September and 10 October and produced an unexpected result: defeat for the National Conference (JKNC) which, as a member of India's ruling BJP-led coalition, supported India's rule. The JKNC took 28 seats, Congress (I) 22, and the People's Democratic Party (PDP) 16. The Hurriyat Conference umbrella group of 23 separatist parties boycotted the poll. Turnout was 46 per cent and unofficial international observers—30 Western diplomats acting as informal monitors—judged the elections freer and fairer than recent Kashmiri polls, although a record 750 people were killed during the campaign. One victim was the state's law minister, Mushtaq Ahmed Lone, gunned down with three others during a campaign rally in Kupwara on 11 September. JKNC leader and central government minister Omar Abdullah, son of outgoing chief minister, Farooq Abdullah, lost his seat. Prime Minister Vajpayee said that the high turnout was a victory for Indian democracy.

Vajpayee renewed charges on 7 October that Pakistan was not honouring the pledge that it had made in August, after talks with US Deputy Secretary of State Richard Armitage, to end cross-border terrorism and was backing attempts to sabotage the elections. But within a week of the Kashmir poll the Indian government on 16 October ordered a phased withdrawal of the 700,000 troops stationed on the border with Pakistan, ending its longest period of high alert. Within hours, Pakistan announced that it was pulling back its troops to "peacetime locations" and that 90 per cent of its 400,000-500,000 troops would stand down in phases. However, India still insisted that it would not hold talks with Pakistan until it stopped cross border terrorism.

Just before the Kashmir elections ended, and ahead of the Pakistani elections (see VIII.2.ii), Pakistan announced on 4 October that it had fired a new Shaheen surface-to-surface missile capable of carrying a warhead to New Delhi. Hours later India tested one of its sophisticated surface-to-air missiles. Both governments said the tests were routine and that they had informed each other in advance.

Political impasse followed the Kashmir elections with both the PDP and Congress (I) wanting their respective leaders to become chief minister. A coalition government was formed on 27 October under Mufti Mohammad Sayeed of the almost wholly Muslim PDP. He quickly promised to apply a "healing touch" to the separatist conflict and offered to talk with the Hurriyat Conference's leaders. The new government also freed a key separatist leader from jail in Jammu on 11 November as part of its policy of conciliation.

Militants attacked a Hindu temple in Gandhinagar, the administrative capital of Gujerat, on 25 September and killed 28 worshippers. Indians were quick to blame Pakistan but the government called for calm. The temple was beseiged for 14 hours until commandos killed the assailants. Police said they had found two letters in Urdu on the militants' bodies. The Pakistan government condemned the raid and denied responsibility. The attack coincided with the second phase of voting in Kashmir and was in the constituency of India's Deputy Prime Minister and Home Affairs Minister L.K. Advani.

India's Finance Minister Yashwant Sinha presented his 2002-03 budget to the legislature on 28 February. It projected planned total spending of R2,702 billion against forecast revenue of R2,358 billion, thus aiming for a fiscal deficit of 5.3 per cent of GDP (reduced from 5.7 per cent of GDP in 2001-02). The budget involved a 4.8 per cent increase in defence spending; a 5 per cent surcharge on income tax to pay for this; cuts in subsidies for fertilisers, cooking gas, and kerosene of 5 per cent, 15 per cent, and 33 per cent respectively; cuts in interest rates on saving schemes; a one rupee cut in the price of petrol; a 20 per cent increase in spending on infrastructure; and an abolition of many controls in the farming sector to liberalise agricultural trading. This was Sinha's fifth successive budget and was judged by most financial analysts as cautious in its reforms and unlikely to provide the necessary stimulus to India's flagging economy. In reply to critics of his failure to make a deeper cut in the huge fiscal deficit, Sinha said that the problem lay not in excessive government spending but in revenue shortfalls.

Prime Minister Atal Behari Vajpayee announced on 1 July a long expected Cabinet reshuffle of which the most striking, and unexpected, feature was the exchange of portfolios between Jaswant Singh and Yashwant Sinha who became, respectively, Finance Minister and Minister of External Affairs. Singh told ministers at the September IMF-World Bank meetings in Washington DC that India was the fastest growing economy in the world, with a doubling in the first quarter of 2002 to 6 per cent thanks to growth in services and information technology and a rebound in agriculture.

Arun Shourie, India's Minister for Disinvestment, announced on 5 February the first major successes in the government's privatisation programme with the sales of stakes in the state-owned IBP petroleum company and the VSNL international telecommunications company. Later in the year, however, open differences between ministers about the way that privatisation was being handled led Shourie on 8 September to announce a three-month freeze on the privatisation scheme. The privatisation of India's two largest oil refineries, Hindustan Petroleum and Bharat Petroleum, was at the centre of these latest differences. Shourie wanted to auction them to strategic bidders in a private sale, as had happened with 30 other state enterprises; but other ministers, notably Petroleum Minister Rama Naik, said that this would encourage a private monopoly and risk putting national assets into foreign hands. The dispute went deeper, with some critics alleging that Naik wanted to keep two lucrative sources of patronage within his ministry's control. Then, on the intervention of Prime Minister Vajpayee, the licences of nearly 4,000 petrol stations and cooking gas outlets were cancelled after accusations that many had been given since January 2000 to people close to the ruling BJP. The opposition Congress (I) party claimed that the licence allocations had been orchestrated by Naik. Inder Malhoutra, the respected veteran political commentator said: "India's politics have become disturbingly criminalised and this has encouraged the spread of corruption elsewhere in society—in the judiciary, the civil service, and the police." Despite this, Vajpayee said on 6 October that privatisation was "on track and irreversible", and approved India's next Five Year Plan that factored in some US$24 billion in revenues from privatisation.

Torrential monsoon rains flooded more than half of Assam and large areas of Bihar at the end of July. Nepal and Bangladesh were also severely affected and an estimated 1,000 people in the region were thought to have died as a consequence of the flooding. Nagaland and Manipur were cut off as roads and railway lines became submerged. By contrast, farmers in northern and western India were in despair at the continued failure of the monsoon in their region, where summer crops had withered in the worst drought for a decade.

On 28 August the Bhopal High Court reinstated charges of culpable homicide laid against Warren Anderson, former chief executive of Union Carbide, the chemical company which leaked deadly gas from its plant in Bhopal in 1984 killing or disabling some 500,000 people (see AR 1984, p. 276) in the worst industrial accident in history.

The first case reported since 1987 of suttee—the ancient Hindu custom of a widow burning herself to death on her husband's funeral pyre—came from a village in Madhya Pradesh in August. The woman's two sons were arrested and faced charges of murder. They were suspected of forcing the widow into self-sacrifice in order to claim their inheritance. The crime of encouraging suttee carried the death penalty.

ii. PAKISTAN

CAPITAL: Islamabad   AREA: 796,000 sq km   POPULATION: 141,500,000
OFFICIAL LANGUAGE: Urdu   POLITICAL SYSTEM: military regime with elected legislature in British Commonwealth
HEAD OF STATE: President (Gen.) Pervez Musharraf (since June '01), formerly Chief Executive Officer of National Security Council (since Oct '99)
RULING PARTY: coalition led by Pakistan Muslim League—Quaid-i-Azam (PML-Q)
PRIME MINISTER: Zafarullah Khan Jamali (PML-Q) (since Nov '02)
MAIN IGO MEMBERSHIPS (NON-UN): OIC, SAARC, ECO, CP, NAM, CWTH (suspended)
CURRENCY: Pakistan rupee (end-'02 £1=PRs93.3864, US$1=PRs58.3100)
GNI PER CAPITA: US$420, US$1,920 at PPP ('01)

PAKISTAN had returned by the end of 2002 to a form of elected government, but the year saw the political system put under very heavy strain by domestic and international developments, especially but not exclusively as a result of terrorist activity.

A referendum was held on 30 April to endorse the candidacy of Gen. Pervez Musharraf for the position of President for a five-year term. The conduct of the referendum was widely criticised for the way that a 98 per cent vote in favour of Musharraf was manufactured. Once the referendum was over, attention turned to the elections that were due in the autumn under the terms of an earlier Supreme Court ruling on the legitimacy of the Musharraf regime (see AR 2000, p. 303). The government issued a Legal Framework Order which set out in advance of the restoration of elected government some major changes to the constitution, although the question of whether it had to be endorsed by the National Assembly (legislature) was left open. The most important was the permanent status given to the National Security Council. Chaired by the President and including key military as well as political leaders, the Council was given the power to dismiss the Prime Minister (a right held by the President directly from 1985 to 1997). A novel change in the electoral law was a provision that all members of the national and provincial assemblies had to be university graduates. There was also increased representation for women. Politically, the Musharraf government found itself obliged, as previous military governments had been, to construct a political party to lend it support. This took the form of a breakaway group from the Pakistan Muslim League (PML-N) which called itself the Pakistan Muslim League-Quaid-e-Azam (PML-Q) and was popularly known as the "King's party". The most prominent figure within it was Chaudhry Shujaat Hussain, a powerful Punjab politician.

The elections, held on 10 October under reasonably peaceful conditions, produced five significant political players. The largest party in terms of seats won was the PML-Q, which initially gained 118 seats; while the Pakistan People's Party (PPP-P, the last P standing for "Parliamentarian" to avoid possible legal complications) came second with 80. In the absence of Benazir Bhutto the party was led by Makhdoom Amin Fahim. The PML-N, deprived of its principal leader Nawaz Sharif, who remained in exile in Saudi Arabia, and of many of its local leaders, who had joined the PML-Q, struggled to reach a total of 19. The Muttahida Qaumi Movement won 17 seats in Karachi and other urban centres in Sindh. The main winner from the elections, however, was the Muttahida Majlis-e-Amal (MMA), a coalition of established religious parties which had never previously made much electoral impact. At the national level it won 60 seats; at the provincial level it won an absolute majority in the North-West Frontier Province and made substantial gains elsewhere, especially in Balochistan. The consensus view among commentators was that the real driving force behind the MMA success was anti-US feeling in the aftermath of operations in Afghanistan and against al-Qaida sympathisers within Pakistan.

The elections thus produced no clear verdict at the national level, and for some weeks thereafter there was intense political manoeuvring, with each of the main groups discussing possible coalition terms with the others. However, in broad terms the question was how closely the government would be willing to work with the President and the army. In the end, with considerable assistance from the President and army, including the temporary suspension of rules that had earlier been brought in to ban defections from one party to another, the PML-Q was able to form a government. Its successful candidate for the post of Prime Minister was Zafarullah Khan Jamali, the first person from Balochistan to achieve this office. Jamali, from a landlord background, had had extensive experience in government posts over many years, although not at the very highest level. He emerged as Prime Minister on 21 November, winning a narrow majority in the National Assembly, and on 30 December he won a vote of confidence with 188 out of 342 votes. This result was achieved by the engineered defection of a group of 10 PPP-P legislators, as well as with the support of the MQM and of some smaller groups. The support of the non-PML-Q members came at a price, however, and a disproportionate number of Cabinet portfolios were allocated to the PPP-P defectors, while the MQM received the provincial governorship in Sindh.

The success of the PML-Q meant that in broad terms there was continuity of policy from the previous government. Musharraf's Finance Minister, Shaukat Aziz, continued as advisor to Jamali, and the governor of the State Bank remained in his post.

While the government continued to lend its support to the USA in its operations in Afghanistan, the success of the MMA in the elections was only one indicator of growing popular resistance both to this and to US policy towards Iraq, as well as concern over the way that US agencies operated within Pakistan itself. Another was a series of terrorist activities, some aimed at foreign targets, which occurred throughout the year. In January a US journalist, Daniel Pearl, was kidnapped and later murdered. In March there was an attack on a church in the diplomatic area of Islamabad which killed five, and in May 17 people died when a group of French engineers working on a government submarine project was attacked by a suicide bomber in Karachi. In June a bomb outside the US consulate killed 12 Pakistani bystanders. There were also attacks on members of the Pakistani Christian minority, including the killing of four nurses at a hospital near Rawalpindi and an attack on a church on Christmas day, in which three children were killed. A number of parcel bombs exploded also in Karachi. Different organisations appeared to be involved in these various activities, even if there were some common threads. Although the government was able to make some high-profile arrests, the problem persisted.

At the official level, relations with the USA were close, as Pakistan continued to play a key role in the ongoing operations in Afghanistan. However, the US administration remained suspicious of the presence within the population of sympathisers with Islamic militancy, and visa restrictions and special registration requirements for Pakistani citizens in the USA were widely resented. Allegations in the US press of Pakistani involvement over the years in exchanging nuclear and missile technology with North Korea pointed to a possible source of future difficulty.

Relations with India were very poor during the year (see VIII.2.i). Both at the beginning of the year, and again in May and June, border tensions rose to the point where armed conflict, with a possible escalation to a nuclear exchange, seemed a definite possibility. Musharraf demonstrated that he was willing to meet some of India's concerns with a strongly worded speech against terrorism at the beginning of the year, and the arrest of some militant leaders connected with the Kashmir struggle. He also relied heavily on pressure from the international community to prevent India from attacking across the line of control within Kashmir. Although tensions subsided in the latter half of the year, India refused to accept that Pakistan was doing all that it could to reduce cross-border infiltration.

There were mixed results on the economic front. Foreign exchange reserves reached record levels during the year, partly because of debt forgiveness and rescheduling by the USA and other donors and partly because of higher levels of remittances from Pakistanis working and living abroad. Interest rates declined, as did inflation. However, industrial and agricultural output did not increase commensurately, and there was little impact on poverty levels, which had increased steadily in the previous decade.

iii. BANGLADESH

CAPITAL: Dhaka   AREA: 144,000 sq km   POPULATION: 133,400,000
OFFICIAL LANGUAGE: Bengali   POLITICAL SYSTEM: multiparty republic in British Commonwealth
HEAD OF STATE: President Iajuddin Ahmed (since Sept '02)
RULING PARTY: Bangladesh Nationalist Party (BNP)-led coalition
HEAD OF GOVERNMENT: Khaleda Zia, Prime Minister (since Nov '01)
MAIN IGO MEMBERSHIPS (NON-UN): SAARC, CP, OIC, CWTH, NAM
CURRENCY: taka (end-'02 £1=Tk92.7298, US$1=Tk57.9000)
GNI PER CAPITA: US$370, US$1,680 at PPP ('01)

THE Bangladesh National Party (BNP), and its leader, Prime Minister Begum Khaleda Zia, consolidated their power throughout 2002 following their election victory of October 2001. They did so despite the challenge of boycotts and strikes encouraged by the main opposition party, the Awami League (AL), and a high incidence of political assaults and other forms of lawlessness. The new BNP-led government comprised a four-party alliance with an overall two-thirds majority in the unicameral Jatiya Sangsad (legislature). Two parties of the coalition were hardline Islamic groupings, but the BNP had an overall majority in its own right.

The heavily confrontational nature of relations between Bangladesh's two main political parties was evident in mid-March when all 58 members of the AL in the Jatiya Sangsad threatened to resign. The threat came in response to a move by Zia to repeal legislation passed by the previous government making it mandatory to display in public offices portraits of Sheikh Mujibur Rahman, the founding father of Bangladesh and the father of the AL's current leader, former Prime Minister Sheikh Hasina Wajed. On 24 March, the day the repeal became law, 50 AL supporters were injured in Dhaka by police during a demonstration against the legislation.

On 21 June President A.Q.M. Badruddoza Chowdhury resigned under pressure from the ruling BNP after failing to visit the grave of former President Maj.-Gen. Ziakr Rahman on the 30 May anniversary of his assassination in 1981 (see AR 1981, pp. 278-79). Rahman had been the husband of Begum Khaleda Zia, and founder of the BNP and President of Bangladesh from 1977 until his death. Chowdhury, 71, had resigned his membership of the BNP upon becoming President in November 2001. He said that he was unsure why he had been asked to resign, and many commentators described the resignation as "unconstitutional". In the same month Zia appointed her son, Tareq Rahman, to be joint secretary-general of the BNP, in a move widely seen as an attempt to strengthen her grip on the party and government.

On 6 September Iajuddin Ahmed, the nominee of the ruling BNP, was sworn in unopposed as the new President after the Election Commission found that the nominations of two other candidates were invalid. Once again, this was widely construed as a move by Zia to consolidate her power.

Pakistan's President Pervez Musharraf visited Bangladesh for three days on 29-31 July, signed a number of agreements with Zia, and expressed several times his regrets at "excesses" committed by Pakistani troops during Bangladesh's 1971 war of independence from Pakistan (see AR 1971, p. 279). Bangladesh claimed that three million people had been killed and 200,000 women raped during Pakistan's attempts to crush the independence movement. An enquiry by Pakistan in 1973 blamed senior military officers for the atrocities, but its findings had been suppressed until 2000 when Musharraf had ordered their release.

A meeting in Paris in mid-March of the Bangladesh Development Forum, the international consortium of aid donors, said that future assistance would depend on significant progress being made to curb corruption and improve law and order. The main attempt to achieve this came in October with "Operation Clean Heart", a nationwide government crackdown on crime, in which the army was used to assist the police. Robbery, extortion, murder, rape, and related crimes had become so commonplace that few felt safe at night in Dhaka's dimly lit and sometimes flooded streets. The police force itself was either a bystander or actually involved in crime out of greed or fear of retribution from better-armed gangsters, some of whom enjoyed protection from local politicians. With the army providing support in the streets, the police rounded up many people on its lists of criminal suspects, and killed a number of notorious criminals. Although the operation raised grave human rights concerns, it was popular among all levels of society and many defended the campaign's excesses, saying that sacrificing individual human rights might be necessary to ensure the safety of the majority. The main question that remained was whether "Clean Heart" would have beneficial lasting results and whether democracy would be undermined if the army were to assume a permanent national guardianship role. A number of commentators observed that it was too much to hope for a dramatic improvement in law and order without deeper changes in society.

Violence against journalists was also on the rise. Reporters Sans Frontiers stated in mid-June that 145 journalists had been assaulted or subjected to death threats and one reporter murdered since the BNP had returned to power in October 2001. Furthermore, the country's only independent television station, ETV, was closed and its founder and managing director, Sumon Dring, expelled from Bangladesh on 3 October. Ministers said that ETV favoured the opposition and that its coverage was biased.

iv. NEPAL

CAPITAL: Kathmandu   AREA: 147,000 sq km   POPULATION: 23,600,000
OFFICIAL LANGUAGE: Nepali   POLITICAL SYSTEM: multiparty monarchy
HEAD OF STATE: King Gyanendra (since June '01)
RULING PARTY: Nepali Congress Party (NCP)
HEAD OF GOVERNMENT: Lokendra Bahadur Chand, interim Prime Minister (since Oct '02)
MAIN IGO MEMBERSHIPS (NON-UN): SAARC, CP, NAM
CURRENCY: Nepalese rupee (end-'02 £1=NRs122.519, US$1=NRs76.5000)
GNI PER CAPITA: US$250, US$1,450 at PPP ('01)

EVENTS in Nepal in 2002, as in immediately preceding years, were characterised by volatile politics in the capital city revolving around personal and factional rivalries and otherwise by the mounting scale of Maoist-led insurgency, which complicated the land-locked Himalayan state's foreign relations.

Since the deployment of the Royal Nepalese Army (RNA) against the rebels from the Communist Party of Nepal (Maoist) in November 2001 (see AR 2001, p. 342), the violence of the seven-year insurgency had escalated dramatically and was much more expensive in terms of deaths and destruction of property in 2002 than in the previous year. Although there were occasional speculative reports of clandestine talks between government and rebel representatives, there was no sign that the government was making any real headway against the insurgency. The Maoists aimed to abolish the monarchy and, by the end of 2002, they controlled about one-third of Nepal's 75 districts. A general strike called for 23-27 April brought Kathmandu and much of Nepal to a standstill, largely because of a campaign of intimidation by the rebels. There were two small bomb explosions in Kathmandu on the night of 22 April, and on 25 April Maoists destroyed the ancestral home of Prime Minister Sher Bahadur Deuba in the town of Assigram, about 450 km north of Kathmandu.

On 17 April, King Gyanendra prorogued the 21st session of the legislature during which 15 bills had been approved, including measures against terrorism and corruption, and bills increasing women's and minorities' rights. But the leader of the main opposition party, the United Communist Party of Nepal (Marxist-Leninist) (UCPN), criticised the Prime Minister for failing to fulfil his promise to introduce a bill to amend the constitution.

The rumbling crisis in Nepal's ruling party came to a climax on 17 September when the Election Commission recognised the faction of the divided Nepali Congress Party (NCP) led by former Prime Minister Girja Prasad Koirala as the legitimate holder of the party title and logo. The minority faction, supporting Prime Minister Deuba, registered as a new political party on 23 September the Nepali Congress Party-Democratic (NPC-D). The Commission made no ruling on which of these two parties could use the NCP's traditional symbol of a tree and four stars.

Nepal's political crisis deepened when on 4 October King Gyanendra dismissed Prime Minister Deuba and his entire Council of Ministers for alleged "incompetence" after the Prime Minister had asked for a one-year postponement of elections due on 13 November for fear of their disruption by the rebels, who had called for a general strike on 11-13 November. The King temporarily assumed executive powers, indefinitely postponed the elections, and appointed an interim government under a monarchist former Prime Minister, Lokendra Bahadur Chand. This was the first dismissal by a King of an elected government since the supersession of absolute monarchy in 1990. Article 127 of the 1990 constitution allowed the King to intervene in the political sphere in order to resolve "difficulties".

On 7 October Gyanendra consulted the leaders of six political parties, including the ruling NCP and the opposition UCPN. The King, however, met the leaders separately, not jointly as they had requested. On 11 October Gyanendra appointed Lokendra Bahadur Chand of the pro-monarchy National Democratic Party (RPP) as head of an interim Cabinet. Chand had served as Prime Minister three times previously: in 1983-86 when political parties were banned, briefly in 1990 during the transition to multi-party democracy, and in 1997 in coalition with the UCPN (see AR 1997, pp. 316-17). Chand said that his priorities were to restore peace and security, reopen dialogue with the Maoists, and prepare for general elections. On 18 November King Gyanendra expanded the interim Cabinet formed in October after consultation with Chand. The new appointments included one defector from the opposition UCPN, as well as businessmen and independents. Chand relinquished 14 of the portfolios which he had assumed personally in October.

Finance Minister Badri Prasad Shrestha on 31 October presented a 10-point package of economic reforms for the next six months in an attempt to revive the ailing economy. These measures concentrated on poverty alleviation, control of corruption, fiscal reform, and improved efficiency in public expenditure.

The long running controversy between the UK and Nepalese governments regarding pension rights and remuneration for ex-Gurkha soldiers took on another aspect in July when Gurkhas who had been held prisoner by the Japanese in World War II took the UK government to court in an attempt to get adequate compensation.

The year ended for Nepal as it had begun with Maoist insurgents occupying much territory and "national" politics in and around Kathmandu being characterised by factiousness, intense personal rivalries, and with the King playing an active role either from front of stage or from the wings.

v. BHUTAN

CAPITAL: Thimphu   AREA: 46,500 sq km   POPULATION: 828,000
OFFICIAL LANGUAGES: Dzongkha, Lhotsan & English   POLITICAL SYSTEM: non-party monarchy
HEAD OF STATE: Dragon King Jigme Singye Wangchuk (since '72)
HEAD OF GOVERNMENT: Lyonpo Kinzang Dorji (since Aug '02)
MAIN IGO MEMBERSHIPS (NON-UN): SAARC, CP, NAM
CURRENCY: ngultrum (end '02 £1=Nu76.8104, US$1=Nu47.9600)
GNI PER CAPITA: US$640, US$1,530 at PPP ('01)

TENTATIVE efforts to modernise Bhutan's autocratic monarchical political and administrative system and to introduce a written constitution continued throughout 2002. Otherwise the main problem was how to deal with the well-armed militant Indian separatist groups—the United Liberation Front of Assam (ULFA) and the National Democratic Front of Bodolaul (NDFB)—that operated on Bhutan's soil near to its border with India.

On 7 August during a visit to Bhutan, India's Minister of External Affairs, Yashwant Sinha, agreed to co-operate closely with the government regarding the problem of camps maintained by the ULFA and the NDFB on Bhutan's territory, although the ULFA's leaders claimed their camps were located on undemarcated territory.

The 80th session of Bhutan's unicameral legislature, the National Assembly, closed on 29 July having endorsed the government's ninth Five Year Plan which proposed major administrative changes. In mid-August, Bhutan's Minister for Trade and Industries, Lyonpo Khandu Wangchuk, gave up the chairmanship of the Council of Ministers in favour of the Minister of Agriculture, Lyonpo Kinzang Dorji, who became the fifth chairman since the post was established by King Jigme Singye Wangchuk in 1998.

The 39-member committee, first set up in late September 2001 to draft a written constitution for Bhutan to replace the royal decree of 1953 under which the country was still ruled, continued its work.

vi. SRI LANKA

CAPITAL: Colombo   AREA: 66,000 sq km   POPULATION: 19,600,000
OFFICIAL LANGUAGES: Sinhala, Tamil, English   POLITICAL SYSTEM: multiparty republic in British Commonwealth
HEAD OF STATE AND GOVERNMENT: President Chandrika Bandaranaike Kumaratunga (since Nov '94)
RULING PARTIES: United National Party (UNP) heads United National Front Coalition
PRIME MINISTER: Ranil Wickremesinghe (since Dec '02)
MAIN IGO MEMBERSHIPS (NON-UN): SAARC, CP, CWTH, NAM
CURRENCY: Sri Lankan rupee (end-'02 £1=SRS154.886, US$1=SRs96.7100)
GNI PER CAPITA: US$830, US$3,560 at PPP ('01)

PROSPECTS for peace in Sri Lanka improved steadily throughout the year under the new United National Front (UNF) government elected the previous December (see AR 2001, p. 345). Diplomatic and political activity towards peace with the Liberation Tigers of Tamil Eelam (LTTE) was complicated, however, by the tension between the new government of Ranil Wickremesinghe and the President, Chandrika Bandaranaike Kumaratunga, a member of the opposition People's

Alliance (PA). The peace process was assisted by the facilitation of Norway and by the transfer of allegiance from the PA to the UNF by Cabinet Minister Gamini Lakshman Peiris who had developed constitutional solutions under the previous government. After nearly 20 years the warfare between the government and the LTTE had exhausted all combatants, damaged the economy, cost many thousands of lives, and achieved very little (see AR 1983, p. 268).

The constitution adopted in 1978, based on an executive President sharing power with an elected government, contained the potential contradiction that these might be controlled by opposing parties (see AR 1978, p. 273). This was the case throughout the year following the election victory of the UNF. The principle of "cohabitation" was urged whereby President Kumaratunga and Prime Minister Wickremesinghe would work together while retaining their partisan roles. In practice, however, this did not work very well and mutual recriminations between the parties continued. The constitution allowed the President to dissolve Parliament after one year and this became an acute issue by December. The government tried to gain support for a constitutional amendment which would remove this power and reduce the President's control over the armed forces. However, this required a two-thirds majority which could only be achieved if several opposition legislators defected to the government. The issue was unresolved by the end of the year, with both sides fearing that the other would control the timing of any future general election.

The Norwegian government took the major role in bringing the government and the LTTE together, culminating in meetings in Thailand in September and an international conference with US participation in Oslo in November. India remained distant from this process because of its determination to extradite and put on trial LTTE leader Vellupillai Prabhakaran for the assassination of Rajiv Gandhi in 1991 (see AR 1991, pp. 309-10). Some opposition parties—notably the Janatha Vimukthi Peramuna (JVP) and Sihala Urumaya—strongly opposed dealing with the LTTE. A memorandum of understanding was signed in February under which the LTTE agreed to end its armed activity pending negotiations about the future status of the Northern and Eastern provinces. Anton Balasingham was the major negotiator for the LTTE, and contacts between the two sides were expedited by the lifting of the proscription of the LTTE on 4 September.

Following the Oslo talks it seemed as though the LTTE was ready to abandon its armed struggle and its goal of independence in return for a degree of federal devolution. This was not, however, the only interpretation of speeches made by Balasingham in London and by Prabhakaran in the northern Wanni region on "heroes day", 27 November. On the assumption that the LTTE favoured federal devolution, some politicians became interested in the British and Swiss systems. As members of the Tamil National Alliance pointed out, their predecessors in the Federal Party had advocated the Swiss model 40 years earlier.

A basic problem in institutionalising devolution, however, was the role of the LTTE in the areas which it controlled. Despite the ceasefire, there were sporadic outbreaks of violence. Muslims on the east coast felt threatened and one objective of the Sri Lanka Muslim Congress was to create a distinct Muslim administration in the area which would avoid LTTE domination. The LTTE also maintained courts, police, and armed units throughout the Wanni and the Jaffna peninsula and objected to "security zones" managed by the Sri Lankan armed forces. It was one role of the Sri Lanka Monitoring Mission, organised by Norway, to ensure a degree of freedom within the LTTE areas. One major dispute involved relations with the Eelam People's Democratic Party (EPDF), which had controlled the island of Delft for 10 years but was being driven out by the LTTE by the end of the year.

In pursuit of its privatisation program the government launched a major advertising campaign lauding the advantages of private enterprise. It also made 135 million shares available to the public in Sri Lanka Telecom. The goods and services tax was replaced by a value added tax in the budget. The prospect of peace improved the hitherto gloomy economic outlook, with improved airline connections being planned or implemented and a tourist facilitation agreement being signed with China. Following the Oslo meetings in December, international aid of US$70 million was extended and promises of further support came from Japan following Wickremesinghe's visit.

Diplomatic activity around the peace negotiations led to many visits to, and excursions from, Sri Lanka by political leaders. Although Prabhakaran remained in his headquarters in the Wanni, the reclusive leader gave his first press conference for many years on 10 April. Prime Minister Wickremesinghe visited India, Japan, Norway, and the USA.

Oswald Thomas Gomis was appointed Catholic Archbishop in July. Party leadership remained fairly stable, with Kumaratunga appointing Mahinda Rajapakse as leader of the opposition in February, the first time that someone not related to the Bandaranaike family had led the Sri Lanka Freedom Party in its 50 year history. The leadership of the Sri Lanka Muslim Congress was being disputed at the end of the year.

3. INDIAN OCEAN STATES

i. MAURITIUS

CAPITAL: Port Louis   AREA: 2,040 sq km   POPULATION: 1,198,000
OFFICIAL LANGUAGE: English   POLITICAL SYSTEM: multiparty republic in British Commonwealth
HEAD OF STATE: President Karl Auguste Offmann (since Feb '02)
RULING PARTIES: Mauritian Socialist Movement (MSM) & Mauritian Militant Movement (MMM)
HEAD OF GOVERNMENT: Sir Aneerood Jugnauth, Prime Minister (since Sept '00)
MAIN IGO MEMBERSHIPS (NON-UN): AU, COMESA, SADC, ACP, CWTH, Francophonie, NAM
CURRENCY: Mauritian rupee (end-'02 £1=MRs47.0215, US$1=MRs29.3600)
GNI PER CAPITA: US$3,830, US$10,410 at PPP ('01)

SINCE the attacks of 11 September 2001 Mauritius had been under pressure to pass a stringent anti-terrorist law which would commit it to co-operate with the USA. President Cassam Uteem, who had close links with the Muslim community in Mauritius, refused to sign the legislation, however, and eventually resigned in February. He was succeeded by Karl Offman from the Mauritian Socialist Movement (MSM). In October the Prime Minister, Sir Anerood Jugnauth, announced that he would step down in September 2003—the plan being that he would take over as President. Uteem, however, announced that he was returning to politics at the head of a pro-Muslim party.

The island of Rodrigues, which had acquired autonomous status, held its first elections in September. The Organisation of the People of Rodrigues (OPR) won 10 of the 18 seats.

Other developments included widespread damage caused in January by cyclone Diana, which destroyed 20 per cent of the country's sugar crop and damaged electricity supplies and textile production. Mauritius was also adversely affected by the scandal at Enron Corp. (see IV.1) which had 43 subsidiary companies registered in Mauritius. Plans were pushed ahead for the creation of a major information technology centre, a so-called CyberCity, at Ebene at a cost of US$50 million.

ii. SEYCHELLES, COMOROS AND MALDIVES

Seychelles

CAPITAL: Victoria   AREA: 454 sq km   POPULATION: 82,000
OFFICIAL LANGUAGES: Seychellois, English & French   POLITICAL SYSTEM: multiparty republic in British Commonwealth
HEAD OF STATE AND GOVERNMENT: President France-Albert René (since June '77)
RULING PARTY: Seychelles People's Progressive Front (SPPF)
MAIN IGO MEMBERSHIPS (NON-UN): AU, COMESA, SADC, OIC, ACP, CWTH, Francophonie, NAM
CURRENCY: Seychelles rupee (end-'02 £1=SRs8.9975, US$1=SRs5.6180)
GNI PER CAPITA: US$7,310 ('00)

Comoros

CAPITAL: Moroni   AREA: 1,860 sq km   POPULATION: 572,000
OFFICIAL LANGUAGES: Arabic & French   POLITICAL SYSTEM: multiparty federal republic
HEAD OF STATE AND GOVERNMENT: Col Assoumani Azali (since April '99); Anjouan President, Mohamed Bacar; Ngazidja (Grande Comore) President, Abdou Soule Elbak; Mohéli President, Mohamed Said Fazul
MAIN IGO MEMBERSHIPS (NON-UN): AU, COMESA, ACP, AL, OIC, Francophonie, NAM
CURRENCY: franc (end-'02 £1=CFr767.833, US$1=CFr479.431)
GNI PER CAPITA: US$380, US$1,610 at PPP ('01)

Maldives

CAPITAL: Malé   AREA: 300 sq km   POPULATION: 283,000
OFFICIAL LANGUAGE: Divehi   POLITICAL SYSTEM: non-party republic in British Commonwealth
HEAD OF STATE AND GOVERNMENT: President Maumoon Abdul Gayoom (since Nov '78)
MAIN IGO MEMBERSHIPS (NON-UN): SAARC, CP, OIC, CWTH, NAM
CURRENCY: rufiya (end-'02 £1=R20.4198, US$1=R12.7500)
GNI PER CAPITA: US$2,040, US$4,520 at PPP ('01)

WITH elections to the SEYCHELLES legislative assembly scheduled for the end of the year, the ruling Seychelles People's Progressive Front (SPPF), the party of Prime Minister Albert René, faced a strong challenge from Wavel Ramkalawan and the opposition Seychelles National Party (SNP). In September Ramkalawan, with backing from Réunion politicians, visited Paris to build bridges with the French government, particularly on the question of debt repayment. In spite of allegations of various electoral malpractice and a potentially sinister purging of the army of SNP supporters, the elections went ahead on 4-6 December and were approved by observers from Francophonie and the European Parliament. The SPPF took 23 of the 34 seats and the SNP only 11, but the voting was much closer with the SNP securing 43 per cent of the votes cast. The Democratic Party, the party of former leader James Mancham, polled only 3 per cent of the vote but had a significant impact on the contest in that it split the opposition vote in many constituencies. As a result of the SNP's strong showing, René agreed to meet the opposition leader for the first time on 10 December in order to try to defuse tension in the islands.

The UN and the Organisation of African Unity (OAU) both suspended Seychelles' voting rights because of arrears in payments.

During the year in COMOROS attempts were made to implement the new constitution of the Union of the three islands of Ngazidja, Anjouan, and Mohéli, which had been agreed by referendum in December 2001 and was intended to reunite the three islands in a loose federation. The agreement made provision for a federal government headed by a Union President who would be elected from each of the three islands in turn, and three regional island governments, also headed by Presidents. Early in 2002 Assoumani Azali, the then head of state, resigned to fight for election to the new office of Union President. An interim administration was eventually formed after the opposition was promised the Finance Ministry. In March presidential elections were held in Anjouan and Mohéli and in April Azali was duly elected first Union President after all of his challengers withdrew in the second round of voting. He formed his government in June.

In May Abdou Soule Elbak was elected as the island President of Ngazidja, defeating Bakari Boina, who had been backed by Azali. The result was that the two Presidents, each residing in Moroni (the federal capital), disputed the effective control of the island. The focus of the dispute was the collection of customs dues in the port of Moroni, as these were the most important source of income for the islands, and two rival customs administrations emerged. The islands' indebtedness rose to the equivalent of its annual GDP but the IMF refused to negotiate a Heavily Indebted Poor Countries (HIPC) agreement until the political confusion was resolved. A meeting with IMF officials in December eventually led to agreement over the partition of the customs revenues between the island administrations.

In September Azali formed a new "presidential" political party, the Convention for the Renewal of the Comores (CRC), to try to strengthen his hold on power. Meanwhile Anjouan's effective independence was demonstrated when Mohamed Bacar appealed directly to the African Union (AU) to intervene in the islands. The lack of any effective Union government had led to Anjouan becoming a centre for offshore and Internet business activity. There were also allegations of Comorian passports being sold to Islamic extremists and to criminals.

Although the three islands were nominally reunited, they now had, in effect, four Presidents with no end in sight to the seemingly endless round of elections, as the legislative assemblies all had to be elected in 2003.

Although in the MALDIVES there had not yet been any serious challenge to the 25 year rule of Maumoon Abdul Gayoom, discontent with the government was clearly rising. Gayoom, who was not only President but head of the government, Commander-in-Chief of the armed forces, Minister of Defence, Minister of Finance, and governor of the Central Bank, held all of the reins of power and, until the terrorist attacks of 11 September 2001, was widely accredited with having presided over an economic miracle in the Maldives. This was based on a systematic growth of tourism and involved the growth of 87 resort islands. The slump in tourism after 11 September, however, brought severe economic problems, which were compounded by fears of war in the Middle East.

Discontent was revealed in May when only 38 per cent of the voters turned out in the capital, Malé, to vote in a by-election caused by the imprisonment and exile of the former legislator. The election was won by the official candidate, Abdullah Kamaluddheen, the Minister of Human Resources. There was further embarrassment for the government when the Independence Day celebrations in July turned into a public relations disaster after a dance display depicting the Maldivian defeat of the Portuguese in the 16th century gravely offended the Portuguese representative.

The main concern of the Maldives in the international arena was to secure the implementation of the 1997 Kyoto Protocol on climate change for which it lobbied hard at the Summit on Sustainable Development in Johannesburg. Gayoom's strategy was to work for international understanding of the Maldivian position making particular use of Maldives' membership of the Commonwealth.

iii. MADAGASCAR

CAPITAL: Antananarivo   AREA: 587,000 sq km   POPULATION: 16,000,000
OFFICIAL LANGUAGES: Malagasy & French   POLITICAL SYSTEM: multiparty republic
HEAD OF STATE: President Marc Ravalomanana (since May '02)
RULING PARTY: I Love Madagascar Party (TIM)
HEAD OF GOVERNMENT: Jacques Sylla (since May '02)
MAIN IGO MEMBERSHIPS (NON-UN): AU, COMESA, OIC, ACP, Francophonie, NAM
CURRENCY: Malagasy franc (end-'02 £1=MFr10201.9, US$1=MFr6370.00)
GNI PER CAPITA: US$260, US$870 at PPP ('01)

IN the wake of the disputed presidential elections of December 2001 (see AR 2001, pp. 349-50), the year was dominated by the struggle for power between the two leading candidates in those elections: the then incumbent President, Didier Ratsiraka, and Marc Ravalomanana, the mayor of Antananarivo. Official figures had given Ravalomanana 46 per cent of the vote, but Ratsiraka, who polled 40 per cent, demanded a second round of voting. Ravalomanana, however, claimed he had won the election on the first round, and refused to participate in a further vote. He had himself sworn in as President in February. Supporters of the new President demonstrated in his favour, and staged strikes which closed businesses and telecommunications and brought the economy to a halt. Ratsiraka initially tried to carry on as President from his power base in Toamasina (Tamatave) and, with the support of some provincial governors, imposed a blockade on the capital but he gradually lost the support of civil servants, the army, the churches, and the donor community. Attempts were made to mediate by the Organisation of African Unity (OAU), the Francophonie Community and even by former US President Jimmy Carter, and eventually it was agreed to recount the votes from the first round of voting.

From this process, which was overseen by officials from Senegal, Ravalomanana, strongly supported by the Tananarive elite, was declared the winner by the High Court with 51.46 per cent of the vote. He was sworn in on 6 May. Ratsiraka at first refused to accept this outcome, but when the USA and Germany led the way in recognising the new President, he fled the country. Although the African Union, newly formed in July (see XI.6.ii), withheld recognition until legislative elections could be held which would confirm Ravalomanana's victory, the new President was invited to attend the Summit on Sustainable Development in Johannesburg. The legislative elections, held in December, witnessed lavish spending by all parties (the presidential coalition having a dozen helicopters at its disposal). Although there were increasingly bitter power struggles within the ruling elite, the President's supporters achieved an emphatic victory.

Ravalomanana, once effectively in power, made the restoration of the economy his highest priority. At a conference of donors in July he promised to prioritise good government and initiated an anti-corruption campaign which included a tenfold rise in ministerial salaries. In September a sceptical World Bank released a US$40 million structural adjustment credit following the promise of budgetary cuts of 60 per cent. A Finance Law approved in December also opened the way for a debt reduction programme under the World Bank's Heavily Indebted Poor Countries scheme. In spite of this, however, the political disturbances of the year resulted in a near collapse of the economy with exports falling by 47 per cent. Only the fishing industry prospered, with shrimps becoming the island's main export.

IX SOUTH-EAST AND EAST ASIA

1. MYANMAR (BURMA)—THAILAND—MALAYSIA—BRUNEI—SINGAPORE—
INDONESIA—EAST TIMOR—PHILIPPINES—VIETNAM—CAMBODIA—LAOS

i. MYANMAR (BURMA)

CAPITAL: Yangon (Rangoon)   AREA: 677,000 sq km   POPULATION: 48,300,000
OFFICIAL LANGUAGE: Burmese   POLITICAL SYSTEM: military regime
HEAD OF STATE AND GOVERNMENT: Gen. Than Shwe, Chairman of State Peace and Development Council and Prime Minister (since April '92)
MAIN IGO MEMBERSHIPS (NON-UN): ASEAN, CP, NAM
CURRENCY: kyat (end-'02 £1=K10.0791, US$1=K6.2933)
GNI PER CAPITA: n/a

DAW Aung San Suu Kyi, the general secretary of the National League for Democracy (NLD), was released from house arrest in May. Subsequently she travelled to Mandalay and the Kayin, Shan, and Rakhine states addressing supporters and opening NLD offices. However, despite this and other signs—such as the release of several hundred political prisoners—that the military State Peace and Development Council (SPDC) was inching its way towards reaching a political accommodation with the NLD, there was no substantive progress toward a more democratic form of government. Tan Sri Razali Ismail, the UN special envoy to Myanmar, attempted to effect a rapprochement between the two sides but made little progress during the year other than to extract a commitment from the SPDC to restart the constitution-drafting process. Despite occasional hints of a softening in its position, the NLD continued to insist that the results of the 1990 election be recognised by the army and that foreigners should not invest in or tour the country.

On 7 March police in Yangon arrested U Aye Zaw Win, the husband of former General Ne Win's daughter Sandar Win, and their three sons for attempting to organise a coup against the government. At the root of the case was a claim that, having lost influence in the government and, therefore, some important business deals as a consequence of the declining power of the Ne Win family, they had sought to change the government by suborning troops assigned to protect Ne Win's villa, kidnapping the three most senior generals, and then forcing them to do their bidding. They were tried later and all sentenced to death. Ne Win himself remained under house arrest until his death in December at the age of 92. His funeral was a small, private gathering (see XVIII).

Myanmar and the International Labour Organisation (ILO) agreed in March to the opening of an ILO Liaison Office in Yangon to work with the government to end the practice of forced labour. The UN Special Rapporteur on Human Rights in Myanmar, Paulo Pinheiro, visited the country twice and submitted lengthy reports calling on the government to grant an amnesty to more than 1,000 political prisoners. While condemning the continued practice of forced labour and arbitrary arrests, he drew attention to some improvements in the human rights situation, including the extension of human rights training for the police and government officers, and efforts to improve police discipline. Pinheiro refused to investigate claims of widespread rape made by two Shan exile groups, calling instead for an independent investigation. The International Committee of the Red Cross (ICRC) expanded its activities in the country, opening offices in the Shan state in order to monitor the human rights situation in remote areas of continuing armed conflict. Previously the ICRC had concentrated on making visits to investigate the condition of prisoners.

The economy faced a difficult year. Inflation was perhaps as high as 50 per cent, though the government, as usual, published no official economic statistics. Food shortages were reported in some rice-deficient regions and market prices went up dramatically during the year. At one point around mid-year, following the closure of the border with Thailand, the local currency, the kyat, was trading on the black market at 1,300 to the US dollar, having been around 800 to the dollar five months earlier and eventually settling at 1,000.

Relations with Thailand deteriorated badly in the middle of the year, leading to the closure of the border, following clashes between drug militias and the Thai military (see IX.1.ii). An anti-Thai campaign ensued during which the country was referred to as "Yodaya" (a former kingdom invaded by Myanmar in the 18th century) and Thai-produced goods were seized. By contrast, relations with China remained warm, as did those with India which had previously shunned Myanmar's military regime. During the course of the year, the USA and the EU renewed their existing sanctions, thus limiting foreign investment and aid flows to the country.

Some aid was received in support of anti-narcotics efforts conducted by the UN drug prevention programme. Myanmar had reduced its production of opium poppy by more than half in recent years and was pledged to end the production of drugs by 2005. Thailand and Japan provided assistance for the anti-drug campaign, while the EU and USA made modest contributions to anti-AIDS/HIV programmes. Japan announced that it was cancelling US$1.25 billion of Myanmar's foreign debt, nearly a quarter of all the country's obligations.

ii. THAILAND

CAPITAL: Bangkok   AREA: 513,000 sq km   POPULATION: 61,200,000
OFFICIAL LANGUAGE: Thai   POLITICAL SYSTEM: multiparty monarchy
HEAD OF STATE: King Bhumibol Adulyadej (Rama IX), since June '46
RULING PARTY: Thai Rak Thai (TRT) party
HEAD OF GOVERNMENT: Thaksin Shinawatra, Prime Minister (since Feb '01)
MAIN IGO MEMBERSHIPS (NON-UN): ASEAN, CP, APEC, NAM
CURRENCY: baht (end-'02 £1=Bt69.3471, US$1=Bt43.3000)
GNI PER CAPITA: US$1,970, US$6,550 at PPP ('01)

THAILAND'S economic recovery continued such that the country was in a position by the end of 2002 to arrange to pay off US$4.8 billion of outstanding debt to the IMF two years ahead of schedule. Finance Minister Somkid Jatusripitak said that the Thai economy grew at an estimated 4.8 per cent in 2002, up from a mere 1.8 per cent in 2001. At the start of the year, Somkid introduced a budget which contained only modest increases in public expenditure.

Thailand's Foreign Minister Surakiat Sathianthai met Myanmar's Foreign Minister Win Aung for the sixth time on 9 January to discuss the repatriation of Myanmar citizens living in Thailand. The stumbling block to agreement was Myanmar's reluctance to accept back into the country 100,000 Karen refugees believed to be supporters of the anti-government Karen National Union (KNU). The KNU was accused of several bomb attacks in Myanmar border towns during the year which killed several people. KNU dissidents also attacked a Thai school bus in Ratchaburi province in June.

In March the Thai government lodged a protest with the government of Myanmar following clashes on the border between Thai forces and the United Wa State Army (UWSA) which exercised a great deal of autonomous power within Myanmar's Shan state. Myanmar replied that the exchange had been prompted by action by the Thai side. Gen. Maung Aye, the second most senior member of the government of Myanmar, visited Bangkok in late April and came away with an apparent agreement to halt such clashes in future. However, relations between the two countries deteriorated further in May when the UWSA clashed on the border with troops of the rebel Shan State Army (South) which Myanmar said was assisted by Thai forces. Both groups were involved in the drug trade in the region. While Defence Minister Chaovalit Yongchaiyudh attempted to calm the situation by offering to proceed to the Myanmar capital, Yangon, for further talks, Thai army commander Gen. Surayud Chulanot exacerbated the border tensions by condemning the UWSA and, by implication, the Myanmar authorities. Border crossing points began to be closed by the Myanmar government, ending trade between the two countries for five months.

The border tensions between Thailand and Myanmar, which continued to escalate until August, led to civilian-military tensions in the Thai government. Whereas Prime Minister Thaksin Shinawatra and Defence Minister Chaovalit called on the Thai military to not overreact following an incident on 20 June when shells were fired into Thailand from Myanmar, Gen. Surayud insisted that his troops were following orders and that there was no difference between the civilian and military arms of government. Surayud was dismissed as military commander on 2 August, with effect from 1 October, and was replaced by Gen. Somdhat Attanand. The Thai Foreign Minister visited Yangon in August and promised to improve relations. Soon afterwards the Thai National Security Council announced that Thailand would no longer be a welcoming base for dissidents from neighbouring countries, and groups opposing Myanmar's military State Peace and Development Council (SDPC) began to complain of harassment as a number of persons were returned to the Myanmar border. Thailand's unofficial buffer zone policy—whereby the government at minimum ignored, and in some cases assisted, anti-Myanmar groups—had effectively been ended but not until relations between the two countries were near breaking point.

The government of Prime Minister Thaksin was criticised for cracking down on the freedom of the press following comments published in foreign media. The visas of two journalists from the *Far Eastern Economic Review* were revoked and a March issue of *The Economist* was banned for publishing implied oblique criticism of the Prime Minister by King Bhumibol Adulyadej. In March, the Anti-Money Laundering Office (AMLO) launched investigations of the finances of opposition politicians and journalists. Though the AMLO was formally separate from the Prime Minister, suspicion grew that Thaksin had prompted the move. At the time, the AMLO was chaired by Deputy Prime Minister and Defence Minister Chaovalit who later resigned from the post.

Three alleged leaders of the Pattani United Liberation Organisation, an Islamist separatist group, were convicted on 15 October of conducting a series of bombings in the country's southern provinces in 1998. Another Islamist group was suspected to be behind three bombs which went off in Pattani as well as arson attacks on five schools on 29 October.

Domestic politics saw little significant change, although the ruling Thai Rak Thai (Thais Love Thais) Party lost five seats in 14 by-elections held in March. The reruns were required under Thailand's tough electoral legislation designed to cut down on excessive spending by candidates. However, the government's large majority was little affected, and in the same month the Chart Pattana Party brought its 23 deputies to join the ruling coalition, prompting a minor Cabinet reshuffle, with another to follow in September. The government easily survived a series of no-confidence motions against its Ministers in May as the 132-strong opposition was unable to attract sufficient support from members of the 500-seat House of Representatives (legislature).

iii. MALAYSIA

CAPITAL: Kuala Lumpur   AREA: 330,000 sq km   POPULATION: 23,800,000
OFFICIAL LANGUAGE: Bahasa Malaysia   POLITICAL SYSTEM: multiparty monarchy in British Commonwealth
HEAD OF STATE: King Syed Sirajuddin Syed Putra Jamalullail, Sultan of Perlis (since April '02)
RULING PARTY: National Front (BN) coalition
HEAD OF GOVERNMENT: Mahathir Mohamad, Prime Minister (since July '81)
MAIN IGO MEMBERSHIPS (NON-UN): ASEAN, APEC, CP, OIC, CWTH, NAM
CURRENCY: ringitt Malaysia (end-'02 £1=RM6.0859, US$1=RM3.8000)
GNI PER CAPITA: US$3,640, US$8,340 at PPP ('01)

THE Prime Minister of Malaysia for the past 22 years, Mahathir Mohamad, announced on 22 June that he would resign with effect from October 2003. The visionary Mahathir, who was credited by many with leading multi-ethnic Malaysia through a period of remarkable economic development while maintaining political stability, would be succeeded by his deputy, Abdullah Ahmed Badawi. The Defence Minister, Najib Razak, was nominated as Badawi's future deputy but many saw him as the chief rival for the top post. The Sultan of Perlis, King Syed Sirajuddin Syed Putra Jamalullail, was installed as the 12th Agong or head of state on 25 April.

Mahathir, who also served as Finance Minister, presented the annual budget in September. Among a range of measures designed to stimulate the economy in the face of declining exports, corporate tax for smaller companies was cut by 8 per cent to 20 per cent. Government employees were also given a one month's pay bonus to stimulate consumption. The government expected the economy to grow by about 4 per cent during the year, a target which was achieved.

In January Malaysian police arrested 20 suspected members of Kumpulan Militan Malaysia (KMM), a group with alleged links to one of the men charged in connection with the 11 September 2001 attacks in the USA. A further 14 were also arrested under the Internal Security Act (ISA) in April, bringing the total to 62 arrests since September 2001. Thirteen were sentenced to two-year terms in June and one was released. Further arrests took place in September and October. KMM was said to have links with Jemaah Islamiah, a group affiliated to the al-Qaida organisation. One of those arrested during the year was deported to the USA in October. Mahathir had met with US President George W. Bush in Washington DC in May to discuss anti-terrorism cooperation. In May the governments of Malaysia, Indonesia, and the Philippines signed an agreement to cooperate in anti-terrorist policing of the region.

The National Justice Party (PKN), led by the wife of the jailed former Deputy Prime Minister Anwar Ibrahim, accused the ruling National Front (BN) of slurring its reputation by linking it in by-election campaigning with the opposition Pan-Malaysian Islamic Party (PAS). When Anwar appeared in court in February to launch an unsuccessful appeal against his 1999 corruption conviction, only a few of his supporters offered their public support. His trial was further delayed in March by a bomb scare in the courthouse for which two men were detained under the ISA.

A rally of PAS supporters which turned violent in February prompted Deputy Prime Minister Badawi to urge the police strictly to enforce a ban on unlawful public demonstrations. The president of PAS, Fadzil Nor, died in June and was succeeded by his more militant deputy Abdul Hadi Awang. The ruling BN candidate won Fadzil Nor's old seat in the Malaysian legislature in a by-election. In April the government changed the election law to ban challenges to the electoral roll which the opposition claimed was inflated with the names of the dead; also, the deposit that candidates were required to make was increased from ringgit 5,000 to ringgit 20,000 at the discretion of the Election Commission, in an attempt to discourage frivolous candidates. The only opposition party in the state assembly of Sabah, the Parti Bersatu Sabah (PBS), rejoined the BN in January, having left it two years earlier.

Malaysia expelled a number of illegal immigrants in 2002. At least half of the nearly one million immigrants in the country were believed to be there illegally. Most were from Indonesia, the Philippines, and Bangladesh. Their expulsion crippled the construction industry and led to diplomatic protests from their home countries. A new scheme for importing much needed labour for Malaysia's factories and construction work was introduced during the year, allowing for an orderly and legal system of entry as well as diversifying the source of such labour to countries such as Myanmar and Vietnam.

iv. BRUNEI

CAPITAL: Bandar Seri Bagawan   AREA: 5,765 sq km   POPULATION: 345,000
OFFICIAL LANGUAGES: Malay & English   POLITICAL SYSTEM: sultanate in British Commonwealth
HEAD OF STATE: Sultan Sir Hassanal Bolkiah (since '67)
MAIN IGO MEMBERSHIPS (NON-UN): ASEAN, APEC, OIC, CWTH, NAM
CURRENCY: Brunei dollar (end-'02 £1=Br$2.7819, US$1=Br$1.7370)
GNI PER CAPITA: US$25,020, US$25,740 at PPP ('00 est.)

THE saga of the financial profligacy of the brother of Sultan Hassannal Bolkiah, Prince Jefri Bolkiah, continued in 2002 as the Sultan attempted to settled with the creditors of the Prince's Amadeo Development Corporation. In May, 13 foreign employees of Global Evergreen, a company set up to resolve the outstanding debt, were confined to the country pending investigation. The lawyers, accountants, and administrators who were attempting to unravel the finances of the Prince when he served as Finance Minister (see AR 2000, p. 322), were eventually returned their passports.

In July Brunei hosted the 35th annual meeting of the Foreign Ministers of the 10-nation regional grouping, the Association of South East Asian Nations (ASEAN), as well as the larger ASEAN Regional Forum of 23 countries (see XI.6.iii). The meeting was noteworthy for the attendance of US Secretary of State Colin Powell, who concluded a joint declaration with the delegates on fighting terrorism.

v. SINGAPORE

CAPITAL: Singapore   AREA: 1,000 sq km   POPULATION: 4,100,000
OFFICIAL LANGUAGES: Malay, Chinese, Tamil & English   POLITICAL SYSTEM: multiparty republic in British Commonwealth
HEAD OF STATE: President S.R. Nathan (since Sept '99)
RULING PARTY: People's Action Party (PAP)
HEAD OF GOVERNMENT: Goh Chok Tong, Prime Minister (since Nov '90)
MAIN IGO MEMBERSHIPS (NON-UN): ASEAN, APEC, CP, CWTH, NAM
CURRENCY: Singapore dollar (end-'02 £1=S$2.7819, US$1=S$1.7370)
GNI PER CAPITA: US$24,740, US$24,970 at PPP ('00)

EXPORT-DEPENDENT Singapore just avoided a double dip recession in 2002. GDP fell by 9.9 per cent in the third quarter but rose 0.1 per cent in the fourth quarter because of improvements in manufacturing. Overall, the economy grew by 2.2 per cent after contracting 2 per cent in 2001. Prime Minister Goh Chok Tong predicted that growth in 2003 would be between 2 and 5 per cent, depending on the international climate.

On 5 January, the government announced that it had arrested 14 Singaporeans and one Malaysian for plotting to bomb the US embassy and US military facilities and businesses in the city state. Thirteen of those arrested were said to be members of Jemaah Islamiah (JI), an Islamic fundamentalist group affiliated with Kumpulan Militan Malaysia (see IX.1.iii) as well as Islamist groups in Indonesia. In August, Singapore sought the extradition of one other individual from the USA and several more from Indonesia on suspicion of being involved in the plot. A further 21 Singaporeans, said to be members of JI, were arrested in August on related charges. Singapore expressed strong concern that Indonesia was not acting swiftly enough to deal with Islamist militants following the 11 September attack on the World Trade Centre and, especially, the Bali bombing in 2002 (see IX.1.vi).

Following fears that the arrests would lead to discrimination against or oppression of Singapore's 15 per cent Malay Muslim population, in January the government established inter-racial "Confidence Circles" of community leaders to forestall such eventualities. Racial and religious tensions were, however, exacerbated when three female students were suspended and one withdrawn from school for wearing a *tudung* (Islamic headscarf) in violation of government uniform codes. Two months later the girls' families announced that they would sue the government on the grounds that banning the *tudung* was unconstitutional.

J. B. Jeyaretnam, a former member of Parliament and leader of the Worker's Party, who had been banned from political office and bankrupted as a result of a series of suits against him by the government, apologised in court in April for defaming Prime Minister Goh Chok Tong in 1997. In return, seven outstanding suits against him over his 1997 remarks were dropped.

Relations with neighbouring Malaysia were once more strained, this time as the result of further land reclamation programmes which, according to the authorities in Malaysia's Johor State, threatened to narrow access to the ports there. Singapore had grown in size by nearly 161 square km as a result of such programmes since the 1960s.

Former President Ong Teng Cheong, the first person elected to the position in 1993 for a six year term (see AR 1993, p. 338), died in February. The 66-year old Ong, who had served as Deputy Prime Minister and had overseen the construction of Singapore's rail transport system, died of cancer.

vi. INDONESIA

CAPITAL: Jakarta   AREA: 1,905,000 sq km   POPULATION: 213,600,000
OFFICIAL LANGUAGE: Bahasa Indonesia   POLITICAL SYSTEM: multiparty republic
HEAD OF STATE AND GOVERNMENT: President Megawati Sukarnoputri (since July '01)
RULING PARTY: Indonesian Democratic Party of Struggle
MAIN IGO MEMBERSHIPS (NON-UN): ASEAN, APEC, CP, OIC, OPEC, NAM
CURRENCY: rupiah (end-'02 £1=Rp14,281.8 US$1=Rp8,917.50)
GNI PER CAPITA: US$680, US$2,940 at PPP ('01)

THE year was characterised by a slightly greater degree of political and economic stability than in the recent past. Major problems of regionalist and inter-ethnic conflict persisted, however, and, in October, Indonesia was thrust into the international limelight as the scene of the worst terrorist atrocity since the 11 September 2001 attacks in the USA with the bombing of a nightclub in Bali (see below).

During the year, President Megawati Sukarnoputri did little to alter the widespread perception of her leadership as lacklustre and indecisive. Yet there may, paradoxically, have been some merit in her style at this particular stage in Indonesia's post-authoritarian development. The coalition of all the major parties of which her government was composed remained largely stable, if not especially innovative in its policies. Such significant political change as occurred during the year was initiated not by the government but by the country's senior constitutional body, the People's Consultative Assembly (MPR). In August a series of amendments to the 1945 constitution determined, over Megawati's objections, that from 2004 there would be direct rather than indirect elections for the presidency. In another highly emblematic break with the past, the MPR abolished the block of seats in the legislature reserved for the military.

On the economic front, the general decline of the previous five years appeared to slow during 2002. Relations with the IMF were repaired after the spats and tensions of the last phase of Gen. Mohamed Suharto's presidency and lending to Indonesia was resumed. The rupiah appeared to have stabilised during the year at an exchange rate of about 10,000 to the US dollar.

Despite these positive signs, however, endemic problems of corruption and malpractice in high places persisted. It was unclear in this, as in other areas of necessary reform, whether Megawati was either willing or able to deliver change. In January the Speaker of the House of Representatives (DPR—the legislature) and leader of Golkar (the still powerful "national" party of the Suharto period), Akbar Tandjung, was accused of misappropriating some US$4 million of development funds and channelling them into party coffers. Initially it appeared as if the government would seek to ride out the scandal. In March, however, Tandjung was formally charged and in September sentenced to three years in prison. This apparent victory for good governance was, however, tempered for many by the fact that Tandjung was one of the country's most able—and genuinely reformist—politicians and a likely presidential candidate in 2004. At the beginning of the year the Central Bank chief, Syahril Sabirin, was also convicted of misappropriation of funds. In this case, however, events took a more predictable turn. In September the conviction was quashed and he remained in office at the end of the year.

One, at least partial, victory for the rule of law came in March when Tommy Suharto (Hutomo Mandala Putra), the son of the former dictator, was finally convicted of organising the murder of a supreme court judge involved in a previous corruption case against him (see AR 2001, p. 359). He was sentenced to 15 years in prison—though it was noted that the two assassins who carried out his orders were given life.

The ends of justice were less well served in the trials of those accused of carrying out the reign of terror and destruction in East Timor in 1999 (see AR 1999, pp. 347-48). The government had acquiesced in the legal process only reluctantly and under considerable external pressure. In the event, no senior military figures were indicted, and the sentences passed on those found guilty (including the former governor, Abílio Soares, and the notorious militia leader, Eurico Guterres) were notably lenient.

The formal independence of East Timor in May of 2002 (see XI.1.vii) drew a line under Indonesia's blood-soaked relationship with the territory. During the year, however, other long-standing micro-nationalist crises remained at boiling point. Upwards of 1,300 people died during 2002 in the insurgent area of Aceh in Sumatra. Here, as previously in East Timor, Megawati's instinctive nationalism, inherited from her father, the country's legendary first President, made her ambivalent towards compromise and a peaceful settlement. A new peace agreement between the government and the Free Aceh Movement (GAM) was signed in December and supplanted the one reached in 2000 which had subsequently unravelled (see AR 2000, p. 324). The centrepiece of the agreement was an arrangement for local autonomy. This meant that GAM compromised on its fundamental commitment to total independence, but it also involved an acceptance by the government of extensive foreign monitoring, which it had previously strongly resisted..

In January, at the other end of the national archipelago, Indonesian New Guinea (Irian Jaya) was formally renamed "Papua" in a gesture to local feeling, and given a significant degree of legislative autonomy. A bicameral assembly was formed and agreement reached that a considerable proportion of the revenues from local mineral exploitation would be returned to the province. It was unclear, however, whether the reforms would make much impact on the small but persistent Free Papua Movement (OPM) which continued to harass Indonesian officials and settlers in the remoter areas of the territory.

In Ambon in the Moluccas—the scene in recent years of some dreadful inter-communal violence between the Christian and Muslim communities which populated the island in roughly equal numbers—2002 began with grounds for optimism (see AR 2000, p. 324). But an inter-communal peace agreement signed in February disintegrated in April when violence re-erupted. A further round of blood-letting followed in September. Similar though smaller scale violence took place in north Sulawesi during the year, another area in which Christians and Muslims lived together in critical demographic balance.

In May, the government had arrested Umar Thalib, leader of the militant Muslim movement Laskar Jihad, and charged him with incitement in Ambon. This caused some mild surprise as the government had hitherto shown itself unwilling to confront radical Islam. Muslims made up about 85 per cent of Indonesia's population and, while the vast majority pursued their religion in a relaxed and tolerant way, caution and self-interest had long deterred politicians from challenging more militant manifestations of Islam. Indonesia's near neighbours, Singapore and Malaysia, as well as the USA, had urged a more robust response from the Indonesian government to what they saw as a mounting Islamic terrorist threat, but to little avail. A major focus of suspicion was the 63-year old Abu Bakar Basyir, leader of the Jemaah Islamiah movement. When, on 12 October, a bomb destroyed the Sari nightclub in Kuta, on Bali, killing about 190 people, most of them Western tourists, the government was forced finally to act and Basyir was arrested along with a number of other suspected militants.

The full circumstances of the bombing, however, remained opaque. Theories about the atrocity ranged from full-scale al-Qaida involvement to suggestions that its roots and motives were purely local rather than global. Whatever the truth of the matter the effects were devastating. Beyond the immediate loss of life and injuries, the bombing went a considerable way towards the destruction of the country's tourist industry which in 2001 had been worth some US$5.4 billion. It was a blow that Indonesia's frail economy struggled to absorb.

IX.1.vi. INDONESIA

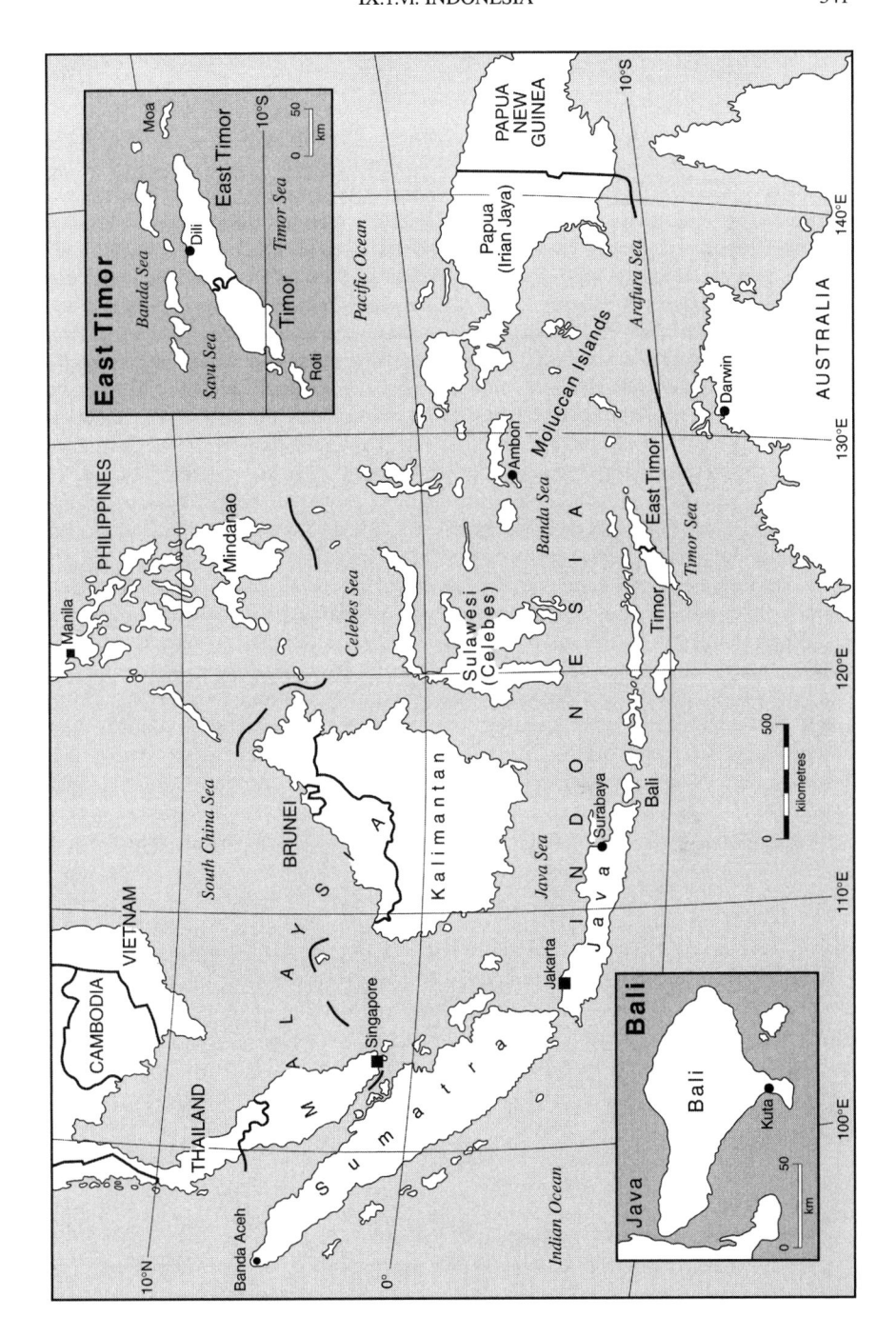

vii. EAST TIMOR

CAPITAL: Dili   AREA: 153,870 sq km   POPULATION: 750,000
OFFICIAL LANGUAGES: Portuguese, Tetum & Bahasa Indonesian   POLITICAL SYSTEM: Transitional government overseen by UNTAET
HEAD OF STATE: President José Alexandre (Xanana) Gusmão (since April '02)
HEAD OF GOVERNMENT: Mari Alkatari
CURRENCY: n/a

ON 20 May 2002 East Timor became independent when the head of the UN administration, Sérgio Vieira de Mello, formally transferred power to the country's newly elected President, Xanana Gusmão. The presidential election had taken place on 14 April when Gusmão had won overwhelmingly—with 82.7 per cent of the 378,538 votes cast—against the only other candidate, Francisco do Amaral. Gusmão had agreed to run only reluctantly and on condition that he would do so as an independent. In the months leading up to independence his relations with his former comrades in Fretilin (Revolutionary Front for the Liberation of East Timor), who formed a majority in the Constituent Assembly elected in August 2001 (see AR 2001, p. 359), had deteriorated sharply. However, initial fears that he might be unable to establish a working relationship with the Chief Minister, Mari Alkatiri, proved unfounded.

Amidst the euphoria generated by the final success of East Timor's long and bloody struggle for independence there lurked some difficult questions. On attaining statehood East Timor became the poorest country in Asia by all significant indicators. Unemployment stood at 70 per cent. Over 40 per cent of the population was illiterate and the average annual income was US$200. However, the new state attracted favourable responses from its key aid donors who agreed a package worth US$440 million for the first three years of independence. The UN was also to maintain a presence in the country to assist with reconstruction and development projects. Eventually, it was hoped, a new revenue stream would be provided by the exploitation of off-shore oil resources in partnership with Australia.

viii. PHILIPPINES

CAPITAL: Manila   AREA: 300,000 sq km   POPULATION: 77,000,000
OFFICIAL LANGUAGE: Filipino   POLITICAL SYSTEM: multiparty republic
HEAD OF STATE AND GOVERNMENT: President Gloria Macapagal-Arroyo (since Jan '01)
RULING PARTY: Lakas ng EDSA-National Union of Christian Democrats (Lakas-NUCD)
MAIN IGO MEMBERSHIPS (NON-UN): ASEAN, APEC, CP, NAM
CURRENCY: Philippine peso (end-'02 £1=PP85.4027, US$1=PP53.3250)
GNI PER CAPITA: US$1,050, US$4,360 at PPP ('01)

IN the Philippines 2002 began and ended with political uncertainty, while throughout the year the long-standing problems of separatism, insurgency, and the relationship with the former colonial power, the USA, took on a new dimension in the context of the so-called "war on terror".

January marked the first anniversary of the "people's power" actions that had elevated Gloria Macapagal Arroyo from the vice presidency to head of state when her predecessor, the populist José Estrada, was effectively removed from power by mass demonstrations (see AR 2001, p. 360). Despite the subsequent electoral legitimisation of Arroyo, however, 2002 began with persistent rumours of a coup which might or might not be calculated to return Estrada to power. The former President still enjoyed considerable support from the urban poor who had been the least questioning of his abilities and probity. The change of style brought by the elegant and sophisticated Arroyo, though originally warmly welcomed, had by the beginning of 2002 come to look suspiciously vacuous as real change was difficult to discern.

A particular problem for Arroyo was her evident pro-US stance. Educated in the USA, she was by far the most enthusiastic of South-East Asian leaders for the post-11 September "war on terror". Beyond her natural sympathies for the US project, however, there was an element of national self-interest in her co-operation with the USA. The government's efforts to resolve the long-standing and intractable problem of Muslim separatism in the southern Philippines could be aided by direct US involvement. In January the first 650 US troops were deployed in the south of the country as part of "Operation Shoulder-to-Shoulder". Their role was to train Philippine forces in the campaign against the separatist Muslim guerrillas. Although they were not to engage in fighting themselves (other than in self-defence) their presence in such numbers inevitably raised problems in a country with such an ambivalent historical relationship with the USA. Reflecting this nationalist sensitivity, Arroyo's Vice President and Foreign Minister, Teofisto Guingona, resigned in July.

Whatever the politics of the US presence, its practical benefits in respect of the performance of local military forces were not obvious. A major objective of the Philippine army was the elimination of the Abu Sayyaf Group which operated in the southern islands. Although linked by the USA to al-Qaida, and thus to international terrorism, other assessments of the group were less inflated. Abu Sayyaf was seen by many as a local criminal gang practising extortion through kidnapping rather than as a dedicated band of Islamic militants. Either way, however, the group posed a serious threat to the government's authority. At the beginning of the year, Abu Sayyaf was holding a US missionary couple and a Filipina nurse as hostages. When, in June, the US-trained army attempted a rescue operation, one of the US citizens and the Filipina were killed and the hostage was wounded. Four of their kidnappers apparently died in the shoot-out but several times that number, including the leaders of the group, escaped. It was a considerable humiliation for both the Philippine armed forces and for their US mentors. The following month US forces began to withdraw.

Meanwhile, in April, bombs in the mainly Christian town of General Santos in predominantly Muslim Mindanao killed 14 people. It was not clear which group was responsible, though blame was ascribed variously to the Abu Sayyaf Group and to the more unequivocally "political" Moro Islamic Liberation Front.

The US practice of assigning the formal status of "terrorist organisation" to specific movements in its "war on terror" caused some difficulty for the Arroyo government in August when the New People's Army (NPA), the armed wing of the communist National Democratic Front (NDF), was so designated. The move threatened further to provoke nationalist suspicions among yet another section of Philippine society. It also jeopardised long-running peace talks between the government and the NDF. In an attempt to defuse the situation Arroyo announced that US forces would not be allowed to pursue the NPA in the national territory.

The Philippine economy enjoyed a period of stability during 2002. In a somewhat self-congratulatory State of the Nation speech in the middle of the year Arroyo pointed to low inflation, a stable currency, and a projected growth rate for the year of 4 per cent. In reality, though, these conditions were typical of the South-East Asian region as a whole. The country's massive budget deficit did not feature in the speech, although it was uppermost in the assessments of many economists.

Arroyo's popularity and approval ratings declined over 2002, and at the end of the year opinion polls were pointing to her likely defeat in the presidential elections scheduled for 2004. Nevertheless, observers were taken by surprise at the end of December when she unexpectedly announced that she would not be a candidate. Speculation began immediately as to whether this was a firm commitment, an emotion of the moment, or a carefully calculated attempt to wrongfoot the opposition.

ix. VIETNAM

CAPITAL: Hanoi   AREA: 332,000 sq km   POPULATION: 79,500,000
OFFICIAL LANGUAGE: Vietnamese   POLITICAL SYSTEM: one-party republic
HEAD OF STATE: President Tran Duc Luong (since Sept '97)
RULING PARTY: Communist Party of Vietnam (CPV)
PARTY LEADER: Nong Duc Manh, CPV secretary general (since April '01)
HEAD OF GOVERNMENT/PRIME MINISTER: Phan Van Khai, Prime Minister (since Sept '97)
MAIN IGO MEMBERSHIPS (NON-UN): ASEAN, APEC, NAM, Francophonie
CURRENCY: dong (end-'02 £1=Vnd24,663.1, US$1=Vnd15,399.5)
GNP PER CAPITA: US$410, US$2,130 at PPP ('01)

IT was announced in early March that elections to an expanded, 498 seat, National Assembly (legislature) would take place on 19 May. A modest degree of choice pertained as there were 759 candidates for the seats. However, all but 51 of those elected were members of the ruling Communist Party of Vietnam (CPV) and all had been vetted by the party. Two of those elected were independents. Over 300 of the deputies were elected for the first time and only 11 per cent were over the age of 40. The overwhelming majority had been university educated and over a quarter were women. Only 25 business people were chosen. At its first session in July, the National Assembly re-elected President Tran Duc Luong for a second term as well as Prime Minister Phan Van Kai; Truong My Hoa was elected Vice-President. The Prime Minister reshuffled his Cabinet in August, bringing in a number of younger members but only one woman.

Accusations that the Vietnamese authorities were continuing to oppress indigenous Christian minorities in the central highlands region (a group known as Montagnards) continued in 2002 (see AR 2001, p. 362). The government denounced as slanderous a report by Human Rights Watch, on the subject, which was echoed by the US-based Montagnard Foundation. This claimed that 200 people were tortured and imprisoned in late December 2001. Four men said to be affiliated with the Foundation were jailed by a Vietnamese court in January for having assisted in smuggling 83 Montagnards into Cambodia the previous year. (Another report on the subject by Human Rights Watch in April was also denounced by the government.) The Vietnamese and Cambodian governments had agreed in January that more than 1,000 individuals should be returned to Vietnam under the auspices of the UN High Commissioner for Refugees (UNHCR). The first 15 returned in February. However, the UNHCR withdrew from the process the following month, saying that the authorities were using unacceptable levels of coercion to force the Montagnards to return. For its part, the Vietnamese government criticised the UNHCR for following external advice. The USA offered to grant asylum to the people involved and, after agreement with the government of Cambodia, 900 were accepted. Cambodia also closed its border to further migration from the highlands into its territory.

Former Prime Minister Vo Van Kiet (1991-97) reportedly came under investigation in 2002 for having released the crime boss of Ho Chi Minh City, Nam Cam, from jail in 1997. Two members of the Central Committee of the CPV were expelled from the party in July for alleged links with Nam Cam. One was a Vice-Minister for Police and former head of police in Ho Chi Minh City, while the other advocated Nam Cam's release through the official media. It was announced in October that the two would be prosecuted, along with more than 80 other people, for accepting bribes from Nam Cam. The government's struggle to control the rampant corruption in the economy was demonstrated by the conviction of 37 people, mainly government employees, in one province alone in the middle of the year. A further 55 people were sentenced to death for drug trafficking.

The US government assisted the Vietnamese authorities in hosting a major international conference in Hanoi in March to discuss the health and environmental consequences of the spraying of large quantities of the dioxin, Agent Orange, by the USA during the Vietnam War. The Russian navy and air force in May abandoned the US-built base at Cam Ran Bay, on which it had a 25-year lease due to expire in 2004, two years ahead of schedule.

Gen. Van Tien Dung, the commander of the North Vietnamese army who led the final successful assault against the South in 1975 (see AR 1975, pp. 275-77) died at the age of 85. Dung, whose memoirs of the war were published in English, later served as Defence Minister for seven years in the 1980s. The Catholic Bishop of Saigon (now Ho Chi Minh City) at the time of Dung's victory over the South, Cardinal Francois Xavier Nguyen Van Thuan, died in Rome in September. He was arrested in 1975 and detained until 1988 when he went into exile at the Vatican (see XVIII).

x. CAMBODIA

CAPITAL: Phnom Penh   AREA: 181,000 sq km   POPULATION: 12,300,000
OFFICIAL LANGUAGE: Khmer   POLITICAL SYSTEM: multiparty monarchy
HEAD OF STATE: King Norodom Sihanouk (elected Sept '93)
RULING PARTIES: Cambodian People's Party (CPP) & United National Front for an Independent, Neutral, Peaceful and Co-operative Cambodia (Funcinpec)
HEAD OF GOVERNMENT: Hun Sen, Prime Minister (since July '97)
MAIN IGO MEMBERSHIPS (NON-UN): ASEAN, CP, Francophonie, NAM
CURRENCY: riel (end-'02 £1=R6141.95, US$1=R3835.00)
GNI PER CAPITA: US$270, US$1,520 at PPP ('01)

IN what was seen as a precursor to national elections in 2003, Cambodia's voters went to the polls in elections to district councils on 3 February. According to UN reports, there were 20 unexplained deaths of candidates and party activists from the junior party in the coalition, Funcinpec, during the campaign, probably at the hands of the police and political rivals. Another candidate, belonging to the opposition Sam Rangis Party (SRP), drowned mysteriously. Government spokesmen and the national human rights commission denied that a climate of fear had been created. In the event, the elections passed off relatively smoothly, with the ruling Cambodian People's Party (CPP) of Prime Minister Hun Sen winning 1,575 councils. The SRP won just 11 with 17 per cent of the vote, while Funcinpec won 10 with 22 per cent. The councils had enhanced powers over local development budgets. In May, the son of King Norodom Sihanouk founded a new political party, known as the Prince Norodom Chakrapong Khmer Soul Party, in advance of the 2003 general election. Chakrapong had been involved in a coup attempt in 1994 (see AR 1994, pp. 364-65).

International donors pledged US$635 million in aid to Cambodia during 2002, nearly US$150 million more than requested. Again, donors insisted that the government carry out reforms to tackle corruption, or face the prospect of reduced aid assistance. Some progress had been achieved in reducing the size of the army and in improving aspects of public management and accounting. In June the government banned 54 publications without explanation. The growth of mob violence, which went largely unchecked by the police, was an increasing concern. On at least 11 occasions in the six months to May mobs attacked and killed individuals in the streets.

The long awaited agreement between the UN and the Cambodian government on the establishment of a tribunal to try members of the Khmer Rouge for genocide and crimes against humanity during their rule over Cambodia (1975-79) was delayed yet again in February (see AR 2001, p. 363). The UN contended that the court, to be established under a Cambodian law passed in 2001, would be insufficiently independent to carry out its mandate. Talks about founding the court had continued for five years, the government apparently reluctant to proceed against a number of now elderly individuals. In a surprise move, Prime Minister Hun Sen announced in July that the government was prepared to compromise with the UN on the court issue, following a visit by UN Human Rights special envoy Peter Leuprecht, but no agreement had been reached by the end of the year.

Widespread flooding displaced 450,000 people in five provinces after the Mekong River burst its banks in the middle of the year. Although at least 14 people died, new flood defences were believed to have saved many lives. The area had been severely affected by drought earlier in the year.

xi. LAOS

CAPITAL: Vientiane   AREA: 237,000 sq km   POPULATION: 5,400,000
OFFICIAL LANGUAGE: Laotian   POLITICAL SYSTEM: one-party republic
HEAD OF STATE: President (Gen.) Khamtay Siphandon (since Feb '98)
RULING PARTY: Lao People's Revolutionary Party (LPRP)
HEAD OF GOVERNMENT: Boungnang Volachit, Prime Minister (since March '01)
MAIN IGO MEMBERSHIPS (NON-UN): ASEAN, CP, Francophonie, NAM
CURRENCY: new kip (end-'02 £1=K12,171.8, US$1=7,600.00)
GNI PER CAPITA: US$310, US$1,610 at PPP ('01)

CONTINUITY remained the hallmark of government in Laos. On 9 April, the fifth National Assembly (109-seat unicameral legislature) re-elected 77-year old President Khamtay Siphandon together with his Vice President and the Prime Minister. Indeed, almost the entire Cabinet was re-elected, putting paid to rumours that, following the general election in February (in which only one of the 166 candidates was not a member of the ruling Lao People's Revolutionary Party), there would be a generational change in the leadership of the country. The former Deputy Minister for the Interior, Maj.-Gen. Soutchay Thammasith, took the newly created Minister for Internal Peacekeeping portfolio when his old ministry was abolished.

Relations between Laos and neighbouring Thailand became strained in the middle of the year when Lao rebels fled across the border after a failed attack in Vientiane province in June. Laos also continued to seek the return of insurgents who had crossed the border in 2000 in another failed attempt to destabilise the Communist regime. However, Thailand refused to comply with a Lao request to return 17 Laotian citizens convicted in March (along with 11 Thais) of raising the former Royal Lao standard at a border post in 2000 (see AR 2000, p. 330). The anti-Communist rebels claimed that they had engaged government forces several times between June and August but with no obvious consequences. These attacks were apparently not connected with a bomb blast in Vientiane city in September which killed one child and injured another. That incident was put down to rivalries between rival groups involved in the annual Khao Dadap Din festival.

At the end of the year, the government announced that GDP was believed to have grown by 5.7 per cent. This masked a number of problems, however, including declining rates of revenue collection, inflation up to 15 per cent, an ailing national currency, the kip, and a major fall off in foreign investment. Despite the failure of the government to carry through its commitments for structural reform, the international community pledged further economic assistance to the country in 2003, amounting to US$409.1 million, which exceed the amount pledged in 2002.

2. CHINA—HONG KONG—TAIWAN—JAPAN—SOUTH KOREA— NORTH KOREA—MONGOLIA

i. PEOPLE'S REPUBLIC OF CHINA

CAPITAL: Beijing   AREA: 9,597,000 sq km   POPULATION: 1,271,900,000
OFFICIAL LANGUAGE: Chinese   POLITICAL SYSTEM: one-party republic
HEAD OF STATE: President Jiang Zemin (since March '93)
RULING PARTY: Chinese Communist Party (CCP)
PARTY LEADER: Hu Jintao, CCP general secretary (since Nov '02)
CCP POLITBURO STANDING COMMITTEE: Hu Jintao, Wu Bangguo, Wen Jiabao, Jia Qinglin, Zeng Qinghong, Huang Ju, Wu Guanzheng, Li Changchun, Luo Gan
CCP CENTRAL COMMITTEE SECRETARIAT: Zeng Qinghong, Liu Yunshan, Zhou Yongkang, He Guoqiang, Wang Gang, Xu Caihou, He Yong
CENTRAL MILITARY COMMISSION: Jiang Zemin, chairman (since Nov '89)
PRIME MINISTER: Zhu Rongji (since March '98)
MAIN IGO MEMBERSHIPS (NON-UN): APEC
CURRENCY: renminbi (RMB) denominated in yuan (end-'02 £1=Y13.2564, US$1=Y8.2772)
GNP PER CAPITA: US$890, US$4,260 at PPP ('01)

THE 16th National Congress of the Chinese Communist Party (CCP), which took place in Beijing in November, dominated events in the People's Republic of China (PRC) in 2002. Speculation was rife in local and international media regarding the significance of the Congress, the expected emergence of a new generation of political leaders, and their potential impact on the direction of economic and political reform in China. The Congress did mark the end of Jiang Zemin's tenure as party secretary, and signalled that he would be stepping down as President in March 2003, but no radical changes in policy or direction emerged. The Chinese economy continued to grow, but not without problems, and 2002 saw the PRC consolidate its major bilateral international relationships as well as deepen its activities within regional co-operative structures.

ECONOMY AND SOCIETY. Headline figures for the Chinese economy indicated another year of significant growth. Industrial production was reported to have increased by 12.6 per cent over 2001 and in May PRC foreign currency reserves became the second largest in the world (after Japan) at US$238.4billion. The UN Conference on Trade and Development (UNCTAD) reported that in 2001 foreign direct investment into the PRC amounted to US$47 billion, the second highest in the world after the USA, and reports speculated that the PRC could surpass the USA as the world's primary recipient of foreign investment by 2010. January saw China's induction into the World Trade Organisation (WTO) and considerable speculation as to how this would help or hinder the growth of the Chinese economy. China's international economic standing was bolstered with the signing of a free trade agreement with the member states of the Association of South East Asian Nations (ASEAN), an event which generated considerable concern in Japan (see IX.2.iv).

However the headline growth figures were accompanied by a number of serious problems in the economy, especially with regard to the financial sector. China's local stock markets continued to perform badly, and were damaged by perceptions that they were poorly regulated centres of excessive speculation not based on underlying economic fundamentals. The stock market problems were highlighted in June when the government had to abandon plans to raise funds for social security spending by selling shares under its control on local markets. There was widespread concern, and informed speculation, that China's four state banks (Bank of China, Industrial and Commercial Bank, China Construction Bank, and Agricultural Bank) had accumulated non-performing loans amounting to as much as US$170 billion. Speeches by Zhu Rongji emphasised expanding domestic demand, and the need to stimulate domestic employment and re-employment through job-creation schemes.

Official figures announced that published defence spending had risen by 17 per cent to US$17.2 billion in 2001. Much of this increase was spent on acquiring modern foreign technology: over half of Russia's US$4billion defence sales in 2001 went to the PRC. A proportion of China's defence capability was also directed towards dealing internal problems. Japanese reports stated that the People's Liberation Army had transferred around 40,000 troops to southern Xinjiang to put down a "Muslim separatist movement". The State Council information office stated that between 1990 and 2001 more than 200 terrorist incidents in Xinjiang had resulted in the deaths of 162 people.

The anti-corruption agenda remained a high priority and was at the heart of an important speech by Zhu Rongji in February. Zhu called for new measures including more rigorous supervision and inspection of party cadres, and greater efforts directed at major corruption cases, especially where they involved finance, securities, real estate, personnel, or the judiciary. Gao Yan, head of the State Power Corporation, disappeared amid allegations of shady dealings and financial arrangements with China Construction Bank; Gao was the only corporate executive on the CCP Central Committee, and was often linked to former Premier Li Peng. The Dutch-Chinese businessman, Yang Bin, one of China's richest men, was appointed to head a new Special Economic Zone in North Korea in the spring, but was arrested in October in the PRC on suspicion of economic crimes and tax evasion in Shenyang, where former mayor Mu Xiuxin had already been convicted of corruption (see AR 2001, p. 367).

The terrible problems of China's basic infrastructure continued to manifest themselves in a series of high profile fatal accidents. Records for 2001 showed that 116,858 people had been killed in accidents; 81.5 per cent of them transport related. An explosion in a coal mine in Heilongjiang killed 115 people, making it the fourth largest single mining disaster in China's history (an estimated 5,000 mine workers were killed in 2001). These tragedies were not confined to the old industrial sectors, however, as illustrated by the deaths of 24 people in a fire at an unlicensed Internet café in Beijing. The Beijing mayor, Liu Qi, ordered all the estimated 2,400 internet cafes in the capital to close, and vowed to allow only 200 to reopen, under licence. Public health also came under the spotlight following the publication of a UN report, "HIV/AIDS: China's Titanic Peril", which estimated that between 800,000 and 1.2 million people in the PRC had contracted the HIV virus and suggested that the number of people infected could reach 10 million by 2010 if current trends continued. Official AIDS/HIV awareness campaigns continued to grow in scale and profile, especially in the coastal regions.

Social unrest was also a growing problem throughout the year. Reliable reports in the Hong Kong press suggested that the number of demonstrations and protests registered by the government had risen from 80 a day in 2001 to more than 700 a day in 2002. The Hong Kong reports suggested that more than 250 rural protests had involved more than 1,000 people, including one report of an organised protest group consisting of up to 80,000 rural workers in Yulin County, Shaanxi, in December. The same reports suggested that the incoming party chairman, Hu Jintao, regarded dealing with the issue of social unrest as a major priority for the new leadership.

The CCP's ongoing conflict with the outlawed religious cult, the Falun Gong, took a new twist in June when Falun Gong activists hacked into the state-owned Sinosat satellite to broadcast pro-Falun Gong propaganda. The cult jammed Sinosat transponders with high powered radio signals and then broadcast their own views, and were also reported to have hacked into cable television networks. The issue generated considerable anger and embarrassment amongst the Chinese leadership.

POLITICS. High level politics in China was dominated by preparations for the 16th Party Congress, which was widely believed to be preparing the way for the retirement of the current "Third Generation" of Chinese leaders, with President Jiang Zemin at their head, and their replacement by a younger "Fourth Generation". The Chinese media were filled with reports of the great successes and advances that had taken place over the previous 13 years, the period during which Jiang had been a part of the core leadership of the PRC. Increasing prominence was also given to the "Three Representations", the controversial ideology of political reform widely attributed to, and associated with, Jiang (see AR 2000, p. 333-34). It became clear in June that the party constitution would be amended to incorporate the "Three Representations", despite the opposition of conservatives within the CCP. The formulation now sat alongside Marxism-Leninism, Mao Zedong Thought, and Deng Xiaoping Theory as the party's guiding ideology.

On the 80th anniversary of the founding of the CCP in July, Jiang called for the party to admit private entrepreneurs. Although in practice this had been happening for some time (since perhaps as early as 1987), the call for open engagement with this issue signalled a significant step toward reforming the party and reorienting its relationship with Chinese society. A widely ranging debate in Chinese journals could be read throughout the spring and summer, with both support and criticism of the proposed admission of "capitalists" in evidence. An important left-wing opponent of Jiang, Deng Liqun, wrote a scathing criticism of both Jiang's proposed revision of the constitution and of Jiang himself.

The Congress, held in early November, saw the 2,114 delegates select around 200 full members and 150 alternate members of the party's Central Committee, to serve for five years. Although much of the process of orchestrating the Party Congress remained secret, it was clear that from July senior party figures were deeply involved in the negotiations to sideline the current leadership. The Congress opened in November, much later than had been expected, representing the latest starting date of any Congress since the reform period began in 1978. The lack of consensus in the senior leadership over the issue of succession was demonstrated by the unexpected announcement that the size of the Politburo Standing Committee was to be increased from seven members to nine.

The new Chinese leader, 59-year old Hu Jintao, was expected to replace current President Jiang Zemin (aged 76) in most of his main roles by March 2003. However, it was reported that Jiang was to keep his position as chairman of the important Central Military Commission, the body that provided leadership and direction to the Peoples' Liberation Army. This was not unexpected, but speculation varied as to whether it represented an attempt by Jiang to continue to wield de facto influence, or a move to ensure that Hu would not have to worry about military opposition to his leadership. The reason given in the local media for Jiang retaining his position was cited as "the treacherous Taiwan situation".

Speculation abounded as to the significance of the various appointments to the new Standing Committee, especially the extent to which Jiang appeared to have been successful in ensuring that political figures loyal to him were in a majority. The two most significant changes were, firstly, the growing power and influence of Zeng Qinghong, who was widely perceived to be very close to the outgoing President and was believed to be number five in the new hierarchy; and, secondly, the retirement of Li Ruihuan (aged 68), formerly number four in the leadership, who had been expected by many to emerge as the new number two in the leadership hierarchy. Li, with a reputation of being one of the more liberal members of the senior leadership, was widely regarded as a rival to Jiang. An increase in size of the Committee from seven to nine members was widely interpreted as a consequence of the inability to find agreement or consensus among the third generation leadership over who should be appointed.

The end of the Congress in November still left many issues unresolved, as appointments to key posts (such as Secretary-General of the State Council) and the composition of the "Leading Small Groups" which determined much vital day-to-day policy were still to be announced. These matters would remain unclear until after the National People's Congress session scheduled for March 2003.

EXTERNAL AFFAIRS. Consistency and conservatism were the hallmarks of China's foreign relations in 2002. Relations with the USA remained the key bilateral diplomatic concern of the Chinese leadership and China's acquiescence with the US-led "war on terror" remained important for the Bush administration. The importance of Sino-US ties was highlighted by a visit to the USA by Hu Jintao on 28 April-1 May 2002. The visit was widely seen as an attempt by Hu to raise his profile within the PRC as well as to familiarise himself with key political figures in the USA. November saw what was likely to be Jiang's last formal meeting as China's head of state with the US President, when he visited George W. Bush at his ranch in Crawford, Texas. Official transcripts of the conversation were not made available, but it was widely held that the two leaders discussed a range of matters including the "war on terror", the Taiwan question, and Sino-US economic ties. The changing international agenda of the USA following the 11 September 2001 attacks was highlighted by the low level of attention given to the publication in July of a controversial report on US-China relations by a Senate committee, the US-China Security Commission. The review, the result of a 12 month investigation by Congress (the US legislature) into the implications of China's growing military and economic strength, was deeply critical of the PRC and called for a much harder economic and security stance to be taken towards it. The review had been initiated after the serious cooling in Sino-US relations following the incident in April 2001 when a Chinese pilot was killed while intercepting a US spy plane over southern China (see AR 2001, p. 368).

China's other main international relationships remained stable, although relations with Japan were soured by a series of incidents in which North Korean refugees attempted to enter Japanese diplomatic compounds, provoking Chinese security forces to remove them (see IX.2.iv). Also, the Japanese Prime Minster Junichiro Koizumi visited the controversial Yasukuni Shrine in Tokyo to Japan's war dead, a move that prompted considerable criticism in the PRC (see IV.2.iv). The Chinese continued to try to engage North Korea over the nuclear issue, but with little obvious success, and relations with the South East Asian nations were bolstered by a number of multilateral trade agreements.

ii. HONG KONG SPECIAL ADMINISTRATIVE REGION

CAPITAL: Victoria   AREA: 1,000 sq km   POPULATION: 6,900,000
STATUS: Special Administrative Region of People's Republic of China (since 1 July 1997)
CHIEF EXECUTIVE: Tung Chee hwa (since July '97)
ADMINISTRATIVE SECRETARY: Donald Tsang Yam Kuen (since Feb '01), previously Chief Secretary (since Sept '93)
MAIN IGO MEMBERSHIPS (NON-UN): APEC
CURRENCY: Hong Kong dollar (end-'02 £1=HK$12.4903, US$1=HK$7.7989)
GNP PER CAPITA: US$25,920 US$26,050 at PPP ('01)

JULY 2002 saw the fifth anniversary of the reversion of Hong Kong to Chinese sovereignty and the creation of the Hong Kong Special Administrative Region (see AR 1997, pp. 350-51). The local economy remained sluggish, and the Chief Executive Tung Chee-hwa came in for criticism from sections of the Hong Kong and international media for his attempts to reduce the influence of the Hong Kong civil service by increasing his role in appointments and also over proposals for a new national security law.

A major controversy developed over proposals for new laws on "treason secession, sedition, subversion against China, treason and theft of state secrets". These were already covered by Article 23 of the Basic Law which governed Hong Kong, but were not defined. Martin Li of the Democratic Party called the government proposals a serious attack on Hong Kong's political freedoms, while defenders of the proposed laws argued that the proposed changes would make little difference to existing or previous practice and were similar to those on the statute books around the world. Hong Kong's ambivalent position with regard to certain forms of expression was highlighted when 16 followers of the Falun Gong religious cult, outlawed in China, were arrested and charged with obstruction in March.

The Chief Executive's political agenda was dominated by attempted to reform the senior levels of the Hong Kong civil service. Chief Executive Tung Chee hwa had complained of the lack of accountability in the system and revised it to allow the Chief Executive to replace the existing tradition—whereby most members of the Executive Council (Cabinet) were civil servants—with one based on relevant ministers from the private sector. The Chief Secretary, Secretary for Justice, and Financial Secretary would also be appointed by the Chief Executive. A new Cabinet reflecting these changes was appointed in June. Tung claimed that this would promote better performance, whereas his critics suggested that the changes were cosmetic or were an attempt by Tung to increase his power over the civil service, which had in the past resisted some of his initiatives.

The local economy remained troubled in 2002. Employment hovered just below 8 per cent for most of the year, and in the period from April to June a record 10,173 cases of personal and corporate bankruptcy were reported.

iii. TAIWAN

CAPITAL: Taipei   AREA: 35,981 sq km   POPULATION: 22,370,000 (est.)
OFFICIAL LANGUAGE: Chinese   POLITICAL SYSTEM: multiparty republic
HEAD OF STATE AND GOVERNMENT: President Chen Shui-bian (since May '00)
RULING PARTY: Democratic Progressive Party (DPP)
PRIME MINISTER: Yu Hsi-kun (since Jan '02)
MAIN IGO MEMBERSHIPS (NON-UN): APEC
CURRENCY: Taiwan dollar (end-'02 £1=NT$55.8621, US$1=NT$34.8800)
GNI PER CAPITA: US$12,974, $17,200 at PPP ('01)

THIS was a year of uncertainty for Taiwan: political problems beset the ruling administration; local elections showed dissatisfaction with the national leadership, but were generally inconclusive; economic problems continued to mount; and relations with the People's Republic of China (PRC) remained mired in controversial debates concerning the status of the island.

President Chen Shui-bian continued to struggle to maintain unity in his ruling administration, with politics frequently deadlocked over issues that were both principled and petty. In January he conducted a major Cabinet reshuffle (in preparation for the opening session of the newly elected Legislative Yuan), which included the appointment of his presidential secretary general and former Vice Premier, Yu Hsi-kun, as Premier. The impasse between the new legislature and the executive was not as divisive as in 2001 (see AR 2001, pp. 370-73), but this was partly because the ruling Democratic Progressive Party (DPP) steered clear of controversial legislation. The biggest crisis of the year was linked to non-performing loans among grass-roots credit unions.

The ruling DPP performed badly, although not catastrophically so, in local elections in December. Ma Ying-jeou, the incumbent mayor of Taipei, standing for the opposition Nationalist Party (KMT), won an easy victory taking 64 per cent of the vote, while his main opponent, the DPP's Lee Ying-yuan, polled just 36 percent. This increased Ma's margin of victory over his opponent by 13 per cent, compared with the 1998 contest. Commentators also remarked that voter turnout had fallen by 10 per cent (to 70.61 per cent) since the previous poll, suggesting a growing disillusionment with electoral politics. Ma's success increased speculation that he would stand as the KMT's candidate in the 2004 presidential election. The DPP also did poorly in the election in Taiwan's second city, Kaohsiung. The DPP incumbent, Frank Hsieh, managed to retain his seat, but polled just 50 per cent of the vote, narrowly beating his KMT opponent, Huang Jun-ying, who won 47 per cent of votes cast. Again, voter turnout was down on 1998.

Relations between Taiwan and the PRC were marked by a series of arguments over Taiwan's status. Cross-Straits relations began on a controversial note in January when the government announced that the English words "Issued in Taiwan" would be added to the cover of Republic of China (ROC) passports from November. The announcement was strongly criticised by the government of the PRC as part of an agenda to promote Taiwan's separation from China. These tensions were exacerbated in August when President Chen stated that there was "one country on either side of the Taiwan Straits", echoing the controversial "special state-to-state" relations speech of former President Lee Teng-hui in 1999 (see AR 1999, pp. 365-67. In comparison to the 1999 incident, the response from the PRC was subdued, with only mild criticism and some warnings about the consequences for the island of any move toward independence. However the statement did cause important complications with Taiwan's relations with the USA; the chairman of the Mainland Affairs Council, Tsai Ying-wen, had to travel to Washington DC to reassure the Bush administration that Taiwan was not about to complicate the US-PRC relationship at a time when the USA strongly wanted Chinese diplomatic goodwill in the face of mounting tensions over Iraq.

Despite the arguments over form and status, there was progress in a number of areas related to cross-Straits relations. Entry into the World Trade Organisation (WTO) by both Taiwan and the PRC in January meant that both countries could now approach each other directly via an international forum; and although disputes over steel tariffs clouded the relationship, Taiwanese investors regarded the new relationship in a positive light. In addition, discussions reached an advanced stage over the possibility of allowing direct flights between Taiwan and China in time for the start of the Chinese New Year in February 2003.

The Taiwanese economy maintained steady growth through 2002, with GDP increasing by a reported 3 per cent, but with unemployment reaching a record high of 5 per cent. In May the government's Council for Economic Planning and Development (CEPD) unveiled its "Challenge 2008" initiative, a plan to spend US$75 billion over the next six years on national projects ranging from infrastructure and public construction plans to information technology development. As part of this plan, in December the Cabinet agreed an economic stimulus package of US$2 billion, mainly to be spent on infrastructure and public construction.

January saw Taiwan's entry into full membership of the WTO, and this generated a number of immediate problems. Taiwan was widely criticised for its failure adequately to address issues of copyright piracy, and relations with the PRC were strained because of the imposition of tariffs on Taiwanese steel exports across the Taiwan Straits. There were also immediate domestic impacts, with the price of fruit and vegetables falling by between 20 and 50 per cent. The changing tariffs on alcohol products saw rice wine increase rapidly in price, which in turn led to bootlegging and illegal production. The deaths of 10 people following consumption of bootlegged wine in November saw widespread panic and more serious attempts by the government to address the issue of illegal production.

Even greater problems in the agricultural sector derived from President Chen's decision in November unilaterally to suspend the Ministry of Finance plan to reform the credit unions of the various farmers' and fishermen's associations The credit associations were in severe financial difficulties because of the growth in non-performing loans, and government plans to reform them and reduce available credit generated considerable anger in the agricultural sector. The dispute was deeply damaging to the credibility of the DPP, disillusioned its grass roots supporters, and led to significant splits within the DPP and among its allies. The Finance Minister, Lee Yung-san, and the chairman of the Council of Agriculture, Fan Chen-tsung, resigned over the matter, and 23 November saw a demonstration by an estimated 120,000 farmers and fishermen in Taipei. Credit issues were particularly acute in 2002 because the floods that came in late 2001 were followed by the worst drought that northern Taiwan had seen in over 20 years, with water levels in the two main reservoirs at their lowest ever recorded levels. Agricultural land was left fallow and water rationing imposed on much of northern Taiwan, including Taipei. The drought in turn led to a serious dispute between the KMT-controlled city government and the DPP Cabinet over control of, and responsibility for water rights to, Taiwan's main reservoir. The crisis eased following the arrival of the first typhoons in July.

The appalling safety record of the main Taiwanese air carrier, China Airlines (CAL), was demonstrated again in May when an ageing CAL aircraft broke up in mid air en route to Hong Kong, killing all 225 people on board. This followed three fatal crashes in the late 1990s. The reputation of CAL was further tarnished as it argued with the relatives of the victims over appropriate levels of compensation and appeared to renege on a promise to improve its maintenance and repair sections.

The relationship with the USA was in the spotlight in 2002. In April, Paul Wolfowitz, the US Deputy Defence Secretary, publicly restated US President Bush's pledge of April 2001 to "protect" Taiwan (see AR 2001, pp. 372-73). This was highly contentious as it could have been seen as marking the end of the policy of "strategic ambiguity" that had been at the core of US policy on the Taiwan question since the early 1970s. In the absence of any official clarification on the Wolfowitz statement, speculation continued as to whether there had been a shift in US policy. A 10-day visit to Washington DC, New York, and Los Angeles in September by Wu Shu-chen, wife of President Chen, was hailed as a breakthrough by sections of the Taiwanese press, but for others it simply highlighted Taiwan's impotence because of its need to rely on informal diplomacy, since the power and influence of the PRC was sufficient to prevent formal diplomatic contacts.

iv. JAPAN

CAPITAL: Tokyo   AREA: 378,000 sq km   POPULATION: 127,100,000
OFFICIAL LANGUAGE: Japanese   POLITICAL SYSTEM: multiparty monarchy
HEAD OF STATE: Emperor Tsugu no Miya Akihito (since Jan '89)
RULING PARTIES: Liberal Democratic Party (LDP) leads coalition with New Komeito & New Conservative (Hoshu Shinto) parties
HEAD OF GOVERNMENT: Junichiro Koizumi, Prime Minister (since April '01)
MAIN IGO MEMBERSHIPS (NON-UN): APEC, CP, OECD, G-8
CURRENCY: yen (end-'02 £1=Y192.186, US$1=Y120.000)
GNI PER CAPITA: US$35,990, US$27,430 at PPP ('01)

THROUGHOUT the year Japan was governed by a coalition Cabinet under Junichiro Koizumi, consisting of the Liberal-Democratic Party (LDP), the New Komeito, and the New Conservative Party (Hoshu Shinto). Koizumi of the LDP had been Prime Minister since April 2001 but his high initial popularity rating was falling. There was continued weakness in the economy and great pessimism about stimulating it despite widely differing remedies for dealing with its major problems. Koizumi was intent on reform which, he reiterated, was a bitter pill that had to be swallowed if declining productivity was to be cured. But he faced an uphill struggle from factions within the LDP who opposed his proposed reforms because, they feared, their radical nature could cause the collapse of the economy, already weakened by the downturn in the global economic situation.

The political and economic gloom was relieved by some successes in international affairs. Though the year was not a good one for the Foreign Ministry, US-Japanese relations remained strong, cemented by US President George W. Bush's visit in February. (Japan was generally supportive of its US ally's efforts in the Indian Ocean area, sending there in December an Aegis-equipped destroyer to provide logistic support for the continuing military campaign against terrorists in Afghanistan.) The co-hosting of the Football World Cup was another highlight which enhanced Japan's reputation abroad and created an enthusiasm at home, which had not been seen since the Tokyo Olympics some 40 years previously (see AR 1964, p. 360).

The year started in Tokyo with an international conference on Afghanistan at which Japan had been asked to take the lead in planning financial aid to the new Afghan state. The conference, which was presided over by Sadako Ogata, the former UN High Commissioner for Refugees, was a great success and a testimony to Japan's capacity to play a large and responsible role in global affairs. But it also generated an unexpected domestic crisis. Two Japanese non-governmental organisations were deliberately prevented from attending by Foreign Ministry action. This was met with a widespread public outcry, and the order was subsequently rescinded. In the enquiry that followed, it seemed to emerge that the Foreign Ministry had responded to pressure from a senior member of the LDP, Muneo Suzuki. In the contentious atmosphere which this created, Koizumi asked for the resignation of Makiko Tanaka from the post of Foreign Minister. Tanaka had hitherto been one of Koizumi's staunchest allies over his reform programme and one of the most popular members of his Cabinet. She, in turn, made a series of bitter attacks on the Prime Minister; and there was speculation that she might try to challenge

Koizumi's leadership. She was, however, suspended from the LDP in July for two years, thereby preventing her from running as a party candidate. Finally, because of allegations that she had misused secretaries' salaries, she resigned from the Diet (the bicameral legislature) in August.

Yoriko Kawaguchi, the former Environment Minister, was appointed as Tanaka's successor as Foreign Minister on 1 February. She spent much of the year reforming the ministry, a process started in radical fashion under Tanaka. One aspect of the reform plan was intended to prevent undue influence being exerted by politicians over ministry bureaucrats. The immediate cause of the trouble, the above-mentioned Suzuki, was arrested in June on bribery charges and eventually resigned from the LDP.

Another senior politician who had to leave the Diet was Koichi Kato, one of Koizumi's closest lieutenants, over a scandal involving political funding. The Speaker of the House of Councillors (the upper chamber), Yutaka Inoue, also resigned in similar circumstances. This series of scandals had its effect on the government's reputation, the LDP losing a by-election in Niigata in May and the mayoral election in Yokohama. It may have been from a desire to restore some popularity to his party that Koizumi decided to pay a surprise visit on 22 April to the Yasukuni shrine, Tokyo, which commemorated the nation's war dead (including some convicted war criminals). This was an act which won him praise from the nationalist lobby but was bitterly criticised in China and South Korea, as it had been in the past when similar visits had been made on the anniversary of the end of World War II (see AR 2001, p. 375).

Instead of the export-driven recovery which the government had been predicting, there was a financial down-turn which was internationally recognised when Moody's and other agencies downgraded Japan's credit-rating on 31 May. The government was deeply upset and complained about this "unjust act", taken despite Finance Ministry protests.

The Foreign Ministry, which had come under attack for the misuse of discretionary funds and its ineptitude in implementing foreign policies, unveiled its wide-ranging reform proposals in August. These included the slimming down of numbers in the ministry, the need for improved co-ordination between it and related ministries particularly trade ones, better promotion prospects for personnel and the elimination of cliques. The fact that the Foreign Ministry was in the spotlight was damaging when many other countries were encouraging Japan to assume a larger diplomatic role.

In May and June Japan co-hosted with South Korea the FIFA World Football Cup, the first time that the event had taken place in Asia (see XVI). This involved the building of new stadia in prefectural capitals around the country and generally improving the infrastructure. Between the time when the opening match was played in South Korea on 31 May and the final in Yokohama on 30 June, the prevailing economic and political gloom evaporated. The games were efficiently organised, no major international incidents occurred, and the Japanese team performed well, reaching the second round. It was a prestige event, important alike for tourism, international media coverage, and national pride.

One of the consequences of the World Cup was that relations with South Korea, traditionally fragile, improved. A much-needed rapprochement took place after years of recrimination. But it was two episodes affecting North Korea that became the focus of attention. Early in May five North Koreans took refuge in the Japanese consulate-general in Shenyang (formerly Mukden), China. Chinese police entered the grounds and forcibly evicted them. This was a violation of diplomatic privilege and was denounced in the Japanese media as a national affront. Japan protested and demanded an apology on the grounds that it was contrary to the Foreign Ministry's stated aims of protecting asylum-seekers that Japan should permit their arrest. Enquiries were launched on both sides but their reports were contradictory.

Secondly, Koizumi took the bold step on 17 September of paying a one-day visit to President Kim Jong-Il of North Korea in the North Korean capital, Pyongyang. There seemed to be evidence that the North Korean regime was seeking better relations with its neighbours. Preparations for the visit had been made over the preceding year and discussed with the USA. Koizumi made clear that he wanted to keep diplomatic protocol to a minimum, would not stay overnight, or expect any official banquet to be arranged. In the joint declaration which was issued after the talks, Japan apologised for her colonial occupation of Korea and offered substantial economic aid in compensation. In return Kim Jong-Il unexpectedly apologised for the abduction of 12 Japanese nationals from Japanese territory which had taken place 24 years earlier. This superseded years of North Korean denials that any kidnappings had occurred. Kim's admission was surprising, both because the apology was given voluntarily and because it was so far-reaching (see IX.2.vi).

Japan hoped to bring North Korea out of the cold and end its diplomatic isolation. Koizumi's gamble paid off and he regained some of his former popularity. But his trip was followed on 25 October by North Korea announcing that it was not going to end its nuclear weapons programme and would reactivate its nuclear reactor, a statement which contradicted some of the key assurances which Koizumi had received on nuclear matters.

The arrangements whereby the five survivors of the kidnappings were permitted to return temporarily to Japan did not work well. The five visited their homeland in October amid a spate of publicity and made tearful contact with their relatives. But the knowledge that so many of the 12 abductees had died aroused the suspicion and anger of the Japanese public to such an extent that Japan would not allow the five survivors to return to North Korea. It was not surprising, then, that the normalisation talks between Japanese and North Korean officials which opened in Kuala Lumpur, Malaysia, at the end of the month ended in deadlock.

A minor Cabinet reshuffle took place in the autumn. The important change was the promotion of Heizo Takenaka, an economist and unelected member of the Cabinet, to a new post as Economic and Financial Services Minister, combining responsibility for economic and fiscal policy. With the country in deep recession this was clearly a critical portfolio. Koizumi's difficulties in obtaining consensus within the LDP meant that his reform proposals encountered massive opposition. Thus, for example, he was unable to push through the reform of the national postal service, one of his favourite programmes. In October Takenaka, who was unpopular with the banks, produced a report on how to use public funds to support those banks which were saddled with non-performing loans, but it was unacceptable to the LDP and members of the ruling coalition. He was forced to modify his proposals substantially on 30 October when he unveiled his package of measures to fight deflation and clean up bad debts in the banking system by stricter evaluation of bad loans and an injection of public funds into the banks.

On the more encouraging front of foreign trade, there were significant developments. In January during his visit to south-east Asian countries, Koizumi signed a Free Trade Agreement with the Singapore government, the first concluded by Japan. He also advocated in a speech "comprehensive economic co-operation between Japan and the states of the Association of Southeast Asian Nations" (ASEAN). In March he clinched a Free Trade Agreement with President Kim Dae-Jung of South Korea. Early in November Japan received from China a proposal for a tripartite free trade arrangement between China, South Korea, and Japan, similar to one already put to ASEAN. Japan was not enthusiastic, seeing it as the start of a struggle for leadership in east Asia.

It was a strange year in politics where the opposition parties were too divided to present a serious challenge to the government and where the Prime Minister found himself out of line with influential members of the LDP and reliant on support from the official opposition. The year ended with two unexpected political mergers. In November Yukio Hatoyama, president of the Democratic Party of Japan (DPJ), agreed a merger with the president of the small Liberal Party in the hope of creating a stronger opposition. When he put the proposal to his party executive, however, it was defeated; Hatoyama was instead forced to resign and was replaced by Naoto Kan. Quite independently of this, a new party was launched in December after a merger between the New Conservative Party (Hoshu Shinto) and defectors from the DPJ. But the number of legislators who finally acceded to it was smaller than expected. So Koizumi's LDP-dominated coalition, in spite of its internal disagreements, was still not seriously challenged. On 27 October the governing coalition had success in five out of seven by-elections which it fought, although the turn out was unprecedentedly low.

Distinguished Japanese who died included Shizue Kato (January), the feminist campaigner for birth control; Koki Ishii (October), member of the opposition DPJ, the victim of a political assassination; and Professor Saburo Ienaga (November), the radical historian famous alike for his long-running legal campaigns against the Ministry of Education over its censorship of textbooks and for his writings on Japan's history in the 1930s and 1940s, particularly his monograph, *The Pacific War, 1931-45*. Prince Takamado, cousin of the current Emperor, who had made a great contribution in the international cultural field, died in November at the age of 47.

The Nobel Prize for Chemistry was awarded to Koichi Tanaka of the Shimazu Corporation and that for Physics to Masatoshi Koshiba, emeritus professor at Tokyo University (in each case shared with two others). The winner of the Tchaikovsky music prize in the piano category was Ayako Uehara, the first Japanese to win the title.

v. SOUTH KOREA

CAPITAL: Seoul   AREA: 99,000 sq km   POPULATION: 47,600,000
OFFICIAL LANGUAGE: Korean   POLITICAL SYSTEM: multiparty republic
HEAD OF STATE AND GOVERNMENT: President Kim Dae Jung (since Feb '98)
PRESIDENT ELECT: Roh Moo Hyun (from Feb '03)
RULING PARTIES: Millennium Democratic Party (MDP), formerly the National Congress for New Politics, and United Liberal Democrats (ULD)
PRIME MINISTER: Kim Suk Soo, since Oct '02
MAIN IGO MEMBERSHIPS (NON-UN): APEC, CP, OECD
CURRENCY: won (end-'02 £1=W1,918.26, US$1=W1197.75)
GNI PER CAPITA: US$9,400, US$18,110 at PPP ('01)

IT was a year of passion and frenzy in South Korea that brought virtually the entire population onto the streets in reaction to one or other major event, be it the presidential elections, the football World Cup, or anti-US demonstrations.

The most significant development in 2002 was the so-called "generational earthquake" that dismantled the foundations of the South Korean political establishment, in which seniority and educational background, rather than merit and vision, were the traditional criteria for leadership. On 19 December Roh Moo Hyun, a self-taught and self-made human rights lawyer, the candidate of the ruling Millennium Democratic Party (MDP), won the presidential elections with 49.9 per cent of the vote. Roh's victory was unprecedented, since he had no university education and, more significantly, owed no debts to any of the country's *chaebols* (family-controlled conglomerates) or any powerful political allies. The following day, Lee Hoi Chang, of the Grand National Party (GNP), who had been Roh's closest rival in the elections (achieving 46.6 per cent of the vote), announced his retirement from politics after having failed in his second attempt on the presidency. President-elect, Roh, was due to take over from President Kim Dae Jung in February 2003.

Another major event in South Korea in 2002 was the finals of the football World Cup that the country co-hosted with Japan (see IX.2.iv; XVI). The frenzy generated by the event, and particularly the national side's outstanding performance in defeating some of the best football teams in the world, engendered passion and zeal for the nation. The mantras *"Daehan Minguk!"* (Republic of Korea!) and *"O, Pilsung Korea!"* (Oh, Victory Korea!) came to assume the status of a national anthem for the "Red Devils", the supporters of the national team in their "Be the Reds" T-shirts. Guus Hiddink, the Dutch coach of the Korean national team, was given a larger-than-life sized statue and was also rewarded with the status of honorary citizenship from the South Korean government.

The third focus of national attention was the strained relationship between South Korea and the USA, evident during the first visit of US President George W. Bush to the country in February which was dogged by student protests. Public concern was centred in particular on the Status of Forces Agreement (SOFA) regarding the stationing of US military forces in South Korea. A further blow to the already discredited image of the USA among the much of the Korean population occurred when, on 13 June, two 13-year old school girls, Shin Hyo-Sun and Shim Mi-Seon, were killed by a US Army truck that was on a training exercise 30 km south of the border with North Korea. Their deaths created uproar as many thousands of people came to vent their grief and anger by demonstrating at all the possible venues. Candlelit rallies commemorating the two girls were organised in all major cities. The two US soldiers involved in the accident were acquitted of charges of negligent homicide by a US court martial five months later, the US authorities having refused to allow them to be tried in a South Korean court. This deeply-unpopular verdict resulted in the outbreak of a nationwide campaign against US attitudes and policies toward the Korean peninsula.

Among other notable developments in 2002 were events that severely damaged President Kim Dae-Jung's policies and reputation. On 1 November, the Seoul District Court sentenced the second of the President's three sons, Kim Hong-Up, to 42 months in prison; on 11 November, the President's youngest son, Kim Hong-Gul, was jailed for two years. Both of them were also heavily fined for accepting bribes from business circles in return for exerting influence to win government contracts. President Kim was also opposed in the National Assembly (the unicameral legislature) for his nomination to the largely ceremonial post of Prime Minister of Chang Sang, the president of Ewha Woman's University, who was the first ever woman to be nominated for the post. Legislators objected to her alleged involvement in real estate speculation and her misrepresentation of her academic credentials. A month later, in August, Kim's second choice for Prime Minister—Chang Dae-Hwan, a former newspaper executive—was also rejected following accusations of tax evasion and embezzlement. Kim Suk Soo, a former Supreme Court judge, was approved as Prime Minister in October. In a separate case, a representative of the opposition GNP, Eom Ho-Sung, alleged that the US$400 million in emergency loans given to Hyundai Merchant Marine by the Korea Development Bank had gone secretly to North Korea before the historic meeting of the two Kims in 2000 (see AR 2000, pp. 345-46).

South Korea suffered from natural disasters during the year. In August a heavy storm and flooding caused enormous damage, both in terms of human lives as well as the destruction of property after the arrival of Typhoon Rusa in Chungcheong and Gangwon provinces. About 270 people were reported dead and missing, and the damage was estimated at US$750 million.

vi. NORTH KOREA

CAPITAL: Pyongyang   AREA: 123,370 sq km   POPULATION: 22,384,000
OFFICIAL LANGUAGE: Korean   POLITICAL SYSTEM: one-party republic
RULING PARTY: Korean Workers' Party (KWP)
PARTY LEADER: Kim Jong Il, KWP general secretary (since Oct '97)
PRIME MINISTER: Hong Song Nam (since Sept '98)
MAIN IGO MEMBERSHIPS (NON-UN): NAM
CURRENCY: won (end-'02 £1=W3.5234, US$1=W2.2000)
GNP PER CAPITA: US$741 ('97 South Korean est.)

NORTH KOREA in 2002 was a source of dramatic developments for observers of the peninsula. The inclusion of the state within the "axis of evil" conjured up in US President George W. Bush's State of the Union address (see IV.1) seemed for many to be realised at the end of the year when the country announced that it had restarted its nuclear programme (see below). On the domestic front, the news about massive adjustments of wages and prices that began on 1 July started to spread. One official source in the capital, Pyongyang, was cited as saying that the official price of rice had gone up from 0.08 won per kilo to 30-35 won. The price rises were also reported to have affected areas such as housing, electricity, fuel, and transport. Whilst this news came as a surprise, it also engendered hopes that the North Korean hermit state was loosening its tightly controlled and centralised economy, and was attempting to rectify the chronic food shortages of recent years.

Observers of politics in the region saw another unexpectedly encouraging development in the ground-breaking visit by Japan's Prime Minister Junichiro Koizumi to North Korea in September (see IX.2.iv). The North Korean leader, Kim Jong-Il, expressed an apology for the abduction of 12 Japanese civilians during the 1970s and 1980s. This was a major breakthrough as Japan had demanded an explanation of the fate of its missing citizens as a precondition for talks. But in terms of inter-Korean relations, North Korea did not hesitate to strike at South Korean President Kim Dae Jung's "Sunshine Policy" of rapprochement when the two Koreas engaged in a 21 minute naval skirmish along the "northern limit line" of the Yellow Sea on 29 June. The incident, which claimed lives on both sides, occurred after a North Korean naval vessel crossed three miles south of the line (a maritime border which the North did not recognise) and opened fire on a South Korean patrol boat that was warning the North Korean ship to retreat.

The international community received a more serious shock when, on 4 October, North Korea confessed that it was secretly continuing its nuclear programme in contravention of the 1994 Framework Agreement with the USA, under which North Korea had agreed to halt all of its nuclear activities and submit to nuclear inspections in return for economic assistance in the form of heating oil and the construction of two light water reactors by an international consortium, the Korean Peninsula Energy Development Organisation, (KEDO—see AR 1994, p. 460). North Korea announced in October, following a visit from a US delegation, that it considered the 1994 agreement "nullified". After the talks, during which the US side had confronted the North Koreans with US intelligence that North Korea was attempted to obtain enriched uranium, the North Korean government admitted pursuing a ballistic missile programme, and also to possessing some "powerful things".

The construction of the first of two light water reactors had been inaugurated at a ceremony in August. However, North Korea, under increasing pressure from the USA to allow comprehensive inspections by the International Atomic Energy Agency (IAEA) of all its nuclear facilities, threatened to withdraw from the project because of what it said were delays in building the reactors caused by the USA.

On 12 December, the government announced that it was going to remove all the equipment seals and monitoring cameras from its nuclear facilities at the Yongbyon complex, 90 km north of Pyongyang, and restart the nuclear power plant. The Yongbyon complex had been monitored by the IAEA since 1994, and was believed by the USA to be capable of producing sufficient plutonium within a year for two nuclear weapons. North Korea claimed that the decision to restart Yongbyon had been taken in response to KEDO's actions in November—the halting of the supply of fuel oil to the country, at the instigation of the USA—and announced that it would henceforth generate electricity at its nuclear reactors. On 27 December North Korea expelled from Yongbyon two IAEA inspectors who had reported to the IAEA the previous day that new fuel rods were being moved to the reactor. North Korea's actions, undertaken at a time when the attention of the USA was focused on Iraq's alleged weapons of mass destruction, caused consternation within the international community.

vii. MONGOLIA

CAPITAL: Ulan Bator   AREA: 1,564,116 sq km   POPULATION: 2,400,000
OFFICIAL LANGUAGE: Halh (Khalkha) Mongolia   POLITICAL SYSTEM: multiparty republic
HEAD OF STATE AND GOVERNMENT: President Natsagiyn Bagabandi (since June '97)
RULING PARTY: Mongolian People's Revolutionary Party (MPRP)
PRIME MINISTER: Nambaryn Enhbayar (since July '00)
MAIN IGO MEMBERSHIPS (NON-UN): NAM, EBRD
CURRENCY: tugrik (end-'02 £1=T1,798.54, US$1=T1,123.00)
GNI PER CAPITA: US$400, US$1,800 at PPP ('01)

PRIME Minister Nambaryn Enhbayar, leader of the ruling Mongolian People's Revolutionary Party (MPRP), faced new challenges as he entered his third year of office. Opposition Democratic Party (DP) member Lamjavyn Gündalay disrupted Enhbayar's opening address to the autumn session of the Great Hural (the unicameral legislature) by displaying a series of slogans before the television cameras. His slogan "I would like to speak!" protested against the MPRP government's June 2001 resolution limiting the right to speak at the opening of Great Hural sessions to legislative parties with eight or more members (there were only four opposition members). Gündalay's slogan "760 million twice is a state bribe!" referred to his accusation that the MPRP government had secretly distributed 10 million tugrik to each of the MPRP members of the Great Hural to spend in their constituencies in 2001, and planned to do the same in 2002. Other slogans included "Stop putting journalists in prison!" and "Stop the land swindle!" The protests forced state television's live coverage of proceedings to be cut. Gündalay later described Mongolia as an "elective dictatorship".

The Laws on Land and on Land Privatisation, adopted in June and scheduled to come into force in 2003, limited the area to be privatised to 1 per cent of the country's territory, but the tradition of common ownership of land made them controversial. In November farmers of the Movement for the Just Privatisation of Land demonstrated in Ulan Bator, the capital, against MPRP land policy. The demonstrators, headed by Erdeniyn Bat-Üül, a DP leader, claimed that land would be bought up by the "oligarchy". When tractors were parked illegally on Sühbaatar Square the police arrested demonstrators and journalists and surrounded the DP's headquarters.

"Justice", a group of dissident MPRP members headed by Galigaagiyn Bayarsayhan, called in May for greater democracy and transparency in the appointment of MPRP leaders, a process that they said was reverting to the practices of the 1970s and 1980s. The MPRP denied the existence of any party group of this name, but "Justice" was supported in the press by victims of political repression in the 1960s, who claimed that Enhbayar was resorting to old "Communist methods".

The government in 2002 declared the 840th anniversary (calculated by 14 60-year cycles of the traditional lunar calendar) of the birth of Genghis Khan, founder of the Mongol Empire. The celebrations included a state ceremony in May to lay the foundations of a new statue and a commemorative session of the 8th congress of the International Association for Mongol Studies in August.

Russian Prime Minister Mikhail Kasyanov's visit in March ended in confusion after Russian press reports that Mongolia had agreed to repay at par with the US dollar its Soviet aid debt of 11.5 billion "transferable roubles" (the Soviet-era international accounting unit). Prime Minister Enhbayar went on Mongolian television to say that, while methods of repaying the debt had been discussed, there was still no agreement with Russia on its dollar equivalent.

UN Secretary General Kofi Annan visited Ulan Bator briefly in October. At the invitation of the Buddhist community, the Dalai Lama spent a week in Mongolia, arriving in early November from Japan. During his visit China closed its border with Mongolia for 33 hours for "technical reasons", holding up several goods and passenger trains.

The July meeting in Ulan Bator of the consultative group on aid for Mongolia agreed a one-year aid package of US$333 million. A 76 per cent share in the Mongolian Trade and Development Bank was bought for some US$12 million by a consortium formed by Banca Commerciale Lugano and the US company Gerald Metals. Economic growth in 2002 reached 3.7 per cent while inflation fell to 3.1 per cent, but the revised budget deficit was US$64.8 million and the foreign trade deficit fell only slightly to US$158 million. The annual livestock census in December showed a further fall to 23.7 million head.

X AUSTRALASIA AND THE PACIFIC

1. AUSTRALIA—PAPUA NEW GUINEA

i. AUSTRALIA

CAPITAL: Canberra AREA: 7,741,000 sq km POPULATION: 19,400,000
OFFICIAL LANGUAGE: English POLITICAL SYSTEM: multiparty system in British Commonwealth
HEAD OF STATE: Queen Elizabeth II (since Feb '52)
GOVERNOR-GENERAL: Peter Hollingworth
RULING PARTIES: Liberal-National coalition
HEAD OF GOVERNMENT: John Howard, Prime Minister (since March '96)
MAIN IGO MEMBERSHIPS (NON-UN): APEC, PC, PIF, CP, ANZUS, OECD, CWTH
CURRENCY: Australian dollar (end-'02 £1=A$2.8553, US$1=A$1.7828)
GNI PER CAPITA: US$19,770, US$25,780 at PPP ('01)

TERRORISM'S impact hit Australia directly for the first time in October when bomb blasts at Kuta, Bali killed 88 mostly young Australian holiday makers (see IX.1.vi). The year was marked by continuing controversy over the detention of asylum seekers, culminating in the burning of most of the mainland centres at the end of the year. The economy continued to be sound. Even the dollar began to rise in value although there was a consistent trade deficit. The May budget went into deficit largely because of increased defence and border protection costs. A severe drought began late in the year, prepared the way for the bushfires which were to ravage much of the country in early 2003.

The central feature of national politics was the consolidation of the popularity of Liberal Prime Minister John Howard and the lacklustre impact of the Australian Labor Party (ALP) leader Simon Crean. Unusually all the eight state and territory governments were controlled by the opposition ALP, while the Liberal and National coalition remained effectively unchallenged at the national level. The Greens continued to enjoy significant support in the polls, eating into the constituency of the Australian Democrats, who were in disarray. The One Nation party continued to fade into oblivion (see AR 2000, p. 355). The national government was able to benefit from the perception that it had defended Australia against unauthorised asylum seekers and would continue to do so against terrorists. However there was some uncertainty about involvement in a US-led war against Iraq, with the ALP opposition firming up its criticism of any participation which was not sanctioned by the UN. The year was also characterised by media speculation about the possible retirement of Howard, but there was no evidence on which to base this and his confidence and popular support only increased as the year advanced.

The success of the Liberal and National parties at the national level was not reflected in the states where there was leadership instability and electoral defeat. In South Australia, the only state under Liberal control at the start of the year, the ALP under Mike Rann achieved a narrow victory on 9 February and formed a minority administration which depended on the support of two independents who had previously been in the Liberal Party.

South Australia election

Party	% of votes	Seats in Legislative Assembly
ALP	36.8	23
Liberal	39.6	20
Independents	14	4
Australian Democrats	7.3	-
Greens	2.3	-

The halving of support for the Australian Democrats in their strongest state began a process which threw the party into increasing disarray. There was acrimony over the independents' support for the ALP, and the outgoing government presented itself for a vote of confidence which it lost by one vote.

Tasmania voted on 20 July with a landslide victory for the sitting government of Jim Bacon.

Tasmania election

Party	% of votes	Seats in Legislative Assembly
ALP	52.3	15
Liberal	26.9	6
Greens	18.2	4
Democrats	0.7	-
Others	1.9	-

Victoria went to the polls on 30 November with another landslide for the government of Steve Bracks.

Victoria election

Party	% of votes	Seats in Legislative Assembly
ALP	47.9	62
Liberals	33.9	17
Nationals	4.3	7
Greens	9.7	-
Others	4.2	2

The ALP won control of the upper chamber in the Victoria legislature, the Council, for the first time with 25 seats compared with 14 for the Liberals and five for the Nationals. This gave it an opportunity to change the electoral system in order to bring it into line with that in other states which used systems based on proportional representation.

A less satisfactory result for the ALP was at the federal by-election for Cunningham in October, where the steel town of Wollongong was considered so safe for the ALP that the Liberals did not contest it. In the event ALP complacency proved unfounded as the Green candidate was elected as the first member from his party to sit in the House of Representatives (the lower chamber of Parliament, the bicameral Australian legislature). The collapse of the Australian Democrat vote again indicated that the party was in serious trouble and was losing its following to the Greens. The ALP loss, when compared with the state-level victories, once again prompted criticism of the national leader, Simon Crean. He was, however, able to steer important organisational changes through a special party conference in October.

These volatile elections paralleled several changes in party leadership, including the overthrow of the Liberal leaders in New South Wales, Victoria, and Tasmania. The national leader of the Democrats, Natasha Stott-Despoja, was forced out in August and replaced by Senator Andrew Bartlett. The party had already lost one Senator when former leader Meg Lees resigned in July.

Corporate Australia continued to be unstable with liquidations and takeovers (see AR 2001, p. 386). The earlier collapse of HIH Insurance led to a royal commission on its affairs which continued throughout the year and heard much critical comment. The long-established two airlines policy finally disappeared with the liquidation of Ansett in March, leaving Qantas facing major competition only from Virgin Blue (see AR 2001, p. 386). United Medical Protection, the largest medical indemnity insurer, was liquidated in May, leaving the government to guarantee its un-funded liabilities. Losses by the state-owned medical insurer Medibank caused an increase in its fees in September.

Lack of control over the Senate frustrated the government on several issues, most importantly in its failure to secure the sale of the remaining 51 per cent of the telecommunication company Telstra. This proposal had already caused some tension within the coalition, with the National Party anxious to protect those of its rural constituents who required uneconomic services. Eventually an alliance between the ALP, the Democrats, and some independents forced Treasurer Peter Costello to announce on 27 November that no sale would be possible before 2004. Offers to use the proceeds for environmental projects failed to influence Democrat or Green senators, although promises of rural subsidies were more attractive to the Nationals. Majority public opinion was recorded in the polls as against the sale.

Important non-economic issues included the legalisation of stem cell research using in vitro embryos. This was opposed by the Catholic Church and by some conservative Ministers, though not by the Prime Minister. A free vote was allowed, cutting across the parties, and the legislation was passed in the House of Representatives by 99 votes to 33 in September and in the Senate by 45 votes to 26 in December. Following the shooting of two students at Monash University the Commonwealth negotiated a buy-back agreement for automatic handguns with the states in December. It was less successful in replacing the

National Crime Authority, however, which also required approval by the states, and had to be content with a new Australian Crime Commission which would lack security and intelligence powers. A similar fate had been suffered by anti-terrorism legislation introduced in April but amended by the Senate to limit the arrest powers of the Australian Security Intelligence Organisation and the right to proscribe organisations.

Australia pursued an active foreign policy during the year, declaring its full support for the USA in its conflict with Iraq and improving its relationship with Indonesia which had been damaged by support for Timorese independence (see AR 1999, p. 380). The Bali bombing in October saw close co-operation between Australian and Indonesian police and intelligence. Howard travelled extensively during the year, visiting the USA twice, China, Germany, Greece, Italy, and Indonesia. His influence in Asia was, however, diminished in December when he stated that Australia had the right to make a "pre-emptive strike" into Asia in pursuit of terrorists. The opposition became increasingly critical of Australia's attitude towards the USA by mid-year, arguing that the priority for Australia was not to the Middle East but the Pacific rim, where instability in the Solomon Islands continued to be the most significant local problem after the threat of Islamic extremism in Indonesia (see X.2.ii).

The "Pacific solution" of interning asylum seekers on Nauru or Manus Island (in Papua New Guinea) continued throughout the year with over 500 still being held on Nauru at the end of the year (see AR 2001, p. 385). With the defeat of the Taliban in Afghanistan, offers of repatriation were made to Afghan asylum seekers, some of which were taken up. Policy towards Iraqi nationals was inhibited by the prospect of military intervention. Only a handful of asylum seekers were accepted by other countries, apart from New Zealand, and Australia began moving some to Australia on temporary protection visas. Those already in Australia became increasingly restive at long delays and conditions in detention centres, especially at Woomera. Riots, demonstrations, and attempts at escape became common and were widely covered in the media. The numbers detained gradually fell as no new boats arrived. Claims made during the 2001 election that some asylum seekers had thrown their children into the water when engaged by Australian warships were shown by a Senate enquiry to be untrue. The ALP opposition modified its previous support for government detention policy, but only in detail and with the aim of humanising conditions, especially by ending the detention of women and children. Popular opinion became polarised but the government assumed it had majority support and made few concessions.

Both the governor general, Peter Hollingworth, and the Catholic Archbishop of Sydney, George Pell, were embarrassed by claims of sexual harassment in their respective churches. Criticism of the governor general by the opposition and the media was ineffective as he had the support of the Prime Minister. New South Wales police commissioner Peter Ryan resigned in April after tension with the state government. In July Gen. Peter Cosgrove became head of the defence forces (see AR 2000, p. 353), while in December Max Moore-Wilton retired as secretary of the Department of Prime Minister and Cabinet. Geoff

Clark was re-elected as chairman of the Aboriginal and Torres Strait Islander Commission in December after a year of public debate about the direction of Aboriginal policy. Among visitors to Australia were Queen Elizabeth II in February and Japanese Prime Minister Junichiro Koizumi in June.

Among those who died during the year were former Prime Minister (1968-71) Sir John Grey Gorton (90) (see XVIII); former New South Wales governor Sir Roden Cutler, VC (85); three academics: Louis Matheson (90), foundation vice-chancellor of Monash University, Heinz Arndt (87), and Sir Leslie Melville (80); two First World War veterans Alec Campbell (103), the last survivor of the Gallipoli landing, and Jack Lockett (111), the oldest man in Australia; two Aboriginal artists Jimmy Pike (62) and Clifford Possum Tjapaltjarri (70); and actors Leo McKern (82) and Ruth Cracknell (76).

ii. PAPUA NEW GUINEA

CAPITAL: Port Moresby   AREA: 463,000 sq km   POPULATION: 5,300,000
OFFICIAL LANGUAGES: Pidgin, Motu & English   POLITICAL SYSTEM: multiparty system in British Commonwealth
HEAD OF STATE: Queen Elizabeth II
GOVERNOR-GENERAL: Sir Sailas Atopare
RULING PARTY: National Alliance Party (NAP)
HEAD OF GOVERNMENT: Sir Michael Somare (NAP), Prime Minister (since August '02)
MAIN IGO MEMBERSHIPS (NON-UN): APEC, CP, PC, PIF, ACP, CWTH, NAM
CURRENCY: kina (end-'02 £1=K6.3203, US$1=K3.9463)
GNI PER CAPITA: US$580, US$2,150 at PPP ('01)

THE dominant event of 2002 in Papua New Guinea (PNG) was the violent and chaotic general election held in June and July. The poll both reflected and intensified the underlying instability and disorder of politics and society in contemporary PNG.

The contest, for the 109-seat National Parliament was scheduled to last for two weeks in the second half of June. In the event, it went on until the end of July and even then the results for many constituencies remained disputed. During the polling period some 30 people died in election-related violence and large areas of the country, particularly in the highland provinces, descended into wholesale communal violence with widespread rape and arson. Polling officials and candidates in many areas were subject to systematic intimidation, polling stations were attacked and ballot boxes stolen and destroyed. Inevitably, the legitimacy of the result was subject to considerable doubt. The troubled election resulted from a combination of poor preparation and organisation, and the country's growing propensity for political violence, particularly in pursuit of the control of state resources.

Early in the electoral process it became clear that the incumbent Prime Minister, Sir Mekere Morauta, would not survive in office. The high turnover of members, long a characteristic of PNG elections, meant that fewer than half of the Cabinet retained their seats. When the new Parliament convened on 5 August to nominate a new Prime Minister, the post went to the 66-year old veteran Sir Michael Somare who had been the country's first head of government after independence in 1975 (see AR 1975, p. 299). Now leader of the National Alliance Party, Somare put together a widely based but inherently unstable coalition government that was typical of the country's political system.

While his innate authority and national standing were seen as useful and necessary stabilising factors, Somare's readiness and ability to push through urgent economic and political reform were questionable. Morauta had been respected among foreign neighbours and aid donors for his commitment to such reform, although this proved to be in inverse proportion to his popularity at home. Early signs suggested that Australia, PNG's former colonial power and principal aid donor, was less than enthusiastic to see Somare back in office. Not the least of Australia's concerns was the new government's attitude to the accommodation of would-be asylum seekers diverted to PNG before their arrival in Australia (see AR 2001, p. 388). In January the Morauta government had agreed to take a further contingent in addition to a group of 200 already detained on Manus island. It was unclear, however, whether the new government would be willing to maintain this arrangement.

Beyond the election-related violence, the country continued to suffer from a high level of what had become routine disorder. January saw a mutiny among a section of troops at the Moem barracks in Wewak, in the north of the country. A varied and rather incoherent list of demands was presented by the mutineers which included the dismissal of the government, the abandonment of the IMF-driven privatisation programme and an end to the reduction of army numbers. The mutiny was eventually suppressed after two weeks, with minimum violence, when loyal troops retook the barracks. But however insignificant the event may have seemed, it represented another incident in a mounting catalogue of misbehaviour on the part of the armed forces (see AR 2001, p. 388).

Some of the worst election-related violence occurred in the Southern Highlands province where the poll merely intensified a destructive tribal war which had been underway since the beginning of the year. At the height of the trouble the central government appeared to have decided simply to abandon the area to anarchy. The province's election results were annulled and the contests had yet to be re-run at the end of the year.

Somewhat more encouraging developments took place in the long drawn out settlement of the Bougainville conflict. In January Parliament passed an organic law introducing a high degree of local autonomy for the island and allowing for a referendum on the question of total independence to be held within 15 years.

2. NEW ZEALAND—PACIFIC ISLAND STATES

i. NEW ZEALAND

CAPITAL: Wellington   AREA: 271,000 sq km   POPULATION: 3,800,000
OFFICIAL LANGUAGE: English   POLITICAL SYSTEM: multiparty system in British Commonwealth
HEAD OF STATE: Queen Elizabeth II (since Feb '52)
GOVERNOR-GENERAL: Dame Silvia Cartwright
RULING PARTIES: New Zealand Labour Party (NZLP) & Progressive Coalition Party (PCP)
HEAD OF GOVERNMENT: Helen Clark, Prime Minister (since Dec '99)
MAIN IGO MEMBERSHIPS (NON-UN): ANZUS (suspended), APEC, PC, PIF, CP, OECD, CWTH
CURRENCY: New Zealand dollar (end-'02 £1=NZ$3.0948, US$1=NZ$1.9324)
GNI PER CAPITA: US$12,380, US$19,130 at PPP ('01)

PRIME Minister Helen Clark won a second term in mid-year elections. The New Zealand Labour Party (NZLP), in power since 1999, again won more parliamentary seats than any of the opposition parties. Labour's main adversary, the National Party (NP), had its worst election result since it was formed in 1936.

The election would have been held in late 2002 if the government had completed its full three-year term. However, the Prime Minister called the poll for 27 July, about four months early, following the collapse in April of Labour's junior coalition partner, the left-wing Alliance Party. The disarray in the Alliance complicated the Prime Minister's efforts to portray her government as stable and coherent, and herself as a leader with a particular gift for coalition management. Her own policies had contributed to the Alliance's split, which was reflected in the discontent of many within the party with Labour's more moderate, pro-business stance and its support for (and participation in) the US-led "war on terror".

The break-up of the Alliance meant that the Labour Prime Minister had two separate Alliance factions participating at the same time in Cabinet meetings. The refusal of the Alliance leader, Deputy Prime Minister Jim Anderton, to resign from Parliament left him open to criticism since his action—or inaction—went against the spirit of legislation that he had initiated, and that was enacted in 2001, requiring members of Parliament who ceased to be members of the party for which they were elected to resign (see AR 2001, p. 391).

Clark cited the opposition's use of parliamentary time to highlight the Alliance's problems as her principal reason for calling an early election. When she did so, in June, she held a clear lead in opinion polls for the public's choice of "preferred Prime Minister". With the NZLP's lead over opposition parties also substantial, the July election offered Labour an opportunity to become the first party to win an outright parliamentary majority since the introduction of a proportional representation voting system in 1996 (see AR 1996, p. 363).

These hopes faded, however, during a brief campaign that saw the Prime Minister's composure weaken on several occasions. Earlier in the year Clark had been embarrassed by revelations that she had signed her name to a painting (sold for charity) that she had not, in fact, painted. It subsequently transpired that she had signed several such works. The result of the police investigation, released during the campaign, suggested that an offence had probably been committed but that there were no plans to prosecute. The Prime Minister rejected aspersions cast upon her integrity, however, initially threatening to sue media outlets that reported criticism of her behaviour by NP leader Bill English. Subsequently Clark also reacted angrily during television interviews in which it was suggested that her government had engaged in a cover-up over the release of genetically modified seed (for corn), prohibited in New Zealand under a moratorium supported by the government. The issue disrupted previously cordial relations between the NZLP and the Green Party, which refused to guarantee support for a Labour-led government without the promise of a permanent moratorium against genetically modified foods. Clark's behaviour during the interviews led some voters to question the desirability of a return to the style of single-party majority government that had been prevalent prior to the change of electoral system.

English had replaced former Prime Minister Jenny Shipley as leader of the NP, and was leading the party into an election for the first time. Earlier in the year he had attempted to raise his profile as leader by taking part in a charity boxing match. At no time, however, was he able to make much of an impression on Clark's lead over him in the polls. Other opposition parties waged more vigorous campaigns, with the right-of-centre Association of Consumers and Taxpayers (ACT) stressing law-and-order, and the populist New Zealand First (NZF) party emphasising immigration as an ostensible threat to the country's way of life. Both parties also attacked what they regarded as excessive and unwarranted settlements given to Maori claimants under New Zealand's Treaty of Waitangi.

The surprise of the 2002 campaign, however, was the performance of the hitherto electorally feeble United Future New Zealand (UFNZ) party. The party had been represented in Parliament by only one MP, Peter Dunne, since 1996. In 2002, however, his "common sense" style of politics proved attractive to voters alarmed by the other smaller parties, particularly the Greens and the Alliance. Dunne's performance during a televised party leaders' debate was highly commended by commentators, making UFNZ a credible party for voters searching for a stable and reliable coalition partner for Labour.

Although Labour lost about a quarter of its support during the campaign, it was still able to claim victory, winning more seats (52) than it had three years earlier (see AR 1999, pp. 385-86). Its previous coalition partner, the Alliance, failed to win any seats and saw its vote fall to only 1.3 per cent. The Alliance's former party leader, Anderton, now campaigning as the leader of a new party, the Progressive Coalition Party (PCP), won his seat; the party finished with a total of two legislators. A Labour-Progressive coalition government was quickly formed, and a 32-person executive, the largest in the country's history, was established. An agreement was also reached with UFNZ, which won eight seats and agreed to act as a "support" party on confidence votes and, subsequently, with the Green Party (with nine seats), which was to be "consulted" on government policy.

The new Parliament saw the NP so depleted in parliamentary strength that it lost its right to occupy the entire front bench of the opposition side of the chamber. Despite a challenge from other opposition parties, however, the NP leader was able to retain the title of "Leader of the Opposition". In the wake of the election defeat—which saw National reduced to only 27 seats—the party's president resigned. The other right-of-centre parties, ACT and NZF, won nine and 13 seats respectively. The new Parliament continued recent trends towards greater diversity, with New Zealand's first ever Muslim MP taking the oath of allegiance on a copy of the Koran.

Although there were few new policy initiatives, Clark sought to close some of the wounds of New Zealand's past. In February she issued a formal apology to New Zealand's Chinese community for the decades of discrimination (including special taxes) imposed upon their forebears during the 19th and early 20th centuries. In June, on a visit to Samoa, Clark apologised to the Samoan people for "inept and incompetent" administration during New Zealand's governance of Western Samoa (which lasted from 1914 to 1962).

New Zealand also continued to make efforts to improve its relations with the USA. The presence of New Zealand's Special Air Service (SAS) troops in Afghanistan—on which the Prime Minister had refused to comment—was confirmed in March by a document posted on the US presidential website. Their 12-month deployment in "Operation Enduring Freedom" (see VIII.1.ii) was ended in December. The Prime Minister stated that New Zealand's participation in a possible war against Iraq was contingent upon UN approval, although a New Zealand frigate was sent to the Gulf region to assist in patrol activities. Clark's March visit to Washington DC to meet US President George W. Bush was the first formal meeting between a Labour Prime Minister and a US President for 27 years. Although US Secretary of State Colin Powell said that New Zealand and the USA were "very, very, very close friends", he confirmed that they were no longer allies, a consequence of New Zealand's anti-nuclear stance. The policy was also identified as an obstacle in the development of a free trade agreement between the two countries.

ii. PACIFIC ISLAND STATES

Federated States of Micronesia
CAPITAL: Palikir (Pohnpei) AREA: 701 sq km POPULATION: 120,000
OFFICIAL LANGUAGE: English POLITICAL SYSTEM: multiparty republic in free association with USA
HEAD OF STATE AND GOVERNMENT: President Leo Falcam (since May '99)
MAIN IGO MEMBERSHIPS (NON-UN): PC, PIF
CURRENCY: US dollar (end-'02 £1=US$1.6016)
GNI PER CAPITA: US$2,150 ('01)

Fiji
CAPITAL: Suva AREA: 18,375 sq km POPULATION: 824,000
OFFICIAL LANGUAGES: Fijian, Hindi & English POLITICAL SYSTEM: multiparty republic in British Commonwealth
HEAD OF STATE: President Ratu Josefa Iloilo (since July '00)
RULING PARTY: United Fiji Party (SDL)
HEAD OF GOVERNMENT: Laisenia Qarase (since July '00)
MAIN IGO MEMBERSHIPS (NON-UN): CWTH (suspended), PC, PIF, CP, ACP
CURRENCY: Fiji dollar (end-'02 £1=F$3.3276, US$1=F$2.0778)
GNI PER CAPITA: US$2,130, US$5,140 at PPP ('01)

Kiribati
CAPITAL: Tarawa AREA: 1,000 sq km POPULATION: 93,000
OFFICIAL LANGUAGES: English & Kiribati POLITICAL SYSTEM: multiparty republic in British Commonwealth
HEAD OF STATE AND GOVERNMENT: President Teburoro Tito (since Sept '94)
MAIN IGO MEMBERSHIPS (NON-UN): CWTH, PC, ACP
CURRENCY: Australian dollar (end-'02 £1=A$2.8553, US$1=A$1.7828)
GNI PER CAPITA: US$830 ('01)

Marshall Islands
CAPITAL: Dalap-Uliga-Darrit AREA: 200 sq km POPULATION: 53,000
OFFICIAL LANGUAGES: English & Marshallese POLITICAL SYSTEM: multiparty republic in free association with the USA
HEAD OF STATE AND GOVERNMENT: President Kessai Note (since Jan '00)
RULING PARTY: United Democratic Party (UDP)
MAIN IGO MEMBERSHIPS (NON-UN): PC, PIF
CURRENCY: US dollar (end-'02 £1=US$1.6016)
GNI PER CAPITA: US$2,190 ('01)

Nauru
CAPITAL: Domaneab AREA: 21.4 sq km POPULATION: 12,100 (est.)
OFFICIAL LANGUAGES: Nauruan & English POLITICAL SYSTEM: one-party republic, special member of the British Commonwealth
HEAD OF STATE AND GOVERNMENT: President Rene Harris (since April '01)
MAIN IGO MEMBERSHIPS (NON-UN): CWTH, PC, PIF
CURRENCY: Australian dollar (see above)
GNI PER CAPITA: n/a

Palau (Belau)

CAPITAL: Koror   AREA: 460 sq km   POPULATION: 20,000
OFFICIAL LANGUAGE: English   POLITICAL SYSTEM: multi-party republic in free association with USA
HEAD OF STATE AND GOVERNMENT: President Tommy Remengesau (since Nov '00)
MAIN IGO MEMBERSHIPS (NON-UN): PC, PIF
CURRENCY: US dollar (end-'02 £1=US$1.6016)
GNI PER CAPITA: n/a

Samoa

CAPITAL: Apia   AREA: 2,842 sq km   POPULATION: 171,000
OFFICIAL LANGUAGES: English & Samoan   POLITICAL SYSTEM: multiparty monarchy in British Commonwealth
HEAD OF STATE: Susuga Malietoa Tanumafili II (since Jan '62)
RULING PARTY: Human Rights Protection Party
HEAD OF GOVERNMENT: Tuila'epa Sa'ilele Malielegaoi, Prime Minister (since Nov '98)
MAIN IGO MEMBERSHIPS (NON-UN): CWTH, PC, PIF, ACP
CURRENCY: tala (end-'02 £1=T5.1830 US$1=T3.2362)
GNI PER CAPITA: US$1,520, US$5,450 ('01)

Solomon Islands

CAPITAL: Honiara   AREA: 28,000 sq km   POPULATION: 432,000
OFFICIAL LANGUAGE: English   POLITICAL SYSTEM: multiparty system in British Commonwealth
HEAD OF STATE: Queen Elizabeth II
GOVERNOR-GENERAL: Sir John Ini Lapli
RULING PARTY: People's Alliance Party (PAP)
HEAD OF GOVERNMENT: Allan Kemakeza, Prime Minister (since Dec '01)
MAIN IGO MEMBERSHIPS (NON-UN): CWTH, PC, PIF, ACP
CURRENCY: Solomon Island dollar (end-'02 £1=SI$12.1606, US$1=SI$7.5930)
GNI PER CAPITA: US$580, US$1,680 at PPP ('01)

Tonga

CAPITAL: Nuku'alofa   AREA: 750 sq km   POPULATION: 101,000
OFFICIAL LANGUAGES: Tongan & English   POLITICAL SYSTEM: non-party monarchy in British Commonwealth
HEAD OF STATE: King Taufa'ahua Tupou IV (since Dec '65)
HEAD OF GOVERNMENT: 'Ulakalala Lavaka Ata, Prime Minister
MAIN IGO MEMBERSHIPS (NON-UN): CWTH, PC, PIF, ACP
CURRENCY: pa'anga (end-'02 £1=P2.8553, US$1=P1.7828)
GNI PER CAPITA: US$1,530 ('01)

Tuvalu

CAPITAL: Fongafle   AREA: 26 sq km   POPULATION: 10,200
OFFICIAL LANGUAGE: English   POLITICAL SYSTEM: non-party monarchy, special member of the British Commonwealth
HEAD OF STATE: Queen Elizabeth II (since Feb '52)
GOVERNOR-GENERAL: Tomasi Puapua
HEAD OF GOVERNMENT: Saufatu Sopoanga, Prime Minister (since Aug '02)
MAIN IGO MEMBERSHIPS (NON-UN): PC, PIF, ACP, CWTH
CURRENCY: Australian dollar (end-'02 £1=A$2.8553, US$1=A$1.7828)
GNI PER CAPITA: n/a

Vanuatu

CAPITAL: Port Vila   AREA: 12,000 sq km   POPULATION: 201,000
OFFICIAL LANGUAGES: English, French & Bislama   POLITICAL SYSTEM: multiparty republic in British Commonwealth
HEAD OF STATE: President John Bani (since March '99)
RULING PARTY: Vanu'aku Pati (VP) and Union of Moderate Parties (UMP) coalition
HEAD OF GOVERNMENT: Edward Natapei (VP), Prime Minister (since April '01)
MAIN IGO MEMBERSHIPS (NON-UN): CWTH, PC, PIF, ACP, Francophonie
CURRENCY: vatu (end-'02 £1=V213.727, US$1=V133.450)
GNI PER CAPITA: US$1,050, US$2,710 at PPP ('01)

THE Pacific Islands Forum held its 33rd meeting, with representatives from 16 countries gathering together at a resort in Suva, Fiji, on 15-17 August. The meeting was attended principally by heads of government, who considered a wide range of economic, political, environmental, and security issues. A special declaration was issued on regional security, highlighting the dangers posed by terrorism and transnational crime, while smaller island states continued to express particular concerns about climate change, global warming, and rising sea levels.

The "war on terror" and the possibility of a war in Iraq had their impact on the region. In the COMMONWEALTH OF THE NORTHERN MARIANAS the USA continued to conduct bombing exercises on Farallon de Mendinilla Island despite objections from environmentalists concerned about the effects on endangered species and migratory birds. The US embassy in Apia, SAMOA was closed briefly during August following reports of a possible terrorist attack. Although GUAM and AMERICAN SAMOA were included in the USA Homeland Security legislation, a federal report categorised these territories (and the Northern Marianas) as ill-prepared to respond to acts of terrorism and weapons of mass destruction.

The effects of international terrorism were complemented by violence within a number of Pacific Island states and territories. In August, in the SOLOMON ISLANDS, on Guadalcanal, a government Minister, Father Augustine Geve, was assassinated. Geve had been the legislator for the region. A rebel leader, Harold Keke, took credit for the killing. Keke had not joined the peace accord, known as the Townsville Agreement, that had ended more than two years of ethnic conflict in the Solomons. Attempts to apprehend Keke, both before and after the assassination, led to the killing by his forces of those seeking to capture him.

Elsewhere in Melanesia, there was unrest in the French territory of NEW CALEDONIA between local Melanesians, known as Kanaks, and immigrants from French-ruled WALLIS AND FUTUNA, with several people being killed in the communal violence. VANUATU experienced another of its periodic mutinies by its police and paramilitary mobile forces. In August Prime Minister Edward Natapei had to go into hiding when heavily armed paramilitary police surrounded police headquarters, arresting the acting police commissioner. His appointment was subsequently ruled invalid in court. Vanuatu was also destabilised by a group protesting against the imprisonment for three years in July of former Prime Minister Barak Sope on corruption charges. Elections held in May returned the coalition of the Vanua'aku Party (led by Natapei) and the Union of Moderate Parties (led by former Prime Minister Serge Vohor).

Elections elsewhere in the Pacific produced political change. In TUVALU, Prime Minister Koloa Talaki lost his seat in the 15-member legislature. In August the country's legislators elected Saufatu Sopoanga as the new Prime Minister on an 8-7 vote. In KIRIBATI elections were held for a new House of Assembly (unicameral legislature) in November and December. President Teburoro Tito was seeking a third term—the limit under the country's constitution—but his government lost 14 of its 25 seats, with seven Cabinet Ministers being defeated. The assembly's election of a new President was to take place in early 2003.

The island of NIUE'S April elections brought former Prime Minister Young Vivian back to power. In the COOK ISLANDS the Deputy Prime Minister, Robert Woonton, became Prime Minister in February when the legislature removed Prime Minister Terepai Maoate on a no-confidence vote. In FRENCH POLYNESIA voters gave strong support to French President Jacques Chirac in France's presidential elections (see II.2.ii), in which the overseas French territories participated. An air crash in May cost the lives of three members of the territory's assembly.

Elections in TONGA produced victory for seven pro-democracy movement members. However, in October all nine of the people's representatives (elected by Tonga's adult population) walked out of the Legislative Assembly in protest after a number of bills that had been proposed by them were voted down. The people's representatives were outweighed by the nine nobles' representatives (elected by the country's 33 hereditary nobles) and a further 12 Cabinet members appointed by the King of Tonga, giving them limited opportunities to influence policy.

In FIJI there was limited progress towards ethnic reconciliation following several coups in recent years. The leader of the Labour Party, former Prime Minister Mahendra Chaudhry, turned down an invitation to be leader of the opposition on the grounds of an alleged constitutional right to be a member of the government. The claim was rejected by Prime Minister Laisenia Qarase, who characterised the divide between Fiji's two communities—the indigenous Fijian and the Indo-Fijian population descended from immigrants from India—as "wider now than it has ever been". George Speight, the man who deposed Chaudhry in May 2000, taking him prisoner (see AR 2000, p. 362), was given a death sentence, subsequently commuted to life imprisonment, after he pleaded guilty to treason. Speight's brother easily won the by-election for the parliamentary seat that the imprisoned Speight had had to vacate.

Fiji's progress towards democracy and constitutional government was recognised by the return of regional and international leaders to the country. In July the African, Caribbean, and Pacific summit was held, bringing together 78 nations, and the following month brought the 16-nation Pacific Island Forum summit to Fiji. The government's legitimacy remained under challenge, however, and protesters were banned from the summit conferences. A plot by Fiji army officers to kidnap Qarase, in order to bring about the release of Speight and gain immunity for others involved in the coup attempt, was foiled. Chaudhry continued to claim that the more important coup planners remained free, with Speight a scapegoat—charges indicative of the substantial distrust still permeating Fiji's politics and society.

Although a lack of democracy, accountability, and good governance had been increasingly identified by international and regional organisations as contributing to the Pacific's economic and political problems, more tangible factors were not hard to identify. Typhoon Chata'an ("rainy" in Chamorro) swept through Chuuk state in the FEDERATED STATES OF MICRONESIA, leaving large numbers of people homeless. At least 47 people were confirmed dead, many in landslides, and emergency assistance (including medical personnel) was provided from Guam and Hawaii. Guam itself was declared a disaster area by US President George W. Bush, with damage estimated at about US$60 million. The Northern Marianas were also affected by Typhoon Chata'an, with damage to agriculture and homes on the island of Rota.

Environmental issues were the subject of a two-day conference held in PALAU in October. Pacific Island leaders issued the Palau Declaration calling for improved water resource management, the application of ocean thermal energy conversion technology, and special assistance to small island states seeking to respond to the adverse effects of climate change and sea level rise. Island leaders also took part in world summits on sustainable development (held in Johannesburg, South Africa, in September) and food (held in Rome, Italy, in June). Here, too, the commitment to shared goals was seen to be placed in jeopardy by climate change, with agricultural production on small islands and atolls threatened by rising seas. The government of Tuvalu announced plans to launch a lawsuit in the International Court of Justice against the USA and Australia over their greenhouse gas emissions. Tuvalu's nine atolls stood only several meters above sea level and were expected to be submerged in about 50 years on present trends. Several Pacific Island countries unilaterally declared Pacific whale sanctuaries, but proposals for the establishment of a South Pacific whaling sanctuary at the International Whaling Commission meeting in Japan in May were not successful, in part due to opposition by two Pacific Island states with close ties to Japan: Palau and the Solomon Islands.

A lack of technical resources and financial expertise was in evidence in some Pacific Island states. The government of Tonga began legal action in an attempt to recover US$24 million lost by the Tonga Trust Fund through investments promoted by the person appointed by the King as his court jester. Additional damage limitation was evident in the decision by Tonga's government to close its international registry of ships following incidents in which Tongan-registered ships were implicated in weapons shipments and the transport of illegal immigrants.

The Niue government's latest scheme to bring in large-scale investment to the island—home to fewer than 2,000 people—also foundered. The government conducted negotiations with a religious group, based in South Korea, that had been seeking to build a walled "holy city" on the island. The plan would have given the group a long-term lease on 150 hectares (375 acres) to build the enclosed religious compound, but was opposed by most Niueans.

There were also some positive developmental signs. Niue and the MARSHALL ISLANDS were removed from the Organisation for Economic Co-operation and Development's (OECD) Financial Action Task Force list of non-co-operating countries and territories, reflecting progress in improving their anti-money laundering systems. In Palau the new Koror-Babeldaob Bridge (funded by Japan) was opened in January, more than five years after the old bridge had collapsed. The span connected the island of Koror, Palau's capital and the centre of government and tourism, with Babeldaob, the country's largest island and the location of much of its natural resources.

Attempts to introduce constitutional change were frustrated in the Federated States of Micronesia (FSM), where each of the 14 constitutional amendments proposed by the 2001 constitutional convention failed to gain the necessary 75 per cent approval in a referendum held on 27 August. The FSM and the Marshall Islands were continuing their protracted negotiations with the USA over new Compacts of Free Association, with the parties divided over funding, accountability, and migration provisions.

The "Pacific Solution" developed by Australia in response to attempts by illegal immigrants to land in that country began to peter out during 2002. With the defeat of the Taliban in Afghanistan, most of the asylum seekers from that country saw their claims for refugee status rejected. The asylum seekers, who had been detained in inhospitable conditions, were leaving NAURU, with most being returned to their country of origin.

Smaller Pacific Island territories gained somewhat greater international scrutiny, with TOKELAU receiving a visit from a UN Decolonisation Mission. The visitors were advised in September that the people of Tokelau "prefer to remain part of New Zealand". American Samoa's request to be removed from the list of non-self-governing territories—reflecting a wish to be considered a part of the USA—was accepted by the UN General Assembly. PITCAIRN ISLAND'S population of 43 people continued to be affected by a worldwide investigation of multiple allegations of sexual offending, first made in 1999. An apparent "tradition" of rape and sexual abuse involving underage girls had been alleged and up to 20 men—half the population—could face charges arising out of the investigations. The first murder in more than 15 years was reported on EASTER ISLAND (also known as RAPA NUI). It was only the third murder in 113 years on the island, the most recent having taken place in 1986.

A poignant reminder of the Pacific War occurred with the discovery by an international team, led by US oceanographer Robert Ballard, of PT-109, former US President John F. Kennedy's torpedo boat. It was found off the Solomon Islands after about a week of searching in waters some 380 km northwest of Honiara, on the sea bed of the Blanket Strait off Gizo Island. Kennedy's boat had been sliced in two by a Japanese destroyer in August 1943, but he and other crew members made their way to a nearby island, from which they were subsequently rescued (see AR 1943, pp. 277-80).

The image of the Pacific as a sort of "paradise" was revived by an unlikely source, the USA State Department, whose annual country-by-country report on human rights singled out Tuvalu as a country with a virtually perfect human rights record. Tuvalu was described as a country without killings, disappearances or torture; a state with an independent judiciary; a society in which violence against women was "rare", domestic violence "infrequent", prostitution illegal, and with no reports of child abuse. The country had few, if any prisoners, apart from overnight stays for drunkenness.

XI INTERNATIONAL ORGANISATIONS

1. UNITED NATIONS AND ITS AGENCIES

DATE OF FOUNDATION: 1945 HEADQUARTERS: New York, USA
OBJECTIVES: To promote international peace, security and cooperation on the basis of the equality of member-states, the right of self-determination of peoples and respect for human rights
MEMBERSHIP (END-'02): 191 sovereign states; those not in membership of the UN itself at end-2002 were the Holy See (Vatican) and Taiwan (Republic of China), although all except Taiwan were members of one or more UN specialised agency
SECRETARY-GENERAL: Kofi Annan (Ghana)

THROUGHOUT 2002 it was a very busy year for the United Nations. The major areas of interest were terrorism, Africa, the Middle East (including Palestine), Iraq, Afghanistan, East Timor, the continuing reform of the UN, and the capital plan for the refurbishment of its headquarters complex in New York city. The Security Council established one new peace office and adjusted another; laid down three peacekeeping operations and created one new one; dissolved one sanctions regime, adjusted one from national to global competence, and strengthened another. An inter-agency unit on Internal Displacement was created. The Human Rights Office in Croatia, which opened in 1993, became the first such mission ever to be closed. The Department of Public Information introduced an e-mail United Nations News Service. The UN celebrated 50 years of guided tours of the United Nations Headquarters in New York, during which there had been over 37 million visitors. The International Criminal Court was formally established. The UK, at the end of its presidency in July, presented the Security Council with the foster care of an elephant called Burra which had been rescued from a snare by a wildlife trust in Nairobi. It was hoped that the young elephant would be a sign of a long memory of the Security Council for things that go both right and wrong in Africa.

APPOINTMENTS. The Secretary General appointed Sergio Vieira de Mello as High Commissioner for Human Rights on 11 September in succession to Mary Robinson; and Catherine Bertini, formerly Executive Director of the United Nations World Food Programme, as Under-Secretary General for Management replacing Joseph Connor on 1 January 2003.

ELECTIONS. The General Assembly established a new precedent when it elected two months earlier than usual Jan Kavan of the Czech Republic as the President of the 57th Session. This early appointment was part of the process of revitalising the work of the General Assembly that had been recommended by Resolution 56/509, which had been passed on 8 July. Acting on the recommendation of the Security Council, the Assembly admitted on 10 September and 27 September respectively Switzerland and East Timor to be the 190th and

191st members of the United Nations. The General Assembly also elected on the first ballot, Angola and Pakistan from the African and Asian Group, Chile from the Latin American and Caribbean Group, and Germany and Spain from the Western Europe and other states Group to be the new non-permanent members of the Security Council for two years from 1 January 2003. They replaced Singapore, Mauritius, Columbia, Norway, and Ireland.

SPECIAL ASSEMBLY SESSIONS. The 27th Special Session of the General Assembly, which met in New York from 8-10 May, adopted without a vote a Declaration and Plan of Action to strengthen international action for the promotion of children's rights into the 21st century. The plan listed specific targets for children in the fields of health, education, protection against abuse, exploitation and violence and AIDS/HIV.

The General Assembly resumed its 10th Emergency Special Session on 7 May when it adopted a resolution (74 in favour, four against, and 54 abstentions), which requested the Secretary General to present a report on the events that took place in Jenin Refugee Camp and other Palestinian cities during a major Israeli offensive against Palestinian areas (see V.1; V.2.i). The Assembly had requested the report after the Secretary General had disbanded his fact-finding team when, after an initial promise of full co-operation by Israel, the Sharon government had raised obstacles to the work of the mission, which made its timely deployment impossible. The Assembly met again on 8 August when, after taking note of the report, it demanded by a vote of 114 in favour, four against, and 11 abstentions, the immediate cessation of military incursions and all acts of violence, terror, provocation, incitement, and destruction in Israel and the occupied Palestinian territories.

THE GENERAL DEBATE. The General Debate was addressed by 187 member states and one observer including 33 heads of state, 14 heads of government, two vice presidents, 14 deputy prime ministers, one crown prince, 100 foreign ministers, two vice ministers, 11 chairs of delegations, and the observer from Palestine. Kirbati, Libya, and the Seychelles did not speak.

There were a number of important developments during the session. The Assembly endorsed the important report of the Secretary General on strengthening the United Nations: an agenda for further change which included a thorough review of the institution's work to ensure that it was concentrating on priorities; detailed proposals for enhancing performance in human rights and public information; the elimination of overlap and duplication which would result in fewer meetings and fewer reports for the secretariat to prepare; the improvement in the co-ordination of technical assistance; changes in the budget and planning system; a review by an independent panel of relations between the United Nations and civil society; and proposals to enhance the secretariat by accelerating recruitment, increasing the retention of qualified people, and improving mobility.

In an attempt to improve the work of the General Assembly and to encourage interactive debate, a panel was convened (in which only the panellists were allowed to make prepared statements) to explore the many facets of the UN's role in Afghanistan.

The Assembly also paid close attention to the problems faced by developing states, particularly those in Africa. This included, at a high level plenary meeting, support for the New Partnership for Africa, and a discussion of the AIDS/HIV pandemic. The Assembly also decided how it would review the implementation of the Millennium Declaration in the future; approved the Optional Protocol to the Covenant against Torture; and endorsed the capital master plan to refurbish the headquarters in New York. The construction of a new 800,000 square foot building was scheduled to begin in October 2004 with a budget of $1.05 billion, plus or minus 10 per cent depending on the actual starting time. In the meantime, major repairs were to be carried out to the existing complex.

FINANCE. Joseph E. Connor reported to the fifth committee in October that his prediction for the UN's financial situation in 2002 was more circumspect than that of 2001.

He believed that at the end of the year the combined cash available for the regular budget, the Tribunals for the former Yugoslavia and Rwanda, and peacekeeping would be about US$1.37 billion. It had been necessary throughout the year to finance the regular budget by cross-borrowing from peacekeeping cash. (It was hoped that this might be avoided in future because the USA —the largest contributor—had announced that from 2003 it would pay its assessed dues at the beginning of the year rather than in October.) He considered that the US$10 million available to the tribunals would possibly allow them to avoid cross-borrowing while awaiting new assessment payments in early 2003; but the higher cash levels for peacekeeping were deceptive because money could now only be borrowed from the cash available in closed missions.

Connor noted that US$2.63 billion had been appropriated for the 2002-03 regular budget. This was slightly above the sum appropriated for 1994-95. Regular budget assessments had been at roughly the same level since 1994. This had been achieved by reducing costs through cutting posts and improving efficiency; by absorbing inflation, special mission costs, and other unforeseen costs relating to peace and security; and, above all, by favourable currency rates. Nevertheless, remaining within the appropriation level continued to be a challenge, partly because appropriations and mandates had not been synchronised. The organisation was struggling to meet the budgetary reductions mandated by the General Assembly of US$75 million for 2002-03. The UN had been forced to curtail meetings, reduce its utilities consumption, and limit further improvements in information technology. Furthermore, new mandates had been approved or anticipated for which there were no appropriations. These would increase the current budget by a further US$300 million to US$2.93 billion. This was due to special political missions (US$114.7 million), security improvements at UN headquarters (US$59.4 million), exchange rate fluctuations (US$49 million), International Civil Service Commission recommendations (UN$29.7 million), the capital master plan (US$22.5 million), unforeseen and extraordinary expenses (US$12 million), funding to offset low vacancy rates (US$8 million), conference and support services for the Counter-Terrorism Committee (US$7.5 million), and other financial implications (US$1.5 million). This increase could not be absorbed within the present regular budget, necessitating new assessments.

PAYMENTS. At the end of September only 105 members had paid their assessments in full; 45 had made partial payments, and 39 had made no payment at all, leaving the UN with a deficit in anticipated income according to past payments patterns of US$12 million. At 30 September the USA owed US$446 million (70 per cent of the total shortfall), although payments of US$255 million were anticipated with a further US$23 million awaiting the approval of Congress. Brazil owed US$44 million (8 per cent), Argentina US$30 million (5 per cent), with the combined debt of a further 81 states standing at US$56 million (10 per cent).

The budgets for the Tribunals for 2002 were about US$200 million. However, increased costs were foreseen for the Tribunals because of the Security Council decision to approve ad litem judges for Rwanda. Further costs could arise from the enforcement of sentences. At the end of September, 56 states had paid their assessments in full for both Tribunals; 35 had made partial payments, and 98 had failed to pay. The largest amount of unpaid assessments was from the USA (33 per cent), Brazil and the Russian Federation (18 per cent each), the Republic of Korea and Argentina (5 per cent each)—a total of 79 per cent from five states. A further 128 states owed collectively 21 per cent. However, tribunal cash at US$43 million was sufficient to fund planned activities until the end of the year.

Peacekeeping assessments for 2002 had been US$2.1 billion. At the end of September outstanding assessments totalled US$1.78 billion. The USA owed US$866 million. Eleven of the other 15 major contributors owed US$537 million and all other member states owed US$373 million.

PEACEKEEPING DEBT. The Secretariat had hoped to pay during 2002 some US$893 million owed to states that had contributed to peacekeeping. It was estimated, however, that only US$629 million would be paid. Thus the organisation would be unable to meet the Secretary-General's goal of paying for all current obligations in the year in which they occurred. Yet despite this reduction in payment, debt too had been reduced. The USA's payments of a significant portion of its peacekeeping arrears were immediately transferred to the troop-contributing states. The USA had also lifted the cap of 25 per cent on its peacekeeping contributions for the years 2001 to 2004 which would prevent the accumulation of new arrears. Payments for contingent-owned equipment were paid up to December 2001 in those missions where cash levels were appropriate. The situation was better for troop payments. Once 2002 reimbursements had been completed, the UN would be only be six months in payment arrears for UNFIL, UNDOF, UNIKOM, UNAMSIL, and UNMEE.

THE SECURITY COUNCIL. The Security Council held 185 meetings and approved 167 resolutions and 42 presidential statements; one third of the meetings discussed Africa at the continental, regional, and national level; another 21 were devoted to the situation in the Middle East. There were also four themed debates: civilians in armed conflict; children and armed conflict; women, peace, and security; and small arms. But these themes and others explored in earlier years were now being regularly discussed and incorporated into relevant resolutions. The USA used its veto twice and abstained twice; Syria did not take part in one vote and abstained twice; Russia, Bulgaria, and Cameroon each abstained on one resolution.

The Council continued to seek greater transparency in its work. There were many more open meetings, on subjects including Palestine and weapons inspection in Iraq, which were often addressed by large numbers of non-members of the Council, and open briefings by the secretariat. Many of the monthly presidents informally briefed the press and non-members on the work of the Council. There were five "wrap up" discussions on the work of the Council: three of these (in February, May, and June) were private but included participation by non-members of the Council, and two (in January and December) were open. The Council changed the format of its annual report to the General Assembly so that it was more analytical, smaller, and cheaper to produce. Furthermore, for the first time the Council had an open meeting on the report before it was submitted to the Assembly.

There were a number of institutional developments. The Council established an ad hoc working group on Africa that reviewed issues, undertook preparatory work for the Council, and prepared recommendations. Members of the Council, of the Economic and Social Council, and the Secretariat undertook a joint working mission to Guinea-Bissau. The President was invited to address the Economic and Social Council High Level Segment on the views of the Security Council on AIDS/HIV. The newly elected members of the Council were invited to attend not only the informal consultations of the whole Council but also the formal meetings of the subsidiary bodies of the Council for the month preceding their term of membership. Additionally, if an incoming member assumed the presidency in the first two months of its term it would be invited to attend the informal consultations for a period of two months.

The Secretariat was asked to distribute a written information note to members the day before an oral briefing to the Council. It was decided that the Council would receive monthly briefings on the Middle East. This would ensure that members were fully informed and could have a regular exchange of views, including dialogue with the Secretary General. During an open meeting of the Council on the issue of children and armed conflict, three children from Liberia, East Timor and Bosnia and Herzegovina addressed the Council on their experiences of being caught in armed conflict. The Council requested the High Commissioner for Human Rights to prepare a report on alleged atrocities in the Democratic Republic of the Congo and then invited her to attend informal consultations for the first time to discuss the report. The Executive Director of the World Food Programme briefed the Council on food insecurity as a threat to international peace and then later submitted detailed written replies to the questions that had been raised.

The Council sent missions to Ethiopia and Eritrea on 21-25 February; to the Great Lakes region of Africa on 27 April-7 May, and to Kosovo and Belgrade (in the Federal Republic of Yugoslavia) on 14-17 December. In March the Council endorsed a working mission to the Horn of Africa by interested Council members and Secretariat staff.

TERRORISM. On 11 September the Security Council held a high level meeting which paid solemn tribute to the memory of the victims of the terrorist attack in New York and Washington DC and urged co-operation with the Counter-Terrorism Committee, established by resolution 1373 in 2001 and designed to ensure that all member states took effective steps to prevent and suppress terrorism anywhere. A total of 178 states reported on their legislative and administrative response to terrorism, but 13 states did not. The committee, drawing upon expert advice, sent confidential letters to those states which had reported, offering, where appropriate, advice and guidance on how to fill in the gaps in implementing the resolution. States had to pay particular attention to legislation which had to cover all aspects of the resolution, including becoming party to the 12 international conventions and protocols relating to terrorism, as well as developing effective executive machinery for countering terrorist financing. The committee had yet to initiate action on paragraph 4 of the resolution, which noted the potential links between terrorism and other forms of international organised crime.

The Council adopted three condemnatory resolutions against specific acts of terrorism: the bomb attack in Bali, Indonesia, on 12 October (see IX.1.vi); the hostage taking in Moscow on 23 October (see III.3.i); and the bomb attack on the Paradise Hotel in Kikamba, Kenya and the attempted missile attack on the Arkia Israeli Airlines flight 583 departing Mombasa on 28 November (see VI.1.ii).

IRAQ AND WEAPONS INSPECTORS. In September the Secretary General received a letter from the Foreign Minister of Iraq in which he invited inspectors, who had left the country in December 1998, to return to establish whether Iraq had complied with UN resolutions for the destruction of its proscribed weapons and delivery systems. (The Secretary General had had a regular dialogue with Iraq on this issue and the USA was threatening to use force for the disarmament of Iraq.)

The Council on 8 November, after many weeks of tough negotiation, among the permanent five in particular, unanimously adopted Resolution 1441, which set out the terms on which the inspectors would return (see XVII.1). There were eight important features: it declared that Iraq was in material breach of previous resolutions; that Iraq had seven days to accept the resolution and 30 days to provide a full declaration of its weapons of mass destruction; that new inspections were to begin within 45 days and an interim progress report was to be submitted within 60 days; that all sites, including presidential palaces, were subject to unfettered inspections; that the United Nations Monitoring, Verification and Inspection Commission (UNMOVIC) had the right to interview Iraqis in private, including taking them outside Iraq; that UNMOVIC could freeze activity at any suspect site; that Iraq was forbidden from taking hostile action against any state upholding UN resolutions; and that UNMOVIC had the authority to report Iraqi non-compliance and that the Security Council had the opportunity to meet to consider how to respond to that non-compliance.

On 25 November the first inspectors arrived in Baghdad. On 7 December Iraq provided a declaration of all aspects of its programmes to develop chemical, biological, and nuclear weapons, ballistic missiles and other delivery systems. Copies of this declaration were initially given only to states on the Council which possessed nuclear weapons. The Executive Chairman of UNMOVIC, Hans Blix, and the Director General of the International Atomic Energy Agency (IAEA), Mohamed El Baradei, provided the Council in closed session with their initial assessment of the declaration and the progress of the inspections.

PALESTINE. The Council discussed the issue of the Middle East peace process and the Palestinian Intifada throughout the year. There were a number of open meetings. The Council adopted five resolutions and three presidential statements. In March the Council adopted resolution 1397 (2002), which for the first time affirmed the Council's vision of a region where two states, Israel and Palestine, lived side by side within secure and recognised borders. As the violence mounted and intensified both in the Palestinian territories and in Israel the Council's central demands in the range of resolutions were: an immediate ceasefire; the withdrawal of Israeli forces from Palestinian cities; an end to all acts of violence; co-operation with the Quartet (the USA, Russia, the UN, and the EU) in their quest for a peaceful settlement via a defined "road map"; the implementation of the Tenet and Mitchell Plans; improvement in the dire humanitarian conditions; and support for the Secretary General's initiative for a fact finding team to investigate what precisely had happened after Israeli forces smashed their way into the Jenin refugee camp. A US veto meant that the Council failed to adopt a resolution in December, proposed by Syria, that sought to condemn the actions of the Israeli armed forces in killing employees of the UN and deliberately destroying a World Food Programme warehouse.

PEACE-BUILDING AND PEACEKEEPING. The Council established one new peace-building mission and reshaped another during 2002. The United Nations Assistance Mission in Afghanistan was established to assist the Afghans to implement the Bonn Agreement (see AR 2001, p. 323) and to help with reconstruction. The Secretary-General stated that this was an integrated mission designed to support the political, governance, and peace-building processes whilst simultaneously responding to urgent humanitarian and recovery needs. The Council monitored Afghanistan through monthly briefings; it commended the establishment of the Transitional Authority; appealed for funds both for reconstruction and for the return of refugees and the internally displaced; endorsed the Kabul Declaration on Good Neighbourly Relations (see VIII.1.ii); and renewed the mandate for the international security force.

The second peace-building mission was the United Nations Mission in Angola, the successor to the United Nations Office in Angola, which was designed to assist the Angolan government to protect and promote human rights, to support the social and professional reintegration of demobilised personnel through appropriate UN agencies, to help mobilise humanitarian assistance, to promote economic recovery, and to provide technical assistance for removing landmines.

Three peacekeeping missions were laid down in 2002: the UN Transitional Administration in East Timor (UNTATET), the UN Mission in Bosnia and Herzegovina (UNMIBH), and the UN Mission of Observers in Prevlaka (UNMOP). The United Nations Mission of Support for East Timor, which had a limited executive capacity and peacekeeping duties and was expected to leave within two years, replaced the first. An EU Police Mission replaced the second. The Council adjusted the mandates of UNIFIL, UNMIK, UNAMSIL, MONUC, and UNMEE. In October the Council supported the establishment of an African Union International Force in the Central African Republic, and in December the Council approved the deployment of an ECOMOG Monitoring Group in Côte d'Ivoire (see VI.3.i).

Following allegations made in a joint survey conducted by the High Commissioner for Refugees and Save the Children Fund that peacekeepers in Sierra Leone had sought sexual favours from children, principally adolescent girls, in camps for refugees and internally displaced people, UNAMSIL required that all newly deployed peacekeepers take a sensitisation programme (which included a briefing on appropriate sexual behaviour) by UNHCR and the mission's human rights office.

The Security Council adopted in March an aide-memoire on the protection of civilians in armed conflict to guide deliberations for the establishment, review, or termination of peacekeeping operations. In June the USA decided to veto the renewal of the mission in Bosnia and Herzegovina because it feared that the coming into effect of the Rome Statute of the International Criminal Court, to which the USA was not a party, might permit US military personnel to be arraigned before the Court. The problem was resolved when the Council decided that if a case involving US peacekeeping personnel arose then the Council would request that consideration of it be deferred for 12 months. There was an intent that such a deferral would be renewed every 12 months thereafter. In August there was a joint meeting between the Working Group on Peacekeeping and the troop-contributing countries. This was a new mechanism, which had been approved by the Council in January. The High Commissioner for Human Rights and the Under-Secretary General for Peacekeeping in November signed an agreement to strengthen and expand their co-operation in Peacekeeping Operations.

The United Nations Peacekeeping Department sponsored a seminar on past, present, and future challenges to Peacekeeping in October. Colombia, the Council President for December, convened an informal but important seminar principally for members of the Council, on the role of the Security Council in establishing and supporting UN peace operations. The Assembly adopted a resolution on the scope of the legal protection offered by the 1994 Convention on the Safety of United Nations and Associated Personnel in response to concerns about the wellbeing of peacekeepers (52 civilian and military personnel lost their lives while on UN peace operations in 2002).

UNITED NATIONS POLITICAL AND PEACE-BUILDING MISSIONS

	Established	Present Strength	Current Authorisation
UNOB: United Nations Office in Burundi	October 1993	Special Representative of the Secretary General and Head of UNOB: Berhanu Dinka (Ethiopia). 28 international civilian; 27 local civilian and 1 military advisor.	Until 31 December 2003
MINUGUA: United Nations Verification Mission in Guatemala	September 1994	Special Representative of the Secretary General and Chief of Mission: Tom Koenigs (Germany) 60 international civilian; 138 local civilian; 6 civil police observers.	Until 31 December 2003
UNPOS: United Nations Political Office for Somalia	April 1995	Representative of the Secretary General and Head of UNPOS: Winston A. Tubman (Liberia). 5 international civilian; 3 local civilian.	Until 31 December 2003
UNOL: United Nations Peace-Building Support Office in Liberia	November 1997	Representative of the Secretary-General and Head of UNOL: Abou Moussa (Chad). 10 international civilian; 15 local civilian.	Until 31 December 2003
Office of the Special Representative of the Secretary-General for the Great Lakes Region	December 1997	Special Representative of the Secretary-General: Ibrahima Fall (Senegal). 7 international civilian; 3 local civilian.	Until 31 December 2003
UNPOB: United Nations Political Office in Bougainvillea	June 1998	Head of Office: Noel Sinclair (Guyana). 4 international civilian; 3 local civilian; 1 military advisor.	Until 31 December 2003
UNOGBIS: United Nations Peace-building Support Office in Guinea-Bissau	March 1999	Representative of the Secretary General and Head of UNOCBIS: David Stephen (UK). 13 international civilian; 2 military advisors;1 civilian police advisor;11 local civilian.	Until 31 December 2003

UNITED NATIONS POLITICAL AND PEACE-BUILDING MISSIONS *continued*

	Established	Present Strength	Current Authorisation
UNSCO: Office of the United Nations Special Co-ordinator for the Middle East.	October 1999	Special Co-ordinator for the Middle East Peace Process and Personal Representative of the Secretary General to the Palestine Liberation Organisation and the Palestinian National Authority: Terje Roed-Larsen (Norway). 23 international civilian; 16 local civilian.	Until 19 September 2003
UNMA: United Nations Mission in Angola	October 1999	48 international civilian; 68 local civilian; 8 military observers.	Until 15 February 2003
BONUCA: United Nations Peace-Building Office in the Central African Republic	February 2000	Representative of the Secretary General and Head of BONUCA: Gen. Lamine Cissé (Senegal), 19 international civilian; 5 military advisors; 6 civilian police; 2 UN volunteers; 29 local civilian.	Until 31 December 2003
UNTOP: United Nations Tajikistan Office of Peace-Building	June 2000	Representative of the Secretary General: Vladimir Sotirov (Bulgaria): 10 international civilian; 18 local civilian; 1 civilian police advisor.	Until 31 May 2003
Office of the Special Representative of the Secretary-General for West Africa	March 2002	Special Representative of the Secretary General: Ahmedou Ould-Abdallah (Mauritania). 5 international civilian; 2 local civilian.	Until 1 June 2003
UNAMA: United Nations Assistance Mission in Afghanistan	March 2002	Special Representative of the Secretary General: Lakhdar Brahimi (Algeria). 166 international civilian; 303 local civilian; 4 military advisors; 4 civilian police.	Until 28 March 2003
Source: United Nations Background Note 15 January 2003.		Total Personnel for the 13 missions: 398 international civilian personnel; 39 military personnel and civilian police and 636 local civilian personnel.	

UNITED NATIONS PEACEKEEPING MISSIONS

	Established	Present Strength	Fatalities	Renewal Date
UNTSO: United Nations Truce Supervision Organisation	June 1948	154 military; 101 international civilian; 111 local civilian.	Fatalities: 38	
UNMOGIP: United Nations Military Observer Group in India and Pakistan	January 1949	44 military; 24 international civilian; 47 local civilian.	Fatalities: 9	
UNFICYP: United Nations Peacekeeping Force in Cyprus	March 1964	1,211 military; 35 civilian police; 42 international civilian; 105 local civilian.	Fatalities: 170	15 June 2003
UNDOF: United Nations Disengagement Observer Force	June 1974	1,043 military; 39 international civilian; 88 local civilian.	Fatalities: 40	30 June 2003
UNIFIL: United Nations Interim Force in the Lebanon	March 1978	2,077 military; 116 international civilian; 314 local civilian.	Fatalities: 246	31 January 2003
UNIKOM: United Nations Iraq Kuwait Observation Mission	April 1991	1,105 military; 63 international civilian; 164 local civilian.	Fatalities: 17	The Security Council reviews the mandate of UNIKOM every six months.
MINURSO: United Nations Mission for the Referendum in Western Sahara	April 1991	217 military; 25 civilian police; 167 international civilian; 123 local civilian.	Fatalities: 10	31 January 2003
UNOMIG: United Nations Observer Mission in Georgia	August 1993	117 military; 91 international civilian; 175 local civilian.	Fatalities: 7	31 January 2003
UNMIK: United Nations Interim Administration Mission in Kosovo	June 1999	4,446 civilian police; 39 military; 1,022 international civilian; 3,243 local civilian.	Fatalities: 20	Established for an initial period of 12 months; to continue unless the Security Council decides otherwise.

UNITED NATIONS PEACEKEEPING MISSIONS *continued*

	Established	Present Strength	Fatalities	Renewal Date
UNAMSIL: United Nations Mission in Sierra Leone	October 1999	16,042 military; 44 civilian police; 298 international civilian; 552 local civilian.	Fatalities: 99	30 March 2003
MONUC: United Nations Organisation Mission in the Democratic Republic of the Congo	December 1999	4,371 military; 49 civilian police; 559 international civilian; 675 local civilian.	Fatalities: 12	30 June 2003
UNMEE: United Nations Mission in Ethiopia and Eritrea	July 2000	4,034 military; 227 international civilian; 263 local civilian.	Fatalities: 3	15 March 2003
UNMISET: United Nations Mission of Support in East Timor	May 2002	3,853 military; 730 civilian police; 895 international civilian; 1,425 local civilian.	Fatalities: 5	20 May 2003

Sources: United Nations: Background note 15 January 2003, and United Nations current peacekeeping operations website.

All figures as of 31 December 2002.

Total Personnel: Contributing states: 89; military personnel and civilian police: 39,636; international civilian personnel: 3,644; and local civilian personnel: 7,285.

Total fatalities since 1948 as of 31 December 2002: 1,778.

Three operations were laid down in 2002: **UNTAET:** United Nations Transitional Administration in East Timor in May 2002; **UNMIBH:** United Nations Mission in Bosnia and Herzegovina; and **UNMOP:** United Nations Mission of Observers in Prevlaka in December 2002.

SANCTIONS. Following the events of 11 September and the overthrow of the Taliban government in Afghanistan, the Security Council in January expanded the sanctions—an asset freeze, a travel ban, and an arms embargo—beyond the territory of Afghanistan to include individuals and entities belonging to or associated with the Taliban, Osama bin Laden, and the al-Qaida organisation regardless of their location. Thus the mandate changed from national to global counter-terrorist measures. The monitoring group was similarly charged to monitor the compliance, implementation, and enforcement by member states. In December the Council introduced humanitarian exemptions regarding the frozen funds of the Taliban and members of al-Qaida.

In Angola the Council, in an attempt to facilitate the transition of the National Union for the Total Independence of Angola (UNITA) from an armed rebel group into a political party and to allow UNITA leaders to travel and negotiate with the government about cessation of hostilities, decided to suspend the travel restrictions against UNITA leaders for two periods of 90 days and then lifted the ban altogether on 14 November. On 9 December it removed the remaining sanctions—the diamond and arms ban and the asset freeze—against UNITA and decided to dissolve the Angola Sanctions Committee. The Council also extended the mandate of the monitoring mission twice until 19 December, at which point it was wound up.

The oil-for-food programme in Iraq was renewed on three occasions. The Council in May adopted a new mechanism for the processing of civilian exports to Iraq which was further refined in December. Its purpose was to increase sharply the flow of these goods while maintaining controls on dual use and other military-related equipment. There was, however, a substantial fall in oil revenue, which reduced the purchase of goods and services.

With regard to Liberia the Council twice asked the Secretary General to re-establish the Panel of Experts, first for five weeks and then for three months, to visit the region and to provide an independent audit of the government's compliance with the arms embargo, and the diamond and travel bans which had been imposed because of its support for rebels in Sierra Leone and elsewhere in the region; and then to conduct a follow up assessment of compliance with the sanctions which had been renewed for a further 12 months in May and to assess the potential economic, humanitarian, and social impact upon the Liberian population of further proposed sanctions. The chairman of the Sanctions Committee wrote letters to states seeking information about alleged violations of the sanctions regime.

The Council in December, concerned that the government of Sierra Leone did not have effective control over the diamond producing areas, decided to extend the prohibition on uncertified rough diamonds from Sierra Leone until 5 June 2003. The chairman of the Sanctions Committee, which lacked a monitoring mechanism, visited the area on a fact-finding mission between 22 June and 4 July and briefed the Security Council upon his return.

The Council decided that the arms embargo on Somalia should be strengthened. First in May it asked the Secretary General to appoint a expert team of two to provide the Sanctions Committee with an action plan which would establish the resources and expertise that a Panel of Experts would require to be able to generate independent information on violations and for improving the enforcement of the embargo. In July the Council asked the Secretary General to establish a Panel of Experts to be based in Nairobi, Kenya, for six months, and it was decided that the chairman would visit the region to examine how the embargo might be further reinforced.

2. DEFENCE AND ECONOMIC ORGANISATIONS

i. DEFENCE ORGANISATIONS

North Atlantic Treaty Organization (NATO)
DATE OF FOUNDATION: 1949   HEADQUARTERS: Brussels, Belgium
OBJECTIVES: To ensure the collective security of member states
MEMBERSHIP (END-'02): Belgium, Canada, Czech Republic, Denmark, France, Germany, Greece, Hungary, Iceland, Italy, Luxembourg, Netherlands, Norway, Poland, Portugal, Spain, Turkey, United Kingdom, United States (total 19)
SECRETARY GENERAL: Lord (George) Robertson of Port Ellen (UK)

Partnership for Peace (PFP)
DATE OF FOUNDATION: 1994   HEADQUARTERS: Brussels, Belgium
OBJECTIVES: To provide a framework for cooperation between NATO and the former communist and neutral states of Europe and ex-Soviet Central Asia
MEMBERSHIP (END-'02): Albania, Armenia, Austria, Azerbaijan, Belarus, Bulgaria, Croatia, Estonia, Finland, Georgia, Hungary, Irish Republic, Kazakhstan, Kyrgyzstan, Latvia, Lithuania, Macedonia, Malta (suspended), Moldova, Romania, Russia, Slovakia, Slovenia, Sweden, Switzerland, Tajikistan, Turkmenistan, Ukraine, Uzbekistan (total 28)

ON 10 September 2001, it was still common, if somewhat unimaginative, to speak of "the post-Cold War world". Since then this phrase had given way to "the post-11 September world", and it remained to be seen how long the new shorthand would remain the point of departure for analysis of international security and defence. Around the world, security and defence organisations—such as the ANZUS Pact, the Andean Pact, the ASEAN Regional Forum, the Council for Security Co-operation in the Asia Pacific, and the Organisation for Security and Co-operation in Europe—were all touched in different ways by the impact of 11 September. These organisations struggled during 2002 to respond formally to the radically changing international security landscape. At the same time, and more importantly, their members struggled to find a common language and common perception of threat around which to cohere. Nowhere was the organisational struggle to adapt more evident than in the efforts of NATO and the EU, and nowhere was the political struggle to cohere more pronounced than between the USA and its European allies.

The year did not begin well for the transatlantic security relationship. In his State of the Union speech in January 2002, President George W. Bush broadened the US campaign against al-Qaida and international terrorism into an assault upon the "axis of evil": alleged terrorist-sponsoring and weapon-proliferating states such as Iran, Iraq and North Korea (see IV.1). For many critics in Europe, Bush's language was exaggerated, simplistic, and inflammatory, and his remarks were condemned as pandering to a domestic political agenda, which was at best uninformed and at worst xenophobic. European critics saw the US administration becoming increasingly unilateralist, in its policies on the Kyoto Protocol and the Anti-Ballistic Missile Treaty, and in its unconditional backing for Israel, as well as alarmingly hegemonic in its calls for "regime change" in Iraq. On the other hand, there were those in the Bush administration who were losing patience with, and interest in, the USA's European allies. From the point of view of the US government, European allies steadfastly refused to commit more resources to defence to keep pace with the US effort—the US$48 billion increase in US defence spending dwarfed any European defence budget—and remained inward-looking and obsessed with the fine detail of institutional arrangements within the EU.

NORTH ATLANTIC TREATY ORGANISATION. In spite of, or perhaps because of, US-European tensions and disagreements, NATO set out in 2002 to meet its Secretary General George Robertson's challenge of "modernisation or marginalisation". NATO's "transformation" agenda would touch upon all aspects of the Alliance: its membership; its relations with Russia; its functional and geographical role and competences; and its operational capabilities.

Having decided in 1999 that its next enlargement would be decided no later than 2002, NATO found itself with a shortlist of 10 applicants, the so-called "Vilnius Group" of Albania, Bulgaria, Croatia, Estonia, Latvia, Lithuania, Macedonia, Romania, Slovakia, and Slovenia. All 10 had participated in NATO's five-part Membership Action Plan, designed after the 1999 enlargement both to correct the impression that the "open door" had slammed shut, and to assist new candidates in their pre-accession preparatory work. But some candidates were always far more likely than others to gain admission. And so the challenge to NATO—as it had been in 1997-99—was to select the candidates that it really wanted, or needed, without discouraging the failures and without showing Article 10 of NATO's Washington Treaty to be hollow rhetoric.

The altered international security environment gave the application and selection process some sense of purpose. Familiar questions could be revisited and discussed more candidly. Why did the candidates want NATO membership? Fear of Russian aggression now seemed exaggerated. Wishing to join the Western "club" of nations was flattering, but hardly urgent, and in any case the EU could probably offer better accommodation. The clever candidates exploited the chink in NATO's armour; the general presumption was for enlargement, so it was more a problem for NATO to rationalise rejection than for the candidates to prove their case for admission. What, then, could each of the candidates bring to NATO's pool of military capability? Some, such as the three Baltic republics, could bring very little, but what military force they had was NATO-

and intervention-oriented (having built their national forces from scratch). Others, such as Bulgaria and Romania, brought very large armed forces still undergoing post-Cold War restructuring, and certainly too much for NATO to digest in their current form. Slovakia had similar problems militarily, but was generally more affluent and economically stable than Bulgaria and Romania. Slovenia, with its small armed forces, could present few problems if admitted. Albania was still considered politically eccentric and an economic liability, and Croatia and Macedonia geopolitically too unpredictable.

The 11 September attacks and their aftermath generated a new criterion for selection: what could the applicants bring to NATO's support for the USA in its "war against terrorism"? In this respect, Bulgaria and Romania became beneficiaries of the September 2001 crisis. Admission of these two could give NATO a coherent and geostrategically significant "southern dimension", connecting Hungary through the Balkans to Greece and Turkey. Not often in agreement on matters of national and regional security, Greece and Turkey shared the view that Bulgaria and Romania should be admitted. Seizing the moment, and exploiting the high level of public support for NATO membership, Romania was energetic in making its military infrastructure useful: two military airports were made available for transit use by friendly foreign expeditionary forces; and the Black Sea port of Constanta was made available as a staging point for US troops en route to operations in Kosovo.

All was decided at NATO's November summit meeting in Prague. Albania, Croatia, and Macedonia were turned down, remaining among the dozen or so European countries outside NATO. But the other seven candidates—the three Baltic republics (Estonia, Latvia, and Lithuania); Slovakia and Slovenia (the "Slo-Slo Duo"); Bulgaria and Romania—were all invited to join, in the Alliance's biggest ever single enlargement. Only a few years earlier, the accession of several of these countries would have been unthinkable. But for many commentators, the real significance of the latest enlargement was the effect that it would have on the functioning of the Alliance. By May 2004, when the current accession process was expected to be complete, NATO's membership would total 26, with several applications pending. In political, bureaucratic, and military terms, could a NATO of 26 members really be efficient and effective? And might enlargement simply exacerbate long-standing and unresolved tensions within NATO? For example, would enlargement make it more or less likely that European NATO members—however many—could keep pace with their US ally in defence spending and military capability? Would the purpose of NATO be made any clearer by enlargement? Several new members viewed NATO in unreconstructed Cold War terms, as a guarantee of collective self-defence, perhaps against a resurgent Russia. But given NATO's improving relations with Russia, some observers found this line of thinking anachronistic, arguing instead that the new NATO could only be rationalised politically, rather than militarily. For them, enlargement was a sufficient demonstration of NATO's vitality, as a union of free-market democracies observing the rule of international law and enjoying peaceful relations with each other. Other commentators tried to occupy the middle ground, seeing in NATO a loosely co-operative political union, but with the capacity for decisive military action when required. That enlargement proceeded without these questions being answered, or indeed even addressed meaningfully, prompted speculation as to why the process had been so straightforward. In short, was the Prague enlargement really testimony to NATO's vitality and relevance, or proof that it no longer mattered much? For some, a decisive shift in the international security landscape had taken place. A new relationship now operated between the USA and Russia, one that was no longer fixated on Europe, and one in which NATO could no longer play a leading role. By this argument, the USA had progressively been losing faith in its European allies as collective military partners, and was now willing to see NATO slip into military obsolescence.

The improved relationship with Russia was high on NATO's transformation agenda during 2002. In large part a reward to Russia's President Vladimir Putin for his support of the Bush administration's military operations in Afghanistan and the broader campaign against terrorism, the long-awaited NATO-Russia Council was inaugurated in May at the NATO foreign ministers meeting in Reykjavik. Superseding the flaccid 1997 Permanent Joint Council, the new body offered Russia an executive, rather than merely consultative role in NATO's deliberations, and was described by Robertson as "historic and even revolutionary". Although not a member of the Alliance, and therefore not in a position to influence NATO's core business—its Article 5 mutual defence pact—Russia would henceforth be involved in the development of joint policy in many areas, including counter-terrorism, arms control and non-proliferation, missile defence, crisis management and peacekeeping, and search and rescue operations.

As well as the high politics of enlargement, and the complex diplomatic relationship with Russia, the definition of a clear strategic mission, with the operational capabilities to match, was a major preoccupation for NATO in 2002. NATO had been sidelined by the USA in Afghanistan, largely because the Alliance did not have sufficient medium-scale, integrated, and deployable forces available at short notice. At Prague, NATO's leaders responded by establishing a new NATO Response Force (NRF). Following Bush's visit to Europe in May 2002, when he spoke of the case for NATO to have a central role in the "war against terrorism", the Alliance also began to examine and improve its capacity for counter-terrorism. And late in the year, the US administration's request to NATO for help in the event of military operations against Iraq, seemed finally to lay the ghost of the US lack of interest in NATO in the days immediately following 11 September. The Prague summit also, finally, gave a boost to the ambitious and by now flagging NATO Defence Capabilities Initiative, launched in 1999. At Prague it was agreed to focus on fewer, but strategically critical capabilities: defence against chemical, biological, radiological, and nuclear attack; superiority in command, control, communications, and intelligence; and improvements in the interoperability, deployability, and sustainment of combat forces.

EUROPEAN SECURITY AND DEFENCE POLICY. For the EU, 2002 was an opportunity to develop the European Security and Defence Policy (ESDP). The 1999 Helsinki European Council had agreed to establish an ESDP bureaucratic infrastructure in Brussels, and to work towards the goal of a 60,000-troop deployable force by the end of 2003. This "European Rapid Reaction Force" would be expected to conduct, simultaneously, a "heavy" operation such as the prevention of a conflict or the separation of belligerent forces, and a "light"' operation such as the evacuation in a crisis of an embassy's civilian staff. An extraordinary meeting of the European Council on 21 September 2001 had also sought to involve the EU in the global fight against terrorism, although it remained unclear late into 2002 as to how best the EU should contribute to this.

In order for the EU force to be effective in any situation—"heavy", "light", or counter-terrorism—it had long been recognised that deficiencies in critical military equipment would have to be addressed: suppression of enemy air defences; precision-guided weapons; un-manned aerial vehicles; reconnaissance, intelligence, surveillance, and target acquisition; combat search and rescue; air-to-air refuelling; and strategic transport. These equipment deficiencies were all too familiar, most of them having been identified in NATO's Defence Capabilities Initiative, and subsequently at the Helsinki European Council. In an effort to invigorate the development of these key capabilities, the EU established its own initiative—the European Capabilities Action Plan (ECAP)—in late 2001. Rather than produce an ambitious and overwhelming list of capability deficiencies, ECAP took a more subtle approach, seeking to identify "bottom-up", multinational projects which had a reasonable prospect of being delivered. ECAP development panels were established, but for some sceptics the initiative made too little progress during 2002.

As well as capabilities, another scarce commodity was practical experience of crisis management and decision-making. Addressing this deficiency, the EU organised its first crisis management exercise in May 2002, testing political-military structures and procedures at an early stage of a crisis. Another important step was taken at the Seville European Council in June, when it was agreed that the EU's first crisis management operation would begin in January 2003, in the form of the deployment of a 500-strong EU Police Mission to Bosnia and Herzegovina. It was ironic that after so much ambitious talk of a large and deployable military capability, the EU's first mission would be a small policing operation. Furthermore, from NATO's perspective it was feared that whatever the political significance for the EU, in practical terms the EU mission would be less helpful than it appeared; the 500-strong EU contingent would replace the 1,500-strong International Police Task Force in Bosnia and Herzegovina, thereby increasing the workload for NATO's military forces in the country.

The EU's lack of practical experience was felt most keenly in the deployment of military forces on peace support and conflict prevention operations. According to the Helsinki timetable, the European Rapid Reaction Force (ERRF) would become progressively more capable and deployable, reaching its full operational capability by the end of 2003. But late in 2001, a controversial analysis by the British Foreign and Commonwealth Office suggested that it might be another decade before the ERRF was ready for peacekeeping and similar operations. In March, leaked documents emphasised the UK's scepticism regarding the capacity of the EU to undertake a major military operation. Undaunted, the March 2002 Barcelona European Council insisted that the EU was indeed ready to take over from NATO's 700-strong "Task Force Fox" in Macedonia, when that commitment concluded in October 2002. It was acknowledged, however, that the EU operation could not take place without agreement with NATO on sharing military and planning assets. Within months, EU planning for the Macedonia commitment (to be renamed "Operation Allied Harmony") was blocked by a dispute between Greece and Turkey over EU access to NATO equipment and planning procedures. This long-standing disagreement appeared to have been resolved in December 2001, when the so-called "Ankara text"—worked out between Turkey, the USA, and the UK—made concessions to Turkey in return for its endorsement of the December 2000 Nice provisions giving EU the access it needed to NATO planning and military assets. But when Greece assumed the European Council Presidency for ESDP matters in July 2002, it objected to what it saw as Turkish oversight on EU operations. Although some commentators despaired of resolving the disagreement while Greece held the presidency, the dispute was finally settled in mid-December 2002 with the long-awaited "Berlin-Plus" arrangement, hailed by George Robertson as the completion of the "great jigsaw" of European defence. "Berlin-Plus"' gave the EU "assured access" to NATO planning capabilities, and provided for NATO support to EU-led operations in which the Atlantic Alliance as a whole was not engaged militarily.

The scarcity of deployable military capability in Europe severely limited the practical capacity of ESDP, encouraging the argument that the best prospects for the EU project lay in areas of so-called "soft security" such as post-conflict judicial reconstruction, policing, and general conflict prevention. Hence, settlement of the "Berlin-Plus" arrangement was an extremely significant milestone in the development of the ESDP: without a close, practical relationship with NATO, the Helsinki project could never amount to much. Other achievements in 2002 included the first ever formal meeting of EU defence ministers on 13 May, and broad agreement on the financing of EU missions. With all of these agreements, 2002 was undoubtedly a good year for the ESDP. It was all the more surprising, therefore, to see old divisions re-emerge in the course of the year. The UK had long resisted the idea of "reinforced co-operation" in the context of ESDP, arguing that NATO was the most suitable organisation for military responses to armed attacks or threats against a member state. When the Spanish government and others argued that the ERRF should be directed explicitly at counter-terrorism, the UK and some Nordic countries extended the earlier argument, claiming that such operations would best be undertaken by NATO. Conflicting expectations of the ESDP were exposed most clearly in the last weeks of the year. A report by the defence working group of the Convention on the Future of Europe discussed, *inter alia*, the establishment of a joint military college, the expansion of the EU's operational agenda to include combating terrorism, the creation of a new defence industrial co-operation organisation, and even the inclusion of something close to a collective defence clause in the 2004 revision of the EU treaty. The last two proposals, in particular, were anathema to the UK government, which argued again that defence industrial and procurement matters should not come under EU legal jurisdiction, and was adamant that defence guarantees should remain the preserve of NATO, which was the only organisation able to meet such guarantees.

PROSPECTS. After many years of often rather circular argument there were encouraging signs in 2002 that the USA and its European allies had at last found a way both to promote NATO's transformation and to encourage the development of the EU's ESDP. For over a decade, the contest between the main European security and defence organisations had been a self-fuelling combustion process, with increasingly hot exhaust driving increasingly extravagant ambitions, none of which were met in practice. In 2002 however, both organisations showed the potential to respond organisationally and operationally to the evolving international security agenda. The most optimistic assessment of the events of 2002 was that these two ambitious projects were at last developing in tandem, enabling the US-European security relationship better to confront the threats and challenges of "the post-11 September world". But the spat over the scope of the European Convention warned of underlying disagreements which might require resolution before substantial progress could be made in either organisation. So far, moreover, neither "new NATO" nor the ESDP had been tested politically or militarily.

ii. ECONOMIC ORGANISATIONS

International Monetary Fund (IMF)

DATE OF FOUNDATION: 1945 HEADQUARTERS: Washington DC, USA
OBJECTIVES: To promote international monetary co-operation and to assist member states in establishing sound budgetary and trading policies
MEMBERSHIP (END-'02): 184 members
MANAGING DIRECTOR: Horst Köhler (Germany)

International Bank for Reconstruction and Development (IBRD/World Bank)

DATE OF FOUNDATION: 1945 HEADQUARTERS: Washington DC, USA
OBJECTIVES: To make loans on reasonable terms to developing countries with the aim of increasing their productive capacity
MEMBERSHIP (END-'02): 184 members
PRESIDENT: James D. Wolfensohn (United States)

World Trade Organisation (WTO)

DATE OF FOUNDATION: 1995 (successor to General Agreement on Tariffs and Trade, GATT)
HEADQUARTERS: Geneva, Switzerland
OBJECTIVES: To eliminate tariffs and other barriers to international trade and to facilitate international financial settlements
MEMBERSHIP (END-'02): 144 acceding parties
DIRECTOR GENERAL: Supachai Panitchpakdi (Thailand)

Organisation for Economic Co-operation and Development (OECD)
DATE OF FOUNDATION: 1965   HEADQUARTERS: Paris, France
OBJECTIVES: To promote economic growth in member states and the sound development of the world economy
MEMBERSHIP (END-'02): Australia, Austria, Belgium, Canada, Czech Republic, Denmark, Finland, France, Germany, Greece, Hungary, Iceland, Ireland, Italy, Japan, South Korea, Luxembourg, Mexico, The Netherlands, New Zealand, Norway, Poland, Portugal, Slovakia, Spain, Sweden, Switzerland, Turkey, United Kingdom, United States (total 30)
SECRETARY GENERAL: Donald Johnston (Canada)

Organisation of the Petroleum Exporting Countries (OPEC)
DATE OF FOUNDATION: 1960   HEADQUARTERS: Vienna, Austria
OBJECTIVES: To unify and co-ordinate member states' oil policies and to safeguard their interests
MEMBERSHIP (END-'02): Algeria, Indonesia, Iran, Iraq, Kuwait, Libya, Nigeria, Qatar, Saudi Arabia, United Arab Emirates, Venezuela (total 11)
SECRETARY GENERAL: Alvaro Silva Calderón (Venezuela)

INTERNATIONAL MONETARY FUND. The financial collapse in Argentina and related "contagion" in neighbouring countries dominated the 2002 agenda for the IMF, which continued to face questions about the effectiveness of its "standard model" for dealing with national economic meltdowns. Despite Argentina's default on more than US$100 billion in loans, the IMF declined throughout the year to approve any new assistance because of the failure of the Argentinian government to adopt the IMF's prescribed economic reforms and banking regulations. The relatively tougher line toward Argentina was seen as the IMF's response to criticism that it had sometimes continued lending for an inappropriate length of time to "delinquent" countries. At the same time, the Fund emphasised that it would strongly support countries which were "victims" of financial crises despite sound economic policies. In that context, a US$30 billion bailout package was endorsed in September for Brazil, perceived as suffering from problems (the difficulties in Argentina) which lay beyond its control.

IMF managing director Horst Köhler acknowledged that the situation in Latin America indicated that the Fund still "has a lot to learn" in trying to mitigate the effects of national economic emergencies. In order to facilitate quick negotiations between creditors and nations facing potential default in the future, the Fund proposed in 2002 that provisions henceforth be attached to loans that would make it easier to reschedule repayments if necessary. Another much more controversial plan called for creation of a Sovereign Debt Restructuring Mechanism (SDRM) within the IMF to arbitrate between creditors and debtor nations. Although IMF members endorsed the proposals "in principle" at the September joint meeting with the World Bank, international commercial banks remained vehemently opposed to forced arbitration through the SDRM.

In other activity in 2002, the IMF called on rich nations to liberalise their trade regimes to help boost the sluggish international economy, criticising recent US protectionist measures in regard to steel tariffs and farm subsidies as antithetical to global development. The Fund also warned several EU countries to rein in projected budget deficits and criticised the burgeoning US trade deficit as a potential source of global economic "instability".

WORLD BANK. In July 2002 donor countries agreed to a US$23 billion, three-year replenishment of the International Development Association (IDA), the arm of the Bank which lent to some 79 poor countries on a highly concessional basis. The accord was reached only after the USA compromised on its initial proposal that 50 per cent of the money be offered in the form of grants rather than loans. The USA, arguing that past Bank lending had "heaped debt" on developing countries whilst doing little to combat poverty, had urged that grants be given directly to health, education, and sanitation projects in developing countries without being channelled through "wasteful" national governments. However, other lenders feared that IDA resources might eventually be depleted through such large-scale use of grants, and the final agreement provided for a grant component of about 20 per cent. For its part, the Bank claimed that the IDA had "sharpened its focus" regarding lending and was positioned to support "good-policy countries". Meanwhile, Bank officials called upon rich nations to provide an additional US$40-60 billion in overall aid to help poor countries reach current development goals. Part of that aid would be earmarked for a new Bank initiative, launched in April, which envisioned full enrolment of elementary school-age children by 2015. According to Bank estimates, as many as 20 per cent of such children in the world currently did not attend school. Twenty-three countries were declared eligible for the educational funding, many of them in Africa, where absenteeism had been exacerbated in recent years by the AIDS epidemic.

The Bank acknowledged in 2002 that initial projections had proved "overly optimistic" regarding the programme that had been adopted in 1996 in conjunction with the IMF to help Heavily Indebted Poor Countries. It was reported that only a handful of the more than 30 countries considered eligible for the programme had been accorded debt forgiveness to date, while falling commodity prices and overall sluggish global economic growth were constraining the ability to establish "sustainable" debt levels for many poor countries. In order to invigorate the international economy, the Bank called upon developed countries to liberalise their trade policies and urged the private sector to invest in infrastructure development in poor countries.

WORLD TRADE ORGANISATION. Entering 2002, supporters of trade liberalisation hoped that swift progress would ensue in the WTO's "Doha Round" negotiations as the result of a perceived renewed commitment to multilateralism emanating from the worldwide response to the attacks in the USA on 11 September 2001 and the subsequent global "war on terrorism". However, momentum in that regard, if it ever really existed, dissipated quickly, in part under the influence of major disputes between the USA and the EU. Only two months after the Doha Round was launched with much fanfare, the WTO's appellate body in January confirmed an earlier ruling from a dispute tribunal that a massive US tax shelter for US companies conducting business overseas was a violation of WTO regulations. The WTO subsequently ruled that the EU could impose some US$4 billion in retaliatory tariffs against the USA, although no action had been taken by the end of the year as efforts continued toward a possible negotiated settlement that would include revising the offending US legislation. The EU was also deeply distressed by the USA's imposition in March of import tariffs of up to 30 per cent on steel in order to protect US producers. Other major manufacturers, including Japan and China, joined the EU in filing a formal complaint with the WTO in regard to the matter. In addition, WTO officials criticised the USA's decision in May to provide US$180 billion in subsidies to its farmers over the next 10 years.

These and other disputes added up to a "long list of headaches" for Supachai Panitchpakdi, the former Deputy Prime Minister of Thailand, who took over as WTO director general in September. (Supachai succeeded Mike Moore of New Zealand as part of an agreement reached after extensive negotiations in 1999 under which the two were to split a six-year term.) Supachai, the first person from a developing country to lead the Organisation, bravely pledged to attempt to rejuvenate the Doha Round talks in order to meet the proposed completion deadline of December 2004. However, progress, such as it was, was mostly limited to procedural rather that substantive matters. A "mini-summit" of 25 prominent WTO members in November agreed to pursue the "political will" necessary to energise the trade talks. However, the difficulty in translating rhetoric into action was again underscored in December when the USA vetoed a proposed WTO accord that would have provided poor countries with access to inexpensive versions of recently patented medicines. (The USA, mindful of the potential effect on its pharmaceutical sector, wanted the list of covered drugs to be significantly more restricted than proposed by the developing countries.)

The new WTO director general, decrying "resurgent protectionist sentiments", also promised to work toward streamlining WTO dispute settlement mechanisms and to provide greater technical assistance to developing countries to help them negotiate more successfully with the highly industrialised nations. At the same time, Supachai generated concern among some developing countries by announcing that he would seek intensified co-operation with the International Labour Organisation as well as international environmental organisations. (Some developing countries saw extensive labour and environmental regulations as weapons that could be used against them by the developed countries.)

ORGANISATION FOR ECONOMIC CO-OPERATION AND DEVELOPMENT. The OECD made significant progress in 2002 in its campaign to eliminate national "tax havens", considered harmful to global trade and investment because they offered low-tax or no-tax options to foreign depositors. Of the 38 countries and territories that were included on the OECD's original list of offenders in 2000, only seven (Andorra, Liberia, Liechtenstein, Marshall Islands, Monaco, Nauru, and Vanuatu) were still deemed "unco-operative" at the end of 2002. The others had either already implemented measures to permit the requested exchange of information among countries to prosecute tax evaders or had agreed to do so. OECD accords early in the year with several Caribbean countries were considered crucial in overcoming resistance to the OECD initiative on the part of many of the jurisdictions involved, some of which had earlier called for "solidarity" in trying to protect the secrecy of their financial institutions. Nevertheless, the matter continued to generate controversy, particularly in regard to the failure of several OECD countries, most notably Switzerland, to adopt the same standards as those required of the "listed" countries. Late in the year the OECD announced that its members would be permitted to address "defects" in their tax regimes on a voluntary basis until April 2003, at which point the Organisation said it would consider imposing sanctions such as those envisioned for any non-OECD countries still being unco-operative.

The financial aspects of the US-led "war on terrorism" in 2002 also focused attention on the anti-money laundering activities of the Financial Action Task Force (FATF), which was formed in 1989 by the Group of Seven countries and subsequently co-operated closely with the OECD. A number of prominent nations (including Hungary, Israel, and Russia) were dropped from the FATF blacklist in 2002, leaving 11 jurisdictions (Cook Islands, Egypt, Grenada, Guatemala, Indonesia, Myanmar, Nauru, Nigeria, Philippines, St. Vincent and the Grenadines, and Ukraine) to face the "name and shame" pressure as of the end of the year. The FATF encouraged governments and corporations not to conduct any business with the financial institutions in those "non-co-operating" countries. (The USA was reportedly considering formal action of that nature in regard to several countries under new powers granted to the federal government as part of the Patriot Act passed in the wake of the 11 September 2001 terrorist attacks.) However, much like the OECD's tax haven initiative, the anti-money laundering campaign also faced criticism from developing countries that "rich countries" were being "let off the hook" and that poor countries were being disproportionately embarrassed by the blacklist. Consequently, in October it was announced that no new countries would be added to the list in 2003 while the IMF, World Bank, and FATF attempted to forge a "universal, co-operative approach" under which recalcitrant countries would be "persuaded" to be more aggressive in attacking money laundering.

In a related vein, the OECD warned that new security measures arising from the global anti-terror campaign could prove costly to the international economy if carried to extremes. For example, the Organisation argued, new border restrictions might impose higher transportation costs or lead to delays that could negatively affect perishable goods. Remittances from overseas workers, an economic mainstay for many poor countries, could also be restricted by more stringent immigration policies.

ORGANISATION OF THE PETROLEUM EXPORTING COUNTRIES. The year was one of high anxiety but little action for OPEC. Faced with a wobbly global economy, two major disruptions in Venezuela's output, surging Russian production, and intractable Middle East tensions, the OPEC ministers, not surprisingly, clung to the status quo for most of 2002. That meant sticking, at least officially, with the production cuts approved at the end of 2001 (effective 1 January 2002) in order to prop up prices which had slipped to US$17 per barrel in late 2001. Prices quickly rebounded in the spring of 2002 to the upper end of OPEC's preferred US$22-28 per barrel range. In fact, the increase was so sharp that some observers urged the cartel to increase production in order to temper the rise lest high prices dampen economic recovery efforts around the world. However, OPEC resisted the pressure, arguing that Middle East issues, particularly the aggressive stance of the Bush administration in the USA toward Iraq, were "distorting" the realities of supply and demand. According to OPEC's analysis (supported by most neutral observers), the so-called "war premium" was adding US$3-4 to the cost of a barrel of oil. OPEC continued to assert that current supplies were sufficient even as the per barrel price edged toward US$30 in the late summer and autumn. However, by that time the Organisation, praised over the past two years for its renewed cohesion, was facing a significant challenge to its credibility. It was estimated that members were "cheating" on their production quotas by as many as 3 million barrels per day over the stated 21.7 million barrel OPEC limit. In a complicated initiative to attempt to rectify the situation, in mid-December OPEC decided to raise its formal quota to 23 million barrels per day, with the hope that members would adhere to the new levels and thereby reduce actual production by some 5 per cent.

In addition to attempting to restore discipline within its own ranks, OPEC also assured the anxious international community in December that it was prepared to increase production immediately if necessary in order to counter unanticipated shortfalls. The most immediate challenge emanated from Venezuela, normally the source of about 2.5 million barrels per day but currently pumping only about 200,000 barrels per day because of a strike by oil workers attempting to force President Hugo Chávez from office (see IV.5.x). Chávez, a strong supporter of OPEC, had also faced a two-day coup attempt in April, following which he had recalled OPEC secretary general Ali Rodríguez Araque to resume leadership of Venezuela's national oil company. Underscoring the importance of Venezuela to the Organisation, OPEC quickly elected Venezuela's Energy Minister Alvaro Silva Calderón to serve as secretary general for the 18 months remaining in Rodríguez's term of office.

OPEC also grappled throughout 2002 with the issue of Iraq, the source of 1.8-2.0 million barrels of oil per day through the UN's "oil-for-food" programme. Especially difficult for OPEC was the decision by Iraq (currently a "non-voting" member of the Organisation and not a participant in its production quotas) in April to halt production for a month in support of the Palestinian cause. Iraq exhorted other Arab states to follow its example, Iran having already voiced, in a separate context, a willingness to use the "oil spigot" as a means of applying pressure to Israel and the USA. However, Iran (as well as Libya, another potential "embargo" candidate) declined to join Saddam Hussein's campaign, a decision that was warmly welcomed by the other OPEC members.

3. OTHER WORLD ORGANISATIONS

i. THE COMMONWEALTH

DATE OF FOUNDATION: 1931   HEADQUARTERS: London, UK
OBJECTIVES: To maintain political, cultural and social links between (mainly English-speaking) countries of the former British Empire and others subscribing to Commonwealth democratic principles and aims
MEMBERSHIP (END-'02): Antigua & Barbuda, Australia, the Bahamas, Bangladesh, Barbados, Belize, Botswana, Brunei, Cameroon, Canada, Cyprus, Dominica, Fiji, the Gambia, Ghana, Grenada, Guyana, India, Jamaica, Kenya, Kiribati, Lesotho, Malawi, Malaysia, Maldives, Malta, Mauritius, Mozambique, Namibia, Nauru, New Zealand, Nigeria, Pakistan (suspended), Papua New Guinea, St Kitts & Nevis, St Lucia, St Vincent & the Grenadines, Samoa, Seychelles, Sierra Leone, Singapore, Solomon Islands, South Africa, Sri Lanka, Swaziland, Tanzania, Tonga, Trinidad & Tobago, Tuvalu, Uganda, United Kingdom, Vanuatu, Zambia, Zimbabwe (suspended) (total 54)
SECRETARY GENERAL: Don McKinnon (New Zealand)

THROUGHOUT 2002 the situation in Zimbabwe remained central to Commonwealth political concerns. When the eight-member Commonwealth Ministerial Action Group (CMAG) met on 30 January it called for an end to violence and intimidation and for all parties to be allowed to campaign freely in the forthcoming elections. The Commonwealth Heads of Government Meeting (CHOGM), postponed from 2001, was rearranged for 2-5 March, in Coolum, north of Brisbane, Australia. Zimbabwean President Robert Mugabe called the presidential elections for 9-11 March, just days after CHOGM, thus limiting the scope for action in Coolum (see VII.2.iii).

As the heads gathered, a 52-strong Commonwealth election group, led by former Nigerian head of state Abdulsalami Abubakar, was already in Zimbabwe. It was by then the only fully international observer group on the ground, EU observers having withdrawn. In the face of growing pressure for the suspension or even expulsion of Zimbabwe from the Commonwealth, CHOGM empowered a committee of three heads of state to decide what action to take as soon as the observers had reported. The three—dubbed "the troika"—were Presidents Thabo Mbeki of South Africa and Olusegun Obasanjo of Nigeria, together with Prime Minister John Howard of Australia.

The observer group report appeared on 14 March. It was unambiguous in that it found that the election "did not adequately allow for a free expression of will by the electors". Mbeki and Obasanjo flew to Harare en route to London to persuade Mugabe to seek to create a government of national unity, but he rejected the idea. In a tense one-day meeting in Marlborough House on 19 March, at which Mbeki showed some hesitancy, the three decided that Zimbabwe should be "suspended from the councils of the Commonwealth" for one year.

Mugabe had not attended Coolum, but sent his Foreign Minister. CHOGM recognised that land was at the core of the crisis and offered help on the issue, but Zimbabwe maintained that the Commonwealth's involvement in its affairs was illegal and outside CMAG's terms of reference. Attempts by secretary general Don McKinnon to open a dialogue with Zimbabwe were rejected.

Despite the postponement, the turnout of heads at the summit was high. Of the

51 leaders in Coolum, 35 were heads of state or government. Pakistan was still suspended and so was absent, but Fiji was there after its restoration to full membership. Antigua and Barbuda, and Grenada did not attend.

The summit's most substantial outcome was adoption of the report of the High Level Review Group established in 1999 to examine the role of the Commonwealth "and advise on how it could respond to the challenges of the new century". The five-month postponement of CHOGM led to an early leak of the draft report, the text of which so disappointed non-governmental organisations (NGOs) that they issued a more robust document entitled *A New Vision for the Commonwealth*. Governments, however, resisted pressure for any substantial change in their draft. An important review proposal was to widen the "good offices" role of the secretary general, allowing him to take up at an earlier stage, with a member country, issues perceived as serious or persistent violations of the Commonwealth Principles. CHOGM also produced a declaration entitled *The Commonwealth in the 21st Century: Continuity and Renewal*, intended to complement the declarations of 1971 (Singapore—see AR 1971, pp. 499-500) and 1991 (Harare—see AR 1991, pp. 392-93).

The Commonwealth was increasingly active in pursuit of good governance. In Pakistan, Commonwealth observers found the October parliamentary elections flawed (see VIII.2.ii) and CMAG decided that the country should remain suspended "pending greater clarity and an assessment of the role and functioning of democratic institutions". It continued to monitor the situation in Solomon Islands, which remained unstable; and in Fiji, where coup threats and racial tensions remained evident. In his "good offices" role, the secretary general sent envoys to Swaziland and Guyana, and in the wake of the chaotic mid-year election in Papua New Guinea (see X.1.ii) an expert team from five countries went to advise on the future conduct of polling there.

The last week of the year ended on an upbeat note with the successful transfer of power in Kenya to President Mwai Kibaki, ending the 24-year rule of Daniel arap Moi and the 40-year supremacy of the Kenya African National Union (see VI.1.ii). In the months leading up to the election on 27 December the Commonwealth had successfully provided advice and technical help to the Electoral Commission of Kenya. Commonwealth observers, led by Adebyao Adedeji, a former UN under secretary general, gave the election and the work of the Commission a good (if still somewhat flawed) bill of health. They reported: "We have no hesitation in saying... the electoral process was credible, the conditions existed for a free expression of the will by the electors and the results reflected the wishes of the people of Kenya."

Leaders of 10 countries attended a Commonwealth round table in Denarau Island, Fiji, on 19-20 August to discuss ways to improve democratic government in the Pacific. The meeting, chaired by Fiji Prime Minister Laisenia Qarase, was along the lines of the exercise carried out by African leaders in Kasane, Botswana, in 1997. It found constitutions based on the Westminster model did not take account of the circumstances and values of Pacific societies and decided that different electoral systems should be considered.

In her golden jubilee year Queen Elizabeth II's Commonwealth-wide travels took her from Nunavut, in northernmost Canada, to Coolum for CHOGM, with the highly successful Commonwealth Games in Manchester, UK, as a culmination.

Commonwealth innovations in 2002 included the first-ever meeting of Foreign Ministers, held in New York (14 September) during the UN General Assembly, and attended by representatives of 37 countries. Another was the participation of NGOs in the Commonwealth Finance Ministers Meeting held in London (25-26 September). They presented the ministers with proposals from six regions to reduce global poverty, and in doing so illustrated the way in which NGOs were steadily winning a role at ministerial meetings.

Two major changes took place in the Commonwealth secretariat. Florence Mugasha of Uganda became deputy secretary general (political) upon the retirement of Kris Srinivasan of India. Mugasha had been the first woman in Africa to serve as a head of the public service. Matthew Neuhaus of Australia, a former High Commissioner in Nigeria, took over from Jon Sheppard, also of Australia, as director of political affairs.

ii. FRANCOPHONE AND PORTUGUESE-SPEAKING COMMUNITIES

International Organisation of Francophonie (OIF)
DATE OF FOUNDATION: 1997   HEADQUARTERS: Paris, France
OBJECTIVES: To promote co-operation and exchange between countries wholly or partly French-speaking and to defend usage of the French language
MEMBERSHIP (END-'02): Albania, Belgium (French-speaking community), Benin, Bulgaria, Burkina Faso, Burundi, Cambodia, Cameroon, Canada, Cape Verde, Central African Republic, Chad, Comoros, Democratic Republic of Congo, Republic of Congo, Côte d'Ivoire, Djibouti, Dominica, Egypt, Equatorial Guinea, France, Gabon, Guinea, Guinea-Bissau, Haiti, Laos, Lebanon, Luxembourg, Macedonia, Madagascar, Mali, Mauritania, Mauritius, Moldova, Monaco, Morocco, New Brunswick (Canada), Niger, Quebec (Canada), Romania, Rwanda, St Lucia, São Tomé & Príncipe, Senegal, Seychelles, Switzerland, Togo, Tunisia, Vanuatu, Vietnam (total 50)
SECRETARY GENERAL: Abdou Diouf (Senegal)

Community of Portuguese-Speaking Countries (CPLP)
DATE OF FOUNDATION: 1996   HEADQUARTERS: Lisbon, Portugal
OBJECTIVES: To promote political, diplomatic, economic, social and cultural co-operation between member-states and to enhance the status of the Portuguese language
MEMBERSHIP (END-'02): Angola, Brazil, Cape Verde, East Timor, Guinea-Bissau, Mozambique, Portugal, São Tomé & Príncipe (total 8)
EXECUTIVE SECRETARY: João Augusto de Médicis (Brazil)

THE central point of the year for the ORGANISATION INTERNATIONALE DE LA FRANCOPHONIE (OIF) was the final holding on 18-20 October in Beirut of the organisation's biennial summit. This had been delayed for a year from 2001 because of the destruction of the World Trade Centre in New York on 11 September of that year. Otherwise there were only a few routine meetings in 2002, such as the annual meeting of the Francophone parliamentary assembly, held in Berne, Switzerland.

To some extent the biennial summit benefited from the year's delay, especially in relation to France's position in the Arab world. This had always been a point that French leaders had liked to emphasise, but this time it seemed as if the long years of trying and diplomatic spadework were paying off. In the tense world situation, the Arab world appeared to be looking for all the friends it could get, and France—with its linguistic sphere of influence represented by the OIF—was an obvious candidate. It was also a major occasion for French President Jacques Chirac to cut an international figure in the wake of his massive victory in the May presidential elections, followed by a victory in parliamentary elections, which meant that he was finally free of the difficulties of cohabitation with the Socialists (see II.2.ii).

The summit was attended by delegations from the OIF's 45 full member states, as well as by three participating governments (two Canadian provinces and the French community of Belgium), two associates (Albania and Macedonia), and several observers, including Poland, Lithuania, Slovenia, the Czech Republic and, for the first time, Algeria. The loose qualification of the OIF was countries or areas "where French is wholly or partly spoken", but the membership could be characterised as representative of areas where France had or was trying to have a measure of influence. Although initially the OIF was focused on Africa, the two preceding summits had been held outside the continent (Vietnam in 1997 and New Brunswick in 1999), as part of a conscious effort to emulate the English-speaking Commonwealth.

Thus, the 2002 summit went ahead in a "seaside hotel in downtown Beirut" (as one US newspaper put it) and was host to over 4,000 delegates, observers, and representatives of the media, gathered amid high-level security arrangements dictated by the participation of over 35 heads of state and government, including Chirac, Canadian Prime Minister Jean Chrétien, over a dozen African leaders, as well as the President of Vietnam Tran Duc Luong.

Whereas prior to 1997 the summits had largely considered questions of culture and language, such as the problems of a "francophone" information technology, the organisation's decision to appoint a secretary general of its own opened up the subject matter of discussions as well obliging a "declaration" in the manner of other summits. The raising of the profile of the organisation fitted in very much with the ambitions of the first secretary general Boutros Boutros-Ghali, whose term of office came to an end with this summit. The favourite candidate for his successor was former Senegalese President Abdou Diouf, but he came up against a surprising level of opposition from other African countries. This was in part because of some resentment at perceived Senegalese "arrogance", and the fact that representatives of Senegal already held several senior international positions, including the prestigious director generalship of the Food and Agriculture Organisation. Diouf's case was also not helped by the high-handed lobbying techniques of President Abdoulaye Wade of Senegal, which at one point caused the Togolese President, Gnassingbe Eyadema, to leave a meeting in a private house, slamming the door behind him. Diouf had originally been proposed by French Premier Lionel Jospin in 2000, but he also received support from Chirac. His rival, Henri Lopes from the Congo, a high functionary in UNESCO, had been a candidate in 1997 when he had lost to Boutros-Ghali. Lopes had strong support from Congolese President Denis Sassou-Nguesso, and also from his son-in-law, Gabonese President Omar Bongo, who resented the way that West African leaders had sabotaged his proposed Ivoirian mediation meeting a few weeks before the Beirut meeting. Bongo recruited Togo to the Congolese side, and Sassou-Nguesso called on the loyalty of his old Marxist friend, President Mathieu Kérékou of Benin. The result was a majority of three for Lopes, and it was only when French Co-operation Minister Pierre-André Wiltzer mentioned possible human rights lawsuits against the Congolese leader in Belgium and France that Congo decided to withdraw. It was not exactly a famous victory.

As this was the first Francophone summit to be held in an Arab country, Middle East politics inevitably made an intrusion, with an Israeli journalist being expelled and some surprise at the presence at the opening ceremony of Hezbollah leader Hassan Nasrallah, currently in favour with the Lebanese government. The presence of President Abdelaziz Bouteflika of Algeria was also a coup for France, as it was the first time that Algeria had attended any meeting of La Francophonie, an institution which the country had consistently criticised. True, Bouteflika attended merely as an observer, but he indicated that Algeria would join the organisation at a future, although unspecified, date.

The pro-Arab tenor of the meeting did not express itself forcefully in the conference's closing declaration, which closely reflected French policy on the Middle East, with the call for a resumption of the peace process based on the principles of the Madrid conference and UN resolutions 242 and 338. There was only a one-line reference to Iraq, when the declaration called on the UN's "collective responsibility to resolve the Iraqi crisis". This was backed up by an oblique statement from President Blaise Compaoré, of Burkina Faso (the country was scheduled to host the next meeting in 2004) who said "preventive wars cannot bring solutions".

Other subjects in a highly political declaration were the violence in Côte d'Ivoire, and the recent Congolese peace accord, while it also praised the New Partnership for Africa's development (NEPAD) to which both France and Canada, as G-8 members, had lent their support. There were also statements more usually associated with the OIF, dealing with cultural diversity, which had been discussed at length in the summit. One sentence in particular drew comment: "We believe, under the present conditions, that the preservation of cultural diversity means abstaining from any liberalisation with the WTO relating to cultural goods and services, in order not to compromise the effectiveness of the instruments designed to promote and support cultural diversity".

The year 2002 was one of fluctuating fortunes for the COMMUNITY OF PORTUGUESE-SPEAKING COUNTRIES (CPLP). The most significant event of the year was the formal granting of independence to the Democratic Republic of East Timor on 20 May (see IX.1.vii) and final dislocation from the terror associated with the territory's annexation by Indonesia in 1974. In a ceremony attended by UN Secretary-General Kofi Annan, and Portugal's President Jorge Sampaio, the UN handed over authority to President José Alexandre (Xanana) Gusmão. Confirming its solidarity with the new state, the CPLP accepted East Timor as the eighth member of the CPLP at the Heads of State Conference in Brasilia, Brazil, on 1 August.

The death of Jonas Savimbi, leader of the rebel National Union for the Total Independence of Angola (UNITA) on 27 February proved highly significant (see VII.1.v). It paved the way for a ceasefire agreement, which was signed on 4 April and a cessation of the civil war that had disrupted Angola since 1975. The CPLP was a critical opponent of Savimbi's activities and warmly welcomed the signing of an agreement on 23 August aimed at implementing the 1994 peace accord, the Lusaka Protocol.

In contrast to these favourable developments, 2002 was also a year in which Portugal's new Social Democratic Party (PSD) government (see II.4.iii) challenged the CPLP to become a more modern and dynamic trading organisation. Speaking at the CPLP's Business Forum in Lisbon on 27 June, Portuguese Foreign Minister Antonio Martins da Cruz highlighted the organisation's ongoing difficulties. Portugal's five African colonies had once accounted for around a quarter of all Portuguese trade, but by 2001 this figure had fallen to less than 1 per cent of Portugal's imports and around 3 per cent of its export market. That decline was blamed on CPLP countries joining regional economic alliances, which then assumed greater importance than membership of the CPLP. Examples included Guinea-Bissau, which as a member of an eight-nation West African Economic Monetary Union shared the same currency and enjoyed lucrative free trade arrangements with its partners. Guinea-Bissau's Economic Minister Rui Duarte Barros responded by highlighting the language difficulties which made the CPLP something of a misnomer. While Portuguese remained the official language, only small minorities of the African member states' populations spoke it in everyday use. This realisation gave renewed gravitas to the construction of the CPLP's flagship project, the Portuguese Language International Institute (IILP) at Cidade da Praia, Cape Verde, which began in the summer of 2002.

iii. NON-ALIGNED MOVEMENT AND DEVELOPING COUNTRIES

Non-Aligned Movement (NAM)
DATE OF FOUNDATION: 1961   HEADQUARTERS: rotating with chair
OBJECTIVES: Originally to promote decolonisation and to avoid domination by either the Western industrialised world or the Communist bloc; since the early 1970s to provide a authoritative forum to set the political and economic priorities of developing countries; in addition, since the end of the Cold War to resist domination of the UN system by the USA
MEMBERSHIP (END-'02): 114 countries (those listed in AR 1995, p. 386, plus Belarus and the Dominican Republic, minus Yugoslavia)
CHAIRMAN: President Thabo Mbeki, South Africa (since June '99); succeeded Nelson Mandela, who had held the post since Sept '98)

Group of 77 (G-77)
DATE OF FOUNDATION: 1964   HEADQUARTERS: UN centres
OBJECTIVES: To act as an international lobbying group for the concerns of developing countries
MEMBERSHIP (END-'02): 134 developing countries (those listed in AR 1996, p. 385, minus South Korea, plus China, Eritrea, Palau & Turkmenistan)
CHAIRMAN: Chairman: Hugo Chávez Frías (Venezuela)

THE Co-ordinating Bureau of the Non-Aligned Movement held a ministerial meeting on 29 April in Durban, South Africa, to prepare for the forthcoming 13th summit conference. Because the Jordanian government withdrew its offer to act as the host, the summit had to be postponed. However, an alternative offer from Malaysia for February 2003 was accepted. As a result, South Africa continued to hold the chairmanship of the Movement throughout 2002, beyond the normal three-year term.

The predominant concern of the Bureau meeting was the deteriorating situation in the Middle East. It issued a special Declaration on Palestine expressing outrage at the Israeli military assault on Palestinian cities, particularly Jenin, and the siege of the Church of the Nativity in Bethlehem (see V.2.i). As the conflict continued to wreck havoc amongst civilians on both sides, the Declaration called for "an end to the application of double standards", with respect to "an Israeli culture of acting with impunity". In response to the siege of President Yassir Arafat's headquarters, the Bureau decided to send a delegation to visit him in Ramallah. Later, on 2 June, the South African Foreign Minister, Nkosazana Dlamini Zuma, led a visit with five other ministers, who were flown in from Amman by helicopter, as an unusual and dramatic affirmation of solidarity with the Palestinians.

The NAM collaborated with the Arab League at the UN to mobilise support for the Palestinians. On 30 March it obtained a Security Council resolution which called for a ceasefire and the withdrawal of Israeli troops from Ramallah. When the Israeli government refused to co-operate with a UN fact-finding team to investigate events in Jenin, the NAM reconvened the UN General Assembly's emergency special session on Palestine. On 7 May it asked the Secretary General to prepare a report on the events, and it convened again on 5 August to receive the report. It did not endorse claims that Israelis had systematically massacred civilians in Jenin, but it did document Israeli violations of the Fourth Geneva Convention. A resolution tabled by the NAM was passed by 114 votes to four (see XI.1).

It demanded both the immediate Israeli withdrawal from Palestinian towns and access for medical and humanitarian organisations. Terrorism by Palestinian groups was condemned indirectly by a general appeal for the safety of civilians and a demand for an end to violence and terror. The most positive development for the NAM was a surprise initiative by the USA. On 12 March the Security Council affirmed "a vision of a region where two states, Israel and Palestine, live side by side" (see XI.1).

In April, the term "axis of evil", used by US President George W. Bush in his State of the Union address, was described by the Bureau as "a form of psychological and political terrorism" against the three NAM members identified (see IV.1). The Bureau reviewed the "threats of aggression" and "affirmed their categorical rejection of assaulting Iraq". In September, the NAM ministers in New York welcomed Iraq's decision to allow the return of UN weapons inspectors. On 10 October South Africa requested a Security Council meeting to discuss their return. The NAM was concerned that elected members of the Council were being excluded from consultations by the permanent members. The resulting debate was an important contribution to Resolution 1441 (2002) which was approved in November (see XVII.1).

The Bureau looked forward to the entry into force of the Rome Statute for the International Criminal Court. It was concerned to push forward the work on defining the crime of aggression, to bring it under the Court's jurisdiction. The conviction in the Netherlands of a Libyan citizen for the destruction of a US airliner over the Scottish town of Lockerbie in December 1988 (see V.4.ii), was rejected on the grounds that it was politically motivated and was "without any valid legal grounds". Extraordinary support was given to President Robert Mugabe, in describing his corrupt re-election (see VII.2.iii) as an expression of the "the will of the people of Zimbabwe" and his capricious land seizures as "social justice". This contradicted the endorsement of the New Partnership for Africa's Development (NEPAD), which included African governments working "with African civil society and people as a whole". The previous year's misgivings about the war in Afghanistan changed to acceptance of the political result and a desire to contribute to the reconstruction. The outcome of the UN-hosted International Conference on Financing for Development, held in Monterrey, Mexico, in March, was welcomed, with great scepticism over the promises for increased aid. An appeal was made to ensure the entry into force in 2002 of the 1997 Kyoto Protocol on Climate Change.

The Group of 77 (G-77) followed up one of the decisions of the South Summit (see AR 2000, p. 394), by holding a Conference on Science and Technology in the United Arab Emirates in October. The priority questions were water and sanitation, biotechnology, and narrowing the digital divide. However, it seemed unlikely the decisions would be implemented, as no commitment of any financial or institutional resources was made to the ideas for joint ventures and information exchanges in the three key fields.

The Non-Aligned Movement and the G-77 held their 26th annual meetings in New York on 18 and 19 September respectively. Both welcomed the endorsement of the NEPAD by a special meeting of the UN earlier the same week. The NAM was encouraged by the positive developments in Africa, with the peace agreements covering the Congo, Rwanda, and Angola. The G-77 welcomed the decision of the World Summit for Sustainable Development in Johannesburg (see XVII.3) to establish the World Solidarity Fund to contribute to the eradication of poverty, but doubted the ability of the UN to fund its activities. The institutional weakness of the G-77 was exposed by the absence of sustained follow-up to the South Summit and by the failure of 80 per cent of its members to pay their contributions in full to their joint office in New York (see AR 2000, p. 394).

At the end of 2002 Venezuela handed the Chair of the G-77 to Morocco for 2003. During the year, the size of the G-77 increased to 134 members, when Palau was admitted at the New York meeting. The strong relations between the developing countries and the Group of 8 industrialised countries that had been developed in Tokyo in 2000 were not repeated in 2001 or 2002 (see AR 2000, pp. 394-5).

iv. ORGANISATION OF THE ISLAMIC CONFERENCE (OIC)

DATE OF FOUNDATION: 1970   HEADQUARTERS: Jeddah, Saudi Arabia
OBJECTIVES: To further co-operation among Islamic countries in the political, economic, social, cultural and scientific spheres
MEMBERSHIP (END-'02): Afghanistan, Albania, Algeria, Azerbaijan, Bahrain, Bangladesh, Benin, Brunei, Burkina Faso, Cameroon, Chad, Comoros, Côte d'Ivoire, Djibouti, Egypt, Gabon, the Gambia, Guinea, Guinea-Bissau, Guyana, Indonesia, Iran, Iraq, Jordan, Kazakhstan, Kuwait, Kyrgyzstan, Lebanon, Libya, Malaysia, Maldives, Mali, Mauritania, Morocco, Mozambique, Niger, Nigeria, Oman, Pakistan, Palestine, Qatar, Saudi Arabia, Senegal, Sierra Leone, Somalia, Sudan, Suriname, Syria, Tajikistan, Togo, Tunisia, Turkey, Turkmenistan, Uganda, United Arab Emirates, Uzbekistan, Yemen (total 57)
SECRETARY GENERAL: Abdelouhed Belkeziz (Morocco)

THE Foreign Ministers of the Organisation of the Islamic Conference and their counterparts from the EU held a landmark meeting in Istanbul, Turkey, in mid-February. The meeting, which brought together representatives of 71 countries, had been called by Turkey in the aftermath of the 11 September 2001 terrorist attacks on the USA and was aimed at fostering inter-cultural dialogue between the West and the Islamic world. Discussions were dominated by the political impact of the attacks on the USA and the worsening situation in the conflict between Israel and the Palestinians. Most participants managed to avoid contentious political statements and focused instead on the need to encourage dialogue and understanding and to develop universal values on such issues as the rights of women, the death penalty, and the right to freedom of religion.

Foreign Ministers held an extraordinary meeting on terrorism in early April in Kuala Lumpur, the Malaysian capital. The session's opening speech by Malaysian Prime Minister Mahathir Mohamed—in which he defined all attacks on civilians as terrorist acts, including suicide bombings by Palestinians and by the Tamil Tiger separatists of Sri Lanka—was not (as was customary) adopted by the OIC. The Foreign Ministers adopted a Kuala Lumpur Declaration affirming their collective resolve to combat the menace of terrorism and to establish a 13-member ministerial committee to recommend measures to strengthen co-operation between OIC members against terrorism. In the Kuala Lumpur Declaration, ministers reaffirmed their "commitment to the principles and true teachings of Islam which abhor aggression, value peace, tolerance and respect as well as prohibiting the killing of innocent people". Furthermore, they rejected "any attempt to link Islam and Muslims to terrorism" and reiterated that "preventive action taken to combat terrorism should not result in ethnic or religious profiling or the targeting of a particular community". Ministers emphasised the importance of addressing "the root causes of international terrorism", and remained "convinced that the war against terrorism will not succeed if the environment that breeds terrorism, including foreign occupation, injustice and exclusion, is allowed to thrive". They rejected any unilateral action taken against any Islamic country under the pretext of combating international terrorism, as this would undermine global co-operation against terrorism, and instead reaffirmed their commitment to "action at national level and through international co-operation in combating terrorism". The conference adopted a separate declaration condemning recent Israeli military action in Palestinian territory.

Foreign Ministers held their 29th regular session in Khartoum, the Sudanese capital, in late June. In his opening address to the conference, Sudanese President Omar Hassan Ahmad al-Bashir said that the Khartoum meeting would send forth "three nos" to the whole world: (i) "no going back on our religion but steadfast attachment to its guidelines with wisdom and sagacity"; (ii) "no terrorism in Islam but peace, tolerance, interaction, and defence of self, land, honour, and religion"; and (iii) "no division or dispersal but unity, solidarity, and dialogue". The conference adopted a number of resolutions aimed at "strengthening Islamic solidarity, preparing the Islamic Ummah to meet contemporary challenges, achieving the aspirations of Muslim communities, and preserving the fundamental religious and cultural values of Islam". The ministers agreed to hold their 30th regular session in Tehran, Iran, at a date to be determined between the host country and the general secretariat.

4. EUROPEAN UNION

DATE OF FOUNDATION: 1952   HEADQUARTERS: Brussels, Belgium
OBJECTIVES: To seek ever-closer union of member states
MEMBERSHIP (END-'02): Austria, Belgium, Denmark, Finland, France, Germany, Greece, Ireland, Italy, Luxembourg, Netherlands, Portugal, Spain, Sweden, United Kingdom (total 15)
PRESIDENT OF EUROPEAN COMMISSION: Romano Prodi (Italy)
CURRENCY: euro, used by 12 countries; Denmark, Sweden & UK not participating (end-'02
£1=€1.61, US$1=€1.00)

THE year began on a positive note, with the smooth introduction of euro notes and coins in the 12 countries of the Eurozone to replace their national currencies. It concluded with the equally upbeat decision to admit 10 new member countries to the European Union (EU) during 2004, promising a transformed economic and political geography for Europe. A specially appointed Convention worked throughout the year to shape a new constitution for the enlarged Union.

These positives were set against a deteriorating economic situation which called into question the respect for the monetary disciplines required by European Monetary Union, plus increasing contention between the member countries over the approach which should be taken to US policy towards the Middle East in general and the drive to war against Iraq in particular.

ENLARGEMENT. "We now shake off the burden of Yalta" was how the Polish Prime Minister Leszek Miller saw the decision taken at the European Council in Copenhagen on 13 December to admit 10 new member countries to the EU as from May 2004. For the Danish Prime Minister, Anders Fogh Rasmussen, president of the Council, Europe was "spreading its wings in freedom, prosperity and in peace". Subject to ratification the new members would be Cyprus, Czech Republic, Estonia, Hungary, Latvia, Lithuania, Malta, Poland, Slovakia, and Slovenia. Bulgaria and Romania were expected to join in 2007, while a decision would be taken in regard to Turkey's future membership in December 2004.

Hopes of reaching agreement by the year's end had frequently been put in doubt over the year. A specific risk was that Ireland's voters would again reject the draft Treaty of Nice (see AR 2000, pp. 397-99) when their referendum was re-run on 19 October. The Treaty set out the institutional procedures for an enlarged EU and its ratification was a precondition for an expanded Union. A positive vote of 63 per cent on a 50 per cent turnout was greeted with intense relief across the EU institutions. "The truly historic enlargement of the European Union can go ahead" said Irish Taoiseach Bertie Ahern. "We want to welcome the people of the applicant countries into the European Union with open hearts as well as open minds."

There were fears that the presidential and parliamentary elections in France in June and the German general election in September would force their governments into taking hard-line positions. Resolving the future of the common agricultural policy and the future budgetary arrangements for an enlarged EU were potential stumbling blocks, reflecting both internal divisions between the 15 existing member states and the demands of the candidate countries themselves—and especially Poland—on both agricultural and budget issues.

When he took up the presidency in June, the Danish Premier warned of the dangers of delay. He recalled the undertakings already made to the candidate countries and foresaw a serious political, economic, and social backlash if these were not respected. Rasmussen stressed that the issues of reform of the common agricultural policy and enlargement should be kept strictly separate, and that agreement on one should not be a precondition for the other, but this analysis involved an element of wishful thinking. The French were insistent that there must be a common position on agriculture before the enlargement negotiations could be finalised. While the German government had favoured a cutback in the agricultural budget, France wanted no change at least until 2006.

For several years there had been much talk of the collapse of the Franco-German axis in formation of European policy. The enlargement issue seemed likely to demonstrate more of the same, so it was all the more surprising when on 23 October, on the eve of a European summit, French President Jacques Chirac and German Chancellor Gerhard Schröder met at the Conrad Hotel in Brussels and agreed a formula which would mean no change in EU farm policy before the end of 2006, an inflation-proofed standstill (but no cut) on spending between 2007 and 2013, and a limit on spending in other areas—a deal which gave the French the assurances that they needed and removed a prime objection to an enlargement settlement, although it seemed to throw into doubt the agricultural reform proposals which had been tabled by the European Commission in the Mid-term Review in July. Much was made of UK Prime Minister Tony Blair's wounded reaction to this deal and the breakdown of relations between himself and Chirac (leading to postponement of a Franco-UK meeting scheduled for December), but the October summit incorporated the Conrad Hotel formula, modified to leave some scope for agricultural reform in the light of the World Trade Organisation Doha trade round.

When it came to the Copenhagen summit on 12-13 December, negotiations were tense but concentrated as the Poles held out for a big increase in transfers. Praise was heaped on the Danish Prime Minister for his presidential skills. It was finally agreed that EU aid amounting to €40,800 million would be allocated to the 10 candidate countries between 2004 and 2006 to allow for their smooth integration into the Union. This figure included some special concessions to Poland—an additional €108 million for improved border controls, the right to advance a further €1,000 million from structural funds to help cash flow, and an improved quota for milk producers. The other candidate countries would share an additional €300 million.

The Turkish membership application provoked strong feelings, not least because of a letter from US Secretary of State Colin Powell on the eve of the summit which demanded that Turkey be given an early date for membership, implying that the state of progress on the Turkish human rights front should not be a precondition and that refusal would confirm a Muslim perception that there was a "clash of civilisations" with the Islamic world. This heavy-handed approach—"unacceptable interference" in the view of diplomats—combined with Turkey's own threats to limit access for German exports, were probably counter-productive. It was again the Schröder-Chirac combination which settled the issue, setting a target date of July 2005 for the possible start of negotiations with Turkey. The final agreement stated that if the summit in December 2004 decided that Turkey fulfilled the human rights criteria of the EU, then "the European Union will open accession negotiations with Turkey without delay". Meantime, further assistance and co-operation would be provided.

Two issues were related to the Turkish accession question: Cyprus and the EU relationship with NATO. In regard to the former, the summit confirmed its "strong preference" for accession by a united Cyprus rather than by the Greek sector alone and welcomed the commitment of Greek and Turkish Cypriots to continue negotiations to reach a settlement by 28 February 2003 for a unified island on the basis of UN proposals (see II.4.vi). Turkish leaders accordingly agreed to encourage Turkish Cypriot President Rauf Denktash to finalise a deal.

Turkey's role was also crucial on EU access to NATO assets, a pre-requirement for the Union if it were to create an effective Rapid Reaction Force under the European Security and Defence Policy. Agreement between the EU and NATO had been held up, first by Turkey, then by Greece. After parallel negotiations in Copenhagen and at the Alliance's headquarters in Brussels, an agreement was reached during the summit, with the detailed arrangements to be finalised by 1 March 2003 (see XI.2.i).

Net recipients and contributors to EU budget*

Recipient	Receipts in millions of euros	Receipts as % of GNP	(Rank by amount receieved)
Greece	4,373.90	3.61	(2)
Portugal	2,112.00	1.93	(3)
Ireland	1,674.60	1.83	(4)
Spain	5,055.90	0.86	(1)
Finland	216.90	0.17	(6)
Denmark	169.10	0.10	(7)
Italy	713.40	0.06	(5)

Contributor	Contributions in millions of euros	Contributions as % of GNP	(Rank by amount contributed)
Sweden	1,177.40	0.50	(5)
Germany	9,273.20	0.47	(1)
Netherlands	1,737.70	0.44	(3)
Luxembourg	65.10	0.35	(8)
Austria	543.50	0.27	(6)
UK**	3,774.70	0.25	(2)
Belgium	327.30	0.13	(7)
France	1,415.30	0.10	(4)

*Budgetary balances in 2000 based on "UK rebate definition".
**Amount contributed after receipt of the UK annual rebate of approximately 4 billion euros per year.

(Source: European Commission.)

INTRODUCTION OF THE EURO. On 1 January 2002 euro notes and coins became the legal tender in 12 European countries—the so-called Eurozone. Of the EU member states, only Denmark, Sweden, and the UK retained their own currencies. The switch constituted a huge logistical operation but was pronounced an "extraordinary success" by European Commission President Romano Prodi. There were problems in handling the huge quantity of old notes and coins which had to be collected and some complaints by retailers about insufficient quantities of some denominations of the new coins and notes, but in general the operation proceeded smoothly and within two weeks of the launch some 90 per cent of transactions within the Eurozone were estimated to be taking place in the euro. Fears of a crime wave associated with the transfer were not realised.

By the end of the year, following a trans-European poll, the Commission was able to argue that the introduction of the new money was strengthening the integration of markets across the EU, abolishing exchange rate risk and transaction costs, and also removing a psychological barrier to cross-border economic interaction. Individuals were increasingly interested in buying goods in other EU countries and 32 per cent of businesses said that they were more interested in selling their goods abroad. The new currency was also widely accepted outside Europe.

The public did link the adoption of the euro with significant increases in prices, although the Commission claimed that only 0.2 per cent of any increases could be attributed to that cause. It was recommending that dual pricing still practised by many retailers should be abandoned in order to accelerate full acceptance of the new currency.

MONETARY UNION. Economic management did not run as smoothly as the currency switch. Faltering growth throughout Europe put increasing pressure on government tax revenues while spending continued to rise. Several member countries in the Eurozone found their public deficits approaching or breaching the 3 per cent limit of gross national product which had been set in the Stability and Growth Pact when the rules of the European Monetary Union had been agreed. A particular irony was that Germany, which had driven through the discipline of the 3 per cent rule in 1996 as a way of keeping in check countries with a less rigorous monetary and fiscal policy (such as Italy), was itself caught as the German economy stagnated, unemployment increased, and public spending rose.

In June at the Seville European Council, European leaders had made a formal commitment to balance their budgets by 2004 at the latest. By July a serious crisis was looming as it became clear that economic growth had slipped and spending was not being controlled. As guardian of the rules, the European Commission was faced with the unenviable task of pointing the finger at those countries which were breaching or threatening to breach the limits, just as it had done the previous year towards Ireland. Fines might have had to have been imposed on those countries with the biggest overshoot.

Prodi stated that the way the Stability and Growth Pact was implemented was "stupid", but otherwise the Commission remained cautious, defending the theory of the Pact. In July it recommended that an early warning be issued to Germany and Portugal. Germany was approaching the 3 per cent level, while new figures from Portugal indicated a deficit of 4.1 per cent. The Council of Ministers closed the procedure when the two countries undertook to implement their stability programmes in full to avoid breaking the ceiling and achieving medium term targets by 2004.

The Commission held back until after the German elections on 22 September. Two days later the Commissioner responsible for Economic and Financial Affairs,

Pedro Solbes, delivered a devastating account to his colleagues of the state of public finances in the member states. There would be no chance of France, Germany, or Italy balancing their budgets at least until 2006, he said, so the deadline would have to be extended. Germany would almost certainly break through the 3 per cent ceiling. Perhaps more worrying for the Commission, some governments were not taking the targets seriously—both President Chirac of France and Prime Minister Silvio Berlusconi in Italy were disdainful of the need to respect them, preferring instead to follow classic Keynesian theory that tax cuts were needed to stimulate the economy by increasing domestic demand. German Finance Minister Hans Eichel, however, did insist on the need to stick to the pledges in the Pact and indicated that his country would accept the launch of the early warning procedure against it.

The Commission was forced to bend to political realities. It re-set 2006 as the target date for returning to balance and announced a new schedule for those governments in breach to achieve budgetary balance, at an improvement rate of 0.5 percentage points each year. However, in the closing months of the year the Stability Pact's defenders became more vociferous. The European Central Bank staunchly defended the rules. In a statement in October it said that "contrary to the claims of its critics, the Stability and Growth Pact provides sufficient flexibility—a necessary complement of a monetary policy geared to price stability". It also sent an important message to countries hoping to join the EU, said the Bank.

Supporters also rallied in the Council. In November a proposal by France and Germany—again working in concert—that the Pact should be fine-tuned to take account of debt, inflation, and employment received short shrift from the Commission, but also from the Greek, Dutch, and Luxembourg Ministers. Austria's Finance Minister hoped that the deficit procedure would be launched soon against the deficit countries.

On 19 November the Commission adopted a report which indicated that Germany's 2002 deficit would be 3.8 per cent of GDP, with gross government debt rising above the 60 per cent limit laid down under the Maastricht rules. An "Excessive Deficit Procedure" was expected to follow. On the same day the Commission recommended that an early warning be sent to France following the autumn forecast which anticipated a deficit at 2.7 per cent of GDP in 2002 and 2.9 per cent in 2003. Both cases were scheduled for discussion by Finance Ministers in January 2003.

EUROPEAN SECURITY AND DEFENCE POLICY. When Spain took over the six-month EU presidency in January it was determined to give an impetus to the Union's security and defence policy. The commitments which had been made to introduce a more effective Common Foreign and Security Policy, backed up by a Rapid Reaction Force of 60,000 men able to operate for up to one year away from home, depended on practical capabilities if they were to be credible. The Spanish Defence Minister, Frederico Trillo, stressed the need to reduce the capabilities gap between Europe and the USA. He underlined the importance of a European armaments policy and called for a single armaments agency and co-ordinated investment. To this end, 12 working panels began work in February to identify the capability gaps, including strategic transport, guided missiles and munitions, attack helicopters, command systems, control, communications and intelligence, and theatre missile defence. Further panels were added later in the year.

On 13 May EU Defence Ministers met formally as the Council of Ministers for the first time. They discussed implementation of a European Capability Action Plan (ECAP) and the need for strengthened co-operation in the armaments field. It was agreed that National Armaments Directors of the EU countries should be involved in finding procurement solutions to the gaps identified by the working panels.

Although Denmark took the presidency for the second half of the year, the country's self-imposed exclusion from the Common Foreign and Security Policy meant that Greece, the next country in line, would be in the chair for this policy area for a full 12 months. The Greek government sought to maintain the policy momentum and combine the diplomatic process with a new reality—managing peace-keeping operations in the Balkans by the end of the year. That reality, however, depended on having the capabilities—for instance to move and control troops—which had hitherto been provided by the USA.

Comparison with the USA was a dominant theme in the capabilities discussions. Greek Defence Minister Yiannos Papantoniou warned that if the gap continued to widen it would have two serious consequences. "On one hand the EU would be dependent upon American armaments and this would have an impact on its security and defence policy", he warned. "Also, if the European arms industry weakens, this will have an effect on the EU's technological and economic development in general."

Since the EU member states were not capable of providing the resources and skills required, EU initiatives would depend on access to NATO assets for dealing with situations where the Alliance was not directly involved. This in turn depended on agreement by all NATO members, including Turkey. It was not until the Copenhagen Council in December that an agreement was finally reached between the Alliance and the Union (see XI.2.i).

Forces from several European countries were already active in the Balkans, reflecting the sense that the region was Europe's responsibility, and the lion's share of reconstruction and development costs was being met by Europe, to the tune of €900 million a year. More than 85 per cent of the peacekeeping troops in the area, numbering 50,000 people, were provided by EU countries. However, all were dependent on the USA for moving forces, command and control, and provisioning.

Following the December agreement with NATO the EU at last saw the possibility of taking responsibility for the Amber Fox peace-keeping operation in Macedonia which it should have taken over when the NATO mandate expired on 26 October. It also announced in Copenhagen that it would be willing to lead a military operation in Bosnia and Herzegovina, taking over NATO's role. This latter proposal came as a surprise to the Alliance, which nonetheless welcomed the possibility, subject to adequate preparation.

EXTERNAL RELATIONS. Relations with the USA became more complex and more strained as the year progressed. After the display of post-11 September solidarity of the previous autumn, many Europeans began to perceive a US administration that was following a unilateralist path.

A number of issues damaged relations, including US President George W. Bush's refusal to sign up to the Kyoto Protocol on global warming, the US rejection of the International Criminal Court, and certain trade issues including steel tariffs and a new US farm bill which increased support to US farmers. The issue of aircraft noise, with the ban on "hush kits", was resolved, but a World Trade Organisation finding against the US Foreign Sales Tax further soured relations. Several European governments became increasingly mistrustful of US policy. The "axis of evil" reference in Bush's State of the Union Address in January (see IV.1), singling out North Korea and Iran as rogue states similar to Iraq, provoked particular irritation since Europe had sought constructive dialogue with both countries. There was also a widening gap over US policy towards Iraq, its partisan attitude towards the Israel-Palestinian conflict, and over its tendency to disregard the role of the UN. On Iraq, Javier Solana, as High Representative for the Common Foreign and Security Policy, said in October that "the Union is not in favour of a change of regime. It is fighting against the proliferation of weapons of mass destruction." The Germans were even more forthright. The Social Democrats fought and won the general election on a platform of outright rejection of a war against Iraq.

For Europe, resolving the Middle East conflict was the highest priority. The December European Council in Copenhagen adopted a declaration calling on the Israeli and Palestinian people "to break the endless cycle of violence". While condemning all acts of terrorism and suicide attacks, and recognising Israel's "legitimate security concerns", the Council called upon Israel to stop its excessive use of force and extra-judicial killings. It also expressed alarm at the continuation of illegal settlements and pledged to continue budgetary support to the Palestinian National Authority, reaffirming that it was determined to continue work within the Quartet to implement the road map for the establishment of two states.

The Copenhagen declaration on Iraq was less robust. It underlined support for UN Resolution 1441 (see XVII.1), noted Iraq's acceptance of the Resolution and expressed its full support for the inspection operations of the United Nations Monitoring, Verification and Inspection Commission (UNMOVIC) and the International Atomic Energy Agency (IAEA), which "should be allowed to proceed with their important task without interference, using the full range of tools available to them". There was no reference to the threat of force contained within the UN Resolution.

THE CONVENTION. A special Convention began work in Brussels on 27 February with the task of drawing up options for a European Union constitution suitable for an EU of 25 or more countries. It was chaired by former French President Valery Giscard d'Estaing, with Italy's Giuliano Amato and Belgium's Jean-Luc Dehaene as vice-chairmen. Sir John Kerr, former head of the British Foreign Office, was appointed secretary general to the Convention. Giscard compared its work with the Philadelphia Convention of 1787 which underpinned the US constitution. Initial scepticism towards the Convention fell away as the year progressed. The Convention's work, done in public and private sessions in twice monthly meetings, began to look convincing, as if it might really determine the shape of a new constitution for Europe. The Italians were even raising hopes that its findings could be translated into a new Treaty for signature in Rome in December 2003. A draft text of the Convention was due to be delivered in April 2003, with a final document ready for the Thessaloniki summit in June 2003.

From the start the UK accepted the idea of a written constitution and its incorporation of the Charter of Fundamental Rights, which had been such a contentious issue in the 1990s. In the autumn France and Germany each appointed its Foreign Minister to attend the Convention, impressed, it was said, by the effectiveness of the UK representative, Europe Minister Peter Hain, in shaping the outcome. "Britain is leading the dance on the Convention" said French Commissioner Pascal Lamy. As expected, the Convention's debates exposed some of the traditional fault lines in discussion over the future of Europe—such as the balance of power between member states and the central institutions, the distribution of power between those institutions, and the relative power of the big countries to dominate their smaller partners. The UK, France, and Spain all favoured the appointment of a full-time EU president chairing the Council of Ministers and therefore serving the interests of the member states, while Germany inclined more to a strong European Commission and Parliament. Some of the smaller countries feared that a strong Council president would allow the large countries to dominate business. Therefore they tended to favour a stronger Commission—a view shared by the Commission itself, which wanted a bigger role in foreign policy issues and called for the EU High Representative to become a member of the Commission college and no longer an official of the Council. Among other sensitive questions was whether the veto should be scrapped for policy areas, such as foreign relations and taxation, and qualified majority voting applied.

JUSTICE AND HOME AFFAIRS. Measures to strengthen the EU's borders were agreed at the European summit in Seville in June. Discussions were to continue on the creation of a European border police force and it was agreed that there should be a common asylum policy by the end of 2003. The heads of government pledged to maintain the closest possible co-ordination with the USA and other partners in the fight against terrorism.

COMPETITION POLICY. New proposals for dealing with large mergers were put forward by the European Commission, spiced by three judgements of the European Court of First Instance where Commission merger decisions had been overturned. It was clear that a more rigorous regulatory procedure would be needed, and Mario Monti, Commissioner for Competition, announced stronger economic analysis with the appointment of a chief economist and a less confrontational approach.

A reformed system of anti-trust control suitable for a Union of 25 or more members was approved by Ministers, involving a new division of labour between the

European Commission and the regulatory authorities in the member states. At the heart of the reform was a network of national competition authorities working closely together under the co-ordination of the Commission—a recipe for private litigation and confusion in the view of many lawyers, but the only way of dealing with anti-trust issues in an enlarged EU, in the view of the policy-makers (see XIV.1.ii).

FINANCIAL SERVICES. Investment services, banking, and insurance lagged behind other business sectors in terms of access to a single European market, so in February the EU embarked on a major programme of legislation under the auspices of a Financial Services Action Plan. A tailor-made procedure was introduced known as the Lamfalussy process which relied on national financial service regulators to work out detailed implementing rules which would then be incorporated in EU legislation. The legislative programme for opening up European markets was flanked by corporate governance issues such as accounting standards which had been highlighted by the Enron Corp. imbroglio (see IV.1) and the extra-territorial aspects of US policy.

5. EUROPEAN ORGANISATIONS

i. THE COUNCIL OF EUROPE

DATE OF FOUNDATION: 1949   HEADQUARTERS: Strasbourg, France
OBJECTIVES: To strengthen pluralist democracy, the rule of law and the maintenance of human rights in Europe and to further political, social and cultural cooperation between member states
MEMBERSHIP (END-'02): Albania, Andorra, Armenia, Austria, Azerbaijan, Belgium, Bosnia & Herzegovina, Bulgaria, Croatia, Cyprus, Czech Republic, Denmark, Estonia, Finland, France, Georgia, Germany, Greece, Hungary, Iceland, Ireland, Italy, Latvia, Liechtenstein, Lithuania, Luxembourg, Macedonia, Malta, Moldova, Netherlands, Norway, Poland, Portugal, Romania, Russia, San Marino, Slovakia, Slovenia, Spain, Sweden, Switzerland, Turkey, Ukraine, United Kingdom (total 44)
SECRETARY GENERAL: Walter Schwimmer (Austria)

THE Council of Europe welcomed another member state with the accession of Bosnia and Herzegovina in April 2002. Meanwhile, Monaco's application for membership made progress with the adoption of a number of constitutional amendments called for by the Council of Europe.

The Federal Republic of Yugoslavia continued its progress in meeting the accession criteria of the organisation, ratifying and implementing several Council of Europe legal instruments. The Parliamentary Assembly of the Council of Europe considered the country's candidacy in September 2002 and agreed that it had made considerable progress towards democracy and political pluralism and in respect for the rule of law and human rights. Accession would be conditional on the implementation by both Serbia and Montenegro of the Constitutional Charter which had been proposed under the terms of an agreement in March which paved the way for a change in the relationship between the constituent parts of the Federal Republic. An improvement in levels of co-operation with the International Criminal Tribunal for the former Yugoslavia, as a mark of the country's commitment to international standards, would also be a precondition for accession. The autumn presidential elections had not been completed by the end of 2002, as the threshold for voter participation had not been reached in successive ballots (see III.2.vi), and the potential political stalemate was cause for some concern.

The application for membership by Belarus had been frozen in January 1997, and the country's special guest status at the Assembly suspended. The re-opening of the office of the Organisation for Security and Co-operation in Europe (OSCE) in the Belarusian capital, Minsk, in December 2002 was welcomed, but the Council of Europe hoped to see further democratic progress there before it would consider the country's application further.

The Council of Europe's monitoring procedure continued in Albania, Armenia, Azerbaijan, Georgia, Moldova, Russia, Turkey, and Ukraine. It continued to work for a solution to the conflict between Armenia and Azerbaijan over Nagorno-Karabakh, tried to ease the political situation in Moldova (which was due to take over the chairmanship-in-office of the organisation in May 2003), and expressed concern over press freedom in Ukraine. It also continued to work for peace in Chechnya, and maintained a presence in the office of Abdul-Khakim Sultygov, who replaced Vladimir Kalamanov as Russian President Vladimir Putin's special representative in Chechnya during the summer. The hostage-taking by Chechen terrorists in a Moscow theatre in October and the bombing in Grozny in December (see III.3.i) dominated efforts to resolve the conflict. The security situation and humanitarian considerations in the area continued to cause grave concern to the Council of Europe; a referendum for a new constitutional settlement was proposed for 2003.

In December 2002 the General Assembly of the UN adopted a resolution on co-operation with the Council of Europe. The Council also continued to work closely with the OSCE and its Office for Democratic Institutions and Human Rights (ODIHR) in missions to monitor elections in Ukraine, the former Yugoslav Republic of Macedonia, Bosnia and Herzegovina, Latvia, Serbia, and Turkey.

During the year, the Convention on the Future of Europe began its work to consider the future institutional structure of the EU as it prepared for enlargement, whilst NATO also prepared to welcome new members. The Committee of Ministers agreed in principle to hold a third Council of Europe summit to discuss the future direction of the organisation in the context of the changing institutional architecture of the continent.

The Council also continued to play an important part in efforts to combat international terrorism. It resolved that intensified efforts to promote legal co-operation against the threat of terrorism must be pursued while ensuring that fundamental values of human rights and the rule of law were respected and democratic principles maintained.

A programme was agreed to increase resources for the European Court of Human Rights to enable it to cope with its escalating workload. The financial provision covered the years 2003-05 and it was hoped that it would maintain the Court's long-term effectiveness. The efficient functioning of the Court would continue to be a priority for the Council in the coming years.

ii. ORGANISATION FOR SECURITY AND CO-OPERATION IN EUROPE (OSCE)

DATE OF FOUNDATION: 1975   HEADQUARTERS: Vienna, Austria
OBJECTIVES: To promote security and co-operation among member states, particularly in respect of the resolution of internal and external conflicts
MEMBERSHIP (END-'02): Albania, Andorra, Armenia, Austria, Azerbaijan, Belarus, Belgium, Bosnia & Herzegovina, Bulgaria, Canada, Croatia, Cyprus, Czech Republic, Denmark, Estonia, Finland, France, Georgia, Germany, Greece, Holy See (Vatican), Hungary, Iceland, Ireland, Italy, Kazakhstan, Kyrgyzstan, Latvia, Liechtenstein, Lithuania, Luxembourg, Macedonia, Malta, Moldova, Monaco, Netherlands, Norway, Poland, Portugal, Romania, Russian Federation, San Marino, Slovakia, Slovenia, Spain, Sweden, Switzerland, Tajikistan, Turkey, Turkmenistan, Ukraine, United Kingdom, United States, Uzbekistan, Yugoslavia (suspended) (total 55)
CHAIRMAN: Antonio Martins da Cruz (Portugal)

THE new Chairman-in-Office of the OSCE for the year 2002 was the Portuguese Foreign Minister, Jaime Gama. In his inaugural speech to the OSCE Permanent Council in Vienna he spelt out his priorities for the forthcoming year. Not surprisingly in the wake of the terrorist attacks against Washington DC and New York on 11 September 2001, he began by underlining the importance of the fight against terrorism. He announced his attention to appoint a Personal Representative on Terrorism who would be responsible "for driving forward the initiatives laid out by the Bucharest Action Plan" (see AR 2001, p. 447), and indicated his interest in drafting a proposal for a possible OSCE Charter on Terrorism.

More generally, Gama emphasised the importance of strengthening the OSCE's comprehensive approach to security "by promoting a greater articulation and complementarity between the three OSCE dimensions: human, politico-military, and economic and environmental". Such a comprehensive approach to security, he argued, was essential to deal with the new challenges facing OSCE member states. The human dimension—understood as the right of all citizens to live in democratic societies which were guaranteed by the rule of law—was to remain the basis of all OSCE activities, Gama insisted, and in this respect the work of the High Commissioner on National Minorities, the Office for Democratic Institutions and Human Rights (ODIHR), and the Representative on the Freedom of the Media were crucial. In terms of the economic and environmental dimension, Gama pointed to the issue of co-operation for the sustainable use and protection of the quality of water as the focus of OSCE concerns in 2002. Finally, as regards the politico-military dimension, he spoke of the need to strengthen synergy between the Forum for Security Co-operation and the Permanent Council, and to develop further the concept of the Platform for Co-operative Security in order to strengthen the OSCE's role in conflict prevention, civil crisis management, and post-conflict rehabilitation.

The fight against terrorism had not been high on the agenda of the OSCE prior to 11 September, but in 2002 it became an issue of central importance. The Chairman-in-Office on 29 January appointed the former Danish Minister of Defence, Jan Troejborg, to be his Personal Representative to co-ordinate OSCE anti-terrorist activities. Troejborg argued that although the OSCE did not have a leading role in the fight against terrorism, it did have a "clear role to play in adding value to the United Nations initiatives" on this issue. His role, he argued, was to co-ordinate OSCE activities on preventing and combating terrorism by implementing the initiatives set out in Bucharest Plan of Action and the follow-up Bishkek Programme of Action, adopted in December 2001. He also noted that the OSCE's work in its three "dimensions" was crucial to an effective fight against terrorism. These covered social issues such as fostering a cultural dialogue, promoting tolerance between religious and ethnic groups, and strengthening human rights; promoting good economic governance; and preventing the proliferation of weapons of mass destruction and the spread of small arms and light weapons. The problem of combining an effective anti-terrorist strategy with the protection of human rights and civic liberties was subsequently addressed by the OSCE Ministerial Council. The director of the ODIHR, Gerard Stoudmann, argued strongly that the protection of human rights should be seen as an integral part of the struggle against terrorism, not as an obstacle to it.

The Permanent Council meeting on 12 April in Vienna provided the opportunity for a stock-taking of OSCE efforts to combat terrorism. One significant new development was the establishment of an anti-terrorism unit within the Secretariat to serve as the "OSCE focal point, database and clearing house" in matters of preventing and tackling terrorism. This included the creation of a database in which participating states could register their needs for assistance in implementing counter-terrorism commitments or to make known their offers to provide assistance. At this meeting, the OSCE secretary general, Jan Kubis, announced his intention to call a meeting on terrorism-related matters to co-ordinate activities amongst a range of international organisations. This meeting was held on 12 June, and included senior officials from the UN, NATO, the EU, and the Council of Europe, as well as the International Committee of the Red Cross, the European Commission, and the UN Office for Drug Control and Crime Prevention. In his address to the meeting, Kubis argued that the OSCE's approach to anti-terrorism was based on three, mutually-reinforcing layers: assistance to its own participating states and facilitation of their activities; promotion of co-operation with sub-regional organisations; and the effective linking up of all these regional efforts on a global platform. OSCE anti-terrorism efforts in 2002 culminated in the adoption of an OSCE Charter on Preventing and Combating Terrorism, agreed at the 10th Meeting of the Ministerial Council in Porto on 7 December. This condemned "in the strongest terms terrorism in all its forms and manifestations" and noted "the links between terrorism and trans-national organised crime, money laundering, trafficking in human beings, [and] drugs and arms". The Porto meeting also adopted a set of agreed guidelines to meet the new challenges to security and agreed to hold an Annual Security Review Conference, beginning in 2003.

The Chairman-in-Office changed in April 2002 following elections in Portugal (see II.4.iii). The new holder of this post was Antonio Martins da Cruz, who made his first address to the Permanent Council on 2 May. He pledged to continue the work of his predecessor and to strengthen the work of the OSCE's missions and field activities. These consumed the bulk of the organisation's resources—approximately 85 per cent of its total budget for 2002 of 187.3 million euros—and constituted the most practical manifestation of the Organisation's mandate to contribute to conflict prevention and post-conflict rehabilitation. In 2002, the OSCE had 3,000 people working in 19 field missions in 17 countries, giving it a significant operational capacity.

Much of the OSCE's activities in this area continued to be focused on southeastern Europe. Macedonia was a particular concern in 2002. The OSCE Mission in Skopje was responsible for six field offices which were engaged in police monitoring and confidence-building work between the ethnic communities. In February, an OSCE-supported Police Academy was opened in Idrizovo, in Macedonia, to train multi-ethnic police officers imbued with an ethos of "democratic policing". In September, parliamentary elections were held in Macedonia which were monitored and observed by the ODIHR (see III.2.iv). Elsewhere in former Yugoslavia, the OSCE field missions continued with their work in post-conflict rehabilitation. In Kosovo, the organisation helped organise municipal elections in October and appointed an official to monitor the work of the Kosovo Assembly to ensure that it complied with the provisions of its constitutional framework. In Bosnia and Herzegovina, the OSCE continued with its task of implementing the 1995 Dayton accords (see AR 1995, pp. 126-28). Its achievements in this respect were formally acknowledged by the outgoing UN High Representative, Ambassador Wolfgang Petritsch, in his final address to the Permanent Council. The organisation had played an "invaluable part" in helping to stabilise Bosnia and Herzegovina, he argued, not least by helping to rebuild civil society, overseeing elections and facilitating the return of refugees and displaced persons.

Finally, with the "war on terror", the international focus on Afghanistan, and the stationing of US forces in Uzbekistan, Kyrgyzstan, and Tajikistan, the OSCE's centre of attention began moving eastwards. The Central Asian republics had become OSCE participating states after the collapse of the Soviet Union in 1991, but they had long been marginal to the activities of the organisation—not least because of their poor human rights record. Yet as US Ambassador Robert Barry argued, "the combination of organised crime, religious extremism, economic collapse and terrorism will create a need for the OSCE to play a greater role in this region" in the coming decade. The OSCE, he suggested, should be "the instrument of choice in multilateral efforts to prevent the spread of terror by promoting civil society, especially in the volatile former Soviet republics of Central Asia bordering Afghanistan". The coming years, therefore, were likely to see a much greater focus of OSCE energies on this hitherto neglected region.

iii. EUROPEAN BANK FOR RECONSTRUCTION AND DEVELOPMENT (EBRD)

DATE OF FOUNDATION: 1991 HEADQUARTERS: London, UK
OBJECTIVES: To promote the economic reconstruction of former Communist-ruled countries on the basis of the free-market system and pluralism
MEMBERSHIP (END-'02): Albania, Armenia, Australia, Austria, Azerbaijan, Belarus, Belgium, Bosnia-Herzegovina, Bulgaria, Canada, Croatia, Cyprus, Czech Republic, Denmark, Egypt, Estonia, European Investment Bank, European Union, Finland, France, Georgia, Germany, Greece, Hungary, Iceland, Ireland, Israel, Italy, Japan, Kazakhstan, Kyrgyzstan, South Korea, Latvia, Liechtenstein, Lithuania, Luxembourg, Macedonia, Malta, Mexico, Moldova, Mongolia, Morocco, Netherlands, New Zealand, Norway, Poland, Portugal, Romania, Russia, Slovakia, Slovenia, Spain, Sweden, Switzerland, Tajikistan, Turkey, Turkmenistan, Ukraine, United Kingdom, United States, Uzbekistan, Yugoslavia (total 62)
PRESIDENT: Jean Lemierre (France)

NEW business by the Bank in the transition economies in 2002 was a record €3,890 million, a 7 per cent rise on 2001. That funding contributed to what the EBRD's annual *Transition Report* estimated as total foreign direct investment in those economies as US$30,970 million, a 27 per cent rise on the previous year. The Bank's disbursements, at €2.4 billion in 2002, were the same as in 2001; this showed that more funding went into the project pipeline than was being implemented. Commitments were to 102 new projects, the same as in 2001, and of these less funding went to the states of central-eastern Europe and the Baltic States which were to join the EU in 2004. Within the EBRD's total commitments, that group's share declined from 44 per cent (€1.6 billion) in 2001 to 31 per cent (€1.27 billion). This followed a policy of offering greater support to countries further away from, or not potential candidates for, EU membership. Russia's share rose from 23 per cent (€0.8 billion) to 33 per cent (€1.3 billion), and the amount offered to those countries in an early or middling stage of transition from 33 per cent (€1.2 billion) to 36 per cent (€1.35 billion). Because those states were less attractive to foreign investors (into the six south-east European states, their inflow was lower in 2002 than in 2001), the overall share of private sector deals in the Bank's new portfolio was 71 per cent in 2002, against 76 per cent in 2001 and 78 per cent in 2000. Within the projects selected during 2000, small and medium enterprises (SMEs) had particular salience. Thus the EBRD joined forces with the International Finance Corporation (IFC) in lending US$147 million to local banks to give credit to SMEs in Central Asia, where the Bank had already helped fund more than 40,000 entrepreneurs, and with the EC and the Austrian Raiffeisen Zentralbank for €45 million for SMEs in Bulgaria, Czech Republic, Poland, and Romania.

Given the changes in the transition landscape, the Bank initiated a review of its country strategies. During the year they were published for Albania, Belarus, Lithuania, Macedonia, Poland, Russia, Slovakia, Slovenia, and Turkmenistan. Visits of the EBRD's President, Jean Lemierre, to Moldova and Romania, a shareholders' delegation to Yugoslavia, and a London seminar—with representatives from Armenia, Azerbaijan, Georgia, Kyrgyzstan, Moldova, Tajikistan, and Uzbekistan—exchanged experience of key issues in the Bank's countries of operation. The annual meeting in Bucharest (19-20 May) was notable for the participation of

Paul O'Neill, the first US Treasury Secretary to attend for 10 years, and for the cloud over international lending to Romania, symbolised by the decision of the IMF the previous week to delay the release of a US$107 million tranche of its US$383 million loan facility (see AR 2001, p. 128) and of the World Bank to postpone a US$300 million restructuring loan, both attributable to the Romanian government's laxity in fulfilling loan conditions.

Controversy surrounded the decision, made in 1999, to hold the 2003 annual meeting in Tashkent, because of Uzbekistan's poor human rights record. The location was retained, however, and arrangements were made to hold the meeting there in May.

iv. NORDIC, BALTIC, AND ARCTIC ORGANISATIONS

Nordic Council
DATE OF FOUNDATION: 1952   HEADQUARTERS: Stockholm, Sweden
OBJECTIVES: To facilitate legislative and governmental cooperation between member states, with particular reference to proposals of the Nordic Council of Ministers
MEMBERSHIP (END-'02): Denmark, Finland, Iceland, Norway, Sweden (total 5)
SECRETARY GENERAL: Soren Christensen (Sweden)

Baltic Council
DATE OF FOUNDATION: 1992   HEADQUARTERS: rotating
OBJECTIVES: To promote political, economic and social cooperation between the three Baltic republics
MEMBERSHIP (END-'02): Estonia, Latvia, Lithuania (total 3)

Council of the Baltic Sea States (CBSS)
DATE OF FOUNDATION: 1992   HEADQUARTERS: Stockholm, Sweden
OBJECTIVES: To promote political, economic and other cooperation between Baltic littoral and adjecent states
MEMBERSHIP (END-'02): Denmark, Estonia, Finland, Germany, Latvia, Lithuania, Norway, Poland, Russia, Sweden (total 10)

Arctic Council (AC)
DATE OF FOUNDATION: 1996   HEADQUARTERS: Ottawa, Canada
OBJECTIVES: To promote co-operation between Arctic states (involving indigenous communities) on environmental issues and on the social and economic development of the region
MEMBERSHIP (END-'02): Canada, Denmark, Finland, Iceland, Norway, Russia, Sweden, United States (total 8)

ON 28-31 October the annual session of the NORDIC COUNCIL was held in Helsinki, Finland. The session marked the 50th anniversary of the founding of the organisation and Prime Ministers from all five member states were present. The main theme of the discussion was the vision of a Nordic area without frontiers. A report presented to the session enumerated many examples of laws and regulations that were obstacles to this goal. Although 40,000 citizens every year moved from one Nordic country to another, substantial differences in the systems of taxation, pensions, and family policy made work, study, and relocation difficult. There were also numerous problems concerning trade and transport. The meeting requested the Nordic Council of Ministers to work out a plan for eliminating such obstacles. This drive towards integration was significant in the context of the increasing co-operation between countries within the EU. The Nordic Council aimed to be more active in order to avoid the region being overshadowed by the enlargement of the EU and the process of European integration as a whole. During the session the Norwegian Inge Lönning (conservative) was appointed President, succeeding Outi Ojala from Finland.

The dominant ethos of consensus in Nordic institutions was overshadowed by the sharp conflicts that characterised the conference on democracy and welfare, arranged by the Nordic Council earlier in the year, during which Danish policy on immigration was strongly criticised by officials from the other Nordic countries. Another controversial issue for Nordic co-operation in general, and the Nordic Council in particular, was the fishing industry, particularly in the context of numerous published reports describing the polluted and depleted nature of the Baltic Sea. The fishing policy adopted by the EU would be crucial for the Nordic area, even for Norway, Iceland, the Faroe Islands, and Greenland which were not members of the EU. Greenland and the Faroe Islands were totally dependent on the fishing industry and there was serious conflict between the Nordic countries concerning the balance between environmental and economic priorities.

On 9-10 October the ARCTIC COUNCIL held its third Ministerial Meeting in Inari, Finland. The meeting was opened by the Finnish Foreign Affairs Minister Erkki Tuomioja. The main theme of the meeting was combating pollution and environmental degradation. Issues relating to Arctic co-operation were also discussed. In the so-called "Inari Declaration" the meeting expressed the commitment of the governments of the Arctic states and indigenous peoples to work together to promote sustainable development and environmental protection.

"Gender, equality and women" was the theme of an Arctic Council conference in Inari on 3-6 August. The participants discussed women and work, women as entrepreneurs, gender in the self-determination of indigenous peoples, and living conditions in the Arctic area.

The EU's Northern Dimension provided a framework for dialogue and co-operation and continued to be a major subject for the COUNCIL OF THE BALTIC SEA STATES (CBSS) which was aiming to become an "umbrella" organisation for all intergovernmental co-operation embracing the Baltic Sea region. The 11th Baltic Sea Parliamentary Conference meeting in St Petersburg (Russia) on 30 September-1 October concentrated on forthcoming EU enlargement. Within the CBSS the promotion of sustainable development in the region also had a strong focus. On 20 November the ministers in charge of energy issues in the Baltic Sea region and the European Commission decided to make the region a testing ground for joint implementation projects for reducing greenhouse gas emissions in the energy sector. Joint implementation was one of the flexible mechanisms of the Kyoto Protocol.

At a meeting in June the heads of government in the member states welcomed their broadening co-operation on a number of issues relating to children at risk, including the large number of street children, children in social care institutions, as well as trafficking in children.

v. OTHER EUROPEAN ORGANISATIONS

European Free Trade Association (EFTA)
DATE OF FOUNDATION: 1960   HEADQUARTERS: Geneva, Switzerland
OBJECTIVES: To eliminate barriers to non-agricultural trade between members
MEMBERSHIP (END-'02): Iceland, Liechtenstein, Norway, Switzerland (total 4)
SECRETARY GENERAL: William Rossier (Switzerland)

Central European Free Trade Association (CEFTA)
DATE OF FOUNDATION: 1992   HEADQUARTERS: rotating
OBJECTIVES: Reducing trade barriers between members with a view to their eventual membership of the European Union
MEMBERSHIP (END-'02): Bulgaria, Czech Republic, Hungary, Poland, Romania, Slovakia, Slovenia (total 7)

Visegrad Group
DATE OF FOUNDATION: 1991   HEADQUARTERS: rotating
OBJECTIVES: Reducing trade barriers between members with a view to their eventual membership of the European Union
MEMBERSHIP (END-'02): Czech Republic, Hungary, Poland, Slovakia (total 4)

Central European Initiative (CEI)
DATE OF FOUNDATION: 1992   HEADQUARTERS: rotating
OBJECTIVES: To promote the harmonisation of economic and other policies of member states
MEMBERSHIP (END-'02): Albania, Armenia, Belarus, Bosnia & Herzegovina, Bulgaria, Croatia, Czech Republic, Hungary, Italy, Macedonia, Moldova, Poland, Romania, Slovakia, Slovenia, Ukraine, Yugoslavia (total 17)
SECRETARY GENERAL: Director General: Harald Kreid

Black Sea Economic Co-operation Organisation (BSECO)
DATE OF FOUNDATION: 1992   HEADQUARTERS: Istanbul, Turkey
OBJECTIVES: To promote economic cooperation between member states
MEMBERSHIP (END-'02): Albania, Armenia, Azerbaijan, Bulgaria, Georgia, Greece, Moldova, Romania, Russia, Turkey, Ukraine (total 11)
SECRETARY GENERAL: Valeri Chechelashvili

THE new Convention of the EUROPEAN FREE TRADE ASSOCIATION (EFTA) entered into force on 1 June. The Convention, which replaced the EFTA Convention of 1960, had been signed by ministers in Vaduz, Switzerland, a year earlier on 21 June 2001. The Vaduz Convention deepened the level of economic integration between the four EFTA countries to the same level as that which existed between Switzerland and the EU. The Convention provided for the liberalisation of trade in goods and services, as well as the movement of capital, investment, and labour between the EFTA countries. It also granted citizens of EFTA countries new rights to reside, work, and claim social security benefits in any EFTA country. In a further major development during the year, EFTA concluded a free trade agreement with Singapore in 2002 which was scheduled to come into force on 1 January 2003. The agreement, signed in Egildstadir, Iceland, on 26 June, was the 19th such agreement between EFTA and a non-EU country.

In an historic development, the European Commission announced on 9 October that 10 of the EU applicant countries were expected to become EU members in 2004 (see XI.4). The 10 candidate countries included the members of the CENTRAL EUROPEAN FREE TRADE ASSOCIATION (CEFTA) with the exceptions of Romania and Bulgaria which were not scheduled to gain EU membership before 2007. The annual summit of the heads of government of CEFTA member states was held in Bratislava, Slovakia, on 13-14 September. The Premiers of the seven member countries issued a declaration which noted that negotiations on the accession of Croatia to CEFTA were almost complete.

The four-country VISEGRAD GROUP, the forerunner to CEFTA, had been established in 1991 and revived in 1998 because of tensions within CEFTA (see AR 1998, p. 449). Relations between the Visegrad members deteriorated to an unprecedented degree during 2002 when Hungary was forced to cancel a meeting of the Visegrad leaders scheduled for 1 March after the governments of the Czech Republic and Slovakia threatened to boycott the meeting in protest at remarks made by Hungarian Prime Minister Viktor Orban in late February. Orban had caused a furore when he suggested that he would not back Slovakia's campaign to join NATO unless the country dropped its opposition to a new Hungarian law—known as the "Status Law"—which offered health and other benefits to some 500,000 ethnic Hungarians who normally lived in neighbouring states but who lived or worked in Hungary on a temporary basis (see III.1.v). The Slovak government objected to the law, which had been enacted in June 2001 (see AR 2001, p. 124), on the grounds that it was racially divisive. Orban, who faced a general election in April, also fuelled tension in the region by suggesting on 20 December that a series of edicts which stripped thousands of ethnic Hungarians and Germans of their land in the Czechoslovak Federation after the World War II (the "Benes decrees") were incompatible with Czech membership of the EU.

The CENTRAL EUROPEAN INITIATIVE (CEI) held its annual heads of government summit, under the auspices of the Macedonian presidency, in Skopje on 14-15 November. The leaders of the 17 member countries adopted a declaration which, amongst other things, welcomed the announcement by the European Commission on 9 October that 10 applicant countries, including five CEI members—the Czech Republic, Hungary, Poland, Slovenia, and Slovakia—were expected to become EU members in 2004. The declaration also encouraged co-operation with CEFTA and endorsed attempts by CEI members to join that body.

The BLACK SEA ECONOMIC CO-OPERATION ORGANISATION held its decennial summit in Istanbul on 25 June. In the summit declaration, the heads of state or government of the 11 member states affirmed the importance of co-operation with the EU and called for the settlement of regional disputes according to the principles of international law. The leaders also condemned terrorism "in all its forms and manifestations" and promised to take all necessary steps, whilst respecting human rights and fundamental freedoms, to counter it.

6. ARAB, AFRICAN, ASIA-PACIFIC, AND AMERICAN ORGANISATIONS

i. ARAB ORGANISATIONS

League of Arab States
DATE OF FOUNDATION: 1945 HEADQUARTERS: Cairo, Egypt
OBJECTIVES: To co-ordinate political, economic, social and cultural co-operation between member states and to mediate in disputes between them
MEMBERSHIP (END-'02): Algeria, Bahrain, Comoros, Djibouti, Egypt, Iraq, Jordan, Kuwait, Lebanon, Mauritania, Morocco, Oman, Palestine, Qatar, Saudi Arabia, Somalia, Sudan, Syria, Tunisia, United Arab Emirates, Yemen (total 22)
SECRETARY GENERAL: Amr Mahmoud Moussa (Egypt)

Gulf Co-operation Council (GCC)
DATE OF FOUNDATION: 1981 HEADQUARTERS: Riyadh, Saudi Arabia
OBJECTIVES: To promote co-operation between member states in all fields with a view to achieving unity
MEMBERSHIP (END-'02): Bahrain, Kuwait, Oman, Qatar, Saudi Arabia, United Arab Emirates (total 6)
SECRETARY GENERAL: Abdulrahman al-Attiya (Qatar)

Arab Maghreb Union (AMU)
DATE OF FOUNDATION: 1989 HEADQUARTERS: Casablanca, Morocco
OBJECTIVES: To strengthen 'the bonds of brotherhood' between member states, particularly in the area of economic development
MEMBERSHIP (END-'02): Algeria, Libya, Mauritania, Morocco, Tunisia (total 5)
SECRETARY GENERAL: Habib Boulares (Tunisia)

HAVING agreed in January 2002 to allow Yemen to join the health, educational, and labour councils of the organisation, as a preparatory step towards full membership, the GULF CO-OPERATION COUNCIL (GCC), during 2002, had to face a series of distractions from its primary objective of creating the conditions to launch its much-heralded common market on 1 January 2003. Tensions between Saudi Arabia and Qatar developed in mid-year over the Amirate's continued toleration of the al-Jazeera satellite television, with Saudi threats of boycotting the annual heads of state meeting which was to be held in Doha, Qatar, at the end of the year. The problem of continued Iranian control and claims on Abu Musa and the demand by the United Arab Emirates (UAE) for the return of the Thunbs island, occupied by Iran in 1971, was not resolved, although the GCC emphasised its determination to seek a peaceful solution to the dispute throughout the year.

The GCC in April also affirmed its belief, according to its secretary general, Abdulrahman al-Attiya, that oil should not be used as a weapon in any conflict with Iraq. The GCC meeting at Jeddah, in June, also reaffirmed its conviction that Iraq should comply with all outstanding UN resolutions and release the Kuwaiti prisoners that it allegedly continued to hold. The meeting also approved the outcome of the Arab League summit in March, at which the Saudi peace plan for the Israeli-Palestinian conflict was adopted. The GCC had previously affirmed its support for Saudi Arabia in March when US accusations of Saudi complicity in the 11 September attacks against Washington DC and New York began to surface. At a subsequent meeting in August, the GCC ministerial council noted its satisfaction with the signature of the border agreement between the UAE and Oman and with the visit of Bahrain's monarch to Iran. At the same meeting, the ministers issued a declaration condemning terrorism.

The major development, however, came at the heads-of-state meeting in Doha on 23 December 2002 when the GCC approved the long-awaited common customs tariff at a rate of 5 per cent from 1 January 2003. Trade within the GCC, currently at US$16 billion, was expected to rise dramatically. This, together with the establishment of uniform standards for manufactured goods, a single quarantine system, and the proposed monetary union by 2005 together with a single currency by 2010, meant that the dream of a Gulf common market was now under way. This also meant that the long-delayed GCC-EU agreement could go ahead, although problems remained over the EU's discriminatory 6 per cent aluminium tariff. The agreement, which partnered a similar agreement signed with European Free Trade Association states in May, would help to balance the EU's trade surplus with the GCC, running at €7 billion on EU exports of €29 billion in 2000, and to counter the decline in EU investments in the region which fell by half to €1.5 billion, compared with GCC investment in Europe which rose by 15 per cent to €4 billion in 2000.

The DAMASCUS DECLARATION GROUP, created in the aftermath of the Second Gulf War in 1991 and designed to provide Syrian and Egyptian military support to the Gulf states in the wake of the Iraqi invasion of Kuwait, appeared to have become defunct. The al-Quds COMMITTEE OF THE ORGANISATION OF THE ISLAMIC CONFERENCE, which was headed by the King of Morocco, met in Morocco at the start of the year to condemn Israeli policy towards the Palestinians on 26 January 2002. The ARAB-MAGHREB UNION, which brought the countries of North Africa together in an economic and security union, met several times during the year in an attempt to revive its programme but with little success.

The LEAGUE OF ARAB STATES, however, was far more active during the year, not least because of the impending crises in the region, particularly over Iraq and the Israeli-Palestinian conflict. The League's new secretary general, the former Egyptian Foreign Minister, Amr Moussa, had to exert all his diplomatic skills to keep the organisation together, particularly in the face of growing anger in Libya at what it saw as the pusillanimous Arab response to the crisis in the Occupied Territories. In October, frustrated by apparent Arab inaction in the face of growing violence, Libya announced its intention to leave the organisation. In the event, it took the combined skills of Amr Moussa and Egypt's President Mohammed Hosi Mubarak to prevent this from happening.

Libya had earlier threatened to leave the League when its leader, Col Moamer Kadhafi was prevented from attending the Arab League's extraordinary summit, held in Beirut at the end of March. The Libyan leader was unable to attend because of threats to his safety from the Shi'a community in Lebanon, which remained incensed over the disappearance of its leader, Imam Musa Sadr, in August 1978 whilst on a visit to Libya. They held Libya responsible for this disappearance despite repeated Libyan denials. Libya's threat to leave the organisation on 3 April was, however, quickly withdrawn after some emollient words from the secretary general.

The meeting itself was the occasion for the presentation of the Saudi plan for peace in the Middle East (see V.2.i). The plan received the unanimous support of the Arab states, although it was quickly over-shadowed by Israeli intransigence and US indifference. The summit was also notable for the final formal reconciliation between Iraq and the Arab Gulf states, particularly Kuwait. Iraq was still required to comply fully with UN resolutions, however, and to free all remaining Kuwaiti prisoners whom it was alleged to hold. In August, the League's secretary general warned, through his spokesman, that the organisation was resolutely opposed to any military action against Iraq. In early November the organisation did, however, approve the return of United Nations Monitoring, Verification and Inspection Commission (UNMOVIC) inspectors to Iraq under UN Security Council Resolution 1441 (2002) (see XVII.1).

The League devoted much of its deliberations to the Israeli-Palestinian issue. In March, the meeting of Arab League foreign ministers in Cairo approved the provision of US$420 million in support to the Palestinian National Authority for the six months until October. Later on, at the end of November, the League condemned, through its spokesman in Cairo, US intentions to provide US$12 billion to Israel in grants and loan guarantees. The League, showing perhaps a greater realism over Arab economic failure than in the past, joined with the UN in sponsoring the Arab Human Development Report, which painted a bleak picture of the Arab world's economic future and which was presented in Cairo on 2 July.

ii. AFRICAN ORGANISATIONS AND CONFERENCES

African Union
DATE OF FOUNDATION: 2001   HEADQUARTERS: Addis Ababa, Ethiopia
OBJECTIVES: To promote the unity, solidarity and co-operation of African states, to defend their sovereignty, to promote democratic principles, human rights and sustainable development and to accelerate the political and socio-economic integration of the continent
MEMBERSHIP (END-'02): Algeria, Angola, Benin, Botswana, Burkina Faso, Burundi, Cameroon, Cape Verde, Central African Republic, Chad, Comoros, Congo, Côte d'Ivoire, Democratic Republic of Congo, Djibouti, Egypt, Equatorial Guinea, Eritrea, Ethiopia, Gabon, the Gambia, Ghana, Guinea, Guinea-Bissau, Kenya, Lesotho, Liberia, Libya, Madagascar, Malawi, Mali, Mauritania, Mauritius, Mozambique, Namibia, Niger, Nigeria, Rwanda, Sahrawi, São Tomé and Príncipe, Senegal, Seychelles, Sierra Leone, Somalia, South Africa, Sudan, Swaziland, Tanzania, Togo, Tunisia, Uganda, Zambia, Zimbabwe (total 53)
CHAIRMAN: President Thabo Mbeki (South Africa); CHAIR OF AU COMMISSION: Amara Essy (Côte d'Ivoire)

Economic Community of West African States (ECOWAS)
DATE OF FOUNDATION: 1975   HEADQUARTERS: Abuja, Nigeria
OBJECTIVES: To seek the creation of an economic union of member states
MEMBERSHIP (END-'02): Benin, Burkina Faso, Cape Verde, Côte d'Ivoire, Gambia, Ghana, Guinea, Guinea-Bissau, Liberia, Mali, Mauritania, Niger, Nigeria, Senegal, Sierra Leone, Togo (total 16)
EXECUTIVE SECRETARY: Lansana Kouyaté (Guinea)

West African Economic and Monetary Union (UEMOA)
DATE OF FOUNDATION: 1994   HEADQUARTERS: Ouagadougou, Burkina Faso
OBJECTIVES: To promote the economic and monetary union of member states
MEMBERSHIP (END-'02): Benin, Burkina Faso, Côte d'Ivoire, Guinea-Bissau, Mali, Mauritania, Niger, Senegal (total 8)

Southern African Development Community (SADC)
DATE OF FOUNDATION: 1992   HEADQUARTERS: Gaboro, Botswana
OBJECTIVES: To work towards the creation of a regional common market
MEMBERSHIP (END-'02): Angola, Botswana, Democratic Republic of Congo, Lesotho, Malawi, Mauritius, Mozambique, Namibia, Seychelles, South Africa, Swaziland, Tanzania, Zambia, Zimbabwe (total 14)
EXECUTIVE SECRETARY: Pakereesamy ("Prega") Ramsamy (Mauritius)

Common Market for Eastern and Southern Africa (COMESA)
DATE OF FOUNDATION: 1993   HEADQUARTERS: Lusaka, Zambia
OBJECTIVES: To establish a full free-trade area
MEMBERSHIP (END-'02): Angola, Burundi, Comoros, Democratic Republic of Congo, Djibouti, Egypt, Eritrea, Ethiopia, Kenya, Madagascar, Malawi, Mauritius, Namibia, Rwanda, Seychelles, Sudan, Swaziland, Uganda, Zambia, Zimbabwe (total 20)
SECRETARY GENERAL: Erastus Mwencha (Kenya)

Economic Community of Central African States (CEEAC)
DATE OF FOUNDATION: 1983   HEADQUARTERS: Libreville, Gabon
OBJECTIVES: To establish a full free-trade area
MEMBERSHIP (END-'02): Angola, Burundi, Cameroon, Central African Republic, Chad, Democratic Republic of Congo, Congo, Equatorial Guinea, Gabon, Rwanda, São Tomé & Príncipe (total 11)
SECRETARY GENERAL: Louis-Sylvain Goma (Congo)

East African Commission (EAC)
DATE OF FOUNDATION: 1996 (reviving former East African Community) HEADQUARTERS: Nairobi, Kenya
OBJECTIVES: To promote economic integration between member states
MEMBERSHIP (END-'02): Kenya, Tanzania, Uganda (total 3)

AFRICAN UNION. The African Union (AU) was launched, to take the place of the Organisation of African Unity, at a summit meeting of almost all African countries held in Durban, South Africa, in July 2002 (see XVII.2). (Madagascar was barred from the summit because the government of Marc Ravalomanana was not regarded as legally constituted.) President Thabo Mbeki of South Africa took office as the first chair of the AU, and Amara Essy remained the acting chair of the AU Commission. The AU agreed that an extraordinary summit would be held early in 2003 to decide on the idea, advanced by Col. Moamer Kadhafi of Libya, that the countries of the continent should move rapidly towards full integration as a United States of Africa.

In the first half of the year Africa's most prominent leaders spent much time promoting the New Partnership for Africa's Development (NEPAD) (see AR 2001, p. 457), with its idea of "good governance". While critics dismissed NEPAD as an unrealistic pipe-dream or condemned it as a top-down plan, drawn up without consultation with civil society or the people of the countries of Africa, its proponents viewed it as a bold initiative for Africa's renewal. In June Mbeki presented it to the World Economic Forum's Africa Economic Summit in Durban. Afterwards Mbeki, together with Presidents Olusegun Obasanjo (Nigeria), Abdelaziz Bouteflika (Algeria), and Abdoulaye Wade (Senegal) took it to the G-8 meeting at Kananaskis, Canada. Although the G-8 accepted the idea, all that the rich countries promised was another US$1 billion in development aid to Africa. Mbeki, the main architect of NEPAD, hoped that in return for increased aid and investment (US$64 billion annually), debt relief and trade opportunities, African states would commit themselves to democracy, good governance, and peace. The hope was that economic growth would increase to 7 per cent per annum. When asked for detailed proposals, Mbeki mentioned the hydroelectric project at the Inga Falls on the Congo River.

In July the AU summit adopted NEPAD as its socio-economic development programme. Much controversy then occurred concerning the "peer review" system that would judge whether a member of the AU was behaving improperly. There was considerable confusion over whether the peer review mechanism included the scrutiny of political governance, or was limited to economic issues. In November Mbeki said that other institutions, still to be established, such as the Court of Justice and the Commission for People's and Human Rights, would monitor political governance. Meanwhile, nothing was done to censure Zimbabwe, and its President, Robert Mugabe, continued to participate in AU and other conferences.

REGIONAL ORGANISATIONS AND CONFERENCES. At its meeting in Australia in March, the Commonwealth gave Presidents Obasanjo of Nigeria and Mbeki of South Africa, together with the chair of the Commonwealth, John Howard of Australia, the task of deciding on action against Zimbabwe (see XI.3.i). After the contested presidential election there later in March, the troika agreed to suspend Zimbabwe from the Commonwealth for a year. The three met again at Abuja, Nigeria, six months later, but decided to take no further action against Zimbabwe. They were to review the situation again in March 2003.

As chair of the Non-Aligned Movement, and of the AU, the South African President was very busy on the international scene. The South African government was very active in trying to bring about peace in the Great Lakes region. Numerous conferences were held to try to bring peace to the Democratic Republic of the Congo (DRC), Rwanda, and Burundi (see VII.1.i; VII.1.ii). South Africa sent peacekeeping forces to the latter, and promised to send troops to the DRC. The largest single meeting held on the continent in 2002 was the World Summit on Sustainable Development (WSSD), held in Johannesburg at the end of August (see XVII.3). President Sam Nujoma of Namibia used the occasion to launch a strong verbal attack on UK Prime Minister Tony Blair for his policy towards Zimbabwe, and the US Secretary of State, Colin Powell, was booed because of the US record on environmental issues. Most people thought that the WSSD established the link between sustainable development and poverty reduction, but whether sufficient action would follow from the conference to justify the large cost involved in staging it remained to be seen.

In West Africa, the Economic Community of West African States (ECOWAS) continued its tradition of offering to mediate in conflicts, but when the stability of Côte d'Ivoire was threatened, it was the French who sent troops to bolster the regime of the incumbent Ivorian President. The Economic Community of Central African States (known by its French acronym CEEAC) followed the lead of ECOWAS and took on a new role for itself when it sent a peacekeeping force to patrol the border between the Central African Republic and Chad, after fighting broke out there early in the year (see VI.3.ii).

iii. ASIA-PACIFIC ORGANISATIONS

Association of South-East Asian Nations (ASEAN)
DATE OF FOUNDATION: 1967   HEADQUARTERS: Jakarta, Indonesia
OBJECTIVES: To accelerate economic growth, social progress and cultural development in the region
MEMBERSHIP (END-'02): Brunei, Cambodia, Indonesia, Laos, Malaysia, Myanmar, Philippines, Singapore, Thailand, Vietnam (total 10)
SECRETARY GENERAL: Rodolfo C. Severino (Philippines)

Asia-Pacific Economic Co-operation (APEC)
DATE OF FOUNDATION: 1989   HEADQUARTERS: Singapore
OBJECTIVES: To promote market-oriented economic development and co-operation in the Pacific Rim countries
MEMBERSHIP (END-'02): Australia, Brunei, Canada, Chile, China, Hong Kong, Indonesia, Japan, South Korea, Malaysia, Mexico, New Zealand, Papua New Guinea, Peru, Philippines, Russia, Singapore, Taiwan, Thailand, United States, Vietnam (total 21)
SECRETARY GENERAL: Executive Director: Zhang Yan (China)

South Asian Association for Regional Co-operation (SAARC)
DATE OF FOUNDATION: 1985   HEADQUARTERS: Kathmandu, Nepal
OBJECTIVES: To promote collaboration and mutual assistance in the economic, social, cultural and technical fields
MEMBERSHIP (END-'02): Bangladesh, Bhutan, India, Maldives, Nepal, Pakistan, Sri Lanka (total 7)
SECRETARY GENERAL: Nihal Rodrigo (Sri Lanka)

Indian Ocean Rim Association for Regional Co-operation (IORARC)
DATE OF FOUNDATION: 1997   HEADQUARTERS:
OBJECTIVES: To promote co-operation in trade, investment, infrastructure, tourism, science, technology and human-resource development in the Indian Ocean region
MEMBERSHIP (END-'02): Australia, Bangladesh, India, Indonesia, Kenya, Madagascar, Malaysia, Mauritius, Mozambique, Oman, Seychelles, Singapore, South Africa, Sri Lanka, Tanzania, Thailand, United Arab Emirates, Yemen (total 18)
DIRECTOR: D. Dusoruth

Pacific Community (PC)
DATE OF FOUNDATION: 1947 (as South Pacific Commission)   HEADQUARTERS: Noumea, New Caledonia
OBJECTIVES: To facilitate political and other co-operation between member states and territories
MEMBERSHIP (END-'02): American Samoa, Australia, Cook Islands, Fiji, France, French Polynesia, Guam, Kiribati, Marshall Islands, Federated States of Micronesia, Nauru, New Caledonia, New Zealand, Niue, Northern Mariana Islands, Palau, Papua New Guinea, Pitcairn Islands, Samoa, Solomon Islands, Tokelau, Tonga, Tuvalu, United Kingdom, United States of America, Vanuatu, Wallis & Futuna Islands (total 27)
DIRECTOR GENERAL: Lourdes Pangelinan (Guam)

Pacific Islands Forum (PIF)
DATE OF FOUNDATION: 1971 (as South Pacific Forum)   HEADQUARTERS: Suva, Fiji
OBJECTIVES: To enhance the economic and social well-being of the people of the Pacific, in support of the efforts of the members' governments
MEMBERSHIP (END-'02): Australia, Cook Islands, Fiji, Kiribati, Marshall Islands, Federated States of Micronesia, Nauru, New Zealand, Niue, Palau, Papua New Guinea, Samoa, Solomon Islands, Tonga, Tuvalu, Vanuatu (total 16)
SECRETARY GENERAL: Noel Levi (Papua New Guinea)

LEADERS of the 10-member ASSOCIATION OF SOUTH-EAST ASIAN NATIONS (ASEAN) in early November held a summit meeting in Phnom Penh, the capital of Cambodia, also attended by China's Premier Zhu Rongji and India's Prime Minister Atal Behari Vajpayee. It was noted that the involvement of China in most of the agreements that were signed reflected the country's economic and military dominance in the region. Whilst committing themselves to co-operate in the suppression of terrorism in the aftermath of the 12 October bomb attacks on the Indonesian holiday resort of Bali (see IX.1.vi), ASEAN leaders criticised "indiscriminate warnings" by Western countries against travel in south-east Asia, saying that such blanket warnings threatened tourism and economic development.
  At the summit meeting ASEAN members and China signed a framework agreement to establish a free trade area by 2010. It was agreed that the four economically weaker ASEAN states—Burma, Cambodia, Laos, and Vietnam—would have until 2015 to achieve targets on eliminating tariff barriers. ASEAN members and China also approved a joint "declaration on the conduct of parties in the South China Sea", where there were long-standing disputes over sover-

eignty of the Spratly Islands—claimed wholly or in part by Brunei, China, Malaysia, the Philippines, Taiwan, and Vietnam—and the Paracel Islands—claimed by China and Vietnam. The agreement fell short of the formal code of conduct that ASEAN members had argued for as a means of avoiding the repetition of past military and diplomatic confrontations. Also at the summit, India and ASEAN announced the establishment of a task force to draft a framework for a free trade agreement for consideration in 2003. India's trade with the ASEAN region was worth some US$10 billion annually compared with China's US$40 billion, but analysts said that some ASEAN members saw India as a potential counterbalance to China's power. Burma, Cambodia, China, Laos, Thailand, and Vietnam also signed an agreement on an ambitious programme of hydroelectric development in the Mekong River region.

ASEAN foreign ministers held their 35th annual meeting at Bandar Seri Bagawan, the capital of Brunei, in late July. The meeting was followed by a meeting of the ASEAN Regional Forum (ARF). The most important item at the ARF was the signing on 1 August by US Secretary of State Colin Powell and ASEAN foreign ministers of a joint declaration for co-operation to combat international terrorism. This agreement provided a formal framework for the involvement of the USA in regional efforts to combat terrorism, including financial and technical assistance, exchange of information, and "capacity building".

Terrorism was again the main topic of discussion at a meeting of ASEAN home and security affairs ministers held in May in the Malaysian capital, Kuala Lumpur. At the end of the meeting the ministers issued a 16-point communiqué reaffirming ASEAN's commitment to forging a cohesive and unified approach to combat terrorism and outlining a work programme of security co-operation. It also emphasised that terrorism "must not be identified with any religion, race, culture, or nationality". Malaysia's Deputy Prime Minister and Home Affairs Minister, Abdullah Ahmed Badawi, said that ASEAN members for the first time recognised the importance of addressing the root causes of terrorism in individual countries.

ASEAN environment ministers meeting in Kuala Lumpur in early June agreed on co-operation in fighting the forest fires that had plagued the region each year, creating severe smoke pollution with heavy environmental and economic costs. ASEAN claimed that the agreement was the first such regional fire-fighting arrangement in the world. It did not, however, include any enforcement mechanism.

Heads of state and government of the 21-member ASIA-PACIFIC ECONOMIC CO-OPERATION (APEC) forum in late October held a summit meeting in Los Cabos, Mexico. The summit's unusually political closing declaration condemned the "mass slaughter of innocents" in the recent bomb attacks in Bali, Indonesia, and expressed the leaders' determination not to let the threat of international terrorism curb international trade and economic development. The declaration said that terrorism was "a direct challenge to APEC's goals of free, open and prosperous economies and an affront to the fundamental values that APEC members share". The declaration reaffirmed APEC members' commitment to the abolition of farm tariffs and the conclusion of the current round of World Trade Organisation (WTO) talks by the start of 2005

The summit had been preceded in early September by a meeting of APEC finance ministers, also at Los Cabos. Ministers endorsed an action plan to combat the financing of terrorism, in co-ordination with the UN, the IMF, the World Bank, and the Financial Action Task Force (FATF) established by the Group of Seven (G-7) and the Organisation for Economic Co-operation and Development (OECD). The closing statement found that the majority of indicators suggested that a global economic recovery was under way, but emphasised the importance of promoting a more open multilateral trade system.

APEC ministers responsible for trade had gathered in Puerto Vallarta, Mexico, in late May to discuss concrete ways to contribute to fostering economic growth in the APEC region. Within this context, ministers reaffirmed APEC member economies' commitment to move forward with the common goal of free and open trade and investment in order to bring about economic recovery and sustainable economic growth in the region.

The fourth ASIA-EUROPE MEETING (ASEM 4) was held in Copenhagen, the capital of Denmark, in late September. The summit was attended by the heads of state and government of 10 Asian and 15 European nations and the President of the European Commission, Romano Prodi. Although the ostensible agenda was trade and economic issues, it was overshadowed by the prospect of a US-led war against Iraq, about which several leaders, including China's Premier Zhu Rongji, expressed grave misgivings.

The leaders underlined their resolve to fight international terrorism, while taking into account "the multiple reasons leading to the emergence of terrorism". They pledged to work closely together to combat this threat to global peace and security, sustainable economic development, and political stability, and emphasised that the fight against terrorism must be based on the leading role of the UN and the principles of the UN Charter. To this end leaders adopted the ASEM Copenhagen Declaration on Co-operation against International Terrorism and the ASEM Copenhagen Co-operation Programme on Fighting International Terrorism. The leaders said that the 11 September 2001, terrorist attacks on the USA had "clearly demonstrated" that the ASEM process, encompassing peoples of various cultures and from different civilisations, was "an asset in international relations that merits further development". In this spirit, leaders held for the first time a retreat session under the heading "Dialogue on Cultures and Civilisations".

The 11th summit meeting of the leaders of the seven-member SOUTH ASIAN ASSOCIATION FOR REGIONAL CO-OPERATION (SAARC) was finally held in Kathmandu, the capital of Nepal, in early January. The meeting had been scheduled to take place in 1999, but had been postponed because of the poor state of relations between India and Pakistan. SAARC had long been frustrated in making progress on greater regional economic and political co-operation by antagonism between the two states. Indian Prime Minister Atal Behari Vajpayee and Pakistan's President Gen. Pervez Musharraf both attended the summit, but they did not enter into direct negotiations, despite Musharraf twice making the gesture of approaching and shaking Vajpayee's hand.

At the summit, the leaders adopted conventions on preventing and combating the trafficking of women and children for the purposes of prostitution and on regional arrangements for the welfare of children. A commitment was made to complete a framework for a South Asia Free Trade Area (SAFTA) and the closing declaration of the summit condemned terrorism "in all its forms and manifestations" as "a challenge to all states and to all humanity". The leaders agreed that terrorism constituted "one of the most serious threats to international peace and security in the 21st century". It was agreed that the organisation's 12th summit would be held in Pakistan in early 2003.

The 16-member PACIFIC ISLANDS FORUM (PIF) held its 33rd meeting in mid-August in Suva, the capital of Fiji. At the meeting, East Timor was welcomed as a special observer. Among the major issues discussed were climate change and rising sea levels (which threatened the existence of small island states such as Tuvalu); the escalating problem of AIDS/HIV transmission in the Pacific; problems of regional security and governance; and trade, development, and environmental matters.

Finance ministers of Asia's leading economies attended the 35th annual meeting of the board of governors of the ASIAN DEVELOPMENT BANK (ADB) in Shangahi, China, in early May. In his closing remarks to the meeting, the ADB president, Tadeo Chino, said that the governors had noted that the world economy was in a modest recovery from the synchronised slowdown of 2001, and that the economy in the Asia-Pacific region was "showing resilience". Chino noted that developing member countries (DMCs) were achieving faster economic recovery than had earlier been anticipated. Nonetheless, he called on DMCs to accelerate policy and structural reforms; invest in human resources, including IT-related capacity building; empower women; and vigorously pursue good governance efforts.

East Timor became the ADB's 61st member country on 24 July. The ADB was managing projects worth US$52.8 million in the country. These projects were financed by the multi-donor Trust Fund for East Timor, established in December 1999 to help rebuild the country after the devastation that followed its vote for independence from Indonesia in August that year (see AR 1999, pp. 347-48).

iv. AMERICAN AND CARIBBEAN ORGANISATIONS

Organisation of American States (OAS)
DATE OF FOUNDATION: 1951 HEADQUARTERS: Washington DC, USA
OBJECTIVES: To facilitate political, economic and other co-operation between member states and to defend their territorial integrity and independence
MEMBERSHIP (END-'02): Antigua & Barbuda, Argentina, Bahamas, Barbados, Belize, Bolivia, Brazil, Canada, Chile, Colombia, Costa Rica, Cuba (suspended), Dominica, Dominican Republic, Ecuador, El Salvador, Grenada, Guatemala, Guyana, Haiti, Honduras, Jamaica, Mexico, Nicaragua, Panama, Paraguay, Peru, St Kitts & Nevis, St Lucia, St Vincent & the Grenadines, Suriname, Trinidad & Tobago, United States of America, Uruguay, Venezuela (total 35)
SECRETARY GENERAL: César Gaviria Trujillo (Columbia)

Rio Group
DATE OF FOUNDATION: 1987 HEADQUARTERS: rotating
OBJECTIVES: To provide a regional mechanism for joint political action
MEMBERSHIP (END-'02): Argentina, Bolivia, Brazil, Chile, Colombia, Costa Rica, Dominican Republic, Ecuador, El Salvador, Guatemala, Guyana, Honduras, Mexico, Nicaragua, Panama, Paraguay, Peru, Uruguay, Venezuela (total 19)

Southern Common Market (Mercosur)
DATE OF FOUNDATION: 1991 HEADQUARTERS: Montevideo, Uruguay
OBJECTIVES: To build a genuine common market between member states
MEMBERSHIP (END-'02): Argentina, Bolivia, Brazil, Chile, Paraguay, Uruguay (total 6)
ADMINISTRATIVE SECRETARY: Santiago Gonzalez Cravino (Argentina)

Andean Community of Nations (Ancom/CA)
DATE OF FOUNDATION: 1969 HEADQUARTERS: Lima, Peru
OBJECTIVES: To promote the economic development and integration of member states
MEMBERSHIP (END-'02): Bolivia, Colombia, Ecuador, Peru, Venezuela (total 5)
SECRETARY GENERAL: Sebastian Alegrett (Venezuela)

Latin American Integration Association (ALADI)
DATE OF FOUNDATION: 1980 (as successor to Latin American Free Trade Association founded in 1960) HEADQUARTERS: Montevideo, Uruguay
OBJECTIVES: To promote Latin American trade and development be economic preference
MEMBERSHIP (END-'02): Argentina, Bolivia, Brazil, Chile, Colombia, Cuba, Ecuador, Mexico, Paraguay, Peru, Uruguay, Venezuela (total 12)
SECRETARY GENERAL: Juan Francisco Rojas Penso (Venezuela)

Latin American Economic System (SELA)
DATE OF FOUNDATION: 1975 HEADQUARTERS: Caracas, Venezuela
OBJECTIVES: To accelerate economic and social development in member states
MEMBERSHIP (END-'02): Argentina, Bahamas, Barbados, Belize, Bolivia, Brazil, Chile, Colombia, Costa Rica, Cuba, Dominican Republic, Ecuador, El Salvador, Grenada, Guatemala, Guyana, Haiti, Honduras, Jamaica, Mexico, Nicaragua, Panama, Paraguay, Peru, Suriname, Trinidad & Tobago, Uruguay, Venezuela (total 28)
SECRETARY GENERAL: Otto Boye Soto (Chile)

Caribbean Community and Common Market (Caricom)
DATE OF FOUNDATION: 1973   HEADQUARTERS: Georgetown, Guyana
OBJECTIVES: To facilitate economic, political and other co-operation between member states and to operate certain regional services
MEMBERSHIP (END-'02): Antigua & Barbuda, Bahamas, Barbados, Belize, Dominica, Grenada, Guyana, Haiti, Jamaica, Montserrat, St Kitts & Nevis, St Lucia, St Vincent & the Grenadines, Suriname, Trinidad & Tobago (total 15)
SECRETARY GENERAL: Edwin Carrington (Trinidad & Tobago)

Association of Caribbean States (ACS)
DATE OF FOUNDATION: 1994   HEADQUARTERS: Port of Spain, Trinidad
OBJECTIVES: To foster economic, social and political co-operation with a view to building a distinctive bloc of Caribbean littoral states
MEMBERSHIP (END-'02): Caricom members plus Colombia, Costa Rica, Cuba, Dominican Republic, El Salvador, Guatemala, Honduras, Mexico, Nicaragua, Venezuela (total 25)
SECRETARY GENERAL: Norman Girvan (Jamaica)

Organisation of Eastern Caribbean States (OECS)
DATE OF FOUNDATION: 1981   HEADQUARTERS: Castries, St Lucia
OBJECTIVES: To co-ordinate the external, defence, trade and monetary policies of member states
MEMBERSHIP (END-'02): Antigua & Barbuda, Dominica, Grenada, Montserrat, St Lucia, St Kitts & Nevis, St Vincent & the Grenadines (total 7)
DIRECTOR GENERAL: Swinburne Lestrade (Dominica)

THE main business of the 32nd annual General Assembly of the ORGANISATION OF AMERICAN STATES (OAS), held on 2-4 June in Bridgetown, Barbados, was the signing by 30 of the member states of the US-sponsored Inter-American Convention against Terrorism. This defined terrorism and criminalised both terrorism and support for it. The situation in Venezuela also exercised OAS members, and representatives of the organisation strongly condemned the abortive coup in the country in May (see IV.5.x). On 13 September a three-person OAS mission, which had been sent to Venezuela to help restore peace, issued a statement calling on all parties to reach a political solution by constitutional means, a call which, however, continued to be resisted by right-wing elements opposed to President Hugo Chávez.

Following the US invocation of the mutual assistance clause of the 1947 Inter-American Treaty of Reciprocal Assistance (TIAR), or "Rio Pact", in September 2001 (see AR 2001, p. 466), Mexico gave notice on 6 September of its intention to withdraw from the Treaty in 2004, becoming the first member (other than Cuba which was excluded in 1964) to do so.

At a meeting of the INTER-AMERICAN DEVELOPMENT BANK (IADB) in Washington DC, on 11-12 February, the Bank, together with other institutions, approved loans and grants totalling US$1,300 million to support the peace process in Guatemala. At the meeting, however, the representative of the UN verification committee criticised the Guatemalan government's failure to implement some of the measures to which it was committed under 1996 agreements.

On 26 March the INTER-AMERICAN COURT OF HUMAN RIGHTS (IACHR) confirmed the preliminary finding of November 2000 that the rights of Efraín Bamaca

Velásquez, the former leader of the leftist guerrilla organisation, the Organisation of the People in Arms (ORPA), had been violated. Bamaca Velásquez had been abducted and tortured by Guatemalan security forces in 1992 and had subsequently "disappeared". The court further ordered the Guatemalan government to pay an indemnity of US$500,000 to the dead man's family.

The 16th presidential summit of the 19-member RIO GROUP, held in San José, Costa Rica, was dominated by the abortive military coup in Venezuela, which had delayed its start. In a joint statement the other 18 leaders condemned the coup. They also agreed to close their borders and to freeze the bank accounts of all known Colombian guerrillas, in conformity with UN Security Council resolution 1373 (2001).

On 15 May the Cayman Islands became the fourth associate member (together with Anguilla, the British Virgin Islands, and the Turks and Caicos) of the CARIBBEAN COMMUNITY AND COMMON MARKET (CARICOM). On 16 June Haiti was finally granted full membership of the organisation, after five years as an associate member. The 23rd annual summit of heads of government, which took place on 3-4 July in Georgetown, Guyana, reaffirmed its support for the Free Trade Area of the Americas (FTAA) proposed by the USA, but warned of the difficulties facing members in opening up their economies to the outside world. A further CARICOM summit, held at Havana on 8 December, called on the USA to end its embargo on trade with Cuba, echoing the earlier resolution to the same effect adopted by the UN General Assembly on 12 November.

The second EU-LATIN AMERICAN SUMMIT, held in Madrid, Spain, on 17-18 May, was dominated by the collapse of the Argentinian economy (see IV.5.ii) and its possible consequences for other countries in the western hemisphere. Many Latin American and Caribbean leaders complained that EU leaders appeared obsessed with the US-led "war on terrorism" and were not moving fast enough to dismantle protectionist barriers. The second Summit of South American Presidents, which took place on 27-28 July in Guayaquil, Ecuador, was also strongly critical of what they saw as the protectionist policies of the EU as well as the USA. They strongly urged the early completion of an agreement between the SOUTHERN COMMON MARKET (Mercosur/Mercosul) and the ANDEAN COMMUNITY (ANCOM), in order to strengthen the hands of both sets of negotiators in talks with the US government. On 6 August the US Congress gave President George W. Bush "fast-track" authority to negotiate trade agreements; at the same time it renewed the Andean Trade Preferences Act, giving trade preferences for all of the member states of ANCOM, except Venezuela, in return for their co-operation in the US-led campaign against the trade in illegal drugs.

The 22nd summit of Mercosur, which was held on 4-5 July in the Argentinian capital, Buenos Aires, agreed to settle the long-running dispute between Argentina and Brazil over restrictions on imports of the products of the automotive industry by reducing tariffs and increasing quotas in order to allow the creation of a free market within Mercosur by 2006. At the 23rd summit, held on 5-6 December in Brasília, members reaffirmed their intention to incorporate Bolivia and Chile as full members of the group.

The 12th IBERO-AMERICAN SUMMIT meeting was held at Punta Cana, Dominican Republic, on 15-16 November. The 19 heads of state and government who attended called on the international community to find an "effective, just and lasting solution" to the problems of Latin American indebtedness.

With effect from 12 March, it was agreed that nationals of the ORGANISATION OF EASTERN CARIBBEAN STATES (OECS) should travel freely within the OECS area, with the exception, for the time being, of Anguilla and the British Virgin Islands. A common passport would be introduced by 1 January 2003. At a meeting in Basseterre, St Kitts and Nevis, on 18-20 June, leaders of the seven member states agreed to improve the regulation of offshore financial transactions.

XII RELIGION

APPOINTMENT OF ARCHBISHOP. A Welsh churchman, Dr Rowan Williams, became leader of the Church of England (see II.1.i), the first appointment from outside the established English Church since the Reformation. He was confirmed in early December as the 104th Archbishop of Canterbury at St Paul's Cathedral in London, and succeeded Dr George Carey. The choice was unpopular with many conservatives because of support by Williams for women bishops, his tolerance of the remarriage of divorcees in church, and his liberal attitude to homosexuality within the church. Perhaps more significantly, the new Archbishop made clear his opposition to the US-led "war on terrorism" and to any possible war against Iraq. According to the *Guardian,* Williams was likely to find himself in conflict with UK Prime Minister Tony Blair: "We will witness a spectacle for which there was no 20th century precedent," predicted the newspaper, "the coexistence of an archbishop and a prime minister with equally pronounced views about the moral impulse of politics." In December, Williams delivered the Richard Dimbleby Lecture 2002, entitled "Nations, Markets and Morals". He spoke from the perspective of the churchman about the dangers of a market-led state in which a sense of community responsibility was superseded by the orthodoxy of individual choice. One way of countering this danger, Williams suggested, was for government to engage with religious communities "in a new way". "Institutional religion," he said, "has a history of violence, of nurturing bitter exclusivism and claiming powers for which it will answer to nobody. So the challenge for religious communities is how we are to offer our visions, not in a bid for social control, but as a way of opening up some of the depth of human choices; offering resources for the construction of growing and critical human identities."

The Welsh heritage of Williams was in evidence at the National Eisteddfod in Wales, where, as a member of the Gorsedd of Bards, he wore the traditional robe of an honorary White Druid. Despite some criticism that he was pandering to neo-paganism, Williams was praised for his contributions to Welsh culture as a bishop, a theologian, and a poet. Many other Welsh Christian leaders had also served as Archdruids and wrote poetry in Welsh.

MARRIAGE OF DIVORCEES. After 20 years of debate the Anglican Church, at its synod in York in July, agreed in principle to allow divorced people to be remarried in church. Although formally prohibited, about 7,500 church marriages each year included already one party who had been divorced and had an ex-partner still living. There was much speculation that the decision would open the way for the marriage of Prince Charles, the Prince of Wales, and his long-standing lover, Camilla Parker Bowles, a divorcée.

PAEDOPHILE PRIESTS. The Roman Catholic Church was further rocked by revelations of the sexual abuse of children by paedophile priests. The scandal lay not only in the numbers of clergy who had betrayed the trust of their parishioners by committing such monstrous crimes, but also in the readiness in many instances of the church authorities to conceal the abuse and to permit its perpetrators to remain in their posts. Worldwide condemnation of the string of abuse revelations had forced Pope John Paul II to apologise on 22 November 2001 to the victims of predatory priests and to acknowledged the Church's failure to confront the issue. He made a further papal statement on 22 March 2002 in which he condemned the sexual abuse of minors by priests as "grievously evil". The Church also took a number of measures to address the crisis during the year, but these were widely perceived as inadequate for both the scale and gravity of the problem. On 8 January the Vatican published new rules on how to deal with allegations of abuse. These stipulated that local Church tribunals of priests, convened in secrecy but under direct Vatican supervision, would decide on an accused priest's future in the Church and whether or not he would be relieved of his ministry. The rules did not preclude initiating civil prosecutions against abusers, but did neither did they make such action mandatory, leading to criticism that the Church was continuing to evade the issue.

Bishops in the USA, Poland, and Ireland resigned over allegations that they had themselves sexually abused minors. From early January a US newspaper, the *Boston Globe*, published over 250 stories of sexual abuse of minors by Catholic priests, followed by thousands of articles in other papers. In addition to focussing on individual abusers, the campaign also highlighted senior church figures who had allegedly permitted priests under their jurisdiction to continue working, often with young people, despite being suspected of abuse. One of the casualties of the revelations was Cardinal Bernard Law, the most senior figure in the Catholic Church in the USA, who resigned as Archbishop of Boston on 13 December. His original offer to resign, at a special summit of 12 US cardinals held in the Vatican on 23-24 April to discuss the problem, had been rejected by the Pope, who told him to remain in his post and resolve the hundreds of lawsuits against the Boston archdiocese by victims of abuse. In June US bishops had drafted a "zero-tolerance" policy which included provision for the removal of priests from active duties immediately upon a sexual abuse allegation being filed against them. It also defined sexual abuse in broad terms and eliminated any statute of limitations for the punishment of past offenders. The Vatican equivocated, however, insisting that there should be due process for accused priests who should not be condemned on the basis of unjust or unproven allegations. Eventually a revised plan was approved by the Vatican on 16 December whereby bishops were charged with conducting a confidential preliminary investigation into abuse allegations before removing a priest from active duties. The revised charter, which also provided for a statue of limitations for prosecuting priests of 10 years beyond the 18th birthday of the victim, was criticised by some for giving too much discretion to senior church figures who had already proved themselves unreliable in dealing with the problem.

The Roman Catholic Church made several controversial canonisations during 2002. These included, on 16 June, Padre Pio, a controversial but immensely popular Capuchin friar; Juan Diego Cuauhtlatoatzin, a 16th-century Aztec Indian whose very existence was open to doubt; and Josemaría Escrivá de Balaguer, the Spanish founder of Opus Dei (see II.3.viii and II.4.i)

RELATIONS WITH ORTHODOX CHURCH. The Russian Orthodox Church continued to protest against alleged "proselytism" in Russia by the Roman Catholic Church, reacting with fury to the Vatican's announcement in February that it was to upgrade its four apostolic administrations in Russia (which were regarded as temporary bodies) to dioceses. Over the course of the year a total of five Roman Catholic clergymen serving in Russia were prevented from re-entering the country on their return from visits abroad. The possibility of a papal visit to Russia seemed ever more remote as far as the two churches were concerned, although it appeared from remarks by President Vladimir Putin in January that the Russian state would welcome such a visit.

In Belarus, a new law "On religious freedom and religious organisations" came into force in November. The new law, which bore similarities to legislation passed in Russia in 1997, elevated the Russian Orthodox Church in Belarus over other religions, assigning to it the leading role in "shaping the spiritual, cultural, and state traditions of the Belarusian people". The law appeared to target non-traditional religions by outlawing unregistered religious activity; requiring prior censorship for all religious literature; banning foreign citizens from leading religious organisations; restricting publishing and education to faiths active in Belarus for at least 20 years and with at least 10 registered communities; and banning most religious meetings in private homes.

THE DIGNITY OF DIFFERENCE. A new book of this title by British Chief Rabbi Jonathan Sacks was praised at home and abroad, but it was denounced by a group of orthodox rabbis as heresy. The subtitle of his new book was "How to avoid the clash of civilisations by recognising that the differences of orthodox faiths were 'essential' parts of creation." In it the Chief Rabbi warned Israel against corrupting its traditions through its military occupation of Arab land and its oppression of Palestinian civilians, conduct which, he argued, was incompatible with the founding ideals of the Jewish state. He stated his conviction that Israel, in order to achieve peace with its Arab neighbours, had to give back the land which it had illegally occupied since the 1967 war. While still supporting the Jewish state, Sacks also made repeated efforts to open avenues of dialogue with Muslims, much to the anger of many in right-wing Israeli circles. The book was widely denounced by Zionists and an advertisement in the *Jewish Chronicle* said that parts of the work were "open to interpretation that is inconsistent with basic Jewish beliefs". One of orthodoxy's greatest authorities forbade Jews to have the book in their homes, and Sacks, apparently bowing to such pressure, disappointed many of his supporters by promising to rewrite some passages in a new edition.

PAPACY AND THE HOLOCAUST. For over 40 years there was debate on the wartime role of Pope Pius XII, and what he did or did not do to save Jews from the Nazi

Holocaust. Dozens of articles in scholarly journals and newspapers addressed this activity, or lack of it, together with allegations of Catholic anti-Semitism. Yet claims that Pius XII actively assisted in persecuting the Jews, and could even be characterised as "Hitler's Pope", had little factual basis. More complex questions concerned how much the Pope had known of the Holocaust, and whether he recognised any obligations to rescue Jews, had this been possible. Despite the anti-Jewish feeling that was widespread in Church circles in the late 19th and early 20th centuries, there was no evidence that Pius XII saw the removal of the Jews from Europe as a benefit for Christianity. Between 1965 and 1981 the Holy See had published 11 volumes of archival material which suggested that the Pope and his aides had done much in secret to help the Jews, as well as making some diplomatic protests about their persecution. There were increasing calls, however, for the Vatican to open its archives fully in order to allow historians to assess the accuracy of the claims and counter-claims concerning the Church's stance towards the Jews during World War II.

THE ISLAMIC WORLD. For the Islamic world, 2002—most of which accorded with the Islamic year 1423 (calculated in lunar years dating back to the Prophet's move from Mecca to Medina in the Christian year 622)—was another difficult year, dominated by the long shadow of the terrorist attacks of 11 September and the looming US-led war against Iraq. For Muslims and non-Muslims alike it seemed as if the combustible mix of Islamic extremism and resurgent US imperialism was conspiring to produced a "clash of civilisations". As war preparations intensified throughout the year key questions about the future shape of Islam and its role within the world were raised but remained unanswered.

Although not the only religion in the Arab world, Islam was by far the most important and claimed the adherence of the overwhelming majority of Arab states and their populations. Yet a UN-sponsored report in 2002, by Arab academics, concluded that of 280 million Arabs in the Middle East region, 65 million were illiterate and 20 per cent were subsisting on less than US$2 per day. The report identified three major causes of this backwardness: a lack of freedom, insufficient rights for women, and poor educational opportunities. Each of these causes could, arguably, be seen as a direct consequence of Islam. Although Muslims had often blamed the decline of the once-great Islamic civilisation on outside forces, particularly Western imperialism and Zionism, for many observers—such as Yale University's authority on Islam, Bernard Lewis—the causes were also internal and included a "lack of freedom of the mind from constraint and indoctrination, to question and inquire and speak; freedom of the economy from corrupt and pervasive mismanagement; freedom of women from male oppression; and freedom of citizens from tyranny". Thus, although Islam continued to grow and to display the hallmark of being one of the world's great religions, it seemed increasingly threatened by the prospect that it would be shaped and defined only in terms of its anachronistic opposition to the remorseless advance of the West.

This was never more true than in the aftermath of 11 September, an attack by extremists which was illustrative of the frustration and powerlessness felt by many

Muslims in the face of US global military and economic might and the US government's support for the crimes against humanity which were being committed almost daily by the state of Israel. The UK author Salman Rushdie used a column in the *New York Times* to lambaste Muslim moderates for their ambivalence over the 11 September attacks. "Where", he demanded, "is the Muslim outrage at these events? As their ancient, deeply civilized culture of love, art and philosophical reflection is hijacked by paranoiacs, racists, liars, male supremacists, tyrants, fanatics and violence junkies, why are they not screaming?" It was a pertinent question, although one which failed to recognise the efforts made by some Muslim moderates to make clear their opposition to fundamentalism. In Iran there were increasing signs of conflict between the radical ruling mullahs and a generation of young people who had attained adulthood since the 1979 Islamic revolution and who, whilst wishing to remain faithful to their Islamic beliefs, were growing restive at the restrictive excesses of the theocracy in which they lived. This was most dramatically demonstrated in the student demonstrations which were triggered by the sentencing to death of university professor, Hashem Aghajeri, who in June had called for a withdrawal of clerical rule from secular affairs (see VIII.1.i). There were also institutional manifestations of moderate Islam, such as the meeting between foreign ministers from the Organisation of the Islamic Conference (OIC) and their counterparts from the EU in Istanbul, Turkey, in mid-February, which attempted to encourage dialogue and understanding and to develop universal values on issues such as the rights of women, the death penalty, and the right to freedom of religion (see XI.3.iv). OIC foreign ministers also met in Kuala Lumpur, the Malaysian capital, in April, and affirmed their collective resolve to combat terrorism in all its guises. The meeting issued the Kuala Lumpur Declaration which reaffirmed their "commitment to the principles and true teachings of Islam which abhor aggression, value peace, tolerance and respect as well as prohibiting the killing of innocent people".

Too often, however, such voices were drowned by the sound of gunfire and bombings perpetrated by Islamic terrorists. These were personified by Osama bin Laden, a spectral presence throughout the year, but one whose message of conflict and hatred was all too audible. In a taped statement purportedly from the al-Qaida leader, produced in November, the day before the first anniversary of the fall of Kabul, he listed the attacks carried out by his followers and told his listeners to "expect more that will distress you. The Islamic nation has started to attack you at the hands of its beloved sons, who pledged to God to continue *jihad* through words and weapons to establish right and expose falsehood." The choice for Muslims could not have been more stark: modernise and find means of living with the West, or engage in a mortal struggle, the outcome of which could not be known but the violence of which was all too certain.

XIII THE SCIENCES

1. SCIENTIFIC, INDUSTRIAL AND MEDICAL RESEARCH

SPACE, ASTRONOMY AND PHYSICAL SCIENCES. Sean O'Keefe, the new administrator of the USA's National Aeronautics and Space Administration (NASA) appointed in December 2002, struck a cautionary note in his first interview with the media on 8 January, emphasising the need, in a time of increasing budgetary pressures, to direct NASA's efforts in space exploration towards more utilitarian and entrepreneurial ends. In contrast with the more visionary ethos espoused by his predecessor Daniel Goldin, O'Keefe questioned the rationale of "pure exploration", saying that space missions should be justified in terms of concrete achievements. O'Keefe, a former Navy Secretary, also said that NASA would need to work more closely with the US Defence Department on research and development, because it was often difficult to differentiate between military and civilian technology. He was expected to restructure the agency to save money and to rein in funding of the orbiting International Space Station (ISS), an international collaboration in which the USA and Russia were the major partners. The major addition to the structure of the ISS during 2002 was the installation of a US$600 million girder called the S-Zero Truss, launched on 8 April aboard the space shuttle *Atlantis* after weeks of delays caused by technical faults. The girder was the first of nine that would form a space railway on the outside of the ISS, while also serving as the armature for an array of solar panels.

Following a mission on 5-19 June by the space shuttle *Endeavour* to take a replacement (fifth) crew to the ISS, NASA announced on 25 June the grounding of all four remaining space shuttles after minute cracks were found in the linings of fuel pipes on both *Atlantis* and *Discovery*. This caused the postponement of the scheduled 19 July flight of *Atlantis* to the ISS, to deliver a 13.5-metre, 15-tonne structural girder packed with computers and communications equipment. The space shuttles were essential to the development of the ISS: routine supplies could be ferried by unmanned Russian Progress spacecraft, and crews could be exchanged by the Russian Soyuz craft, but the shuttle alone was able to transport the structural members and heavy equipment needed to fulfil the space station's potential as an orbiting laboratory. Yet the shuttles had become veteran spacecraft, the oldest, *Columbia*, being 22 years old, and with no replacements in sight. Eventually on 18 September NASA cleared the shuttles to resume operations, and the *Atlantis* mission on 8-18 October went without a hitch. It was reported in September that Canada had joined the other 14 members of the ISS consortium in putting pressure on the USA to restore funding that it had unilaterally cut from the ISS budget to recoup massive cost-overruns. The USA had effectively scaled back the space station's crew from the planned seven to three astronauts, who had little time to spare from maintenance duties for scientific research. Canada, which had contributed US$1.4 billion to the project, currently had only 30 minutes' research time per week. Construction of the ISS, the last remaining manned space project, had begun in November 1998 with the launch of the first (Russian) module (see AR 1998, p. 473). The only notable independent Russian contribution to manned space flight during the year was to carry on 25 April the second paying "space tourist", Mark Shuttleworth, a South African, for a 10-day stay aboard the ISS, following the example of Dennis Tito in 2001 (see AR 2001, p. 474).

The space shuttle *Columbia* lifted off from Cape Canaveral on 28 February to rendezvous with the orbiting Hubble optical telescope. The crew of *Columbia* would perform perhaps the most ambitious, sustained and complex space mission of 2002 as they renovated Hubble over a period of 10 days. The seven-astronaut crew installed, repaired and replaced equipment, including replacing the solar arrays and the power unit of the telescope. They left Hubble with its imaging capability 10 times more powerful than before. The telescope's last refit had taken place in December 1999, when faulty gyroscopes had been replaced.

There were notable unmanned contributions to space exploration during the year. NASA put into orbit on 5 February the High Energy Solar Spectroscopic Imager (HESSI), which was designed to study solar flares and to send back the first high-resolution colour pictures of the flares during their peak energy emissions. The European Space Agency (ESA) in October launched its *Integral* gamma ray observatory on a Russian Proton rocket from Baikonur cosmodrome in Kazakhstan. *Integral*'s IBIS imager (Imager on Board the *Integral* Satellite) was the most sensitive instrument of its kind ever produced, and in December it transmitted its first image of a gamma ray burst from a source 5,000 light years from Earth. NASA suffered a major setback on 15 August when it lost contact with the ambitious Comet Nucleus Tour (CONTOUR) spacecraft launched on 3 July. CONTOUR had been designed to rendezvous with two comets, in 2003 and 2006, making a close approach to the nucleus of each and taking detailed photographs to determine their chemical composition. An investigation was begun into the failure later in August. A contribution to the long-standing debate on the presence of water on Mars was reported in February. Images transmitted by the *Mars Global Surveyor* spacecraft provided evidence of floods of water issuing from volcanic fissures some 10 million years ago. An observation overlapping the fields of astronomy and physics was announced by NASA on 10 April. Images from the orbiting Chandra X-ray observatory, launched in 1999 (see AR 1999, p. 465), of two previously undiscovered neutron stars showed anomalies that suggested that the super-dense stars might not be composed of neutrons but of an even more extreme form of matter, called strange quark matter. It was reported in December that NASA had succeeded in reactivating a data recorder on the veteran spacecraft *Galileo* that had been damaged when *Galileo* passed through Jupiter's radiation belt in November. The probe's last relay of data would close down in mid-January 2003. *Galileo*, which was launched on 18 October 1989, was expected to burn up in Jupiter's atmosphere in September 2003.

Earthbound astronomy was not entirely eclipsed by such developments. The opening ceremony took place on 18 January for the Gemini South telescope in the Chilean Andes. Together with its twin, Gemini North in Hawaii (which had been in operation for more than a year), it offered astronomers an unparalleled view of the entire sky, and the telescopes' eight-metre diameter mirrors had a light-gathering power 10 times that of the mirror of the Hubble telescope. Observing at the infrared end of the spectrum, Gemini enabled astronomers to see through the dust clouds obscuring the centres of galaxies. It was reported in March that Australian and UK astronomers had found evidence in the analysis of the clustering pattern of 250,000 galaxies that the universe was expanding at an ever-increasing rate. This appeared to support earlier evidence of "negative gravity" and a force referred to as "dark energy". An announcement on 10 April at the annual conference of the UK Royal Astronomical Society confirmed again how intimately entwined were the disciplines of astronomy and physics. An analysis by the Institute of Astronomy at Cambridge of a three-dimensional map of 220,000 galaxies had resulted in a calculation of the mass of the smallest and most elusive subatomic particle, the neutrino, to be 1.8×10^{-36} kg. Until recently it had been thought that neutrinos had no mass, but their possession of mass had been confirmed by research at the underground heavy water Sudbury Neutrino Observatory (SNO) in Canada. The SNO research also found that many of the electron neutrinos emitted by the Sun were changed to tau or muon neutrinos en route to Earth, thus clearing up the long-standing mystery of the paucity of detected electron neutrinos. The Sudbury results were named in December by the journal *Science* as one of the 10 most significant scientific discoveries of the year. Also amongst *Science*'s top 10 was the announcement in May that a study employing the Cosmic Background Imager (CBI)—an array of 13 microwave telescopes in the Chilean Atacama desert—had provided insights into the early state of the universe through detection of fluctuations in the cosmic microwave background left over from the Big Bang. The observations showed the first clusters of matter that were seeds of galaxies, confirmed the existence of "dark matter" and "dark energy", and supported the inflation theory of rapid early expansion of the universe.

The ESA's heavy-lift Ariane-5 rocket successfully launched Envisat, an eight-tonne advanced meteorological satellite, into orbit from the ESA's launch site at Kourou, French Guyana. The operation ended eight months of uncertainty since Ariane-5's last, failed launch. Envisat was expected to orbit the Earth 14 times a day for five years in order to build up a comprehensive picture of the atmosphere, oceans, land masses, and polar ice caps, with the aim of enabling European scientists to detect climatic and environmental change. In August the ESA successfully launched the first of a new generation of meteorological satellites, the Meteosat Second Generation (MSG-1), which took up a geostationary orbit 35,000 km above the equator. MSG-1's most sensitive instrument measured incoming radiation from the Sun against outgoing radiation from the Earth, a major factor in climate change. Repeated successful performances of Ariane-5 appeared to confirm the rocket's viability in the overcrowded commercial satellite launcher market. The Russian space agency Rosaviakosmos was currently negotiating to transfer commercial satellite launches by its medium-lift Soyuz rocket to Kourou from the Baikonur cosmodrome. However, the ESA suffered a serious setback on 11 December when an advanced version of Ariane-5 veered off course during its inaugural flight from Kourou and was exploded by remote control, with the loss of two communications satellites worth US$600 million. It was announced on 31 December that the launch of the ESA's *Rosetta* spacecraft (planned to rendezvous with a comet) in January 2003 would be delayed until the investigation of the Ariane-5 malfunction was complete. In March 2002 EU leaders agreed on the finance of the ESA's Galileo project for a network of civilian navigational satellites, in the teeth of strong opposition from the USA, which feared that Galileo might interfere with its own rival military Global Positioning System (GPS).

China demonstrated its continuing commitment to space exploration by successfully launching into orbit the *Shenzhou III* spacecraft in March and the *Shenzhou IV* in December. Both were unmanned, but the Chinese space agency stressed that the *Shenzhou* could carry a crew. The flight of *Shenzhou IV*, launched on 30 December, was intended to test control and life support systems, giving rise to speculation that China planned a manned space flight in 2003.

It was reported in February that scientists at the Max Planck Institute in Heidelberg, Germany, had claimed the observation of a rare neutrinoless double-beta decay. Such an event would represent a breakthrough in nuclear physics because it would violate a fundamental principle of the Standard Theory of physics, the conservation of lepton number. However, other researchers argued that the claim was based on a flawed analysis of the data in the experiment. The question of scientific fraud or dubious interpretation of results was raised more than once during the year. The Lawrence Berkeley National Laboratory in the USA admitted in July that a claim by a team of its scientists in 1999 to have discovered a new element, ununoctium (number 118), which was retracted in August 2001 for lack of corroboration (see AR 2001, p. 476), had actually been based on evidence fabricated by one of its researchers, who had subsequently been dismissed. In September Jan Hendrik Schön, a scientist working for US Bell Laboratories, admitted that apparently ground-breaking work in the miniaturisation of computers, for which some had predicted he would be nominated for the Nobel Prize for Physics, had in fact been partly fraudulent. Schön's research had culminated in the claim that he had created a transistor using a single molecule. His results had been impossible to reproduce and Schön's use of identical graphs of data relating to different parts of the experiment eventually led to his work being discredited by peer review.

Genuine advances in nanotechnology were reported in different studies published in the journal *Nature* on 13 June. Teams of scientists at Cornell and Harvard universities in the USA had succeeded in creating a transistor from, respectively, a cobalt atom and two atoms of vanadium attached to gold atoms as electrodes. Perhaps the most exotic scientific development was announced on 17 June by the Australian National Laboratory in Canberra. A team of researchers had teleported a laser beam and regenerated it one metre away, using a subatomic phenomenon known as "quantum entanglement".

MEDICAL AND BIOLOGICAL SCIENCES. The research hailed by *Science* as the most significant scientific advance of the year was represented in a study published in September by a team of scientists led by Jo Milner of York University, UK, into the properties of the ribonucleic acid (RNA) molecule. Previously thought to be merely the messenger carrying genetic instructions for protein-building produced by the more celebrated deoxyribonucleic acid (DNA), the study found that RNA was much more versatile and controlled many of the processes in the individual cell, including switching genes on and off. The researchers, using a technique known as RNA interference (RNAi), succeeded in destroying cancer cells in the laboratory by "silencing" genes of the papilloma virus. The research pointed to a new approach to understanding cell processes, and RNAi was thought to be more powerful and more specific than any other technique of gene therapy yet used.

There were other significant developments in genetic research during the year, notably the publication in April of the full genetic sequence, or genome, of rice; in October of the decoded genome of the malaria-carrying mosquito; and in December that of the mouse. Researchers hoped that deciphering the genetic composition of rice would lead to the development of strains that were more nutritious and more resistant to pests, drought, and disease. The results would also be applicable to other cereal crops. In fact two different strains of rice were sequenced. A publicly funded collaboration between scientific institutions in the USA and China decoded the genome of the *indica* rice strain, commonly grown in eastern Asia and the Pacific region. Unrestricted public access was given to the genetic data. The *japonica* strain, grown in temperate or arid climates, was sequenced by the Swiss-based biotechnology company, Sygenta, which restricted access to its research data. In October separate teams of researchers published the complete genomes of the malarial parasite *Plasmodium falciparum* and of the malarial mosquito *Anopheles gambiae*. It was expected that the genetic information would help scientists to design new drugs and insecticides to replace some current treatments to which both parasite and mosquito had begun to develop immunity. According to UN World Health Organisation (WHO) statistics malaria still infected some 300 million people each year, of whom at least 1 million died. The publication of the complete mouse genome by US and UK researchers in December was expected to accelerate research into human diseases, including cancer, because the mouse, the most commonly used mammal in laboratory research, shared 99 per cent of its 30,000 genes with human beings.

There were a number of developments in cloning and stem cell research. Following a legal ruling in January in the UK on the remit of the Human Fertilisation and Embryology Act to regulate research into cloning techniques, the government's regulatory body in March awarded the first two licences to conduct embryonic stem cell research for therapeutic rather than reproductive purposes. The debate continued inconclusively over whether adult stem cells could effectively be used to repair and regenerate tissue, thus obviating the controversial practice of extracting primordial stem cells from unwanted embryos. It was reported in June that a team of scientists at the University of Minnesota, USA, had succeeded in using engineered stem cells from adult mice to create a wide variety of cell types in mouse embryos. The weight of scientific opinion still leaned, however, to the view that embryonic cells held the most potential. It was reported on 14 February in *Nature* that the first cloned kitten had been born in December 2001 at Texas A&M University, USA, representing the first successful attempt to clone a domestic pet. In the same month, however, a study by researchers at Japan's National Institute of Infectious Diseases in Tokyo found that in a batch of 12 cloned mice 10 had died prematurely, and all were afflicted with degraded immune systems. Deficiencies in the immune system had been found in other cloned mammals, such as cows and goats. The most dramatic development in the science of cloning, if it could be verified, came at the end of the year, when on 27 December a company called Clonaid announced in Hollywood, Florida, USA, that the world's first cloned baby had been born to a US citizen. Clonaid was established by the founder of a quasi-religious cult called the Raelians, which believed that human beings had been created by the cloning of aliens. The claim was received with almost universal scepticism by reputable biotechnology researchers and re-ignited the debate over the ethical issues involved in human reproductive cloning, which was already banned in some 30 countries, including the USA.

The most striking discovery in the field of palaeontology was that announced in the journal *Nature* on 11 July of what appeared to be the oldest known hominid skull, some 6 to 7 million years old, which was about 1 million years older than the previously identified oldest human ancestor. The skull was found in the Djurab desert in Chad, some 1,500 km west of the sites in Ethiopia and the Rift Valley in Kenya where most early hominid remains had been excavated, which appeared to indicate that human evolution was more complex than previously thought. The new species, which had a problematic mix of hominid and simian features, was widely regarded as highly significant and was named *Sahelanthropus tchadensis*. Some scientists were sceptical, however, that the discovery was truly a hominid, and critics even took the view that the skull was that of a gorilla. The fossil nevertheless featured in *Science*'s list of the 10 most important scientific breakthroughs of the year.

NOBEL PRIZES. The award of the 2002 Nobel Prize for Chemistry was shared by John Fenn (USA) and Koichi Tanaka (Japan) for developing methods of determining the mass of proteins and other large biological molecules, and by Kurt Wüthrich (Switzerland) for using magnetic resonance imaging techniques to create three-dimensional images of long protein chains. The Prize for Medicine was won by Sydney Brenner (UK), Robert Horvitz (USA), and Sir John Sulston (UK) for discoveries in the genetic regulation of organ development and programmed cell death, deriving from research into the nematode worm (*Caenorhabditis elegans*). The Prize for Physics was awarded jointly to Ray Davis (USA) and Masatoshi Koshiba (Japan) for devising underground chambers to detect neutrino radiation from the Sun, and to Riccardo Giacconi (USA) for building the first orbital telescopes to detect cosmic X-ray sources.

2. INFORMATION TECHNOLOGY

FOR the Information Technology (IT) industry, 2002 ended with a sense of cautious optimism. An exit from the crash which had followed the boom of previous years finally seemed to have begun, heralding a return to a less volatile business landscape. Although the year began with the collapse of industry giants such as WorldCom, Global Crossing, and Tyco in false accounting scandals that exceeded even the one which had brought down Enron Corp.—WorldCom's US$3.8 billion profit overstatement being one of the largest cases of accounting fraud in history—the year ended with a few surviving companies emerging from the dust and edging into profitability. The biggest names in online retailing and services, Yahoo, Ebay, Amazon, and Expedia all posted their first ever profits.

MICROSOFT. An end to Microsoft's five year court battle with the US Department of Justice at last seemed likely as US District Court Judge Colleen Kollar-Kotelly rejected the action brought by nine US states for tougher sanctions against Microsoft. Kollar-Kotelly ruled that the sanctions accepted by Microsoft and the Department of Justice in November 2001 would last for five years, unless extended by the court. These sanctions required greater and more timely disclosure to software developers of the functioning of key elements of Microsoft operating systems. They also imposed restrictions on the bundling with operating systems of so called "middle-ware" applications (such as the Internet browser "Internet Explorer"). Still, they were considerably less stringent than the measures contained within the original ruling—later overturned (see AR 2001, p. 482)—by US District Judge Thomas Penfield Jackson, which had called for the break up of Microsoft into two separate companies.

Outside the courts, Microsoft made changes to its software licensing model which signalled a move away from the one-off purchase of a software product towards something more akin to a subscription-based service. The change was poorly received by customers, who saw it as being good for Microsoft (in that it guaranteed the company a steady cash flow) but bad for them (in that it reduced choice as to when to upgrade a programme and increased costs). The research and advisory firm Gartner estimated that medium-sized businesses with a policy of upgrading software every three years would pay between 33 and 77 per cent more under the new plan than they did currently. Those upgrading every four years would pay 68-107 per cent more.

OPEN SOURCE/FREE SOFTWARE AND THE DIGITAL DIVIDE. Anger at Microsoft's new licensing model gave a boost to its greatest threat: the loose alliance of software movements often collectively referred to as Open Source. The description Open Source was generally—and erroneously—applied to both the open-source software development methodology and the Free Software movement These two groups advocated approximately the same aim—that software developers should be able to view, modify, and distribute the source code of computer programmes—but for different reasons (the former as a method of producing better software, the latter as a means of ensuring individual liberty). The two groups were often confused as they shared an important common feature—their software could almost always be legally obtained free of charge—and a common enemy: proprietary software. Because of its founding principles of open source code and individual freedom and, of course, its low cost, the Open Source alliance continued to gain momentum in 2002, particularly in developing countries which were seeking to build the IT infrastructure that would enable them to compete in an increasingly information-based world economy.

A number of countries in the developing world introduced measures supportive of Open Source software during the year. The starting point for most of these was education. In May Pakistan's Ministry of Science and Technology revealed plans to install some 50,000 low-cost computers in schools and colleges throughout the country. These computers, at a cost of less than US$100 each, would run the free, open-source operating system GNU/Linux. "Don't be surprised if we become the first country in the world to say that all (government-run) services are going to be GNU/Linux based," said Ministry of Science and Technology advisor Salman Ansari. In Thailand, the ambitious SchoolNet experiment, an initiative seeking to provide universal access to teachers and students in schools, also began using GNU/Linux. It had developed a Linux School Internet Server (Linux SIS) to be promoted and distributed to schools "as a cheaper alternative to using expensive server software". In Nepal an initiative named "Ganesha's Project" was launched. The project would use donated machines and open-source software in order to cut the costs of acquiring software licences for "an already impoverished school system".

In addition to education, the state backing of Open Source software throughout all public services was seen in its most extreme form in South America, where the governments of Peru, Mexico, Venezuela, and Colombia all drew up preliminary legislation which would make the use of Open Source software in government agencies obligatory wherever possible. Similar proposals were being considered by the EU and Ukraine. Microsoft reacted by sending its chairman Bill Gates to each country considering such legislation, where he made donations of cash, software, and training services in an effort to win a reconsideration. Proprietary software vendors (including Microsoft) formed the Initiative for Software Choice (ISC) in May to lobby against the mandatory use of Open Source software and to argue for the selection of software based on its merits (an argument with which many Open Source supporters also agreed).

Most governments in any case pursued a dual strategy whereby they continued to encourage the use of Open Source software, whilst accepting largesse from Microsoft. In India, where Open Source was very popular, the government accepted a US$400 million donation from Microsoft towards computer literacy programmes. Visiting Bangalore, India's technology hub, Richard Stallman, founder of the Free Software Foundation and a leading Open Source advocate, likened Microsoft's donation to that of cigarette manufacturing companies giving sample packs to students "to encourage addiction".

PEER-TO-PEER FILE SHARING. Naptster, the company that brought peer-to-peer music file sharing to the mainstream (see AR 2000, pp. 446-47), and in so doing opened a Pandora's box of copyright questions and legal actions, finally closed in 2002. After losing the legal action brought against it by the Recording Industry Association of America (RIAA) and being subsequently purchased by recording giant Bertlesmann Music Group (BMG) Entertainment, whereupon the site moved to a paid subscription model, Napster failed to hold even a tiny fraction of the 38 million subscribers which it had enjoyed at its peak. The vulnerability of the Napster service was its reliance on centralised servers that listed the contents of users' computers in order to allow files to be shared. New, alternative applications that were more truly peer-to-peer, such as Morpheus and Kazza, by avoiding the need for a centralised content directory were able to take over where Napster left off and they continued to augment the popularity of peer-to-peer file sharing. Although the RIAA had a number of high profile legal actions already underway against the companies behind this new breed of software, which they claimed were engaged in a "21st century piratical bazaar", it was not clear that closing the companies down would stop the service, because of the absence of any central element on which the activity depended. In a year in which, according to the International Federation of the Phonographic Industry (IFPI), music sales declined in value by 5 per cent despite there having been no fall in the popularity of recorded music, both Internet piracy and the mass illegal copying of CDs were considered to be directly replacing CD sales. Again, as with Napster, many music industry experts maintained that the only successful response to this phenomenon that the Recording Industry could make would be the provision of their own copyrighted music via paid Internet services, services which nearly all the major record companies launched during the year.

BLOGGING. Easy-to-use web publishing tools moved the Internet away from being just a passively accessed library to becoming a popular publishing platform accessible to just about anyone with a web browser. Personal and frequently updated web sites known as Blogs (WeB LOGS) brought web publishing to the masses and, without the need for either editor or publisher, created thousands of amateur journalists. Blogs could also be made interactive, allowing any visitor to post an opinion. The result of this new, increasingly popular pass-time (dubbed "blogging") was the development of entire online communities, centred around every niche interest imaginable. There were few firm statistics for the number of active blogs, but most experts agreed on around 500,000 and growing.

SPAM. Unsolicited Commercial Email (UCE, commonly known as spam) reached levels which threatened to make electronic mail systems unusable. Research carried out by the email filtering company Brightmail, showed that the number of spam emails had soared in 2002, with four in 10 emails received by computers being classed as unwanted junk. Some junk emails were genuine adverts that worked on the principle that if just a tiny percentage of the millions who received the email (which cost very little to send) responded, then the exercise was worthwhile. Many junk emails, however, were either attempts to defraud recipients by trying to extract bank details in return for fictitious rewards, or adverts for pornographic websites. To combat this flood, Internet service providers such as Microsoft Network (MSN), America Online (AOL), and Yahoo began providing premium rate spam protection as a way of attracting new users. However, the senders of junk email became increasingly sophisticated in their attempts to avoid detection by filtering software, typically sending the emails from addresses unrelated to their organisation or forging the sender's identity entirely. Legislation passed by the EU, which required that users agree to receive marketing emails, seemed unlikely to stem the flow since the vast majority of junk emails were being sent from outside the EU.

MOBILE TECHNOLOGY. The struggle around the development and launching of Third Generation (3G) mobile telephone networks, which would allow fast video and data access from mobile handsets, continued in Europe and south east Asia. In March nearly 2,000 European business leaders signed a petition demanding that governments (including Germany, UK, France, and Italy) return the €214.4billion which had already been paid for 3G licences and resell the 3G spectrum in a cheaper, fairer manner. No such move was made before the year's end. At the same time, leading analysts urged telecommunications companies to cut their losses and simply abandon their 3G licences. Some companies had already done so: Spanish Telefonica and Finnish Sonera abandoned their joint German 3G licence and another German 3G licence holder, MobilCom, was facing insolvency. In Sweden, Tele2 (the country's second biggest operator) wrote off its €45 million investment in a Norwegian 3G license, handing it back to the Norwegian government. Orange, Hi3G, and Vodafone all asked the Swedish telecoms authorities to extend the deadline for full 3G rollout, but the Orange and Vodafone requests were quickly rejected. Even in Japan, where new mobile technologies had already proved marketable, the birth of 3G went less well than had been hoped. NTT DoCoMo, which had over the last few years become the world's largest Internet service provider on the back of the 30 million subscribers to its 'i-mode' wireless Internet service based on existing (2G) mobile phone technology, launched its FOMA 3G service during the year but experienced poor take-up. In Europe, Hutchison seemed likely to be the first to launch commercial 3G services in the UK and Italy, but postponed the launch till 2003.

3. THE ENVIRONMENT

THROUGHOUT 2001, newly elected US President George W. Bush had dominated environmental issues, but from an environmentalist perspective, for all the wrong reasons. Early fears that Bush would follow both his right-wing instincts and his father's example and act in the interests of his oil industry sponsors had been proven fully justified, the abrogation of the Kyoto Protocol being the single most destructive example of this stance. As 2002 began, the question was not whether Bush would continue in the same vein, but whether the rest of the world could act in concert with sufficient resolve and coherence to sideline US policy. One significant political grouping committed to oppose the USA was the EU. At the Laeken conference at the end of 2001, the EU had committed itself to sustaining the 1997 Kyoto Protocol on Climate Change. EU policy was also at odds with US demands over the licensing and labelling of genetically modified (GM) foods.

It was not long before the US administration confirmed its environmental credentials, or lack of them. In January it announced three dramatic policy shifts: US power stations would not be subject to the clean-up legislation planned by Bush's predecessor, President Bill Clinton; nuclear waste would after all be dumped in a huge cave in the Yucca mountains in Nevada, even though after 20 years of research many geologists remained convinced that the site was hopelessly inadequate; and the administration would cease funding research into improving the efficiency of car engines, the ostensible reason being a shift of focus to research a more promising technology, hydrogen power. Hydrogen engines produced no pollution at the point of use, but as the fuel had to be made somehow, they offered little more than very local benefits. Perhaps more important was the fact that no such technology could reasonably be expected to be viable in the next two presidential terms, the suspicion being that this policy change was simply a recipe for burning more oil in the interim.

That other focus for conflict between environmentalists and big business, the World Economic Forum (WEF), resurfaced at the end of January when the meeting which had been planned to take place in Davos, Switzerland, was abruptly moved to the Waldorf Astoria in New York, where the US administration promised that the meeting between world leaders and the heads of major trans-national companies could take place in "a unique club atmosphere". The theme of the conference was to be "Leadership in Fragile Times: A Vision for a Shared Future". Greens protested that this vision clearly excluded dissenting voices, crucially those which focussed on sustainable development.

February began with a warning from the Potsdam Institute in Germany which reported on research into Dansgaard-Oeschger events: rapid global warmings which had occurred during the last ice age. Computer models by Andrey Ganolpolski and Stefan Rahmsdorf tied these events to a natural 1,500-year cycle, possibly linked to solar fluctuations and to the state of circulatory currents in the Atlantic. These currents, driven by high salinity in the waters near Greenland, helped to keep the planet cool. However if the circulation faltered, the solar cycle was sufficient to trigger climate change. Whilst not a cause for immediate alarm, the research provided another insight into climate instability, and suggested that as the world warmed, and the ice caps melted, conditions could be right for a major global warming early in the 22nd century.

Of more immediate concern was research by English Nature on weeds in Canada. The research showed that volunteer plants—crop plants growing wild—were accumulating genetic modifications, a process known as gene stacking. The result was the appearance of plants which were resistant to a wide variety of herbicides with the consequence that farmers would have to use extra chemicals to control them. The work prompted environmental groups to call again for increased separation between fields of GM and non-GM varieties: five km instead of the current 50 metre norm.

A study co-funded by the environmental pressure group Greenpeace challenged the assumption that organic farming practices were a luxury affordable only by developed nations. On the contrary, the report concluded, developing countries could benefit more as the cost of imported agrochemicals was greater than in developed countries. Nicolas Parrott, of Cardiff University, told the Nuremberg conference on organic farming that a reluctant shift to organic methods had resulted in significant increases in production with lower costs. Cuba, deprived of cheap pesticides and fertilisers by the collapse of the Soviet Union, had been forced to turn to biological methods of pest control, resulting in over half the country's rice and vegetables being produced organically. Madagascan rice farmers had more than trebled their yields; Brazilian maize crops had more than doubled through using rotation and crop residues to improve soils; and Indian cotton farmers had rescued an industry blighted by pesticide-resistant whitefly by using decoy crops to control the pests.

February did not conclude without another blow from Bush. The US administration announced its revised targets for curbing greenhouse emissions following its withdrawal from the Kyoto Protocol: an 18 per cent cut, per unit of GDP, to be achieved by 2012. Although superficially a reasonable target, it was seen as wholly inadequate for the world's largest polluter. Moreover, by linking the cut to GDP, a thriving US economy could massively increase its emissions whilst still achieving its stated goals. The administration claimed in justification that to meet the 7 per cent absolute cut promised by Clinton would have cost some US$700 billion and five million US jobs.

By contrast, a UK government study concluded that even large cuts in emissions would have little effect either on the UK economy or on the number of unemployed, and so proposed a 20 per cent improvement in energy efficiency by 2010, with much of the improvement coming from enhanced use of renewable energy sources. Of concern to the green activists, however, was the refusal to eliminate nuclear energy from the proposals. In the UK capital, London, mayor Ken Livingstone announced that the world's biggest congestion charging scheme would begin in early 2003.

Fulfilling its promise, the EU took the legal steps necessary to ratify the Kyoto Protocol in mid-March. Although insufficient to effect the treaty—Russia, Japan, and the rest of Europe would also have to ratify for it to come into effect—the move served as a signal that the world could continue to press ahead with the measure despite the opposition of the USA.

At Yokohama in Japan, the 226 delegates at the Codex Alimentarius Commission of the UN Food and Agriculture Organisation (FAO) and the World Health Organisation (WHO) reached agreement on a framework for evaluating the safety of GM foods, defining the need for pre-market safety assessments and requiring post-market monitoring. It also called for improvements in the capabilities of regulatory authorities, especially those in developing countries, to manage the safety of GM foods. This placed the FAO and the WHO in conflict with US (and, potentially, World Trade Organisation—WTO) expectations that there should be no trade restrictions on GM products.

In April India joined the list of countries approving the use of transgenic crops. Approved trials included mustard, soya, and corn as well as a variety of cotton patented by the US giant Monsanto. Some farmers' groups hailed it as a major step forward whilst others condemned the move. Devinder Sharma of the Indian Forum for Biotechnology and Food Security claimed that it was "a recipe for environmental disaster".

Bush continued his programme to weaken the environmental movement by engineering the removal of Bob Watson as chair of the Inter-governmental Panel on Climate Change (IPCC). Watson was acknowledged to be an effective leader of the IPCC and a scientist committed to pursuing the logic of the IPCC's conclusions: that impending climate change required effective contrary measures. Next Bush targeted Brazilian José Bustani, the head of the Organisation for the Prohibition of Chemical Weapons (OPCW). The USA claimed it had been unfairly targeted by the body but the OPCW countered that a spate of inspections in the USA had occurred only because the USA had been three years late in submitting its list of facilities covered by the OPCW remit.

On the eve of an important climate change meeting, the UN Environment Programme (UNEP), working with the International Centre for Integrated Mountain Development (ICIMOD), underlined the need for action by releasing predictions that nearly 50 lakes in the Himalayas, swollen by increased melt waters, could burst their banks in the ensuing decade, flooding entire communities and threatening not just major loss of life but also massive damage to property, infrastructure, and economies. The Regional Co-ordinator in Asia for UNEP's Division of Early Warning and Assessment, Surendra Shrestha, said: "Our findings indicate that 20 glacial lakes in Nepal and 24 in Bhutan have become potentially dangerous as a result of climate change. We have evidence that any one of these could, unless urgent action is taken, burst its banks in five to 10 years time with potentially catastrophic results. Who knows how many others, elsewhere in the Himalayas and across the world, are in a similar critical state?"

In Australia, an extensive survey of the corals in the Great Barrier Reef revealed an alarming level of bleaching, a symptom of excessive water temperatures caused by the loss of the algae within the corals. Whilst the effects could be temporary, bleaching could also prove fatal for the corals. Reports of similar bleaching across the South Pacific served to exacerbate concerns amongst coral conservationists.

The Third Global Environment Outlook was published in May. A synthesis of the views of a great many specialists involved in both environmental and developmental issues, the report described the planet as being at a cross roads and called upon countries to take effective action at the forthcoming UN World Summit on Sustainable Development (WSSD) scheduled to open in Johannesburg in August. Klaus Toepfer, executive director of the UNEP, commented: "We need concrete actions, we need concrete timetables and we need an iron will from all sides." In an earlier publication, the UNEP had concluded that major corporations were continuing "business as usual" and that a "sustainability first" approach was called for; it was clear that the UNEP at least had not been cowed by US tactics, instead stating that unless effective action was taken, the world faced disaster by 2030. June saw the gathering of government representatives in Bali intended to prepare the ground for smooth progress at the WSSD. It failed. What emerged was disagreement over all the major questions, including issues such as the debt burden, Kyoto Protocol, globalisation and sustainability, controlling multi-national corporations, and whether to apply the precautionary principle in policy making.

Acrylamide, a chemical used in the manufacture of plastics and a known carcinogen, came under the spotlight at a WHO/FAO joint meeting in June. Swedish research, and subsequent studies in Norway, Switzerland, the UK, and the USA, found that acrylamide levels in certain starch-based foods, such as potato chips, french fries, biscuits, cereals, and bread, were well above the acceptable level given in the WHO's *Guideline Values for Drinking Water Quality*. Whilst the meeting concluded that not enough was known either about the chemical, its toxicity, its sources, or the amounts needed to cause cancer in humans, it did conclude on the need for further study with some urgency.

In the run up to the WSSD a new pan-European inter-governmental body, the Transport, Health and Environment Pan-European Programme (THE PEP) was established at a meeting in Geneva. Recognising the rapid growth in passenger and freight transport in the EU (it had doubled in 25 years) and the resultant health costs (100,000 premature deaths per year were attributed to particulate pollution, and a similar number caused by traffic accidents), Brigita Schmögnerová, Executive Secretary of the UN Economic Commission for Europe (UNECE), opened the second high-level meeting on Transport, Environment and Health saying "Efficient transport is essential for the development of international trade. At the same time, it is clear that the continuing expansion of transport demand, heavily dominated by road transport, raises serious concerns about the long term sustainability of present mobility trends."

As Johannesburg prepared for the arrival of the largest number of delegates ever to an environmental summit, the FAO warned of growing food shortages in Southern Africa and launched an appeal for US$25 million of aid. In desperate need of help were Lesotho, Malawi, Swaziland, Zambia, and Zimbabwe, with an estimated 10 million people facing severe food shortages. For the second consecutive year food supplies had been hit by both drought and floods and the situation had been exacerbated by poor management of reserves, inadequate financial resources, land degradation, and damaging land reforms, in particular the redistribution of land in Zimbabwe. AIDS/HIV was also contributing to the problem: the high prevalence of the disease removed crucial workers, absorbed public funds, and crippled both agriculture and administration. The FAO reported a more encouraging picture emerging from Afghanistan, recovering from the damage caused both by the war and by drought. Whilst aid would continue to be needed for a while at least, food production had increased. Essential for long-term recovery was continued investment by aid agencies in order to rebuild both communities and infrastructure such as irrigation schemes.

The smogs across south east Asia, identified by the UNEP as one of the world's most pernicious environmental hazards which killed hundreds of thousands each year, were fuelled by forest fires which began in July and peaked in August. This annual event, triggered largely by plantation companies and forestry activities, contributed to choking smog spreading across the region, closing airports in its path. Combined with emissions from other sources such as factories, power stations, and vehicles, the smoke formed pollution clouds which spread as far afield as Nepal, Afghanistan, and south east China.

The WSSD was held on 26 August-4 September and, as predicted, little of any substance was agreed during the discussions. A minor victory for the anti-globalisation lobby—the inclusion of a text to promote inter-governmental agreements on corporate accountability—was immediately undermined by the USA which sought to alter its meaning via a "letter of interpretation". The only other new commitments were to improve access to basic sanitation globally, and to establish marine protected networks. The summit did not impress the green movement. Charles Secrett, director of Friends of the Earth, said that the summit "should have been about protecting the environment and fighting poverty and social destruction. Instead it has been hijacked by free market ideology, by a backward-looking US administration, and by the global corporations that help keep reactionary politicians in business." The Kyoto Protocol, however, survived, not as a result of international consensus at the conference, but as a result of commitments announced in Johannesburg by the Prime Ministers of Russia and Canada that their respective countries would ratify the agreement. Also at the conference the UNEP revealed its plans to promote a global network of "sustainable energy" centres. The USA, negative almost to the last, did announce one positive move at the summit—the US Agency for International Development (USAID) and the United Nations Foundation said that they would give a total of US$3 million to support the International Coral Reef Action Network (ICRAN). However, the funding was not for global research, it was to be targeted at the Mesoamerican reef, the largest barrier reef system in the Atlantic Ocean and the second largest in the world.

Desertification was at one time a favourite buzz-word for environmental movements as the apparently relentless expansion of deserts gave an early boost to the green lobby. But during the 1990s evidence had begun to emerge that the process was neither one way nor irreversible. In September evidence was released that the desertification of Burkina Faso, the world's poorest country, was in retreat to the extent that families who had fled degraded lands decades earlier were returning to their ancestral homes. Analysis of satellite images showed this to be not merely a local phenomenon. Possible explanations included the end of the droughts of the 1970s and 1980s, a reduction in land use which allowed it to recover naturally, and the application of farming techniques designed to conserve what little water was available. In any event the "re-greening" of marginal desert regions promised to lock up carbon and to compensate for forest loss elsewhere.

Australian research also brought positive news: the ban on Chlorofluorocarbons (CFCs) had begun to have the intended effect and the ozone hole over the Antarctic was set to begin shrinking; a 50 year process but proof that international environmental protocols could work. However many Inuit who had been forced to leave their lands could take little comfort. The loss of ice cover had resulted in a catastrophic reduction in the numbers of whale, walrus, seal, and waterfowl that formed the foundation of the local economy. Polar bears, it transpired, were faring little better. At the top of the food chain, the polar bear was most at risk from toxins which accumulated in body tissues. A report by the Norwegian Arctic Monitoring and Assessment programme revealed the discovery of bears with both male and female organs—a result of so called "gender bender" chemicals such as PCBs and of organic mercury in the food chain. The findings added to fears, voiced earlier in the year by the World Wide Fund for Nature, that Polar bears were under threat of extinction through the loss of habitat.

More species were added to the "Red List" (the list of species judged to be in real danger of extinction) published in October. A total of 121 species of all varieties, from a breed of small water mouse to a type of antelope, achieved this dubious distinction. But the Red List was not all bad news: a few species though to have been eradicated returned, including the Bavarian pine vole which was thought to have died out in the 1960s. A community of the creatures was discovered during 2002 in the Northern Tyrol in Austria. However, from the USA, it emerged that attempts to save the condor had failed. Whilst birds bred in captivity had survived after release, their own attempts at breeding in the wild had failed—the deaths of the first chicks born in the wild being attributed to pollution. Smaller birds featured in another extinction scare: Darwin's famous finches were under threat from an alien invasion. The mangrove finches (*Camarhynchus heliobates*) were suffering from infestations by larvae of the warble fly (*Philoros Downsi*) which sucked the blood of fledgling birds. With only around 100 breeding pairs of the finches surviving, any loss of breeding stock threatened to have serious consequences.

At the November meeting of the UN Convention on International Trade in Endangered Species (CITES) held in Santiago, Chile, the whale shark and the basking shark—both threatened because of their highly prized fins—were accorded protected status. The big leaf mahogany, a tree which was a major victim of illegal logging, was also added to the protected list, as was the sea horse.

Before the year was out, GM food was once again in the news. The UK's Environment Minister, Michael Meacher, described the USA as "wicked" for attempting to force countries where people were starving to accept GM food. Zambia, Malawi, and Mozambique had all requested that food aid supplies should be guaranteed free from GM crops: Zambia, for example, had refused to accept GM foods on the basis of the precautionary principle, fearing that its grain stock could be contaminated and it could subsequently find itself unable to export to important markets, including Europe. However, the USA retorted that "beggars can't be choosers", a stance which led to accusations that it was using the famine to force GM seed onto countries which did not want it.

In December Canada delivered on its commitment to ratify the Kyoto Protocol. At the same time, the UK's Meteorological Office released data which showed that the world had seen the second warmest year since records began 140 years previously—the highest overall temperatures were recorded in 1998—with nine of the 10 hottest years all having occurred since 1990. Nor was that the end of the story: analysis of the prospects for 2003 suggested that it would prove to be warmer still, with average temperatures over half a degree warmer than for the period 1961-90.

As the year ended, environmentalists were relieved that, despite the implacable opposition of the USA, the Kyoto Protocol had survived. In that sense at least, US antagonism towards the environmental consensus had been contained. But with the Kyoto Protocol considered by most as being an entirely inadequate response to the impending threat to the planet, it was a small victory indeed.

XIV THE LAW

1. INTERNATIONAL LAW—EU LAW

i. INTERNATIONAL LAW

THE "war against terrorism" continued to raise many legal questions. One of the most controversial was whether the right to use force in self-defence against terrorism, as claimed in the ongoing campaign by the USA in Afghanistan, could be extended to cover the use of force against other states such as Iran, Iraq, and North Korea—the three states identified as the "axis of evil" by US President George W. Bush in his State of the Union Address of 29 January (see IV.1). The US National Security Strategy produced in September put forward a wide new doctrine of pre-emptive self-defence against rogue states and terrorists said to pose a threat because of their potential use of weapons of mass destruction. The question also arose in many states how far the "war against terrorism" justified restrictions on human rights. A petition was brought to the Inter-American Human Rights Commission on behalf of the hundreds of persons allegedly associated with the Taliban or al-Qaida who were detained in the US naval station at Guantanamo Bay in Cuba. The US position was that they were not entitled to prisoner of war status. In February the Commission requested the USA to take urgent measures to have the legal status of the detainees determined by a competent tribunal. The special UN Security Council Committee, established after the 11 September attacks, received information from many states on the steps taken to implement anti-terrorism measures, as required in Resolution 1373 (2001) (see XI.1). The International Convention for the Suppression of the Financing of Terrorism came into force on 10 April.

The Rome Statute of the INTERNATIONAL CRIMINAL COURT (ICC) entered into force on 1 July, a landmark in the history of international relations. Eighty-seven states had ratified the statute by the end of the year. The ICC was a permanent court with the power to bring to justice individuals who, after 1 July 2002, committed the most serious crimes of concern to the international community, such as genocide, war crimes, and crimes against humanity. The process to nominate and elect judges and the prosecutor began. However, in May the USA had informed the UN that it did not intend to become a party to the treaty and, accordingly, had no legal obligation arising out of its earlier signature of the Statute on 31 December 2000. The USA said that it was concerned about politically motivated prosecutions; there were problems relating to jurisdiction and due process, since the power of the tribunal was independent of consent; and that the statute provided insufficient opportunity for Security Council supervision. Therefore the USA would not cooperate with the ICC and sought immunity for US peacekeepers involved in UN operations. When other members of the Security Council initially refused to accept its demand, the USA in June vetoed the renewal of the mandate of the UN peacekeeping mission in Bosnia and Herzegovina (UNMIBH). After protracted negotiations a compromise was worked out on the basis of Article 16 of the Rome Statute. The Security Council adopted Resolution 1422 requesting the ICC not to investigate or prosecute forces from states that had not ratified the Rome Statute. After 12 months the exemption could be extended (see XI.1). Many argued that US concern was unjustified as there were sufficient safeguards in the Rome Statute. Resolution 1422 was an erosion of the statute which risked discrediting the Security Council; it permitted the possibility of impunity for genocide, crimes against humanity, and war crimes. The USA also made bilateral agreements with states such as Israel and Romania which prohibited the surrender of US citizens to the ICC.

Another development in the area of international criminal jurisdiction was the agreement between the UN and Sierra Leone on 16 January to establish a Special Court for Sierra Leone with jurisdiction to try individuals bearing the greatest responsibility for offences committed during the country's 10-year civil war. This was the first tribunal where UN and local judges would sit side by side. The Trial Chamber and Appeals Chamber were set up in July; the judges were sworn in in December. In contrast, UN negotiations with the government of Cambodia to establish a special tribunal to try Khmer Rouge leaders for genocide and crimes against humanity committed between 1975 and 1979 broke down in February.

The trial of former President Slobodan Milosevic before the INTERNATIONAL CRIMINAL TRIBUNAL FOR THE FORMER YUGOSLAVIA (ICTY) opened on 13 February. Milosevic was the first former head of state to stand trial for genocide, crimes against humanity, and war crimes. Although in 2001 he had refused to plead or to be represented by counsel because he did not recognise the authority of the ICTY, he subsequently defended himself at length. The trial was repeatedly suspended on the grounds of his ill-health. In September the first phase of the trial on Serb atrocities in Kosovo in 1999 ended; the Court then began to hear evidence about the 1991-95 conflicts in Bosnia and Herzegovina and Croatia. The ICTY experienced some problems in securing co operation from Yugoslavia and Croatia, but its large-scale reforms succeeded in expediting the resolution of cases, with the long term aim of completing the tribunal's mission by 2010. The tribunal came to operate at full capacity with six simultaneous trials being held daily. Bosnian Serbs were convicted in three cases arising out of events in 1992-93 for a range of crimes against humanity. In *Kunarac, Kovac and Vukovic* the Appeals Chamber upheld the sentences for rape, enslavement, and torture of Muslim women in the area of Foca in 1992; it clarified the law on crimes against humanity with regard to the requirement of the existence of an armed conflict, the nexus between armed conflict and the criminal behaviour, and the definition of enslavement and rape as crimes under international law. The Appeals Chamber also gave a judgment on the right of the tribunal to compel the testimony of a war correspondent. A *Washington Post* journalist who had interviewed Radislav Brdjanin, later indicted for crimes against humanity, resisted a subpoena to appear before the ICTY. The Appeal Chamber established a test to be applied in balancing the interests of justice against the public interest in the work of war correspondents.

The INTERNATIONAL CRIMINAL TRIBUNAL FOR RWANDA (ICTR) continued to make slow progress. Some of the abuses by defence lawyers such as over-billing, fee-splitting, and gift-giving between defence lawyers and their clients were addressed, but there were still serious concerns about rocketing defence costs. There were also problems in increasing the number of judges and in securing the presence of witnesses. The Trial Chambers were fully engaged in the ongoing trials of 22 accused persons, but few cases were completed. In March Lt Samuel Imanishimwe was acquitted of conspiracy to commit genocide, the first time that the tribunal had ordered acquittal before the end of a trial. However, he still faced seven counts of genocide, crimes against humanity, and war crimes. In the ongoing *Media* case the Trial Chamber acquitted Ferdinand Nahimana on one count of crimes against humanity and Jean-Bosco Barayagwiza on three counts of crimes against humanity and war crimes. The Appeals Chamber unanimously rejected the prosecution's appeal and confirmed the acquittal of Ignace Bagilshema in July. There were concerns over the lengthy period of pre-trial detention; the prosecutor therefore drastically revised her investigation programme from 136 new suspects to 16, to be concluded by the end of 2004.

The INTERNATIONAL COURT OF JUSTICE gave judgments on the merits in three cases. The first, *Arrest Warrant of 11 April 2000,* concerned the scope of immunity for international crimes. A Belgian court had issued an international arrest warrant against the then Foreign Minister of the Democratic Republic of Congo (DRC) for incitement of racial hatred against the Tutsis leading to the genocide of 1994. The DRC argued, first, that Belgium had no jurisdiction over crimes committed abroad by non-nationals and, second, that the Foreign Minister had immunity. The Court was divided on the question of universal jurisdiction and avoided a decision by limiting its judgment to the question of immunity. In its first pronouncement on this subject the Court found on the basis of customary international law that the immunities of Foreign Ministers were granted to ensure the effective performance of their functions on behalf of their states. Therefore a Foreign Minister enjoyed full immunity from criminal jurisdiction and inviolability; no distinction could be drawn between private and official acts; and this immunity extended even to war crimes and crimes against humanity.

The next two cases concerned boundary delimitation; both involved the interpretation and determination of the validity of colonial treaties. In *Cameroon/Nigeria* the Court decided on the contested land boundary in the Bakassi peninsula, Lake Chad, and other areas; it broadly affirmed the colonial boundaries challenged by Nigeria. It held that Nigerian actions on the ground were not sufficient to undermine Cameroon's legal title and that Nigeria should accordingly withdraw its military and administrative forces from those areas to which it did not have title. However, the Court refused to pronounce on the claims of Cameroon (and the counterclaims of Nigeria) with regard to state responsibility for the illegal use of force because neither side had adequately proved its claims. As for the maritime boundary, Nigeria was more successful. The Court applied the 1982 Law of the Sea Convention, to which both states were parties, and broadly followed the equidistance line in its delimitation of the single maritime boundary.

In *Indonesia/Malaysia* the Court found by 16 votes to one that sovereignty over the contested islands of Ligitan and Sipadan off the northeast coast of Borneo belonged to Malaysia. Indonesia had based its claim on an 1891 convention between the then colonial powers, the Netherlands and the UK. Malaysia argued that the Convention did not cover the relevant area. On the basis of the preparatory works and the subsequent conduct of the parties the Court accepted Malaysia's position. It then considered whether the activities of the parties evidenced an actual exercise of authority over the islands. Malaysia's actions in applying a Turtle Preservation Ordinance and in constructing lighthouses on both islands, although modest, were diverse in character and included legislative, administrative, and quasi-judicial acts. They covered a considerable period of time, and Indonesia had not expressed a protest.

Four new cases were taken to the Court. El Salvador applied for revision of the judgment of 11 September 1992 in the land, island, and maritime frontier case between El Salvador and Honduras. Benin and Niger jointly submitted a boundary dispute. Both these cases were to go to Special Chambers of the Court, the first use of such chambers for many years. The DRC brought two new cases, but in both the basis of the Court's jurisdiction seemed tenuous. The case against France for illegal assertion of jurisdiction was unlikely to proceed further as France had not accepted the Court's jurisdiction. The DRC also brought a new case against Rwanda, although it had withdrawn a similar case only the year before. This new case concerned allegations of massive violations of human rights on Congolese territory resulting from acts of armed aggression since 1998; the DRC made a request for provisional measures, but this was refused on grounds of probable lack of jurisdiction on the merits.

Five judges were elected for nine-year terms: Judges Shi Jiuyong (China) and Abdul Koroma (Sierra Leone) were re-elected; Hiasashi Owada (Japan), Bruno Simma (Germany), and Peter Tomka (Slovakia) were elected for the first time.

The PERMANENT COURT OF ARBITRATION (PCA) was involved in several interstate cases; it had significantly increased its activities in recent years, especially since its centenary was celebrated in 1999. Under its auspices the *Ethiopia/Eritrea* Boundary Commission, established under the peace settlement after the war between the two states, announced its ruling on the delimitation and demarcation of the boundary in April. A claims commission was also created to decide all claims by the two governments and their nationals for loss, damage, or injury related to the conflict and resulting from violations of international humanitarian law. The PCA was also engaged in the *Ireland/UK* arbitration under the 1992 Convention for the Protection of the Marine Environment of the North-East

Atlantic (the OSPAR Convention) concerning access to information in relation to the mixed oxide (Mox) plant at Sellafield. Another case brought by Ireland against the UK over the Mox plant was before an arbitral tribunal under the 1982 Convention on the Law of the Sea (see also AR 2001, p. 495).

The EUROPEAN COURT OF HUMAN RIGHTS gave several landmark decisions, many in cases against the UK. In *Pretty* the applicant, who suffered from an incurable degenerative disease, failed in her claim that the UK prohibition on assisted suicide violated her rights; the Court held that Article 2 on the right to life did not cover a right to die. In *Goodwin* the Grand Chamber modified its own previous position on the rights of transsexuals. The applicant complained that lack of legal recognition of her change of sex constituted an interference with her right to marry. In the light of the continuing international trend in favour of increased social acceptance of transsexuals and of legal recognition of a new sexual identity the UK Government's position was no longer tenable. The power of the UK Home Secretary to determine the length of life sentences was also successfully challenged in a number of cases. A striking feature of the Court's caseload was the increasing number of cases on the human rights of companies, including one in which a company's right to protection of its "home" was upheld.

There were several developments with regard to the death penalty. In Europe Protocol 13 to the European Convention for the Protection of Human Rights and Fundamental Freedoms concerning the Abolition of the Death Penalty was opened for signature on 2-3 May; the earlier Protocol 6 had not excluded the death penalty for acts committed in time of war or imminent threat of war. Both the UN Human Rights Committee and the Inter-American Court of Human Rights held that Trinidad and Tobago had violated human rights through its mandatory death penalty for murder.

The UN General Assembly adopted an Optional Protocol to the Convention against Torture, to establish a preventive system of visits to places of detention to strengthen protection for persons deprived of their liberty against torture. In September the UN held a Treaty-Signing Event to encourage wider acceptance of treaties relating to sustainable development.

ii. EUROPEAN UNION LAW

OF the two most significant developments at state level for lawyers in 2002, neither came to fruition during the year. On the one hand, the Treaty of Nice was finally ratified by Ireland, after a second referendum, thus enabling its far-reaching provisions on the European Court of Justice (ECJ) to come into force early in the following year. The ECJ and the European Commission had already begun work on drafting some of the texts which would implement the Nice changes. These included a new set of Rules of Procedure that were required to take into account the merger of the two separate statutes of the Court into a single document (after the expiry and non-renewal earlier, in July, of the European Coal and Steel Community (ECSC) Treaty of April 1951—see AR 1951, p. 164, the number of statutes had been reduced from three).

More importantly, the Treaty up-graded the Court of First Instance (CFI), giving it fully autonomous status, although it was still located in the by now massive court complex on the Kirchberg Plateau just outside Luxembourg city. The autonomy of the CFI would prepare the way for further development of the EU's judicial system, increasing the role of the Court, perhaps by transferring to it some of the references from national courts under Article 234 of the EC Treaty. The changes at Nice, while of major importance, were thus only a stage in the deeper and wider reform which continued to be widely advocated.

Indeed, of far more significance than even these changes were the completely new Treaty provisions allowing the creation of "judicial panels" under the ECJ. These would not be merely specialised chambers of the Court under a new name but would be new courts altogether, each concerned with a special subject jurisdiction. The first of these to be prepared was to be, in effect, an EU civil service labour tribunal to which all "staff cases" would be transferred from the CFI: work on this was far advanced by the year's end. Other potential candidates under discussion included a panel for competition cases and another for intellectual property cases, but no firm consensus on these emerged.

On the other hand, much progress was made on a new Patent Regulation, the old Community Patent Convention being moribund as it had never received the necessary ratifications. If eventually adopted, the new Regulation would fit with the well-established Trade Mark Regulation/Directive and the new Design Right Regulation. Particularly relevant was its inclusion of provisions for the creation of an EU Patent Court, an innovation which was raising concern among the English patent Judges. It was expected that the new Patent Regulation would probably constitute a *sui generis* court rather than be subsumed into one of the new judicial panels, most obviously an intellectual property panel, which it might replace.

The pattern emerging at the year's end thus appeared to be a three-tier court system with judicial panels at first instance; the CFI as intermediate appellate court from the judicial panels with an extended jurisdiction to try direct actions for judicial review of EU administrative acts and a new jurisdiction to reply to national courts requesting interpretation of EU laws and the Treaties under Article 234; and the ECJ gradually moving closer to being a more remote High Constitutional Court and ultimate court of appeal in important cases. The Treaty of Nice did not specifically make these changes itself, but rather changed many of the key provisions in order to enable them to be made later by a lower level decision, thereby avoiding the need for yet further Treaty amendment in the future. Underlying all of these developments was the awareness that they were taking place in the context of the forthcoming Intergovernmental Conference (IGC) in 2004 at which the EU and EC Treaties would probably be fundamentally re-shaped.

Preparation for that event was pursued during the year by the newly created Convention on the Future of Europe (see XI.4). The aim of this body was to draft a fundamental revision of the existing three basic Treaties—EU, EC, and Euratom—and replace them by a single text, a "constitution". This would embody the essentials of the existing documents but would incorporate substantive and textual changes essential to the new state-like polity that the new European Union was becoming. The Convention itself was not a treaty (like that of the Berne Copyright Convention) but a group of legislators of varied character openly modelled on the 18th century Philadelphia Convention which had drafted the Constitution of the USA. This assemblage was organised in three parts: the plenary Convention comprising all the members; a Presidium consisting of a president, two vice-chairmen, and nine other members who acted somewhat like a government, directing proceedings and putting forward proposals to the plenary; and 11 working groups (committees) which examined special areas in detail and submitted reports, also to the plenary. By the end of the year, all the working groups had produced their final reports, and on the basis of these, and the debates which accompanied them, the Presidium was beginning to draft its proposals for the precisely worded individual articles of the new "constitution". No draft articles had been published by the year's end, but the Presidium had in September issued an outline "table of contents" setting out its view of the forthcoming "constitution's" structure and content to form the basis for the articles as they emerged. The working groups were naturally focussed particularly on political and economic matters. Those with a particular interest to lawyers formed two clusters: (i) constitutional law and legislative processes (working groups I Subsidiarity and IX Simplification of types of legislation); and (ii) hard law (working groups II Charter of Fundamental Rights and the European Convention on Human Rights, III Legal personality of the EU, and X Freedom, security and justice).

Part of the motivation of the Convention, as indeed of the political (as opposed to the judicial) parts of the Treaty of Nice, was to provide an updated constitutional framework for a greatly enlarged EU. Negotiations on the 5th enlargement culminated in the approval by the European Council in December of the applications to join the EU made by 10 further European states (see XI.4). The detailed terms of the enlargement (from 15 to 25 member states) were not released, indeed had not been drafted, at that time. As for the other events outlined above, 2002 was the preparatory year: the precise legal texts (the Treaty and Act of Accession) would not appear until the following year, with actual accession planned for 2004 coincident with the new IGC. For lawyers, then, the December decision on enlargement was not a particularly significant event: it merely increased the area and the scope of existing law without adding new content to it. More noticeable would doubtless be the involvement of large numbers of lawyers and judges from Eastern Europe in the practice of EU law both domestically and in the European Court system.

Against this background of huge structural change, ordinary day-to-day law might have seemed tame. However, equally major changes were taking place, not least being the gradual repatriation of EU competition law (or at least the antitrust part of it) to the member states now that they had nearly all adopted national laws which duplicated the EU rules. This was being done through a systematic reworking of the block exemption regulations. That process culminated just before Christmas in the adoption of a replacement (Regulation 1/2003) for the keystone text on which the whole antitrust edifice, and much of the work of EU lawyers, depended: the famous Regulation 17 which dated back to 1962 and embodied the working procedure without which the system could not function.

Less dramatic, but equally significant, was a series of directives on the financial services (particularly insurance) industry. In particular, these completed the free internal market in life assurance (Dir. 2002/83); provided for harmonised regulation of insurance brokers and other intermediaries (Dir. 2002/92); extended harmonised supervision of banks, insurance companies etc. which formed part of a financial conglomerate (Dir. 2002/87); and made compulsory for all publicly traded companies the adoption of International Accounting Standards (IAS) and International Financial Reporting Standards (IFRS) insofar as the Commission had decided to that effect (Reg. 1606/2002).

In the burgeoning field of criminal law, the Council adopted in June two far-reaching framework decisions (a new legislative form applicable to third pillar acts, with an effect equivalent to that of directives but without direct effect), both of which followed decisions taken the previous December. The first defined and criminalised "terrorism" (Fr. Dec. 2002/475/JHA); the other introduced a European Arrest Warrant and in effect abolished extradition between member states, replacing it with automatic surrender of the requested person (Fr. Dec. 2002/584/JHA). Two further framework decisions strengthened the criminalisation of trafficking in people, whether for forced or compulsory labour or for sexual exploitation (Fr. Dec. 2002/629/JHA) and regulated police joint investigation teams (Fr. Dec. 2002/465/JHA).

2. LAW IN THE UNITED KINGDOM

THE Treaty of Nice, altering the operation of the EU after the accession of new members, was ratified as part of English Law in the European Communities (Amendment) Act, while the European Parliamentary Elections Act consolidated the rules relating to elections to the European Parliament. The Electoral Fraud (Northern Ireland) Act aimed to reduce electoral fraud in Northern Ireland, and the Sex Discrimination (Election Candidates) Act that legalised gender-based positive discrimination in the selection of candidates for election aimed to increase the number of women members of the House of Commons. In a claim arising from the destruction of aircraft during the 1991 Gulf War, the House of Lords clarified the operation of the tort of conversion at the same time as resolving questions relating to the relations between international law and the law of England. The Court of Appeal declined to examine whether legal proceedings in the Netherlands had been properly conducted, and the House of Lords refused to hold that

Germany would be in breach of its human rights obligations in its treatment of applicants for political asylum.

The politicisation of the judicial process, especially as a consequence of the enactment of the Human Rights Act 1988, was increasingly marked. Challenge was made to the practice of detaining asylum seekers at reception centres, but the House of Lords resolved that it did not constitute a breach of human rights; the Court of Appeal refused to require the Foreign Secretary to intervene on behalf of a UK citizen captured in Afghanistan and imprisoned in Cuba by the authorities of the USA; a penalty scheme involving fixed penalties for drivers bringing illegal immigrants into the UK was held in principle to breach the drivers' right to a fair trial, though their claim was dismissed on other grounds. The Home Secretary was held to have acted lawfully in determining not to allow entry to the UK to a foreign religious leader when he had had reason to believe that this might lead to public disorder. In an application for political asylum, it was held that a foreign politician was entitled to a hearing by an Immigration Appeal Tribunal to determine whether or not he had a well-grounded fear of persecution in his home country despite its being clear that such persecution would have been illegal; but it was stressed that when an applicant sought asylum on the grounds that he was at risk of persecution for his political beliefs, it was essential that the persecution should stem from his beliefs and not because, as in the instant case, he was believed to have been a witness to criminal behaviour by an organ of the state. Asylum seekers who were both infirm and destitute were held entitled to demand that accommodation be found for them by a local authority.

In the Nationality, Immigration and Asylum Act, Parliament introduced more stringent conditions for granting British nationality, and placed greater restrictions on the conditions for foreign nationals seeking asylum. Balancing this, the International Development Act made greater provision to fund development and the relief of poverty abroad.

In an apparently supremely trivial case involving the prosecution of a market trader for selling vegetables by non-metric weights, the Queen's Bench Divisional Court introduced into the law a fundamental distinction between constitutional statutes and ordinary statutes, holding that the former could only be repealed by express words in a later Act of Parliament, whereas the latter were susceptible to repeal by implication. A provision in the Finance Act 1989 under which an Inspector of Taxes could require disclosure of documents was held not to authorise a demand to produce documents between legal adviser and client; the rules of legal professional privilege were well entrenched and could only have been displaced by express words in the statute. A restriction order preventing a football supporter attending matches, under the terms of the Football Spectators Act 1989, was held not to constitute a breach of his human rights; but as a consequence of the right to life enshrined in the Human Rights Act the state did have a duty properly to investigate any deaths occurring in prison. A more speculative attempt to persuade the Court of Session to determine that the Scottish Parliament's ban on foxhunting was contrary to the European Convention on Human Rights was unsuccessful.

The law relating to adoption was updated by the Adoption and Children Act, with the aim both of streamlining the adoption service and of promoting the greater use of adoption; in particular, and most controversially, it allowed the possibility of adoption by same-sex couples. Problems arising from the interrelationship of civil and religious divorces, particularly in situations involving orthodox Jews, were resolved by the Divorce (Religious Marriages) Act, providing that in certain cases the a decree absolute of divorce should only be given once the marriage had been properly dissolved by the appropriate religious authority. Two important decisions in the Court of Appeal touched on the operation of the Mental Health Review Tribunals: a mother was held entitled to demand disclosure of medical information relating to her adult son, in order to allow her to make a reasoned decision whether or not to seek his discharge from the guardianship of the Local Authority under the Mental Health Act 1983; and the whole procedure for reviewing decisions of Mental Health Review Tribunals was trenchantly criticised.

The Enterprise Act altered the criteria determining whether or not a corporate merger should be permitted, put the Office of Fair Trading on a statutory footing, and eased the law relating to bankruptcy. More stringent enforcement processes were introduced to deal with cases involving breaches of copyright and other forms of intellectual property rights; but the rights of copyright holders were restricted through the Copyright (Visually Impaired Persons) Act in order to permit the production of copies of works for the visually impaired. The Employee Share Schemes Act made amendments to the taxation regime applicable to company share schemes; and the Employment Act amended the law entitling mothers to maternity leave and extended it to provide rights to paid paternity and adoption leave. The system of granting export licences—and hence of restricting the export of cultural objects, arms, and other property—was updated through the Export Control Act in the light of changing global conditions. In the courts, the application of well-established legal principles was clarified: the Court of Appeal held that a customer entitled to raise a defence of estoppel to a claim by a bank to recover a payment made by mistake could only retain the payment in so far as it was fair and equitable to do so, and that an equitable assignment of shares had been validly completed on the signature of a share transfer form; there was no necessity for the form to have been delivered to the company. The House of Lords held that the settlement of a contractual claim against one defendant did not automatically prevent the pursuit of a claim against another defendant: all depended on the wording of the initial settlement and the intention behind it. The Court of Appeal held that the requirement in the Insolvency Act 1986 that a person should be required to account for any loss which had been incurred was not self-incriminatory and therefore unlawful. The conviction of a journal and its editor who had published material contrary to the terms of an injunction was upheld in the House of Lords, notwithstanding that there was no proof that their publication infringed the interest which the injunction had been designed to protect. The House of Lords also upheld a decision of the Court of Appeal that it was in the interests of justice that the identity of a hospital employee who had disclosed to the press confidential information relating to medical treatment should be revealed.

The Commonhold and Leasehold Reform Act introduced wide-ranging reforms to the law relating to the holding and occupation of residential leasehold property, allowing leaseholders to designate a company to manage blocks of flats independently of the landlords and creating a new form of landholding, designated as commonhold, under which the owners of individual units of property would be able to form associations to manage the common parts of the property. Very substantial changes were made to the law relating to the transfer of title to land through the Land Registration Act, in particular facilitating the use of electronic conveyancing. The Homelessness Act placed additional statutory obligations on local authorities to tackle the problems of homelessness. The procedures for determining whether a refusal of accommodation by a homeless person was reasonable were held to satisfy the conditions laid down by the Human Rights Act, as were those adopted by a planning authority considering a redevelopment application. The law relating to adverse possession of land was clarified by the House of Lords.

In a case of potentially enormous significance, the House of Lords held that in an action for negligently caused personal injuries the claimant would not be prevented from recovering damages simply because he was unable to prove which of a number of potential causes was the true cause of his injury; the burden of proof was held to be satisfied where it was shown that the defendant's conduct had materially increased the risk of injury or illness and that the current state of medical knowledge was such that definitive proof of causation would be impossible to achieve. In other decisions expanding the scope of liability, a hospital was held liable for the negligent act of an uninsured independent contractor using its premises, since it was the hospital's duty to ensure that the contractor was properly insured; and failure by a doctor to warn a patient of a slight risk of injury from an operation was held to ground a claim in negligence when the risk eventuated. The Court of Appeal, assessing damages for loss of earnings in a personal injury claim, held that it was proper to take into account the value of services that the claimant had, prior to his injury, performed gratuitously for his disabled brother; but where a mother had been killed it was said that damages should not take account of the support that she had provided for the family without offsetting the value of services provided thereafter by her partner. A restrictive view was taken of the circumstances in which a jury's award of damages for defamation should be reduced, though in one case involving a well-known professional footballer accused of match-fixing the House of Lords did reduce a substantial award to a nominal £1. A similarly restrictive approach was taken to the requirement of the Civil Liability (Contribution) Act 1978 that an order for contribution could be made only if two defendants were liable for the "same" loss.

A number of cases touched on the emergent law relating to the protection of privacy: in *Wainwright* v. *Home Office* it was decided that the Common law itself knew no tort of interference with privacy, nor had one been introduced by the Human Rights Act; in *A* v. *B plc* the Court of Appeal, reversing a decision of the

High Court, held that a professional footballer should not be entitled to a injunction preventing a newspaper publishing details of an extra-marital dalliance; and information that a well-known fashion model was receiving medical treatment was held not to be confidential information whose publication should be prevented by injunction, nor did its disclosure by a newspaper constitute a breach of the Data Protection Act 1998.

Three decisions sharpened the boundary between private law and public law. Hospital managers were held to be exercising a public function, and their decisions were therefore amenable to proceedings for judicial review; in a very carefully crafted judgment, the Court of Appeal explained why the denial of a claim in tort to a crown employee did not involve any breach of the injured person's right to a fair trial; and an application for an anti-social behaviour order was held to constitute civil rather than criminal proceedings, so that hearsay evidence might properly be admitted.

New guidelines were laid down for sentencing in cases of rape and burglary, the latter attracting considerable publicity and criticism. In an attempt to reduce the attraction of the theft of mobile telephones, it was made a criminal offence to re-programme any such device; and refusal on the part of the driver of a private hire vehicle to carry a disabled passenger was also criminalised. The Justice (Northern Ireland) Act overhauled the operation of the criminal law in Northern Ireland. The range of statutory rules relating to the confiscation of the proceeds of crime and money-laundering were consolidated and extended; and an Assets Recovery Agency was set up under the Proceeds of Crime Act. The Court of Appeal approved the Parole Board's practice of reviewing without an oral hearing judges' impositions of extended sentences; the Human Rights Act's requirement of a fair trial was satisfied so long as the judge's initial determination had been fair. The statutory mandatory life sentence for murder was held not to be disproportionate and so not in breach of the requirements of the Human Rights Act, though the Privy Council resolved that mandatory death sentences for murder in Jamaica and St Kitts and Nevis were unconstitutional. The provision of the Crime (Sentences) Act 1997 giving authority to the Home Secretary to fix the appropriate tariff for prisoners sentenced to life imprisonment was declared to be incompatible with the Human Rights Act. On the other hand there was held to be no breach of the Act by police who retained the fingerprints and DNA of a person who had been the subject of a criminal investigation but had not been charged with any offence; and the House of Lords held that the Common law recognised a right of search and seizure pursuant to a warrant of arrest for extradition, which did not constitute an infringement of the human rights of the person arrested; and that the trial of a civil offence by a Court Martial did not involve a breach of the right to a fair trial guaranteed by the Human Rights Act. In sharp contrast to the normal rules relating to pleas of guilty to criminal offences, the Court of Appeal decided that it was appropriate to set aside such a plea where the prosecution had been culpable in failing to disclose material matters to the defence and prosecution witnesses had committed perjury.

The House of Lords held that the Crown Court had a power to make a confiscation order against a defendant who had been sent to it for sentencing after conviction in a Magistrates' Court. Witness evidence taken by video recording was held to have been properly admitted, notwithstanding that a question had been raised about the mental competence of the witness.

The operation of the civil justice system after the introduction of the new system embodied in the Civil Procedure Rules 1999 was clarified. Guidance on the circumstances in which a wasted costs order could be made against counsel in a case was given by the House of Lords; and the importance of the role of the Court of Appeal in supervising the operation of conditional fee agreements and related devices was emphasised. The Court of Appeal outlined the principles relating to the award of costs on an indemnity basis, and elucidated the requirement that the costs of litigation should be proportionate to what was at stake in the litigation. The fact that a judge had received free legal services from one party's solicitor was held not to raise any suspicion of bias.

In the wake of the outbreak of foot and mouth disease in 2001, the Animal Health Act gave new powers to the Secretary of State for the Environment to order the slaughter of infected animals, and also to restrict the breeding of certain genotypes of animal thought to be particularly susceptible to diseases which might infect humans. Further reforms of the education system were made by the Education Act, introducing a new framework for school governance and increasing the powers of the Secretary of State for Education to intervene where necessary to deal with particular weaknesses or to impose special measures. The structural framework of the National Health Service was similarly reformed by the National Health Service Reform and Health Care Professions Act. Changes in the regulatory framework of the communications industry were prefigured by the Office of Communications Act; a Communications Bill was introduced into Parliament to bring about the substantive changes. Reforms in the management of the police force were brought in by the Police Reform Act, widening the powers of the Home Secretary to intervene to remedy cases of perceived inefficiency or ineffectiveness. The powers of the Historic Buildings and Monuments Commission were expanded by the National Heritage Act to include historic wrecks under its remit. The Tobacco Advertising and Promotion Act made tobacco advertising illegal with effect from February 2003.

3. LAW IN THE USA

A decision of the US Supreme Court in 2002 continued a trend that had begun with a 1995 Supreme Court decision that limited the powers of the federal government. In *Federal Maritime Commission v. South Carolina State Ports Authority* the Court ruled that the South Carolina ports authority, as a state instrumentality, could not be required to appear before the Federal Maritime Commission to respond to a claim that it had violated federal maritime laws when it refused to allow two ships that offered casino gambling to berth at its docks. The state government's sovereign immunity was unconstitutionally "affronted" by the requirement that it respond to complaints by individuals and private companies before a federal agency. As in past cases upholding state sovereign immunity, the Court decided the case by a vote of five to four.

Unprecedented anti-terrorism measures by federal agencies were reviewed by the courts in 2002 for their constitutional and statutory propriety. A US federal district court held that Jose Padilla, a US citizen arrested as an "enemy combatant" and accused, but not charged with, conspiring with al-Qaida operatives to detonate a radiological weapon within the USA, was entitled to have counsel represent him in his challenge to his detention without being charged or tried. Two federal appeals courts reached different conclusions concerning the authority of the federal government to hold secret deportation hearings of more than 600 immigrants arrested in response to the events on 11 September 2001. The Third Circuit Court of Appeals, in Philadelphia, held that "at a time when our nation is faced with threats of such profound and unknown dimensions" such hearings could be held secretly, while the Sixth Circuit Court of Appeals, in Cincinnati, held that they could not be so held. The federal district court and appeals court decisions were appealed against. For the first time since its establishment under the Foreign Intelligence Act of 1978, the FISA (Foreign Intelligence Surveillance Act) court, which met and conducted its proceedings entirely in secret, denied an application by the federal government for an order to conduct electronic surveillance on a person in the USA, because the purpose of the order was not clearly for the purpose of collecting intelligence on foreign agents and appeared to be related to a criminal investigation by the criminal division of the Federal Bureau of Investigation. The Court of Review, also established by the 1978 law but never previously convened, reversed the FISA court's ruling, holding that the USA Patriot Act, enacted in response to the events on 11 September 2001, had amended the 1978 law to permit the exchange of information between criminal and other divisions, and that the government was no longer required to show that its purpose in conducting electronic eavesdropping was other than for the purpose of criminal investigation.

Decisions in two cases expanded the criminal suspect's right to counsel. In *Shelton v. Alabama* the Supreme Court held, by a vote of five to four, that a defendant upon whom a court imposed a 30-day suspended sentence had a right to have counsel appointed to represent him at his trial. The decisions were the most significant extension of two prior decisions of the Court in 1966 and 1972. In *Chavez v. Martinez* the Ninth Circuit Court of Appeal held that a suspect could sue the police for coercive interrogation where the police officer repeatedly questioned the suspect after he had been shot five times in a struggle with police. The decision was significant because the right to be free from coercive interrogation was previously asserted as a defence in a criminal prosecution and not as an independent claim against the police. The decision was appealed against because it could be used to bar interrogation of suspected terrorists.

In two cases the Court established new limitations on the death penalty. In *Atkins v. Virginia* the Court, by a six to three vote, ruled that the execution of mentally retarded offenders offended "evolving standards of decency" and constituted cruel and unusual punishment. In *Ring v. Arizona* the Court, in a seven to two vote, held that juries, not judges, must make the factual findings on which the decision to impose the death penalty was based.

A federal district court reached the final decision in *USA v. Microsoft*, which substantially endorsed a settlement agreed between the Justice Department and the giant computer software company, Microsoft. The decision avoided the division of Microsoft into separate businesses, which had been ordered previously by the court; that previous decision had been reversed on appeal (see XIII.2).

In three decisions the Supreme Court limited the definition of "disability" under the Americans with Disabilities Act—a federal law prohibiting discrimination against disabled persons in employment, public housing, and public transportation. The Court held that an employee with a work-related injury did not have a right to another position she was capable of performing. In a second case, the Court held that an employer could prefer an employee with seniority to a person with a disability. In a third case, the Court held that the employer could refuse employment to a person whose condition might be aggravated by the conditions in which he would be working.

Jury verdicts in individual lawsuits against tobacco companies resulted in unprecedented judgments that were expected to be reversed or reduced on appeal. A jury in California awarded US$28,000 million against Philip Morris in punitive damages to a cancer victim. An Oregon jury awarded US$115 million in punitive damages, also against Philip Morris, for fraudulent marketing of its cigarettes. A jury in a federal court in Florida awarded US$5.5 million to a flight attendant for the effects suffered from cigarette smoke inhaled while working in smoky cabins. This last case was the first following a settlement, in 1997, of a class action between flight attendants and tobacco companies concerning the effects of "secondhand" smoke. The judge ruled, in the present case, that, as a result of the 1997 settlement, the flight attendants did not have to prove that the tobacco companies had been negligent or had produced a defective product. The tobacco companies appealed against all of these verdicts. Through such appeals the tobacco companies had avoided paying these and all previous awards against them in cases brought by individuals, except for the payment of US$1.1 million, in 2001, in response to a judgment made in 1996.

XV THE ARTS

1. OPERA—MUSIC—BALLET & DANCE—THEATRE—CINEMA—TELEVISION & RADIO

i. OPERA

THE Royal Opera began the year by alternating Franco Zeffirelli's seemingly ageless production of Puccini's *Tosca* with Britten's *The Turn of the Screw* in a not very atmospheric staging by Deborah Warner. In *Tosca* the indomitable Luciano Pavarotti sang and acted splendidly on the first night, only 24 hours after his mother had died, and the attractive US soprano Carol Vaness was a more convincing Tosca than any other exponent of the role since Maria Callas. The cast of *The Turn of the Screw* all sang and acted vividly, especially Joan Rodgers as the Governess and Ian Bostridge as the evil Peter Quint. The conductor Daniel Harding, making his Royal Opera debut, moved the action along briskly. Puccini and Britten were followed by Mozart, a new production of whose *Don Giovanni* starred the popular Welsh baritone Bryn Terfel as the licentious nobleman. Terfel made Giovanni much too thuggish a character, but he sang the role ebulliently. Rebecca Evans was the most delightful Zerlina imaginable, and the rest of the cast was never less than excellent, with Rainer Trost singing Ottavio's two arias elegantly, and Colin Davis conducting with confidence and flair. A second group of performances, with a different cast and conductor, offered Simon Keenlyside as a stylish, elegant yet dangerous Giovanni, with Charles Mackerras conducting even more impressively than Colin Davis.

Five other new productions were presented by the Royal Opera. Marco Arturo Marelli, directing Bellini's *La Sonnambula*, chose to have the action take place not in the early 19th century Swiss village envisaged by Bellini and his librettist but in a 21st century sanatorium. Fortunately, a first-rate cast was on hand to do justice to the composer, with Elena Kelessidi and Juan Diego Florcz singing and acting superbly as the young lovers. Puccini's *La Rondine*, not seen in London since 1974, was directed intelligently by Nicolas Joel, and sung ravishingly by opera's popular married couple, Roberto Alagna and Angela Gheorghiu. *I Masnadieri*, the opera that Verdi wrote for London and which was first performed there in 1847 at Her Majesty's Theatre in the Haymarket, joined the Royal Opera's repertoire in a somewhat lacklustre staging by Elijah Moshinsky, who was roundly booed on the first night. The singers, however, were excellent, with the Russian baritone Dmitri Hvorostovsky giving a stylish portrayal of the villainous Francesco. Edward Downes conducted an electrifying account of Verdi's magnificent score. Strauss's *Ariadne auf Naxos* was conducted stylishly by Antonio Pappano, at the beginning of his term as the Royal Opera's music director, and a superb multi-national cast was assembled from the USA, Australia, France, Germany, Sweden, and Lithuania.

Christof Loy's witty staging was aided enormously by Herbert Murauer's complex, multi-level décor.

The Royal Opera's final new production was the eagerly awaited world premiere of *Sophie's Choice* by Nicholas Maw, an opera based on William Styron's novel about a Polish Catholic woman who, upon being consigned to Auschwitz, is forced to choose one of her two children to be sent to the gas chamber. Unfortunately, Maw's opera was disappointing. It was far too long—four acts of about an hour each—and its story could have been told in less than half that time were it not for the unmemorable music which simply meandered along, adding very little of interest to the stage action.

Two of English National Opera's new productions were unsuccessful: Spontini's *La Vestale* because its music was characterless, with Jane Eaglen unconvincing as the eponymous heroine, and Verdi's *Un Ballo in Maschera* (sung in English as *A Masked Ball*) because of its absurd production by Calixto Bieto who attempted to shock ENO's audience by setting the first scene not in an 18th century royal court but in a modern public lavatory occupied by 14 male choristers sitting on the seats with their underpants around their ankles. Much more interesting was Richard Jones's imaginative staging of Alban Berg's *Lulu*, with US soprano Lisa Saffer singing and acting the title-role expressively, and the rest of a large cast all outstanding.

The Death of Klinghoffer, an opera by the US composer John Adams, whose subject was the hijacking by Palestinians of the cruise-liner *Achille Lauro* in the Mediterranean in 1985, was given its UK premiere, not in an opera house, but as a concert performance at the Barbican concert hall in London. The work, which was widely (but perhaps unfairly) perceived as being tainted by anti-Semitism, was burdened with unmemorable music and a libretto which was both confused and pretentious.

Glyndebourne opened its summer season with a revival of Graham Vick's mistreatment of *Don Giovanni*, and continued with Gluck's rarely encountered *Iphigénie en Aulide* in a staging by Christof Loy that proved to be just another example of a director considering himself a rival creator instead of an interpreter. However, it was well sung and conducted. Much more enjoyable was Weber's *Euryanthe*, a piece not often staged, perhaps because its plot was more than usually imbecilic. It contained much beautiful music, with a superb overture and arias that were sometimes romantic, sometimes demonic. Anne Schwanewilms, a German soprano making her Glyndebourne debut, was stunning in the title-role, and Mark Elder secured marvellous playing from the Orchestra of the Age of Enlightenment.

Country house opera began to proliferate during the year. Longborough staged a truncated *Ring*, while Grange Park extended its definition of opera to take in Cole Porter's *Anything Goes*. The highlight of Garsington's season was Rossini's *La Gazza Ladra*.

British Youth Opera staged Offenbach's *Orpheus in the Underworld* in London's Queen Elizabeth Hall, with some of the opera stars of the future, and the Guildhall School of Music and Drama performed Chabrier's *L'Etoile*, the student cast and orchestra making it go with a swing under the experienced baton of Clive Timms.

ii. MUSIC

CLASSICAL music in the UK in 2002 encompassed not only the total range of performances, covering all traditions and all periods, but also, running through it like a golden thread, the minority of those UK composers whose music was successfully performed, thereby contributing collectively to the living UK tradition. All musicians, composers and performers alike, faced a contracting market in 2002. The performance of classical music as a whole continued the worldwide slump of previous years, and formed only a tiny fraction of the overall maelstrom of activity of the UK music industry, which consisted for the most part of commercial pop music. Successful performances occurred not so much during the regular, recurring presentations of established classics, as at festivals and special events, at which innovatory work was looked for; and particularly in recordings, which in 2002 reached new levels of achievement, largely in the case of the smaller labels.

Among the UK festivals, however, the older, more established ones—Aldeburgh, Cheltenham, Edinburgh, Huddersfield, London Promenade Concerts—had a nondescript year in 2002. They seemed to be locked into a bureaucratic, somewhat cosy conservation of past formulae, normally fatal in classical concerts, even more so in the case of unfamiliar or new music. First, and probably last, performances were given of David Sawer's *Piano Concerto*, Joseph Phibbs's *La noche amolladone*, Anthony Payne's *Visions and Journeys*, and John Harle's *The Little Death Machine*. The Three Choirs Festival, the UK's oldest, was also the least adventurous.

The living tradition of cathedral music was better served in 2002 when Maxwell Davies's new *Mass* was sung at Westminster Cathedral. The composer employed such traditional means as *a capella* choir and plainchant, which he had used and parodied many times in earlier, more iconoclastic works, but which in this case seemed to reach a conclusion. He addressed directly the aesthetics of a new tonality, as his recent *Antarctic Symphony* had demonstrated, and as he stated in a note to the *Second Symphony:* "To support a complex structure... an extremely basic unifying hypothesis is necessary if the ear is to be able to relate surface detail."

Little-known composers fared better when they were heard in more than one concert, and when they revealed a clear creative impulse. UK composers Maxwell Davies and James MacMillan featured at the St Magnus Festival, directed by Davies. Among other composers, Per Norgard's work featured both at a Promenade Concert (*Sixth Symphony*) and at Cheltenham and Huddersfield (*Violin Concerto*). Festivals were mounted on London's South Bank to promote Magnus Lindberg in January, and Louis Andriessen in October, in which *La Passione*, for solo voice, solo cello and ensemble, was notably successful. The Barbican responded with a festival devoted to the US minimalist John Adams, and a series entitled *New Music at the Barbican*, promoted by the BBC, which included some middle-generation UK composers: Colin Matthews, Oliver Knussen, and Dominic Muldowney. The only London orchestra to promote a UK composer was the London Symphony Orchestra, which, under the direction of Pierre Boulez, spread works by George Benjamin over several concerts in the season.

The UK concert scene reflected the global network. The world culture of music manifested itself in ethnic characteristics of the greatest diversity, and the most internationally promoted composer of 2002 was the Korean Unsuk Chin. Her residency with the Deutsches Symphonie-Orchester led to the Berlin premiere of her *Violin Concerto* under Kent Nagano, repeated later in Seoul and Helsinki. Further works, heard in Oslo, Copenhagen, and London, included *Piano Concerto* (for orchestra), *Acrostic-Wordplay* (for ensemble), and *Kala* (for choir and orchestra). In the same way Magnus Lindberg's *Parada*, with the Philharmonia under Esa-Pekka Salonen, was first heard at the Stockholm Festival, and then later in London, Paris, and Brussels.

If there was one leading conductor who did most to promote UK composers it was Simon Rattle. His championship of Mark-Anthony Turnage led to many performances of Turnage's work in 2002, while his support for Nicholas Maw (see AR 1991, p. 482) led to the premiere at Covent Garden in December of Maw's new opera *Sophie's Choice*. It came in a year of outstanding success for the Royal Opera, marked by spectacular productions of *Wozzeck* and *Die Meistersinger*. *Sophie's Choice* was the first new UK opera since Covent Garden was re-opened in 1999, and was conducted by Rattle, the best known of all UK conductors, whose appointment to that most prestigious of orchestras—the Berlin Philharmonic—had just been celebrated with his definitive recording with that orchestra of Gustav Mahler's *Fifth Symphony*. Indeed if promotion and performance and a glittering occasion alone were enough to ensure artistic success, this would have been the musical event of the year. It fell short on aesthetic grounds. The opera lacked dramatic flair, the music being technically uncertain in idiom, inconsistent in tonality, and indistinctive in structure. The libretto, from the novel by William Styron, was complex, unfocussed and, at over four hours, far too long (see XV.1.i).

Greater success on a much smaller scale was achieved by the Forum for Suppressed Music, under which title two concerts were given at the Wigmore Hall in June of chamber music by composers who had come to the UK to escape from Nazi Europe, which gave them a shared creative impulse: Hans Gal, Berthold Goldschmidt, Karl Rankl, Franz Reizenstein, Matyas Seiber, Leopold Spinner, and Egon Wellesz. These performances were recorded on a new label, Andante, ensuring for them the additional exposure that was not to be had from a single public performance. Indeed the unflawed standard of performance of a CD, and the high fidelity reproduction, facilitated the search for that elusive musical aesthetic, about which there was an absence of generally accepted standards. New and unfamiliar music particularly was seen to benefit from recording, and 2002 was marked by some striking successes.

Notable single-composer releases included Andrzej Panufnik's *Symphony 8, Violin Concerto, Concertino* (Hyperion), Mark-Anthony Turnage's *Fractured Lines, Four Horned Fandango* (Chandos), Francis Routh's *Piano Music* (Redcliffe Recordings), and music by Edwin Roxburgh (Warehouse). The most revelatory was the British Musical Heritage recording of music by the 18th century composer Samuel Wesley. It was a definitive, premiere performance of newly published music 200 years old, by an important composer of the classical period in England. Wesley's music had been ignored by the Victorians, and only began to be re-discovered much later, in the 1970s (see AR 1997, pp. 491-92) .

Further discoveries were made by smaller labels such as Metier, Riverrun, Meridian, Nonesuch, Global Music, Sanctuary Classics, and Sargasso, which promoted both little known composers—Christopher Fox, Andrew Keeler, George Nicholson, Geoffrey Poole, Anthony Powers, David Stoll, Piers Hellawell, Mark Gentworth, and David Horne; and those more familiar—Harrison Birtwistle, Michael Nyman, Mark-Anthony Turnage, and James MacMillan.

As the pattern of 2002 showed, UK music entered the 21st century with two characteristic features most prominent. One, at the compositional level, which it shared with other Western traditions, was the aesthetic uncertainty caused by the plurality of musical styles; and, arising from this, the search for a new tonality to replace the common musical language based on the diatonic scale, which Western music had previously enjoyed. The other, at the practical, financial level, and more deep-rooted in the UK than in other Western countries, was the marked tendency on the part of patrons and promoters to support and promote performers at the expense of composers. This trend went back a long way. When after 1945 the principle of public funding for the arts was established, with the creation of the Arts Council of Great Britain, financial support was promised to orchestras, opera houses, and performing bodies rather than to composers. Performances were to be publicly supported; composers were not. This dichotomy between the two sides of the musical art was to lead to profound consequences, and to a lopsided musical culture in the UK. It lay at the root of the well-known reluctance on the part of UK officialdom to back native talent; that much-vaunted English reserve. So it was that the proportion allotted to British composers, out of the total musical activity in 2002, was less than 4 per cent.

Those who died in 2002 included the composers Daniel-Lesur and Anthony Milner; the conductors Mark Ermler and Yevgeny Svetlanov; the singer Martha Modl; the pianist Leo Ornstein; the cellist Alan Shulman; and the musicologist Philip Brett.

BOOKS OF THE YEAR. *In Search of Opera*, by Carolyn Abbate; *Serial Music Serial Aesthetics: Compositional theory in post-war Europe*, by M.J. Grant; *From Classicism to Modernism*, by Brian K. Etter; *Béla Bartók, Life and Work*, by Benjamin Suchoff; *Symphony of Dreams: The conductor and patron Paul Sacher*, by Lesley Stephenson; *The New York Schools of Music and Visual Arts*, edited by Steven Johnson; *Stravinsky and Balanchine: A journey of invention*, by Charles M. Joseph; *Stravinsky Inside Out*, by Charles M. Joseph.

iii. BALLET & DANCE

REMARKS about the demise of classical ballet that recurred in 2002 seemed premature as a group of choreographers, all of whom trained at the Royal Ballet School when Norman Morrice was head of choreographic studies, showed a rich and varied range of creations throughout the world. The three choreographers of the group who were most in evidence in 2002 were Christopher Wheeldon, Christopher Hampson, and Cathy Marston. Wheeldon, who was resident choreographer at both New York City Ballet and Boston Ballet, also created ballets for San Francisco Ballet and The Royal Ballet. *Tryst*, his creation for the latter, with a central *pas de deux* for Darcey Bussell and Jonathan Cope, was the highlight of the Royal Ballet's year. A bold work with sinuous movement to a challenging score by James MacMillan, it provided a ray of hope in an otherwise bleak season. The Royal Ballet's Artistic Director, Ross Stretton, made no attempt to understand The Royal Ballet's position in the UK dance scene and imported productions that had been well received in Australia over the past two decades but which were out of date in London. Stretton's unpopular style of direction resulted in his departure 13 months into a three-year contract and Monica Mason's appointment, as his replacement, was cause for universal cheers. Mason's involvement with the company stretched back over 40 years, having recently been an admired coach of the dancers and an inspiring ambassador for dance.

Wheeldon's *Polyphonia* was seen in London for the first time in the acclaimed chamber programme, "Danse Concertante". Ten dancers from New York City Ballet, accompanied by three musicians, performed four ballets. The group was led by superb dancers, Peter Boal, Wendy Whelan, and Jock Soto, and the choice of repertory—including the *Triple Duet* for Alexandra Ansanelli and Craig Hall, specially created by Benjamin Millepied—showed them to advantage.

Gerald Scarfe's concept and designs initially swamped Christopher Hampson's *The Nutcracker* for English National Ballet (ENB), but once the dancers had discovered their characters and the production had settled down it made more impact. Cathy Marston favoured literary subjects for her creations. The most interesting of these was *Facing Viv* to music by John Adams in which six dancers (led by Gary Avis and Cindy Jourdain) played facets of T.S. Eliot and his wife, Vivienne. This production was indicative of ENB's more creative range under the directorship of Matz Skoog. In the autumn both The Royal Ballet and ENB acquired works by Mark Morris. Morris created separate works for classical companies rather than passing on productions from his own company's repertoire, and both ballets had been created for American Ballet Theatre. The Royal presented *Gong*, a gamelan-inspired work, which seemed rather routine, but ENB acquired the witty and challenging, *Drink To Me Only With Thine Eyes* to piano music by Virgil Thompson which the company performed engagingly. In respect of other acquisitions by The Royal, the most interesting was Mats Ek's *Carmen*, a collage of memories at the point of Don José's death.

The dancers involved, including Sylvie Guillem in the title role, Jonathan Cope as the flamboyant Escamillo, and Zenaida Yanowsky as "M", clearly enjoyed the eccentricities of the choreography.

Three other choreographers, based on different continents, made a positive contribution to dance in 2002. Merce Cunningham, celebrating 50 years of choreography, hardly rested on his laurels. Of the five works shown at the Barbican, four were created in the last two years, with *Fluid Canvas* premiered as part of Dance Umbrella. Of these, *Interscape*, with music by John Cage and designs by Robert Rauschenberg, was the most imaginative but the highlights of the season (and his first London residency) were works from the past. In *How to Pass, Kick, Fall and Run* (from 1965) Robert Swinston assumed Cunningham's original central role and was joined by eight other dancers. Cunningham himself, with the droll David Vaughan, delivered one-minute stories which accompanied the work. Also fascinating was the 1942 solo, *Totem Ancestor*, reconstructed and performed by Daniel Roberts. Both were valuable reminders of company's rich past. At the same time Rambert Dance Company performed *Ground Level Overlay* superbly. One of Cunningham's masterpieces, the work contrasted moments of stillness with flurries of movement in a burnished ambience.

Rambert also performed Wayne McGregor's exciting *PreSentient*, created for Christopher Bruce's farewell season as Artistic Director of the company. Formal in structure, and danced to Steve Reich's *Triple Quartet*, *PreSentient* presented a fresh lexicon of movement albeit drawn from McGregor's extreme and liquid vocabulary. For his own company, Random, McGregor created *Nemesis* for video and live dancers but the gimmicky use of prosthetic limbs, created in collaboration with Jim Henson's Workshop, limited the effect of this 70-minute work.

The third choreographer who generated real excitement was Graeme Murphy, who took a fresh approach to *Swan Lake* for Australian Ballet in a production that was technically demanding and theatrically seductive. Different women, Margaret Illmann and Simone Goldsmith, danced the black and white aspects of the heroine, with Steven Heathcote as the Prince. This version of *Swan Lake*, using Kristian Fredrikson's elegant Edwardian costumes, made the ballet less of a fantasy and more of a tragedy.

The highlight of American Ballet Theatre's year was the presentation of two of Frederick Ashton's masterworks, *The Dream* and *La Fille mal gardée*. The former received quite the best all-round performances seen in years, with Ethan Steifel and Carlos Acosta as Oberon, Julie Kent as Titania, and the mercurial Herman Cornejo as Puck. In this ballet the dancers, carefully coached by Anthony Dowell, captured the Victorian essence of the production and never overplayed the comedy of the lovers or the mechanicals. Elsewhere, Ashton's choreography was performed by the Royal Swedish Ballet. In *Scènes de Ballet* they showed an ability to cope with the fast, precise footwork and rich épaulement that Ashton's choreography demanded. *Scènes de Ballet* was the centrepiece of a curious, wide-ranging programme that also included duets by Angelin

Preljocaj and Vasilie Vainonen, and the rock-ballet *Unreal Estate* for which earplugs were supplied to the audience. At American Ballet Theatre the lovely artist, Susan Jaffé, retired from the stage with a last *Giselle* on 24 June. This had a once in a life-time cast, for not only was Jose Manuel Carreño her partner (Albrecht) but other principals, Angel Corella and Julio Bocca, played Wilfred and Hilarion respectively. Kathleen Moore returned to the company to mime Berthe, Giselle's mother, and Gillian Murphy danced Myrta.

Throughout the world companies revived ballets by Kenneth MacMillan to mark the 10th anniversary of his death. While most performed the three-act works, *Mayerling* (in which Johan Kobborg was a powerful Prince Rudolf for The Royal Ballet) and *Manon*, a small group led by Adam Cooper and Sarah Wildor presented less well-known ballets helping to remind audiences, and indeed companies, of the real range of MacMillan's choreography.

Dance works by certain choreographers, notably Pina Bauch and Matthew Bourne, attracted wide audiences. Bourne had focused on choreography for musicals in the last two years while reorganising his own company, but his New Adventures provided the performers for his *Play Without Words: The House-warming* at the National Theatre. Inspired by the 1963 Harold Pinter-Joseph Losey film, *The Servant*, most roles were performed in triplicate. For a while it was interesting but in this, as in his enlarged and revived *Nutcracker!*, Bourne failed to develop his ideas. Pina Bauch was a much more entertaining choreographer although, whatever the theme and however imaginative the setting, each production appeared constructed to a formula. *Masurca Fogo* (Portuguese for "Fiery Mazurka") was the more novel of the two sold-out productions shown in London which, with her projections of waves, visually looked back to productions created 100 years earlier.

A similar fascination with the past could be seen in *Excelsior*, presented by the ballet of La Scala, Milan, at the Paris Opéra. Created in 1881, this once hugely popular "ballo grande", a presentation of technological progress and international harmony, seemed comic to many viewers but it provided an insight into late 19th century ballet production with its effective use of travesty and pointe-work for the telegraph messengers. Similarly the Kirov's reconstruction of the 1900 staging of *La Bayadère* emphasised the importance of spectacle and restored the long-lost final act to something like Marius Petipa's intention. In London the Kirov performed two galas, including a refreshing variety of ballets overlooked on recent overseas tours such as *Leningrad Symphony*. Finally London saw a curious presentation of *Romeo and Juliet* by the Lithuanian Ballet choreographed by Vladimir Vasiliev. This old-fashioned staging needed more space than was possible on two platforms at the Barbican concert hall. Nevertheless the end provided a powerful piece of theatre. As the last chords were heard conductor Mstislav Rostropovich (in whose honour the work was performed) left the podium around which the orchestra was gathered to walk to where Romeo and Juliet lay, and united their hands in death.

iv. THEATRE

It was back to business as usual for the theatre during 2002, following the terrorist atrocities of 11 September 2001 which had so disrupted live performances on both sides of the Atlantic. With the resilience of a street that had not been called "the fabulous invalid" for nothing, Broadway rebounded by the end of 2002 to near-record levels of business and attendance, alongside a diversity of fare that threatened, for the first time in years, to render the London theatre an "also-ran".

How could this be? Partly, London was a victim of various circumstances, among them the closure during much of 2002 of two of the capital's most important playhouses, the Almeida and the Hampstead, both of which were being renovated. Added to this was the Royal Shakespeare Company's abandonment of what for 20 years had been its London base, the Barbican Centre. The result was a city oddly depleted of its usual dramatic output, with the Royal National, the Donmar, and the Royal Court left to fly the not-for-profit flag. Of these three theatres, two were entering a defining period of transition. The National was in its last full season under Sir Trevor Nunn, who was due to hand over artistic control of the English-language theatre's most important single venue to Nicholas Hytner in early 2003. Over at the tiny Donmar (seating capacity: a scant 251), Oscar-winner Sam Mendes (*American Beauty*) had announced that he was going freelance as of 1 December, after 10 years of turning a former banana ripening warehouse into a theatre whose international renown existed disproportionately to its size.

What, then, to do for a final season? In the case of Mendes, the Donmar programming for five months of the year honoured the theatre's ties to the USA over the 10-year tenure of a Cambridge graduate who had always shown a particular affinity for US work. And so a playhouse that had begun its new life under the then 27-year old director in October 1992, with the premiere of the scabrous Stephen Sondheim-John Weidman off-Broadway musical *Assassins*, would go out as it came in, this time showcasing a sequence of work that included several UK premieres of already acknowledged US plays—Kenneth Lonergan's *Lobby Hero*, Stephen Adly Guirgis' *Jesus Hopped the 'A' Train*, and David Auburn's *Proof*—as well as two world premieres by New York dramatists: Richard Greenberg's *Take Me Out* and Keith Reddin's *Frame 312*. Of the quintet of plays, *Frame 312* was the only outright flop, a meditation on the John F. Kennedy assassination that was almost shockingly undramatic, especially in light of its subject matter. (The same play would later get a second chance, albeit in a separate production, at the Alley Theatre in Houston, Texas.) And though one could argue that both *Proof* and *Lobby Hero* were better served in their original New York incarnations, the former pleased the London press because it starred the Oscar-winning US actress Gwyneth Paltrow in her UK stage debut. Her role was that of a mentally unbalanced young woman from Chicago who also happened to be a mathematics genius. The latter play showcased Scottish actor David Tennant playing the role of the shy yet morally scrupulous building employee in a typically faceless Manhattan apartment block, and Lonergan's piece evidently struck enough of a nerve with UK viewers that it was snapped up for a commercial West End transfer—an achievement *Proof*, due in no small measure to Paltrow's prior filming commitments, never managed. (Paltrow, however, was expected to return to the material in the slow-burning film version of the play, to be directed, as was the London incarnation of the work, by John Madden, who had guided Paltrow to her Oscar for *Shakespeare In Love*).

But it was in the autumn that the Donmar really came to define the London theatrical landscape, with Mendes himself directing two classic plays in a sellout repertory season that early in 2003 would transfer to New York. Both plays, *Uncle Vanya* and *Twelfth Night*, were frequently performed in London but rarely with the shimmering affinity that comes with seeing Chekhov and Shakespeare produced in tandem and sharing the same cast. The result reaped particular benefits as regards *Twelfth Night*, that most mysterious and melancholic of Shakespeare plays, a comedy flecked throughout with tragedy. In Mendes' hands, this director's favourite took on a rewardingly painful hue, its tale of disguise and deceit acted with a real awareness of the spectre of death, not least those numerous emotional deaths, large and small, that are part of our daily lives. Theatregoers thriving on "compare and contrast" could set Mendes' interpretation of the play—situated on a mostly bare Anthony Ward set dominated by a forest of flickering candles—against an all-male al fresco production of the play that same summer at Shakespeare's Globe. That version played to capacity houses and garnered special cheers for Mark Rylance's Olivia, a grieving figure in black who tripped weightlessly across the stage; by contrast, Helen McCrory, inhabiting the same part for Mendes, played Olivia as an earthy tease, her seductress not a million miles removed from the erotic siren that this accomplished actress so carefully cut as Yelena in *Uncle Vanya*.

London was fond of classic theatre, and why not, since a familiar play could achieve a fiercely renewed power when wedded to a director's fresh voice. Sometimes, however, the desire to invigorate tilted towards indulgence: reprising Shakespeare's *The Winter's Tale* for the Royal Shakespeare Company at north London's Roundhouse, director Matthew Warchus hit on the idea of having his mostly UK cast speak the entire play in US accents, an acting device that seemed to distance a hit-and-miss company even further from this wondrous play. (Perhaps Warchus, newly married at the time to US actress Lauren Ward, merely wanted to prove that, accents aside, he and his new wife spoke the same language.) Over at the National, a lively *Tartuffe*, starring a stringy-haired Martin Clunes, ceded the Lyttelton auditorium later in the year to an utterly bizarre reappraisal of *A Streetcar Named Desire*, in which both the Stanley Kowalski (Scottish actor Iain Glen) and the Blanche du Bois (theatre-trained Hollywood star Glenn Close, in her UK stage debut) seemed totally miscast. Instead, the evening's virtues landed squarely at the feet of visiting Australian performer Essie Davis, as Blanche's younger sister Stella. Indeed, watching Davis career harrowingly between an abusive husband and a mentally disturbed sister was to witness a major co-option of a classic Tennessee Williams drama such as had not been seen in London since the decade before, when then-unknown Sara Crowe (playing Sibyl) stole an Aldwych Theatre production of Sir Noel Coward's *Private Lives* from under the nose of Joan Collins, playing Amanda.

Not content with an operatic *Streetcar*, the production's director, Trevor Nunn, ensured that his last full year running the National would be a personally exhausting one. Over the summer, he opened all nine-hours-plus of Sir Tom Stoppard's trilogy of plays, *The Coast of Utopia*, a huge achievement that was somewhat churlishly received by the London press. An anatomy of the various mindsets behind the major European revolutions of the 19th century, not to mention a specific biographical drama of the socialist writer and thinker Alexander Herzen, Stoppard's plays blazed with an ambition that one had thought was all but lost—even if few could deny that such a daunting enterprise for actor and audience alike could probably and profitably have been pruned for the benefit of both. Perhaps it was in response to such self-evident epics that at least a few of the year's most successfully reviewed new plays were notably short. Among those none was as bracing as the ever-unpredictable Caryl Churchill's latest Royal Court play, *A Number*, a four-character work for two actors that gave Sir Michael Gambon and Daniel Craig a mutually unforgettable chance to shine under the alert eye of the Court's onetime artistic director, Stephen Daldry. Nominally inspired by the current debate surrounding cloning, Churchill went beyond contemporary headlines to forge her own timeless enquiry into the ongoing mystery of human behaviour in all its manifestations. In *The Breath of Life* (Haymarket), the year's greatest commercial success, the UK's best-known theatrical Dames, Judi Dench and Maggie Smith, locked horns in a deceptively elegant play from Sir David Hare that dared to fold the potentially hoariest of situations—ex-wife meets her former husband's mistress—into an examination of what Smith's character referred to as "the wreck of memory". In these actress's hands it was a most ravishing wreck, too.

Throughout 2002 the London theatre fared least well where New York looked stronger than ever—namely, in the realm of the musical, which remained any commercial theatre's economic mainstay. London offered up show after show which included well-known songs in new, sometimes scenically spectacular surroundings. (*We Will Rock You*, the Dominion Theatre extravaganza set to the pounding sonorities of the much-beloved rock group Queen, was as astonishing a physical achievement as, in script terms, it was empty and banal.) *The Full Monty* (Prince of Wales) travelled over from New York to the West End to the apparent confusion of Londoners who did not understand why Broadway had cannibalised a popular small-scale UK movie and then transported the results back, as it were, to the source. The New York dance musical *Contact* (Queen's) seemed chillier and less sophisticated on Shaftesbury Avenue than it had seemed during its long Lincoln Centre Theatre engagement across the Atlantic. Or maybe it was simply that the work of US director-choreographer Susan Stroman did not look quite so lustrous when set against a UK equivalent such as director-choreographer Matthew Bourne, whose experimental National Theatre pastiche of swinging 1960s London, *Play Without Words*, seemed both witty and wise. The season's noisiest musical, *Chitty Chitty Bang Bang*, drew for inspiration from a forgettable film (and relied for effect upon a none-too-reliable airborne car), while a competitor like *Bombay Dreams* took as its source a film industry, namely Bollywood, that the Western stage musical had never before approached. The latter was good news for its London producer, Andrew Lloyd Webber, the composer who put his song writing skills aside in order to create what looked like being his first substantial hit for some time.

And yet, none of the London musicals could compare with the big three that caused Broadway to celebrate all autumn, a typically moribund time of year that was instead leaving theatregoers in thrall. Away from the musicals, Broadway offered the eternal enticements of stars. These included relatively new ones—like Edie Falco and Stanley Tucci in the hit revival of Terrence McNally's *Frankie and Johnny in the Clair de Lune* (Belasco)—as well as living legends like 78-year old Paul Newman, back on Broadway for the first time in decades as a commendably vinegary Stage Manager in Thornton Wilder's enduring *Our Town* (Booth). (Newman's Oscar-winning wife, actress Joanne Woodward, was the play's producer.)

But it was at musicals like *La Bohème* (Broadway) and *Movin' Out* (Richard Rodgers)—leaving aside the anodyne *Thoroughly Modern Millie* (Marquis), which won the Tony for Best Musical against scant competition in June—that one felt a real celebration of the new. Puccini's *La Bohème* showed the determination of Australian director Baz Luhrmann (*Moulin Rouge*) to bring to his Broadway debut the same youthfulness and brio that he had long applied to film. Watching the two-act dance piece *Movin' Out*, one looked on in awe at the artistic wedding of two seemingly disparate people—the populist songwriter Billy Joel and the veteran pioneer of modern dance, director-choreographer Twyla Tharp. Here, one realised, was a brilliant way to exploit a singer-songwriter's extant back catalogue, free of the lazy karaoke posturing of works such as the ABBA-inspired *Mamma Mia!* As an impressive cast leapt across the stage to tell a Vietnam-era tale with startling immediacy and verve, no theatre lover's heart could fail to do its own jeté. Broadway most definitely was back.

v. CINEMA

IF economic hard times did not much affect the cinema's box-office returns (since going to the movies was still one of the cheapest forms of entertainment outside the home), world recessions made financing films more precarious. Fewer risks were taken, and the result was often a general lack of quality. Yet, considering everything, the commercial cinema had a good year in 2002 and the so-called art cinema, appealing to minorities, did not have a bad one either.

The commercial sector was given a large present by two films in particular, both of them sequels to their highly successful predecessors. Chris Columbus' *Harry Potter and the Chamber of Secrets*, the successor to his *Harry Potter and the*

Philosopher's Stone, and Peter Jackson's *The Two Towers*, successor to *The Fellowship of the Ring*, made almost a billion dollars between them, proving that films based on books (by J.K. Rowling and J.R.R. Tolkien, respectively) were still a huge attraction, provided that the books were best-sellers also. There were other big successes during the year, like Steven Spielberg's *Minority Report*, and the latest James Bond extravaganza, but none came near to these two.

In the field of more upmarket products were some good US films such as Alexander Payne's *About Schmidt*, Spike Jonze's *Adaptation*, Stephen Daldry's *The Hours*, Todd Haynes' *Far From Heaven*, and Rob Marshall's *Chicago*; highly praised UK films like Len Loach's *Sweet Sixteen*, Mike Leigh's *All or Nothing*, Peter Mullan's *The Magdalene Sisters*, Stephen Frears' *Dirty Pretty Things*, and Michael Winterbottom's *In This World*. There was also a whole group of Latin-American films—among which were Mexico's *Japon* and Brazil's *City of God*; the Bollywood blockbuster *Lagaan*; the Chinese epic *Hero*; the Spanish *Talk To Me*; and the Finnish *Man Without A Past*. Not all of these made money (although almost all of them would eventually go into profit), but the prestige gathered was considerable and Pedro Almodovar's *Talk To Me* duly won the European Film Award of the year.

It seemed to prove that good films could emanate from almost anywhere and that the ascendancy of Hollywood, whose films could be seen almost everywhere, supported by much expensive publicity, was not necessarily as complete as a sometimes despairing non-US film world would suppose. Nevertheless, it remained a dispiriting fact that in almost every country it was increasingly difficult to see anything other than totally commercial films, most of which were US in origin. The rise of DVD was a hopeful sign but by no means yet one which would suggest that either the classics of the past or the best films of the present were regularly accorded a release on the new medium.

As for the classics of the past, the film magazine *Sight and Sound* again produced its once-a-decade critical poll of the world's top 10 films. They were, in order, Welles' *Citizen Kane*, Hitchcock's *Vertigo*, Renoir's *La Règle du Jeu*, Coppola's *The Godfather, parts 1 and 2*, Ozu's *Tokyo Story*, Kubrick's *2001: A Space Odyssey*, Eistenstein's *Battleship Potemkin*, Murnau's *Sunrise*, Fellini's *8 and a Half*, and Donen's *Singin' in the Rain*.

It was only the film festivals, still proliferating throughout the world and claiming excellent audiences, that sustained film-making that was not largely of entertainment value only. However, the problem remained that people were prepared to take risks at festivals which they would not take outside the atmosphere of such heady film jamborees, so that a big success at Cannes or elsewhere often did not translate into a triumph in the outside world.

The two areas where Hollywood did not have the whip hand were China, where the USA was making significant inroads but had not yet overcome the vagaries of either the bureaucracy or the distribution system, and India, where Bollywood still reigned supreme. Indeed, it was during 2002 that Bollywood became fashionable not just among the Indian diaspora throughout the world (so that Bollywood filmmakers could make as much money abroad as at home), but in the non-Indian

West too. It was not that the films were successful among Europeans and in the USA, with the exception of *Lagaan*, a tall but rousing tale about Indian villagers who learned to play cricket and then beat the British land-owners at their own game. Rather it was that the media began to take note of the music, costumes, and general colour in the films, which seemed in some way to remind everybody of the Hollywood musicals of yesteryear. Unfortunately, several epics, among them *Ashoka*, about India's favourite Emperor, and *Devdas*, a musical romance shown within the competition at the Cannes Festival, proved that Bollywood still had a lot to do to attract non-Indian audiences, notably by desisting from making their films almost three hours long. In India itself, *Lagaan* and *Devdas* did well but few other Bollywood spectaculars justified their cost, and smaller films like the UK's *Bend It Like Beckham*, about a young woman determined to be a footballer despite her parents' objections, seemed of greater appeal to the burgeoning middle-class audiences than the melodramatic excesses of Bombay's star vehicles.

The rise of Latin-American cinema, once the envy of the world in the heady revolutionary days of the 1960s but then stamped out by the continent's various military dictatorships, was particularly surprising, since Hollywood films had swamped Latin-American cinemas for several decades. But here, as elsewhere, people were beginning to want films that were recognisably of their own world—another hope for the future. Generally, such developments were initially created by the work of either one or a whole group of new film-makers and this seemed to be the case in both Mexico and Brazil. Cuba, however, afflicted by the continuing US boycott but once a leader in this field, managed to produce nothing of note. In the East, Japan produced popular but few prestigious films, giving way to South Korea whose film-makers came up with a wide range of good work, including Lee Chang-Dong's *Oasis*, a provocative study of disabled lovers in a hostile Seoul, which won the Best Director award at Venice.

Unfortunately, little stirred in Africa, largely because African film-makers had little or no money. But one film was made during the year which achieved deserved success at film festivals—Mahamat Saleh Haroun's *Abouna*, a delicate and poignant study of parental loss set in the Chadian bush.

Iran continued to produce excellent films, led by the work of Abbas Kiarostami, Mohsen Makmalbaf, and Samira Makmalbaf, Mohsen's daughter. Kiarostami once again astonished everyone by making a film called *Ten*, entirely set in a Teheran taxi carrying various women, one of them a prostitute, about their business. (A film definitely not suitable for the country's religious mullahs.) These films were celebrated by the festivals, but few were allowed to be shown, except privately, in Iran itself, much to the chagrin of their makers.

Russia's once glorious cinema still seemed crippled by its lack of funds, the Russian Mafia's desire to finance films resembling those made in the USA, and the loss of many of the country's cinemas. But there were glimmers, notably the superb work of Alexander Sokurov (the natural successor to the great Tarkovsky) whose *Russian Ark* took him around the treasures of the Hermitage in St Petersburg—90 minutes accomplished in a single, uncut steadycam shot. It was a tragedy for the Russian industry that Sergei Bodrov Jr, actor and film-maker son of a film-maker father, died in a landslide with 30 others as they filmed the single scene that was to be set in that area in the mountains. Such a talent could ill be spared.

Among those who also died during 2002 were the veteran Hollywood actor James Coburn; UK star of the 1940s and 1950s Phyllis Calvert; UK comedian and musician turned Hollywood star Dudley Moore; post-war German star Hildegard Knef; dominant Hollywood producer of the 1970s Julia Phillips; maverick Hungarian director André de Toth; Mexican star Katy Jurado; Hollywood star Rod Steiger; UK director J. Lee Thompson; UK actress Katrin Cartlidge; Belgian director André Delvaux; Indian star Naseem Banu; Irish actor Richard Harris; UK director Jack Lee; Spanish director Juan Bardem; US star Eddie Bracken; UK director Karel Reisz; French star Daniel Gelin; and US director George Roy Hill. (For Coburn, Moore, Steiger, Harris, and Reisz see XVIII.)

vi. TELEVISION AND RADIO

DURING the year the chickens came home to roost and many of the international media tycoons who had wagered the future of their business on the world of the Internet and the convergence between the media, computers, and telecommunications lost their bets.

The most spectacular crash was that of the flamboyant French "master of the universe", Jean-Marie Messier, who through a rapid programme of acquisitions turned a French water and sewage company into Vivendi Universal, one of the world's media groups. Debt and falling media share values finally caught up with Messier in July, when the new chief executive of Vivendi, Jean-René Fourtou, a pharmaceutical executive, accepted his resignation. A sale of assets at the group, which owned Universal studios in Hollywood, then began to reduce debt. The sale included Messier's US$20 million New York apartment.

Later that month the family owners of Bertelsmann, the German media group whose interests included a controlling stake in the UK's Channel 5, moved against its chief executive Thomas Middelhoff. The Bertelsmann chief executive was committed to modernising and seeking a stock exchange quotation for the media company, which was one of the world's largest book publishers and music groups, and expanding within the UK. His successor, Gunter Thielen, was much less interested in the UK and seemed more committed to consolidation than innovation.

July also saw further shake-ups in the management structure of AOL Time Warner, the world's largest media company, formed in 2000 from the merger of Internet company America On Line and the traditional media organisation, Time Warner (see AR 2000, p. 486). The hoped for "synergies" between the two groups had not materialised and the share price of the merged company had collapsed with the result that there was a record US$60 billion loss in the value of the company's assets. The management changes saw AOL executives on the board being largely sidelined and Time Warner executives reasserting their authority, led by new chief executive Richard Parsons.

Earlier the disarray in the ranks of the media moguls had been exposed when Leo Kirch, owner of the largest media group in Germany, and one of the largest in Europe, was forced out of the company that he had founded. KirchMedia held a majority stake in Formula One motor racing, the largest stake in ProSiebenSat (the main German commercial channel), and owned the largest film library outside the USA. The company filed for insolvency in April and a "fire sale" of the various parts of the empire began.

One of the few established media moguls to emerge relatively unscathed from the recession (which was exacerbated by the 11 September 2001 attacks on the USA), was Rupert Murdoch, chairman and chief executive of The News Corporation, owners of Twentieth Century Fox studios and *The Times* and the *Sun* newspapers in the UK. Murdoch cut costs and spending early in order to ride out the recession. As a result, in October he was able to buy Telepiu, Vivendi's loss-making pay television service in Italy in a UK£590 million deal. In the US things also appeared to be going Murdoch's way as regulatory opposition grew to the merger of two US satellite companies, DirecTV and EchoStar. The development cleared the way for News Corp. to acquire DirecTV and thereby achieve the long-term dream of Murdoch to own a satellite television venture covering all of North America.

The new sense of reality also led to senior executives losing their jobs in the UK broadcasting industry, many as result of the final collapse in April of ITV Digital, the digital terrestrial television service which folded with losses totalling more than UK£1.3 billion. An immediate casualty was Stuart Prebble, chief executive of both ITV Digital and the ITV network centre. His departure was followed later in the year by that of Steve Morrison, chief executive of Granada, and Gerry Murphy, chief executive of Carlton, the two large TV companies that owned ITV Digital. The two chief executives left because there was no place for them in the management structure of a new merged Carlton and Granada. The new company to be created, subject to the approval of the competition authorities, was likely to be called ITV plc. It would be chaired by Michael Green of Carton and run by chief executive Charles Allen, chairman of Granada.

The ability to merge, at least in theory, would be created by the Communications Bill which was finally published during the year and began its Parliamentary passage. The Bill sought to give widespread powers to Ofcom (the Office of Communication), a super-regulatory body comprising five existing regulators. They were: the Independent Television Commission, the telecommunications regulator Oftel, the Radio Authority, the Broadcasting Standards Commission, and the Radiocommunications Agency—the body responsible for the management of the radio spectrum. A separate bill had already been passed providing for the formation of Ofcom which would be chaired by economist Lord Currie and run by Stephen Carter, former managing director of cable group NTL. The Comunications Bill would enable non-European Union broadcasters to buy ITV companies for the first time. It also freed large newspaper groups such as News Corporation and Trinity Mirror (publishers of the *Daily Mirror*), to take control of Channel 5, which re-branded itself as FIVE during the year.

The Bill was scrutinised in advance by a House of Lords committee chaired by Lord Puttnam, the distinguished film producer. The committee noted that little attention had been given to the programme production market, particularly the role, and complaints of, the UK's independent production sector. Culture Secretary Tessa Jowell accepted the committee's point and asked the ITC to carry out a rapid investigation. The independents were happy with the outcome. There would be a code of practice covering the relationships between independents and broadcasters, particularly the BBC, to be monitored by Ofcom. The existing 25 per cent programme quota would apply separately to BBC One and BBC Two and Ofcom had the power to decide that the quota could apply to programme budgets as well as broadcasting hours if it believed this to be necessary.

During discussions on the Bill the government also changed its mind on rules for radio ownership. The initial plan was to make sure there were three different radio owners in large metropolitan markets, in addition to the BBC. After arguments from the radio industry that this was too restrictive, however, the government liberalised the rules to allow a minimum of two owners plus the BBC. Critics complained that the relaxation of ownership rules for radio and commercial television had changed the nature of a bill designed to decrease regulation. Instead the final version had moved away from "light regulation" to "appropriate" regulation, mainly to ensure that programme quality would not be damaged by ownership changes.

During a year of recession the BBC was able to plough ahead with one of the most remarkable periods of expansion in its history because of a generous licence fee settlement that was linked to retail prices plus 1.5 per cent. Two new digital television services for children, Ceebies and CBBC, were launched and BBC Four, a new digital channel devoted to arts and documentaries, finally got under way. After long delays and government doubts, permission was given to launch the UK£100 million a year BBC Three, a channel aimed at the 25-34 age range. Stringent public service conditions were applied and Jowell warned that the new channel was "on probation".

The BBC also launched no fewer than five new national radio networks, including a black music station, an Asian network, and Radio 7—a station produced largely from the BBC archives. Not many people could hear the new services, however, and by the end of the year there were only around 120,000 listeners with digital radio sets. (Even at Christmas there were too few sets available in the shops to satisfy demand.) Permission to launch a BBC online education service was also expected, albeit with stringent conditions following sustained complaints from private educational publishers. The BBC was also centrally involved in making sure that something, at least, would rise from the ashes of ITV Digital. At the end of October broadcasters, including both the BBC and BSkyB, launched Freeview, a 35-channel free-to-air service available to those buying a receiver costing around UK£100. By the end of 2002 more than 1 million homes were watching Freeview, most of them old ITV Digital subscribers.

The accusation that the BBC was "dumbing down", or at the least placing too great an emphasis on populism and ratings, did not diminish during the year. The BBC chairman, Gavyn Davies, did not help matters by attacking those who made the accusation as being "southern, white, middle-class, middle-aged and well educated". He later said he greatly regretted giving the impression that he was either taking the BBC's heartland for granted or was in favour of dumbing down. In an interview with *The Times* Davies acknowledged that critics of the disappearance of the arts from BBC One had a point and that "we should do something to bring the arts back into the centre of the schedule".

There were also the first hints of trouble over the licence fee as a number of campaigners claimed it was illegal under Article 10 of the Human Rights Act. The resulting cases had yet to come to court but BBC lawyers said they were confident of winning.

During the year the BBC was criticised for its coverage of the death of Queen Elizabeth The Queen Mother (see XVIII) when the news-reader on duty at the time, Peter Sissons, wore a burgundy, rather than a black, tie. However, the Corporation was praised for coverage of the funeral itself. There was also praise for its coverage of the football World Cup tournament in Japan and South Korea, the Commonwealth Games in Manchester, and the Queen's Jubilee Party at Buckingham Palace (see II.1.i). Other programme highlights were dramas such as *The Gathering Storm* on Churchill and *Crime and Punishment*. But all broadcasters expressed worries that the young appeared less and less interested in conventional political and current affairs programming.

As the year ended the BBC was starting to think about how it would make its case for a new Royal Charter running from 2006. At the same time the government was thinking about a wide-ranging review of what the BBC's future role and function should be.

A former managing director of BBC Television, Mark Thompson, currently chief executive of Channel 4, issued a challenge to all of the UK's broadcasters in his MacTaggart lecture at the Edinburgh Television Festival. Thompson said British programmes had become dull and predictable compared with the best of US television. The executive claimed that only Channel 4, together with the independent sector, could "blaze a trail back to creativity". Owing to the recession, however, Channel 4 announced a loss of more than UK£20 million, only the second loss in its history. Around 200 jobs were cut and the channel greatly reduced its presence in feature film making. The popularity of Channel 4's *Big Brother* continued unabated with audiences, and revenue, up from the second series in 2001.

ITV showed signs of recovery with the continuing popularity of formats such as *Pop Stars-The Rivals*, although for the second year running it had a smaller share of total viewing than BBC One. The network also failed to land the new chief executive of its choice. Dawn Airey, chief executive of FIVE, decided instead to go to the satellite broadcaster BSkyB, where she was placed in charge of all channels apart from sport. Instead Nigel Pickard, who had successfully launched the new BBC digital channels for children, became ITV director of programmes.

Meanwhile BSkyB continued to add new subscribers. By the end of the year it had 6.6 million satellite subscribers (compared with 5.7 million a year earlier) and was on course to reach its target of 7 million by the end of 2003. BSkyB was partly able to progress so quickly because of the relative weakness of the two big cable groups, Telewest and NTL. Both had to restructure their finances during the year, a process which meant that their shareholders lost virtually everything and the companies became controlled by banks and other bond holders. There was further positive news for BSkyB in December when the Office of Fair Trading caused considerable surprise by clearing the satellite broadcaster of breaching competition law. The main complainants had been ITV Digital and the cable companies.

During 2002, for the first time, more than 50 per cent of the UK population had access to multi-channel television from satellite, cable, or digital terrestrial sources. The changing nature of the UK broadcasting market and the British audience was best symbolised by the Christmas ratings. For the first time ever, viewers of all of the new channels combined totalled more than those watching ITV.

2. VISUAL ARTS—ARCHITECTURE

i. VISUAL ARTS

THE 11 September 2001 attack on the World Trade Centre and the general downturn of the world economy which followed it made themselves felt in all institutional aspects of the art world. Tourism was down everywhere, but especially in New York and the Middle East. The Guggenheim Museum announced that it had lost 25 per cent of its visitors. Some artists in New York organised free exhibitions and gave away their work, or sold it for next to nothing, while galleries cut prices by up to 50 per cent for pieces by the less famous. Egypt, which was heavily dependant on tourism as a means of earning foreign currency, estimated in July that since 11 September its tourist industry had shrunk by US$1 billion compared with the US$4.3 billion earned in 2000. This prompted the Culture Ministry to arrange a large exhibition of ancient Egyptian artefacts to go on a five-year tour of 13 centres in north America for an overall fee of US$24 million.

Such charges contributed only a little, however, to the tight squeeze felt by museums in the USA, UK, and France. The collapse of the financial markets meant that there was less corporate money for sponsorship, without which many of the activities which attracted the public tended to atrophy. The British Museum was particularly affected by this problem and by the decline in tourism, and faced an unprecedented deficit of UK£3.4 million. It announced cuts to the tune of UK£6 million during the summer, which involved the closing in rotation of many galleries, the reduction of the acquisitions budget from UK£500,000 to UK£100,000 and the loss of curators and conservators, the last provoking the first strike in the museum's history. In Paris, accusations in the newspapers of mismanagement at the Louvre by the Minister of Culture, Catherine Tasca, shocked an establishment more used to discretion in its high-level bureaucrats, and provoked an angry response from the Louvre's new director, Henri Loyrette.

By contrast, in Russia, the first signs of a sponsorship culture made themselves felt, with one of the biggest companies, Yukos Oil, under Mikhail Khodorovsky, setting up a philanthropic fund to distribute UK£10 million in grants for cultural activities.

In Italy, the right-wing government of Prime Minister Silvio Berlusconi rushed through legislation to create a public company called Patrimonio dello Stato spa (State Heritage Ltd) into which state property, including land, public buildings, monuments, museums, archives, and libraries, could be transferred to allow them "to be turned to better advantage". This provoked an outcry at the prospect of the Coliseum or Uffizi gallery being sold off, and while there were conditions in the bill which made that almost impossible, there was a strong risk that large tracts of countryside could be privatised.

The internationalisation of the art world accelerated, the museums following where the freelance curators of contemporary art had led: a Spaniard, Vicente Todoli, was appointed head of Tate Modern in London; James Cuno, director of the Harvard Museums, was made director of the Courtauld Institute and Gallery, also in London; Julian Raby of Oxford University became director of the Freer Gallery of Art and Arthur M. Sackler Gallery in Washington DC; while the former director of the Courtauld Gallery, John Murdoch, was made director of the Huntington Museum in California.

At Documenta, the huge quinquennial exhibition in Kassel, Germany, of international contemporary art, the Nigerian curator, Okwui Enwezor, assisted by an international team of specialists, put together an enormously successful (in terms of visitor numbers) show, in which video, documentary film, and photography were dominant, united by the common rejection of violence and a sympathy for the alienated and excluded. Many of the artists were almost unknown to the art trade (only 5 per cent of the 121 came from the USA, which was the leading market). Among works that stood out were a film by the Israeli, Eyal Sival, about the Rwandan genocide and another by Amar Anwar about the tensions on the border between India and Pakistan. The very few artists working in traditional media were included for their subject matter. For example, the US painter Leon Golub was there because his figurative art depicted acts of violence. Some art critics found this Documenta too politically correct, too little about art in the strict sense of the word, even too miserable, but others praised it for being an art event that at long last took into consideration the perilous state of the world and that was strengthened by its unifying theme.

So far as the dealers were concerned, the art market went into the doldrums, with little buying and selling between themselves, and quiet sales at the ever more numerous art fairs. Only top level auction sales defied this trend as buyers sought to take the limited opportunities to buy particular masterpieces. Thus, Sotheby's in London saw Lord Thomson, the Canadian press baron and collector, bid UK£49.5 million for the brilliantly composed if horrifying Massacre of the Innocents by Rubens, which had been estimated at only UK£6 million. Very good Impressionist and Modern works also held firm, with UK£7,153,750 paid in London for a Fauvist Vlaminck, US$18 million in New York for a Brancusi brass head, and US$12.6 million for a surrealist work by Magritte of simultaneous night and day. Anything second-rate or already hawked around the market failed to find a buyer, however. Contemporary art did well at auction, bearing in mind that only well-established artists were accepted for sale. Artists working with photography, especially Germans such as Thomas Struth and Andreas Gursky, were especially in demand. Works by Gerhard Richter, the painter whose show was visited by 333,695 people while at the Museum of Modern Art in New York, achieved prices which reflected the popularity that the artist commanded from both the intellectuals of contemporary art and the public.

Sotheby's remained in the red throughout the year, and the new auction house, Phillips de Pury Luxembourg, continued to lose money at such a rate that its original backer, Bernard Arnauld of LVMH (Louis Vuitton Moet Hennessy), sold his 70 per cent shareholding in it, thus ending the 1990s flirtation between luxury goods and the art trade.

It was a bad year for the chairman and majority shareholder of Sotheby's, A. Alfred Taubman, who began his sentence of a year and a day in prison for breaking US anti-trust laws by colluding with Christie's over vendors' commission. Christie's was spared punishment because it had co-operated with the US Justice Department. Frederick Schultz, the established New York antiquities dealer, also found himself facing a 33-month prison sentence for dealing in recently excavated and smuggled Egyptian antiquities, and the Federal judge told him that he was "no better than an ordinary thief".

Aware that London had become an entrepot for the trade in illegally excavated or exported goods, the government set up an advisory panel, whose work came to fruition when on 1 August the UK signed the UN Educational, Scientific and Cultural Organisation (UNESCO) Convention on the Means of Prohibiting and Preventing the Illicit Import, Export and Transfer of Ownership of Cultural Property. Japan and Switzerland, both countries with a strong market in antiquities, were debating the changes in national legislation required before they too could sign the convention.

Elsewhere, UNESCO debated but rejected the idea of trying to rebuild the giant Bamiyan Buddhas of Afghanistan, destroyed by the Taleban in 2001 (see AR 2001, p. 319). This was largely on the grounds that what remained was too fragmentary to be saved and that there were more urgent priorities for funds, such as restoring the Kabul Museum. Prague and Dresden were both severely affected in August by the flooding of the Elbe, but while the Dresden opera house and the Zwinger were filled with water, the incomparable collections of painting, porcelain, and arms in the latter were all taken to safety. The exquisite 18th-century park with follies at Dessau-Wörlitz suffered badly, and the bill overall for the region ran into many hundreds of millions of euros. On 6 September, an earthquake shook western Sicily, damaging the Norman Cappella Palatina with its precious mosaics.

Towards the end of the year, archaeologists and lawyers in the USA, led by a former curator at the Getty Museum, began to lobby the US Defence Department to take into account the many thousands of archaeological sites in Iraq when planning any attack upon the country.

In December, some 30 of the world's most prestigious museums—led by the Metropolitan Museum of Art, the Louvre, the State Museums of Berlin, the Hermitage, and the British Museum—issued a declaration of the value and importance of universal museums. It followed increasing concern over the politicisation of the Greek campaign for the return of the Parthenon Marbles from the British Museum, and stressed that "museums serve not just the citizens of one nation, but the people of all nations". The declaration was greeted by reproaches from a number of third world countries, which declared it to be self-serving.

Deaths during the year included: the Swiss collector, Hans Heinrich von Thyssen Bornemisza (see XVIII); the US museum director, J. Carter Brown; the US artists, Niki de Saint Phalle and Larry Rivers; the Spanish artist, Eduardo Chillida; the Mexican photographer, Manuel Alvarez Bravo; and the British art historians Nicolai Rubinstein and his wife Ruth.

ii. ARCHITECTURE

THE year in architecture provided a reminder that out of disaster springs opportunity. A building destroyed reveals the site for a new one. Following a well-organised public debate, the Lower Manhattan Development Corporation in New York brought forward six outline proposals of designs to replace the "twin towers" of the World Trade Centre (WTC) which had been destroyed in the terrorist attack of 11 September 2001. The shortlisted firms were mainly from the USA. However, the plans were undistinguished and were rejected by the public. They were criticised for displaying too much commercial space, for overlooking community and cultural use, and for insufficiently considering energy and local transport needs.

Meanwhile, the site was cleared of debris and viewing points were constructed. Thousands of people, including amateurs and professional architects and artists, began to submit designs for a permanent memorial. (They were logged on the Internet, which showed its potential to become a global notice board for impromptu design.) The memorial would commemorate the deaths of the thousands of people of varying nationalities who had died in the WTC, the Pentagon, and in the hijacked aircraft which had been used to perpetrate the attacks (see AR 2001, pp. 1-2). In response, the Development Corporation decided to hold a new contest for the WTC site, informed by a better brief. It said that any memorial would be the subject of a separate competition. In the USA, work continued to revise building engineering codes that would allow for the progressive collapse of tall structures. This attempt to mitigate disasters caused by terrorism might yet prove one of the enduring legacies of the attacks on the WTC. The architectural consequences would take time to emerge.

Fear of global economic slowdown in the wake of the terrible events of 11 September meant that many projects were delayed or deferred. Others, however, commissioned earlier, began to take shape. A tall, phallic tower for commercial occupation in the City of London designed by Foster and Partners (and christened "The Gherkin") rose from the ground. Its distinctive lattice structure loomed over the Tower of London and would be visible across the UK capital. Dampeners installed to correct the excited dynamic movement of the pedestrian "wobbly bridge" (the Millennium bridge—see AR 2000, p. 492) across the Thames in London, also by Foster and Partners, proved effective.

Another Thames pedestrian river crossing opened to the public, two years late but to general acclaim. The twin Hungerford footbridges between Charing Cross and Waterloo ran parallel to the 19th century engineer Brunel's original suspension bridge, which was now a railway bridge. The UK structural engineer, Ron Slade, conceived the new bridges' cable-stay mast design, which supported steady concrete decks. The architects were Lifschutz Davidson with engineers WSP Group. Westminster City Council on behalf of the London Cross-River Partnership managed the complex construction project heroically. Ken Livingstone, the mayor of London, helped to finance the project. It was estimated that the twin bridges would carry 7 million pedestrians each year to and from the south bank of the Thames. The bridges also revealed new views to the Palace of Westminster, the UK Parliament.

London's South Bank arts complex did not take full advantage of the footbridges, which landed outside its front door. Progress on the south bank development master plan, by US architect Rick Mather, was deferred by a combination of public opposition, management lethargy, and official timidity. The plans (the third set in a decade, the first two abandoned at public expense) included a new concert hall and open spaces, and the refurbishment by UK architects Allies and Morrison of the Royal Festival Hall of 1951. Elsewhere in the capital, the Royal College of Art produced plans by the architect Nicholas Grimshaw to extend its building next to the Royal Albert Hall. Critics complained that these did not respect the thoughtful 1960s composition of Cadbury Brown and Sir Hugh Casson. Meanwhile, the decade-long restoration of the Albert Hall by Building Design Partnership culminated in the completion of new service tunnels and the start of construction of the new South Porch, designed in keeping with the rest.

Outside London, the new Scottish parliament in Edinburgh took shape to a posthumous design by Enrico Miralles. Concerns about cost gave way to growing approval of its distinctive "upturned boat" design. A new library opened in Alexandria, Egypt, to replace the city's legendary library which had been destroyed by fire 1,600 years earlier. Designed by Austrian-born architect Christoph Kapeller, with the Norwegian practice Snohetta, the new building aspired to match its fabled predecessor. It contained 240,000 volumes and was paid for by international aid. A new cathedral opened in Los Angeles, USA, designed by Rafael Moneo with landscape architects Campbell and Campbell of Santa Monica. The US architect Rafael Viñoly won his first commission in Europe to design new theatres in Leicester, a provincial UK city notable for an early work by the architect Sir James Stirling. A proposal by the Dutch architect Eric Van Egeraat to redesign the Royal Shakespeare Company's (RSC) theatres in Stratford-upon-Avon, the playwright's birthplace, met with a cool reception. National opinion was divided over whether to demolish or retain the "listed" (protected) 1930s Shakespeare theatre by Elisabeth Scott. (The site lay in a flood plain on the banks of the river Avon.) The RSC announced its intention to create a "theatre village" in Stratford, a phrase regarded as a public relations blunder; the idea of creating a greater thespian enclave did not go down well in the English market town.

Other cultural projects were also delayed. There was little progress on realizing US architect Daniel Liebskind's eccentric "spiral" design for an extension to London's Victoria and Albert Museum. In Venice, Italy, the rebuilding of La Fenice, the opera house destroyed by fire in 1996, continued at a snail's pace, having been dogged by contractual disputes. The Greek government continued to plan hopefully for the return of the Parthenon (Elgin) marbles, in a new, empty museum. The British Museum once more declined to return them from their current location in the Museum. The Science Museum in London revealed ambitious proposals to convert a redundant airbase in Swindon, Wiltshire, into a national centre for sustainable development. US architect William McDonough, WSP and Arup were among teams commissioned to carry out initial studies of the 650 acre site, where the museum stored large objects.

The £7 billion UK lottery capital programme reached its peak, whereupon a revenue funding famine promptly replaced the lottery feast. Some projects opened their doors to the public and were promptly threatened with closure, either through management difficulties or lack of visitor receipts. These included the earth centre in Doncaster, Yorkshire, and the science centre in Glasgow, Scotland. The UK government (through the lottery distributor bodies which it controlled) diverted lottery money to "soft" community projects and small-scale initiatives. It said that the move was in response to public opinion; the amount of lottery capital invested in the art of architecture declined as a result.

The UK commission for architecture lobbied for better design in an alternative source of funds for architectural patronage, the "private finance initiative" (PFI). Bidding firms were encouraged to include reputable architects in teams formed to design, finance, and operate PFI schools, hospitals, and prisons. The Lord Chancellor's department offered a novel approach. It paid architects to enter a design competition for a new PFI civil justice centre in Manchester. They were the Richard Rogers partnership, Pringle, Richards Sherratt, and the Australian practice Denton, Corker, Marshall. The Australians won.

UK government ministers staged an "urban summit" in Birmingham. The conference debate, at which no opposition party spokesmen were invited to speak, was on the prospects for an urban renaissance. It showed that better design was a necessary but insufficient condition of success. For this, investment in public transport and in safer streets was also necessary.

In the world of design, Sir Terence Conran, the restaurateur and inventor of Habitat furnishings and eponymous design shops across the world, who had influenced the taste of generations of home-makers in the late 20th century, staged a revival. He designed a range of furniture for lower-income homemakers which aimed to rival the successful IKEA brand.

The Royal Institute of British Architects (RIBA) Stirling Prize was won by Wilkinson Eyre for their bridge across the river Tyne between Newcastle and Gateshead. It was shaped like an eyelid and tilted to allow shipping through. The RIBA Gold Medal was won by a group of theoreticians from the 1960s called Archigram. They were influenced by pop music and space travel, and proposed "plug-in cities" and "living pods". However, these were not taken up, and the group built nothing together.

3. LITERATURE

THROUGHOUT 2002 the world struggled to come to terms with the devastating terrorist attacks of 11 September 2001. It was inevitable, therefore, that many hastily produced analyses of their impact—not just upon the "twin towers" of the World Trade Centre in New York, but also on how society would develop in the aftermath—should flood bookshops in almost every Western country. None of them had any lasting literary merit, but this was perhaps the year in which the divide between marketable commissioned journalism and serious writing became obvious to all.

A new cynicism, which some called commercial realism, dominated publishing almost everywhere. If a book failed to make a profit quickly, or at least to hold its place on the bookshelves, then it was pulped. The reader was increasingly thought to want publications born out of a television series, novels that were versions of screenplays, and biographies and autobiographies of celebrities who were still in mid-career. The measured pace of traditional publishing, under pressure both from the philosophy of the modern market economy and from the speed of world events, appeared to be disappearing. The risk was that it was being replaced by superficial and instantaneous values.

In such an environment works by serious authors struggled for attention. The book that sold the most copies in the UK was a guide to style and fashion called *What Not to Wear*, a spin-off from a television series of the same name, written by the programme's presenters, Susannah Constantine and Trinny Woodall. In both the USA and the UK the popular sellers in fiction were by the likes of Tom Clancy, Martina Cole, John Grisham, and James Patterson, not one of which was taken seriously by literary critics. An account by his wife Pamela Stephenson of the life of the television comedian Billy Connolly stayed in the best-seller lists for months longer than Roy Jenkins' masterly life of Winston Churchill, published in the second half of 2001. This was despite a television poll which voted Churchill the "greatest Briton" of all time.

Though philistinism seemed to be eating into the heartland of the great publishing houses, many fine books nevertheless came out and new reputations were established. The award of the Commonwealth Writers Prize to the Australian novelist Richard Flanagan for *Gould's Book of Fish* gave an international accolade to a relatively unknown writer. The same was true when the Booker Prize for Fiction went to the French Canadian Yann Martel for his picaresque tale *The Life of Pi*, although a minor squall followed this decision because the author was accused of plagiarism.

It was difficult to anticipate which, if any, of the 12,000 new novels published in the USA and the UK would be remembered in a decade's time. The most talked about new novel was *The Corrections* by Jonathan Franzen, though its assertively US tone did not travel quite as well as its promoters had hoped. The French novelist Michel Houellebecq had a great success with *Platform*, the role of the translator Frank Wynne perhaps being the key to this. Though some of the great names of world fiction, such as Umberto Eco, Carlos Fuentes, Milan Kundera, José Saramago, and Mario Vargas Llosa, produced new novels, none of them was felt to be writing at the top of his form. One of UK's most prominent novelists A.S. Byatt, with *A Whistling Woman,* completed a trilogy which she had begun more than 20 years earlier, but the book, honourable in intention and earnest in execution, was not regarded as the masterpiece that it clearly aspired to be. However, another veteran author, Michael Frayn, was at the peak of his powers with *Spies*.

The writing of a second novel presents a particular challenge to any author who had achieved great success with a first. Donna Tartt was thought to have met the challenge successfully and found herself promoting *The Little Friend* in many countries. Zadie Smith, after the exceptional and almost hyperbolic reputation she had earned the previous year with *White Teeth*, followed her debut novel with *The Autograph Man*, a less linguistically innovative and less socially comprehensive book than its predecessor. Two African novelists made a mark with their first books: Tatamkhulu Afrika with *Bitter Eden*, which the 80-year old writer drew from his wartime experiences, and Helon Habila, a young author whose *Waiting for an Angel* confirmed earlier promise when he had been awarded the Caine Prize for African writing.

It was not considered an exceptional year for new poetry. Strong new collections by John Fuller, Paul Muldoon, and Tom Paulin, and two by Mark Doty, were well received. In the UK the revelation that the incoming Archbishop of Canterbury, Rowan Williams, was a highly competent poet, caused considerable interest (see XII). Another figure in the official tapestry of the state, the Poet Laureate Andrew Motion, brought out a new collection called *Public Poetry*, in which the responsibilities of his post were partly the subject matter. The posthumous publication of Samuel Beckett's complete poems caused much interest.

Growing public interest in the lives of celebrities fortunately meant not only a plethora of books about footballers and pop stars but also some well-researched biographies of true originality. Claire Tomalin's life of the diarist Samuel Pepys was particularly praised. Fiona MacCarthy, in her study of Byron, re-appraised the poet's notorious sexuality, suggesting that the legendary lover was more fond of boys than women. Peter Conradi took another writer's life, Iris Murdoch's, and again surprised scholars and readers alike by the complexity of his subject's sexuality. The Murdoch biography went hand-in-hand with Richard Eyre's film, in which Dame Judi Dench's portrayal of the novelist was widely admired. It was a good year for literary biography, with Dominic Hibberd's revaluation of Wilfred Owen, and Stanley Wells drawing from a lifetime's experience in his book on Shakespeare.

The publishing industry appeared to head both in the UK and the USA towards a uniform corporate identity. John Murray, a family firm for 250 years, was taken over by Hodder Headline. The year also saw the demise of Harvill and Everyman's Library as independent companies. After fears in previous years that young people would simply stop reading, thus eventually forcing many publishing firms out of business, some contrary evidence emerged in the form of a survey among teenagers. This suggested that people aged 15 to 16 actually watched videos and played on computer games for fewer hours than they had done at the age of 11. Even at this earlier age, reading was enjoyed by no fewer than 81 per cent of those polled.

It became clear from such surveys that the link between films and reading was very strong. *Lord of the Rings*, by J.R.R. Tolkien, enjoyed huge new sales worldwide as a result of the commercial success of the first two films made of the trilogy. Equally popular was the second of what promised to be at least a seven-part series of cinematic realisations of J.K. Rowling's Harry Potter books (see XV.1.v). The phenomenal sales of these books had preceded the launch of a film version, but they now took on a commercial profitability that broke all known records in almost every country, including China.

The year saw the death of the Swedish author and illustrator Astrid Lindgren. One of the most popular children's writers of all time, whose literary reputation seemed much stronger than Rowling's, Lindgren created in 1945 an enduring favourite character for children, Pippi Långstrump, or Pippi Longstocking. Senior poets who died included the socially committed Spaniard José Hierro, the Scottish writer George Bruce, the US lyricist Adolph Green, and the English academic poet D.J. Enright. The biographer Elizabeth Longford, author of the most distinguished life of Queen Victoria, died, as did the novelists William Cooper (pseudonym for Harry Hoff), Timothy Findley, and Mary Wesley (the latter having published her first book when she was 70). The great US philosopher John Rawls, the Scottish socialist playwright John McGrath, and the publisher Max Reinhardt were among the famous figures in the literary world who also passed on. (For Longford, Wesley and Rawls see XVIII).

The Nobel Prize for Literature was won by Imre Kertész. This Hungarian novelist's best-known work was published in 1975 and translated into English in 1992 as *Fateless*. The choice of a writer so connected to the horrors of the Holocaust showed how long was the reach of 20th century shadows into the new century. Indeed, within those shadows perhaps fell the most publicised and politically influential publications of the year: the dossiers on Iraq's weapons of mass destruction. The paradox was that although hardly anyone read them in their entirety, almost everyone was aware of their contents. It was as though reading by remove had become a standard practice for the whole world.

In a darkening world it was sometimes trivial absurdities which kept the human spirit buoyant. Jeffrey Archer's antics in prison, or more often out of prison as he persistently abused his leave privileges, led to the publication of a surprisingly well-received prison diary. The theft, probably to order, of three first edition copies of *A Christmas Carol* from Charles Dickens's house in London showed that nefarious behaviour in the literary world had not ceased with Lord Archer's incarceration.
Among the books published in 2002 were the following:

FICTION Tatamkhulu Afrika, *Bitter Eden* (Arcadia); Paul Bailey, *Uncle Rudolf* (Fourth Estate); Iain Banks, *Dear Air* (Little, Brown); John Banville, *Shroud* (Picador); William Boyd, *Any Human Heart* (Hamish Hamilton); Anita Brookner, *The Next Big Thing* (Viking); James Lee Burke, *Jolie Blon's Bounce* (Orion); A.S. Byatt, *A Whistling Woman* (Chatto and Windus); Justin Cartwright, *White Lightning* (Sceptre); J.M. Coetzee, *Youth* (Secker & Warburg); David Davidar, *The House of Blue Mangoes* (Weidenfeld & Nicolson); Margaret Drabble, *The Seven Sisters* (Viking); Umberto Eco, (trans. William Weaver) *Baudolino* (Secker and Warburg); Anne Enright, *The Pleasure of Eliza Lynch* (Cape); Jeffrey Eugenides, *Middlesex* (Bloomsbury); Michael Faber, *The Crimson Petal and the White* (Canongate); Timothy Findley, *Spadework* (Faber); Richard Flanagan, *Gould's Book of Fish* (Atlantic Books); Giles Foden, *Zanzibar* (Faber); Michael Frayn, *Spies* (Faber); Janice Galloway, *Clara* (Cape); Maggie Gee, *The White Family* (Saqi Books); Linda Grant, *Still Here* (Little, Brown); Norbert Gstrein (trans. Andrea Bell), *The English Years* (Harvill); Helon Habila, *Waiting for an Angel* (Hamish Hamilton); Georgina Hammick, *Green Man Running* (Chatto); Philip Hensher, *The Mulberry Empire* (Flamingo); Christopher Hope, *Heaven Forbid* (Macmillan); Michel Houellebecq (trans. Frank Wynne), *Platform* (Heinemann); A.L. Kennedy, *Indelible Acts* (Cape); Jamaica Kincaid, *Mr. Potter* (Chatto); Kumpfmüller (trans. Anthea Bell), *The Adventures of a Bed Salesman* (Weidenfeld); Milan Kundera (trans. Linda Asher), *Ignorance* (Faber); Hanif Kureishi, *The Body* (Faber); John Lanchester, *Fragrant Harbour* (Faber); Philip Larkin (ed. James Booth), *Trouble at Willow Gables and Other Fictions* (Faber); Toby Litt, *Exhibitionism* (Hamish Hamilton); Manuel Vargas Llosa, (trans. Edith Grossman) *The Feast of the Goat* (Faber); Arnošt Lustig (trans. Ewald Osers), *Lovely Green Eyes* (Harvill); Amin Malouf (trans. Barbara Bray), *Balthasar's Odyssey* (Harvill); Yann Martel, *Life of Pi* (Canongate); Rohinton Mistry, *Family Matters* (Faber); Courttia Newland, *Snakeskin* (Abacus); Edna O'Brien, *In the Forest* (Weidenfeld & Nicolson); Ben Okri, *In Arcadia* (Weidenfeld & Nicolson); Ian Pears, *The Dream of Scipio* (Cape); Julian Rathbone, *A Very English Agent* (Little, Brown); José Saramago (trans. Margaret Jull Costa), *The Cave* (Harvill); Alice Sebold, *The Lovely Bones* (Picador); Kamila Shamsie, *Kartography* (Bloomsbury); Sam Shepard, *Great Dream of Heaven* (Secker); Carol Shields, *Unless* (Fourth Estate); Zadie Smith, *The Autograph Man* (Hamish Hamilton); David Storey, *As It Happened* (Cape); Luke Sutherland, *Sweetmeat* (Doubleday); Donna Tartt, *The Little Friend* (Bloomsbury); William Trevor, *The Story of Lucy Gault* (Viking); Barry Unsworth, *The Songs of the Kings* (Hamish Hamilton); Alan Warner, *The Man Who Walks* (Cape); Marina Warner, *Murderers I Have Known* (Chatto); Sarah Waters, *Fingersmith* (Virago); Irvine Welsh, *Porno* (Cape); Tim Winton, *Dirt Music* (Picador).

POETRY Samuel Beckett, (ed. John Calder) *Poems 1930-1989* (Calder); Angus Calder, *Colours of Grief* (Shoestring Press); David Constantine, *Something for the Ghosts* (Bloodaxe); Mark Doty, *Source* (Cape); Mark Doty, *Still Life with Oysters and Lemon* (Beacon); Carol Ann Duffy, *Feminine Gospels* (Picador); Ruth Fainlight, *Burning Wire* (Bloodaxe); James Fenton, *An Introduction to English Poetry* (Viking); John Fuller, *Now and for a Time* (Chatto & Windus); Linton Kwesi Johnson, *Mi Revalueshanary Fren* (Penguin); Mimi Khalvati, *The Chine* (Carcanet); E.A. Markham, *A Rough Climate* (Anvil); Glyn Maxwell, *The Nerve* (Picador); Andrew Motion, *Public Property* (Faber); Paul Muldoon, *Moy Sand and Gravel* (Faber); Ruth Padel, *Voodoo Shop* (Chatto); Tom Paulin, *The Invasion Handbook* (Faber); Jem Poster, *Brought to Light* (Bloodaxe); Peter Reading, *Faunal* (Bloodaxe); Jeremy Reed, *Heartbreak Hotel* (Orion); Robin Robertson, *Slow Air* (Picador); Neil Rollinson, *Spanish Fly* (Cape); Carol Rumens, *Hex* (Bloodaxe); Lawrence Sail, *The World Returning* (Bloodaxe*)*; Peter Scupham, *Collected Poems* (Carcanet Oxford); Greta Stoddart, *At Home in the Dark* (Anvil); Matthew Sweeney, *Selected Poems* (Cape); John Wilkinson, *Effigies against the Light* (Salt); Rowan Williams, *The Poems of Rowan Williams* (The Perpetua Press).

BIOGRAPHY AND AUTOBIOGRAPHY Peter Ackroyd, *Dickens: Public Life and Private Passion* (BBC); Carole Angier, *The Double Bond: Primo Levi - a Biography* (Viking); David Attenborough, *Life on Air* (BBC); Julia

Blackburn, *Old Man Goya* (Cape); T.J. Binyon, *Pushkin* (HarperCollins); Peter Clarke, *The Cripps Version: the Life of Sir Stafford Cripps, 1889-1952* (Allen Lane); Sally Cline, *Zelda Fitzgerald: Her Voice in Paradise* (John Murray); Peter Conradi, *Iris Murdoch: A Life* (HarperCollins); Robert Fraser, *The Chameleon Poet: A Life of George Barker* (Cape); Jonathan Gregson, *Blood against the Snows: the Tragic Story of Nepal's Royal Dynasty* (Fourth Estate); John Grigg, *Lloyd George: War Leader* (Penguin); N. John Hall, *Max Beerbohm: A Kind of Life* (Yale); Dominic Hibberd, *Wilfred Owen: A new biography* (Orion); Christopher Hitchens, *Orwell's Victory* (Allen Lane/Penguin); Eric Hobsbawm, *Interesting Times: A 20th-Century Life* (Allen Lane); Lisa Jardine, *On a Grander Scale: The Outstanding Career of Sir Christopher Wren* (HarperCollins); Anja Klabunde, *Magda Goebbels* (Little, Brown); Hermann Kurzke (trans. Leslie Willson), *Thomas Mann: A Biography* (Allen Lane/ Penguin); Adam LeBor, *Milosevic: A Biography* (Bloomsbury); Roger Lewis, *Anthony Burgess: A Life* (Faber); Simon Louvish, *Stan and Ollie: The Roots of Comedy* (Faber); Fiona MacCarthy, *Byron: Life and Legend* (John Murray); Nicholas Murray, *Aldous Huxley* (Little, Brown); Ira Nadel, *Double Act: A Life of Tom Stoppard* (Methuen); C.S. Nicholls, *Elspeth Huxley: A Biography* (HarperCollins); Fanny Parkes, *Begums, Thugs and White Mughals: The Journals of Fanny Parkes* (Sickle Moon); Jane Ridley, *The Architect and His Wife: A Life of Edwin Lutyens* (Chatto & Windus); Ann Saddlemyer, *Becoming George: The Life of Mrs W.B. Yeats* (OUP); Ed Sikov, *Mr Strangelove: A Biography of Peter Sellers* (Sidgwick & Jackson); Garry Sobers, with Bob Harris, *Garry Sobers: My Autobiography* (Headline); Hilary Spurling, *The Girl from the Fiction Department: a Portrait of Sonia Orwell* (Hamish Hamilton); Pamela Stephenson, *Billy* (HarperCollins); T.J. Stiles, *Jesse James: Last Rebel of the Civil War* (Cape); Ian Thomson, *Primo Levi* (Hutchinson); Gillian Tindall, *The Man Who Drew London: Wenceslaus Hollar in Reality and Imagination* (Chatto and Windus); Claire Tomalin, *Samuel Pepys: The Unequalled Self* (Viking); Ursula Vaughan Williams, *Paradise Remembered* (Albion Music).

OTHER Martin Amis, *Koba the Dread: Laughter and the Twenty Million* (Cape); Antony Beevor, *Berlin* (Viking); Paula Byrne, *Jane Austen and the Theatre* (Hambledon & London); Humphrey Carpenter, *The Angry Young Men* (Allen Lane); Linda Colley, *Captives: Britain, Empire and the World 1600-1850* (Cape); William Dalrymple, *White Mughals: Love and betrayal in eighteenth-century India* (HarperCollins); Alain de Botton, *The Art of Travel* (Hamish Hamilton); Nick Groom, *The Forger's Shadow: How Forgery Changed the Course of Literature* (Picador); Alethea Hayter, *The Wreck of the Abergavenny* (Macmillan); Seamus Heaney, *Finder's Keepers: Selected Prose 1971-2001* (Carcanet); Blake Morrison, *Things My Mother Never Told Me* (Chatto & Windus); V.S. Naipaul, *The Writer and the World: Essays* (Picador); Jody Rosen, *White Christmas: The Story of a Song* (Fourth Estate); Arundhati Roy, *The Algebra of Infinite Justice* (Flamingo); Salman Rushdie, *Step Across This Line: Collected Nonfiction 1992-2002* (Cape); Jeremy Seal, *The Wreck at Sharpnose Point* (Picador); Ronald Segal, *Islam's Black Slaves: A History of Africa's Other Black Diaspora* (Atlantic Books); Marina Warner, *Fantastic Metamorphoses, Other Worlds* (OUP); Richard Weight, *Patriots: National Identity in Britain 1940-2000* (Macmillan); Stanley Wells, *Shakespeare for all Time* (Macmillan); A.N. Wilson, *The Victorians* (Hutchinson).

XVI SPORT

ASSOCIATION FOOTBALL. Although it ended with a classic confrontation between two of the game's traditional superpowers, the 2002 World Cup represented a significant shift in football's global order. Brazil, who beat Germany 2-0 in the final, remained the world's most successful national team, but this World Cup would be remembered mostly for the fall of France, Argentina, and Italy and for the emergence of South Korea, Senegal, Turkey, and the USA. The tournament broke new ground by being held in Asia. Japan and South Korea were perfect co-hosts: the stadiums and playing surfaces were excellent, the hospitality warm and, most pleasing of all, hooliganism almost non-existent. Both host countries had much to cheer on the pitch. Japan's fluent football was a joy to watch, though their feat in reaching the second round was eclipsed by South Korea, whose supremely fit and well-organised team reached the semi-finals before losing 1-0 to Germany. Although the Germans rarely shone, their disciplined performances were typified by their goalkeeper, the outstanding Oliver Kahn, whose copybook was blotted only by a rare error which gifted Brazil a goal in the final. Senegal, who had lost to Cameroon in the African Nations Cup final, were playing in their first World Cup and shocked the holders, France, by winning the opening game en route to the quarter-finals. The USA also made it to the last eight, while Turkey went one better before bowing out to a single Ronaldo goal in the semi-finals. The first-round casualties included the holders, France—whose humiliation was exacerbated by their team's failure to score a goal during the tournament—Argentina, and Portugal. Italy scraped through to the second round but paid for their negativity when they went out to South Korea. Ronaldo was the individual hero of the tournament, scoring both goals against Germany in the final to take his tally for the tournament to eight, and putting behind him the misery of the 1998 final, when he performed poorly in the defeat against France after suffering a fit before the game (see AR 1998, p. 549).

Brazil had ended the hopes of England in the quarter-finals when Ronaldinho's audacious free-kick dropped over David Seaman, the goalkeeper, for the winning goal. Although England enjoyed a memorable victory over Argentina, David Beckham's penalty helping to erase the memory of his sending-off against the same opponents four years earlier, Sven-Goran Eriksson's team performed fitfully. The Republic of Ireland's preparations were disrupted by an extraordinary row between the manager, Mick McCarthy, and his captain, Roy Keane, who was sent home before the tournament began. The Irish responded magnificently in his absence before losing on penalties to Spain in the second round. One concern for Fifa, the governing body, was the number of poor refereeing decisions. Italy had what appeared to be five good goals disallowed during the tournament, while the Spanish were angered by two bad decisions which denied them what would have been crucial goals against South Korea.

After the World Cup, Europe's attention turned to the qualification process for the 2004 European Championship to be held in Portugal. England got off to a fortunate winning start in Slovakia and followed it up with a patchy 2-2 draw at home to Macedonia. McCarthy resigned as Republic of Ireland manager after a poor opening to the campaign, but Wales, who were continuing to improve under the managership of Mark Hughes, made a flying start and claimed a notable scalp with a thoroughly deserved 2-1 home win over Italy. Scotland, having failed to reach the 2002 World Cup, appointed the former German national coach, Berti Vogts, to succeed Craig Brown as manager, but the results in his first year were mostly disappointing, especially a humiliating 2-2 draw away to the Faroe Islands. Northern Ireland's year was clouded by Neil Lennon's retirement from international football after he received death threats from loyalist extremists before a friendly against Cyprus. Lennon played for Celtic, a predominantly Catholic club. Real Madrid were again the world's outstanding club side, winning the Champions League with a wonderful goal by Zinédine Zidane in the final in Glasgow against Bayer Leverkusen. The Germans were the year's surprise package and accounted for Liverpool in the quarter-finals and Manchester United in the semi-finals. Arsenal went out after the second phase. In the 2002-03 competition Manchester United, Arsenal, and Newcastle United all qualified for the second phase but Liverpool missed out.

The English Premiership saw Arsenal overcome Manchester United and Liverpool in a thrilling three-way battle for the title. Arsenal were irresistible in the second half of the season and won the elusive "Double" by beating Chelsea in the FA Cup final. Blackburn Rovers won the Worthington Cup, Andy Cole hitting the winner against Tottenham Hotspur. Manchester United's year had been disrupted by speculation over the future of their manager, Sir Alex Ferguson, who initially said he would step down at the end of the 2001-02 season. However, he later reversed the decision and signed a new three-year contract. United signalled their intent to continue challenging for all the major honours by paying Leeds United UK£30 million for Rio Ferdinand, the sixth highest transfer fee of all time and the highest involving English clubs. The transfer was arranged against the wishes of Terry Venables, the new Leeds manager, who had taken up the job after the unexpected dismissal of David O'Leary prior to the start of the 2002-03 season. Although Venables was a veteran manager at club and national level, his Leeds team made a poor start to the new season and were forced to begin selling key players to ease the club's mountain of debt.

Adam Crozier, chief executive of the Football Association, was forced out in a power struggle with leading Premiership clubs, while senior Football League officials also departed in the wake of the collapse of the ITV Digital television channel, which put paid to the remaining UK£178 million of their three-year deal with the League. Although a new TV agreement was signed with Sky worth UK£95 million over four years, many clubs were left in dire financial straits, Leicester City and Bradford City among those forced into administration.

Rangers, revived by the management of Alex McLeish, won both the Scottish League Cup—beating Ayr United in the final after disposing of Celtic in the semi-finals—and the Scottish Cup, beating Celtic 3-2. Celtic won the league title by 18 points, losing only once all season and winning 18 out of their 19 home matches.

WINTER OLYMPICS. In an age where politics played an increasingly major role in sport, it should perhaps have been no surprise that the biggest headlines from the Winter Olympics were about officials rather than competitors. While there were many sparkling performances in Salt Lake City, USA, a controversy over the judging in figure skating overshadowed everything. The issue exploded after the Russians, Anton Sikharulidze and Yelena Berezhnaya, won the gold in the pairs event, leaving the Canadian pair, David Pelletier and Jamie Salé, with the silver. It was alleged that the French judge, Marie Reine Le Gougne, had been pressured into voting for the Russians in exchange for support for the French ice dance pair later in the week. Le Gougne denied this and claimed that she had in fact resisted pressure to vote for the Canadians. The International Olympic Committee responded by awarding gold to both the Russians and the Canadians. Many saw this as a dangerous precedent and it upset Russia, which had already been angered by the exclusion of its top cross-country skier, Larissa Lazutina, following a pre-event blood screening. The Russians talked of boycotting the Games, though they did not carry out this threat. Before the Games were over there was more controversy as the skier Johann Muehlegg, Spain's adopted German, failed a drugs test.

The Games took place amid high-level security following the 11 September attacks in New York only five months previously. In such an atmosphere it was no surprise that US triumphs—like that of 16-year-old Sarah Hughes in the women's figure skating—were greeted with high-octane fervour by the crowds, although the continuing winter domination of Germany and Norway left the USA in third place in the final medals table. Canada ended a wait of more than half a century to secure the Olympic ice hockey title, while a Croatian enjoyed arguably the greatest individual success, Janica Kostelic winning three golds and a silver to become the first Alpine skier to win four medals at one Olympics. There was more controversy in the short track speed skating, where South Korea's defending 1500 metres champion, Kim Dong-Sung, lost the gold after he was adjudged to have impeded the USA's Apolo Anton Ohno. The 1,000 metres short track final featured perhaps the most extraordinary moment of the Games, the leading four men (including Ohno) crashing just before the finish to hand the gold to the unheralded Steven Bradbury, who took Australia's first winter gold medal. Britain won its first winter gold medal for 18 years when its women's curling team beat Switzerland in a dramatic final. Rhona Martin's team had qualified from the round-robin stage only after two closely contested play-offs. Alex Coomber secured bronze for Britain in the skeleton bobsleigh, but British joy at Alain Baxter's skiing bronze in the slalom turned to despair when he failed a drugs test. Baxter had used an inhaler that he had bought in the USA, and which contained an illegal drug which was not used in the UK version of the device. The Scot's appeal failed.

COMMONWEALTH GAMES. After the fiascos over the rebuilding of Wembley and the non-building of a new athletics stadium at Picketts Lock, there had been fears that the Commonwealth Games in Manchester would be another embarrassment to UK sport. However, nothing could have been further from the truth. The Games were an outstanding success, superbly organised, magnificently supported, and crowned by sporting excellence. The individual hero was Ian Thorpe. The Australian swimming sensation won six golds and broke his own world record in the 400 metres freestyle. However, the English were delighted with their 32 swimming medals. The English athletes also had an excellent Games, finishing with 12 golds, six silver, and 11 bronze medals, although the most anticipated showdown ended in disappointment for England when Dwain Chambers and Mark Lewis-Francis both pulled up injured in the 100 metres final, which was won by Kim Collins of St Kitts and Nevis. Paula Radcliffe ran away with the 5,000 metres, while Jonathan Edwards added the Commonwealth triple jump crown to his Olympic, World, and European titles. It made Edwards only the third British athlete—the others being Daley Thompson and Sally Gunnell—ever to hold all four major championship titles and the world record at the same time. Other English gold medal winners ranged from 15-year-old Charlotte Kerwood in shooting's double trap to 70-year-old Ruth Small, a blind lawn bowler. Australia headed the final medals table with 82 golds, followed by England (54) and India (32). New Zealand retained its rugby sevens crown, Australia and India took the men's and women's hockey titles respectively, Australia beat New Zealand in a gripping netball final, and the Australians enjoyed the most success in the boxing ring, taking home three golds. The triathlon made its Games debut, Canada celebrating a double triumph through Simon Whitfield and Carol Montgomery.

ATHLETICS. The athlete of the year was Paula Radcliffe, who began it in spectacular fashion by winning the London Marathon in the second fastest time by a woman (overshadowing, remarkably, Khalid Khannouchi's men's world marathon record on the same day). After victories in the Commonwealth Games 5,000 metres in Manchester and the European Championships 10,000 metres in Munich, where she set a European record, Radcliffe ended the year with victory and a world record in the Chicago Marathon. Little wonder that she won the BBC's Sports Personality of the Year award. It was a good year for Britain, which won seven golds at the European Championships. Steve Backley and Colin Jackson claimed record-breaking fourth consecutive European golds in the javelin and 100 metres hurdles respectively; Dwain Chambers won the 100 metres title and the British men won the 4 x 100 metres and 4 x 400 metres relays; Ashia Hansen won gold in the women's triple jump. Earlier in the year Britain had won seven medals at the European Indoor Championships in Vienna and had regained the Europa Cup with a fine performance in Annecy, holding off the challenge of Germany. Chambers beat Maurice Greene, the Olympic champion, five times during the year, but it was another US athlete, Tim Montgomery, who broke the 100 metres world record with a time of 9.78 seconds in Paris.

CRICKET. Australia were again the world's outstanding team and started the year with a double triumph over South Africa. After completing a 3-0 home series victory, the Australians also won in South Africa. Nowhere was their dominance better illustrated than in Johannesburg, where Australia won by an innings and 360 runs, the second biggest winning margin in Test history. It was a mixed year for England, who began with a fighting 3-3 draw in a one-day series in India, followed by a narrow 3-2 defeat in a one-day series in New Zealand. The Test series in New Zealand ended 1-1. After winning the first Test, England failed to push home their advantage in the second, which was drawn, and faded on the last day of the third Test to lose by 78 runs. The first Test had been notable for Nathan Astle's double hundred for New Zealand off only 153 balls, the fastest in Test history. The previous fastest had been scored a few days earlier by Australia's Adam Gilchrist, off 212 balls, against South Africa in Johannesburg. Back in England, Nasser Hussain's men crushed Sri Lanka in a three-Test series. Sri Lanka were also the losers in a triangular one-day tournament, won by India in a thrilling final at Lord's. England's home Test series against India ended 1-1, with two Tests drawn, but again it was a contest that Hussain's team should have won after dominating the first two matches. England failed to make any significant progress in the Champions Trophy in Sri Lanka—where the final between the hosts and India was washed out—and ended the year by suffering a comprehensive defeat "Down Under". Australia went into the Ashes fresh from a crushing series victory over Pakistan and the writing was on the wall on day one of the first Test, when England's Simon Jones suffered a horrific tour-ending knee injury and Australia ended on 364 for two after Hussain had chosen to field. England suffered a series of injuries but had not helped their cause by selecting players with fitness problems. However, England could take cheer from the form of Michael Vaughan, who in 2002 scored six centuries from his 14 Test innings and was the world's highest Test run scorer in the year. His total of 1,536 runs was also the highest annual total by an England Test player.

Surrey won their third county championship title in four years, while Yorkshire were relegated to the Second Division, 12 months after winning the First Division. Yorkshire found consolation with a six-wicket victory over Somerset in the Cheltenham and Gloucester Trophy final, while Warwickshire beat Essex in a one-sided Benson and Hedges Cup final. Glamorgan won the Norwich Union League championship. The most remarkable day's cricket was at the Oval, where Surrey beat Glamorgan in a Cheltenham and Gloucester Trophy match by nine runs on a day when 867 runs were scored, a one-day record. Surrey's Ally Brown scored 268 off 160 balls, smashing the individual world one-day record. Lord MacLaurin, the innovative chairman of the England and Wales Cricket Board, stepped down to be replaced by David Morgan, the former chairman of Glamorgan, while two untimely deaths shocked the sport. Hansie Cronje, the disgraced former South African captain, died in an air crash (see XVIII), while the young England player Ben Hollioake was killed in a motor accident in Australia.

Rugby. France won the Six Nations' Championship in style, crushing Ireland 44-5 in Paris to complete the Grand Slam. It rewarded the brave policies of Bernard Laporte, the French coach, who put his faith in a new generation of skilful, athletic players. The crucial game was England's 20-15 defeat to France, also in Paris, as Clive Woodward's team had to settle for second place and the Triple Crown. Wales had a miserable year, the coach Graham Henry departing in the wake of a 54-10 defeat to Ireland on the opening weekend of the championship, to be replaced by his fellow New Zealander, Steve Hansen. South Africa won the Tri-Nations trophy with a tense 33-31 victory over Australia. However, the tournament was marred by an incident during South Africa's home defeat to New Zealand when a fan ran on to the pitch and attacked David McHugh, the referee, who suffered a dislocated shoulder. With the World Cup fast approaching—the 2003 event would be staged only in Australia after New Zealand could not reach agreement on co-hosting—the autumn internationals gave a chance to assess world form. The northern hemisphere looked in good shape: England struck psychological blows with wins over Australia, South Africa, and New Zealand, while Ireland and Scotland were encouraged by victories over Australia and South Africa respectively.

Leicester were again the outstanding club side in Europe, winning the Heineken Cup by beating Munster in the final. In an extraordinary finish to their semi-final, Leicester beat Llanelli 13-12 thanks to a 58-metre last-minute penalty by Tim Stimpson which hit the woodwork twice before going over. Sale beat Pontypridd in the Parker Pen Shield final. Leicester matched Bath's achievement of winning four successive league titles, while Gloucester beat Bristol in the Zurich Championship final in June at the end of a gruelling season. London Irish won the Powergen Cup, crushing Northampton in a high-quality final; Pontypridd lifted the Principality Cup by beating Llanelli; and Leinster overcame Munster in the Celtic League final.

In rugby league Great Britain drew a home Test series against New Zealand, a good recovery after losing the first match 30-16. Wigan overturned the odds to win the Challenge Cup, beating St Helens 21-12 at Murrayfield, but the Saints ended the season on a high, beating the Bradford Bulls 19-18 thanks to Sean Long's last-minute drop kick in the Grand Final at Old Trafford.

Tennis. An outstanding performance saw Pete Sampras defy the years to win the US Open in New York. The US player's career had seemed in decline but he raised his game to lift his home title after a final against Andre Agassi. The two men, with a combined age of 63, were the oldest finalists in the event's history. Lleyton Hewitt began and ended the year as world number 1 and lived up to his billing at Wimbledon, where he beat the number 28 seed, Argentina's David Nalbandian, in the final. Thomas Johansson won his first Grand Slam event, beating Marat Safin in the Australian Open final, while the French Open produced another unlikely champion, Albert Costa beating Juan Carlos Ferrero in an all-Spanish final.

The UK's Tim Henman had a good 2002, despite losing to Hewitt in his fourth Wimbledon semi-final in five years. The UK number 1 won the Australian Hard-court Championship and beat his fellow countryman, Greg Rusedski, in the Australian Open before losing to Jonas Bjorkman in the fourth round. Rusedski reached the second week of Wimbledon, losing a five-set thriller to Xavier Malisse, but the two Britons both went out of the US Open in the third round. Henman, troubled by a shoulder injury which required surgery later in the year, lost to Juan Ignacio Chela while Rusedski lost to Sampras. Russia overcame the odds to beat France in the Davis Cup final in Paris. Britain lost in the first round to Sweden but retained its place in the World Group by beating Thailand thanks to a heroic performance by Henman.

Jennifer Capriati won the Australian Open, recovering from a set and 0-4 down to beat Martina Hingis, whose year was subsequently wrecked by injury. Thereafter the women's season was dominated by the sisters Serena and Venus Williams, the former beating the latter in the finals of the three subsequent Grand Slam tournaments. Although she won the US Open in 1999, Serena Williams had generally been outshone by her sister until her remarkable run in 2002.

GOLF. Paul McGinley was an unlikely hero, but the Irishman was at centre stage for arguably the most dramatic day of the sporting year as Europe beat the USA in the Ryder Cup at the Belfry. Europe won by $15\frac{1}{2}$ points to $12\frac{1}{2}$, McGinley sinking the winning putt. The teams had been all square at the end of day two, the US golfers fighting back after Europe, inspired by three wins out of four from the partnership of Lee Westwood and Sergio Garcia, had set the pace. Sam Torrance, Europe's captain, decided on a gung-ho approach in the final day's singles, traditionally the USA's strongest hand. Torrance sent out all his best players early and they responded magnificently. There were also some unexpected heroes as McGinley halved with Jim Furyk and Philip Price, ranked 119th in the world, beat Phil Mickelson, the number 2. Colin Montgomerie was Europe's highest scorer in the match, with $4\frac{1}{2}$ points. Tiger Woods remained the world's number 1. He won his third Masters title, finishing three strokes clear of Retief Goosen after the South African (who later in the year retained the European Order of Merit) faded on the final day. Woods won the US Open at Farmingdale by the same margin, this time against Mickelson, but in the US PGA he was runner-up to an outsider, 31-year old Rich Beem. Woods also came unstuck at the Open at Muirfield on the third day, when the leaders played in appalling weather. He recorded an 81, his worst score as a professional. A nerve-wracking final day saw Ernie Els win a four-way play-off against Thomas Levet, Stuart Appleby, and Steve Elkington.

The USA's women golfers came from behind to take the Solheim Cup back from Europe at Edina, Minnesota. The USA also won the Curtis Cup in Pittsburgh, beating Great Britain and Ireland 11-7. Sweden's Annika Sorenstam was player of the year in the USA, winning 11 of her 23 tournaments and, remarkably, recording 20 top 10 finishes, while Australia's Karrie Webb won the Women's British Open at Turnberry.

MOTOR SPORT. Michael Schumacher utterly dominated the Formula One season. The German won his fifth drivers' title, his third in a row, breaking several records. His 11 victories beat the record of nine in a season which he had shared with Nigel Mansell and he won the crown in record time, with six races to go. The Ferrari driver also became the first to finish on the podium in every race. The year began with Schumacher winning in front of a 127,000 crowd in Melbourne, after a crash at the first corner halved the field. Unfortunately, public interest in the championship rapidly declined from there because of the German's domination. At the Austrian Grand Prix there was outrage as Rubens Barrichello was ordered by his Ferrari team to let his teammate Schumacher through to win. Ferrari were fined US$1 million for their drivers' behaviour on the podium, where Schumacher insisted that Barrichello should stand on top.

Marcus Gronholm won the world rally title, while on two wheels Colin Edwards regained the world superbikes title and Valentino Rossi ran away with the World MotoGP crown.

RACING. As if Manchester United's manager had not enjoyed enough sporting success, Sir Alex Ferguson enjoyed a remarkable season as part-owner of the horse of the year, Rock Of Gibraltar. Trained by Aidan O'Brien, Rock Of Gibraltar won the 2,000 Guineas and made history with seven successive Group One wins. He was finally beaten in the Breeders' Cup at Arlington Park, where his stablemate High Chaparral's victory in the Turf race was overshadowed by the death of Landseer, who shattered his off-fore in the Mile. O'Brien saddled the first two home in the Epsom Derby, High Chaparral and Hawk Wing, and the first three in the Irish Derby, won by High Chaparral. The Godolphin stable and Frankie Dettori won the Oaks with Kazzia and the Arc de Triomphe with Marienbard. Tim Easterby's Bollin Eric won the St Leger, while Michael Stoute's Golan held off Nayef to win a thrilling King George VI and Queen Elizabeth Diamond Stakes at Ascot. The jockey Tony McCoy broke Sir Gordon Richards' record of 269 winners in a season, finishing the National Hunt campaign with 289 wins, and then surpassed Richard Dunwoody's career record of 1,699 winners over fences. Best Mate, ridden by Jim Culloty, won the Cheltenham Gold Cup, while Hors La Loi III won the Champion Hurdle, which would be remembered for two horses which failed to make it to the finish: Istabraq, attempting a record fourth win, was pulled up after two flights, while Valiramix, the favourite, broke his back in a fall at the penultimate hurdle when seemingly heading for victory. Bindaree, ridden by Culloty, won the Grand National, holding off What's Up Boys in a tight finish.

ELSEWHERE. Lennox Lewis confirmed his status as the world's best heavyweight boxer, knocking out Mike Tyson in their world title fight in Memphis. Lewis had waited for years to meet Tyson and the two men had brawled at a prefight press conference. Of the other leading UK boxers, Joe Calzaghe and Ricky Hatton remained WBO super-middleweight and WBU welterweight world champions respectively, while Naseem Hamed failed to impress in a comeback against Manuel Calvo. Audley Harrison stayed unbeaten in his fledgling professional career but was criticised for the poor quality of his opponents.

In an eventful year on the high seas, Bruno Peyron sailed round the world in 64 days, breaking the record, while John Kostecki's *Illbruck* won the Volvo Ocean Race. The America's Cup began in New Zealand, where Chris Dickson's *Oracle* and Russell Coutts' *Alinghi* qualified for the final of the Louis Vuitton Cup. The winners would go on to race their fellow countrymen from Team New Zealand for the America's Cup itself. Britain lost in the quarter-finals to Dennis Conner's *Stars & Stripes*, but there was British joy in the Route du Rhum, won by Ellen MacArthur. Matthew Pinsent and James Cracknell's 25-race winning streak in rowing's coxless pairs ended with two defeats in the World Cup series in Lucerne, but the British pair bounced back, winning at the world championships in world record time. The British men's coxed four and women's lightweight coxless pair also won golds in Seville. Oxford won the Boat Race, edging out Cambridge by two-thirds of a length in a thrilling finish.

Lance Armstrong continued to dominate the Tour de France, winning for the fourth successive year. Joseba Beloki was runner-up, but Armstrong rarely looked in trouble. Peter Ebdon won the world snooker championship for the first time, beating Stephen Hendry 18-17 in a dramatic final. At the World Equestrian Games in Jerez the USA took the three-day event team title and France the showjumping championship. Britain's showjumpers finished 16th, their worst ever performance. Dermott Lennon became the first Irish rider to win the individual showjumping title. Pippa Funnell and Supreme Rock won Badminton.

Super Bowl XXXVI was decided in dramatic fashion, Adam Vinatieri's field goal from 48 yards giving the New England Patriots a 20-17 victory over the St Louis Rams, who had been clear favourites. The Los Angeles Lakers won the National Basketball Association title for the third year in succession, beating the New Jersey Nets in the play-offs final. Shaquille O'Neal was the Most Valuable Player, also for the third year in succession. The Detroit Redwings beat the Carolina Hurricanes to win ice hockey's Stanley Cup, while the Anaheim Angels won baseball's World Series, defeating the San Francisco Giants 4-1.

XVII DOCUMENTS AND REFERENCE

1. UN SECURITY COUNCIL RESOLUTION ON IRAQ

Published below is Resolution 1441 (2002) on disarming Iraq, adopted by the Security Council at its 4644th meeting, on 8 November 2002

The Security Council,

Recalling all its previous relevant resolutions, in particular its resolutions 661 (1990) of 6 August 1990, 678 (1990) of 29 November 1990, 686 (1991) of 2 March 1991, 687 (1991) of 3 April 1991, 688 (1991) of 5 April 1991, 707 (1991) of 15 August 1991, 715 (1991) of 11 October 1991, 986 (1995) of 14 April 1995, and 1284 (1999) of 17 December 1999, and all the relevant statements of its President,

Recalling also its resolution 1382 (2001) of 29 November 2001 and its intention to implement it fully,

Recognizing the threat Iraq's non-compliance with Council resolutions and proliferation of weapons of mass destruction and long-range missiles poses to international peace and security,

Recalling that its resolution 678 (1990) authorized Member States to use all necessary means to uphold and implement its resolution 660 (1990) of 2 August 1990 and all relevant resolutions subsequent to resolution 660 (1990) and to restore international peace and security in the area,

Further recalling that its resolution 687 (1991) imposed obligations on Iraq as a necessary step for achievement of its stated objective of restoring international peace and security in the area,

Deploring the fact that Iraq has not provided an accurate, full, final, and complete disclosure, as required by resolution 687 (1991), of all aspects of its programmes to develop weapons of mass destruction and ballistic missiles with a range greater than one hundred and fifty kilometres, and of all holdings of such weapons, their components and production facilities and locations, as well as all other nuclear programmes, including any which it claims are for purposes not related to nuclear-weapons-usable material,

Deploring further that Iraq repeatedly obstructed immediate, unconditional, and unrestricted access to sites designated by the United Nations Special Commission (UNSCOM) and the International Atomic Energy Agency (IAEA), failed to cooperate fully and unconditionally with UNSCOM and IAEA weapons inspectors, as required by resolution 687 (1991), and ultimately ceased all cooperation with UNSCOM and the IAEA in 1998,

Deploring the absence, since December 1998, in Iraq of international monitoring, inspection, and verification, as required by relevant resolutions, of weapons of mass destruction and ballistic missiles, in spite of the Council's repeated demands that Iraq provide immediate, unconditional, and unrestricted access to the United Nations Monitoring, Verification and Inspection Commission (UNMOVIC), established in resolution 1284 (1999) as the successor organization to UNSCOM, and the IAEA, and regretting the consequent prolonging of the crisis in the region and the suffering of the Iraqi people,

Deploring also that the Government of Iraq has failed to comply with its commitments pursuant to resolution 687 (1991) with regard to terrorism, pursuant to resolution 688 (1991) to end repression of its civilian population and to provide access by international humanitarian organizations to all those in need of assistance in Iraq, and pursuant to resolutions 686 (1991), 687 (1991), and 1284 (1999) to return or cooperate in accounting for Kuwaiti and third country nationals wrongfully detained by Iraq, or to return Kuwaiti property wrongfully seized by Iraq,

Recalling that in its resolution 687 (1991) the Council declared that a ceasefire would be based on acceptance by Iraq of the provisions of that resolution, including the obligations on Iraq contained therein,

Determined to ensure full and immediate compliance by Iraq without conditions or restrictions with its obligations under resolution 687 (1991) and other relevant resolutions and recalling that the resolutions of the Council constitute the governing standard of Iraqi compliance,

Recalling that the effective operation of UNMOVIC, as the successor organization to the Special Commission, and the IAEA is essential for the implementation of resolution 687 (1991) and other relevant resolutions,

Noting that the letter dated 16 September 2002 from the Minister for Foreign Affairs of Iraq addressed to the Secretary-General is a necessary first step toward rectifying Iraq's continued failure to comply with relevant Council resolutions,

Noting further the letter dated 8 October 2002 from the Executive Chairman of UNMOVIC and the Director-General of the IAEA to General Al-Saadi of the Government of Iraq laying out the practical arrangements, as a follow-up to their meeting in Vienna, that are prerequisites for the resumption of inspections in Iraq by UNMOVIC and the IAEA, and expressing the gravest concern at the continued failure by the Government of Iraq to provide confirmation of the arrangements as laid out in that letter,

Reaffirming the commitment of all Member States to the sovereignty and territorial integrity of Iraq, Kuwait, and the neighbouring States,

Commending the Secretary-General and members of the League of Arab States and its Secretary-General for their efforts in this regard,

Determined to secure full compliance with its decisions,

Acting under Chapter VII of the Charter of the United Nations,

1. Decides that Iraq has been and remains in material breach of its obligations under relevant resolutions, including resolution 687 (1991), in particular through Iraq's failure to cooperate with United Nations inspectors and the IAEA, and to complete the actions required under paragraphs 8 to 13 of resolution 687 (1991);

2. Decides, while acknowledging paragraph 1 above, to afford Iraq, by this resolution, a final opportunity to comply with its disarmament obligations under relevant resolutions of the Council; and accordingly decides to set up an enhanced inspection regime with the aim of bringing to full and verified completion the disarmament process established by resolution 687 (1991) and subsequent resolutions of the Council;

3. Decides that, in order to begin to comply with its disarmament obligations, in addition to submitting the required biannual declarations, the Government of Iraq shall provide to UNMOVIC, the IAEA, and the Council, not later than 30 days from the date of this resolution, a currently accurate, full, and complete declaration of all aspects of its programmes to develop chemical, biological, and nuclear weapons, ballistic missiles, and other delivery systems such as unmanned aerial vehicles and dispersal systems designed for use on aircraft, including any holdings and precise locations of such weapons, components, subcomponents, stocks of agents, and related material and equipment, the locations and work of its research, development and production facilities, as well as all other chemical, biological, and nuclear programmes, including any which it claims are for purposes not related to weapon production or material;

4. Decides that false statements or omissions in the declarations submitted by Iraq pursuant to this resolution and failure by Iraq at any time to comply with, and cooperate fully in the implementation of, this resolution shall constitute a further material breach of Iraq's obligations and will be reported to the Council for assessment in accordance with paragraphs 11 and 12 below;

5. Decides that Iraq shall provide UNMOVIC and the IAEA immediate, unimpeded, unconditional, and unrestricted access to any and all, including underground, areas, facilities, buildings, equipment, records, and means of transport which they wish to inspect, as well as immediate, unimpeded, unrestricted, and private access to all officials and other persons whom UNMOVIC or the IAEA wish to interview in the mode or location of UNMOVIC's or the IAEA's choice pursuant to any aspect of their mandates; further decides that UNMOVIC and the IAEA may at their discretion conduct interviews inside or outside of Iraq, may facilitate the travel of those interviewed and family members outside of Iraq, and that, at the sole discretion of UNMOVIC and the IAEA, such interviews may occur without the presence of observers from the Iraqi Government; and instructs UNMOVIC and requests the IAEA to resume inspections no later than 45 days following adoption of this resolution and to update the Council 60 days thereafter;

6. Endorses the 8 October 2002 letter from the Executive Chairman of UNMOVIC and the Director-General of the IAEA to General Al-Saadi of the Government of Iraq, which is annexed hereto, and decides that the contents of the letter shall be binding upon Iraq;

7. Decides further that, in view of the prolonged interruption by Iraq of the presence of UNMOVIC and the IAEA and in order for them to accomplish the tasks set forth in this resolution and all previous relevant resolutions and notwithstanding prior understandings, the Council hereby establishes the following revised or additional authorities, which shall be binding upon Iraq, to facilitate their work in Iraq:
- UNMOVIC and the IAEA shall determine the composition of their inspection teams and ensure that these teams are composed of the most qualified and experienced experts available;
- All UNMOVIC and IAEA personnel shall enjoy the privileges and immunities, corresponding to those of experts on mission, provided in the Convention on Privileges and Immunities of the United Nations and the Agreement on the Privileges and Immunities of the IAEA;
- UNMOVIC and the IAEA shall have unrestricted rights of entry into and out of Iraq, the right to free, unrestricted, and immediate movement to and from inspection sites, and the right to inspect any sites and buildings, including immediate, unimpeded, unconditional, and unrestricted access to Presidential Sites equal to that at other sites, notwithstanding the provisions of resolution 1154 (1998) of 2 March 1998;
- UNMOVIC and the IAEA shall have the right to be provided by Iraq the names of all personnel currently and formerly associated with Iraq's chemical, biological, nuclear, and bal-

listic missile programmes and the associated research, development, and production facilities;
- Security of UNMOVIC and IAEA facilities shall be ensured by sufficient United Nations security guards;
- UNMOVIC and the IAEA shall have the right to declare, for the purposes of freezing a site to be inspected, exclusion zones, including surrounding areas and transit corridors, in which Iraq will suspend ground and aerial movement so that nothing is changed in or taken out of a site being inspected;
- UNMOVIC and the IAEA shall have the free and unrestricted use and landing of fixed- and rotary-winged aircraft, including manned and unmanned reconnaissance vehicles;
- UNMOVIC and the IAEA shall have the right at their sole discretion verifiably to remove, destroy, or render harmless all prohibited weapons, subsystems, components, records, materials, and other related items, and the right to impound or close any facilities or equipment for the production thereof; and
- UNMOVIC and the IAEA shall have the right to free import and use of equipment or materials for inspections and to seize and export any equipment, materials, or documents taken during inspections, without search of UNMOVIC or IAEA personnel or official or personal baggage;

8. Decides further that Iraq shall not take or threaten hostile acts directed against any representative or personnel of the United Nations or the IAEA or of any Member State taking action to uphold any Council resolution;

9. Requests the Secretary-General immediately to notify Iraq of this resolution, which is binding on Iraq; demands that Iraq confirm within seven days of that notification its intention to comply fully with this resolution; and demands further that Iraq cooperate immediately, unconditionally, and actively with UNMOVIC and the IAEA;

10. Requests all Member States to give full support to UNMOVIC and the IAEA in the discharge of their mandates, including by providing any information related to prohibited programmes or other aspects of their mandates, including on Iraqi attempts since 1998 to acquire prohibited items, and by recommending sites to be inspected, persons to be interviewed, conditions of such interviews, and data to be collected, the results of which shall be reported to the Council by UNMOVIC and the IAEA;

11. Directs the Executive Chairman of UNMOVIC and the Director-General of the IAEA to report immediately to the Council any interference by Iraq with inspection activities, as well as any failure by Iraq to comply with its disarmament obligations, including its obligations regarding inspections under this resolution;

12. Decides to convene immediately upon receipt of a report in accordance with paragraphs 4 or 11 above, in order to consider the situation and the need for full compliance with all of the relevant Council resolutions in order to secure international peace and security;

13. Recalls, in that context, that the Council has repeatedly warned Iraq that it will face serious consequences as a result of its continued violations of its obligations;

14. Decides to remain seized of the matter.

Annex:

Text of Blix/El-Baradei letter

H.E. General Amir H. Al-Saadi
Advisor
Presidential Office
Baghdad
Iraq

8 October 2002

Dear General Al-Saadi,

During our recent meeting in Vienna, we discussed practical arrangements that are prerequisites for the resumption of inspections in Iraq by UNMOVIC and the IAEA. As you recall, at the end of our meeting in Vienna we agreed on a statement which listed some of the principal results achieved, particularly Iraq's acceptance of all the rights of inspection provided for in all of the relevant Security Council resolutions. This acceptance was stated to be without any conditions attached.

During our 3 October 2002 briefing to the Security Council, members of the Council suggested that we prepare a written document on all of the conclusions we reached in Vienna. This letter lists those conclusions and seeks your confirmation thereof. We shall report accordingly to the Security Council.

In the statement at the end of the meeting, it was clarified that UNMOVIC and the IAEA will be granted immediate, unconditional and unrestricted access to sites, including what was termed "sensitive sites" in the past.

As we noted, however, eight presidential sites have been the subject of special procedures under a Memorandum of Understanding of 1998. Should these sites be subject, as all other sites, to immediate, unconditional and unrestricted access, UNMOVIC and the IAEA would conduct inspections there with the same professionalism.

We confirm our understanding that UNMOVIC and the IAEA have the right to determine the number of inspectors required for access to any particular site. This determination will be made on the basis of the size and complexity of the site being inspected. We also confirm that Iraq will be informed of the designation of additional sites, i.e. sites not declared by Iraq or previously inspected by either UNSCOM or the IAEA, through a Notification of Inspection (NIS) provided upon arrival of the inspectors at such sites.

Iraq will ensure that no proscribed material, equipment, records or other relevant items will be destroyed except in the presence of UNMOVIC and/or IAEA inspectors, as appropriate, and at their request.

UNMOVIC and the IAEA may conduct interviews with any person in Iraq whom they believe may have information relevant to their mandate. Iraq will facilitate such interviews. It is for UNMOVIC and the IAEA to choose the mode and location for interviews.

The National Monitoring Directorate (NMD) will, as in the past, serve as the Iraqi counterpart for the inspectors. The Baghdad Ongoing Monitoring and Verification Centre (BOMVIC) will be maintained on the same premises and under the same conditions as was the former Baghdad Monitoring and Verification Centre. The NMD will make available services as before, cost free, for the refurbishment of the premises.

The NMD will provide free of cost: (a) escorts to facilitate access to sites to be inspected and communication with personnel to be interviewed; (b) a hotline for BOMVIC which will be staffed by an English speaking person on a 24 hour a day/seven days a week basis; (c) support in terms of personnel and ground transportation within the country, as requested; and (d) assistance in the movement of materials and equipment at inspectors' request (construction, excavation equipment, etc.). NMD will also ensure that escorts are available in the event of inspections outside normal working hours, including at night and on holidays.

Regional UNMOVIC/IAEA offices may be established, for example, in Basra and Mosul, for the use of their inspectors. For this purpose, Iraq will provide, without cost, adequate office buildings, staff accommodation, and appropriate escort personnel.

UNMOVIC and the IAEA may use any type of voice or data transmission, including satellite and/or inland networks, with or without encryption capability. UNMOVIC and the IAEA may also install equipment in the field with the capability for transmission of data directly to the BOMVIC, New York and Vienna (e.g. sensors, surveillance cameras). This will be facilitated by Iraq and there will be no interference by Iraq with UNMOVIC or IAEA communications.

Iraq will provide, without cost, physical protection of all surveillance equipment, and construct antennae for remote transmission of data, at the request of UNMOVIC and the IAEA. Upon request by UNMOVIC through the NMD, Iraq will allocate frequencies for communications equipment.

Iraq will provide security for all UNMOVIC and IAEA personnel. Secure and suitable accommodations will be designated at normal rates by Iraq for these personnel. For their part, UNMOVIC and the IAEA will require that their staff not stay at any accommodation other than those identified in consultation with Iraq.

On the use of fixed-wing aircraft for transport of personnel and equipment and for inspection purposes, it was clarified that aircraft used by UNMOVIC and IAEA staff arriving in Baghdad may land at Saddam International Airport. The points of departure of incoming aircraft will be decided by UNMOVIC. The Rasheed airbase will continue to be used for UNMOVIC and IAEA helicopter operations. UNMOVIC and Iraq will establish air liaison offices at the airbase. At both Saddam International Airport and Rasheed airbase, Iraq will provide the necessary support premises and facilities. Aircraft fuel will be provided by Iraq, as before, free of charge.

On the wider issue of air operations in Iraq, both fixed-wing and rotary, Iraq will guarantee the safety of air operations in its air space outside the no-fly zones. With regard to air operations in the no-fly zones, Iraq will take all steps within its control to ensure the safety of such operations.

Helicopter flights may be used, as needed, during inspections and for technical activities, such as gamma detection, without limitation in all parts of Iraq and without any area excluded. Helicopters may also be used for medical evacuation.

On the question of aerial imagery, UNMOVIC may wish to resume the use of U-2 or Mirage overflights. The relevant practical arrangements would be similar to those implemented in the past.

As before, visas for all arriving staff will be issued at the point of entry on the basis of the UN Laissez-Passer or UN Certificate; no other entry or exit formalities will be required. The aircraft passenger manifest will be provided one hour in advance of the arrival of the aircraft in Baghdad. There will be no searching of UNMOVIC or IAEA personnel or of official or personal baggage. UNMOVIC and the IAEA will ensure that their personnel respect the laws of Iraq restricting the export of certain items, for example, those related to Iraq's national cultural heritage. UNMOVIC and the IAEA may bring into, and remove from, Iraq all of the items and materials they require, including satellite phones and other equipment. With respect to samples, UNMOVIC and IAEA will, where feasible, split samples so that Iraq may receive a portion while another portion is kept for reference purposes. Where appropriate, the organizations will send the samples to more than one laboratory for analysis.

We would appreciate your confirmation of the above as a correct reflection of our talks in Vienna.

Naturally, we may need other practical arrangements when proceeding with inspections. We would expect in such matters, as with the above, Iraq's co-operation in all respect.

Yours sincerely,

(Signed)
Hans Blix
Executive Chairman
United Nations Monitoring Verification and
  Inspection Commission

(Signed)
Mohamed ElBaradei
Director General
International Atomic
Energy Agency

Source: *UN Press Office.*

2. DURBAN DECLARATION ON LAUNCH OF AFRICAN UNION

Published below is the declaration which marked the launch of the African Union (AU) as the successor to the Organisation of African Unity (OAU), Durban, South Africa, 10 July 2002.

We, the Heads of State and Government of the Assembly of the African Union, meeting in our inaugural session in Durban, South Africa, have adopted the following declaration in tribute to the Organisation of African Unity:

1. Thirty nine years ago, the Heads of State and Government of the then independent African Countries gathered in Addis Ababa, Ethiopia to found the Organisation of African Unity.

2. The main objectives for establishing the organisation were, inter alia, to rid the continent of the remaining vestiges of colonisation and apartheid; to promote unity and solidarity among African States; co-ordinate and intensify co-operation for development; for the defence of sovereignty, territorial integrity and consolidation of the independence of African States, as well as promoting international co-operation within the framework of the United Nations.

3. The common identity and unity of purpose engendered by the OAU, became a dynamic force at the service of the African people in the pursuit of the struggle for the total emancipation of the African Continent in the political, economic and social fields. Nowhere has that dynamic force proved more decisive than in the African struggle for decolonisation. Through the OAU Co-ordinating Committee for the Liberation of Africa, the Continent worked and spoke as one with undivided determination in forging an international consensus in support of the liberation struggle. Today, we celebrate a fully decolonised Africa and Apartheid has been consigned to the ignominy of history.

4. Pursuant to one of the major objective of its Charter, the OAU has strived to address Africa's problem of poverty and under development and adopted strategies in this regard, including the 1980 Lagos Plan of Action and the Final Act of Lagos which continue to be the blue print for Africa's integration and development.

5. In June 1991, the Treaty establishing the African Economic Community was signed and is now in force. The Treaty seeks to build the African Economic Community through a Common Market built on the Regional Economic Communities. Today, Regional Economic Communities are consolidating and proving to be engines for integration. ECCAS, SADC, COMESA, UMA, ECOWAS, IGAD and CENSAD are making great effort at economic development and integration as well as at promoting peace through conflict resolution in their region. We remain committed to continental and global co-operation including the strengthening of Afro-Arab co-operation.

6. In the political realm, the OAU Declaration on the Political and Socio-economic Situation in Africa and the Fundamental Changes taking place in the World of 1900, underscored Africa's resolve to seize the initiative, to determine its destiny and to address the challenges to peace, democracy and security. The Mechanism for Conflict Prevention, Management and Resolution that was established in 1993 was a practical expression of that determination to begin in earnest, the task of promoting peace and stability in Africa.

7. Through the Mechanism, the OAU has managed to address constructively many of the conflicts which have and continue to afflict our Continent. The Mechanism has made a funda-

mental difference, not only in its political significance of our determination to strive for peace, but more so in the practical framework it has provided for the continent to address conflicts and conflict situations.

8. The OAU has been on the vanguard in the promotion of the observance of human and people's rights. The OAU Charter on Human and People's Rights and the Grand Bay Declaration and Plan of Action on Human Rights are among the instruments adopted by the Organisation to promote human rights. Underlying these instruments is a determination to ensure that Africa responds to the challenge of observing, promoting and protecting human rights and the rule of Law.

9. The OAU has also responded to the yearning of the African people for greater political freedoms inherent in democratic government. To this effect, it was at the forefront in galvanising governments around a new determination to progressively place the people at the centre of decision making. The Charter on Popular Participation adopted in 1990 was a testimony to this new determination.

10. Today, Africa is firmly on the road to democratisation. In our Algiers decision on unconstitutional changes of Government and our Lomé Declaration on the Framework for an OAU Response to Unconstitutional Changes adopted in 1999 and 2000 respectively, we reiterated our determination to see Africa governed on the basis of democracy and by governments emanating from the will of the people expressed through transparent, free and fair elections.

11. Similarly, in our 2000 Solemn Declaration on the Conference on Security, Stability, Development and Co-operation, we agreed on fundamental principles to govern our co-operation in security, and development and in the promotion of Democracy and Good Governance in the Continent.

12. Through the OAU, Africa has been able to respond to the many other challenges it faces. Whether in the protection of the environment, in fighting international terrorism, in combating the scourge of the HIV/AIDS pandemic, malaria and tuberculosis or dealing with humanitarian issues such as refugees and displaced persons, landmines, small and light weapons among others, Africa has found collective action through the OAU.

13. We, the Heads of State and Government meeting in the inaugural session of the Assembly of our African Union, honour the founding leaders of the OAU and pay tribute to their tenacity, resilience and commitment to African Unity. They stood firm in the face of the divisive manipulations of the detractors of Africa and fought for the integrity of Africa and the human dignity of all the peoples of the continent. In the same vein, we pay tribute to all the Secretaries General and all the men and women who served the OAU with dedication and commitment.

14. As we hail the achievements of the OAU, we rededicate ourselves more resolutely to its principles and objectives and to the ideals of freedom, unity and development which the founding leaders sought to achieve in establishing the Organisation thirty-nine years ago. As we bid farewell to the OAU, we rededicate ourselves to its memory as a pioneer, a liberator, a unifier, an organiser, and the soul of our continent. We pledge to strive more resolutely in pursuing the ultimate goals of the OAU and in furthering the cause of Africa and its people under the African Union.

15. We reiterate our continuing commitment to the objectives of the African Union which was initiated at the fourth extraordinary session of the OAU Assembly of Heads of State and

Government in the Great Socialist People's Libyan Arab Jamahiriya and as embodied in our 9.9.99 Sirte Declaration. We further rededicate ourselves to the objectives on the New Partnership of Africa's Development (NEPAD), as a programme of the African Union for strengthening inter-African co-operation and integration in a globalising world and to overcome the prevalence of poverty and strive for a better quality of life for all the peoples of Africa.

16. We commit ourselves to urgently establish all institutional structures to advance the agenda of the African Union and call on all Member States to honour their political and financial commitments and to take all the necessary actions to give unwavering support to all the Union's initiatives aimed at promoting peace, security, stability, sustainable development, democracy and human rights in our continent.

17. In order to ensure the involvement of our peoples and their civil society organisations in the activities of the Union, we recommit ourselves to the early establishment of the Pan African Parliament and the Economic, Social and Cultural Council (ECOSOCC) as envisaged in the Constitutive Act of our Union.

18. We welcome and recognise the important contribution of the youth, women, business community, parliamentary representatives and civil society and call upon these stakeholders to continue participating fully as partners in the regeneration of the African Continent through the programmes of the African Union. We reaffirm, in particular, the pivotal role of women in all levels of society and recognise that the objectives of the African Union cannot be achieved without the full involvement and participation of women at all levels and structures of the Union.

19. We note the importance of continuing to co-operate with Africa's partners as well as regional and continental organisations in the furtherance of the objectives of the African Union.

20. As we enter a new era in the history of our continent, we commit ourselves to the principles and objectives that we set out in the Constitutive Act of our Union in order to ensure that our peoples live in peace and prosperity. We also rededicate ourselves to implementing all programmes, policies and decisions of the African Union.

Source: *African Union News Service.*

3. KEY OUTCOMES OF THE UN WORLD SUMMIT ON SUSTAINABLE DEVELOPMENT

Published below is an extract from the official summary of the outcomes of the United Nations World Summit on Sustainable Development, Johannesburg, South Africa, 26 August-4 September 2002.

The Summit reaffirmed sustainable development as a central element of the international agenda and gave new impetus to global action to fight poverty and protect the environment.

The understanding of sustainable development was broadened and strengthened as a result of the Summit, particularly the important linkages between poverty, the environment and the use of natural resources.

Governments agreed to and reaffirmed a wide range of concrete commitments and targets for action to achieve more effective implementation of sustainable development objectives.

Energy and sanitation issues were critical elements of the negotiations and outcomes to a greater degree than in previous international meetings on sustainable development.

Support for the establishment of a world solidarity fund for the eradication of poverty was a positive step forward.

Africa and NEPAD were identified for special attention and support by the international community to better focus efforts to address the development needs of Africa.

The views of civil society were given prominence at the Summit in recognition of the key role of civil society in implementing the outcomes and in promoting partnership initiatives. Over 8,000 civil society participants attended the Summit, reinforced by parallel events which included major groups, such as, NGOs, women, indigenous people, youth, farmers, trade unions, business leaders, the scientific and technological community and local authorities as well as Chief Justices from various countries.

The concept of partnerships between governments, business and civil society was given a large boost by the Summit and the Plan of Implementation. Over 220 partnerships (with $235 million in resources) were identified in advance of the Summit and around 60 partnerships were announced during the Summit by a variety of countries.

Key Commitments, Targets and Timetables from the Johannesburg Plan of Implementation

1. Poverty Eradication

(a) Halve, by the year 2015, the proportion of the world's people whose income is less than $1 a day and the proportion of people who suffer from hunger *(reaffirmation of Millennium Development Goals).*
(b) By 2020, achieve a significant improvement in the lives of at least 100 million slum dwellers, as proposed in the "Cities without slums" initiative *(reaffirmation of Millennium Development Goal).*
(c) Establish a world solidarity fund to eradicate poverty and to promote social and human development in the developing countries.

2. Water and Sanitation

(a) Halve, by the year 2015, the proportion of people without access to safe drinking water *(reaffirmation of Millennium Development Goal)*.
(b) Halve, by the year 2015, the proportion of people who do not have access to basic sanitation.

3. Sustainable Production and Consumption

Encourage and promote the development of a 10-year framework of programmes to accelerate the shift towards sustainable consumption and production.

4. Energy

Renewable energy
(a) Diversify energy supply and substantially increase the global share of renewable energy sources in order to increase its contribution to total energy supply.

Access to Energy
(b) Improve access to reliable, affordable, economically viable, socially acceptable and environmentally sound energy services and resources, sufficient to achieve the Millennium Development Goals, including the goal of halving the proportion of people in poverty by 2015.

Energy Markets
(c) Remove market distortions including the restructuring of taxes and the phasing out of harmful subsidies.
(d) Support efforts to improve the functioning, transparency and information about energy markets with respect to both supply and demand, with the aim of achieving greater stability and to ensure consumer access to energy services.

Energy efficiency
(e) Establish domestic programmes for energy efficiency with the support of the international community. Accelerate the development and dissemination of energy efficiency and energy conservation technologies, including the promotion of research and development.

5. Chemicals

(a) Aim, by 2020, to use and produce chemicals in ways that do not lead to significant adverse effects on human health and the environment.
(b) Renew the commitment to the sound management of chemicals and of hazardous wastes throughout their life cycle.
(c) Promote the ratification and implementation of relevant international instruments on chemicals and hazardous waste, including the Rotterdam Convention so that it can enter into force by 2003 and the Stockholm Convention so that it can enter into force by 2004.
(d) Further develop a strategic approach to international chemicals management, based on the Bahia Declaration and Priorities for Action beyond 2000, by 2005.
(e) Encourage countries to implement the new globally harmonized system for the classification and labeling of chemicals as soon as possible, with a view to having the system fully operational by 2008.

6. Management of the natural resource base

Water
(a) Develop integrated water resources management and water efficiency plans by 2005.

Oceans and fisheries
(b) Encourage the application by 2010 of the ecosystem approach for the sustainable development of the oceans.
(c) On an urgent basis and where possible by 2015, maintain or restore depleted fish stocks to levels that can produce the maximum sustainable yield.
(d) Put into effect the FAO international plans of action by the agreed dates:
 - for the management of fishing capacity by 2005; and
 - to prevent, deter and eliminate illegal, unreported and unregulated fishing by 2004.
(e) Develop and facilitate the use of diverse approaches and tools, including the ecosystem approach, the elimination of destructive fishing practices, the establishment of marine protected areas consistent with international law and based on scientific information, including representative networks by 2012.
(f) Establish by 2004 a regular process under the United Nations for global reporting and assessment of the state of the marine environment.
(g) Eliminate subsidies that contribute to illegal, unreported and unregulated fishing and to overcapacity.

Atmosphere
(h) Facilitate implementation of the Montreal Protocol on Substances that Deplete the Ozone Layer by ensuring adequate replenishment of its fund by 2003/2005.
(i) Improve access by developing countries to alternatives to ozone-depleting substances by 2010, and assist them in complying with the phase-out schedule under the Montreal Protocol.

Biodiversity
(j) Achieve by 2010 a significant reduction in the current rate of loss of biological diversity.

Forests
(k) Accelerate implementation of the IPF/IFF proposals for action by countries and by the Collaborative Partnership on Forests, and intensify efforts on reporting to the United Nations Forum on Forests, to contribute to an assessment of progress in 2005.

7. Corporate responsibility

Actively promote corporate responsibility and accountability, including through the full development and effective implementation of intergovernmental agreements and measures, international initiatives and public-private partnerships, and appropriate national regulations.

8. Health

(a) Enhance health education with the objective of achieving improved health literacy on a global basis by 2010.
(b) Reduce, by 2015, mortality rates for infants and children under 5 by two thirds, and maternal mortality rates by three quarters, of the prevailing rate in 2000 *(reaffirmation of Millennium Development Goal).*

(c) Reduce HIV prevalence among young men and women aged 15-24 by 25 per cent in the most affected countries by 2005 and globally by 2010, as well as combat malaria, tuberculosis and other diseases (*reaffirmation of General Assembly resolution*).

9. Sustainable development of small island developing States

(a) Undertake initiatives by 2004 aimed at implementing the Global Programme of Action for the Protection of the Marine Environment from Land-based Activities to reduce, prevent and control waste and pollution and their health-related impacts.
(b) Develop community-based initiatives on sustainable tourism by 2004.
(c) Support the availability of adequate, affordable and environmentally sound energy services for the sustainable development of small island developing States, including through strengthening efforts on energy supply and services by 2004.
(d) Review implementation of the Barbados Programme of Action for the Sustainable Development of Small Island Developing States in 2004.

10. Sustainable development for Africa

(a) Improve sustainable agricultural productivity and food security in accordance with the Millennium Development Goals, in particular to halve by 2015 the proportion of people who suffer from hunger.
(b) Support African countries in developing and implementing food security strategies by 2005.
(c) Support Africa's efforts to implement NEPAD objectives on energy, which seek to secure access for at least 35 per cent of the African population within 20 years, especially in rural areas.

11. Means of implementation

(a) Ensure that, by 2015, all children will be able to complete a full course of primary schooling and that girls and boys will have equal access to all levels of education relevant to national needs (*reaffirmation of Millennium Development Goal*).
(b) Eliminate gender disparity in primary and secondary education by 2005 (*reaffirmation of Dakar Framework for Action on Education for All*).
(c) Recommend to the UN General Assembly that it consider adopting a decade of education for sustainable development, starting in 2005.

12. Institutional Framework for sustainable development

(a) Adopt new measures to strengthen institutional arrangements for sustainable development at international, regional and national levels.
(b) Enhance the role of the Commission on Sustainable Development, including through reviewing and monitoring progress in the implementation of Agenda 21 and fostering coherence of implementation, initiatives and partnerships.
(c) Facilitate and promote the integration of the environmental, social and economic dimensions of sustainable development into the work programs UN regional commissions.
(d) Establish an effective, transparent and regular inter-agency coordination mechanism on ocean and coastal issues within the United Nations system.
(e) Take immediate steps to make progress in the formulation and elaboration of national strategies for sustainable development and begin their implementation by 2005.

Source: *UN Press Office*.

4. PREAMBLE TO THE CONSTITUTION OF THE DEMOCRATIC REPUBLIC OF EAST TIMOR

Published below is the preamble to the Constitution of the Democratic Republic of East Timor (Timor Leste) which came into effect on 20 May 2002.

Following the liberation of the Timorese People from colonisation and illegal occupation of the Maubere Motherland by foreign powers, the independence of East Timor, proclaimed on the 28th of November 1975 by Frente Revolucionária do Timor-Leste Independente (FRETILIN), is recognised internationally on the 20th of May 2002.

The preparation and adoption of the Constitution of the Democratic Republic of East Timor is the culmination of the historical resistance of the Timorese People intensified following the invasion of the 7th of December 1975.

The struggle waged against the enemy, initially under the leadership of FRETILIN, gave way to more comprehensive forms of political participation, particularly in the wake of the establishment of the National Council of the Maubere Resistance (CNRM) in 1987 and the National Council of Timorese Resistance (CNRT) in 1998.

The Resistance was divided into three fronts.

The armed front was carried out by the glorious Forças Armadas de Libertação Nacional de Timor-Leste (FALINTIL) whose historical undertaking is to be praised.

The action of the clandestine front, astutely unleashed in hostile territory, involved the sacrifice of thousands of lives of women and men, especially the youth, who fought with abnegation for freedom and independence.

The diplomatic front, harmoniously carried out all over the world, enabled the paving of the way for definitive liberation.

In its cultural and humane perspective, the Catholic Church in East Timor has always been able to take on the suffering of all the People with dignity, placing itself on their side in the defence of their most fundamental rights.

Ultimately, the present Constitution represents a heart-felt tribute to all martyrs of the Motherland.

Thus, the Members of the Constituent Assembly, in their capacity as legitimate representatives of the People elected on the 30th of August 2001,

Based on the results of the referendum of the 30th of August 1999 organised under the auspices of the United Nations which confirmed the self-determined will for independence;

Fully conscious of the need to build a democratic and institutional culture proper appropriate to a State based on the rule of law where respect for the Constitution, for the laws and for democratically elected institutions constitute its unquestionable foundation;

Interpreting the profound sentiments, the aspirations and the faith in God of the People of East Timor;

Solemnly reaffirm their determination to fight all forms of tyranny, oppression, social, cultural or religious domination and segregation, to defend national independence, to respect and guarantee human rights and the fundamental rights of the citizen, to ensure the principle of the separation of powers in the organisation of the State, and to establish the essential rules of multi-party democracy, with a view to building a just and prosperous nation and developing a society of solidarity and fraternity.

The Constituent Assembly, meeting in plenary session on the 22nd of March 2002, approves and decrees the following Constitution of the Democratic Republic of East Timor:

5. UNITED KINGDOM LABOUR GOVERNMENT
(as at 31 December 2002)

Members of the Cabinet

Prime Minister, First Lord of the Treasury and Minister for the Civil Service	Rt. Hon. Tony Blair, MP
Deputy Prime Minister	Rt. Hon. John Prescott, MP
Chancellor of the Exchequer	Rt. Hon. Gordon Brown, MP
President of the Council and Leader of the House of Commons	Rt. Hon. Robin Cook, MP
Lord Chancellor	Rt. Hon. The Lord Irvine of Lairg QC
Secretary of State for Foreign and Commonwealth Affairs	Rt. Hon. Jack Straw, MP
Secretary of State for the Home Department	Rt. Hon. David Blunkett, MP
Secretary of State for Environment, Food and Rural Affairs	Rt. Hon. Margaret Beckett, MP
Secretary of State for International Development	Rt. Hon. Clare Short, MP
Secretary of State for Transport	Rt. Hon. Alistair Darling, MP
Secretary of State for Health	Rt. Hon. Alan Milburn, MP
Minister without Portfolio and Party Chair	Rt. Hon. Dr John Reid, MP
Secretary of State for Northern Ireland	Rt. Hon. Paul Murphy, MP
Secretary of State for Defence	Rt. Hon. Geoff Hoon, MP
Secretary of State for Work and Pensions	Rt. Hon. Andrew Smith, MP
Secretary of State for Scotland	Rt. Hon. Helen Liddell, MP
Leader of the House of Lords	Rt. Hon. The Lord Williams of Mostyn, QC
Secretary of State for Trade and Industry	Rt. Hon. Patricia Hewitt, MP
Secretary of State for Culture, Media and Sport	Rt. Hon. Tessa Jowell, MP
Parliamentary Secretary, Treasury and Chief Whip	Rt. Hon. Hilary Armstrong, MP
Secretary of State for Education and Skills	Rt. Hon. Charles Clarke, MP
Chief Secretary to the Treasury	Rt. Hon. Paul Boateng, MP
Secretary of State for Wales	Rt. Hon. Peter Hain, MP

Also attending Cabinet

Minister of State for Work	Rt. Hon. Nick Brown, MP
Lords Chief Whip and Captain of the Gentlemen at Arms	Lord Grocott

Other Senior Ministers

Minister of State for Local Government and the Regions	Rt. Hon. Nick Raynsford, MP
Minister of State for Housing and Planning	Rt. Hon. Lord Rooker
Minister of State for Social Exclusion and Deputy Minister for Women	Barbara Roche, MP
Minister for the Cabinet Office and Chancellor of the Duchy of Lancaster	Rt. Hon. Lord Macdonald of Tradeston
Minister of State in the Cabinet Office	Douglas Alexander, MP
Paymaster General	Dawn Primarolo, MP
Financial Secretary to the Treasury	Ruth Kelly, MP
Economic Secretary to the Treasury	John Healey, MP

Parliamentary Secretary in the Privy Council Office	Ben Bradshaw, MP
Minister of State for Trade	Rt. Hon. Baroness Symons of Vernham Dean
Minister for Europe	Dr Denis MacShane, MP
Minister of State for Police and Crime Reduction	Rt. Hon. John Denham, MP
Minister of State for the Criminal Justice System	Lord Falconer of Thoroton, QC
Minister of State for Citizenship and Immigration	Bev Hughes, MP
Minister of State for the Environment	Rt. Hon. Michael Meacher, MP
Minister of State for Rural Affairs	Rt. Hon. Alun Michael, MP
Minister for Pensions	Rt. Hon. Ian McCartney, MP
Minister of State for Transport	Rt. Hon. John Spellar, MP
Minister of State for Health	Rt. Hon. John Hutton, MP
Minister of State for Health	Jacqui Smith, MP
Minister of State for Northern Ireland	Jane Kennedy, MP
Minister of State for Defence	Rt. Hon. Adam Ingram, MP
Minister of State for E-Commerce	Stephen Timms, MP
Minister of State for Energy	Brian Wilson, MP
Minister of State for Employment, Manufacturing, and Regions	Alan Johnson, MP
Minister of State for Schools	David Miliband, MP
Minister of State for Universities and Lifelong Learning	Margaret Hodge, MP
Minister of State for Sport	Rt. Hon. Richard Caborn, MP
Minister of State for the Arts	Rt. Hon. Baroness Blackstone

Law Officers

Attorney General	Rt. Hon. Lord Goldsmith QC
Solicitor General	Rt. Hon. Harriet Harman, QC, MP
Advocate General for Scotland	Dr Lynda Clark, QC, MP

6. UNITED STATES REPUBLICAN ADMINISTRATION
(as at 31 December 2002)

Members of the Cabinet

President	George W. Bush
Vice President	Richard B. Cheney
Secretary of State	Colin Powell
Secretary of the Treasury	John Snow
Secretary of Defence	Donald Rumsfeld
Secretary of the Interior	Gale Norton
Secretary of Agriculture	Ann Veneman
Secretary of Commerce	Donald Evans
Secretary of Housing and Urban Development	Mel Martinez
Secretary of Transportation	Norman Mineta
Secretary of Health and Human Services	Tommy Thompson
Attorney General	John Ashcroft
Secretary of Labour	Elaine Chao
Secretary of Energy	Spencer Abraham
Secretary of Education	Roderick Paige
Secretary of Veterans' Affairs	Anthony J. Principi

Cabinet Rank Members

President's Chief of Staff	Andrew H. Card Jr
Administrator of Environmental Protection Agency	Christine Todd Whitman
Director of Office of Homeland Security	Tom Ridge
Director of Office of Management and Budget	Mitchell E. Daniels Jr
Director of Office of National Drug Control Policy	John Walters
United States Trade Representative	Robert B. Zoellick

Other Leading Executive Branch Officials

Chairman of Council of Economic Advisers	R. Glen Hubbard
National Security Adviser	Condoleeza Rice
Director of Central Intelligence Agency	George J. Tenet
Ambassador to United Nations	John D. Negroponte
Director of National Economic Council	Stephen Friedman
Director of Small Business Administration	Hector V. Barreto

7. INTERNATIONAL COMPARISONS: POPULATION, GDP AND GROWTH

The following table gives population, gross domestic product (GDP) and growth data for the main member states of the Organisation for Economic Co-operation and Development plus selected other countries. (Source: World Bank, Washington)

	Population 2001mn	Avg. annual %growth 1990-2001	GDP ($000mn) 2000	GDP ($000mn) 2001	GDP growth % 2001	Avg. annual %growth 1990-2001
Algeria	30.9	1.9	53.8	53.0	-1.5	2.0
Argentina	37.5	1.3	285.5	268.8	-5.8	3.7
Australia	19.4	1.2	394.0	368.6	-6.5	4.0
Austria	8.1	0.5	191.0	188.7	-1.2	2.1
Bangladesh	133.4	1.8	47.9	46.7	-2.5	4.9
Belgium	10.3	0.3	231.0	227.6	-1.5	2.1
Brazil	172.6	1.4	587.6	502.5	-14.5	2.8
Canada	31.0	1.0	689.5	677.2	-1.8	3.0
Chile	15.4	1.5	70.7	63.5	-10.1	6.4
China	1,271.9	1.0	1,080.0	1,159.0	7.3	10.0
Colombia	43.0	1.9	82.8	83.4	0.7	2.7
Denmark	5.4	0.4	160.8	162.8	1.3	2.5
Egypt	65.2	2.0	98.3	97.5	-0.8	4.6
Finland	5.2	0.4	119.8	122.0	1.8	4.5
France	59.2	0.4	1,286.3	1,302.8	1.3	1.8
Germany	82.2	0.3	1,870.1	1,874.0	0.2	1.5
Greece	10.6	0.4	112.0	116.3	3.9	2.3
Hungary	10.2	-0.2	45.7	52.4	14.5	1.9
India	1,033.4	1.8	479.4	477.6	-0.4	5.9
Indonesia	213.6	1.6	153.3	145.3	-5.2	3.8
Iran	64.7	1.6	99.0	118.9	20.1	3.6
Irish Republic	3.8	0.8	94.4	101.2	7.2	7.6
Italy	57.7	0.2	1,068.5	1,090.9	2.1	1.6
Japan	127.1	0.3	4,677.1	4,245.2	-9.2	1.3
Kenya	30.7	2.5	10.4	10.4	0.1	2.0
South Korea	47.6	1.0	457.2	422.2	-7.7	5.7
Malaysia	23.8	2.4	89.3	87.5	-2.0	6.5
Mexico	99.4	1.6	574.5	617.8	7.5	3.1
Netherlands	16.0	0.6	364.9	375.0	2.7	2.8
New Zealand	3.8	1.0	50.0	48.3	-3.4	2.9
Nigeria	129.9	2.7	41.2	41.2	-0.03	2.5
Norway	4.5	0.6	149.3	165.5	10.8	3.5
Pakistan	141.5	2.5	61.7	59.6	-3.4	3.7
Philippines	77.0	2.1	75.2	71.4	-5.0	3.3
Poland	38.7	0.1	158.9	174.6	9.9	4.5
Portugal	10.2	0.3	103.9	108.5	4.4	2.7
Russia	144.8	-0.2	251.1	310.0	23.4	-3.7
South Africa	43.2	1.9	125.9	113.3	-10.0	2.1
Spain	39.5	0.2	555.0	577.5	4.1	2.6
Sweden	8.9	0.3	227.4	210.1	-7.6	2.0
Switzerland	7.2	0.6	240.3	247.4	2.9	0.9
Thailand	61.2	0.9	121.9	114.8	-5.9	3.8
Turkey	66.2	1.5	199.9	147.6	-26.2	3.3
United Kingdom	59.8	0.4	1,413.4	1,406.3	-0.5	2.6
USA	284.0	1.2	9,882.8	10,171.4	2.9	3.5
Venezuela	24.6	2.1	120.5	124.9	3.7	1.5
Vietnam	79.5	1.7	31.3	32.9	5.0	7.6

XVIII OBITUARY

Anger, Per (b. 1913), Swedish diplomat who, as a member of the Swedish legation in Budapest when the Germans invaded Hungary in 1944, helped to save many thousands of Jews from concentration camps. Born in Gothenburg, Anger studied law at the universities of Stockholm and Uppsala and within a few months of graduating was sent as a trainee to the legation in Berlin, where he learnt of the impending German invasion of Denmark and Norway. He was posted to Budapest in 1942, where his main initial task was the promotion of Swedish trade with Hungary. Following the German invasion and the imposition of a Fascist government pursuing Nazi policies, Anger became almost totally concerned with the issuing of provisional Swedish passports to Jews, identifying them as Swedish citizens and offering them some protection against arrest and deportation. As the work of this rescue mission increased, the legation was joined by Raoul Wallenberg, sent by an international delegation to lead the operation. Wallenberg disappeared soon after Soviet troops arrived in Budapest and was never seen again, though Anger spent much time in later years trying to find him and making a number of direct appeals to Soviet leaders who, he suspected, knew of Wallenberg's fate. Anger continued with his diplomatic career after the war, serving as his country's ambassador to Australia, and later to Canada. He received a "Righteous among the Nations" award from Israel for risking his life rescuing Jews during the war, and received other distinctions for his work with Wallenberg from Hungary, the USA, and from his own country. Died 26 August.

Annenberg, Walter (b. 1908), US publisher and philanthropist who was, from 1969-75, US Ambassador to the UK. Born in Milwaukee, Walter was the only son of eight children of Jewish immigrants from Prussia. His father, Moses Annenberg, established a publishing empire, Triangle Publications, which included the purchase of the *Philadelphia Inquirer*, by dubious means which led eventually to imprisonment for criminal tax evasion. On his father's death Walter Annenberg inherited a business deep in debt but turned it around so successfully that he soon became one of his country's wealthiest businessmen. He used his money to support many charities and to establish a life-style that included the acquisition of numerous works of art, including paintings by Monet, Renoir, Van Gogh, Cézanne and Picasso, a collection which he left to the Metropolitan Museum in New York. As an influential publisher he was also courted by politicians, one of whom, Richard Nixon, became a friend whose political career Annenberg supported financially as well as through his newspapers and magazines. His reward, when Nixon became President, was to be sent to the UK as Ambassador, an appointment which had an inauspicious beginning in London. A television documentary filmed the presentation of his credentials, when his heavily formal and circumlocutory response to a simple question from the Queen made him something of a laughing stock. He proved to be a hard-working and popular ambassador, however, generously contributing to many British institutions and leaving behind an embassy that had been stylishly refurbished at his own expense. On his departure the Queen awarded him an honorary KBE.

Back in his own country he sold Triangle Publications to Rupert Murdoch and concentrated on increasing his wealth and his philanthropy. Died 1 October.

Augstein, Rudolf (b. 1923) was founder, publisher and editor-in-chief of the influential German news magazine *Der Spiegel*. Born in Hanover, he trained as a journalist on a local paper but was soon called up and sent to fight with the artillery on the eastern front, where he was wounded and eventually taken prisoner by the US forces. Returning to Hanover after the war he was appointed by the British occupation forces to work on a news magazine, *Dies Woche*, and in 1947 was allowed to buy the publication, which was renamed *Der Spiegel* and moved to Hamburg. Augstein liked to refer to his magazine as the "artillery of democracy", and it quickly established a reputation for hard-hitting investigative journalism. Its first major crisis came in 1962, when the magazine upset Franz Josef Strauss, then Minister of Defence, by running a story about a NATO military exercise which revealed that there was little chance of the West effectively repelling a Soviet attack in Europe, which Strauss wanted to counter by acquiring nuclear weapons. The offices of *Der Spiegel* were raided by the police and three staff arrested, including Augstein, who was held in prison while allegations that he was publishing state secrets and threatening German security were investigated. After nearly four months he was released without charge, partly as a result of growing public pressure in support of press freedom. The success of *Der Spiegel* was now assured, the magazine soon selling more than a million copies a week and making its proprietor a wealthy man. Augstein developed other media interests and was elected to the Bundestag (the lower chamber of the legislature), but resigned after a few weeks and continued to be active in providing ideas and opinions to *Der Spiegel*, contributing columns even after becoming blind. He was married five times. Died 7 November.

Bagnall, Field Marshal Sir Nigel, GCB, CVO, MC and Bar (b. 1927), was Chief of the General Staff from 1985-88 and a popular soldier with a distinguished service record. Born in India in 1927, Bagnall was educated at Wellington before joining the Army at the age of 18. Commissioned in the Green Howards in 1946 he transferred to the Parachute Regiment to serve in Palestine during the Stern Gang terrorist campaign. In 1950 he rejoined the Green Howards and was posted to Malaya, where he won the Military Cross for his bravery in fighting terrorists in the jungle, later winning a Bar to his medal in the same campaign. He subsequently served in the Suez Canal Zone and in Cyprus, where he was again active in counter-insurgency operations, and in Germany, where he commanded the Royal Armoured Corps 1st (British) Corps and developed a more flexible approach to the deployment of armoured units. This led to a defence fellowship at Balliol College, Oxford, before he returned to Germany in command of the 4th Armoured Division with the Rhine Army. In 1983 he was promoted to General in command of NATO's Northern Army Group. He was brought back to London in 1985 as Chief of the General Staff, to find himself at once concerned with the problems created by defence cuts and political reforms involving the centralisation of power in Whitehall. He worked successfully to remove some of the more impractical proposals, but his strongly expressed arguments were not always appreciated by his political superiors. In his retirement he wrote a history of the Punic Wars (published in 1991). Died 8 April.

Balaguer Ricardo, Joaquin, (b. 1907), President of the Dominican Republic for six terms between 1960 and 1996. Born in the province of Santiago, Balaguer studied law at the University of Santo Domingo and at the Sorbonne in Paris. He joined the foreign service in Madrid 1932-35 before returning home as Under-Secretary of Foreign Affairs. He was Ambassador to Colombia from 1940-46 and Alternate Representative to the UN from 1947 until returning to his university as Professor of Law and Rector of the university. In 1954 he was brought back into politics by the country's dictator, Rafael Trujillo, who appointed him Minister of Foreign Affairs in 1955, Minister for Education and the Arts in 1956, and Vice-President of the Republic in 1957, when Trujillo's son Hector was nominally President. In 1960, when Hector Trujillo resigned, Balaguer became President. When the dictator was assassinated in 1961 Balaguer emerged as the Republic's dominant political figure, sending the remaining Trujillo family into exile. He founded the Reform Party and organised a democratic election, but lost it to Juan Bosch, who was deposed after seven months by a military coup supported by the US government, nervous of his apparent leanings towards Cuban communism. Balaguer returned to win the presidency in the election of 1966. His new policies of supporting business, privatising properties seized from the Trujillos, setting up welfare programmes and securing US aid, proved popular and he went on to win two more elections before being defeated in 1978. He returned to power again in 1986 and won two further elections in 1990 and 1994, finally leaving office in 1996, when he formed a new party with his old opponent, Bosch. Their candidate won the election. Although frail and blind Balaguer made a further attempt to regain power in the election of 2000, at the age of 93, but he finished in third place. Died 14 July.

Banzer Suárez, General Hugo (b. 1926), President of Bolivia who won power first as a military dictator and subsequently as a democratic politician. Born in Santa Cruz, the son of a farmer and grandson of a German immigrant, Banzer was educated at the military school in La Paz and at staff college in Argentina. His first experience of politics came in 1964, when he was appointed Minister of Education and Culture in the military government run by General René Barrientos. He served as military attaché, first in Argentina and then in the USA, before taking over as director of the military school in La Paz. In 1971 he was a leading member of the military junta that seized power from the government of General Juan Jose Torres, and became President for the first time. During his seven years as dictator Banzer presided over a period of growing prosperity for Bolivia, encouraging free enterprise and attracting foreign investment, but he did not tolerate serious opposition. He held elections in 1978, which he won, but they were generally seen as fraudulent and there was no great surprise when he was ousted by another military coup. In 1980 he founded the National Democratic Action Party and in 1985 won the presidential election, though deprived of office by the electoral system then in force. He stood as presidential candidate four more times, finally being successful in 1997. His second term as President was preoccupied with a largely successful attempt to stop the illegal growth of coca, which formed the basis of cocaine, and with the development of the country's large reserves of natural gas. Illness forced him to hand over the presidency to his deputy in 2001. Died 5 May.

Bedford, Duke of (b. 1917) was a pioneer among British aristocrats opening their historic houses to members of the public and adding new attractions to increase the number of visitors. Born in London as John Robert Russell, he was known to family and friends as Ian and had an unconventional upbringing. He never went to school but was educated by a succession of tutors, and though he had the title of Lord Howland was not aware that he was heir to the dukedom until he was 16. Disinherited by his father in 1939 for marrying a divorcée, he worked for a time as a rent collector, enlisted in the Coldstream Guards when war came but was soon invalided out, then worked briefly as a reporter on the *Sunday Express*. In 1940, when his father succeeded as 12th Duke, Howland became Marquess of Tavistock, but gave up work to look after his sick wife, who died in 1945. His second marriage, to a daughter of Lord Churston, brought a reconciliation with his father, but soon after the Tavistocks had settled in South Africa his father died in a shooting accident and Tavistock returned to the ancestral home of Woburn Abbey as 13th Duke, to be faced with death duties of some UK£5 million. Determined to retain Woburn, he sold some of the family's estates in London, opened the Abbey and its treasures, and added to the grounds a fun fair, wild animal safari park, and souvenir shop. His marketing skills kept the stately home in the family, but after 20 years Bedford decided to hand it on to his son and heir and went to live abroad with his third wife. Died 25 October.

Belaûnde Terry, Fernando (b. 1913), twice President of Peru and champion of democracy in a country where military rule had become the norm. Born in Lima, Belaûnde was educated locally before going to France and the USA to study architecture. He established a successful practice in Lima, but was diverted into politics in 1943, when he became a founder member of the National Democratic Front. He was elected to the Chamber of Deputies in 1945 but returned to architecture following the military coup of 1948. Eight years later he formed his own political party, the Popular Action Party, running unsuccessfully in two presidential election campaigns before finally becoming President in 1963, having won some 40 per cent of the popular vote and the support of the armed forces. He at once launched into an extensive programme of social, economic and land reforms, but the cost of his grand schemes for new roads and dams, paid for largely by foreign loans, created a balance of payments crisis which eventually resulted in the devaluation of the currency and, in 1968, his overthrow by a military coup. Belaûnde fled to the USA, but returned for new democratic elections in 1980, when he won a landslide victory, supported by majorities in both houses of Congress, but soon found that the climate for expansive projects was no better than it had been during his first term. As the economy declined and inflation raged Belaûnde's ambitions shrank. He became preoccupied with ensuring that political power should be democratically handed on at the elections of 1985, and in this he succeeded, though his own party was defeated and the constitution was later suspended. Died 4 June.

Castle, Baroness (Barbara) of Blackburn, PC (b. 1910), former Labour MP, Cabinet Minister and Member of the European Parliament, she was one of the best-known politicians of her time, renowned for her fiery temperament and dedicated socialist principals. Born in Bradford as Barbara Betts, daughter of an inspector of taxes, she was educated at the local grammar school and at St Hugh's, Oxford. Her first job was in journalism, but the local paper for which she worked closed down and she spent an unhappy time working in a department store in London, finally getting the sack and being rescued from despair by a chance meeting with William Mellor, with whom she had an affair. He gave her a job on a local government magazine and later on *Tribune*, which he edited when it was founded in 1937. When Mellor died in 1942 Barbara Betts got a job with the Ministry of Food and then joined the *Daily Mirror*, where she met Ted Castle, then the paper's night editor. They married in 1944, a marriage that lasted until his death in 1979. Barbara Castle entered Parliament as Member for Blackburn in the 1945 election, gravitating naturally to the left of her party and becoming one of the disparate group led by Aneurin Bevan, commonly known as the Bevanites. She was elected to the party's National Executive Committee in 1950 and, when Labour finally returned to power in 1964, was appointed to Harold Wilson's Cabinet as Minister of Overseas Development. A year later she became Minister of Transport, which brought her to the forefront of popular attention, particularly when she introduced the breathalyser to combat drunken driving. In 1968 she was appointed Secretary of State for Employment and Productivity, with the rank of First Secretary, and was spoken of as likely to become the UK's first woman Prime Minister. In fact the job put paid to any such ambition, entailing as it did the introduction of a Prices and Incomes Bill, which she called "In Place of Strife", and which led to bitter opposition among Labour MPs and the trades unions, to a lost general election, and to Castle being voted off the Shadow Cabinet. She was appointed Secretary of State for Health and Security by Wilson when Labour was returned to power in 1974, but she was sacked by James Callaghan following Wilson's resignation in 1976. She left Parliament in 1979 and was elected instead to the European Parliament, where she was Leader of the British Labour Group and vice-chairman of the Socialist Group. When she retired in 1989 she was appointed a life peer and was soon making her presence felt both in the House of Lords and at Labour Party conferences, particularly as she grew more critical of the policies of New Labour, although increasing blindness began to limit her activities. Died 3 May.

Claus, Prince of the Netherlands (b. 1926), consort of Queen Beatrix and former German diplomat whose marriage in 1966 provoked protests among the Dutch people. Born Claus von Amsberg in Dotzingen on the Elbe, he was a member of a minor German family that was forced to take up farming in Africa during the depression, though Claus returned to Germany for his education. He became a member of the Hitler Youth and during World War II served first in the German Navy and then with a Panzer division in Italy. He was cleared by the Allies' denazification tribunal after the war, which enabled him to take a degree at Hamburg University and embark on a diplomatic career. He met his future wife while on a skiing holiday in Switzerland in 1965, and when rumours of an impending engagement with the Crown Princess began to surface there was a crisis in the Netherlands and the Prime Minister of the time sent a protest to the palace. Eventually the match was approved by both houses of parliament and the couple were married in 1966, Claus being awarded the title of Prince and granted Dutch citizenship. Gradually he became a popular royal figure, concerned with problems of the environment and nature conservation, and being appointed a special adviser on development aid by his wife when she became Queen following the abdication of Queen Juliana in 1980. Prince Claus found the role of consort more difficult, and began a series of treatments for depression before developing Parkinson's disease. Died 6 October.

Coburn, James (b. 1928), US actor. Born in Nebraska and raised in Los Angeles, Coburn served as a radio operator during World War II, and then studied acting. After working in the theatre and television he made an impressive screen debut in Budd Boetticher's elegiac western, *Ride Lonesome* in 1959. Further films followed and in 1965 he made *Major Dundee*, his first film with the director Sam Peckinpah who would later become a close friend. Other collaborations with Peckinpah—most notably *Pat Garrett and Billy the Kid* (1973), in which he gave a haunting performance as the lawman who kills his erstwhile outlaw friend, and *Cross of Iron* (1977), a powerful anti-war film set on the Eastern Front (which he co-wrote with Peckinpah)—were amongst his most memorable performances. Although he continued to work, and was second-unit director on Peckinpah's *Convoy* (1978), in the 1980s he was increasingly crippled by rheumatoid arthritis. After overcoming the disease he returned to acting in the 1990s and in 1999 won an Oscar for best supporting actor in Paul Schraer's *Affliction*. He continued to make films until his sudden death from a heart attack. Died 18 November.

Cooper, Sir Frank GCB, CMG, PC (b. 1922), British civil servant. Born in Manchester, he was educated at Manchester Grammar School and Pembroke College, Oxford and articled to a firm of chartered accountants before joining the RAF during the war and becoming a Spitfire pilot. During service in Italy he was shot down and held prisoner for 24 hours before making his escape. After the war he joined the Air Ministry, where he remained for 16 years until the ministry was merged with the War Office and Admiralty to form the Ministry of Defence. After a spell as deputy secretary in the Civil Service Department Cooper became, in 1973, permanent under-secretary in the Northern Ireland Office, setting up the new department to take over the running—with the introduction of direct rule—of police, fire and other departments, and taking part in talks with Sinn Féin which led to a Provisional ceasefire in 1975. In 1976 he took charge of the Ministry of Defence, where his aggressive managerial style was notably successful in reducing manpower without any substantial cuts in defence commitments, and in taking on, and ultimately winning, a battle with the Treasury over procurement policy. His major challenge came in 1982, when he was able to prove that the operation that he had overhauled was capable of winning back the Falkland Islands, although he later admitted that sending a British task force some 8,000 miles to fight the Argentinians had been something of a gamble. When he retired soon after the campaign he took up a number of appointments with private industry, some of which—notably the chairmanship of United Scientific Holdings—were regarded as too sensitive for a civil servant of his experience, controversy to which he cheerfully added by continuing to comment publicly on defence matters. Died 26 January.

Cronje, Hansie (b. 1969) South African cricket captain whose career ended abruptly when he admitted taking bribes. Born in Bloemfontein, he was encouraged in his youth to be an all-round games player, captaining the Orange Free State's under-19 rugby side and its cricket team when he was 20. He concentrated on cricket once South Africa had been readmitted to the international arena after the years of apartheid, playing in the country's first Test against the West Indies in 1992. In the third Test, against India, he scored 135, but at a very slow rate, a characteristic anchor-man's innings that became very much his style. In all test matches for his country he scored 3,714 runs, with six centuries. He was also a useful medium-paced bowler of great accuracy, an excellent fielder and an astute captain whose authority as leader of a successful team was never questioned until allegations of cheating were made following a tour of India in 1999. He was accused of rigging the outcome of one-day matches in return for money. He denied the charges but admitted that he had taken money "for information and forecasting" of one-day matches. He was banned for life by the South African cricket authorities. Died in an air crash, 1 June.

Cunningham, Group Captain John, CBE, DSO and two Bars, DFC and Bar, AE (b. 1917) was a British wartime night-fighter and peacetime test pilot whose success in shooting down enemy aircraft in the dark earned him the nickname "Cat's Eyes". Born in Croydon and educated at Whitgift School, Cunningham at the age of 18 joined the Royal Auxiliary Air Force and, having taken a degree in aeronautical engineering, was appointed a test pilot with de Havilland. He was called up in August 1939, flying Bristol Blenheim night fighters, and his squadron was the first to be fitted with the new airborne interception radar in 1940. As he moved on to Bristol Beaufighters and de Havilland Mosquitos his night-flying prowess (said to derive from a fondness for carrots) became well known and his nickname was officially encouraged as the radar system was still top secret. By the end of the war Cunningham had shot down at least 20 German aircraft and had collected three DSOs, two DFCs and the Air Efficiency Award as well as a Silver Star from the USA and the Order of Patriotic War from the USSR. After the war Cunningham returned to de Havilland and was appointed the company's chief test pilot when Geoffrey de Havilland was killed attempting to beat the world air speed record. His first task was to establish why de Havilland's DH108 (a model for the future Comet airliner) had broken up. After more than 150 flights Cunningham reported that the aircraft had become unstable because of its lack of a tail plane. The Comet was redesigned to incorporate one, and Cunningham flew the world's first jet airliner at Hatfield in 1949. When the airliner was grounded following two fatal accidents he spent four years testing modified versions until the new Comet 4 began operating the first transatlantic service in 1958. Later he worked on the development of the Trident, remaining chief test pilot when de Havilland merged with British Aerospace, for which he became an executive director until his retirement in 1981. Died 21 July.

de Leon Carpio, Ramiro (b. 1942), President of Guatemala 1993-96. Born in Guatemala City, de Leon studied law at the Rafael Landivar University and was legal consultant to the Ministry of Education before being appointed manager of the Sugar Association of Guatemala in 1981. He soon became actively involved in politics, founding with his cousin the National Centre Party, which within a few years became the country's main political opposition to the military government of that time. When General José Efrain Rios Montt was ousted from the presidency in 1984, de Leon was elected to the new Constituent Assembly and helped to draft the country's new constitution establishing a representative democratic system of government, after which he was elected human rights ombudsman during the troubled period when rebels of the United National Revolutionary Party (URNG) were engaged in guerrilla warfare against the military, which ultimately led to the suspension of the constitution by President Jorge Serrano. The adverse international reaction to this persuaded the military to withdraw its support for Serrano, who went into exile. When de Leon was elected to succeed him as President in 1993, to serve out the remainder of Serrano's term, his major preoccupation was to end the long-running conflict between the military and the Indian rebels of the URNG. His efforts met with some success in 1995, when the URNG agreed a ceasefire and urged its supporters to vote in the election of the following year. When his presidency ended, de Leon became a member of the Central American Parliament, the six-nation forum based in Guatemala, and of which he became president. Died 16 April.

Dung, Van Tien (b. 1917), North Vietnamese general. Born into a poor peasant family in French Indochina, Dung had little education and no formal military training. He joined the Communist Party and participated in the guerrilla struggle against the French colonial authorities and spent several spells in prison. After a series of promotions he rose to become chief of staff to General Vo Ngyuyen Giap who decisively defeated the French at the battle of Dien Bien Phu in 1954. After Vietnamese independence, and its division into the communist North and the capitalist South, Dung continued to serve with Giap, directing the guerrilla struggle against South Vietnam and its US ally. By the time of the 1973 Paris Peace Accords Giap was Minister of Defence in North Vietnam and Dung had become Army Chief of Staff. In this capacity Dung planned the final offensive against the South in 1975, decisively defeating its forces in the central highlands in a classic campaign based on speed of manoeuvre which opened the road to Saigon. With the South's defeat Dung was rewarded with ministerial office in the newly unified Vietnam, serving as Defence Minister from 1980 to 1987. His implacable opposition to moves towards a market economy in the 1980s, however, led to his dismissal. Thereafter he lived the remainder of his life in obscurity. Died 17 March.

Eban, Abba (b. 1915), was Deputy Prime Minister of Israel 1963-66 and Foreign Minister 1966-74. Born Aubrey Solomon Meir in Cape Town, South Africa, he took his stepfather's name and was brought up and educated in England, becoming a research fellow and tutor in oriental languages at Pembroke College, Cambridge, in 1938. During the Second World War he joined the staff of the British Minister in Cairo and was sent to Jerusalem to train Jewish volunteers in methods of resistance should there be a German invasion. When war ended he took up the Zionist cause, becoming its political information officer and, in 1947, the Jewish Agency liaison officer with the UN Special Committee in Palestine. In the following year, when the state of Israel was proclaimed, Eban became its UN delegate, later combining the post with that of Ambassador to the USA in Washington DC. He left for Israel in 1959 and was appointed Minister of Education until

1963, when he became Deputy Prime Minister to Levi Eshkol. Three years later he was appointed Foreign Minister and was almost at once involved with the crisis that erupted when President Gamal Abdel Nasser moved Egyptian troops into the Sinai Peninsula. Working for a diplomatic solution he flew to Paris, London, and Washington to urge support in opening the blockaded straits of Tiran to Israeli shipping. When Israel attacked its Arab neighbours in 1967 Eban defended his country's actions and resisted demands for its withdrawal from the occupied territories with great eloquence, but when Eshkol died and was replaced by Golda Meir he began to lose influence and support at home. Meir and her Washington ambassador, Yitzhak Rabin, tended to deal directly with each other, and when Rabin succeeded as Prime Minister in 1974 Eban lost his job. He did not hold office again, being too much of a loner, an intellectual and a dove to be regarded by others as a potential leader of his country. He retired from the Knesset in 1988, becoming Professor of International Affairs in Washington, continuing to write books and deliver lectures which were less in demand at home than they were in other countries. Died 17 November.

Fortuyn, Pim (b. 1948), flamboyant and provocative Dutch politician who seemed to be gaining an increasing amount of support when he was shot dead. Born in Velsen, in the north-west of the Netherlands, Fortuyn was educated locally, at the Universiteit Nyenrode in Breuelen, at the University of Amsterdam and finally at Groningen, where for a time he taught sociology and began making his name by writing books (one with the title *Soulless Europe* and another *Suffocating Netherlands*) and controversial columns and newspaper articles arguing for an end to immigration, supporting personal liberty, opposing socialism, and openly acknowledging his homosexuality. In 2001 he declared that he intended to reshape Dutch politics, joining the newly-formed Leefbaar Nederland movement which elected him leader but had to disown him a few months later when he campaigned for the repeal of the first article of the constitution, which outlawed discrimination. Fortuyn at once set up his own party and won 17 of the 45 seats in the Rotterdam city election in March 2002. Opinion polls suggested that he might have been on his way to winning a substantial number of seats in the Dutch parliament, for which he was campaigning when he was assassinated. Died 6 May.

Ginsburg, Alexander (b. 1936), Russian dissident. Born in Moscow, Ginsburg studied journalism at Moscow University, from which he was expelled and sentenced to two years in a labour camp in 1960 for taking part in demonstrations and for editing and publishing poetry for the underground magazine *Sintaksis*. In 1966-67 he studied at the Moscow Historical Archive Institute, but ran into trouble again when he published a book on the trial of the dissident Andrei Sinyavsky. He was sent to prison for five years and was subsequently forced to live outside Moscow before again being arrested, having caused further disapproval for his work on administering the covert fund set up to help Soviet prisoners and their families, the money coming from royalties from Alexander Solzhenitsyn's book *The Gulag Archipelago*. Ginsburg had also offended by becoming a founder member of the group which monitored breaches of the Helsinki human rights agreement. After his arrest he was interrogated for more than a year before being tried and convicted of anti-Soviet agitation. Sentenced to eight years' imprisonment, he and four other dissidents were exchanged in 1979 for two Soviet citizens who were serving sentences in New York for spying against the USA. Ginsburg went to live with Solzhenitsyn in Vermont, but soon left the USA to live in Paris, remaining there after the collapse of the Soviet Union and becoming a French citizen in 1998. Died 19 July.

Gorton, Sir John, GCMG, AC, CH, PC (b. 1911), Prime Minister of Australia 1968-71. Born in Melbourne, Gorton was the illegitimate son of a British-born businessman and a young Irishwoman who died when he was nine. He was educated at Geelong Grammar School and Brasenose College, Oxford, and ran his father's fruit farm before enlisting in the Royal Australian Air Force, becoming a fighter pilot. He was badly injured when his Hurricane crash-landed near Singapore, and was medically discharged after another crash in New Guinea. In 1948 he joined the Liberal Party and was elected senator for Victoria in the following year. He was a member of the joint parliamentary committee of foreign affairs from 1952-58 before taking office as Minister of the Navy and, for short spells, Minister of the Interior, Minister of Works, and Minister for Education and Science. In 1968 he was elected to lead his party as Prime Minister when his predecessor, Harold Holt, disappeared and was presumed drowned. Gorton proved to be something of a buccaneering leader. Though his nationalism was popular his crude and unorthodox style, disdain of formality, and eye for pretty women shocked many of his supporters, and his immediate and drastic reform of the public service upset those upon whom he should have depended. He grew restive at Australia's support for the USA in the Vietnam war, and when he returned to office in the 1969 election he announced that Australian troops would be withdrawn from the conflict. Some of his other measures were also popular, including increased social security and arts funding, but his unorthodoxy won him many enemies. In 1971 he sought a vote of confidence from his parliamentary party, and promptly resigned when the returns proved to be even. He continued to serve as deputy to the new Prime Minister, William McMahon, until he was returned to the back benches. He retired from politics in 1975, having been appointed a Companion of Honour in 1971. He was appointed GCMG in 1977 and a Companion of the Order of Australia in 1988. Died 19 May.

Gotti, John (b. 1940), the most famous US Mafia figure since Al Capone. Brought up in a poor family in New York, Gotti became a gang leader and by the age of 25 had convictions for a range of crimes. He joined the Gambinos, one of New York's five major organised crime families, in 1966 and quickly established a reputation for ruthless violence and the ability to evade conviction for his crimes. In December 1985 the leader of the Gambino family, Paul Castellano, was gunned down in the street and Gotti became the new boss of the family. Nicknamed the "Dapper Don", Gotti escaped conviction on three further occasions, often by bribing or intimidating jurors and witnesses. Arrested in 1990, however, he was eventually convicted of racketeering and murder after his right-hand man, Salvatore Gravano, testified for the prosecution. In June 1992 Gotti was sentenced to life imprisonment (upheld by the Supreme Court in 1994) and served his sentence in a maximum security federal prison in Marion, Illinois. Diagnosed with cancer in 1998, he was moved to a prison hospital in Springfield, Missouri, where he spent the remainder of his life. Died 10 June.

Guei, General Robert (b. 1941) was military ruler of Côte d'Ivoire for 10 months after seizing power in December 1999. Born in the village of Kabakouma, he received military training in Upper Volta and at the Saint Cyr officers' training college in France, and when only a colonel was appointed leader of the armed forces by President Houphouet-Boigny in 1990, following a failed army mutiny. When the President died in 1993 Guei found himself at odds with his successor, Henri Konan Bedie, who wanted the army to curb opposition activity during the elections of 1995. Guei refused and was placed under house arrest on suspicion of planning a coup. He was freed and given a Cabinet post when no evidence against him was produced, but was later dismissed from the army on charges of misconduct. On Christmas Eve 1999 he came to power in a military coup, maintaining that he did so reluctantly, having agreed only to be spokesman for the junta that had removed Bedie from office. Guei's short presidency was marked by unrest in Abidjan and other towns, and when elections were held in 2000 Guei was heavily defeated by Laurent Gbagbo. Guei retired to the country but agreed to support Gbagbo's broad-based government. He withdrew his support after a few days and was found dead in the streets of Abidjan when government troops moved in to quell an army mutiny. Died 19 September.

Hampton, Lionel (b. 1909), US jazz band leader who continued to tour well into his eighties. Born in Chicago, Hampton was introduced to jazz at an early age and played in his school band, where he played the drums. After leaving school he moved to Los Angeles in search of work and joined Louis Armstrong's backing band, taking up the vibraphone, an electric version of the xylophone, while playing at the Los Angeles Cotton Club In 1936 he was offered a contract by Benny Goodman, and played in some of the memorable swing and jazz recordings made by the quartet at that time as well as producing the Flying Home number which became his signature tune. In 1940 Hampton formed his own band which was soon renowned for its rhythm and stridency as well as for Hampton's drumming, xylophone, and vibraphone playing. Between his big band gigs he continued to play in small groups, notably with the Benny Goodman quartet, taking part in the group's last concert in 1973, shortly before the drummer Gene Krupa's death. Off-stage Hampton was a generous supporter of many charities, funding musical scholarships and endowing an annual jazz festival at the University of Idaho, which subsequently bore his name. He often took his band to play for Presidents in the White House, from Harry S. Truman to Bill Clinton, the latter awarding him the National Medal of the Arts in 1997. Died 31 August.

Harris, Richard (b. 1930), stage and screen actor. Born in Limerick, in the Republic of Ireland, the son of a miller who died a bankrupt, Harris trained as an actor at the London Academy of Music and Dramatic Art. His first stage appearance was in Brendan Behan's *The Quare Fellow* at the Comedy Theatre in London in 1956, in a production by Joan Littlewood. He stayed with her company for six productions at the Theatre Royal, Stratford, including *Fings Ain't Wot They Used T'Be* and J.P. Donleavy's *The Ginger Man*. He also began to make his mark in films, notably in *The Mutiny on the Bounty*, for which he won an award at the Cannes film festival, and *This Sporting Life*, for which he won an Oscar nomination. At the same time he was earning a reputation as a difficult, hard-drinking and aggressive man, and apart from *Camelot* in 1967 his later films did not match his obvious talent. He also disappointed many of his admirers by failing to fulfil his early promise on the stage, tackling none of the great classical roles until he played the title role in Pirandello's *Henry IV* in London in 1990. Instead, concerned about money (he was more than once declared bankrupt), he took over the stage role of King Arthur in the musical *Camelot* from Richard Burton, acquiring the stage rights and taking it on tour round the world. It made him rich and, it was suggested, sapped his ambition. He returned to the cinema to play Professor Dumbledore in *Harry Potter and the Philosopher's Stone* and *Harry Potter and the Chamber of Secrets*, but did not live long enough to take part in the third of the film series. Died 25 October.

Hayes, Bob (b. 1942), US athlete and footballer. Born in Jacksonville, Florida, Hayes attended local school before going to Florida Agricultural and Mechanical University in Tallahassee, where he played football but also equalled Jesse Owens's world record of 9.3 seconds for the 100 yards sprint. In 1963 he was selected for the US track and field team, setting a world record time of 9.1 seconds for the 100 yards, a record that stood for 11 years. At the 1964 Tokyo Olympics he won the 100 metres in 10 seconds to equal the world and Olympic records, and then ran in the final leg of the 4x100 metres relay. The US team lay fourth when he received the baton, but he turned a two-metre deficit into a three-metre margin of victory. His time for the leg was unofficially recorded at 8.6 seconds. In 1965 he joined the Dallas Cowboys football team, playing with them for 10 seasons, which included the winning of the Super Bowl in 1971. In his retirement he battled with illness and with drugs, serving a term of imprisonment after pleading guilty of attempting to sell drugs to an undercover policeman. Died 18 September.

Helms, Richard (b. 1913), was Director of the US Central Intelligence Agency (CIA) 1966-73. Born in Pennsylvania, Helms grew up in New Jersey, spending two of his high school years in Germany and Switzerland before going on to Williams College, Massachusetts. He became a reporter for the United Press news agency, working in Europe where he covered the 1936 Berlin Olympics and obtained an exclusive interview with Adolf Hitler. Returning to the USA he worked for Scripps Howard newspapers until joining the US Navy in 1942. He was soon recruited to the Office of Strategic Studies, working for US intelligence in London and Paris, and after the war in Berlin. He returned to Washington DC to help with the creation of the CIA in 1947, soon making his mark through espionage and covert operations such as the overthrow of the Iranian Prime Minister Mohammed Mossadeq and the digging of a tunnel between East and West Berlin to tap telephone lines with Moscow. After the failure of the Bay of Pigs operation in Cuba, Helms was appointed deputy director in charge of CIA operations in the field, though he had doubts about ongoing plans to assassinate Fidel Castro and appointed another agent to run what was known as Operation Mongoose, which proved a disaster. The CIA restored its reputation by discovering the nuclear weapon sites in Cuba, and in 1966 Helms was appointed director of the agency by President Lyndon B Johnson. He advised against further involvement in Vietnam, and found it difficult to gain the confidence of Johnson's successor, Richard Nixon, the relationship coming to breaking point during the Watergate cover-up, in which Helms refused to let the CIA become involved. He was dismissed and appointed as US ambassador to Tehran, but resigned in 1977 when it was revealed that, under his leadership, the CIA had been involved in the overthrow of Salvador Allende, the elected Marxist President of Chile, which Helms had previously denied. Died 22 October.

Heyerdahl, Thor (b. 1914), Norwegian anthropologist who became well-known for his adventurous voyages in craft made of materials available to primitive man, notably the *Kon-Tiki* in which he sailed from Peru to Polynesia. Born in Larvik, Heyerdahl was educated at Oslo University, where he took degrees in zoology and geography. He first demonstrated his unusual approach to anthropology with his marriage in 1937, when he took his bride to honeymoon on a remote Pacific island and observed that the prevailing winds and currents were easterly, suggesting to him that the first migrants to Polynesia might have come from Peru. He developed his ideas after serving in England with the Free Norwegian Army during the war, building a raft of balsa wood which he named after a Peruvian Indian king and a legendary Polynesian hero. In 1947 he set sail from Peru in the *Kon-Tiki* with five companions, the craft drifting across the Pacific for 101 days before landing on the island of Tuamotu in Polynesia after a journey of some 4,000 miles. His account of the voyage, *The Kon-Tiki Expedition*, published in 1948, sold many millions of copies, and the documentary film of the voyage was awarded an Oscar. Heyerdahl four years later published a serious scientific work, *American Indians in the Pacific*, but anthropologists remained unconvinced that early South American migrants had indeed made the hazardous crossing to Polynesia. Heyerdahl then took expeditions to a number of South American countries, and to Easter Island, before launching another sea voyage designed to test possible links between Pharoic Egyptians and the Incas. He built two reed vessels, *Ra I* and *Ra II*, the first setting sail from Morocco in 1969 but which he abandoned when it became waterlogged in the Atlantic. The second reached Barbados in 1970. In 1977 Heyerdahl planned a further voyage, designed to show Arabian influences in Africa and Asia, but dramatically burnt his boat in Djibouti in protest at the state of the world as demonstrated by the war in the Horn of Africa. He published an autobiography, *In the Footsteps of Adam*, in 2000, but shortly afterwards was found to have a brain tumour. Died 18 April.

Jatti, Basappa Danappa (b. 1912), Indian politician who became acting President during the difficult period following the electoral defeat of Indira Gandhi in 1977. Born in the state of Karnataka, Jatti was educated locally and at Rajaram College in Kolhapur. He worked actively in support of the campaign for India's independence, eventually being appointed Chief Minister of the state of Jamakhandi. After independence he became Health and Labour Minister in Mysore province, and Chief Minister in 1958. He supported Indira Gandhi during the challenge to her leadership of the Congress party, and in 1974 she appointed him Vice-President of India. A quiet and unassuming man, he was thrust into the midst of political crisis when the Janata Party came to power in 1977 and demanded that the nine Congress governments in the provinces be dissolved. The provincial chief ministers refused, and the Supreme Court declined to intervene.

When the Janata leaders asked Jatti, as acting President, to dismiss the nine state governments he declined on the grounds that it would be unconstitutional. Janata responded by demanding his resignation, with which Jatti had to comply, resuming the vice-presidency until his term ended in 1979. Died 7 June.

Junge, Traudl (b. 1920), personal secretary to Adolf Hitler. Born Gertraud Humps in Munich, she became a secretary at the German Chancellery. In December 1942 she was appointed as the youngest of Hitler's personal secretaries, and said of their first meeting that he was "a pleasant older man who welcomed us with real friendliness". She married Hans Junge in 1943 but he was killed in action in France a year later. In the face of intensive Allied bombing of Berlin, Junge moved with Hitler and his staff into an underground bunker in January 1945 and remained with the German leader until his suicide in April. One of her last acts of service was to take down Hitler's last will and testament, and she later admitted feeling disappointment that it contained no revelatory explanation of Germany's catastrophic defeat. After the war Junge was interrogated and spent six months in prison before resuming work as a secretary and, later, as a science reporter. Throughout her life she maintained that she had had no knowledge of Nazi war crimes, and expressed guilt that she had liked "the greatest criminal who had ever lived". At the end of her life, suffering from cancer, she published a book, *Through the Final Hours*, based on notes which she had compiled in 1946. This was made into a widely-publicised documentary—*Blind Spot*, by André Heller—which received its premier at the Berlin Film Festival. After telling Heller that "Now I've let go of my story, I can let go of my life," she died within hours of the film's screening. Died 10 February.

Karsh, Yousuf (b. 1908), Portrait photographer who memorably captured the fighting spirit of Winston Churchill by plucking the cigar from his mouth. Born in Mardin, Armenia, Karsh's family escaped to Syria when Armenians were being massacred in Turkey, and shortly afterwards Yousuf was sent to live with an uncle in Canada, where he was educated. He was apprenticed to a photographer in Boston before returning to Canada to set up a studio in Ottawa, from which many of his portraits were published in magazines such as *The Illustrated London News*. In 1941 Churchill visited Ottawa to address the Canadian parliament, and it was after this speech that the celebrated Karsh photograph was taken. Churchill had just lit a cigar, but as Karsh later recalled he did not want to use this prop: "I said, 'Forgive me, Sir' and plucked the cigar from his mouth. By the time I got back to my camera he looked so belligerent he could have devoured me." From that time on a portrait by Karsh became a mark of distinction. He regularly travelled abroad taking portraits of the famous, but it was his studio portraits in Ottawa that really made his mark, using an 8-by-10 inch plate which gave great definition but limited the style, which remained static and somewhat uncritical. He was accorded exhibitions in many countries, received many honorary degrees, and had many books of his work published. He was appointed a Companion of the Order of Canada in 1990. Died 13 July.

Kilpatrick, Dame Judith (b. 1952), head teacher of City of Portsmouth Girls' School, was widely recognised in the UK as setting an example of how city comprehensive schools should be run. Born Judith Foxley in St Helens, Lancashire, she was educated at Cowley Grammar School for Girls and the University of Kent before taking a postgraduate certificate of Education at Southampton. She taught at Regents Park Girls' School in Southampton, was deputy head teacher at King Richard School, Portsmouth, from 1989 and head teacher at the Wavell School, Farnborough from 1993. She married Andrew Kilpatrick in 1994 (the marriage was dissolved in 1998), and joined the City of Portsmouth Girls' School in 1995. Under her leadership the school achieved the best state sector GCSE results in the area, was designated a "beacon school" and was used for the training of student teachers, and its success led to Kilpatrick's appointment to many committees, including the Home Office Advisory Council for the Misuse of Drugs, the Southern Strategic Partnership, and the executive council of the Teacher Training Agency. She was appointed DBE in 2000. Died 5 September.

Kyprianou, Spyros (b. 1932), President of Cyprus 1977-89 who inherited a divided island and was never able to accept international proposals for resolving the dispute between Greece and Turkey and the Greek and Turkish Cypriots, though he took part in many meetings. Born in Limassol, Kyprianou was educated locally and at the City of London College before being called to the Bar at Gray's Inn in 1954. During his time in England he had been appointed London secretary to Archbishop Makarios, charged with furthering the campaign for enosis (union with Greece). When Eoka launched its guerrilla war against the British Kyprianou left for Athens and New York, returning to London in 1957 as the Archbishop's representative, leading up to the island's independence in 1960. Kyprianou returned to Cyprus to become first Minister of Justice and then Foreign Minister, a post which he held until 1972, when he was dismissed as a result of pressure from the Greek military junta. He began to practice law, but when Makarios's government was overthrown and Turkey invaded Cyprus Kyprianou returned to politics and formed a new party, the Democratic Front. In 1976 he was elected President of the House of Representatives, and on the death of Makarios in the following year succeeded as President of the Republic. He was elected unopposed in 1978, agreeing to meet the Turkish Cypriot leader, Rauf Denktash, under UN auspices, but the talks quickly broke down. After winning a further five-year term in 1983 Kyprianou rejected a new UN attempt to reach a settlement, but when the Turkish Cypriots unilaterally declared independence in 1985 he agreed to meet Denktash in New York but rejected the UN's proposals. He was strongly criticised for the failure of these meetings, suffered a heart attack in 1987 and failed to win re-election in the following year. Died 12 March.

Lebed, Aleksandr (b. 1950), Russian general and politician. Born in Novocherkassk, Lebed served as a prominent paratroop commander during the Soviet war in Afghanistan in the early 1980s, and was promoted to the rank of general in 1990. In August 1991 he became a hero of Russia's fledgling democracy when he refused to lead his elite Tula paratroop division against the then Russian President Boris Yeltsin during the attempted coup against Soviet President Mikhail Gorbachev. In 1992 Lebed commanded the Russian 14th Army during the conflict in Moldova over the ethnic Russian territory of Dnestr, and helped broker a peace deal. In 1995 he was retired from the military after voicing sharp criticism of the army's treatment by the Russian authorities. He entered the State Duma, observing that it had not taken long for capitalism, bereft of free competition, to reduce much of the country's population to "beggars". The high-water mark of his political career occurred in the following year when he came third in the first round of the presidential elections. He endorsed Yeltsin's candidacy in the second round, for which he was rewarded with the post of secretary of the Security Council by the new President. In this capacity, he negotiated the Khasavyurt agreement which ended the first war in Chechnya in 1996, but was dismissed from the Security Council in October of that year after only four months. In 1998 he won the governorship of Krasnoyarsk oblast. Although a relentless critic of corruption, Lebed's autocratic style of leadership alienated many and his record in government was less impressive than his supporters had hoped. He was killed when a helicopter in which he was travelling to open a new ski resort in Krasnoyarsk crashed into power lines. Died 28 April.

Lee, Peggy (b. 1920), US singer and songwriter. Born Norma Egstrom in Jamestown, North Dakota, into a family of Norwegian and Swedish descent, she changed her name to Peggy Lee when singing with a local radio station, which she combined with working as a waitress. Success came in 1941 when she was recruited by Benny Goodman to sing in his band. She recorded many popular songs, including *I Got it Bad and That Ain't Good*, and made her film debut in *Stage Door Canteen*, in which she sang *Why Don't You Do Right?* In 1943 she married Goodman's guitarist, Dave Barbour, giving up her career for two years when she had a daughter. In 1945 she made a series of recordings for Capitol Records and then a number of films, including *Mr Music* with Bing Crosby and *Pete Kelly's Blues*, for which she won an Oscar nomination in 1955. In the same year she wrote some of the songs and recorded some of the voices for the cartoon characters in *Lady and the Tramp*. During this period she also made some of her most successful records, including *Lover* and *Fever* and then began a series of successful seasons at the Basin Street East club in New York. Her health began to deteriorate following the break-up of her marriage and a series of failed romances and other marriages. She made no more films and fewer public engagements, but retained her popularity with live audiences, who understood the pain that now seemed to underlie her performances. Died 21 January.

Littlewood, Joan (b. 1914), English theatre director whose rebellious nature transformed British theatre in the 1950s, but not wholly in the way that she wished. Born in Stockwell, south London, the illegitimate daughter of a girl of 16, Littlewood was educated at a local convent school. She won a scholarship to the Royal Academy of Dramatic Art but left before completing the course because, she said, it was "full of debs learning elocution". She went to Manchester, where she met and married the writer and poet Jimmie Miller, who later became better known under the name Ewan MacColl and who at that time was running a company called Theatre of Action, which performed mainly in the streets. Together they set up another company, Theatre Union, which was disbanded in World War II, when Littlewood worked for the BBC until she was dismissed for being too left-wing. At the end of the war Theatre Union was re-created as Theatre Workshop, Littlewood directing a version of *Lysistrata* by Miller and an original play by him called *Uranium 235*, both of which transferred to London. By this time Littlewood had transferred her affections to another member of the company, Gerry Raffles, whom she married when her first marriage was dissolved, and together they set up a permanent home for Theatre Workshop at the derelict Theatre Royal in Stratford, east London. Their first success there was with Brendan Behan's *The Quare Fellow*, which was followed by a series of other plays which transferred to the West End, notably Shelagh Delaney's *A Taste of Honey*, Lionel Bart's *Fings Ain't Wot They Used T'Be*, Stephen Lewis's *Sparrers Can't Sing* and *Oh! What A Lovely War*, a compilation of World War I songs which typified Littlewood's style of extemporising and developing ideas during rehearsals but which also, in transferring to the West End and being made into a film, emphasised the fact that it was not in Stratford East that, in spite of her best intentions, Littlewood's natural audiences lay. When Raffles died in 1975 Littlewood left the Theatre Royal and went to live in France, where she collaborated on a book, *Milady Vine*, with Baron Philippe de Rothschild and wrote her autobiography, *Joan's Book*, (1994). Died 20 September.

Longford, Elizabeth Countess of, CBE (b. 1906), historian and biographer who was also matriarch of a prolific literary family. Born Elizabeth Harman, daughter of a Harley Street surgeon and Katherine Chamberlain, niece of Joseph Chamberlain, she was educated at Headington School and at Lady Margaret Hall, Oxford, then lectured in English, politics and economics for the Workers Education Association from 1929 to 1935, having married Frank Pakenham, whom she first met at Oxford, in 1931. She had ambitions to become a Labour MP, standing for Cheltenham in 1935, for King's Norton in Birmingham in 1943, and for Oxford City in 1950, but she was never elected, though she persuaded her husband to switch allegiance from Conservative to Labour, and he became a Labour peer in 1945. After rearing eight children, Elizabeth channelled her ambition into writing, publishing her first book, *Jameson's Raid*, in 1960 and the book that established her reputation as a sympathetic biographer, *Victoria R.I.*, for which she was awarded the James Tait Black Memorial Prize, in 1964 (by which time she had become Elizabeth Longford on her husband's succession to the earldom). She followed this with a two-volume biography of the Duke of Wellington: *Wellington: Years of the Sword,* with its memorable account of the battle of Waterloo, in 1969 and *Wellington: Pillar of State* in 1972. Though never quite matching these works she continued to write and publish regularly for the rest of her life, many of her later books—including biographies of Queen Elizabeth II and Queen Elizabeth The Queen Mother—focusing on royal subjects. Her autobiography, *The Pebbled Shore*, was published in 1986. Four of her seven surviving children were writers. Died 23 October.

Lovelace, Linda (b. 1949), pornography star and later anti-porn crusader. Born Linda Boreman in the Bronx in 1949, she had a strict Catholic upbringing and was frequently beaten by her mother. She married Chuck Traynor, under whose management she adopted the name Lovelace and began appearing in low budget pornographic films. She became the first internationally famous porn star when she appeared in *Deep Throat* (1972), a film which sought to redefine the genre by adding a plot (albeit a ludicrous one) to the graphic sex scenes. The film was most remembered, however, for Lovelace's capacity for deeply penetrative fellatio, an act which thereafter took its name from the film's title. The movie was hugely popular, playing to mainstream audiences in over 70 US cities and in many countries throughout the world. Having been made for US$25,000, it grossed over US$500 million, although Lovelace received only US$1,250, most of which was apparently kept by Traynor. Lovelace enjoyed celebrity status in the early 1970s, promoting and making porn films, (including *Deep Throat II* (1973)), posing for *Playboy* magazine, and appearing on chat shows and in commercials. During this period she left Traynor and claimed to be a libidinous free-sprit. She later severed her connection with the porn industry, however, and in 1979 published her autobiography, *Ordeal*, in which she claimed that her films had been made under duress as a result of Traynor's violence and intimidation. Following the book's publication she campaigned against the adult entertainment industry, testifying before the US Senate's Meese inquiry into the dangers of pornography, and publishing a second memoir, *Out of Bondage* (1986). Died 22 April.

Luns, Dr Joseph (b. 1911) Dutch politician who was Secretary General of NATO from 1971-84. Born in Rotterdam, Luns was educated at schools in Amsterdam and Brussels and at the London School of Economics and at the University of Berlin before joining the Foreign Ministry in 1938. During the war he was posted to London with The Netherlands Government-in-exile, remaining there until 1949, when he was sent to the UN in New York. He was appointed Minister without Portfolio in his country's coalition government in 1952 and Minister for Foreign Affairs in 1956, signing the Treaty of Rome in the following year. He retained his ministry, through many changes of administration, working hard to get the UK into the European Community in spite of General de Gaulle's fierce opposition, until 1971, when he was invited to become Secretary General of NATO. In this post he was wholly committed to the Atlantic military alliance, maintaining that the Soviet Union could only be contained by Western strength, and he was strongly critical of individual NATO countries seeking to cut their military spending. He was equally outspoken when NATO countries showed their strength, describing the UK's action in recapturing the Falkland Islands in 1982 as "a boon for NATO". He retired in 1984 having been awarded many honours, including the Knight Grand Cross of the Order of the Netherlands, an honorary British GCMG and an honorary CH. Died 17 July.

Margaret, HRH Princess, Countess of Snowdon, CI, GCVO (b. 1930), was sister of Queen Elizabeth II and younger daughter of King George VI and Queen Elizabeth The Queen Mother. Born at Glamis in Scotland and christened Margaret Rose, Princess Margaret was educated privately and, unlike her older sister, did not have to live with the knowledge that she would one day become Queen. She grew up a fun-loving and slightly rebellious child, interested in art and music but not trained for any role outside what was known as "the family firm". As a beautiful young woman she enjoyed London high-life but was plunged into controversy when, soon after her sister became Queen, she took up with Group Captain Peter Townsend, a member of the Queen Mother's personal staff and a married man who was just becoming divorced. To her family she declared her desire to marry him, but accepted that at the age of 23 she could not do so for two years without the Queen's permission. Much pressure was put upon her during this time, both within the family and from outside advisers such as the Archbishop of Canterbury, to abandon the idea of marrying a divorced man. When it was also revealed that she would lose her royal status if she went ahead with the marriage, she finally decided against it. In 1960 Princess Margaret married the photographer Antony Armstrong-Jones who shared her sense of fun and artistic bent, and who in 1961, shortly before the birth of their first child, was created Earl of Snowdon. A second child was born in 1964, but the marriage later ran into difficulties and the couple were separated in 1976 and divorced two years later. Princess Margaret's royal engagements were reduced, she spent more time in her Caribbean retreat on the island of Mustique, and began to be troubled by ill-health. She suffered several strokes but continued to keep in daily touch with the Queen and other members of her family, making one of her final public appearances in a wheelchair at her mother's 101st birthday party. Died 9 February.

Martin, Archer, CBE, FRS (b. 1910), English chemist whose work on chromatographic techniques and the physical principles of separation won him the Nobel Prize in 1952. Educated at Bedford School and Peterhouse, Cambridge, Martin initially intended to become a chemical engineer but turned to biochemistry, later obtaining a doctorate on the isolation of Vitamin E while working at the Dunn Nutritional Laboratory in Cambridge. He then turned to developing an automatic machine capable of splitting crude Vitamin E into three separate fractions, later developing the machine for the Woollen Industries Research Association to separate amino acid derivatives. Working with R.L.M. Synge, with whom he jointly won the Nobel Prize, Martin developed a new form of chromatography, developing his machine greatly to improve the separation of acetylated amino acids. Subsequently he invented paper chromatography, which made it possible for the first time to separate and determine closely related chemical substances. Martin was head of the Physical Chemistry Division of the National Institute of Medical Research at Mill Hill from 1952-56, director of the Abbotsbury Laboratories from 1959-70, and consultant to the Wellcome Institute from 1970-73. During this time he continued to work on separation science, developing techniques which revolutionised the methods of drug-testing in sport and for testing atmospheric pollution. For his scientific work he was awarded many honours, fellowships and prizes, in addition to his Nobel and CBE. Died 28 July.

Milligan, Spike (b. 1918), comedian and writer whose surrealist, chaotic and anarchic humour, reflected most memorably in *The Goon Show*, inspired a new wave of British comedy. Born Terence Alan Milligan in Ahmednagar, India, he was educated at the Convent of Jesus and Mary in Poona and a number of other Roman Catholic schools in India until the family returned to London in 1931. He taught himself to play the drums, trumpet and other instruments, performing with a number of dance hall bands until the outbreak of World War II, when he enlisted in the Royal Artillery (later describing his experiences in six volumes of comic memoirs beginning with *Adolf Hitler: My Part in his Downfall*, published in 1971). After the war, in which he was nearly killed by a mortar shell and suffered a nervous breakdown, he embarked on a number of musical tours in Europe before meeting Harry Secombe, Peter Sellers, and Michael Bentine, with whom he launched a show for BBC radio, initially called *Those Crazy People, The Goons*, in 1951. It became one of the most popular weekly programmes, running for eight years, but it put an immense strain on Milligan, who wrote most of the scripts. During the third series he was put in a straitjacket and kept in an isolation ward for several months after a series of rows with the BBC drove him into temporary insanity. The strain also cost him his marriage, but did not stop him creating a new style of television comedy, *A Show Called Fred*, for which he won a British Academy award in 1956, and a series called *Q5*, later extended to *Q6*, *Q7*, *Q8*, and *Q9*. After making a short film, *The Running, Jumping and Standing Still Film*, he embarked on a productive period of book writing. In his lifetime he wrote some 50 books, including his memoirs, collections of nonsense, many children's books, and several volumes of verse. He also took up many causes, particularly in defence of animals, in favour of nuclear disarmament, and against pornography and smoking. He wrote hundreds of letters, including one to *The Times* in 1990 asking the paper to make sure his obituary was ready "as I have not been feeling well lately". A citizen of the Irish Republic, he was appointed Honorary KBE in 2000. Died 27 February.

Moore, Dudley, CBE (b. 1935), comic actor and musician who starred in stage and television shows and in films but could never quite shake off his own sense of failure. Born in Dagenham, Essex, he was educated at Dagenham County High School and studied music at the Guildhall School of Music before winning a scholarship to Magdalen College, Oxford, where he composed, acted in cabaret and played jazz, staying on after gaining his degree to take a Bachelor of Music course in composition. He then played jazz with Johnny Dankworth and toured the USA with the Vic Lewis Band before being recruited for a show, *Beyond the Fringe*, for the Edinburgh Festival, together with Alan Bennett, Peter Cook, and Jonathan Miller. After Edinburgh the show ran for two years in London's West End and a further two years on Broadway in New York and its success brought a measure of fame to all four Oxbridge graduates. Returning from New York Moore featured successfully on a BBC TV music show, *Offbeat*, and then began three series of programmes, *Not Only...But Also* with Peter Cook. The success of these led them into a couple of films, *The Wrong Box* (1966) and *Bedazzled* (1967), after which Moore broke out on his own, scripting, composing, and starring in the film *Thirty is a Dangerous Age, Cynthia* and playing the Woody Allen role in *Play It Again, Sam* on stage in the West End. He joined again with Peter Cook in another stage review, *Behind the Fridge*, which was particularly successful, with the revised title of *Good Evening*, in the USA, where they were awarded Tony awards. His subordinate relationship with Cook (who was by then drinking very heavily) soured, however, and Moore went to Hollywood, playing a small part in the film *Foul Play* and then starring roles in *10*, with Julie Andrews and Bo Derek and its follow-up *Arthur* with Liza Minelli and John Gielgud, for which both Moore and Gielgud won the critics' Golden Globe awards. He made a succession of rather less successful films before returning to music, giving a piano concert in New York, which was poorly received, and presenting a series of BBC TV programmes on classical music. In 1997, after suffering a number of strokes, he was diagnosed as suffering from a rare and debilitating neurological disorder, progressive supranuclear palsy, which eventually proved fatal. Died 27 March.

Moyola, Lord (b. 1923), was, as James Chichester-Clark, Prime Minister of Northern Ireland 1969-71. A descendant of Thomas Dawson, who bought the Moyola Estate in Co. Londonderry in the 17th century, James Dawson Chichester-Clark was educated at Eton and served in the Irish Guards during World War II. Injured at Anzio in 1944 he was later appointed ADC to Field Marshal Earl Alexander of Tunis, then Governor-General of Canada, and retired from the army as major in 1960, when he was elected to the Ulster Commons as member for South Londonderry. He became Chief Whip in 1963, Leader of the House in 1966, and Minister of Agriculture in 1967. He resigned from the Cabinet in April 1969 over the timing of Prime Minister Terence O'Neill's reforms, but when O'Neill himself resigned was within days elected Prime Minister, beating William Faulkner by one vote. He took office in violent times, and within months asked the British government to send in troops to help control the rioting between Protestant and Catholic extremists. As the violence continued more British troops were sent to the province, but Chichester-Clark found himself under attack from within the Unionist Party both for his reforming programme and for not being tough enough on suspected terrorists, while having to defend British government's policies which in his view failed to take full account of the collapsing security situation. In despair he resigned as Prime Minister in 1971. He was created a life peer as Baron Moyola of Castledown, and spoke in the House of Lords in support of subsequent British government attempts to bring peace to Northern Ireland. Died 17 May.

Ne Win, General (b. 1911), Burmese soldier who seized power and presided over his country's economic collapse for more than 20 years. Born Maung Shu Maung in Paungdale, a town in central Burma, he was educated at Rangoon University but left when he became involved with the nationalist movement. In 1940 he went to Japan for military training, taking the name Ne Win ("Brilliant as the Sun") and becoming a commander in the Burma National Army. Soon after Japan invaded Burma in 1941 Ne Win returned to Burma and was appointed Commander-in-Chief of the Army in the puppet Burmese government. When the British arrived in 1944 Ne Win changed sides, bringing his army with him and commanding a unit under General Slim's 14th Army as it advanced through the country. When Burma became independent outside the Commonwealth Ne Win became the strong man behind U Nu's government and Deputy Prime Minister and Defence Minister as well as C-in-C. As security problems increased, Ne Win in 1962 abrogated the constitution, declared martial law, placed U Nu under house arrest and took over the running of the country. Publishing a manifesto entitled *The Burmese Way to Socialism*, which promised to end the nation's "pernicious" economic system, Ne Win in fact wrecked the economy by isolating the country, nationalising foreign assets, excluding overseas investment and trade, and by capricious legislation such as the division of all the country's banknotes by nine. Many hundreds of people were killed as demonstrations were ruthlessly put down. Ne Win officially retired in 1988, but kept close watch on the military junta that succeeded him until he was placed under house arrest in 2002. Died 5 December.

Norfolk, The Duke of, KG, GCVO, CB, CBE, MC (b. 1915) soldier who became premier Duke and Earl Marshal of England in 1975. Born Miles Francis Stapleton Fitzalan-Howard, he was educated at Ampleforth and Christ Church, Oxford, before joining the Grenadier Guards in 1937. He served with his regiment in France, North Africa, Sicily, Italy, and in the Normandy landings, winning the Military Cross for bravery during the crossing of the Sangro river in Italy in 1943. He stayed in the Army after the war, becoming head of the British military mission to the Soviet forces in Germany in 1957 and GOC 1st Division in BAOR in 1963. He was appointed to the Ministry of Defence in 1965, becoming director of service intelligence in 1966. Retiring from the Army in 1967, he joined the merchant bank Robert Fleming as a director, continuing in the job after succeeding as 17th Duke on the death of his cousin. As Duke he inherited Arundel Castle, which had been saved from death duties and opened to the public but still needed substantial funds for repairs and upkeep. Norfolk formed an independent charitable trust to protect it, which meant that he had to pay £10 a night to stay in the small flat that he kept there. As Duke he was senior British layman in the Roman Catholic Church, representing the Queen at the funerals and installations of Popes, and helping to prepare her visit to the Vatican. His advice was also sought by Rome in the appointment of English Cardinals, but though a devout Roman Catholic he was often critical of the Church's stand on a number of issues, including birth control. He was a family man, marrying Anne Constantine-Maxwell in 1949. They had two sons and three daughters and 35 nephews and nieces. "We are not short of heirs in our family," he once said. Died 24 June.

Parker, Sir Peter, KBE, LVO (b. 1924), was chairman of British Rail 1976-83 and of many other public and private companies during his business career. Born in France, the son of English parents, he was educated in China and France before the family returned to England, when he went to Bedford School. He served in the Intelligence Corps during the war and in 1947 went to Lincoln College, Oxford, where he was active in the dramatic society and in the university Labour Club, subsequently receiving a Commonwealth Fund Fellowship to study industrial relations at Cornell and Harvard universities. He stood unsuccessfully as Labour candidate for Bedford in 1951 then worked for Philips Electrical before running the overseas department of the Industrial Society and organising the Duke of Edinburgh's study conference on the human problems of industry (1954-56). He then joined the sugar company Booker McConnell. Asked to take on British Rail in 1947, he turned it down because he regarded the salary as too low. In 1970 he left the Booker board to become chairman-designate of the new National Ports Authority, but when Labour lost the election this did not happen and he took on directorships with the Rockware Group, the Dawnay Day Group, and with Curtis Brown until in 1976 he was again asked to be chairman of British Rail. This time the salary was acceptable, but for all his natural optimism, self-confidence, and capacity for hard work he found the task of persuading the rail unions to accept reforms, and successive governments to provide sufficient investment, a challenge too far. It was with some relief that, when his contract ended in 1983, he returned to private industry as chairman of Rockware and of Mitsubishi UK and Europe. He also chaired the governors of the London School of Economics and served in many voluntary organisations. He was appointed LVO in 1957, knighted in 1978, and appointed KBE in 1993. Died 28 April.

Peake, Dame Felicity, DBE (b. 1913), became first director of the Women's Royal Air Force in 1949. Born Felicity Hyde Watts in Cheadle Hulme, Cheshire, she was educated at St Winifred's, Eastbourne, and at Les Grands Huguenots, Vaucreson, France. In 1935 she married Jock Hanbury, taking flying lessons and obtaining a pilot's licence with him while on honeymoon in Monte Carlo. When war came her husband joined up as a fighter pilot but was killed in a crash in October 1939. Felicity Hanbury meanwhile had volunteered for the ATS and was posted to Biggin Hill during the Battle of Britain. In charge of some 250 women, she was there when the station suffered a surprise attack by German bombers and she was subsequently awarded an MBE. She then joined the Women's Auxiliary Air Force, working at the Air Ministry before being posted to Bomber Command in 1943 as deputy WAAF administration staff officer. She was given command of the WAAF officers' school in Windermere for two years before being appointed Senior WAAF staff officer to the Commander-in-Chief Mediterranean and Middle East Command. In 1946 she was appointed director of the WAAF, when she was only 32. Her service there brought her the honour of directing the WRAF when it was set up in 1949. She retired in the following year, and in 1952 married Sir Harald Peake, chairman of Lloyds Bank, whom she had first met during the war when, as Air Commodore, he had been in charge of RAF public relations. During her retirement Felicity Peake did much work for the RAF Benevolent Fund and was a Trustee of the Imperial War Museum (chairman 1986-88). She published an autobiography, *Pure Chance*, in 1993. Died 2 November.

Perutz, Professor Max, OM, CH, CBE, FRS (b. 1914), scientist who won the Nobel Prize for work on the structure of haemoglobin and was founder and first chairman of the Medical Research Council's Laboratory of Molecular Biology in Cambridge. Born in Vienna, he was educated at the Theresianum and the University of Vienna, where he studied chemistry. He then went to Peterhouse, Cambridge and to the Cavendish Laboratory as a research student, where he learnt X-ray crystallography and began the study of haemoglobin. He remained in Cambridge after Austria's incorporation into Nazi Germany, but in 1940 Perutz and his father, who had come to live in the UK, were interned by the British and sent to a camp in Canada. His Cambridge friends eventually secured his release and after the war he returned to his studies at the MRC's Unit for Molecular Biology. In 1954 he became Reader in Chemistry at the Davy Faraday Research Laboratory in London and in 1962 shared the Nobel Prize for Chemistry with Sir John Kendrew for their work on the structure of the biological macromolecules—Perutz for haemoglobin (the respiratory proteins of red blood cells) and Kendrew for myoglobin (carrying and storing oxygen in muscle cells). In the same year Perutz set up the Laboratory of Molecular Biology, remaining its chairman until 1979. Although running the laboratory and constantly lecturing in many parts of the world, he continued to spend most of his time on research work at the bench until the end of his career. He was an honorary fellow of most scientific academies, made a Fellow of the Royal Society in 1954, appointed CBE in 1963, CH in 1975, and OM in 1989. Died 6 February.

Porter of Luddenham, Lord, OM, FRS (b. 1920), scientist who won the Nobel

Prize for Chemistry in 1967. Born in Stainforth, Yorkshire, he was educated at Thorne Grammar School and Leeds University. He served as a radar operator in the Royal Navy Volunteer Reserve during the war, and on demobilisation went to Cambridge to study with Ronald Norrish, who was working on photochemistry, specifically trying to capture fragments of molecules made when chemicals were exposed to intense beams of light. Porter thought that using short flashes of light, instead of a continuous beam, might do the trick: the first flash would create the fragment, known as a free radical, and later flashes would photograph its brief existence. He and Norrish built an apparatus for the purpose, and began the process known as flash photolysis for the study of gaseous free radicals and combustion, subsequently developed for many chemical, physical, and biological problems. For this work Porter, Norrish, and Manfred Eigen of Germany shared the Nobel Prize. In 1968 Porter became director of the Royal Institution, a post from which he became widely known as a lecturer and broadcaster on science, regularly appearing on the televised children's Christmas lectures. When he was elected President of the Royal Society in 1985 he campaigned to improve the status of science and for greater government funding, warning in a BBC Dimbleby Lecture in 1986 that if the government continued to downgrade science the UK would become part of the "third world of science". He served on many other scientific bodies, received many honorary degrees and fellowships, was knighted in 1972 and appointed OM in 1989. Died 25 July.

Porter, Professor Roy (b. 1946), unconventional historian whose scholarship was worn lightly and communicated with ease in books, papers, articles, lectures, and on radio and TV. Born in Hitchin, he was educated (by means of scholarships) at Wilson's Grammar School in Camberwell and at Christ's College, Cambridge, where he achieved a starred double first in history. He stayed on to write a doctoral thesis on *The Making of Geology: Earth Science in Britain 1660-1815* (published in 1977) and to lecture on the British Enlightenment, which was one of his enduring interests. He collaborated with Mikulas Teich to produce a collection of essays, *The Enlightenment in National Context* in 1982 and, much later, wrote *Enlightenment: Britain and the Creation of the Modern World*, which won the Wolfson Prize for history in 2001 and was made into a TV programme. His other major historical concerns were medicine and science. He left Cambridge to return to London in 1979, working at the Wellcome Institute, writing many books including *Disease, Medicine and Society in England 1550-1860*; *A Social History of Madness*; *Patients' Progress: Doctors and Doctoring in 18th century England*; *Gout: the Patricians Malady*; and *Bodies Politic: Disease, Death and Doctors in Britain 1650-1900*. He retired from the Wellcome in 2002, when he was 55, declaring that he wanted to take up a musical instrument and get many things done. Died 3 March.

Qadeer, Haji Abdul (b. about 1951), Afghan warlord appointed one of three Vice-Presidents of his country in 2002. Born in Jalalabad, Qadir was educated locally and joined the resistance against the Soviet occupation as soon as he left school. When the mujahideen came to power in 1992 Qadir became governor of the eastern province of Nangahar, a large opium-producing area, from which he benefited financially, though he later supported attempts to reduce the drug's production. When Osama bin Laden returned to

Afghanistan in 1996 Qadir welcomed him, but was later forced to flee the country when the Taliban came to power. He returned when the Taliban regime was overthrown and he was reappointed governor of Nangahar, taking a prominent part in the Northern Alliance and in the setting up of the transitional government headed by President Hamid Karzai. He disrupted events by walking out of the UN-sponsored conference in Bonn, complaining that the Pashtuns were under-represented, but was nonetheless appointed Housing Minister and named one of the three Vice-Presidents at the *Loya Jirga*. He was shot dead in Kabul a month later. Died 6 July.

Queen Elizabeth The Queen Mother (b. 1900), consort of King George VI and mother of Queen Elizabeth II who continued to make an exceptional contribution to the work of the monarchy and the life of the UK and Commonwealth throughout her 51 years of widowhood. Born Elizabeth Angela Margaret Bowes-Lyon, ninth of 10 children born to Lord and Lady Glamis, she became Lady Elizabeth when her father succeeded to the earldom of Strathmore and inherited Glamis Castle. Elizabeth was taught to read and write, and the rudiments of music, dancing and drawing, by her mother, with later education from governesses. When World War I broke out she travelled with her mother to Scotland, where Glamis Castle was converted into a hospital and where she stayed, helping with the wounded as best she could, throughout the war. In 1920 she attended a dance in London, at which Prince Albert, Duke of York, second son of King George V, was also present. They married in 1923 and she began her first experience of royal duties. Their first child, Princess Elizabeth, was born in 1926 and their second, Princess Margaret Rose, in 1930. The death of the king in 1936 plunged the royal family into crisis when his successor, King Edward VIII, declared his intention to marry Wallis Simpson and abdicated the throne in order to do so, leaving his younger brother to become king as George VI. As Queen and consort, and mother of the new heir to the throne, Elizabeth embarked on the problem of establishing Buckingham Palace as her home as well as accompanying the King on formal visits to France and Canada. When World War II broke out Queen Elizabeth continued to spend most of her time in London, was indefatigable in visiting bombed cities, factories and dockyards and, when Buckingham Palace was bombed, she declared that she was glad as it enabled her "to look the East End in the face". When war ended the family paid a three-month visit to South Africa, after which she saw her older daughter happily married to Philip Mountbatten, created the Duke of Edinburgh. In 1951 the young couple set off on a tour that was intended to take them to Australia, but which ended abruptly when the King, who had developed cancer, died. Under the constitution a Queen Consort's place was well defined, but as a widow she was accorded no particular status. The former Queen, then 51, had already established a solid place in the nation's affection, and she set about securing this by taking on a vast number of public engagements. It was agreed that she should be called Queen Elizabeth The Queen Mother, and she was appointed a Counsellor of State, which enabled her to stand in on occasion for her daughter, the new Queen. Among many other activities the Queen Mother became president or patron of some 300 organisations, colonel-in-chief of many regiments, the first female Warden of the Cinque Ports, owner of horses and keen supporter of racing. In later life she became a little frail, undergoing a number of hip operations, but she continued to fulfil public engagements, her hundredth year proving to be particularly active. Died 30 March.

Rawls, John (b. 1921), US eminent political philosopher whose influential books on justice brought philosophy back to fundamental questions of ethics and society, freedom and responsibility. Born in Baltimore, Maryland, Rawls was educated at Kent School in Connecticut and at Princeton University. After graduating in 1943 he enlisted in the US army and fought in the Pacific. He was horrified by the US use of atomic weapons against Japan, an act against which he spoke out in later years. After completing his doctorate at Princeton in 1950, he went to Oxford for a year before going to Cornell University in 1953 as assistant professor of philosophy. He moved to Harvard for a year in 1959 and then joined the Massachusetts Institute of Technology before returning to Harvard in 1962 as professor of philosophy, where he remained for the rest of his academic career. In 1971 he completed and published his major work, *A Theory of Justice*, in which he sought to provide an appropriate moral concept of justice in a democratic society, arguing that a just society would be one whose constitutive principles were the outcome of a fair and impartial decision-making process. To some extent this challenged fashionable utilitarianism and revived and updated the ideas of the social contract. The book sold more than 250,000 copies in English and was translated into many languages. Some of its ideas were taken up by the Social Democratic Party when it split from the Labour Party in the UK, and copies of it were seen in the hands of Chinese students assembling in protest in Tiananmen Square in 1989. An extremely modest and gentle man, Rawls was astonished by the book's success, and consistently avoided the accolades and attention that ensued. His later books were *Political Liberalism* (1993), addressing the difficulties raised by conflicting religious and moral views in free societies, and *The Law of Peoples* (1999), which dealt with the problems of international justice. His later writings also reflected some shift in his views, suggesting a rejecting of the capitalist welfare state and contending that liberal principles could only be achieved in a property-owning democracy or market-socialist state. He was awarded a National Humanities Medal and the Rolf Schock Prize in Logic and Philosophy. In 1995 he was incapacitated by a stroke. Died 24 November.

Reisz, Karel (b. 1926), film and theatre director who first made his mark with the film *Saturday Night and Sunday Morning*. Born in Czechoslovakia, he began his education in his own country but went to England as a refugee when Czechoslovakia was invaded by Germany in 1938, continuing his education at Leighton Park School in Reading. He served in the Czech air force during the war, afterwards going to Emmanuel College, Cambridge, where he read chemistry. Always interested in the cinema, he made some 16mm films while at school and upon going down from university joined the magazine *Sequence*. He wrote a book on the techniques of film editing and made a number of documentaries, including *Momma Don't Allow*, which he directed with Tony Richardson. His first feature film, *Saturday Night and Sunday Morning*, starring Albert Finney and based on Alan Sillitoe's novel about the working class in the Midlands, was released in 1960. It was the first of many 1960s films on similar themes, though few were directed by Reisz. He was producer for Lindsay Anderson's *This Sporting Life* in 1963, directed an unmemorable remake of *Night Must Fall* in 1964, a psychological comedy called *Morgan, A Suitable Case for Treatment* in 1966, and *Isadora* in 1968. This was so badly received that Reisz gave up film making until 1981, when he directed a successful film version of *The French Lieutenant's Woman*. Died 25 November.

Rostow, Eugene (b. 1913), Professor of Law who served in various capacities under four US Presidents. Born in Brooklyn, New York, Rostow trained as an academic lawyer, graduating from Yale at the age of 19 and passing the New York State Bar exam in 1937. He became an associate professor of law at Yale in the following year, and as a lawyer remained at Yale for the rest of his academic life (though he was at one point close to being nominated to the Supreme Court). He was equally at home in public affairs, serving as an adviser in the State Department during the war, as assistant executive secretary to the UN Economic Commission for Europe in 1949-50, and later turning his attention to the growing threat from the Soviet Union. He left his post as Dean of the Law School at Yale in 1966, when he was appointed Under-Secretary for Political Affairs at the State Department, defending US policies in Vietnam on legal grounds (the US being bound by the SEATO treaty to defend the area against communist aggression). In 1976 Rostow was co-founder of the Committee on Present Danger, set up to oppose the second SALT agreement limiting nuclear weapons, serving as chairman until 1981 and again from 1986-91. He was appointed director of the Arms Control and Disarmament Agency in 1981 but resigned two years later, mainly as a result of Senate opposition. He published a number of books on the subject of peace, including *Law, Power and the Pursuit of Peace* (1968), *Peace in the Balance* (1972), and *Towards Managed Peace* (1993). Died 25 November.

Sabri al-Banna (b. 1937), Palestinian terrorist who adopted the name Abu Nidal and was, directly and indirectly, responsible for the deaths of thousands in many countries of the world. Born in Jaffa during the British mandate of Palestine, Sabri was educated at local schools until the family was forced to move during the Arab-Israeli war of 1948, when he went to Cairo to study engineering. In the 1950s he worked for a time in Saudi Arabia, where he was recruited into Fatah, the guerrilla organisation set up by Yassir Arafat and took the name of Abu Nidal ("Father of the Struggle"), moving to Jordan where he set up a trading company. In 1970 he was sent to Baghdad as PLO representative, where he associated with Abu Da'ud, a member of the Fatah terrorist arm which killed Israeli hostages at the Munich Olympics in 1972. Abu Nidal then set himself up with a terrorist organisation called "Black June" which operated initially against enemies of Iraq but whose main targets came to be moderate Arab regimes and Palestinian leaders such as Arafat who were deemed to be traitors to true Palestinian nationalism. In fact his operations generally did far more harm to the Arab cause, by prompting, for example, Israel's invasion of Lebanon following the attempted assassination of Israel's ambassador to London in 1982. Later attacks for which he was responsible included the killing of 19 people at El Al check-in points at Rome and Vienna airports in 1985 and the bombing, in 1988, of an Istanbul synagogue when 22 people were killed. In his later years he spent much of his time in hiding, suffering from various illnesses, and was ultimately reported to have been found dead, apparently by his own hand, from gunshot wounds in his apartment in Baghdad. Died 16 August.

Savimbi, Jonas (b. 1934), Angolan guerrilla leader. Born in Munhangoa, where his father was a stationmaster and a Protestant preacher, Savimbi was a bright student who went to Lisbon (the capital of Portugal, the colonial power in Angola) in 1958 to study medicine. There he became active in the struggle for Angolan independence but, after attracting the attention of the Portuguese secret police, he fled to Switzerland, where he changed his field of study to politics. He received his doctorate in 1965. Infiltrating back into Angola in 1966, Savimbi founded the National Union for the Total Independence of Angola (UNITA) in Moxico province and led the group in a guerrilla war against the Portuguese. After the Portuguese withdrawal from Angola in 1975, Savimbi proclaimed himself "President" of the People's Democratic Republic of Angola, in opposition to the socialist Popular Movement for the Liberation of Angola (MPLA) government. He launched a war to overthrow the MPLA and establish a multi-party capitalist-orientated democracy. Initially, UNITA operations were concentrated in the movement's heartlands in the centre and south-east of the country. After 1981, with South African military and logistical support and covert aid from the USA, UNITA operations extended to most of the country, causing serious disruption to the Angolan economy and large-scale displacement of its population. The reorientation of South African foreign policy after 1988, leading to its withdrawal from Angola and then, in 1989, to agreement on Namibian independence and the ending of direct support for Savimbi, increased the importance of US support for UNITA. The MPLA government was also under pressure from a reforming Soviet government and a collapsing economy, and in June 1989 the two sides came together to agree a ceasefire and begin moves towards national reconciliation. UN peace efforts led to presidential and legislative elections in September 1992, but after UNITA and Savimbi lost the contest fresh fighting erupted and the country was plunged back into civil war. Seemingly facing military defeat in 1994, UNITA signed a peace agreement (the Lusaka protocol) with the government but then consistently refused to comply with its terms. Using arms funded from smuggled diamonds from central and eastern Angola, Savimbi continued to fight an increasingly pointless personal war in which hundreds of thousands of already impoverished peasants were killed, wounded, or displaced. His death, during fighting with government forces in Moxico, was the cause of celebration in Luanda and heralded the final collapse of UNITA's violent campaign. Died 22 February.

Shaker Sharif Zaid ibn (b. 1934), diplomat and three times Prime Minister of Jordan who also commanded an armoured brigade during the 1967 Six Day War. With family ties to the Hashemite dynasty, Shaker was a childhood friend of the future King Hussein, being educated with him at Victoria College in Alexandria and subsequently at the Royal Military Academy, Sandhurst. He served as assistant military attaché in London in 1957 before returning to Jordan for active service on a number of battlefields, including the Six Day War and the Black September War of 1970. He was Commander-in-Chief of the Armed Forces 1976-99, Chief of the Royal Court 1988-89 and again in 1993, and became Prime Minister for the first time in 1989 when, having suspended a 10-year period of martial law, he presided over the first democratic elections for the House of Deputies for many years. He began a second term as Prime Minister in 1991, when his main concern was to re-establish relations with other Arab countries following Jordan's support of Iraq during the Kuwait crisis; and his third in 1995, when he reached an agreement with Yassir Arafat, whose Palestine Liberation Organisation he had previously driven from the country. Shaker resigned the premiership in the following year prompted, it was suggested, by a difference of opinion with the King over the severance of ties with Iraq. On his resignation he was appointed emir, which precluded further political activity, though he continued to be influential in Jordan's affairs. Died August 30.

Snead, Sam (b. 1912), US golfer who won more than 135 tournaments in a playing career that lasted more than 30 years. Born in West Virginia, Samuel Jackson Snead showed himself to be a natural athlete at school, able to run 100 yards in 10 seconds and nurturing an early ambition to play American football. He turned to golf when a back injury put an end to that idea, developing a smooth but powerful swing which was the envy of golfers everywhere, which could carry the ball 270 yards and which earned for him the nickname of "Slammin' Sam". In 1936, when he turned professional, he won the West Virginia championship, taking only 61 for one of his rounds, a record for the course which he broke with a 59 more than 20 years later. He won his first PGA tour event in 1937 and the Vardon Memorial Trophy as best golfer of the year in 1938, when he also became a member of the US Ryder Cup team (he took part in seven of these matches, captaining the team twice). He won the US PGA in 1942, 1949 and 1951 as well as the Masters on three occasions, in 1954 beating Ben Hogan in an 18-hole play-off. He came second in the British Open at St Andrews in 1939, and won it when it was next played in 1946. The only major he failed to win was the US Open, though he was runner-up four times. In his fifties his putting, always the least reliable part of his game, began seriously to let him down, though as a senior he won 11 more titles and was world senior champion five times. Died 23 May.

Steiger, Rod (b. 1925), US film and stage actor who played his roles with an intensity that sometimes went out of control. Born in Westhampton, Long Island, Steiger was brought up by his mother in New Jersey, his parents having divorced when he was an infant. He started to act at Newark High School, but then joined the US Navy in which he served for four years. He returned to study acting in New York after the war, and after a spell at the Actors' Studio, where he was introduced to the "method" style of acting, he appeared on Broadway in a revival of Clifford Odets's play *Night Music*. In 1953 he took the lead in the original TV production of *Marty* and in 1954 played Marlon Brando's brother in the film *On the Waterfront*. His memorable performance in this brought him many other film roles, not all of them as successful. Cast as Judd Fry in the film version of *Oklahoma!*, for example, he hopelessly overloaded the part with method-inspired psychological problems and later, in the film *Waterloo*, persuaded himself that Napoleon had overdosed on drugs on the eve of the battle. He was more convincing as a crooked boxing promoter in *The Harder They Fall* (1956), as Al Capone in the film of 1959, and as a police captain in *The Heat of the Night* (1967), for which he won an Oscar. He appeared in many other films, including *Dr Zhivago* in 1965 and *The Loved One* in the same year, but generally in character parts rather than leading roles. His later career suffered from bouts of illness and depression. Died 9 July.

Stassinopoulos, Michael (b. 1905), Greek university professor, poet, judge, and politician who was President of his country for six months. Born in Calamata, he was educated locally and at Athens University, where he was lecturer in administrative law from 1937-68. He was also Professor of Administrative Law at the High School of Political Sciences in Athens from 1939-68. He served as a State Council Adviser in 1943-58, was appointed Minister for the Press and Minister of Labour in 1953, also chairing national boards for opera and broadcasting during this time. In 1966 he was appointed President of the Council of State, the legal body charged with safeguarding the rights of Greek citizens, coming up against the country's military dictatorship at that time when the Council reinstated judges and other officials who had been dismissed. Stassinopoulos was dismissed—officially declared to have resigned, because members of the Council were appointed for life—but announced that he had not resigned and did not intend to. He was nonetheless replaced. In December 1974, after the fall of the colonels' government, he was proposed by Konstantinos Karamanlis to be head of the new government of national unity as temporary President of Greece until a new constitution had been approved. He served until the first President of the new Greek Republic was elected in June 1975, subsequently becoming an ad hoc judge at the International Court of Justice at The Hague from 1976-78. During his life he wrote several books on politics and the law, as well as books of poetry, including *Poems* (1949), *Harmonia* (1956), and *Two Seasons* (1979). Died 31 October.

Thaw, John, CBE (b. 1942), English actor best known for the television characters he created, first in *The Sweeney* and later in *Morse* and *Kavanagh QC*. Born in Manchester, he attended high school there, emerging with one O level, in English. He began performing at a local youth club and was persuaded to apply to the Royal Academy of Dramatic Art in London, which he joined two years before the normal eligible age. In 1965 he was given the lead in a TV series called *Redcap* but it was *The Sweeney*, in which he played Detective Inspector Jack Regan, that brought him stardom. The series ran for four years, totalling 53 episodes and was translated into two films sold to some 40 countries. When the series ended Thaw appeared in a revival of John Arden's *Sergeant Musgrave's Dance* at the National theatre and joined the Royal Shakespeare Company for a season, playing Sir Toby Belch in *Twelfth Night* and Cardinal Wolsey in *King Henry VIII*. In 1987 he began the Inspector Morse series, in which he created the slightly grumpy Oxford policeman with a fondness for classical music and real ale whose investigations in and around Oxford colleges attracted viewing figures of some 18 million in Britain. The series, based on novels by Colin Dexter, ran to 33 films over a period of 13 years, but it neither exhausted nor type-casted Thaw, who went on to play a north country barrister in another successful TV series, *Kavanagh QC*, after starring in an unsuccessful adaptation of Peter Mayle's *A Year in Provence*. In 1993 he returned to the stage to give a memorable performance as the Labour Party leader in David Hare's play *The Absence of War* at the National Theatre. He was appointed

CBE in the same year. He was twice married, his second wife being the actress Sheila Hancock. Died 21 February.

Thom, René (b. 1923), French mathematician and creator of catastrophe theory. Born the son of a shopkeeper near the Swiss border, Thom studied mathematics in Paris and Strasbourg, writing a doctoral thesis in algebraic topology under the distinguished academic Henri Cartan. During the 1950s he was the co-founder (together with Hassler Whitney) of the mathematical fields of differential topology and singularity theory, and created cobordism theory and classified generic singularities of smooth maps. For this pioneering work he was awarded a Fields Medal (the equivalent in mathematics of a Nobel Prize) in 1958, after which in addition to topology he also began to write extensively on linguistics, philosophy, and theoretical biology. His studies resulted in a book published in 1972 entitled *Structural Stability and Morphogenesis*, which contained catastrophe theory: an explanation of situations in which gradually changing forces could lead to sudden dramatic change. Although the theory was widely developed by other mathematicians, it did not prove as useful in predicting disastrous phenomena (such as earthquakes, flooding, or war) as Thom had hoped. It did, however, assist with the later emergence of chaos theory, which sought to understand unpredictability by examining how small changes to the initial conditions of a deterministic system could result in large variations in the ensuing motion. Although still in its infancy, some scientists believed that chaos theory would one day be recognised as the third great theory of the 20th century, alongside relativity and quantum mechanics. Died 25 October.

Thuan, Cardinal Nguyen Van (b. 1928), Roman Catholic Archbishop of Saigon who was imprisoned for 13 years. Born in Hue, Vietnam, Thuan was ordained in 1953 and obtained a doctorate in canon law at the Gregorian University in Rome in 1959. On his return to Vietnam he became rector of the seminary at Nha Trang, a maritime city north of Saigon, and was appointed bishop of the city in 1967. In 1975 he was appointed coadjutor archbishop of Saigon but was arrested three months later when the Communists seized the city. Thuan was offered the choice of imprisonment or resigning his priesthood. He chose prison. Moved between various prisons and re-education camps, and spending nine of the years in solitary confinement, he followed the example of St Paul and wrote daily messages which were smuggled out to local Catholics. He also contrived to celebrate Mass every day, sending out a request for medicine for a stomach ache and having bread and wine smuggled back. When he was finally released in 1988 he spent another three years under house arrest in Hanoi before being sent into exile to Australia. He went to Rome, where three years later he was appointed vice-president of the Pontifical Council for Justice and Peace, becoming its president in 1998. He was appointed Cardinal in 2001. His messages from prison were published as a book, *The Road to Hope*, as was a collection of Lenten talks he gave in the papacy in 2000, published with the title *Testimony to Hope*. Died 16 September.

Thyssen-Bornemisza de Kaszon, Baron Hans Heinrich (b. 1921), industrialist and art collector. Grandson of August Thyssen, who built up the iron, steel and armaments conglomerate upon which the family's fortune was based, "Heini" Thyssen was born in Scheveningen, near

The Hague, and educated at the Realgymnsium in The Hague and at Fribourg University in Switzerland, where he was sent following the German invasion of Holland. In 1944, when he was 23, his father transferred to him ownership of all of the family's German companies, assets which with considerable skill Thyssen managed to retain and develop. When his father died in 1947 he inherited 60 per cent of the estate, estimated to be worth about US$8 billion, and full control of the business empire. He also inherited his father's art collection of some 500 Old Masters, though this was broken up when the will was challenged by his brother, two sisters, and his father's widow. This setback inspired Thyssen to form his own collection, buying back some works acquired by other members of the family and adding some 900 more modern paintings, including the Renoir, Monet, Manet, Cézanne, Morisot, Pissarro, and Toulouse-Lautrec with which he furnished his bedroom and study in his father's old villa on Lake Lugano. The Tintorettos and Titians were housed in the museum alongside. In time the collection became too large, but Thyssen wanted it to be kept together and asked the Swiss to fund an enlargement of the museum. The sum offered failed to satisfy him and he then enjoyed the process of seeking an alternative site outside Switzerland. Among those who courted him were Disney World in Orlando, the Getty Museum in California, and the UK government, which proposed a site in London Docklands. He finally chose Madrid in Spain, where the Villahermose Palace was redesigned to become the Thyssen-Bornemizsa Museum. Thyssen's other passion was for beautiful women. It was said that he collected them rather as he collected works of art, but found old mistresses more troublesome than Old Masters. He was married five times, first to a princess, second and third to English models, fourth to a Brazilian banker's daughter, and finally to a Spanish beauty queen. Died 27 April.

Tobin, James (b. 1918), US economist who won the Nobel Prize and was adviser to President John F. Kennedy. Born in Champain, Illinois, he was educated at high school in Urbana and at Harvard University, where he wrote a thesis inspired largely by the ideas of John Maynard Keynes, though in later work he generally modified some of Keynes's views, believing that they were too inflationary. After graduating in 1939 and taking a masters degree in economics in the following year he began work in the Office of Price Administration, but enlisted in the US Navy following the attack on Pearl Harbour. Returning to Harvard he completed his doctorate on *The Theoretical and Statistical Study of Consumption Function*, remaining there until 1950, when he was appointed an associate professor at Yale, becoming a full professor in 1955 and Sterling Professor of Economics in 1957. During these years he also edited the journals *Econometrica* and the *Review of Economic Studies*. He served as Director of the Cowles Foundation for Research in Economics in 1955-61, at one point writing an article criticising the Federal Reserve Board's tight monetarism. When this was published he received a call from President Kennedy asking him to join his Council of Economic Advisers. The Council urged full employment, a faster growth rate for the economy, and increased competition, but Tobin soon wanted to return to what he described as his ivory tower at Yale and resigned in 1962. He later became associated with what was called "the Tobin tax", a proposed levy on foreign currency transactions to counter the risks that currency flows posed to financial growth. This was subsequently taken up by anti-globalisation groups working to reduce poverty in developing countries, but Tobin declared that he was not against globalisation. When he was awarded the Nobel Prize in 1981 the committee noted that his work had inspired substantial research during the 1970s "on the effect of monetary policy, the implications of government budget deficits and stabilisation policy in general". Among his last publications was a fourth and final volume of a series *Essays in Economics* (1996). Died 11 March.

Todd, Sir Garfield (b. 1908), missionary who became Prime Minister of Southern Rhodesia 1953-58 but was later imprisoned for supporting black majority rule. Born in Invercargill, New Zealand, he was educated at Otago University, at Glen Leith Theological College, and at the University of Witwatersrand in South Africa, where he spent a year on a medical course. He went to Southern Rhodesia as a missionary of the Church of Christ in 1934, working first at Mashoko and then at Dadaya, where he was superintendent until 1953. He was elected to Parliament as member for Shabani in 1946, and in 1953 became Prime Minister when Sir Godfrey Huggins (later Viscount Malvern) became Prime Minister of the newly-created Federation of Rhodesia and Nyasaland. Though Todd won an overwhelming majority for the United Rhodesia Party in the elections of 1954, opposition began to build up within the party when he amended the Land Apportionment Act to allow hotels, restaurants, and clubs to become multiracial, and in 1958 he lost the leadership and the subsequent general election to Sir Edward Whitehead. Out of office he began to campaign for majority rule, and when Ian Smith became Prime Minister and declared unilateral independence Todd was first confined to his ranch and later for a short time imprisoned for encouraging extremist black leaders such as Joshua Nkomo and Robert Mugabe. When the latter became President of an independent Zimbabwe Todd was rewarded with a seat in the Senate, but he quickly became disillusioned as the country's economy began to be destroyed by corruption and incompetence. He was not reappointed to the Senate and shortly before his death an attempt was made to deny him a vote in the general election on the grounds that, born in New Zealand, he was disqualified from Zimbabwean citizenship. Died 13 October.

Unitas, Johnny (b. 1933), US footballer who held 22 National Football League records at the time of his retirement and was voted the greatest quarterback of all time while still a player. Born in Pittsburg, Pennsylvania, he began his career playing semi-professional football in his home town for US$6 a game. He was recruited to the Baltimore Colts in 1955 and became part of the most successful team of the time. As quarterback he controlled the team's play with assurance and authority, leading them to the NFL Championships in 1958 and 1959 and victory in the Super Bowl in 1970. At one point he completed at least one touchdown in 47 straight games, a record that no one has since approached, and among his other superlatives were the most passes achieved and completed, most touchdown passes, and most yards gained in passing. During his career he completed 2,830 of 5,186 passes for 40,239 yards and 290 touchdowns. He retired in 1974 and was inducted into the NFL Hall of Fame in 1979. He had a triple by-pass in 1993 following a heart attack, but did not survive a second attack in 2002. Died 11 September.

Vance, Cyrus (b. 1917), US Secretary of State who resigned in 1980 in protest at the attempt to rescue 52 US hostages held in Tehran. Born in Clarksburg, West Virginia, Vance was educated at Kent School, Connecticut, and Yale University, where he read economics. After serving in the US Navy in World War II he was called to the Bar and joined the New York law firm of Simpson, Thacher and Bartlett. In 1959-60 he served as associate counsel for Senate sub-committees investigating the comparative strengths of US and Soviet nuclear forces and satellite programmes, and became general counsel to the Defence Department. In 1962 he was appointed Secretary of the Army by President John F. Kennedy and in 1964 Deputy Secretary of Defence by President Lyndon B. Johnson, who sent him on a number of trouble-shooting missions overseas, notably to Panama, South Vietnam, Cyprus, and South Korea. Vance also took a major part in a special delegation sent to Detroit after race riots had broken out in the city in 1967, and his handling of the situation and subsequent report were highly praised. In 1968 he went to Paris as deputy chief US delegate under Averell Harriman to begin talks which ultimately led to the ceasefire in Vietnam and to the withdrawal of US forces. When Jimmy Carter was elected President in 1976 Vance was appointed Secretary of State. During his first two years in the post he worked to improve relations with China, and to improve the chances of peace in the Middle East, culminating in the Camp David agreement and the signing of the peace treaty between Egypt and Israel in1978. When Iranians seized hostages in the US embassy in Tehran in 1979 he advocated a policy of quiet and patient diplomacy to resolve the crisis, but the President authorised a military operation which proved abortive. After his resignation Vance on occasion served as a peace broker for the UN, seeking to end civil strife in Yugoslavia, working for a ceasefire in Croatia, and endeavouring to find peaceful settlements to the disputes that broke out following the collapse of the Soviet Union. He was awarded the Medal of Freedom in 1969 and published his autobiography, *Hard Choices*, in 1983. Died 12 January.

Weinstock, Lord (b. 1924), industrialist who as managing director of the General Electric Company for 33 years developed it into a large conglomerate that disintegrated after his retirement. Arnold Weinstock was born in London, the son of Jewish refugees from Poland, and educated at the London School of Economics, where he took a degree in statistics. He was called up in 1944 to work as an administrative officer in the Admiralty, and on release worked in property development. In 1947 he married Netta, daughter of Michael Sobell, and in the 1950s joined his father-in-law's company, Radio & Allied Industries, to run the television manufacturing side of the business. The company went public in 1958 and three years later joined with GEC in what was in effect a reverse takeover arranged by Weinstock. In 1963 he became managing director and within five years had increased its profits by 200 per cent, partly because of his careful financial control. In 1967 he began the growth of the company by acquiring Associated Electrical Industries, English Electric, and Elliott-Automation, creating an industrial group that was involved in electronics, telecommunications, heavy electrical plant, and consumer goods, with many defence and other government contracts, and which involved Weinstock in a huge programme of reorganisation and rationalisation. This he did by a process that was compared to a spider's web: management being devolved along the outer circles, with Weinstock sitting at the centre, scrutinising the performances of each of more than 150 companies, with a particularly keen eye on costs. It was a system that worked successfully to control a conglomerate achieving a turnover of UK£1 billion, to which, in 1973, was added the construction of the nation's nuclear industry. During the 1980s GEC ran into a series of difficulties, being sued for faults in the design of the high speed train (which was ultimately abandoned), and castigated for the costly failure of the Nimrod Early Warning contract, on which GEC's subsidiary, Marconi, had been working for nine years. There were a number of attempts to take over and break up GEC, but Weinstock managed to keep it intact, and when he finally, and reluctantly, retired in 1996 he was able to hand over a business worth UK£10 billion and with cash reserves of more than UK£3 billion. He then had to watch as his successors crippled the business so that shares which had once been worth more than UK£12 each fell to 4p by the time of his death. Apart from business Weinstock's only other major preoccupation was horse racing. The first horse he bought, London Cry, won the Cambridgeshire in 1958 at odds of 20-1, and later Classic successes included the Derby with Troy in 1979 and the Oaks and St Leger with Sun Princess in 1983. He was a trustee of the British Museum and of the Royal Philharmonic Orchestra. He was knighted in 1970 and made a life peer in 1980. Died 23 July.

Werner, Pierre (b. 1913) was Prime Minister of Luxembourg from 1959-74 and 1979-84 who played a major part in the early promotion of a single European currency. Born at Saint André near Lille in France, Werner was educated at schools in Luxembourg and at the University of Paris (where he studied law). He worked with the Banque Générale du Luxembourg during the war but then moved into politics. He was elected to Luxembourg's parliament as a member of the Christian Social People's Party, becoming government commissioner for bank control in 1946. He was appointed Minister of Finance and of the Armed Forces in 1953, elected leader of his party in 1954, and became Prime Minister and Minister of Finance in the coalition government of 1959. In a speech in Strasbourg in 1960 he urged that a single currency (which he named the "euror") be adopted as soon as possible. Though the idea was referred to in the 1957 Treaty of Rome it had not been seriously considered until brought forward by Werner. It was formally agreed as a European goal in 1969, when Werner was appointed to lead a committee to report on how monetary union could be achieved. His report did not propose the introduction of a new currency or the setting up of a central bank, but it did recommend the total and irreversible convertibility of currencies, fixing of parity rates, and the elimination of exchange rate fluctuations. It also recognised that economic and fiscal policy, including the size and financing of national budgets, would have to be determined by the EEC. Werner's report was adopted by the six Community countries and endorsed by those negotiating entry, but its implementation did not take place until 2002. Meanwhile in Luxembourg Werner had successfully developed his small country as a profitable centre for banking and finance, but he lost the 1974 election. He returned to power in 1979, but lost again in 1984, when he retired from politics to pursue a business career. His work for Europe was recognised by the award of a Robert Schuman gold medal in 1971 and the Prince of Asturias prize in 1998. Died 24 June.

Wesley, Mary (b. 1912), writer whose first novel was published when she was 71, after which she produced a series of best-sellers for the rest of her life. Born Mary Farmer, daughter of a colonel and descendant of the Duke of Wellington on her mother's side (from whose family name, Wellesley, she adopted her pen name), she was educated informally by a series of governesses. In 1937 she married an Irish peer, Lord Swinfen, but when war came she enlisted in the signals deciphering unit, which brought her to London, where she was caught up in the social and sexual whirl of the time and which she was later to describe so vividly in some of her novels, while her family remained in Cornwall. The marriage was dissolved in 1945 and some years later she married Eric Siepmann, a journalist and unsuccessful novelist who encouraged his wife to write, which she enjoyed, having two children's books published in 1968. When Siepmann died in 1970 she found it hard to live on a widow's pension and turned more seriously to writing, having a third children's book published in 1983 and her first novel, *Jumping the Queue*, in the same year. Her second and most successful novel, *The Camomile Lawn*, was published in 1984 and later adapted and produced for TV by Peter Hall. After that there followed a novel a year for the next four years, and a further four between 1990-97. All concentrated on the lives of women, generally from start to finish of their lives, and all were described with brutal frankness, particularly in their sexual encounters. Died 30 December.

Wilder, Billy (b. 1906), film director and screenwriter whose films won many Oscars. Born in Sucha, then part of Austria, Wilder was educated in Vienna, enrolling at the university but dropping out after a year to become a journalist. As such he worked for papers in Vienna and in Berlin, where he also began scriptwriting. He left Germany when Hitler came to power in 1933, arriving in Hollywood where he was eventually taken on as a scriptwriter by Paramount, where he worked with the novelist Charles Brackett on a number of successful comedies, including *Ninotchka* which starred Greta Garbo. He turned to directing in 1942, beginning with a comedy, *The Major and the Minor*, and a war film, *Five Graves to Cairo*, before making a succession of films that established his reputation—*Double Indemnity* (1944), *The Lost Weekend* (1945), and *Sunset Boulevard* (1950), for which he and Brackett won Oscars for the best screenplay. Not all his later films were so successful, but he had a box office winner with *The Seven Year Itch*, starring Marilyn Monroe, and though he found her hard to work with Wilder cast her again in what was to become his most successful and enduring comedy, *Some Like It Hot* (1959), which also starred Jack Lemmon and Tony Curtis. In the following year he made another successful comedy, *The Apartment*, which won him two more Oscars. None of his later films reached such high standards, and a few of them embarrassed even his most devoted fans. Died 27 March.

Wolstenholme, Kenneth, DFC and Bar (b. 1920), sports commentator. Born in Worsley, near Bolton, Wolstenholme worked in local newspapers until joining the RAF in 1938. After distinguished wartime service, in which he flew more than 100 combat missions and was decorated, he entered broadcasting and commentated on his first televised football match in 1948. In 1964 he became famous as the presenter of the new BBC *Match of the Day* programme screened on Saturday nights. Although his commentary was largely pedestrian, and frequently ridiculed, it was also boyishly keen and reflective of Wolstenholme's patriotism and obvious love of the game. Amongst the numerous matches which he covered in his career were 23 FA Cup finals, 16 European Cup finals, and five World Cup finals. It was at Wembley in 1966, however, during the World Cup final between England and West Germany, that his most memorable moment occurred. With only minutes of extra time left to run in a tense match, England led 3-2 but the West Germans were pressing for a late equaliser. Even as England striker Geoff Hurst broke with the ball some members of the crowd had advanced onto the pitch in anticipation of the final whistle. Encapsulating the moment perfectly, Wolstenholme spontaneously stated: "Some people are on the pitch. They think it's all over." (At which point Hurst's searing shot flew into the top corner of the opposition goal.) "It is now." It was a soundbite which defined England's moment of victory, and which was subsequently used extensively in programmes, advertisements, and records. Such was its exposure that it entered the collective memory and Wolstenholme later described it as his "pension". Despite this, the BBC dispensed with Wolstenholme's services in 1971, although he continued to make sporadic forays into football commentary for Channel 4 and local radio in the 1980s and 1990s. He also made regular appearances as an after-dinner speaker and chat show guest. Died 26 March.

Wu Cheng-chung, John Baptist (b. 1925), Hong Kong Cardinal who safely protected his Roman Catholic diocese during the transition to Chinese communist rule in 1997. Born in Ho Hau village in the Guangdong province of China, Wu entered the South Regional Seminary in Hong Kong, where he was ordained in 1952. He went to Rome to obtain a doctorate in canon law, then to the USA where he worked in the chanceries of New York, Boston, and Chicago before taking up a post in 1957 as a parish priest in Taiwan. While there in 1975 the Pope appointed him Bishop of Hong Kong, rejecting the names suggested by the Hong Kong clergy and ignoring the strained relationship that existed between China and Taiwan. However in 1986 Wu was invited to lead a church delegation to visit China (the first to visit the country since 1949), which also gave him the opportunity of meeting his mother for the first time in 40 years. When he was made Cardinal in 1988 he set about trying to avert the duplication of the church system then operating in China, where there was an officially recognised Catholic Church controlled by the government and an illegal one, whose bishops were appointed by the Vatican. He built up communities of lay Catholics in Hong Kong capable of carrying on should Catholic bishops be imprisoned when China resumed sovereignty, and urged Catholic schools in the territory to teach in Chinese. His efforts were rewarded when China decided to allow a two systems rule for Hong Kong, effectively allowing the Catholic church its independence. Died 23 September.

Young, Baroness, PC (b. 1926) was first woman Leader of the House of Lords and, apart from the Prime Minister herself, the only woman in Margaret Thatcher's Cabinet. Born Janet Mary Baker, she was educated at the Dragon School in Oxford and at Headington School before being evacuated during the war to the USA, where she attended Mount Holyoke College in Massachusetts. On returning to Oxford she went to St Anne's College. In 1950 she married Geoffrey Young, and they had three daughters. Concerned about the erosion of family values she took up politics and was elected to Oxford City Council in 1957. She was created a life peer in 1971, becoming a junior whip in the House of Lords, and in 1973 Under Secretary of State in the Department of the Environment. After the government's fall in 1974 she remained active in opposition, becoming deputy chairman of the Conservative Party Organisation in 1977. When the party returned to power under Margaret Thatcher in 1979, Young was appointed Minister of State in the Department of Education and Science, then Chancellor of the Duchy of Lancaster and, in 1981, Leader of the House of Lords. She had to yield the post to William Whitelaw, and leave the Cabinet, two years later, but went to the Foreign and Commonwealth Office as Minister of State until 1987. In that year she became a director of NatWest Bank and of Marks & Spencer (in both cases their first woman director), but returned fiercely to politics in 1997 to fight the Labour government's proposals to repeal section 28 of the Local Government Act, which prohibited the promotion of homosexuality in English and Welsh schools, and to lower the age of consent for homosexuals from 18 to 16. The Lords supported her on section 28, and the government backed down after its second defeat, but she failed to stop the reduction in the homosexual age of consent. Died 6 September.

Young of Dartington, Lord (b. 1915), UK sociologist who founded many organisations, some of which, such as the Consumers' Association, became national institutions. Born in Manchester, Michael Young was educated at Dartington Hall School in Devon (where he came under the influence of its founders, Leonard and Dorothy Elmhirst), and at the London School of Economics. During the war he worked at Political and Economic Planning, a non-party research organisation, becoming its director in 1941. In 1945 he became secretary of the Labour Party's research department, drafting the party's manifesto for its triumphant election of that year, but left the post in 1951 to take up sociology, setting up the Institute of Community Studies with Peter Wilmore and publishing, in 1957, *Family and Kinship in East London*, a study of the influence of slum clearance on inner-city communities. In the following year Young published a totally different kind of book, *The Rise of the Meritocracy*, which was intended as a satirical parody, though the word "meritocracy", which he coined as a nasty elitist term on a par with "aristocracy", was taken more seriously than he intended. More successfully in 1958 he founded the Consumers' Association and its magazine *Which?*, following up in 1960 with the Advisory Centre for Education and its magazine *Where?* In 1962 he founded the National Extension College, an open learning institution that paved the way for the Open University, and he followed this up with other educational innovations, including an International Extension College, the Open College of the Arts, and the Open School. He was made a life peer in 1978, became a founder member of the Social Democratic Party in 1981, and was appointed its spokesman on education in the House of Lords. Among his other publications was a history of the Elmhirsts at Dartington, which he subtitled *The Creation of a Utopian Community* (1982), *The Metronomic Society* (1988), *Life after Work* (1991) and, with his second wife Sasha Moorsom, a collection of poems *Your Head in Mine* (1994). Died 14 January.

XIX CHRONICLE OF PRINCIPAL EVENTS IN 2002

JANUARY

1 **Argentina:** Eduardo Duhalde was elected President by a joint assembly of federal congressmen and provincial governors. Duhalde, the fifth Argentinian President since the deepening of the country's economic crisis in December 2001, appointed a new Cabinet and abandoned the convertibility of the peso to the US dollar.
EU: The euro, the European Union's single currency, became legal tender in the 12 member states that had adopted it. All the former national currencies that it replaced would cease to be legal tender after 28 February. Only Denmark, Sweden, and the UK had elected to retain their national currencies and remain outside the euro zone.
Spain: the government formally ended military conscription.

2 **Zambia:** Levy Mwanawasa of the ruling Movement for Multiparty Democracy (MMD) was sworn in as President after narrowly winning the highest share of the vote in the presidential election of 27 December 2001. In legislative elections, also held on 27 December, the MMD won the largest number of seats in the National Assembly but lost its majority.

3 **Middle East:** Israel seized a ship in the Red Sea containing 50 tonnes of weapons that it said were being delivered to the Palestinian National Authority. The interception happened on the day that US envoy Gen. (retd) Anthony Zinni returned to the region in an attempt to renew negotiations and bring about a cessation of violence between Israel and the Palestinians.

5 **Singapore:** the government announced that in December it had arrested 15 members of a cell of Islamic extremists linked to the al-Qaida network who were suspected of plotting bomb attacks on the US embassy as well as other embassies and military facilities.

10 **Afghanistan:** final agreement was reached on the command structure of the UN-mandated and UK-led multinational International Security Assistance Force (ISAF) charged with providing security for Kabul, the capital.
Chad: President Idriss Déby described a peace agreement signed between the government and the rebel Movement for Democracy and Justice in Chad (MDJC) as "a victory for the Chadian people".
USA: US military authorities began transferring Taliban and al-Qaida prisoners captured in the war in Afghanistan to a detention centre at the US military base at Guantanamo Bay, Cuba, dubbed "Camp X-Ray".
Hong Kong: the Court of Final Appeal ended a three-year legal battle over the rights of immigrants from mainland China to live in Hong Kong in a ruling that disappointed 90 per cent of the applicants.

12 **Pakistan:** in a landmark television broadcast President Gen. Pervez Musharraf announced the banning of several prominent Islamic militant organisations and offered the country a choice between a progressive, moderate Islamic society founded on law, tolerance, and modernity and the divisiveness and destructiveness of sectarian extremism.

15 **Iran:** supreme spiritual leader Ayatollah Seyed Ali Khamenei defused a political crisis by issuing a pardon for Hossein Loqmanian, a member of the Majlis (the unicameral legislature), who had been imprisoned in December 2001 for libel of the judicial system.

17 **Democratic Republic of Congo:** the volcano Mt Nyiragongo erupted, forcing 400,000 people to flee the nearby town of Goma, which was largely destroyed. At least 105 people died in the eruption and its aftermath, and at least 13 looters were shot dead by troops.
The Gambia: President Yahya Jammeh's ruling Alliance for Patriotic Reorientation and Con-

struction (APRC) won an overwhelming victory in legislative elections after the main opposition United Democratic Party (UDP) boycotted the poll.

18 **Sierra Leone:** President Ahmad Tejan Kabbah presided over a ceremony that marked the completion of the process of disarming the rebel Revolutionary United Front (RUF) and pro-government militias.

Netherlands Antilles: the ruling coalition led by Prime Minister Miguel Pourier was returned to power in elections to the 22-member Staten (the unicameral legislature).

20 **Congo:** in a referendum that was boycotted by opposition parties 84 per cent of voters approved a new constitution.

21 **Afghanistan:** a two-day donor conference in Tokyo, Japan, pledged US$4.5 billion for the reconstruction of Afghanistan.

Cyprus: President Glafkos Clerides and President Rauf Denktash of the self-proclaimed Turkish Republic of Northern Cyprus launched their first direct negotiations since 1997 aimed at resolving the conflict that had divided the island since 1974.

Russia: TV-6, the country's last independent television station, was closed down by the authorities after a court had put its holding company into liquidation. Critics claimed that the decision had been engineered by the state to extend its control over broadcasting.

Taiwan: President Chen Shui-bian appointed a new Premier, Yu Hsi-kun, amid a major Cabinet reshuffle intended to revitalize the ailing economy.

22 **Northern Ireland:** a special criminal court in Dublin, capital of the Republic of Ireland, convicted Colm Murphy of conspiracy in the 1998 Omagh bombing, Northern Ireland's worst terrorist atrocity, in which 29 people died. Murphy was the first person to be convicted in connection with the bombing.

24 **Lebanon:** former militia commander Elie Hobeika, leader of the forces that carried out the 1982 massacre of Palestinian civilians in the Sabra and Chatila refugee camps, was assassinated by a car bomb.

28 **Kazakhstan:** Prime Minister Qasymzhomart Toqayev resigned, to be replaced by Imangali Tasmagambetov.

29 **USA:** in his first State of the Union address President George W. Bush said that the USA would act against an "axis of evil" consisting of Iraq, Iran, and North Korea.

31 **Philippines:** some 650 US troops began an exercise in counter-terrorism alongside the Philippines army in the southern island of Basilan. The exercise was related to a conflict with an Islamic separatist group.

FEBRUARY

1 **Argentina:** the Supreme Court ruled that draconian restrictions on banking withdrawals imposed in December 2001 to prevent the collapse of the financial system were unconstitutional. Members of the Chamber of Deputies (the lower house of the bicameral legislature) from both the ruling and opposition parties on 5 February initiated impeachment proceedings against the six Supreme Court judges.

3 **Costa Rica:** in presidential elections no candidate secured the 40 per cent of the vote necessary for victory. The two leading candidates, Abel Pacheco de la Espriella of the ruling Social Christian Unity Party (PUSC) and Rolando Araya Monge of the National Liberation Party (PLN), would run in a second round on 7 April. In legislative elections held on the same day, PUSC was the leading party, with 19 seats in the 57-member Legislative Assembly.

4 **USA:** US President George W. Bush presented to Congress (the bicameral legislature) his administration's proposed US$2,130 billion budget for the fiscal year 2003. The most notable item was a 13.7 per cent increase in defence spending to US$378.6 billion.

6 **Democratic Republic of Congo:** the government of Belgium expressed its "profound regret" for Belgium's role in the 1961 murder of Prime Minister Patrice Lumumba of the then Belgian Congo.
7 **Albania:** President Rexhep Mejdani invited Pandeli Majko of the ruling Socialist party of Albania (PSS) to form a new government after the resignation of Prime Minister Ilir Meta.
United Kingdom: Home Secretary David Blunkett published a White Paper proposing new legislation on immigration which included the introduction of a mandatory UK citizenship pledge.
8 **Liberia:** President Charles Taylor declared a state of emergency after a series of attacks around the capital, Monrovia, by forces of the rebel group, Liberians United for Reconciliation and Democracy (LURD).
12 **Indonesia:** leaders of the Christian and Muslim communities in the eastern Molucca islands signed a peace agreement to end three years of sectarian conflict in which at least 5,000 people had been killed.
Cook Islands: the government of Prime Minister Terepai Maoate was brought down by a no-confidence vote in Parliament. Robert Woonton was elected Prime Minister and formed a government the following day.
13 **Yugoslavia:** the trial of Slobodan Milosevic, former Yugoslav President, began at the International Criminal Tribunal for the Former Yugoslavia in The Hague. Milosevic was charged with genocide, crimes against humanity, and war crimes.
15 **Mauritius:** President Cassam Uteem resigned, having refused to sign an anti-terrorism bill, finding many of its clauses "contrary to our democratic life". Uteem was replaced by interim President Aritanga Pillay, who signed the bill into law.
16 **Nepal:** a rebellion by Maoist guerrillas escalated dramatically when a series of attacks by the rebels in the western district of Accham killed at least 129 people, the highest losses in a single day since the insurrection began in 1996. The government claimed on 27 February that the army had killed 189 guerrillas since the Accham attacks.
18 **Zimbabwe:** EU foreign ministers decided to withdraw an observer mission for forthcoming presidential elections because of conditions imposed by Zimbabwe. The EU also imposed an arms embargo on the country and "smart sanctions" against President Robert Mugabe and 19 of his associates because of continuing political violence and human rights violations.
Fiji: George Speight, leader of a May 2000 coup that brought down the government of Prime Minister Mahendra Chaudhry, pleaded guilty on the first day of his trial for treason. He was sentenced to death but this was quickly commuted to life imprisonment. It was widely thought that Speight had pleaded guilty to prevent the exposure of the backers of the coup.
Cameroon: the International Court of Justice (ICJ) in The Hague began a hearing on a maritime border dispute dating from 1994 in which Cameroon claimed that Nigeria was occupying part of its territory.
20 **Colombia:** following the intensification of a bombing campaign by the leftist Colombian Revolutionary Armed Forces (FARC) and the kidnapping of a senator, President Andrés Pastrana Arango ordered the army to invade the 42,000 sq. km safe haven that had been granted to FARC in 1998 in the interests of peace negotiations.
Egypt: a fire aboard a train travelling from Cairo to Aswan caused by an exploding gas canister killed 263 people. The disaster resulted in the resignation of the Transport Minister and the head of the railways authority.
22 **Angola:** Jonas Savimbi, veteran leader of the rebel National Union for the Total Independence of Angola (UNITA), was killed in combat with government troops in the eastern province of Moxico.
Ecuador: President Gustavo Noboa Bejarano declared a state of emergency in two Amazonian departments after the serious disruption of the activities of the oil industry by a loose coalition

of indigenous farmers and environmental protesters.

Madagascar: Marc Ravalomanana declared himself President and attempted to form a government, despite there having been no second round to decide the inconclusive presidential election of December 2001. Incumbent President Didier Ratsiraka declared a national state of emergency.

Pakistan: a videotape handed to US consular officials confirmed that a US journalist, Daniel Pearl, who had been abducted in January, had been murdered by his kidnappers.

Sri Lanka: the government and the separatist Liberation Tigers of Tamil Eelam (LTTE) signed an agreement on an internationally monitored indefinite ceasefire beginning the following day, giving rise to hopes that an end could be negotiated to a civil war that had begun in 1983.

27 **India:** an arson attack on a train full of Hindu activists halted at Godhra in the western state of Gujarat—in which 58 people, the majority of them women and children, were killed—sparked a wave of sectarian violence across the state by Hindus against the Muslim minority, leading to at least 60 more deaths.

Georgia: the USA announced plans to expand its "war against terrorism" to Georgia because of its suspicion that guerrillas from the al-Qaida network headed by Islamic militant Osama bin Laden had fled Afghanistan and had taken refuge in the breakaway region of Abkhazia.

28 **EU:** the EU launched a constitutional convention that had been agreed in the December 2001 Laeken declaration, with the purpose of drawing up proposals for the future shape of the EU's institutions before the admission of up to 10 new members.

Palestine: in the culmination of a month of escalating violence between Israelis and Palestinians in the West Bank and the Gaza Strip the Israeli army invaded and occupied two refugee camps—at Jenin and Balata (near Nablus) in the West Bank—that Israel claimed harboured terrorists.

MARCH

1 **Sierra Leone:** President Ahmad Tejan Kabbah announced the lifting of the state of emergency imposed in January 1998 during the country's civil war. Former rebel leader Foday Sankoh appeared in court on 4 March charged with robbery and murder.

India: Hindu mobs continued a pogrom against Muslims in the western state of Gujarat; by 12 March an estimated 700 people had died in sectarian attacks. The intervention of large numbers of troops began to quell the violence in the latter part of the month.

2 **Palestine:** a month of continuing heavy violence between Israelis and Palestinians began with two days of attacks by Palestinian suicide bombers and snipers that killed 22 Israelis in Jerusalem, the Gaza Strip, and the West Bank.

3 **São Tomé and Príncipe:** The Movement for the Liberation of São Tomé and Príncipe-Social Democratic Party (MLSTP-PSD) won a narrow victory in legislative elections and attempted to form a coalition government. However, it was announced on 26 March that an independent, Gabriel Costa, had been appointed Prime Minister.

Switzerland: some 54.1 per cent of voters and 12 of the country's 23 cantons voted in favour of a government proposal to apply for full membership of the UN.

7 **Myanmar (Burma):** former military ruler Gen. Ne Win was placed under house arrest and several of his relatives detained over an alleged plot to overthrow the government.

Ireland: in a referendum voters narrowly rejected a constitutional proposal to close a loophole in the country's already strict law on abortion. The proposal would have removed the risk of suicide by the prospective mother as grounds for an abortion.

Netherlands: in municipal elections in Rotterdam the newly formed Leefbar Rotterdam (LR) party, led by right-wing, anti-immigration politician Pim Fortuyn, won power in the city.

9 **France:** the government reopened the trans-Alpine Mont Blanc tunnel linking France and Italy to cars and light vehicles. It had been three years since the tunnel was closed in 1999 following a devastating fire in which 40 people died.

10 **Colombia:** in elections to the bicameral legislature the leading party was the opposition Liberal Party (PL), winning 54 seats in the 161-seat House of Representatives and 28 seats in the 102-seat Senate. A total of 38 minor parties secured 71 seats in the lower house and 49 seats in the Senate, preventing any of the major parties from achieving a majority.

Congo: incumbent President Denis Sassou-Nguesso was re-elected for a seven-year term, receiving over 89 per cent of the votes.

11 **USA:** President George W. Bush outlined a "second stage of the war on terror", intended to prevent the Islamist al-Qaida network from regrouping in other countries following its defeat in Afghanistan and to prevent "rogue states" and "terrorist organisations" from developing weapons of mass destruction.

12 **Palestine:** the UN Security Council approved resolution 1397, which for the first time unambiguously endorsed the idea of a Palestinian state.

14 **Yugoslavia:** the leaders of Serbia, Montenegro, and the Federal Republic of Yugoslavia (FRY) agreed "in principle" on the establishment of a new state of Serbia and Montenegro to replace the current federation. The agreement was subject to ratification by the legislatures of the two republics.

15 **India:** the government deployed some 37,000 paramilitaries in Ayodhya, Uttar Pradesh state, to prevent the performance of a Hindu religious rite at the former site of the Babri Masjid mosque, destroyed by Hindu militants in 1992. The rite had been banned by the Supreme Court pending the resolution of legal disputes over the site. Following the destruction of the mosque in 1992 some 3,000 people had been killed in sectarian riots.

EU: heads of government began a two-day summit meeting in Barcelona, Spain, at which they agreed on measures including the liberalisation of the energy market and an increase in development aid for the world's poorest countries.

17 **Zimbabwe:** Robert Mugabe was sworn in for a third six-year term as President following controversial elections on 9-11 March. Defeated challenger Morgan Tsvangirai of the Movement for Democratic Change (MDC) claimed that the government had rigged the poll and disenfranchised thousands of opposition supporters.

Comoros: the first round of presidential elections for the new Union of the Comoros was held, with Col Assoumani Azali securing the largest share of the vote.

Pakistan: five people died in a grenade attack on a Christian church in the diplomatic quarter of Islamabad, the capital. Among the dead were a US diplomat and her daughter and it was thought that the attack was aimed by Islamic extremists both at Westerners and at the government of President Gen. Pervez Musharraf, in order to undermine his support for the US "war against terrorism".

Portugal: the opposition Social Democratic Party (PSD) narrowly defeated the governing Socialist Party (PS) in elections to the 230-seat Assembly of the Republic (the unicameral legislature) but failed to secure an overall majority. The PSD on 29 March signed a coalition agreement with the conservative People's Party (PP), with PSD leader José Manuel Durão Barraso named as Prime Minister.

19 **Italy:** Marco Biagi, an economist who acted as an adviser to the government on labour reforms, was shot dead in Bologna. The extreme left-wing Red Brigades, last active in 1999, claimed responsibility for the murder, which coincided with a rise in labour unrest.

20 **China:** some 5,000 demonstrators clashed with military police in the north-eastern city of Daqing,

part of an unprecedented wave of industrial unrest in the region.

France: the Paris Appeals Court refused an application by an aide of President Jacques Chirac for a halt to judicial inquiries into alleged corruption during Chirac's tenure as mayor of Paris in 1977-95.

22 **Germany:** the government narrowly secured the passage through the Bundesrat (the upper house of the bicameral legislature) of a controversial immigration bill allowing controlled immigration by skilled workers whilst cracking down on illegal immigration.

26 **Madagascar:** a government appointed by Marc Ravalomanana, one of the candidates in the disputed December 2001 presidential election, submitted its programme to the National Assembly (the lower house of the bicameral legislature). However, incumbent President Didier Ratsiraka maintained that he still held power. At least 12 people were killed during March in clashes between rival supporters.

27 **Arab League:** the 22 members of the League began a two-day summit meeting in Beirut, the Lebanese capital. The two main items at the summit were the endorsement of Saudi Arabia's "land-for-peace" plan to end the Israeli-Palestinian conflict and Iraq's pledge to respect the sovereignty of Kuwait.

29 **Palestine:** in response to an attack by a suicide bomber in the Israeli resort of Netanya on 27 March in which 22 people were killed, the Israeli army launched an attack on the besieged compound of Palestinian leader Yassir Arafat in Ramallah in the West Bank, destroying several buildings, killing seven Palestinians and taking 70 prisoner.

30 **UK:** Queen Elizabeth The Queen Mother, the mother of Queen Elizabeth II, died at Windsor, aged 101, seven weeks after the death on 9 February of her younger daughter Princess Margaret, aged 71.

31 **Ukraine:** in elections held to the 450-seat Supreme Council (the unicameral legislature) the Our Ukraine bloc of opposition parties won 112 seats, narrowly ahead of parties and independents supporting President Leonid Kuchma.

APRIL

4 **Angola:** the government signed a formal ceasefire agreement with the rebel National Union for the Total Independence of Angola (UNITA) to end the country's 27-year civil war. Previous peace agreements reached in 1994, 1991, and 1975 had all collapsed.

Palestine: as part of a major offensive during April in which Israel occupied all major towns and refugee camps in the West Bank, Israeli troops fought a six-day battle for control of Jenin camp during which vast swathes of the camp were destroyed by the invaders. Israel was accused by Palestinians of killing hundreds of civilians in the devastated camp.

7 **Costa Rica:** in the second round of a presidential election commenced in February, Abel Pacheco de la Espriella, candidate of the ruling Social Christian Unity Party (PUSC), defeated Rolando Araya Monge of the National Liberation Party (PNL). The turnout of 60 per cent was reportedly the lowest since 1948.

8 **Algeria:** the National People's Assembly (the legislature) approved a constitutional reform giving the Berber language, Tamazight, equal status with Arabic.

9 **UK:** 10 days of national mourning culminated in the funeral of Queen Elizabeth The Queen Mother, who died on 30 March. An estimated 1 million people gathered in London for her funeral procession.

11 **Tunisia:** the explosion of a natural gas tanker outside the ancient Ghriba synagogue on the island of Djerba killed 17 people, including 12 tourists, most of whom were German. The explosion was at first described by the Tunisian authorities as an accident but later the German government said that it was a terrorist attack by al-Qaida.

12 **Venezuela:** a group of 10 senior military commanders announced that they had ousted President Hugo Chávez Frías in an apparently successful coup and replaced him with Pedro Carmona as provisional President. Carmona attempted to dissolve the legislature and the Supreme Court. However, Chávez was rescued by loyal elements of the armed forces and returned to the presidency on 14 April. There were subsequent reports that agencies within the USA were involved in the attempted coup.

16 **East Timor:** veteran independence leader José Xanana Gusmão was elected the first internationally recognised President of East Timor with 82.7 per cent of the vote. The former Portuguese colony was due to gain full independence in May.

Netherlands: the government of Prime Minister Wim Kok symbolically resigned in response to a Dutch report criticising the Dutch government and Dutch UN peacekeeping troops for their share of responsibility in the failure in July 1995 to protect thousands of Bosnian Muslims in the "safe haven" of Srebrenica from massacre by Bosnian Serb forces. The government would continue, however, as a caretaker administration until general elections in May.

17 **UK:** Chancellor of the Exchequer Gordon Brown presented a budget for the financial year 2002-03 which for the first time since the Labour Party came to power in 1997 included increases in direct taxation, largely to fund a major increase in spending on the National Health Service.

18 **Afghanistan:** former King Mohammed Zahir Shah, exiled since 1973, returned to the capital, Kabul.

19 **USA:** the Democratic Party-controlled Senate (the upper house of the bicameral legislature) passed a comprehensive energy bill but effectively rejected a controversial amendment, opposed by environmentalists, that would have allowed drilling for oil in the Arctic national Wildlife Refuge in Alaska.

21 **France:** in the first round of a presidential election the incumbent President Jacques Chirac of the Rally for the Republic (RPR) led a record field of 16 candidates with 19.83 per cent of the vote. Second place was unexpectedly taken by Jean-Marie Le Pen of the far-right National Front (FN), putting Prime Minister Lionel Jospin of the Socialist Party (PS) into third place and thus eliminating him from the second round. Le Pen's success caused widespread dismay both domestically and abroad.

Hungary: the opposition Hungarian Socialist Party (MSzP) emerged from the second round of legislative elections as the largest single party in the 386-seat National Assembly (the legislature), with 178 seats. The first round had been held on 7 April.

Niue: legislative elections left the 20-seat Fono equally divided between government and opposition but by 25 April Young Vivian had been chosen to replace Sani Lakatani as Prime Minister.

29 **Madagascar:** a recount of December 2001's disputed presidential election, the aftermath of which had brought the country close to civil war, gave victory to opposition candidate Marc Ravalomanana over incumbent President Didier Ratsiraka.

30 **India:** reports prepared for embassies of EU countries claimed that the death toll in sectarian violence in the western state of Gujarat had passed 2,000 and that the massacre of Muslims was not spontaneous but a long-prepared pogrom in which state officials had connived.

Pakistan: a referendum in which 97.7 per cent of voters endorsed the extension of the term of President Gen. Pervez Musharraf by a further five years was widely condemned by opposition parties, the independent Human Rights Commission, and the domestic and foreign press as a stage-managed and fraudulent exercise.

Palestine: the UN effectively abandoned its attempt to send a fact-finding team to Jenin refugee camp, to examine claims of Israeli human rights abuses, after Israel withdrew its earlier offer to co-operate with the investigation.

UK: Queen Elizabeth II made a speech to Parliament to inaugurate Golden Jubilee celebrations of the 50th anniversary of her accession.

MAY

1 **Palestine:** with the transfer of six Palestinian militants to a prison in Jericho the Israeli army lifted the siege of the headquarters of Yassir Arafat, President of the Palestinian National Authority (PNA), which had begun in late March.

2 **Bahamas:** in a general election the opposition Progressive Liberal Party (PLP) won an unexpected landslide victory, securing 29 seats in the 40-member House of Assembly (the lower house of Parliament). A new Cabinet led by Prime Minister Perry Christie of the PLP assumed office on 22 May.

3 **Somalia:** President Mohamed Ibrahim Egal, of the self-declared Republic of Somaliland died, aged 73. Senior officials inaugurated Dahir Riyale Kahin as his replacement.

4 **Nigeria:** an airliner crashed in the northern city of Kano killing 149 people, including all 76 people on board the aircraft.

5 **France:** incumbent President Jacques Chirac won an overwhelming victory in the second round of the presidential elections, securing over 82 per cent of the vote to defeat Jean-Marie Le Pen of the far-right National Front (FN). Chirac on 6 May appointed Jean-Pierre Raffarin of the centrist Liberal Democracy (DL) as Prime Minister of an interim Cabinet, succeeding Lionel Jospin of the Socialist Party (PS), who had announced his retirement from politics after being beaten into third place in the April first round of the presidential election.

Burkina Faso: in legislative elections the ruling Congress for Democracy and Progress emerged as the largest of the 13 contesting parties with 57 seats but only a narrow overall majority in the 111-seat National Assembly (the lower house of the bicameral legislature).

Bolivia: former President Hugo Bánzer Suarez, who had ruled as military dictator (1971-78) and as elected President (1997-2001), died, aged 75.

6 **Myanmar (Burma):** Daw Aung San Suu Kyi, leader of the opposition National League for Democracy (NLD), was released from the house arrest to which she had been confined since September 2000, as a result of prolonged secret negotiations with the ruling State Peace and Development Council (SPDC—the military government) and foreign diplomatic pressure channelled through the UN. Suu Kyi's previous period of house arrest had lasted from 1989 to 1995.

8 **Pakistan:** a suicide bomber in the port city of Karachi detonated an explosion that killed 17 people including 11 French naval engineers working on a project to build submarines for Pakistan's navy. The bombing was blamed on Islamic extremists allied to the Islamic militant al-Qaida network.

10 **Palestine:** the Israeli army's siege of the Church of the Nativity in Bethlehem, which began in April, was lifted with the evacuation and eventual exile of 39 Palestinian militants, after mediation by the EU and the USA.

12 **Mali:** in the second round of a presidential election Gen. (retd) Amadou Toumani Touré was elected President with 65.01 per cent of the vote. The first round had been held on 28 April.

Cuba: former US President Jimmy Carter began a private visit lasting until 17 May, the most prominent US political figure to visit the island since President Calvin Coolidge in 1928.

14 **India:** an attack by Islamic militant separatists on an army camp in the northern state of Jammu and Kashmir in which 34 people, mainly women and children, were killed brought India and Pakistan close to war. The Indian government accused Pakistan of arming, training and infiltrating terrorists into Kashmir.

15 **Netherlands:** in a general election overshadowed by the assassination on 6 May of Pim Fortuyn, leader of the anti-immigration Lijst Pim Fortuyn (LPF), the Christian Democratic Appeal (CDA) secured 43 seats in the Tweede Kamer (the lower house of the bicameral legislature), followed by the LPF with 26 seats. The Labour Party's representation fell from 45 seats to 23.

16 **Dominican Republic:** in legislative elections the ruling Dominican Revolutionary Party (PRD)

lost its majority in the 150-member Chamber of Deputies (the lower house of the bicameral legislature), being reduced to 73 seats. However, the PRD increased its majority in the Senate (the upper house).

17 **Ireland:** in a general election Prime Minister Bertie Ahern's Fianna Fáil (FF) party won 81 seats, the largest number in the Dáil (the lower house of the bicameral legislature), but short of an overall majority.

19 **Chad:** final results were announced of the 21 April elections to the 155-seat National Assembly (the legislature), with the ruling Patriotic Salvation Movement (MPS) of President Idriss Déby winning 108 seats.

Vietnam: in elections to the 498-member 11th National Assembly (the legislature) all but 51 deputies were members of the Communist Party of Vietnam (CPV) and only two were independents.

20 **East Timor:** the former Portuguese colony, occupied by Indonesia 1975-99 and administered by the UN since September 1999, gained formal independence in a ceremony attended by UN Secretary-General Kofi Annan and representatives of 92 countries.

Sierra Leone: President Ahmad Tejan Kabbah was sworn in for a second term, having won a presidential election earlier in the month with over 70 per cent of the vote. In legislative elections Kabbah's Sierra Leone People's party won 83 seats in the 112-seat National Assembly. The UN-sponsored elections were seen as an important step in the recovery of the country from a decade of civil war.

22 **China:** the government imposed heavy tariffs on a range of US steel products in retaliation against US tariffs imposed in March on steel imports. The EU, China and several other countries had already filed complaints at the World Trade Organisation (WTO) against the US tariffs.

Kyrgyzstan: following 13 days of anti-government protests Prime Minister Kurmanbek Bakiev and his entire Cabinet resigned. The principal cause of the protests was the ratification by the legislature of a border treaty signed in 1999 that ceded territory to China.

Nepal: King Gyanendra dissolved the legislature on the advice of Prime Minister Sher Bahadur Deuba after a split in the ruling Nepali Congress Party (NCP).

24 **Disarmament:** US President George W. Bush and Russian President Vladimir Putin signed the Strategic Offensive Reduction Treaty (SORT), in Moscow, intended to reduce the number of nuclear warheads deployed by each state to between 1,700 and 2,200 by 31 December 2012.

25 **Lesotho:** the ruling Lesotho Congress for Democracy (LCD) won 77 seats in elections to the 120-member National Assembly (the legislature). Its nearest challenger was the Basotho National Party with 21 seats. This was the first election in which 40 seats were elected by proportional representation.

Taiwan: an airliner of the state-owned China Airlines crashed in the sea on a flight to Hong Kong, killing all 225 passengers and crew. It was the airline's fourth fatal crash since the beginning of 1994.

26 **Colombia:** Alavro Uribe Velez of the Colombia First party won a presidential election with 53.04 per cent of the vote. Uribe was a defector from the Liberal Party (PL), whose candidate Horacio Serpa Uribe came second with 31.72 per cent. A low turnout reflected widespread intimidation by leftist guerrillas and right-wing paramilitaries.

Hungary: following victory in the April general election Peter Medgyessy, leader of the Hungarian Socialist Party (MSzP), signed a formal coalition agreement with the Alliance of Free Democrats (SzDSz) and the following day presented a new Cabinet.

Tunisia: in the country's first ever referendum 99.52 per cent of voters approved numerous constitutional changes, among them provisions that would enable President Zine el-Abidine Ben Ali to prolong his tenure of power.

28 **NATO:** at a ceremony near Rome the north Atlantic Treaty organisation (NATO) and Russia

signed an agreement on establishing a new relationship through the NATO-Russia Council (NRC).

Vanuatu: it was announced that after negotiations following elections on 2 May to the 52-seat National Assembly, Edward Natapei would be reappointed Prime Minister.

29 **Malawi:** the UN's World Food Programme (WFP) and the Food and Agriculture Organisation (FAO) warned that 10 million people in Malawi, Zimbabwe, Lesotho, and Swaziland were at risk of starvation because of the worst food shortages in the region for a decade. It was estimated that 10,000 Malawians had already died of hunger-related diseases since late 2001.

USA: Robert Mueller, director of the Federal Bureau of Investigation (FBI), announced a series of reforms of the agency intended to improve the FBI's ability to prevent terrorist attacks on the USA.

30 **Algeria:** in elections to the 389-member National Assembly (the lower house of the bicameral legislature) the pro-government National Liberation Front (FLN) won an absolute majority with 199 seats. Two moderate Islamic parties won a combined total of 81 seats. A record low turnout of 46 per cent was partly caused by a boycott of the election in the north-eastern Berber region of Kabylie.

31 **Denmark:** the Folketing (the unicameral legislature) passed controversial legislation to make it much harder for foreign nationals to gain residency permits or to seek political asylum.

JUNE

2 **Switzerland:** in a national referendum a decisive majority voted to relax the country's strict abortion laws.

3 **Vanuatu:** meeting for the first time since legislative elections in April, the National Assembly re-elected Edward Natapei as Prime Minister.

5 **Iran:** it was reported that the Majlis (the unicameral legislature) had passed the country's first foreign investment law since the 1950s as part of reforms intended to open up the economy.

6 **USA:** President George W. Bush called on Congress (the bicameral legislature) to pass legislation establishing a Cabinet-level Department of Homeland Security. The new department would subsume some 22 federal agencies and would review and co-ordinate intelligence data and defence measures at both the federal and state levels.

Burkina Faso: Paramanga Ernest Yoli was reappointed Prime Minister following elections to the National Assembly (the lower house of the bicameral legislature) held in May.

Ireland: following the general election in May, incumbent Prime Minister Bertie Ahern, leader of the Fianna Fáil (FF) party, announced a new Cabinet in coalition with the Progressive Democrats (PD).

9 **Palestine:** President Yassir Arafat unveiled a new Cabinet, reduced from 31 ministers to 21, as a first step towards reforms in the Palestinian National Authority (PNA) demanded by Israel.

10 **FAO:** the UN's Food and Agricultural Organisation (FAO) hosted a four-day World Food Summit in Rome that was poorly attended by heads of state or government from rich countries. At the first World Food Summit in 1996 world leaders had pledged to halve the number of people in the world suffering from hunger and malnourishment. By 2002 the total had been reduced by just over 3 per cent.

13 **Afghanistan:** a *Loya Jirga*, or council of tribal elders, elected Hamid Karzai, head of the interim government, as interim President with over 80 per cent of the vote. Karzai announced a new Cabinet list on 19 June.

Brazil: Finance Minister Pedro Malan announced a range of measures, including the drawing-down of US$10 billion of an IMF facility, to counter a sharp loss of confidence in the economy, which was adversely affected by the continuing economic crisis in Argentina. The IMF on 25 June approved a credit of US$875 million to shield Uruguay from the "contagion effect" of the Argentinian crisis.

Disarmament: the USA's withdrawal from the 1972 Anti-Ballistic Missile (ABM) treaty, announced in December 2001, came into formal effect.

14 **Pakistan:** in the fourth attack on foreign targets in the country since the beginning of the year a car bomb exploded outside the US consulate in Karachi, killing 13 people and injuring more than 40.

15 **Czech Republic:** two days of legislative elections concluded with the leftist Czech Social Democratic Party (CSSD) as the largest party in the 200-member Chamber of Deputies (the lower house of the bicameral legislature), with 70 seats but short of an overall majority. Turnout at 58 per cent was the lowest since 1989.

16 **France:** in a second round of legislative elections the centre-right Union for the Presidential Majority (UMP) won a decisive majority with 355 seats in the 577-member National Assembly (the lower house of the bicameral legislature), thus consolidating incumbent President Jacques Chirac's electoral victory in May.

19 **Kyrgyzstan:** following the resignation in May of the previous government, the new Prime Minister, Nikolay Tanayev, announced a new Cabinet but did not broaden the administration into the coalition that the opposition had expected.

Macedonia: the 120-member Sobranje (the unicameral legislature) approved legislation recognising Albanian as an official language, a condition of the August 2001 peace accords that had ended the conflict with separatist ethnic Albanian guerrillas.

20 **Spain:** a general strike against controversial new labour laws led to the closure of most heavy industry and the worst disruption to the country's transport system since the general strike of 1994.

21 **EU:** a two-day summit meeting of EU heads of government began in Seville, Spain. The leaders agreed new measures against illegal immigration, to implement a common asylum policy by the end of 2003, and a commitment to prepare for the enlargement of the EU in 2004 by 10 new members. Plans were also introduced to reform the European Commission and the Common Agricultural Policy (CAP).

Bangladesh: President A.Q.M. Badruddoza Chowdhury resigned under pressure from the ruling Bangladesh Nationalist Party (BNP) after failing to visit the grave of the BNP's founder. Chowdhury's forced resignation was widely regarded as unconstitutional.

24 **Albania:** the People's Assembly (the unicameral legislature) elected Gen. (retd) Alfred Moisiu, 74, as President, replacing Rexhep Mejdani, who had held the post since 1997. Moisiu was a consensus choice of both the ruling and opposition parties.

Hong Kong: Chief Executive Tung Chee-hwa announced membership of a new Executive Council (Cabinet), incorporating the most radical restructuring of government since the restoration of Chinese sovereignty in 1997.

Palestine: in a speech on the Middle East, US President George W. Bush called on the Palestinian people to elect new leaders, create institutions and reach new security arrangements with Israel as preconditions for achieving statehood.

Tanzania: at least 281 people were killed and 800 injured in a crash between a passenger train and a freight train some 50 km south-east of Dodoma, the capital. The government declared two days of official mourning for the worst railway disaster in Tanzania's history.

25 **G-7:** leaders of the G-7 (Group of Seven) advanced industrialised countries and Russia began a three-day summit meeting at Kananaskis, Canada. At the meeting Russia was admitted as a full member of the group and would host a G-8 meeting in 2006. The leaders adopted a G-8 Action Plan for Africa, increased debt relief for Heavily Indebted Poor Countries, and reached agreement on new nuclear security and anti-terrorism measures.

XIX CHRONICLE OF PRINCIPAL EVENTS IN 2002

Malaysia: Prime Minister Mahathir Mohamad, who had held power since 1981, announced that he would resign in October 2003.
South Africa: the National Assembly (the lower house of the bicameral legislature) approved the controversial Mineral and Petroleum Resources Development Bill abolishing private ownership of mineral rights and returning them to the state.
Zimbabwe: some 2,900 white farmers whose land was to be seized and given to blacks became legally obliged to stop farming following a directive from President Robert Mugabe.

26 **Cuba:** the National Assembly (the unicameral legislature) voted unanimously to adopt a constitutional amendment declaring Cuba's socialist system to be permanent and "irrevocable".
Russia: the State Duma (the lower house of the bicameral legislature) voted 258-149 to pass a law allowing the sale and purchase of farmland. However, an amendment to the bill forbade the sale of farmland to foreigners or to companies in which foreigners held a majority stake.

27 **UK:** Transport Secretary Alistair Darling announced that the bankrupt private railway infrastructure company Railtrack would be succeeded by a new not-for-profit company named Network Rail.

30 **Bolivia:** in inconclusive presidential elections former President Gonzálo Sánchez de Lozada led with just over 22 per cent of the vote. In simultaneous elections to Congress (the bicameral legislature) no party was able to secure a majority in either house.
Guinea: in elections to the 114-seat National Assembly (the unicameral legislature) the ruling Party of Unity and Progress (PUP) won 85 seats, increasing its majority.
North-South Korea: a South Korean patrol boat was sunk with the loss of five crew members in the most serious naval clash between the two countries since 1999.

JULY

1 **Chile:** the Supreme Court suspended human rights proceedings against the former dictator Gen. (retd) Augusto Pinochet Ugarte, ruling that Pinochet was suffering from incurable and irreversible dementia.
Russia: major changes to Russia's criminal justice system were introduced, replacing the 1960 criminal code with one intended to be closer to Western standards of justice.

5 **Madagascar:** the battle for the presidency, ongoing since disputed elections in December 2001, was finally resolved in favour of Marc Ravalomanana when former President Didier Ratsiraka fled with his core supporters to France. Ravalomanana's legitimacy had been boosted on 3 July when France, the former colonial power, had joined the USA in recognising him as President.

6 **Afghanistan:** unidentified gunmen assassinated Vice President Haji Abdul Qadeer in Kabul, the capital, throwing the stability of the interim government into question.
African Union: the African Union (AU), successor organisation to the Organisation of African Unity (OAU), was officially launched at a two-day meeting in Durban, South Africa.
EU: European Commissioner for Agriculture and Rural Development Franz Fischler unveiled far-reaching proposals for reform of the Common Agricultural Policy (CAP).

7 **UN:** the UN's 14th International AIDS conference was held until 12 July in Barcelona, Spain.

10 **Iran:** in a letter of resignation Ayatollah Jalaleddin Taheri, one of the most senior liberal clerics, issued a damning indictment of the conservative establishment and the state of the country.

11 **Argentina:** former dictator Gen. (retd) Leopoldo Galtieri was arrested on a warrant issued by a judge investigating the abduction, torture and murder of 18 left-wing guerrilla leaders in 1980.
Czech Republic: President Václav Havel appointed Vladimir Spidla, leader of the Czech Social Democratic Party (CSSD), to the post of Prime Minister. Spidla had assembled a coalition with the narrowest of majorities in the 200-seat Chamber of Deputies (the lower house of the bicameral legislature) following elections in June.

Morocco: Moroccan soldiers occupied a small, uninhabited offshore island, precipitating a diplomatic crisis with Spain, as both countries claimed sovereignty. Spanish forces seized the island on 17 July but later withdrew. US diplomacy persuaded both sides to lower tensions but the status of the island remained unresolved.

12 **Bosnia and Herzegovina:** a compromise deal on the USA's desire to exempt its personnel from the jurisdiction of the International Criminal Court (ICC) enabled the UN to renew the mandates of the military and civilian missions in Bosnia until the end of the year.

14 **France:** a lone right-wing gunman attempted to assassinate President Jacques Chirac during the Bastille Day parade in Paris. Chirac was unharmed and the attacker quickly apprehended.

15 **Bosnia and Herzegovina:** the Presidents of Bosnia, Croatia, and Yugoslavia held a landmark summit meeting in Sarajevo, the Bosnian capital, reaffirming their commitment to the 1995 Dayton peace agreement.

Pakistan: four men were convicted in an anti-terrorist court in Karachi, the capital of Sind province, of the abduction and murder in January of the US journalist Daniel Pearl. Of the convicts, said to be Islamic militants, one was sentenced to death, the others to life imprisonment.

16 **Zambia:** the National Assembly (the unicameral legislature) voted unanimously to lift former President Frederick Chiluba's immunity from prosecution in order to allow an investigation into allegations of corruption made against him.

19 **Cameroon:** the Supreme Court announced the final results of a general election held on 30 June, awarding the ruling Cameroon People's Democratic Movement (RDPC) 133 seats in the 180-member National Assembly (the unicameral legislature).

20 **Sudan:** a breakthrough was announced in peace talks between the government and the southern rebel Sudan People's Liberation Movement (SPLM), recognising the right of predominantly Christian southern Sudan to self-determination and exemption from Islamic law. The agreement did not include a ceasefire in the country's civil war.

21 **Greece:** the authorities charged a member of the notorious left-wing November 17 group with the assassination in June 2000 of British defence attaché Brig. Stephen Saunders. Since late June police had arrested some 14 members of November 17, a group responsible for at least 24 murders since 1975.

22 **Netherlands:** following protracted coalition negotiations in the wake of the general election in May, the Christian Democratic Alliance (CDA) formed a government with Lijst Pim Fortuyn (LPF) and the People's Party for Freedom and Democracy (VVD).

Zimbabwe: the EU broadened the range of sanctions imposed on Zimbabwe to include a visa ban and asset freeze on all Cabinet ministers and some senior officials.

23 **Palestine:** a bombing raid by an Israeli aircraft that assassinated Salah Shihada, leader of the military wing of Hamas, also killed 12 other people, including nine children, and injured 140. There was widespread international criticism of the raid, even from the USA. Previously some progress had been reported in diplomatic initiatives, including proposals by Hamas for a ceasefire.

26 **Indonesia:** a court convicted Tommy Suharto (Hutomo Mandala Putra), son of the former President Suharto, of conspiracy to murder a Supreme Court judge, sentencing him to 15 years' imprisonment. He was the first member of Suharto's family, widely believed to have embezzled billions of dollars of public money, to be tried and convicted.

30 **Democratic Republic of Congo (DRC):** a peace agreement with Rwanda was signed in Pretoria, South Africa. The agreement provided for the withdrawal of Rwandan troops from the DRC in exchange for the disbanding of forces such as Hutu militias hostile to the Rwandan government.

USA: President George W. Bush signed into law a bill on corporate fraud already approved by both houses of Congress (the bicameral federal legislature). The legislation, which was tougher in its provisions than the bill proposed by the administration, was a response to revelations of fraudulent or irregular accounting practices at major US corporations such as Enron, World-Com, and Xerox.

Uruguay: the government declared an emergency banking holiday to stem a run on the banks begun by Argentinian depositors attempting to circumvent banking restrictions imposed in neighbouring Argentina to control the Argentinian economic crisis.

AUGUST

1 **Iraq:** Foreign Minister Naji Sabri Ahmad al-Hadithi wrote to Hans Blix, head of the UN's weapons inspection agency, inviting him to talks on the possible resumption of inspections of Iraq's suspected programmes of weapons of mass destruction, suspended since late 1998. UN Secretary-General Kofi Annan on 5 August declined the offer, saying that Iraq must first accept the Security Council's terms for the resumption of inspections.

2 **Tuvalu:** following a general election held on 25 July legislators elected Saufatu Sopoanga as Prime Minister.

4 **Bolivia:** following an inconclusive popular presidential election in June, members of both houses of Congress (the bicameral legislature) elected Gonzálo Sánchez de Lozada, candidate of the centre-right Nationalist Revolutionary Movement (MNR), President for the second time. Final results of simultaneous legislative elections in June showed the MNR to be the leading party in both houses of Congress, but without a majority in either.

Georgia: tension with Russia mounted after Georgian border guards claimed that they had been bombed by Russian aircraft pursuing rebels from the Russian republic of Chechnya believed to be hiding in the Pankisi Gorge in the Georgian breakaway republic of Abkhazia.

5 **Papua New Guinea:** following a protracted, chaotic general election begun in June that was plagued by violence and allegations of malpractice, legislators in the National Parliament (the unicameral legislature) elected Sir Michael Somare as Prime Minister to replace Sir Mekere Morauta. Somare, who had served as the country's first prime minister upon achieving independence in 1975, on 13 August announced a Cabinet that largely consisted of newly elected MPs.

7 **Libya:** UK junior foreign minister Mike O'Brien began a two-day visit, the first UK minister to visit Libya since 1983.

8 **New Zealand:** following a general election held on 27 July in which her Labour party had failed to gain a majority in the 120-seat House of Representatives, Prime Minister Helen Clark formed an alliance with the United Future (UFNZ) party, Labour's previous alliance with the Green Party having broken down. Clark announced her new Cabinet on 14 August.

Zimbabwe: this day was set by President Robert Mugabe as the deadline for some 2,900 white farmers to vacate their farms as part of the government's land reform programme.

9 **Mali:** the Constitutional Court reversed a number of results in a general election held in July to the 147-seat National Assembly (the unicameral legislature) because of electoral malpractice, awarding former Prime Minister Ibrahim Boubacar Keita's Hope 2002 coalition 66 seats. The decision meant that the Alliance for Democracy in Mali (ADEMA) was relegated into second place with 51 seats. The Interior Ministry had previously awarded ADEMA 62 seats, against 53 seats for Hope 2002.

11 **Indonesia:** the annual session of the People's Consultative Assembly (MPR—the highest authority of the state) concluded with the passing of constitutional amendments providing for the direct election of the president from 2004 and the abolition in the same year of seats for the military in the legislature.

12 **Colombia:** President Alvaro Uribe Velez decreed a 90-day state of emergency following attacks on government buildings in Bogota, the capital, by the rebel Colombian Revolutionary Armed Forces (FARC).

13 **Nigeria:** the House of Representatives (the lower house of the bicameral legislature) passed a resolution calling on President Olusegun Obasanjo to resign within two weeks or face impeachment.

Indonesia: a human rights tribunal set up to try crimes against humanity committed in East Timor before the territory's independence delivered its first verdict, sentencing a former civilian governor of East Timor to three years' imprisonment. The following day the tribunal acquitted six military and police officers.

16 **Palestine:** the notorious radical guerrilla leader Abu Nidal, responsible for many terrorist attacks since the 1970s, although apparently quiescent for more than 10 years, died in Baghdad, the Iraqi capital, aged 65. The circumstances of his death were unclear, although he was reported to have shot himself.

18 **Germany:** Chancellor Gerhard Schröder hosted a summit in Berlin for the EU and central European countries affected by the worst floods in living memory, which had killed at least 112 people and caused massive damage in 12 countries.

Poland: Pope John Paul II, 82, concluded a four-day visit to his homeland that was thought likely to be his last.

19 **Russia:** rebels in the separatist republic of Chechnya shot down a Russian military helicopter, killing 114 of the 147 people on board. The crash was the worst single loss of life on the Russian side since the start of the war in 1999.

21 **Canada:** Prime Minister Jean Chrétien, who had led the Liberal Party to three successive election victories, announced that he would step down as Prime Minister in February 2004.

Pakistan: President Gen. Pervez Musharraf passed a series of constitutional amendments that ensured a continuing role for the military in government despite a return to democracy in elections scheduled for October.

26 **Spain:** the legislature voted to petition the Supreme Court to ban Herri Batasuna (HB), the former political arm of the militant Basque separatist group ETA, following outrage over the refusal of HB to condemn an ETA bomb attack on 4 August in which a young girl was killed.

27 **Japan:** the District Court in Tokyo dismissed a law suit filed by 180 Chinese plaintiffs claiming compensation for alleged biological warfare atrocities carried out by Japan during World War II.

SEPTEMBER

2 **Iran:** President Mohammed Khatami presented a bill to the Majlis (the unicameral legislature) curtailing the powers of the conservative Council of Guardians in vetting candidates in general and presidential elections. A second bill, presented on 24 September, extended the President's constitutional powers.

4 **UN:** the UN World Summit on Sustainable Development (WSSD), begun on August 26, ended in Johannesburg, South Africa. Its closing declaration contained few major new commitments towards fulfilling the goal of reconciling economic growth in developing countries with protection of the environment. The summit had been intended as the successor to the 1992 Earth Summit in Rio.

5 **Afghanistan:** interim President Hamid Karzai survived an assassination attempt unscathed when a security guard fired on his vehicle in the southern city of Kandahar.

6 **Bangladesh:** Iajuddin Ahmed was sworn in as President, replacing A.Q.M. Badruddoza Chowdhury, who had resigned under pressure in June.

China: a government report admitted for the first time the scale of the health problem posed to the country by HIV/AIDS, estimating that by the end of 2002 some 1 million people would be infected by the virus.

Democratic Republic of Congo (DRC): President Joseph Kabila and Ugandan President Yoweri Museveni signed a peace agreement providing for the withdrawal of Ugandan forces from the north of the DRC.

9 **Burundi:** government troops in pursuit of rebel forces massacred 173 civilians in Itaba, central Gitega province.

12 **Iraq:** US President George W. Bush made a speech to the UN General Assembly saying that he would work with the Security Council to secure a resolution authorizing the use of force against Iraq if it did not allow the "unfettered" return of UN weapons inspectors.

Tibet: it was announced that a delegation representing the Tibetan spiritual leader, the Dalai Lama, was holding talks with the Chinese authorities in Beijing, the Chinese capital. It was the first high-level contact between China and the Dalai Lama's representatives since 1993.

15 **India:** the first of four rounds of elections to a state assembly was held in the disputed northern state of Jammu and Kashmir, claimed by Pakistan. Muslim separatist parties boycotted the elections, saying that they were meaningless without conducting a prior referendum on independence for the state.

Macedonia: in a general election to the 120-seat Sobranje (the unicameral legislature) the opposition Together for Macedonia coalition won 59 seats, beating the ruling coalition under Prime Minister Ljubco Georgievski into second place.

Sweden: in a general election the ruling Social Democratic Labour Party (SAP) increased its share of the vote and won the largest number of seats (but not a majority) in the Riksdag (the unicameral legislature). It was expected that Prime Minister Göran Persson would maintain his coalition with the Left Party (Vp) and the Green Party (MpG), but the MpG withdrew its support after being denied Cabinet seats.

16 **Iraq:** in a letter to UN Secretary-General Kofi Annan, Iraq agreed to the unconditional return of the UN's agency to inspect suspected sites of weapons of mass destruction: the UN Monitoring, Verification and Inspection Commission (UNMOVIC).

Sri Lanka: the government began a first three-day round of peace talks with the separatist Liberation Tigers of Tamil Eelam (LTTE) to consolidate a ceasefire that had held since February and end a civil war that began in 1983.

17 **Democratic Republic of Congo (DRC):** Rwanda began withdrawing the first of its estimated 20,000 troops from the country in accordance with the peace agreement signed in July.

North Korea: during an unprecedented visit by Japanese Prime Minister Junichiro Koizumi, North Korea's leader Kim Jong Il for the first time admitted that North Korea had abducted at least 12 Japanese citizens during the 1970s and 1980s.

18 **Zimbabwe:** the House of Assembly (the unicameral legislature) passed an amendment to the 1992 Land Acquisition Act in order to accelerate the government's requisition of the land of white commercial farmers.

19 **Côte d'Ivoire:** fighting broke out in the capital, Abidjan, between government forces and rebel soldiers protesting at their impending forced retirement. Former military ruler Gen. Robert Guëi, whom the government blamed for the rebellion, was killed in an early clash. The conflict—which attracted both African and European diplomatic intervention—spread, with rebels claiming to control the important cities of Bouaké and Korogho by the end of the month.

USA: the government submitted to Congress (the bicameral legislature) a draft resolution authorizing President Bush to use all "appropriate" means, including force, to counter "the threat posed by Iraq".

Venezuela: the government announced the establishment of eight security zones in response to calls from military and business factions for the forcible overthrow of President Hugo Chávez Frías.

21 **Slovakia:** the results of a two-day general election showed the nationalist Movement for a Democratic Slovakia (HZDS) to have won the largest share of the vote (19.5 per cent) and

the largest number of seats (36) in the 150-member National Council (the unicameral legislature). However, HZDS leader Vladimir Meciar was unable to form a coalition and on 27 September President Rudolf Schuster asked Prime Minister Mikulas Dzurinda to form a new coalition without the HZDS.

22 **Germany:** legislative elections returned Chancellor Gerhard Schröder to office with a narrow majority. Although Schröder's Social Democratic Party (SPD) lost 47 seats from its 1998 total of 298, the SPD's coalition allies—the Greens—achieved their best ever result with 55 seats in the Bundestag (the lower house of the bicameral federal legislature).

24 **EU:** the European Commission abandoned the 2004 deadline for member states to achieve balanced budgets imposed by the EU's stability and growth pact, and allowed France, Germany, Italy, and Portugal extensions until 2006.

Israel: the UN Security Council passed resolution 1435 demanding that Israel should immediately cease military measures around the Palestinian town of Ramallah, including the siege of the headquarters of Palestinian leader Yassir Arafat. Israel lifted the siege on 29 September but did not withdraw its troops from the area.

UK: Parliament was recalled for a one-day debate on the possibility of UK participation in a US-led war against Iraq. Although the House of Commons (the lower house) had the opportunity to vote only on a procedural rather than a substantive motion, backbenchers from the ruling Labour Party mounted one of their biggest rebellions since 1997 against the government, with 53 members joining 11 from other parties to register their opposition to the prospect of UK military action against Iraq.

26 **Myanmar (Burma):** four members of the family of former dictator Gen. Ne Win were sentenced to death for allegedly attempting in March to mount a coup against the current military government. Earlier in the month, a secret military tribunal had sentenced 83 soldiers to prison terms for their participation in the plot.

27 **Morocco:** elections were held to the 325-member House of Representatives (the lower house of the bicameral legislature). Prime Minister Abderrahmane el-Yousifi's Socialist Union of Popular Forces (USFP), won 50 seats to become the largest party in the new legislature; coalition negotiations were still in progress at the end of the month.

Senegal: an overcrowded ferry heading towards Dakar, the capital, capsized in a storm killing nearly 1,000 people.

OCTOBER

2 **SADC:** heads of state and government of the Southern African Development Community (SADC) began a two-day summit meeting in Luanda, the capital of Angola. The leaders noted with "great concern" the humanitarian disaster developing in six member-states that were affected by severe food shortages.

3 **Namibia:** Foreign Minister Hidipo Hanutenya announced that the government was considering confiscating white-owned farmland for redistribution to landless blacks if white farmers continued to resist a voluntary redistribution scheme. Namibia's close ally President Robert Mugabe of Zimbabwe was already implementing a comparable compulsory redistribution programme.

4 **Nepal:** King Gyanendra sacked the government of Prime Minister Sher Bahadur Deuba for "incompetence" and appointed an interim Cabinet of pro-monarchy ministers led by Prime Minister Lokendra Bahadur Chand. Deuba had asked for a one-year postponement of general elections due in November for fear of disruption by guerrillas of the underground Communist Party of Nepal (Maoist). The King's dismissal of the government—the first since the end of absolute monarchy in 1990—was criticised as unconstitutional by the major political parties.

5 **Bosnia and Herzegovina:** general elections to the various representative bodies in Bosnia saw gains for the ethnic nationalist parties—the (Muslim) Party of Democratic Action (SDA), the Serb Democratic Party (SDS), and the Croatian Democratic Community (HDZ). Turnout in the first locally-organised election since the end of the civil war in 1995 was 55 per cent, the lowest since 1995.

6 **Yemen:** a large explosion damaged the French oil tanker *Limburg* off the coast of Yemen, killing one crew member. It was later determined that the explosion was the result of a terrorist attack, responsibility for which was claimed by a group named the Islamic Army of Aden-Abyan.

7 **Trinidad and Tobago:** the ruling People's National Movement (PNM), led by Prime Minister Patrick Manning, was returned to power in a general election in which it won 20 seats in the 36-member House of Representatives (the lower house of the bicameral Parliament). The result ended a period of political deadlock following a tied general election in December 2001.

8 **India:** in completed elections begun in September to the state assembly of Jammu and Kashmir, the National Conference (JKNC) party, traditionally the dominant political force in Kashmir, lost power to a coalition of the People's Democratic Party (PDP) and the Congress (I) party. The new Chief Minister, Mufti Mohammad Sayeed, said that in order to end a separatist conflict that had claimed at least 35,000 lives he would release some political prisoners and seek negotiations with separatist groups.

Slovakia: negotiations following inconclusive general elections in September resulted in a coalition government of four centre-right parties led by Prime Minister Mikulas Dzurinda of the Slovak Democratic and Christian Union (SDKU).

9 **EU:** The European Commission announced that 10 out of 13 applicant countries were expected to become EU members in 2004.

10 **Cameroon:** the International Court of Justice at The Hague ruled in favour of Cameroon in a border dispute with Nigeria about sovereignty over the oil-rich Bakassi peninsula.

Pakistan: legislative elections were held to the National Assembly (the lower house of the bicameral federal legislature), fulfilling a Supreme Court order to President Gen. Pervez Musharraf to hold national elections within three years of the October 1999 coup in which Musharraf had taken power. The pro-Musharraf Pakistan Muslim League—Qaid-i-Azam (PML-Q) emerged as the largest party with 118 seats in the 342-seat Assembly.

11 **Nobel Prizes:** The Nobel Committee of the Storting awarded the 2002 Nobel Peace Prize to former US President Jimmy Carter.

USA: the Senate (the upper house of Congress, the federal bicameral legislature) approved by 77 votes to 23 a resolution authorizing President George W. Bush to take military action against Iraq if peaceful efforts to deprive Iraq of weapons of mass destruction under the auspices of the UN failed. The resolution had been passed by the House of Representatives (the lower house of Congress) on the previous day by 296 votes to 133.

12 **Indonesia:** a massive bomb blast at a holiday resort on the island of Bali killed more than 190 people and injured 300, the majority of them foreign tourists. At least 18 nationalities were represented among the casualties, but nearly half of the dead were Australian. Suspicion of responsibility quickly fell on the Jemaah Islamiah (JI) regional Islamist group thought to be linked to the al-Qaida militant network and to have carried out or planned a number of other terrorist attacks in south-east Asia.

13 **Kenya:** four Cabinet ministers resigned in protest against President Daniel arap Moi's choice of Minister of Local Government Uhuru Kenyatta as his successor.

Yugoslavia: an inconclusive second round of presidential elections was held for the republic of Serbia, following a first round in September. Although current federal Yugoslav President Vojislav Kostunica won 67 per cent of the vote, the turnout (45.5 per cent) was lower than the 50 per cent required for the election to be valid.

14 **Northern Ireland:** the UK government suspended the Northern Ireland Assembly and executive and re-imposed direct rule in the province for the fourth time since the devolution of power in 1999. The suspension of the institutions followed the exposure of an alleged Irish Republican Army (IRA) spy ring in Northern Ireland government offices.

16 **Jamaica:** in a general election, the ruling People's National Party (PNP) led by Prime Minister Percival J. Patterson won 35 seats in the 60-member House of Representatives (the lower house of the bicameral Parliament), securing an unprecedented fourth successive term in power.

Netherlands: the government led by Prime Minister Jan Pieter Balkenende resigned when the government became paralysed by ministerial resignations caused by feuding within the junior coalition partner, the Lijst Pim Fortuyn (LPF).

17 **Côte d'Ivoire:** the leader of the rebel Patriotic Movement of Côte d'Ivoire (MPCI) signed a cease-fire agreement that the government said it would also accept. Hundreds of people had died in the rebellion, which began as an army mutiny in September, and thousands of immigrants from Mali and Burkina Faso had been turned into refugees by the hostilities. Peace talks began in neighbouring Togo on 30 October under the auspices of the Economic Community of West African States (ECOWAS).

North Korea: the USA announced that during a visit to North Korea by US Assistant Secretary of State James Kelly earlier in the month, North Korean officials had admitted to the existence of a programme to build nuclear weapons based on enriched uranium. It was unclear whether North Korea had succeeded in producing any such weapons.

18 **Macedonia:** following a general election in September, the former communist Social Democratic Alliance for Macedonia (SDSM) and the ethnic Albanian Democratic Union for Integration (BDI) announced agreement on forming a coalition government.

20 **Ecuador:** Col Lucio Gutiérrez emerged unexpectedly as the leading candidate in the first round of a presidential election with 20.3 per cent of the popular vote. Gutiérrez was the joint candidate of the Popular Socialist Party (PSP) and the New Country-Pachauri Movement (NMN-PP).

Ireland: in a referendum on the Treaty of Nice on EU integration and enlargement 62.9 per cent of votes favoured ratification of the treaty, reversing the result of a June 2001 referendum.

Yugoslavia: Legislative elections held in the republic of Montenegro gave an absolute majority to the pro-independence Democratic List for a European Montenegro, led by President Milo Djukanovic, which won 39 seats in the 75-member legislature.

21 **China:** President Jiang Zemin began a seven-day official visit to the USA for a summit meeting with US President Bush on what was expected to be Jiang's last foreign trip as general secretary of the Chinese Communist Party (CCP).

Sweden: Prime Minister Göran Persson of the Social Democratic Labour Party (SAP) presented a new Cabinet, having reached agreement with the Left Party (Vp) and the Green Party (MpG) following a general election in September.

22 **Germany:** the Bundestag (the lower house of the bicameral federal legislature) re-elected Gerhard Schröder of the Social Democratic Party (SPD) as Chancellor, following a general election in September. Schröder's Cabinet was a renewed SPD-Green coalition.

23 **Iraq:** the USA presented to the full UN Security Council a draft resolution on disarming Iraq of weapons of mass destruction.

Russia: about 40 heavily armed Chechen separatists captured a theatre in Moscow, the capital, during the performance of a popular musical show. The Chechen rebels threatened to blow up the theatre, killing their 850 hostages, if Russia did not immediately withdraw its forces from Chechnya. The siege ended violently on 26 October when Russian special forces stormed the theatre, having first pumped in a paralysing gas. Most of the hostage-takers were shot, and it later emerged that at least 119 hostages had also died, all but two from the effects of the gas.

UK: the radical Muslim cleric known as Abu Qatada was arrested under the 2001 Anti-Terrorism Act. Qatada, widely believed to be a key figure in the Islamist al-Qaida network, had disappeared in London in December 2001.

24 **Bahrain:** the first legislative elections since 1975 were held, with 174 candidates (including eight women) standing for election to 37 seats in the newly created House of Representatives. Turnout was 53.2 per cent.

25 **Central African Republic:** rebel troops loyal to exiled former armed forces chief of general staff Gen. François Bozize occupied part of Bangui, the capital, but were driven out after five days by government forces.

27 **Brazil:** Luiz Inácio "Lula" da Silva, candidate of the Workers' Party (PT), won the second round of a presidential election with 61.2 per cent of the vote, beating José Serra, candidate of the Brazilian Social Democratic Party (PSDB), who gained 38 per cent. Da Silva had also led in the first round with 46.4 per cent of the vote. A former union leader, da Silva had lost three previous presidential elections. In simultaneous legislative elections, the PT became the largest single party in the Chamber of Deputies, but without an overall majority.

Togo: elections to the National Assembly (the unicameral legislature) resulted in an overwhelming victory for President Gnassingbe Eyadema's ruling Togolese People's Rally (RPT), which won 72 of the Assembly's 81 seats. The elections were boycotted by the leading opposition parties.

29 **UK:** the House of Commons (the lower house of Parliament) adopted a package of procedural reforms intended to improve its ability to hold the executive to account and to make the chamber's hours more "family friendly".

30 **Israel:** the Likud-led "national unity" government collapsed when the Labour Party withdrew from the coalition because of its opposition to the funding of Jewish settlements in the West Bank and Gaza Strip in the 2003 budget.

NOVEMBER

1 **Macedonia:** the Sobranje (the unicameral legislature) formally approved by 72 votes to 28 a coalition government headed by Prime Minister Branko Crvenkovski, leader of the former communist Social Democratic Alliance of Macedonia (SDSM).

2 **Czech Republic:** in biennial elections for 27 seats in the 81-member Senate (the upper house of the bicameral legislature) the ruling centre-left coalition lost its overall majority, its representation being reduced from 41 to 34 seats.

3 **ASEAN:** leaders of the 10-member Association of South-East Asian Nations (ASEAN) began a three-day summit meeting during which a declaration was agreed with China on the conduct of parties to the long-running disputes over the sovereignty of the Spratly and Paracel islands in the South China Sea. The Spratlys were claimed wholly or in part by four ASEAN members, China, and Taiwan, whilst the Paracels were disputed by China and Vietnam.

Russia: following the mass hostage-taking in a Moscow theatre by Chechen rebels in October, Russia launched a new military offensive in Chechnya.

Turkey: The Justice and Development Party (AKP), led by Recep Tayyip Erdogan, secured an overall majority in a general election, winning 363 seats in the 550-seat Grand National Assembly (the unicameral legislature). The former ruling Democratic Left Party (DSP) won only 1.23 per cent of the vote and failed to gain any seats. President Ahmet Necdet Sezer on 16 November invited AKP deputy leader Abdullah Gül to form a government (Erdogan having been legally barred from running for election).

4 **Senegal:** President Abdoulaye Wade dismissed Prime Minister Mame Madior Boye and her entire Cabinet in response to the September ferry disaster in which an estimated 1,200 people drowned. Wade appointed a new Cabinet on 6 November under Prime Minister Idrissa Seck.

5 **USA:** in mid-term Congressional elections, the Republican Party made gains in the House of Representatives (the lower house of the bicameral federal legislature) and regained control of the Senate (the upper house). When Congress reconvened in January 2003 the Republican Party would control both houses and the presidency for the first time since 1954.

6 **Western Sahara:** King Mohammed VI dismissed the long-deadlocked UN plan to hold a referendum on the future of the disputed territory as "null" and "out of date".

7 **Latvia:** the Saeima (the unicameral legislature) approved by 55 votes to 43 the formation of a four-party coalition government under Prime Minister Einars Repse of the centre-right New Era party.

Morocco: King Mohammed VI appointed a new government led by non-party figure Prime Minister Driss Jettou.

8 **Iraq:** the UN Security Council unanimously approved Resolution 1441 (2002) demanding that Iraq co-operate with UN weapons inspectors or face "serious consequences". Iraq had already agreed in September to the return of the UN Monitoring, Verification and Inspection Commission (UNMOVIC). Iraq on 13 November formally accepted the conditions of the resolution.

11 **Cyprus:** UN Special Envoy Alvaro de Soto presented a new peace plan for the reunification of the island to Greek Cypriot President Glafkos Clerides and Turkish Cypriot leader Rauf Denktash. The two leaders agreed to use the plan, partly modelled on the political structure of Switzerland, as a basis for negotiations.

Kazakhstan: President Nursultan Nazarbayev signed legislation to ratify an agreement with Russia over the division of the northern part of the Caspian Sea.

Russia: at a summit meeting in Brussels, the Belgian capital, Russia and the EU reached an agreement to settle a dispute over travel documents for inhabitants of the Russian enclave of Kaliningrad, which would be surrounded by EU members once Lithuania and Poland joined the EU in 2004.

Sweden: the government announced that two Russian diplomats had been expelled for engaging in industrial espionage.

13 **UK:** the Queen's Speech to Parliament set out the legislative programme of the Labour government led by Prime Minister Tony Blair, which included a controversial criminal justice bill, a bill to establish autonomous hospitals within the National Health Service, and measures on local and regional government.

14 **Argentina:** the government announced that it would repay only a small proportion of a US$805 million loan repayment due to the World Bank, thus putting the country into a state of default under World Bank rules.

15 **China:** the 16th central committee of the Chinese Communist Party (CCP)—elected on the last day of the 16th CCP congress (8-14 November)—elected Hu Jintao as general secretary of the CCP in succession to President Jiang Zemin.

North Korea: the USA persuaded the other members of the Korean Peninsula Energy Development Organisation (KEDO—South Korea, Japan, and the EU) to suspend from December monthly shipments of fuel oil to North Korea as punishment for the clandestine nuclear arms programme disclosed by North Korea in October.

Palestine: Palestinian gunmen killed at least 12 Israelis, mostly soldiers or police, in an attack in the West Bank city of Hebron. Earlier, on 10 November, a Palestinian gunman killed five Israeli civilians in a kibbutz in northern Israel. A Palestinian suicide bomber killed 11 Israelis on 21 November when he detonated a bomb on board a bus in Jerusalem.

16 **Nigeria:** the publication of a newspaper article suggesting that the Prophet Mohammed might have chosen one of the contestants in the Miss World beauty pageant (scheduled to be held in Nigeria on 7 December) as a wife exacerbated Muslim feeling against the contest, sparking Muslim-Christian violence in the northern city of Kaduna in which more than 200 people died.

Ukraine: President Leonid Kuchma dismissed the government of Prime Minister Anatolii Kinakh. Kuchma's nomination of Viktor Yanukovych as Prime Minister was confirmed in the Supreme Council (the unicameral legislature) on 21 November and a new government was appointed by 30 November.

17 **France:** the centre-right alliance, the Union for the Presidential Majority (UMP), that won legislative and presidential elections earlier in the year was formally converted into the Union for a Popular Movement, retaining the same initials.

Italy: an appeals court in Perugia shocked the political establishment by convicting former Prime Minister Giulio Andreotti of ordering the murder in 1979 of an investigative journalist; it sentenced Andreotti to 24 years' imprisonment. Andreotti had originally been acquitted of the crime in 1999.

18 **UK:** three Algerian suspected members of the al-Qaida network were charged in London under the 2000 Anti-Terrorism Act, but no details of the charges were made public.

19 **Belarus:** EU foreign ministers banned Belarusian President Alyaksandr Lukashenka from entering 14 out of 15 EU states (the exception being Portugal) because of his government's poor record on human rights and democracy. The USA on 26 November imposed a similar ban.

21 **Indonesia:** police in north-western Java arrested Imam Samudra, thought to have planned the October bomb atrocity in Bali.

Pakistan: after prolonged wrangling amongst the major political parties, the National Assembly (the lower house of the bicameral federal legislature) which had been elected in October convened to choose a new Prime Minister, electing Zafarullah Khan Jamali, candidate of the Pakistan Muslim League—Qaid-i-Azam (PML-Q) and an ally of President Gen. Pervez Musharraf. Jamali's new Cabinet was sworn in on 23 November.

22 **NATO:** at the end of a three-day summit meeting in Prague, the Czech capital, the 19-member North Atlantic Treaty Organisation (NATO) invited Bulgaria, Estonia, Latvia, Lithuania, Romania, Slovakia, and Slovenia to join NATO in 2004.

24 **Austria:** in elections to the Nationalrat (the lower house of the bicameral legislature) the People's Party (ÖVP)—the dominant member in the outgoing coalition—won the largest number of seats (79), but was unable immediately to form a new coalition government. Support for the right-wing Freedom Party (FPÖ) fell from nearly 27 per cent in 1999 to just over 10 per cent.

Ecuador: Col Lucio Gutiérrez, candidate of the leftist Popular Socialist Party (PSP) and of the New Country—Pachakutik United Movement (NMN—PP), won the second round of the presidential elections with over 54 per cent of the popular vote, defeating banana tycoon Alvaro Fernando Noboa Pontón of the New Party for Nationalist Action (PRIAN).

25 **Yugoslavia:** Milo Djukanovic resigned as President of the Republic of Montenegro. Presidential elections were scheduled for 22 December.

Turkmenistan: President Saparmurat Niyazov survived an alleged assassination attempt in Ashgabat, the capital. Niyazov named four exiled former ministers whom he believed were behind the attack and police arrested over 100 alleged conspirators.

27 **Sri Lanka:** following a second round of talks held from 31 October to 3 November between negotiating teams representing the government and the separatist Liberation Tigers of Tamil Eelam (LTTE), Vellupillai Prabhakaran, the LTTE leader, said in a speech that the Tigers were willing to accept a form of regional autonomy in place of their long-held ambition for an independent Tamil state.

28 **Côte d'Ivoire:** a six week truce in the country's civil war broke down when government troops moved against rebels around the town of Vavoua.

Kenya: a car bomb wrecked an Israeli-owned hotel in the city of Mombasa, killing 10 Kenyans and three Israeli tourists. Simultaneously an attack from shoulder-fired anti-aircraft missiles narrowly missed an Israeli passenger jet carrying 261 passengers as it took off from Mombasa airport. Both attacks were blamed on the Islamist al-Qaida network.

DECEMBER

1 **Slovenia:** Prime Minister Janez Drnovsek of the Liberal Democracy of Slovenia (LDS) won the second round of a presidential election, beating independent candidate Barbara Brezigar. Drnovsek was sworn in as the new President on 22 December.

2 **Venezuela:** a long-running crisis over President Hugo Chávez Frías's allegedly dictatorial abuse of power deepened when the Venezuelan Workers' Confederation (CTV) called a general strike in an attempt to force Chávez to resign. Key workers at the state oil monopoly joined the strike on 4 December, quickly causing petrol and food shortages. An unidentified sniper killed three opposition demonstrators on 6 December in Caracas, the capital.

3 **Burundi:** the government signed a ceasefire agreement with the main Hutu rebel group, the National Council for the Defence of Democracy—Forces for the Defence of Democracy (CNDD—FDD), effective from 30 December.

Greenland: a surprisingly strong showing in legislative elections for the opposition left-wing pro-independence Inuit Brotherhood (Inuit Ataqatigiit—IA) brought the IA into a coalition government with the Forward (Siumut) party, replacing the Community (Atassut) party.

Indonesia: among further arrests made of suspects for the October bombing in Bali, in which over 190 people were killed, was that of Ali Ghufron, believed to be operational chief of the Jemaah Islamiah (JI) regional Islamic militant network.

5 **Myanmar (Burma):** Gen. Ne Win, the former military dictator who ruled Burma from 1962 to 1988, died aged 91.

6 **Seychelles:** the ruling Seychelles People's Progressive Front (SPPF) was returned to power with a reduced majority in elections to the 34-seat National Assembly (the unicameral legislature).

8 **Iraq:** Iraqi government officials handed over to the UN Monitoring, Verification and Inspection Commission (UNMOVIC) a 12,000-page declaration on weapons of mass destruction. Whilst Iraq said that the "complete and accurate" declaration proved that it was pursuing no illegal weapons programmes, the USA claimed on 19 December that the documentation "completely failed" to meet the UN's demands.

Yugoslavia: a third round of voting in a presidential election for Serbia, the larger of Yugoslavia's two constituent republics, failed to produce a valid result because the turnout, as in the second round held in October, fell below the required 50 per cent of the electorate. Federal Yugoslav President Vojislav Kostunica led the poll with 57.66 per cent of the vote. Serbia's President Milan Milutinovic's term expired on 19 December and Natasa Micic, Speaker of the Serbian legislature, on 30 December assumed the position of Acting President.

9 **Cyprus:** a revised version of a UN plan for the peaceful reunification of Cyprus was immediately rejected by Rauf Denktash, leader of the self-declared Turkish Republic of Northern Cyprus (TRNC). On 26 December 30,000 Turkish Cypriots marched through the streets of Nicosia, the island's divided capital, expressing their support for reunification and calling on Denktash to resign.

Indonesia: the government and the separatist Free Aceh Movement (GAM) signed an agreement in Geneva, Switzerland, to end a rebellion in the Sumatran province of Aceh that had begun in 1976.

10 **Croatia**: the governments of Croatia and Yugoslavia signed a temporary protocol agreeing on the continued demilitarisation of the disputed Prevlaka peninsula after the expiry on 15 December of the mandate of a UN monitoring mission.

11 **Chile:** Chilean and US officials signed a free trade agreement between the two countries follow-

ing 10 years of negotiations. The agreement would come into effect after being approved by the respective legislatures of the two countries.

Côte d'Ivoire: France announced that it was sending more troops to join the 1,500 already attempting to supervise a truce in the civil conflict in Côte d'Ivoire. At least two new rebel factions emerged during the month.

12 **India:** the Bharatiya Janata Party (BJP), the leading party in the federal government, won a landslide victory in elections to the assembly in the western state of Gujarat, the only major state still controlled by the BJP. In his campaign the controversial chief minister Narendra Modi exploited the Hindu nationalist sentiments that had fuelled anti-Muslim riots earlier in the year.

North Korea: in an escalation of its confrontation with the USA over North Korea's alleged nuclear weapons programme the government announced that it would restart a nuclear power plant at the Yongbyon nuclear complex that was thought to produce weapons grade plutonium. On 22 December North Korea announced that it had begun removing equipment seals and surveillance cameras installed at Yongbyon in 1994 by the UN International Atomic Energy Agency (IAEA) and on 27 December that it was expelling IAEA inspectors monitoring the complex.

Uzbekistan: the Oli Majlis (the unicameral legislature) adopted a bill to create a bicameral legislature. The term of the Oli Majlis was due to expire in December 2004.

13 **EU:** at the conclusion of a two-day summit in Copenhagen, the Danish capital, EU members approved a timetable for the enlargement of the Union to include 10 candidate countries for formal admission on May 1, 2004. The candidates were: Cyprus, the Czech Republic, Estonia, Hungary, Latvia, Lithuania, Malta, Poland, Slovakia, and Slovenia.

Nicaragua: former President Arnaldo Alemán Lacayo was formally charged with money-laundering and theft of state funds after the National Assembly (the unicameral legislature) had on 12 December voted 47-45 to strip him of his parliamentary immunity to prosecution.

15 **Equatorial Guinea:** incumbent President Teodoro Obiang Nguema Mbasogo won a presidential election with 99.5 per cent of the vote. However, four opposition parties had withdrawn their candidates from the election, saying that the polling process was deeply flawed and that voters had been intimidated.

Hong Kong: up to 50,000 people joined a demonstration against a proposed anti-subversion law that critics feared would undermine political and civil liberties and make the territory's administration a puppet of the central government of mainland China.

Madagascar: President Marc Ravalomanana's I Love Madagascar (Tiako I Madagasikara—TIM) party won 103 seats in elections to the expanded 160-seat National Assembly (the lower house of the bicameral legislature).

16 **Germany:** the Federal Constitutional Court ruled that the government's key immigration law was null and void, not having been properly passed by the Bundesrat (the upper house of the federal legislature).

17 **Democratic Republic of Congo (DRC):** the government and opposition groups including the major rebel factions, the Rwanda-supported Congolese Rally for Democracy (RCD) and the Uganda-supported Congolese Liberation Movement (MLC), signed a power-sharing agreement intended to end the country's civil war. A transitional government would prepare the country for elections within 30 months.

USA: President George W. Bush announced that the USA would deploy its proposed missile defence system (MDS), with the initial installation of 10 missile interceptors in Alaska.

19 **South Korea:** Roh Moo Hyun, 56, of the ruling Millennium Democratic Party (MDP), narrowly won a presidential election, defeating Lee Hoi Chang of the conservative Grand National Party (GNP), the favourite for most of the campaign.

22 **Yugoslavia:** a presidential election in Montenegro, the smaller of Yugoslavia's two constituent

republics, was declared invalid after it failed to achieve the requisite 50 per cent turnout. Filip Vujanovic, candidate for the pro-independence Democratic List for a European Montenegro (DLEM), won over 83 per cent of the vote, but two major parties had boycotted the election.

24 **Uganda:** the government and the rebel Uganda National Rescue Front (UNRF II) signed a peace deal under which rebels would be resettled with government help or be integrated into the Ugandan army.

27 **Kenya:** presidential and legislative elections brought to an end 24 years of rule by President Daniel arap Moi and his Kenya African National Union (KANU) party. Mwai Kibaki of the National Rainbow Coalition (NARC) won the presidential contest with 62.3 per cent of the vote, beating Moi's chosen successor, Uhuru Kenyatta, into second place with 31.3 per cent. NARC won an outright majority in elections to the 224 seat-National Assembly (the unicameral legislature) with 132 seats, while KANU won only 68 seats.

Russia: suicide bombers destroyed the headquarters of the Russian-backed administration in Grozny, the capital of Chechnya, killing at least 80 people. Russia's President Vladimir Putin had signed a decree on 12 December calling for a referendum on a constitution establishing Chechnya as an autonomous republic within the Russian Federation.

30 **Philippines:** President Gloria Macapagal-Arroyo, who gained the presidency in a "People Power" uprising in January 2001, announced that she would not seek a second term in presidential elections due by 2004.

Togo: the National Assembly (the unicameral legislature) approved 36 constitutional amendments, including the creation of a second chamber (the Senate) and the removal of the limitation of a president to two five-year terms.

Turkmenistan: opposition leader and former Foreign Minister Boris Shikhmuradov was sentenced to life imprisonment for attempting to assassinate President Saparmurat Niyazov in November. There was widespread speculation that the charges were fabricated and that the assassination attempt was a fiction.

INDEX

Page references in bold indicate location of main coverage.

11 September, 9, 21, 24, 29, 34, 47, 52, 72, 138, 140-2, 144, 146, 148, 150, 152-3, 155, 159, 168, 172-3, 176, 205, 208-9, 212, 219, 224-6, 305, 327, 330, 336, 338, 343, 352, 393, 395, 401, 403, 407, 413, 421, 425, 434, 441, 450, 469, 482, 492, 499, 502, 505-6, 508, 515
Abacha, Mohammed, 258
Abacha, Sani, 258
Abbate, Carolyn, 488
Abdullah ibn Abdul Aziz, Crown Prince of Saudi Arabia, 206, 219, 225
Abdullah ibn al-Husain, King of Jordan, 4, 212-3
Abdullah, Farooq, 316
Abdullah, Omar, 316
Ablyazov, Mukhtar, 312
Abou Ghaith, Soulaiman, 238
Abraham, Spencer, 538
Abramovich, Roman, 128
Abshir Farah, Hassan, 249
Abu Nidal, 566 (obit.), 592
Abu Sayyaf Group, 343
Abu Sayyaf, 213
Abu Tourab, Rachid, 240
Abubakar, Abdulsalami, 405
Abuchakra, Ivonne Leyla Juez, 195
Acebes, Ángel, 80
Acosta, Carlos, 490
Adair, Johnny, 43
Adamkus, Valdas, 102
Adams, Gerry, 45
Adams, John, 485-6, 489
Adedeji, Adebayo, 406
Advani, L.K., 317
Aelvoet, Magda, 63
Aferwerki, Issayas, 247-8
Afghanistan, 2, 35-6, 38, 61, 112, 116, 140, 151, 155, 160, 168, 212, 217, 226, 228, 303, **304-8**, 310-1, 314, 320-1, 356, 368, 373, 379-80, 382, 386, 392, 396, 412, 427, 466, 469, 477, 504, 578-9, 581-2, 584, 587, 589, 592
African Union (AU), 7, 236, 275, 298, 331, **436-7**, *(document)* 528-30, 589
Afrika, Tatamkhulu, 509
Agabi, Kanu Godwin, 256
Agar, Mehmet, 94
Agassi, Andre, 518
Aghajeri, Hashem, 304, 451
Agnew, Spiro, 144
Agyeman, Hackman Owusu, 255
Ahern, Bertie, 48-9, 415, 586-7
Ahmed, Iajuddin, 322, 592
Ahmeti, Ali, 121
Ahrens, Geert-Hinrich, 115
AIDS/HIV, 5, 168, 173, 246, 248, 252, 281, 283, 287, 292-3, 295-7, 299, 333, 350, 381-2, 401, 442, 466
Airey, Dawn, 501
Akayev, Askar, 313
Akol, Lam, 235
al-Assad, Bashar, 38, 214, 217
al-Attiya, Abdulrahman, 434
al-Banna, Sabri, see Abu Nidal
al-Baradei, Muhammad, 222
al-Bashir, Omar Hasan Ahmed, 233-4, 414
al-Bunni, Walid, 216
al-Dumayri, Ibrahim, 210
al-Hada, Sameer Mohamed Ahmed, 226
al-Hadithi, Naji Sabri Ahmad, 591
al-Harithi, Qaed Salim Sinan, 227
al-Homsi, Mamum, 215
al-Hudaybi, Ma'mun, 211
al-Khattab, Omar ibn, 129
al-Khatib, Abdul Illah, 213
Al-Megrahi, Abdel Baset, 39, 235
al-Mujahir, Abdullah, 149
al-Qaida, 1, 35, 59, 129, 151, 155, 219, 225-8, 240, 261, 320, 336, 340, 343, 392, 394, 451; and Afghanistan, 155, 305-6, 310, 469; and alleged links to Iraq, 2, 157, 224; and attack on Tunisia, 52, 238-9; and arrests of suspects, 2, 151, 212, 217, 225-8, 239, 243, 306, 469, 482
al-Ragheb, Ali Abu, 213
al-Saadi, Amer, 222
al-Sharif, Ahmad, 210
al-Shibhi, Ramzi bin, 226
al-Turk, Riyad, 215
al-Turabi, Hasan, 235
Alagna, Roberto, 484
Albania, **114-6**, 394-5, 408, 424, 428, 580, 588
Albert, Duke of York, 564
Alberto Gasser Vargas, 193
Alemán Lacayo, Arnaldo, 165, 601
Alencar, José, 182

Alexander of Tunis, Field Marshal Earl, 560
Alexander, Douglas, 536
Alexander, Wendy, 40
Algeria, 2, **239-41**, 243-4, 408-9, 437, 583, 587
Aliyev, Geidar, 138-9
Alkatiri, Mari, 342
Allawi, Ayad, 223
Allen, Charles, 499
Allen, Woody, 559
Allende, Salvador, 552
Alliot-Marie, Michèle, 56
Almodovar, Pedro, 496
Alois, Hereditary Prince of Liechtenstein, 79
Alvarado, Arturo, 165
Alvarez, Oscar, 165
Alwaleed ibn Talal, Prince, 216
Amaral, Francisco do, 342
Amato, Giuliano, 61, 421
Amdi Petersen, Mogens, 68
American Samoa, 376, 379
Amery, Dick, 167
Amini, Ibrahim, 304
Amnesty International, 265
Amory, Vance, 172
Andani, Imoro, 255
Andean Community of Nations (Ancom/CA), 445
Anderson, Lindsay, 566
Anderson, Warren, 318
Anderton, Jim, 371-2
Andorra, 77-8, 402
Andreotti, Giulio, 60, 599
Andrews, Julie, 559
Andriessen, Louis, 486
Anger, Per, 540 (obit.)
Angola, 1, 267, 279, 281-2, **284-6**, 292, 295, 297, 381, 386, 392, 410, 413, 580, 583
Anguilla, 177-8, 445-6
Anne, the Princess Royal, 24
Annan, Kofi, 90-1, 95, 219-21, 234, 243, 261, 271, 280, 310, 364, 410, 586, 591, 593
Annenberg, Moses, 540
Annenberg, Walter, 540
Ansanelli, Alexandra, 489
Ansari, Salmann, 459
Anthony, Kenny, 172
Anthrax, 3, 149, 222
Antigua and Barbuda, 171-2, 406
Antunovic, Zeljka, 118
Anwar Ibrahim, 336
Anwar, Amar, 503
Aparicio Pérez, Juan Carlos, 80
Appleby, Stuart, 519
Arab League, 219, 228, 233, 237, 411, **433-5**, 583

Arab Maghreb Union, 239, **433-4**
Arafat, Yassir, 4, 155-6, 202, 204-5, 207, 217, 411, 566, 568, 583, 585, 587, 594
Araya Monge, Rolando, 166, 579, 583
Archer, Jeffrey, 511
Architecture, 505-8
Arctic Council (AC), 430
Arden, John, 569
Arévalo Lacs, Eduardo, 164
Argaña Ferraro, Luis Maria, 188
Argentina, 7, 13, 43, **184-7**, 189-90, 383, 400, 445, 513, 578-90, 598
Aristide, Jean-Bertrand, 170
Armenia, 137-8, 424, 428
Armitage, Richard, 316
Armstrong, Hilary, 536
Armstrong, Lance, 521
Armstrong, Louis, 550
Armstrong-Jones, Antony, 558
Arnauld, Bernard, 504
Arndt, Heinz, 369
Arosemena, Francisco, 194
Arrellano Félix, Benjamín, 162
Arrellano Félix, Ramón, 162
Arroyo, Gloria Macapagal, 342-4, 602
Aruba, 179
Asamoah, Obed, 255
Ashcroft, John, 147-9, 151, 538
Ashdown, Paddy, 116-7
Ashton, Frederick, 490
Asia-Pacific Economic Co-operation (APEC), 440-1
Asian Development Bank (ADB), 442
Aslan, Lt-Gen. Ali, 215
Association of Caribbean States (ACS), 444
Association of South East Asian Nations (ASEAN), 337, 348, **438-40**, 597
Astle, Nathan, 517
Atatürk, Mustafa Kemal, 94
Atchugarray, Alejandro, 189
Auburn, David, 492
Augstein, Rudolf, 541 (obit.)
Aung San Suu Kyi, Daw, 332, 585
Australia, 38, 153, 218, 244, 289, 342, **365-9**, 370, 378-9, 405, 407, 437, 454-5, 464, 467, 484, 489, 515-8
Austria, 66, **73-5**, 119, 419, 467, 520, 599
Avis, Gary, 489
Awang, Abdul Hadi, 336
Aye Zaw Win, U, 332
Azali, Col Assoumani, 329, 582
Azerbaijan, 137-9, 312, 424, 428
Aziz, Shaukat, 320
Aziz, Tariq, 220
Aznar López, Jose María, 80-2

Bacar, Mohamed, 328-9
Bachelet, Michelle, 190
Backley, Steve, 516
Bacon, Jim, 366
Badawi, Abdullah Ahmed, 335-6, 440
Baduel, José Raúl, 200
Bagilshema, Ignace, 471
Bagnall, Field Marshal Sir Nigel, 541 (obit.)
Bahamas, **174-5**, 585
Bahçeli, Devlet, 93-4
Bahrain, 226, **228-32**, 434, 597
Bain, Sir George, 26
Bakassi Peninsula, 471
Baker, James, 244
Bakiev, Kurmanbek, 586
Bakogianni, Dora, 89
Balaguer Ricardo, Joaquin, 170, 542 (obit.)
Balasingham, Anton, 326
Balcerowicz, Leszek, 98
Balkenende, Jan Pieter, 64, 596
Ballard, Robert, 379
Ballet and Dance, **489-91**
Baltic Council, **429**
Balyel, Mekki Ali, 235
Bamaca Velásquez, Efraín, 444
Bangladesh, 12-3, 318, **321-3**, 336, 588, 592
Bannani, Amin, 235
Banu, Naseem, 498
Banzer Suárez, General Hugo, 193, 542 (obit.), 585
Baraev, Movsar, 130
Barak, Ehud, 204
Barayagwiza, Jean-Bosco, 471
Barbados, **173**, 444
Barber, Brendan, 26
Barbour, Dave, 555
Barco Isakson, Carolina, 197
Bardem, Juan, 498
Barnes, Roy, 144
Barniol, Rodolfo, 194
Barreto, Hector V., 538
Barrichello, Rubens, 520
Barrientes, Byron, 163
Barrientos, General Rene, 542
Barry, Robert, 427
Bart, Lionel, 556
Bartlett, Andrew, 367
Barzani, Masoud, 224
Basyir, Abu Bakar, 340
Bat-Üül, Erdeniyn, 363
Batlle Ibáñez, Jorge, 189
Bauch, Pina, 491
Bawden, Nina, 29
Baxter, Alain, 515
Baxter, Clifford, 147

Bayarsayhan, Galigaagiyn, 363
Baykal, Deniz, 94
Beatrix, Queen of the Netherlands, 65, 544
Beckett, Margaret, 536
Beckett, Samuel, 509
Beckham, David, 513
Bedford, Duke of, 543 (obit.)
Bedie, Henri Konan, 550
Beem, Rich, 519
Behan, Brendan, 550, 556
Behn, Ari, 70
Beknazarov, Azimbek, 313
Belarus, 97, **131-3**, 135, 424, 428, 449, 599
Belaúnde Terry, Fernando, 192, 543 (obit.)
Belgium, **63-4**, 66, 218, 279, 408-9, 471, 580
Belize, **176**
Beloki, Joseba, 521
Bemba, Jean-Pierre, 274
Ben Ali, Zine el-Abidine, 237-9, 586
Ben Jaafer, Mustapha, 238
Ben-Eliezer, Binyamin, 204
Benflis, Ali, 239-40
Benin, **263-9**, 409, 472
Benisón, Alberto, 189
Benjamin, George, 487
Bennett, Alan, 559
Bentine, Michael, 558
Beradino, Joseph, 147
Bercow, John, 19
Berezhnaya, Yelena, 515
Berezovsky, Boris, 128
Bergier, Jean-François, 75
Berisha, Sali, 114
Berlusconi, Silvio, 59-62, 107, 214, 419, 503
Bermuda, **177-8**
Bermúdez, Jesús, 200
Bertini, Catherine, 380
Berzins, Andris, 101
Besigye, Kizza, 254
Betancourt, Ingrid, 196
Bevan, Aneurin, 544
Bhumibol Adulyadej, King of Thailand, 335
Bhutan, **325**, 464
Bhutto, Benazir, 319
Biagi, Marco, 59-60, 582
Bieto, Calixto, 485
bin Abdul Aziz, Prince Sultan, 224
bin Faisal, Turki, 224
bin Laden, Osama, 2, 59, 146, 151, 212, 217, 219, 224, 228, 261, 305, 392, 451, 563, 581
Bird, Lester, 172
Birt, Lord, 28
Birtwistle, Harrison, 488
Bishop, Charles, 146

Biya, Paul, 271
Bizimungu, Augustin, 279
Bizimungu, Pasteur, 278
Björk, 68
Björklund, Leni, 71
Bjorkman, Jonas, 519
Black Sea Economic Co-operation Organisation (BSECO), 433
Blackstone, Baroness, 537
Blair, Cherie, 20
Blair, Tony, 19, 24, 27, 36-9, 42, 45-6, 207, 214, 218, 236, 259, 416, 438, 447, 536, 598
Blix, Hans, 219, 222, 386, 591
Blunkett, David, 27-8, 536, 580
Boal, Peter, 489
Boateng, Paul, 19, 536
Bobetko, Janko, 119
Bocca, Julio, 491
Bodrov Jr, Sergei, 497
Boetticher, Budd, 545
Boina, Bakari, 329
Bolanos, Enrique, 165
Bolanos, Jorge Walter, 166
Bolivia, 14, **192-4**, 446, 585, 589, 591
Bolkiah, Prince Jefri, 337
Bolton, John, 168
Bomhoff, Eduard, 64
Bongo, Omar, 272, 409
Bosch, Juan, 542
Bosnia and Herzegovina, 6, 36, 65, **116-8**, 125, 156, 161, 384, 387, 397, 420, 423-4, 427, 470, 590, 595
Bossi, Umberto, 62
Bostridge, Ian, 484
Botswana, 274, **291-4**, 406
Boucher, Richard, 303
Bougainville, 370
Boulares, Habib, 239
Boulez, Pierre, 487
Boulkheir, Messaoud Ould, 265
Bourn, Sir John, 41
Bourne, Matthew, 491, 494
Bouteflika, Abdelaziz, 241, 244, 409, 437
Boutros-Ghali, Boutros, 408
Bowes-Lyon, Elizabeth Angela Margaret, see Queen Elizabeth, The Queen Mother
Boyce, Sir Michael, 26
Boye, Mame Madior, 264, 597
Bozizé, Gen. François, 271-2, 597
Bracken, Eddie, 498
Brackett, Charles, 575
Bracks, Steve, 366
Bradbury, Steven, 515
Bradshaw, Ben, 537

Brando, Marlon, 568
Bravo Mena, Luis Felipe, 162
Bravo, Manuel Alvarez, 505
Brazauskas, Algirdas, 102
Brazil, 13, 86, **180-4**, 188, 218, 383, 400, 410, 445, 463, 496-7, 513, 587; presidential election, 14, 180-2, 597
Brazill, Nathan, 152
Brdjanin, Radislav, 470
Brennan, Seamus, 48
Brenner, Sydney, 457
Brett, Philip, 488
Brezigar, Barbara, 122, 600
British Virgin Islands, **177-8**, 445-6
Brown, Ally, 517
Brown, Cadbury, 506
Brown, Craig, 514
Brown, Gordon, 25, 32, 35, 536, 584
Brown, Harold, 24
Brown, J. Carter, 505
Brown, Nick, 536
Bruce, Christopher, 490
Bruce, George, 510
Brunei, **337**, 440
Bucaram, Jacobo, 195
Buckovski, Vlado, 121
Budisa, Drazen, 118
Bührer, Gerold, 76
Bulgaria, 11, 111, **112-4**, 384, 394-5, 415, 428, 432, 599
Bullock, Betty, 152
Burjak, Lt-Col Ali, 212
Burkina Faso, 261, 266, **267-8**, 409, 467, 585, 587, 596
Burma, see Myanmar
Burrell, Paul, 23
Burton, Richard, 551
Burundi, 252, **277-8**, 298, 438, 593, 600
Bush, George W., domestic affairs, 3, 10, 15, 140-4, 146-7, 153-4, 538, 579, 587, 590; external relations, 3-4, 7, 14-5, 36-7, 52, 111, 130, 140-1, 143-4, 148, 153, 155-7, 161, 167-8, 180, 191, 197, 200, 203, 206-9, 218-21, 223, 229, 234, 236, 247, 302-3, 306, 336, 351, 354-6, 360-1, 373, 378, 393-4, 396, 404, 412, 421, 445, 462-4, 469, 582, 586, 588, 593, 595-6, 601
Bush, Jeb, 143-4
Bussell, Darcey, 489
Bustani, José, 464
Buyoya, Pierre, 277-8
Byatt, A.S., 509
Byers, Stephen, 28-9
Byron, 509
Cabanillas, Pío, 80

INDEX

Cabello, Diosdado, 199-200
Caborn, Richard, 537
Cage, John, 490
Caldera Cardenal, Norman, 165
Calderón, Sila María, 180
Callaghan, James, 544
Callas, Maria, 484
Calmy-Rey, Micheline, 76
Calvert, Phyllis, 498
Calvo, Manuel, 520
Calzaghe, Joe, 520
Cambodia, 144, 345, **346-7**, 439, 470
Cameroon, 258, 264, **271-2**, 279, 384, 471, 513, 580, 590, 595
Cammaert, Patrick, 247
Campbell, Alec, 369
Campo Gomez, Teodoro, 197
Canada, 8, 36, 38, 79, **158-61**, 162, 172, 407, 409, 437, 452, 454, 463, 466, 468, 515-6, 592
Cape Verde, 280, **281-2**, 410
Capitanich, Jorge, 184
Caplin, Carole, 20
Capone, Al, 568
Capriati, Jennifer, 519
Card Jr, Andrew H., 538
Cardoso, Carlos, 283
Cardoso, Fernando Henrique, 180
Carey, George, 24, 447
Caribbean Community and Common Market (Caricom), **445**
Carlos Antonio, 195
Carmona, Pedro, 198-200, 584
Carreño, Jose Manuel, 491
Carrió, Elisa, 186
Cartan, Henri, 570
Carter, Jimmy, 144, 167, 200, 331, 573, 585, 595
Carter, Stephen, 499
Cartlidge, Katrin, 498
Caruana, Peter, 84
Caspian Sea Littoral States, 303
Casson, Hugh, 506
Castañeda, Jorge, 163
Castaño, Carlos, 197
Castellano, Paul, 549
Castle, Baroness (Barbara) of Blackburn, 21, 543 (obit.)
Castle, Ted, 544
Castro, Fidel, 167, 551
Castro, Raul, 168
Cavallo, Domingo, 186
Cayman Islands, **177-8**, 445
Cecchetti, Alberto, 79
Cem, Ismail, 93-4

Central African Republic, 236, 271, **272**, 387, 438, 597
Central Asian Co-operation Organisation, 311
Central Europe Free Trade Association (CEFTA), **432**
Central European Initiative (CEI), **432**
Cevallos, Rodrigo Borja, 195
Chad, **270-1**, 438, 457, 578, 586
Chakrapong, Prince Norodom, 346
Chalabi, Ahmed, 223
Chalgam, Mohammed, 236
Chamberlain, Joseph, 556
Chambers, Dwain, 516
Chand, Lokendra Bahadur, 324, 594
Chang Dae-Hwan, 361
Chang Sang, 361
Chang-Dong, Lee, 497
Chao, Elaine, 538
Chaovalit Yongchaiyudh, 334-5
Charles, Pierre, 172
Charles, Prince of Wales, 22-3, 447
Chatty, Kerim, 71
Chaudhry, Mahendra, 377, 580
Chaverri, Danilo, 166
Chávez Frías, Hugo, 14, 169, 195, 198-200, 404, 444, 584, 593, 600
Chea, Daniel, 261
Chechnya, 1, 5, 7, 68, 128-30, (*map*) 136, 138, 424, 591-2, 596-7, 602
Chee hwa, Tun, 352-3
Chela, Juan Ignacio, 519
Chen Shui-bian, 353-5, 579
Chen-tsung, Fa, 355
Cheney, Dick, 142, 147-8, 156, 226, 538
Chiaruzzi, Mauro, 79
Chile, 13, 15, 144, **190**, 381, 446, 454, 467, 589, 601
Chillida, Eduardo, 505
Chiluba, Frederick, 286, 590
China, People's Republic of, **348-52**, accidents, 349, AIDS/HIV, 349, 592; border agreements, 311, 586; cinema, 496, 510; Dalai Lama, 364; dissent, 1, 315, 349, 582; economy, 8, 11-2, 172, 348-49, 442; environment, 466; external relations, 5, 8, 131, 135, 153, 172, 220, 308, 315, 327, 333, 351-2, 357-8, 368, 439-41, 596, 598; trade, 153, 348, 359, 402, 439, 586, 440; **Hong Kong**, **352-3**, 578, 601; politics, 348, 350, 598; science, 455-6; **Taiwan**, **353-4**
Chino, Tadeo, 442
Chirac, Jacques, 6, 37, 54-8, 61, 240, 268, 272, 377, 408-9, 416, 419, 583-5, 588, 590

Chissano, Joachim, 284
Chissano, Nyimpine, 284
Chowdhury, A.Q.M. Badruddoza, 322, 588, 592
Chrétien, Jean, 158-9, 161, 408, 592
Christie, Perry, 174, 585
Christodoulos, Archbishop, 89
Chronicle of 2002, 578-602
Chubais, Anatolii, 128
Churchill, Caryl, 494
Churchill, Winston, 508, 553
Churston, Lord, 543
Chygyr, Aleksander, 132
Chygyr, Mikhail, 132
Ciampi, Carlo Azeglio, 59-60, 214
Çiller, Tansu, 94
Cinema, 495-98
Cissé, Soumaila, 265
Clancy, Tom, 508
Clark, Geoff, 369
Clark, Helen, 371-3, 591
Clark, Joe, 159
Clark, Lynda, 537
Clarke, Charles, 31-2, 536
Clarke, Kenneth, 19
Claus, Prince of the Netherlands, 65, 544 (obit.)
Clerides, Glafkos, 90, 95, 579, 598
Clinton, Bill, 37, 143, 190, 462-3, 550
Close, Glenn, 493
Clunes, Martin, 493
Coburn, James, 498, 545
Cofferati, Sergio, 60, 62
Cole, Andy, 514
Cole, Martina, 508
Collins, Joan, 494
Collins, Kim, 516
Colombia, 7, 45, 153, 179, 191, **196-198**, 200, 381, 387, 459, 580, 582, 586, 591
Columbus, Chris, 495
Comboni, Javier, 193
Comiskey, Brendan, 48
Common Market for Eastern and Southern Africa (COMESA), 436
Commonwealth of Independent States (CIS), 311
Commonwealth of the Northern Marianas, 376
Commonwealth, The, 7, 23, 36, 38, 289-90, 330, 367, **405-7**, 408, 437, 560, 564
Community of Portuguese-Speaking Countries (CPLP), 409-10
Comoros, 329, 582
Compaoré, Blaise, 268, 409
Condit, Gary, 149

Congo, Democratic Republic of (DRC), 6, 14, 252-3, 272, **274-6**, 278-9, 289, 297-8, 384, 438, 471-2, 578, 580, 590, 593, 601
Congo, Republic of, **272**, 409, 413, 579, 582
Connell, Cardinal Desmond, 48
Conner, Dennis, 521
Connolly, Billy, 508
Connor, Joseph E., 380, 382
Conradi, Peter, 509
Conran, Terence, 507
Constantine, former King of Greece, 89
Constantine, Susannah, 508
Constantine, Tom, 44
Constantine-Maxwell, Anne, 561
Conté, Lansana, 266
Cook Islands, 377, 403, 580
Cook, Peter, 559
Cook, Robin, 536
Coolidge, Calvin, 585
Cools, André, 64
Coomber, Alex, 515
Cooper, Adam, 491
Cooper, Sir Frank, 545 (obit.)
Cooper, William, 510
Cope, Jonathan, 489-90
Corella, Angel, 491
Cornejo, Herman, 490
Corsica, 1, 55, 58
Cosgrove, Peter, 368
Costa Rica, **166**, 445, 579, 583
Costa Santolalla, Gino, 191
Costa, Albert, 518
Costa, Cesar Augusto Alarcon, 195
Costa, Gabriel, 282, 581
Costello, Peter, 367
Côte d'Ivoire, 6, 58, 63, 255, **266-7**, 272, 387, 409, 438, 593, 596, 599, 601
Couchepin, Pascal, 76
Coufoudinas, Dimitris, 88
Council of Europe, 108, 127, 135, **423-4**, 426
Council of the Baltic Sea States (CBSS), 430-1
Coutts, Russell, 521
Covic, Dragovan, 117
Coward, Noel, 494
Cracknell, James, 521
Cracknell, Ruth, 369
Craig, Daniel, 494
Crean, Simon, 365, 367
Croatia, 11, 116, **118-20**, 186, 380, 394-5, 432, 470, 515, 590, 600
Cronje, Hansie, 517, 545 (obit.)
Crosby, Bing, 555
Crowe, Sara, 494

Crozier, Adam, 514
Crvenkovski, Branko, 120, 597
Csurka, István, 107
Cuauhtlatoatzin, Juan Diego, 79, 449
Cuba, 45, 155, **167-8**, 173, 199, 226, 306, 314, 444-5, 463, 469, 477, 497, 585, 589
Cubas Grau, Raúl, 188
Culloty, Jim, 520
Cunningham, Group Captain John, 546 (obit.)
Cunningham, Merce, 490
Cuno, James, 503
Currie, Edwina, 20
Currie, Lord, 499
Curtis, Tony, 575
Cutler, Roden, 369
Cyprus, 5, 37, 89, **90-2**, 93, 415-6, 514, 579, 598, 600-1
Czech Republic, 36, 43, 74, **103-5**, 380, 408, 415, 428, 432, 588-9, 597, 601

da Costa, Guilherme Posser, 281
da Silva, Luiz Inácio "Lula", 180-3, 597
Da'ud, Abu, 566
Dada, Arte, 115
Daddah, Ahmed Ould, 265
Dalai Lama, 364, 593
Daldry, Stephen, 494, 496
Dalhousie, Lord, 22
Dalila, Arif, 216
Danforth, John, 233
Daniel, Celso, 181
Daniel-Lesur, 488
Daniels Jr, Mitchell E., 538
Dankworth, Johnny, 559
Darboe, Ousainou, 260
Darling, Alistair, 28, 30, 536, 589
das Neves, Maria, 282
Daschle, Tom, 143
Däubler-Gmelin, Herta, 52
Davidson, Jane, 41
Davies, Gavyn, 501
Davies, Maxwell, 486
Davis, Colin, 484
Davis, David, 18
Davis, Essie, 493
Davis, Ray, 457
Dawson, Thomas, 560
Day, Stockwell, 159
De Almeida, José Maria, 182
de Gaulle, General, 557
de Havilland, Geoffrey, 546
De la Rúa Bruno, Fernando, 184
de Leon Carpio, Ramiro, 164, 546 (obit.)
de Menezes, Fradique, 281-2
de Rothschild, Baron Philippe, 556

de Saint Phalle, Niki, 505
de Soto, Alvaro, 90, 598
de Toth, André, 498
de Villepin, Dominique, 56, 236, 241
Déby, Idriss, 578, 586
Dehaene, Jean-Luc, 421
Deiss, Joseph, 76
Delaney, Shelagh, 556
DeLay, Tom, 144
Delvaux, André, 498
Dembo, Antonio, 284
Dench, Dame Judi, 494, 510
Deng Liqun, 350
Denham, John, 537
Denktash, Rauf, 90, 92, 95, 417, 554, 579, 598, 600
Denmark, **67-8**, 417, 420, 441, 578, 587
Derek, Bo, 559
Dervish, Kemal, 94
Dettori, Frankie, 520
Deuba, Sher Bahadur, 323, 586, 594
Dexter, Colin, 569
Dhina, Mourad, 240
Dhlakama, Alfonso, 284
Diallo, Siradiou, 266
Diana, Princess of Wales, 23
Dickens, Charles, 511
Dickson, Chris, 521
Diego, Juan, 163
Diouf, Abdou, 408
Disarmament, see Strategic Offensive Reduction Treaty, Weapons of Mass Destruction
Disasters & Accidents (see also 11 September, AIDS/HIV, environment), air crashes, 76, 355, 377, 585-6; cyclone, 328; earthquakes, 59, 308, 504; famine, 6, 285, 287, 295, 297, 587, 594; floods, 52, 59, 103, 318, 347, 355, 361, 504, 592; forest fires, 440; train crash, 210, 253, 580, 588; tsunami, 59; storms, 59, 361; typhoon, 361, 378; volcanic eruptions, 59, 274, 578
Djaballah, Sheikh Abdallah, 239
Djibouti, 233, 248, **249**
Djindjic, Zoran, 124
Djukanovic, Milo, 125, 596, 599
Dlamini, Sibusiso, 298
Documents and Reference, **522-39**
Doe, Samuel, 261
Dole, Elizabeth, 144
Dole, Robert, 144
Dominica, **172**
Dominican Republic, **169-70**, 446, 585-6
Donaldson, Denis, 21

Donaldson, William, 154
Donleavy, J.P., 550
Donnelly, Brian, 39
dos Santos, Anibal, 283
dos Santos, Jose Eduardo, 285-6
Doty, Mark, 509
Doudou, Emile Boga, 266
Douglas, Denzil, 172
Dowell, Anthony, 490
Downes, Edward, 484
Dreyfus, Ruth, 76
Dring, Sumon, 323
Drnovsek, Janez, 122, 600
Drummond, Stuart, 18
Duarte Barros, Rui, 410
Duarte Cancino, Isaias, 198
Duhalde, Eduardo, 184, 187, 578
Duncan Smith, Iain, 17-9
Duncan, David, 147
Dung, Van Tien, 345, 547 (obit.)
Dunne, Peter, 372
Dunwoody, Gwyneth, 28
Dunwoody, Richard, 520
Durão Barroso, José Manuel, 85, 582
Duvanov, Sergei, 313
Dzurinda, Mikulas, 105-6, 594-5

Eaglen, Jane, 485
East African Commission, 253, **437**
East Timor, 1, 339, **342**, 380, 384, 409, 442, (*document*) 535, 584, 586, 592
Easter Island, 379
Easterby, Tim, 520
Eban, Abba, 547 (obit.)
Ebdon, Peter, 521
Ecevit, Bülent, 93-4
Eco, Umberto, 509
Economic Community of Central African States (CEEAC), 438
Economic Community of West African States (ECOWAS), 264, 267, **438**, 596
Ecuador, 14, 169, 186, **194-5**, 197, 445, 580, 596, 599
Edinburgh, Duke of, 561
Edward VIII, King, 564
Edwards, Colin, 520
Edwards, Jonathan, 516
Egal, Mohamed Ibrahim, 249, 585
Egypt, 38, 207, **208-11**, 233-5, 403, 502, 506, 580
Ehrlich, Robert, 144
Eichel, Hans, 50, 419
Eigen, Manfred, 563
Ek, Mats, 489
El Baradei, Mohamed, 386

El Salvador, 164, 200, 472
el-Yousifi, Abderrahmane, 241-2, 594
Elbak, Abdou Soule, 328-9
Elder, Mark, 485
Elizabeth II, Queen, 17, 22, 24, 40, 369, 407, 556-7, 564, 583-4
Elkington, Steve, 519
Elmhirst, Dorothy, 577
Elmhirst, Leonard, 577
Els, Ernie, 519
Emanuel, Carlos Julio, 194
English, Bill, 372
Enhbayar, Nambaryn, 363-4
Enright, D.J., 510
Enron Corp., 9, 33, 142, 147, 149-50, 178, 328, 423, 458
Environment, 463-8, aircraft noise, 421; birds, 87; climate change, 376, 378, 442, 463-4; drought, 248, 283, 287, 297, 318, 355, 365; endangered species, 376; fishing, 40, 70-1, 430; floods, 52, 103, 318, 347, 355, 504, 592; GM organisms, 287, 372, 462-4, 468; greenhouse gas emissions, 378, 430, 463; hydroelectric power, 68-9; missiles, 112; nuclear waste, 462; oil, 82-3, 194, 303; pollution, 430, 465, 467; sustainable development, 430, 462, 473; transport, 29-30; water, 378, 425; whales, 69, 378, 467; see also Kyoto Protocol, nuclear energy, World Summit on Sustainable Development
Enwezor, Okwui, 503
Eom Ho-Sung, 361
Equatorial Guinea, 273, 601
Erdogan, Recep Tayyip, 94-5, 597
Eriksson, Sven-Goran, 513
Eritrea, 233, 235, 246, **247-8**, 385
Ermler, Mark, 488
Escrivá de Balaguer, Josemaría, 79, 83, 449
Eshkol, Levi, 548
Espersen, Lene, 68
Essy, Amara, 437
Estonia, 100-1, 130, 394-5, 415, 599, 601
Estrada, José, 343
ETA, 5, 45, 81-2
Ethiopia, 6, 233, **245-7**, 248, 385, 457
Etter, Brian K., 488
Eurasian Economic Community (EEC), 311
Euro, 6, 35, 50, 54, 72, 84, 88, 102, 104, 153, 414, 417-8
European Bank for Reconstruction and Development (EBRD), 11, **428-9**
European Central Bank (ECB), 11, 419
European Commission, 11, 40, 54, 57, 83-4, 86, 97, 108-9, 135, 416, 418, 426, 430, 432, 441, 473, 588, 594-5

European Council, 61, 415, 421, 475
European Court of Human Rights, 89, 424, 473
European Court of Justice, 473-4
European Free Trade Association (EFTA), **431-2**, 434
European Monetary Union (EMU), 11, 71, 415, 418
European Parliament, 21, 80, 111, 168, 208, 247, 329, 476,
European Union (EU), **414-23**, agriculture/fishing, 6, 15, 37, 40, 58, 97-8, 109, 416, 430, 462, 588-9; economies/euro, 10-11, 32, 47, 50, 54, 57, 66-7, 71-2, 75, 84-6, 88, 123, 126, 153, 400-2, 414-9, 422-3, 431-2, 434, 459, 461, 463, 465, 475-6, 578, 582, 586, 594; enlargement, 6, 37, 67-8, 74, 86-7, 89-95, 97-100, 102-6, 108-13, 123, 414-6, 421-2, 424, 428, 430, 432, 581, 588, 595, 601; external relations, 7, 11, 14, 38, 75, 121-3, 130, 132-3, 135, 202, 208-9, 234, 243, 256, 268, 286-7, 289-90, 303, 308, 333, 386, 405, 413, 421, 433-4, 445, 451, 455, 580, 585, 587, 590, 598-9; law, **473-6**, member states' attitudes, 6, 58, 60-1, 67, 71, 418, 422, 596; security/defence/peacekeeping, 58, 117, 126, 387, 393-4, 397-9, 417-20, 422, 425; presidency, 67, 80; Treaty of Nice, 49, 415, 473-6, 596
Euthanasia, 64
Evans, Donald, 538
Evans, Rebecca, 484
Eyadéma, Gnassingbe, 264, 268, 408, 597
Eyre, Richard, 510
Eyzaguirre, Nicolás, 190

Fadlallah, Sheikh Allamah Mohammed Husayn, 217
Fahim, Makhdoom Amin, 319
Fahim, Mohammad, 306
Falco, Edie, 495
Falconer of Thoroton, Lord, 537
Falkland Islands, 187
Fanego, Julio César, 188
Faroe Islands, 68, 514
Fastow, Andrew, 150
Faulkner, William, 560
Faysal, Tujan, 213
Fazul, Mohamed Said, 328
Federated States of Micronesia, **378**
Fenn, John, 457
Ferdinand, Rio, 514
Ferguson, Sir Alex, 514, 520
Ferreira Leite, Manuela, 85-6
Ferrero, Juan Carlos, 518

Ferro Rodrigues, Eduardo, 84
Ferry, Luc, 56
Fiji, 337, 406, 442, 580
Filipos, Abune, 248
Financial Action Task Force (FATF), 172-4, 403, 441
Findley, Timothy, 510
Finland, 13, 36, **72-3**, 429-30
Finney, Albert, 565
Fischer, Joschka, 53
Fischler, Franz, 589
FitzGerald, Garret, 49
Flanagan, Richard, 509
Flego, Gvozden, 118
Florez, Juan Diego, 484
Fogh Rasmussen, Anders, 67, 415
Foley, Lawrence, 212
Food and Agriculture Organisation (FAO), 408, 464-6, 587
Foot and mouth disease, 34, 42, 481
Fortuyn, Pim, 65, 548 (obit.), 582, 585
Foss, Per-Kristian, 69
Foster, Peter, 20
Fourtou, Jean-René, 498
Fox Quesada, Vicente, 162-3
Fox, Christopher, 488
France, 2, 11, 28, 37, **54-8**, 66, 156, 220-1, 236, 239, 264, 267, 328, 408-9, 415, 419, 422, 461, 472, 484, 502, 513, 518-9, 521, 582-3, 588-90, 594, 601; presidential election, 6, 54-6, 240, 377, 408, 584-5
Franco y Bahamonde, Gen. Francisco, 83
Franco, Julio César, 187
Francophonie Community, see International Organisation of Francophonie
Franks, Tommy, 311
Franzen, Jonathan, 509
Frattini, Franco, 60
Frayn, Michael, 509
Frears, Stephen, 496
Fredrikson, Kristian, 490
French Polynesia, **377**
Fridleifsdottir, Siv, 68
Friedman, Stephen, 154, 538
Frist, David, 146
Fuentes, Carlos, 509
Fujimori, Alberto Keinya, 192
Fuller, John, 509
Funnell, Pippa, 521
Furyk, Jim, 519

Gabon, **272-3**
Gal, Hans, 487
Galab, Yacin Yabeh, 249
Galtieri, Gen. (retd) Leopoldo, 589

Gama, Jaime, 84, 425
Gambia, The, 260, 264, 280-1, 578-9
Gambon, Michael, 494
Gandhi, Indira, 552
Gandhi, Rajiv, 326
Ganolpolski, Andrey, 462
Gao Yan, 349
Garang, John, 233-4
Garba, Joseph, 258
Garbo, Greta, 575
García, Alan, 191
García, José Guillermo, 164
Garcia, Sergio, 519
Garfa, Mahamat, 270
Garotinho, Anthony, 182
Garzón, Baltasar, 82
Gates, Bill, 459
Gatete, Jean-Baptiste, 279
Gayoom, Maumoon Abdul, 330
Gbagbo, Laurent, 63, 266-8, 550
Geaney, Donal, 47
Gechem Turbay, Jorge Eduardo, 196
Geingob, Hage, 295
Gelin, Daniel, 498
Gennimata, Fofi, 89
Gentworth, Mark, 488
Geoghan, John, 152
George V, King, 564
George VI, King, 22, 557, 564
Georgia, 2, 43, (*map*) 136, **137-8**, 424, 428, 581, 591
Georgievski, Ljubco, 593
Gephardt, Dick, 144
German, Mike, 41
Germany, 2, 6, 10, 37, 43, **50-4**, 58, 73, 75-6, 102, 156, 225, 239, 331, 368, 381, 418-9, 422, 455, 461-2, 477, 485, 499, 503, 513, 515-6, 583, 592, 601; presidential election, 51-4, 594, 596
Geve, Father Augustine, 376
Ghai, Yash, 251
Ghana, 127, **254-55**, 267-8
Ghazali, Col Rustum, 215
Gheorghiu, Angela, 484
Ghufron, Ali, 600
Giacconi, Riccardo, 457
Gibraltar, 84, 243
Gielgud, John, 559
Gil Díaz, Francisco, 162
Gilchrist, Adam, 517
Gilchrist, Andy, 25-6
Ginsburg, Alexander, 548 (obit.)
Giordiani, Jorge, 200
Giovagnoli, Gino, 79
Giscard d'Estaing, Valery, 421

Glamis, Lady, 564
Glen, Iain, 493
Goh Chok Tong, 337-8
Goica, Pedro Julio, 170
Goldin, Daniel, 452
Goldschmidt, Berthold, 487
Goldsmith, Lord, 537
Goldsmith, Simone, 490
Golub, Leon, 503
Gomes, Ciro, 182
Gomis, Oswald Thomas, 327
Goncharik, Vladimir, 132
Gongadze, Heorhiy, 134
González Macchi, Luís, 187-8
Goodman, Benny, 550, 555
Goosen, Retief, 519
Gorbachev, Mikhail, 554
Gore, Al, 143, 146
Gorton, Sir John, 369, 549 (obit.)
Gotti, John, 549 (obit.)
Grant, M.J., 488
Grasser, Karl-Heinz, 75
Gravano, Salvatore, 549
Greece, 6, 37, **88-90**, 115, 368, 395, 398, 417, 420, 590
Green, Adolph, 510
Green, Michael, 499
Greenberg, Richard, 492
Greene, Maurice, 516
Greenland, 68, 430, 462, 600
Gremah, Lawal Ari, 269
Grenada, 173-4, 403, 406
Grimshaw, Nicholas, 506
Grisham, John, 508
Grocott, Lord, 536
Gronholm, Marcus, 520
Grossman, Mark, 96
Group of 77 (G-77), 199, **411-3**
Group of Eight (G-8), 409, 437
Group of Seven (G-7), 160-1, 403, 441, 588
Grunow, Pam, 152
Guam, 376, 378
Guatemala, 79, **163-4**, 167, 176, 403, 444
Guebuza, Armando Emilio, 284
Gueï, Gen. Robert, 266-7, 550 (obit.), 593
Guellah, Ismail Omar, 249
Guillem, Sylvie, 490
Guinea, 258, **266**, 589
Guinea-Bissau, 267, **280-1**, 384, 410
Guingona, Teofisto, 343
Guirgis, Stephen Adly, 492
Gukasyan, Arkadii, 139
Gül, Abdullah, 95, 597
Gulf Co-operation Council (GCC), 433-4
Gulf War, 4, 203, 220, 434, 476

INDEX

Gündalay, Lamjavyn, 363
Gunnell, Sally, 516
Gurirab, Theo-Ben, 295
Gursky, Andreas, 504
Gusinsky, Vladimir, 127
Gusmão, José Alexandre (Xanana), 342, 410, 584
Guterres, António, 84
Guterres, Eurico, 339
Gutiérrez, Col. Lucio, 195, 596, 599
Guyana, 175-6, 178, 406, 445
Gyanendra, King of Nepal, 323-4, 586, 594

Habila, Helon, 509
Habsade, Muhammad Ibrahim, 249
Hadayet, Hesham Mohamed, 150
Hagen, Carl, 69
Hagos, Mesfin, 247
Haider, Jörg, 74-5
Hain, Peter, 21, 42, 422, 536
Haiti, 169-70, 175, 445
Hakim, Abdelaziz, 223
Hakim, Ayatollah Baqir, 223
Hall, Craig, 489
Hall, Peter, 575
Halonen, Tarja, 72
Hamas, 202-3, 206, 210-11, 590
Hamed, Naseem, 520
Hammami, Hamma, 238
Hampson, Christopher, 489
Hampton, Lionel, 550 (obit.)
Hanbury, Jock, 562
Hancock, Sheila, 570
Hanekom, Derek, 301
Hans-Adam II, Prince of Liechtenstein, 79
Hansen, Ashia, 516
Hansen, Steve, 518
Hanssen, Robert, 149
Hanutenya, Hidipo, 594
Haouari, Mokhtar, 146
Harding, Daniel, 484
Hare, David, 494, 569
Harle, John, 486
Harman, Harriet, 537
Haroun, Mahamat Saleh, 497
Harper, Stephen, 159
Harriman, Averell, 573
Harris, Richard, 498, 550 (obit.)
Harrison, Audley, 520
Hart, Gary, 146
Hasan, Adnan Badr, 215
Hassan, King of Morocco, 242
Hassannal Bolkiah, Sultan, 337
Hatfill, Steven, 149
Hatoyama, Yukio, 359

Hatton, Ricky, 520
Havel, Václav, 103, 157, 589
Hayes, Bob, 551
Haynes, Todd, 496
Healey, John, 536
Heathcote, Steven, 490
Heavily Indebted Poor Countries Initiative (HIPC), 165, 253, 401
Heinsbroek, Herman, 64
Hellawell, Piers, 488
Heller, André, 553
Helms, Jesse, 144
Helms, Richard, 551-2 (obit.)
Hendry, Stephen, 521
Henman, Tim, 518
Henry, Graham, 518
Herzen, Alexander, 494
Hewitt, Lleyton, 518
Hewitt, Patricia, 536
Hewitt, Penelope, 24
Heyerdahl, Thor, 552 (obit.)
Hezbollah, 215-7, 409
Hibberd, Dominic, 510
Hiddink, Guus, 360
Hierro, José, 510
Hill, Michael, 25
Hingis, Martina, 519
Hitler, Adolf, 551, 553
Hobeika, Elie, 218, 579
Hodge, Margaret, 537
Hoff, Harry, 510
Hogan, Ben, 568
Hollingworth, Peter, 368
Hollioake, Ben, 517
Holocaust, 109, 450, 510
Holt, Harold, 549
Holy See, see Vatican
Honduras, 165, 472
Hong Kong, 350, **352-3**, 355, 578, 586, 588, 601
Hoon, Geoff, 536
Horne, David, 488
Horvitz, Robert, 457
Houellebecq, Michel, 509
Houphouet-Boigny, 550
Howard, John, 38, 289, 365, 368, 405, 437
Hoyte, Desmond, 175-6
Hsi-kun, Yu, 353, 579
Hsieh, Frank, 354
Hu Jintao, 8, 350-1, 598
Hubbard, R. Glen, 538
Hue, Robert, 56
Hughes, Bev, 537
Hughes, Mark, 43, 514
Hughes, Sarah, 515

Hull, Edward, 227
Human Rights Watch, 236, 247, 314, 345
Hun Sen, 346
Hungary, 107-9, 395, 403, 415, 432, 584, 586, 601
Hurst, Geoff, 576
Hurtado Larrea, Osvalso, 195
Hussain, Chaudhry Shujaat, 319
Hussain, Nasser, 517
Hussein, King of Jordan, 567
Hussein, Saddam, 2-5, 36-7, 74, 156-7, 161, 218-23, 302, 404
Hussey, Gillian, 49
Hutchinson, Tim, 144
Hutt, Jane, 41
Hutton, John, 537
Hvorostovsky, Dmitri, 484
Hytner, Nicholas, 492

Ibarretxe, Juan José, 82
ibn Shaker, Field Marshal Sharid Zaid, 214, 567
Ibrahim, Izzat, 219
Iceland, 68-9, 70, 430, 432
Iddrisu, Alhaji, 255
Idris, Abdullah, 248
Ienaga, Saburo, 359
Iliescu, Ion, 109, 111
Illmann, Margaret, 490
Ilves, Toomas Hendrik, 100
Imanishimwe, Lt Samuel, 471
India, 1, 5, 12, 22, 131, 283, 310-11, **315-8**, 321, 325-7, 333, 377, 407, 439-41, 459, 463-4, 496-7, 503, 516-7, 581-2, 584-5, 593, 595, 601
Indian Ocean Rim Association for Regional Co-operation (IORARC), 439
Indonesia, 2, 5, 12, 336-8, **338-40**, (*map*) 341, 368, 403, 410, 442, 472, 580, 586, 591-2, 600; Bali bombing, 1, 7, 368, 385, 439-40, 595, 599-600
Information technology, 231, 328, 354, 442, **458-61**
Ingram, Adam, 537
Inoue, Yutaka, 357
Inter-American Development Bank (IADB), 444
Inter-governmental Authority for Development (IGAD), 233
International Court of Justice, 229, 258, 271, 378, **471-2**, 569, 580
International Criminal Court, 111, 156, 380, 387, 412, 421, **469-70**, 590
International Criminal Tribunal for Rwanda, 279, 382-3, **471**

International Criminal Tribunal for the former Yugoslavia (ICTY), 119, 382-3, 423, **470-1**, 580
International Labour Organisation (ILO), 332
International Monetary Fund (IMF), 9, 13, 15, 93-5, 115, 120, 122, 125, 164, 176, 178, 181-2, 184-7, 189, 194, 214, 225, 254, 257, 259, 271, 275, 287, 294, 299, 317, 329, 333, 339, 370, **399-400**, 429, 441, 587-8
International Organisation of Francophonie (OIF), 331, 329, **407-9**
International Whaling Commission (IWC), 69-70, 378
Intifada, 1, 4, 13, 202, 205, 386
IRA (Provisional Irish Republican Army), 21, 45-6, 596
Iran, 2-3, 36, 45, 96, 130, 139-40, 155, 218, 229, **302-4**, 308, 310-2, 394, 404, 414, 421, 434, 451, 469, 497, 578, 587, 590, 592
Iraq, 218-24, alleged links to al-Qaida, 2, 157, 224; economy/sanctions, 36, 114, 117, 125, 135, 222, 392, 404, 434; external relations, 74, 199, 204, 207-8, 210, 213-4, 219, 225, 228-9, 368, 435, 583; Kurds, 223-4, 303; threat of US/UK military action, 2-3, 15, 17, 26, 33, 35-7, 50, 52, 54, 58, 96, 140, 143, 153-8, 161, 203, 212, 218-9, 222-3, 302-3, 320, 354, 365, 368, 373, 376, 394, 396, 404, 409, 412, 415, 421, 441, 447, 450, 469, 505, 579, 593-5; UN weapons inspections, 3, 5, 37, 131, 155, 157, 214, 219-22, 229, 380, 384-6, 412, 434-5, (*document*) 522-7, 591, 593, 596, 598, 600; see also Weapons of Mass Destruction
Ireland, 47-9, 78, 87, 381, 415, 418, 448, 473, 513, 518-9, 581, 586-7, 596
Irvine of Lairg, Lord, 536
Ishii, Koki, 359
Islamic Jihad, 203, 210-1
Israel, 1, 3-4, 13, 24, 38, 61, 63, 155-6, **202-5**, 206-8, 210-2, 215-6, 218-9, 225, 227-9, 237, 252, 311, 381, 386, 394, 403-4, 411-4, 421, 434-5, 449, 451, 470
Issa, Habib, 216
Italy, 11, 37, 43, **59-62**, 115-6, 119, 135, 156, 214, 237, 247, 307, 368, 418-9, 461, 499, 503, 507, 513, 582, 594, 599
Ivanov, Igor, 138, 220
Ivanov, Sergei, 130
Ivory Coast, see Côte d'Ivoire

Jackson, Colin, 516
Jackson, Jesse, 143
Jackson, Peter, 496

Jackson, Thomas Penfield, 458
Jaffé, Susan, 491
Jagdeo, Bharrat, 175
Jama, Jama Ali, 249
Jamaica, 38, **168-9**, 178, 480, 596
Jamali, Zafarullah Khan, 308, 320, 599
Jammeh, Yahya, 260, 578
Japan, 8, 11-2, 70, 86, 127-8, 153, 264, 308, 310, 327, 333, 348, 352, **356-9**, 362, 364, 378, 402, 457, 461, 463, 497, 504, 513, 592-3, 596
Jatti, Basappa Danappa, 552-3 (obit.)
Jawara, Dawda Kairaba, 260
Jemaah Islamiah, 336-7, 340, 595, 600
Jenkins, Roy, 508
Jettou, Driss, 241-3, 598
Jeyaretnam, J. B., 338
Jiang Zemin, 348, 350-1, 596, 598
Jibril, Ahmed, 218
Jibril, Jihad, 218
Jiménez, Tucapel, 190
Jiuyong, Shi, 472
Joel, Billy, 495
Joel, Nicolas, 484
Johansson, Thomas, 518
John Paul II, Pope, 7-9, 98, 114, 139, 152, 163, 448, 592
Johnson, Alan, 537
Johnson, Hilde Frafjord, 233
Johnson, Lyndon B., 551, 573
Johnson, Steven, 488
Jones, Richard, 485
Jones, Simon, 517
Jongwe, Learnmore, 290
Jonze, Spike, 496
Jordan, 1, 38, 207, **212-4**, 230, 411
José, Don, 489
Joseph, Charles M., 488
Jospin, Lionel, 54-7, 408, 584-5
Jourdain, Cindy, 489
Jowell, Tessa, 500, 536
Jugnauth, Sir Aneerood, 328
Juliana, Queen of the Netherlands, 545
Julu, Charles, 261
Jun-ying, Huan, 354
Junge, Hans, 553
Junge, Traudl, 553 (obit.)
Junguito Bonnet, Roberto, 197
Juppé, Alain, 56
Jurado, Katy, 498
Jurcic, Ljubo, 118

Kabbah, Ahmad Tejan, 258-9, 579, 581, 586
Kabila, Joseph, 274-6, 593
Kadhafi, Col Moamer, 236-7, 435, 437

Kagame, Paul, 275-6, 278
Kahin, Dahir Riyale, 249, 585
Kahn, Oliver, 513
Kahneman, Daniel, 15
Kalam, A.P.J. Abdul, 316
Kalamanov, Vladimir, 424
Kallas, Siim, 100
Kallsberg, Anfínn, 68
Kamaluddheen, Abdullah, 330
Kamilov, Abdulaziz, 310
Kan'an, Lt-Gen. Ghazi, 215
Kan, Naoto, 359
Kapeller, Christoph, 506
Karadzic, Radovan, 117
Karamanlis, Konstantinos, 569
Karatzaferis, Georgios, 89
Karimov, Islam, 310-1, 314
Kark, Austen, 29
Karsh, Yousuf, 553 (obit.)
Karzai, Hamid, 304-6, 308, 564, 587, 592
Kashmir, 1, 5, 315-7, 321, 585, 593, 595
Kasyanov, Mikhail, 364
Kato, Koichi, 357
Kato, Shizue, 359
Kavan, Jan, 380
Kawaguchi, Yoriko, 357
Kazakhstan, **309-14**, 453, 579, 598
Keane, Roy, 49, 513
Keeler, Andrew, 488
Keenlyside, Simon, 484
Keita, Ibrahim Boubacar, 265, 591
Keke, Harold, 376
Kelessidi, Elena, 484
Kelly, James, 596
Kelly, Pete, 555
Kelly, Ruth, 536
Kendrew, Sir John, 562
Kennedy, Charles, 18
Kennedy, Jane, 537
Kennedy, John F., 379, 492, 571, 573
Kennedy, Robert, 144
Kenny, Enda, 48
Kent, Julie, 490
Kenya, 1, 7, 233, 248, **250-2**, 253, 279, 406, 457, 595, 599, 602
Kenyatta, Uhuru, 250, 595, 602
Kérékou, Mathieu, 268, 409
Kerr, John, 421
Kerry, John, 146
Kertesz, Imre, 109, 510
Kerwood, Charlotte, 516
Kesete, Semere, 248
Keynes, John Maynard, 571
Khalayla, Fadel Nazzal, 212
Khalili, Abdul Karim, 306

616 INDEX

Khamenei, Ayatollah Seyed Ali, 578
Khamtay Siphandon, 347
Khan, Genghis, 364
Khandu Wangchuk, 325
Khannouchi, Khalid, 516
Kharrazi, Kamal, 303
Khatami, Mohammad, 229, 304, 310, 592
Khattab, see al-Khattab
Khodorovsky, Mikhail, 503
Khulayfat, Awad, 213
Kiarostami, Abbas, 497
Kibaki, Mwai, 250, 406, 602
Kiley, Robert, 30
Kilpatrick, Dame Judith, 553-4 (obit.)
Kim Dae Jung, 359-62
Kim Dong-Sung, 515
Kim Hong-Gul, 361
Kim Hong-Up, 361
Kim Jong Il, 358, 362, 593
Kim Suk Soo, 361
Kinakh, Anatolii, 134, 599
Kinzang Dorji, 325
Kirbati, 381, 374, **377**
Kirch, Leo, 499
Kiselev, Evgenii, 128
Kissinger, Henry, 144
Klaus, Vaclav, 104
Knef, Hildegard, 49 8
Knussen, Oliver, 486
Kobborg, Johan, 491
Kocharian, Robert, 137
Kodjo, Agbeyome, 268
Kohl, Helmut, 107
Köhler, Horst, 254, 400
Koirala, Girja Prasad, 324
Koizumi, Junichiro, 12, 352, 356-9, 362, 369, 593
Kok, Wim, 65, 584
Kolélas, Bernard, 272
Kollar-Kotelly, Colleen, 458
Korea, Democratic People's Republic of (North Korea), 3, 5, 8, 15, 36, 140, 151, 155, 218, 227, 321, 349, 352, 358, **361-3**, 394, 421, 469, 579, 589, 593, 596, 598, 601
Korea, Republic of (South Korea), 8, 12, 86, 264, 357, 359, **360-61**, 362, 378, 383, 497, 513, 515, 589, 598, 601
Koroma, Abdul, 472
Koroma, Ernest, 259
Koroma, Johnny Paul, 259
Koshiba, Masatoshi, 359, 457
Kosovo, 6, 35, 121, 124-5, 385, 427, 470
Kostecki, John, 521
Kostelic, Janica, 515
Kostov, Hari, 121

Kostunica, Vojislav, 124-5, 595, 600
Koutoubi, Sani, 269
Kozik, Leanid, 132
Krupa, Gene, 550
Kubis, Jan, 426
Kuchma, Leonid, 133-4, 583, 599
Kufuor, John, 255
Kulov, Feliks, 313
Kumaratunga, Chandrika Bandaranaike, 325-7
Kundera, Milan, 509
Kurds, 93-5, 223, 303
Kuwait, 173, 219, **227-32**, 434-5, 583
Kwasniewski, Aleksander, 97
Kyoto Protocol, 156, 159, 161, 330, 394, 412, 421, 430, 462-3, 465-6, 468
Kyprianou, Spyros, 554 (obit.)
Kyrgyzstan, **309-14**, 427-8, 586, 588

Laar, Mart, 100
Labus, Miroljub, 124
Labwani, Kamal, 216
Lagos, Ricardo, 190
Lahoud, Emile, 215, 217
Lakatani, Sani, 584
Lamy, Pascal, 422
Laos, **347**, 439
Laporte, Bernard, 518
Latin American Economic System (SELA), 443
Latin American Integration Association (ALADI), 443
Latvia, **101**, 130, 394-5, 415, 424, 598-9, 601
Lautenberg, Frank, 144
Lavagna, Roberto, 185, 187
Law, Cardinal Bernard, 78, 152, 448
Law, (see also European Court of Human Rights, International Court of Justice, International Criminal Tribunal for the Former Yugoslavia, International Criminal Tribunal for Rwanda, Permanent Court of Arbitration), **469-83**; European Union Law, **473-6**; International Law, **469-73**; UK Law, **476-81**; USA Law, **481-3**
Lawal, Amina, 256
Lay, Kenneth, 147
Lazutina, Larissa, 515
Le Gougne, Marie Reine, 515
Le Pen, Jean-Marie, 55-6, 584-5
League of Arab States, see Arab League
Lebanon, 206-7, 214-5, **216-8**, 435, 579
Lebed, Aleksandr, 554 (obit.)
Lee Hoi Chang, 360, 601
Lee, Jack, 498
Lee, Peggy, 555 (obit.)
Lees, Meg, 367

Leigh, Mike, 496
Leijonborg, Lars, 67, 71
Lemierre, Jean, 428
Lemmon, Jack, 575
Lennon, Dermott, 521
Lennon, Neil, 44, 514
Lepper, Andrzej, 98
Lesotho, 294-5, 465, 586-7
Leuprecht, Peter, 346
Levet, Thomas, 519
Levy, Chandra, 149
Lewis, Bernard, 450
Lewis, Lennox, 520
Lewis, Stephen, 556
Lewis, Vic, 559
Lewis-Francis, Mark, 516
Li Peng, 349
Li Ruihuan, 351
Li, Martin, 352
Liberia, 258-9, **261**, 266-7, 392, 402, 580
Libya, 2, 207, 232-3, **235-7**, 272-3, 290, 381, 384, 404, 412, 435, 437, 591
Liddell, Helen, 536
Liebskind, Daniel, 507
Liechtenstein, 79, 402
Lindberg, Magnus, 486-7
Lindgren, Astrid, 510
Lindh, John Walker, 151
Lindsey, Larry, 154
Lippone, Paavo, 72
Literature, 505-12
Lithuania, 102, 130, 157, 394-5, 408, 428, 485, 598-9, 601
Littlewood, Joan, 550, 555
Liu Qi, 349
Livingstone, Ken, 30, 463, 506
Llosa, Mario Vargas, 509
Lloyd Webber, Andrew, 495
Loach, Len, 496
Lockerbie, 39, 235-6
Lockett, Jack, 369
Lone, Mushtaq Ahmed, 316
Lonergan, Kenneth, 492
Long, Sean, 518
Longford, Elizabeth Countess of, 510, 556 (obit.)
Lönning, Inge, 430
Lopes, Henri, 409
Loqmanian, Hossein, 578
Loret de Mola, Aurelio, 191
Losey, Joseph, 491
Lott, Trent, 144, 146
Lovelace, Linda, 556 (obit.)
Loy, Christof, 485
Loyrette, Henri, 503

Lubbes, Ruud, 244
Luhrmann, Baz, 495
Lukamba "Gato", 286
Lukashenka, Alyaksandr, 131-3, 599
Lula, see da Silva
Lumumba, Patrice, 63, 580
Lundgren, Bo, 71
Luns, Joseph, 557
Luxembourg, 66, 78
Luzhkov, Yuri, 128
Lytvyn, Volodymyr, 134

MacArthur, Ellen, 521
MacCarthy, Fiona, 509
MacColl, Ewan, 555
Macdonald of Tradeston, Lord, 536
Macedonia, 1, 58, 116, **120-22**, 394-5, 408, 420, 424, 427-8, 514, 588, 593, 596-7
Machar, Riek, 233
Mackerras, Charles, 484
MacLaurin, Lord, 517
MacMillan, James, 486, 488-9
MacMillan, Kenneth, 491
MacShane, Denis, 537
Madagascar, 264, **330-1**, 437, 463, 581, 583-4, 589, 601
Madden, John, 493
Made, Joseph, 291
Madl, Ferenc, 107
Madobe, Shaykh Adan, 249
Madrazo Pintado, Roberto, 162
Maduro, Ricardo, 165
Mahathir Mohamad, 335-6, 413, 589
Maher, Theodore "Ted", 79
Mahler, Gustav, 487
Mahuad Witt, Jamil, 195
Majali, Qaftan, 213
Majko, Pandeli, 114-5, 580
Major, John, 20, 23
Makarios, Archbishop, 554
Makmalbaf, Mohsen, 497
Makmalbaf, Samira, 497
Makoni, Simba, 291
Malan, Pedro, 181, 587
Malawi, 6, **287-8**, 465, 468, 587
Malaysia, 12, 291, **335-6**, 338, 340, 358, 411, 413, 440, 472, 589
Malhoutra, Inder, 318
Maldives, 330
Mali, 265, 267, 585, 591, 596
Malisse, Xavier, 519
Malta, 86-8, 235, 415, 601
Malvern, Viscount, 572
Malvo, John Lee, 151
Manasievski, Jovan, 121

Mancham, James, 329
Mandala Putra, Hutomo, 339, 590
Mandela, Nelson, 300
Mangulama, Leonard, 288
Manley, John, 159-60
Manning, Patrick, 174, 595
Mansell, Nigel, 520
Manus Island, 368
Maoate, Terepai, 377, 580
Marelli, Marco Arturo, 484
Margaret, HRH Princess, Countess of Snowdon, 20, 22-3, 38, 557, 564, 583
Marshall Islands, **378**, 402
Marshall, Rob, 496
Marston, Cathy, 489
Martel, Yann, 509
Märtha Louise, Princess of Norway, 70
Martin, Archer, 558 (obit.)
Martin, Paul, 158-60
Martin, Rhona, 515
Martinez, Mel, 538
Martins da Cruz, Antonio, 410, 426
Martins-Kuye, Djibril, 257
Marvanova, Hana, 103
Mashhur, Mustafa, 211
Masire, Ketumile, 274
Maskhadov, Aslan, 68, 130
Mason, Monica, 489
Mather, Rick, 506
Matheson, Louis, 369
Matthews, Colin, 486
Maung Aye, 334
Mauritania, **265**
Mauritius, **327-8**, 381, 580
Maw, Nicholas, 485, 487
May, Brian, 23
May, Theresa, 19
Mayle, Peter, 569
Mbeki, Thabo, 38, 274, 276, 289, 291, 298, 300, 405, 437
McBride, Bob, 143
McCarthy, Mick, 49, 513
McCartney, Ian, 537
McColl, Major General, 35
McConnell, Jack, 21, 40
McCoy, Tony, 520
McCreevy, Charlie, 48
McCrory, Helen, 493
McDonough, Alexa, 160
McDonough, William, 507
McDowell, Michael, 49
McGinley, Paul, 519
McGrath, John, 510
McGregor, Wayne, 490
McHugh, David, 518

McKern, Leo, 369
McKinnon, Don, 405
McLeish, Alex, 514
McLone, Ron, 30
McMahon, William, 549
McManus, Liz, 48
McNally, Terrence, 495
Meacher, Michael, 468, 537
Meciar, Vladimir, 105, 594
Medgyessy, Peter, 108-9, 586
Medina Gómez, Enrique, 201
Medrano, Adán, 163
Medvedchuk, Viktor, 134
Megawati Sukarnoputri, 338-9
Meir, Golda, 548
Mejdani, Rexhep, 115, 580, 588
Mejía, Hipólito, 169-70
Mellor, William, 544
Melville, Leslie, 369
Mendes, Sam, 492-3
Mendez Estrada, Alvaro, 164
Menendez, Antonio Xavier Neira, 195
Mer, Francis, 56-7
Merentes, Nelson, 199
Merkel, Angela, 50
Merlo, Marcelo, 194
Mesic, Stipe, 118
Messaoudi, Khalida, 240
Messier, Jean-Marie, 57, 498
Meta, Ilir, 114, 580
Mexico, 12, 79, **162-3**, 440-1, 444, 459, 496-7
Michael, Alun, 27, 537
Michel, Louis, 63
Micic, Natasa, 124, 600
Mickelson, Phil, 519
Micronesia, see Federated States of Micronesia
Middelhoff, Thomas, 498
Milburn, Alan, 536
Miliband, David, 537
Millepied, Benjamin, 489
Miller, Jimmie, 555
Miller, Jonathan, 559
Miller, Leszek, 415
Milligan, Spike, 558-9 (obit.)
Milner, Anthony, 488
Milner, Jo, 456
Milongo, André, 272
Milosevic, Slobodan, 124, 470, 580
Milutinovic, Milan, 600
Minelli, Liza, 559
Mineta, Norman, 538
Mintoff, Dom, 87
Miquilena, Luis, 199
Miralles, Enrico, 506

Mitchell, George, 144
Mitreva, Ilinka, 121
Mitzna, Maj.-Gen. (retd) Avraham, 204
Mkapa, Benjamin, 252-3
Mnangagwa, Emmerson, 291
Modi, Narendra, 316, 601
Modl, Martha, 488
Moeller, Heinz, 194
Mofaz, Lt-Gen. Shaul, 204
Mogae, Festus, 294
Mohammed VI, King of Morocco, 207, 241-4, 598
Moi, Daniel arap, 250, 406, 595, 602
Moisiu, Gen. (retd) Alfred, 115-6, 588
Moldova, 135, 424, 428
Molina Tamayo, Carlos, 199-200
Möllemann, Jürgen, 51, 53
Monaco, 78, **79**, 402, 423
Mondale, Walter, 144
Moneo, Rafael, 506
Mongolia, 363-4
Monks, John, 25-6
Monroe, Marilyn, 575
Montealegre Rivas, Eduardo, 165
Montenegro, 123-5, 423, 582, 596, 599, 601-2
Montesinos, Vladimiro, 192
Montgomerie, Colin, 519
Montgomery, Carol, 516
Montgomery, Tim, 516
Monti, Mario, 422
Montserrat, 178
Moore, Dudley, 498, 559 (obit.)
Moore, Jo, 20
Moore, Kathleen, 491
Moore, Mike, 402
Moore-Wilton, Max, 368
Moorsom, Sasha, 577
Moose, Charles, 151
Morales, Evo, 192
Moran Muñoz, Robin, 164
Morauta, Sir Mekere, 369-70, 591
Morgan, David, 517
Morgan, Rhodri, 21, 41-2
Morganti, Giuseppe Maria, 79
Morocco, 2, 42, 83, 135, 207, **241-3**, 244, 272, 413, 434, 590, 594, 598
Morrice, Norman, 489
Morris, Estelle, 21, 30-1
Morris, Mark, 489
Morrison, Steve, 499
Moshinsky, Elijah, 484
Moss, Richard, 194
Mossadeq, Mohammed, 551
Motion, Andrew, 509
Mountbatten, Philip, 564

Moussa, Amr, 237, 435
Moussaoui, Zacarias, 146, 148
Moyo, Jonathan, 291
Moyol, Lord, 560 (obit.)
Mozambique, 282-4, 468
Mramba, Basil, 253
Mramor, Dusan, 122
Mswati III, King of Swaziland, 297-8
Mu Xiuxin, 349
Muasher, Marwan, 213
Mubarak, Gamal, 211
Mubarak, Mohammed Hosni, 207-11, 435
Mudede, Tobaiwa, 289
Muehlegg, Johann, 515
Mueller, Robert, 148, 587
Mugabe, Grace, 290
Mugabe, Robert, 6-7, 38-9, 252, 288-91, 294-6, 405, 412, 437, 572, 580, 582, 589, 591, 594
Mugasha, Florence, 407
Mugford, Roger, 24
Muhammad, John Allen, 151
Muldoon, Paul, 509
Muldowney, Dominic, 486
Mullan, Peter, 496
Mulroney, Brian, 159
Muluzi, Bakili, 288
Muñoz, Gil, 163
Murauer, Herbert, 485
Murdoch, Iris, 509
Murdoch, John, 503
Murdoch, Rupert, 499, 541
Murphy, Colm, 579
Murphy, Gerry, 499
Murphy, Gillian, 491
Murphy, Graeme, 490
Murphy, Paul, 42, 46, 536
Murphy-O'Connor, Cormac, 25
Murray, John, 510
Musa Sadr, Imam, 435
Museveni, Yoweri, 254, 278, 593
Musharraf, Gen. Pervez, 319-22, 442, 578, 582, 584, 592, 595, 598-9
Music, 486-8
Musonge, Peter Mafany, 271
Mutasa, Didymus, 290
Mwanawasa, Levy, 286, 578
Myanmar (Burma), 12, **332-3**, 334, 336, 403, 439, 581, 585, 594, 600
Myers, Gen. Richard, 315

Naal, Haitham, 216
Nagano, Kent, 487
Nagorno-Karabakh, 139, 424
Nahimana, Ferdinand, 471

Naik, Rama, 318
Nalbandian, David, 518
Nam Cam, 345
Namibia, 285, 292-3, **295-7**, 438, 594
Nano, Fatos, 114-5
Nasrallah, Hassan, 409
Nasraoui, Radia, 238
Nasser, Gamal Abdel, 548
Nasser, Michael, 218
Nastase, Adrian, 109-11
Natapei, Edward, 376, 587
Naumova, Marija, 101
Nauru, 368, **379**, 402-3
Nazarbayev, Nursultan, 311-3, 598
Nazarov, Muhammad, 314
Ndayizeye, Domitien, 277
Ne Win, Gen., 332, 560 (obit.), 581, 594, 600
Negroponte, John D., 538
Nepal, 63, 318, **323-4**, 441, 459, 464, 466, 580, 586, 594
Netanyahu, Binyamin, 204
Netherlands Antilles, 179, 579
Netherlands, The, 6, 36, 39, **64-5**, 98, 412, 472, 476, 582, 584-5, 590, 596
Neuhaus, Matthew, 407
New Caledonia, 376-7
New Zealand, 38, 153, 368, **371-3**, 379, 402, 516-8, 521, 591
Newman, Paul, 495
Ng'ethe, David, 251
Nhasse, Alamara, 281
Nicholson, George, 488
Nicol, Walter, 258
Niger, 267, **269**, 472
Nigeria, 13, 255, **256-8**, 271, 281, 285, 289-90, 403, 405, 407, 437, 471, 580, 585, 592, 595, 598
Niue, 377-8, 584
Nixon, Richard, 144, 540, 552
Niyazov, Saparmurat, 308, 312, 314, 599, 602
Nkomo, Joshua, 572
Nkurunziza, Pierre, 278
Nobel Prizes, Chemistry, 359, 457, 562; Economics, 15; Literature, 109, 510; Medicine, 457; Peace, 595; Physics, 455, 457
Noboa Bejarano, Gustavo, 194, 580
Noboa Pontón, Alvaro Fernando, 194-5, 599
Nóbrega, Tobías, 200
Non-Aligned Movement (NAM), 411-3, 438
Noonan, Michael, 48
Nor, Fadzil, 336
Nordic Council, 429-30
Norfolk, Duke of, 560-1 (obit.)

Norgard, Per, 486
Norodom Sihanouk, King of Cambodia, 346
Norrish, Ronald, 563
North Atlantic Treaty Organisation (NATO), 7, 58, 61, 72, 99, 102, 104-6, 109-14, 116, 123-4, 126, 130, 138, 157, **393-6**, 416-7, 420, 424, 426, 432, 541, 557, 586-7, 599
Northern Ireland, 21, **43-6**, 514, 579, 596
Northern Marianas, 376, 378
Norton, Gale, 538
Norway, 36, **69-70**, 234, 326-7, 381, 430, 465, 515
Nuclear energy, 72, 74, 113, 130, 236, 362-3
Nuclear weapons, see Weapons of Mass Destruction
Nujoma, Sam, 295-6, 438
Nunn, Trevor, 492, 494
Nuss, Bela, 148
Nyachae, Simeon, 251
Nyman, Michael, 488

O'Brien, Aidan, 520
O'Brien, Mike, 591
O'Connell, Anthony, 152
O'Keefe, Sean, 452
O'Leary, David, 514
O'Neal, Shaquille, 521
O'Neill, Paul, 154, 181, 189, 429
O'Neill, Terence, 560
Obasanjo, Olusegun, 38, 256-7, 271, 289, 405, 437, 592
Obiang Nguema, Teodoro, 273, 601
Obituaries, 540-77
Obure, Chris, 251
Öcalan, Abdullah, 94
Oddsson, David, 69
Odets, Clifford, 568
Odinga, Raila, 250
Oduber, Nelson, 179
Offman, Karl, 327
Ogata, Sadako, 356
Ohno, Apolo Anton, 515
Ojala, Outi, 430
Oman, 229, 434
Omar, Mullah Mohammed, 305
Ong Teng Cheong, 338
Onyia, Dubem, 256
Opera, 484-5
Orban, Viktor, 107-9, 432
Orde, Hugh, 44
Orengo, James, 251
Organisation for Economic Co-operation and Development (OECD), 54, 77-8, 378, **402-3**, 441

INDEX

Organisation for Security and Co-operation in Europe (OSCE), 115, 132, 311, 313, 424, **425-7**
Organisation of African Unity (OAU), 7, 329, 331
Organisation of American States (OAS), **444**
Organisation of Eastern Caribbean States (OECS), 446
Organisation of the Islamic Conference (OIC), 233, **413-4**, 451
Organisation of the Petroleum Exporting Countries (OPEC), 199, 225, 231, 257, **403-4**
Ornstein, Leo, 488
Ortega Saavedra, Daniel, 166
Ortiz, Jacobo Bucaram, 195
Osborne, Ozzy, 23
Ospina Ovalle, Carlos Alberto, 197
Ouattara, Alassane, 267
Oviedo, Francisco, 188
Oviedo, Lino César, 188
Owada, Hiasashi, 472
Owen, Wilfred, 510
Owens, Jesse, 551

Pacheco de la Espriella, Abel, 166, 579, 583
Pacific Community (PC), 439
Pacific Island Forum (PIF), 376-7, **442**
Padilla, Jose, 149, 482
Padmanabhan, Gen. S., 315
Paige, Roderick, 538
Pakenham, Frank, 556
Pakistan, 1, 2, 4, 58, 147, 149, 226, 308, 311, 316-7, **319-21**, 381, 406, 441, 459, 503, 517, 578, 581-2, 584-5, 588, 590, 592-3, 595, 599
Paksas, Rolandas, 102
Palacio, Ana, 80
Palau, 378
Palestine and Palestinians, 1, 2, 4, 38, 63, 155-6, 202, **205-8**, 210-2, 214, 216, 219, 225, 229, 237, 239, 242, 380-1, 384, 386, 404, 411-4, 421, 434, 485, 581-5, 587-8, 590, 592, 598
Palestine National Authority (PNA), 156, 202, 421, 435
Paltrow, Gwyneth, 492
Paniagua, Luis Arturo, 163
Panitchpakdi, Supachai, 402
Panting Peñalba, Reginaldo, 165
Panufnik, Andrzej, 487
Panama, 167
Papandreou, George, 89
Papantoniou, Yiannos, 420

Pappano, Antonio, 484
Papua New Guinea, 368, **369-70**, 406, 591
Paracel Islands, 440, 597
Paraguay, 13, **187-8**
Paris Club, 125, 257
Parker Bowles, Camilla, 447
Parker, Sir Peter, 561 (obit.)
Parrott, Nicolas, 463
Parsons, Richard, 499
Partnership for Peace (PFP), 393
Parts, Juhan, 100
Pasalic, Ivic, 118
Pasi, Solomon, 112
Pasko, Grigorii, 128
Pastrana Arango, Andrés, 196, 580
Patassé, Ange-Félix, 236, 272
Patten, Chris, 115-6
Patterson, Anne, 197
Patterson, James, 508
Patterson, Percival J., 168, 596
Paulauskas, Arturas, 102
Paulin, Tom, 509
Pavarotti, Luciano, 484
Payá, Oswaldo, 168
Payne, Alexander, 496
Payne, Anthony, 486
Paz Zamora, Jaime, 192
Peake, Dame Felicity, 562 (obit.)
Peake, Harald, 562
Pearl, Daniel, 147, 320, 581, 590
Peckinpah, Sam, 545
Peiris, Gamini Lakshman, 326
Pell, George, 368
Pelletier, David, 515
Pelosi, Nancy, 144
Pepys, Samuel, 509
Perdue, Sonny, 144
Peres, Shimon, 204
Pérez, Felipe, 200
Perez, Guillermo, 165
Permanent Court of Arbitration, **472-3**
Persson, Göran, 70, 593, 596
Peru, 7, 14, 190, **191-2**, 459
Perutz, Professor Max, 562 (obit.)
Petipa, Marius, 491
Petritsch, Wolfgang, 116, 427
Peyron, Bruno, 521
Phan Van Kai, 344
Phibbs, Joseph, 486
Philippines, 2, 336, **342-4**, 403, 440, 579, 602
Phillips, Julia, 498
Pickard, Nigel, 501
Pike, Jimmy, 369
Pillay, Aritanga, 580
Pimenta, Rui Costa, 182

Pinheiro, Paulo, 332
Pinochet Ugarte, Gen. (retd) Augusto, 190, 589
Pinsent, Matthew, 521
Pinter, Harold, 491
Pio, Padre, 78, 448
Piqué i Camps, Josep, 80
Pires, Mario, 281
Pires, Pedro, 281
Pitt, Harvey, 154
Pius XII, Pope, 449
Poland, 11, 78-9, **97-9**, 231, 408, 415-6, 428, 432, 448, 592, 598, 601
Polisario, 243
Politkovskaya, Anna, 128
Poole, Geoffrey, 488
Portas, Paulo, 85
Porter of Luddenham, Lord, 562-3 (obit.)
Porter, Professor Roy, 563 (obit.)
Portillo, Alfonso, 164
Portillo, Michael, 19
Portugal, 66, **84-6**, 126, 282, 330, 410, 418, 426, 513, 582, 594, 599
Potocnik, Vika, 122
Pourier, Miguel, 579
Powell, Colin, 3, 14, 155-6, 200, 207-8, 216, 222, 242, 286, 310, 337, 373, 416, 438, 440, 538
Powers, Anthony, 488
Prabhakaran, Vellupillai, 326-7, 599
Prabhu, Suresh, 316
Prebble, Stuart, 499
Preljocaj, Angelin, 491
Prescott, John, 18, 26, 29, 536
Previti, Cesare, 61
Prevlaka Peninsula, 387, 391, 600
Price, Philip, 519
Prieto, José Luis, 200
Primarolo, Dawn, 536
Principi, Anthony J., 538
Prodi, Romano, 135, 417-8, 441
Prosper, Pierre-Richard, 279
Pryor, Mark, 144
Puerto Rico, 179-80
Pûrvanov, Georgi, 113
Putin, Vladimir, 7, 8, 61, 70, 98, 126-30, 133, 139, 156, 220, 312, 396, 424, 449, 586, 602
Puttnam, Lord, 500
Qaboos, Sultan, 229
Qadeer, Haji Abdul, 306, 563 (obit.), 589
Qanouni, Mohammad Yunis, 35
Qarase, Laisenia, 377, 406
Qatada, Abu, 597
Qatar, 15, **228-32**, 233, 433

Québec, 158-60
Queen Elizabeth, The Queen Mother, 22, 40, 501, 556-7 (obit.), 564, 583
Quinn, Rory, 48
Quintero Meraz, Jesús Albino, 163

Rabbitte, Pat, 48
Rabin, Yitzhak, 548
Raby, Julian, 503
Racan, Ivica, 118-9
Radcliffe, Paula, 516
Raffarin, Jean-Pierre, 56, 585
Raffles, Gerry, 556
Rahim Wardak, Abdul, 306
Rahman, Sheikh Mujibur, 322
Rahman, Tareq, 322
Rahman, Maj.-Gen. Ziakr, 322
Rahmonov, Imamoli, 311, 314
Rahmsdorf, Stefan, 462
Rajapakse, Mahinda, 327
Rajoy Brey, Mariano, 80
Rakipi, Arben, 115
Ramírez, Marta Lucía, 197
Ramkalawan, Wavel, 328
Randerson, Jenny, 41
Rangel, José Vicente, 200
Rankl, Karl, 487
Rann, Mike, 365
Rapa Nui, see Easter Island
Ratsiraka, Didier, 330-1, 581, 583-4, 589
Rattle, Simon, 487
Rauschenberg, Robert, 490
Ravalomanana, Marc, 330-1, 437, 581, 583-4, 589, 601
Rawlings, Jerry, 255
Rawls, John, 510, 565 (obit.)
Raynsford, Nick, 536
Razak, Najib, 335
Razali Ismail, Tan Sri, 332
Reagan, Ronald, 154
Real IRA, 44
Red Brigades, 59
Red Cross, International Committee of the, 28, 333, 426
Reddin, Keith, 492
Reich, Steve, 490
Reichhold, Mathias, 75
Reid, John, 21, 46, 536
Reid, Richard, 146, 151
Reinhardt, Max, 510
Reisz, Karel, 498, 565-6 (obit.)
Reizenstein, Franz, 487
Religion, 447-51
Remes Lenicov, Jorge, 184-5
René, Albert, 328

Reno, Janet, 143
Renzaho, Tharcisse, 279
Repse, Einars, 101, 598
Restrepo, Juan Camilo, 196
Reyes Villa, Manfred, 192
Reyes, Matias, 152
Rice, Condoleeza, 538
Richards, Sir Gordon, 520
Richardson, Tony, 565
Richter, Gerhard, 504
Ridge, Tom, 538
Riess-Passer, Susanne, 75
Rigas, John, 150
Rincón, Lucas, 198, 200
Rio Group, 445
Rios Montt, General Jose Efrain, 547
Rios, Patricio, 190
Rivera Cardona, Ennio, 163
Rivers, Larry, 505
Roberts, Daniel, 490
Robertson, George, 398
Robinson, Mary, 380
Roche, Barbara, 536
Rodgers, Joan, 484
Rodríguez Araque, Ali, 199, 404
Rodríguez Chacín, Ramón, 199-200
Rodríguez Iturbe, José, 199
Rodríguez Zapatero, José Luis, 81
Rodríguez, Jorge, 190
Roh Moo Hyun, 360, 601
Roldos Aguilera, Leon, 195
Roma, 108, 110, 112, 120
Romania, 11, 107, **109-12**, 157, 394-5, 415, 428, 432, 470
Romanov, Roy, 160
Ronaldinho, 513
Ronaldo, 513
Rooker, Lord, 536
Rop, Anton, 122
Rosal Zea, Jorge, 164
Rosario, Humberto Rivero, 173
Rosengren, Björn, 71
Rospigliosi, Fernando, 191
Rossi, Valentino, 520
Rostow, Eugene, 566
Rostropovich, Mstislav, 491
Routh, Francis, 487
Rowley, Coleen, 148
Rowling, J.K., 496, 510
Roxburgh, Edwin, 487
Roy Hill, George, 498
Rubinstein, Nicolai, 505
Ruckauf, Carlos, 184, 187
Ruggiero, Renato, 60
Rugova, Ibrahim, 125

Rumsfeld, Donald, 52, 123, 223-4, 247, 250, 302, 310, 538
Rumyantsev, Aleksandr, 303
Rusedski, Greg, 519
Rushdie, Salman, 451
Russian Federation, AIDS/HIV, 5; air crash, 76; arts, 497, 503; Chechnya/security, 1, 5, 8, 67-8, 127-30, 138, 424, 591, 596-7, 602; defence/disarmament, 345, 349, 394-6, 586-7; economy, 7, 11, 123, 126, 130, 161, 364, 403, 428, 588; environment, 463, 466; external relations, 7-8, 11, 38, 61, 70, 98, 130-3, 135, 137-9, 156-7, 235, 303, 311-2, 315, 349, 364, 383-4, 386, 394, 591, 598; Iraq 220-2, 131; politics, 126-30, 579, 589; religion, 449; space, 452-4; sport, 515, 519
Rwanda, 252, 274-6, **278-9**, 299, 382-3, 413, 438, 472, 503, 590, 593, 601
Ryan, Peter, 368
Rylance, Mark, 493

Sa'dun, Hassan, 216
Saavedra Bruno, Carlos, 193
Sabirin, Syahril, 339
Sabri Ahmad al-Hadithi, Naji, 219, 221
Sacks, Jonathan, 24, 449
Saffer, Lisa, 485
Safin, Marat, 518
Safra, Edmond, 79
Sahlin, Mona, 67
Sakho, Youssouph, 264
Salé, Jamie, 515
Saleh, Habib, 215
Salih, Ali Abdullah, 226
Salonen, Esa-Pekka, 487
Sama, Kofi, 268
Sambou, Youba, 264
Samoa, 373, **376**
Sampaio, Jorge, 85, 410
Sampras, Pete, 519
Samudra, Imam, 599
San Marino, **79**
Sanader, Ivo, 118
Sánchez de Lozada, Gonzálo, 192, 589, 591
Sandar Win, 332
Sankoh, Foday, 259, 581
Sanussi, Joseph, 257
São Tomé and Príncipe, **281-2**, 581, 583
Saramago, José, 509
Saravic, Mirko, 117
Sarkozy, Nicolas, 56-8
Sarney, Roseana, 181
Sarukhan Kermez, José, 162
Sassou-Nguesso, Denis, 272, 409, 582

Saudi Arabia, 2, 4, 38, 144, 206, 217, **224-5**, 229-30, 243, 308, 319, 433-4, 583
Saunders, Brig. Stephen, 590
Savimbi, Jonas, 284, 286, 410, 567 (obit.), 580
Savisaar, Edgar, 100
Sawer, David, 486
Saxecoburggotski, Simeon (former King of Bulgaria), 112
Sayeed, Mufti Mohammad, 317, 595
Sayf, Riyad, 215
Scajola, Claudio, 60
Scarfe, Gerald, 489
Scharping, Rudolf, 52
Schmögnerová, Brigita, 465
Schön, Jan Hendrik, 455
Schori, Pierre, 290
Schraer, Paul, 545
Schröder, Gerhard, 6, 50, 52, 54, 416, 592, 594, 596
Schultz, Frederick, 504
Schumacher, Michael, 519
Schüssel, Wolfgang, 73, 75
Schuster, Rudolf, 594
Schwanewilms, Anne, 485
Scientific, Medical and Industrial Research, 452-7
Scolari, Luiz Felipe, 86
Scotland, 39-41, 507, 514, 518
Scott, Elisabeth, 507
Seaga, Edward, 169
Seaman, David, 513
Seck, Idrissa, 264, 597
Secombe, Harry, 558
Secrett, Charles, 466
Seglins, Mareks, 101
Seiber, Matyas, 487
Sekerinska, Radmila, 121
Seleznev, Gennadii, 129
Sellers, Peter, 558
Senegal, 263-4, 331, 437, 513
Serbia, 36, **123-5**, 423-4, 582, 595, 600
Serpa Uribe, Horacio, 196, 586
Serra, José, 181-2, 597
Serrano Elías, Jorge, 167, 547
Seselj, Vojislav, 124
Seychelles, 328-9, 381, 600
Sezer, Ahmet Necdet, 94-5, 597
Shaikh, Ahmad Omar Sayeed, 147
Shalabi, Mohammed, 213
Shamir, Yitzhak, 203
Shamkhani, Ali, 302
Shanghai Co-operation Organisation (SCO), 311
Sharif, Nawaz, 319

Sharma, Devinder, 464
Sharon, Ariel, 4, 63, 202, 205-7, 215, 217, 228
Sharon, Omri, 205
Shatigudud, Mohamed Nur, 249
Shaw, Peter, 43
Sheppard, Jon, 407
Shevardnadze, Eduard, 138
Shihada, Salah, 203, 590
Shikhmuradov, Boris, 314, 602
Shim Mi-Seon, 360
Shin Hyo-Sun, 360
Shining Path, 7, 191
Shipley, Jenny, 372
Short, Clare, 37, 233, 536
Shourie, Arun, 318
Shrestha, Badri Prasad, 324
Shrestha, Surendra, 464
Shu-chen, Wu, 355
Shulman, Alan, 488
Shuttleworth, Mark, 453
Siepmann, Eric, 575
Sierra Leone, 258-9, 261, 266, 387, 392, 470, 579, 581, 586
Sikharulidze, Anton, 515
Silanyo, Ahmed Mohamed, 249
Sillitoe, Alan, 565
Silva Calderón, Alvaro, 404
Silva Ruete, Javier, 191
Simma, Bruno, 472
Simonic, Ante, 118
Simpson, Wallis, 564
Simsic, Danica, 122
Singapore, 2, 12, 15, **337-8**, 340, 359, 381, 432, 578
Singh, Duleep, 22
Singh, Jaswant, 317
Sinha, Yashwant, 317, 325
Sinyavsky, Andrei, 548
Sissons, Peter, 22, 501
Sival, Eyal, 503
Sixsmith, Martin, 20
Skele, Andris, 101
Skoog, Matz, 489
Slade, Ron, 506
Slim, General, 560
Slovakia, 11, **105-6**, 108, 394-5, 415, 428, 432, 514, 593, 595, 599, 601
Slovenia, 122-3, 394-5, 408, 415, 428, 432, 599, 601
Small, Ruth, 516
Smith, Andrew, 536
Smith, Ian, 572
Smith, Jacqui, 537
Smith, Maggie, 494

Smith, Vernon L., 15
Smith, Zadie, 509
Snead, Sam, 568 (obit.)
Snow, John, 154, 538
Snowdon, Earl of, 558
Soares, Abílio, 339
Sobell, Michael, 573
Sobell, Netta, 573
Soglo, Nicéphore, 268
Sokurov, Alexander, 497
Solá, Felipe, 185
Solana, Javier, 123, 421
Solari de la Fuente, Luis María, 191
Solbes, Pedro, 419
Sole, Masupha Ephraim, 294
Solís Fallas, Ottón, 166
Solomon Islands, 368, **376**, 378, 406
Solzhenitsyn, Alexander, 548
Somalia, 6, 233, **248-9**, 392, 585
Somare, Sir Michael, 370, 591
Somdhat Attanand, 334
Somkid Jatusripitak, 333
Sondheim, Stephen, 492
Sope, Barak, 376
Sopoanga, Saufatu, 377, 591
Sorenstam, Annika, 519
Soro, Guillaume, 267
Sosa, Lizardo, 164
Sotiropoulou, Angeliki, 88
Soto, Jock, 489
Souane, Abdel Khader, 240
Sousa Santos, Gen. Alvarenga, 86
Soutchay Thammasith, 347
South Africa, 1, 236, 249, 255, 259, 267, 274-7, 281, 283, 289-90, 293-4, **298-301**, 405, 411-2, 437, 517-8, 589-90, 592
South Asian Association for Regional Co-operation (SAARC), 441-2
Southern Africa Development Community (SADC), 285, **436**, 594
Southern Common Market (Mercosur), 445
Space exploration, 178, 452-3
Spain, 5, 37, 66, **80-3**, 84, 207, 241, 243, 381, 419, 422, 445, 513, 515, 578, 582, 588-90, 592
Spalding, James, 188
Speight, George, 377, 580
Spellar, John, 537
Spidla, Vladimir, 103, 589
Spielberg, Steven, 496
Spinner, Leopold, 487
Sport, 513-21
Spratly Islands, 440, 597
Sri Lanka, 1, **325-7**, 413, 517, 581, 593, 599

Srinivasan, Kris, 407
Ssendawula, Gerald, 254
St Kitts and Nevis, **171-2**, 446, 480, 516
St Vincent and the Grenadines, **173**, 403
Staderini, Marco, 62
Stallman, Richard, 459
Stassinopoulos, Michael, 569 (obit.)
Steifel, Ethan, 490
Steiger, Rod, 498, 568 (obit.)
Steiner, Michael, 126
Stenbeck, Jan, 71
Stephenson, Lesley, 488
Stephenson, Pamela, 508
Stimpson, Tim, 518
Stirling, James, 506
Stoiber, Edmund, 50, 52
Stoll, David, 488
Stolojan, Theodor, 110
Stoltenberg, Jens, 69
Stoppard, Tom, 494
Stott-Despoja, Natasha, 367
Stoudmann, Gerard, 426
Stoute, Michael, 520
Strategic Offensive Reduction Treaty, 130, 156, 586
Strauss, Franz Josef, 541
Straw, Jack, 36, 536
Stretton, Ross, 489
Stroman, Susan, 494
Struth, Thomas, 504
Stubbs, Sir William, 30
Styron, William, 485, 487
Suchoff, Benjamin, 488
Sudan, **233-5**, 248, 253, 270, 282, 414, 590
Suharto, Mohamed, 339
Suharto, Tommy (Hutomo Mandala Putra), 339, 590
Sulayman, Omar, 211
Sullivan, Scott, 150
Sulston, Sir John, 457
Sultan, Hidaya, 230
Sultygov, Abdul-Khakim, 424
Sumbeiyow, Lazaro, 234
Sumner, Clare, 22
Surakiat Sathianthai, 334
Surayud Chulanot, 334
Suriname, 176
Suzman, Helen, 289
Suzuki, Muneo, 356-7
Svetlanov, Yevgeny, 488
Swaziland, 292, **297-8**, 406, 465, 587
Sweden, 36, 69, **70-2**, 417, 461, 485, 519, 578, 593, 596, 598
Swinfen, Lord, 575
Swinston, Robert, 490

626   INDEX

Switzerland, 61, 66, **75-6**, 78, 233, 380, 403, 431, 462, 465, 504, 515, 581, 587, 598, 600
Syed Sirajuddin Syed Putra Jamalullail, King, 335
Symonenko, Petro, 133
Symons of Vernham Dean, Baroness, 537
Synge, R.L.M., 558
Syria, 38, 114, 207, **214-6**, 217-8, 221-2, 384

Taheri, Ayatollah Jalaleddin, 304, 589
Taiwan, 8, 12, 172, 281, 351-2, **353-5**, 440
Tajikistan, 308, **309-14**, 427-8
Takamado, Prince, 359
Takenaka, Heizo, 358
Talabani, Jalal, 224
Talaki, Koloa, 377
Taliban, 2, 35, 155, 212, 304-5, 308, 310, 314, 368, 379, 392, 469
Tanaka, Koichi, 359, 457
Tanaka, Makiko, 356-7
Tanayev, Nikolay, 588
Tandja, Mamadou, 269
Tandjung, Akbar, 339
Tantawi, Shaykh Mohammed Seyyed, 210
Tanzania, **252-3**, 274, 277, 279
Tarlev, Vasile, 135
Tartt, Donna, 509
Tasca, Catherine, 503
Tasmagambetov, Imangali, 312, 579
Taubman, A. Alfred, 504
Taylor, Charles, 261, 267, 580
Tedla Bairu, Herui, 248
Teich, Mikulas, 563
Television and Radio, **498-502**
Tenet, George J., 538
Teng-hui, Lee, 354
Tennant, David, 492
Terfel, Bryn, 484
Thackeray, Bal, 316
Thailand, 1, 12, 326, **333-5**, 347, 402, 440, 459, 519
Thaksin Shinawatra, 334
Thalib, Umar, 340
Tharp, Twyla, 495
Thatcher, Margaret, 576
Thaw, John, 569 (obit.)
Theatre, **492-5**
Thielen, Gunter, 498
Thom, René, 570 (obit.)
Thompson, Daley, 516
Thompson, J. Lee, 498
Thompson, Larry, 142, 147
Thompson, Mark, 501
Thompson, Tommy, 538

Thompson, Virgil, 489
Thomson, Lord, 503
Thorpe, Ian, 516
Thuan, Cardinal Nguyen Van, 345, 570 (obit.)
Thunbs Islands and Abu Musa, 229, 433-4
Thurmond, Strom, 144
Thyssen, August, 570
Thyssen-Bornemisza de Kaszon, Baron Hans Heinrich, 505, 570 (obit.)
Tibbetts, Kurt, 178
Tihic, Sulejman, 117
Tillu, Fawaz, 216
Timms, Clive, 485
Timms, Stephen, 537
Tito, Dennis, 453
Tito, Teburoro, 377
Tizón, Allan Wagner, 191
Tjapaltjarri, Clifford Possum, 369
Tobin, James, 571
Todd Whitman, Christine, 538
Todd, Sir Garfield, 572 (obit.)
Todoli, Vicente, 503
Toepfer, Klaus, 465
Togo, 263-4, **268**, 409, 596-7, 602
Togoïmi, Youssouf, 270
Tokelau, **379**
Toledo, Alejandro, 190-1
Tolkien, J.R.R., 496, 510
Tomalin, Claire, 509
Tomka, Peter, 472
Tomlinson, Mike, 30
Tonga, 375, **377-8**
Topolanek, Mirek, 104
Toqayev, Qasymzhomart, 312, 579
Torrance, Sam, 519
Torres, General Juan Jose, 542
Torricelli, Robert, 143
Touré, Gen. (retd) Amadou Toumani, 265, 585
Touré, Sidya, 266
Townsend, Kathleen Kennedy, 144
Townsend, Peter, 557
Tran Duc Luong, 344, 408
Transdniester, 135
Traynor, Chuck, 556
Treaty of Nice, 49, 415, 473-6, 596
Trifi, Mokhtar, 238
Trillo, Frederico, 419
Trimble, David, 21, 45-6
Trinidad and Tobago, **174**, 473, 595
Troejborg, Jan, 425
Trost, Rainer, 484
Trujillo, Hector, 542
Trujillo, Rafael, 542
Truman, Harry S., 550
Truong My Hoa, 344

Tshisekedi, Etienne, 275
Tsvangirai, Morgan, 237, 288-91, 582
Tsvetkov, Valentin, 127
Tucci, Stanley, 495
Tudor, Corneliu Vadim, 110
Tung Chee-hwa, 588
Tunisia, 52, 71, **237-9**
Tuomioja, Erkki, 430
Turkey, 2, 6, 35, 37, 90, **93-6**, 303, 306, 395, 398, 413, 415-7, 420, 424, 451, 513
Turkmani, Lt-Gen. Hasan, 215
Turkmenistan, 308, **309-14**, 428
Turks and Caicos, **178**, 445
Turnage, Mark-Anthony, 487-8
Turnbull, Charles, 180
Tutu, Desmond, 289, 300
Tuvalu, 375, **377**, 378-9, 442
Tversky, Amos, 16
Tyson, Mike, 520
Tzannetakis, Yannis, 89

U Nu, 560
Uehara, Ayako, 359
Uganda, 233, 235, 252, **253-4**, 274-6, 278, 407
Ugolini, Giovanni Francesco, 79
Ukraine, 97, 131, **133-5**, 403, 424, 459, 583, 599
Unitas, Johnny, 572
United Arab Emirates, 227, **228-9**, 412, 433-4
United Kingdom (UK) (see also Northern Ireland, Scotland, Wales), **17-46**, accidents, 29, 39; agriculture, 27; arts, 484-95, 498-512; crime/trials, 23-4, 39, 43-6; dependencies, 177-8; diplomacy/external relations, 17, 35-9, 66, 163, 187, 207, 214, 218, 221-3, 225, 228, 234-6, 252, 258-9, 298, 305, 324, 398, 578, 591, 594; economy, 17, 25-6, 32-5, 40, 42, 584; elections, 17-8; EU, 37, 416-7, 422, 578; environment, 463, 465, 468; Gibraltar, **84**; government list, 536-7; immigration, 27-8, 580; Iraq, 5, 36-8, 214, 218, 221-3, 228; law, 472-3, **476-81**, overseas aid/loans, 20; peacekeeping forces, 35-6, 258-9, 305-6; politics, 17-22, 27, 39, 41-6, 597-8; public services, 19-20, 25-6, 28-32, 40-1, 589; race relations, 18, 24-5; religion, 24-5, 42-3, 447; royal family, 22-4, 38, 40-1, 407, 583-4; scandals, 20, 110; science, 454, 456, 461; security and defence, 2, 71, 35-7, 43-6, 209, 398, 597, 599; sport, 41, 43, 513-21; UN, 380; USA, 2, 4-5, 17, 36-8, 207, 218, 221-3

United Nations (UN), **380-93**, Afghanistan, 306-7, 382, 386, 392, 578; AIDS, 248, 293, 295-6, 349, 381, 384, 589; American Samoa, 379; Angola, 286, 386-7; appointments/elections, 380-1; Bosnia & Herzegovina, 36, 65, 117, 156, 387, 427, 470, 584, 590; budget/finance, 382-3; Cambodia, 346, 470; Central African Republic, 387; Central Asia, 310; China, 349; Colombia, 387, 445; Côte d'Ivoire, 387; Council of Europe, 424; Cuba, 445; Cyprus, 89-92, 95, 416-7, 598, 600; Democratic Republic of Congo, 14, 274-6, 384; development, 13, 15, 382, 412-3, 592; drugs, 300, 307-8, 333, 426; East Timor, 342-3, 380, 387, 410, 586; environment, 464-7, 473; Ethiopia and Eritrea, 246-8, 385; Guatemala, 444; Guinea Bissau, 280, 384; headquarters, 380, 382; international courts, 63, 156, 469-70, 590; Iraq, 3-5, 36-7, 52, 54, 131, 143, 155, 157, 161, 214, 219-22, 225, 228-9, 302, 365, 373, 385-6, 392, 404, 409, 412, 421, 434-5, *(document)* 522-7, 591, 593, 595-6, 598, 600; Israel/Palestine, 38, 202, 206, 381, 386, 411, 582, 584, 594; Kosovo, 36, 125-6, 385; Kuwait, 229; Liberia, 261, 392; Libya, 236; Mongolia, 364; Myanmar (Burma), 332-3, 585; Nigeria and Cameroon, 258, 271-2; North Korea, 8, 151, 601; peacekeeping/building missions *(table)*, 388-91; Prevlaka, 387, 600; reform, 381; religion, 24, 450; refugees, 27-8, 253, 259, 345; sanctions, 14, 219, 222, 229, 236, 261, 286, 392-3; Seychelles, 329; Sierra Leone, 258-9, 261, 387, 392, 470, 586; Somalia, 249, 392-3; South Africa, 300; Sudan, 233-4; Swaziland, 298; Switzerland, 75-6, 380, 581; Syria, 214; terrorism, 385, 392, 426, 441, 469; Tokelau, 379; torture, 382, 473; Trinidad & Tobago, 473; UNESCO, 157, 504; Vietnam, 345; Western Sahara, 243-4, 598; World Food Programme, 281, 285, 287, 295, 384, 587
United States of America (USA), **140-57**, 11 September (see also 11 September), 72, 138, 140, 148, 150, 153, 155, 159, 172-3, 176, 212, 219, 224, 226, 305, 327, 336, 338, 401, 413, 434, 441, 482; Afghanistan, 2, 140, 155, 160-1, 168, 226, 304-6, 310, 320, 396, 469, 477, 578; arms, 3, 141, 154, 190, 204, 229, 241, 315, 345, 360-1, 394-6, 419-20, 427, 464, 601; arts, 70, 484-6, 492-4, 496-9, 501-10; **dependencies**, **179-80**; 379; diplomacy/external relations, 4, 7-

8, 45, 47, 52, 54, 58, 61, 68, 83, 95-6, 98, 111, 123, 125, 128, 130, 132-3, 135, 155-7, 159-61, 163-4, 167-8, 173-5, 178, 180-1, 189, 191-3, 198-200, 207, 224-9, 233-4, 236, 242-4, 256, 279, 281, 286-7, 289-90, 298, 302-3, 310-1, 314, 316, 320-1, 326-7, 331, 343, 345, 351-2, 354-6, 358, 360, 362-3, 368, 373, 376, 379, 393-4, 396, 398-9, 416, 421-2, 444, 470, 596, 601; domestic events, 140, 151-2; economy, 9-10, 12, 102, 140-2, 152-5, 160, 184, 198, 285, 348, 402, 579; environment, 7, 15, 142, 156, 376, 378, 394, 421, 438, 462-8, 584; foreign aid, 14-5, 135, 165, 209, 213, 308, 310, 321, 333, 364, 378, 401, 429, 468; internal security, 2, 142, 146, 148-50, 376, 469, 482, 587; Iraq, 2-4, 15, 37, 52, 54, 58, 96, 135, 140, 143, 154, 157-8, 161, 203, 208, 212-4, 218-25, 228-9, 302-3, 354, 363, 365, 368, 376, 385, 396, 404, 415, 441, 450, 593, 595-6, 600; Israel/Palestine, 4, 13, 38, 155-6, 202-8, 211-2, 215-6, 228, 386, 394, 412, 435, 451, 588; law, 150, 152, 155, 458, 469-70, **481-3**; politics, 140-6, (*map*) 145, 154, (*document*) 538, 584, 598; presidential address, 3, 36, 140-1, 155, 168, 218, 236, 302-3, 361, 393-4, 412, 469, 579; scandals, 10, 25, 33, 47, 78, 142, 147, 149-50, 160, 178, 423, 448, 590-1; science, 452-3, 455-7; sport, 513, 515-6, 518-9, 521; trade, 15, 33, 142, 153, 161, 167-8, 225, 232, 293-4, 352, 400-2, 421, 445, 586, 600-1; "war on terror", 2, 132, 138, 140, 155, 168, 192, 197, 209-11, 214, 224, 226, 241, 243, 247, 249-50, 327, 336-7, 340, 342-4, 351-2, 371, 376, 395, 401, 403, 422, 440, 444-5, 447, 469, 482, 581-2; UK, 4, 17, 37, 218, 221-3; UN, 4, 157, 214, 220-2, 302, 382-6
Unsuk Chin, 487
Uribe Velez, Alvaro, 196-7, 586, 591
Ursón, Francisco, 199
Uruguay, 13, **189**, 601
US Virgin Islands, 179-80
Uteem, Cassam, 327-8, 580
Uzan, Cem, 95
Uzbekistan, 308, **309-14**, 427, 428, 588, 591

Vainonen, Vasilie, 491
Vajpayee, Atal Behari, 310, 316-8, 439, 441
Van der Biest, Alain, 64
van der Graaf, Volkert, 65
Van Egeraat, Eric, 507
Vance, Cyrus, 572-3 (obit.)

Vancea, Ilie, 135
Vaness, Carol, 484
Vanuatu, 376, 402, 587
Vargas Guatatuca, Carlos Antonio, 195
Vasiliev, Vladimir, 491
Vatican, 77, **78-9**, 345, 448-9, 450
Vaughan, David, 490
Vaughan, Michael, 517
Velazquez Herrera, Jacinto, 195
Velchev, Milen, 114
Venables, Terry, 514
Veneman, Ann, 538
Venezuela, 7, 13-5, 169, 179, 195, **198-201**, 403-4, 413, 444-5, 459, 584, 594, 600
Verheugen, Guenther, 112-3
Verhofstadt, Guy, 63
Vick, Graham, 485
Victoria, Queen, 22
Vides Casanova, Eugenio, 164
Vieira de Mello, Sérgio, 342, 380
Vietnam, 144, 146, 336, **344-5**, 408, 439, 586, 597
Vinatieri, Adam, 521
Viñoly, Rafael, 506
Vintu, Sorin Ovidiu, 110
Visegrad Group, 107, **432**
Visual Arts, 502-5
Vitorino, António, 84
Vivian, Young, 377, 584
Vo Ngyuyen Giap, 547
Vo Van Kiet, 345
Vogts, Berti, 514
Vohor, Serge, 376
Volpinari, Antonio Lazzaro, 79
von Amsberg, Claus, 65
von Sydow, Björn, 71
Voronin, Vladimir, 135
Voynet, Dominique, 56
Vujanovic, Filip, 125, 602

Wade, Abdoulaye, 264, 408, 437, 597
Waisman, David, 191
Wajed, Hasina, 322
Wales, 21, 24, 27, **41-3**, 447, 514, 518
Walesa, Lech, 98
Wallenberg, Raoul, 540
Wallis and Futuna, 376
Walters, John, 538
Wangchuk, Jigme Singye, 325
War Crimes Tribunals, see International Criminal Tribunal for the former Yugoslavia, International Criminal Tribunal for Rwanda
Waraabe, Faisal Ali, 249
Warchus, Matthew, 493

Ward, Anthony, 493
Ward, Lauren, 493
Wardak, Taj Mohammad, 307
Warner, Deborah, 484
Wasel, Shaykh Nasser Farid, 210
Watkins, Sherron, 147
Watson, Bob, 464
Watson, Harlan, 156
Weakland, Rembert, 152
Weapons of Mass Destruction, 2-3, 5, 36-7, 140, 146, 151, 155-7, 218-22, 229, 236, 363, 376, 421, 426, 469, 582; biological, 3, 36, 149, 168, 204, 220, 222; chemical, 157, 220, 222, 236; Iraq, 3, 5, 36-7, 157, 161, 218-22, 228, 510, *(document)* 522-7, 591, 593, 595-6, 600; North Korea, 5, 8, 321, 352, 362-3, 596, 598, 601; nuclear, 3, 5, 36, 130, 156, 161, 236, 303, 358, 362-3, 541
Weatherall, Bonnie, 218
Webb, Karrie, 519
Weidman, John, 492
Weinstock, Lord, 573-4 (obit.)
Wellesz, Egon, 487
Wellington, Duke of, 575
Wells, Stanley, 510
Wellstone, Paul, 144
Werner, Pierre, 66, 574 (obit.)
Wesley, Mary, 510, 574 (obit.)
Wesley, Samuel, 488
West African Economic Monetary Union (UEMOA), **436**, 410
Western Sahara, 83, **243-4**, 598
Westerthaler, Peter, 75
Westerwelle, Guido, 51
Westwood, Lee, 519
Wheatley, L. Allen, 178
Wheeldon, Christopher, 489
Whelan, Wendy, 489
Whitehead, Edward, 572
Whitelaw, William, 577
Whitfield, Simon, 516
Whitney, Hassler, 570
Wickremesinghe, Ranil, 325-7
Wieck, Hans-Georg, 132
Wijnschenk, Harry, 64
Wilder, Billy, 575 (obit.)
Wilder, Thornton, 495
Wildor, Sarah, 491
Willcocks, Sir Michael, 22
William, Prince, 23
Williams of Mostyn, Lord, 536
Williams, Rowan, 24, 42, 447, 509
Williams, Serena, 519
Williams, Tennessee, 493

Williams, Venus, 519
Wilmore, Peter, 577
Wilson, Brian, 537
Wilson, Harold, 21, 544
Wiltzer, Pierre-André, 409
Win Aung, 334
Winterbottom, Michael, 496
Wolfowitz, Paul, 96, 243, 355
Wolstenholme, Kenneth, 575 (obit.)
Woodall, Trinny, 508
Woods, Tiger, 519
Woodward, Clive, 518
Woodward, Joanne, 495
Woonton, Robert, 377, 580
World Bank, 9, 15, 111, 115, 135, 173, 252, 254, 257, 259, 271, 275, 317, 331, 399-400, **401**, 403, 429, 441, 598
World Economic Forum (WEF), 437, 462
World Health Organisation (WHO), 456, 464-5
World Summit on Sustainable Development (WSSD), 7, 15, 220, 298, 330-1, 378, 413, 438, 465, *(document)* 531-4, 592
World Trade Organisation (WTO), 12, 15, 122, 138, 153, 161, 185, 232, 237, 348, 399, **401-2**, 409, 416, 421, 441, 464, 586
World War I, 369
World War II, 73-5, 99, 105, 107, 324, 357, 378, 432, 450
World Wide Fund for Nature, 467
Wowereit, Klaus, 51
Wu Cheng-chung, John Baptist, 576 (obit.)
Wüthrich, Kurt, 457
Wynne, Frank, 509

Xhaferi, Musa, 121
Xyros, Savvas, 88

Yacob, Abune, 248
Yahyaoui, Zouhair, 238
Yakubu, Malik al-Hassan, 255
Yalla, Kumba, 280
Yang Bin, 349
Yanowsky, Zenaida, 490
Yanukovych, Viktor, 134, 599
Yates, Buford, 150
Yeltsin, Boris, 128, 133, 554
Yemen, 1, 8, 58, 207, **226-7**, 228, 433, 595
Yilmaz, Mesut, 93-4
Ying-jeou, Ma, 353
Ying-wen, Tsa, 354
Ying-yuan, Lee, 353
Yoli, Paramanga Ernest, 587
Yorongar, Ngarléjy, 271

Yotopoulos, Alexandros, 88
Young of Dartington, Lord, 577 (obit.)
Young, Baroness, 22, 576-7 (obit.)
Young, Geoffrey, 576
Yu Hsi-kun, 579
Yugoslavia, Federal Republic of, 123-6, 382, 385, 423, 428, 470, 580, 582, 590, 595-6, 599-601
Yung-san, Lee, 355
Yushchenko, Viktor, 133
Yusuf, Abdullahi, 249

Zahir Shah, Mohammed, former King of Afghanistan, 307, 584
Zakayev, Akhmed, 67
Zambia, 6, 274, 285, **286-7,** 465, 468, 578, 590
Zaplana, Eduardo, 80
Zarqawi, Abu Misab, 212

Zeffirelli, Franco, 484
Zelezny, Vladimir, 104
Zeman, Milos, 74
Zenawi, Meles, 245-6
Zeng Qinghong, 351
Zhakiyanov, Ghalymzhan, 312
Zhu Rongji, 315, 349, 439, 441
Zia, Begum Khaleda, 321-2
Zidane, Zinédine, 514
Zimbabwe, 6-7, 14, 38-9, 236, 252, 275, 287, **288-91,** 292, 294, 296, 299, 301, 405, 437-8, 465, 580, 582, 587, 589, 590-91, 593-94
Zinni, Gen. (retd) Anthony, 578
Zoellick, Robert B., 538
Zouabri, Antar, 240
Zuma, Jacob, 298, 300
Zuma, Nkosazana Dlamini, 411